AF580765

INTERNATIONAL HANDBOOK OF CONTEMPORARY DEVELOPMENTS IN ARCHITECTURE

INTERNATIONAL HANDBOOK OF CONTEMPORARY DEVELOPMENTS IN ARCHITECTURE

EDITED BY
WARREN SANDERSON

GREENWOOD PRESS
WESTPORT, CONNECTICUT • LONDON, ENGLAND

Library of Congress Cataloging in Publication Data
Main entry under title:

International handbook of contemporary developments in architecture.

Bibliography: p.
Includes indexes.
1. Architecture, Modern—20th century—Addresses, essays, lectures. 2. City planning—1945 —Addresses, essays, lectures. I. Sanderson, Warren.
NA680.I48 724.9'1 80-24794
ISBN 0-313-21439-5 (lib. bdg.)

Library of Congress Catalog Card Number: 80-24794
ISBN: 0-313-21439-5

First published in 1981

Greenwood Press
A division of Congressional Information Service, Inc.
88 Post Road West, Westport, Connecticut 06881

Distributed in the United Kingdom and Europe by
Aldwych Press, Ltd., London

Printed in the United States of America

10 9 8 7 6 5 4 3 2 1

CONTENTS

ILLUSTRATIONS

PREFACE

Architecture consists essentially in the provision of distinguished shelters to serve many specific human needs. The bonds between man and his built environment reflect and further the character of thought and daily life in every age. The architecture of the Modern Movement, introduced almost at the outset of this century, set into tangible forms modes of social thought that were pursued into the decades following the Second World War. In some parts of the globe these forms are still being replicated.

There is abroad now the feeling that architecture changed drastically during the 1960s—that stormy decade of impressive political upheaval. Many observers of modern architecture recognize that a departure, in the sixties, from the precepts of the Modern Movement has left architecture today in a fragmented, sometimes chaotic, condition. Relatively idiosyncratic, at times narrowly localized, architectural innovations and introspections into a multiplicity of pasts abound. It is time for a global summing up and sifting of the myriad of movements that have occurred in the field since the sixties. It is time, too, to try to come to some meaningful awareness of the relationships of recent directions in architecture to the flurry of achievements of Modernism that took place in the wake of the destruction of the late thirties and the early forties. The observations and reasoned opinions of architects, planners, and architectural historians and critics in this volume provide the reader with an opportunity to assess a great many recent directions in architecture. By bringing together a wide diversity of views and approaches to contemporary developments in architecture, I have tried to encourage a broadening of our bases of discussion.

Since Greenwood Press invited me to put together a book on recent developments in architecture around the world, it has been my intention to help provide an array of selective data from which we may begin to answer the questions of "From where do we come?" "Who are we?" and "Where are we going?" In the widely dispersed corners of our narrowing world, each of us may at first tend to find different answers to these questions. However, considering world and regional economics, the spread of technology, and the almost instantaneous nature of the information explosion, particular patterns of consensus concerning our architecture will ultimately surface. Indeed, even now they are emerging and may be informed by, as well as tested against, the manifold contents of this book.

Part I presents selective overviews of recent trends, theories, technology, preservation and restoration, and urban and regional planning. Part II consists of compilations and interpretations of the architectural developments in several nations. Rather than molding these into some monolithic unity, I have encouraged each author to put forward his or her judgments in the manner with which he or she is most comfortable; in my editing I have tried to maintain a respect for a consequent variety of viewpoints. My personal perceptions of what has happened in architecture throughout the world, particularly since 1945-1946, have been confined, I hope, to the necessarily rather synoptic discussions in the pages of my own chapter.

Major accomplishments of architectural talents around the globe are identified in this handbook—some almost to the moment of publication. Partisan presentations of specific buildings, complexes, architectural movements, and individual architects lead us into pathways that we may prefer to pursue or to reject. If we are to choose our directions and enrich those to which we may already be committed, however, we must be aware of the existence of many new, stimulating and thought-provoking architectural landmarks; a number of which are discussed in this volume. Though by and large the texts of the thirty-eight chapters that follow are concerned with developments since the mid-1940s, in some few cases a brief look toward earlier decades was required to provide an adequate context within which to understand more recent architecture. Along with most of the contributing authors, I would have appreciated the opportunity to have included more information, more fully elaborated discussions, and more illustrations. Given the physical and practical limitations to which we all agreed, this was impossible: it would have led to a work of far greater size, one that would also have been far less readily accessible. The reader will recognize, I am sure, that in a volume of such broad scope and size inevitably some inaccuracies or misstatements may have eluded detection. I urge that these be brought to my attention speedily so that they may be corrected as practically as possible. Inevitably, too, some countries that I would like to have included have been omitted for reasons beyond my control.

Architects, critics, historians, urbanists, students, and general readers will find in the *International Handbook of Contemporary Developments in Architecture* an unusual wealth of information and ideas with which to expand their immediate frames of reference, the mind-sets from which decisions are made that affect our built environments and, consequently, our daily lives. I hope the many strengths of this volume will make it as useful to its readers as they have made it for me in bringing it to completion.

Montréal
August 1981

ACKNOWLEDGMENTS

Many more people than I can possibly thank individually have made this book possible. For arousing the interest of a budding medievalist in the architecture of the twentieth century, I am much indebted to several faculty members and students affiliated, in the later 1960s, with the Department of Architecture of the University of Illinois' Chicago Circle campus, and particularly to A. Frederick Koieper and Niklaus Morgenthaler. For support during a particularly problematic moment in the preparation of the final manuscript, I am grateful to Alfred Pinsky, formerly Dean of the Faculty of Fine Arts at Concordia University.

For having invited me to undertake such a book and for her good counsel during its formulation in 1977, special thanks go to Marilyn Brownstein of Greenwood Press. For assistance and advice during the editing and production of this book I am indebted to Cynthia Harris, James Sabin, and especially Anne Kugielsky. Professor Günter Grimm of the University of Trier in the Federal Republic of Germany generously provided facilities and assistance in the difficult initial stages of searching out contributing authors during my successive visiting professorships in the spring semesters of 1977 and 1978. Architect, professor, and author, Sten Samuelson of Lund, Sweden, was enthusiastic in his help during this and later phases.

The thirty-eight authors of the following pages were recruited from the ranks of architects, critics, urban planners, and historians of architecture the world over. For their patient forbearance with my sometimes burdensome editorial recommendations in a world of occasionally irregular postal services, I am sincerely indebted to them. I should like to recognize here also the considered recommendations of Mr. Joachim Maynard and Mrs. Lorna Scherzer of Montreal. In the same city special thanks go to Laura L. Greco for her extraordinary work with some of the photographic materials and for her continuing enthusiastic encouragement. Helpful too was the staff of McGill University's Blackader Library. And Dorothy Atkinson is especially appreciated for her yeoman's work in typing (and sometimes deciphering) the final manuscript.

It is particularly to my wife, however, that I am indebted for sharing and airing with me a wide variety of specific issues of substance concerning worldwide developments in architecture; her careful consideration of points of translation in their contexts, her editorial and research assistance, and her objective criticisms have been invaluable.

Every reasonable effort has been made to verify the information received by the editor and to trace the owners of copyright materials in this book, but in a few instances this has proved impossible. The publishers will be glad to receive information leading to more complete acknowledgments in subsequent printings of this book. In the meantime we extend our apologies for any omissions.

PART I

WORLDWIDE DEVELOPMENTS

1

TRENDS IN CONTEMPORARY ARCHITECTURE

WARREN SANDERSON

Many contemporary trends in architecture stem from developments that had their beginnings during the first decades of the century and continued, with an interruption between 1939 and 1946, almost unbroken into the sixties. In the aftermath of the Second World War European architects had to reestablish their links with those developments before they could proceed to rebuild effectively. In Japan architects did the same, though their previous relationship to a truly modern architecture had hardly been as secure. And in the Americas, with the dangers of trade upon the oceans lifted, architectural developments resumed in full.

During the sixties the prewar trends were seriously challenged and the realignments of architectural thinking that occurred then play a substantial role in the directions that architectural development is now taking. For us to recognize major trends abroad in architecture during the last decade or more, we must begin with a clarification of the prewar development of the Modern Movement and follow its ebbs and flows across the war years, the decades of reconstruction, and into the 1960s. The chapter will conclude with a consideration of some important recent trends.*

The Modern Movement into the 1930s

Since the nineteenth century, creative epochs often seem to have had archfiends against which their avant-gardes have reacted. For the Modern Movement that retained its vigor and bridged the chasm caused by the violent interruption of a world in battle between 1939 and 1946, the prime architectural villain was the Movement's nineteenth-century inheritance with its obscurant decorations. A host of new beginnings (neo-Romanesque, neo-Gothic, neo-Renaissance, and neo-Classical manners) had become the stylistic inheritance of the new century and it was from this that the Modern Movement broke away especially during the 1920s. In their protests against the past, the Modernists—Functionalist, Rationalist, avant-garde architects and critics—were reacting particularly often to the neo-Classical architecture that had constituted their heritage from the Graeco-Roman era, a heritage that had been renewed since the fifteenth century in each succeeding century. The avant-garde position was straightforward: neo-Classicism was anathema. Even with the success of the Modern Movement *qua* movement the strength of that Classical tradition remains evident, for only relatively recently has the plague of mostly mediocre repetitions of neo-Classical architecture tended to disappear from banks and various other public buildings.

In the absolutism of their protests the architects of the avant-garde were carrying a new idealism forward to an end point. They purified and absolved form of most of its decoration so that form in itself became the basic stuff of architectural design. This purification is evident in virtually all of the buildings of Mies van der Rohe and in hundreds if not thousands of essentially Miesan echoes throughout the world. With the discipline of Le Corbusier's

*EDITOR'S NOTE: When illustrations of buildings discussed in this chapter appear neither here nor elsewhere in this volume, the reader may often find them in A. Drexler, *Transformations in Modern Architecture* (1979), J. Joedicke, *Architecture since 1945* (1969), or, D. Sharp, ed., *A Visual History of Twentieth Century Architecture* (1972).

modular conception and his pronouncements that architectural design was to be based on ''universal views," it is evident the working process of this preeminent poetic Functionalist was to start from "fixed" points,'' or ''implacable laws.'' Though the ideals of form of the Classical Greeks and the purist Rationalists were different, an absolutism common to both was clearly inherent in their idealizing and perfecting. In this sense the Modern Movement and its International Style may be understood as having continued the essence of Classicism, though railing against its more recent outer trappings in neo-Classicism.

RATIONALIST ARCHITECTURE AND LE CORBUSIER

Rationalism in modern architecture was basically rooted in precepts of a higher order that recall those of the Classical Greeks while proclaiming differences. Though usually seemingly simple at first in its emphasis upon rectilinear surfaces in cubical and slablike designs, the architecture of the Rationalist trend required a high degree of precision in planning and in construction. Its beginnings early in this century in Holland, Germany, and France spread as an International Style during the 1920s appearing by the 1930s in the more technologically advanced countries of Europe, Asia, and North America.

South America had been made well aware of the new style of buildings by Le Corbusier himself during his lecture tour of that continent in 1929. Architects in Argentina, Brazil, and Uruguay were especially receptive to his ideas, and in 1936 he was invited to Brazil as a consultant for what became a landmark of modern architecture in South America, the Ministry of Education and Health building in Rio de Janeiro [1936-1943]. This had effects not only during the forties in South America but also in the fifties in the Republic of South Africa where the Meat Board Building in Pretoria [1951] by Stauch and Partners is related to it, according to I. Prinsloo.

The Corbusian idea of a building as a ''machine-for-living'' expressed a relationship of architecture with technology that cannot be too strongly stressed. Particularly as the need for new structures to replace those destroyed during the Second World War forced a faster pace of industrialization upon what had been the less technologically developed countries, regional and national variations upon the International Style appeared haltingly first during the fifties in other European countries such as Greece, Poland, and the Union of Soviet Socialist Republics; in the Near East in Turkey; in the Orient, particularly in Australia, less so in Japan, and a bit later in the People's Republic of China; and finally in South America, by then as an importation from the United States.

ORGANIC ARCHITECTURE, FRANK LLOYD WRIGHT, AND EXPRESSIONISM

A second major modern movement, not to be confused with the International Style so often termed the Modern Movement, was the drive toward organic expression manifested particularly in the work of Frank Lloyd Wright. In Europe, this offered an alternative to Rationalism; and as the Rationalist International Style grew stronger immediately after the Second World War, a polemic of Organicism developed in reaction to it. As early as 1898 Wright had built the River Forest Golf Club [River Forest, Illinois; enlarged in 1901] to parallel the flat site upon which it was located. The sense that the designer of a building should take his cues from the landscape, harmonizing his structure with nature in a vital continuity between both, became one of the guiding tenets of Wright's sixty years of practice. Perhaps surprisingly, this is an attitude very much related to ancient Greek practices of seeing in the setting of a site certain natural characteristics that bespeak aspects of one or another deity and building a temple there to that god.[1]

Unknowingly and with a down-to-earth, insightful approach, Wright had reframed a Classical concept quite remote from his own immediate frame of reference. (The Rationalists' relationship with the Classical past was much more conscious, as we have seen.) In Europe particularly during the twenties it was not so much the notion of any continuity between landscape and architecture but rather the idea of an organic continuity or wholeness of architectural space and form that took hold in the work of Erich Mendelsohn [Potsdam, Einstein Observatory Tower, 1919-1921], Hugo Häring [Garkau Farm Cowshed, 1923-1925], and the designs of Hans Scharoun [Hostel building, 1929 Werkbund Exhibition, Breslau, now Wroclaw in Poland]. So few were the opportunities of building in this manner then that not until the postwar decades did the work of Scharoun become widely known.

Unlike Wright, Häring saw the house as an expressive extension of man's internal organic structure; a house was an external organ or as he himself put it in 1930 "man's second skin." All of these architects, having broken away from the restrictions of the Rationalist cage, created buildings of varied forms combining curving facades with straight surfaces as if one grew out of the other. Their buildings seemed to move in irregular serpentine fashion within or across a site, whether the terrain was flat or hilly, and were considered as both irrational and Expressionist.

Wright's views of Organic architecture were introduced into Europe immediately after the Second World War by Bruno Zevi[2] and with the formation in Rome of the Associazione per l'Architettura Organica. Zevi, who became an outstanding exponent of this viewpoint, was largely responsible for introducing it into South America during a lecture tour in 1951. In those lectures Zevi urged a recognition of the ramifications of an Organic approach in urban planning as well as in architecture.

FUNCTIONALIST ARCHITECTURE

Despite Giedion's formulation of the "Rational-Functional" versus the "irrational-Organic,"[3] the notion of "Functionalism" seems to have provided a common meeting-ground for the Rationalists and the Expressionists, within which latter group we may include the closely related practitioners of Organic architecture. Their differences resided in their relative orientation toward man: for the Rationalists man was a generic objective reality whose various functionings were to be accommodated in perfected enclosures, the all-purpose spaces for instance of Mies van der Rohe; for the Expressionists man was more personal, more idiosyncratic, and his buildings were to reflect greater varieties of surface treatments and spatial solutions interacting with their environments, as in Hugo Häring's Fritz Schminke House at Labau, 1933.

To present architecture in terms of such a doctrinal polarization is a convenient exaggeration that helps us to understand alternative positions. The qualities of both Rationalist and Organic-Expressionist poles were in some measure resident within works of each of the major architects of Modernism. In Le Corbusier an interaction of expressively rounded, elongated, and rectangular masses and spaces occurs *within* the Rationalist cubic framework of his villas of the late 1920s and 1930s. The terrace roof-garden level of the Villa Savoye at Poissy [1929-1931], the introduction of barrel vaulting in his Weekend House at Boulogne-sur-Seine [1935], and the grand sculpturally curved chimneys and play areas atop the Unité d'Habitation, Marseille [1948-1952] all lead toward the monumental expressive transformation into a powerful hyperboloid form above the roofline of Chandigarh, India's Ministries' Building of 1958. And more importantly, this development led to perhaps his most marvelous creation, the animated yet iconic Ronchamp Chapel [1950-1954], where broad but twisted and curving walls were so plastically conceived as to deny the existence of any homage to the Rationalists' cube. Mies van der Rohe employed a semicircular partition that functionally enclosed half of a dining area around a round table in his 1930 Tugendhat House at Brno, Czechoslovakia, but this remains the exception and he never consistently nor fully developed the idea of rounded moving spaces and corresponding masses. In Frank Lloyd Wright's Price Tower [1953-1956] at Bartlesville, Oklahoma [important to many architects; and compare Juan Carlos Calderón's Pinilla Building, La Paz, Bolivia, 1975-1978 (fig. 11.3)] the plan of each floor is determined not as much by organic interrelationships of space as by an abstract, *rational* device of design: the rotation upon a square of a large pinwheel-like cross element in which small rooms and the service areas are concentrated. Though the plan displays a simple but strongly geometric counterplay of volumes, the four arms of the cross element are less saliently expressed upon the exterior. They appear as angled masses rising with the skyscraper, enlivening its appearance, and breaking any of its resemblance to a box. Particularly in their varied heights and their parallelism, these tall elements seem to insist upon suggesting the growth one finds in Organic architecture.

From this very brief accounting, then, we may speak of organic and expressive aspects of predominantly Rationalist architecture, and we may likewise find rationalist aspects of predominantly Organic and Expressionist architecture. The issue appears to be based upon the approach of architects to the functional realities of the architectural problems at hand. Before we leave this consideration of the philosophical and stylistic dichotomy that has existed even to our own day between the Rationalists and the exponents of Organic architecture, two more facets of the latter remain to be introduced: the approaches of the Scandinavians and of the Japanese to solving architectural and, by extension, urban building problems.

PREWAR FINNISH AND JAPANESE STYLES

In addition to Wright's Organic theories, European architects recognized as an alternative to Rationalism the eminently humanistic architecture best exemplified in the work of Alvar Aalto of Finland. Infusing his work with a wealth of natural materials he made it respond to human requirements. For instance he led the way with an undulating wooden ceiling in the lecture hall of the Viipuri Library

[1927-1935], a ceiling that seemed quite irrational and yet was so well based upon scientific studies of acoustics that it enhanced human hearing. There, as in his Tuberculosis Sanatorium at Paimio in southern Finland [1929-1933], his enclosures opened through large glass surfaces to the natural surroundings; and, sometimes undisturbedly, sometimes by landscaping gradations, his formal inventories became part of the context of nature. Before the war his work was known as far south as Italy but hardly at all outside Europe.

Before the war, too, especially in the thirties, Japan had been the recipient of Western ideas of architecture even as she had become increasingly nationalistic. Traditionally, Japanese architecture had been elegant, yet simple and serene in design, employing natural material without concealment and respecting the qualities of the landscape of its site. In Tokyo, Frank Lloyd Wright built the earthquake-proof Imperial Hotel [1916-1922; demolished 1968]; and finding in Japan a sympathetic view of an architecture that was "of the earth," he returned to the United States much influenced himself. Antonin Raymond, who had been associated with Wright but favored the International Style, set up his atelier in Tokyo during the twenties and became there one of the immediate sources of Western building design and technology. Important Japanese architects such as Kunio Maekawa (with whom Kenzo Tange apprenticed for twelve years) and Junzo Sakakura worked with Le Corbusier in Paris during the late twenties and thirties. It was only after the Second World War that the Japanese aesthetic, translated in part into the technological and urbanistic terms understood in Europe and America, had its effects in the West.

Non-Modern Movement Architecture Before the Second World War

Having focused upon trends existing in modern architecture before the war, we run the risk of believing that this architecture was characteristic of the period. But that is surely not the case. The most-advanced buildings constituted but a slight percentage of the total constructed and therefore must be thought of as largely atypical. The norms of the world's architecture from the twenties through the forties may be found in the various long-established national and regional traditions of building. In fact, during the thirties and into the fifties in many countries there occurred a romantic reaction to the Modern Movement. Most strikingly, for example, in Greece the International Style was almost totally abandoned after the 1930s until about 1954 for a neo-Classical style that actually originated in early nineteenth-century Germany. In Hungary, neo-Baroque style became popular [Gyula Walder's Cistercian church, Budapest, 1930] together with reevocations of a folk manner [Agricultural School at Rackeve, 1941, by Janos Wanner] and in Turkey around 1940 an old Anatolian idiom came to the fore in residential building. In the United States (where in 1932 Henry-Russell Hitchcock and Philip Johnson had formulated the name "International Style") a panoply of local and pseudohistorical architectural styles for the most part obtained, rather than the manners of Modernism.

With the notable exceptions of Brazil's Rio de Janeiro and São Paulo where there were strong avant-garde movements, in most countries of South America still lacking modern technology and materials in the thirties and forties, colonial, neo-Baroque, neo-Classical, and indigenous adobe constructions were the orders of the day. Occasional modernist buildings appeared in Venezuela [Carlos Raúl Villanueva's Corbusian Gran Colombia School, Caracas, 1939] and in Colombia [the immigrant German architect Leopoldo Rother planned and began building the campus of the National University at Bogotá, 1936-1938]; but in Argentina with the ascendance of the Peron government (1946-1955) colonial and folk architecture were so strongly supported that such talented young architects as Horacio Caminos and Eduardo Catalano left the country.

In Japan dominant militarism's call for a return to traditional architecture was answered among others by Kenzo Tange's winning project [1942] in a competition for a monument to commemorate the Greater East Asia Co-Prosperity Sphere; while in the Germany of the thirties and early forties only the large scale of construction introduced by the International Style survived in an overbearingly totalitarian fascist architecture [Albert Speer's Party Congress precinct at Nuremberg, 1943].[4]

In the Union of Soviet Socialist Republics the great promise of the Constructivist architects of the twenties such as Ivan Leonidov [Project for the Lenin Institute, Moscow, 1927], Ivan Golossov [Club Zouiev building, Moscow, 1926-1927], Leonard and Victor Vesnine [Project for the Pravda building on the Leningradskaya, Moscow, 1924] and Constantine Melnikov [Roussakov Club building, Moscow, 1927-1929] was cut short. The doctrine of Social Realism was imposed in its stead in 1934, and a blend of pseudo-Classical, vernacular Russian, and a broad-base skyscraper architecture quickly dominated the Stalinist era. With technology and industrialization on the one hand and the architectural imagination on the other, modern architecture continued to grow and make its way in the world against these more reactionary trends. But this was interrupted for more than six years.

The Modern Movement During the Second World War

The architectural situation when war broke out in 1938/39 may be briefly summarized. Would-be innovators, whatever the sources of their enthusiasm and whatever their causes, had to contend with long-established traditional ways of seeing architecture and ways of building. The architectural avant-garde for the most part agreed upon the need for some sort of functional approach and opposed the nonfunctional, unyielding, and decorative modes of previous architectural styles. Within the avant-garde were two major avenues to the solution of functional problems: the Rationalist that resulted in what came to be called the International Style, and the Expressionist-Organic that some considered as irrational. Within the International Style (also called the Modern Movement) were several Rationalist variations such as De Stijl (Netherlands), the Bauhaus (Germany), and Constructivism (Germany and the USSR).[5] Virtually all movements of the International Style were European in their origin. An effort was rightly made to fit Wright into this context because of the strong geometry of such designs as his Unity Church [Oak Park, Illinois, 1906] that so impressed visiting European architects. Given his philosophy of Organic architecture, his work would seem to express *both* the Rationalist and the Organic, with the latter having become ever stronger as his life progressed.

Formal geometric aspects of Organic architecture were more apparent in the Expressionist buildings of Europe during the first third of this century than in Wright's own works; they appeared as well before the Second World War in the architecture of Aalto, while in Japan's traditions there was also an incipient organicism. Finally, there was the work of the structural engineers that developed the dictates of materials and systems in and of themselves, leaning more often in the direction of the Rationalists, while simultaneously helping to make possible the expressive forms of Expressionist-Organic architecture. We are confronted, then, with essentially three major trends by 1940: the Rationalist, the Expressionist-Organic, and the primarily technological.

During the global warfare of 1938/39-1945/46, the creative energies of most of the participating countries were channeled into efforts other than architectural. In the Americas, meanwhile relatively unaffected physically by the European and Asian conflagrations, there was some interesting building activity. Wright continued to construct private residences in the United States, and that country began to feel the influence of such displaced Europeans as Mies van der Rohe (in Chicago from 1938), Walter Gropius (at Harvard University from 1937) who was the founder of the Bauhaus at Weimar, Germany from 1919, Marcel Breuer (from France in 1937, also at Harvard), and José Luis Sert (who arrived from Spain in 1939 and in 1958 became Dean of the Harvard Graduate School of Design). The response of the American public generally to "Modernism" in architecture in those years is typified in the attacks of local journalists upon Gropius's and Breuer's Defense Housing compound [New Kensington, Pennsylvania, near Pittsburgh, 1941-1942]. Despite innovative elimination of partitions to create an open living-dining-kitchen space on the ground floor, despite the uses of natural materials and a sensitive siting, it was the geometric regularity of their external shapes that was particularly perceived; and this conformity made for buildings considered as little more than chicken coops.

In South America, from the group that had been engaged in the Corbusian Ministry of Education and Health building at Rio de Janeiro, Oscar Niemeyer's career as an architect of worldwide standing was launched with such expressive plastic interpretations as the Church of St. Francis [Pampulha, Brazil, 1943]. Here the dominant parabolic concrete tunnel-vaulted nave is joined by a series of parallel, lesser, concrete tunnel vaults to echo the traditional T-plan churches. From that same group Eduardo Affonso Reidy, known since his 1933 orphanage building in Rio, went on to several important projects. After the conclusion of the war, he achieved prominence with, for instance, the low-income residential complex of Pedregulho (fig. 12.1) that beautifully accommodates a long seven-story building on *pilotis* to the undulations of a hillside [1950]. Reidy's Pedregulho development was but one reflection of a concern with low-cost mass housing that had occupied European architects for most of the century and that became a major realm of architectural endeavor after 1945. In Argentina Amancio Williams's design for his brother's home (fig. 7.1) at Mar Del Plata [1945] mounted an oblong box with strip windows upon a curved slab of reinforced concrete, recalling the lessons of Robert Maillart. During the forties too, the Austral (Southern) Group (1939), consisting of Antonio Bonet, Jorge Ferrari Hardoy, and others, provided a nucleus of impetus for new ideas in

Argentina's architecture until Peron's adverse policies became effective after 1943. At the same time, in Colombia, Leopoldo Rother collaborated with Bruno Violi in the International Style School of Engineering building [Bogotá, 1941-1942] and later worked with the engineer Guillermo González Zuleta in the National University Press building [1946].

In Europe only the Iberian peninsular countries on the west, Sweden in the north, and Switzerland were nonbelligerents. Many of Spain's leading architects had left during or soon after the Spanish civil war ended in 1939. In Sweden and Switzerland the economic effects of the European war and a lack of raw materials were considerable. What little was built often were weakly romantic revivals with a folklike character, and, in all, construction in these countries consisted for the most part of completions of what had been begun earlier rather than of new starts.

Technological Progress in Architecture

Whatever the aesthetic impulse, the social or philosophical outlook of the architect, it was the technological and industrial reality, the possibilities permitted by structural engineering, that enabled him to build as he wished. The constructional means available for architectural expression have grown so rapidly that at least since the mid-sixties architects have been able to build in almost whatever fashion they have wished. How rapid indeed has been the development of steel as a structural element! From its tentative introduction in the form of girders in parts of the ten-story cast-iron frame Home Insurance Company building in Chicago [1883-1885] by William Le Baron Jenney it led to such multistory, steel framework and glass structures as the Lake Shore Drive apartment towers [1949-1951] in that same city by Mies van der Rohe. Mies's sophisticated use of the I-beam and his extraordinary detailing in steel structures have by now become legendary. The lines between engineers of genuine sensitivity and architects are blurred in the development of modern architecture.

In the reinforced-concrete structures of the Swiss engineer Robert Maillart (1872-1940), stripped to the minimum for economy and function while sacrificing no load-bearing aspects, there is a lightness and often an elegance of curvatures as well that proclaims the art of architecture. The slab construction that he employed in such early bridges as that over the Rhine at Tavanasa [1905; destroyed 1927] was basic to the adaptation in 1925 of precast-concrete slab construction for mass-produced housing by Ernst May, the city architect of Frankfurt, Germany. In turn this led to the industrialized prefabrication of reinforced concrete that became basic in large-scale housing projects throughout the world after 1945.

The *architecte-ingénieur* Auguste Perret, born in Burgundy two years after Maillart, outlived him by fifteen years, long enough to have received a fitting reward for his pioneering efforts in the use of reinforced concrete. From his apartment building at 25 bis rue Franklin in Paris, in which for the first time [1903!] a reinforced-concrete skeleton was used openly for architectural expression, to the docks at Casablanca with their remarkable, most unusually thin, brick vaultings [1916], to the magnificent church of Notre Dame at Raincy [1922] with its wondrously slim columns bearing light, shallow tunnel vaults more airy and illuminated than a Gothic hall church, Perret opened new pathways. In 1945 at the age of 71, his efforts were crowned with a call out of retirement to oversee the reconstruction of the port city of Le Havre (fig. 21.1). Ultimately, Perret's explorations with reinforced concrete were seminal to those of the Spanish engineer Eduardo Torroja [hyperboloid shell vault series, cantilevered above the grandstands at the Zarzuela Racetrack, Madrid, 1935]; to his younger compatriot Félix Canédela's eggshell-thin concrete vaults in Mexico [Cosmic Ray Pavilion, University City, Mexico, 1951, fig. 29.2]; to Le Corbusier and the European Brutalists in the 1960s; and to the dramatically scaled sequence of shell-thin concrete vaults that crowns the Sydney Opera House by Jorn Utzøn [1957-1974, fig. 8.4].

With the outstandingly gifted Italian engineer Pier Luigi Nervi (1891-1979), a talent of no less an order than Maillart's and Perret's and perhaps one of the greatest builders of all time, we enter into a generation that bridged the modern and contemporary decades. Though he preferred to work with reinforced concrete, he brought to it whatever materials were appropriate and logical to realize the fullest structural and functional potentials of the building problems at hand [compare his *Costruire Corettamente,* 1956]. And in doing so he imbued his architecture with a beauty and grace inherent in its structure and immediately apparent even to the casual observer. With such an engineer-architect it is difficult to become concerned about the sequential development of his work. Each structure is unto itself a universe of mathematics and geometry imaginatively transcended, from the early Giovanni Berta Stadium in Florence [1930-1932], with its dramatically but ever-so-lightly and freely thrust concrete shell sheltering the grandstand; to the Small Sports Palace in Rome [1956-1957] with its shell roofing, braced by an integral radiating myriad of interlacing, sinuous, shallow members; to what many consider his most beautiful project, the "Italia 1961" Palace in Turin. His collaborations with other distinguished builders as a consulting structural engineer were of considerable importance far beyond Italy's borders and will be taken up later.

When to reinforced concrete and steel we add such materials as glass, wood, stone, bricks, and plaster, and when all of these and more are available for whatever structural systems man's industry and technology may devise, then we may begin to appreciate the enormous breadth of possibilities of what was to come after 1945 in the architecture of the more contemporary world.

Initial Postwar Trends

AALTO'S BAKER HOUSE DORMITORY

To my vivid personal recollection it was first in the work of Alvar Aalto that the opposing poles that exist within both human and architectural realities were linked. I refer to the cool intellectuality of the Rationalists as opposed to the more evident emotionality of the Expressionist-Organicists. In a heroic statement that presaged significantly the content of the thirty-odd years that followed the Second World War, and at a time when Boston and neighboring Cambridge, Massachusetts, were for the most part still deeply mired within distant architectural traditions, Aalto's Baker House Dormitory was erected [1947-1948] at the Massachusetts Institute of Technology on the Cambridge side of the Charles River. To fulfill his intention of giving each room a view of the river while avoiding an awareness of the large brickwork expanse of that side of the building, Aalto designed an undulating serpentine structure six stories high around a reinforced concrete frame. Within the dormitory, natural materials including unplastered rough brick walls were used as seldom before in the United States. Though the building is sited in parallel with the roadway before it, its wavelike main facade's frame of reference is not the road but rather the Charles River beyond.

The opposite facade consists of a series of large, flat walls that contain and mask rather than reflect the undulating plan of the building. These walls are tied together in design by a projecting, enclosed staircase descending from either end toward the central entry. Banks of windows are coordinated with the staircase enclosure in which there are none. Thus, the reverse facade is composed in angular accents and is altogether different in character from the riverside facade. Across a large athletic field is a bricolage of miscellaneous utilitarian buildings, small factories, warehouses, and occasional residences, all relatively low-rise, boxlike structures of various heights forming a polyglot angular cityscape. The rear facade reflects in kind the city of Cambridge beyond it as the front followed the idea of the river flowing before it.

The Baker Dormitory participates in its locale contextually by offering to it interpretations of the two predominant images of its ambience. It is neither an imposition nor an intervention. Instead it is integrated topographically and geographically in its *quartier* and here appropriately enough lacks historical references just as its environs do. Humanistically and organically it recreates its own neighborhood, all the while asserting its own existence. The notions of contextualism in urban design of which we have heard so much, and much more recently, are stated here with subtlety and with clarity by one of the great master architects of our time. To my recollection the Baker Dormitory was the object of curious onlooking and of assorted witticisms soon after it was built, but it was neither scorned nor rejected as an intrusion by the public. The contrast of this reaction with that which accompanied the completion of Le Corbusier's Carpenter Center for the Visual Arts at Harvard University [1961-1963] is striking. Physical and imagistic contextualism became a major factor in postwar architectural thought and construction.

PLANNING FOR URBAN RENEWAL

In the countries devastated by the war the immediate need after 1945/46 obviously was for the reconstruction of housing and industrial facilities, and as the population grew there was an increasing move toward building new towns. The heightenings of social consciousness inherent in the planning and erection of new and mass housing in Europe had ramifications in other parts of the world as well, and a wide variety of solutions appeared, particularly in the fifties and sixties. There were ample models available with which city planners could work. Gropius and Breuer had collaborated to propose slablike eight- to twelve-story blocks at right angles to the roadway and paralleling one another with considerable open space between them [Haselhorst project, Berlin, 1929]. Le Corbusier had offered various plans for apartment slabs often built at right angles to one another, sometimes attached and always in spacious settings [*La Ville Radieuse*, Boulogne, 1934]; Frank Lloyd Wright had offered his spaciously suburban concepts with few high rises in a variegated package [Broadacre City, exhibited 1935] and there were a great many more. A goodly number of new towns and sections of cities had been built before the war, especially in the Netherlands, Germany, and England, based upon ideas that reached back into the nineteenth century. It is no accident that Ebenezer Howard's *Garden Cities of Tomorrow*, London, 1898, was published in new editions during 1964 and 1965. Le Corbusier's *Radiant City* was reissued in French in 1946 and in an English translation when urban and suburban planning developed a remarkable crescendo. The range of precedents was enormous.

Before we consider just what was built in the postwar world, two factors must be recognized as preeminent. First, the restoration of the destroyed industrial bases of countries with previously advanced technology had to be accomplished. With the Marshall Plan passed by the Congress of the United States in 1947, massive infusions of American dollars (some twelve billion) in loans and subsidies were earmarked specifically for rebuilding the industrial bases of western European economies so that, in turn, each war-ravaged country could generate its own wealth. In this way control of social decisions, including the construction of massive public housing, was maintained by the individual national governments rather than becoming dictated by the funding nation. Many countries that sought to enjoy the fruits of technology had to build new industrial capacities: for example, in Eastern Europe, Hungary, Poland, and Roumania; in South America, Chile, Bolivia, and Colombia; and in Asia, China, and India. The Eastern European countries and the USSR rebuilt and expanded their prewar industrial capacities under different circumstances from those in Western Europe. In the Orient with the notable exception of Japan and in South America, excepting Argentina and Brazil for the most part, industrialization had hardly begun even by 1950.

Second, the traditional concept that from a few highly important centers of architectural creativity innovations would gradually radiate to the far corners of the earth was drastically altered. This resulted from the information explosion's rapid, worldwide distribution of architectural journals with their theoretical formulations, their photos, and their detailed drawings of new buildings. New buildings and complexes of distinction as well as technological innovations could be known in most urban centers within a few months or even weeks of their announcement. The character of architectural exclusivity gave way to a broader engagement with the new: we were and are confronted with virtually worldwide movements in the field, such as the megastructure of the sixties or the user-participation in design of the sixties and seventies. The polarization of Rationalism versus the Organic movement (discussed above) was inevitably weakened and positions that more evenhandedly encompassed both came forward. Technological advances of significant magnitude, including new developments in the manufacture of glass and prefabrication of building systems, became the province of all who could afford them. In essence, the nature of the avant-garde in architecture became democratized.

Architects of the Modern Movement believed that through architecture society could be changed for the better, but, as is so often the case, in their generic perceptions of "society" they tended to neglect the specific, the idiosyncratic needs and wishes of individuals, despite proclamations to the contrary. In 1928 the Congrès Internationaux d'Architecture Moderne (CIAM) had been formed in Switzerland, bringing together some of the most distinguished architects in the world; and their worldwide representation grew as the organization continued in existence until its transmutation and fragmentation in the late fifties.[6]

The principles set forth during the 1933 CIAM conference, the Charter of Athens, formed the basis for postwar urban planning after their publication by Le Corbusier in 1941. There were four considerations: housing, work, recreation during leisure hours, and traffic. Housing was to be built in "places in which space, fresh air, and sunshine are plentifully guaranteed." Work was to be organized so that it would "regain its character as a natural human activity." "Installations necessary for the good use of leisure" were to be built so that it would become "beneficial and productive." And between the architectural entities for housing, work, and leisure there was to be "a traffic network that facilitates movement . . . while respecting the rights of all." By constructing tall apartment buildings there would be an opening up of spaces to be used for leisure. (And yet somehow all measurements were to be based on a human scale.) Later a fifth functioning principle was added: historicism, particularly in the urban core.[7]

Working from these five tenets a whole host of new urban developments came into existence during the quarter-century following the war. Indeed, the fully planned city, town, or housing development has been one of the major trends of postwar architecture, subsuming a variety of architectural styles and raising anew by the 1960s questions of imagery and meaning in architecture.

The Scandinavian countries were highly influential with such housing estates at Stockholm as the Gröndal project just after the war was concluded and Vällingby, planned during the war years with its first phase finished in 1954. At Gröndal Sven Backström and Leif Reinius used point buildings with groups of lower, terraced housing in a varied, organically composed, basic design. That variety of building, though mostly reflecting International Style types, was necessarily greater in Sven Markelius's plan for Vällingby, a community for twenty-five thousand people that included recreational, cultural, and business facilities to serve the area beyond its own limits. In Denmark Arne Jacobsen (fig. 19.2) built at Gentofte [1947]; and in Søholm at Klampenborg outside Copenhagen [1950] his clusters of small individual homes with terraces and common grounds effectively fused the spatial continuities and geometric-rectilinear vocabulary of Rationalism with the material and shed roofs of the local vernacular. Though these homes are much alike in setting their parallel facades in sequence, one behind the other, an idea that was apparent only in plan in Aalto's Sunila housing [1937-1939], each offers a sense of privacy rather than seeming part of any monolithic unity. Jørn Utzen's Kingohusene Court development of Elsinore in Denmark [designed 1953; completed 1960] achieved a more elaborate, looser, more organic unity with its sixty-three homes of the same yellow brick, sited undulatingly in the landscape. Far to the south, for the village of La Martella in southern Italy, Ludovico Quaroni's townplanning approach from 1949 clearly reflected the Scandinavian efforts of the forties.

In Great Britain soon after 1945 Scandinavian influence in the planning of large-scale housing was significant. We see a version of the small Danish court home, for instance, in the low buildings with terraces at the Ackroydon Estate, Wimbledon, London; and at the same complex the combination of terraced homes and eleven-story towers recalls such a development as Backström's and Reinius's Gröndal housing. Le Corbusier's *Ville Radieuse* ideas became important again in the Alton Estates, Roehampton, London [1952/53; erected 1955/59] built for some sixty-five hundred residents. A series of five ten-story slabs on columns is arranged as parallel diagonals on one side of a sloping, curving, central green, complemented on the other side by two widely separated groups of twelve-story apartment buildings. With their limited variety of International Style solutions repeated in varied groupings of buildings in a spacious landscape setting, an open urban environment was created that realized the first four principles of the CIAM's Athens Charter. Both Alton and Ackroydon Estates were planned by the housing division of the London County Council (LCC) that employed a staff of some three hundred architects, many of whom flourished in their own practices during the sixties.

In the USSR large residential buildings four- or five-stories high, but of dubious constructional quality, had appeared soon after the war (by 1948) in Moscow and other large cities. In their quest for standardized housing formulae Soviet architects were ignorant of the marvelous and sometimes grandiose statements of the "reactionary" Russian Constructivist architects of the twenties and early thirties. The buildings of Melnikov, Leonidev, and others had been destroyed and their working drawings banished to the depths of various state archives and forgotten. Thus, there appeared in the New Cheremushki area of Moscow in 1956 (three years after the death of Joseph Stalin) horizontal four- or five-story, gray, slab buildings and vertical nine-story structures, all apartment houses. Their arrangement on the site echoed the precepts of the CIAM, whether intentionally or not, rather than the more unusual recommendations of the Russian architects and planners of the twenties and early thirties. Very soon after 1956 the New Cheremushki types were built throughout the USSR and appeared as well in Eastern Europe, wherever massive low-cost housing was required.

Indeed, this very generalized concept (of combinations of horizontal and vertical apartment dwellings distributed broadly in a landscape) has remained from the time of the Athens Charter as an instrument for new-town planners and developers throughout the world. The following examples illustrate the variety that can be gained by working with these simple orientations. The complex of three twenty-story high rises, eight eleven-story slabs, and a block-long, three-story largely glass-enclosed shopping center—built 1960-1969 on the east side of Marszalkowska Street in Warsaw (fig. 32.1) according to the master plan of Zbigniew Karpiński[8]—is an excellent urban solution. It maintains the geometric vocabulary of the International Style without sinking to the commonplace statements made by many real estate developers around the world. The same functional combination of high- and low-rise buildings with a shopping center in Budapest's Kelenfold estate [1967-1968] though pleasant in its arrangement (fig. 25.2) lacks the lustre of the Warsaw construction. Complexes such as the Ciudad Tlatelolco project [1960-1974] in Mexico City by architect Mario Pani and Associates present immense developments (fig. 29.4) with some interesting variety introduced in the high-rise groupings and seem to encourage a minimalist view of individual human differences. Much the same may be said for the very abstractly beautiful, totally new city of Brasilia, begun in 1956. Caracas's Parque Central urban-renewal complex (fig. 38.4) recently completed by Siso, Shaw and Associates, is on a smaller scale. Even with seven very large slab buildings and two towering skyscrapers an elegance and humane interaction have been achieved, in spite of its mammoth dimensions. The slab structures taper out toward the bottom on their broader sides and are given a slanted roof; the skyscrapers are treated to an inventive variety of formal vertical articulations coursing from top to bottom; some of the landscaping has been by that master of landscape architecture, Roberto Burle-Marx of Brazil.

By the late 1950s the rejection of the spacious layouts of the Athens Charter was beautifully epitomized in the Halen Housing complex [1959-1960] nestled in a forested hilly site near Berne, Switzerland. Atelier 5 (Erwin Fritz, Samuel Gerber, Rolf Hesterberg, Hans Hostettler, Alfredo Pini, Fritz Thormann, and Niklaus Morgenthaler) succeeded eminently well in arranging seventy-nine three-story houses in five narrow, unequal, and closely set, terraced blocks. These blocks around a small rectangular community square for shopping, with a club room, service buildings, and swimming pool comprise an independent, highly compact settlement. Each house is narrow but long, finished in concrete, and has an enclosed walled garden. There is a unity and repetition that tends to characterize International Style projects, and though the vocabulary is essentially geometric there is an unexpected and pleasant diversity and variety of appearance to the whole. So compact an arrangement was made possible in part by the slope of the hillside into which the complex was built. Though virtually an ideal solution for urban building, without this immediate advantage of a hilly variation from the horizontal, the Halen arrangement was not easily repeatable in a city. In Switzerland variations upon this scheme of terraced hillside housing occurred at Umiken by Hans Ulrich Scherer with Team 2000 as architects and the Metron group as builders [1963-1965] and at Visp in André Studer's development [1964-1967].

Clearly, the planned community (advocated almost continuously in various forms since at least the nineteenth century, argued sometimes heatedly by the CIAM and its progeny such as Team X) is one of the most important trends in architecture actually built since the end of the Second World War, whether constructed for private or public use, for housing alone or for mixed usage, or for rural, suburban, or urban locations.

Long before the forties Le Corbusier had proposed a modern rebuilding of Paris that would start with the razing of extant quarters of the city [Plan Voisin, 1922]. Fortunately, this approach was rejected. Unhappily, however, many cities of Europe were confronted with so ruinous a condition after 1945, that it seemed more economic in terms of monetary value to clear away the rubble and begin anew. The entire central city of Rotterdam, having been savagely reduced to rubble during the early part of the war, was completely rebuilt, especially during the fifties, into a thriving modern metropolis. The reconstruction avoided the pitfalls of a stylistically uniform architecture by favoring varied versions of the International Style's geometry [Johannes H. Van den Broek and Jacob B. Bakema (fig. 30.2), Lijnbaan Shopping Center, 1949-1953; and compare the massive De Bijenkorf building nearby].

In the city centers of the world where land values have been perennially at a premium, economics once again was a determining factor. Consequently, coupled with the bulldozer complex, came the skyscraper, the high rise, and the massive block and slablike low rises. These buildings gradually encroached upon the once airy, sometimes broad, city streets and squares. During the postwar period not only was it natural to turn toward a politically benevolent, productive country for models, but vast and very much needed economic assistance had been forthcoming from that same land to both Europe and the Orient. The promise of similar assistance for South America was made with the Allianza para Progresso announced by President John F. Kennedy in 1962. The building technology of the United States was exported throughout the world, beginning in the 1940s, and combined more assuredly with local and regional inspiration and interpretation.

Subsequent Postwar Trends

SKYSCRAPERS AND ALTERNATIVES

In part for economic and political reasons, but more significantly because of the intrinsic talent of those who practiced and taught the profession of architecture in the United States, that country became the forge of the avant-garde for nearly two decades. This was particularly true of its applications of the International Style, which Frank Lloyd Wright (probably not apocryphally) called an architecture of "those glass cages." We should not lose sight of the fact that Ludwig Mies van der Rohe and Konrad Wachsmann, both having fled Nazi Germany, were teaching at the Illinois Institute of Technology in the 1940s and 1950s and that Mies's concepts of design found fertile ground not only in Chicago but also in New York [Seagram building with Philip Johnson, 1955-1958], Montreal [Westmount Square, 1965] and many other North American cities, either directly or through the work of his disciples.

Konrad Wachsmann, a pioneer in reinforced-concrete industrialized building and modular coordination, was sent abroad by the government of the United States to acquaint architects with the technological advances made in his new country. His Rationalist, structurist teaching was very eagerly received in the Federal Republic of Germany (during a single year of teaching at Ulm), in Austria (through summer seminars at Salzburg), and in Japan and Israel. With the seeds for a variety of vast structures effectively planted in this manner, the American proclivity for very tall buildings caused excitement, admiration, some theoretical discussion, and little else at first in Europe, with some few exceptions. Instead of European firms erecting skyscrapers, it was particularly the American firm of Skidmore, Owings and Merrill that spread the lofty gospel of the tall steel frame and the curtain wall in a series of technically demanding, tall buildings that eventually have girdled a good part of the world.

Such high rises as the Lever Brothers building in New York [1951-1952] and the Inland Steel building in Chicago [1956-1958] had their effects, for example, upon Arne Jacobsen in Denmark [SAS Air Terminal and Hotel, Copenhagen, 1960 (fig. 19.3)] and on the German firm of Helmut Hentrich and Hubert Petschnigg [Phoenix Rheinrohr AG Offices, Düsseldorf, 1956-1960]. The idea of separate parallel towers united in a simple design at the Inland Steel building (where service functions were clearly separated) was worked into the three slender unequal slabs of the Düsseldorf office building (shared functions) and appeared at virtually the same time in the twin slabs of Brasilia's Parliament Building [1956-1960] by Oscar Niemeyer. By the seventies not only Skidmore, Owings and Merrill but also Hentrich and Petschnigg were erecting skyscrapers in South Africa [Hentrich and Petschnigg's Standard Bank Headquarters building, Johannesburg, 1971] alongside the works of local architects that continued to employ the idiom [Colyn and Meiring's Trust Bank Centre, Cape Town, 1970; Philip Dowson et al., IBM building, Johannesburg, 1975]. And virtually isolated in the midst of far lower buildings, the Credit Lyonnais Tower [built by Cossutta and Associates in Lyons, France, 1972-1974] signals a distinctly non-American, European interpretation of the skyscraper.

One place in which the International Style skyscraper was metamorphosed into distinctive, locally favored forms as early as the late 1950s deserves special mention. In the nexus of Italian Rationalist theoreticians, indeed at their very hub in Milan, three major skyscrapers erected from 1956 into the 1960s, exemplify striking differences in design concepts. The twenty-six-story Velasca Tower [1956-1958] by Lodovico Belgioioso, Enrico Peressutti, and Ernesto N. Rogers (BBPR) first was developed from the International Style upon the drawing board and then was altered to the final "Medieval" tower (fig. 27.3) that rises today so high above the cityscape. The second skyscraper, the Galfa Tower [1957-1959] by Melchiorre Bega, sweeps swiftly upward in a light and delicate, glass curtain-wall pattern that lends a new subtlety to Rationalist thinking. But the most refined concepts are the result of collaboration between the architect (and publisher) Gio Ponti and that supreme structural engineer, Pier Luigi Nervi. In their thirty-four-story Pirelli Tower [1956-1959] an unusual, boat-shaped polygonal plan is recessed at either end to form shafts of shadow framed by solid, triangular-in-plan, end buttresses; the dark shafts contrast with the brilliant play of light that bathes the taut, glass-skinned, curtain wall of the broader segments of the building (fig. 27.4).

We should recognize that some forays into skyscrapers—or at least high-rise architecture—were made by architects beyond the bounds of the Rationalists. Two of the most prominent, Hans Scharoun and Alvar Aalto, both identified with more expressive trends, are represented, respectively, by the tamely eccentric "Romeo" flats tower [1954-1957], part of a larger complex at Stuttgart-Zuffenhausen that is lower in elevation; and by the Schönbühl apartment building, Lucerne [1965-1967], with its arching plan and facade broken into flat segments, some recessed in balconies, some with a broad, curving segment that opposes the building's shape.

Distinctive skyscrapers rather than high rises appear in the USSR from the late forties [Ministry of Foreign Affairs Building on Smolensky Square, 1948-1952, by V. G. Gilfreikh et al.], consisting of a build-up of tower elements toward a massive central tower that seems to be a more broadly conceived expression of some of the designs of prewar New

York City. Moscow skyscrapers became the models for buildings in many other cities of the USSR and Eastern Europe into the fifties (fig. 36.1). After Stalin's death (1953) their use diminished, and by the sixties interpretations upon International Style skyscrapers could be found [twenty-two- to twenty-six-story apartment houses on Kalininsky Prospect, Moscow, 1964-1969 (fig. 36.3) by M. V. Posokhin, A. A. Mdoyants and V. A. Svirskyl] throughout the Soviet Union and in Eastern Europe.

Though one finds skyscrapers in most large European cities, their concentration is rarely as great as, nor are they as tall as, in the cities of North America. Europe and most of the rest of the world outside of North America seems to have preferred a more moderate form, the high rise. The distinction in height between the high rise and the skyscraper cannot be generalized, for such terms are relative. But the proportions of the skyscraper are more elongated, whether in a central or rectangular plan building.

Rather than the skyscraper or the high rise, the low rise building has found worldwide favor in both residential and office buildings, stemming from the practicalities of building technologies and from the widespread ramifications of Le Corbusier's Unité d'Habitation slab block at Marseille [1947-1952 (fig. 21.2)]. This prewar design by the great master, though anticipated almost a decade earlier by him in Rio de Janeiro's Ministry of Health and Education building, did not come into full flower until the Marseille Unité was in place. Le Corbusier's basic building vocabulary articulated in these buildings sets forth in a multidwelling scale the logical consequences of his early notion (1914) of the independent skeletal structure: 1) free planning of space, 2) *pilotis* (supporting piers), 3) glass or curtain wall, 4) *brise-soleil* (sunbreaks), and 5) the roof terrace. The low-rise block and slab with many or all of Le Corbusier's five points have provided a basis for lively experimentation on every continent: whether marshalled in supercuadros or regular low-cost housing arrangements or contrasted with high rises; whether raised into a high rise itself or turned into a sweeping Y-shaped plan structure (Breuer et al.); whether built in one or another material or of prefabricated sections. Compared with the social intentions and architectural vocabulary of Le Corbusier's Unité, Carlo Aymonino's Gallaratese area buildings (fig. 27.2), a generation later at Milan [1967-1974], represent so much of a step forward in *formal* inventiveness and overall arrangements as to transcend their ultimate Marseille origin and lead in new directions.

BRUTALIST ATTITUDES AND PLASTIC RAMIFICATIONS

Concerns with materials as positive elements in architectural design had received new life in Europe and America early in the fifties thanks to the wide recognition afforded particularly to the Finns and especially to such efforts as Aalto's Säynätsalo Civic Center [1950-1952] in which bold brickwork outside is only occasionally dressed within and contrasts with the wood of ceilings, trusses, and furnishings. Between 1956 and 1961, Giovanni Michelucci's Autostrada church at Florence combined a concrete that displayed the imprint of the wooden grain of its temporary formers with small-stone-facing upon its interior and exterior wall surfaces. At Säynätsalo and in the Autostrada church, materials could be read in terms of their structural functioning. In many countries, too, during the forties and fifties an emphasis upon local materials in building had been part of a nationalistic romantic vernacular revival. Thus by the fifties there was a widely diffused underlying receptive attitude toward coarse materials and visibility of structure.

In theoretical terms, this attitude was first given an intellectual impact by Alison and Peter Smithson around 1953, under the banner of the "new Brutalism." Their thinking, as Jürgen Joedicke has pointed out " . . . revolved round a number of complementary ideas like responsibility, truth, objectivity, material and structural honesty and visibility," but their buildings present their theory only with a great deal of inconsistency.[9] The Smithson's New Brutalism stressed the openness not only of structure but also of the functioning parts of a building such as electrical and telephone conduits, heating and air conditioning ducts and plumbing systems. The machine-for-living became a reality in more than the spatial functioning of the building, as perhaps best exemplified in the brightly colored systems of the Centre Pompidou at the Place Beaubourg in Paris [1969-1976] by Richard Rogers, Renzo Piano, and Franchini and Young. This aspect of the New Brutalism grew out of and was inextricably wedded to the "old" Functionalism and the Rationalist's approach to architecture, not only in theory but also in buildings.

But the rapid spread of Brutalism in the late fifties and through most of the sixties is probably not traceable in the great workaday world to such intellectual formulations of an avant-garde, though no doubt they helped. Instead, once more we must look to Le Corbusier and his economically practical use of *béton brut* (rough concrete) throughout his Unité d'Habitation at Marseille [1947-1952] as a visible structural element—less economically used in combination with roughly finished brickwork in his Maisons-Jaoul of Neuilly, Paris [1954-1956]. It was from the easily understood term *béton brut* together with the relatively low cost of reinforced concrete that Brutalism came to have such a wide appeal through most of the 1960s. In more Rationalist manifestations it appears in Paul Rudolph's Yale University Art and Architecture Building (fig. 37.3), New Haven, Connecticut [1959-1963], and Ahrends, Burton and Koralek's Residential Building for Chichester Theological College, Chichester, England [1962-1968], both of which are heavily massed, open-structural statements. But Le Corbusier's handling of reinforced concrete had ramifications that went beyond Rationalism.

The formal Functionalism of the International Style that had most significantly yielded to the plastic pliability of reinforced concrete at Ronchamp [1954] was reinterpreted in Le Corbusier's more monumental work at Chandigarh, India [1951-1956]. Though on either of its ends the High Court Building (fig. 1.1) may resemble a great concrete box, that impression is quickly dispelled by the dramatic treatment of its recessed facade in staggered, open, *brise-soleil* boxes turning en masse outward toward the great space above, a facade broken asymmetrically by a group of three great upright pylons, with all of this protected by the immense continuity of the roof overhang. Ronchamp's sculptural quality, though irrational, was in that very manner an expression of the spiritual nature of the building. The drama of Chandigarh's Law Courts Building was a function of the necessary protection from the heat of a fierce sun. Nonetheless, above all else it is the plasticity of both buildings and their use of reinforced concrete to gain their effects that became the message for the sixties.

Any doubts of this must have been set aside when, at the end of the fifties, architects and critics recognized that even at the monastery of Sainte Marie de La Tourette [1956-1959]—where Le Corbusier returned to his Rationalist, rectilinear, geometric vocabulary—there was a forceful, even aggressive sculptural impact, for within its massive overall framework each body of design-elements

1.1. Le Corbusier, architect. High Court Building, view with principal façade. Chandigarh, India, 1951-1956. (Photograph: M. M. Puri, courtesy of the Director, Public Relations and Cultural Affairs, Chandigarh Administration)

vigorously asserted its own existence. And concrete left rough provided a textural effect that spoke further of vigor. The line between rational containment and irrational (?) projection of the building's "self" began to shatter, and the sixties saw a flood of ponderous ambitious architecture, broken into less ponderous pieces, all of which (or nearly so) served their functions even as they were caught up in emotion-provoking, exciting compositions.

The character of spaces changed. There was excitement inside as one discovered anew that space need not be taken for granted, but could stimulate, could even seem overpowering in its grandeur, and could still reserve for us familiar, closer confines into which, if we wished, we might retreat or from which we might view what we had experienced. Such spaces are Giovanni Michelucci's Autostrada church (of St. John the Baptist) outside of Florence [1956-1961] with its vast reverse tunnel vaults so tentlike within and without; the City Hall in Boston, Massachusetts [1962-1969] by Gerhard Kallmann, Noel McKinnell, and Edward Knowles, a free-standing building (fig. 37.4) fronting a large plaza with a facade very much in the mold of La Tourette and an interior with varying levels and exaggerated spatial contrasts; Kenzo Tange's Cultural Center at Nichinan, Japan [1961-1963], a kind of interlocking geometry of "action'' architecture in concept; and, finished in 1963, Hans Scharoun's masterpiece, the Philharmonic Concert Hall in Berlin.

To grasp the essence of Scharoun's space in the Berlin Philharmonic Concert Hall [1956-1963] requires of us an unusual effort to make visible the invisible. We may understand the foyer in its several interrelated levels of space from the sculpturesque struts and staircases, from close galleries that project into it and change direction, and from the changes in ceiling systems and levels as we traverse these various areas. But within the auditorium (fig. 22.3) it is quite a different matter: we are not meant to move; we sit and listen. The orchestra located in the center *is* the center of attention, and we look down upon it, while above it a canopylike section of ceiling shelters it. The seating is arranged in a great many geometric sections moving up and out from the orchestra so that the audience is—as it were—given a series of neighborhoods of colisteners. We do not attend en masse, but rather as individuals. The sharp bounds of many of the multileveled listening neighborhoods should each be read as ground plans with transparent enclosing planes rising on diagonals back over us and toward the walls beyond the reverse-canopied ceiling but dissolving before they reach that high. In this way we may reconstruct phantom, crystalline, cubistic, spaces clustering around the orchestra, so that the audience may find its special places within the hall while relating to the music. The treatment of space thus evokes a sculptural conception of solids akin to the aggressive agglomerations of much of the architecture of the sixties, but within it we are attuned to the transparency of sound—the purpose for which it was designed.

The highly plastic, emotive spaces that were built from Ronchamp through the sixties, with or without intended references to Mendelsohn, Häring, Scharoun, or Aalto, attest in themselves to the confident triumph of an Organic Expressionism in a time of political and economic optimism. Space, after all, is the primary architectural consideration, and from that architecture's solid manifestation sculptural form is developed. Considered spatially, we may view the TWA Terminal at Kennedy Airport, New York [1956-1962, by Eero Saarinen and Associates] in the context of an expressionist plasticity though not of Brutalism. Structurally aggressive and plastically graceful, its organization and evocation of the idea of flight in space moves us boldly and dynamically through the terminal.

Brutalism introduced a new sense of plastic solidity and spatial vitality into the modern architecture of the Americas, Europe, and Japan. An array of formal inventions is one of its bequests to us, from the unexpectedly simple, massive geometries of Marcel Breuer and Hamilton Smith at New York University's Bronx Campus [1957-1961] and the lively agglomerations of space around and within the open central areas of the Bank of London and South America in Buenos Aires (figs. 7.2 and 7.3) by Clorindo Testa and the architectural firm SEPRA [1960-1966] or Gustavo Medeiros's ''primordial'' clusters at the University of Oruro [1970] in Bolivia (fig. 11.2), to the heavy concrete, cubistically intricate forms of Walter Förderer (fig. 1.2) with an in-

1.2. Walter Förderer, architect. Church of St. Nicolas, interior. Hérémence, Switzerland, 1967-1971. (Photograph: Courtesy of Oswald Ruppen)

terior brilliantly transmuted by sunlight in his Church of St. Nicolas [1962-1971] at Hérémence, Switzerland. In Mexico Brutalism informed and reinforced the efforts of such architects as Pedro Ramírez Vázquez, Rafael Mijares, and Ricardo Legorreta to reestablish links with their national, pre-Hispanic aesthetics. And Brutalist expression such as Arata Isozaki's early Oita Prefectural Library, with its array of bold, reinforced-concrete geometries, constitutes one side of the new leading role that Japan came to play in the sixties.

SYSTEMS APPROACHES TO ARCHITECTURE

The rationalization of planning for housing, when predicated upon a strong industrial base and a mass market, must lead to prefabrication and reproductibility of parts for construction, as gradually and inevitably it did, most notably and most broadly in the Eastern European countries and the USSR from the decade of the fifties. For that part of the world reinforced concrete, especially, made possible the standardization of high- and low-rise slabs, mentioned above in the discussion of planning for urban renewal. The systematization of reinforced concrete and of steel construction, and sometimes of other materials as well, has occupied architects and fired their imaginations at least since the fifties and particularly from the sixties into the seventies. The plasticity of technological possibilities to reach out and shape man's environment has been explored in physical actuality.

The American inventor and universal planner Buckminster Fuller has emphasized systematic planning and growth in his clear-space-enclosure, geodesic-dome designs for the Union Tank Car Company [Baton Rouge, Louisiana, 1958] and for the USA Exhibition at Montreal's Expo '67, both of which still stand as impressive works, and in his proposal for a two-mile hemispherical dome to enclose central Manhattan, New York. However, despite his words and grandiloquent concepts of scale, the geodesic dome is, in its regular geometric configuration and its structure, a system that is closed rather than open and continuous. This would remain so even if the New York project were built and multiplied: the city would become segmented rather than continuous. Not only an inventor and planner, but also an excellent lecturer, Buckminster Fuller was his own best spokesman and presented his ideas throughout the United States, in Europe, and in Japan during the 1950s and 1960s. When Fuller's dome designs were first realized in the 1950s their magnitude alone was mind-boggling. But what was to come alongside of this during the 1960s and into the 1970s was equally so.

Le Corbusier *Ville Radieuse*, Wright's Broadacre City, Hilbersheimer's *Grosstadtarchitektur* and a host of earlier utopian proposals (often the springboards for later developments) were profoundly modified by the new technologies of the postwar era. In the Megastructure and Metabolism movements of the 1960s the essentially sequential and segmented nature of earlier utopian proposals was replaced by a new continuity that emphasized as its major binding element the transportation-communication axes of dense settlements.

MEGASTRUCTURES. As Reyner Banham has shown so well, megastructures—that is, huge interconnected structures that have a flexible, adaptive capacity, include a variety of different functions and are usually linear in the core of their plans—have been with us for a long time; but he maintains that "no deliberately designed megastructures existed in concrete fact before 1966."[10] Indeed one could probably reach back to Roman or even ancient Egyptian architecture for precedents. But this is hindsight, for in the ahistorical thinking of the majority of architectural-technologist-planners of the fifties and sixties such a return was unlikely. Instead, the advent of the megastructure was more immediately preceded and paralleled by an array of theoretical and sometimes whimsical proposals. Among the most notable were Louis Kahn's for urban revivifications in Philadelphia [Center City project, 1952; Viaduct plan, 1964]; Yona Friedman's "space frames in the air" suggested for Algiers, Paris, and New York [1957-1963];[11] the Archigram group's Walking City project [1963 by Ron Herron and Brian Harvey] and the same group's Plug-In City projects [1963-1964 by Peter Cook]. The last of these is the most interesting in its assortment of units formed by modern technology that are "plugged-in" to the whole.[12]

Projects in the form of drawings and models proliferated throughout the world from the Austrians Günther Domenig and Eilfried Huth's prize-winning (Cannes, 1969) Graz-Ragnitz model [1966-1969] that commanded so much attention throughout Europe, to the many projections of Japan's Metabolism group and to Paul Rudolph's Lower Manhattan Expressway scheme [1970]. The Brazilian Eduardo Affonso Reidy's large Pedregulho housing project [1947-1950], beautifully built in accord with the landscape (fig. 12.1) comes very close to being the first modern megastructure. Influenced no doubt by Le Corbusier's "Project 'A'" of 1931 for Algiers, it lacks the assertiveness and hardware usually associated with megastructures. For the Tucumán University project of Horacio Caminos in Argentina [begun 1951-1952 upon a mountain top but unfortunately not finished] Cesar Pelli—himself the architect of more than one megastructure candidate [Pacific Design Center, Los Angeles, 1976]—advocates precedence as the first megastructure. Less well known is the partially completed Helicoide project [1956] for the Roca Tarpeya, a mountain that divides the city of Caracas, Venezuela. Employing a design that recalls the forms of Frank Lloyd Wright's Pittsburgh, Pennsylvania, Civic Center project [1947] as a unifying device, Jorge Romero Gutiérrez, Pedro Neuberger, and Dirk Bornhorst terraced the mountain with cantilivered roads and the stores of a shopping center, all linked with a superhighway that connects both halves of the city. Whether or not one or another is the first, the avant-garde in South America seriously anticipated megastructural thinking and building elsewhere by more than a decade.

Outstanding among megastructures actually constructed with a built-in extensibility—one of the defining features of the type—are John Andrews's Scarborough College of the University of Toronto [1964-1966, fig. 13.8], a Brutalist design; Simon Fraser University in British Columbia, Canada, with its elegant open "social crossroads" space-frame by Arthur C. Erickson [1963-1965] with some buildings by others; and the projects realized by Ralph Erskine at Newcastle-on-Tyne (the Byker development, a "rustic" example according to Banham) and at Svappavaara, Sweden [1963-1964] north of the polar circle (figs. 1.3 and 1.4). There is a theoretical basis of systematic, additive, mechanistic design in the megastructure as built in the Occident that merges there with the high technology Pop display of the late sixties and the early seventies.

METABOLISM. Japan's Metabolist group, though it joined in the Occidental visions of the megastructure that were constructed from the mid-1960s, rested upon a different theoretical basis as its name suggests. Before the end of the 1950s Arata Isozaki and Kisho Kurokawa, both of whom had been working with Kenzo Tange on urban planning for Tokyo, began exchanging ideas informally with Kiyonori Kikutake, Fumihiko Maki, Masato Otaka, all architects then in their early thirties. They were joined by the journalist, Noboru Kawazoe. In 1960 they published a collection of their writings under the title, *Metabolism 1960*, and the name took hold almost immediately. At a time of rapid economic progress their central theme was maximum urban adaptation, recognizing that the perfecting of cities was impossible since new construction and replacement of worn-out architecture is a continuing process.

Tange had articulated the biological analogy upon which Metabolist theory was constructed at the Otterloo CIAM-Team X meeting the previous year. Introducing two urban-planning schemes of Kiyonori Kikutake, he stated that, "the structural element is thought of as a tree—a permanent element, with the dwelling units as leaves—temporary elements that fall down and are renewed. . . . The building can grow within this structure and die and grow again—but the structure remains."[13] This analogy is reflected in Tange's Tokyo Bay Plan (fig. 28.1)

1.3. Ralph Erskine, architect. Proposal for new town center of Svappavaara, northern Sweden, 1961. Rowhouses (1), theater meeting hall (2), various shelters (3), library (4), café (5), kitchen (6), school cafeteria (7), school (8), gymnasium and swimming pool (9), and residential megastructure as windbreak. (Photograph: Courtesy of Ralph Erskine from his sketch)

1.4. Ralph Erskine, architect. View of residential megastructure (detail) from sheltered side. Svappavaara, northern Sweden, 1963. (Photograph: Courtesy of Rolf Dahlström)

[published 1960] where the key to the problem of continuing overpopulation was the development of an appropriate transportation axis system, the "trunk and branches" of the urban "tree," that could expand or contract when necessary.

The organic precepts of Japanese traditional thought were brought to bear upon the modern urban situation and led beyond the Tokyo Bay Plan through the unfulfilled Tsukiji Plan [1961], with its remarkable skyscrapers linked by bridges and horizontal buildings at various levels, to his Yamanashi Communications Center [1966] at Kufu (fig. 28.2), the first fully built megastructure in Japan and perhaps the world. Grids of large vertical core shafts, containing service elements, root the Yamanashi center firmly to the earth, rise several stories, and are bridged by horizontal floors into which suites of rooms were built as required. Some floor sections are left out, providing dramatically great open spaces; some elements project from the grid system's vertical core shafts, and simply by adding such shafts the building may be expanded as the need occurs. (In this particular case, however, the neighboring structures made expansion quite unlikely, if not altogether impossible.) In the Yamanashi Communications Center only the single spine, the single axis element of Occidental megastructures, is lacking. But clearly in the megastructure, as a concept being realized, the architecture of Occident and Orient has become one. And just as clearly the CIAM ideal of a quiet order, that tended to create closed designs, whether of buildings or cities, was relinquished in favor of open structures. From this viewpoint the 1960s marked a highpoint of expansive postwar optimism in architecture as in other economic realities.

In one important sense Metabolism and Kenzo Tange denied the very nature of their basic analogy. Though aiming for growth in an organic fashion, though designing "open" structural arrangements, their structures were in *sequences* that confronted the possibilities of change. Sequential or systematic design has been a dominant mode, then, within both megastructural and Metabolist thinking.

THE RESULTS OF MEGASTRUCTURE AND METABOLISM. Though miles of large, essentially indoor, spaces in the city of Montreal are linked by broad underground passages as well as by the characteristic spine or transportation axis (the metro lines) of a megastructure and though we may point to megastructures throughout the world, particularly in universities and town centers, the *idea* of the megastructure had a greater impact than the frequency with which they were built. As with much contemporaneous avant-garde painting, such structures were very large and expansive: our concept of architectural scale was changed. It gained a megastep over the twenties. This raised questions again of contextual interrelationships in urban and natural environments, answers to which had in part been posed by, among others, Aalto's MIT dormitory, on a smaller scale, and by planners such as Giancarlo de Carlo in his renovation of the historic city center at Urbino [1956].

The expansiveness breathed into the architecture of the sixties and seventies by the visionaries of Metabolism and megastructure was expressed especially in the dominant stylistic attitude, Brutalism, of the late fifties and sixties. The Rationally interpreted Brutalism of Paul Rudolph's magnificent megastructural Government Service Center in Boston, Massachusetts [1962-1971] contrasts with the menacingly looming, Expressionist character of Gottfried Böhm's Pilgrimmage Church at Neviges, Germany [1966-1968] and the same architect's more controlled horizontality and still irrational angularity in the City Hall at Bensberg, Germany (fig. 22.3) [1965-1967]. Within the fabric of the city, the Boston City Hall [1969] is complemented by Rudolph's Government Service Center two blocks away. With other buildings, they each frame civic plazas of irregular form. The Bensberg City Hall dominates its surroundings, and, spread upon a hillside, it is more organically related to the preserved ruins of stone walls beneath it and the lower, saddleback roofs clustered near it.

This expansionist architectural aspect also found expression in a new range of modular construction, developed in its niceties, often in relation to a technology of prefabrication, by such people as Aldo van Eyck with square precast-concrete units in his Amsterdam Orphanage [1955-1960] and Louis Kahn in his University of Pennsylvania Richards Medical Research Center, Philadelphia [1957-1961], where an iconography of "served" and "servant" parts was articulated to comprise each modular unit. Kisho Kurokawa's Nakagin Capsule Building [1972] in Tokyo (fig. 28.4) is a prototype for a modular megastructural totality of concrete service-towers around which welded-steel, mass-produced rooms (capsules) are arranged, a prototype that has found no bright future. At Montreal's Expo '67 Moshe Safdie's Habitat caused a great deal of excitement whether or not one terms it a megastructure. A three-dimensional modular building system developed by him first as a student at McGill University, it consists of standardized precast-concrete room units attached to a horizontal zigzagging segment of a support system. With its tic-tac-toe buildup of apartments in space and its open man-made terraced hills, it recalled the panorama of Italian hill towns. Habitat remains a monument to the concept of a flexible and open, modular, residential system, the practical reality of which in the West has proven questionable. Toward 1970 Justus Dahinden in Switzerland formulated polyvalent modular residential building systems ["Trigon" Village at Doldertal, 1966-1969] of standardized prefabricated parts ("Heliopolis"), but there was a limited market and they were without adequate financial justification.

Particularly in office, hospital, and industrial building, however, systematization on a large scale has been finding wide acceptance [Centraal Beheer Office Complex, Apeldoorn, the Netherlands, 1968-1972, by Herman Hertzberger]. That the practicality of large-scale modular construction of dwellings rests with low costs and an all-too-anonymous mass market continues to be shown with its appearance in the East from Constantine Doxiadis's Bagdad, Iraq, housing colony to Vastu-Shilpa and B. V. Doshi's Hyderabad housing, India [1974].

Intrinsically, any systems-approach to architecture and urban planning imposes a modulus upon Man instead of taking Man as the modulus. With this approach, then, we have had a continuation of, and a series of variations upon, Man as the group rather than Man as the individual, Man as the rational and functional but apparently with little vent for Man as the irrational. It may well be, and this is an optimistic assessment indeed, that at least in architecture the emotionality of "Man" the generic and "man" the individual found its place within the rational but visionary developments of the sixties under the rubric of social concerns.

Summary of Postwar Trends

Throughout the decades since the Second World War we have questioned architecture's identities and this has taken on a more humanistic, individualizing tone.

In this essay we have considered the polar roots of modern architecture in the prewar period and the technological developments that enabled their expression in building. We have also taken into account the reaction to "Modernism" as in the public taste for anachronistic "revivals" and their continuations—evidently an attitude toward architecture handed down from the "neo's" of the nineteenth century. We have turned to the postwar period and its aftermath, finding in the establishment of *planning* throughout the world a realization of many of the goals of the prewar CIAM and, for the most part, a continuation of the International Style's formal vocabulary. We have seen that the export of the American *skyscraper* was not immediately successful, took hold only sporadically into the sixties, and showed signs of becoming better established during the seventies. Its main effect was in its compromised form, the *high rise*, a kind of building that reinforced CIAM and International Style concepts. Le Corbusier's influence after the war, in his Unité d'Habitation and in his amazing romance with a *new plasticity* at Ronchamp, was profound. The immediately wide appeal of *Brutalism* later, in the fifties and sixties, so largely attributable to his influence and probably secondarily to Aalto's—rather than to the intellectualizations of the Smithsons—was a manifestation of the new plastic trend in architecture, a trend broad enough to encompass both the Rationalist and Expressionist-Organic persuasions. In retrospect the argument could be made that this reuniting of the two major approaches to Functionalism would appear to have completed an historic cycle that began in the twenties, the result of which was to humanize architectural and functional form. And in so doing contemporary architecture was ready for a new departure. It was not long in coming, for Metabolism and Megastructure lent a new sense of scale and open, expansive progression to the field by the sixties. Since the fifties, with increasing intensity and vigor, systematic modular organization of buildings ("Structuralism") also was intensively and dynamically pursued, especially in Holland.

Continuing Trends

While all this was occurring, the nature of architectural thinking had been changing from the attractive abstractions of Modernism to more humanistic concerns.

CULTURAL-HISTORICAL CONTEXTUALISM

By the time that Aalto's MIT dormitory joined with the Cambridge environment without disrupting it [1948], the flight from the cities of America to the bright, grassy new suburbs had begun, and reconstruction of the cities destroyed between 1938 and 1946 was underway in other parts of the world. Sigfried Giedion's *Space, Time and Architecture* (1941), with its orientation toward the CIAM, Rationalism, and the history of architectural technology, most effectively synthesized ". . . human activities and the similarity of methods . . . in architecture, construction, painting, city planning, and science."[14] The book went into a second edition in 1949 and has remained vital for generations of students of architecture. Colin Rowe's essay, "The Mathematics of the Ideal Villa" (1947), followed by his "Mannerism and Modern Architecture" (1950) (both published in the *Architectural Review*, London) had the seminal effects of directing contemporary architects' imaginations to consider the relationships of the Modern Movement with sixteenth-century Italian architecture and of provoking a greater engagement with historical meanings beyond the stylistic and the technological.

By the early fifties Louis Kahn and Robert Venturi were both "roaming around Italy," looking at both the old and the new; they were followed by hordes of American tourists some of whom were or became architects. American architectural thinkers recognized not only history but cultures different from theirs, and turned these interests toward their own work and to a reassessment of their American environments.

Reconstruction brought with it much more than the bulldozer complex that we have mentioned. Whole sections of London and Amsterdam, for instance, were recycled during the 1950s and 1960s: that is, buildings that had been residences were fitted out for new uses, usually commercial. Their external appearances at least were retained so that they continued to fit into the fabric of the city. In European cities and in countryside villages as well, buildings in ruinous conditions were restored; or upon their sites detailed precise reproductions of prewar buildings were erected. The Gothic city hall of Trier, Germany, totally demolished in 1945, reappeared replete with statuary and brightly painted by the 1960s but recycled in its use. In the same city nearly half of a huge, late-Roman, Imperial Audience Hall was rebuilt and restored (by the Roman archaeologist Wilhelm Reusch) and is now used as a Protestant church. In Poland, eighteenth-century panoramic landscape paintings by visiting Venetians were employed as sources for reconstructions of ravaged quarters. In Rome, Mario Ridolfi, Ludovico Quaroni, and Mario Fiorentino saved the Tiburtino quarter [1949-1950] in an effort (fig. 27.1) that would have its effects upon later architects of the urban environment. These are typical of the activities that rescued much of Western Europe's architectural heritage. In Central and South America, generally, neo-Colonial and neo-Baroque-styled buildings continued to be erected.

The same may also be said generally for the United States into the air-conditioning revolution of the mid-1950s, while in the southeastern states there remains even now a predilection for the neo-Classical in many quarters. Contrasting with all of this were developments in and around the urban centers of North America. The fashionable move to the new suburbs left behind in the city centers a larger number of older neighborhoods than it was practical to convert to business usages: the Amsterdam model would not do. Indeed, until the sixties "recycling" was hardly ever recognized as a possibility for Canadian and American cities, outside of very limited circles. The entire physical character of downtown Montreal was changed from the early sixties as skyscrapers and high rises quickly followed where bulldozers' treads had been. In Chicago, Detroit, Saint Louis and elsewhere, buildings that would have remained derelict and withered in the encroaching "area of transition," between the city core and the nearby suburbs, dropped in value and were sold or rented to less economically advantaged people. In the midst of such neighborhoods and in the active downtown cores, buildings of historic value were razed and/or went unrecognized by public administrators.

In part this was a reflection of the tenor of the times, but in Chicago there can be no doubt that it also proceeded to extremes because of that city's particular obsession with the "new." In the 1950s and 1960s for Chicago the "new" was the Mies van der Rohe-Bauhaus-International Style brand of Functionalism and Rationalism, with Frank Lloyd Wright's Organic architecture still holding on but in the background. In so rich an array of successive waves of avant-garde buildings as existed in Chicago, concern for architecture's cultural past was largely excluded. In New York, where many new skyscrapers quickly replaced older skyscrapers and mammoth, utilitarian, public-housing blocks despoiled the fringe neighborhoods or created them, the past concerned architects even less, other than from a distant, rather academic, vantage point.

Inevitably, decisions on which buildings and neighborhoods were to be razed came to rest upon questions of historical and cultural symbolic values. Conversely, when new buildings or developments were to be erected questions were raised concerning their relationships to the urban fabric in terms of their physical presence and their functional and symbolic sociocultural values. Thus, born in the fifties and grown to early maturity by the late sixties, contextualism continued to play an important role in architecture and urban planning through the seventies. A building's meaning is more than its structure, function, or use: its image resides as well in the intricate systems of associations that it may trigger. As in a work of literature, music, painting, or sculpture, the richness of the responsive associative network has to do with cultural judgments of the quality as well as the imagery of architecture.

THE NEW ECLECTICISM

Robert Venturi's book *Complexity and Contradiction*, written in 1962, may be viewed as a response to the questions that are summed up in the word *contextualism*. Referring to the "varying heights and styles" of the buildings surrounding the Piazza San Marco in Venice, he asked, "Is there not a similar validity to the vitality of Times Square in which the jarring inconsistencies of buildings and billboards are contained within the consistent order of space itself?" And " . . . is not Main Street almost all right?"[15] He pursued his advocacy of taking to heart the lessons of the best of "ordinary buildings around us" and of Pop Art in architectural and urban design in *Learning from Las Vegas* (1972).[16] By then the contemporary architectural scene had changed.

One way in which it was deeply altered, if not permanently so, was in the very practice of architecture. Before 1960 Ralph Erskine was among the first to espouse the participation of prospective users in the designing of buildings, believing that "the built environment must express human presence." In effect this pushed to the fore one aspect of what had often been normal, for the architect to consult with his client, but extended it through much if not all of the design process. Erskine has demonstrated the effectiveness of user participation in his developments at Kiruna [1959-1961] in northernmost Sweden, in the Byker "wall" at Newcastle-on-Tyne [from 1968], and more recently in his very-much-altered project for Resolute Bay in Canada's Northwest Territory [1978], as well as in his smaller scale projects. The catchwords *user participation* helped bring about a newly vital social and political consciousness among architects and students of architecture, but it also demoralized many faculties of architectural schools and contributed to making political activists of many students by 1968.

The broad appeal of Venturi's emphasis upon integrating new architecture with, and creating from, the vernacular may have been derived from the continuing engagement of people around the world with their past styles, whether local, regional, or international and with the warm familiarity of their own immediate surroundings. In any case it provided a theory that, when exaggerated, became a lever that opened a Pandora's box of architectural hybrids and kitsch statements from the mid-1960s to the present.

Eclecticism (or *ad hocism*) came to be fashionable, and architects borrowed "images" and "reintegrated" them with their own thoughts in a virtual frenzy of uncertain directions that came to be called *Post-Modernism*, a positive term for the evidently negatively valued word, *eclecticism*. Many of these manners were short-lived so only those few *ad hocisms* that seem to have had some consequence for today will be considered here.

With a vast array of stylistic constituents admissible from so much of history's architecture (including folk expressions, each of which carried various meanings) new methods were sought to understand the complexities of architectural imagery. The relatively recently developed field of linguistics became a source of critical and structural analogies for "knowing" the significance of architectural works. The building took on a sometimes bewildering wealth of almost subliminal literary (semiotic) meanings, differing from critic to critic in their niceties, but—and so the theory goes—maintaining and projecting central imagistic contents. The fallacy here resides in the assumption of a similar background existing among all or nearly all who would wish to "read" a building.

An eclectic approach to architecture was clearly articulated as early as 1962-1965 in Vincenzo, Fausto, and Lucio Passarelli's bizarre multiuse building on Rome's via Romagna. There, a cubical, black, glass, curtain-wall structure some three-stories high (with a three-story parking area in exposed concrete beneath ground) is topped by a vastly different four-story superstructure of concrete with vines trailing from it. The shock created seeing it seems intentional, for the aggressive upper portion is set askew from the regular geometric form. Imagewise, the message from this is clear: apartments above—office building beneath. A few years later [1969] Wimmenauer, Szabo, Kaspar, and Meyer (in a model for a project that was never built) posed two huge linked glass tubes in parallel as a habitable structure upon an eighteenth-century building in Düsseldorf. Neither the vernacular styles available nor historic styles outside of the Modern Movement were used in Rome nor in the addition at Düsseldorf. That both used the current vocabulary of the Modern Movement should be stressed, since the compatibility of purist juxtapositions of forms seems to have been put in question.

Historic and geographically distant styles appeared in many buildings elsewhere. The exterior of the Casa Baldi [1959-1961] at Rome, by Paolo Portoghesi, architect, historian, and critic, recalls the well-known Hellenistic Temple of Venus at Baalbek [third century A.D.]. The sensitive Carlo Scarpa, a master at augmenting and renovating older buildings with structures in his own manner [Museum at Possagno, 1956-1957], skillfully incorporated Oriental split-circular and elliptical windows into shop designs in

Bologna and Venice, respectively. Charles Moore's fountain environment for the Piazza d'Italia in New Orleans [1975] used a time-honored Italian classical vocabulary in a new and surprisingly refreshing, colorful way; but not so with Philip Johnson's AT&T tower in New York [1977-1980], a farcical effort in which Brunelleschi's Pazzi Chapel facade-design of the Italian Renaissance is "quoted" in a grossly distorted scale at street level, while far above a neoclassically inspired broken pediment serves as the roofline.

In the United States during the 1960s and 1970s Robert Venturi, Robert Rauch, Robert A. M. Stern, John Hagman, and James Righter, among others, excerpted such elements as overhanging eaves, Palladian windows, semicircular dormer windows, dormers, pitched roofs, and occasionally the wood shingling of early twentieth-century American houses and created modern versions of the vernacular (fig. 37.6), informed with new spatial and sculptural interrelationships. The ongoing vernacular tradition continued quietly in Japan, for instance with Kiyonori Kikutake's Tokoen Hotel at Kaike Spa, Yonago [1963-1964] in which a high-rise design remains typically Japanese, employing tatami proportions but in concrete rather than wood. And an eighteenth-century South-German-Austrian vernacular, of oblong five- or six-story structures with steeply pitched roofs, was assimilated in concrete into the Lapin d'Or building [1969-1971] in Tokyo by the Takenaka Komuten [Construction] Company. The American redesigning of a vernacular tradition was looked upon with surprise by European avant-garde architects who had considered past and present as distinct. By the seventies outstandingly up-to-date combinations of their respective traditional architectural elements could be found in England [Robert Matthew and others, Hillingdon Civic Centre offices, Uxbridge, London, 1971-1976], France [M. T. A. Marot Tremblot, La Verrerie Housing at Amboise, 1970-1974] and the Netherlands [Abe Bonnema at Leeuwarde, 1972-1975, and Aldo van Eyck's Zwolle Housing, 1975].

Pop Art too came within the purview of architecture in the uses of huge graphic decorations (supergraphics) imposed upon and within buildings, as in Venturi's restaurant renovation in West Philadelphia [1962] and in a residence in Lourenço Marques by Amancio d'Alpoim Guedes. On a much larger scale, colorful supergraphics, such as bull's-eyes and industrial symbols, add greatly to the tightly clustered diverse masses of Minoru Takeyama's Ni-Ban-Kan highrise in Tokyo [1970]. Or consider the large "M" and colorful Pop Art decor of your local McDonald's restaurant.

Pop-realistic decoration was turned deliberately to surreal effect by Emile Aillaud in housing he accomplished at Nanterre, France [1969-1970]. Particularly in his Assembly Buildings at Dacca in Bangladesh [from 1962], Louis Kahn seems to come to the border of surrealistic composition in an associative, dreamlike series of forms. In 1967 he wrote of "meaning being answerable to belief" and that rather than a work of architecture being merely pleasant " . . . feeling must be in the back of it. . . ."[17] Indirectly, this suggests the subconscious. But more to the point is the evidence of the buildings themselves: their simple, geometric, solid forms on an unexpectedly large scale; the cutting-out, sometimes at odd angles, of circular, semicircular, and triangular sections from cubes and cylinders; screens formed by successions of large circular cutouts and placed nonconcentrically behind one another; and long, dark, cavernous series of tunnel vaulting. Dislocations of scale and sequence as well as formal simplifications are consistent with the artistic vocabulary of a great many surrealist painters. Whether or not this suggestion of a surrealist content in Kahn's highly plastic geometry seems likely, that there has been a distinctively surrealist trend abroad in some architectural circles at least since the seventies is indisputable. We need only look at: the elegantly evocative break down the center of a facade by Hans Hollein [1975] leading us into a Viennese jewelery shop; the crumpled tinfoil-like facades of Günther Domenig's Favoriten branch office (fig. 9.6) of the Central Savings Bank of Vienna [1975-1979]; the "54 Windows" house and clinic of Hiratsuka City in Kanagawa Prefecture, Japan, by Kazuhiro Ishii [1973-1975]; and Chicago architect Thomas Hall Beeby's "House of Virgil" project in Wisconsin [1981] with its return to a preindustrial "Golden Age" expressed not as much formally as in ornamentation. It is difficult to predict how widespread surrealism (as opposed to such visionary or even sci-fi architecture as Agustín Hernández's own atelier [1976-1977], in Mexico, fig. 29.9) will be in the architecture of the 1980s and 1990s.

THE RENEWAL OF MODERNISM

At approximately the time, during the sixties, when this eclectic, seeming fragmentation and apparent reversal of the Modern Movement came to the fore and throughout the so-called Post-Modern period, mainstream, Modern-Movement, formal geometric designs have continued to pour forth from innumerable creative quarters. Perhaps it would be best to attempt to chart the sequence in which a new monumentality seems to have come toward fruition.

We have already mentioned the new expansiveness

of architecture sparked by Metabolism and the short-lived megastructure mania. The notions of growth integral to both used a biological idiom, derived, for instance, from minute studies of insects' wing structures, as in the huge, almost amorphous "tents" of Frei Otto (fig. 22.5). But size notwithstanding, their "soft" effects prevent these fascinating structures from qualifying as monumental. At Expo '67 in Montreal, Carlos Raúl Villanueva's very beautiful Venezuela Pavilion (fig. 38.3) was for his own personal development—a clarifying work in a severe, disciplined, minimal, geometric formulation resembling minimalist sculptures. The minimal art and architecture that explored very simple forms may have provided both a pause and an alternative to the rash of idiosyncratic developments of the 1960s. In essence, stylistically we have a clarification of formalism in the midst of eclecticism and Brutalism. At that same time projects underway included Marcel Breuer's inverted-stepping of solid cubical form in the Whitney Museum, New York [1963-1965], I. M. Pei's Everson Museum of Art at Syracuse, New York [1962-1968], and Arthur C. Erickson's glass wedges at Osaka's Expo '70 [1967-1969], all basically simple, yet sophisticatedly proportioned, formalist solutions.

It was particularly with the advancing technology of glass that mostly geometric, formalist solutions took precedence over the figurative, allegorical imagery of buildings in the second-half of the sixties and strongly into the seventies and to the present. There were neither vernacular nor Pop nor any other literary messages included in Cambridge University's History Faculty Building [1964-1968] by James Stirling, in the Barcelona office buildings [1965-1972] of José Antonio Coderch, in Skidmore, Owings and Merrill's Equibank Building (fig. 1.5) at Pittsburgh [1973-1976], nor in Welton Becket Associates' Hyatt Regency Hotel and Reunion Tower in Dallas, Texas [1973-1978]. They seem instead to have celebrated a rebirth on a grand scale of the abstractions of architecture put forth during the earlier prewar years of the Modern Movement. The Dallas Hyatt Regency with its clustered vertical forms building up to futuristic towers and its breadth on a grand scale, and the Pittsburgh Equibank Building with its polygonal towers joined as a unit, point to formal explorations that go beyond the realm of mass to realize anew spatial volumes as well. Not only the reflective factor of glass but actually the building's formal situation within urban space seem part of a design philosophy that fuses the building with the context of its surroundings.

The drama of the new monumentality is very evident in the juxtaposition of multiple wedge-forms in I. M. Pei's East Building for the National Gallery of Art (figs. 1.6 and 1.7) [Washington, D.C., 1971-1978]. Monumentality in Andrault and Parat's University of Paris, Faculté de Tolbiac at Paris [1971-1973] and in Arata Isozaki's Kitakyushu City Art Museum is based upon an activation, or potential for activation, built into their compositions. Movement is implied by diagonal thrusts and diagonally contrasting masses and spaces in the Pei building. In the Paris building clear and simple glass cubes, horizontally separated and pierced by slim concrete towers, cluster around more substantial, though still slim towers unequal in height. Rooted to a podium, they are partly encircled by a series of low, broad cylinders. The tensions of formal interplays here force upon us a realization of motion as a threatening possibility. Finally, in the Kitakyushu Museum twin very substantial, long and parallel building elements, although brought together as parts of one building, are also thrust daringly out beyond their visible supporting structures in a forceful cantilevering.

1.5 Skidmore, Owings and Merrill, architects. Equibank Building. Pittsburgh, 1973-1976. (Photograph: Courtesy of Ezra Stoller © ESTO)

1.6. I. M. Pei, architect. The National Gallery of Art, entry façade. Washington, D.C., 1971-1978. (Photograph: Courtesy of Edith S. Sanderson)

One of two more factors inevitably contributing to a new monumentalism is the neo-Rationalist movement exemplified in the grand projects of Leon and Rob Krier in London and Vienna and in the work of Aldo Rossi in Italy. Rossi's contribution to the Gallaratese housing area at Milan [1969-1973] is coldly and remarkably beautiful (fig. 1.8) in its parallelism with the central, long building of the complex by Carlo Aymonino. It exists as a much more highly abstract, very long, cubiform structure. Though articulated in sections, with rows of *pilotis* framing a seemingly endless portico and square windows aligned in two and three stories above, it has so great a sense of refined, unadorned surface, so great an abstracted regularity of form, that it seems fragilely but hermetically sealed off from its immediate neighbor. One wants to whisper, and who would dare to hang out laundry? Rossi in all of his work seems to prefer pure geometric forms in alignment [project for a municipal building at Scandicci, Florence, 1969, with Massimo Scolari] or otherwise simply arranged. His is a focus on ideology that relates to absolutism, whatever the social and political views he espouses.

One of the most important contributions to the rebirth of Modernism and to the new monumentality has been the rediscovery of space as something more than a mere background or foil for defining forms that have mass and tangible substance. When Le Corbusier created the thick walls of Ronchamp's church he did so by piercing them with splayed windows and by warping their surfaces, among other things, so that we became aware of their animated existence: he breathed life not only into the wall but also into the ceiling (as vaulting) and this was a part of what Brutalism came to be about, though few architects took him up on his ceiling "proposals." Space at Ronchamp is whatever the movement of walls and ceiling make of it: it is essentially pushed into being, for it was and has remained largely a kind of nonfactor—it is merely there, so to speak. Ronchamp's capturing of space, indeed space's subservience to the solidity of walls, ceilings, and floors, is essentially different from the proud and assertive, even heavy, quality of space that we sense in the Pantheon [second century A.D.] at Rome, or in the Audience Hall [fourth century A.D.] at Trier. In these Roman buildings space is virtually tangible.

1.7 I. M. Pei, architect. The National Gallery of Art, interior view of the great hall. Washington, D.C., 1971-1978. (Photograph: Courtesy of Edith S. Sanderson)

The Japanese, I believe, are particulary responsible for changing our assumption of passive space in architecture. Traditionally, in Japan space had not only a physical presence but also an image: it was something—not nothing. Hence, it was and is today a positive factor in Japanese architectural design. Hiromi Fujii, a member of the so-called Japanese New Wave, refers for example to the "quasi-quadratic elements that repeatedly appear in the walls of certain space compositions" and to "hollow forms."[18] For him architecture is composition of spaces; and forms need not be tangible. This is evident in his Marutake Building [1976] in Saitama Prefecture (fig. 1.9), where our interest passes through the quite flat, neutral walls that frame space: it is space contained immediately behind the huge windowlike frames that engages our attention.

Among others, Steven Kent Peterson of the New York firm Chimacoff/Peterson would seem to have approached an understanding of architecture in which the traditional Western values of wall versus space have been reversed in his firm's Lo Ho II house [1974] at Morristown, New Jersey. He states that its general configuration " . . . is distorted to wrap around formed external geometric spaces . . . [and it] is conceived of as background walls to a garden of volumetric space."[19]

The recognition of space as a factor in architectural composition is expressed within buildings as well as outside of them, for example, in the quite complex designs of Peter Eisenman, Michael Graves,

1.8. Aldo Rossi, architect. Gallaratese Housing. Milan, 1969-1973. (Photograph: Courtesy of the architect, Centro Di, and Francesco Maschini)

1.9. Hiromi Fujii, architect. Marutake Building, Saitama Prefecture. Japan, 1976. (Photograph: Courtesy of the architect)

Charles Gwathmey, John Hejduk, and Richard Meier. But one cannot speak of space as a prime factor in their work: a sense of geometric structure motivates their architectural discourses; and space, though finally cubistically mannered, is more traditionally Western than in Peterson's work. It is neither palpable nor monumental. Part of the impressiveness of Aldo Rossi's Gallaratese building and his small courtyard of the Broni school [1971] and also of Mario Botta's secondary school at Morbio Inferiore, Switzerland [1972-1976], is in the presence of an almost tangible space. These are part of the new monumentality, despite their different scales. When an understanding of space as coequal in importance with mass exists [Skidmore, Owings and Merrill's National Commercial Bank project, 1977-1980, Jeddah, Saudi Arabia], when space is shaped as an architectural element in a delicate but full relationship with mass [I. M. Pei's Kennedy Library, 1979, Boston], and when the building exists as part of and integrated with space around it [Arata Isozaki's Shukosha Building, 1973-1975, Fukuoka City, Japan], then the expression of monumentality will appear not overbearing as we often understand it to be but instead fitting and proper [Kisho Kurokawa and Associates, Fukuoka Bank Headquarters Building, Fukuoka Prefecture, 1971-1975].

Of all the trends mentioned in this essay, perhaps the most important has not yet been singled out: the full entrance of an architectural sensitivity different from that of the prewar Modernists—that of the architects of Japan—into contemporary avant-garde architecture. The cross-fertilization of ideas between cultures grown toward one another lends a new understanding and will continue to revitalize architecture in the eighties.

Notes

1. Vincent Scully, *The Earth, the Temple and the Gods. Greek Sacred Architecture* (New Haven: Yale University Press, 1962) discusses this ancient practice.
2. Bruno Zevi, *Verso un Architettura Organica* (Turin: Einaudi, 1945).
3. Sigfried Giedion, *Space, Time and Architecture*, 5th ed. (Cambridge, Mass.: Harvard University Press, 1967), p. 872ff.
4. Cf. H. Brenner, *Die Kunstpolitik des Nationalsozialismus* (Hamburg, 1963).
5. These variations are discussed at some length within still other classifications in Charles Jencks, *Modern Movements in Architecture* (New York: Anchor Press/Doubleday, 1973).
6. Giedion, *Space, Time and Architecture*, pp. 696-704.
7. "CIAM: Charter of Athens: Tenets," reprinted from Le Corbusier's 1941 publication in Ulrich Conrads, ed., *Programs and Manifestoes on Twentieth-Century Architecture* (Cambridge, Mass.: MIT Press), pp. 137-45.
8. Among the architects involved in designing these buildings were Jerzy Waclawek, Jan Klewin, Marcin and Jan Boguslaroski, Jerzy Kowarski, and Jerzy Jakubowicz.
9. Jürgen Joedicke, *Architecture since 1945, Sources and Directions* (New York: Praeger, 1969), p. 109.
10. Reyner Banham, *Megastructure, Urban Futures of the Recent Past* (New York: Harper and Row, 1976), p. 13.
11. *See also* Yona Friedman, *Towards a Scientific Architecture* (Cambridge, Mass.: MIT Press, 1980) for an exposition of a humanized "universal" systems architecture.
12. Peter Cook, ed., *Archigram* (London: Studio Vista, 1972).
13. Oscar Newman, ed., *CIAM '59 in Otterloo* (London and New York: 1961), p. 186.
14. Giedion, *Space, Time and Architecture*, p. vi.
15. Robert Venturi, *Complexity and Contradiction in Architecture* (New York: Museum of Modern Art, 1977), p. 54.
16. Robert Venturi, Steven Izenour, and Denise Scott Brown, *Learning from Las Vegas* (Cambridge, Mass.: MIT Press, 1972).
17. Louis Kahn, *Perspecta 10/11* (New Haven: Yale University Press, 1967), p. 305.
18. Kenneth Frampton, ed., *New Wave of Japanese Ar-*

chitecture (New York: Institute for Architecture and Urban Studies, 1978), catalog 10, p. 30.

19. Steven Kent Peterson, "Space and Anti-Space," *The Harvard Architecture Review* 1 (Spring, 1980): 111.

Bibliography

BOOKS

The New City: Architecture and Urban Renewal. Catalog of an Exhibition. New York: Museum of Modern Art, 1967.

Ambasz, Emilio. *The Architecture of Luis Barragán.* New York: Museum of Modern Art, 1976.

Bächer, Max, ed. *Walter M. Förderer: Architecture, Sculpture.* Neuchâtel: Editions du Griffon, 1975.

Bachmann, Jul and von Moos, Stanislaus. *New Directions in Swiss Architecture.* New York: George Braziller, 1969.

Banham, Reyner. *Megastructure, Urban Futures of the Recent Past.* New York: Harper and Row, 1976.

______. *The New Brutalism.* New York: Reinhold, 1966.

Benevolo, Leonardo. *Storia dell'archittetura moderna.* Vol. 2. Bari: Editioni Laterza, 1960.

Bohigas, Oriol. *Arquitectura Modernista.* Barcelona: Lumen, 1968.

Bush-Brown, Harold. *Beaux-Arts to Bauhaus and Beyond.* New York: Whitney Library of Design, Watson-Guptill, 1976.

Cetto, Max L. *Modern Architecture in Mexico.* London: Alec Tiranti, Ltd., 1961.

Cohen, J. L.; De Michelis, M.; and Tafuri, M. *La Città, L'architettura URSS, 1917-1978.* Rome: Officina Edizioni, and Paris: L'Equerre, 1979.

Conrads, Ulrich, ed. *Programs and Manifestoes on 20th-Century Architecture.* Cambridge, Mass.: MIT Press, 1970.

Cook, Peter, ed. *Archigram.* London: Studio Vista, 1972.

Dahinden, Justus. *Thinking, Feeling, Acting.* Pully Lausanne: Anthony Kraft, 1973.

Delevoy, Robert I. *Rational Architecture.* Brussels: Archives d'Architecture Moderne, 1978.

Drew, Philip. *Third Generation, the Changing Meaning of Architecture.* New York: Praeger, 1972.

Drexler, Arthur. *Transformations in Modern Architecture.* New York: Museum of Modern Art, 1979.

Flores, Carlos. *Arquitectura Española Contemporanea.* Bilboa: Aquilar, 1961.

Frampton, Kenneth; Drexler, Arthur; and Rowe, Colin. *Five Architects: Eisenman, Graves, Gwathmey, Hejduk, Meier.* New York: Oxford University Press, 1975.

Frampton, Kenneth, ed. *New Wave of Japanese Architecture.* Catalog 10. New York: Institute for Architecture and Urban Studies, 1978.

Friedman, Yona. *Towards a Scientific Architecture.* Cambridge, Mass.: MIT Press, 1980.

Giedion, Sigfried. *Space, Time and Architecture.* 5th ed. Cambridge, Mass.: Harvard University Press, 1967.

Glaeser, Ludwig. *The Work of Frei Otto.* New York: Museum of Modern Art, 1972.

Gregotti, Vittorio, ed. *Architettura, Urbanistica e Disegno Industriale.* Vols. 31, 32, 33. L'Arte Moderna series. Milan: Fratelli Fabbri, 1967.

Harvard Graduate School of Design Students. *The Harvard Architecture Review* 1 (Spring). Cambridge, Mass.: MIT Press, 1980.

Hitchcock, Henry-Russell. *Architecture: Nineteenth and Twentieth Centuries.* Harmondsworth: Pelican History of Art, 1958.

Howard, Ebenezer. *Garden Cities of Tomorrow.* London: S. Sonnenschein & Co., 1902 (orig. pub. as *Tomorrow,* 1898.

Jacobs, Jane. *The Death and Life of Great American Cities.* New York: Random House, 1961.

Jacobus, John. *Twentieth Century Architecture: The Middle Years, 1940-65.* New York: Praeger, 1966.

Jencks, Charles. *The Language of Post-Modern Architecture.* New York: Rizzoli, 1977.

______. *Modern Movements in Architecture.* Garden City, N.Y: Anchor Press/Doubleday, 1973.

Joedicke, Jürgen. *Architektur und Städtebau—Das Werk der Architekten van den Broek und Bakema.* Stuttgart: Gerd Hatje Verlag, 1963.

______. *Architecture since 1945, Sources and Directions.* New York: Praeger, 1969.

Kellen, D., van der and Blanklenstijn, H. *Illustrated International Architecture.* Vol. 1, 1967: Vol. 2, n.d.; Vol. 3, 1969. The Hague: Ten Hagen, N.V.

Koenig, Giovanni Klaus. *Analisi strutturale delle sette invarianti zeviane.* Florence: Fiorentina, 1976.

Krenz, Gerhard. *Architektur Zwischen Gestern und Morgen: ein Vierteljahrhundert Architekturentwicklung in der DDR.* Stuttgart: Deutsche Verlag Anstalt, 1975.

Kulterman, Udo. *New Architecture in Africa.* London: Thames and Hudson, 1963.

______. *New Architecture in the World.* Rev. ed. Boulder, Colo.: Westview, 1976.

Pehnt, Wolfgang, ed. and Hatje, Gerd, general ed. *Encyclopaedia of Modern Architecture.* London: Thames and Hudson, 1963.

Ragon, Michel. *The Aesthetics of Contemporary Architecture,* Neuchâtel: Editions du Griffon, 1968.

Richards, J. M., ed. *Who's Who in Architecture.* London: Weidenfeld and Nicolson, 1977.

Ross, Michael Franklin. *Beyond Metabolism. The New Japanese Architecture.* New York: McGraw-Hill, 1978.

Rowe, Colin. *Mathematics of the Ideal Villa and Other Essays.* Cambridge, Mass.: MIT Press, 1976.

Schück, Armin. *Altersheime, Altersiedlungen, Alterswohnungen.* Rüschlikon: Schück Söhne Verlag des Schweizer Baublatt, 1976.

Sharp, Dennis, ed. *The Rationalists: Theory and Design in the Modern Movement.* London: Architectural Press, 1978.

______. *A Visual History of Twentieth Century Archi-*

tecture. Greenwich, Conn.: New York Graphic Society, 1972.

Sivo, Benito de. *L'Architettura in Svizzera Oggi*, Naples: Edizione Scientifiche Italiane, 1968.

Smithson, Alison, ed. *Team Ten Primer*. Cambridge, Mass.: MIT Press, 1968.

Tafuri, Manfredo. *Architecture and Utopia*. Cambridge, Mass.: MIT Press, 1975.

Venturi, Robert. *Complexity and Contradiction in Architecture*. New York: Museum of Modern Art, 1977.

Waetzoldt, Stephan and Haas, Verena, general eds. *Tendenzen der Zwanziger Jahre, 15: Europäische Kunstaustellung*. Berlin: Dietrich Reimes Verlag, 1977.

Zevi, Bruno. *Architecture as Space*. Translated by Milton Gendel. Edited by Joseph A. Barry. Rev. ed. New York: Horizon Press, 1974.

______. *The Modern Language of Architecture*. Seattle: University of Washington Press, 1978.

JOURNALS

"Dolf Schnebli." *Architecture and Urbanism* 98 (November 1978): 3-40.

"Suisse," *L'Architecture d'Aujourd'hui* 121 (June 1965): xxi-xxxi, 1-100.

"Le Corbusier, 1910-1934." *Architecture, Mouvement, Continuité* 49, special issue (September 1979).

"Les Années 70 de Carlo Scarpa." *Architecture, Mouvement, Continuité* 50, special issue (December 1979).

"Ein Reisebericht ans Barcelona." *Bauen and Wohnen* 32 (January 1978): 9-28.

"Recent Architecture in the Countries of the Arabian Gulf." *Domus* 595 (June 1979): 1-47.

"Mexican Architecture 1968-78" [in French]. *Techniques et Architecture* 320 (June 1978): 119-46.

"60 Jahre Werk." *Werk* 60, jubilee issue (December 1973).

Alba, A. F. (Introduction). "Espagne: Madrid, Barcelone." *L'Architecture d'Aujourd'hui* 149 (1970): xi-xlii, 105.

Bense, Max. "Architecture et sémiotique." *L'Architecture d'Aujourd'hui* 178 (March-April 1975): 107-112.

Lüchinger, Arnulf; Hertzberger, Herman; van Eyck, Aldo; et al. "Strukturalismus—eine neue Strömung in der Architektur." *Bauen und Wohnen* 30, no. 1 (1976): 5-40.

Mechkat, Cyrus and Socratides, Costas. "Export—Architektur." *Werk—Archithese* 29-30 (May 1979): 1-60.

Pommer, Richard. "The New Architectural Supremacists." *Architectural Forum* (October 1976): 38-43.

2

ARCHITECTURAL THEORY AND CRITICISM SINCE 1945

BRUNO ZEVI

Sigfried Giedion's book, *Space, Time and Architecture*, was published in 1941 and had an immediate and vast success in the English-speaking countries. After the Second World War, it was translated into many languages and remained a basic text for almost two decades. Even the historians who did not agree with Giedion's interpretation of the birth and development of the Modern Movement were ready to recognize that his book was a fundamental, though very controversial, contribution. In 1945 the author of the present essay wrote a book, *Towards an Organic Architecture*. It was fully "anti-Giedion," and for it to be so it depended very much on Giedion's work.

Architectural theory and criticism since 1945 may well start with *Space, Time and Architecture* because for a long time (since his position was quite clear) virtually all new architectural theories and interpretations were meant either to integrate or to oppose Giedion's thesis. Giedion felt that all that was valid in the Modern Movement derived from Cubism, and everything which did not derive from Cubism—namely, Expressionism, Constructivism, post-Cubism in general—was rather insignificant or essentially negative. In his book, he neither mentioned Antonio Gaudí and Erich Mendelsohn, nor did he find any relevance in Erik Gunnar Asplund and the Scandinavian development since the Stockholm Exhibition of 1930. Of course, writing in the United States, he had to take into consideration the genius of Frank Lloyd Wright, but he treated it as an isolated phenomenon. It is worthwhile to remember that, in the first edition of the book, not even Alvar Aalto was considered; the Finnish architect was too "Organic" or too "Expressionist" for his taste. For Giorgio Vasari, art history ended with Michelangelo; for Giedion, the Modern Movement achieved its perfection with Le Corbusier and the Bauhaus.

For about a decade, historians and critics tried to correct Giedion's vision. On the urban scale, the humanistic ideas of Lewis Mumford were very influential, as was the theme analyzed during the seventh International Congress for Modern Architecture, held at Bergamo in 1949: "The Heart of the City." On the strictly architectural scale, the tendency was to emphasize the importance of space and comfort, against mere volumes and technics. Some important books that reflected these trends are: *Art and the Nature of Architecture* by Allsopp Bruce, *Architecture as Space* by Bruno Zevi, *Theory and Design in the First Machine Age* by Reyner Banham, *Intentions in Architecture* by Christian Norberg-Schultz.[1] In this period many theories formulated in Europe between the two world wars, and particularly the ideas of the Dutch group, "De Stijl," were diffused beyond the limited circles of specialists.

Around 1955, in a sudden change of taste, Expressionism was rediscovered. Eero Saarinen in the United States, Hans Scharoun in Germany and Oscar Niemeyer in Brazil flatly refused the boxlike solutions of Cubism, as Wright and Aalto had already done. More surprisingly, in the Chapelle de Ronchamp [1950-1954] Le Corbusier himself had repudiated the famous "five principles" of 1921: that is, the *pilotis*, the free plan, the strip window, the free facade, and the roof garden. The International Style architects thus lost their father and God, whose approach seemed to become quite similar to that of the Expressionists. In the Chapelle de Ronchamp was the rediscovery of both Gaudí and Mendelsohn. In May 1962 the Department of Art

History and Archaeology and the Avery Architectural Library of Columbia University organized a symposium on the theme "From the Novembergruppe to the C.I.A.M." In October 1964 the XXVII Maggio Musicale Fiorentino held an international congress on Expressionism. The congress became almost a nemesis of the International Style, which was violently criticized. People began to consider the crisis of the Modern Movement; and the confusion that ensued led Robin Boyd to write his book, *The Puzzle of Architecture.*

Robert Venturi's essay, *Complexity and Contradiction in Architecture,* appeared in 1966, one year after Boyd's *Puzzle.* Its theory was based on the experience of sixteenth-century Mannerism, with which, in fact, the modern situation was rather analogous. The masters of the Modern Movement were disappearing. Mendelsohn died in 1953, Wright in 1959, Le Corbusier in 1965. Gropius and Mies van der Rohe died in 1969, but creatively they had disappeared before: the former falling back into the eclecticism of the Bagdad University project [1960] and the Classicism of the American Embassy in Athens [1961], and the latter collaborating with Philip Johnson in the static, symmetrical Seagram Building in New York [1958]. Young architects lost their guides and felt orphaned. What were they to do? In the first place, they tried to invent a new father, Louis Kahn. Then, it was Kahn's pupil, Venturi, who promoted the same operation that had been accomplished by the heirs of Michelangelo, Raphael, and Leonardo da Vinci, namely a combining of styles. Instead of the "pure," doctrinaire, uniform approach of the International Style, there arose a tendency that was highly intellectual but open to historical memories and heterogeneous impulses. It may be useful to remember that Arnold Hauser's book, *Mannerism—The Crisis of the Renaissance and the Origin of Modern Art,* had just been published in 1965. And in the same year Marcus Whiffen edited for the MIT Press *The History, Theory and Criticism of Architecture* in which he collected essays by Stanford Anderson, Reyner Banham, Serge Chermayeff, Peter Collins, Stephen W. Jacobs, Sibyl Moholy-Nagy, and Bruno Zevi. The illusion was synthesized in the slogan, "The Future of the Past." Since 1961, Jane Jacobs's *The Death and Life of Great American Cities* had meant a revolt against urban renewal: decayed quarters and even slums could be regenerated and there was no need to destroy them. In a similar way, past architecture with its diversity of forms could provide some blood for the anemic contemporary idiom. Many felt that inspiration should not be derived from the great works of the past but from the *Architecture without Architects,* the anonymous building that Bernard Rudofsky was exalting.

In the late 1960s and in the 1970s, semiology and linguistics invaded the architectural field. The manneristic experience continued but was not satisfactory. Something more solid and scientific was needed and therefore research on verbal and behavioral communication was extended to cities and buildings. Among the most interesting contributions, we can mention: *Meaning in Architecture* edited by Charles Jencks and George Baird in 1969, *Architettura come mass medium* by Renato De Fusco, *Teoria e storia dell'architettura* by Manfredo Tafuri, *Architettura e comunicazione* by Giovanni Klaus Koenig, *Appunti per una semiologia delle comunicazioni visive* by Umberto Eco, *The Modern Language of Architecture* by Bruno Zevi, *The Language of Post-Modern Architecture* by Charles Jencks,[2] and many writings published in the American magazines *Perspecta* and *Oppositions* and the Italian magazine *Op. cit.* The last significant event to be registered is the International Symposium on Organic Architecture, held in London in September 1978, an attempt to revitalize the Modern Movement against the suicidal trend of the "post-Modern."

After this brief and necessarily incomplete panorama, we may examine the main principles of architecture today, as they derive both from the creative works of building and from theory and criticism. Our purpose is to show that crisis and confusion in architecture are much less relevant than is generally felt. In reality, since 1945 a method of architectural communication has been developed, even if many architects and critics are not yet quite conscious of it.

Destructuring Architectural Grammar and Syntax

Theories developed since 1945 confirm that William Morris's philosophy is at the basis of modern aesthetics in architecture. A building is no longer a closed image, a performance to be contemplated from outside, an object having its own formal equilibrium, achieved through a synthesis either a priori or a posteriori. The machinery of the Classical "orders," from Vitruvius to Palladio, is totally dismissed, together with the apparatus of decorations. All past modes and notions are refused. The zero degree of architectural "writing" has thus been reached.

The range of architectural activity has been so broadened that it includes the entire environment of human life. For Morris all modifications of the earth, and especially alterations of the landscape, concern architecture. A new task, a new challenge has come into being which makes almost grotesque the abstract values of "beauty," "symmetry," "rhythm," "golden proportion," "style," "balance," and "harmony." Architects are called to a responsibility concerning town and country, something much bigger than "fine arts." They have to invent not the building but the kind of life that goes on in it. Since this invention must have a social, democratic approach, it cannot use the preconceived rules of the academy.

The problem consists in a destructuring of the conventional patterns of architectural speech. No prefabricated phrases are allowed. Every word—that means every window, door, corner, room—has to have its own justification. Mechanical repetition of modules, openings, dimensions is condemned. Function and content are the keys of design and forms will follow. As in the Middle Ages, adjectives and often verbs are eliminated. The list, the inventory of functions and contents, becomes the technique of communication, without any concern for the final result. Actually, a final result should not exist. All relevance is given to process, which is supposed to remain open in order to accept all vital changes and variations.

The Conquest of Dissonance

The zero degree, atonalism, destructuring, the method of listing, all imply a resemantization of the architectural dictionary. In the Middle Ages a language had to be reconstructed on the ruins of the Roman and Byzantine worlds. In our age an alternative form of communication must be developed: it should be able to annihilate the rules of its own game at any moment and go back to origins, to the inventory of functions. This language should consider all departures or derogations not as exceptions to the rules but as rules in their own right. Dissonance in architecture goes back to Art Nouveau, but only recent theories have clarified its meaning. In music, the notion of dissonance is by now fully accepted because Arnold Schönberg not only used it but also codified the language of dissonance. In architecture, on the contrary, while all real artists have used dissonances, from Victor Horta to Aalto, Safdie, and Johansen, nobody, not even Wright nor Le Corbusier, formulated a code of architectural dissonances or antirules.

Tonality, according to Schönberg, is against freedom because each note depends on the preceding one and conditions the next. And Roland Barthes adds that classical writing is a class writing, accomplished through dogmatic resolutions, and as such it excludes all the spontaneous proceedings of the popular soul; political authoritarianism and classical writing are faces of the same historical phenomenon. As for symmetry, the most neurotic version of consonance, Georg Simmel in an essay dated 1896 stated that it is a symptom of all despotic societies. He opposed to it the principle of anomaly, according to which each element should develop independently, following its natural growth, and the whole should not satisfy any rule.

In architecture, dissonance integrates the entire list of functions. If every man is different, every house should be functionally different and a code of dissonances is just what is needed for that purpose. Linguists say that it is not we who speak a language, but "the language speaks us." Therefore, a language of dissonances may be very useful for the method of designing by listing functions and contents. During the epoch of the Enlightenment, there were theoreticians like Carlo Lodoli who preached strict functionalism. However, the Enlightenment ended with the dictatorship of neo-Classicism. Why? A free language was not codified, and human freedom cannot stand consonance and symmetry. Schönberg codified dodecaphony. Le Corbusier and the Bauhaus stimulated an architectural method of dissonances, without codifying it.

Three-Dimensionality Without Perspective

Einstein's Theory of Relativity and Bergson's thoughts on the *durée réelle* are reflected in architectural aesthetics. They bring to its final consequences the crisis of Renaissance vision, which had already been recognized in the age of Mannerism. To conceive of a building statically, according to the three dimensions of Euclidian geometry, and to favor a single viewpoint over all others is no longer bearable. The perspectival scheme implies a rigid hierarchy between the main facade, the sides, and the back. The destructuring ensuing from the listing principle and the code of dissonances has demolished such hierarchies. Modern architectural science has no use for the fixed or unique viewpoint; it desires a mobile viewpoint, able to control the building in all its aspects, from above, from below, outside and inside, because they are all equally important. Mobility in turn means time, the "fourth" dimension.

For Giedion, architectural space-time was strictly connected with European experiences based on Cubism, that is to say, with Le Corbusier's school and the Bauhaus. This is rather absurd, considering that the architect of the Einstein tower was Erich Mendelsohn, the most important figure of Expressionism. The fact is that space-time could be interpreted in two completely different ways. According to Cubist theory, as we shall see in the next section, three-dimensionality should be destroyed by breaking the volume and, above all, killing its mass. According to Expressionist thought, three-dimensionality could well be preserved under the condition that mass, and consequently building materials, be conceived as energy in a most dynamic and dramatic manner.

Mendelsohn, the creator of the Einstein tower at Potsdam, writes: "Architecture grasps the space, encloses the space, becomes space. . . . Architectural vitality refers both to the tactile and to the visual sense: in the weight of masses bound to the earth and in the bodiless hovering in light. Architecture establishes the conditions of masses in movement. . . ." For the Cubists, space-time is a formula, or an a priori given, in any case a mechanism to get rid of perspective. The Expressionists, on the contrary, know that perspective can be eliminated in the conflict between tactile and visual values, between spaces within and their containers, between light and mass.

Four-Dimensional Decomposition

The seventeen "fundamental principles" of architecture, enunciated by the founder of the Stijl group, Theo van Doesburg, in 1925 but widely diffused only after the Second World War, are the most mature contribution of cubist research. For coherence they may best be reorganized into three nuclei,[3] as follows:

1) The modern architect, instead of starting with an a priori form for every new theme tackles ex novo the design problem. Form is a posteriori (I). The new architecture is formless, even if well determined. It does not accept preordered schemes—molds where functional spaces can be poured. The division and subdivision of internal and external spaces are made through planes which do not have an individual form. Therefore, these planes can be extended to the infinite, in every direction and without interruption. There exists a relation between the different planes and the external space (V).

2) The new architecture has abolished monotonous repetition and has destroyed the equality of the two halves, the symmetry. Equilibrium and symmetry are quite different notions. Instead of symmetry, the new architecture suggests the well-balanced relation of unequal parts, that is of paths which are different (in position, measure, proportion, etc.) because of their functional character. The new architecture does not separate an "in front of" (facade) from a "back," a "right" from a "left" and, if possible, an "on top of" from a "below" (XIV). The new architecture, instead of being monumental, is an architecture of transformation, light, and the transparent (VI).

3) The new architecture does not recognize passive components: it has defeated the hole. The window is no longer a hole in the wall. The window plays an active role (VII). The new architecture has destroyed the wall, crossing out the dualism between inside and outside. Walls do not support anymore. Thus we have a new plan, an open plan, totally different from the classical one, because inside and outside spaces interpenetrate (VIII). The new architecture consists of a general space, divided into different spaces which refer to the comfort of the inhabitants. This division is made through planes which separate (inside) and planes which enclose (outside). The first can be mobile (as doors are already). In a future stage of architectural development, the plan will disappear. For the spatial composition projected in two dimensions on a horizontal section (the plan) there can be substituted an exact calculus of the construction. Euclidian mathematics will not be of any use, while non-Euclidian four-dimensional calculus will simplify such an operation (IX). The new architecture is anticubic: its various spaces are no longer compressed in a closed cube. On the contrary, the different spatial cells are developed in an eccentric way from the center to the periphery of the cube, so that the dimensions of height, width, and depth acquire a newly plastic expression (XII).

These few statements of van Doesburg's "principles" are enough for us to understand that here is a most serious attempt to formulate a new architectural syntax. There are, of course, some contradictions: why should the "formless" be "well-determined"? why do the "unequal parts" need to have a "well-balanced equilibrium"? However, these are residues of the Enlightenment which do not invalidate De Stijl's revolutionary message. The position of De Stijl is quite clear. In order to extirpate the cancer of perspective, it is necessary to destroy the third dimension, and that can be done only by decomposing the "box" into two-dimensional planes and then by *proceeding to their four-dimensional reassemblage*. Practically, this is a game of free planes in space, played in such a way that the old, closed volume is never reborn.

Because the advantages of the De Stijl syntax are quite evident, it has been discussed a great deal in architectural theory and criticism since 1945. However, it implies at least four heavy costs: (a) free planes in space must reduce or even annihilate depth; (b) building structure must be hidden so as not to compete with planes; (c) spaces to be lived in cannot be freely molded, as they belong to "a general space," later "divided into different spaces"; (d) finally, these planes "can be extended to the infinite, in every direction and without interruption."

Objection to (a) was made, as we have seen, by the Expressionists and later by the Futurists, especially by Umberto Boccioni (as discovered only in 1972 in his architectural manifesto). Structural engineering opposed condition (b); while Frank Lloyd Wright protested against (c). The urban approach was contrary to (d), the option concerned with continuity, since it is rather difficult to imagine an urban texture composed only of free planes. However, four-dimensional decomposition is a principle, or "invariant," that cannot be eliminated from the modern code of architecture. It occupies a central position between, on the one hand, the principles of listing, dissonance, and three-dimensionality without perspective and, on the other, three more principles that we shall discuss.

Organic Structural Involvement

Vitruvius's *soliditas* has always formed a basic component of the architectural equation, but it was never satisfactorily related to two other components, namely function and beauty. Positivism exalted *soliditas* in connection with the new technology and its materials: iron, steel, reinforced concrete. In 1747 the schism between engineering and architecture was ratified in Paris with the foundation of the Ecole des Ponts et Chaussées. With the beginning of the twentieth century, and even in the preceding decades, the most progressive architects proclaimed that "true" architecture was that produced by engineers. And engineers were surprised and shocked by the artistic results of their work.

The famous French engineer Eugène Freyssinet (1879-1962) wrote:

> The questions of art are totally extraneous to me. My technical curriculum has made of me an engineer passionately concerned with his own profession, but ignorant in all other fields, especially in architecture. In my Hangars at Orly, the contrast between the absence of artistic intentions and the potency of the effect is striking. I have not thought for a single minute of artistic results, and still they are impressive. There is a sensation of equilibrium, harmony, order, a certainty that each element is just what it should be, a feeling quite similar to the one we feel in front of a true work of art. How does it happen that such results can come from mechanical means used only for utilitarian purposes.

It should be noted that engineers, speaking of aesthetic values, refer to concepts like "equilibrium," "order," "certainty," which are typical of the classical apparatus, while architects extol the opposite values: daring cantilevers, asymmetric effects, sensations of instability.

"The great buildings of our age have a bone structure, in steel or reinforced concrete. This bone structure is to the building as the skeleton is to the animal. Those who hide even a part of the bone structure take away from architecture its most beautiful ornament, the only legitimate one. Those who hide a pillar make a mistake. Those who build a false pillar commit a crime," stated Auguste Perret (1874-1954), reechoing the theories of the Enlightenment and of Viollet-le-Duc. The dichotomy between skeleton and skin implies that the skeleton is the engineer's business, while the skin belongs to the architect. A building thus equals its skeleton plus its skin, forgetting all the complex systems of living organisms.

With such a mentality, the reintegration of technology and art is impossible. And architecture remains in a tragic situation of structural backwardness. A ship floats, an airplane flies, while buildings continue to weigh much more than is necessary, because too many of their portions are just carried.

The modern science of construction suggests the way to surmount this impasse. It states that the resistance of a structure does not depend on the quantity of its materials but on their forms. Mathematical calculus can verify the form but cannot invent it. The invention of structural forms is the architect's task, and creative engineers are architects. But it is essential that a maximum number of architectural forms be involved in the structural play. Only thus will building engineering stop being Classical and receive the principles of listing, dissonance, three-dimensionality without perspective, and four-dimensional decomposition.

Timing Architectural Space

The three "reminders to architects" promulgated by Le Corbusier in 1920 concerned volumes, surfaces, and plan. Purism, the most Enlightenment-bound of all Cubist filiations, is unaware of space or considers it only as "universal space." We have seen that De Stijl conceived space merely as a result of the four-dimensional game of planes. The Expressionists did have a clear understanding of space-time. But only the genius of Frank Lloyd Wright was able to translate in architectural terms the concept of "spatial field" as Einstein developed it.

With Wright the space within, where people live, becomes the motive and the motor of the architectural process. Such space is fluid, fluent, and dynamic, continuous with and belonging to the fluid, fluent, and dynamic space of the environment. As for Einstein, so for Wright "empty space" does not exist. All elements are in a state of flux: man, life, building, landscape, materials. Change is the only law that we may know. The individual must recognize that he is no longer master of the universe; but once he gets rid of the absolute laws he himself has created, he is free to break them and to reconquer his dignity and independence. Events are related no longer only to time but also to space. So architecture can register human events and stimulate their enrichment. Wright's space-time was a feedback for both Cubists and Expressionists, but it is neither Cubist nor Expressionist and not even Cubist plus Expressionist. It is an Einsteinian space-time where environment and human space meet together with the notions of "field" and of energy-materials.

Urban and Natural Continuum

The separation between buildings and urban "empty spaces" is typical of the Classical approach. Modern planning, with Camillo Sitte as its theoretician, looked back into the medieval city in order to find a continuum in building structure and, at the same time, a continuity of open spaces, streets, and plazas. There was one more reason for the modern interest in the Middle Ages: the search for the right dimension of the city, against the hypertrophic expansion of the metropolis. Thus, the idea of the garden city arose. These are satellite nuclei of 32,000 inhabitants that were supposed to reproduce, in the framework of an industrial economy, what in the past had been achieved by the distribution of settlements in the rural countryside. In spite of its advantages, such a method reiterates the separation between urban compactness and the emptiness of the countryside around it.

At the end of the last century, Ebenezer Howard proclaimed that city and country should be united and saw in their union a new hope, a new life, a new civilization. In reality, however, his garden city substituted for the old city walls an agricultural "ring" with the same purpose of avoiding the habitat's growth. In 1929 El Lissitzky stated: "Today cities do not satisfy our needs. We live in rigid chrysalides. What is at stake is fundamental: either 'geometry' or 'organicity.' When society is in a state of anarchic conflicts, the imposed order becomes the only factor of cohesion, and geometry is the most useful solution. But when the community generates a vital organism, where each individual is an indivisible part, then we have the basis of a new urban system."[4] It is quite clear that the dilemma of the city—geometry or organicism, repressive order or free arrangement—repeats in a larger scale the dilemma of architecture.

In spite of the illusions of many theorists, cities and countries have reached a unity; cars and airplanes have narrowed distances. Through radio and television, the whole earth has become an urban amalgam, and Lewis Mumford speaks of a continuous "invisible city." However, in order to achieve a real continuum in visual terms, it is necessary that each component of the whole remain somehow unfinished, so as to need integration with the other components. Modern planners insist on the "open" plan, the opposite of the "closed" one of Classicism; they want a plan that can change and even contradict itself to meet new requirements. But we have to recognize that the continuum of architecture-city-landscape is still an intention. The most important attempt to overcome the contrast between town and country was made by the American landscapists, especially by Frederick Law Olmsted. Hostile to the authoritarian metropolis of European origin, they neither hated the town nor made a myth of the country. They looked for a democratic, aleatory habitat based on an open dialogue between built zones and green areas, with immense parks in the very heart of the metropolis, as in New York. The neo-Classical reaction defeated them but could not kill the aspiration to an alternative scheme of human settlements that led later on to Broadacre City, the ideal of Wright.

The "unfinished" is a rather old architectural instrument that was used by Brunelleschi and, in a methodical way, by Michelangelo. No total environment can be designed with simple isolated objects. If integration is needed, no object should be complete in itself. To be sure, thinking again of the six preceding principles or "invariants" of the modern architectural code, we find that each one of them implies the philosophy of the "unfinished." The list of functions is, by definition, unfinished. So are dissonance, three-dimensionality without perspective, four-dimensional decomposition, structural involvement, and timing of space. This is quite logical because the modern language of architecture was evolved in opposition to classical completeness.

The seven principles we have discussed thus far are

based on the experiences of old and new architecture, of the creative building of all ages. Theory and criticism since 1945 have accomplished a tremendous amount of work to identify them, to free both the architect and the user of his buildings from the tyranny of the academy.

Democratizing Architecture

Renaissance humanism and neoclassic doctrine imagined "ideal cities" that could be entirely controlled by a demiurge, the architect-planner. A somewhat similar attitude existed in the International Style of the 1920s and 1930s. The slogan of the Bauhaus, "from the spoon to the town," meant that design was the supreme master on all levels and scales of the environment. In the 1950s, this self-proclaimed "universalism" of architecture was vigorously questioned. In 1958, Friedrich Hundertwasser wrote one of his iconoclastic manifestos, preaching that architecture should stop being rational and go moldy:

> In our countries, architecture today is censored the same way painting is in the Soviet Union. What can it produce? Only pitiful compromises. . . . Every man has the right to build his own four walls as he likes, and be responsible for them. The material unlivableness of the slums is much better than the spiritual unlivableness of our functional buildings. In most poor sectors of the city, it is only man's body that can be ruined, but in the architecture designed for men, it is their soul that collapses. . . . It is time that people revolt against being pigeon-holed in building boxes, like cockerels and hares. . . . The use of the T-square in architecture is criminal; today, we live in a chaos of straight lines. If you don't believe it, try to count how many straight lines surround us, you will never get to an end. . . . All modern architecture in which the T-square or the compass have played some role, even for a single minute, has to be rejected. . . . To save functional architecture from decay, we should throw over its shiny glass walls and its smooth surfaces some elements that would make them go mouldy. Industry should recognize its fundamental mission: creative mouldiness![5]

During the years of "informal" painting, designer William Katavolos fought for an architecture based on the "self-making" principle and not on a priori projects and believed that this was possible through the use of new chemical materials. In 1960 he wrote:

> We should build no more with such fatigue. Architecture should be just an event. . . . It should free itself from the traditional models, and become organic. The new discoveries in the field of chemistry make it possible to produce materials that can expand quite a lot, and then solidify. . . . Buildings could expand up to a determined dimension, and then be divided up or blend in order to achieve gigantic complexes. . . . In the morning, suburbs could unite with the city; at night, they could move to another site and satisfy the cultural needs of contemporary living.[6]

In different keys, ideological, technical, and psychological, architecture is involved in a process of democratization. Combating Classicism, not only has it developed the seven principles that we have examined—seven "nays" to academic laws—but mainly it recognizes that there exists a reality which cannot be controlled by the architect. An extraordinary opening of the aesthetic horizons is occurring, the most relevant aspects of which are:

ARCHITECTURE WITHOUT ARCHITECTS

The world of primitive, vernacular, spontaneous building, free from all academic dogmas and therefore excluded up to now from the history of art, is recovered. The seven principles of modern architectural language, it is discovered, may be found in peasants' homes much more than in princes' palaces. The class attitude that separated a "major" from a "minor" architecture, or architecture as an art from building as a profession, comes to an end. As in music, an exchange is effected between the highflown and the popular, between dialect and language.

ENVIRONMENTAL CACOPHONY

Pop Art teaches us to perceive the aesthetic aspects of the ugly, the vulgar, the dreary. Slums, barracks, bidonvilles, barriadas, and favelas are passionately investigated, and quite a few identify in them the "architecture of democracy." Even environmental decay is interpreted as a symptom of an era of popular mass consumption, as the apotheosis of the common man in the democratic desert. Robert Venturi and Denise Scott Brown revalue signs and symbols of the American "main street" and extol Las Vegas's cityscape, comparing its hypnotic power to that of Rome's plazas.

MULTIFUNCTIONAL BRICOLAGE

Moshe Safdie, architect of Habitat '67 at Montreal, states that we must reject the bidimensional city divided between land and prisms and develop the three-dimensional one that would articulate space and integrate residences, offices, recreative and green areas in one organism in which each function would be complemented by the others, thus offering a free environment with full mobility. In other words, we should break the buildings into their basic components, well enough for industrial production, and then reassemble them with a flexible technology, in order to stimulate in their users the search for their own identities. Safdie repeats that every house should be different, because each person is different.

TASTE FOR THE ALEATORY

"Three 'components' with 'subcomponents' attached, plugged into one 'chassis' or 'gate,' and then connected by four 'circuiting systems' superimposed at separate levels to avoid cross-circuiting"—this is how John Johansen defines his Mummers Theater [1966-1970] at Oklahoma City.[7] He writes:

As McLuhan has said, ". . . all that is required as a basis for a work of art is the brush of one idea against another idea"—in the case of habitable structure . . . function against function. It is action: the infusion of human beings and the distribution of services, which is expressed clearly, usually directly from one point to another. It is the surprise, unexpected juxtaposition, superimposition, crowding, segregation, and confrontation of elements which accommodates the human movement patterns which give whatever architectural quality this construction may have. The concern is that of reality, immediacy, honesty, economy. . . . The actual and final appearance is unpredictable. Elevations, if one can say they exist, cannot be drawn or studied: in fact, facets of wall, roof, and soffit are so numerous, with interface so prevalent, that their relationship may as well be left to chance. As in the new mathematics, we deal with "sets" of symbols or images; we recognize group effects, unplanned peripheral sensations, along with selected views. . . . The impression is generally . . . what Norbert Wiener called "organic incompleteness." . . . Facets, not facades, result in bombardment of composite images; yet they are held together by the ordering device. Permutation, flux, change, whether by actual reassemblage in future years, or by suggestion of this possibility in concept, give the structure an aspect of "in-process." By making this vivid, the occupants may feel they participate, . . . are involved, feel empathy, identify with, have, in fact, become part of the process. Not only is the axially fixed station-point of the Renaissance out of date, but the moving station-point of Sigfried Giedion's space-time is out of date also, in favor of multiple simultaneous station points, consistent with our present-experience world. . . . The assemblage is volatile; elements may relate back to the same thing, yet not to each other. The relationship is organizational, not formal. Slang, not eloquence, is foremost.[8]

DE-ARCHITECTURIZATION

This is the watchword of the American group SITE Projects, Inc., led by James Wines.

With the accelerated deterioration of our social, economic, and political institutions we are witnessing the development of a new "iconography of disaster." Nowhere is this entropic imagery more conspicuously manifested than in the recent proliferation of disaster films. Their fundamental attraction has been to provide a disillusioned generation, weary of political deception and technological folly, with a means of vicarious revenge. This is particularly true of the movies representing urban and architectural calamity. For the ill-housed, re-mortgaged, and unemployed, an evening spent watching the bank towers go up in smoke and the perpetrators destroyed is redeeming satisfaction in an otherwise frustrating existence. . . . A similar aesthetic of destruction and a distrust of traditional prerogatives has affected the environmental arts. Formalism, expressionism, and the International Style have been challenged by areas of hybrid endeavor emerging internationally. These anti-formal, anti-institutional ideas constitute a form of "de-architecturization" comparable in their criticism of rhetorical assumptions in architecture to the "Technosplat" sensibility confirming our doubts about science and engineering. De-architecturization refers to a condition (or attitude) of reversing or removing some quality or element from architecture. . . . Entropy represents the threat of "chance," the very opposite of an objectified, rational, world. As the legacy of formalism and functionalism is clearly a failure, a new iconography is evolving from contradictions to the programatic view of architecture and environment. . . . It is understandable that an iconography growing out of a state of indeterminacy will, of necessity, be diverse, personalized, and less specific than its institutional predecessors. Its consolidating strength must derive from an appeal to the reflexive, subconscious response of the public to changing phenomena in place of fixed ideologies. This becomes a reversal of the traditional purpose of iconography and communicative facade. . . . In our age when the monolithic institutions are crumbling under their own weight, it is really "missing parts" and fragmentary pieces, that represent the real vitality of urban life. Missing parts are humanizing questions to replace intransigent answers, the positive interpretation of the negative, the search for less in a world committed to more. . . . The fascination with missing parts is universal. Witness the magnetism of demolition or construction sites and archeological ruins. Their attraction is a visual dialogue requiring the spectator to reconcile the known and the void as interactive events, to accept a dialectic of entropy and equivocation as the bridge between architecture and environment.[9]

Wines feels that architecture urgently needs a Marcel Duchamp.

TECHNOLOGICAL EQUIPMENT AS AESTHETIC MATERIAL

Technics, in architectural history, has always meant structural technology, *soliditas* or *firmitas.* The International Style of the 1930s made a myth of steel and reinforced concrete structures, as if their expression were a guarantee of good architecture.

Lighting, hydraulics, heating, ventilating, and air-conditioning plants were forgotten. According to Mies van der Rohe, it was impossible to produce quality architecture showing the installation's pipes. On the contrary, it is quite possible, as the Centre Georges Pompidou in Paris has demonstrated. Its inspiration does not derive from steamships, motorcars, and airplanes but instead from missile stations like Cape Kennedy or from sea towers for the drilling of oil. Equipment = comfort was a notion almost unknown, even in the most sumptuous palaces of the Renaissance. Now comfort means use-value instead of contemplative-value.

NEO-MANNERISM

The revaluation of architecture born from the crisis of Renaissance Classicism has enriched the aesthetic horizon, bound for too long to the taboo of "stylistic purity." Complexity, contradiction, contamination, even the worst eclecticism are rather functional to an epoch that wants to accumulate before choosing. Moreover, Mannerism responds to the need of mediating the contrasting inheritances of the great masters. After Wright, Le Corbusier, Mies, Gropius, Mendelsohn, Aalto, the urge for such mediation is strongly felt, and this is why figures like Hugo Häring, Hans Scharoun, Rudolf Schindler, Giuseppe Terragni are so much appreciated. Mannerism includes two quite different attitudes: one introverted, sophisticated, intellectual, a "speech upon the speech" of the masters, good enough for an elite; the other, on the contrary, mingles various languages to serve a larger audience. In any case, both refuse homogeneity.

REREADING HISTORY

In the Bauhaus curriculum, the teaching of architectural history did not exist, because it was felt that it would negatively condition avant-garde impulses. Since 1945, however, historiography, dismissing academic interpretations, has been able to read the past with new, modern eyes. Today, figures like Arnolfo di Cambio, Brunelleschi, Borromini, Gaudí, works like the Erechtheion, Hadrian's Villa, the Temple of Minerva Medica, the Siena plaza, towns like Ferrara or Bologna are no longer quoted as traditional "models," but as stimuli for courageous and original proposals; that is, for the future.

ADVOCACY PLANNING

Populist ideology postulates the idea of user sovereignty. Housing should be designed not for the people, but by the people. The power of the architect should be limited, in order to integrate the inhabitants into the conception of every plan. According to John F. C. Turner, a British architect who worked for many years in the squatters' settlements of Peru, housing should be "a process which the users themselves must be free to manipulate through the support of institutionalized services."[10] In other words, "professional imperialism" should come to a stop. Pluralism must prevail. The architect's role is not to make the final decisions, but simply to understand the various opinions among people and help in weighing them against each other. Advocacy planning attacks the Affluent Society, the Welfare State, the behavioral patterns established by the bureaucratic power, the fetishistic character of the individualized products of design, the universal norms, and, consequently, authoritarian regimentation. It implies a revolution in the habits of the architectural profession, a transfusion of popular blood into an elitist culture.

The New Aesthetic of Architecture

Theory and criticism since 1945 have deeply changed our vision of architecture. Many factors of this change had appeared in the second half of the last century and during the first four decades of our century. Some factors are even older, coming from Mannerism and the Enlightenment period. But only since 1945 was the theoretical and critical work undertaken that has brought about the formulation of a democratic approach to architecture. The seven principles of modern architectural language have led to the dismantling of the apparatus of Classicism. The functionalist ideology was dismantled by many researchers, including Christopher Alexander. Up to the 1950s faith in the building "program" was indiscriminate. Later, it was found that long-term projects for hospitals, university campuses, airports, and even residential districts became quickly anachronistic. The suspicion arises that, paradoxically, we should design without a program in order not only to suffer change but to stimulate it.

Some scholars believe that architecture is a mass medium, because its message is persuasive, received without attention, ready to be filled with heterogeneous meanings, subject to rapid obsolescence and to market fluctuations, oscillating between the maximum of coercion and the maximum of irresponsibility. Consequently, the need is felt for an architectural aesthetics able to decodify the architects' messages for the people and, even more, to involve people in the making and conveying of the messages. One of the Paris 1968 slogans called for an art that would refuse segregation in the museums and come down into the streets to be enjoyed by everybody. Well, buildings are already in the streets, and they are containers of human behavior. Today's problem is to provoke more differentiated behaviors. It is a problem that concerns not objects but the quality of individual and collective life. The pleasure of the text in architecture is given, as both Einstein and Wright have shown, by the dialectics between environmental field and space within, where man in movement can recognize and question himself.

Notes

1. For full reference data *see* Bibliography to Chapter 2, below.

2. *See* note 1.

3. Within each nucleus the specific "principles" of Doesburg that I employ are indicated appropriately in roman numerals.

4. El Lissitzky, "Russland-Rekonstruktion der Architektur in der Sowjetunion," *Neues Bauen in der Welt* 1 (Vienna, 1920): 38ff.

5. Friedrich Hundertwasser, *Verschimmelungs-Manifest (Mould Manifesto)* Schrift der Galerie Renate Boukes, Reinhard Kaufman, ed. (Wiesbaden, 1959).

6. William Katavolos. Quoted from *Quadrat Blatt*, de Jong and Co., Hilversum 1961; cited also in a different translation in U. Conrads, editor. *Programs and manifestoes on 20th-century architects*, Cambridge, Mass., MIT Press, 1975, 163-64.

7. John Johansen. In *Architectural Forum*, May 1968.

8. Ibid.

9. James Wines. In *L'Architecturra. Cronache e Storia* 236, June 1975.

10. John F. C. Turner. In *Housing by People. Towards Autonomy in Building Design Environments*, London: Boyars, 1976.

Bibliography

Argan, Giulio Carlo. *Progetto e destino*. Milan: Il Saggiatore, 1965.

Banham, Reyner. *Theory and Design in the First Machine Age*. London: Architectural Press, 1960.

Boudon, Philippe. *Sur l'espace architectural—Essai d'épistémologie de l'architecture*. Paris: Dunod, 1971.

Boyd, Robin. *The Puzzle of Architecture*. Melbourne: Melbourne University Press, 1965.

Brandi, Cesare. *Struttura e architettura*. Turin: Einaudi, 1967.

Bruce, Allsopp. *Art and the Nature of Architecture*. London: Pitman, 1952.

CIAM 8. *The Heart of the City: towards the humanisation of urban life*. London: Humphries, 1952.

Collins, George R. and Crasemann, Christiane. *Camillo Sitte and the Birth of Modern City Planning*. London: Phaidon Press, 1975.

Conrads, Ulrich. *Programme und Manifeste zur Architektur des 20. Jahrhunderts*. Berlin: Ullstein GmbH, 1964.

De Fusco, Renato. *Architettura come mass medium. Note per una semiologia architettonica*. Bari: Dedalo, 1967.

Eco, Umberto. *Appunti per una semiologia delle comunicazioni visive*. Milan: Bompiani, 1967.

______. *La struttura assente. Introduzione alla ricerca semiologica*. Milan: Bompiani, 1968.

Giedion, Sigfried. *Space, Time and Architecture. The growth of a new tradition*. Cambridge, Mass.: Harvard University Press, 1941.

Hauser, Arnold. *Mannerism—The Crisis of the Renaissance and the Origin of Modern Art*. London: 1965.

Jacobs, Jane. *The Death and Life of Great American Cities*. New York: Random House, 1961.

Jammer, Max. *Concepts of Space. The History and Theories of Space in Physics*. Cambridge, Mass.: Harvard University Press, 1954.

Jencks, Charles. *The Language of Post-Modern Architecture*. London: Academy Editions, 1977.

______ and Baird, George. *Meaning in Architecture*. London: Cresset, 1969.

Koenig, Giovanni Klaus. *Analisi del linguaggio architettonico*. Florence: Editrice Fiorentina, 1964.

______. *Analisi strutturale delle sette invarianti zeviane*. Florence: Editrice Fiorentina, 1976.

Nicco-Fasola, Giusta. *Ragionamenti sull' architettura*. Città di Castello: Macri, 1949.

Norberg-Schulz, Christian. *Intentions in Architecture*. London: Allen & Unwin, 1963.

Rudofsky, Bernard. *Architecture without Architects*. New York: Museum of Modern Art, 1964.

Tafuri, Manfredo. *Teoria e storia dell' architettura*. Bari: Laterza, 1968.

Toccafondi, Lucia. *Le forme sorgono*. Turin: Paravia, 1975.

Turner, John F. C. *Housing by People. Towards Autonomy in Building Design Environments*. London: Boyars, 1976.

Tzonis, A. "In the name of the People." *Forum* 25:3.

Van de Ven, Cornelis. *Space in Architecture*. Amsterdam: Gorcum, 1978.

Venturi, Robert. *Complexity and Contradiction in Architecture*. New York: Museum of Modern Art, 1966.

Whiffen, Marcus, ed. *The History, Theory and Criticism of Architecture*, 1964 AIA-ACSA Teacher Seminar. Cambridge, Mass.: MIT Press, 1965.

Zevi, Bruno. *Architecture as Space: how to look at Architecture*. Translated by Milton Gendel. Edited by Joseph Barry. New York: Horizon Press, 1974.

______. *Architettura in Nuce*. Florence: Sansoni, 1960.

______. *Editoriali di architettura*. Turin: Einaudi, 1979.

______. *Il linguaggio moderno dell' architettura*. Turin: Einaudi, 1973.

______. *The Modern Language of Architecture*. Seattle: University of Washington Press, 1978.

______. *Saper vedere d'architettura*. Turin: Einaudi, 1948.

______. *Verso un'architettura organica*. Turin: Einaudi, 1945.

3

TECHNOLOGY AND ARCHITECTURAL DESIGN

ROBERT W. WHITE

Introduction

The changes in the technology of building since World War II have been extensive and varied, but simply to catalog them, either in relationship to their inventors or with respect to some other taxonomic system, is to miss the more interesting ideas about architecture that have been happening. These ideas have often been transitory, important in only some parts of the world, culture-bound and inseparable from seemingly nontechnological interests, such as social or political programs. There are few architectural ideas that don't encompass both technology and social programs (or progess), aesthetics, and history. It is in the relationship of one of these aspects to another that architectural ideas are unique.

Charles Jencks, in *Modern Movements in Architecture*,[1] showed a continuous "field of thought" delineated by logical, intuitive, and unselfconscious categories, wherein he located each particular (well-known) architect. He seems to have assumed that there was some type of logical progression from one level to another and that someone in systems-building would have few interests in semiology. It wouldn't be very difficult to make nonsense of this theory with a few well-chosen examples. For example, the works of Le Corbusier, Saarinen, Wright, Kahn, and to a lesser extent many other architects cannot be neatly categorized. Even if the architects themselves were self-conscious about their work in the sense of claiming one line of thought, the results are invariably expressive of many aspects of life. Thus, a Marxist critique of suburban housing—hardly great architecture—transcends the example of an individual dwelling in order to consider the larger economy which sustains the housing type.[2] A semiotic reading of the same subject finds symbolic meaning relating to patriotism, hearth, display, dreams, and so forth.[3]

Another system, such as Paczowski's,[4] sees a balance between "firmness," "commodity," and "delight," a modern update of the old Vitruvian idea. Any architectural movement is a "mixture," much the way columns are composed of structural reinforcing, mass, and decoration. None of these schemes seems satisfactory because it does not allow multiple, strong readings of the same building or architect. Most buildings, and all the best ones, can simultaneously engage several ideas at the same time. The more multivalent a building is, in Jencks's sense, the more interesting it becomes and the less neatly it fits convenient critical categories. It is through the relationships between buildings and the multiple ways a building can be understood that one learns how diverse and resonant with meaning even uncelebrated buildings may be. Technology in all its manifestations, as one critical category, can be useful in understanding contemporary building; conversely, any critical theory of contemporary architecture which does not include technology is inadequate.

If Jencks's categories are decidedly unrigorous and univalent in themselves, he is right to say that some architects and their work do not show an explicit interest in technology. For example, the Venturis, Charles Moore, and Robert Stern say they care most about aesthetic ideas of architectural form, and we should take them at their word. When they create these forms, their concerns are with the bank of historical images and relationships they know, and which they expect a more-or-less limited audience will know—a sort of "museum without walls," to use Malraux's concept.

But self-conscious unconcern with technology does

not mean that these architects stand outside technological development in the postwar period. For example, Venturi's work is often sympathetic to the engineer's interests, for his "decorated sheds" are cheap, straightforward, and easily analyzed mathematically. The questions to put to the Venturis's work are: "Could it have been done at any other time than now? What necessary conditions are required for it?" It is clear that their dialogue with American strip development and suburban cultural mythologies (*Learning from Las Vegas*) is preconditioned by the automobile and the rapid communications of the "global village," both technological products of the postwar period. Their version of Post-Modernism is, thus, less concerned with the explicit effects of technology than with it as an implicit resource for contemporary culture. Western capitalistic society running on the engine of economic growth which requires new products, inventions, and their consumption produces these effects but few plans. The Post-Modernists then consider these technological artifacts (the consumer goods) as empty of meaning in themselves but find the accumulated effects of the society as being worthy of extended analysis and imitation—making visible Adam Smith's invisible hand. Paradoxically, however, their "fixup" that would convert co-op city from being "almost" all right[5] to completely all right might come from sixteenth-century Italian Mannerist sources. If one rejects building technology as inappropriate to sustain the depth of meaning architecture should express, should one also reject the influence of other nonarchitectural technologies of the society? Or does architecture need to concern itself with this at all: that is, do architectural ideas transcend their particular time and society?

Clearly, they are connected to a society and perhaps most tangibly in the area of construction. The means and manner used for a building's construction are important aids to understanding the context and raison d'être for that building.

Technological issues, while often inseparable from economic, social, and aesthetic concerns, are an accessible way for the public and professionals alike to understand architectural work. Of particular interest to us are the expressive uses of building technology; the relationship of building technology to contemporary developments in other fields; the relationship of technology to aesthetic concerns, particularly in the Post-Modern movement as we have just seen; and finally the current and potential evolutions caused by both the cost escalation and the shortages of energy supplies. These worldwide trends have been due to the extraordinary influence of the media, especially the glossy magazines, and the international linkage of monetary and energy supplies. There were, however, notable exceptions to these movements in the Communist bloc countries and the Third World, where the romance of technology never lost its bloom and for which these economic links were not important.

Building and Social Programs

It is surely no accident that most important historical or contemporary utopian schemes proposed elaborate new kinds of building and often novel ways of constructing, even if the creator of the utopia was not an architect. Architectural plans illustrate written utopian relationships and must necessarily integrate, compromise, and resolve conflicts. They situate a utopia and, by making a special place for it, make it seem real or possible.

Ehrmann's perceptive essay relating utopia to architecture also makes the converse connection that many, if not all, architectural plans share the utopian imagination and are thereby limited by their hermetic possiblities.[6] The Unité d'Habitation, at Marseilles [1947-1952] of Le Corbusier, is an explicit example which is now quite desirable, although it was initially an economic as well as a political disaster. It embodied all the latest technology, such as prefabricated parts, modular construction, experimental mechanical systems, novel acoustical isolation, and, in addition, was part of a large urban-planning scheme to be replicated during the postwar reconstruction (fig. 21.2).

It was essential to Le Corbusier's utopian idea that the Marseilles block be the first of many others to form whole *quartiers* and cities—the *ville radieuse*—and that replication could only happen if modern prefab technology could produce these buildings from factories. Indeed, the Marseilles block was originally conceived in steel, a material requiring the most exact and highly technical means of manufacture.[7]

If architectural form is in part an exploration of how ideas, especially utopian ones, interact, then the technology of how the form is produced will inevitably reflect those ideas.

Since 1945 the interaction of architectural ideas and technology has become more elaborate. While there were many ideas in the Modern Movement, particularly in prefabricated construction, there were few which facilitated technology; but during the postwar period technological developments have made almost any building idea feasible. With the sophistication of technology comes a diminished sense of its importance. A broken barrier no longer looks as formidable nor as important as it once did.

Today, barriers to building visionary schemes are more likely to include political and social issues, commitments of money and resources, and possibly the aesthetic aims of the project—in short, the ideology of the visionary scheme or utopia. Coupled to scientific progress is the fact that further unknowns must be examined. The very achievement of building technology then is a step towards the diminishing of its importance.

Since all architects build, they cannot avoid the technological problems their forms impose. Indeed, some 50 to 60 percent of any architectural office's time is spent in the construction process, establishing a procedure to physically make the conceptual design. While much of this work is assigned to partners or assistants with an interest in construction, the best designers must themselves be involved in the construction process. Design and preparation for construction help develop expertise in every architect, even if one's education stressed only design.

The direct result of a new technology or bit of hardware is that it creates possibilities. Large space-frames or geodesic structures make covering huge areas, such as a whole city or region, a reality. The seminal work of Buckminster Fuller, both before and after the war, shows the relationship between a new technique and profound changes in the scope of an architectural imagination. If we immediately see that collections of light space-frame pyramids are inherently stable and very strong, or that the light cable tents of Frei Otto (fig. 22.6) can span great distances, then the function of the component can be grasped. Other analogies, for example, a cable bridge, help to convince the viewer, especially if the new technology is left uncovered. The cliché of honesty in structure, so common in the forties, fifties and into the sixties, may have been due in part to the desire to persuade the viewer that new ways of lightly enclosing space with thin screens and supports actually were safe and logically arranged; for if they were covered how would one know they were safe?

The Expression of Technology

We shall consider three means to express technology in architecture: 1) the direct expression of the technical fact; 2) indirect expression as a cipher for important technical work hidden from direct view; 3) mythology as expressive of an absent or unconnected image or idea about technology.

DIRECT EXPRESSION

The direct expression of a concrete column supporting a load, a duct carrying air, or a conduit of electricity, tells us how things work. Often the evidence is inferred: we know that electricity ''flows'' in a wire (which is presumably in a conduit) to heat a filament in a lamp to make light. A minimal education in science is usually sufficient to understand these relationships. However, there is much contemporary unease with technology because recent inventions don't obey the old scientific principles. A computer or a laser will remain mysterious for most people, whether or not the enclosure around it is stripped away. Thus, even if we could directly express these devices, the information would be of little use.

Direct expression of technology happens infrequently in most buildings, although it carries the highest "moral" value of "honesty" in the Modern Movement's polemics. It is very difficult to accomplish and impossible to do consistently for every part of a building. If, by this rationale, one needs to demonstrate the column-and-beam structure, does their moment connection also need expression even if it can be accomplished with hidden reinforcing steel? Should varying load conditions and their effects on the sizes of structural parts also be described? In a laboratory building, should all ducts and mechanical pipes be exposed? What if they change year by year? Is it more honest to show them even if they collect dust and dirt by being exposed? Does one need to see the hoist machinery every time one uses an elevator? Plainly, all of this would interest a building engineer, but who else? Even if it were possible, in many areas building codes would prevent it. In practice, then, we see only what the designer intends us to see.

The direct expression of structure was a common ideal during the fifties and sixties, especially in those buildings with dominant structural problems, like stadia and buildings with large spans. Pier Luigi Nervi's elegant works, such as the Small Sports Palace in Rome [1955-1957], show fluid, almost dynamic structures balanced on the edge of collapse.[8] In his Gatti Wool Factory, Rome [1951-1953], isostatic lines of stress determine the orthogonal ribs and beams as they might be graphed from a structural analysis.[9] Eduardo Torroja and Félix Candela exploited thin warped surfaces of reinforced concrete to span huge distances with very lightweight structures. In countries where materials were expensive and the carpentry labor to make formwork was cheap, these works were economical. Even when they were not the cheapest solution they were often built for the sheer exhilaration of doing it. Buckminster Fuller's emphasis on weight reduction, as in his U.S. Pavilion at Montreal's Expo '67, was almost a postwar canon. Other lightweight-material, structural systems such as cable tents and fabric tents were and still are being extensively researched by Frei Otto in Germany before being constructed in such places as the German Pavilion at Montreal's Expo '67 or in Munich (fig. 22.5) for the Olympic Stadium [1969-1972]. In the USSR, Oleg Vartagnian has extended the spatial and structural limits of pure form with origamilike, folded plate structures (fig. 3.1) that may easily be shipped and relatively rapidly assembled.

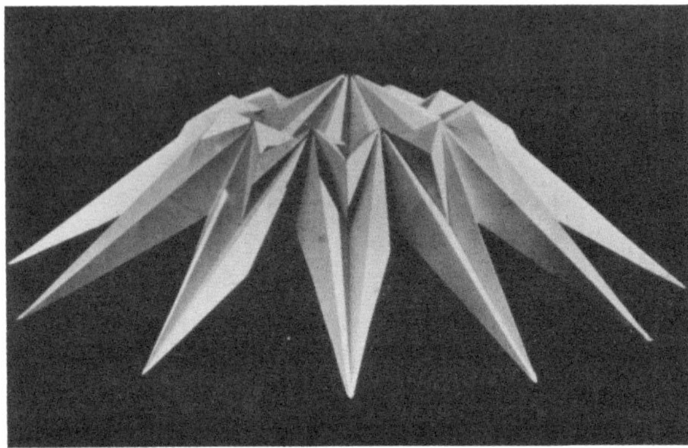

3.1. Oleg Vartagnian. Model of variable folded plate structure formed from a flat sheet. Moscow, 1978. (Photograph: Courtesy of Robert W. White)

Extending the limits of tall buildings was of particular interest in the 1960s. Since the Empire State Building's record height in 1932, skyscrapers were built more modestly to conform to an economic formula determined by rental income and land value. The relationships were so clear that a computer program could design the building, as was done at several firms including Skidmore, Owings and Merrill.[10] The few extraordinarily high buildings were of mixed quality. The World Trade Center [1962-1975], by Minoru Yamasaki and Associates and Emery Roth and Sons, consists of two identical towers whose chief virtue seems to lie in their size alone. In Chicago, birthplace of the tall building, the record-breaking Sears Tower [1972-1974] by Skidmore, Owings and Merrill had an interesting city-scale sculptural quality that directly reflected the relationship of elevator planning and optimal rental floor plans.

In tall buildings, the problem of lateral bracing to resist winds and earthquakes is crucial: thus, several buildings had an X-bracing cage-structure enclosing their floor areas, as in the Hancock Center building, Chicago [1965-1970] by Skidmore, Owings and Merrill. The Hancock tower captured the height-limit prize for a time and by its tapered and cross-braced profile showed the effort made to reach this height. In fact, its structure was concealed by metal and fireproofing.[11] The more prosaic, stiff, central elevator and service core was equally as important for bracing as the exterior, yet it was so hidden from view as to be invisible.

In other tall buildings, difficult but artificial structural problems were set by the designers to be "solved" with novel structural means. For the Federal Reserve Bank [1973] in Minneapolis, Minnesota, Gunnar Birkerts wanted a clear exterior open space under the raised first floor. The entire building is supported on suspended cables, carried by two end piers, much like suspension bridges. The cable itself is seen on the exterior as a change in fenestration detail above and below the cable catenary. A future vertical extension will have a reverse compression arch acting in an analogous way to support more floors. Marcel Breuer and Robert Gatje solved a similar "problem" at the Firestone office building in New Haven, Connecticut [1968].

Engineers might argue that the most interesting features of these buildings were in their foundations or in the elevator designs and controls. In fact, the majority of the design work in such a project is done by engineers, since the architectural coverings are repetitious from floor to floor. The architect acts primarily as a coordinator to broker conflicts between various engineers. Recent buildings of this genre have been more concerned with energy conservation than structure, and thus their mechanical systems have become the new field of interest.

In the 1960s direct expression of mechanical systems received much attention, especially in the New Brutalism buildings of England, North America, and Japan. Piping and ductwork, as architectural form and decoration, were first used by Le Corbusier in La Tourette [1956-1961] because of the economic constraint which did not allow extra ceiling or wall finishes. Exposed ductwork, in its later clichés, was usually painted in bright colors to make a three-dimensional supergraphic that zipped through and around a space. Of course, designers tried to control the engineering necessity of these systems by turning easily made rectangular ducts with ugly irregular ribs and hangers into round tubes of a constant profile. To a public accustomed to smooth plastered finishes with concealed air grills or water taps set into a tile wall, all this exposed "plumbing" was a shock, especially when it was so big. So dominant were the color coding and form that it was often easier to find one's way to the mechanical room than to the front door or auditorium. However, these mechanical "guts" were the most interestingly designed parts of many buildings and their exposed vitality saved many schools and restaurants from appearing boring.

Whether, in fact, it was cheaper to build this way is debatable. Exposing building services requires that they be coordinated very carefully with other trade and building systems, that piping installers and sheet-metal workers be concerned with appearance and visual alignment, that the systems' pieces be made more uniform and elegantly jointed together, and that they all be finished. Ductwork with a very large irregular surface area is hard to reach and very difficult to paint. When designed by Louis Kahn, for example in the Exeter Library, Andover, New Hampshire [1972] or at Yale's Mellon Gallery [1976], ductwork and services were elegant beyond compare (fig. 3.2). While structure and ductwork were the primary objects to be demonstrated within buildings, other systems such as elevators and escalators, as in John Portman's Hyatt Regency Hotel of the late 1960s in Atlanta, or ventilation and lighting, as in Stirling's Leicester Labs [1959-1963], were designed with a direct expressive intent.

These systems were not very advanced when compared to other contemporary technology in aerospace or communications and were really only envelopes for the technological work going on inside them. They were in fact the visible manifestations of forces, velocity, viscosity, or momentum which are impossible to see literally. The building, as a technical expression, is thus not the same thing at all as an experiment which would show accurately what is really happening within a building. What we are really seeing is the expression of the assembly of surfaces as containers of activity. The danger of this direct technological expression is that it may become hermetic, self-referential, and not understood by the public. For contemporary users of any technology, it should be there and work. One doesn't care what happens in detail when pressing the button to start a motor; so too in a building, most users who want cool air don't care to see the air-conditioning system.

Thus, what is meant by a direct expression of technology is unclear, for to be literal about all the physical phenomena and the technology associated with them is beyond the possibility of any building. To show all building systems in their raw state as designed by the engineer is visually chaotic: to choose some with more elegantly designed shapes and jointing is to make them transcend their functional raison d'être toward an aesthetics of form and composition. Moreover, there is no clear distinction between direct and indirect expressions of technology and a more transcendent mythology of technology in a rigorous literal sense. It seems fair to say that a direct and complete ("honest") expression of building technology is logically beyond the abilities of any architect. The choices made about the system-design are concerned with appropriate form, not technology, and they refer to how technology should look rather than what it is.

3.2. Louis Kahn. Library, view with air conditioning ducts, Phillips Exeter Academy. Exeter, New Hampshire, 1962-1972. (Photograph: Courtesy of Robert W. White)

INDIRECT EXPRESSION

Much of the expressive technology in buildings is a symbol for the real work going on behind the exterior surfaces. Mies's famous corner at IIT (Illinois Institute of Technology) in Chicago [1945], which looks like a support, is a mask for a more prosaic steel column inside. Steel almost always has to be fireproofed so that any visible steel, as in the trusses at Piano and Rogers's Place Beaubourg [1969-1976], is a covering to protect the real structural steel behind. The decision of what to express and what to leave out is the architect's prerogative. Referring to the hidden bracing in the Seagram building, Louis Kahn likened it to a beautiful lady in a corset, and indeed all we ever see is a bit or more of lace now and then, carefully controlled for effect.

Because architecture is a visible art we expect and want to see its technology working, but many important inventions remain invisible to us. In structural design, new computational techniques of limit-state analysis[12] and the use of computers have made possible constructions today that could have been conceived of but never properly engineered before. New alloys and connection techniques may never be seen but are responsible for major reductions in cost and increased speed of construction. In fact, the computer makes possible many things that are quite subtle and would have been inconceivable before. It is possible for instance to continuously monitor the temperature and air quality in hundreds of locations throughout a building. The overheating influence of the sun on a wall can stimulate systems that will cause that heat to be removed to a cool wall. Total energy consumption can be compared with other years and against predicted values for a simulated building; and if excesses occur they can be traced through monitors to the leak. Tracking collectors can be programmed to follow the sun for any time of the year. These primitive "intelligent" sensate buildings are of a "higher" order than traditional ones, and yet the formal implications of this information-processing are completely hidden.

Other invisible but important techniques have been in the organization of the design and construction process. Borrowing many of the techniques from the military, such as the critical-path-method, economies of labor, materials, and money, all of which can be converted to monetary values, have dramatically changed the organization of construction and often the design of buildings. If technological effects are not visual as, for example, in information processing, acoustics, or air conditioning, they are not usually the province of the architectural designer but more often of a consultant, such as an engineer.

There are several means of expressing technology indirectly in architectural form. In one case, the problem may not be visual by nature but may have a solution that is visually unusual. The function of the undulating ceiling of Alvar Aalto's lecture hall in the Central Finnish Museum at Jyväskylä [1960-1962] (fig. 3.3) is understood as the expression of an acoustical problem and its solution. There are other ways of doing the same job which would not have been visible, but it seems clear that Aalto, acting as his own acoustical engineer, chose the visually expressive way of indicating the acoustic problem. In

3.3. Alvar Aalto. Lecture room with undulating acoustic reflective ceiling, Central Finnish Museum. Jyväskylä, Finland, 1960-1962. (Photograph: Courtesy of Robert W. White)

another case, the precise Miesian box of the Watson Computer Center at Yale by Skidmore, Owings and Merrill [1961] says by its detailing that a high-precision activity is going on inside. The computer itself was exposed, visible through the exterior glass in case the building was too ambiguous. However, the most interesting part of the computer is not the central memory-processing unit which does the computing, but rather the peripheral tape-drives and printers, themselves indirectly expressive of the computer. The building did not respond well to rapid technological change and the computer was soon moved to larger quarters. Building programs or functions concerned with high technology were often excuses to make the building itself suggest high technology. The sense of the building program or type requiring a particular look or "architecture parlant" is an ancient idea in architectural theory which took on a strange, moralistic character during the nineteenth century. In the twentieth century building programs became more complex and ambiguous. Mixed-use complexes often included underground malls, housing, offices, parking, and theaters, such as Westmount Square in Montreal, Canada [1965-1968], by Mies van der Rohe, or Skidmore, Owings and Merrill's Hancock tower in Chicago. Often layered vertically or intermixed without clear boundaries, it was difficult to "read" them without graphics and floor plans. Wrappings of similar curtain walls obscured their legibility further.

Many building systems can be seen only indirectly since they need to be weather- or fire-protected or because they are too dangerous or unclean to be exposed directly. In the Richards Medical Research Laboratories at the University of Pennsylvania [1957-1964] Louis Kahn expressed the exhaust ducts with vertical brick towers within which metal ductwork contained the waste gases. His early sketches showed a literal directness of increasing shaft profile corresponding to the accumulated ductwork; however, he later made the shape simpler and more abstract.[13] The structure for these same labs was, on the whole, very direct, for there is little concealment of any kind and with some understanding one can read the entire beam- and prefabricated-floor support system easily. So important was his desire for literalness that the consequent major problems of large heat loss and thermal expansion were left uncontrolled. Thus, we see that some technology structure is much more appropriate for direct expression than others (mechanical services).

The designer must respond to problems of scale, proportion, and legibility for buildings which are necessarily made of layers, each of which serves a particular function. It is rare that one layer may work more than one way except in mild climates. What one sees and what the architect has to ''express,'' whether it is the technology or anything else, is in the extreme outer layer. With all these choices and constraints, it is little wonder that rarely in architecture is technology directly expressed.

MYTHOLOGY

Architectural design, so intimately entwined with culture, business, religion, and the social order, is committed to technology, if one believes the most well-known polemics of the Modern Movement. The dominance of technology seemed pervasive in the postwar period when economies expanded at phenomenal growth rates. In architecture, such essential technologies as steel and concrete frame construction, metal and glass curtain walls, air-conditioning systems, efficient illumination by fluorescent lighting, rapid reliable elevators and rapid construction techniques, were already known and only needed to be used on a large scale. Most postwar discoveries were not breakthroughs but refinements that aided the spread of modern architecture and left us with the sense that the real action in technology had shifted elsewhere, to the space programs or to large civil works.[14]

The first attempt at creating a mythology of technology was completed before 1940 with the growth of the Modern Movement in Europe. Buildings shared the same qualities as did contemporary machines of smoothness, precise connections and joints, interchangeability and complexity of planning. While their actual building-technology was primitive compared to other fields, buildings did look modern, that is different, and that was all that was important in order for them to work as signs connoting ''technology.'' Following rapid advances in war-technology (the atom bomb, airplanes, radar, and other communications such as TV) most building-technology seemed even more primitive. However, buildings are large and when the size of buildings was extended in the form of skyscrapers or large column-free spans, their overwhelming scale made their technology seem magical.

Whole cities were transformed very soon after the war by ill-fated urban renewal programs in the United States, while in similar European programs highways almost exactly as in Le Corbusier's *Ville Radieuse* schemes ''organized'' city centers. Little by little, each of the ideas of Mies and Corbusier became possible. In 1950 Lever House established the Miesian glass curtain wall as the corporate style preferred. Public-housing schemes in large cities showed mean versions of the *Ville Radieuse*.[15] North America had gained much European talent that would influence future generations of architects through the professional schools and design offices. In a sense, the technology of the postwar period could justify the claims made for it during the earlier years of the twenties and thirties. We should think of postwar design then as an elaboration of earlier ideas that were developed and extended to their limits. Finally these developed ideas were declared emptied of meaning in the late sixties and early seventies by adherents of a recherché aesthetic movement, the Post-Modernists, who questioned the disproportionate role of technology in architectural design theory.

What does "mythology" mean, as we are using it here? A " . . . myth is a system of communication, that is a message."[16] As distinguished from direct and indirect technological expression, the mythological expression of technology is concerned with a modern iconography. The interesting aspect of this mythology is the influence it had on architectural form, that is, the way the idea or magic of technology was expressed, irrespective of the actual technology of the building. This could take several modes. One way was for the building to look like a machine or a part or product of one. Another was for the building to embody a characteristic of a machine or of an advanced technological object (speed, intricacy, delicacy, power, or smooth finish).

Buildings that look like machines are common in many industrial processes, notably in the chemical and power-operating industries. The Archigram group in London in the 1960s showed a number of schemes which looked remarkably like oil refineries, as does the Centre Pompidou at Place Beaubourg by Piano and Rogers. In Toronto, Craig, Zeidler and Strong designed Ontario Place (fig. 3.4) as a series of platforms in a lagoon that seem to be an abstraction of drilling platforms. In Berlin, the Umlauftank [1968], by Ludwig Leo looks like some gigantic processing machine. Leon Krier said about this project: " . . . technology for him [is] more a matter of passion of the soul than of objective necessity. His knowledge of technical matters will not lead him to a deductive design method but rather to something like technological lyricism."[17] "Holiday Machine," Superstudio's project on the Calabrian coast near Tropea [1968], shows a building becoming a dam, borrowing an aura of power from the scale of the great civil work and its site. Superstudio said: "Myths, the old motives for all activities, are still with us: architecture is a machine also functioning symbolically. From industrial processes, architecture takes methods of composition (assembly, repetition, change of scale) and demonstrates them. The machine producing objects gives birth to an architecture in the image of the machine."[18] The mythological quality of these buildings is in the excess of their technique. We don't need all those pipes to show us the building services (Beaubourg), nor does the building need to be located in the water (Ontario Place) with a living platform raised high in the air connected to others by steel bridges that call forth very industrial analogies (fig. 3.4).

3.4. Craig, Zeidler and Strong. Architecture based upon the structural design of oil drilling rigs. Ontario Place, Toronto, Ontario, 1970. (Photograph: Courtesy of Robert W. White)

It is easier mythologically to recall technology if we refer to a building-type or an object-type that carries a built-in set of images and meanings. Once the configuration of a well-drilling platform and its attendant technology becomes well known as an artifact, then it can stand as a sign for some highly complicated function and, by extension, for advanced technology. It doesn't matter whether the object-type is for drilling oil or coal or for crossing the ocean—its primary use in architecture is to signify complicated technology to which the imitative building aspires. The mythological connection is clear if the building-type is recalled through imitation. Only the essential features of a well-drilling platform need be imitated, and they can be pared down, simplified, and made more abstract. The mythological building is a system of interrelated signs which need to be economical and easily read. A placard which said "I am like an oil-drilling platform" might be easiest, but chances are it wouldn't work since mythological expression in a building must be subtle and indirect. Myth is the description of the result, rather than necessarily the designer's intention.

Roland Barthes believed that the preeminent model for a building or a component to emulate was the automobile: "I think that cars today are almost the exact equivalent of the great Gothic Cathedrals. I mean the supreme creation of an era, conceived with passion by unknown artists and consumed in image, if not in usage, by a whole population which appropriates them as a purely magical object."[19] Making buildings that resembled machine products was common in the 1950s and 1960s. One type was a precisely made object, such as a box supported over the ground or podium level by the most minimal piers. These seemingly weightless box forms with their attendant repetitive modules were like blown-up industrial objects that could have come from an assembly line. The Beinecke Library at Yale by Gordon Bunshaft of Skidmore, Owings and Merrill [1961] shows this motive most clearly, especially in its complete incongruity with neighboring traditional buildings that nest fully upon the ground and indeed have a base, a middle, and a top. Other examples illustrating this trend are the Law School Group by Saarinen [1958-1960] and the Lutheran School of Theology [1966-1967] by Perkins and Will, both at the University of Chicago. These "industrially designed" buildings, often out of scale with their contexts and with unfamiliar materials, seem to transcend a particular time and place and respond to their own internal needs, much as industrially designed objects do.

Prefabricated wall panels are designed to look like machined products in Stirling's Olivetti Training Building at Haslemere, England [1969-1972]. The perfection, finish, and color of his glass-fiber reinforced plastic pieces have a strange look that says as much about technology in general as about that building in particular. We feel that this building has nothing to do with traditional building. It seems like something which has landed from another planet and might take off again at any time, especially when seen with the adjacent old mansion.

The connection between industrial design and architecture is explicitly made by the industrial design and graphics exhibit at the Museum of Modern Art in New York City, a prelude to the architecture exhibit, wherein the very best refined *objêts retrouvés* from industry are collected as reminders of a larger and potentially more perfect world (salvation through design). Furniture, which every great architect is supposed to be able to design well, is prominently displayed to make the connection even more apparent.

Buildings which embody characteristics of a machine are more difficult to classify than those that actually look like something else, especially since most technology is not visually intended. With attributes from concept to process to design we can progress from speed to air resistance to smooth horizontal rounded shapes (streamlining) and, by reversing the sequence, smooth rounded shapes can be read as signs of technology. The Johnson's Wax Building by Frank Lloyd Wright [1936-1939; 1946-1949] does this in an ambiguous way, since the streamlined shapes are made from bricks and glass. In a clearer instance Jean and Claude Prouvé's Palais des Expositions in Grenoble [1968] is made of gasketed glass and enamelled steel panels with rounded corners. The BMW (Bavarian Motor Works) Headquarters Building by Karl Schwanzer in Munich [designed 1968; erected 1970-1973] is streamlined not only in its four, twenty-two-story cyindrical forms and its finely worked steel and glass skin, but also in its constructional technique. Once its service core was completed a system of steel bars served to hydraulically lift prefabricated suspended sections of the fourfold cylinder into place at a rate of one floor a week. The building, then, was finished from top to bottom, adding to the mythology of "streamlining" in terms of process as well as form. In the Marseilles block, Le Corbusier showed the great weight from the community above carried on pairs of exaggerated tapered muscular concrete "thighs," theatrically playing out a precarious drama.[20] Later, he grew tired of that game and in Nantes, Berlin, and Firminy reduced the piers to their required structural sizes. When the later piers were made less substantial, the sense of structural drama was strangely absent.

These examples illustrate only a cursory analysis of one mode of discussing postwar architecture. It is not the only critical method, nor the best for every situation but it does help in making sense out of the curious shapes that may seem so strange to contemporary, Post-Modern-oriented eyes. These mythologies are meant for both the creator—the architectural designer—and the lay observer, for they justify, clarify, or make excuses for a form. While some buildings are almost literary with a set of coded symbols available with an explicit text (Michael Graves, Rodolfo Machado), others, though lacking formal guides, nevertheless have sufficient content in them for us to build a mythology.

Economics and Technology

To incorporate technology into buildings, one must want to construct something difficult and do it cheaply. The curtain wall's wide dissemination required cheap extruded aluminum for ease of maintenance, glazing systems to support large glass surfaces, and air-conditioning systems to moderate large fluctuations in heating and cooling loads. Each of these aspects for the curtain wall required a large market to justify further improvements in component design or manufacturing processes in order to lower costs. This market was largely created by standardization of components that limited the choice of profiles and yet allowed customizing lengths and connections for individual projects. Many other building systems shared the limitations in component configuration and assembly procedure but allowed some flexibility of dimensions. These systems of curtain walls, metal ceilings, panelized "lay in" ceiling tiles and light fixtures, wall panels, elevators and escalators, metal and wooden partition studs, steel beams and columns became very popular. Lengths were restricted to two-foot increments for most preengineered structures and finishes; and although most systems would allow intermediate trimming, that implied waste and increased labor costs. Thus, a tacit standardization of building element-sizes was accepted to reduce costs in order to increase the collective market.

Associated with the standardization of some aspects of partially prefabricated building elements was a change in component sizes, finish, and material. Before the Modern Movement and through the first postwar years, most exposed building components were quite small (brick, tile, stone, glass, wood boards) or were continuous surfaces of concrete or plaster or a combination of these. Building with such small units is labor-intensive, slow, and craftsmanlike. Even the early houses of Le Corbusier were technically primitive. It was not until some few years after the war that the use of panelized building was taken seriously by the majority of architects dealing with such problems as mass housing. Again it was Le Corbusier who showed the way, perhaps not because of particular originality but because of the publicity and drama he created about such ideas, chiefly at the Marseille project [1952].

The problem with large panel construction is the size of the market for the panel. Either a whole building can become the market or one building-type is standardized from building to building so that many buildings repeated comprise an aggregate market. Because public housing can be controlled in program and design from site to site, and since it is usually planned (sadly) in large blocks, it is the likeliest type of building in which to use large prefabricated panels and modules. Several systems, such as the Reema System of England, Descon of Canada and Camus, Coignet, Tracoba, and Costamagna systems from France are marketed or licensed throughout the world. Each has formed a catalog of parts to be assembled on site, as for example in Brunswick Centre, Bloomsbury, London [1960-1972] by Patrick Hodgkinson. This systems-approach to construction values speed, low labor skill levels, and large size. The planning and design options given the architect are few, the major design work being site-massing and landscaping.

Where building authorities are responsible for many buildings, the systems-approach has also been tried, for instance, in schools (SCSD—Schools Construction System Development by Ehrenkrantz late in the 1960s). This approach to design and construction has not been as widespread as its early advocates might have hoped. In the early 1970s poor economic conditions made large multibuilding projects uncertain, diminishing a prospective long-term market and thus limiting the capitalization investment required to market the off-site factories. The large regular building blocks organized for construction needs first, and human long-term accommodation second, were rejected by a public that wanted to live in houses, not projects such as Pruitt-Igoe Housing, St. Louis [1952-1955; destroyed 1972], and have something unique to identify their dwelling. Recent, more subtle reworkings of systems-building have resurfaced in the schemes of Mitchell and Stirling in Lima, Peru [1969]. The most extensive of such schemes are for those underdeveloped countries like Peru and India, where huge migrations to the cities led to squatter housing. Groups of the poor can create a large market for simple building services and components sufficient to warrant construction of factory-produced dwelling structures but leave much of the finishing labor and future extensions to the owner. By strictly limiting the role of outside authorities, such housing is affordable with "sweat equity" and is individualized by its residents to accommodate to different family needs, tastes, and social and economic circumstances. The competition for housing in Manila [1976] won by Athalson, of New Zealand, shows just such a scheme.

There was, again following the war, a great interest in using not only the partially prefabricated building components we have already discussed but also whole building components which were simply bolted or fixed together like a construction toy set. Outstanding examples of this approach may be seen in Archigram's (Peter Cook's) "Plug-in City" project [1964], Shadrack Woods and Jean Prouvé's Berlin Free University building [1970] and Kisho Kurokawa's Nakagin Capsule Tower, Tokyo [1970-1972]. The ideas for this type of construction date back to James Bogardus in the United States during the 1850s and to John Paxton's Crystal Palace [1851].

Making the least intervention with technological means is a notion akin to the appropriate technology movement that was prominent in the United States and elsewhere during the Vietnam War and continues today. Largely a rural antiurban philosophy, it saw architecture estranged from its inhabitants, designed by an elite professional class employing wasteful means and unnatural materials for questionable ends. These values of the corporate establishment were seen to be profit-oriented, resource and energy intensive, and hierarchically socially structured. Many young architectural graduates, some of whom were involved with antiwar and social protest, either worked on imaginary projects or found no chance to build their own large buildings and so went back to nature to construct structures that were handcrafted, naturally finished, and heated with wood-burning stoves. Technology in this case was used in a found and combined ad hoc way that went farther than it had in the hands of Bruce Goff during the fifties [see his Bavinger House, Norman, Oklahoma, 1957]. It was the architect as a bricoleur, discovering wood stoves and wind generators and forming sculpture out of plumbing fixtures. See for example the collection of unusual houses on Prickly Mountain near Warren, Vermont, done in the late sixties and early seventies by Yale University graduates David Sellers, William Rienecke, Tom Luckey, Louis Mackel, Ted Judson, and others. By making simple technology accessible, they unwittingly showed one response to the energy crisis that began in 1973. The alternative technology movement was primarily in domestic architecture where the building's equipment, exposed and low-cost, was of some importance with respect to the total structure.

Constrictions in energy supplies and rapid escalations in prices of oil and gas have caused profound changes in the design of new buildings. Architects and engineers have been forced to conserve energy and prove that their buildings are economical. The first accusatory reaction that the energy crisis evoked was about wasteful practices in industries, transportation, and buildings in developed countries. Buildings were conspicuous offenders by their large expanses of glass, by lights operating at all times and by excessive air-conditioning temperatures. It was not uncommon to find offices consuming energy at 400,000 BTU/ft^2/yr., as Dr. Charles Lawrence discovered in 1972 in a survey of 180 buildings in New York City.[21] Although with cheap energy this was never a design issue, it was easily shown that this consumption could be reduced by half. Recently, in many cases it has in fact been reduced to 80,000 BTU/ft^2/yr. and less, for instance in Toronto's all-glass-surfaced Ontario Hydro building [1972-1976] that employs Gerhard Moog's ENCOM energy-savings system.

Architects and their engineers needed to make substantial savings in consumption. The first step emphasized turning off lights, setting back thermostats in the winter, plugging leaks, fixing faulty insulation, and instituting heat recovery schemes, none of which had any effect on architectural design. Solar collectors affected designs very little, since they were applied to flat roofs and as an engineering fix-up they were largely a public-relations-oriented response by the building professions. The truth was that most architectural designers simply did not know how to design buildings to conserve energy. For large buildings with cheap energy, there had been no need to consider siting for maximum solar gain, efficient shade design, heat storage, or efficient lighting. Buildings as long-term future commitments now need to adjust to strict energy-consumption criteria, whether imposed by regulation or economics. Equipment and appliances, however, become obsolete in five to ten years and must be redesigned to accommodate to new requirements.

If structural expressions and the allied technology of structural engineering typified much of the 1950s architecture, then heating, air-conditioning engineering, and conservation were the dominant themes in the technology of the 1970s and will continue to be in the near future. Large buildings emphasize computer-controlled energy monitoring, off-peak energy storage, low-energy lighting design, and improved building-wall design, all of which excepting the last are designed by consulting engineers. A more careful response to site conditions has emphasized underground building, atria to reduce wall exposure, and careful orientation to the sun and winds to reduce or enhance heating, depending on the exterior climate, all of which are within the area of the architect's decision. When pursued with a vengeance, new building forms have resulted, such as the SERI Building (Solar Energy Research Institute) in

Boulder, Colorado, by Caudill, Rowlett and Scott [1979], an earth-buried structure with active solar collectors and carefully designed devices to distribute daylight. Among the definers of architectural ideas, however, those forms have not been recognized as having special aesthetic qualities. To date, energy considerations have had only a limited impact on contemporary aesthetic ideas in architectural design. Furthermore, few architectural critics have any technical background and thus they cannot be expected to recognize these relationships.

The individual house has always been a laboratory for new ideas in architectural design and now is being used for solar energy research. There are in this new field hundreds of ways to capture, store, and distribute heat. Because exterior surface area is large in relation to floor area, and since building layouts are flexible, the home can be manipulated in a variety of configurations. With many combinations of materials to store, transmit, or reflect heat, and with a variety of components to capture and distribute heat, the ways of making energy-efficient houses seem almost infinite (fig. 3.5)

3.5. "The Ark": Experimental closed ecological system powered by alternative energy sources including vertical solar collectors and windmills. Prince Edward Island, Canada. (Photograph: Courtesy of Robert W. White)

Solar house designs have much in common with the alternative houses of the late 1960s and early 1970s. There are many logical contradictions however. With the exception of some developments in Israel, most solar houses are rural retreats rather than attached in a dense urban configuration. They require long commutes for supplies or services and instead of becoming models for a mass population are sometimes utopian in program. These experiments are informed by much deeper understanding of the physical laws of heat transfer, material properties, solar movement, and climatology. The designers take their building procedures seriously and make tight, well-insulated, and often rather expensive homes. There is a messianic quality to much of this work that is refreshing and naive. It is as if houses are being designed for the first time, for though they often may lack the elegant formal vocabulary that architects like Graves, Gwathmey or Meier can manipulate, their aesthetic qualities are more tactile, nostalgic, and unsophisticated, even if a computer monitors the house and describes the temperature profile in the rock-bed storage area. One feels the sun warm a surface, hears the circulating pump turn on, and watches the temperature/humidity recorder so that technological expression is more than visual.

Technological achievements have been the responses to a perceived need or a problem to be solved. The Vertical Assembly Building by the office of Max O. Urbahn in Cape Kennedy, Florida, the largest enclosed volume in the world, was possible, for example, only when the space program created a need for it. Its subsequent influence on the English architects such as the Archigram group or James Stirling had shock effects apparently throughout the profession, as is evident in Stirling and Gowan's Leicester University Engineering Building [1963] and the Condor Branch of the Bank of the City of Buenos Aires, Argentina [1969] by Manteola, Peterchesky, Sanchez-Gomez, Santos, Solsona, and Viñoly. There were few interesting problems for which technology was essential, except for the ongoing incremental issues of saving time and money. The lack of technological need in architecture, while the rest of society was intimately entwined with and determined by technical change, made for a kind of crisis in the architecture of the late 1960s.

The image of a Western technologically based war in Vietnam, and the corruption of a consumer-goods-oriented society which would not distribute benefits equitably, caused a revolt among the young and disadvantaged in Newark, New Jersey; Watts, California; Haight-Asbury section of San Francisco; Paris; Poland, and throughout those parts of the world that rejected technology and the economic and political systems that it supported. Indeed, building projects were often the direct causes of riots, as in Morningside Heights in New York City where a sports center proposal for Columbia University provoked the wrath of residents and students. More dramatically in 1967 in Newark, New Jersey, riots were due in no small part to the designs for a proposed medical center that would have caused wholesale destruction of a black neighborhood while ignoring urgent health problems in the area. Architectural aesthetic theoreticians could at once reject all by rejecting the antihistorical underpinnings of the Modern Movement and at the same time rediscover the traditional sources of European architecture, especially those of the eighteenth and nineteenth centuries. Having both history and technology, architects could choose to limit their interest, especially since technical needs were of secondary importance. When the importance of technology became evident following the energy crisis in the mid-1970s, the technological solutions became curiously combined with dissimilar values, especially the simple rural self-sufficient ideals of the back-to-earth movements, as in the works of the Total Environmental Action Group in Harris Hill, New Hampshire (U.S.) and Nick Nicholson in Ayers Cliff, Quebec (Canada).

There are many ideas that may not prove economical or practical but now are being tried and measured, and an excitement that, like it or not, architecture will be quite different because of the energy crisis. The influence and growth of technology was extensive and pervasive throughout the postwar period, affecting architectural design in countless direct and indirect ways. As described above, technology's influence on architectural ideas was profound. When architectural designers without an extensive technical education were unable to adequately describe this technology their indirect and mythological expressions were evasions, however well meant. This situation many change. The forces in the world's societies are equal to those of the twenties, but with optimism replaced by a melancholy suspicion that "progress" either peaked years ago or never existed. The economics of material and energy scarcities, disparities between Third World and developed countries, and vast shifts in capital, as well as complex communication networks can in the near future cause urban and architectural form to be radically different from what we now know. Certainly if, with what seems to have been a tame and naive view of the future, the world's economy and society were sufficient to prompt the visions of a Gropius and a Le Corbusier, then the current situation must call for even more considerable change.

Notes

1. Charles Jencks, *Modern Movements in Architecture* (London: Pelican, 1973), p. 28.
2. J. Grant Wanzel, "Postwar Housing in the Atlantic Region . . . Architecture as Counter Revolution" (Paper delivered at the Annual Meeting of the Society for the Study of Architecture in Canada, University of Quebec at Montreal, May 29-June 2, 1980).
3. D. Scott Brown et al., "Suburban Space, Scale and Symbol," VIA III. *Ornament* (1977): 41-47.
4. Bohdan Paczowski, "Classical Split," *Architectural Review* 166, no. 944 (December 1979): 341-46.
5. D. Scott Brown and R. Venturi, "Co-op City: Learning to Like It," *Progressive Architecture*, February 1970, pp. 64-73.
6. Jacques Ehrmann, "Habiter L'Utopia?," *Perspecta, Yale Architectural Journal* 13/14 (1971): 209.
7. Charles Jencks, *Le Corbusier and the Tragic View of Architecture* (Cambridge, Mass.: Harvard University Press, 1973), p. 144.
8. Pier Luigi Nervi, *Aesthetics and Technology in Building* (Cambridge, Mass.: Harvard University Press, 1965), p. 136.
9. Nervi, *Aesthetics*, pp. 66-67.
10. Bruce Graham, "Computer Graphics in Architectural Practice" in Murray Milne, ed., *Computer Graphics in Architecture* (New Haven: Yale University Press, 1968), p. 24.
11. Carl Condit, *Chicago: 1930-1970* (Chicago: University of Chicago Press, 1974), p. 110.
12. D. E. Allen, "Limit States Design—A Probabilistic Study," *Canadian Journal of Civil Engineering* 2, no. 1 pp. 36-49.
13. Romaldo Giurgola and Jaimini Mehta, *Louis I. Kahn* (Boulder, Colo.: Westview Press, 1975), pp. 194-201.
14. Superstudio, "Tropea," *Perspecta, Yale Architectural Journal* 13/14 (1971): 306-7.
15. Jane Jacobs, *Death and Life of Great American Cities* (New York: Vintage Books, 1961), part 4.
16. Roland Barthes, *Mythologies* (London: Phaidon Press, 1955), p. 109.
17. Leon Krier, "Ludwig Leo: A Most Unusual Architect," *Act Net*, London, 1975.
18. Superstudio, "Tropea," *Perspecta, Yale Architectural Journal* 13/14 (1971): 314.
19. Roland Barthes, *Mythologies*, p. 109.
20. Le Corbusier, *Oeuvres Complètes*, vol. 5 (Zurich: Artemis, 1953).
21. D. E. Abrahamson and S. Emmings, eds., "Energy Conservation: Implications for Building Design and Operation" (Papers delivered at the *Energy Conference, University of Minnesota*, May 1973).

Bibliography

BOOKS

Ambasz, E. *Italy: The New Domestic Landscape*. New York: Museum of Modern Art, 1972.

Banham, R. *Theory and Design in the First Machine Age*. London: Architectural Press, 1960.

______. *The Architecture of the Well-Tempered Environment*. London: Architectural Press, 1960.

Boyle, G. and Harper, P., eds. *Radical Technology*. London: Wildwood House, 1976.

Condit, C. W. *American Building Art, The Twentieth Century*. New York: Oxford University Press, 1961.

______. *Technology and Culture* 9 (1968): 1-33.

Cooke, P. *Experimental Architecture*. New York: Universe Books, 1970.

Cowan, H. J. *An Historical Outline of Architectural Science*. Amsterdam: Elsevier, 1966.

Drew, Philip and Lockwood, Crosby. *Frei Otto: Form and Structure*. Staples, 1976.

Drexler, Arthur. *Transformations in Modern Architecture*. New York: Museum of Modern Art, 1979.

Fazio, P. and Haider, G., eds. *Proceedings*: Third International Symposium on Lower Cost Housing Problems. Montreal: Centre de Recherches sur le Batiment, Concordia University, May 27-31, 1974.

Hutchings, R. *Soviet Science, Technology, Design: Interaction and Convergence*. New York: Oxford University Press, 1976.

Joedicke, J. *Shell Architecture*. London: Tiranti, 1963.

Kranzberg, M. and Davenport, W. H., eds. *Technology and Culture*. New York: New American Library, 1975.

Mainstone, R. J. *Developments in Structural Form*. London: Allen Lane, 1975.

Maré, De E., ed. *New Ways of Building*. London: Architectural Press, 1948.

Marks, R. W. *The Dymaxion World of Buckminster Fuller*. New York: Reinhold, 1960.

Michaels, L. *Contemporary Structure in Architecture*. New York: Reinhold, 1950.

Nervi, Pier Luigi. *Structures*. New York: F. W. Dodge, 1956.

Otto, Frei, ed. *Tensile Structures*. Cambridge, Mass.: MIT Press, 1973.

Steadman, Philip. *Energy, Environment and Building*. Cambridge: At the University Press, 1975.

Torroja, E. *Philosophy of Structures*. Berkeley: University of California Press, 1958.

______. *The Structures of Eduardo Torroja*. New York: F. W. Dodge, 1958.

Turner, John F. C. *Housing by People*. New York: Architectural Design, 1976.

Vartagnian, Oleg. *Folded Structural Surfaces*. Montreal: Center for Building Studies, Concordia University, 1979.

Wachsmann, K. *The Turning Point of Building*. New York: Reinhold, 1961.

Watson, Donald, ed. *Energy Conservation through Building Design*. New York: McGraw-Hill, 1979.

White, R. B. *Prefabrication: A History of its Development in Great Britain*. London: National Building Studies Special Report no. 36, H.M.S.O., 1965.

JOURNALS

Agrest, Diana. ''Design versus Non Design,'' *Oppositions* 6 (Fall 1976): 45-68.

Anderson, Bruce. *Architectural Forum* 95: 144-51.

Bryan, V. and Sauer, R., eds. ''Structures Implicit and Explicit.'' *VIA II*. (1973). Graduate School of Fine Arts, University of Pennsylvania.

Dugdale, T., Elder, H., et al. ''Hand Built Hornby.'' *Architectural Design Profiles* no. 14 (1978).

Pawley, Martin. "We Shall Not Bulldoze Westminster Abbey." *Oppositions* (Winter 1976-1977): 27-33.

Rush, Richard. "The Era of Swoops and Billows." *Progressive Architecture* (June 1980): 110-20.

Stirling, James. ''The Functional Tradition and Expression,'' *Perspecta: Yale Architectural Journal* 6 (1960).

4

PRESERVATION, RESTORATION, AND CONSERVATION

ROBERT BRUEGMANN

The idea of preserving a building or a part of the urban fabric for its historical importance or architectural merit is a modern notion that grew out of the Enlightenment and Industrial Revolution. It became a distinct activity late in the eighteenth century when society's needs and technology began to change so quickly that buildings became functionally obsolete before they were structurally untenable. The first organizations for preservation were established in the early nineteenth century, and by the end of the century a wide range of theoretical positions had been explored, largely in France and Britain. Early in the twentieth century, concurrently with a great acceleration in the rate of destruction of old buildings, the importance of preserving important architectural landmarks gained a wider acceptance. Since World War II, however, the scope and direction of preservation have changed dramatically to meet wholly new demands. From today's vantage point it appears that the preservation of old buildings will be increasingly important. Preservation, restoration, and conservation have become increasingly complex and controversial topics of discussion, which include a wide range of attitudes current since 1945, some of which have in common only the premise that old buildings should be saved.[1]

Preservation

POSTWAR RECONSTRUCTION

The physical destruction caused by World War II was unprecedented. Large areas of major cities including historic city centers were leveled, posing reconstruction problems for which old guidelines were no longer adequate. In Rotterdam for instance, the decision was made to discard earlier building patterns and to reconstruct a new city center employing current ideas of urban planning, modern materials, and contemporary architectural styles. Elsewhere, as in Budapest, Leningrad, Dresden, St. Malo, and Nürnberg, an effort was made to follow old street patterns and to reconstruct historic buildings reproducing as closely as possible, prewar appearances.

Probably the largest single campaign was in Warsaw, where ninety percent of all the historic buildings had been destroyed. The historic city center was such an important symbol of national pride that immediately after the war the Polish legislature voted to reconstruct it as completely as possible. All land in the area was expropriated by the city, a large state appropriation was passed, and the clearing of the rubble was made a national priority. Because new facilities were so desperately needed, there was little time to consider the philosophical problems raised by such a restoration. When photos and drawings were available they were used, but for many structures and most interiors there was very little documentary evidence; for some buildings the most reliable information was obtained from views painted during the eighteenth century by Canaletto. Even in cities where the task of rebuilding was less daunting, decisions had to be made quickly and many buildings, even historically important ones, were reconstructed on the basis of little evidence.[2]

The needs of postwar rebuilding brought about major experiments with new restoration technology, as in the reconstruction in steel of the roof of the Cathedral of St. Stephan in Vienna or that of St. Pierre at Verdun in reinforced concrete. In a few cases damaged buildings were deliberately left as ruins, most notably the Kaiser Wilhelm-Gedächtniskirche in Berlin (fig. 4.1), a late nineteenth-century building by Franz Schwechten. Here architect Egon Eiermann juxtaposed with its blackened ruins a resolutely modern church and bell tower, to form a striking contrast and provide an eloquent visual commentary on recent history. Ironically, this rigorous honesty in the preservation of original materials probably was possible only because the church itself was of the late nineteenth century, in a revival style, and not considered architecturally important in 1956, the time of the design competition that determined its fate.[3]

4.1. Egon Eiermann, architect. Kaiser-Wilhelm-Memorial Church. Post-World War II addition to ruins of Franz Schwechten's late ninteenth-century church. Berlin, 1956-1961. (Photograph: Courtesy of C. W. Westfall, 1958)

PRESERVATION AND THE "MODERN MOVEMENT"

Historic buildings usually were reconstructed following World War II because of patriotic feeling and popular sentiment rather than at the insistence of architects. Many progressive designers of the "Modern Movement," in fact, saw the destruction caused by the war as a golden opportunity, for rarely had there been the opportunity for large-scale rebuilding before the war. With large sectors of major cities destroyed it suddenly appeared possible to put into effect the urbanistic notions that had been succinctly stated in the Charter of Athens. This important document, drawn up at the fourth meeting of the International Congress of Modern Architecture (CIAM) in 1933 but published only in 1941, summarized advanced architectural thought at the beginning of the postwar period. The charter contains an entire section entitled "The Historic Heritage of Cities" that begins with the statement: "Architectural assets must be protected, whether found in isolated buildings or in urban aggregations," but each succeeding point set forth considerably qualifies this broad statement. Monuments will be protected, the charter explains, only if they are still serviceable, of universal interest, and do not cause sanitary or social problems. In one sentence especially the charter reveals underlying assumptions: "Certain people, more concerned for aestheticism than social solidarity, militate for the preservation of certain picturesque old districts unmindful of the poverty, promiscuity and diseases that these districts harbor." It is implied here that the cause of social and moral problems is the physical design of the town, and that the means to improve these conditions is to remove the old buildings, while those who favor the preservation of these structures are elitist, interested only in aesthetic matters.[4]

Although not always heeded in the immediate postwar rebuildings, the statements of the Athens Charter and the example of Le Corbusier's urban projects became dominant in planning doctrine by the mid-1950s. In the following decade, whole sectors of European and American cities were demolished, "modern" buildings erected, and great roadways thrust into the center of densely populated areas. New office buildings and housing projects in the International Style were erected on cleared sites in complete disregard of existing street patterns and building stock. From South America to Eastern Europe high office and residential buildings in the hearts of cities came to be equated with "progress." Even in Paris, despite fierce opposition, disruptive highways and tall buildings were constructed, such as the enormous Tour Montparnasse complex that displaced a nineteenth-century railroad station.

THE OLD REVALUED

By the late 1960s a major change was taking place. First, it became clear that the new buildings, for all their up-to-date plumbing and increased light and air, could not by themselves lower crime, increase income, or solve other basic problems. In fact, instead of the rich mixture of occupations and income levels found in traditional European cities, single-purpose buildings, an increased use of zoning, and the construction of "public" housing tended to segregate groups by income level making social mobility difficult and intensifying urban conflicts. The bulldozer approach to "urban renewal" brought a sharp backlash first from the people who were displaced from their homes by demolition and then from the academic arm of the planning profession. In Jane Jacobs's classic *The Death and Life of Great*

American Cities (1961), an entire chapter, entitled "The Need for Aged Buildings," argued not only for the preservation of great monuments but also for ordinary, old buildings which had value as "bargain" spaces. Jacobs showed how cultural and aesthetic vitality were related to diversity. Such epigrams as, "Old ideas can sometimes use new buildings. New ideas must use old buildings" have exerted a tremendous influence on city planning.[5]

Gaping holes in the urban fabric caused by postwar renewal schemes spurred a new interest in the preservation of entire historic districts rather than single monuments, an interest that became evident in a document pointedly called the Venice Charter drawn up in 1964 by the International Congress of Architects and Technicians of Historic Monuments. This change in emphasis has been clearly reflected in legislative and administrative actions for preservation. In the period between the early nineteenth century and World War II almost every major European country had passed legislation establishing a national policy for the classification and protection of individual landmark structures. In the postwar period the new concept of urban preservation on a wider basis, covering districts, or whole towns, became increasingly popular. France's celebrated *Loi Malraux* of 1962 provided the model, followed by Great Britain's Civic Amenities Act of 1967 and similar laws in most other European countries. Examples of major districts subject to legislative controls include: the Marais district in Paris; the entire cities of Bath, Chichester, York, and Chester in Britain; the historic centers of Bologna, Venice, and Urbino in Italy; Fribourg in Switzerland; Tübingen in Germany; the Gamla Stan section of Stockholm; the historic areas of Cuzco, Peru; Kyoto, Japan; Isphahan, Iran; Dubrovnik, Yugoslavia; and the Tunis Medinah in Tunisia. The studies of Giancarlo de Carlo in Urbino and the work of Gustav Peichl in the Freyung in Vienna have been models of careful investigation and sensitive redesign of historic areas.[6] In the United States, although a few laws protecting districts were passed very early in cities like Charleston and New Orleans, progress has been somewhat slower.

On the architectural side, the gap between new and old was being bridged by architects who started to borrow heavily from historic buildings. The relation of new buildings to the existing fabric, or contextualism, became a major issue in the works of Robert Venturi in the United States and the Smithsons in Britain. A concern with existing urban spaces and building typology has become a dominant theme in the work of European architects of as widely divergent philosophies as Leon and Rob Krier, Aldo Rossi, Maurice Culot, Oswald Mathias Ungers, and Ricardo Bofill.[7]

The rise in interest in historic buildings had coincided with a major redefinition of what is historic. During the 1960s and 1970s the entire nineteenth century, previously dismissed in standard histories, was reexamined and found to be worthy of study and preservation. This has probably more than doubled the stock of "historic" buildings especially in the United States which suddenly found itself, for the first time, with an important architectural history. As the pace of construction quickened after World War II, moreover, the rate of demolitions increased, demanding action on behalf of important buildings even of relatively recent vintage. Within the last two decades (since 1960) Paris lost Baltard's Les Halles sheds; London lost the Euston Station and Bunning's Corn Exchange; Tokyo lost the Imperial Hotel of Frank Lloyd Wright. In the United States the toll has been appalling, including single buildings like McKim, Mead and White's Pennsylvania Station in New York and the majority of all buildings designed by less fortunate architects, such as Louis Sullivan. This trend has made necessary governmental interventions to save and restore buildings, even buildings as recent as Walter Gropius's Bauhaus in Dessau [1926] and the Villa Savoye at Poissy by Le Corbusier [1928-1930] and it has led to the paradox of listing Eero Saarinen's Dulles Airport in Chantilly, Virginia, finished in 1968, in the National Register of Historic Places. This speeding up of history has become especially apparent in the United States where Philip Johnson already has made arrangements for the donation of his own house complex in New Canaan, Connecticut, started in 1949, to the National Trust for Historic Preservation.

Finally, and perhaps most important, basic economic changes made preservation an increasingly attractive alternative to new construction. Labor and materials costs rose dramatically in most parts of the Western world during the entire postwar period; the series of energy crises of the 1970s and the rapid increases in fuel costs frequently made thermally light, International Style glass boxes more expensive to operate than the masonry structures of earlier periods. For economic reasons alone it seems that renovation will increase at the expense of new construction for the foreseeable future.

LEGAL AND ADMINISTRATIVE BASES

Today, the legal and administrative apparatus for preservation varies widely from country to country. In France, for example, there is a great deal of centralization in administering the national system of classification, while in the Federal Republic of Germany the individual states, or "Länder," instead have broad powers in this area. Almost every country is now concerned with forming a systematic survey of landmark buildings and districts and with creating legislation to protect these buildings. Since in most Western countries the government is unable to purchase all of the designated structures, each has had to adopt a system of incentives and subsidies that would motivate and enable private owners to maintain them properly. Complicated governmental machinery often is augmented by a proliferation of private and semipublic preservation organizations.

Internationally, since the fifties the United Nations Educational, Scientific, and Cultural Organization (UNESCO) has frequently advised and aided in the case of extremely important monuments like the city of Angkor Wat in Cambodia, the Mayan site of Tikal in Guatemala, the temple of Borobudur in Indonesia, and numerous sites in Iran. UNESCO has also afforded assistance in emergency situations like the flooding of Venice and Florence in 1966 and the earthquake of May 1970 in Peru. It undertook the moving of the temples of Abu Simbel in Egypt in the mid-1960s to prevent their flooding by the new Aswan High Dam, and contributed in 1956, 1961, 1964 and more recently to the protection of Mohenjo Daro, capital of the Indus River Valley civilization, likewise threatened by flooding. To help provide a high level of available expertise UNESCO also established an educational institution in 1958 in Rome, the International Center for the Study of the Preservation and Conservation of Cultural Property (ICCROM), which deals with technical aspects of preservation. Among other organizations that continue to function effectively in these fields are the International Council on Monuments and Sites (ICOMOS), established in 1965, publisher of the magazine *Monumentum*, and the Council of Europe's Council on Cultural Cooperation.[8]

RECONSTRUCTION

Ironically, as preservation has become increasingly attractive economically and has gained wide support first in Europe and then in America, many of the theoretical controversies which first surfaced in the nineteenth century have reappeared. These problems would not have been raised if buildings had simply been left in a deteriorated condition. The very use of the word "preservation" has, since the early nineteenth century, referred specifically to those cases in which intervention was necessary to save structures that otherwise would have been demolished. Since the Second World War there has been a trend in all of the visual arts to minimize intervention into works of art and when such intervention occurs to make it both easily distinguishable from the original and reversible. It has proven quite difficult in architecture especially to establish firm guidelines. The frequent attempts by preservation groups to do so have been doomed to failure.

The position of William Morris and his "Anti-scrape" followers, that any restoration at all is inadmissible, has occasionally been voiced but for most people this stance has been untenable, particularly in the aftermath of events such as the Second World War. The opposite position, that any amount of intervention, even total reconstruction, is permissible has claimed hardly a single proponent, although, perversely enough, there have been a substantial number of total reconstructions which include: the early twentieth-century work of Gaetano Morelli on the campanile in the Piazza of San Marco at Venice; the Capitol and Governor's Palace at Colonial Williamsburg, Virginia; the Stoa of Attalus in Athens, reconstructed 1956-1960 by John Travelos; and hundreds of new "historic" buildings erected in preservation districts.[9] Frequently it is the preservationists, who might be expected to have the strictest stance on distinguishing between the old and the new, who most vehemently demand reconstruction. Frederick Gibberd Associates, hired by Coutts Bank as architects for the conversion of a nineteenth-century London building designed by John Nash, was obliged, for example, to demolish later additions and rebuild [1970-1979] in their place reconstructions imitating the original Nash design, reportedly at the insistence of the local preservation groups.[10]

One of the most interesting "reconstruction" schemes is by Robert Venturi. Hired to reconstruct the eighteenth-century buildings of Franklin's court in Philadelphia, Venturi declined to design a new eighteenth-century building and instead arranged to exhibit on the site evidence which related to the original appearance of the building. Over the remains of foundation walls and displays of quotations and drawings from pertinent documentary texts, he erected a steel outline of the building [1976]. This is a particularly gratifying solution since his client, the United States government's National Park Service, had compiled a remarkably negative record in the previous two decades in Philadelphia, consistently destroying important nineteenth-century buildings in order to provide space for reconstructions of eighteenth-century structures in the newly created fields of grass around Independence Hall.[11]

Restoration

INTERVENTION

Most writers on restoration in recent years have taken a moderate position, leaning heavily, however, toward minimal intervention. This still requires decisions on how new elements should be added to original building fabrics. The so called "restoration" of many Medieval churches in the nineteenth century, for instance, has considerably complicated the task of the present-day viewer or scholar in trying to determine the building's original appearance and later development because the restoration architect often succeeded in matching the original materials. Increasingly, since the late fifties, it has become accepted practice in painting and sculpture to make new materials easily distinguishable from the old, to avoid confusion between what is the product of the original designer and craftsman and what has been added in the restoration. The practice of "infill" has been used only to a limited extent in architecture and mostly in structures of the Classical period.

Though almost all the literature on restoration now condemns the removal of structurally sound additions and remodelings to turn back the clock, the practice continues to be widespread. It was very common after World War II to remove Renaissance and Baroque decorations, some quite elaborate, on Medieval buildings, as at the Cathedral of St. Mary and St. Adalbert at Gniezno in Poland, to cite an outstanding example. Almost all critics of the restoration of the Hotel de Sully [mid-1950s] in the Marais area of Paris praise the removal there of a great deal of the nineteenth-century structure and the reconstruction of a large amount of seventeenth-century design to allow an appreciation of the appearance of the original building, but three centuries of history have been lost in the process. This technique is probably justified when dealing with extremely important monuments with very poor later alterations, but much of the nineteenth-century work is of extremely high quality, as the restorations of Viollet-le-Duc at Pierrefonds and elsewhere in France and those of G. G. Scott in Britain demonstrate. Many of these "restorations" contain features that have little precedent in the period of the original structure but are excellent pieces of nineteenth-century design and deserve to be kept for their own merit. Similarly it is a great shame that the Rotunda of the University of Virginia, designed by Thomas Jefferson, was "restored" in 1976, for this resulted in the destruction of a good McKim, Mead, and White remodelling in favor of an unsuccessful reconstruction of the presumed original. Finally, the restorers of the Frank Lloyd Wright home and studio in Oak Park, Illinois, have specified in their operating plan the removal of later alterations actually designed by Frank Lloyd Wright himself: considerable reconstruction will return the building to its presumed appearance of about 1910.[12]

An extreme approach that seems difficult to justify from any accepted point of view involves the arbitrary alteration of monuments. At the Reichstag Building in Berlin designed by Paul Wallot and built 1887-1898, architect Paul Baumgarten [1976] removed the entire central dome, drastically altered the interior configuration, presumably with the intention of destroying the imperial iconographic content and, thereby, wiping out the historical associations of half a century. Unsuccessful in killing the strong symbolic content of the building, the design only mutilated one of the most important of late nineteenth-century monuments.[13]

In restoration the conflict between the desire to keep as much of the building fabric as possible as documentary evidence and the desire to maintain the buildings's visual integrity as a work of art will continue to be of central concern.

REMODELLING

Unlike paintings which may be considered as having been completed and need only restoration, buildings frequently require modifications over the years to maintain their utility. Some architects have exploited this by making their remodelling contrast with the old fabric. Good examples of this approach are the elegant museums of Franco Albini at Genoa, one in the Palazzo Bianco [1951], the other the Museo del Tesoro di San Lorenzo [1954-1956], and the gleaming white, multileveled Institute of Contemporary Art in Boston, installed by Graham Gund [1975] in the heavy brownstone shell of a nineteenth-century police station.[14] In other cases the contrast is on the exterior. An 1845 railway terminal in Braunschweig designed by Carl Theodor Ottmer has been transformed into a bank headquarters by Architect Hannes Westermann, who during the sixties added to the old shell of the building an aluminum and glass curtain wall between the rear wings. A similar solution was proposed by Emilio Ambasz [1975] for the conversion of an early twentieth-century courthouse in Grand Rapids, Michigan, into an arts center by the insertion of a cascade of glass between the rear wings. Giancarlo de Carlo of Urbino has approached the problem in a more subtle manner and with more respect for the old buildings.

Since the fifties he has converted a number of buildings in Urbino's central area for university use, adding new elements largely within the old walls in a modern style sympathetic to but contrasting with the older structures.[15]

Unusual conditions have led to a number of extraordinary designs. When it became necessary to provide a roof for the Medieval church ruins at Bad Hersfeld, Frei Otto [1968] designed a retractable tension structure held in place by cables. The result is a light tent almost completely independent of the original structure and in sharp contrast with the heavy masonry of the old walls. Gustav Peichl prepared an equally interesting scheme [1977] for an unusued nineteenth-century mill complex on the Giudecca in Venice, where the chief feature involves the transformation of all the roof surfaces into an elaborate set of hanging gardens.[16]

The conservation of districts or whole cities also raises aesthetic problems in reconciling old and new. A few cities have attempted to enforce a stylistic unity: for example, Santa Barbara, California, passed an ordinance requiring Spanish colonial revival-style architecture, while in Ulm, Germany, the city specified steeply pitched roofs. Infill in whole areas has also been well accomplished, for example along the Arno River embankment in Florence where, in new construction to replace structures destroyed in World War II, modern materials were employed, but buildings were kept very close to the historic forms, allowing them to harmonize with but not imitate the remaining historic buildings.

Currently, the favored practice seems to be to design new buildings in frankly modern style and materials that contrast with the old, while maintaining some sense of related scale and massing. The History Museum, Am Hohen Ufer, in Hannover, a good example by architect Dieter Oesterlen [1967], incorporated fragments of the Medieval city wall into a resolutely modern building that preserves a continuity along an historic street. Le Corbusier's Venice hospital project [1964] would have been equally at home in its surroundings.[17]

Ironically, as the idea of the historical pastiche as a solution for new construction in historic areas has come to be almost completely discredited in the eyes of preservationists, a new generation of architects has been edging closer to this same notion, for example in the Zwolle housing project of Aldo van Eyck or the projects of Belgian architect Maurice Culot and his students at La Cambre School in Brussels, and in certain works of Ricardo Bofill's Taller de Arquitectura, notably the cloisterlike arcade in the prize-winning competition design [1975] for the Les Halles area of Paris.[18]

Some of the most interesting remodellings start with fragments of the original buildings and incorporate them into a wholly new context. In a striking example of this, the Gas Works project [1975] in Seattle, Washington, landscape architect Richard Haag left standing an abandoned early twentieth-century industrial facility, demolished subsidiary structures to expose generator towers, pipes, and stacks, and used them as sculptural objects in a newly created park.[19] Increasingly, architects have taken the fragment and have treated it in an ironic manner. Architects Mitchell-Giurgola when required to maintain a four-story Egyptian revival facade on the site of a new office building for the Penn Mutual Insurance Company opposite Independence Hall in Philadelphia, chose [1976] not to integrate it into the wall of the new building. Instead they let it stand freely in front of the building, a solution posed between a serious intent to preserve the nineteenth-century streetscape on the one hand and a parody of preservation on the other. In the case of the Derby Civic Centre project (fig. 4.2) by James Stirling [1970] the decision to take an eighteenth-century facade and tilt it backwards was clearly an ironic act, one calculated to wrench the fragment from its context and present it in a new, rather humorous way.[20]

Conservation

ADAPTIVE REUSE

One of the most striking aspects of preservation since the sixties has been the popularity of "adaptive reuse." Though the reuse of old buildings for new purposes has been common throughout history, it usually consisted of a downward spiral of building use consistent with a gradual deterioration of structures. A palace might be converted into workers' lodgings and this in turn could become a factory, but hardly ever was this sequence reversed. By far the most conspicuous and successful postwar examples of adaptive reuse, on the other hand, involve the conversion of utilitarian structures into prestigious institutions like museums, university buildings, and luxury commercial establishments. The appearance of many books on adaptive reuse demonstrates that an interest exists in upgrading the social and economic status of buildings.[21]

Large-scale interest in this process came to the fore in the United States in San Francisco during the fifties when a number of nineteenth-century industrial buildings in Jackson Square were converted into

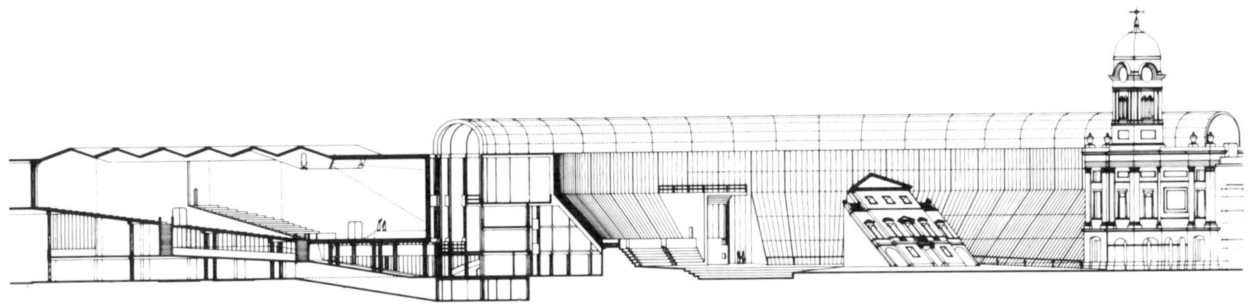

4.2. James Stirling, architect. Civic Center project. Derby, England, 1970. (Photograph: Courtesy of the architect)

shops and offices, followed in 1964-1968 by the conversion of the Ghiradelli Square factory complex (Bernardi, Wurster, and Emmons, architects) and the Cannery (Esherick, Homsey, Dodge, and Davis, architects) into restaurants and shops. A similar interest in adaptive reuse developed at about the same time in Boston where a number of wharves, industrial buildings, and the Old City Hall were converted to serve more lucrative functions. In the most significant of these, a set of early nineteenth-century market buildings was turned into a complex of elegant shops and restaurants, called Faneuil Market (fig. 4.3), by the Boston architect Benjamin Thompson. Significantly, the developer was the Rouse Company, one of America's largest and most respected development firms, previously known for new suburban work. Developers started to turn back to the city, and the examples of San Francisco and Boston inspired a flood of imitators ranging from Canal Square in Washington, D.C., by Moore Associates [1971] to the Trolley Barn in Salt Lake City by Albert L. Christensen [1975]. Several important firms, notably Hardy-Holzman-Pfeiffer of New York, Anderson-Notter of Boston, and Arthur Cotton Moore in Washington, D.C., have become well known for their efforts in designing for adaptive reuse.[22]

European examples have tended to be more subdued and to respect somewhat more the old buildings' original designs, as in the conversion of an entire complex of old structures in Urbino for university use, begun by Giancarlo de Carlo in the fifties. Elsewhere, the Augustiner church in Munich was converted in 1962 into offices and shops; the famous saltworks in Ledoux at Arc et Senans in France became a conference center in 1970; St. Catherine's Docks, London, was turned into an apartment and commercial complex [1970-1974]; a printing works in Hannover, Germany, became temporarily an architecture faculty's building [1965]; the Beguinage at Louvain, Belgium, was changed into dormitories [1964-1968], and a whole chain of castles in Spain was converted into remarkable tourist hotels (paradors). There is a great deal of irony in all this for the very names of the new establishments, "The Factory" for a fancy restaurant, the "Warehouse" for a collection of elegant boutiques, indicate a curiously romantic attitude toward the safely obsolete products of the Industrial Revolution and a desire to turn totally upside down the old hierarchy of building types with their corresponding iconographic programs. Not only individual buildings but whole districts have undergone similar modifications with a splendid example being the Soho or cast-iron district in New York City where an industrial area was transformed into an elegant district of expensive loft apartments and art galleries. The seeming incongruity of successive uses provides much novelty and charm.

THE LARGER URBAN PROBLEMS

New interest in the conservation of districts and whole areas of cities has brought with it corresponding concern for major unresolved social and political problems. While the rehabilitation of city centers undoubtedly contributes heavily to their continued economic viability, the investment of large amounts of money in areas like the Marais in Paris, Covent Garden in London, or the Capitol Hill sec-

4.3. Benjamin Thompson, architect. Faneuil Hall Market, nineteenth century; restored by the Rouse Company. Boston, 1970s. (Photograph: Courtesy of the Rouse Company)

tion of Washington, D.C., almost always brings with it considerable social change involving the displacement of people who can no longer afford the new rent or property taxes. The displaced population is usually obliged to move to other marginal areas, in turn straining further the housing stock available there. It seems possible also that large scale reinvestment in old buildings, rather than in new, may simply provoke a short-circuiting of the age-old downward cycle of building uses, in which case the preserved districts may themselves be at the beginning of another downward cycle.

If preservation has come to mean the safeguarding of structures for cultural reasons, conservation has proved to be a useful term for the notion of saving buildings for economic and social reasons. The rehabilitation of old residential units in city centers is not always less expensive than erecting new building, but it has the great advantage of reusing existing utilities and transportation systems and of minimizing the disruption of neighborhoods caused by displacement. Conservation is quickly becoming the accepted method of providing public housing in Europe and, at a slower rate, in the United States.

Preservation remains, by and large, an activity of the affluent middle class. This has sometimes been obscured in recent times by a concentration on the technical means of restoration, producing a feeling that there is a kind of objectivity in the process which does not exist in other kinds of architectural design. In fact, what usually passes for objectivity is aesthetic timidity, and preservation legislation is often a disguise for aesthetic control, an attempt to legislate good taste. As Sherban Cantacuzino has observed: "Buildings may be perfectly restored, but any feeling of a living city has evaporated, sunk without a trace beneath a pile of tourist trinkets or a blanket of middle-class gentility, expressed not by the so-called vulgarity of the neon lights or commerce but by the pallid pink glow from the carriage light."[23] Moreover, it has become clear that the preservation of a building's aesthetic character is often incompatible with economical conversion. The use of tinted and reflective glass, for example, is often more economical in the long run than the continued use of standard clear glass. Likewise, the use of various synthetic roofing and siding materials, while anathema to the preservationist, can significantly reduce the maintenance costs of a building.

For the fundamental question of displacement the only solutions seem to be either the establishment of massive subsidies to allow occupants to live in buildings in which they otherwise could not afford to live or the abolition of the free market in real estate. The closest approach in the Western world to the latter alternative is found from the 1960s onward in Bologna, where a long-term Communist administration pledged itself to the preservation of the city's historic center for the continued use of the residents already in place. The initial plan in Bologna was to expropriate all buildings in the historic center, rehabilitate them, and turn them over to tenant cooperatives. This approach proved impractical and a system including purchases and long-term contracts was substituted. Still, the unified approach did allow for comprehensive planning, stopped private speculation, and made possible the vigorous participation of neighborhood councils, labor unions, and other groups. Bologna has also been exemplary in its thorough and intelligent survey of existing building stock, its method of classification of building types (fig. 4.4), its pedestrian precincts, and its heavily subsidized mass-transit system.[24]

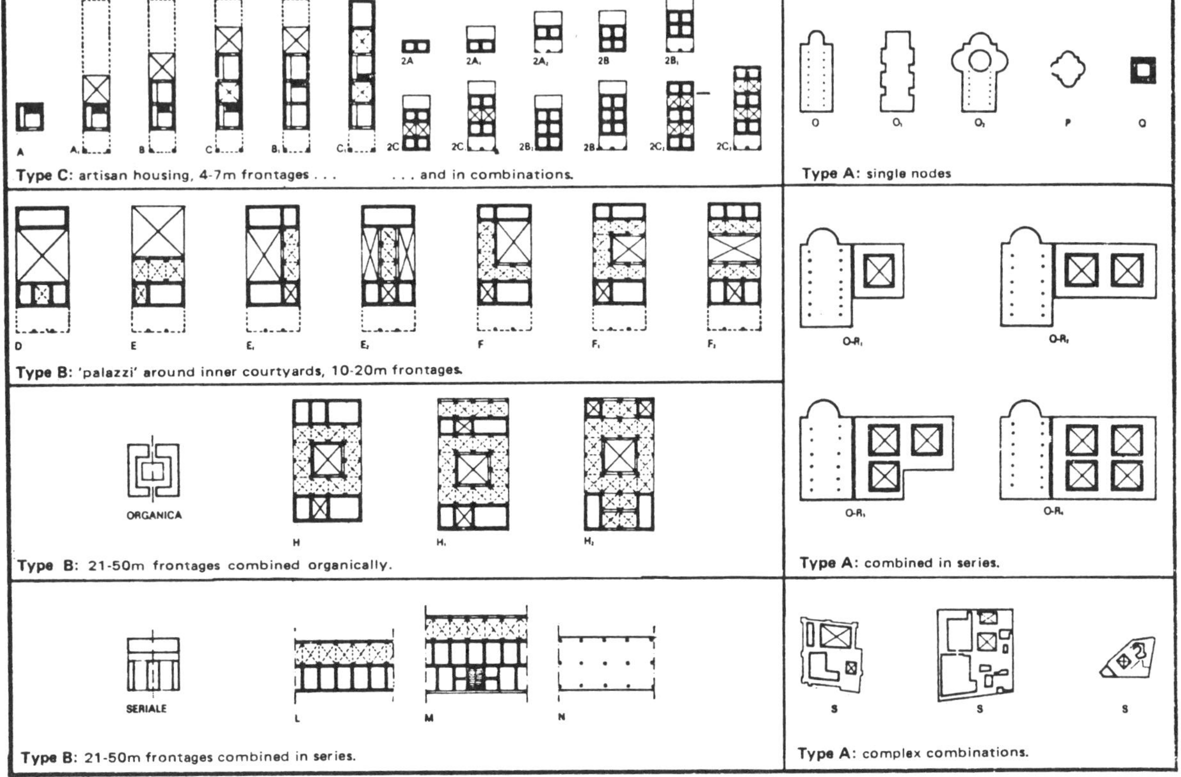

4.4. Restoration plan for Bologna, Italy. Diagram of building types: A. large containers (churches, etc.) suitable for public use; B. small containers (*palazzi* built on a central courtyard) to be used by the university; C. small residential units. (Photograph: Courtesy of *Architectural Design*, January 1976, Angotti and Dale)

Any realistic preservation program demands that profound urban problems be solved. If Bologna seems to have been a positive experiment, many of the underlying assumptions, especially the degree of governmental intervention necessary to make it work, also make it impractical for most Western cities. Even if this were not an obstacle, other problems abound. Venice is the most drastic case, for there conservation will be a final and relatively easy step if the basic problems of a stagnant economy, pollution, and flooding can be solved. Otherwise preservation would simply produce a museum city for affluent tourists, destroying the very nature of the place which has survived for so many centuries. Successful conservation requires a political structure which allows for responsible decision-making, usually a long and painful process. The problem of the automobile, for example, seems to find no easy solutions: the pedestrian precinct, an idea which has enjoyed a huge vogue, has often drained rather than contributed to the vitality of the town center and has led to widespread demolition in contiguous precincts to accommodate the banned vehicles. Political and social clashes have become common now with the recognition that the financial stakes in conservation and preservation have been raised: bitter debates over the areas of Les Halles in Paris or Covent Garden in London, for example, have been erupting for a number of years and show no signs of subsiding.

Preservation and conservation, despite their correlative social problems, are powerful ideas that gather under their banners a diverse following, including some who genuinely love old buildings, some who foresee great profits, and others who are displeased by the technology of modern architecture and contemporary society. As André Corboz has observed, there now exists an alliance between those on the right who have a nostalgic regard for the preindustrial society and those on the left who support soft technology.[25] It is clear that in the realm of planning policy, preservation and conservation have succeeded urban renewal. It remains to be seen whether they will lose their elitist associations and be flexible enough to maintain both the great museum monument and the hundreds of useful but ordinary old buildings which make up the fabric of the world's diverse urban centers.

Notes

1. *See* John F. Smith, *A Critical Bibliography of Building Conservation* (London: Mansell, 1978). Good general studies include Sherban Cantacuzino, *Architectural Conservation in Europe* (New York: Watson-Guptill, 1975); A. D. N. Papageorgiou, *Stadtkerne in Konflikt. Die historische Stadtkerne und ihre Rolle im künftigen Räumgefüge* (Berlin, 1970); and P. Ward, ed., *Conservation and Development in Historic Towns* (Newcastle-Upon-Tyne, 1968).

2. On the restoration of monuments following World War II, *see* Roberto Pane, "La Restoration des monuments historiques depuis la guerre," *Museum* 3 (1950): 36-48, 78-89. On Warsaw, *see* Adolf Ciborowski, *Warsaw, A City Destroyed and Rebuilt* (Warsaw: Interpress, 1964). Cf. also his discussion, Chapter 5, below.

3. *Architectural Forum* 125 (March 1966): 76-83.

4. *La Charte d'Athènes* appeared anonymously in Paris in 1941. The quotations are taken from C.-E. Jeanneret-Gris, *The Athens Charter*, trans. Anthony Eardley (New York, 1973), pp. 86-89.

5. Jane Jacobs, *The Death and Life of Great American Cities* (New York: Random House, 1961), pp. 187-99.

6. Gustav Peichl, "Die Freyung zu Wien," *Bauen und Wohnen*, October 1975, pp. 386-89.

7. An important source for many of these ideas is the December 1976 issue of *Lotus* magazine devoted to "Old Buildings and Modern Functions." *See* especially the discussions of the Berlin Kreuzberg design symposium and the Paris La Villette competition.

8. On national and international organizations, *see* United Nations Educational, Scientific and Cultural Organization, *The Conservation of Cities* (London and Paris: St. Martin's Press, 1975).

9. The Italians have dealt most extensively with preservation history and theory. *See* Renato Bonelli, "Restauro," *Enciclopedia universale dell' arte*, 10: 344-51; Giovanni Carbonara, *La Reintegrazione dell' imagine: probleme di restauro dei monumenti* (Rome: c. 1976); Francesco Gurrieri, *Teoria e cultura del restauro dei monumenti e dei centri antichi* (Florence, 1974). There are also interesting comments in Jane Fawcett, ed., *The Future of the Past: Attitudes to Conservation, 1147-1974* (New York, 1976).

10. *American Institute of Architects Journal* 166 (23 November 1977): 1037-40.

11. On the Venturi project, *see* the *American Institute of Architects Journal*, May 1977, pp. 69-70.

12. On the University of Virginia work *see Progressive Architecture*, 1976, pp. 62-63. Apparently no detailed report on this restoration has appeared. On the Frank Lloyd Wright home and studio the decision to remove later additions was made after a detailed investigation, and very thorough documentation of the removed features is planned. *See* the *Plan for the Adaptive Use of the Frank Lloyd Wright Home and Studio*, by the Restoration Committee of the Frank Lloyd Wright Home and Studio Foundation (Chicago: University of Chicago Press, 1977).

13. On the Reichstag, *see Architecture*, October 1976, pp. 24-28.

14. Albini's museums are discussed in *Domus*, December 1952, pp. 22-26; and *L'Architettura. Cronache e Storia*,

December 1956, pp. 556-65. For the Boston Institute of Contemporary Art *see* Massachusetts Department of Community Affairs, *Built to Last, a Handbook on Recycling Old Buildings* (Washington: Preservation Press, 1977), pp. 31-33.

15. Giancarlo de Carlo, *Urbino, la Storia di una città e il piano della sua evoluzione urbanistica* (Padua, 1966). *See also Architectural Review*, April 1979, pp. 206-14. The Braunschweig bank is discussed in *Architecture Plus*, March/April 1974, p. 55 and the Grand Rapids project in *Progressive Architecture*, January 1976, pp. 60-61.

16. The Frei Otto project was published in *Bauwelt*, 15 July 1968, pp. 880-81, and in Ludwig Glaeser, *The Work of Frei Otto* (New York: Museum of Modern Art, 1972), p. 114. The Peichl scheme can be found in *Architecture d'Aujourd'hui*, December 1977, pp. 38-39.

17. For the Hannover Museum *see Baumeister*, March 1968, pp. 232-34; Le Corbusier's hospital is discussed in Willy Boesiger and H. Girsberger, eds., *Le Corbusier 1910-1965* (New York: Museum Books), pp. 176-83.

18. Maurice Culot, "The Right Wing in Disguise," *Lotus* 13 (December 1976): 94-102.

19. On the Gas Works in Seattle, *see* Walter D. Kidney, *Working Places, the Adaptive Reuse of Industrial Buildings* (Pittsburgh, 1976), pp. 135-37.

20. The Mitchell-Giurgola project is found in *Progressive Architecture*, April 1976, pp. 73-75. The Stirling scheme appears in James Stirling, *Buildings and Projects, 1950-1975* (Oxford: Oxford University Press, 1975), pp. 163-67.

21. Frédérique Boucher, "Rénovation, Réhabilitation ou Restauration," *L'Architecture d'Aujourd'hui*, April 1979, pp. 2-6.

22. On adaptive reuse the best book is Sherban Cantacuzino, *New Uses for Old Buildings* (New York: Watson-Guptill, 1975). For the United States *see* Elizabeth Thompson, *Recycling Buildings* (New York: McGraw-Hill, 1976), and Barbaralee Diamondstein, *Buildings Reborn, New Uses, Old Places* (New York: Harper and Row, 1978).

23. Cantacuzino, *Architectural Conservation in Europe*, p. 19.

24. There is an extensive bibliography on Bologna. *See* P. L. Cervallati and R. Scannavini, eds., *Bologna: Politica e metodologia del restauro nei centri storici* (Bologna, 1973); Paola Ceccarelli and Francesco Incovino, eds., *Risanamento e speculazione nei centri storici* (Milan, 1974); Thomas Angotti and Bruce Dale, "Bologna, Conservative Plans for a Communist City," *Architectural Design*, January 1976, pp. 12-17. On the social problems of conservation *see* Massimo Gennari, "Il problema dei centri storici in Italia," *Domus*, October 1977, pp. 17-24.

25. André Corboz, "Old Buildings and Modern Functions," *Lotus* 13 (December 1976): 68-79.

Bibliography

Bonelli, Renato. "Principles of Architectural and Urban Restoration and Conservation." *Encyclopedia of World Art*. Vol. 12. New York: McGraw-Hill, 1963, 194-97.

Cantacuzino, Sherban. *Architectural Conservation in Europe*. New York: Watson-Guptill, 1975.

______. *New Uses for Old Buildings*. New York: Watson-Guptill, 1975.

Carbonara, Giovanni. *La reintegrazione dell' immagine: problemi di restauro dei monumenti*. Rome, c.1976.

Gurrieri, Francesco. *Culture and Safeguard of the Historical City Centers*. Florence, 1973.

Papageorgiou, A. D. N. *Continuity and Change: Preservation in City Planning*. New York, 1971.

Rath, Frederick and O'Connell, Merrilyn Rogers. *Historic Preservation*. Nashville: AASLH, 1975.

Smith, John F. *A Critical Bibliography of Building Conservation*. London: Mansell, 1978.

Thompson, Elizabeth K. *Recycling Buildings*. New York: McGraw-Hill, 1976.

UNESCO. *Conservation of Cities*. London: St. Martin's Press, 1976.

______. *Preserving and Restoring Monuments and Historic Buildings*. New York: Unipub, 1972.

Ward, Pamela, ed. *Conservation and Development in Historic Towns*. Newcastle-Upon Tyne, 1968.

5

URBAN PLANNING IN EUROPE SINCE 1945

ADOLF CIBOROWSKI

At present it appears that no one has undertaken the task of comprehensively summarizing and critically evaluating the complex problems encountered, the methodologies applied, and the results achieved in the development of European urban settlements since World War II. The numerous publications which concern themselves with selected and often narrow issues cannot serve as a substitute for a general overview dealing with the changes that have occurred in the European network of settlements. The cause of such a lack of up-to-date professional literature in the field of urban planning is probably related to the magnitude of the problem as well as to the too narrow perspective through which a sufficient breadth of generalization may be reached. On the other hand, the lack of such an overview is a pity.

The experiment of building a new Europe in the past thirty-five years as well as the experience gained from that experiment are unique in contemporary human history. Taken as a whole, they serve as an excellent case study for all those encountering the present challenges of urbanization and rapid growth in developing countries. There remains yet perhaps one more practical reason for initiating a study of this topic now. This is the very last opportunity to gather information not only from archives or from field observations but also directly from those people who participated in the planning, designing, and implementation of such projects throughout Europe.

The time available for the preparation of this chapter did not permit me to undertake a broad study or to elaborate in depth on all of the problems and examples of postwar European town planning. Therefore, the thoughts presented in this essay are based primarily on my direct observations, experience, and participation and must be confined to the most typical issues and to selected examples.

The General Picture of Postwar Urban Development

TRENDS AND ISSUES

The consequences of World War II for further processes of social and economic development as well as for developmental patterns of settlements were numerous. The end of the war marks the beginning of a new era in European urban development, a new era in physical development-planning as well as in the restructuring of urban and rural patterns of settlement. Simultaneously, the challenge of reconstruction as well as of accelerated development demanded revision of former theories and methodologies in urban design and physical planning.

The major challenge was the direct result of the scale and scope of war destruction which directly affected more than two-thirds of Europe. Accompanying this was the need for restoration of basic facilities and services for the survivors of the war. The second challenge resulted from the effects of an accelerated industrialization of less-developed European countries, especially in the eastern and southern parts of the Continent. Those areas of Europe which had already achieved a significantly higher level of urbanization and industrialization before the war were faced with the task of modernizing their economies in conjunction with reconstruction.

DRIVING FORCES

From the very first days after World War II, two major driving forces are noticeable which served to stimulate physical reconstruction and, later, further development and expansion in Europe. One force is represented by social and political changes that followed the breakdown of prewar Continental structure in individual nations. These changes were characterized by a general shift towards the recognition of human rights as related to various social groups and classes; by a shift towards state control of some general aspects of development and of economic life; and by a shift towards comprehensive planning of physical development and some components of economic development. The shift towards planned systems never had the same character in each country. The planned-economy systems have been developed in the Eastern European countries while the Scandinavian countries have developed advanced systems of planning within the framework of market economies. Other Western European countries have developed various levels of advanced physical planning as well as sectorial economic planning on the basis of market economy guidelines. Although these systems and their levels of comprehensiveness vary from country to country and subregion to subregion throughout the Continent, the whole process of reconstruction and further development occurred within a much more institutionalized framework of social and physical planning than had any of the prewar experiences and activities, save for the unique exception of the European part of the USSR.

The second driving force can be explained in terms of social changes that expedited social revolution and the development of new patterns of social structures and life. The recognition of everyone's right to housing and basic social services was a cornerstone of newly formulated policies on housing and settlement development in many European countries. This heightened social consciousness was often the major stimulating factor. In some countries it was the force pressuring governmental responsibility for the control of reconstruction, development, and expansion of human settlements; for the control of public resources channelled into urban development; and for the development of comprehensive programs of housing, varied public facilities, places of work, and services.

Some few other driving forces should be noted. Among these were speedily increasing social expectations in relation to the standards and quality of the man-made environment; the rapid evolution of preferences regarding forms of reconstructed and newly built cities and, finally, the increasingly egalitarian character of those demands and expectations as reflected in urban patterns and in the architectural forms of mass development programs.

These egalitarian demands were first satisfied through urban and housing design with standards and norms applied in many European countries. Later the results were expressed by both a unification of architectural forms and a search for mass production in building technology. The ever-increasing quantity of new structures in urban as well as rural settlements called for mass-production systems and factory-made components. As a result, the cityscape of the majority of reconstructed, expanded, or newly built cities has been widely changed.

LIMITATIONS

Through the whole process of urban development in Europe after World War II, certain limitations forced patterns of development and influenced many ideas of design and layout. Generally, these limitations are expressed by the relation of needs and demands to means and resources.

In the first years after the war, these limitations were extremely acute due to the scale of destruction. War damage created a very high building demand while, at the same time, financial and technological means had been undermined because of the shattered and weakened economies. It was after this situation had been overcome that pressures arose for a rapid increase in the quality of living conditions as well as in the quality of life. In many countries this caused a continuous gap between actual building construction and growing market demand. The architectural and town planning race with time that ensued may be interpreted as a factor causing patterns to develop which led to the mass production of new settlements, residential quarters, and cities. There are, of course, some exceptions to this generalization. Since some European countries suffered little or no war damage, their starting point at the beginning of this period was quite different. Therefore, the architectural and town-planning achievements of those countries (for instance, Sweden and the Iberian peninsula) do not always reflect the problems and trends of development encountered across the rest of Europe.

The challenges of reconstruction and of mass production of new housing were dealt with on the basis of a number of preconditions recognized by many European nations. These preconditions were:

Establishment of national settlement policies as a tool to control the tempo of reconstruction and development of components of the settlement system.

Control of the distribution of public resources aimed at reconstruction and urban development.

Centralization of the decision-making process as a component of policy implementation related to mass housing programs and to the expansion of urban areas.

Mobilization of public resources for reconstruction and development programs.

Public participation and involvement in the planning, design, and implementation process.

The forms in which these preconditions have been met naturally differ from country to country. In planned-economy countries, the centralized planning and decision-making activities were placed at the level of the central government and were executed by a system of state agencies. In other countries, parastate organizations or nonprofit corporations were established to handle, for example, mass housing programs.

A majority of countries introduced various systems of state subsidies for "low-cost" housing programs and for various programs of social service and community facilities development. In every one of these programs some rights and responsibilities for controlling the overall concepts and programs of urban development remained with central governmental authorities.

In many European countries public participation and public control were incorporated into planning and implementation procedures either as some statutory requirement or as a political activity. The population at large gained rights to discuss and evaluate every urban development scheme and thus to influence their execution. The issues of reconstruction, of expanded housing programs, of urban expansion, and even of spatial and architectural forms for those programs became important political issues for ruling bodies and political parties.

TYPICAL BASIC TASKS

Urban development in Europe over the past thirty-five years can be subdivided into the following distinguishable types of development and planning activity:

1) Reconstruction of a city as a result of war damage, with an extension of this being the reconstruction of cities devastated by natural disasters.

2) New towns designed and built for two general reasons: namely, within the development of new growth-poles as important components of a nationwide settlement network; or to establish satellite towns for the purposes of easing pressure on existing metropolitan areas, arresting their growth, and decreasing their population densities. Every one of the new towns presented different problems for planners and developers and represented different socioeconomic models.

3) Expansion of existing cities. This has been the most common type of activity in Europe especially during the second period of postwar activity that began when basic reconstruction had already been completed.

4) Urban renewal and modernization. This type of planning activity has grown in importance in recent years partially due to a growing gap between environmental conditions and living conditions within old city cores and newly expanded modern districts.

The magnitude and complexity of all the above urban-development tasks depended on the overall national developmental trends and the nationwide distribution of productive forces and population. The distribution of productive forces and population necessitated the development of large-scale physical planning at the national level as well as at the subnational level of individual regions. This overall planning approach was dependent upon international cooperation as well as upon advanced forms of international economic systems. Thus, it came to be expanded to encompass a number of cooperating countries in commonly conceived physical development plans either for groups of nations or for border regions of two or three neighboring countries.

The forms of national and regional physical planning differed, once again, between countries and in accordance with their political systems. The most advanced and most comprehensive national physical development plans were elaborated in the socialist countries, among which Poland's in 1946 was the very first. In Western Europe, the development of physical planning on a regional scale took place somewhat later and varied greatly in its content from the Eastern European model. The most advanced of Western European regional plans, that of Holland, originated with the need for reclaiming new land from the North Sea. The regional planning systems in the United Kingdom, France, and West Germany are also especially highly advanced.

FOUNDATIONS

Although the postwar period in Europe signified the beginning of a new era in physical planning and urban design, it was some of the philosophical and professional achievements of earlier periods that constituted the cornerstones upon which the newly developed postwar philosophies of urban design and building activity were based. Thus we may clearly see the continuity between the postwar philosophies in general and ideas formulated in the first half of the twentieth century. Among these cornerstones of urban design are:

The British theory and philosophy of garden cities and the very first experiences of the British school of town planning in the development of these cities and in the design of other residential areas.

The CIAM philosophy of the modern city based on the thinking and ideas of Le Corbusier and an international group of architects cooperating with him.

The Charter of Athens, adopted in 1933 by the CIAM group, which is the very first declaration on the substance, structure, and social significance of the modern city and modern town planning.

The experience of the Soviet Union in the field of distribution of productive forces throughout the country and in design of new towns conceived as new economic growth poles.

In addition to these four major cornerstones, one more, of a totally different character, should be included. This pertains to the development of a modern approach to the history of architecture as expounded after the war by the Warsaw School of Architecture. The Warsaw School laid the foundation for postwar reconstruction of historic quarters of cities, first in Poland and later in many other European countries.

Thirty-five years have passed since the end of World War II and the formulating of this manuscript. In this time-frame a very deep restructuring of forms and patterns of settlement networks occurred in Europe. This time span may be subdivided into three periods:

1945 to 1955 (or in some countries to 1960) was a period of reconstruction all over the continent. During this period, too, construction of British new towns and Swedish satellite settlements was initiated.

1955 (or 1960) to 1970 was a period characterized by major expansion of existing cities and towns, interrelated with ongoing processes of urbanization, especially in Eastern and Southern Europe. In this time span, towns that would serve as new growth-poles were initiated in those European countries which were less developed before the war.

The third period, the 1970s, saw further growth of cities resulting mainly from demands for greater improvement in the quality of life and for upgrading living standards, while further processes of urbanization were slowed down to balance rural and urban sectors of the population. This last period can be characterized in many countries, furthermore, by the feedback process between urban and rural areas expressed by the transfer of urban facilities to former rural settlements as well as by the equalization of living conditions throughout many countries. The best examples of this process are those of some central and northern European countries. Another feature of this period was an expanding program of urban renewal expressed by wide-range town planning and building intervention within the cores of many cities.

Reconstruction

Three zones of intensity of war destruction may be differentiated throughout Europe, in each of which there were somewhat different tasks of urban design and reconstruction. The zone of the highest level of destruction included the European part of the Soviet Union, Poland, Germany, Holland, northern France, and part of Belgium. The second zone, with a somewhat lesser destruction of its urban tissue, consisted of the rest of Eastern Europe, the Balkan peninsula, Italy, the southern part of England, and the Scandinavian countries with the exception of Sweden. Finally, the third zone comprised those few countries unaffected by war damage, namely Sweden, Switzerland, Spain, and Portugal.

THE CHARACTER OF DESTRUCTION

In this part of my chapter, I would first like to interject some remarks based on my personal observations and experiences. A city may be destroyed by man during a war, but it may also be destroyed by nature through such catastrophic events as earthquakes and floods. The way that these two types of destruction strike and their results differ. First, in cities destroyed by man the losses in human life are generally much higher in proportion to the whole affected population. Very rarely do losses in population reach the level of 20 to 25 percent of the inhabitants in cities destroyed by nature. In cities destroyed by war, often that part of the population killed amounts to 50 percent or more. In natural disasters, losses of life are mostly at the level of one to five percent, as was the case at Skopie.

Second, both man and nature are selective in their respective choices of physical targets for destruction. Nature selects the weakest, the less resistant and usually the less valuable components of a city so that the more valuable structures have a chance to survive. Man, on the other hand, first attacks the most valuable and most important components of a city. He strikes at new industrial parks, city centers, residential districts, and the most importantly engineered structures. We could say then that man in his destruction is infinitely less human than is nature.

This difference presents, of course, quite different challenges in redesigning and reconstructing a city. The initial capital is quite different in each case; and the possibilities of satisfying the immediate needs of the surviving population differ as well. This is reflected in the reconstruction patterns of various European cities.

Another differentiation that may be made concerning destruction patterns and therefore influencing urban design solutions is based on the way in which a city was destroyed during war. There are three distinct kinds of destruction: by air raids, as for instance, at Coventry, Dresden, and Hannover; as a result of the area having been a battlefield, exemplified by Stalingrad, Berlin, and partially Warsaw; and by planned destruction implemented not only for military but primarily for political reasons, the most dramatic and recent example of which is Warsaw. In more distant history this type of destruction is also represented notably at Carthage and Tenochtitlan.

The first of these three kinds of destruction presents the selective elimination of the most important parts of the city while the second represents an eradication to an even more dramatic degree. In both cases damage to the urban infrastructure was not usually very great. In Warsaw however, the object of planned destruction, the urban infrastructure, was subjected to the same destructive measures as was the city's superstructure.

A destroyed city is not only a human disaster and an economic loss, but it also poses a kind of paradox in its reconstruction. It demands, first, quick reconstruction to provide shelter for every surviving resident. Second, it offers an opportunity for improvement of the physical and functional patterns of the city's shape. The conflicts present within this paradox are heightened by an ever increasing lack of available financial resources. Nevertheless, the European experience indicates that an awareness on the part of both planners and the authorities of a unique opportunity to improve the city is essential to building a better city. The lack of such an awareness, as well as of a deep commitment to improvement, results in a repetition in the rebuilt city of all the shortcomings of the functional and environmental character of the destroyed city.

Some of the best examples of a far-reaching restructuring of downtowns in reconstructed cities are offered by the new city centers of Coventry and Rotterdam. The most advanced and complex example, however, is presented by Warsaw. Other examples are Kiev, Minsk, and Stalingrad. The West German cities, many of which were heavily destroyed, represent a rather modest effort at restructuring due to various limitations imposed on authorities and designers. Nevertheless, one of the best examples of a comprehensive design of a West German inner city is Hannover.

One of the most constraining limitations on freedom for the reshaping and redesigning of cities was that component of city structure that was the most resistant to time and damage—the land ownership pattern and the subdivision of land into separate parcels. The pattern of land ownership survived the historical processes of urban development as well as all war destruction. Almost never destroyed or nullified, land ownership and individual building-lot mortgages were the strongest and first barrier for town planners in their effort to have an impact on rebuilding policies and strategies. These constraints usually resulted in the restoration of street and development patterns similar to those existing before the destruction. In some Western European cities the extremely high costs of land acquisition or the expected costs of rent for land tenure made downtown building-lot mortgages so expensive that the redevelopment process was delayed.

In a number of countries and cities, this was one of the very first problems handled in the process of planning for reconstruction. In the Soviet Union, where land is public property, this issue did not exist. In some other socialist countries, various systems of land control or nationalization of land were introduced. In Warsaw all the land within the city's administrative boundaries was communalized, that is, expropriated for the benefit of the community. The city remained the sole proprietor of land and was therefore the only one to decide how that land would be used. Former owners received compensation in the form defined by law (for example, a building lot for a detached one-family house).

In some Western European countries the problem was solved in a variety of ways based on temporary limited rights such as expropriation or temporary acquisition of land by the reconstruction authorities and the resale of it in accordance with new urban-development land-use patterns. This was exactly the system followed in the most successful of Western European reconstruction plans, at Coventry, Rotterdam, Le Havre, and Hannover.

Generally we may conclude that only in those cases where full control of land was executed by a public body was it possible to introduce and to implement imaginative plans for reconstruction and for far-reaching modernization of former, often outdated, urban patterns.

WARSAW: A CASE STUDY

Warsaw, established in the thirteenth century as the residential city of the Prince of Mazovia, became the capital of a larger Poland at the end of the sixteenth century. The center of national resistance against the German, Austrian, and Russian invaders who partitioned Poland at the end of the eighteenth century, Warsaw grew through the nineteenth century as an important industrial center as well as a center of cultural activity. When Poland regained its national identity and independence in 1918, Warsaw recovered its role as the capital city of the nation and began developing into a modern metropolis. In the mid-1930s, a regional study was undertaken for Warsaw, the so-called "Functional Warsaw" by J. Chmielewski and S. Cyrkus. The development of the city on two axes, along the banks of the Vistula River from north to south and across the city in an east-west fashion, would enable the creation of a system of settlements on a huge cruciform plan with Warsaw's historical center at its focal point.

In 1939 Warsaw began its resistance against the Nazi-German invasion. The unarmed city fought the invaders for a period of roughly three weeks, truly marking the beginning of resistance against fascism and the Nazis. In the first round of resistance Warsaw's damage amounted to 15 percent of its physical stock.

From the very first days of the war, the city of Warsaw had been condemned by Hitler to total destruction since it was a symbol of the Polish nation and culture and a barrier to the expansionist politics of the German Reich. In 1940 a group of German town planners, at the order of the German government, prepared a plan called the master plan of the new German city of Warschau. It proposed the liquidation of the existing city of 1.3 million inhabitants and the substitution in its stead of a city of 150,000 on the left bank of the Vistula. On the river's right bank was to be a concentration camp for the "native" population. A systematic extermination of the Polish and Polish-Jewish population continued throughout the period of Nazi occupation. Besides this policy of extermination, further steps were taken to level the physical structures in the city. This was accomplished especially after the Uprising in the Jewish quarter of the city in 1943 and after the General Uprising in August and September 1944.

Following the collapse of that Uprising and the removal of the surviving population (partially to concentration camps) the last stage of destruction was organized according to previously formulated plans. All buildings were blown up and the infrastructure was either damaged or destroyed. The final tally of destruction in Warsaw was 850,000 people killed; 87 percent of the physical structure of the city completely destroyed; 100 percent of historical buildings and landmarks destroyed; over 20 million cubic meters of rubble left in the form of a huge desert covering the central parts of the city; over 200,000 mines left within the ruins as a welcome-home gift to the population.

When Warsaw was liberated on 17 January 1945 the population of the city amounted to only 140,000. The Polish government made the decision to rebuild it as the capital of Poland, a decision endorsed by the survivors returning to the ruins. At the end of the first year of reconstruction 400,000 people were living in Warsaw once again. The general concept of the reconstructed city was based on the following assumptions:

1) As the capital of Poland, Warsaw will remain the center of its cultural, political, and scientific life.
2) Continuing its former tradition, Warsaw will grow as an important industrial center with priorities for the development of more sophisticated modern industries (such as tools, machinery, automobiles, and electronics, as well as pharmaceutical and graphic industries).
3) The growth of Warsaw will be controlled by the stimulation of the growth of other, medium-sized Polish cities, to reach a population of 2 million by the year 2000.
4) The patterns of urban development must provide improved living conditions and equal housing standards for every citizen with emphasis on the development of social and cultural facilities.
5) Environmental conditions must be enhanced by restricting densities of development and by introducing a system of green and open spaces to ventilate the whole urban area.
6) The functional land-use patterns will follow the rule of separation of housing functions from industrial functions, to result in the design of a number of residential districts which will spread radially from the urban core and be interspersed with industrial parks.
7) The transportation network will be restructured and a new road network as well as railway junctions will be created.

The very first draft of the new master plan for the reconstruction of Warsaw was prepared in a relatively short time. Three months after the liberation of the city, in April 1945, the master plan was presented to the government. This study was, of course, based to some degree on prewar planning studies prepared for Warsaw as well as on some design work conducted in secret during the Nazi occupation.

The main concepts of the new plan followed the lines of the general pattern of development and the approach taken in the "Functional Warsaw" study, while at the same time introducing far-reaching changes in functional and land-use patterns. In the new plan the central core of the city, which in 1939 housed some 800,000 inhabitants, was designated as the central business and cultural district with a very limited number of residential facilities surrounding it. New residential districts were proposed in a corridorlike fashion to the north and south of the central district along the banks of the Vistula River, as well as along other corridors (that is, along the prewar directions of development on the east-west and northeast-southwest axes). Industrial parks were placed in functional interrelations with those districts in which environmental conditions (such as prevailing winds vis-à-vis the level of noxiousness of various industries) suggested a specialization of production. In this way five major industrial districts were proposed which together with the city core composed six major concentrations of working places.

In studies for the master plan a very extensive amount of open and green space was proposed. The major green belt followed the river and separated the city center and residential zones from the river bank. It was supposed to serve as a main ventilation corridor that would be joined by a number of green corridors crossing the city and perpendicular to the river. The city center was to be surrounded by another green belt joined by even more green areas which would run from the outskirts of the city to connect the city with three major forest reserves. Two of the reserves had the status of national parks, while the third was to be expanded into a more extensive forest area.

The general idea of how the city should develop has been retained throughout the whole period of reconstruction and development to the present, and has been retained in the most recent generation of the master plan, for development to 1995. Although the general concept has been incorporated into the latest master plan, it has naturally undergone some evolutionary changes. Indeed, some changes were made in the first years of planning for the reconstruction of Warsaw. Later, when planning began to be perceived as an ongoing process, the master plan was updated every five years, in accord with certain major lines of evolution:

Changes in the estimated size of the city and its tempo of growth were required. The first plan had envisioned that the whole city would reach the level of 700,000 inhabitants during the 20 year period of full reconstruction. However, in that span of time, the city attained a population of one million and, by 1975, it surpassed the prewar population of 1.3 million.

The economic model of the city evolved towards a higher proportion of manufacturing and of workers in the overall employment structure, as well as towards a higher level of development of selected industries (new mill for high-grade steel, expansion of the car and tractor industry, and expansion of electronic manufacturing).

Revision of the proportion of open space in the general land-use patterns resulted from the realization that urban land has a high social and economic value (that is, the cost of infrastructure, the cost of city maintenance, and the social costs of commuting due to the city's expansion) which cannot be neglected.

Revision of the city center's functions and the introduction of a residential program to that area occurred for two reasons: to avoid a "dead" central business district and to lessen the number of people commuting to the downtown area.

A major improvement in environmental conditions compared to the prewar situation was achieved by a very substantial reduction in the density of development and by the expansion of urban territory from 130 square kilometers to over 450. The density of development in 1939 as expressed by lot ratio in the central city district amounted to 4.0 or even 5.0 while the population in some central residential districts was at the level of two to three thousand inhabitants per hectare. In the new plan laid out for the downtown area, the highest plot ratio was at the level of 2.0 with the exception of a few central blocks with business-development programs. The population density in residential areas is generally at the level of 300 to 500 inhabitants per hectare with a couple of central city blocks at the level of 1,100. The plot ratio is generally below 1.0, mostly around 0.5 or 0.7. These figures may be compared with figures for some reconstructed areas in London such as the Barbican area with a plot ratio of 3.5, St. Paul's with 4.2, and the largest area, Stepney-Poplar, where the population density was decreased from roughly 700 to roughly 300 inhabitants per hectare.

Another environmental improvement is represented by a new system of urban heating. Over 80 percent of the housing stock in present Warsaw as well as all other buildings in the central core are heated centrally by four heating and power stations.

The road network was totally redesigned with the introduction of modern through-highways and underpasses. Similarly, the railroad system was modernized, electrified, and developed as two independent systems, long-distance and local. The main fault in the development of the transportation system has been the failure to construct a sorely needed subway system for the city. Although a subway system was planned and designed in the first years of reconstruction and although construction was begun, the whole plan had to be delayed due to serious geological problems and escalating costs.

From the first days of reconstruction, planners were concerned with Warsaw's particular problem: the restoration of destroyed historic buildings and monuments. The task involved retaining the continuity of the city's past for future generations while still building a fully modern city in both functional and architectural terms.

The historical monuments and landmarks of Warsaw, approximately 800 buildings, were totally destroyed by the Nazi occupiers as part of their policy of exterminating the Polish nation. The invaders, as well as the Poles, realized fully that a nation without its history and its culture loses its identity and its ability to resist extermination. The Poles realized it was the duty of the generation rebuilding the city of Warsaw to restore all landmarks and historic buildings as documents of a national heritage to be preserved for following generations. And so they undertook a project that was itself unique in scale and character, the reconstruction not only of the Old Town of Warsaw, but of all the historic palaces, churches, and other miscellaneous monuments scattered throughout the city. The last of these monuments, the Royal Castle, was in its final stages of reconstruction in 1979. The architectural conception of the whole project was based on survey drawings of buildings made by students of the Faculty of Architecture at the Warsaw Polytechnic before the war. Another documentary source was found in the paintings of Canaletto and Bernardo Bellotto which depicted Warsaw's cityscape at the end of the eighteenth century. Since the reconstruction plan for Warsaw recognized that the historical part of the city must participate in full with modern currents of urban activity, some interiors were adapted or modernized to fulfill contemporary expectations and functional demands.

By the end of the 1970s Warsaw was an important industrial center, generating nine percent of Poland's gross national product. At the same time, it was a complex, modern, metropolitan area with extensive new residential districts, a well-developed system of parks and green belts, as well as a broad program of cultural, scientific, and educational activities concentrated in the urban core.

POSTWAR CITY CORES RECONSTRUCTED

The experiences of Coventry and Rotterdam, both nearly totally destroyed in 1940 by the Nazis, provided the cornerstones for the whole process and philosophy of design and reconstruction of European city cores. In both cities the decision was made that the rebuilt central area should follow a fully modern and functional approach to the design of civic centers. The main problem encountered, however, was that the structure of land ownership had to be superseded.

Rotterdam, the second largest city of Holland and its second most important seaport, with 600,000 inhabitants in 1939, was attacked by the Nazis in May 1940. As a result of that attack close to 300 hectares of the central city and dock area were totally destroyed and 11,000 buildings were devastated. Over 3,000 people were killed with about 80,000 left homeless.

Much of the initial planning for Rotterdam's reconstruction was done secretly during the Nazi occupation of Holland. The basic plan, adopted by the authorities in May of 1946, envisioned a wide extension and modernization of the harbor and construction of a brand new central core, representing totally new spatial and functional ideas. The backbone of the new shopping and business district was built in the form of a pedestrian mall that begins with a monumental sculpture by Ossip Zadkine symbolizing the destruction of the city. The main traffic system was redesigned to bypass the central area, thus creating the first example in modern town planning of a traffic-free pedestrian area where shopping, cultural, and other facilities are concentrated. The Rotterdam reconstruction project was completed in the early fifties and, thanks to its innovative approach to spatial and functional arrangements, it had a very broad impact on the development of urban design in Europe during the whole reconstruction period.

Before the war the city of Coventry had been an important industrial center with a quarter of a million inhabitants. On 11 November 1940 Coventry was terrorized by a surprise air attack that totally destroyed its central area, including a number of historical buildings and the famous Gothic cathedral.

The work of design for the reconstruction, undertaken immediately after the attack, was completed in February 1941 when the comprehensive development plan was presented for approval. As in Rotterdam, but on a smaller scale, the newly proposed pattern of development discontinued the old urban configuration and substituted a modern conception of a central square and pedestrian mall surrounded by a circular access road. The controversial issue in this scheme was the proposed treatment of the remaining ruins of the cathedral. Sir Basil Spence, the designer of the new cathedral, decided that the ruins should be retained. The interior of the preserved ruin was to serve as a kind of entrance patio attached to a new modern cathedral. Time proved that the designer's decision was right. The whole complex of the destroyed and new cathedral is one of the most dramatic yet picturesque architectural landmarks built in European cities during the reconstruction period.

While Coventry should be seen as one of the most successful examples of comprehensive planning of a redevelopment project, we should recognize that its implementation was accomplished because the authorities adhered to the design principles involved. Some other European projects are less spectacular.

London, also heavily bombed in 1940, continued to sustain damage to the end of the war by V-1 and V-2 missile attacks. Some important parts of the city center such as the area around St. Paul's Cathedral and the South Bank of the Thames River as well as many others, were destroyed. More than a half-million people were left homeless and part of the central city's life was paralyzed. The Town and Country Planning Act, adopted in 1944, spelled out conditions for the reconstruction of eight different areas in London: Stepney-Poplar, Bermondsay, Barbican, City, South Bank, Elephant and Castle, Bunhill Fields, and St. Paul.

Although the general approach in all those areas was based upon the idea that reconstruction design must introduce improvement in functional and environmental terms, there proved to be a number of factors limiting the freedom of designers and redevelopers. The most important of these factors was probably the value of land and the calculations of the expected returns on reconstruction investments. This resulted, in most cases, in high densities of development and in the introduction of building sizes and heights in direct contradiction to the architectural traditions of the prospective areas. The most striking example of this, the new development around St. Paul's Cathedral, overwhelms some of the smaller remaining historical buildings and closely approximates the impressive scale of the cathedral's architecture. The South Bank of the Thames was developed as a chain of administrative and cultural facilities, creating a new element in the city core across the river from and in some contrast to the historical nuclei of Westminster and Parliament. The Barbican area was one of the first European examples of designs for high-density residential areas which included the separation of vehicular traffic and pedestrian traffic. Stepney-Poplar, an area of roughly 800 hectares, is the major reconstructed residential project in which the number of inhabitants was reduced from 120,000 to 100,000.

Although some of the reconstruction plans in the London area did not take full advantage of their chance for improvement, their layouts played an important role in the overall development of postwar urban planning. England was the only country in Europe which in spite of suffering substantial war damage was never occupied. Thus, even with the hardship of war, British architects and local authorities were better able to start working on reconstruction plans than were their colleagues in the rest of Europe. British universities, fully operational during the war, were training not only the British but also a number of foreign students who had escaped from the Continent. These younger architects and builders returned to their own countries after the war, bringing with them some of the British philosophy and experiences of urban design.

By the end of the war thousands of cities of all sizes and tens of thousands of villages were heavily damaged, while tens of millions of urban dwellers were homeless. Rebuilding activities spread throughout Europe with the understanding that reconstruction must be accomplished quickly and that some improvement in functional and land-use patterns should be incorporated into the final plans. The magnitude of this task often resulted in somewhat schematic or simplified approaches. In many cases, the old traditional scales of the urban environment were neglected and new buildings provided a sharp contrast of scale and form with traditional and surviving parts of cities. This phenomenon may be observed in many reconstruction projects in France where the old central area was developed anew in accordance with modern environmental and functional demands but without regard for the finesse of its former spatial and architectural arrangements. Maubeuge, Calais, and Amiens among others received layouts on a new scale. Some plans presented fresh approaches while in others such as Boulogne-sur-Mer a new scale was consciously introduced for contrast and to express changing times and conditions. The well-known plan for Le Havre, elaborated soon after the war by Auguste Perret, had a broad impact on many other reconstruction and redevelopment projects in Europe. It deserves recognition not only because of the simplicity of its design but also because of its advanced architectural form and its appropriate use of building technology.

It is very difficult to characterize all of the problems, achievements, and/or failures among the reconstructed cities of Europe. In many cases, as for example in West Germany, the control and ownership of land, reconstruction costs, and the desire to retain land values limited the scope and character of changes introduced to land use, density patterns, and spatial composition. Such fully comprehensive plans as those for Hannover and Karlsruhe are rather exceptional, while Frankfurt's or Cologne's, as well as those of many smaller towns, are not too far removed from their traditional layouts. This does not imply that the plans for these cities represent cultural or architectural continuities, for while their urban patterns remained more or less the same, the form and scale of the buildings were changed.

The reconstruction of cities in East Germany was more advanced in revising functional and spatial arrangements, even though the scale of architecture was not always compatible with surrounding environments. One of the more interesting East German examples is the already implemented plan for downtown East Berlin. The traditional backbone of the city, Unter den Linden, has been impressively expanded to include a system of plazas, groups of important governmental buildings, and a shopping area. The complex, including the classic Schinkel architecture of the museums, the reconstructed cathedral church, and the glass and steel architecture of the new parliament, is a well-coordinated arrangement of buildings and open spaces that has evolved throughout history.

The enormous task of reconstructing hundreds of cities in the European part of the Soviet Union was implemented during a period when Russian designers were following Classical rules of spatial and architectural composition. The general layouts of such cities as Stalingrad, Minsk, Sevastopol, and others have undergone very substantial changes characterized by lower densities, the introduction of green and open spaces, and the improvement of transportation. At the same time, central city spatial composition has remained very Classical in form with monumental large-scale architecture. Most picturesque is the reconstructed main street of Kiev, an extremely vivid space, always crowded and full of life. Pedestrian space is accompanied by very rich and ornate architecture which continues the tradition of old buildings, although it has been adapted for a new scale of urban and architectural environment.

SKOPIE

The most dramatic and spectacular of European examples of the reconstruction of a city destroyed by natural disaster is offered by Skopie. The capital city of the Republic of Macedonia, the southernmost republic of Yugoslavia, was hit by an earthquake on 26 July 1963. The city was developing rapidly as an industrial, cultural, and political center after World War II, and had some 170,000 inhabitants on the day of the catastrophe. Over 65 percent of its urban housing stock along with a majority of its services and facilities were destroyed, while the death toll reached 1,200. The tragedy brought worldwide attention and many nations were bent on taking a hand in the rebuilding. The United Nations made its own special contribution to this international effort. It alone was able to provide the sort of many-sided scientific and technical assistance needed for prompt and technically sound reconstruction planning and for further development of that city.

To accomplish the very broad and complex planning required, the United States and the Yugoslav government brought together an international team of planners and scientists representing various disciplines related to building in earthquake-prone areas. The team was composed of the international consulting firms of Doxiadis (Greece), Polservice (Poland), Wilbur Smith (USA), Kenzo Tange (Japan), and of Town Planning Institutes from Skopie and from Zagreb. In addition, a number of individual experts were invited to participate. The general management of the whole operation was the responsibility of this author, Adolf Ciborowski.

The entire planning operation, in terms of its international character and very broad professional scope, was unique and the first on such a scale in the United Nations's experience of technical assistance. The outcome of that exercise offered many, later generalized, principles for urban design in seismically active zones and for the organization of planning and building activities in cases of acute emergency.

First considered by the planners was the problem of how to design the city to decrease the risks and limit the eventual consequences of another earthquake. The solutions adopted in the Skopie master plan were reflected later in some amendments to the Yugoslav building code and were generalized in some manuals published by UNDRO (Geneva 1976). The whole city, planned for a population of 350,000, was totally restructured. The areas indicated by a seismic microregionalization study as the most sensitive and of the highest risk were excluded from any kind of development and left as green and open spaces. Development densities were put at generally low levels, while the road network was not only modernized but also expanded to offer double access to every one of the urban districts. The height and form of buildings were subordinated to the demands of shock-resistance, as gauged from local seismic and soil conditions. A tridimensional model of the city center was examined in the wind tunnel to define the best pattern of spatial organization, taking microclimatic, fire-limitation, and other points of view into account.

The strong commitment of the Yugoslav government and of the local authorities to build the new Skopie fully in accordance with the master plan's program and spatial concepts permitted us to state after ten years of building activities that the initial vision of the resurgent city had been almost 100 percent accomplished!

As a result, Skopie continues to grow as the most modern and functionally sound city on the Balkan peninsula.

New Towns

Since 1945, population growth, economic development, urbanization processes, and the growth of cities have had to be reconsidered; new policies and strategies have been formulated to deal with these phenomena and their effects on the evolution of settlement systems and patterns. New towns have gained interest and popularity as one of the possible strategies of spatial and economic development within the context of national and regional planning. The definition of what kind of settlement could be called a new town was never precisely formulated and therefore there are many differences in national reports concerning the European new town experience. Nevertheless, the most prevalent view is that a new town is a settlement of urban character which is built from scratch and in accordance with a master plan of development formulated at the time of the town's birth. A new town may also be defined as an existing settlement which expands within a given period—usually a short time in planning terms of approximately twenty to twenty-five years, during which the new urban organism will grow to be twice as large as the initial one. Experience has shown that the scale of growth is usually eight to ten times that of the original town, and that the existing settlement serves only as a starting point to be incorporated later into the new structure of the city as a minor or marginal part.

Analyzing the new towns planned and built across Europe in the past three decades, we may distinguish three major types. The first involves new towns built as new nuclei of economic growth. Such towns are primarily in underdeveloped regions of a country or within already developing regions. They function as new or additional production centers close to natural resources and a large rural population that would otherwise have constituted an idle labor force. New towns that provided new job opportunities in rural areas have been typical of Poland and the Soviet Union. A second type consists of those which have been developed as satellite towns in existing metropolitan areas, large cities, or industrial regions to help disperse or slow the further growth of major urban areas by diverting population growth. This new town development is most typical for Great Britain but is also found in Poland's largest new towns and in a number of other European countries. The general concept of a social and economic model for such towns evolved from the concept of dormitory settlements in which people were supposed to live but not work, to the concept of self-sustained towns with sufficient manufacturing and related establishments to provide ample job opportunities. In some models between these two extremes, part of the population is employed in the new towns while the rest commutes elsewhere to work. The most recent view holds that the dormitory type of satellite town is functionally and socially unhealthy and that both the self-sustained model and the new economic growth-pole models are more desirable. The third type of new town development is a settlement that directly extends an existing metropolitan area and is strongly linked functionally and spatially to it. A semantic confusion often arises here, since in some countries, for example Poland, these are considered simply as new districts of an existing city, while in others, especially in Sweden and France, they are identified as new towns.

I am inclined to see this type as an example of natural growth and expansion of existing cities rather than necessarily as a new town. Though quite often in the past this kind of development was designed as a residential complex with necessary services and facilities but without a sufficient number of job opportunities, recently this attitude towards programming and design has changed. New districts or towns in France, Sweden, and Poland for instance, are designed as more or less self-contained units, equipped with necessary working places of almost every kind.

BRITISH NEW TOWNS

The British new towns represent an unusual experience thanks to the comprehensiveness of their philosophy and policy. The first concept was originated by Ebenezer Howard in his idea of a Garden City [1898] and implemented in a model demonstration project of an urban garden city at Letchworth [1904] and then in Welwyn [1920]. Because of its proximity to London, Welwyn was truly the first satellite town of that city. Even under the hardships, economic demands, and pressures of World War II British politicians were searching for imaginative alternatives to improve living conditions in the period that would follow the war. One of the ideas proposed was the concept of satellite towns for various metropolitan areas—first London, then other districts throughout England and Scotland. Legislation enacted after the war, the "New Towns Act" (1946), provided governmental sanctions and financial backing for their construction. From the passage of this act to the mid-1970s, 32 new towns were built, housing approximately, 2,000,000 people with an eventual projected population of 3,250,000. Factories, shopping centers, educational and pleasure facilities were provided within the framework of new design patterns related to land use, functional distribution, and spatial composition.

The first group of British new towns established between 1946 and 1950 was concentrated around London. In this group of eight, the most well-known towns are New Harbor (which grew from 5,000 to 85,000 people), Stevenage (from 7,000 to 76,000 people), and Crawley (from 9,000 to 73,000 people). At the same time Welwyn Garden City grew from 19,000 to a population of 40,000. In this same period among the seven other new towns begun were East Kilbride, growing from 2,000 to 74,000, and Glenrothe, growing from 1,000 to 32,000. Both of these towns, located in Scotland, were developed as urban support systems for the two poles of Edinburgh and Glasgow. In northeast England the two towns of Aycliff and Peterlee were built. Both were developed from scratch with a slower planned tempo of population growth. Since 1950 two other major groups of new towns were started, among which were Cumbernauld and Livingston in Scotland and a number of towns such as Washington [1964] and Runcorn [1967] in northwest England servicing an important industrial region.

The most recent group of new towns has been located mostly in the Midlands. This group, mostly resembling the new growth-pole type of development had a new approach in both size and urban design. At first the size of Mark I towns was limited to a population of 60,000 with a central shopping mall designed to serve them. In time, however, many of these cities surpassed their initially projected population figures to reach 80,000 and even 100,000 residents. Mark II new towns were designed in the first half of the 1960s with a higher population level in mind. Considering the growth trends of the Mark I group, they were planned in a more flexible way so as to include possibilities for further expansion. Mark III towns designed in the late 1960s and early 1970s have been planned for populations of about a quarter million each, with even greater flexibility incorporated into them.

The first group of new towns created not only attractive new living environments but also focal points for their surrounding areas. New civic and shopping centers also blended in the best of the old British town-planning tradition, especially in the spatial dimensions of their pedestrian malls and squares. Such spaces, easily accessible to new town residents and to commuters from the surrounding regions, provided a pleasant atmosphere enabling easier social contacts and causing mounting interest and pressure for their expansion. In some new towns, of course, expansion was restricted by a fixed pattern of development evident in the spatial restrictions of the civic center. Some new towns' centers such as in Stevenage and Harlow have been extended but partially at the cost of revisions in building scales and development densities.

The concept of necessary flexibility built into the latter groups gave Cumbernauld an entirely different civic center. All shopping, cultural, and similar functions were concentrated within one compact structure which contains in its design provisions for future expansion along its main axis. That design created broad interest and controversy at the time of its origin but does not seem to meet all of the designers' expectations. Very compact in pattern with narrow internal malls that lack the urban character of squares and streets, it does not satisfy its users. Therefore, this approach has been changed in more recent new towns.

From the Mark I, British new towns consist typically of a series of villagelike neighborhoods grouped around the town center. Each neighborhood is furnished with basic facilities and services such as a primary school, a community center, a clinic, and shops which are located within easy walking distance of all houses. The town, as a whole, has separate road and footpath systems, with the road pattern excluding any through traffic. These first designs had a broad impact on postwar urban design throughout Europe not only for new towns but also in the reconstruction and expansion of existing cities. The latest generation of new towns, with much higher projected population figures is often based on the expansion of already existing settlements such as Peterborough, Northampton, and Worthington. These developments, contrary to previous ones, will be implemented not only by new town corporations but also in partnership with the local authorities of the existing towns.

SWEDISH NEW TOWNS

The patterns of spatial and functional composition of Swedish developmental projects indicate a close connection with the British conception of new towns. However, their experience has been different since the Swedish new towns developed primarily as an expansion of the metropolitan Stockholm area. They thus reflect the character of the third major type of new towns indicated in the first part of this section.

Although Sweden was not directly involved in World War II and even benefited from it economically, the hardships of war did have an impact on this country. During the war housing production diminished so much that the city of Stockholm experienced a housing shortage, and in the mid-1940s residential construction was begun on a scale then unprecedented in Sweden. In June 1945 a plan entitled the "Principles of the Outline for Stockholm" set guidelines for the development of a system of satellite towns linked with central Stockholm by a rapid-transit rail system. The new developments were to consist initially of housing units for 10,000 to 15,000 residents. In the 1950s the size of each town was increased to accommodate up to 25,000 inhabitants, enough to support a complex range of shopping facilities concentrated within a civic center. Beginning in 1948 such new towns were developed along railways extending north, west, and south of Stockholm's core. By 1975 seventeen spatially and functionally distinguishable new towns had been completed.

Unlike London's satellite towns which were located at a distance of fifty to eighty kilometers from the city, Vällingby, the first Swedish new town, was located at a commuting distance of twenty minutes from Stockholm. As the Swedes called it, Vällingby was an ABC (corresponding to "Work, Housing, and Civic Center") city close to the old city core. With a population of 50,000 Vällingby has all sorts of job opportunities, including industrial. Vällingby, planned largely by Sven Markelius, may be regarded as one of the topmost achievements of modern European urban planning. The design of such residential districts together with the British experience very much influenced the thinking of modern town planners.

Two features of Vällingby should be mentioned. The whole town is arranged around a civic center located on a mass-transit line. The civic center, containing shopping, cultural, and entertainment facilities as well as some housing for bachelors and students, is composed of a pedestrian square and short pedestrian streets. Its design was complete, even down to every piece of furniture and pavement. While its streets had very appropriate spatial proportions to create a feeling of proximity but avoid overcrowding, the square seems to be both overscaled and underused. (That oversizing was rectified in another design for the civic center of Årsta, the new town planned by Uno Åhrén and constructed after Vällingby.) The central area of Vällingby is surrounded by a group of point blocks containing small apartments while the rest of the town has been developed with low- and medium-rise housing of the block, terraced, and semidetached types. The land-use patterns were designed carefully so as to protect valuable features of the landscape such as gentle slopes, groves of trees, and small forests. This environmentally conscious design was an inspiration for a number of topnotch achievements in residential design, as in Finland's new town of Tapiola, a satellite of Helsinki by Aarne Ervi and a dozen other architects. Tapiola, built roughly ten years later than Vällingby, achieved the highest standard of harmonious coordination of the natural and man-made environments.

Vällingby, in my opinion, has not been surpassed by any other Swedish new town. More recent developments around Stockholm have been to some degree retrogressive. Criticism of Vällingby pointed to an apparent overly luxurious use of land. Furthermore, it was deemed necessary to simplify newer layouts to accommodate the demands of modern mass-production technologies. Others sought a more urban cityscape for newer new town developments. These various factors resulted in the evolution of urban design towards higher densities, simplified geometrical patterns of spatial composition, and towards more compact streetlike layouts for civic centers, all of which are well exemplified in the new town of Tensta, begun in 1966. The most recent designs, from the mid-1970s, go even farther in situating groups of buildings in straightforward rows, while seeking a new way of enriching the architectural image through broad and imaginative uses of building colors. Whole groups of buildings have been painted according to a very colorful composition coordinated with the natural colors of accompanying greenery and taking into account seasonal changes in color.

THE NETHERLANDS' NEW TOWNS

There is a unique aspect of new town development in the Dutch experience because of its tradition of reclamation of land from the sea. Following World War II, an extremely ambitious plan for further reclamation was developed as a continuation of work undertaken in the 1930s on a group of new polders: Wieringermeer (20,000 hectares), followed by the Noordoostpolder (48,000 hectares), and then Eastern Flevoland (54,000 hectares). Those polders on which the two new towns of Allmere and Lelystad have been built have extremely rich and well-developed farm lands. These two cities, designed to absorb part of the overspill from Amsterdam, serve also as new urban centers for the surrounding farms.

The city of Lelystad was planned for a population of 100,000 by the year 2000, while Allmere was to have no less than 125,000 inhabitants by that same time. Some reports, however, indicate growth possibilities of up to a quarter of a million people. Both cities were designed to be self-contained with all necessary kinds of job opportunities. Being located on ideally flat but expensive land, it was necessary to adopt rather rigid and very matter-of-fact patterns of spatial organization. Both cities have a central longitudinal zone with two separate levels: one for cars, the other for pedestrian traffic. The residential units, situated around and along the central area, have their own small service centers located on a kind of circular road that unifies the whole development and links the city to access roads.

POLISH NEW TOWNS

During this period, Poland was one of those European countries which was still undergoing an intensive process of urbanization combined with reconstruction, industrialization, and agricultural modernization. Urban population in 1946 amounted to 7.5 million, some 30 percent of the total population, and increased to 19.5 million by 1976, representing 57.5 percent of the total population. The bulk of the increase has been accommodated in developments of medium-sized prewar cities as well as in some small towns designated as new growth poles. The national physical development plan, promulgated in its first version in 1946, spelled out the guidelines for a national settlement policy. As a consequence of the stimulation of growth in new and existing urban centers in less developed regions and of the control of growth in existing major cities a harmonious development of an urban settlement system has been implemented across the whole country. The main tool for controlling growth was the locating of productive forces. While mining and processing industries have been developed mostly in areas of newly found natural resources (copper, sulfur, lignite, and coal), other manufacturing industries were located in areas where the need to stimulate development arose, where a surplus labor force existed, and where environmental conditions were favorable to planned manufacturing activity. Though in most cases the urbanization process was expressed by the growth and expansion of existing cities, in some instances the existing network of cities and towns became insufficient for supporting new opportunities and demands.

As a consequence of the general process, the highest rates of population growth were in over 120 cities of medium size where populations rose from 30,000 and 100,000 to 75,000 and 250,000. However, there are about fifty new towns functioning as new growth poles or satellite towns in addition to new districts developed as parts of existing metropolitan areas throughout the country. Most of these new towns are based on some already existing small settlements.

A group of new towns that serve as growth poles was developed in southeastern and eastern Poland. Zambrow, Dębica, Mielec, Świdnik, and others are all based on textile, chemical fertilizer, or metal industries in those areas. In the heavily industrialized Silesia region (coal mining and black metallurgy) some satellite towns had been designed as early as the early 1950s. Some of them, retaining their former function as dormitory towns, actually slowed in growth, while others were growing and becoming self-contained urban organisms. The most interesting example of the latter is Nowe Tychy, located in the southern part of Silesia. Nowe Tychy is surrounded by a system of forested land and an artificial lake which serves as a major water supply for the whole industrial region.

The city of Nowe Tychy was projected to grow from 8,000 inhabitants to 160,000 with an initial layout, however, that was designed to accommodate only 100,000. Nowe Tychy is well linked to industrial areas by roads and rail connections. In later stages of the evolution of its plan, Nowe Tychy received its own industrial area with a car factory as its main industry. The city was designed along a series of axes . . . *ośe krysztalizujace* . . . closely following the spatial conception of the designer. The town's central facilities are found along the main axis and in turn are surrounded by a series of open spaces. Each subunit of the town is built along an axis where secondary or local centers are located. The case study of Nowe Tychy is probably the most interesting in Poland because the city was designed and built during a twenty-five-year period under the supervision of the same team of architects. This pemitted the retention of the general concept for Nowe Tychy but allowed a continuous evolution of the planning process to incorporate changing demands, preferences, and expectations of society as well as new technology.

Jastrzębie, another new town in Silesia, is much more recent than Nowe Tychy. Built in the 1970s to meet the housing needs of employees of a group of newly opened coal mines, Jastrzębie is projected to grow from 10,000 to 150,000 inhabitants.

Nowa Huta, located some fifteen kilometers to the east of the ancient city of Crakow in southern Poland, is the most interesting example of new town development in the first period of postwar planning. Established in 1951, it was to serve the housing needs of employees of a newly built steel mill that was at that time the largest in Poland. This area was chosen for the location of the mill for a variety of reasons. It could absorb the spillover of rural population in the southern area of Poland. Since it was relatively close (seventy kilometers) to the Silesian industrial region, it could expect cooperation from the older industrial area. Furthermore, Crakow's tradition as the oldest Polish academic center and its prewar industrial expertise assured appropriate professional and academic support for the new mill.

Nowa Huta grew at a somewhat faster rate than had initially been projected, so that by the mid-1960s together with Crakow it comprised a large metropolitan area. Liquidation of an old airport formerly located between Crakow and Nowa Huta enabled the expansion of both cities towards each other creating, as a result, a bifocal urban system. The design of Nowa Huta, especially in its early stages, was a mix of formalized, classic, axial composition containing a central square, residential areas grouped along the line of the neighborhood unit, and a hierarchy of service centers. The new town is fairly well supplied with green and open spaces. A major green belt, for example, separates the residential areas of the town from the steel mill.

With the discovery of large deposits of coal in eastern Poland during the mid-1970s, research and design was undertaken for the development of a system of new towns in that region. This system of new towns is envisioned as functionally related to the existing city of Lublin, an old historical city, and presently designated as a growth-pole for eastern Poland. This system of settlements has been designed in such a way as to take into account the protection of all aspects of the existing natural environment. At the same time, the settlements are grouped in functional interrelation with the mines so that commuting will be facilitated, residential areas will be protected from the noxious impact of this industry, and the processing of coal will be easier.

The density of the urban settlement network in Poland seems to be sufficient for present and future (twenty years hence) needs. The latest series of national development and regional plans (1977) does not foresee the construction of more new towns. Future urban population growth will be accommodated in the expansion of existing cities with an emphasis on a limited development of major metropolitan areas and the strengthening of regional and local growth-poles.

THE SOVIET UNION'S NEW TOWNS

Between 1918 and 1978 the urban population of the Soviet Union increased from 26 to 150 million people. Roughly 40 million of that increase has been accommodated in newly built cities. Depending on the definition of what constitutes a new town, we may estimate that the total number of new cities built in that sixty year period was between 1,000 and 1,200. In 1967, roughly 50 percent of all new cities were located in the European sector of the USSR where they represent a comparatively minor component of the overall Soviet urban settlement system. In the Asian republics, new cities constitute 70 to 80 percent of the total number of urban settlements.

The major new towns in the Soviet Union are of the new growth-pole type. In the Asian part, new growth-poles are usually built from scratch while in the European part they are accelerated expansion types of small, old urban settlements. Although the average size of a new town is at the level of 30,000 to 150,000 residents, there are some cities, especially those developed before World War II, which have already surpassed the half-million mark.

In analyzing Soviet new towns, it is possible to distinguish some further types. For example, a number of the smallest new towns represent new centers servicing agricultural and rural areas, including huge and modern collective and state farms. Medium-sized cities are for the most part somewhat homogeneous in terms of manufacturing, often being based on a single industry or group of interrelated production establishments. The largest new cities are very complex yet comprehensive models in terms of productive facilities, services, and administrative functions as well as scientific, research, and educational facilities.

A group of new towns, distinguished by special scientific and research functions, includes, for example Dubna, Pushkino and Akademgorod near Novosibirsk. Such cities with special functions, for instance the exploration of space, were built in the recent period. Two leading examples of the latest large new towns characterize the trends of the current generation. These are Naberezhnye Chelny and Togliatti, the center of a new automobile industry producing modified Fiat (Lada) cars. These towns increased in population from 61,000 in 1959 to 500,000 by 1975. In their spatial organization they are based on an appropriate functional linkage between the industrial, residential, central city, and recreational zones. Residential areas are structured basically as micro-units, consisting of 12,000 to 15,000 people, and each of these units has its own network and center of services. The next grouping, consisting of 25,000 to 30,000 inhabitants, is equipped with a wider range of recreational, cultural, and shopping facilities. Finally, the core of the city is not only the administrative and social center but also contains many cultural amenities.

FRANCE'S NEW TOWNS

The new town policy in France emerged rather late. The first period after the war was dedicated to the reconstruction of cities and towns in northern and eastern areas of the country. That activity was followed, for some period of time, by a somewhat haphazard yet spontaneous growth of existing cities with especially fast developmental trends in Paris and environs.

The master plan study of Paris noted that Paris would grow from 8.4 million people in 1972 to approximately 14 million people by the year 2000. At the time of the plan's preparation the major problems of the Paris region were: the disappearance of open spaces due to expansion of zones of urban sprawl; the development of suburban housing with inadequate provision for services; the congestion of central Paris due to a lack of suburban areas; and the need for the modernization of older areas in central Paris and its inner suburbs. Thus began a search for a new approach to the planned development of the whole metropolitan area. The sixth national plan for the years 1971-1975 established four goals for a new town policy:

1) To restructure the suburbs by organizing new concentrations of employment, housing, and services.
2) To reduce commuting.
3) To create self-contained cities with balance between jobs and housing by providing housing and supporting services, by creating urban centers, and by considering recreational facilities and environmental protection.
4) To serve as laboratories for experimentation in urban planning and design.

Following this plan, eight new towns were designed along two development corridors within the Paris metropolitan zone. Both corridors run southeast to northwest tangent to the north and south sides of the existing built-up area of Paris. This pattern of spatial development was proposed to break the traditional concentric urban structure and to help develop two new transportation corridors servicing all new developments without entering the already overcrowded city core. Of these eight towns, the five under construction were: Cergy-Pontoise, Evry, Marne-la-Vallée, Melun-Sénart, and Saint Quentin. Two of the proposed new towns were eliminated due to vehement local opposition while the third one was combined with the town of Saint Quentin. The actual plan, therefore, consisted of five new cities and clearly did not resemble the original conception of the development. Other new towns with projected populations ranging from 140,000 to 375,000 were planned in the 1970s to support the existing metropolitan regions of Lille, Lyon, Marseille, and Rouen.

The basic difference between the concept of these nine French new towns and all the others previously discussed is that the French stress that all of theirs have been conceived as new downtown areas. Each new town will be characterized by a downtown area much larger than the needs of the local community and will have a wide range of commercial and business activity. The downtowns are designed with high densities, with the most modern architectural expression of dense cityscapes and with multilevel transport systems, all of which are expected to make the new towns animated regional centers for both residents and nonresidents.

In the first generation of French new towns a new approach to the overall development of urban settlement networks has arisen. These are not truly new towns according to the present definition and experience but rather new central poles which may transfer some of the city-center functions towards new development areas within the complex process of restructuring metropolitan areas.

Bibliography

Bakema, J. B. *Van Stoel Tot Stad.* Antwerp: N. V. Standaard Boekhandel, 1964.

Ciborowski, Adolf. "National Settlements Policy." *Habitat*

International 3, nos. 3-4. New York: Pergamon Press, 1978.

______. "Planning for Urban Renewal." *Theory Into Practice* 9, no. 3 (June 1970). Ohio State University.

______. "Settlement Problems in Europe." *Habitat* 19, nos. 3-4 (1976). Ottawa.

______. "Some Aspects of Town Reconstruction." *IMPACT* (UNESCO) 17, no. 1 Paris (1967).

______. *Town Planning in Poland 1946-55*. Warsaw: Polonia, 1956.

______. *Warsaw—The City Destroyed and Rebuilt*. Warsaw: Interpress, 1970.

Le Corbusier. *The City of Tomorrow*. London: Architectural Press, 1947.

Department of the Environment. *New Towns*. London: Her Majesty's Stationery Office, 1973.

______. *An Outline of Planning in the United Kingdom*. London: Her Majesty's Stationery Office, 1976.

"Les Dommages de la Guerre." *Urbanisme* nos. 45-48, Paris (1956).

Doxiadis, Constantine. *Ekistics: An Introduction to the Science of Human Settlements*. New York: Oxford University Press, 1968.

Duggar, George S. *Urban Renewal Objectives and Practices of Local Governments* (International Union of Local Authorities). The Hague: Martinus Nijhoff, 1965.

Ekistics. Vol. 37, no. 219 (February 1974).

Fisher, Jack C., ed. *City and Regional Planning in Poland*. Ithaca: Cornell University Press, 1966.

Gibberd, Frederick. *Town Design*. London: Architectural Press, 1953.

Golany, Gideon, ed. *International Urban Growth Policies*. New York: A. Wiley-Interscience Publication, 1978.

Goldzamt, Edmund. *Urbanistyka krajów socjalistycznych*. Warsaw: Arkady, 1971.

Hauck Walsh, Annmarie. *The Urban Challenge to Government*. New York: Praeger, 1969.

Jankowski, Stanislaw and Ciborowski, Adolf. *Warsaw*. Warsaw: Interpress, 1978.

Johnson-Marshall, Percy. *Rebuilding Cities*. Edinburgh: At the University Press, 1966.

Ostrowski, Waclaw. *L'Urbanisme Contemporain*. Paris: Centre de Recherche d'Urbanisme, 1970.

Pereny, Imre. *A Varos Kospontja—Tervezes Es Rekonstrukcio*. Budapest: Muszaki Konywkiado, 1970.

Principles of Town Planning in the Soviet Union. Vols. 1-2. Moscow: Stroyisdat, 1976.

Senior, Derek, ed. *The Regional City*. London: Longmans, 1966.

Smoliar, I. M. *Generalnye Plany Nowykh Gorodov*. Moscow: Strojizdat, 1973.

Tinker, Irene and Bucinic, Mayra, eds. *The Many Facets of Human Settlements*. Oxford: Pergamon Press, 1977.

United Nations. *Global Review of Human Settlements*. (Document of United Nations Habitat Conference, Vancouver) (A/Conf.70/A/1), May 1976.

______. *Planning of Metropolitan Areas and New Towns*. (No. 67. 4.5), New York, 1967.

United Nations Economic Commission for Europe. *Human Settlements in Europe: Post-War Trends and Policies*. (ECE/HBP/18), New York, 1976.

United Nations Development Program. *Interregional New Towns, Final Report*. (DP/UN/INT-72-053), New York, 1974.

______. *Skopie Resurgent*. DP/SF/UN/17-YUG), New York, 1970.

U.S., Congress. House Committee on Banking and Currency, Subcommittee on Housing and Urban Affairs. *Urban Growth Policies in Six European Countries*, November 1972.

U.S., Department of Housing and Urban Development. *International Review*. Vol. 1, issue 1 (HUD-503-1-LA), November 1978.

Ward, Barbara. *The Home of Man*. New York: W. W. Norton, 1976.

Wsieobszczaja Istoria Architekturi, 12 (Architektura Zarubieznych Socialisticzeskich Stran). Moscow: Izdatielstwo Architektury Po Stroitielstwu, 1977.

6

URBAN AND REGIONAL PLANNING IN SOUTH AMERICA

JOSÉ M. F. PASTOR

Before 1940 there had been practically no governmental policies of urban and regional development in South America. The present movement of public opinion, which supports much of the governmental concern with rearranging the human habitat in the cities and countryside of South America, originated from the ensemble of ideas about man's productive and destructive occupation of the land that concerned Western European geographers, engineers, and geopoliticians at the beginning of the twentieth century. These ideas entered South America in varying degrees of intensity, but remained confined to the technical and scientific fields (with the exception of those concepts which pertained to provisions for the protection of flora and fauna); to laws regulating national parks and national reserves; to rules about the subdivision of rural lands to be converted into urban zones; to regulations for the parcelling of private lands and their division into lots ready to be developed; and to rules governing the planning of roads and open public spaces.

The worldwide phenomenon of urbanism, foretold by Oswald Spengler in *The Decline of the West* (1918) and later in *Man and His Technique* (1931) and recognized by the Spaniard José Ortega y Gasset in *The Revolt of the Masses* (1930), was intensively researched in the 1930s by Lewis Mumford in *The Culture of Cities* (1938). This universal sociocultural and socioeconomic phenomenon manifested itself in the decade of the 1940s as the "glut of the cities" (Ortega), "the petrification of the countryside" (Spengler), and the "megalopolis" (Mumford). More than a simple rural exodus, it may be defined as a not necessarily negative tendency toward a minimal settling of the countryside furthered by growth in the technology of agricultural production and leading to a gathering of different peoples in urban areas. As a consequence of this, an increasingly complicated and conflicting kind of neighborhood behavior is established in cities that, whether old or new, have been unprepared to receive the influx. The newly arrived population is regarded as intruders instead of as new neighbors, contributors, and participants in the general well-being.

With the awareness of problems of urbanism growing, questions of how to design and plan in order to accommodate rapidly developing urban neighborhoods came to concern many. With Le Corbusier at their head, in 1933 the membership of the Congrès Internationaux d'Architecture Moderne (CIAM) proclaimed the "Charter of Athens," recommending that governments adopt urgent urban-design policies in their regional and national planning. Some South American members of CIAM published the Charter of Athens in their respective countries to help move public opinion towards its precepts. In Argentina, Carlos Maria Della Paolera, an *urbaniste* graduated from the Sorbonne, Paris, led a campaign to pressure the municipality of Buenos Aires and as a result of his recommendations became the first chairman of the newly created Urban Planning Office.

Representatives from different American countries issued many warnings at the national and international levels. For instance at the Argentinian Urbanism Congress of 1936 and the Pan-American

Translated from the original Spanish text by Fernando Montserrat, Montreal.

Congress of Public Housing of 1938, both held in Buenos Aires, the urgency of determining housing and urban-development policies in the Americas was established. With this repertoire of anthropoecological ideas, small groups of professionals and public administrators started to become influential in South American governments toward the end of the 1930s, just as preparations for war were becoming increasingly evident in Europe and the Far East.

Postwar Planning Policies

In Europe and a great part of the United States, urbanism, that is to say, the flux of rural inhabitants toward the cities, resulted in relatively even demodynamic redistributions. [Editor's note: "Demodynamic," a word introduced by Mr. Pastor in this essay, refers to the dynamic character of demographic change.] In South America, on the contrary, the centers of attraction were few—consisting of the old colonial capitals such as Buenos Aires and Santiago and secondary cities (Maldonado, Uruguay; Charcas, Bolivia) in which large groups of new settlers created serious imbalances between agricultural and urban areas. Excessive metropolitan concentrations led to sociocultural and economic impoverishment not only in hundreds of small and medium-sized cities but also for thousands of rural communities. To define "megalopolic metropolism" in terms of the territorial and sociopolitical development of South American countries, the Argentine thinker Ezequiel Martinez Estrada, in his *Radiography of the Pampa* (1933) coined the phrase "Goliath's head." For him this was a hypertrophic "capital," overly crowded, immense, and crowning a semicultivated body which was the national territory. Though related particularly to Argentina and Buenos Aires, this image can be applied as well to the largest cities in all of the South American countries.

The war of 1939-1945 led to an awareness at all levels that there are no longer isolated human communities: the entire planet is humanity's *oikos*. The terrific effort that the countries in conflict had to make in rigorous and integral strategic planning and operational organization with warlike ends, left in the population of each country after the war a strong sense of the need to continue to carefully plan actions that would anticipate each nation's own tasks in partnerships with the international community. The problem became how to reconcile, on the one hand, the liberal feeling of unrestricted free will and spontaneous laissez-faire development, which easily degenerates into man's abuse of land and society with, on the other hand, the social responsibility which all must assume in defense of natural resources and the general well-being.

In effect, world public opinion and that of the young countries in particular was suddenly confronted with the dilemma of opting for one of two methods: "planning with slavery," which the Nobel prize-winning Austrian expert in political economy, Frederik von Hayek, associated with fascist or communist totalitarian regimes; or "planning with freedom," which was encouraged by the German epistemologist, Karl Mannheim, of the University of London. The latter doctrine influenced legislation in urban and rural planning being formulated in Great Britain and soon spread beyond that country's borders. Von Hayek in his book, *The Road to Serfdom* (1944), and Mannheim with his *Diagnosis of Our Times* (1943) constituted, together with the works of Spengler, Ortega, and Mumford, the theoretical bases of planning which were to inspire methods and policies of national development-planning throughout the western world.

With the founding of the United Nations in San Francisco in 1945, its Economic and Social Council was organized. From within the council there arose economic commissions for Europe, Asia, and Latin America. The latter, known by the acronym CEPAL, played an important role in the training of young functionaries, to help the member-states' governments in formulating development plans at the regional and national levels. Unfortunately the predominating concept in this training was more financial than "economic." Social aspects were considered only incidentally and emphasis was placed on national budgets as basic instruments of planning.

The concept of global planning, technically, judicially, and administratively accommodating land-space to the requirements of man's life under optimal conditions of urban and rural coexistence, was ignored for a long time. The biased, restricted approaches of monetary and financial techniques were in the ascendancy, in spite of Karl Mannheim's warning that planning should deal with things and men at the same time.

During the six long years of world war in Europe, news had continued to arrive in Latin America, especially from Great Britain, about plans being prepared, to confront the great tasks of the physical and socioeconomic rebuilding of Europe. The struggle ended in 1945 and the preparatory tasks of rehabilitation were begun. Two years later the United States announced its Marshall Plan, the statute establishing economic cooperation voted by Congress in 1947. By means of the Marshall Plan twelve billion dollars in loans and subsidies were to be distributed to the European countries between 1948 and 1952 through the International Bank for Reconstruction and Development that had been created by the United Nations in 1945. With this aid, national programs with plans already prepared were immediately undertaken. The rapid rehabilitation of agricultural and mining areas, and a spectacular urban reconstruction in cities already cleared of rubble soon became visible. The socialist countries, excluded from the plan by their own decisions, were not left behind: they followed a different rhythm and different operational procedures. Planning procedures were as varied as were political, bureaucratic, and technical apparatuses, from the militant democrats praised by Mannheim to the totalitarians hated by von Hayek. Spain, excluded from the plan, undertook its own effort with a mixed method assimilating the new European experience to its old urban and regional traditions, which subsisted to a good extent also in South America.

Concerned with modernizing, some Latin American governments commissioned studies of the situation that would arise once the war ended. In 1944 Argentina set up the National Postwar Council which inventoried existing and necessary public works and in 1947 carried out the first general census of the population since 1914. In 1944 the Argentine Congress also approved a bill creating the San Juan Rebuilding Council immediately following the earthquake that devastated that region in January of that same year. The council was given planning and operating powers to rebuild in a vast area affected by the earthquake. Considered "the touchstone of national planning," this bill constituted a prototype for regional plans and for several urban plans that the council would formulate.

After four years of governmental indecision about the rehabilitation plan for the area destroyed by the 1944 earthquake, the San Juan Rebuilding Council presented in April 1948 at the Provincial Legislature and at the National Executive Authority a plan for the reconstruction and expansion of the city. The plan was approved immediately and a few months later the council put into practice a part of the first medium-term, 1949-1959 program, that also included projects for the long term (1959-1979), beginning a selected group of public works. The San Juan Rebuilding Council by a federal-provincial agreement administered a reconstruction fund, formed from the proceeds of a national voluntary collection plus a sum voted by the Congress. The programs that implemented the 1948 plan were completed after some interruptions caused by political and administrative changes in the last three decades. The city of San Juan with 40,000 inhabitants in 1948, today has a population near 120,000 and its urban economy formerly based on an agrarian exploitation of the soil with vineyards, has been converted into a mixed mining-agro-industrial structure in a new local economy and society. [Editor's note: The author of both the town plan and its working program as well as the supervisor for the plan's starting stage between 1949 and 1952 was the writer of this essay.] All buildings after 1948 had antiseismic structures. When in 1977 another earthquake entirely destroyed the small city of Caucete some twenty miles to the southeast, San Juan's population felt uneasiness, but there were no consequences for its buildings.

Once the original planning mission was accomplished, the San Juan Rebuilding Council was dissolved and its functions reverted to the normal municipal authorities. Now the first plan is in its last stage, with the finishing of major works like the Civic Center, and with the ring road around the old *casco urbano* completely remodeled into a wide new central avenue as an urban axis of composition for the functional structure of the urban core. One of the five railway restructurings recommended in 1948 is near completion, after the merger of the private Buenos Aires Pacific Railway Company and the government's National Railways Agency.

Earthquakes have caused considerable destruction in other South American urban areas, mostly as a consequence of the precarious construction of many buildings made of adobe (mud bricks, sun-dried) and plain roofs with wooden beams, thick clay covers, and heavy ceramic tile Chillá'n (Chile) was destroyed in 1939 and partially rebuilt in the 1940 decade without a real town reconstruction plan. After Cuzco (Peru) was destroyed partially by an earthquake, the Cuzco Reconstruction Corporation in 1956 began its plan for urban rehabilitation and restoration of many ancient buildings of great architectural interest and built new neighborhoods as well in surrounding municipalities.

Economic and planning organizations appeared in other South American countries, while some like Chile's Corporation for the Improvement of Production (CORFO) and Brazil's technical bureaus concerned with studies of watersheds were early efforts that predated Argentina's council. Brazil's *Commissao Interestadual da Bacia Parana—Uruguay*, formed to consider problems of the Parana and Uruguay rivers' basin, was a precursor of today's International Commission for the Plata Basin; in Colombia the Cauca Valley Corporation was created in order to plan the urban and rural development of an immense region, and in Ecuador there is a similar regional agency for the Rio Guayas Basin.

In its early stages groups of young South American employees or assistants within CEPAL, the United Nations's Economic Commission for Latin America, familiarized themselves with economic planning. The triple blending of laissez-faire pricing, Marxist, and Keynesian theories, with which economists of the time dealt in European and North American universities, was reflected in their training at CEPAL. This formed a basis for initial studies that led to the drafting of national plans of economic development for several South American governments. None of these plans seriously took into account the spatial locations of socioeconomic activities nor the contexts of urban and rural physical structures and infrastructures. Moreover there was no consideration of the impact on national economies of chronic municipal deficits caused by the disorganized growth and use of urban land, nor was there any far-sighted planning for the problems of urbanism.

Requirements for Urban and Regional Development in South America

Since 1940 South American demographic dynamics, added to that of Central America, present a challenge to the governments of all Latin American countries from the Rio Grande at Mexico's border with the United States, to the tip of Cape Horn which divides the oceans between Chile and Argentina. This challenge can be summed up by recognizing that, with the rates of increase recorded in the 1960s and presumably continued through the 1970s, the current population of almost 300 million in Central and South America will double in the next twenty to twenty-five years. The estimated 207.5 million South Americans in 1978 could become 415 million by the year 2000.

This leads one to think about the sheer mass of humanity that must be housed, clothed, fed, educated, and kept healthy; and which must also be given adequate opportunities, both in the countryside and in the city, to make good use of leisure time. For each square meter of housing introduced in a city it is necessary to create a greater and more self-sufficient infrastructure of urban community services than is required by rural housing. Considerable capital investments are required to answer the need of the growing population in reasonable stages beyond the end of the century. By then, the urban population will exceed in proportion the doubling of the total population of South America. Thus, by the year 2000 we must build more than double the present amount of housing and its complementary urban infrastructure. To resolve this problem in South America, we must overcome the purely economic-financial ideology of urban planning, since economists consider this problem to be insoluble with current financial techniques.

South American housing is so intimately tied to the family structure and requires such special attention to sociocultural circumstances that imitation of international architectural norms would be inappropriate. Instead, different notions of spatial distribution in habitable regions, formal designing, building structures, and the uses of materials and manual labor must be employed. In several South American countries many achievements from 1940 to the present show the error of having had meager and arbitrarily uniform norms of habitability applied to design and construction. In the majority of cases, submission to the demands of national and international credit programs, whether in single-family row units or in multifamily, multiple-story units, condemns thousands of South Americans to develop only with great difficulty the normal family life of each anthropogeographical region. They are pigeonholed by universalizing rules that condemn them to see similar urban structures repeated in very different natural and cultural landscapes.

One indication of a concern for the requirements of popular housing which has had a notable influence on the appearance of our cities was the *Unidada Vecinal* (neighborhood unit) No. 1 of Lima, built in 1950 and designed under the inspiration of a group of architects led by Fernando Belaúnde Terry. Belaúnde Terry many years later became president of the Republic and launched Peru's national but unsuccessful development plan with the National Jungle Highway as its basis. Returned to the presidency of Peru in 1980, his ideas concerning regional development took on new life and may act as a link between the Andean countries and those of the La Plata basin. That neighborhood unit, a group of simple, multifamily dwellings, was continuously observed for its effectiveness as a family and social habitat over a span of several years. From this came our first recorded experiences concerning local problems in South American housing.

Almost simultaneously with the Peruvian planning initiatives, in Brazil the urbanist José Luis Sert's preliminary plans for the *Cidade dos Motores* (1942) had developed the thesis of a modern urban structure respecting the traditions of the Laws of the Indies, the fourth book of which contains procedures for the founding and population of cities in Spanish America. The centers of the colonial capitals (i.e., Asunción, Paraguay; Quito, Ecuador; Lima, Peru), once formed of urban shells, belts of villas, and isolated farms that now are within greater urban agglomerations, were planned following these methods. Throughout South America hundreds of small cities preserve their colonial planning almost unchanged, plans that had as their points of departure the square or plaza (i.e., Cochabamba, Bolivia; Valdivia, Chile; La Rioja and Catamarca, Argentina). This initial requirement of South American urban design has been neglected in hundreds of new housing units and urban expansions. With squares omitted altogether or replaced by innocuous green spaces, recent new towns (Punta del Este, Uruguay; Chimpote, Peru; Comodoro Rivadivia, Argentina) are often without the sociocultural significance and functions handed down from the tradition of the Greek agora, transferred to Roman urbanism and thence to Indian legislation.

Popular housing hinges upon such an unquestionable reality as the ability of interested parties to build their own homes quickly, whether well or poorly, or by means of their own efforts or by those of a third party, as the speed with which emergency towns (termed variously "barriadas," "callampas," "villas miseria," "favelas") are put up attests. If they happen to be illegal developments, it is due to the lack of governmental foresight in legalizing such urban efforts. The consideration that South American families develop their lives better in single-family houses is fundamental and must predominate in the planning of housing.

After forty years of experience these basic ideas of regional, country, and urban development are starting to influence South American urban and regional planning. They permit a better evaluation of the demands of the growing population and of the possibilities for each stage of fulfillment of regional and urban development plans.

Governmental Answers to Urban and Rural Needs

The geopolitical ideas that in the first third of this century exercised an influence upon the elite and the governing members of authoritarian and democratic countries gave rise to another group of ideas dealing with land use. Planning for the spatial organization of land use was first tried in rural areas, and the idea was quickly expanded to virgin areas. Intellectual groups in every South American country initiated various movements to warn their governments to stand firm against the simultaneous effects of accelerated population growth, greater demands for fixed and consumer benefits arising from that growth, and against unscrupulous land consumption and the tendency of the burgeoning population to settle in one or some very few disproportionately large cities.

The governments that were eager to modernize acted upon these warnings, but generally without much conviction, to create technical and administrative organisms in imitation of European and North American governments. The new agencies were advisory to the executive powers on economic planning matters and on problems of housing and urban development. A common characteristic of the national postwar development councils, planning committees, and even planning ministries from 1945 to 1980 has been the carrying out of a great many analyses, however hypothetical, of current situations with sophisticated methods of evaluation, strongly saturated by dominant economic theories. From these analyses definitions of broad objectives arose. These were endorsed by a philosophy of development in which the social aspect appears invariably as an appendix to the economic, just as Medina Echevarria of CEPAL had warned. New planners defined a great many goals to be achieved and drew up plans of national development that were hardly more than the usual lists of public works and national budgets, and, in fact, could have been worked out within the normal technical and administrative structure of any country. Private initiative was considered as lagging behind "indicative" planning, especially in housing, the most urgent and politically exploitable of issues.

The direct import of philosophies and planning procedures that were originally European (particularly French) and North American (from the United States exclusively) overlooked differences between political systems, between technically highly developed industrial nations and developing agricultural and cattle-raising or mining-oriented nations, and differences between countries with long years of experience in land-use regulations and nations with hardly two centuries of occupation of lands still largely virgin. As a logical consequence no imitation, not even that so spectacularly unveiled in the program of the Alliance for Progress (compare below), had the desired success. There was no adequate governmental answer to the challenges of national development and urbanism in South America, even in such countries as Argentina and Uruguay, which with the smallest rates of population increase still felt the pressures of urban growth.

A precursory National Coordinating and Planning

Committee was created in Bolivia as early as the 1930s, and in Chile the Corporaton for the Improvement of Production (CORFO) was established with regional committees. Brazil tried out the management planning method as an instrument of the *Estado Novo*, in the fashion of the new European economic policies, and kept it in effect until the 1954 advent of the "new" developmental policy of the Kubitschek government. Argentina transformed its National Postwar Council into the Ministry of Technical Affairs (1945-1955), in charge of working out its first two five-year plans.

All plans that arose from these organizations enumerated lists containing impressive numbers of public and private works to be carried out and defined specific dialectically irreproachable aims. The problem of carrying out plans in a coordinated and synchronized way, however, remained unresolved since the planners left out consideration of the available human potential which, through education, would prepare the planning personnel for immediate and successive stages of development.

Public consciousness today is sufficiently informed and experienced in its own right to support government initiatives that tend to regulate the use of land, whether rural or urban, along planning guide lines. The demands of the countryside differ greatly in each South American nation and between each region of the larger ones, like Argentina and Brazil. This is easily demonstrated when we try to define "agrarian economic unit" for individual regions and countries. Chile's CORFO has tried to achieve its "agrarian reform" with approaches that have differed with the doctrines of successive governmental authorities since 1940; the same has occurred in Peru, where the traditional community is rooted to those of the pre-Columbian and colonial periods.

Typically in the South American countryside, the rural family requires the opportunity for a life of comfortable physical isolation in its respective agricultural and cattle-raising establishments; and it requires a fluid sociocultural intercommunication with the closest city and the country as a whole. The governmental response consists of an adequate infrastructure of roads, the extension of electricity and telecommunications to rural areas, and the political incorporation of rural neighborhoods into municipalities. In some countries this latter objective has been fully achieved by means of organic municipal laws. According to such municipal codes, all of the national territory, or that of a province or state, is made up of areas under municipal jurisdiction. Without the intermediaries of national, provincial, or state territories, however, settlers lack a voice in the local government and are dependent on the remote controls of a provincial, state, or national capital.

For the requirements of the present urban populations, all South American countries now have legislation that stimulates the formulation and execution of regulatory plans with proper initiative under municipal responsibility. With reference to new cities, there is a difference between such cities as Brasilia, created by the national state's own decision (with more or less provincial or state consent in federal countries), and those cities that arise without warning from regulations for the subdivision of land into urban lots and from real estate speculation.

It can be said generally that governmental answers to the requirements of the rural and urban populations are not yet as coherent as they must become. Keeping in mind that the needs originated coincidentally with the phenomenon of urbanism, responses for each urban-regional context may be integrated into an urban system. The concept of an urban system was stated in 1960 by the Institute of Regional and Urban Planning of Buenos Aires (IPRU), a private entity which issued a manifesto proposing to Latin American governments that Operation SUAL (Urban Systems for Latin America) be carried out in their respective national territories. This would start out from municipal bases which would organize the geographic space in each region by means of a coherent planning structure that, in turn, would regulate and promote urban and rural development. Within such a framework there could be located, in a coordinated and synchronized way, the physical works and stimulating social and economic operations announced in the national development plans promoted by the Alliance for Progress.

Governmental Answers to Urban Needs

New ideas concerning the architectural habitat and urban design were brought to South America in 1929 by Le Corbusier during his memorable tour and had their impacts particularly in Buenos Aires and Rio de Janeiro. Years later, through his disciples and followers, Le Corbusier influenced urban-planning projects especially in Brazil where the most far-reaching result has been the design of Brasilia, realized with the direction of Lucio Costa and Oscar Niemeyer, from 1956 through the 1960s. Professionals who acted together with Le Corbusier implanted the recommendations of the 1933 Charter of Athens for city planning in their respective countries but generally found no adequate responses. When some of them came to occupy important positions in public organizations, they could not achieve the acceptance and application of the Le Corbusier designs that they planned. In the official plans for cities like Buenos Aires, Bogotá, and Lima they attempted to impose new housing forms upon existing urban schemes by expropriating entire suburbs, demolishing extant quarters, and constructing a novo in the areas razed.

The drastic alternative of reconstruction proposed was in reality a novo construction upon a tabula rasa. With its manifest economic impracticality, and with its constructive ingenuity based on unusual design models till then untried in South American cities, it provoked disbelief in the viability of urban planning. In public and governmental opinion this helped to reinforce the tradition of spontaneous growth without state control, but for housing regulations for real estate in the name of the public good. The national governments, as they had until then, left decisions on urban land use to local authorities, especially the municipalities, giving them unrestricted freedom to enlarge the cities under their direction, without establishing logical relations in space and time between real demands for land settlement and permits to create new parcels of land for urban use. The rural periphery of existing cities and the environs of areas benefited by great regional public works, such as dikes, dams, or road crossings, were fertile areas for division into lots.

In this way, while legal regulations concerning the subdivision of land were enforced, thousands of acres of productive countryside became unnecessary urban extensions and areas to be newly urbanized. Characteristic of these expansions was an excess of up to five times more parcels of land than was necessary to assure integrated arrangements of housing and all its complements for the rising urban population. The thousands, even perhaps millions, of "interposed uncultivated lands" in urban sites and "dead lots" of South American cities constitute today an oppressive socioeconomic weight for the great majority of municipalities with total deficits that seriously affect national economies.

This inorganic way of unnecessarily expanding urban areas plus a total lack of economic and financial ability to carry out the costly public works that such dispersions of cities require created a chronic deficit of municipal services. That very inability was often emphasized by the draining of local resources by the metropolitan Goliath's Head. The most notable reaction took place in Petropolis, Brazil, in 1950 where the National Congress of Municipalities proclaimed a charter supported by 2,500 towns and cities, which sums up municipal aspirations and suggestions for perfecting the federal system. Reiterated four years later at another municipal congress held in São Lourenço (State of Minas Geraes, Brazil), the charter proposed that the central government confront Operation Municipality as an important element in national development-planning. Two basic means of action were recommended: 1) formulation of a national plan of works and services with its comptroller in charge of an administrative entity with specific funds, and 2) the immediate introduction of an emergency plan, with the assignment of 3 billion cruzeiros to it as an advance upon the total investment in the program.

Araujo Cavalcanti, one of the driving forces of Operation Municipality, saw what its effects were to be. The totality of achievements in urban and rural municipal ambiences would create chain reactions that were to have repercussions in the network of the nation, strengthening its basic structure by expanding local productive potential and improving the coefficients of well-being and general development. The "O. M." would mobilize resources and local initiatives against the imbalances of which one is aware, and that threaten national unity itself. On the one hand one sees capitals of privileged states, while on the other hand thre are thousands of despoiled towns, zones of settlement dispossessed of prestige, and of conditions of survival within the federation.

On the eve (1954) of exciting elections to change the government, this movement of municipalities and towns of the interior began to acquire strength as an answer to the national government's Salte Plan, which proceeded from the federal summit to the interior and considered municipal authorities last. The plan made an impression when its principles were presented, under the motto Operation Municipality, at the Fifth Inter-American Congress of Municipalities in San Juan, Puerto Rico, where the contrast between centralist planning and that inspired in the national coordination of local plans was made evident. The essence of the operation proposed consisted of a permanent tripartite agreement between municipalites, states (in the case of Brazil and other federated countries), and the national government, in order to redistribute the resources of a national fund, to be established from the contributions of some few levels of government by common agreement. The plan would be developed from the bottom towards the top under the technical guidance of a national planning body, whose basic tasks would be to fit together the different parts of locally conceived urban and regional regulatory plans, with municipal plans foremost in consideration.

In Brazil this movement was supported by President Kubitschek (1956-1960), whose government turned its attention toward the vast interior with programs of road-making, hydroelectric complexes, and the relocation of basic industry, culminating in the beginning of work on Brasilia, the new capital. The president's prior municipal association (he had been municipal administrator of Belo Horizonte) and the extranational repercussions of Operation Municipality moved him to raise his concern to a continental level. He launched an initiative, the Pan-American Operation, in the form of a vast cooperative-development action to reinforce the socioeconomic progress of all South American countries, with substantial North American aid, putting into practice "a policy of ardent brotherhood and indestructible continental unity." In July 1960, shortly before the end of Kubitschek's presidency, President Eisenhower made public in his Newport Declaration the wish of the United States to cooperate in the development of Latin America. President Kennedy (1960-1963) supported the idea, which fit into the New Frontier external-affairs policy, and proposed the creation of a special fund at the meeting of the Organization of American States (OAS) in Bogotá, at which the program of social development that an ad hoc committee had formulated was approved. This program recommended rapid action to attend to the urgent socioeconomic needs of the lesser developed countries, since the interests of the American republics were viewed as so interrelated that adequate social and economic progress in each was of great importance to all.

Influence of the Alliance for Progress

On 13 May 1961 President Kennedy proposed that all American countries unite their efforts in an alliance for progress, whose purpose would be to satisfy the basic requirements of the American peoples in terms of housing, jobs, agricultural land, health, and education. Fourteen days later the Congress of the United States voted 500 million dollars to be distributed between the Social Progress Fund (394 million), the International Cooperation Administration, later known as the Agency for International Development (100 million), and 6 million to the OAS in order to stimulate member countries to formulate their respective national development plans. Shortly after, in August 1961, in Punta del Este (Uruguay) the Inter-American Socio-Economic Council defined the objectives that the first ten-year plan of the Alliance for Progress was to reach and entrusted a Committee of the Nine (made up of four South Americans, three Central Americans, one North American and one Briton) to review the national plans submitted.

The Alliance for Progress was an ensemble of Latin American ideas accepted by the United States, rather than a program imposed on Latin America by the United States. It sought to be a working association, oriented within the framework of the genuinely Pan-American operation that the Brazilians proposed to the OAS, just as years before municipalities had made proposals to the Brazilian federal government. In this operation the member countries would mobilize their potential resources in order to jointly carry out vast works of regional, urban, and rural development, progressively confronted in stages, the first of which would be carried out at an accelerated pace over ten years. There was perhaps a lack of sensitivity on the part of the program's proponents in explaining this intention and in orienting public opinion to it, and too much susceptibility on the part of its opponents—whether interested or not—in emphasizing the U.S. "leadership." Its opponents presented the program as one which interfered with national sovereignty and defined it as bilateral aid, rather than as a joint, multilateral effort of an eminently cooperative nature intended to stimulate self-effort and resulting from a genuinely South American initiative.

The program lacked popular support due to the lack of communication between planners, statesmen, and their peoples. As with any plan of development organically oriented toward concrete objectives and starting from a currently critical situation, the Alliance for Progress required almost all countries to honestly face up to the need for reforms in their political economies and in their technical and administrative bureaucracies.

On the proposal of the Brazilian president, Kubitschek, the United States had agreed to act in what was at first dubbed the Pan American Operation, an international projection of Operation Municipality with the spirit of helping to help oneself. In the August 1961 Conference of Punta del Este (Uruguay), the OAS had solidified the Pan-American Operation, the agreement by which the United States, as with the Marshall Plan in Europe fourteen years earlier, made financial aid available to twenty-two American nations. Under the conditions that a) the democratic system of government be maintained and b) there be progress made in social and economic development, Cuba abstained from voting and did not form part of the Alliance for Progress, as it was decided to call the agreement. It was estimated that about 20 billion dollars were needed, with the United States agreeing to contribute most of it and the rest being negotiated with foreign, public, and private sources of credit. The term of fulfillment of the plan was fixed at ten years. Its global goals were expressed in terms of increases in the average internal gross product of all the nations involved and in other statistical parameters, such as population, public health, illiteracy, and so on.

Heedful of these events, the United Nations Economic and Social Council authorized CEPAL within a few months (1962) to establish the Latin American Institute of Economic and Social Planning (ILPES) which was to offer advice to governments in creating planning organizations, training the functionaries making up these organizations, and studying whatever concerned national development. As for the Alliance for Progress, it created the Inter-American Committee (CIAP) the following year as a coordinating agent between member governments and the aggregation of international moneylenders who made up the fund for social progress (1963). The Inter-American Development Bank (BID) founded four years earlier in 1959 was designated as the fund's financial agent. The CIAP was responsible for the annual review of each member nation's policies and plans of national development and for determining whether external financing was necessary and feasible in order to carry them out. Even though the CIAP was made up of representatives from the member nations, many of them felt that to submit to a certain extent to an extranational power clashed with their sense of sovereignty.

The Alliance for Progress successfully helped some countries to develop specific programs of school and hospital construction among other work projects. However, it was unable to achieve the broad goals it set for itself, losing prestige before each of the member nations, discouraging the United States from contributing more funds, and thereby giving the United States reason in the latter years of the 1960s to diminish the contribution initially promised. Colombia was a typical example of the practical inoperability of the theories of planning development that ILPES and CIAP supported, for it worked predominantly in the economic-financial terms of banking operations with the social aspect included more as a matter of compromise than from conviction.

On the other hand, the majority of the countries involved created national development councils and formulated long- and medium-range plans, carrying out their formulations in order to get the CIAP's approval. Later on they gave up trying to effect changes in the financial, monetary, and tax structures, so that from 1970 on the alliance practically ceased to exist.

The contrast between the Marshall Plan and the Alliance for Progress deserves an objective evaluation. The former consisted of aid in the physical rebuilding and moral stimulation of countries which were coming out of a war and were badly off. It was an eminently healing plan. The alliance was characterized by its preventative nature in seeking to help countries that, undamaged by war, ran—and still run—the risk of serious disturbances as destructive as war. In the former case it was a question of trying at least to recover and perhaps even surpass a lost level of well-being, while in the latter situation it was an attempt to approach as much as possible a level never before attained.

Notwithstanding that the alliance has left a positive balance of experiences in all the formerly participant countries with regard to doctrine and practice in planning matters, its unsatisfactory results showed that the social and political sciences have a role to play as important as that of economics, if not more so. It showed too that, besides the assistance and guidance of an ensemble of scientific techniques, it is necessary to be able to count on the support of a strong, well-informed public opinion and on statesmen who have integrated goals and are trained in planning, promotional and executive-management operational practices.

The torch of the alliance was picked up by the United Nations with the Vancouver Conference on Human Settlements (May-June 1976)), called right after the Stockholm Conference on the Human Environment (1972), under the aegis of its global development program (PNVD). The year 1976 also saw the creation of the United Nations Foundation for Human Settlements and Habitat, with headquarters in Nairobi (Kenya), which acts on the request of any of the member nations including all the South American nations that are also OAS members.

An exhaustive evaluation of the reasons why the Alliance for Progress functioned without the efficiency it was supposed to have had when it was created can prove very useful for the future. There is nothing more logical and just than to require efforts from the assisted party in proportion to aid received. But it is evident that the conditions imposed did not manage to create a stimulus for the seemingly beneficiary countries. Why this happened must be investigated before considering that the operational idea has irrevocably failed. Whatever name be given to it, the positive, future development of the South American peoples requires that an alliance be renewed. Such an alliance can further a united and reciprocal progress since appropriate sites, physical works, and promotional operations have already been located by means of regional and district planning that has emphasized the structuring of national urban systems. Not only will it be possible to settle the cities and countryside evenly by such planning, but the increasing communities and families as well as each individual of South America will have the opportunity to move into worthy human habitats, living together in a social environment of Augustinian peace in order.

The Present Situation and a Look at the Future

During the last four decades in South America, many broad peripheral belts of urban settlement have grown up, sometimes as inorganic suburbs resulting from the nonurbanistic orientations of the real estate market, sometimes from lack of governmental policy and vision. Rarely, however, have planned cities been established de novo. Of these few the most notable are Brasilia, Ciudad Guyana, and Nueva Federación. Nueva Federación in Argentina is the result of international cooperation in which two cities, the remains of which now are beneath the waters of the Salto Grande Dam, were relocated to become one. An Uruguayan-Argentine committee supervised the carefully planned urban replacement to include virtually all of the dwellings, schools, and public buildings of the former two cities. With work begun in 1976 now well underway, as part of a vast regional plan intended to influence the area around the Salto Grande Hydroelectric Complex on the Uruguay River, Nueva Federación itself is expected to reach a demodynamic level of 30,000. Some few new cities that more or less generally followed precepts of urban planning but were primarily the outgrowths of great mining and new industrial establishments are Chimbote in Peru, El Teniente in Chile, Caleta Olivia in Argentina and Itaipú in Brazil. But these cannot be considered as thoroughly planned new cities.

In the field of urban renewal most important large cities and many medium-sized and small Latin American cities have now formulated and put into force urbanistic schemes to regulate physical development. Building codes and plans for housing were coordinated and eventually integrated with consistent urban-renewal projects that became parts of urban master plans. São Paulo and Caracas have combined important remodeling works with the construction of housing precincts in the core of the city. In Buenos Aires urban renewal is also interrelated with motorways. Elevated avenues around the city *centro* form an inner ring from which various radial motorways reach another ring where the eight main national highways converge, after passing through populated, surrounding urban areas of Greater Buenos Aires.

Greater Buenos Aires, with ten million people in twenty-two municipal areas, including the three million of the federal capital, is an unusually complicated case among the major Latin American population centers. The physical development of this conglomeration has been governed by the urban planning code since 1977 in the federal capital and the land-use law since 1978 in the remaining, more peripheral municipalities. At the moment a coordinating mechanism for the twenty-two master plans is lacking in the federal and provincial governments. Nevertheless, the president's planning secretariat is preparing legislation to accomplish this purpose, without any coordination in time and space, with responsibility for urban planning remaining within each municipality.

São Paolo and its suburbs today constitute another great center of population growth like that of greater Buenos Aires. Already surpassing Buenos Aires in size and in its complexity of urban problems, São Paolo is developing with extensions de novo such as Campinhas and in large urban remodelings outside of the congested city proper. Rio de Janeiro and Lima are other such areas of population growth at the level of São Paolo and Buenos Aires. The problems of how to confront the development of the great metropolises are being studied in Buenos Aires, Lima, and São Paolo among others, without as yet their posing an adequate functional solution for the necessary political and administrative restructuring of their respective countries.

With specialists in regional and sectorial planning coming, in the 1970s, from the various national development councils, each country set forth its national development system of territories divided into regions and subregions to help identify areas of urban and rural planning or zones and poles of economic development. Some countries juxtaposed the views of socio-urbanist and financial-economic planners. In Venezuela, for instance, the national planning office (ODEPLAN) created eleven regions in 1967 that were reorganized by its national development council in 1971 into five.

In 1968 Brazil was divided into several micro regions upon statistical bases with the expectation of later identifying urban and rural areas in these and with a view toward a later political administrative reorganization. The Bahia-Recife region of Brazil, for example, long in decline economically as well as in terms of planning, is now the responsibility of the Sueprintendency for Development of the Northeast. The creation of thirteen regions in 1976 in Peru led to the beginning of a pilot experiment for rural development in 1977 in the jungle, where the Inca-Hispanic tradition of the indigenous communities remains vital. In this area the pre-Hispanic Inca institution of "minka," the tradition of self-supporting cooperation between these communities, is latent. The Venezuela-Guyana Corporation operates in the area of the new Ciudad Guyana in El Tablazo and in the Tuy Medio Valley. The Cauca Valley Corporation in Colombia has in progress a five-year plan (1977-1982) for the urban development of Buenaventura, a port city through which fifty-five percent of the goods of the country pass. Thus, there has been considerable progress in recent years.

The starting point for surveying South America's future settlement and agro-urban development is in the present state of affairs; and that can be summarized as follows:

1) There is quantitatively considerable demographic growth in the majority of countries (excepting Uruguay, Argentina, and the Guyanas). A doubling of population every twenty-five years, projected from the annual rhythm maintained over the last twenty years must be anticipated with a geographical distribution inclined to urbanism, and a generally excessive metropolism.
2) Economic growth, while providing a large amount of food and clothing requirements, fails to meet the requirements of housing and the infrastructure of urban and regional public services necessary for growing neighborhoods.
3) There is sufficient territorial capacity, suitable climate, and available natural resources for housing and all its complementary building for at least four times the current population (with optimum habitability, nutrition, and clothing, considering only the potential productivity of soil and subsoil developed by contemporary mining and agricultural techniques and omitting the potential productivity of the Atlantic and Pacific oceans).
4) A high degree of sociocultural homogeneity (linguistic, traditional, historical, urbanistic, and architectural) with varied folkloric, racial, topographical, and geoeconomic shades underlies the realm of ideas and popular sentiment. This commonality is more favorable to Pan-American complementing and integration than to nationalist separatism, despite some distracting points of slight friction at international boundaries.
5) Significant deficiencies and lacunae exist in the area of education which combine against the provision of an adequate education and mental-spiritual development for the average citizen, as well as against his training to participate cooperatively in the development of his city, region, and country.
6) A growing popular consciousness of urban and regional planning supports the numerous, diverse governmental initiatives toward a methodical organization of civil and technical processes of development for cities, regions, and territories. But there has been little decision-making and continuity of operational responses on the part of municipal, provincial, or national authorities.
7) A univocal municipal, European, colonial tradition, stifled within political and administrative structures unequal to the times, persists in the centralized control of remote metropolitan areas, even in countries having a federal make-up.

This synthesized panorama of the present South American situation, insofar as it directly pertains to the development of the cities (with the majority of the population) and the countryside (with increasingly fewer inhabitants) describes the basis upon which each country and its urban and regional authorities must forcefully and imaginatively frame programs to regulate and promote urban, territorial, and regional development. In order to achieve such programs it is necessary for countries to agree to undertake simultaneously and sustainedly a South American operation that progressively structures urban systems—that is to say, consistent constellations of metropolises' lesser cities, towns, and villages—to receive demodynamic increases within countries and internationally and to favor the best of societal living in the strong urban and rural neighborhoods. The essence of the movement of public opinion and governmental action lies in the Brazilian-inspired Pan-American operation and in the urban-systems-for-Latin-America operation of the Argentine, with its historical reminiscences of Bolivar's proposed association of states.

With human intelligence and industriousness, South America's future can, by the beginning of the twenty-first century, be a magnificent reality of beautiful, efficient cities set in vast rural landscapes, alternating with broad vistas of intentionally protected virgin nature. These will serve as excellent habitats for twice the current population, while leaving a margin of habitability that duplicates that doubling. One of the probable consequences to anticipate may be a stabilization in the rate of demographic increase that will render the demand for more housing and services less urgent by the year 2000.

It is late in this century for us to start carrying out such a program. Now for the first time in the history of mankind, as Toynbee observed a few years ago, it is possible to adequately satisfy worldwide demands for housing, food, and clothing. This can be achieved by modifying the distribution of capital that is used today for the destruction of man and nature, directing it into national budgets for urban, territorial, and regional developments, toward tangible economic and financial goals.

Complicated and inconsistent financial, tax, and investment arrangements in the last forty years have produced the conflicting urban and rural panoramas that currently prevail in the cities and countrysides of South America. If this continues, with only a few worthwhile urban and regional developmental initiatives that some South American countries and municipalities have rarely put into effect, the panorama of the first years of the twenty-first century—in less than twenty years—will be dramatically negative. All the prospects formulated will vary only in their assumptions as to what the millions of badly lodged, fed, and clothed men, women, and children wandering along streets and roads will do, while other, apparently more fortunate, millions live in fear in the cities and the countryside.

The decision whether to let oneself be and let events pass or to take the reins of a great policy of urban and regional development firmly in hand, depends on the degree of social responsibility assumed by the present generation of statesmen and technicians, and their ability to serve as positive examples for the already blossoming generation that will succeed them.

Sociocultural publications and public education, especially education for development, play the main roles in this vast operation, enabling the majority of the little more than 200 million South Americans to become aware of the tasks to be carried out in each country in the immediate decades to come. There can be a surplus of resources as urban and rural communities, social promotional groups, governing personnel, and labor forces become organized. The planning and programming of physical and economic development are the inseparable, irreplaceable tools that our society has at its disposal. The political and administrative structures must be receptive to them. With an adequate education toward development, the governors and the governed alike will be able to utilize to the fullest the planning and working ability of socially responsible technicians and scientists, who will be able to integrate efforts in time and space within each city, territory, and region in the southern subcontinent of the Americas.

Bibliography

Journal of the American Planning Society, Series no. 1 (1967) to no. 52 (1979). All issues published between 1967-1979 are useful for planning information.

Araujo Gomes, Francelino de and Araujo Calvacanti. *Operacao Municipio*. Rio de Janeiro: Instituto Internacional de Ciencias Administrativas. Secao Brasileira, 1955.

Latin America (ILPES document CPRD B/22). 79-8-1850.

International Union of Local Authorities. *Urbanization in developing countries* (Report of Symposium at Noordwijk, Netherlands, 1967). The Hague: IVLA, 1968.

United Nations Social Affairs Committee. *Urbanization Problems in Latin America* (Report of Symposium at Santiago de Chile). U.N.O.—S.A.C., 1959.

Urban Reform and Development in Latin America, Regional and Urban Implementation. Cambridge, Mass.: Harvard University Press, 1964.

PART II

NATIONAL DEVELOPMENTS

7

ARGENTINA

ELIZABETH D. HARRIS

The history of Argentina's modern architecture unfolds through a series of iconoclasts who initiated technological innovations and explored the plastic potential of new materials. Among her most prominent architects, Amancio Williams, Horacio Baliero, Raphael Iglesia, Clorindo Testa, and Justo Solsona have refused to follow established modes of architectural design. Others, while deriving their ideals from European precedents, sought to solve problems reflecting Argentina's particular needs. Often they formed working associations such as the Austral Group, Grupo Urbis, and the important architectural firm of Manteola, Petechersky, Sanchez-Gomez, Solsona and Viñoly, which served as the vanguard for major developments from Functionalism to Brutalism to Post-Modern endeavors, interpreting modern forms subjectively.

Argentina's colonial history helps to explain the emergence of an iconoclastic approach in her architecture. In the sixteenth century the Spanish colonized Argentina, intermarrying with her native Indians to produce eventually the gaucho, a hardy cowboy who rode the pampas, Argentina's vast northern grasslands. Buenos Aires, however, often considered the Paris of South America, saw influxes of English, French, Italian, and Spanish immigrants. From these came reflections of northern European traditions which set Argentina apart from its predominantly Spanish and Portuguese neighbors. Independent in spirit, the gauchos reigned over their territory, resisting control by the European-dominated government of Buenos Aires, until they gained political power during the nineteenth century. Thereafter, Argentina's personality blended European sophistication with the ruggedness of her roaming cowboys. Though the political fusion was complete by the mid-nineteenth century, the cultural life, including architectural design, continued to be controlled by European sources. Throughout the century, government mandates dictated an architectural development closely following French Beaux-Arts designs.

Since the turn of the century, when the first private school of architecture was established, architectural design in Argentina has enjoyed relative independence from governmental control. Second Empire eclectism gave way to Art Nouveau once architects were free to pursue their own interests. In 1929, soon after these changes had taken hold in Argentina, Le Corbusier visited the country and urged architects to put into practice rational European formulae for architectural conceptions, to discard unnecessary ornament in favor of structural purity and to make use of reinforced concrete. Argentina could not easily provide the steel and other materials needed for such a revolution in construction. Nevertheless, architects built expensive adaptations of Europe's International Style, often influenced by Gaudí's emotional Art Nouveau and Erich Mendelsohn's Expressionism. Investigation into the sculptural qualities of modern materials was begun; but without ready access to new materials, architectural development was stifled and new building frequently lacked originality.

Many young architects, unable to secure architectural degrees in South America, had gone to Paris to obtain formal training, often studying directly with Le Corbusier. Though he visited Latin America only twice before 1947, Le Corbusier was most influential. In 1929 he had lectured in Argentina and also in Brazil and Uruguay. In 1936 he returned to work with Brazilian architects in planning the Ministry of

Education and Health building in Rio de Janeiro.[1] The Brazilian ministry structure (now known as the Ministry of Education and Culture [MEC]) gave three-dimensional immediacy to Le Corbusier's ideas, which slowly became influential in Latin America, mostly through his former students. Indeed, the Brazilian Ministry of Education and Health building initiated a truly modern approach to building design throughout South America by incorporating Le Corbusier's five points: *pilotis*, strip windows, free plan, free facade, and roof garden. In addition, *brise-soleil* were attached to the sun-drenched north side of the ministry building, shading the interior from direct sunlight while allowing fresh air to enter. These were the constructive elements of the sixteen-story building in Rio and, furthermore, demonstrated principles that could be manipulated and applied at other projects according to specific requirements of site and cost. Le Corbusier's innovation lay in his explicit structural vocabulary and his simple, efficient use of new materials, such as reinforced concrete that diminished the number of load-bearing columns and cut the size of the walls to provide support-free interiors. Such tenets established the foundations of modern architecture in Argentina, foundations which lent themselves to interpretation by independent architects who defined form and structure in unique and personal ways.

Le Corbusier also designed Dr. Currutchet's residence in La Plata [1949-1954], with the esteemed Argentine architect Amancio Williams supervising construction. Again, the five points with exterior *brise-soleil* were incorporated into the design but in a plan on a diagonal axis adapted to a restricted urban site. The somewhat mannered house exemplified the transition from smooth to rough concrete popularized in Le Corbusier's Brutalist phase, which served as a point of departure for many Argentine architects.

Amancio Williams and the Austral Group were the first to implement Le Corbusier's theories themselves, and thus it is with them in the 1940s that the actual story of modern architecture in Argentina may be said to have begun. Williams, the most independent member of his generation, admitted no alliances with organized groups and his architecture, not surprisingly, exhibits a rugged individualism. He studied engineering at the Federal University of Buenos Aires until 1941 when the first official school of architecture opened. When offered a professorship at the university, Williams refused, not wanting to be restricted by the government's reluctance to sanction unusual ideas in architectural design. In his career he adhered to particular principles: "Work in total freedom in space, liberally maintaining three dimensions; look to technology for your true expression; work for a feeling of unity; work for a synthesis; work for the feeling of that which is permanent."[2]

A technical innovator, two of his most imaginative designs appear to have been inspired by bridge construction. For his brother's summer home (fig. 7.1)

7.1 Amancio Williams, architect. Roberto Williams Summer House. Mar del Plata, 1945. (Photograph: Courtesy of Grete Stern)

built in 1945 south of Buenos Aires at the beach resort of Mar del Plata, he mounted an oblong box on a bridgelike curved slab of reinforced concrete which not only carried the weight of the entire house but also raised the living area to allow picturesque views from strip windows along the length and width of the house. Williams's plastic application of modern structural materials, which effectively adapted technology to nature, has rarely been surpassed. A visionary plan of 1948 for a high-rise office building was also derived from bridge construction. With three, eight-story blocks suspended on cables from an overhead steel frame, the design would have been most spectacular had it been executed.

In 1939 the Austral Group brought together Antonio Bonet, Jorge Ferrari Hardoy, Juan Kurchan, Alberto Le Pera, Helario Zalba, and others in the first of many architectural associations in Argentina. The group became interested in the publication *Tecné* and ultimately published in it, diffusing their philosophy throughout Latin America. All were admirers or former students of Le Corbusier, but they objected to the then current application of his principles in Argentina. Their 1939 manifesto "Will and Action" was published in the magazine *Nuestra Arquitectura*, criticizing the philosophy of Functional orthodoxy for misunderstanding Le Corbusier's "machine-for-living" concept and for excluding the human element in architectural design. "By misunderstanding the *machine à habiter* and by consciously ignoring individual psychology, Functional architecture with all its aesthetic prejudices and infantile intransigencies, has arrived at intellectual and inhuman solutions."[3] Indeed, Le Corbusier never meant to have his machine-for-living interpreted as a mechanical formula repetitiously applied to any location, though unfortunately this happened when his principles were not completely understood. In their manifesto they also called for a nationalistic architecture which would consider the needs and industrial limitations of Argentina in preference to a thoughtless application of the most recent stylistic innovations from Europe.

The Austral Group stimulated the implementation of Le Corbusier's theories rather than his style. Applying Corbusian principles locally involved conscious consideration of available materials and resources, integrating this knowledge into design conceptions. Therefore, the group's architectural pursuits remained structurally simple and easy to build, based on Le Corbusier's Functional theories, but stressing a regionalism that considered Argentina's social, economic, and cultural necessities unencumbered by stylistic doctrines. In particular the architecture of Antonio Bonet and Jorge Ferrari Hardoy exemplified their fresh approach to Le Corbusier's theories.

Antonio Bonet, a Spanish-born architect and spokesman for the Austral Group, had worked with Le Corbusier on several projects while participating in the design for the Spanish Pavilion at the 1937 International Exhibition in Paris before moving to Argentina in 1939. His development for Punta Ballena, Uruguay, a resort frequented by Argentines, contained ideas evident later in designs by the Austral Group.[4] Two of the buildings from Punta Ballena integrated man with nature by using the machine as a mediator: the Berlingieri House [1946] and the nearby restaurant-hotel La Solana del Mar [1947]. Continuity between structure and landscape together with a use of natural materials defined Bonet's particular approach. Both irregular sites near the beach utilized local stone called *lagarena*, reinforced concrete accented with different colors, and touches of wood. An L-shaped space, roofed with shallow barrel vaults, extends laterally from a hillside to form the body of the house, its volumes connected by terraces and covered walkways that face the beach. Plastic in feeling, the house projects a clean and direct use of form and structure. The long, low restaurant and hotel, one-story of glass and brick, duplicates the direct use of natural materials and integrates them into the seaside terrain.

Jorge Ferrari Hardoy teamed with another member of the Austral Group, Juan Kurchan, in the early 1940s to build an apartment building [1943] with a traditional Corbusian-type plan. A nine-story vertical apartment block on Virrey del Pino in Buenos Aires was raised on slender columns (*pilotis*) and faced with movable vertical louvres (*brisee-soleil*) on each story above the ground floor. An asymmetrical frontal facade resulted from recessing two-fifths of the enclosed building, providing the volumes framed by simple structural elements that extended from the facade. Two large trees grow out of the space thus formed, ironically contrasting nature with the mechanical geometry of architecture and echoing Le Corbusier. Planned for middle-income families in 1943, this experimental urbanization project served as a model for others which soon followed.

The Austral Group's activity as a unified entity continued through the forties, but thereafter the original members drifted apart, some to form new groups while others pursued their careers individually. All of these architects remained innovators in Argentina well into the 1960s.

Politically, the decade of the forties was tumultuous, though it brought promise of change with stability in the rise to power of Juan Domingo Peron. Ambitious architects supported Peron's governmental reforms, but they were quickly disappointed when Peron failed to carry out his cultural platform and continued to encourage anachronistic revivals of colonial architecture and folkloric traditions in art. His government stimulated a revivalist period which mixed modern construction methods with stuccoed facades reminiscent of Spanish colonial architecture. Many of the architects who helped elect Peron for his social reforms did not accept the antiquated styles he sponsored. Polemics often stopped government projects under construction, but most architects continued to pursue Modernism in their designs. Finally, after World War II, several young talented Argentine architects, for instance Horacio Caminos and Eduardo Catalano, left the country because of the restraints of the Peron regime.

The growth and experimentation of the forties blossomed in the early fifties with an influx of modern equipment which radically changed construction methods. The utilization of new building-systems reduced costs and made greater standardization of production possible. This surge to modernize initiated essential changes, enabling modern materials and methods to be utilized more frequently. At the same time, Argentines shifted more toward nature, using local materials as Frank Lloyd Wright or Alvar Aalto preferred; and they stressed engineering, following Pier Luigi Nervi's ideas or the pristine Formalism of Marcel Breuer and Mies van der Rohe. In 1951 eagerness for further knowledge of new techniques inspired the architecture department at the Federal University to invite to Buenos Aires distinguished lecturers such as the Italian architect Bruno Zevi. His lectures not only increased architects' and students' awareness of the then-current work of European and American architects, but also pointed to the importance of interior construction and divisions of space. Furthermore, Zevi emphasized the growing interest in architecture as an urban tool as well as the importance of a thoughtful approach to each specific project.

From 1950 on, three different tendencies emerged in Argentina. First was the logical extension of the principles of the Austral Group into Formalism which reflected Mies van der Rohe's influence rather than Le Corbusier's. Second, architectural production became characterized in large part by a rich use of materials which retained an unfinished quality. This second path, often referred to as Brutalism and derived in part from Le Corbusier's experimentation with *béton brut* (rough concrete), was employed by a number of architects including Horacio Baliero and the Grupo Harpa. Third, the attraction to the rich stock of local materials led to a return to nature and thereupon to a striking out against Rationalism. The anti-rationalists reflected Frank Lloyd Wright's discipline combined with the spirit of colonialism. These three major trends dominated Argentine architecture from 1950 through the 1960s.

When the Austral Group disbanded, Argentine architects of a younger generation were establishing their reputations by concentrating on simplification of structure, reflecting Mies van der Rohe's Formalism, as defined in the first trend described above. The Haras Black Beauty Farm [1954] and the San Fernando Housing Project [1954], both in the province of Buenos Aires, condense architectural motifs into great forms of broad, smooth concrete by which the intense sunlight of two treeless locations was controlled directly and economically.

José Rey Pastor, E. Aubone, and Leonardo Aizemberg exhibit an abstract geometric vocabulary at the Haras Black Beauty Farm in Ituzaingo, with a residence and stable for race horses. Almost cubistic in composition, its U-shaped arrangement rises on one side with superimposed, interpenetrating layers that jut out beyond a base structure and are supported by large, round columns. Cubes of space seem to grow from the interior to an exterior articulated in brick outlined with concrete. Forms and materials are subordinated, however, to a sense of structure that gives an overall unity to the program.

A group of government architects, evidently aware of the Haras Black Beauty Farm, is responsible for a similar design for the San Fernando housing project. Though relying on the abstract motifs of Mies van der Rohe, concrete was used instead of glass because of the long hours of bright sunlight. Neither the intent nor the effect of the complex is sacrificed thereby, and both are perhaps enhanced by this substitution of materials. Apartment blocks are raised on *pilotis* with cantilevered balustrades irregularly connected on two levels which act as *brise-soleil.* High canopy platforms partially shade the flat roof intensifying the play of light and shade of recessed and extended forms in an economical use of modern materials that proved to be a workable solution for low-cost housing. This development may be seen as the beginning of a transition from formalist to brutalist ideas, since the concrete is still smooth here and does not yet display the coarser textures of brutalist surfaces.

Formalism also emerged in the rhetoric of Antonio Bonet's work, such as the Casa Oks of 1958 in Buenos Aires where a Miesian sense of geometry pervades the L-shaped two-story plan. The house starts with a rectangle, repetitiously used to encompass space. On the interior and exterior, I-beam skeletal construction outlines the modular rectangles as movable partitions subdivide the lower level's space and the upper story's bedrooms are separated into equal dimensions. Exposed I-beams and finely finished materials further reveal Mies's influence. Finally, colored tiles of yellow, red, and brown on the exterior animate the planar surfaces of this simple, clean, yet subjectively designed, steel frame house.

Mies van der Rohe's Crown Hall at Chicago's Illinois Institute of Technology is basic to the less dramatic 1960 Pavilion of Fine Arts in Buenos Aires by Ruben Frail, Jorge Gomez, Alais and Cesar Jannelo. A raised glass box, suspended from steel stanchions with the external steel frame fully visible, provides a free-flowing interior exhibition space framed characteristically by clear glass walls. The strong sunlight creates a problem which can only be remedied by the use of venetian blinds which mar this otherwise fine and pure design.

Another architect who initiated his career with interpretations of Mies van der Rohe's vocabulary and then quickly proceeded beyond this is Horacio Baliero. For a house at San Isidro [1961] on a site which overlooks the Rio de la Plata River near Buenos Aires, Baliero collaborated with Eugenio Muarate. The L-shaped plan of interconnecting planes of textured concrete rises two stories with ribbon windows outlined by dark mullions. Cantilevered projections complement the fluid horizontality and recall Frank Lloyd Wright as they reach out into space from a central core similar to the Robie House. Here, Baliero's Formalism moves from the geometric unity of machine-finished materials to a new concern for textures which define separate volumes of space. Various European and American stylistic influences coalesce here to inform Baliero's fine feeling for tectonic construction and manipulation of materials.

From Formalism this first phase of post-1950 Argentine architecture moved toward Brutalism because of a growing interest in the varied uses of reinforced concrete. Grupo Harpa, formed under the direction of former Austral Group member Jorge Ferrari Hardoy, explored the plastic potential of unfinished concrete, brick, and other natural materials in some innovatively engineered buildings during the 1960s.

In 1962 Grupo Harpa designed a primary school in Alcindar, providing separate classrooms and modern educational facilities for a rural area of Argentina. Covered walks link three diagonal rows of cubical sheds, and each cube forms an individual classroom topped by a truncated, star-shaped dome with a central skylight. Recessed glass facades permit even more light, controlled by extended frames that delineate each window and door, functioning like immovable *brise-soleil*. The domes facilitate the covering of a large area free of supports through the sculptural manipulation of reinforced concrete. Local brick and partially finished concrete complement the rough, natural rather than mechanical sense of organization of these thoughtfully designed well-lit and spacious classrooms.

In the 1950s Le Corbusier, by shaping brick and rough concrete into barrel vaults [the Jaoul Houses, Neuilly, 1954-1956], helped create a new structural language that metamorphosed his machine-for-living into a more organic entity. Bruno Zevi's lectures at the Federal University in Buenos Aires (1951) had inspired adaptations of Wright's implementation of natural materials, and Bonet's naturalism in Uruguay had incorporated vaults and local stone. Thus, the bases for architectural styles that echoed a more Organic approach were in place during the fifties.

Those who followed the third architectural trend in Argentina in the 1950s, wanted to express nationalism by a return to natural stone and simpler forms of construction. Initiated during Peron's push for a neo-Colonial revival, anti-Rationalism was at first only associated with the aristocracy. In the late 1950s many progressive architects were attracted not by neo-Colonial styles as much as by a vague longing for reestablishing the aesthetics of the past. The cold rationalism of functionalist architecture lacked some of the intensely human quality experienced in earlier buildings. In a reaction against the persistence of Rationalism, several architects including Claudio Caveri, Eduardo Ellis, and Raphael Iglesia reinstated the human touch and added a regional flavor to the severe geometric purity of Rationalism. Generally, the anti-Rationalists aligned themselves philosophically with neo-Colonialism but not technically. They employed rough concrete or textural stucco, leaving these raw materials natural or painted white. Domes, vaults, arches, and pitched roofs emphasized the human qualities of the early pioneers of Argentina through an unfinished roughness rather than through machinelike precision.

Anti-Rationalist architecture sometimes adopted antiquated techniques as a practical and economic means of modern production for the less industrialized areas of Argentina. In 1958 Claudio Caveri carried to its limits this pragmatic response to need by building a communally oriented village for four families in San Miguel, 150 kilometers from Buenos Aires. Simple homes of brick, covered with white stucco, were built in a cooperative effort by the families themselves. Though somewhat reminiscent of Spanish colonial architecture, their homes incorporated the sophisticated mathematical formula of the hyperbolic parabola. In general there were few colonial sources for such modern adaptations in Argentina and the designs resemble "Spanish Mediterranean," or, more closely, Le Corbusier's brutalist forms, rather than any national heritage. Thus, they cannot be seen as revivalist, but instead as an architectural reevaluation in order to create a new vocabulary oriented idiosyncratically toward humanistic viewpoints.

Claudio Caveri pursued his organic approach to architecture and attained a new unity in the anti-Rationalist Church of Our Lady of Fatima in Martinez in the province of Buenos Aires [1957]. Eduardo Ellis joined Caveri on this project where a simple cruciform plan evolved from elegantly combined local materials delineated by sharp geometric angles. Yet, the red tiled roof and white stucco surfaces of the church lent it a colonial flavor. Other works by architects influenced by anti-Rationalist ideas are nonobjective in presentation, yet spontaneous and direct (as, for example, Caveri's own house at San Miguel and Casa Fernandes, also in the province of Buenos Aires and built by Miguel Ascencio, Carlos

Fracchia, Jorge Garat, Lorenzo Gigli, and Raphael Iglesia [1965]), faced in stucco or rough concrete, with juxtaposing round and angular edges. These homes expressed the thinking of a new generation of architects in Argentina that consciously evolved modern yet nationalistically sensitive forms.

Rather than concerning himself with neo-Colonial aspects of style, Ruben O. Pesci used an anti-Rationalist repertoire of motifs to reinterpret Frank Lloyd Wright. White stucco serves to latinize Wrightian homes that focus on a space which surrounds a centralized hearth, include built-in furniture, and whose entrances are hidden from the street. Horizontal planes reach from the interior to the exterior moving out like extensions of the vast pampas. The most inventive adaptation of a Wrightian motif is the architect's own home at La Plata [1968], where he squared off Wright's dendriform columns, which widen at the top to support a patio roof above. Other Pesci homes of the sixties in this vernacular are the Casa Cottier at Magdalena in Buenos Aires, Casa Holzer, and Casa Ferrari in La Plata.

A generation exposed to instruction in diverse international architectural ideas and philosophies in the 1950s became influential by the late 1960s. With Functionalism rejected here and abroad and Brutalism being preferred, a new heroic monumentalism arose that was emotionally expressive but also determinist. Since form no longer needed to follow function, the exterior no longer ordered the interior; lack of ornamentation became itself a substitute for ornamentation; and the flexibility of new materials brought artistry back into architecture. Though architecture inherently performs a function, modern technology allowed the architect freedom in which to solve programmatic and structural problems. With a new, free spirit in architectural design, Argentine architects reached for the sublime. Novel designs were created by Horacio Baliero, Clorindo Testa, Justo Solsona, and many others for a wide range of projects from mausoleums to bus stations.

In the 1960s concrete maintained its importance in Argentina, but architects moved away from its weighty textural effects toward plastic exploitation of its intrinsic sculptural qualities. Traditionally urban cemeteries in Argentina offered occasions for experimental designs by talented sculptors and architects, and we can see the beginning of a new movement in a small work by Horacio Baliero and C. C. de Baliero, the Israeli Pantheon at the cemetery in Mar del Plata [1965]. Similar to the Brazilian architect Oscar Niemeyer's style in Brasilia, Baliero swirled smooth reinforced concrete into the shape of a snail to produce a unified solemn composition appropriate for quiet prayer.

Clorindo Testa boldly established his prolific career with the Provincial Government House at Santa Rosa, La Pampa [1956-1963], a government commission built in collaboration with Francisco Rossi, Augusto Gaido, and Boris Dabinovic. Not confined by a city, the architect had the freedom in this rural area to create a truly monumental edifice. His building adds variety and depth to the brutalist language with a lively use of cutout concrete frames which encase glassed-in offices and open walkways. At the same Santa Rosa location, Testa worked from 1956 to 1961 with the same group of architects in building a bus terminal. To cover large areas economically he borrowed the reinforced concrete vault, predicated on the geometry of the hyperbolic parabola, from the esteemed Mexican architect-engineer Félix Candela. This engineering technique was of paramount importance for Testa's concrete umbrellas that shaded the terminal area of the bus station. Cantilevered, textural concrete enhanced the terminal structurally and served as a sun deflector in this warm and humid part of the country.

A difficult problem led to an unusual design by Clorindo Testa, in collaboration with Santiago Sanchez Elia, Ferico Peralto Ramos, and Alfredo Agostini (SEPRA) for the handsome Bank of London and South America, Harrod's Branch, begun in 1960 and finished in 1966 (fig. 7.2) in Buenos Aires. The problem of building a large structure facing a narrow, well-travelled street, crowded with pedestrians and overdecorated government offices remaining from Argentina's Beaux-Arts eclectic period, required careful consideration. A concrete box would have overwhelmed the tiny street, whereas a glass building would have contrasted too sharply with adjacent heavily stuccoed Beaux-Arts structures. The architects, cognizant of brutalist motifs, chose a monumental glass-skinned box superimposed with a perforated concrete frame. Acclaimed for its well-balanced unique design of sculptured concrete, the exterior appears closed yet not overpowering, with a variety of cutouts that give relief to the heavy concrete facade and lighten its frame. Highly sculptural in conception, the frame's concrete slabs form a pattern with vertical, oblong shapes of gigantic dimensions that have been cut out at rhythmical intervals. The interior (fig. 7.3) totally contradicts the exterior, since its space is open, with broad balconies supported by the concrete frame. The multiple levels are cantilevered or hung from the ceiling and interlocked by ramps, stairs, and elevators. Here the dichotomy between the spontaneous, mazelike space of the interior and the sculptural exterior offers daily an inspiring architectural experience for the bank's many patrons.

7.2. Clorindo Testa with Santiago Sanchez Elia, Ferico Peralto Ramos and Alfredo Agostini, architects. Head Office, Bank of London and South America, exterior. Buenos Aires, 1960-1966. (Photograph: Courtesy of the Bank of London and South America)

7.3. Clorindo Testa with Santiago Sanchez Elia, Ferico Peralto Ramos and Alfredo Agostini, architects. Head Office, Bank of London and South America, interior. Buenos Aires, 1960-1966. (Photograph: Courtesy of the Bank of London and South America)

During the 1960s the interplay between architecture and art culminated in the house-object of Jorge Romero Brest. As a critic and founder (1964) of the Center for the Visual Arts until the government closed it in 1969, Brest had been instrumental in fostering the arts in Argentina and appraising artists of new international trends. Jorge and his wife Marta asked the architect Edgardo Giminez to build them a house [1969] upon which the three worked together to produce a physical embodiment of Pop Art. The house, sometimes referred to as the "Blue Mosque" for its deep sky-blue color and rounded facade extensions, has been designed so that reflection and action form a fantasy world with mirrors and water, which also add to the ambiguity between interior and exterior spaces.

An architect who dramatically departed from European precedents during the 1960s to narrow the gap between architecture and sculpture is Justo J. Solsona. In a deeply personal approach to architecture, he formalized brutalist grammar into a "wrapped look," by arranging his materials to form redundant stylized overall patterns. In his Sierchuk House (fig. 7.4) in the province of Buenos Aires [1960], roof and facade alike are covered with traditional half-cylindrical, red roofing tiles. Dynamic interest is introduced when, because of an irregular placement of windows and doors, asymmetry

7.4. Justo J. Solsona, architect. Sierchuk Residence. Buenos Aires, 1960. (Photograph: Courtesy of the architect)

ironically dislodges unity. Again sculptural, Solsona's FATE building in Buenos Aires [1966] bundles an office building in concrete, enlivening the exterior with a superimposed raised grid and large geometric window boxes that project at intervals to add a staccatoed effect of vertical accents. Architecture here has become art in its exterior, while the interior environment is isolated from the outside world.

In 1967 Solsona joined forces with a dynamic group of young architects who built on his ideas, developing new ones for the 1970s. With Solsona content to remain in the background, Ignacio Petechersky, Flora Manteola, Javier Sanchez-Gomez, Justo Solsona, Josepha Santos, and Rafael Viñoly became the large cooperative, MGSSV, whose spontaneous and unique endeavors often exemplify architecture for architecture's sake, not in the frivolous sense of nineteenth-century art, but as a twentieth-century rejection of that historicism in architecture which insists upon architecture *qua* architecture rather than as art. They were characterized by an "openness to discussion, vitality, enthusiasm and faith in architecture that means faith in their own capacity to make good architecture."[5] Their ages ranged from twenty-seven to thirty-seven when they met as students and professors at the Federal University of Buenos Aires, where they remained until 1967. Then political opposition to their avant-garde ideas compelled them to leave.

With an intuitive freshness MGSSV continues to evaluate each project according to its specific needs and prefers to seek out challenging public competitions with thought-provoking problems. No one formula or style defines their undertakings, but a few themes tend to recur. A separation of interior from exterior, as in Testa's and Solsona's earlier works, comes into focus. Usually simplified, the exterior construction material is manipulated into abstract molded forms as an extension of interior space; yet it never controls the distribution of volumes on the interior. Often their spaces seem suddenly explosive, surprising and delighting with an imaginative use of volumes, color, and texture. Sometimes reminiscent of ships' interiors, stairs, fixtures, and pipes remain exposed, perhaps hung from chains and painted to highlight their intrinsic sculptural quality; rounded corners and doors reinforce a shiplike arrangement; and the great variety of materials throughout adds to the liveliness of their work.

Art and architecture work together in MGSSV's designs. Their interiors frequently refer to Op Art, with repetitive combinations of color and geometry, as in their first commission, the restructuring of the headquarters of Banco de la Ciudad [1968] in Buenos Aires. The interior had been decorated in a Beaux-Arts eclecticism which was stripped away and replaced by a multilayered work area. Burnt-orange glass tiles now line the walls and floors, while only a clear glass partition separates the banking area from the street. The remodeling of the Banco de la Ciudad, one of the oldest buildings in the city, set the pace for other commissions that followed in rapid succession. The directors of the bank were so pleased with the results that the group went on to remodel branch offices in colorful variations upon the original theme.

Other projects, such as the Condor Branch of Banco de la Ciudad, also in Buenos Aires, recall the sublime precision, angular simplicity, and unity of Minimal Art upon their exteriors, while contrasting with a maximum of design within. While MGSSV appears to have been inspired by European developments that culminated with Richard Rogers's and Renzo Piano's Pompidou Center in Paris [1977], the group's unique juxtapositions of form deny specific influences. The Headquarters Building of the Industrial Confederation of Argentina [1968-1976] harmoniously adapts to surrounding skyscrapers as a formalist glass box juxtaposed to a concrete box to form a 120-meter-high office tower. Though MGSSV suddenly lost one of its members, Ignacio Petechersky, in 1973, that year it produced two of its most original structures, the Condor Branch of Banco de la Ciudad at Buenos Aires and a house in La Lucila.

The Condor Branch of the Banco de la Ciudad de Buenos Aires displays a playful, entertaining approach, satisfying programmatic requirements with an imaginative use of structure and material long overdue in twentieth-century architecture. In a residential area void of tall high rises the group constructed a dramatically free-standing ten-story building that consists of two prismatic glass towers joined at an extended obtuse angle. Faced in dark-green glass bricks that shade the interior from intense sunlight, the exterior contrasts sharply with a surprisingly simplified high-tech interior animated in steel. Open spaces are subdivided into irregular yet efficient public and private banking areas that accord with specific office needs and are never boring, unlike the regular machinelike divisions of traditional office buildings.

Privacy seems paramount in the design of a "Roman" house for an engineer, his wife, and four children at La Lucila [1973] (fig. 7.5). The squared site is completely enclosed by a concrete wall, eight meters in height, niched on one side for entrance and exit. Sliced diagonally in half, the garden occupies one triangular division of the square plan, while the living quarters (fig. 7.6) occupy the other. The roof of the fortresslike residence slopes inward to meet the garden level and is itself surfaced with grass. Glassed-in boxes project from the sloping roof to light the interior of the house and provide exits into the garden. Architecture and nature literally blend together with spaces focused inwardly in this remarkably innovative, personalized home. The versatility of MGSSV is again demonstrated in the apartment project for employees of the Banco de la Ciudad. Working from detailed queries concerning the living requirements and financial capabilities of the prospective residents, MGSSV responded with five distinct types of living quarters unified in one apartment complex with shops, parking, and a kindergarten easily accessible to all. Unlike the often predictable designs for high rises abundant in the sixties, at this complex a sense of expressive variety prevails.

Post-Modern "isms" emerged with the onset of the seventies and brought reactions to the classicizing

7.5. Manteola, Sanchez Gomez, Santos, Solsona, and Viñoly, architects. Casa in La Lucila, view from garden. Buenos Aires, 1973. (Photograph: Courtesy of the architects)

7.6. Manteola, Sanchez Gomez, Santos, Solsona, and Viñoly, architects. Casa in La Lucila, interior. Buenos Aires, 1973. (Photograph: Courtesy of the architects)

of forms that had persisted even during Brutalism's ascendancy in Argentina. Robert Venturi's attacks on modern architecture during the 1960s made architects more aware of everyday environment, with its constant media blasts, rapid movements, extremes of diversity, and apparently inherent chaos. A variety of styles evolved, emphasizing art and individuality. Charles Jencks, among others, has proffered several new "isms" for these difficult-to-define styles, such as "ad hocism," "supereclecticism," and "traditionalesque." In Argentina MGSSV remains outstanding because of the group's ability to integrate a diversity of architectural directions and achieve sophisticated architectural products.

Though our discussion has been mostly of Buenos Aires as the center of architectural development, the second largest city of Argentina, Cordoba, has grown extensively since 1965. Here the work of Miguel Angel Roca provides us with good examples. In housing projects in and around Cordoba he concentrates on satisfying structural and human demands economically, by employing materials on the basis of their availability and adaptability in order to create distinguished designs, rich in texture and pure in geometry. For homes he prefers brick, while for office buildings, he chooses concrete and metal. For banks and other single-purpose structures he prefers monumental, heroic interpretations that seem to be derived from Testa's work.

Roca's most interesting housing project groups individual dwellings around communal service units in a community planned especially for university professors and built between 1973 and 1975. Two-story brick homes pose circular shafts against squared bases that are surmounted by triangular second-story elevations. The brick work molds these pieces, stressing their vertical or horizontal orientation. Warm, rich, natural materials, arranged in conjunction with a strict mathematical formula and set in forestlike surroundings, reiterate a theme taken up by young Colombian architects such as Fernando Martinez and Guillermo Avedaño in their recent designs for domiciles.

Just outside of Cordoba in the town of Rio Tercero, Roca's use of advanced engineering techniques in the branch office for the Cordoba bank recalls work being done in Buenos Aires. Based on the concept of A-frame construction, a glass-enclosed triangle is encased within an aluminum cage, which guards the interior from direct sunlight with immovable horizontal slats, not unlike the double shell of Testa's Bank of London and South America. The raking sides are supported by structural slabs that rise from the center to partition the space of the bank into two separate triangles and then rise above the building. Thus, in Rio Tercero, one again sees the inventiveness of Argentina's young architects.

Modern architecture in Argentina began with Le Corbusier's visit in 1929 and remained in the shadow of this European master through the 1940s, though the Austral Group had tried to turn Corbusier's theories toward an architecture of Argentina's national consciousness as early as 1939. During the ensuing decades Argentina's architects became increasingly aware of and worked actively with a variety of models in an ever more independent manner. Upon the revisionist soil of neo-Colonial styles, Le Corbusier's Functionalism, Mies van der Rohe's notions of purity, and Frank Lloyd Wright's Organic architecture, Argentines were led to learn and to innovate, though more the former than the latter, until the 1960s. A vigorous use of concrete, as introduced by Brutalism, seems to have sparked a freer, more original variety of solutions to architectural problems in Buenos Aires especially by the end of the 1960s. In the architecture of Clorindo Testa and his associates, Horacio Baliero, Justo Solsona, and the MGSSV cooperative, to cite a few, Argentina's maturity is assured. In its richness and originality of ideas it has begun to set precedents for other nations.

Notes

1. *See* chapter 12 Brazil.
2. Amancio Williams, "An Interview and a Speech," *Zodiac* 16 (1966): 36.
3. Francisco Bullrich, *New Directions in Latin American Architecture* (New York: George Braziller, 1969), p. 30.
4. According to Bullrich, architectural communication between Argentina and Uruguay has been constant during the twentieth century. Francisco Bullrich, *Arquitectura Argentina Contemporánea* (Buenos Aires: Ediciones Nueva Visión, 1963), p. 24.
5. "Buenos Aires," *Domus* 519 (February 1973): 14.

Bibliography

BOOKS

Bullrich, Francisco, *Arquitectura Argentina Contemporánea.* Buenos Aires: Ediciones Nueva Visión, 1963.

______. *Arquitectura Latinoamericana* 1930/70. Barcelona: Editorial Gustavo gili, s.a., 1970.

______. *New Directions in Latin American Architecture.* New York: George Braziller, 1969.

Hitchcock, Henry Russell. *Latin American Architecture Since 1945.* New York: Museum of Modern Art, 1955.

JOURNALS

Bottero, Maria. "Architects in Buenos Aires." *Domus* 487 (June 1970): 7-16.

"Cooperative Terra." *Progressive Architecture* 47 (May 1966): 182-83.

Gagniano, Eduardo. "Miguel Angel Roca, Architecte en Argentina." *L'Architecture d'Aujourd'hui* 183 (January 1976): 81-92.

Gimenez, E. "Une Mosque Pop." *Domus* 534 (May 1974): 42.

Iglesia, Rafael. "La Réaccion Antirracionalista en Argentina." *Zodiac* 14 (1965): 146-62.

Pesci, Rubin O. "Un Opera Inedita di Le Corbusier en Argentina." *L'Architettura* 16 (May 1970): 32-38.

Rossi, L. M. and Rossi, H. A. "Quattro Case di Ispira zione Wrightiana dell'Architetto Rubin O. Pesci." *L'Architettura* 14 (October 1968): 448-49.

Rubine, Luciano. "Banco di Londres e dell'America del Sud a Buenos Aires." *L'Architettura* 13 (October 1967): 378-86.

"Une Torre Argentina." *Domus* 572 (July 1977): 20-23.

"Viviendas Rioja Flats." *Domus* 535 (June 1974): 19-21.

Waisman, M. "Architecture in Argentina Today." *Domus* 525 (August 1973).

Williams, Amancio. "An Interview and a Speech." *Zodiac* 16 (1966): 36-74.

Williams, Amancio and de Williams, Delfinia G. "Residencia a Mar del Plata." *L'Architecture d'Aujourd'hui* (June 1948): 62.

OTHER USEFUL JOURNALS

Revista de Arquitectura, Technologia y Diseño, (Buenos Aires)

Nuestra Arquitectura (Buenos Aires)

SUMMA (Buenos Aires)

8

AUSTRALIA

JENNIFER TAYLOR

During the years since World War II Australian architecture, particularly that in the major cities, passed through a transformation unequalled in the relatively short history of about 200 years of European settlement.

Most evident are changes in the size and scale of the man-made environment, brought about by a combination of rapid population increase, investments of overseas funds, and the general financial prosperity of the 1950s and 1960s. Of greater significance for the future is a growing maturity of attitude towards the geographical and situational reality of the country as a unique place with particular problems and its own special quality.

The history of Australia, and therefore of its architecture, has been characterized by a dependency, first on England and in this century also on America. Federation in 1901 brought independence and World War I brought adulthood, but ingrained cultural attitudes are not easily changed. It was not until after World War II that Australia felt sufficiently mature and secure in her own abilities to stand back and appraise herself for what she was and to assess the results of past actions.

The Australian view has been a mixed one. As can be expected in a remote insular settlement, it was quite parochial and things foreign naturally were suspect. Yet at the same time this was contradicted by a reliance on overseas models and ideas. Australia is growing up and her architecture is becoming less dependent and increasingly relevant to local conditions.

Post-World War II architecture in this country falls into three distinct phases. First was the time of austerity when a shortage of materials and skilled labor was combined with a building demand, especially for houses. The new dwellings added to the vast spread of the suburbs which grew in response to the Australian dream of each man to his own house and land, regardless of how small or remote. This was a period of trying to cope with a taxing strain on the building industry. Architecture tended to step backwards rather than forwards as far as the average standard of building was concerned, although in isolated places there were portents of better things to come.

Progress and economic return were the key words of the building boom of the second phase, from the 1950s through the early 1970s. In 1957 the tallest building in Sydney was 170 feet high; in 1977 the tallest building stood at 800 feet. Large areas of old detached houses were replaced with blocks of three-story walk-up flats. The policy of "clear the old and develop the new" resulted in the demolition of many old buildings of character in the urban core, with the consequent destruction of the varied nature of the streetscape. Together with this, perhaps as a reaction, a romantic urge appeared on the part of several leading architects to seek an alternative architecture. These buildings rejected the display and high technology of the time and sought their identity in the local geography and traditional building practices. This was paralleled by a positive reassessment of the desirable qualities of the Australian landscape that, for the most part, previously had been rejected in favor of European garden styles and imported plants.

By the late 1960s a social and cultural consciousness also began to make itself felt. Public opinion rose against the prevalent destruction of workers' homes and historical structures. Buildings for education and cultural use received high priority in state and federal budgets, and the need for a closer study of the building requirements of the aboriginal was given long overdue recognition.

The ills of the cities were noted. Strategic plans with action priorities have been prepared for the central districts of the capital cities of the states over the last ten years. Decentralization became a popular cure for urban overload and much of the new architecture of Australia is to be found in areas well removed from the central cores. Within the cities the priority afforded the motor car was questioned and the pedestrian once again was given due consideration.

The third phase was that of the recession. By the time this struck in 1975 Australia was at least aware of, and had started to move towards, ways of overcoming the mediocrity of much that had preceded the war and the damage caused by the following "renewal" phase.

The recent architecture of Australia is sound, sometimes; but rarely inspiring. Overall the profession is best described as conscientious and competent. The standard of housing, hospitals, and educational facilities by world standards is high. There are no urban areas that could be regarded as slums, and environmentally the average Australian has little of which to complain. While Australia has yet to reach cultural maturity and to take its place with the leading architectural countries of the world, the particular circumstances of its unique physical context and the events of the last thirty years have given rise to developments of considerable significance within the country. Some of these hold promise as lasting contributions towards the improvement of living conditions generally.

Australia is primarily a middle-class society, which values above all the individual home. Given these circumstances it is not surprising that the house has received considerable attention from the architectural profession, and that many of the advances towards buildings in accord with living in this country have been developed first in domestic design. The problems of the immediate postwar period resulted in the construction of the most basic, acceptable houses. These had pitched, usually tiled roofs, brick or fibre asbestos sheeting as cladding, and were of minimal area, approximately 1,200 square feet. Stripped of the vernacular additions, such as verandas, these dwellings were most unsuitable for the climate. A handful of progressive architects were determined to overcome the limitations imposed by the standard house plan and the accepted image of "house."

The buildings of the International Style were slow to gain acceptance, in part due to conservative attitudes, but also because of some healthy questioning as to their suitability for Australian conditions. The first fully fledged International Style house was built at Turramurra, Sydney, 1949. Designed by Harry Seidler, a Viennese-born architect who had studied under Gropius at Harvard before coming to Australia, this house had a marked influence, particularly on the work in Melbourne. The pioneer houses that utilized the flat roof, open plan, surrounding patios, and covered verandas were those designed by Sir Roy Grounds and the architect-critic Robin Boyd, in Melbourne, and by Sydney Ancher in Sydney, at the end of the 1940s and early 1950s. These houses established a spatial organization suitable for the climate and way of life and in these respects remain as the prototypes of housing today.

Between 1953 and 1963 a romantic movement in house design emerged in Sydney—the so-called "Sydney School." These houses, primarily designed by architects for their own use, represented a conscious attempt to realize an Australian identity in domestic construction. Chiefly found on the bushland slopes of the north shore of the harbor, the buildings, usually of cheap clinker bricks and off-saw timbers, step down the inclines in multilevels. The fractured forms of the heavy, tiled roofs echo the slopes and admit high lighting. Where possible rooms open on to patios and verandas on the various levels. Usually the sites were left in the natural condition and the buildings were hidden among the trees and rocks. With the completion of the Ken Woolley house [1962] and the Peter Johnson house [1963] (fig. 8.1) the style reached its maturity.

At this time a major step was taken to improve the quality of dwellings being erected by housing developers. Collaboration between the leading architects and the developers occurred, giving rise to what is now known as "project" housing. With this relationship, architect-designed and modified houses became available to a wide range of prospective house purchasers who would normally have been unable to afford the services of an architect. This liaison made possible a most enviable quality of dwelling for the average Australian buyer. The Sydney School houses proved suitable for adoption to inexpensive solutions and have become part of a countrywide vernacular. Grouped private houses, with shared site amenities, such as open space, are gaining in favor. Winter Park, Doncaster, Victoria, by Graeme Gunn, shows a subtle integration of site planning, building form and texture, and planting.

8.1. Peter Johnson, architect. Peter Johnson House. Sydney, 1963. (Photograph: Courtesy of David Moore)

A consciousness of the past building tradition and an increasing awareness of the need to build sensibly for the climate has, in recent years, created a small revolution in domestic design. In Queensland the buildings by John Dalton exhibit a rational response, with the use of breezeways, vents, verandas, and elevated floors. Philip Cox of Sydney is providing harmonious buildings that are sensitively scaled and related to their use and setting. Lessons learned from unassuming local nineteenth century architecture are evident in his work. Outstanding examples of meticulously designed and crafted, yet simple and sensible, responses to domestic needs are found in the houses of Glenn Murcutt, also of Sydney. The importance of such buildings for the future of housing in this country cannot be overstressed.

But while the individual house is the aim of most Australian families, the need for denser development in the cities becomes increasingly evident. Inner-city low-income housing, constructed by the various state housing commissions, initially was provided in high slab towers. Apart from some fine examples of precast-concrete construction in Melbourne, they warrant little acclaim, since most often they proved to be socially disruptive and inadequate for community life. Lately the housing commissions have addressed themselves to the problem and pursued alternative solutions. In suburban locations the answer has been sought in medium-density, individual or cluster dwellings. The higher densities required for central urban areas have still to be adequately met. "City Edge," Melbourne, a private development by Daryl Jackson [1974-1975] is the first high-density, medium-rise, inner-city development to offer a viable alternative to the tower blocks. The Little Bay Scheme, Sydney, prepared for the New South Wales Housing Commission by the John Andrews Office, commenced construction during 1978. Despite a density of ninety persons per acre, the units are provided with related private open space and covered car parking. Each unit has its own front door on ground level. The low-rise solution augurs well for a rich and varied environment for the low-income aged, families, singles, and young couples it was designed to house.

For the more affluent, handsome and comfortable walk-up units and town houses are taking their place among the single family houses. This is most evident in Sydney where the problem is greatest, and sloping harborside sites offer compatible locations for such development. Quality of design and construction is high. Many of the finest examples have been designed in the offices of Ancher, Mortlock, Murray and Woolley, and of Allen, Jack and Cottier, with "The Penthouses," Sydney [1967], by the former firm being of particular note.

Church groups, with financial assistance from the federal government, assume a major responsibility for the housing of the aged. Some of the most pleasant residential areas of any kind in the country can be seen in intimate, domestic-scaled "village," that provide accommodations for those still able to cater for their own welfare, through to full hospitalization. Private and shared gardens and sporting facilities such as bowling greens are commonly available. The state housing commissions also cater for the needy aged. The Matavai and Turanga tower blocks in Sydney completed in 1978 are proving successful despite pessimistic predictions. Apart from shared community spaces, these blocks provide "floor" lounge areas outside the liftwells and manifest a strongly individual character on each level.

Student residences in this country have traditionally been conventional college buildings of an institutional nature. Costs of servicing, combined with student demands for more freedom, have resulted in independent mixed-sex, small group, cluster housing becoming more readily available. Innovative solutions can be seen in the student residences for Kelvin Grove College of Advanced Education, Brisbane, by John Dalton; Mitchell College of Advanced Education, Bathurst, by Edwards, Madigan, Torzillo and Briggs; and Australian Naitonal University and Canberra College of Advanced Education, both in Canberra, by John Andrews.

Public facilities such as schools and hospitals are almost exclusively designed by the State Department of Public Works. Australia has greatly extended her educational facilities in recent years with a variety of experimental methods of organization, as a rule based on overseas prototypes. Of interest is the use of concrete pneumoformed "Bini Shells," domes designed by Bini who came to Australia after developing them in Italy and elsewhere. The New South Wales Public Works Department has encouraged the investigation of their use for school buildings, and several examples for use as special facilities structures, such as libraries, have been constructed.

The largest project yet undertaken by any government agency in the country is the $166,000,000 (estimated completion cost), 925-bed, Westmead Hospital in the western suburbs of Sydney. For this building, the first stage of which was completed in 1978, the department employed the fast-track system of design and construction. In this the external elements of precast-concrete frame-construction on a double column grid are independent of the internal planning. Without delays caused by particular design decisions, the frame progressed well on schedule, with explicit solutions for the specific spaces being resolved as required.

Significant changes to the cities have resulted from the construction of high-rise structures and the appearance of major feeder roads and bypasses. The problems associated with the tall buldings have been primarily climatic, both from the point of view of the performance of the buildings and the microclimate generated in their near surrounds. Principal advances in building performance have arisen from efforts to prevent solar gain by applied sunshields, and by the use of structural frames which in themselves act as shading. With a highly advanced concrete industry, this material has played a major role both as structure and shield. The first modular curtainwall structures, the M.L.C. Buildings in Melbourne and North Sydney, completed in 1957 by Bates, Smart and McCutcheon, were closely followed by others. Apart from double-glazed, heat-resisting glass with adjustable venetian blinds between skins, such buildings showed little adaption for adjustment to heat, rapid fluctuations in temperature of as much as 25° Fahrenheit in a few hours, and the long sun hours of an Australian summer. Expansion caused structural problems and air-conditioning bills were exorbitant.

The history of the tall buildings in this country can almost be written in terms of how to keep the economy and prestige image of the glass wall, together with the views it affords, and yet defeat the sun. The projecting hoods on the IBM Building, Sydney [1964] by Stephenson and Turner, which gave the building a pagodalike appearance, constituted one of the earliest and most efficient solutions, while the Water Board Building, Sydney, [1965], by McConnel, Smith and Johnson, overcame the sun problem by the use of hung, precast-concrete sheathing panels that allowed adequate sheltered slits of views only on its north and south faces. This was a rational, successful solution. Similar precast elements have been employed as sun control screens by this firm in the Sydney University Law School and the Commonwealth State Law Courts, Sydney. They are now commonly found on work by others as well. The quality and precision of the exposed aggregate precast panels gives these structures an elegant yet solid appearance, in marked contrast to the lightweight curtain walls of the 1950s. The most recent innovative solution is to be seen in John Andrews's King George Tower in Sydney [1977]. The truncated triangular plan of this building with its peripheral service cores greatly reduced the exposed building surface. The total glass skin of the building is sheathed with an aluminum space-frame, supporting translucent polycarbonate panels angled in accord with the incidence of the sun's rays on the various faces of the building. While solar absorbent glass is commonly used, reflective glass has been rarely employed in this country. The first large structure to utilize reflective glass extensively as the building skin, the A.M.P. Tower, Brisbane, by Peddle, Thorp and Walker, was not completed until the end of 1977.

The destruction of the quality of the streetscape of the inner cities, first by the sidewalk-hugging office towers and later by the windswept "podium" buildings, was slow to be recognized. Australia Square and Tower, Sydney, by Harry Seidler and Associates [1967], was the first significant private development to make a responsible gesture to the city by providing on its site a mix of uses and a sheltered sunny public open space. The sophisticated structure of its circular concrete tower provided an important example of advanced engineering. But even greater lessons were to be learnt from the benefits gained from the amalgamation of the approximately eighty individual land titles purchased for this scheme. Though not large in size, Australia Square is a fine space that provided a clear demonstration of what could be done to enhance the urban setting.

Far more ambitious was the M.L.C. development (fig. 8.2) in central Sydney, 1978, also by Seidler. This scheme, which clearly shows the recent formalist phase of Seidler's work, is a multilevel radially organized orchestration of theaters, shops, restaurants, terraces, and plazas that cluster around the base of the sculptured form of the tower. Generous public open spaces here are remote from the street and generate their own mood. The M.L.C. Tower is of interest also as an example of the buildings with deeply recessed glass within projecting steel or concrete frames that are to be found in the large blocks of all cities. The structure of this truncated, square-plan tower is a variant on the tube-in-tube concept. It consists of an inner service core and the outer tube of eight massive peripheral columns joined by six-feet-deep spandrel beams at each level. The three-feet, three-inch-wide spandrel beams shade its double-glazed ribbon windows. Following the construction principles of the earlier Australia Square Tower, the precast units form the permanent formwork for in situ poured concrete. Standing at 800 feet, the M.L.C. Tower is one of the tallest concrete frame buildings in the world.

The antithesis of Seidler's resolved composition for the M.L.C., is the bold, contextual statement of Andrews's King George Tower [1977] which, rather than creating a haven cut off from the street, turns its forecourt into a part of the mainstream of the life of the city. This distinctive, rugged tower of board-marked textured concrete makes a welcome visual as well as social contribution to the city of Sydney.

8.2. Harry Seidler and Associates, architects. M.L.C. Office Tower. Sydney, 1978. (Photograph: Max Dupain, courtesy of the architects)

Public squares and streets are also being transformed into pedestrian precincts. City Hall Plaza, Brisbane; Martin Plaza, Sydney; and the Malls of Perth and Adelaide are among the most successful undertakings. Apart from these large schemes, the upgrading of small pockets of public land, such as Macquarie Place, Sydney, are adding to the enriched quality of the urban street levels. In Sydney recently constructed enclosed pedestrian overpasses link the major retail stores, and the council propose a further extended system of underground connections throughout the central city.

Among the positive benefits to the cities has been the appearance of cultural centers in all capital cities, with the exception of Hobart. In Melbourne the first stage of the project by Sir Roy Grounds, the National Gallery of Victoria, has been in use since 1968. Work is in progress towards the construction of the Concert Hall, one of three performing arts centers, to be associated with the Gallery. The Festival Centre, Adelaide, by Hassel and Partners [1970-1976] stands on the banks of the Torrens River in the central city. Its principal auditoriums, which are roofed with white plastic-coated concrete slabs supported on a steel frame, are partially sunken below the elevated plaza which covers other facilities and acts as a vast sculpture garden. Perth boasts an Entertainment Centre, 1974, by Hobbs, Winning, Leighton and Partners, which joins the earlier Concert Hall by Howlett and Bailey [1972].

In Brisbane work was commenced in 1979 on the inner-city banks of the Brisbane River for a large, mixed-use, cultural center by Robin Gibson (fig. 8.3). The design, which steps the buildings towards the water, shows a sensitive handling of indoor, outdoor, and linkage spaces, grouped over and around a water mall. Gibson's concern for climatic control and his resolution of the clear yet subtle circulation patterns make this a rational and elegant solution. It promises well as a valuable future addition to the city. Sydney's Opera House, 1959-1973 (fig. 8.4) by the Dane, Jorn Utzon, completed by Hall, Todd and Littlemore after 1966, is one of the world's most imaginative and poetic modern buildings. The drama and beauty of the white tiled shells of the roof-forms create a memorable image on its harborside in the center of the city. Their ingeniously designed pointed-arch roof vaults of segmented precast-

8.3. Robin Gibson, architect. Model, Queensland Cultural Centre. Brisbane, begun 1979. (Photograph: Courtesy of the architect)

8.4. Jørn Utzon, architect. The Opera House. Sydney, 1973. (Photograph: Courtesy of Sidney Opera House Trust)

concrete ribs by Utzon in collaboration with Ove Arup and Partners, Engineers, demonstrated the potential flexibility of precast-concrete construction. Too often, the advances in engineering evidenced by this building are overlooked. The possibilities of prefabrication, for instance, were explored further, in particular with the use of plywood for inner cladding. Also not always appreciated is the important role this complex plays in providing a waterfront promenade that connects the passenger ferry terminals of Circular Quay to the west with the Botanical Gardens to the east. In every respect the Sydney Opera House has masterfully enhanced its setting.

While the popular image of Australians as "outback" country dwellers is incorrect, that of a nation of sports lovers is true. Swimming pools, both private and public, constitute the highest numbers of sporting facilities built. The Harold Holt Swimming Pool, Melbourne, designed by Daryl Jackson in association with Keven Borland [1959], remains the finest public pool in the country. The sports stadium, constructed in Canberra for the 1977 Pacific Games, provides an interesting example of the subtle architecture of Philip Cox and Partners, with a clearly expressed concrete structural system rising with an organic continuity from the supportive earthworks that bank its sides. By the merging of the engineering of the earth and the engineering of the concrete, this large structure retains a low profile and a related human scale.

Changes to the inner cities were at first mutely accepted and later confronted with outrage. Concerned and well-organized resident action groups emerged during the early 1970s in many inner areas to protest policies that condoned the destruction of buildings and open spaces they considered of value. These action groups did much to stir the conscience of local government bodies. During 1971-1975, Sydney was the setting for a unique Australian occurrence—the "Green Ban" movement. In the absence of adequate legislation to protect the existing environment, resident groups called on the assistance of the Communist-led New South Wales Builders Labourers Federation (BLF), and later other unions joined in support of the movement. The "Green Ban" is ostensibly a withholding of labor from a job until agreement is reached between those undertaking the project and those opposing the work. Over forty bans were imposed during the first four years, and work was halted on projects worth $3,000 million. The protests included those against local government sales of natural bushland for housing development, a proposed sporting stadium in a large natural suburban park, the removal of old Moreton Bay fig trees in a central park to make way for a car-parking station, and the demolition of extensive tracts of historic areas of the inner city. The issues were both social and environmental, and were concerned with the safekeeping of community as well as building structures. It is difficult to ascertain to what extent the search for political advantage determined the Green Ban movement, but whatever the motives, before long the BLF became the champion of threatened environments.

It is unfortunate when government legislation is so inadequate that environmental conservation can only be achieved by such strong-arm tactics. The Green Ban movement saved much of worth, and was in many ways responsible for increasing public involvement in the planning of local environment. Before long the developers, badly affected by the bans, joined the protesters in the demand for legislation to clarify the question of preservation. Since this time a federal government body has been instigated to record and conserve the national estate. Victoria now has legislation to prevent demolition without enquiry, and a similar bill has recently been passed by New South Wales' Parliament. No action has been taken by the other states.

Before the emergence in the seventies of the protest groups, run-down, late Victorian inner-city suburban-like enclaves, for example, Carlton in Melbourne and Paddington in Sydney, were being revived by those who rediscovered the beauty of the old terraces with their decorative cast-iron verandas and those for whom the daily travel from their far-flung suburban homes was becoming untenable. These areas now are among the prime residential zones. But in Paddington and Carlton, increased real estate values drove out the original residents to an extent almost equal to that threatened by the development proposals. The need to keep low-income inner-residential areas became apparent. The purchase by the federal government of a large segment of Church of England land and housing stock in the Sydney region of Glebe was the most forward-looking event to emerge from this realization. Government owned properties in this area are being restored and renovated. House occupants are relocated during renovation and then returned to their own home on marginally increased rents. Further state and government supported projects involving advocacy planning and citizen participation are in progress, again primarily in Sydney and Melbourne. The present indication speaks well of the future results of these undertakings.

Australia is one of the most urban countries in the world, with 40 percent of the total population living in Sydney and Melbourne, and a further 25 percent in other major towns. The large urban centers of Australia, with their far-flung boundaries, are unwieldy. The intensive immigration policies that brought 2.2 million persons to Australia between 1946 and 1971 vastly increased the urban population. This increase combined with the general drift from the country to the city, taxed urban resources. As city life becomes increasingly trying for many, there are some signs of a reversion of this pattern, and decentralization is now a matter of government policy. Several new growth centers were designated—the major ones being the existing twin towns of Orange-Bathurst and Albury-Wodonga. The selected centers became the recipients of national aid to stimulate industry and to improve amenity in order to draw population from Sydney and Melbourne in particular. Despite major cutbacks in government expenditure that have curtailed development since 1975, the move to the new growth centers has been successful. Within the existing cities decentralization follows the American pattern of regional hospital, school, entertainment, and shopping development, and many of the new tertiary educational complexes are located on the fringes and even outside of the urban zones.

Space is something of which Australia is not short, and the character of the new universities and colleges has been conditioned to a marked extent by the generous bushlands in which they are located. Recent new universities include the University of Newcastle, outside that city; James Cook University, Townsville; and Griffith University outside Brisbane.

All have natural bush settings with which the planning and architecture is in accord. Some of the finest new buildings in the country are to be found on these recently founded campuses. A notable example, the Kuring-Gai College of Advanced Education, by the New South Wales government architect [David Turner, design architect, 1969-1976], combines many of the best features of much recent work. It has an intimate relationship with the formation and vegetation of its site and evidences a sensible response to the climate, excluding the unwanted aspects but exploiting the benefits. The liberal and sympathetic attitude to the needs of the users has given rise to an interesting and involving internal arrangement. Outstanding among the distinctive campus buildings by Robin Gibson (Brisbane), the Library and Humanities Building for Griffith University is in close harmony with its rather untamed setting despite the formal order of its structure. The propylaea it forms to unite two areas of the campus has a majesty of scale and progression rarely encountered in twentieth-century work.

While the large cities have their problems, Australia has its own model city: the national capital, Canberra. The plan of Canberra was designed by Walter Burley Griffin, the winner of the international competition of 1911. The topography was the dominant element that determined the structure of the city. Central Canberra, which is encircled by mountains, is laid out on a generous scale around a man-made lake created by damming a local river. The inner pattern focuses on the axially divided Parliamentary Triangle, ringed by concentric roads crossed by radial arteries. The inner housing is almost exclusively found in low-density garden communities of intentionally restricted size. This central area is surrounded by a wide green belt and beyond that, in the branching valleys, lie the satellite towns linked to the center by fast highways.

Canberra was still in its infancy in the 1940s and much of the present city is the result of construction undertaken since that time. The population expanded from 39,000 in 1958 to 190,000 in 1975. All land in the federal territory is owned by the national government and leased on long-term holdings. Planning and development of the Canberra area is under the control of the National Capital Development Commission which generally engages private architects to undertake specific projects. Rarely have even the principal buildings required by this small nation been large, and the extensive space of the mountain-encircled central Canberra, with its major vistas and parklands, has proved daunting to most architects. Monuments, such as the Australian War Memorial, are satisfactorily scaled to their setting, but while scale is not necessarily a matter of size, most buildings of Canberra are disappointingly lost. An exception to this is the recent Trade Office Building [1970-1974] by Harry Seidler, which is admirably scaled and sited for its location near the parklands of Lake Burley Griffin. The building is constructed of huge precast concrete elements, the largest of which are the 160-foot post-tensioned facade beams that each weigh eighty tons. The units were placed using three-legged steel gantries on rails, designed to allow for rotation at the corners. With this building Seidler again demonstrated his capacity for handling this material and his mastery of drawing on the potential of the order of such structures to create imposing sculptural building compositions.

Major civic buildings are emerging in the inner core of Canberra: the High Court of Australia and the National Art Gallery, both by Edwards, Madigan, Torzillo and Briggs (fig. 8.5) were under construction in 1979 on the shores of Lake Burley Griffin. Also during 1979, the Family Law Courts, by Philip Cox and Partners, was reaching final design-stage, and debate over the selection of an architect for the new Parliament House was in process. The High Court of Australia and the National Art Gallery form a complementary linked pair of buildings within the Parliamentary Triangle on the shore of the lake. Special-use spaces in both buildings relate to the pivotal visual reference point of the foyers. In the High Court this area, with a ceiling height of seventy-three feet, assumes an imposing scale which is given a dynamic quality through the use of large diagonal ramps and overhanging gallery spaces. Their imposing and expressive concrete forms strongly pronounce their nature, both in function and status. When completed, the presence of these two commanding buildings will have a major impact on the visual qualities of their settings. The Family Law Courts adopt a quite different approach from that evident in the High Court. A sympathetic, poetic, solution unites a brick podium and low, partially enclosing walls with the almost weightless quality of glass vaults over glass walls. The plan, with its organization of courtrooms related to open courtyards, reflects a similar relationship of enclosure and openness.

The outer towns surrounding Canberra's core provide a laboratory of community development with few equals. These fast-growing areas are assisted by federal funds. High-, medium- and low-density housing is to be found in Australia's version of Letchworth, Radburn, Cumbernauld, and Milton Keynes. Among the most interesting recent proposals

8.5. Edwards, Madigan, Torzillo and Briggs, architects. High Court of Australia (right) and National Art Gallery (left). Canberra, 1979-. (Photograph: Courtesy of the architects)

for housing in the Canberra area are those prepared by Philip Cox and Partners. These include lake-edge housing for Belconnen which blends the land and water by weaving the units across the two zones; Reid housing that contains the highest residential densities in the Canberra area in a terraced terrain that closely ties buildings and landscape; and the Tuggeranong East Knoll development, a hillside "Citadel" complex based on the integration of housing and other uses along a dense, varied pedestrian path. While radical departures from the past prototypes have rarely been undertaken, the new center of Belconnen is innovative in its design, organized around two major megastructural office blocks—John Andrews's Cameron Office [1977] for 4,000 government employees and McConnel, Smith and Johnson's Belconnen West Offices, housing 3,500 similarly employed workers.

Cameron, the first major building in the center, was seen to hold the potential to be more than just a building but a major component of the urban, pedestrian-based plan. By aligning the structure horizontally and arranging its spaces around an elevated, covered, yet open circulation spine, the building offered itself as the connection between the proposed medium-density housing planned for the north and the retail area and transportation interchange to the south. East-west pedestrian routes were planned to make connections in future developments along this path. In accord with this concept the later Belconnen West Offices also offer a pedestrian throughpath as part of the central circulation network. Although recent planning changes have caused some disruption to the initial concept of Belconnen, the potential of the unique concept on which the planning of this center was based is clearly evident.

The Cameron Office building warrants mention, not solely for its planning principles, but also as the most illuminating example of Andrews's work yet constructed. It is a heroic work of architecture with an ingenious structural system supporting the low-profile branching office wings that enclose deep garden courtyards. Cameron's services include a computerized telerail delivery network, a heating and cooling plant that will serve other buildings in the area, and a suction garbage collection service that draws rubbish to the central service area where it is shredded, bailed, and dispatched. With the design of this building Andrews explored many issues regarding people in buildings, and buildings in cities. The built solution and the many challenging questions it raises place the Cameron Office among the most significant buildings of its time.

With its open spaces and generous hours of sunshine, it might be expected that Australia would be at the forefront of experimental low-energy architecture. However, while government and university bodies are pursuing this direction in laboratory and small prototype situations, no major application has been undertaken. Most promising was the proposed design for Monarto, a new growth center (fig. 8.6) in an arid region outside Adelaide. This scheme utilized sun, wind, and water pressure from the pipeline, its sole water supply, to the interior for heating, power, and evaporative cooling, but government financial cuts coupled with greater need in other areas prevented its realization.

The mining towns in the desert environment of Australia generate special requirements that demand unique solutions. Stressful conditions are caused by extreme climatic conditions, isolation, and the impermanent nature of the townships. After a period of no rain, two inches may fall within the hour; 120 mile-per-hour winds and sun temperatures of 180 degrees are not uncommon. Among the most progressive of these towns is Lawrence Howroyd's Shay Gap [1970] near Port Hedland and on the fringe of the Great Sandy Desert of Western Australia. A predicted life span of only ten years called for economical short-term architecture that provided psychological and

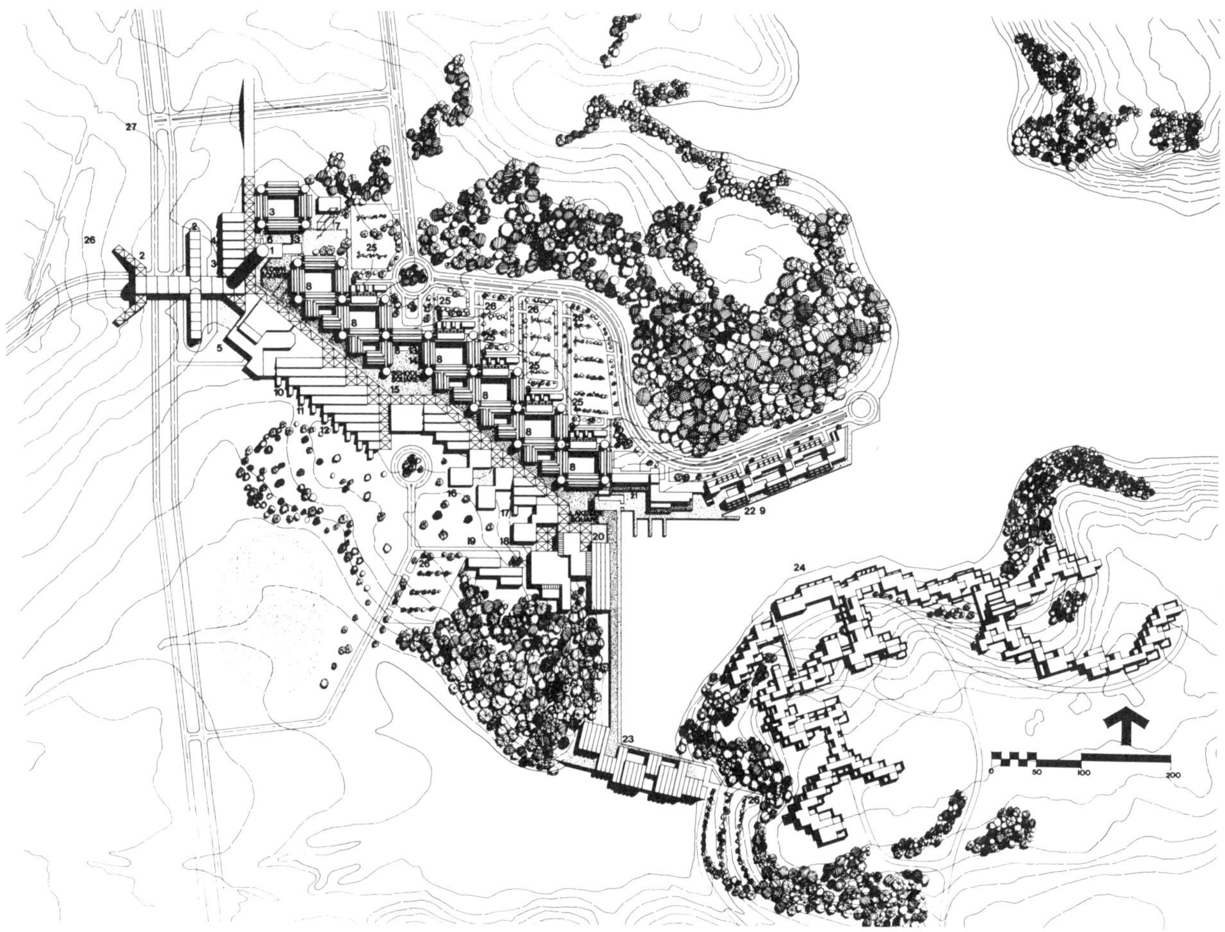

8.6. John Andrews International, urban designers. Monarto City Centre Project, Stage I. South Australia (planned but discontinued). (Photograph: Courtesy of John Andrews International)

MONARTO LEGEND			
	1 WATER TOWER	10 APPLIED ARTS	19 PRE-SCHOOL
	2 TRANSPORTATION TERMINAL	11 TECHNICAL STUDIES	20 INDOOR SPORTS CENTRE
	3 RETAIL	12 ENVIRONMENTAL STUDIES	21 HOTEL
	4 POLICE, FIRE, AMBULANCE	13 BUSINESS & GENERAL STUDIES	22 MDC OFFICES
	5 PERFORMING ARTS CENTRE	14 SCHOOLS ADMINISTRATION	23 SCIENCE CENTRE
	6 HEALTH AND WELFARE	15 LIBRARY RESOURCE CENTRE	24 LAKESIDE HOUSING
	7 CHURCH PRECINCT	16 PRIMARY SCHOOL	25 SHORT TERM PARKING
	8 OFFICES	17 SCIENCE CENTRE (SCHOOLS)	26 LONG TERM PARKING
	9 CITY CENTRE HOUSING	18 SECONDARY SCHOOL	27 SERVICE STATION

physiological protection. Notable advances have been made here with modular steel-framed, polyurethane-panelled constructions serviced by an advanced technology including air-transported sewage and reticulated refrigerants. The buildings are grouped around traffic-free courts which provide shade and stimulate social contact.

The humid north, particularly those areas in the cyclone belt, pose particular problems. The devastation of the port of Darwin, in December 1974, drew national attention to the unsuitability of much of the architecture in these parts. Since then the federal government, especially, has accelerated its experimental program for building in the cyclone zone, with studies that have led to improvements in heat/humidity control and building performance in high winds, particularly in pilot schemes for the rebuilding of Darwin.

Over the last ten years, the neglected area of Aboriginal settlement, and in particular housing, has been the subject of intensive study. The Aborigine is normally referred to as belonging to a nomadic race, which before white intervention wandered this country erecting applicable shelters from available materials at the camping spots. A major design problem arises from the often encountered conflict of the desire to occupy a home akin to that of the white settlers and the unsuitability of such dwellings for their way of life. Due to the wide range of climatic conditions in this country, the habits and social structures of the Aboriginal groups can be at polar opposites. These distinct tribal group differences, and the various stages of cultural loss suffered by the Aboriginal, preclude a universal panacea. Solutions to the problems of housing the Aborigines have ranged from providing typical suburban dwellings to minimal self-help programs. The most successful results have occurred where the tribal group is still strong and the culture little tarnished.

A federal undertaking to give priority to a "vigorous housing scheme" to properly house all Aboriginal families within ten years was instigated in 1973. With a level of social investigation far in excess of that afforded housing for the white population, studies concentrated on examining, from first principles, the relationships between the dwelling, the ecology, and the way of life of the inhabitants. Criteria were established, prototypes of individual homes and entire villages were constructed and subjected to intensive post-occupation evaluation. The results of the various prototypes have, nevertheless, been most disappointing, and there have even been incidences of the entire abandonment of settlements.

Lately the policy has moved in the direction of more self-help housing, with funds supplied to tribal groups (Aboriginal Housing Cooperatives), usually contingent upon the employment of an architect and an accountant. Growing in strength is the Homeland Movement which is ostensibly a return to the land. Tribal groups of about seventy-five to one hundred persons who wish to break from the white settlements to work out their own problems are receiving support for their practical needs. Achievement of the goal of the Homeland Movement is far in the future and will require perhaps a generation or more to resolve the complex social and material conditions. The return to the ethnic pattern of living is seen as a move forward to self-support and independence.

Considering the spectrum of recent work produced in this country, it becomes evident that, while Australia can boast a significant number of buildings equal to, and sometimes excelling, any of their kind throughout the world, the most important changes have arisen from the persuasive general effect of certain events. Among these must be counted, first, the arrival of Harry Seidler in 1948; second, the positive change in attitude towards the local culture, landscape, and climate that occurred in the late 1950s, with the wide-ranging influence of Sydney Ancher as an innovative regional architect, Bruce Mackenzie as a landscape designer, and Robin Boyd, primarily as a critic especially noted; third, the swing in values of the Australian people following a recognition of the negative effects of the economic boom; and fourth, the return from Canada of the Australian-born architect, John Andrews, in 1969. The construction of the Sydney Opera House, apart from stimulating local industry and building technology, has had little direct influence on local design. Its major significance lies in its impact on the consciousness of the Australian population in general, for it has created an awareness of the potential greatness of architecture which must have a profound effect on the future. While the factors influencing architecture are many and complex, these appear as the major milestones along the path towards the evolution of an architecture that speaks in the cultural language of this country, yet contributes to the solution of the commonly shared problems of the environment today.

Bibliography

Blake, Peter. *Architecture for the New World: The Work of Harry Seidler*. Cammeray: Horwitz Australia, 1973.

Boyd, Robin. *Australia's Home*. Melbourne: Melbourne University Press, 1952.

Freeland, J. M. *Architecture in Australia*. Melbourne: F. W. Cheshire Publishing Pty., 1968.

McKay, Ian; Boyd, Robin; Stretton, Hugh; and Mort, John. *Living and Partly Living*. Thomas Nelson Australia Pty., 1971.

Sowden, Harry. *Towards an Australian Architecture*. Sydney: Ure Smith, 1968.

Stretton, Hugh. *Ideas for Australian Cities*. Sydney: Griffith Press, 1970.

Tanner, Howard. *Australian Housing in the Seventies*. Sydney: Ure Smith, 1976.

Taylor, Jennifer. *An Australian Identity: Houses for Sydney 1953-1963*. Sydney: Department of Architecture, University of Sydney, 1972.

9

AUSTRIA

FRIEDRICH ACHLEITNER

The cultural situation of architecture in Austria is determined largely by the fact that one quarter of its people live in Vienna, and that, despite its loss of historical importance, Vienna possesses a great many fascinating buildings which have continuously influenced the thought and plans of architects. As late as the 1930s, Vienna played an absolutely dominating role in Austria's architectural developments. After the Second World War, however, in response to economic, cultural, and political developments, regional centers were formed which now are developing their own particular characteristics. Not without importance for this development was the artificial division of Austria into four zones of occupation, each with its own sometimes very different cultural activities. The dynamics peculiar to the individual provinces (from west to east: Vorarlberg, Tyrol, Salzburg, Upper Austria, Carinthia, Styria, Lower Austria, Vienna, and the Burgenland) continue to become more pronounced so that it will become ever more difficult to speak of an Austrian architecture. Since it would be too much to go into these developments here and to describe this spectrum precisely, we shall instead consider the more conspicuous aspects of recent architecture in Austria.

In the various provinces symbols of architectural progress are accepted freely and without criticism, probably because of a certain feeling of competition with Vienna. Vienna cultivates its sense of the historical as a kind of feeling for life and awareness of itself, which is understandable considering its abundance of a fertile psychologizing and semanticizing soil. This orientation toward history, however, is not necessarily to be considered as the equivalent of historicism, that is, as the equivalent of a plastic reproduction of history. It most certainly does not represent a nostalgic use of history. It may be explained instead as a critical ability to see the present from a distance that is based on an awareness of history; an inevitable relativizing of the immediate present, if one will; a standard or an opposing force tending to overcome the new against which it has to exist. Thus, innovation occurs more slowly and must be more decisively articulated.

In 1940 Austria was part of the Third Reich. Construction was limited to the implementation of Hitler's armament industry, manifesting itself for the most part in factories and industrial workers' residences. Thus, in the wake of the construction of the "Hermann Göring-Werke" in Linz (now VÖEST—Alpine AG, steelworks) large residential complexes were developed: in Salzburg, the Tyrol, and Vorarlberg large developments were built to house Italians who had been resettled from the South Tyrol. Until 1945 one cannot speak of a specifically Austrian architecture.

The collapse of Austrian modern, however, had occurred before the annexation of Austria to Germany. Leonardo Benevolo, in his *Geschichte der Architektur des 19. und 20. Jahrhunderts* (*History of Modern Architecture*), refers to the "irritating compromise" that existed in the Austrian (or Viennese) development in the compromise between Classicism and modernism. After the death of Adolf Loos in 1933 and the immigration of Josef Frank in 1934, a variation of modern traditionalism (Heimatar-

Translated from the original German text by Edith and Warren Sanderson.

chitektur) was promoted under the political regime of Austrian fascism, which was clearly related to the conservative wing of the fascist architecture of Italy. As early as the twenties the most vital phase of Modernism had already been played out in Vienna. Certainly the Social-Democratic city administration of Vienna which had been very liberal in matters of architecture had aided the Otto Wagner school to reach a dominant position in the construction of municipal buildings. However, it was precisely in this school that a broad spectrum of historicism later developed. Thus, despite political differences there was a certain readiness for the architectural ideologies of National Socialism, strengthened by the circumstance that in Vienna (with the exceptions of Adolf Loos and Josef Frank) these not exactly shiningly logical nor theoretically formulated positions were neither seen nor even suspected as at all connected.

It is understandable that these historical encumbrances made it very difficult to pursue a uniquely Austrian manner. The majority of the leading architects of the thirties had emigrated or had died. The Austrian self-censorship resulting from Hitler's cultural politics had created above all else a great paucity of information. In addition, of central interest for young architects was the rapid rebuilding of cities destroyed by the war. The immense range of necessary building provided opportunities, especially for those architects working with ponderous architectural concepts and a trivial vocabulary. This trend to establish "normal conditions" as quickly as possible created an antiexperimental and antiarchitectural climate that confronted the younger generation of architects from 1945.

The decade after the Second World War, that is, until the Austrian treaty with the Allied powers and the withdrawal of the armies of occupation, was characterized on the one hand by simple rebuilding and on the other by the reconstruction of some richly symbolic architecture of considerable importance for the political and especially the cultural identity of the new state. Among these the Cathedral of St. Stephan in Vienna, the "Burgtheater," the State Opera, and, also in Vienna, some striking buildings and plazas such as the Heinrichshof and Stephansplatz were of greater than average interest. Characteristic of the architectural situation of that time is the fact that none of Austria's most prominent contemporary living architects (such as Josef Hoffmann, Clemens Holzmeister, Lois Welzenbacher, Max Fellerer, Oswald Haerdtl, or Franz Schuster) took part in the design of these symbolically significant projects. With the exception of Josef Hoffmann, who however was 75 years old in 1945, all of these architects had their effect as teachers. Particularly in the school of Clemens Holzmeister a climate was developed that was to lead to essential changes in the architectural scene. It has become clearer in retrospect that the romantic, somewhat historicizing architecture of Holzmeister created a good basis for a "school." In this "school" the reasonable (developed from the architectural drawing, often transformed by historical models, usually proceeding from a concrete sense of place and taking account of a particular situation) played its role, rather than the antirational, the emotional, and the sensual. On the one hand Holzmeister had the ability to inspire his students through the medium of architecture; on the other, his dynamic but thoughtless commitment provoked criticism and contradiction. When we consider that his outstanding but nonverbal manner of teaching was carried on in a context that was ignorant of and intolerant of international architectural developments, and that Holzmeister's generation had developed a kind of protective shield against this development, it is not unfounded to maintain that the younger Austrian architects of the 1950s had to begin once again from ground zero.

When we speak of tendencies which should be of greater interest, we must speak essentially of two camps that formed the basis of opposition to the dominant situation in the fifties, two trends that have continued to develop separately to today. One is represented by the work of Roland Rainer (born 1910); the other by the *Arbeitsgruppe 4* (Workgroup 4) of Wilhelm Holzbauer, Friedrich Kurrent, and Johannes Spalt (born about 1930 with the exception of Spalt).

Roland Rainer was the only architect who, because of his contact with the Austrian modern style of the 1930s (and with Josef Frank), strove to further a continuity with prewar modern architecture. He believed that the time following the period of the pioneers was concerned with solidifying and spreading the inheritance of the architectural revolution. His doctrine of "the single-story residence" comes out of the tradition of the garden city movement which, though very much opposed in Vienna, was a trend that he pursued consistently, trying to solidify and enrich it with his studies of the architecture of such cultures as those found in the Balkans and the Near East. During the fifties in addition to this posture on the architecture of the city there was the conflict with prefabrication in residential building that focused upon the single-story house, for which there were few precedents in Austria. As the city planner for Vienna between 1958 and 1963, in a time of great changes in the architectural climate, Rainer's doctrine was confronted by the architectural reality of the metropolis. This led to a marked change in his constructional models and finally to a break with the municipal administration. In the Puchenau development near Linz, built in stages from 1966, Rainer realized his conception of urban construction in its purest form. Here Rainer succeeded in demonstrating that at least a part of today's housing requirements can be satisfied by older but still richly variegated forms, and that the primary needs of man remain constant even in the rapidly changing world of architecture. Rainer's architectural work is diverse and varied, oriented toward Scandinavian functionalism and yet shows many aspects which stem from a continuing concern with the architecture of earlier cultures. His architectural range is perhaps most visible in his city halls at Bremen, Ludwigshafen, and Vienna in which constructive concepts are unified with semantic and symbolic concepts.

While Roland Rainer's architectural doctrine reflects in principle the Functional landscape of the 1950s and 1960s and consciously represents the inheritance of modernity, in the *Arbeitsgruppe 4* of Holzbauer, Kurrent, and Spalt the independence of a young and critical generation is visible—an independence that was shared by their contemporaries. To this generation of architects educated in the 1940s and 1950s fell the tasks of reestablishing contacts with international developments, and of trying to reestablish as well the lost traditions of their country by laying bare its own roots. One can maintain that this generation, which prepared the change of scene with an idealistic guerrilla warfare of sorts, assumed very special characteristics based on the historical situation.

Typical of these architects was an enthusiastic relationship to the history of the Modern Movement, a certain hero-worshipping of the pioneers, a naiveté toward the theory of architecture, a disturbed attitude toward politics as well as toward architectural politics, and an emphatic sense of the ethics of one's work and of the role of the architect. Their enthusiastic attitude toward the history of the modern movement resulted from the fact that this generation had to rediscover it against the opposition of the older generation. This was not only an exciting adventure but also brought welcome arguments against the prevailing state of affairs. A naive attitude to architectural theory, with characteristic overvaluing and undervaluing of methodological or analytical thought is a generally Austrian quality that perhaps is related to a predilection for contemplative or intuitive thinking. Their disturbed attitude toward politics was an inheritance from the previous generation, from the "country that no one wanted." Thus, from the political fanaticism of the First Republic, or the so-called interregnum between the wars, came an inheritance that even today leaves much to be fulfilled. Finally an ethical, even moralizing emphasis upon the role of the architect and the purposes of architecture may be considered as a traditional phenomenon, when one thinks how the writings of Adolf Loos became a kind of bible for this generation.

The rediscovery of Karl Kraus and Ludwig Wittgenstein also belongs in this context. The *Arbeitsgruppe 4* was exemplary for various reasons. Not only did its projects and publications lead to broad discussions but above all else its refusal to accept an architecture of compromise, as for example in the municipal buildings in Vienna, provided encouragement and moral support for many of its contemporaries. Apart from reflecting contemporary problems, the rational, positivist, and structural architectural perspectives of Otto Wagner were continued. To be more specific, in principle his system of values, including his interpretation of history and progress, was adopted and fitted to the new situation. The decisive reference to the city's tradition, with the simultaneous building upon architectural achievements from the Wagner school to Loos, Frank, and Plischke, stiffened the resolve of Vienna's situation against the sequences of international styles and currents.

The years following the peace treaty (1945) formed without doubt the prelude for a rather radical change of scene. By 1958 there was an upward turn. Roland Rainer finished his construction of the Vienna City Hall and became city planner of Vienna. Karl Schwanzer demonstrated to the world the first signs of life in Austrian architecture with his pavilion at the Brussels World's Fair. In Salzburg, Clemens Holzmeister documented the vitality of his traditionalism with his music festival complex (fig. 9.1),

9.1. Clemens Holzmeister, architect. Salzburg Music Festival Complex. 1926-1937 and 1953-1971. (Photograph: Courtesy of Friedrich Achleitner)

while in the same city Konrad Wachsmann through his summer academy seminars exerted such great influence upon the younger generation of architects that great changes took place in their conceptions of the aims of architecture. The first works of *Arbeitsgruppe 4*, by Johann Gsteu, Josef Lackner, Gerhard Garstenauer, Hans Puchhammer, Gunther Wawrik, and Ottokar Uhl, all of whom are representative of today's architecture, developed under this influence. Nor should one forget that in the romantic school (for instance of Lois Welzenbacher as well as Holzmeister) there existed an intellectual hunger for rationalist methods, for precision and control, for argumentation and reasoning, and that the teaching and working methods of Wachsmann transmitted if nothing else at least a belief in these truths. Because of the lack of industrial capacity and perhaps also because of an excessive skepticism concerning his views, the dreams of Wachsmann could not even partially have been realized. Yet they prepared the groundwork for very important discussions of architectural theory that offered some architects occasion to articulate their ideas. So, in the final analysis, his influence was quite fruitful.

As early as 1958 the growing peremptory decisiveness of some architects and groups, whose optimism was furthered by technological progress, brought forth certain countercurrents. This was the time of Friedrich Hundertwasser's creative "Mold Manifesto" (*Verschimmelungsmanifest*) and Günther Feuerstein's first edition of *Incidental Architecture* (*Inzidente Architektur*).

Now regarded as almost legendary, the vital and prosperous 1960s, when viewed more precisely in terms of architectural history, extend from 1958 to the energy crisis. Even before the end of the building boom, the year of the student rebellions, 1968, represented a shock for the theoretical independence of architecture.

One could designate this decade, on the one hand, as one of consolidation, when the younger generation of architects began to build, found international connections, and was able to define itself with many key buildings. On the other hand, it may be viewed as the beginning of conflict at a newly attained level. It is difficult to offer even a summary presentation of the issues in conflict, for since they tend to cancel one another out their contexts and their relationships to preceding views are hardly recognizable.

Certainly the difficulty here has also to do with the well-known lateness with which events seem to occur in Austria. For example, the phase of self-realization of the younger generation at the beginning of the sixties began so timidly and so late that reflections upon it and reactions to it occurred almost simultaneously. In the same manner the international reaction to the modern academicism of Mies van der Rohe's followers was coincidental with the first realizations of Austrian constructivism, while the first waves of the New Brutalism occurred with the beginning of discussion concerning the urbanistic movement.

The conquest of the architectural scene was barely begun when it was complicated by a concern with technological and urban utopias. Though the realization that buildings were objects unto themselves had found only scant acceptance, the individuality of buildings was put into question by a shift of interest toward the complex interrelationships involved in urban planning. One thing remained as before, however: architecture was seen as art. Considered with the totality of its environment once again, its scope was broadened to include the conceptual, the psychological, and the sublime. Architectural designers and developers turned their attention toward the art market.

With an exhibition in the Gallery St. Stephan in Vienna in 1963, Hans Hollein's and Walter Pichler's works were introduced to the public. Their visions provoked protests: the claim that "all is architecture" was scarcely taken seriously. And with that event criticism of Functionalism began, even before it had been consolidated in building. Groups such as *Haus-Rucker-Co*, *Coop Himmelbau* and *Zünd-Up* ("Salt of the Earth") broke off from Feuerstein's "Club Seminar," and moved in part to somewhere between the fields of influence of *Archigram* and *Wiener Aktionismus*. One has the impression that somehow, from the middle 1960s, this poetically individualistic (*Haus-Rucker-Co*) and aggressively hectic (*Coop Himmelbau*) phase proclaimed a deep crisis, the most lively manifestation of which was at another level, in the politics of the student rebellions. Since then, discussion of architecture in Austria has entered into a new arena at a new level that, on the one hand, made accessible new areas and relationships, while, on the other hand, it brought uncertainty and resignation to an entire generation of students.

Having considered major trends and developments thus far, we shall try now to make the topography of the architectural landscape more clearly visible by considering representative architects, their work, and their interrelationships.

Roland Rainer, because of his more than twenty years of effective teaching and his strong ideas about education, had created a school which made itself felt in all of Austria but especially in the western part of the country. This school was effective, for example, in Vorarlberg, particularly in private residences and housing developments where there were regional precedents such as the tradition of building in wood. *Arbeitsgruppe 4* represented a kind of cooperative for its members, architects of the same generation, including Johann Georg Gsteu, Josef Lackner, Gustav Peichl, Hans Puchhammer, Gunther Wawrik, Anton Schweighofer and Ottokar Uhl. Holzbauer, Kurrent, and Spalt worked as a group for a full decade, for instance in the church at Parsch, Salzburg [1953-1956]; at St. Josef's College (fig. 9.2) in Salzburg [1961-1964]; and at the retreat of Steyr-Ennsleiten [1958-1970]. The latter, an emphatically constructivist building, was developed in cooperation with J. G. Gsteu. In 1964 Wilhelm Holzbauer left the group, having chosen a different direction after several sojourns in America, while Johannes Spalt and Friedrich Kurrent furthered the aims of the group, bringing them to a rather successful conclusion in buildings such as the Central Savings Bank branch office (fig. 9.3) at Floridsdorfer Spitz, Vienna [1970-1974]. Holzbauer never departed from the basic "Vienna traditionalism," that is, the tendency toward an inclusive and well-balanced concept of architecture, shunning, however, an emphasis upon constructivist Structuralism in favor of a more spatial architectonic interpretation. He was more interested, so to speak, in a dialectic of effects, a mannerism of comparative forms that makes a building habitable,even in a way independent of its function. In just that way the St. Virgil Educational Center at Salzburg [1965-1976] proceeds beyond its actual functional requirements to create a dialogue with the Mannerist, Baroque tradition of Salzburg without making use of architectural collage or quotation (fig. 9.4). Holzbauer avoids literary or psychological levels of understanding so that his Mannerism remains in the framework of pure architectonic statement. Johann Georg Gsteu, who had begun to build in the fifties, also as a constructivist purist, as in the chapel on the Baumgärtner Spitz in Vienna [1960-1965] (fig. 9.5), advanced his "myth of

9.2. Wilhelm Holzbauer, Friedrich Kurrent, and Johannes Spalt, architects. Arbeitsgruppe 4, St. Josef's College. Salzburg-Aigen, 1961-1964. (Photograph: Courtesy of Friedrich Achleitner)

9.3. Friedrich Kurrent and Johannes Spalt, architects. Central Savings Bank, Floridsdorfer Spitz Branch Office. Vienna, 1970-1974. (Photograph: Courtesy of Friedrich Achleitner)

9.4. Wilhelm Holzbauer, architect. Rendering of St. Virgil's Educational Center. Salzburg-Aigen, 1965-1976. (Photograph: Courtesy of the architect)

9.5. Johann Georg Gsteu, architect. Chapel on the Baumgärtner Summit. Vienna, 1960-1965. (Photograph: Courtesy of Friedrich Achleitner)

modular organization'' directly into the realm of the irrational, for instance in his church at Hohenems Vorarlberg [1965-1974]. His strong spatial and plastic formal vocabulary manifestly requires systems of order which in their final, built appearance may be immediately deprived of their logical bases, much as in the work of Kafka, if the comparison may be allowed, in which the irrational consists of a buildup of small rational steps. In any case, whether Gsteu's architecture is concerned with residential buildings of the Vienna community [Aderklaaerstrasse, 1973-1978] or the renovation of old buildings, it is full of vitality and original statements.

Josef Lackner, a Tyrolian who resides in the Tyrol, is perhaps the only student of Holzmeister who carries on the folklorish, expressive, strikingly emphatic architecture of his teacher, and yet brings other factors into play. Lackner formulates architectural ideas, whether in his works for the young or for the church, that proceed to a realm beyond the strong rhetoric of his formal vocabulary. Outstanding examples of this may be seen in his Neu-Arzl church near Innsbruck [1958-1960]; the Völs Church in the Tyrol [1965-1967]; and the School and Boarding School of the Ursulines at Innsbruck [1971-1979].

Gustav Peichl, aside from his work as a caricaturist (*Ironismus*), became known chiefly for his regional broadcasting studios for Austrian radio (ORF-Landestudios) in Linz, Salzburg, Innsbruck, and Dornbrin from 1968 to 1973. Their futuristic styling is on the one hand the last instance of the nostalgia for a technological architecture apparent during the 1960s, and on the other an impressive aesthetic interpretation of the radio station's power of information. A historical connection with Futurism can be taken altogether literally; the glorification of technical progress even permits association with the idea of a battleship, so that these buildings not only represent working equipment but, beyond that, symbolize technical might.

Anton Schweighofer, although also a Holzmeister student like those mentioned above, is the most difficult to fit into the traditional Viennese context since his architectural vocabulary reflects, instead, international trends. The meaning of his work resides for the most part in strongly sociologically and anthropologically motivated interpretations of building requirements [City for Children at Vienna, 1969-1974, Zwettl Hospital, 1970-1979] that show a kind of humanization for which there are few examples in Viennese conceptions of architecture.

In the context of the generation of architects who are now in their fifties we must mention Hans Puchhammer and Gunther Wawrik as well as Ottokar Uhl. Although coming from different schools, they share in the architectural spectrum of the 1960s. In his early church buildings, such as the assembly churches (*Montagekirchen*) in Vienna [Siemenstrasse, 1963-1968; Kundratstrasse, 1967] Uhl strove towards a nonsacred, demystified, demonumentalized, and desymbolized architecture which, in its denial of semantics, arrived almost automatically at an antihistorical and antiarchitectonic position. Therefore, it is probably also consistent that, in residential building, his efforts to obtain extensive input from his clients were so important as to become a preoccupation for him and led to such highly disreputable results as his badly built residential project at Hollabrun [1971-1977]. The buildings of Puchhammer and Wawrik are less controversial and formally almost indefinable. They are all oriented toward the same sort of problems and show an emphasized but not formalized sense of the technology of building. Their entire wavelength is visible in a difficult augmentation of the Burgenland Landesmuseum in the former Jewish ghetto of Eisenstadt [1966-1976]

The most important of the regional developments, with the exception of the Tyrol where Lackner, Parson, Hörmann, and Norer, among others, are active is in Graz, Styria, which during the 1960s was the site of an especially active technical university where teachers such as Ferdinand Schuster and Hubert Hoffman, especially, had a great influence. Contrary to Vienna, the Graz milieu reacted more quickly and more decisively to international currents, but at the cost of a certain discontinuity of development. While the *Werkgruppe Graz*, including Eugen Gross and Friedrich Gross-Rannsbach, Werner Holomey, and Hermann Pichler, was inspired from the first by

Konrad Wachsmann, the early works of Günther Domenig and Eilfried Huth were outgrowths of the Swiss wave of the late fifties, in particular of the work of Walter Förderer [for example, the Commercial College, St. Gall, 1957-1963; and the Secondary School at Aesch near Basel, 1958-1962]. The emphatically spatial-plastic direction of this architecture, however, was soon superseded by a technical, structural phase in which an expressive sense of architectural space was further intensified, as in Trigon '67 and the restaurant pavilion of the Olympic swimming pool building in Munich [1972]. The paths of Domenig and Huth diverged in the early 1970s. Domenig pursued his sublime visions of space with enormous perseverance, as in the branch offices of the Central Savings Bank of Vienna (fig. 9.6) at Favoriten [1975-1979]; while Huth was engaged in problems of client participation in housing development, as at the *Deutschlandsberg* [1974-1978].

Linz with its own economy represents another regional center. Next to heavy industry such as the steelworks of VÖEST – Alpine AG, the proximity of the Federal Republic of Germany is decisive for architecture here. A strong practical orientation and a certain openness toward technical problems is characteristic of architects in this area. Thus, relatively early, one finds there a coming-to-grips with problems posed by synthetic materials in building, for instance in the work of Karl Odorizzi [the Koch commercial firm, Grieskirchen, 1968-1969 and the School Center, Härter Plateau, Leonding, 1971-1975]; and a stronger concern with prefabrication and flexibility in residential housing, for example in projects by the *Werkgruppe Linz* (Helmut Frohnwieser, Heinz Pammer, Edgar Telesko, Helmut Werthgarner) as at the development (*Wohnanlage*) *Flexibles Wohnen* [Linz, 1976-1978].

Generally, one can claim that in the provinces of Austria, since buildings were more easily perceived in the broader surroundings, and since more dynamic economic changes occurred there, architects had greater opportunities to articulate their ideas of building. At the same time their colleagues in Vienna, who would not accommodate to conditions, built hardly anything. This situation, however, resulted in the fact that in the Vienna milieu there were more lively, many-sided discussions of architectural theory. More skeptical, more remote from nature, and perhaps more cynical, the architect had less occasion to experiment with reality and to make mistakes. This resulted often in his overloading small building commissions with ideas, for instance Hans Hollein's Candle Shop in Retti, since whenever the architect had occasion to realize a project he wanted to demonstrate all of his thinking exhaustively.

9.6. Günther Domenig, architect. Central Savings Bank of Vienna, Favoriten Branch Office. Vienna, 1975-1979. (Photograph: Courtesy of Margherita Krischanitz)

If the 1960s may be characterized by dynamic building activity and by a diversity of architectonic statements, then the 1970s reflected in part a much changed situation. Not only the decline in building activity and the beginnings of a dominance of architecture "factories," which have receded somewhat in importance since then, but also a new understanding of architecture by the younger generation are responsible for this change. For a large group of students and young architects, the politicization of architecture at least theoretically and its related verbalization, their radical questioning and denunciation of architecture as "the instrument of bourgeois domination," led in part into the cognate fields of spatial planning, basic research, and sociology. And so, there was a rekindling of interest in architectural history that again stimulated architectural discussion.

One can state expressly that in Vienna from the start there was a considerable willingness to define architecture anew, as was being attempted chiefly in America and Italy in the wake of the criticism of Functionalism. In Vienna one had, so to speak, always practiced this expanded conception of architecture, without, and that is also typical, making theoretical capital out of it.

Furthermore, one may state that the so-called Post-Modern scene in Vienna is very lively. If one looks forward from the viewpoint of the progenitors such as Günther Feuerstein or Hans Hollein and the "tradition" reaching back into the fifties, to a line of thought linked with that of Josef Frank and once again topical in the late seventies, then the bases of contemporary discussions may be found in the sixties. Hans Hollein, with his "ritualizing aesthetics," his method of montage, his arrangements of meanings and constellations of quotations, created a kind of unreality that had had its societal function in the psychological mechanism of repression in Vienna since the Baroque era. But the history and wealth of buildings of Vienna offer an inexhaustible reservoir of realities, so that no boundaries are set to limit an "expanded range of vision." Thus, the "ironic quotations" of Hermann Czech [Kleines Café, 1973-1974 and Wunder-Bar, 1974-1975, both in Vienna] presuppose the theory of an Adolf Loos, the ambivalence of his precise statements, indeed even their multiplicity in a new context. The works of the "Missing Link" group, Adi Krischanitz and Otto Kapfinger, which consist of different means of expression that arise from a "constant overlapping, intersection and opposition," show their fascination with the phenomenology of Viennese historical reality. Another team, "Igirien," that includes Werner Appelt, Eberhard Kneissl, and Elsa Prochazka, tries to include the range of the aesthetic of everyday life and commerce in their projects, such as the multipurpose hall of the church on Rennbahngasse [Vienna 1977]. Their theme is "pretty monotony," perhaps a Post-Modern variation of Uhl's position against an academic conception of architecture.

Helmut Grimmer, who died in 1975, and Heinz Tesar take a decidedly different position. Grimmer, who left us only drawings, emphatically warned against the autonomy of an architecture that did not serve the world but rather represented a world of its own. Just as decidedly, Heinz Tesar attempts to effect a total architecture, the role of which is derived from the dialectics of autonomy and dependence, society and the individual, law and freedom, responsibility and the ironic, reality and interpretation, and in the realm of building, the typical and the exceptional. In other words, he tries to see architecture again in its entire complexity of relationships and interconnections [for example, in his Sound Studio Pier, Steinach am Brenner, Tyrol, 1974-1976; in a house in Riedenthal, southern quarter of Vienna, 1974-1980; and in the Unternberg Church, Salzburg, 1976-1979].

The Vienna scene has been further enriched in recent years since Rob Krier accepted a teaching position in that city. Undoubtedly because of this a new frame of reference is nascent in Vienna, one which as yet has hardly been reflected in the works of others. In the ongoing discusison of architecture changes have already taken place, even though, in all likelihood, we must still await their realizations.

Vienna has a long tradition of creating opposing realities. Building and building industry go their separate ways, dictated by different laws. Architects see their field as an artistic one, in the foreground of which lies an interest in effects, symbols, and meanings. Scenarios of destruction here have always generated new life. In this the architectural scene remains unchanged and promises to remain so for a long time to come.

*Bibliography**

BOOKS

Österreichische Architektur. Exhibition Catalog of the Zentralvereinigung der Architekten Österreichs. Vienna: *Der Bau*, 1961.

Achleitner, Friedrich et al. *Neue Architektur in Österreich, 1945-1970*. Edited by Johannes M. Treytl. Vienna: Bohmann, 1970.

______. *Österreichische Architektur im 20. Jahrhundert*. 3 vols. Vol. 1: *Oberösterreich, Salzburg, Tirol, Vorarlberg*. Salzburg: Residenz Verlag, June 1980.

______. "Vorwort." *Heinz Tesar, Vorformen, Entwürfe, Verwirklichungen*. 1978.

Feuerstein, Günther. *Vienna, Present and Past*. Edited by Vienna Tourist Board. Vienna: Jugend and Volk, 1974.

Holzmeister, Clemens. *Architekt in der Zeitenwende: Clemens Holzmeister*. Zürich: Verlag das Bergland Buch, 1976.

Schwanzer, Karl and Feuerstein, Günther *Wiener Bauten, 1900 bis Heute*. Vienna, 1964.

Uhl, Ottokar. *Moderne Architektur in Wien*. Vienna: Schrollverlag, 1966.

JOURNALS

Achleitner, Friedrich, ed. "Österreich." (with English summary) *Bauen und Wohnen* 19,9 (1965): 335-78.

______. "Österreichische Architektur im 20. Jahrhundert," 1, 2," *Deutsches Architektenblatt* 10, 11, (1978).

______. "Österreichische Architektur der Gegenwart." *Österrerichische Architektur 1945-1975*. Catalog, 1976.

"Josef Hoffman" (in Japanese). *Architecture and Urbanism* 2, no. 4 (April 1972): 79-94.

"Junge Architekten in Österreich." *Bauen und Wohnen* 30, no. 4 (April 1976): 113-52.

Pontoizeau, Yvetley and Cousin, Jean-Pierre, eds. "Autriche." *L'Architecture d'Aujourd'hui* 151 (August 1970): 2-53, 65-72, 76-79, 86-106.

*Augmented by the Montreal editorial staff.

10

BELGIUM

JEAN BARTHELEMY

Belgium is no doubt one of the Western European countries most resistant to objective analysis. Rarely are her split communities, her arcane sociopolitical scenes, and her cultural ambiguities accurately perceived by outside observers. Could this be the price paid by a small, relatively artificially created state, whose history and geographic situation have placed it in the middle of English pragmatism, German efficiency, and French cerebralism? This heterogeneity results in advantages as well as disadvantages. A melting pot where divergent points of view confront each other, Belgium is rich in its efforts to assimilate and harmonize contradictory influences. Architecture, a faithful reflection of this complexity, is full of such influences. Regions that gather together so many "architectural models" from the most mediocre to the most remarkable, from the most pretentious to the most subdued, must be rare in the world.

Research into the underlying reasons for this situation is surely interesting, but for those who live daily with the incongruities and contradictions of Belgium, concern and engagement with the inevitable accompanying polemic discourse and scathing slogans are necessary. "Belgium is the ugliest country in the world" proclaimed Renaat Braem.[1] If this awareness of the generalized damage to our environment is fully justified, its harsh phraseology is exaggerated—the ardent cry of a man in revolt rather than the quiet conclusion of an analytic mind. There are many countries that could legitimately compete with Belgium for this hardly enviable claim to fame. Chaos, unhappily, is universal. In comparing, for example, the world image of Belgium with that of Holland or of Germany, the disorder here is more flagrant and widespread. On the other hand, space is allocated on a much more sensitive, personal basis and diversification is more attractive. Compared with French chaos, it is less brutal, even less rudimentary. A variety of structures and a picturesque quality in their ornamentation often express by their very naiveté, a sort of sympathetic tenderness toward the physical environment.

In any case, Belgian architecture is struggling in a manifestly difficult cultural context. Though historical eclecticism can only be found in the form of a few antiquated facades, a geographic eclecticism still enjoys great prestige. The desire to build a Provençal villa beneath the evergreens of the Ardennes or a Swiss chalet on the coast remains vital, fed in fact by many attractive magazine presentations and the prospectuses of real estate promoters. The sometimes insoluble administrative difficulties and the increasing politicization of public commissions certainly do nothing to clear the atmosphere. That remarkable architectural works surge forth from this cauldron is miraculous and may be explained only by the stubbornness of man, made more combative and often less dogmatic by the difficulties of the situation.

Prisoner to this ambience of incessant confrontation and subject to such a variety of diverse constraints, it is not surprising that Belgian architecture at its most innovative does not project the coherent strength of, for instance, Danish and Swiss schools. Is this the reason that international architectural

Translated from the French by Elise Bernatchez.

criticism, naturally more inclined toward Cartesian classifications than toward complex analysis, seems to have frozen the Belgian contribution to the development of contemporary architecture at the Art Nouveau stage, as if Victor Horta and Henry van der Velde had managed mysteriously to suspend time? For example, G. E. Kidder Smith judges Belgian architecture in a very rudimentary manner; three multistoried buildings attracted his attention in a very brief overview. The rest seemed insignificant to him. "Several other buildings are of general interest and merit a cursory glance but the total situation is lamentable."[2] Such an opinion without nuance is without depth and can only be based on preconceived ideas and insufficient information. In his defense, it must be admitted that, without reference to one or another guidebook or journal article that would draw one's attention to some few among the more current architectural works, one is very much deprived, whatever the country being visited. Very rarely does a chance excursion lead to the convent of La Tourette! And in 1961, when Kidder Smith wrote, Belgium was noticeably poor in architectural monographs. Happily, since then many serious works have helped fill this grievous gap.

In view of the almost complete lack of information on Belgian architecture between the two world wars, a few historical reminders seem necessary for us to understand the more recent movements. The creation in 1926, under the direction of Henry van der Velde, of the Institut Supérieur des Arts Décoratif, better known as *La Cambre*, was a major event in the development of Belgian architecture, for it was there that most of the architects who became prominent after 1945 were trained. Each of their professors, whether Victor Bourgeois, Antoine Pompe,[3] Jean Eggericx, or Louis Herman De Koninck, participated actively and directly in the Modern Movement in architecture. Each affected the actions of his disciples profoundly in two ways: imparting a seemingly unshakable confidence in Modernism and a meticulous approach to building studies. Let us remember that, as early as 1924, Louis Herman De Koninck[4] built a villa on Fond'Roy avenue in which everything was novel, from the astonishing quality of its interior spaces to its quite original central-heating system. The residence for the painter Lenglet, built in 1926, with its standard kitchen that became a model for industrialization in 1930, and its system of modular construction constitute proofs of continuous research actualized. Long ignored outside a limited circle, his contribution was recently reinstated by Michel Ragon[5] and Dennis Sharp.[6] The homage paid by Walter Gropius to Victor Bourgeois is also worthy of mention: "The members of the CIAM knew his 'Cité Moderne,' built in 1922, and considered it as an avant-garde complex that already applied many progressive ideas in the field of urbanism and the physical environment, ideas for which the CIAM was working and fighting. . . . His work as an architect and as an urbanist should be recognized as a creative contribution of permanent value for the human habitat of modern times."[7]

The decade following the war of 1940-1945 should, in retrospect, be considered as the most somber for Belgian architecture and the only one that can justify G. E. Kidder Smith's severity. Whether one looks at the construction of public buildings, at the development of new areas, or at the theoretical bases for action, the same uniformly neutral picture appears. The malaise was total. It seems that the faith that had animated the leading lights of the prewar period was extinguished. Comparison between two works of Léon Stijnen, who was Director of *La Cambre* for many years and who, in his position, could have transmitted the "van der Velde spirit," bears witness to its loss. The Elsdonck residence at Wilrijk, built in 1933, carries within it a great many characteristics of nobility and conceptual freshness, while the Meirburg administrative building at Antwerp, built in 1949, breathes boredom. For many, Gaston Eysselinck's Main Post Office at Ostende [built 1939, completed after 1951] is practically the only example of an architecture without compromise in the period immediately following the war. Commenting on the difficulties he encountered during the development of this project, the architect himself was surprised at the disenchantment of his colleagues. "I had to face," he writes, "opposition from the city-planning consultant of Ostende, the architect Eggericx, which is all the more disappointing because he used to be part of a revolutionary group in matters of architecture. . . . I would have been willing to accept criticism from the architect he once was, but not from the one he had become."[8]

The construction of community housing followed the same process. Before the war, a number of collective settlements, the Kappelleveld Garden City in Woluwé-Saint Lambert by Antoine Pompe [1922]-1926] and those of Boitsfort by Louis Van der Swaelmen and Jean-J. Eggericx [1921-1930][9] show a sensitivity in their constant awareness of the scale of constructed volumes and of the configuration of the landscape. The period immediately after the war leaves us only with soulless stereotypes of cities; administrative establishments dependent on the chance availability of building sites; and the reduction of projects to the strict execution of the banal "model" and hundredfold repetition.

This period was also characterized by a phenomenon which, upon reflection, is akin to geographic eclecticism. It was the awe with which progressive architects looked upon some few great international models that they discovered from 1952 on, such as the Lever House by Skidmore, Owings and Merrill [1951-1952], dazzling symbol of economic success, and the Unité d'Habitation at Marseille [1947-1952], the ultimate result of a complete theory of the habitat created by the magic of Le Corbusier. A point of departure for the curtain-wall technique in Belgium, the National Insurance building [1956] in Brussels, the work of Antwerp architect Hugo van Kuyck, affected the imagination of a large number of promoters because of the brilliant reflections of its aluminum and because of its blue balustrades. They immediately perceived, in this gaudy disguise, an infallible method to entice their clientele. On the other hand, city planning consistent with the Charter of Athens was to be practiced with more or less success in some new zones added to the cities. The Droixhe Plain, at Liège, begun in 1951 by the Egau group of Charles Carlier, Hyacinthe Lhoest, and Jules Mozin; and the Cité Kiel at Antwerp, erected since 1950 by Renaat Braem (who had worked, and we emphasize this, in Le Corbusier's studio in 1936) in association with the architects Victor Maeremans and Henri Maes, are two of the most coherent examples of the urbanist apartment building model, a model which has been rightly questioned since then. The apartment house built by Willy Van der Meeren in 1954 at Evere is worthy of particular attention. Not much of a conformist, he understood the dangers to one's individuality of a system that was intractable and, making use of the motto of the Société Commanditaire (Credit Bank), "To each his own dwelling," he took the prerogative of including in his design all that could give an enclosure a sense of independent, diversified space, such as private interior staircases, pathways, set-back terraces, and so forth.[10]

Finally, until 1958, the year of the Brussels World's Fair, the most important architectural event would go unnoticed—that is, the meeting of two cultured and enthusiastic Walloon architects, Jacques Dupuis and Roger Bastin, the former from the Borinage, the other from the Namur area. The same age, both had studied under Jean Eggericx and Victor Bourgeois at *La Cambre* a few years before the war. They remained faithful to the van der Velde message of keeping an open mind, avoiding prejudgments, and remaining honest in all one's dealings. From the active intellectual emulation of these two strong personalities the original architecture missing in Belgium gradually began to appear—an art of synthesis that, without ignoring any of the most recent international tendencies, remained above all faithful to its own roots and environment. Roger Bastin expressed the spirit of their inquiry perfectly:

> Before the war I felt the impact of the religious architecture of the Rhineland [Rudolf Schwarz, Dominikus Böhm]. After the war, I travelled to Scandinavia with Jacques Dupuis. Nordic architecture [Erik Gunnar Asplund and then Alvar Aalto] was a revelation. Furthermore, the general postwar climate was marked by the haunting presence of the inaccessible Le Corbusier. All these influences were tempered by a love for rural buildings, for the value of their integration with the site, their unity and their unpretentiousness.[11]

Their first significant collaborative realization was at Malmédy in 1948 with two groups of modest housing in which the vocabulary of regional architecture was resuscitated.[12] At a time when others, clouded by cubistic aesthetics, continued to impose aggressive forms whatever the environment, both Bastin and Dupuis continued to seek an architecture of high quality that was responsive to the countryside. At a time when Le Corbusier, with all his prestige, was ridiculing sloping roofs in the name of liberated roofing, whatever one says today, much intelligence and courage was needed to resist the fiat of the Modern Movement.

Roger Bastin's studio at Namur was, during this period, a privileged place where young Walloon architects—notable among the most gifted, Charles Vandenhove and Lucien Kroll—came not to find prescriptions but to forge an attitude of honesty and depth. Bastin's very important work, the church of Sart-en-Fagne constructed in 1965, particularly reveals his originality. It may be that today, under the pressure of superficial reactions, we would have wanted to save the neo-Gothic construction which towered above the village and keep it unchanged at all costs. The solution adopted was certainly more radical but, far from being a break with the neighborhood, it became largely a reinsertion of the church into the structural fabric of the physical environment. The church was built in proper scale, jutting out over the roofs, but not disproportionately so. The surface of the roof harmonizes with the usual roofing in the vicinity, the walls are in accord with nearby masonries, and it would seem that this form has been timelessly crystallized in the style of the surrounding buildings.[13]

Jacques Dupuis occupies a privileged position among Walloon architects because of the originality of his thinking and the elegance of his talent.[14] After the period of collaboration with Roger Bastin, he built a kindergarten at Frameries in 1953[15] and a series of very interesting individual houses in the vicinity of Mons between 1952 and 1962. Especially striking in these are, on the one hand, the suppleness and variety of their organic composition and, on the other, an almost filial submission to the great tradition of rural architecture of the Hainault. Here volumes are articulated with whitened bricks under slate roofs; subtleties of the details of the edges give the roofing delicacy and lightness; poetic dialogue takes place with the natural surroundings; and the interior spaces, always unexpectedly different in their plays of light, are tailored to the needs of each family. Cubism no longer constrains. Jacques Dupuis does not yield to any aesthetic dogma, accepting only respect for the site and the fluidity of spaces as guides for his fertile inspirations.[16]

From 1956 a parallel movement appeared at the other end of the country, at Nieuport. Peter Callebout built a sort of little holiday village in the rear dunes. Here the Nordic influence is particularly evident, with subtle trails through the trees, long horizontal lines emphasizing the flatlands, unconstrained interior spaces, and natural wood railings.[17] Not far away, a few years later, another settlement was erected at St. André, near Bruges, with the same concern for essentials, intimacy, and accommodation to the natural setting. In one of these houses, built by Paul Félix for the sculptor Bonduel [1963], the exposed concrete ceilings abruptly disengage from the walls of the facade to allow light to penetrate completely into the studio.[18] In another, the Brys house [1961], Jean Tanghe developed an organic construction which was slipped horizontally in beneath the tree foliage and showed a clarity of planning and an excellence of structure in which exterior spaces harmoniously prolonged its internal composition.[19] The convent of the Clarist nuns, Het Zonnelied, at Mariakerke, built in 1957 by Paul Félix, may also be considered as an important stage in the development of architecture in Belgium.[20] Its rather austere exterior appearance scarcely distinguishes it from the poverty of the surrounding neighborhood, while on the interior the bricks and the natural concrete harmonize in an unpolished accord, in keeping with the Franciscan spirit. The general design, simple and orderly, defines a series of interior gardens of various dimensions. But the most impressive lesson in this building is the exemplary dialogue which during the two years of construction saw a perfect understanding between the architect and his clients.

That the Brussels World's Fair of 1958 had an impact is unquestionable. But that such impact was not always positive was itself predictable from the ambiguity of this type of exercise, which usually has more to do with stunning than with educating. Typically enough, a very well-conducted survey showed that the French Pavilion, an enormous mastodon based on superfluous structural acrobatics, was the most appreciated by the public. On the other hand, the very subtle urbanistic experimentations of the Italian Pavilion by Ernesto N. Rogers, Enrico Peressutti, and Lodovico Barbiano di Belgioioso, with its tangle of volumes and open urban density, held the attention of only some few curious people. The exhibition was, nevertheless, the occasion that a few young Belgian architects seized upon to distinguish themselves. The group formed by Robert Courtois, Henry Montois, Thierry Hoet, Frédérique Seghers, Jacques Goossens-Bara, and Albert Moens de Hase in association with the engineer Abraham Lipski received the Reynolds Prize for the very airy structure of the Transportation Pavilion;[21] while the architects Lucien Baucher, Jean-Pierre Blondel, and Odette Filippone, with engineer René Sarger, conceived for Marie Thumas a pavilion made of sheets and steel chains which gained the admiration of the specialists.[22] Numerous national distinctions (Van de Ven Prize, 1958; National Prize for Lodgings, 1960, and more) and several publications in foreign magazines have very justly pointed out the interest in houses constructed by this group in the vicinity of Brussels. These houses are lively, well-articulated, pleasant to live in, and installed without damage to their site. A style responds, when all is said and done, to the main features of the geographical and cultural environment.[23]

However, aside from these satisfactions, "the period after Expo, in the 60's, is characterized in Belgium, as everywhere else, by the invasion of modern design. Modern buildings were erected everywhere and in complete disorder. These included apartment buildings, modern villas and factories; all marked, some more than others, by architectonic ambitions which, *grosso modo*, reduced them all to a ridiculous search for prestige."[24]

In this very incongruous group of office buildings, among the several that could be cited in Brussels to exemplify an abundant panoply of international models, the Banque Lambert [1959] by Skidmore, Owings and Merrill, the Headquarters of Glaverbel [1967], Watermael-Boitsfort by André Jacqmain, Victor Mulpas, Pierre Guilissen, and Renaat Braem, and the Headquarters of the United Cement and Brickworkers [1970], opposite the Glaverbel building, by Constantin L. Brodzki and Marcel Lambrichts have in fact been included in many exhibitions and presentations abroad. However, one must also mention the incomparable Foncolin Building on Montoyer Street, by André Jacqmain and Jules Wabbes, since, as the oldest of them all [1958], and after more than twenty years, this building is so perfectly integrated into the business district that it remains an object of admiration.[25] Inside one appreciates the play of lines and reliefs, the rightness of its proportions and its binary rhythm. For the first time, the design of the concrete galleries supported by elegant metal tie-beams accompanied by planks of exotic wood created the same dynamism of the facades which ensured the success of the Banque Lambert.

Especially notable is that almost inscrutable personality, André Jacqmain, an elegant aesthete, always surprising, always prepared for the paradoxical. "Immense space, this is what interests me, that is to say beyond our ordinary world. The extent of this space is thus not what we usually deal with; it is related to man, and sublimely to the natural environment. Inordinate space is beyond measure, as architects say, and more exactly beyond our everyday scale and normal conventions."[26] In a work that tackles the most varied of programs, the realistic argument is blurred when faced with problems of form. The architect likes to please himself, and his intelligence often permits him to please others as well. The private museum and Urvater dwelling at Rhode-St.-Genèse, built in 1960, a sort of explosion of spaces and staggered levels, illustrates this formal exuberance that so impresses some but also irritates others.[27]

One really must contrast a work by Constantin L. Brodzki,[28] the Gallo-Roman lapidary museum at Montauban-Buzenol,[29] with the Urvater Museum. Situated on a wooded promontory in the extreme south of Belgium, this tiny building was included by the Museum of Modern Art in New York in a 1963 exhibition of museums round the world from the previous decade. Here the architecture is so discreet, so precise, and so natural that one is unaware of it when viewing the museum's Roman remains, leaving these with all of their fascinating and meditative strengths.

Could this tendency toward an extreme reduction of essentials signify a return to the so-called "architecture without architects"? Undoubtedly, yet not exactly, for one could only contemplate such a return at the price of a coherent collective effort that would have to be titanic after decades of individualism, regulations, specialization, and commercialism. But one cannot doubt that it is the testimony of a new awareness of the architect who, without renouncing his artistic mission, tries to respond more to a social project that surpasses daily consideration than to anecdotal formalist aspirations. In any case, this is the main thesis supported by Geert Bekaert in the very fine monograph he devoted to Charles Vandenhove. In its frontispiece we read: "There is no more architecture since architects have entered upon the scene."[30] This is paradoxical for all who know the work of Charles Vandenhove. Always thoroughly thought through, carefully structured and polished, his work is so very well accomplished and complex that it must depend upon a transcendental professional competence, a sort of quintessence of the profession.

In fact, it is less in the definitive form than in the architectural process that one finds the key to this paradox. The architecture of the architect is by definition one in which the personality of the planner immediately imposes itself. Any references to whatever could interfere with this imposition are immediately rejected. By a reductive method, the program is schematized to become no more than a pretext for plastic invention. The creative process of Charles Vandenhove is dramatically opposed to this method. It is, on the contrary, with an exemplary conscientiousness that he devotes himself to the proposed program. He dismantles it, dissects it, submits each one of its elements to his analytic screening, and evaluates the program in terms of the timeless and the universal. He discards any and all anecdotal aspects. He refines it, and when, with his indefatigable patience, he has managed to discover all of the program's resources and all of its interrelationships, he recomposes it and develops it into a system whose aim is to transcend time. Obstinately, he seeks the right nuance which, in his mind, means a flawless authenticity, an overpowering presence and, finally, an internal coherence within the project down to its smallest details.

The work of Charles Vandenhove can be considered in successive phases that constitute the stages of a long development of thought. A first phase dating from 1958 was the mortuary clinic at Liège that was soon augmented and completed [1962] with the addition of a blood-transfusion center. Their long ochre walls, their copper finishing and their natural teak woodwork set the tone of an organic, sobre, and refined architecture.[31] A second phase may be associated most notably with the Headquarters of the National Institute of the Coal Industry at Liège [designed 1960, built 1962-1965][32] and his private residence on Chauve-Souris Street [Li6ege, 1963].[33] The concern with flexibility in adapting a building to its site, the attention paid to regulations affecting public ways, and the care taken to emphasize these by means of flawless staircases, is confirmed; and at the Student Residence Lucien Brull, Liège [designed 1962, built 1964-1967], a rigor of very geometric planes is added, organizing the space without constraining it.[34] Then from 1963, a third phase (fig. 10.1) included the University Institute of Physical Education

10.1. Charles Vandenhove, architect. University Institute of Physical Education. Liège, 1963-1969. (Photograph: Courtesy of the architect)

[1969], in which a series of large basilicalike hall buildings was developed in successive levels on one of the slopes of the Sart Tilman.[35] A masterwork, this building has solid concrete windbreaking gables arranged in a sequence inspired by the terrain, Long roofs, after rising to catch the light better at their summit, fall onto long rhythmic panels of glass. The Schoffeniels house [1969] at Olne[36] and the Standard omnisports hall at Aúgrée [1968],[37] conceived on vastly differing scales, demonstrate all the potentialities of a central plan and of pyramidal space. The enlargement of his own home in 1974 (fig. 10.2)

10.2. Charles Vandenhove, architect. Interior of the architect's home. Liège, 1974. (Photograph: Courtesy of François Her/Viva)

marks still another experience.[38] Breaking with the original architectonic system, the new glass roofing, supported by an original tubular structure, crowns the house with such ease that the first phase of construction seems to have been nothing more than a preliminary base. The University Medical Center at Sart Tilman [1978-1981] will become, without doubt, a landmark that will take its place in the evolution of hospitals.[39] Some young architects around Charles Vandenhove have been inspired by the same philosophy and the the same love for work well done. In this way a sort of school has been created in which Bruno Albert has the major role.[40] Furthermore, one must mention the fundamental contribution of the engineer and architect René Greisch to the spirit that animates this entire group and to the structural design of its projects.

By concerning ourselves with some works by Jan Tanghe, André Jacqmain, Constantin Brodzki, and Charles Vandenhove we have clearly entered the present. Thus, it is necessary to try to clarify somewhat a situation that the perspective of time does not yet permit us to understand easily. To facilitate this, it is worthwhile to inquire into the major preoccupations that motivate the Belgian architectural milieu, ignoring, of course, various current squabbles.

The passion caused by the issue of industrialization of construction more than ten years ago, has calmed down. Many of the projects of Jean Englebert,[41] for instance, embodying all of his convictions concerning rebuilding and industrialization, have faded away. Perhaps they will become evident again, though many doubt this because the necessary demographic conditions no longer exist and much of our architectural heritage no longer appears to be unsuitable for contemporary use. Since large prestigious constructions no longer figure prominently in the broad urbanistic context, they are no longer compelling issues. The despoiling of urban and rural sites was so flagrant and the memory of the aesthetic reasons invoked to justify so many architectural urbanistic crimes is still so fresh that this continuing disaffection with large constructions is particularly justified.

It is in the shifting of public opinion that the major concerns of Belgium's architects in the early 1980s must be found. In fact, many private associations, spontaneously created since 1968, are trying to improve the environment; and in 1975, the European architectural heritage year, many local committees were formed. These associations and committees threw themselves into the battle at an opportune moment in order to reanimate architectural research, assigning to it three objectives: integration of architecture with its sites; revitalization of historic centers; democratization of urbanism. All of this implies a greater participation in all aspects of the architectural process by those who are to use the finished structures.

Of course research into better ways of inserting architecture into its site is not new. But suddenly, the theories of Jean François, which were neglected for too long a time, are resurgent and the merits of architectural discretion are finally being widely recognized.[42] In Belgium, whenever the dialogue between architecture and its natural environment is brought up, one must mention the name of Jean Cosse,[43] for he defined his concept of architecture very clearly, summarizing it in these words: "an idea that tends to create a specific architecture is like the emanation of a place; an architecture that plunges its roots into the subsoil from which we all come."[44] Many private houses built in Wallonia, such as the Toussaint house at Waterloo [1965], perfectly exemplify this. But some more developed rural and religious programs have confirmed the continuity and authenticity of an approach profoundly sensitive to the characteristics of "place": the public stables at Arville [Van de Ven Prize, 1962];[45] the agricultural estate at Glabais [Maison Européenne Prize, 1965];[46] a grouping of houses at Ciney [1967]; and the church of St. Paul at Waterloo [1968].[47] The St. André of Clerlande Monastery[48] at Ottignies particularly exemplifies an organic architecture (fig. 10.3) that emphasizes a sequence of hospitable interior spaces, a sobriety of means, and the harmonizing of forms within their site. The rhythm of its glass windows answers the tight vertical sequence of pine trees, and the leather color of its bricks extends the surrounding ochres of the underbrush. But this unity with the countryside should not make one forget how much the sculptural intent of this composition is strongly centered on the creation of an atmosphere for active prayer.

10.3. Jean Cosse, architect. Monastery St. André de Clerlande. Ottignies, 1970. (Photograph: Courtesy of the architect)

The Antwerp architect, Georges Baines,[49] follows a parallel road with a similar respect for the environment in, for example, the Gentils home and studio and the Reypens house [Van de Ven Prize, 1968].[50] In 1977 another house built between party walls, at Wilrijk, was awarded the Maskens Prize (fig. 10.4). The complex geometry of its interior spaces and the transparency of its large veranda facing the garden give this work a character of luminosity and freedom that is astonishing for a house of this type. In Corsica, faced with a completely different site dominated by stone, Claude Strebelle[51] built the Oceanographic Research Station of the University of Liège,[52] following an organic development which provided yet another very sculptural facet of the renewed association between architecture and nature.

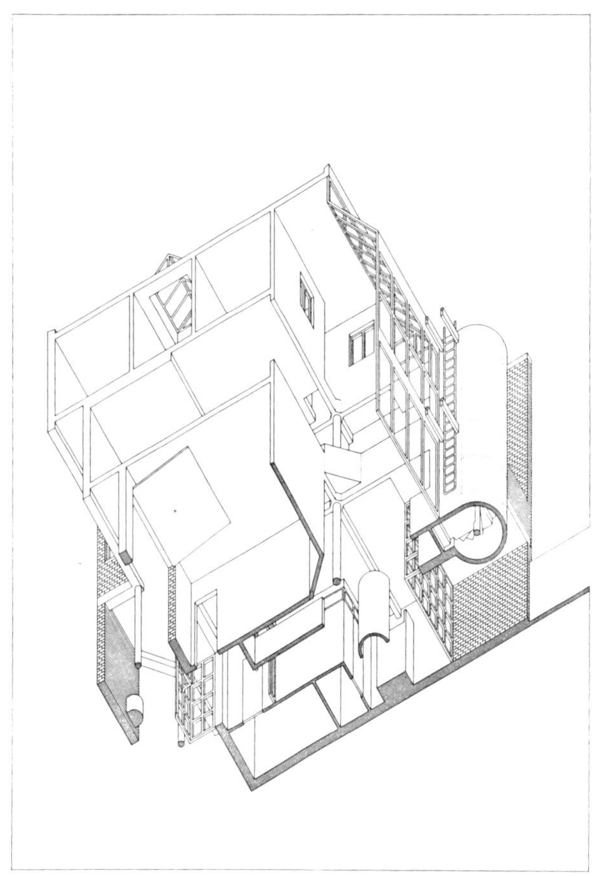

10.4. Georges Baines, architect. House at Wilrijk, orthogonal drawing, 1977. (Photograph: Courtesy of the architect)

The reutilization of historical centers constitutes a second research theme which manifestly interested many architects, particularly the younger ones. In 1964 the restoration of the Grand Beguinage of Louvain (fig. 10.5) was started under the direction of Raymond Lemaire.[53] The reutilization of this monumental complex, which had been destined for demolition, as student dormitories certainly played a decisive psychological role in affecting the new awareness of the potential of our architectural heritage. On the outside, the signs of our era appear only in small discreet touches such as concrete lintels and new fenestration, but, inside, the space has been completely modernized. The marvelous framework of the old infirmary, for instance, is visible over panels of polished wood, which are not far from a perfectly designed open concrete fireplace. The colors are cheerful. A new life begins. In its turn the Grand Hornu, majestic testimony to nineteenth-

10.5. Raymond Lemaire, architect. Restoration of the Grand Beguinage of Louvain; 1964. (Photograph: Courtesy of the architect)

century industrial architecture, has been saved thanks to the intervention of the architect Henri Guchez. Since then, architects like André Godart,[54] Jan Tanghe,[55] Bob Van Reeth,[56] Paul Van Aerschot,[57] Michel Lemmens,[58] Benoît Jonet [59] and Bruno Albert have brought their talents to bear on this type of problem. Charles Vandenhove also threw himself enthusiastically into the struggle for urban rehabilitation and presently is working on an ambitious project combining restoration and new construction in the historic quarter of Hors-Château at Liège.[60] The movement is gaining momentum.

In the urbanistic field, the city of Bruges, under pressure from a dynamic alderman, Dries van den Abeele, commissioned the Group Planning, headed by Jan Tanghe, for a study of its structural plan.[61] The excitement generated for the realization of this plan by the urban planners confers upon it the quality of a new model which, surpassing the principles of the Charter of Athens, seeks to encourage continuity in the urbanistic process while taking care not to smother its dynamism. It is symptomatic to note that, in order to establish the masterplan of the university city of Louvain-la-Neuve, another exceptional recent experiment, Raymond Lemaire, collaborating with Jean-Pierre Blondel, was largely inspired by the concept of the historic city, even clinging single-mindedly to the definition and scale of open spaces.[62] In 1978 the International Union of Architects took special note of this conception of urban design.

Apart from certain ecological projects,[63] the process of establishing master plans constitutes the latest area of research that has been of especial interest in Belgian architectural circles during the past few years. Lucien Kroll[64] is the unquestioned leader of all who are venturing into this difficult area. The intelligence and conviction he brings to this struggle command admiration. Difficulties and setbacks are certainly not unknown to him. His student dormitories[65] at Woluwé-St. Lambert [1974] are notable as the objects of a controversy which extends well beyond the borders of Belgium. Was user-participation here really authentic? Didn't the wish to radically oppose the dryness and inhumanity of barracks architecture with an architecture of chance take precedence over research that would have adapted to the wishes expressed by the future occupants? There are many questions that have plausible explanations only when we remember the extraordinary effervescence of ideas of May 1968. Neither the goal of better user-participation, nor the designing talents of Lucien Kroll may be doubted. On the contrary, the sociocultural distance still to be travelled in order to attain serenity and equilibrium in the sharing of tasks and responsibilities in architecture takes on its true dimensions. Kroll recognized that "collective creativity" will not come about spontaneously, but can only result from a long process of exercises, observations, examples, apprenticeships, and education.[66]

At the end of this view of recent developments in Belgian architecture there are many reasons for optimism. Recent and promising currents are developing that can bring greater coherence to the physical environment. Defiance is yielding to continuity and harmony. Who would not rejoice?

Notes

1. Renaat Braem, *Het lelijkste land ter wereld* (Louvain: Davidsfonds, 1968.)

2. G. E. Kidder Smith, *The New Architecture of Europe* (New York: World Publishing Company, 1961), p. 21.

3. Maurice Culot and François Terlinden, *Antoine Pompe et l'effort moderne en Belgique 1890-1940* (Ixelles: Editions Musée d'Ixelles, 1969).

4. Robert L. Delevoy and Maurice Culot, *L. H. De Koninck, architecte* (London: Architectural Association, 1973).

5. Michel Ragon, *Histoire mondiale de l'Architecture et l'Urbanisme moderne*, vol. 2 (Paris, 1972), pp. 203-4.

6. Dennis Sharp, *Visual History of Twentieth-Century Architecture* (Greenwich, Conn.: N.Y. Graphic Society, 1972), p. 83.

7. Culot and Terlinden, *Pompe*, p. 108.

8. W. Enzinck, "Interview avec G. Eysselinck," *Architecture* 1 (1948), p. 1.

9. Marcel Smets, *L'avènement de la cité-jardin en Belgique* (Brussels: Editions Pierre Mardaga, 1976), p. 128.

10. Gaston Esselinck, "Appartements 'jeder zijn huis,' Evere," *Architecture* 38 (1961), p. 689.

11. Geert Bekaert and Francis Strauven, *La Construction en Belgique 1945-1970* (Editions Confédération Nationale de la Construction, 1971), p. 263.

12. "Cité Mon Bijou, à Malmédy," *Architecture* 39-40 (1961), p. 733.

13. Jean Barthélemy, "Innovation et continuité," *A* + 53 (November 1978): 16.

14. Albert Bontridder, "Jacques Dupuis, ou l'architecture perdue et retrouvée" (special issue), *Architecture* (1955).

15. "Jardin d'enfants, Frameries," *Architecture* 39-40 (1961), p. 737.

16. "Habitations P. H. Franeau et G. Camus," *Architecture* 51 (1963), pp. 118-22.

17. Pierre Puttemans, *Architecture moderne en Belgique* (Brussels: Edition Vokaer, 1974), p. 186.

18. "Maison pour un artiste près de Bruges," *Architecture* 44 (1962), p. 42.

19. Ibid., p. 48.

20. "Monastère des Clarisses d'Ostende," *L'Architecture d'Aujourd'hui* 96 (June/July 1962): 62-65.

21. "Pavillon des transports," *La Maison* 7 (1958), p. 233.

22. "Pavillon Marie Thumas," *L'Architecture d'Aujour'hui* 78 (1958); Puttemans, *Architecture moderne*, p. 159.

23. "Sept Fontaines, Rhode-St-Genèse," *L'Architecture d'Aujourd'hui* 86 (1959); *La Maison* 11 (1959), pp. 364-65.

24. Bekaert and Strauven, *Construction*, p. 69.

25. André Jacqmain, *Zodiac* 2 (1958), p. 172; *Architecture* 27 (1959), pp. 160-61.

26. André Jacqmain, "Volumes intérieurs, en hauteur," *La Maison* 7-8 (1969).

27. "Musée privé et habitation Urvater, à Rhode-St-Genèse," *L'oeil* 88 (1962); and *Domus* 401 (1963).

28. R. L. D., "Constantin L. Brodzki," *Zodiac* 2 (1958).

29. "Musée lapidaire gallo-romain à Montauban-Buzenol (1959)," *Architecture* 44 (1962).

30. Geert Bekaert, *Charles Vandenhove* (Brussels: Editions Pierre Mardaga, 1976), p. iii.

31. "Clinique Mortuaire, rue Dos-Fauchon, à Liège (1958-1961)," *Architecture* 82 (1968), pp. 83-85.

32. "Bâtiments de l'Institut National de L'Industrie Charbonnière, rue Ch'bra, à Liège," *Domus* 451 (1967); *Architecture* 75 (1967), p. 556.

33. "Habitation personnelle, 60, rue Chauve-Souris, à Liège," *Casabella* 332 (1969), p. 20.

34. "Home pour étudiants Résidence Brull, quai G. Kurth, à Liège," *L'Architettura* (1968), p. 147.

35. "Institut d'Education Physique au Sart-Tilman, à Angleur Tilff," *Casabella* 332 (1969), p. 34.

36. "Maison Scoffeniels, Roiessonsart, à Olne," *Casabella* 346 (1970): Bekaert and Strauven, *Construction*, pp. 96-99.

37. "Halle Omnisport du Standard, ave. du Centenaire, à Augrée," *Casabella* 346 (1970); *Architecture* 93 (1970), p. 683.

38. "Agrandissement de l'habitation personnelle, à Liège," *A* + 17 (1975); Bekaert and Strauven, *Construction*, pp. 92-95.

39. "Centre Hospitalier Universitaire au Sart-Tilman, d'Angleur-Tilff," *L'Architecture d'Aujourd'hui* 150 (1970); *Architecture* 93 (1970), p. 676.

40. Bekaert and Strauven, *Construction*, p. 253.

41. Jean Englebert, "Logement évolutif totalement industrialisé," *Neuf* 23 (1970).

42. Jean François, *Paysage et Architecture, Cahiers d'urbanisme* 41-42 (Paris: Editions Art et Technique, 1962). 41-42.

43. Jean Cosse, *Des maisons pour vivre* (Paris: Editions Art, Vie, Esprit, 1975).

44. Bekaert and Strauven, *Construction*, p. 289.

45. "Fermes à stabulation libre à Arville," *La Maison* 3 (1972), p. 73.

46. "La Maison Européenne," *Architecture* 66 (1965), p. 100.

47. "Eglise St-Paul à Waterloo," *La Maison* 12 (1968), p. 480.

48. "Monastère St.-André de Clerland, à Ottignies," *Art d'Eglise* 157 (special issue) (1971), pp. 225-56.

49. Bekaert and Strauven, *Construction*, p. 256.

50. "Soleil en profondeur," *Architect action* 6 (1978), pp. 29-31.

51. Bekaert and Strauven, *Construction*, p. 351.

52. "Peut-on encore être un box architecte aujourd'hui?," *Architect action* 5 (1977).

53. Bekaert and Strauven, *Construction*, p. 332.

54. Jean Barthélemy, "L'avenir du patrimoine architectural dans le Hainaut," *A* + 36 (1977), p. 142.

55. "Centre des services 'De Gilde,' à Bruges (1977-1979)," *A* + 58 (1979), pp. 16-23.

56. "Collège Onze-Lieve-Vrouw à Anvers," *A* + 53 (1978), pp. 8-11.

57. Bekaert and Strauven, *Construction*, p. 352.

58. "Magasin de fleure, rue Vinàve d'Ile, à Liège," *A* + 17 (1975).

59. "Maison et atelier d'architecture à Silly," *A* + 59 (1979), p. 28.

60. "Projet de renovation en Hors-Château, à Liège, 1979," *A* + 52 (1978), p. 23.

61. "Plan de structure de la ville ancienne de Bruges," *A* + 1 (1973), pp. 30-72.

62. "Louvain-la-Neuve ou l'université, moteur d'une ville nouvelle," *Environment* (January 1971): 21-56.

63. Luc Schuiten, "Un habitat bio-solaire de ville," *Architecture Belgium* 9 (1979).

64. Bekaert and Strauven, *Construction*, p. 328.
65. Puttemans, *Architecture Moderne*, p. 251.
66. Bekaert and Strauven, *Construction*, p. 330.

*Bibliography**

BOOKS

Bekaert, Geert. *Charles Vandenhove.* (Brussels: Editions Pierre Mardaga, 1976).

Bekaert, Geert and Strauven, Francis. *La construction en Belgique 1945-1970.* Brussels: Editions Confédération Nationale de la Construction, 1971.

Braem, Renaat. *Het lelijkste land ter wereld.* Louvain: Davidsfonds, 1968.

Cosse, Jean. *Des Maisons pour vivre.* Paris: Art, vie, esprit 1975.

Culot, Maurice and Terlinden, François. *Antoine Pompe et l'Effort Moderne en Belgique 1890-1940.* Ixelles: Ixelles Museum, 1969.

Delevoy, Robert L. and Culot, Maurice. *L. H. de Koninck.* London, 1973.

Modern Architecture in Belgium. Brussels: Marc Voekaer, 1976.

Puttemans, Pierre. *Architecture Moderne en Belgique.* Brussels: Editions Voekaer, 1974.

Ragon, Michel. *Histoire mondiale de l'Architecture et de l'Urbanisme moderne.* Paris, 1972.

Smets, Marcel. *l'Avènement de la cité-jardin en Belgique.* Brussels: Editions Pierre Mardaga, 1976.

Victor Bourgeois: Architectures 1922-1952. Brussels: Art et Technique, 1952.

Watelet, G.; Baudon, J.; Delatte, E.; Eggericx, J.; Kroll, L.; and Puttemans, P. *Bruxelles Guide d'Architecture 1890-1972.* Brussels: Ministère de la Culture Française, 1972.

JOURNALS

"Architectes d'après guerre." *Zodiac* 2 (1958): 159 ff.

"Architettura di Charles Vandenhove dal Belgio." *Domus* 451 (June 1967): 7-10.

"The Alibi of Architecture: The Work of Bob van Reeth." *Forum* 26, no. 3 (1977): 4-57.

Biscogli, Luigi. "Recent Works by Charles Vandenhove." *Casabella* 332 (January 1969): 18-35.

______. "Vandenhove 2." *Casabella* 346 (March 1970): 14-19.

"Brussels, 17th-20th Century Buildings." *Architectural Design* 41 (February 1971): 96-99.

"Complexe Hospitalier Universitaire, Sart Tilman, Ch. Vandenhove et al." *l'Architecture d'Aujourd'hui* 150 (June-July 1970): 16-20.

Culot, Maurice. "Antoine Pompe, The Architecture of Sentiment" (in Japanese). *Architecture and Urbanism* 10, no. 97 (October 1978): 105-12.

Félix, Paul. "Architecture religieuse: Belgique." *l'Architecture d'Aujourd'hui* 196 (June-July 1961): 62-65.

Kjelberg, J. "Louvain fera école; le grand béguinage de Louvain." *Connaissance des Arts* 209 (July 1969): 54-59.

Vinson, R. J. "Bruxelles Construit." *Connaissance des Arts* 228 (February 1971): 72-77.

Williams, Stephanie. "Ecological Architecture of Lucien Kroll." *Architectural Review* 165, no. 984 (February 1979): 94-101.

"Wohnhaus and Privatmuseum J. B. Urvater, Rhode-Saint-Genèse; Brüssel; A. Jacqmain, arch." *Deutsche Bauzeitung* 69 (November 1964): 876-80.

OTHER USEFUL JOURNALS

A +, architecture, urbanism, design.

Architect Action.

Architecture, Belgium.

Environnment.

La Maison.

Neuf.

* Prepared by the Montreal editorial staff.

11

BOLIVIA

GUSTAVO MEDEIROS

Bolivia is a remote country, largely unknown beyond its borders, with sometimes fascinating and often baffling contrasts. It is a country in which geography opposes the tallest mountains to the deepest valleys and torrid prairies; a country in which villages seem to grow out of inaccessible folds of nature, isolated from the world and from each other by thousands of kilometers. One can travel for hours, explore an abandoned villa and perhaps a fine church with a fabulous gilded altarpiece, all without seeing a soul. Some five million inhabitants occupy approximately a million square kilometers of rather rugged terrain. Its more populated cities may be no more distant from one another than a half-hour's flight, but also a twelve-hour drive! The indigenous population communicates in one or two native languages along with a rudimentary form of Castillian. In the cities *quechua* and *aimara*, which were common before the Agricultural Reform of 1953, have been virtually forgotten languages; the populace speaks Castillian and generally a foreign language. In a country that has had as many as six presidents in a single day, frequent and disturbing changes of government with a consequent political instability are characteristic. Democratic representation in past elections is reflected in the appearance of no less than some fifty legal, political parties, of which two represent approximately 70 percent of the native population. The rural population produces only 20 percent of all exports, while requiring the importing of wheat and other foodstuffs. Though Bolivia is the world's second largest producer of tin, it exports little else and is disadvantaged by its dependence upon commercial imports and its landlocked position. Economic and social reforms have proceeded at a rapid pace, conceptually, but have not been satisfactory in terms of the general equilibrium and their integral effects in society. All these contrasts, their ideals and frustrations, are the stuff of the everyday life of Bolivians and of the architect and the student of architecture.

Geographic isolation, difficult roads, lack of diversified construction systems and materials, together with a relatively low volume of building have contributed to a lag in the development of architectural technology in comparison with the technologies of neighboring countries. In Bolivia the most ambitious of residential-complex planning, destined for the new town of Los Pinos in La Paz, aims at construction of 3,000 residences over a span of eight years, while in other countries 30,000 residences may be constructed in a year. Contributing further to the limitation of technological development in Bolivia are the pace of the working routine, the high margin of utility that construction firms obtain without the need to compete in methods of rationalizing their systems and controls of work, and the distrust of promoters and financiers towards changes in technology. Since no permission is given to use "their money" for constructional systems that are without precedent in Bolivia, planning of a type or on a scale that would justify changes in technology cannot be introduced.

At the moment the material most widely employed is adobe, sun-dried clay, fabricated in situ in blocks 10 cm. x 20 cm. x 40 cm. Since the clay of the im-

The editor is indebted to Ms. Heydee Venegas, Directress of the Museo de la Fundación Arqueológica, Antropológica e Histórica de Puerto Rico, for her invaluable assistance in translating this chapter from the original Spanish text.

mediate surroundings is used by the builders themselves, they pay neither for the cost of the material nor for the cost of energy but only for the salary of one man, the *adobero*. Though professional architects are prejudiced against this material and tend to disregard it, more than 70 percent of the population uses adobe. The way in which this material is produced effectively discourages the manufacture, transport, and sale of any other. The capability of the population to build their own homes with their own hands, using this material and without recourse to technical or financial assistance, stands as the major obstacle to establishing industrialized lines of materials. Nevertheless, there are now facilities for manufacturing bricks, ceramic tiles, PVC (plastic: polyvinyl-chloride), ducts, cement blocks and rudimentary prefabricated beams, corrugated zinc plates called *calaminas*, and artistic lines of stucco plaques. There are also factories for cement which is distributed by means of cement mixing trucks.

Brick, widely manufactured in the cities and used in the tropical plains where stone is unknown, has been reduced in its use mainly to wall-partitioning. The structural possibilities of brick so evident in colonial works have been forgotten, and its production lacks the quality control that would permit its employment in such improved constructional modes as arches, vaulting, domes, and structural or bearing walls. Reinforced concrete, introduced into architecture in the twenties, is most frequently used on construction overseen by engineers or architects in countries where there is a lack of steel. Its use in Bolivia is so indiscriminate that there are examples of large constructions in places quite removed from the tropics, where cement was brought in along Bolivian waterways by ship from Israel since this was more feasible economically than transporting it from La Paz. Paradoxically, at the end of the seventies, cement factories in Bolivia maintained prices three times higher than the worldwide level, thus reducing the use of this material and limiting their market.

Bolivian engineers are permitted more technical innovation in bridge construction than architects are in their buildings. Many architectural projects that would have employed prestressed concrete have been rejected or forced to adopt more common structural systems while the smallest bridges are erected with prefabricated prestressed voussoirs. There have been exceptions to the rule, of course, such as Emilio Villanueva's stadium [1928, destroyed 1974] at the University of La Paz that introduced reinforced concrete to Bolivia; and thirty years later some buildings by the engineer Mario Galindo, most prominent of which are his churches at San Miguel and Miraflores and the Olympic Pool, all in La Paz. The structures by Galindo are highly refined designs that employ a daring technology of parabolic, laminated, very thin forms and suspended reinforced concrete.

As a result of the concentration of constructional activity in buildings of twenty to thirty stories in La Paz over the last decade, there are now some new technical possibilities available. Among these are constructional elements such as lightweight flooring, wooden and/or metallic molded plank linings and scaffolding; distribution and making of concrete with special trucks; and the use of such devices as elevators and cranes. Even air conditioning has been introduced, and there are new materials for carpentry and glass-making to say nothing of new finishing materials that give a more sophisticated and better finished appearance. No doubt such "pyrotechnics" can be criticized for responding only to an image of "progress," "comfort," and "prestige," an image for those who forget that there should be a sense of social and environmental equilibrium. We shall look into this problem later (compare below) when we analyze the evolution of architectural thought as it relates especially to studies on the preservation and the restructuring of the historic centers of cities.

Finally, for certain projects, particularly large, spacious sports facilities with roofs, designs such as the Oruro sports complex (compare below) are being introduced that are intended for construction in systems of metallic stereometric structures. Because of lightweight quality, these can compete effectively with poured concrete and thus break the longstanding Bolivian taboo against metallic structures. Designers and analysts are up-to-date enough in the managing of advanced techniques and in their abilities to contribute to decisions on adopting or adapting the possibilities that can most prudently be executed in the medium. It would be desirable if the same technical capacities were carried over to confront and explore other technological means of resolving in their turn the most pressing if less spectacular needs that exist in Third World countries. In other words, one must ask why certain large projects achieve an architectonic level of quality while complying with the exigencies of well-known economic restrictions and for other works of a social character, such as schools, hospitals, and housing, the same effort to achieve high quality is not demanded.

Architectural education began in 1943 when the first School of Architecture was founded at La Paz's Universidad Mayor de San Andrés. To the end of the fifties there were no more than ten students per course enrolled, while by the early seventies registration reached 1,500. By then, too, the Faculty of Architecture founded at the Universidad Mayor de San Simón at Cochabamba in the fifties enrolled some 800 students. Architecture seems suddenly to have become fashionable, and the repercussions of greatly increased enrollments were felt in the organization of the faculties and in professional practice. Without doubt, this increase in the numbers of students was in response to the noteworthy increase of construction in La Paz by the seventies and to a specific political situation that obtained, as well as to a new social mobility combined with the lack of more diversified means of education.

The faculty, itself also growing, bore the pressures of numbers and the dominion of mediocrity. What a contrast between the "old school" of the first architectural engineers with the rigidly functional vision and the architects of the future! Affected by today's crises in the scope and concepts of architecture, they ignore or distrust the great modern masters and are bound to the new socioeconomic theories. They understand their work to be in planning and often miss the chance to acquire even the basics of their trade. It is wrong to excel! Every connotation of cultural and personal development is to be avoided. The language of design is transformed by the wordiness of sociological pseudoinvestigation, maintained by certain contemporary European authors who offer guidelines for interpreting all Latin American phenomena in terms of design, eventually negating solutions put forth in architectonic terms.

This current had manifested itself in the faculties at La Paz around 1970, a very special time. The traditional system ruptured, there was a despicable laying-off of older professors in favor of their former students, occurring against the framework of a fervor and enthusiasm for socialism. The beginning of an educational focusing upon social aims that this signified ended in guerrilla barricades and death far up in the mountains. Unfortunately, political repression followed this. Schools and universities were closed and simultaneously a suprauniversity coordinating body sought to impose a restructuring of professional education through the country. Just as in 1970 when a new mode of teaching, confused with political indoctrination, had been experimented with, students eight years later rejected the modality planned by the National Council on Higher Education (Consejo Nacional de Educación Superior; CNES), though it was academically objective, interpreting it as an instrument of the government and therefore negatively. The result of all of this has been a continuing confusion on the part of both the left- and right-wing political forces toward higher educational teaching and academic structuring. For the education of today's restless youth, faculties of architecture must present their courses with special dedication, group consensus, and a degree of faith and hope in the future.

There are and have been substantial differences between the architectural faculties at La Paz and Cochabamba. At Cochabamba, the arrival of young architects educated abroad, the assimilation of views espoused at the Third Conference of Latin American Schools and Faculties of Architecture (1964), the presence of professors invited from Córdoba and Montevideo together with American Peace Corps architects such as Professor Stephen Jacobs (1964-1966) all led toward the creation of a dynamic Faculty of Architecture under the auspices and direction of Franklin Anaya as dean. Substantial modifications of the curricula and of course-plans ensued, with a growth in levels of experience and realizations unknown before in the region. These ranged from the day-to-day interaction of a community of professors and students, to teaching by involvement in local and national problems of architecture and planning, to the actual designing and construction of university buildings such as the Central Library, the School of Agronomy building, and the expansion of the Faculty of Architecture buildings under the supervision of architect and professor Jorge Aramburo.

During the crises of the early 1970s, the architectural faculty at La Paz continued on its way with the calm and confidence offered by a system totally untouched by the physical and social aspects of its local environment and impervious to the experiences, achievements, and crises of other Latin American schools and faculties of architecture. Later the La Paz faculty became interested in the experiences of Cochabamba that had preceded the revolutionary acts of 1970. Today the differences that exist between the two faculties are substantially derived from their different circumstances of location. Cochabamba, situated appropriately in physical terms but much less so economically, has a very dedicated educational atmosphere but offers very little work for young architects. La Paz, on the other hand, has for its fifteen-hundred students today the same physical facilities it had for sixty students quite some time ago. Bureaucracy and the growth of construction in the city keep both professors and students so busy that studying seems to become nearly a collateral and relatively insignificant activity. Inspired by the academic continuity of Cochabamba, efforts have been made to establish much the same curriculum at La Paz, but the vastly different conditions there have mitigated against this.

With few exceptions professional architects are concentrated in three cities: La Paz (population, 700,000), Cochabamba (160,000), and Santa Cruz (150,000). As in neighboring countries, the architect, usually considered as liberal, must divide his time between functioning as a businessman, as a professor, or in some relation to the new forms of work afforded by the governmental bureaucratic system. Some 90 percent of employed architects work for the national and municipal bureaucracy, which could be interesting were it not for the constraints of political uncertainties and unsteadiness that result in chance decisions and improvisations. To avoid this, a system of multidisciplinary consulting groups primarily led by engineers and economists has grown up. In such groups architects are sometimes influential, though they prefer to maintain their traditional level of independence. It has become recognized that after each governmental crisis a former ministerial group of qualified professionals can become the next consulting firm.

In the realm of large architectural projects and urban planning, given the individualism of architects, firms of consulting engineers usually receive the major commissions, though their experience is predominantly in the construction of bridges, roads, and sewer systems. Since at some point in developing their projects they require the services of professional architects, in response to this situation such architectural consulting firms as Consultex (Jorge Romero, Alfonso Frias, Alberto Marquez) and Centro de Estudios y Proyectos Nueva Visión (directed by Gustavo Medeiros) have been formed. Both governmental and private clients in Bolivia also tend often to favor foreign consulting firms for their larger projects, despite the exorbitant fees charged and despite the turning of these firms to local professionals for their understanding of local sociocultural problems in the contexts of their projects.

With so much confusion on the part of the authorities, of various institutions and of the public throughout the country concerning the related activities of architects and engineers; with an almost complete lack of awareness that the planners so much in vogue now need not be only economists but may be architects as well; and with the number of architectural graduates of Bolivian universities greatly increased, possibilities of unemployment seem imminent in the architectural profession. Few architects can attend to their work of building and urban and regional planning, publish, and teach at much the same time. Thus, the field of commercial construction with its easy yet widely accepted designs remains predominant.

Aside from the many publications of the architect Emilio Villanueva, for the forties into the sixties there is an almost total lack of publications concerning the development of architectural theory and practice in Bolivia. Villanueva was the most renowned and influential architectural personality of his time (1886-1970). Most of his work had been accomplished between 1916 [the La Paz General Hospital] and 1928 [Hernando Siles Stadium, La Paz], but the thirteen-story central tower block of the University of San Andrés, La Paz [constructed between 1941 and 1948] is the most representative of his architecture and was also the first "skyscraper" in Bolivia. [fig. 11.1] In 1930 he served as Minister of Education, having been rector of the university the previous year. After publishing several books of which two were devoted to city planning, and after founding the School of Architecture of the University of San Andrés (1943), the first in the country, Villanueva served as editor of the journal *Arquitectura y Planificación* between 1944 and 1949. One of the more important Bolivian architects and critics of his generation, his influence upon the architectural students and architects of the 1940s and 1950s was immeasurable. There were other architects of intuition and creativity like Villanueva. However, to understand the currents of architecture in Bolivia we must understand that, though there was some small influx of magazines and some outside travel—as well as a trend by a number of young professionals to seek an education outside the country—the general processes for building in Bolivia often worked to discourage new ideas.

One of the most important events in Bolivian history, the Chaco War with Paraguay from 1932 to 1935, represents a turning point in architectural history for us: the few architects from the time before this conflict usually had studied in Paris, while after the war and until the early 1950s architects for the most part were educated in Santiago, Chile, and in La Paz. The blockade of the Atlantic during World War II impeded but did not prevent the Bolivians who were in Chile in particular and Latin American students in general from dedicating themselves to almost autodidactically learning the Functionalist and urbanistic concepts of the CIAM, outside of the typical academic programs of that time. Their pressure resulted in one of the first urban regulatory plans in the hemisphere, that of Cochabamba elaborated between 1942 and 1950 by architects Jorge Urquidi, Gustavo Knaudt, Franklin Anaya Arze, Daniel Bustos, and Gustavo Urquidi. Inescapable in

11.1. Emilio Villanueva, architect. Entrance to the Tower Building of the Universidad Mayor de San Andrés. La Paz, 1948. (Photograph: Courtesy of Gustavo Medeiros)

this is the influence of Le Corbusier by whom it is still said a preliminary sketch for the city plan was made.

But the place where this influence and that of the entire Rationalist movement was undoubtedly felt the most was in the construction of entirely residential neighborhoods (*barrios*) in the city of La Paz. There, designs of "white houses" of cubic forms emerged at fairs for miniatures, called *Alacitas*, where people could buy small scale models of whatever they hoped to have during the course of the year. Then popular artisans copied the white cubiform buildings in miniature and their designs spread widely. An incredible result of this custom is that today the dominant image in many urban neighborhoods is none other than that of the *Alacitas* house in full-size. Clearly these cubiform homes are not built in any orthodox manner. In their imitational forms a dominolike structure is suppressed, and the terrace garden is replaced by a corrugated zinc (*calamina*) roof hidden from the street below but visible from the street above within the topographic configuration of La Paz.

More representative of the modern architecture of La Paz, the Hotel La Paz [1939] on Camacho Avenue by the Krsul firm and the tower building of the University of San Andrés by Emilio Villanueva [1948] retain their strong identities today. The Hotel La Paz is an almost Mendelsohnian design. Begun as part of an experiment in urban renovation in the center of the city, it stamped the character of Camacho Avenue and remains an important example of what may be done to modernize an urban area by creating a new, unified image. Villanueva's tower block stood out as very different with its forceful, monolithic design and its thirteen-story height until the recent surge of skyscraper construction in La Paz. With Villanueva there was initiated a current that sought to fuse the modern technology of reinforced concrete (with its established Formalism) and the yearning for a cultural identity in the archaeological character of Tihuanacu. Villanueva explained this quite clearly:

> The necessity of linking traditions with architecture does not imply an adoption of yesterday's forms. . . . The University tower block doesn't have a particular style. If it has any, it is that which is manifested in every product of this epoch, of this civilization, when it is elaborated without the premeditated intention of imitating past models. . . . Now surely, independently of style, there is the rubric that conditions of locale and origin impose. In order to imprint this physiognomy, two figurations of Tihuanacan archaeology have been insinuated; the "stepped sign" and the sign of the sun. These allusions pretend neither to set a tone for the structure nor for its details.[1]

In the forties official governmental works in an academic manner, such as the Palace of Justice at Sucre, coexisted with others that were totally international (by the Krsul contractors) and with buildings such as those we have considered by Villanueva. The latter were linked also by a neo-Colonial stylistic current, then much in vogue in Argentina, in which "colonial" twelve-story towers were built. Franklin Anaya Arze's works of the 1950s at Cochabamba such as his plan for University City, continued to reflect the ideas of Le Corbusier that had been embodied in that city's master plan developed since the 1940s. Among individual buildings his Polytechnic Hall of the Cochabamba University adapted the vocabulary of *pilotis*, ramps, and *brise-soleil* to the climate and the landscape setting. One cannot speculate on the directions in which these currents would have moved had there not been a period of twelve years in which architecture and all other constructional activity was almost paralyzed. Between 1952 and 1964 the political and economic changes of the Nationalist Revolutionary Movement were effected. Instead of architecture, during this period mural painters such as Walter Solón Romero, the Imaná brothers, Lorgio Vaca, and Miguel Alandia Pantoja made use of parts of governmental and university buildings to show their enthusiasm for political and revolutionary ideals. At Cochabamba's university, nevertheless, Franklin Anaya continued to build, as exemplified by his structure for the Faculty of Architecture; and in La Paz among the few avant-garde buildings erected, one of the most outstanding is the Worker's Hospital building.

During the second half of the 1960s, Bolivia went through a time of economic boom in which concepts of planning played a role. Two areas of architectural activity became important: one with the creation of the National Housing Council (CONAVI, Consejo Nacional de Vivienda); the other with new university construction. CONAVI raised prospects for architects since from time to time it considered urban and architectural designs that were linked with technological efforts of architects outside of the bureaucratic system. Inevitably and invariably, however, the mold of very mediocre solutions prevailed. The development of this field is very closely related to questions of financial funding sources; and decisions concerning matters of management, processing, and legal adjudication take precedence over ample and intensive studies of urban and constructive designs. The ideas of the young and inexperienced professional architects regularly employed by CONAVI are easily rejected by their more experienced bureaucratic superiors, so that the city planning set forth by this agency is little more than a simple parceling of 64-square-meters per individual home without a full complement of services, much less buildings with urban conveniences. Under the direction of this governmental entity no more than 538 housing units were constructed annually in all of Bolivia.

Solutions for "minimal" housing are conceived in the same forms as residential housing; designs are not substantially different whether construction is planned for the tropics or for a mountainous area; housing is erected without thought for the future growth of the internal space; traditional technology is employed without any effort towards its rationalization or systematization, and the motives and policies of the National Housing Council remain self-sustaining.

The second area of activity that opened up to architects in the latter part of the 1960s was in university design and construction at Oruro and Cochabamba, in 1966 and 1969 respectively. Both projects involved planning in order to develop overall facilities, reorienting academic structures in a certain way and redefining the functions of universities. Let us consider in detail the development at Oruro, located not far from Lake Poopo in the mountains at an altitude of some 3,700 meters above sea level.

The planning of University City at Oruro, begun in 1966 by Franklin Anaya Arze and Gustavo Medeiros, was focused around fundamental propositions that ranged from regional, urban, and university concerns to the concretizing of an architectonic formulation that would arouse national and international interest with its content and expression.[2] Franklin Anaya, after his architectural studies in Chile, had established himself in Cochabamba, where in 1956-1957 he was a member of the Regulatory Planning Board and also in the 1950s had designed the plan of the University of San Simon of Cochabamba. Between 1966 and 1968 he collaborated with Medeiros at Oruro. Gustavo Medeiros had distinguished himself in his architectural studies at the Argentine's National University of Córdoba, where he was awarded the Gold Medal for his efforts in 1964. Immediately after that he accepted a teaching post at the university in Cochabamba and remained there until 1969. His work on the University City at Oruro, however, continued to occupy him in both designing and constructional supervision until 1977.

For Bolivia the establishing of Oruro's University city is representative of a time of intensive resumption of architectural activities. In our day it is the city, in its sense of urban planning, that is the instrument and the goal of development. When the Bolivian high plateau required a capital, "it was Oruro—with its central regional location, its expeditious rail and road communication systems, its industrial, mining and metallurgical facilities, the agricultural potential of its nearby fields, its university's activities and its folkloric tradition—that was accredited as the most multivalent center with appropriate potential to become the major city of the region."[3] The issue of urbanism was complemented in 1967 with the integration of a neighborhood apartment unit, the Unidad Vecinal, of the University City into the expanding texture of the city of Oruro. The objective of the Unidad Vecinal, by Gustavo Medeiros, was not only to help remedy a housing shortage but to provide, from the characteristics of its design, models for a new way of life in the area that would relate countryside to the neighborhood; and with a modicum of comfort and a constructive sense would give the idea of a less transitory settlement. These became the first steps in moving from the concept of a mining encampment to that of the capital city of the region.

Between 1931 and 1966 there had been no changes in the university's functioning systems of organization and development, which were similar to those of the time of Abelard. Nor was there any approved norm for approaching the problems of university architectural design—and, indeed, today that is still the case in La Paz. Since architecture seeks to create new modes of order for the future, and in order there is beauty, it must be based upon a full, substantial, and objective comprehension of the problems to be resolved. For the architecture of the university at Oruro development was based upon the following premises: a) the provision of growth in space and time by means of flexibility in utilization, with a modular growth of spaces adaptable to unforeseeable new demands of function and size; b) the convenience of adapting and taking advantage of the landscape and climate of the high plateau, adjusting to the terrain by stepping and horizontally grouping buildings, linking volumes and intervening spaces in turn to patios that are graduated in scale; by carefully designing the area so that architectural forms (fig. 11.2) are compatible and harmonically fused with their surroundings; all to afford the only solution that will avoid domination by the immensity and natural strength of the place; c) the necessity of finding a way to modulate and normalize natural structures in terms of constructed forms that may coexist with them; and d) the development of a reasonable technology that does not seek the impossible, that combines systems to permit a great deal of light and a total freedom in the use of the physical plant, concording with the volumetric plasticity and expressive clarity of the materials and constructive systems employed.

11.2. Gustavo Medeiros and Franklin Anaya, architects. University of Oruro, roof of Mineralogical Museum; stairway; street; laboratory buildings, 1966-1970. (Photograph: Jean Pierre Tumoine, courtesy of the architect)

At the university in Oruro emphasis was placed upon the clarity of volumetric expression of particular enclosed spaces as well as upon the visual qualities of materials and their accord with structural functions. In the forms that constructions of concrete, iron, or wood manifest there is an almost didactic intent to show not only what but also how they bear. All is molded into vigorous volumes, pyramidal forms for example, vibrant structures of concrete and ceramics, where the natural colors of the materials express the various parts, and all becomes one with the landscape.

The buildings of the University of Oruro have reached a new level in the evolution of that current in Bolivian architectural theory that seeks an identity between architecture and its social, cultural, and physical environments. They move toward providing a cultural continuity in architectural expression, progressing subtly from the works of earlier epochs to extend the limits of a Bolivian nationalism that would usually have been expressed by an application of Tihuanacan motives upon the facades of buildings. An architectural language that embodies vigorous forms and materials together with a dynamic interplay of textures and structural logic, all in a symbiotic relationship with its surroundings, has been developed at Oruro by interpreting the life of the high plateau. In a solution uniquely suited to its place rather than to the tropics or valleys this language represents some of the constants in Bolivian culture.

In the years of the sixties, while the university at Oruro was under development, Jorge Aramburo became Dean of the Faculty of Architecture at Cochabamba and Oscar Gonzales Tellez was appointed Professor of Architecture, both having studied at Córdoba, Argentina. Working together with their students late in the decade, they designed Cochabamba's Central Library and Agronomy Faculty. Constructed between 1970 and 1973, this is characterized by a technology of brick and wood enclosing spatial interplays that have been occasionally criticized for departing from the strictly functional needs of the university library building. Also during the 1960s Juan Luis Zuñiga took up practice in his native Bolivia after years of study in Brazil and Japan. Already having been singled out for praise by the Association of Architects of Osaka and Tokyo and by Kenzo Tange for his student projects, in La Paz he won a competition for the important Mutual La Primera office building. In 1969 he proposed for this a construction of large prestressed beams that daringly approached the normal limitations of the structural design of buildings. With the technological vicissitudes that confronted him it took nine years for the building to be constructed—and then in 1978 it was executed in a more conventional system. During the 1970s Zuñiga also distinguished himself with the erection of the Bank of Brazil building and the Progresso apartment building, both in La Paz, while in Santa Cruz's Escuela Normal Superior Enrique Finot he conceived a design essentially of lightweight concrete conical vaults posed upon a base, the outline of which was determined by a system of concentric radii.

During the 1970s there was a boom in institutional construction and in large, horizontally oriented designs of apartment buildings for sale or rental. With a great deal of pride La Paz saw a surging of towering buildings of between twenty and thirty stories upon the same lots that had been occupied previously by tranquil, single-family residences. It is no surprise to us that this construction fever did not always result in an interesting level of accomplishment. Though there was a great deal of building, there was little that could be called architecture, and still less of urban planning. We have already mentioned some exceptions to this situation, and there are others, fortunately. Rodolfo Alborta, for instance, studied in Brazil and after returning was responsible for the interesting design and construction of the Escuela Normal Superior Simon Bolivar in La Paz. A system of integrated volumes executed in concrete trapezoidal forms upon a geometry of crosses and rectangles is very much related here to an Andean, telluric manner of expressive intent. Often very much misunderstood at first glance, this building challenges the present by proposing an architectonic language that requires a great deal of attention. For the University of Oruro, Gustavo Medeiros designed two important projects in the seventies: the Department of Mining and Metallurgical Research Complex and the Sports Complex. The former consists of a grouping of modular pavilions that permit a maximum of flexibility within and exterior expansion, while the latter brings together spaces and structures of swimming pools and roofed colosseums in an architectural language continuing and further developing that of the sixties at Oruro by the same architect. Again in La Paz, in addition to the Sheraton Hotel or the National Bank of Argentina, both of which were accomplished by Argentine architects, some few works by Bolivian architects such as Juan Carlos Barrientos and Juan Carlos Calderón remain to be mentioned for the 1970s.

Juan Carlos Calderón has been especially prolific since his return to Bolivia from the United States in 1972. During his studies at Oklahoma State University and his long association with the California firm of Royston, Hanamoto, Beck and Abey with which he became director of design, he assimilated into his own style the Organic manner of Frank Lloyd Wright. Calderón's *Toward a Quatridimensional Architecture* reflects some of the theoretical bases of his architectural thinking: He states that nothing in the universe just happens, that no planet, nor seashell suddenly "is." Everything has developed over time and time is of the essence of all existence. Nature, he says, has a basic pattern of structure which is apparent at sight. There is a beginning, a pathway, and an end. The pathway points out the general direction of growth. Though the growth may take many shapes, all the pathways may be traced to their points of origin. Calderón believes that if an architect can express the process of development that a building must undergo, visually as well as structurally, he will have included time as a dimension in the realization of the construction and will have expanded the concept of structural honesty in the direction of a new concept of developmental honesty. Two dynamic systems, one objective and the other subjective, could intertwine as a result of a meeting of their pathways of movement, and a new grammar of design would include both. The understanding of this new vocabulary could be as important for this century as the assimilation of the laws of perspective, in other words, as the third dimension was to the Renaissance.

Such ideas, presented in lectures and exhibitions by Calderón, are manifested in his architectural works. For instance his handling of contrasts is evident in the ENTEL building in La Paz in long courses of balconies over which all traffic converges toward an entry that is a single spatial entity in the height of the entire building. Or we may cite the visual play of a battery of transparent elevators arranged along one of the blind facades of the Communications Building in La Paz. Among the other notable buildings that he has accomplished since 1972 are the ENTEL building in Oruro, post office buildings in La Paz and Santa Cruz, commercial buildings for Hansa and the Plaza Hotel together with the apartment dwellings denominated Pinilla, Illimani, Santa Teresa, and Cobana, all in La Paz. The Pinilla building, designed in 1975 and erected in 1978 (fig. 11.3) rises swiftly in

11.3. Juan Carlos Calderón, architect. Pinilla Condominium Building. La Paz, 1975-1978. (Photograph: Felipe Sanjines, courtesy of Gustavo Medeiros)

its almost twenty-story height, with drama built into its design in terms of a predominant sense of vertical articulation of screened and windowed sections. The broad horizontal surface strips between bands of windows at each story assert themselves only in the two uppermost floors, moving out and across the tightly spaced vertical screens to arrest their upward movement. In all, the design of this building has a sense of movement and logic deriving ultimately from Wright's H. C. Price tower at Bartlesville, Oklahoma [1956], a skyscraper that Calderón would have known well from his student days. Finally, his latest projects include a pedestrian passage and parking lot on the Choqueyapu River, a hotel for a tennis club, the Community Church, and the Coca Cola Administration Building, all in La Paz.

In the realm of planning, urban groups of interrelated apartment buildings were constructed as responses to and coextant with individualistic, isolated solutions. The former may be seen in the Los Pinos complex at La Paz (fig. 11.4), the first stage of which was formulated by Mario Galindo, Alcides Torres, Osman Birced, and Gustavo Medeiros in 1971-1972 and built between 1974 and 1977. Some 16,000 inhabitants are accommodated in technologically conservative low-rise buildings that integrate an architecture of reinforced concrete and brickwork with features of the rugged landscape. The success of this group of dwellings led to the designing of a second and third stage during 1977-1978 by the Centro de Estudios y Proyectos Nueva Visión, under the supervision of Gustavo Medeiros. At this center students and architects as well as planners come together to formulate ideas and advance proposals for urban and architectural projects particularly but not exclusively for La Paz. In 1973 Medeiros, collaborating with the architect Rolando Carranza, developed an urban plan for the Laykacota section of the center of La Paz at the Centro de Estudios y Proyectos Nueva Vision. The Laykacota quarter, some fifty hectares of wasteland, was to have been built up (fig. 11.5) with a principal

11.4. Gustavo Medeiros, Mario Galindo, Alcides Torres, and Osman Bírced, architects. Los Pinos Development, phase I. La Paz, 1971-1977. (Photograph: Courtesy of Gustavo Medeiros)

11.5. Gustavo Medeiros and Rolando Carrazana, architects. Section and General View, Urban Renewal Project for the Laykacota area. La Paz, 1973. (Photograph: Centro Nueva Vision, courtesy of G. Medeiros)

axial roadway, a mass-transit monorail system, a national governmental center with stepped buildings and circular towers of a civic esplanade, conjoined by bridgelike multiple-purpose buildings that would function as high-density administrative, commercial, and residential structures, and finally a green area. With the multiple functional buildings raised upon substantial, hollowed *pilotis* as circulation nuclei that would have resolved the geotechnical stability of the area, the entire plan took on the aspect of a megastructure that by 1990 would have permitted the decongestion of the historic center and the preservation and recycling of its structures. In all, some 55,000 inhabitants could have resided in or near the governmental center, had this study been effected.

During the 1970s there was considerable activity not only in urban but also in regional planning in Bolivia. Architects Carlos Calvimontes, Jorge Romero, Alfonso Frias, Alberto Marquez, and Jorge Otero at the Centro Profesional Multidisciplinario (CPM) worked out regional development and urban master plans for Potosí, Sucre, and Oruro. Consultex, a firm consisting of Romero, Frias and Marquez, branched off from CPM to develop plans for Tarija. Prudencio-Claros and Associates (PCA) was responsible for planning at Montero; and the Ministry of City Planning and Housing itself began studies of master plans for smaller towns throughout the land. The city of Santa Cruz employed its master plan developed in the 1950s, updating it during the 1960s. But during the 1970s it was La Paz that continued to offer the greatest challenges.

The management of the mayor's office assisted exceptionally by an architect, Adolfo Navarro, as major technological advisor, commissioned successive important studies of La Paz, studies that we may summarize here only briefly. In 1976 Jorge Saravia and Jorge Otero elaborated a developmental model (*Modelo de Crecimiento*) that took the strains of urban expansion into consideration and recommended certain guidelines, in a publication of that same year. Also that year, the Centro de Estudios y Proyectos Nueva Visión (Center of Studies and Projects New Vision) made a study of the downtown area of La

Paz, integrating analyses of historical and environmental evaluations with sociological urban planning and legislational analyses. The goal of the study was to evolve a plan that would balance concepts of the preservation and revitalization of the historical center with proposals for urban construction that would permit the city to develop in the future without destroying its past.[4] In 1977-1978 two French firms charged with looking into the geological and city-planning problems of the city collaborated with the Bolivian firm of Prudencio-Claros and Associates to produce a more complex study entitled the *Plan for the Urban Development of La Paz* (*Plan de Desarrollo Urbano de la Paz*). Fundamental directions for the future of the city are presented, taking into account its different villages with their languages, customs, and activities that form an almost undecipherable sociocultural mix, yet which are physically so close to one another. The study takes into account such geological and social differences as are encountered between those who construct adobe homes with their own hands along the river banks and those who commission architects wherever their homes are to be; between those who live at an altitude of some 4,150 meters above sea level and those who live in the city 900 meters lower; between those who speak Aimara and those who speak Castillian. It may well be that in order to understand, predict, and interpret the phenomena of this city, not only the most sophisticated data-processing techniques and methods of urban planning but also a goodly amount of imagination and sensibility are necessary (beyond recognition of spatial availabilities, village activities, and population movements) on a plane that in reality represents a three-dimensional spiral.

AUTHOR'S NOTE: To present in their implicit value the many works in the panorama of contemporary Bolivian architecture totally unknown elsewhere—as unknown as the country itself is beyond its boundaries—demands the impartial vision of a critic or perhaps a historian. This task has been taken up, nevertheless, by a professor and practicing architect. The scope of this chapter, therefore, is predetermined, or at lease influenced, by the prejudiced vision of an architect in search of, and preoccupied with the limited opportunities of realizing better-conceived works as opposed to the pretentious excesses of only "profitable" buildings, so often accompanied by a total disdain for the socially balanced and humanly dignified habitat.

Notes

1. Carlos D. Mesa, "Emilio Villanueva el arquitecto más importante del Siglo 20 en Bolivia," *Arte y Arqueologia*, nos. 5, 6, p. 123.
2. Cf. "Amérique Latine, Stop. Problèmes et Méthodes," *L'Architecture d'Aujourd'hui* 173 (May/June 1974).
3. G. Medeiros Anaya, *Oruro: Su Ciudad Universitaria Como Factor del Desarrollo Regional y Urbano* (La Paz: Centro de Estudios y Proyectos Nueva Visión, 1975).
4. Cf. Medeiros Anaya et al., *La Paz: Casco Urbano Central* (La Paz: Honorable Alcadía Municipal de la Paz, 1977).

Bibliography

BOOKS

Documentos de Arte Colonial Sudamericano: Bolivia. La Villa Imperial de Potosí. Vol. 1. Buenos Aires: Academia Nacional de Bellas Artes de la Republica Argentina, 1944.

Documentos de Arte Colonial Sudamericano: Bolivia. Chuquisaca. Vol. 2. Buenos Aires: Academia Nacional de Bellas Artes de la Republica Argentina, 1944.

Plan de Desarrollo Urbano de la Ciudad de La Paz. Orleans, 1978.

Kirchhoff, Herbert. *Bolivia en Accion—1949.* Buenos Aires, 1949.

Medeiros Anaya, Gustavo. *Oruro: Su Ciudad Universitaria Como Factor del Desarrollo Regional y Urbano.* Vol. 1, La Paz: Centro de Estudios y Proyectos Nueva Visión, 1975.

Medeiros Anaya, Gustavo; Clark, Evelyn; Gisberg, Teresa; and Bedregal, Ramiro. *La Paz: Casco Urbano Central.* Vol. 2. La Paz: Honorable Alcadía Municipal de La Paz, 1977.

Mesa, José de and Gisbert, Teresa. *Iglesias Con Atrio y Posas en Bolivia.* La Paz, 1961.

______. *Contribuciones Al Estudio de la Arquitectura Andina.* La Paz, 1966.

______. *Bolivia: Monumentos Historicos y Arqueologicos.* Mexico, 1970.

______. *Monumentos de Bolivia.* La Paz, 1978.

Savaria, Jorge and Otero, Jorge. *Ciudad de La Paz Modelo de Crecimiento.* La Paz, 1976.

Urquidi Zambrana, Jorge. *La Urbanizacion de la Ciudad de Cochabamba.* Síntesis del estudio, documentos y antecedentes. Cochabamba, 1967.

Vignale, Pedreo Juan. *La Casa Real de Moneda de Potosí.* Buenos Aires, 1944.

Villanueva, Emilio. *Motivos Coloniales.* (Unpublished work). 1924.

______. *Urbanismo, esquema de la evolución urbana en Europa y America.* 1939. Translated by Paul Wadingler. La Paz, 1968.

______. *Urbanistica Practica—Tecnica.* La Paz, 1967.

Villarroel Claure, Rigoberto. *Teorias Esteticas y otros estudios*. La Paz, 1976.

Wethey, Harold. *Arquitectura Virreinal en Bolivia*. La Paz, 1961.

JOURNALS

"Amerique Latine, Stop. Problèmes et Méthodes." *L'Architecture d'Aujourd'hui* 173 (May/June 1974). (English summary cxix-cxxii): 2-108. *See* especially, "Université Technique d'Oruro, Bolivie. F. Anaya, G. Medeiros, architectes." xxvii-lviii.

Arquitectura y Planifación. Journal of the School of Architecture of the Universidad Mayor de San Andrés de La Paz. Edited by Emilio Villanueva. Nos. 1-9 (1944-1949).

"Urbitecturas y monorrieles para La Paz, Bolivia." *Summa* 115 (Buenos Aires, August 1977): 110.

"Viviendas unifamiliares." *Summa* 120, special issue, Buenos Aires, January 1978. *See* especially "Casa Medeiros Anaya, La Paz, Bolivia," p. 52.

Anaya, Franklin and Medeiros, Gustavo. "Una solución arquitectónica para un problema regional." *Cultura Boliviana* 34 (June 1969).

Galindo, Mauricio and Medeiros, Gustavo. "La arquitectura en Bolivia, un esquema tragiocómico." *Mundo Nuevo* 28 (October 1969). (Journal of Ilari)

Ibañez Cuellar, Aquino and Suárez Salas, Virgilio. "Experiencias de un estudio urbano-arquitectónico." *Chiquitos. Misiones Jesuiticas*. 1976.

Jorge, Lazcano. "El edificio de la Universidad señala una norma de la nueva edificación." *La Razon* (La Paz, 19 September 1948).

Mesa, Carlos D. "Emilio Villanueva el arquitecto más importante del Siglo XX en Bolivia." *Arte y Arqueologia* nos. 5, 6, 1978. (Journal of the Instituto de Estudios Bolivianos, Academia Nacional de Ciencias, de Bolivia.)

Mesa, José and Gisbert, Teresa. "Arquitectura Boliviana en los siglos XXIX y XX." *Cultura Boliviana* 21. (Monthly publication of the Technical University of Oruro.)

12

BRAZIL

MARLENE MILAN ACAYABA
and SYLVIA FICHER

The Early Development of Modern Architecture

Brazilian architecture subsisted within the framework of colonialism until the assimilation of Rationalists architecture, mainly the work of Le Corbusier, made possible the coexistence of two contradictory aspirations—the overcoming of cultural dependence and the raising of Brazilian art and architecture to an equivalence with the most advanced European levels. Le Corbusier's ideas, with their somewhat oversimplified Cartesian rigor and prophetic enthusiasm, fulfilled the need for an architectural theory that could be adapted to Brazilian underdevelopment, while fostering independent creativity. Other theories, such as the central European Functionalism of Gropius and Hilberseimer, required technical standards not available in the country, while Frank Lloyd Wright's organicism, identifiable with the existing rural structure of Brazil, could not provide a theoretical background for urban development.

The expression *Rationalist architecture* finally came to have an ample and flexible meaning among Brazilian architects: it would be, succinctly, the architecture espoused by Gropius, Mies van der Rohe, Le Corbusier, and Oud. One could add that, besides the characteristics noted by Hitchcock and Philip Johnson in *The International Style*,[1] Brazilian architects gave preference, during the early days of modern Brazilian architecture, to clearly outlined geometric forms, to a distinction between structure and cladding allowing more freedom in the internal management of space, to the insistent use of *pilotis*, to wide glass screens instead of traditional windows, and to the integration of architecture with the other plastic arts, applied decoration being replaced by murals, glazed tile panels, and sculpture.

Although the influence of the European pioneers of the modern movement was felt in the São Paulo avant-garde as early as the early 1920s, the first modern building in Brazil, designed in 1927 by the architect Gregory Warchavchik, had only a moderate local repercussion.[2] The Modern Movement came to affect Rio de Janeiro as a consequence of the young architect Lucio Costa's personal contact with Le Corbusier in 1929. Costa, appointed dean of the Institute of Fine Arts[3] in 1930, reformed the school's curriculum, till then centered on a Brazilian colonial revival, giving it a Rationalist orientation; the experiment, however, lasted for less than one year.[4] Nevertheless, European theories and projects of the period were the main influence on a group of architects known as the Brazilian Modern pioneers—Attílio Correa de Lima, Eduardo Affonso Reidy, Ernani Vasconcelos, Jorge Moreira, Marcelo and Milton Roberto, Oscar Niemeyer, Paulo Antunes Ribeiro, and Raphael Galvão—who soon started their own lines of research. For instance, Attílio Correa de Lima's 1933 plan for Goiania, the new capital of the State of Goiás,[5] clearly shows his awareness of the climate of argument that prevailed since 1928, as a consequence of the International Congresses of Modern Architecture (CIAM).[6] Within the same context, in 1936 Marcelo and Milton Roberto won the competition for the ABI Building,[7] and in 1937 presented their successful design for the Santos Dumont Airport in Rio.[8]

The invaluable assistance of Dr. Paolo Vanzolini of the Museu de Zoologia, Universidade de São Paulo, with the English translation as well as his patient and careful reading of this chapter are most gratefully acknowledged by the authors.

The first real opportunity of national import was the project for the Ministry of Education and Health building [1936-1943], for which Lucio Costa led a team made up of Carlos Leão, Eduardo Affonso Reidy, Ernani Vasconcelos, Jorge Moreira, and Oscar Niemeyer. Gustavo Capanema, then Minister of Education, invited Le Corbusier to direct the project, but the final design, while based on Le Corbusier's proposal, was a result of the Brazilian group's work.[9] The building consists of two parts: a high volume on *pilotis*, housing the offices, and a perpendicular lower one, comprising the auditorium and the exhibition hall. The ensemble, occupying a whole city block, was placed in such a way as to create a plaza in the thickly built Rio downtown. The treatment of the facades was meant to fit the insulation pattern. One exposure was paneled in glass from top to bottom; on the opposite side, a *brise-soleil* was built of fixed vertical and movable horizontal concrete slats. The internal space was also organized along entirely original lines for the time: the plan is free—wooden partitions may be adapted at will to administrative needs and are low enough to ensure adequate cross-ventilation—and the circulation of public and staff is kept separate. In the spirit of integrating plastic arts and architecture, its auditorium is faced with glazed tile designed by the distinguished contemporary painter Candido Portinari and the gardens are complemented with works of vanguard sculptors, Lipschitz, Bruno Giorgi, and Antonio Celso.[10] The building received wide professional and popular acclaim, and sparked a mood of creativity, the immediate products of which achieved international recognition at the New York Museum of Modern Art show in 1943, documented in *Brazil Builds*.[11]

In 1940, Oscar Niemeyer started a series of government-sponsored projects, the first being the tourist hotel at Ouro Preto.[12] A little later, between 1942 and 1943, he designed the leisure and tourist area, Pampulha Park,[13] on a commission from Juscelino Kubitschek de Oliveira, later president of Brazil and builder of Brasilia. This park, within easy reach of the city, stands by an artificial lake specially dammed for the project, and includes a *casa do baile*, a casino, a yacht club, and a chapel. The *casa do baile* (a small restaurant and public dance hall on an island reached by a footbridge) is circular, but the crescent shape of the built-in service areas converts the floor plan to an oval. The roof is a concrete slab, prolonged in flowing lines along the island's shores. The casino, on a promontory jutting out from the lakeside, includes lounges, gaming rooms, bar and restaurant, with a dance floor and stage, arranged in three definite connected masses. The function of each part is clearly outlined architecturally as form follows function. The search for new forms suitable to contemporary techniques reached a high level of achievement in the design of the Pampulha Yacht Club. The cross-section of the inverted double-sloped roof corresponds precisely to the two different volumes in the upper story, which comprises a restaurant on one side and a large lounge on the other. The Chapel of Saint Francis of Assisi, also on the edge of the lake, is Niemeyer's more controversial project of the period. The nave is roofed by a paraboloid that slopes down toward the altar, roofed by another paraboloid. The vestry and other annexes are under three additional roofs of the same shape, one to the left and two to the right of the altar. The tile mural on the rear facade, depicting episodes of the life of Saint Francis of Assisi, is by Portinari, who also painted the Stations of the Cross and the great altar fresco.

The Ibirapuera Park,[14] designed by Niemeyer beween 1951 and 1955, on the occasion of the fourth centennial of the foundation of the city of São Paulo, is a set of four buildings joined by a sprawling marquee of reinforced concrete supported on slender columns, a covered promenade for visitors, linking all buildings and stressing the unity of the whole. Freely designed in flowing lines, it contrasts with the quiet stability of the various blocks. At one end is the Palace of Industry, a large building 205 meters long. The Palace of Arts, specially designed for sculpture exhibits, is a partly sunken dome whose interior is illuminated by skylights at ground level. The Palace of Nations and the Palace of the States (of Brazil) are located at right angles to one another and were originally intended for plastic arts exhibits.

Still in the line of descent from the Ministry of Education and Health building, the Guinle Park [1948-1954] by Lucio Costa in one of the most beautiful neighborhoods of Rio, represented at the time an entirely new type of housing project.[15] It is small, comprising only three apartment buildings on *pilotis* with garages in the basement. The first building faces the main street leading to the park and the other two are on a street cut through the property, the intent being to keep intact as much of the park as possible. The facades are protected against excess insulation by fixed vertical slats and pierced tile-work (the *combogó*), both aiming for an unimpeded scenic view. The use of traditional materials such as the *combogó*, reminiscent of Arab influence on Portuguese architecture, together with *pilotis, brise-soleil*, and other elements of modern architecture, is part of Costa's continuing effort to develop an architecture on a par with the most advanced international trends while at the same time reflecting a local and regional personality.

As director of the Department of Architecture and

Urban Affairs of the city of Rio de Janeiro, Eduardo Affonso Reidy was responsible for several public projects. In the low-income family, residential complex of Pedregulho [1950] (fig. 12.1)[16], Reidy proposed a seven-story building resting on *pilotis* with ramps that link the structure to the hillside, avoiding elevators. He adopted a curved plan that follows the

12.1. Eduardo Affonso Reidy. Pedregulho Housing, Rio de Janeiro, 1950. (Photograph: Courtesy of the Ministry of Foreign Affairs of Brazil)

landscape, to afford a view of Guanabara Bay for all apartments and to save on earth-moving. His Flamengo Landfill project [1954][17] included, besides the construction of an expressway linking Rio's downtown to its south side, gardens of park dimensions, a new beach, the memorial to the dead of World War II, and the Modern Art Museum [1954-1967]. Reidy was in charge of almost all projects, the most complex being the museum.[18] The main structure, made of large trapezoidal concrete porticos closed by glass screens, assures an indispensable flexibility in the use of inner spaces; concrete slabs hung from the roof by iron cables form a series of mezzanines. The program also included an auditorium, an art school, and a restaurant, articulated to the larger horizontal body of the exhibition area as autonomous volumes. In spite of its rigid geometry, the building blends with the landscape and is beautifully complemented by gardens designed by landscape architect Roberto Burle-Marx.

As a result of the reconciliation of European Rationalist architecture principles with the indegeneous heritage, a freer architectural language was born in Rio de Janeiro. Some factors that decisively contributed to the formation of this language must be emphasized. First, the investigations on sunlight and the architectural devices to enhance and avoid it resulted in the dissemination of one of the elements advocated by Le Corbusier, the *brise-soleil*. Movable or fixed, vertical or horizontal, the *brise-soleil* was applied in a variety of materials, according to the orientation of the building, adding an undoubtedly new plastic asset to it. The *brise-soleil* frequently incorporated variations on the colonial screen and shutters (*muxarabi*), native tradition emerging in the new language in the shape of open-work panels of pierced tiles or precast concrete. Another way in which the colonial tradition has been adequately adapted is in the use of glazed tiles (*azulejos*) as a wall facing. The generally hot and humid climate, with heavy rainfall, makes impractical less-resistent facings such as stucco. The use of *azulejos* was stressed in all colors and shades, especially to accent the nonsupporting character of vertical claddings. The development of advanced techniques for reinforced-concrete construction resulted in light, elegant, and inexpensive structures; unencumbered ground floors, made possible by *pilotis*, afford a better integration of interior and exterior space, so important in a tropical environment. But it is in plasticity, so well exemplified by Niemeyer's work, that the most characteristic element of this language lies. Moving away from strict Functionalism, he tried to invent a new form for each design, unusual and without precedent, the emphasis given to curved surfaces as in the Saint Francis of Assisi Chapel or to the interplay and counterpoint of orthogonal volumes and free-forms as in the Ibirapuera Park. These aspects of his work, which came to be identified by American critics with the new Formalism,[19] were further evolved, as will be seen, in the projects for Brasilia.

The Diffusion of Modern Architecture

The period which extends to the early 1950s represents the most prolific and unified stage in the development of modern Brazilian architecture. This achievement was disseminated by the exodus of architects from Rio to other cities, mainly Recife and Salvador, which stimulated the spread of the language. Contemporary architectural renewal in São Paulo, however, presents a distinctive panorama due to local tendencies started earlier by Warchavchik, Flávio de Carvalho, and Rino Levi and stressed by the arrival of several European architects before and after World War II. Additionally, in São Paulo, instead of at a fine arts institute, architects took their degree at the School of Engineering after completing a course focused on technical capability.

RECIFE

Recife, spread on several islands of the Capibaribe River delta, has a very hot and humid climate moderated by steady ocean breezes. It is the capital of the State of Pernambuco and the main commercial and industrial center of the Northeast, with a population of some two million. Luis Nunes, one of Lucio Costa's former students at Rio's Institute of Fine Arts, is responsible for the first modern designs in the city, where he worked between 1934 and 1937. Nunes had to improve and refine local building techniques in order to undertake his projects, the Olinda water reservoir [1936] being his best-known work. In this pioneer example of the use of reinforced concrete in Pernambuco, the pillar-and-beam structure was left apparent and the spans filled with *combogós* in different patterns on each face of the tower. His Army Hospital [1935] is formed by two longitudinal blocks, for wards and medical services, linked by a third perpendicular one, housing the general services.[20] The latter block, on higher *pilotis*, articulates the complex without interrupting the garden space, incorporated into the building through glass panels. Besides promoting the harmony between traditional features and advanced techniques, Nunes was one of the early innovators of climate control.

SALVADOR

Salvador, the first capital of Brazil, founded in the sixteenth century on a topographically uneven site, is today the capital of the State of Bahia. With its one million inhabitants, it is second only to Recife as a commercial and industrial center of the Northeast. In 1942 the creation of the city's Office for Urban Planning led to an awareness of the possibilities of modern architecture in this old Baroque setting. Paulo Antunes Ribeiro, graduated in Rio, designed the Caramuru Building in 1946, which was particularly well known for its *brise-soleil*.[21] Taking into consideration the warm climate and the exposure of the facades on two streets, both enjoying pleasant views, the architect proposed a system of light iron grills attached at a distance from the wall and covered with bronze wire mesh, thus breaking the monotony of the massive rectangular block. The ground floor and mezzanine occupy the whole area of the lot, whereas the seven-story-high office block is set back to ensure ventilation and light on all sides. A little later, the architect Diógenes Rebouças designed various buildings in the same Rationalist tendency, including the Radiology Institute, the Fonte Nova Stadium, the Estados Unidos Building, and the Bahia Hotel [1951].[22] This latter building comprises service rooms in the basement, a grillroom, nightclub and small shops on the ground floor, an ample lounge, restaurant and kitchen on the second floor, and five stories of bedrooms. Contrasting with the modulated treatment of the upper stories, the public areas display an exuberant diversity further enhanced by the interior decoration, with tile motifs by Paulo Antunes Ribeiro and a large mural by Genaro de Carvalho. In 1957 José Bina Fonyat designed Salvador's Castro Alves Theater, a building of marked sculptural character in which stage and audience are unified within two great interpenetrating triangular prisms.[23]

SÃO PAULO

On the southern highlands, sixty kilometers from the Atlantic Ocean, on an uneven terrain and with a very moist subtropical climate, São Paulo, capital of the state of São Paulo, is the largest city in the country, having some eight million inhabitants (ten to eleven million in Greater São Paulo). While in Rio de Janeiro much activity developed along the lines of Le Corbusier's doctrine, mainly in institutional buildings, in São Paulo modern architecture was accepted more slowly and largely through the efforts of Rino Levi and João Batista Vilanova Artigas in residential projects. Levi's careful choice of building materials, rigorous construction techniques, and thorough analyses of functional aspects are ever-present features of his works, such as the School of Philosophy, Letters, and Sciences (*Sedes Sapientiae*) of the Catholic University of São Paulo [1940], the Seguradora Brasileira building [1948], the Antonio Prudente hospital [1947-1954], and the Parahyba factory [1956].[24] In the *Sedes Sapientiae* project, Levi organized classrooms and administration areas around an inner patio surrounded by a marquee, a contemporary interpretation of the traditional convent cloister. This patio serves as a gradual transition between the outside and the inside, emphasized by diffuse lighting through glass brick walls. Leaning toward a more Organic language in residential designs such as the Milton Guper and the Castor Delgado Perez homes, both projects from 1951 to 1953,[25] he employed shaded patios to control sunlight, achieving a fine balance between architecture and nature. The Guper house, on a corner lot, is enhanced by gardens reaching from the sidewalk towards the house. The facades clearly reflect the inner organization and almost disappear amidst the vegetation. The social areas open on an inner patio partly covered by an arbor. The space is divided by custom-designed furniture, even to the bedroom partitions, brick masonry being avoided whenever possible. Rino Levi, through his work and his teaching, deeply influenced young São Paulo architects such as Carlos Millan and Joaquim Guedes.

The first projects of Vilanova Artigas reflected his adherence to Frank Lloyd Wright's Organic architecture as well as his search for spatial unity. In the Paranhos home [1942-1944] the architect made use of the natural slope and programmed the house in independent overlapping volumes jutting out in the open.[26] The wooden beam-work that supports the roof was left exposed, furthering an integration of the several internal spaces. Building materials—brick, wood, and clay tiles—were unadorned. However, by the mid-1940s Vilanova Artigas shifted toward Rationalism, as had contemporary architects in Rio. In the Mario Bittencourt residence [1948] all activities were planned for one single space and distributed along different levels around a central tower housing the water tank and the bathrooms. This internal organization is reflected by the well-defined geometric shapes of the external volume. For the bus depot in the city of Londrina [1951] Vilanova Artigas used a sharp geometry, articulating the building in two sections: a trapezoidal prism containing ticket booths, checkrooms, restaurant, and so on, in several floors linked by ramps; and a series of vaults on *pilotis* as roofing over the bus platforms. The contrast among all parts is further emphasized by the opposition of straight and curved lines in the facades.[27]

These first steps of modern architecture in São Paulo reveal a trend that became progressively more pronounced, the turning of buildings inwards, closing them to the urban environment whose industrial character does not invite the enjoyment of open spaces.

The Development of Brasilia, 1956-1960

After World War II, industrialization accelerated change and Brazil entered into a phase of new vitality. Architectural discussion was stimulated by the arrival of foreign architects, by the opening of new schools, and by international exchanges of publications. The School of Architecture of Mackenzie University opened in 1945, the School of Architecture and Planning of the University of São Paulo in 1948, and the School of Architecture of the University of Rio Grande do Sul in 1949. Of new topics that arose and were argued heatedly the most important and controversial was the projected new Brazilian federal capital to be built in the central highlands.

The intention of moving the capital from Rio de Janeiro to the midwestern region of the country dates from the beginning of the nineteenth century, when Brazil won its independence from Portugal. Finally in 1956, President Juscelino Kubitschek de Oliveira created the Company of the Urbanization of the New Capital—NOVACAP—in charge of the construction of the new city and entrusted to Oscar Niemeyer the direction of all architectural design. As a pioneering effort in the heart of the sparsely inhabited central plateau, the construction of Brasilia assumed from the beginning a double role: it attracted people from northeastern Brazil, who had not been able to participate in the benefits of the economic processes of the large urban centers, and marked a starting point in the conquest of an immense, underexploited region. In a national contest held to select a plan, competing projects reflected the profound influence of Rationalist urbanism, as stated in the functional principles of the 1933 Charter of Athens (CIAM-IV).[28] Lucio Costa's winning project was limited to the layout for the initial settlement of the city after which regional planning would follow. His proposal was probably the most feasible, considering existing technological conditions and the remarkably short span of three years in which construction was to be completed.

Costa arranged the city's zoning in two perpendicular axes as a direct function of the planned transit system.[29] Residential areas are disposed in large aligned blocks (*superquadras*) made of four square subblocks along a broadly curved north-south axis and separated by wide green belts. In these blocks the multiple habitational units are orthogonally arranged with a maximum of six floors on *pilotis*. Local commerce and parking lots are situated in areas accessible to the *superquadras*, with vehicular and pedestrian circulation strictly separated. For each four-block unit, there is a church, a school, a playground, and an athletic field. The east-west, or monumental axis, is adapted to the slope of the terrain, gradually descending eastward to the lake in broad terraces. Municipal administration buildings are located in the west beyond the sports area, to either side of which are the botanical and zoological gardens. East of the sports area, at the highest point of the terrain and close to the intersection of the two axes, stands the television tower.

The junction of the two axes is masterfully arranged in three *niveaux*: the upper level houses the entertainment quarters of the city including cinemas, theaters, restaurants, hotels, and the opera house; the intermediate level is reserved for the central bus station and parking lots and serves as a thoroughfare for slow-moving traffic; the lowest level is a subterranean thoroughfare for fast-moving vehicles, connecting the two wings of the north-south axis. From the upper niveau, the perspective of the Ministries Esplanade opens up revealing the cathedral, in the east, just to the north of the axis, and in the center, a group of buildings which house the several governmental ministries. The Plaza of the Three Powers situated at the far eastern end of the monumental axis houses the Supreme Court, the Government Palace, and the Congress.

In Brasilia, Lucio Costa carried the urbanistic principles of the twentieth century to extremes: he abandoned the traditional concept of a street, enforced a hierarchy of urban functions, introduced vast areas of greenery between isolated buildings, and separated traffic circulation according to its different functions. His plan granted Oscar Niemeyer total freedom in the design of the major office buildings. Niemeyer enlisted the help of a few young architects, and in less than two years of remarkably intense effort, sketches, plans, final conceptions, and drawings were completed. The Presidential Alvorada Palace, designed before Costa's overall plan was defined, is a rectangular building with a distinctive arcade resting upon a ground-level base of very low, broad, and shallow arches.[30] Aligned with these, inverted arches are drawn upward into tall, tapering forms that diminish in section as they rise, to recall inverted columns and support the broadly projecting roof of the palace. This beautifully plastic invention has become a symbol of the city. For the principal area of the monumental axis, the triangular Plaza of the Three Powers,[31] Niemeyer brought into harmony the differing scales of the buildings and of the city. He adopted unprecedented forms for each building, differentiating functions and creating varied plastic elements which brighten one's impression of the plaza. The Palace of Congress defines the principal side of the plaza and separates it from the Ministries Esplanade without interrupting the perspective of the monumental axis.[32] The oblong palace is surmounted by a vast platform from which two low forms emerge, the dome of the Senate and the larger inverted dome of the House of Representatives. A short distance from the west facade of the Congress, just south of its shorter axis, two very tall, slablike office buildings comprising the Secretariat are composed in tandem confronting one another closely as mirror images. The contrast between this pair rising skyward and the plaza's horizontality is so stark and the scale of construction so vast that the result, as intended, is very dramatic. At the remaining corners of the plaza, the Government Palace and the Supreme Court repeat, with differently shaped colonnades, the geometeric mass enclosed by the covered gallery found in the Alvorada Palace.[33]

The regularity of the Ministries Esplanade is broken by two palaces: the Ministry of Foreign Affairs and the Ministry of Justice. The former, also called the Palace of the Arches, is a regular volume enclosed by four loggias with identical facades composed in a sucession of full arches.[34] Jointly, the deep loggias, their facades, and an encircling reflecting pool guarantee control over excessive heat in the building. For the Palace of Justice, Niemeyer developed variations of the arched motif: they appear only in the front and rear facades, while the sides consist of vertical sheets.[35] Water flows in cascades from curved concrete slabs between the arches of the main facade which have the same function in climatic control as the reflecting pool.

Niemeyer's innovative ideas are best seen in the cathedral [1970] (fig. 12.2), whose circular plan expresses his concept of the structure as a sculpture.[36] Dispensing with the tradition of a facade altogether, a subterranean passage leads to the cathedral floor, which is lower than the exterior. Visible above the plaza are only the thin elegantly curved ribs of the roofscape that soar upward. An outstanding effect is created by the contrast between the penumbra at the entrance of the cathedral and the luminosity which filters into it through the glass surfaces between the rising ribs.

After the extraordinary architectural tour de force that is Brasilia, Niemeyer went on to achieve international recognition as one of the leading architects of the postwar era.

Regional Trends since 1960

The population of Brazil, during the three centuries of its colonial history, was distributed among scattered little towns along its extensive coast line. Settlements and architecture closely followed Portuguese traditions all over the country, a vast tropical area with little climatic regional differentiation. Colonization in all its aspects was a Portuguese monopoly. The relative homogeneity of colonial times broke up, first under the influence of the opening of Brazilian ports to international trade (1810), then of the proclamation of independence (1822) with the subsequent transfer to Brazil of its own administration and management, and finally with an intensive flow of European immigrants. Regional cultural differences became more pronounced as the nineteenth century progressed, but not enough to mark the architectural production that continued to follow European models.

The first stage of modern Brazilian architecture, from the Ministry of Education and Health buildings to the development of Brasilia, did not reflect cultural differences. Le Corbusier's internationalist influence contradictorily allied to the political nationalism of the time reinforced the creation of a single architectural language. At that time architects appeared in the field of culture as united in the struggle for a definition of the profession as such and for adequate teaching standards. With Brasilia as a full assertion of this effort, theories both assimilated and enriched are made concrete in buildings and urban design, to become contributions of international importance.

However, simultaneously with the construction of Brasilia, and due to the process of industrialization that spread throughout the country, the architectural language of common origins had to fit into a new

12.2. Oscar Niemeyer. Interior, Cathedral at Brasília, model 1959, completed 1970. (Photograph: Michel Moch, courtesy of the Ministry of Foreign Affairs of Brazil)

context: economic, climatic, technological, and programmatic differences led to a process of regionalization. While it is possible to speak about a tropical architecture all the way from Rio to Fortaleza and Manaus, contrasts between the industrialized South and the rural and impoverished Northeast reflect insurmountable social differences. Architecture throughout the country has lost its monumental character, the city as a whole has become a focus of interest, and architects have become more concerned with the practices of city planning. The demiurgic role of the Rio de Janeiro architect, a builder of new cities, has vanished. A unified Brazilian architecture no longer exists; substituted has been a fragmentary production, whose logic must be sought out in each region.

THE SOUTHERN REGION: SÃO PAULO, CURITIBA, AND PORTO ALEGRE

The architecture of São Paulo since the mid-1950s abides by the principle of strict Functionalism and a technological interest in the industrialization of construction. Yet, an expressive esthetic element also exists in which the strength of contrasting masses and the extensive use of exposed reinforced concrete resulted in a dramatic new architecture. The São Paulo Museum of Art [1957] by Lina Bo Bardi is an example (fig. 12.3).[37] Located on one of the highest points of the city, the museum is a rectangular cage suspended in midair by two enormous concrete porticos spanning sixty-two meters. Such a forceful technical approach accentuates the monumental character of the building without insisting on its formal aspects.

But it is the School of Architecture and Planning of the University of São Paulo, designed in 1961 by Vilanova Artigas in collaboration with Carlos Cascaldi, that best synthesizes the paths to be followed by architecture in São Paulo during the next decades.[38] From the outside, the building, with its equal opposite facades, is organized in a manner that might be said to be Classical, due to the trapezoidal columns carrying the heavy gable that completely closes the upper floors. The inner space of this box-like structure, covered by a concrete grill, is organized into several levels designed around eccentrically located ramps. The building is livened by the central void on the ground-level plaza that is lighted by broad skylights and into which the different floors open. An essential characteristic is the use of concrete without facing as the only building material. In this work Vilanova Artigas uses closed volumes again, on a broader scale, and gables supported by tapering piers, such as can be seen in his earlier projects, for example, the Baeta [1956] and Mendonça [1957] houses,[39] and the Itanhaém [1960][40] and Guarulhos [1961] public schools.[41] In later projects,

12.3. Lina Bo Bardi. Museum of Art of São Paulo, 1957-1969. (Photograph: Courtesy of Romulo Fernando Fialdini)

such as the boathouse of the Santa Paula Yacht Club [1960][42] he develops further the idea of a concrete grid within which the space is organized independently of the structure in accordance with the needs of the program. Both in São Paulo and other areas, architects were influenced by his preference for dynamic balances, for daring structures, and especially for unfaced concrete.

Paulo Mendes da Rocha, in his first designs in collaboration with João Eduardo de Gennaro, adopted formalist solutions, as for instance in his gymnasium of the Club Paulistano in 1961, which displays a sense of pure form and a quality of aerial lightness.[43] Soon after, he turned toward the use of solid concrete walls, with emphasis on internal space rather than outward shape, showing the impact of Artigas's work even among practicing professionals. For the Butantan homes [1964] he arranged all the living areas on a single floor and enclosed them in a mass of exposed, untreated concrete in the manner of *architecture brut*.[44] Mendes da Rocha's design for the Brazilian pavilion at the Osaka Fair in 1970 well embodies the principles of São Paulo architecture at the time.[45] The project comprises a lightly posed rigidly geometrical roof with many skylights which is worked into uneven undulations. Extending beyond, the projection of the roof integrates the pavilion with the ensemble of the fair. The covering is supported by two large prestressed concrete beams, each on two props but with different spans. Three of these props consist only of artificial rubber cushions on rises of the ground; the fourth one is made of two perpendicular round arches. A ramp gives access to the pavilion that comprises an auditorium, offices, restrooms, and so forth, all below ground level. His art museum at the University of São Paulo, designed in 1975 and unhappily not built as yet, follows much the same principles.[46]

Architect Joaquim Guedes in his early works experimented with different alternatives for the definition of space. For the Cunha Lima home [1958] he employed a reinforced concrete structure with large superimposed concrete slabs supported by four central thin pillars and concrete brackets.[47] The lot being narrow, the house is disposed lengthwise, its linear character emphasized by windowless brick side walls. The house is cantilevered over the slope of the back of the lot; the facade, turned towards the valley, is protected only by a *brise-soleil* and the several levels are joined by a graceful flying staircase. In the Itabira courthouse [1958] Guedes works with the interplay of individualized and clearly defined volumes sitting directly on the ground.[48] Oblique lines are emphasized, as are irregularly shaped windows and heavy walls reminiscent of Scandinavian trends. In his later projects, as the Dalton Toledo's [1963] and Sergio Ferreira Leite's [1963] residences, Guedes shows his interest in the exploration of technical alternatives employing concrete and brick vaults.[49] In recent years he has turned to town planning and is now working on large-scale projects for the new cities of Carajás in the State of Pará and Caraíba in the State of Bahia.

Most striking of the projects of architect Carlos Millan are the Morumbi [1960] and the Roberto Millan [1961] homes; the former in a single-level, parallelepiped, elevated upon thin pillars; the latter characterized by a central void around which various functions are developed.[50] The Harmonia Tennis Club designed by Fabio Penteado in 1960, is a very large spatial umbrella, housing all social areas with terraces that create a broad visual field, from the main hall through the building and beyond to the swimming pool.[51] On the facades of the clubhouse Penteado used large panels of colored canvas, an original device for protection from the sun.

Improvisations upon the age-old idea of vaulting have been recurrent in the fairly recent work of several of São Paulo's architects. Sergio Ferro and Rodrigo Lefevre have always sought constructive solutions leading to mass production and cost reduction. For the Cotia house [1965], they proposed a barrel vault sitting directly on the foundations, easily built through the use of precast curved members of concrete filled with bricks.[52] The unencumbered space is divided by plywood partitions; the bedrooms were projected with built-in beds. The great simplicity of the finishing does not harm the project's artistic value. The concern with the integration of his house [1971] with the gardens around it, led architect Marcos Acayaba to place a 270-square-meter parabolic shell over the terraced lot sheltering the internal spaces that open fully towards the outside.[53] Architect Eduardo Longo has devoted himself since 1974 to the construction of spheric houses where all elements, including furniture and bathrooms, were molded by hand in lightweight concrete and coated with epoxy resin (fig. 12.4).[54] This prototype house, with an area of about 100 square meters, has three floors joined by a central staircase and is a model which can be industrially produced.

The urban environment has also been a concern of São Paulo's architects. The Fifth Avenida office building [1959] by Pedro Paulo de Melo Saraiva and Miguel Juliano, for instance, presented a new orientation in the utilization of the urban lot.[55] The principal volume is set perpendicularly to the street, the Paulista Avenue, keeping the building from touching neighbors. In the space freed in this way, a broadened *porte-cochère* for vehicular entrance creates a

12.4. Eduardo Longo. Spheric House prototype. São Paulo, from 1974. (Photograph: Courtesy of Marilyn Ficher and Marlene Milan Acayaba)

12.5. João Batista Vilanova Artigas, architect. Jaú Bus Depot. View of the lateral façade, City of Jaú, S.P., 1973. (Photograph: Courtesy of the architect)

dynamic link between the building and the urban network, while a semisubterranean access for pedestrians forms a gradual transition between exterior and interior. Above there are seventeen floors. The structure being external, the floor plans are completely free, except, of course, for elevators, staircases, and restrooms. The facade is protected by an adjustable *brise-soleil* forming a continuous screen from top to bottom. The southeastern facade has glass curtains. Rino Levi and his collaborator Roberto Cerqueira Cesar used a similar solution for the Itáu Bank building [1961-1965] on the same avenue.[56] The ground floor, occupying all of a corner lot, contains the public areas. A series of vertical concrete sheets along the facades creates a loggia which separates the bank from the busy avenue. The adjustable aluminum *brise-soleil*, protecting the northeastern facade, and the round staircase jutting out from the regular free-standing volume on the southeastern facade results in a sculptural quality. These two projects, which undeniably remind one of the Ministry of Education and Health, are two among the few examples of real interest in Paulista Avenue, one of the main arteries of the city, on which many high-rise buildings have been built during the last ten years. These constructions naively reflect recent international trends, simply copied and forming an underdeveloped catalogue of contemporary architecture.

Vilanova Artigas's bus station in Jaú[57] (figs. 12.5, 12.6, and 12.7), designed in 1973, must also be con-

12.6. João Batista Vilanova Artigas, architect. Jaú Bus Depot. Interior view from upper level towards bus platforms, City of Jaú, S.P., 1973. (Photograph: Courtesy of the architect)

12.7. João Batista Vilanova Artigas, architect. Jaú Bus Depot. Interior view at the rear street level (ticket booth level), City of Jaú, S.P., 1973. (Photograph: Courtesy of the architect)

sidered from the viewpoint of its relationship with the urban environment, in this case a city in the interior of the State of São Paulo. It consists only of a set of horizontals vaulted over by a reinforced concrete grid resting on large tree-shaped columns, the building's sole formal element. By the use of passageways the circulation of buses is isolated and people are encouraged to move spontaneously in this functional wall-less structure that has become a new covered square for the town.

The Zezinho Magalhães Prado low-income housing complex [1968][58] by Vilanova Artigas, Fabio Penteado, and Paulo Mendes da Rocha represents one of the few occasions in which architects had an opportunity to contribute to a large project of social relevance (fig. 12.8). Comprising ten thousand residential units in a suburb of São Paulo, the apartment buildings in the complex are joined in pairs by common staircases, creating an outside intermediate space, more private and richer in comparison with the customary series of monotonous buildings. Each building, with only three stories on *pilotis*, has no need for elevators; the staircase common to a pair of buildings serves only two flats per floor, making hallways unnecessary. As a consequence each apartment faces to longitudinal facades. The flats, each an area of about sixty square meters, contain a living room, three bedrooms, a bathroom, a kitchen, and a little service area. The interior plywood divisions in the bedrooms can be removed in the case of smaller families. The walls between apartments are made of concrete blocks strengthened with iron rods, thus doing away with the need for vertical structural members. The external enclosure consists of cantilevered precast-concrete boxes, reaching half the height of the floor and functioning as cupboards. Above these runs a continuous belt of iron-framed windows. Schools, entertainment and leisure centers, commercial areas, and other perquisites of urban life are included in the project's conception, as in the Brasilia *superquadras* some ten years earlier. This project, sponsored by the State of São Paulo Office for Low-Income Housing (CECAP) has been quite successful, inevitably serving as a model for other programs, such as the Jundiaí housing complex by Abrahão Sanovicz.

In order to expand the State of São Paulo's system of public schools, a program of low-cost construction was devised in 1975. In a school for the town of Vicente de Carvalho [1976] Vilanova Artigas revived his earlier interest in the interplay of materials and textures, combining concrete blocks with a wooden structural system and a roofing of clay tiles. The unconventional admixture of construction techniques of different origins, such as brick archways with wooden trestles, points to changes in the character of

12.8. Paulo Mendes da Rocha, Fabio Penteado and João Batista Vilanova Artigas, architects. "Zezinho Magalhães Prado" Housing complex. View of residential buildings and Health Care Service in the foreground. Guarulhos, São Paulo, 1968. (Photograph: Courtesy of the architect)

São Paulo's architecture, towards more informal and less monumental designs, away from the stern Brutalism of the last two decades.

Curitiba—capital of the State of Paraná, with one million inhabitants, located in a subtropical southern plateau about a hundred kilometers inland—is the main urban center of an important agricultural area of the country that has been, for a decade or so, undergoing a rapid process of industrialization. The introduction of modern architecture to Curitiba occurred at first, as in other Brazilian cities, through the activity of a few isolated professionals and was strengthened in 1958 by the foundation of the School of Architecture of the University of Paraná. A little later, the arrival of architects from São Paulo, such as Luis Forte and José Maria Gandolfi in the mid-1960s, brought about a great influence on this architectural output. However, given the subtropical climate and the ethnic composition of the population, with a strong contribution from Eastern and Northern Europe, the residential projects show a leaning towards Organic architecture, mainly of Finnish inspiration, with a predominance of untreated natural materials, of wooden structures, and of intersecting volumes.

Curitiba is set apart from other Brazilian cities by the thoroughness with which planning and urban design are jointly carried out. The process began in 1965, with a city master plan by São Paulo architect Jorge Wilheim working with a team of architects from Curitiba. The plan was initially conducted by the city's Department of Urban Planning and later by the newly created Institute for Urban Research and Planning (IPPUC). Thanks to the latter's autonomy from the city administration the plan was developed by members of the original staff, thus assuring its continuity in all aspects. In 1971 architect Jaime Lerner, director of the IPPUC at the time, was appointed mayor of Curitiba and vigorously started the implementation of the project.[59] The master plan had anticipated a series of measures (zoning, traffic circulation, and a system of mass transportation) capable of orienting the growth of the city without recourse to urban renewal and without leading to the decay of underprivileged areas. At the same time the plan aimed at a policy of development through industrialization, including an industrial district adapted to the region's economic potential. The real originality of Jaime Lerner and coworkers is in the solutions adopted to rapidly provide a mass-transport system and the urban amenities that had been lacking in the city. The traffic network avoids expensive underground tracks and consists of exclusive bus expressways. Embarkation platforms above sidewalk level are now being considered in order to expedite traffic. Traffic around the downtown district follows a low-speed ring; the streets within it are closed to vehicular traffic and turned into broad walks lined with urban facilities, such as street coffee shops, flower markets, phone booths, book and magazine stalls, all in an environment of flower beds and benches. Some city streets were also closed to traffic and remodelled into playgrounds and sports facilities for the neighborhood. Parks were quickly developed by the identification of green areas through aerial photographs and their immediate expropriation. Emphasis was given to the preservation of a still undecayed urban environment and to the improvement of living standards. A steady refusal to use solely technocratic solutions permitted the maintenance of traditional values during a phase of demographic growth, an extreme conceptual position in Brazilian contemporary history.

Porto Alegre, capital of the State of Rio Grande do Sul, is the main urban center (population 1,300,000) in the extreme South of the country. In 1945 the architecture curriculum of the Institute of Fine Arts was started by architects Edgar Graeff and Demetrio Ribeiro, who had studied, respectively, in Rio de Janeiro and Montevideo. A peculiar overtone to architectural teaching at Porto Alegre, reflecting Montevideo's proximity and cultural importance, was introduced with the discussion of Socialist Realism and Soviet Constructivism to complement the study of Le Corbusier and the Brazilian pioneers.

Edgar Graeff, with an important contribution in the field of architectural teaching and criticism, has dedicated himself mainly to urban planning. His best-known works are the master plans for the cities of Caxias, Alvorada do Norte, and Uraçu in the State of Rio Grande do Sul. Among his recent projects are the designs for the official residence of the minister of mines and energy in Brasilia and the Laje da Pedra Hotel in Canela (RGS). Architect Carlos Fayet always adopts new construction techniques in his designs, such as the precast elements of the Petrobrás building at Canoas [1962] or the metallic structure of the Vitória City bus depot [1978]. For the CEASA [1970], the wholesale food market of Porto Alegre (fig. 12.9), he conceived an undulated covering spanning the 45 meter by 330 meter hall.[60] This roof is composed of overlapping brick vaults with sheds of lighting and is supported only by the longitudinal facades. Finally, Miguel Pereira began his career in Porto Alegre during the 1960s with two projects: the Concordia School and the Pasqualini refinery.[61] In 1969 he accepted the post of Dean of the Department of Architecture at the University of Brasilia and more recently has become well known through his participation in various professional organizations in Brazil and abroad. Given the dearth of published informa-

12.9. Carlos Fayet, architect. CEASA (wholesale food market), view of the interior brick vaults, Porto Alegre, 1970. (Photograph: Courtesy of "Projeto")

tion on Porto Alegre architecture, that should become the object of more specific research.

RIO DE JANEIRO

In São Paulo, a predominant tenor, starting in the 1950s and accomplishing a language of its own in the following decades, was evident not only in the work of Vilanova Artigas but also in the rise of a local group of professionals. The process in Rio de Janeiro was different altogether. From relative unity in the 1930s and 1940s, there was a transition to a fragmentary and variegated production in the 1950s. The project for Brasilia marks a turning point. Conceived by Lucio Costa and Oscar Niemeyer as representative of the whole of Brazilian architecture, the actual contribution to it by other architects was ignored. In the 1960s, the basic theses of Brasilia, long taken as unquestioned truths, were subjected to reevaluation and criticism, and new experimental paths were explored. Nevertheless, in Rio there were the many advantages of being associated with a privileged urban site, on the seashore, hemmed in by mountains covered with an exuberant tropical forest. In this setting architecture became overwhelmingly scenic with buildings almost always making use of the landscape in a symbiotic integration, either employing scenery as a backdrop or simply constituting a frame for it.

The first generation of modern Rio architects, including Jorge Moreira and Marcelo and Milton Roberto, as well as others such as Eduardo Affonso Reidy, followed Le Corbusier's ideals more or less faithfully. Jorge Moreira continued in his Rationalist orientation, as seen in such major projects as his Institute of Puericulture [1953] and the Antonio Cappas residence [1958].[62] The institute was clearly articulated in three parallel blocks adjoining a fourth transverse block, all of which opened into a garden and were most advantageously sited upon a gentle slope. Milton and Marcelo Roberto had developed their own architectural language with emphasis on plastic aspects that differed from Oscar Niemeyer's works. Their first projects, already cited, consisted of pure volumes in which the interplay of masses and voids followed a Rationalist esthetic. In the Samambaia plantation [1954][63] they achieved a closer link between contemporary technique and traditional materials with a dramatic pavilion that projects from a steep slope and is supported by precast beams, resting on five walls of rough stone masonry. During this period, they planned several office and apartment buildings in the downtown district and on the affluent South Side, featuring undulating facades to break a sense of geometric order. In the Marques de Herval office building an especially dynamic effect is seen in the treatment of facades with aluminum blinds secured to a metallic frame with overlapping horizontally curved beams.[64] In the Souza Cruz building about a decade later [1962-1964] the facade was enlivened with a metallic *brise-soleil* on concrete brackets.[65] Recently the Robertos have finished an impressive exhibition hall at Salvador, Bahia.

Henrique Mindlin, an architect who began his career in São Paulo and worked extensively in Rio after 1942, introduced Mies van der Rohe's imposing steel and glass structures into Brazil with his Avenida Central building [1958].[66] His books *Brazilian Architecture* (1943) and *Modern Architecture in Brazil* (1956) were very important in publicizing Brazil's achievements abroad.[67]

Sergio Bernardes is well known for his varied production. In his Brazilian pavilion at the International Fair in Brussels [1958] a temporary character was enhanced by the use of a light metallic structure that could be easily disassembled.[68] The roof is held under tension by steel cables anchored on four metallic trestles, and the floor is a broadly spiralling ramp, surrounding the garden (by Burle-Marx) where the exhibits were held. In his own home in 1960,[69] influenced by Bruno Zevi,[70] he adopted concepts of Organic architecture. The house is situated on a rocky bluff over the sea and organized in two levels. The entrance level, built on a natural stone floor, contains the living areas and stands out with an orthogonal architecture of concrete and glass, conceived in relation to the bay. The lower level, integrated into the hill with rough stone walls, comprises the bedrooms and bathrooms. Bernardes achieved synthesis of Organic and Rationalist concepts in the siting of the building and in the technical solutions adopted. A preference for hi-tech construction and few if any theoretical prejudices has led Sergio Bernardes to recent designs, such as a hotel in Manaus and the Brazilian Institute of Coffee, but because of their visionary character they will probably never be built.

Although in the 1960s Rio lost some of its national importance with the transfer of the federal capital to Brasilia, its architectural output continued to display a great richness, as some few significant examples illustrate. Helio Ribas Marinho's and Marcos Konder Neto's World War II Memorial project [1956-1960] at the Flamengo Landfill is an early example of the influence of Niemeyer's Brasilia.[71] The architects arranged the complex design as a half-sunken horizontal structure facing the bay. In order to enhance its monumental character, they designed twin slender concrete slats joined at the top by a curved plate, the outline of which reminds one of the Congress Palace at Brasilia. Completing the composition is a sculptural group by Alfredo Ceschiatti. At the new campus of Rio de Janeiro State University [1973][72] architects Flavio Marinho Rego and Luis Paulo Conde returned to the idea of an urban campus that was contrary to the Rationalist solution of isolation from the city. Given the limited space available, they adopted a solution of relatively high buildings with interconnected blocks.

Zanine Caldas, a dynamic figure in Rio architecture, began as a plastic artist, executing scale models for Niemeyer. In the last fifteen years he has devoted himself to furniture design and home building, becoming expert in wood and its application to construction. Lately he has begun a thorough survey of urban slums and dwellings constructed on piles in order to study spontaneous technical solutions and since 1977 has worked on Portinho de Massaró, a private-housing condominium he conceived. Caldas has also set up a small factory in Nova Viçosa, State of Bahia, employing local artisans to manufacture and assemble the structure for houses entirely from local woods. Modular elements are transported to the Portinho site and there set upon stone or concrete piers to minimize dampness. Although constructed completely of modular elements, each house is unique.

Oscar Niemeyer must be numbered among Rio professionals, even though much of his work has consisted of exceptional projects executed abroad. Few architects in this century have had the opportunity of being the sole architect for so many monumental works, from palaces and mosques to universities and whole cities.[73] Between 1964 and 1965 he realized several projects in Israel such as a town in the Negev, Haifa University, and a residence for the Rothschilds. In 1967 he began a series of projects in France that included the French Communist Party building in Paris and the Dominicans' Spiritual Center in Sainte-Baume. During the following years he worked in Algeria on important projects such as the Mosque, the Algiers Civic Center, and Constantine University. In the Mondadori Publishing Headquarters in Milan [1973-1976] Niemeyer has created a new structural and design dynamic by building an immensely long, open, arcuated concrete structure and suspending within most of its length a conventional steel and glass building. New, too, for him is the pronounced, repeated variation of intercolumniations, breaking the design into rhythmic sections seen against the regularity of the building within. At either of the short ends, instead of arches a rectilinear design prevails, giving us a sense of finality. This reinterpretation of themes thought to have been exhausted reveals the extent of his inventive abilities once again. In recent years, after a period of exile due to political problems, he returned to work in Brazil. He designed the National Hotel, the first in a series of round towers built in Rio, and the Musical Center in the Flamengo Landfill [1978]. At the same time, his work abroad continued. In France, the Bobigny Exchange was opened and projects are under way for three areas to be developed (*zacs*), Grasse, Dieppe, and Villejuif.[74] Among his latest projects are the new building for Fata Engineering in Turin, Italy, in collaboration with Massimo Germari,[75] the State of São Paulo Electric Centrals building,[76] and the Algiers Ecologic Park.[77]

BRASILIA SINCE 1960

Since the inauguration of Brasilia on 21 April 1960 the NOVACAP has overseen the completion of many federal administration buildings. Generally monumental, these reflected Niemeyer's earlier works for the new city. During the 1960s and into the 1970s, the campus of the University of Brasilia, northeast of the intersection of the city's two axes, has been built with assistance of numerous collaborators associated with the School of Architecture there.[78] All schools of the university were joined in a single three-story building, the Central Institute, while the remaining facilities were located in adjacent areas around the campus's main square. The Central Institute [1961] by Niemeyer and João Filgueiras Lima avoids an overbearing monumentality and is integrated into the landscape by hugging the natural curves of the terrain along its 720-meter length. A low curved volume, called "the big earthworm" by students, consists of a precast structure of two longitudinal wings connected by means of roofed 15-meter-wide sidewalks. Its eastern facade is covered by *brise-soleil*. The wider eastern wing houses departmental quarters, classrooms, ateliers, and laboratories while the western one is reserved for the larger auditoriums. Other campus buildings constructed between 1963 and 1968 are the Colina Teachers Dormitory and the Engineering Department laboratories by Filgueiras Lima; the Student Dormitories by

Leo Bonfim and Alberto Xavier; the Rectory by Paulo Zimbres; the Central Library by José Galbinski and Miguel Pereira; the University Dining Hall by José Galbinski; and the Sports Center by Ricardo Farret and Paulo Zimbres.

Apart from the NOVACAP projects, designs concluded at Brasilia in this period are the Amazon Bank by Mauricio Roberto; the National Development Bank by Alcides da Rocha Miranda; the National Federation of Industry building by Pedro Paulo de Melo Saraiva and Paulo Mendes da Rocha; and the Itamaraty *superquadra* by Sérgio Souža Lima. Constructed since 1968 are the Sports Center by Ícaro Castro Melo and the Graduate School for Public Servants [1973] by Pedro Paul de Melo Saraiva in collaboration with Sergio Ficher and Henrique Cambiaghi Filho.[79] The School for Public Servants with its 32,000 square meters of built area, includes classrooms, laboratories, a TV studio, a computer center, library, and auditorium as well as student dormitories and a complete recreation and sports center. To integrate such a complex program, the project was developed in several blocks covered by a single structure of stunted arches 30 meters in span. Shaded internal gardens between the blocks contribute to the spatial unity of the school while at the middle the auditorium is a truncated cone that contrasts with a general rectilinearity. With arcades on its principal facades and elimination of conflict between vehicular and pedestrian circulation, the project fits well into the city's architectural and urbanistic principles.

In Brasilia, the large scale of projects and the availability of funds permitted experiments in industrial construction. Joáo Filgueiras Lima, who joined Oscar Niemeyer's team at NOVACAP soon after the inauguration of the city, deserves special mention for his research into precasting techniques. In his most recent designs, such as the Taguatinga Hospital [1970] and the Camargo Correa building, his studies facilitated processes for the casting, assembling, and fixing of concrete elements.[80] At the Taguatinga Hospital the slope of the terrain accommodates four main levels, each with a one-story block and each with ample room for expansion. On the lower level are the in-patient wards; on the next, general services and laboratories; on the third, surgical and obstetrics rooms, medical archives, emergency wards, and so on; and on the top are the out-patient clinics. All blocks are connected by wide inclined galleries that allow for an efficient flow of patients and personnel with a minimum of vertical circulation. Each stage has garden terraces that serve as solaria. In all blocks the precast structure is roofed in a cellular system of partly fenestrated tunnel vaults that permit lighting and ventilation, while the whole is enclosed by movable steel-framed glass panelling.

The administrative center for the State of Bahia was to have been built in only eighteen months. When Filgueiras Lima was called in [1972-1974], fifteen very different buildings were already planned in an often discordant arrangement. His proposal consisted of six well-aligned elongated buildings that impart a degree of unity to the ensemble yet allow for expansion. The need to construct quickly led him to a repetitive design that made use of precast modular elements. Each building is supported by a bridgelike structure on immense square piers and is set upon a slope, thus freeing the level spaces for plazas and parking. On the highest ground, an area of great natural beauty, Filgueiras Lima placed the chapel. A central space, generated around a pier and enclosed by stone walls, it is roofed in a succession of individual "petals" that spiral around the single central pier. To complete the ensemble the architect designed a building to house an information center and an exhibition hall that functions as a landmark.

THE NORTHEAST: SALVADOR, RECIFE, AND FORTALEZA

To achieve a satisfactory level of architectural efficiency in the Northeast, it was necessary partly at least to abandon the Rationalist repertory in favor of better adaptation to local sociocultural and climatic conditions. While at these latitudes there is reason for solutions like *brise-soleil* and *pilotis*, it is inadvisable to make use of pure geometrical volumes, flat roofs, or wide openings with glass screens. Rectangular volumes allow direct rays of sunlight on facades, unavoidably increasing temperatures inside. Roof gardens also receive extra radiation and so do not afford the same levels of ventilation and thermic insolation as the undulating and pierced surfaces of tiled roofs. Large glass panes besides permitting direct insolation also produce a "greenhouse" effect that is especially inconvenient during the rainy season, with its high temperatures and humidity. Salient elements, such as the *muxarabi* of colonial tradition or the *brise-soleil*, permit diffused lighting within and free air circulation. Other elements that help in climatic control are high ceilings, spaces that continue over low walls or through pierced elements, and patios with arbors. The Northeast's two-season climate (wet and dry) if neglected as a design factor may lead to disastrous results; duly taken into account, it may spark some very creative solutions.

Throughout his extensive career in Salvador, Francisco Assis Reis has sought to integrate the tropical climate and landscape with his architecture. Aside from many private residences, among his most important works in which this unifying is evident are the "Ginário Humanístico" at Pojuca [1965], the Baptist Communitarian Center of Salvador, and the General Hospital of Canela. For the Albert Schweitzer Medical Center [1969] he utilized reinforced concrete for some original, intentional irregularities, such as floors composed of uneven sections, ceilings set at different angles, framed gaps in the walls, and unexpected openings in the floors.[81] All of these features, derived from his awareness of prevailing wind currents and the effects of insolation, permit a constancy of air circulation and a pleasant atmosphere that does not require air conditioning. In seeking a balance between traditional techniques and contemporary aesthetics, Assis Reis has often employed straightforward brick masonry in his smaller buildings. The José Paixão [1971] house in Itapoã, set among sand dunes, was developed around a swimming pool that served as a climate-tempering device. The living and service areas are disposed within a longitudinal block that faces the pool and are linked with the bedroom block, which also opens towards the pool, by means of a volume that houses a studio. Assis Reis's achievements as a planner include the revision of the building code of Salvador in 1974 and the creation of that city's Urban Development Council (CONDURB) in 1975. A recipient of many awards and a teacher at the School of Architecture of the University of Bahia, Assis Reis has also influenced the younger generation of architects.

At Recife, in the early 1950s, Delfim Amorim and Acácio Gil Borsoi were leading architects. Amorim's first works reveal a strong affinity for Le Corbusier's early Rationalist approach. Recife's conditions of temperature and humidity and the need for constant aeration, however, called for new alternatives. Amorim thus became an innovator, for instance in the use of glazed tiles to finish sun-exposed walls, in experiments with reinforced concrete for high-temperature areas, and eventually in the perfecting of roofing slabs for construction. Among his most influential projects are Recife's Acaiaca and Santa Rita buildings, both built between 1962 and 1964. The Acaiaca at Boa Viagem beach, posed on *pilotis*, displays on its two main facades a beautiful alternation of glazed tile surfaces and salient concrete volumes. Amorim, unlike his Rio colleagues, used glazed tiles (*azulejos*) with repeated blue-and-white geometrical patterns, thus clearly alluding to some still remarkably perfect facades of nineteenth-century buildings in the city.

The works of Acácio Gil Borsoi, a graduate of the Institute of Fine Arts of Rio, emphasize variegated materials—bricks, wood, and glazed terra-cotta tiles—to complement reinforced-concrete structures. The Clovis Rolim home [1958], one of the best of his earlier works, is still influenced by Lucio Costa, as seen in its *pilotis* and clear distribution of internal spaces. Borsoi created an integrated plan with an original circulation pattern on different levels to ensure complete separation between the several areas of the house. An integration of the interior spaces with the gardens and his colorful finishing point to his later lavish development of materials. In the Cajueiro Seco program [1961-1963][82] he worked directly with the marginal population of Recife to solve housing problems through *mutirão* construction employing wattle (*taipa de mão*) mud walls. *Mutirão* is an old Brazilian tradition. Neighbors get together to help with work that demands the efforts of more than one family, receiving food and drink as their only pay. Brick or concrete-block masonry requires special tools and materials; the *taipa de mão* does not, which makes the *mutirão* easier. For the walls Borsoi created modules made of wattled bamboo panels that can be industrially produced and assembled by each family according to its needs. Finally, straw mats are used for roofing. With the costs of technology circumvented, simple crafts and cooperative labor provided people with inexpensive dwellings. For the last few years Borsoi has dedicated himself to institutional projects such as the recently completed Courthouse of Teresina and the Treasury Department offices in Fortaleza, still under construction. In Boa Viagem beach, a new residential suburb of Recife, he designed many apartment buildings which stand out because of their excellence of detail and their fine overall quality of execution. The unpretentious Clovis Rolim beach house [1974] in Fortaleza is carefully arranged in uneven levels so that all rooms have a view of the ocean (fig. 12.10).[83] Bricks are employed as the structural element, clay tiles for the roofing, and concrete appears solely for decorative purposes in this building. A square volume with the living area is enclosed by a vast veranda, and a separate rectangular volume con-

12.10. Acádio Gil Borsoi, architect. Clovis Rolim Beach House. Fortaleza, 1974. (Photograph: Courtesy of the architect)

tains bedrooms, bathrooms, and kitchen, while a low concrete slab over the dining room links the two distinct blocks of this house. Borsoi managed to create here a contemporary architectural language using extremely refined vernacular forms. Considering the high quality of his achievements, it is not surprising to find that he has been the most active architect in Brazil's Northeast.

At Recife's School of Architecture, Delfim Amorim and Acácio Gil Borsoi have contributed much to the formation of such local architects as Armando de Holanda, Vital Pessoa de Melo, Jório Cruz, and Elvio Polito. Their designs usually take effectively into account the local climate, the availability of materials, and the employment of an unskilled labor force. Let us pursue briefly the work of one architect of this new generation, Armando de Holanda, in his plan for the Guararapes National Park [1975] of the city of Recife.[84] Holanda developed public facilities for this historic early seventeenth-century battleground against the Dutch invader upon which, incidentally, a late Baroque chapel had been built. To guarantee integration with the existing building, he provided a light and informal architecture that virtually loses itself in the rich vegetation. A family of roofs of different shapes was erected using concrete shells each resting on two pillars. Holanda's project was simple and economic to execute, employing repeated standard moldings. It created large, covered areas that cast shadows, provided protection from the sun, and with the separation of walks and roofs allowed for cross-ventilation. In his book, *Roteiro para construir no Nordeste*, Holanda discusses these devices and others as he tries to define architectural solutions fitted to man and nature in the Northeast.[85]

The first architects with modern training to work at Fortaleza were José Liberal de Castro and Neudson Braga, both graduates of Rio de Janeiro's School of Architecture. In 1965 they founded the School of Architecture of the State of Ceará University. Some 1,300,000 inhabitants reside in Fortaleza, the capital of the State of Ceará, set in a hot and dry climate where temperatures vary only slightly. Liberal de Castro has worked for the National Institute for Historic and Artistic Property (IPHAN) and is one of Brazil's most renowned architectural historians. Braga is responsible for a vast number of projects, ranging from schools, office buildings, hospitals, and homes to administrative and public buildings. Of his most recent works such as the State of Ceará Bank [1970], the Hemotherapy Center [1975], and the campus of the Federal University of Ceará [1966-1979], the last two were planned in collaboration with Liberal de Castro. In the State of Ceará Bank building in downtown Fortaleza, the first five stories house public areas, on a corner lot, while above and set back, a high-rise slab contains the offices and administrative quarters. With its external structural-support-system a free layout became possible on all floors and circulation was skillfully arranged to avoid the congestion anticipated normally on paydays.

A constant concern with climate control is present in the work of Nicia and Gerhard Bormann, who moved from Rio to Fortaleza in 1965. Nicia designs beach and country houses in the local vernacular manner using, for instance, material from the trunks of an abundant local palm, the *carnaúba*, in these structures. Gerhard Bormann has designed large works such as the Northeast Bank's branches in João Pessoa [1969] and Natal [1970],[86] and the Fortaleza Soccer Stadium, as well as many residences. Also in Fortaleza is the State Congress building [1971] by Roberto Castelo, a graduate of Brasilia's architectural school, and José Furtado, of São Paulo's. Office and public areas are arranged on its several floors to afford the visitor a full view of the building's internal space from any position. Its low rectilinear volume plays as a counterpoint to the prismatic shape of the legislative hall and brings to mind such Niemeyer projects as Algiers University and the Dominicans' Spiritual Center. An extensive use of unfinished concrete and, especially, the internal organization of the building on the other hand are reminiscent of Artigas's school projects.

Among architects who took their degree at Fortaleza's School of Architecture, Paulo Cardoso, Fausto Nilo, Nelson Serra, and José Alberto de Almeida are most active. In Paulo Cardoso's many projects for branch offices of the Northeast Bank throughout the State of Ceará, he often circumvents air conditioning by using reflecting pools, water screens, and double roofings. For the design of his own house in 1972 his inventiveness was expressed in a new technique for casting vaults in situ. Fausto Nilo was influenced markedly by Paulo Mendes da Rocha. In many residential projects he uses a dramatic cantilevering to join space with its surroundings; and he exposes concrete in large variable-section beams which, besides their structural functions, serve as walls for more isolated facades. The Morada Nova Residential Center by Nelson Serra and José Alberto de Almeida [1977] (fig. 12.11) was the first project built reflecting a new policy of the National Drought Department (CNOCS)[87] to encourage implementation of social welfare, sanitational, and educational programs for local peasant populations with construction of rural communities in reclaimed areas. Each family has a house at the Morada Nova Residential Center and its own com-

12.11. Nelson Serra and José Alberto de Almeida, architects. Community, Morada Nova Project. State of Ceará, 1977. (Photograph: Courtesy of Marilyn Ficher and Marlene Milan Acayaba)

munally irrigated garden. A community center for educational and recreational activities and a service center for technical help are provided. The architecture of the ensemble does not diverge much from folk traditions, though there are such basic urban utilities as running water and sewage disposal. All housing units are alike, with two bedrooms, a bathroom, and an open veranda; walls are of load-bearing masonry, and are surmounted by *carnaúba* beams that support the clay-tiled roofs. Among other buildings, designed in different shapes to express their identities more directly, is the community center where one can see the lintels and beams, formed of two palm trunks, supported by brick piers.[88]

Fortaleza architects hold no specific theoretical positions. This has resulted in an eclectic output, in which architectural languages are mixed without achieving a new aesthetic. Influences from Rio and São Paulo, though strong, are not unifying factors. Fortaleza's architects have shown innovative skills particularly in dealing with devices for climate control employing, for instance, arbor-roofed spaces which do not completely close interiors, verandas and expansive patios that are continuous with the interior, unencumbered by partitions even of glass since rain water is always welcome in the semiarid region. Indeed, it is common to let rain fall in gardens adjoining bedrooms and sitting rooms. In construction techniques the Bormanns were traditional, using brickwork and wooden frames. Fausto Nilo prefers exposed concrete, and Nelson Serra and José Alberto de Almeida have aimed at contrasts between concrete and brightly colored finishes. A diversity, rather than a sense of one or two regional styles, prevails in Fortaleza.

NORTHERN REGION: MANAUS

Attempts to settle and exploit the underdeveloped Amazon region, with its 2,000,000 square kilometers of humid tropical forest have left a long history of destruction and failure. The lack of adequate technology combined with the senseless copying of foreign models and the shabby ethics of exploitation may yet change the largest green area in the world into a vast desert unless architects can effect clear pertinent principles of environmental protection.

In Manaus (capital of Amazonas State and at the mouth of the Negro river on the Amazon, 1,800 kilometers from the Atlantic coast) Severiano Mario Porto is trying to create an architecture that will overcome the constraints of an equatorial climate. He has evolved highly architectural solutions employing cross-ventilation, in which a high-pressure area is created in front of a building and a low-pressure one behind it; masonry walls substituting for wooden panels, which have better thermal properties and are cheaper and faster to apply; and using independent double-shelled roofs, designed to attenuate the penetration of radiant energy.

To emphasize the beauty of a neck of land jutting into the Negro river, Severiano Porto surrounded his Portobrás Administrative Headquarters building [1969] with a stone wall where boats may dock at flood tide but that is visible at low tide.[89] Around a broad central patio, the circular concrete building is composed in two concentric paths of circulation—one bordering the patio and offices, the other between the offices and the retaining wall. Air conditioning is unnecessary thanks to the careful design and placement of openings to catch the river breezes. For the Superintendency of the Free Port of Manaus [1971][90] Porto proposed seven interconnected pyramidal modules, each 15 meters by 15 meters, that function as cowls to facilitate air circulation in a building that can be enlarged simply by adding new modules. In the plan for the Amazonas University campus [1973][91] he gathered the departments, research and teaching laboratories, library and administrative quarters into a gridlike modular system with gardens arranged between buildings and an especially spacious, shaded, central garden meeting place for students and teachers.

A variety of woods brought from the forest—several laurels, maçaranduba, black, red, and yellow sucupira, cedar, mahogany, and macacauba—contribute to an intricacy of detailing in Severiano Porto's works, as attested in his own home of 1971.[92] In 1978 Porto received the Brazilian Architect's Association award for his Robert Schuster country house of that same year (fig. 12.12) in Tarumã-Açu.[93] Required to use a clearing of minimum size, he adopted a vertical design with large openings for air circulation. Employing the talent and draftsmanship of local artisans, the structure that

12.12. Severiano Mario Porto, architect. Roberto Schuster Residence at Tarumã-Acu, 1978. (Photograph: Courtesy of the architect)

was built, partially on *pilotis*, was made of hand-worked wood with floors and walls of wooden planks, and the pitched roof of shingles was set on round rafters. Among the free-standing *pilotis* on the ground floor are enclosures for the bathroom and pantry and an open area for hanging hammocks, while from a central living space there is access to bedrooms and to a large balcony.

Concluding Statements

The study of contemporary Brazilian architecture suffers from the lack of historical texts. *Brazil Builds* (1943), Henrique Mindlin's books (1943, 1956), several articles by Lucio Costa, all written before 1960, and some scattered essays by architects have only recently been substantially augmented by Yves Bruand's *L'Architecture contemporaine au Brésil*, a doctoral thesis published in 1973, exhaustively covering the field from 1900 to 1968. These important sources are complemented by architectural journals of a usually short or intermittent life in which there has been a notable absence of criticism and an exaggeratedly high valuation of architectural output. Perhaps in part this may be explained by the fact that Brazilian law does not clearly define the architect's profession which overlaps with the civil engineer's. Another contributing factor to this situation may well be that the cultural activity we know as architecture, after giving Brazil some international renown during the 1940s and 1950s, came to be viewed with suspicion during the 1960s concurrently with certain internal political changes.

From the work of the three principal Brazilian architects, Lucio Costa, pioneer of urban planning and teaching, Oscar Niemeyer, proponent of plastic formal values, and Vilanova Artigas, who proposed a new teaching model, Brazilian architecture has developed formal dialects that have fostered a diversity of designs and that may eventually come to mirror regional characteristics in a country still being built.

Notes

1. Henry-Russell Hitchcock and Philip Johnson, *The International Style* (New York: Norton, 1932), p. 22. "The principles are few and broad . . . . There is, first, a new conception of architecture as volume rather than as mass. Secondly, regularity rather than axial symmetry serves as the chief means of ordering design. These two principles with a third proscribing arbitrary applied decoration, mark the production of the international style."

2. Geraldo Ferraz, *Warchavchik e a introdução da nova arquitetura no Brasil 1925 a 1940* (São Paulo: Museu de Arte, 1965).

3. The Institute of Fine Arts was founded by the French architect Grandjean de Montigny in 1816. Due to his influence, Rio de Janeiro has an important group of Beaux-Arts buildings.

4. Lucio Costa, "Uma escola viva de Belas Artes," *O Jornal* [Rio de Janeiro], 31 July 1931.

5. Attílio Correa de Lima, "Plano de Goiania," *Arquitetura*, no. 14 (August 1963).

6. CIAM (Congrès Internationaux d'Architecture Moderne), held in Europe from 1928 to 1956.

7. *L'Architecture d'Aujourd'hui*, no. 13-14 (September 1947): 60-61 and Henrique Mindlin, *Modern Architecture in Brazil* (São Paulo: Colibris, 1956), pp. 194-95.

8. *L'Architecture d'Aujourd'hui*, no. 13-14 (September 1947): 66-69 and Mindlin, *Brazil*, pp. 226-27.

9. Lucio Costa, *Sobre Arquitetura* (Porto Alegre, 1962), pp. 57-62.

10. Stamo Papadaki, *The Work of Oscar Niemeyer*, 2d ed. (New York, 1951), pp. 50-51.

11. Philip L. Goodwin, *Brazil Builds: Architecture New and Old, 1652-1942* (New York: Museum of Modern Art, 1943).

12. *L'Architecture d'Aujourd'hui*, no. 13-14 (September 1947): 46-47; Papadaki, *Niemeyer*, pp. 22-29; and Mindlin, *Brazil*, pp. 104-5.

13. *L'Architecture d'Aujourd'hui*, no. 13-14 (September 1947): 22-35; Papadaki, *Niemeyer*, pp. 70-111; and Mindlin, *Brazil*, pp. 160-61, 166-71.

14. Mindlin, *Brazil*, pp. 184-92.

15. Mindlin, *Brazil*, pp. 90-93.

16. *L'Architecture d'Aujourd'hui*, no. 33 (December 1950): 56-70 and no. 43-45 (August 1952): 124-28; *Domus*, no. 254 (January 1951): 2-4; Mindlin, *Brazil*, pp. 120-29; and Klaus Franck and Sigfried Giedion, *Eduardo Affonso Reidy—Bauten und Projekte* (Stuttgart: G. Hatje, 1960), pp. 96-117.

17. *Módulo*, no. 37 (August 1964): 30-51; *Arquitetura*, no. 29 (November 1964): 13-16.

18. *L'Architecture d'Aujourd'hui*, no. 52 (January 1954):

100-101 and no. 67-68 (October 1956): 152-67; Giedion and Franck, *Reidy*, pp. 66-85.

19. Marcus Whiffen, *American Architecture Since 1780, a Guide to the Styles* (Cambridge, Mass.: MIT Press, 1969), p. 260.

20. *P.D.F.* 3, no. 1 (January 1963): 10-14.

21. *L'Architecture d'Aujourd'hui,* no. 42-43 (August 1952): 24-26 and Mindlin, *Brazil*, pp. 212-13.

22. *L'Architecture d'Aujourd'hui*, no. 27 (December 1949): 88-90.

23. *Habitat*, no. 48 (May/June 1958): 2-7 and *Acrópole*, no. 261 (July 1960): 232-37.

24. P. H. Goodwin, *Brazil Builds* (New York, 1943) [for Rino Levi's college]; *L'Architecture d'Aujourd'hui*, no. 31 (September 1950): 16-17 and no. 74 (October and November 1957): 94-95, also *Domus*, no. 287 (October 1953): 5-8 [for the Seguradora Brasileira building]; *L'Architecture d'Auhourd'hui*, no. 27 (December 1949): 51a-51h and nos. 43-44 (August 1952): 90; and Mindlin, *Brazil,* pp. 154-57 [for the hospital]; and *Arquitetura*, no. 42 (December 1965): 16-17 [for the Parahyba factory].

25. *L'Architecture d'Aujourd'hui*, no. 52 (January 1954): 4-5 and *Domus*, no. 292 (March 1954): 16-19 [for the Milton Guper home]; *L'Architecture d'Aujourd'hui*, no. 90 (June/July 1960): 62-63 [for the Castor Delgado Perez home].

26. L. Bardi, "Casa de Vilanova Artigas," *Habitat*, no. 1 (October/December 1950): 2-16.

27. *L'Architecture d'Aujourd'hui*, no. 42-43 (July/August 1952): 77 [for the Mario Bittencourt house]. For the Londrina Central Bus Station *see* Mindlin, *Brazil*, pp. 228-29. Vilanova Artigas continued to grow in importance, and it was in his Morumbi Stadium of 1953 that exposed concrete was introduced to Brazil.

28. *La Carta de Atenas, el Urbanismo de los CIAM* (Buenos Aires: *Editorial Contempora*, 1950), *passim*.

29. Costa, *Arquitetura*, pp. 264-78.

30. *L'Architecture d'Aujourd'hui*, no. 80 (October 1958): 56-58.

31. *Acrópole, São Paulo*, no. 256/57 (February/March 1960) and no. 275/76 (July/August 1980): 6-80.

32. *L'Architecture d'Aujourd'hui*, no. 76 (February 1958): 78-79; no. 80 (October 1958): 60-62; no. 90 (June/-July 1960); and Willy Staubli, *Brasilia* (Stuttgart: Koch, 1965), pp. 80-91.

33. *L'Architecture d'Aujourd'hui*, no. 80 (October 1958): 63-65; no. 90, (June/July 1960): 13-15; and Staubli, *Brasilia*, pp. 64-79.

34. Staubli, *Brasilia,* pp. 100-101.

35. Oscar Niemeyer, *Oscar Niemeyer* (Milan: Arnaldo Mondadori, 1975).

36. *L'Architecture d'Aujourd'hui*, no. 80 (October 1958): 70-71; no. 90 (June/July 1960): 30; and Staubli, *Brasilia*, pp. 116-18.

37. *Mirante das Artes*, no. 5 (September/October 1967): 20-23.

38. *Acrópole*, no. 377 (September 1970): 15-17.

39. *Zodiac*, no. 6 (May 1960): 106-7 and 100-101, respectively.

40. *Zodiac*, no. 6 (May 1960): 98-99.

41. *Acrópole*, no. 259 (May 1960): 171-73 and no. 281 (April 1962): 156-57.

42. *Acrópole*, no. 331 (August 1966): 23-27.

43. *Acrópole*, no. 276 (November 1961): 410-12 and no 342 (August 1967): 16-20.

44. *Acrópole*, no. 343 (September 1967): 32-37.

45. *Acrópole*, no. 372 (April 1970): 27-31.

46. *Módulo*, no. 42 (March 1976): 58-60.

47. *Acrópole*, no. 347 (February 1968): 18-23.

48. Yves Bruand, *L'Architecture Contemporaine au Brésil* (Lille: Services de Reproduction des Thèses, Université de Lille III, 1973), p. 862.

49. *Acrópole*, no. 347 (February 1968): 15-17 and 30-33, respectively.

50. Acrópole, no. 317 (May 1965): 36-39 [for the Morumbi home]; no. 276 (November 1961): 420-23 and no. 317 (May 1965): 28-32 [for the Millan house].

51. *Acrópole*, no. 340 (June 1967): 30-33.

52. *Acrópole*, no. 319 (July 1969): 38-39.

53. *Casa Claudia* 185-A (February/March 1976): 16-19.

54. *Casa Claudia* 218-A (November 1979): 14-19.

55. *Acrópole*, no. 255 (January 1960): 88-91.

56. *Habitat*, no. 74 (December 1963): 15-20 and *Acrópole*, no. 334 (November 1966): 22-37.

57. *Módulo*, no. 42 (March 1976).

58. *Acrópole*, no. 372 (April 1970): 32-37.

59. J. Lerner, *Curitiba uma experiência em planejamento urbano* (Curitiba, January 1975) and *A cidade: cenário de encontro* (Curitiba, 1977).

60. *Projeto*, no. 12 (May 1979): 16-17.

61. *Módulo*, no. 7(31) (December 1962): 29-37.

62. Mindlin, *Brazil*, pp. 148-53 [for the Institute of Puericulture] and *Acrópole*, no. 276 (November 1961): 416-19 [for the Cappas house].

63. *Zodiac*, no. 6 (May 1960): 114-15.

64. Ibid., 110-13.

65. *Acrópole*, no. 306 (May 1964): 31-33.

66. *Acrópole*, no. 277 (December 1961): 5-9.

67. Rome: Brazilian Embassy, 1943, and Rio de Janeiro: Colibris, 1956.

68. *Módulo*, no. 9 (February 1958): 22-25.

69. *Zodiac*, no. 11 (November 1962): 48-55.

70. Bruno Zevi, Italian architect and professor, during the 1959 International Congress of Art Critics in Brasilia marked his presence by attacks on the new capital, starting a controversy in professional circles. Some architects, among them Bernardes, receptive to Zevi's Organicist convictions, questioned the Rationalist orientation.

71. *Acrópole*, no. 276 (November 1961): 431-33.

72. *Projeto e Construção*, no. 26 (January 1973): 22-26.

73. O. Niemeyer, *Oscar Niemeyer*, *passim*.

74. *Módulo*, no. 53 (March/April 1979): 76-89.

75. *Módulo*, no. 46 (July/September 1977): 44-49.

76. *Módulo*, no. 54 (July 1979): 70-85.

77. *Módulo*, no. 55 (September 1979): 68-76.

78. *Acrópole*, no. 369/70 (January/February 1970): 47-50.

79. *Construção em São Paulo*, no. 1339, (October 1973): 4-7.

80. *Módulo*, no. 57 (February 1980): 78-93 for both projects.
81. *Acrópole*, no. 366 (October 1969): 28.
82. *Arquitetura*, no. 40 (October 1965): 6-9.
83. *Casa Claudia* 185-A (February/March 1976): 36.
84. Armando de Holanda, *Parque Nacional dos Guararapes: Projeto Físico* (Recife: UFPE, 1975).
85. Armando de Holanda, *Roteiro para construir no Nordeste* (Recife: Universidade Federal de Pernambuco, 1976).
86. *Acrópole*, no. 373 (May 1970): 34-35.
87. The *Department Nacional de Obras Contra a Seca* (DNOCS) is the federal agency in charge of the planning and execution of irrigation projects in the drought areas of the Northeastern region.
88. N. S. Neves, *Projeto Morada Nova, Planejamento Físico Rural* (Fortaleza: DNOCS, 1977).
89. "Casa e Jardim Arquitetura," *Amazonia*, no. 20 (December 1978): 44-45.
90. "Casa e Jardim," pp. 40-42.
91. "Casa e Jardim," pp. 26-36.
92. "Casa e Jardim," pp. 36-40.
93. *Módulo*, no. 53 (March/April 1979): 60-68.

Bibliography

BOOKS

Bardi, Pietro Maria. *The Tropical Gardens of Burle-Marx*. Amsterdam: Colibris, 1964.

Bruand, Yves. *L'Architecture Contemporaine au Brésil*. Lille: Services de Reproduction des Thèses, Université de Lille III, 1973.

Castilho, Maria Stella and Ribeiro Costa, Eunice R., *Índice de Arquitetura Brasileira 1950-1970*. São Paulo: FAUUSP, 1974.

Corona, Eduardo and Lemos, Carlos. *Dicionário da Arquitetura Brasileira*. São Paulo: Edart, 1972.

Costa, Lucio. *Sobre Arquitetura*. Porto Alegre: Centro de Estudantes Universitários de Arquitetura, 1962.

Ferro, Sergio. *O Canteiro e o Desenho*. São Paulo: Projeto, IBA, 1979.

Franck, Klaus and Giedion, Sigfried. *Eduardo Affonso Reidy—Bauten und Projekte*. Stuttgart: Hatje, 1960.

Futagawa, Yukio. *Oscar Niemeyer*. New York: Simon and Schuster, 1971.

Goodwin, Philip. *Brazil Builds: Architecture New and Old, 1652-1942*. New York: Museum of Modern Art, 1943.

Mindlin, Henrique. *Brazilian Architecture*. Rome: Brazilian Embassy, 1943.

______. *Modern Architecture in Brazil*. São Paulo: Calibris, 1956.

Niemeyer, Oscar. *Minha Experiência em Brasília*. Rio de Janeiro: Vitória, 1961.

______. *Oscar Niemeyer*. Milan: Arnaldo Mondadori Editori, 1975.

Papadaki, Stamo. *The Work of Oscar Niemeyer*. 2d ed. New York: Rheinhold, 1951.

Prado, Yan de Almeida et al. *Depoimentos I*. São Paulo: CEB-GFAU, 1960.

Santos, Paulo. "Quatro séculos de arquitetura." In *Quatro Séculos de Cultura*. Rio de Janeiro: Universidade do Brasil, 1966.

Staubli, Willy. *Brasilia*. Stuttgart: Koch, 1965.,

JOURNALS

AB–Arquitetura Brasileira, Rio de Janeiro, RJ, 1967/68-1976: 1-9.

AC–Arquitetura e Construção, São Paulo, SP, 1966/67: 0-4.

Acrópole, São Paulo, SP, 1938-1971: 1-390/1.

Architecture d'Aujourd'hui, Boulogne-sur-Seine, France, after 1929.

Special number on Brazil, no. 13-14 (September 1947) with the following articles: "Pampulha," 22-35; "Hotel d'Ouro Preto (Niemeyer)," 46-47; "ABI (M. M. Roberto)," 60-61; "Aeroporte Santos Dumont (M. M. Roberto)," 66-69; "Sedes Sapientiae (Rino Levi)," 80-81.

Special number on Brazil, no. 42-43 (August 1952) with the following articles: "Edifice Caramuru à Bahai (P. Antunes Ribeiro)," 24-25; "Deux Villas à São Paulo (Vilanova Artigas)," 76-77; "Hospital A. C. de Camargo à São Paulo (Rino Levi)," 90; "L'Unité d'habitation de Pedregulho à Rio de Janeiro (Reidy)," 124-29.

Special number, no. 90, "Brésil, Brasilia, Actualités" (June 1960): "Le palais du Congrès National," 10-13; "Le Palais Habitation à São Paulo (Rino Levi)," 62-63.

"Oscar Niemeyer," no. 171 (January/February 1974).

Arquitetura, Rio de Janeiro, RJ, IAB, 1961-1969.

Arquitetura Brasileira após Brasilia/Depoimentos, IAB, RJ, Rio de Janeiro, after 1978.

Casa e Jardim, Rio de Janeiro, after 1966.

C. J. Arquitetura, after 1973.

Habitat, São Paulo, SP, 1950-1965.

Módulo, Rio de Janeiro, RJ, after 1955.

Projeto, São Paulo, SP, after 1978.

13

CANADA

CLAUDE BERGERON

DEVELOPMENTS IN ARCHITECTURE IN CANADA

The term development is so broad that a study of architecture dealing with all its meanings would embrace a very large number of buildings. Developments in architecture may refer to an evolution or to the results of that evolution. The centralized plan and Bramante's design for St. Peter's can both be termed major developments in Renaissance architecture. One refers to a series of achievements, all linked by common characteristics, while the second considers the isolated work to be a well-known example of the category to which it belongs. An outstanding building can also be called an architectural development, even though it cannot be situated in a specific evolution.

In recent Canadian architecture, the Festival Theatre of Stratford, Ontario, and Terminal I at the Toronto International Airport fall into that last category. The Stratford Theatre (1957) by Rounthwaite & Fairfield is a landmark in theater design. It has a circular plan and, thanks to its 220 degree amphitheater, none of the 2,192 spectators sits farther than 70 feet from its Elizabethan stage. When the Festival Theatre was inaugurated in 1957, the firm of John B. Parkin Associates was already involved in the studies for the Toronto International Airport. These too display a remarkable solution for handling the traffic of airplanes, cars and people generated by an airport. This satellite concept directly influenced the design of the Charles de Gaulle Airport in Paris of a decade later. In Canada, however, that solution had little impact, and after Terminal I was inaugurated in 1964 the Department of Transport reverted to the linear concept after the model of J. F. Dulles Airport in Washington, D.C. for later terminals and even for the enlargement of the Toronto airport.

The Toronto City Hall, in a sense, is also a unique building, although it certainly cannot be said that it exerted an influence on Canadian architecture. Again the name of Parkin is associated with this building, although its conception is by Viljo Revell of Finland, the winner of the 1958 competition. With its twin office towers flanking the council chamber, all three raised on a podium containing the public access area, it recalls the Oslo City Hall completed in 1950. The functionalists have criticized both the eye-catching forms endowed with the symbolism of a democratic government and the lack of clarity of the concrete structure which supports the crescent-shaped towers and the mushroom of the council chamber. Nonetheless, the Toronto City Hall has since its completion in 1965 been an unmistakable landmark, especially due to its civic square, known as Nathan Phillips Square. It is this square, planned and built at the same time as the city hall, which was influential, and not the city hall itself. This vast open space in the heart of the city, with its refreshing pool in the summer which becomes a skating rink in the winter, has been so successful in attracting crowds that it has naturally become the gathering place for all sorts of public manifestations, either political, cultural or simply recreative. Thus the Toronto City Hall and its square have worked extremely well as both an instrument and a symbol of civic life.

This was Canada's first modern civic square, and its success initiated a new trend in the conception of public buildings in this country. For years, a park setting was considered the most appropriate for public buildings like parliaments and city halls in Canada. As late as 1958, the Ottawa City Hall, by Bland, Rother and Trudeau, was built to stand all by itself on its verdant Green Island. Since the early sixties, on the contrary, the tendency has been to complement these public buildings with the construction of terraced plazas. Notable examples of that trend, besides Nathan Phillips Square, are the National Arts Centre in Ottawa, designed by Affleck, Desbarats, Dimakopoulos, Lebensold and Sise, and Robson Square in Vancouver by Arthur Erickson Architects, Cornelia Hahn Oberlander and Raoul Robillard. The National Arts Centre (1969) comprises one large concert hall, two smaller theaters, and one row of shops which border one of the city's main streets, while on the other side terraces overlook the Rideau Canal.

The more recent Robson Square, begun in 1972 and completed in 1979, promises to be as successful as Toronto's Nathan Phillips Square. Like the latter, it is located in the heart of the commercial district, forming a 11,148 m^2 plaza between the old courthouse, which will house the Vancouver Art Gallery, and the new law courts building also designed by Arthur Erickson as part of the same project. Several levels of terraces are connected by monumental steps. The main feature of the top terrace is a large rectangular reflecting pool cascading down the next two levels. The lowest level is lower than street level. Partly covered, this level is planned as an entertainment area, with a skating rink bordered on each side by shops and cafés. Between these extreme levels, shrubbery and small parks contrast happily with the rectilinear geometry of the concrete terraces and stairs.

In this essay, the emphasis will not be on such exceptional works of architecture and works of landscaping. I have chosen rather to concentrate on buildings which, often without being less remarkable than the ones I have just discussed, share essential characteristics with many other buildings, characteristics whose development can be observed over a good number of years, so that they can be said to constitute a trend. I have not tried either to reconstitute the detailed history of the trends I have selected, but I indicate what seems to me the outline of their evolution.

This study encompasses three different developments of varying importance. My reasons for selecting them also vary from one development to the other. Each represents a fairly large number of buildings, but two out of three are local or regional developments. These are the detached house in British Columbia and row houses in Toronto. Being local developments does not however diminish their importance. The architects who designed houses in British Columbia during the 1940's were pioneers of modern architecture in Canada, and it is chiefly their accomplishments in domestic architecture which were admired by their colleagues in other parts of the country who had not yet adhered to the new idiom. Thus, this development, apart from having produced some of the most remarkable private houses in Canada, can be identified as a landmark of contemporary Canadian architecture. Row housing is also an architectural development of national significance. This study concentrates on the Toronto region because of historical circumstances which will be explained later. From Toronto the movement has spread throughout the country, largely helped by the rising costs of housing and energy. Only the last development, introverted architecture, is treated as a nation-wide movement.

This selection of two local or regional developments followed by a national one portrays, even if in a sketchy manner, the origins and the evolution pattern of modern architecture in Canada. The movement began on the West Coast, especially with the construction of private houses. Architects in Toronto were second shooters, but it is not before the early fifties that significant examples of contemporary architecture began to appear in that city, albeit row houses were not yet among them. Finally, when introverted architecture began its successful career, shortly after the mid-fifties, the modern language had been adopted by architects throughout the country.

By themselves, these three developments cannot pretend to illustrate all the major trends of post-war architecture in Canada. Office towers, for instance, could be counted as one of them. They certainly represent a large percentage of the building activity as in most western countries. As in most western countries, too, the glass tower, as established by Mies van der Rohe and Skidmore, Owings & Merrill, was pretty much a standard solution. These great names in commercial architecture were themselves often active in Canadian cities to help to promote that international style of architecture. Taking all this into account, I have chosen to concentrate on developments more specifically distinctive of Canada.

The British Columbia House

The single family dwelling has played a pioneer role in the history of architecture in Canada since the outbreak of the Second World War. In the second half of the thirties, almost every large Canadian city could boast of one or two houses in the modern cubic style. The Swiss-born architect, Robert Blatter, who had known Le Corbusier during the *Esprit Nouveau* period, gave Quebec City a relatively early start in that style with the Bourdon house of 1934. The

Laroque house (1937) in Outremont by Marcel Parizeau and the E. W. Shore house (1937) in Vancouver by an unknown architect suffice to indicate that the modern style of architecture had already pretty well made its debut across the country, although very superficially. Houses such as these possess most of the vocabulary of the International Style, but in general they do not express themselves very convincingly in that language. They have the flat roof, the stuccoed walls, and even the open plan, but most have a heavy appearance alien to the International Style. They are less radical than their prototypes, often lacking the clear-cut geometry of the latter. Geometry was not so much a principle of design and composition as a surface treatment. In any case, the examples are scarce and scattered, and when construction resumed after the war they were, like the first generation of the International Style in Europe, regarded as belonging to another age.

Beginning around 1940, a new style of domestic architecture emerged in British Columbia. It is often mentioned that these houses in the westernmost province of the country were influenced by domestic architecture on the West Coast of the United States. Without denying that influence, it is much more relevant to see them as strictly rational answers to the specific problems of site, of climate, and of available materials. In that respect, British Columbia houses are deeply rooted in their land. On the one hand, they retain a certain number of elements from earlier domestic architecture in that province while, on the other hand, their most distinguishing characteristics show a remarkable continuity up to this day. Whether it be a simple two-bedroom house or a more costly construction composed of several wings dramatically spread out ever different levels, most are characterized by an air of rusticity due mainly to the materials.

The circumstances surrounding the construction of the earliest examples were conducive to the development of an unpretentious, casual, and often rustic style. According to Charles E. Pratt, an associate of the firm of Sharp & Thompson, Berwick, Pratt which is largely responsible for the birth and the spread of this new architecture, the early clients at least were mainly people with limited financial means and a taste for simplicity. That situation encouraged both a rational approach to design and the exploitation of the natural characteristics of the materials. Unpainted cedar left untreated to weather is the usual sheathing material, and non-planed structural members are often prominently exposed. Because of the scarcity of brick and masons on the West Coast, rough masonry is used only occasionally and for limited areas, either a floor, a wall, or a chimney. Finally it is relevant to stress that a remarkably large number of these early houses, and also of the later ones, were the architects' own homes.

There is another factor which, in addition to being of paramount importance for the lay-out and the general arrangement of these houses, must have strongly stimulated the architects to develop a rustic treatment. It is the site, an almost untouched country of steep mountains, tall fir trees, and large expanses of water, even in West Vancouver where the majority of these houses are to be found. Although not far from downtown Vancouver, West Vancouver was at the outbreak of the war still practically virgin land with its rocky cliffs and its steep thickly wooded slopes. While the luxuriant vegetation assured privacy, the breathtaking southern exposure was an incentive to open the house widely. The site and the view are undeniably the most influential factors responsible for the long-lasting character of the postwar British Columbia house. Arthur Erickson, who designed many of them, claims that the site made up half the house. Each one has a definite orientation, and whether firmly settled on the ground or raised on stilts and thrust forward on cantilevers, it appears like a look-out post in the midst of thick foliage.

The houses Robert A. D. Berwick and his associate Charles E. Pratt built for themselves in 1939 and 1947 respectively can be picked to mark the beginning and the end of the first phase of modern domestic architecture in British Columbia. The houses of that period are compact with their rectangular plan and elevations. Open planning permits the enjoyment of the view from most of the interior, with practically all the rooms looking toward the sea or a mountain: the bedrooms upstairs and the living quarters on the ground floor which continues outdoors becoming a terrace. These early houses are firmly settled on the soil, and all practical problems were treated rationally. In order to guarantee the maximum enjoyment of outdoor living in a part of the country where the climate is the mildest but where rainfalls are frequent, the architects were much concerned with providing shelters around the house. The carport, an essential component of British Columbia houses, was planned as a play area for children during the wet weather. The access to the house from the carport is also sheltered, and large overhangs of the roof or terraces projecting out of the second floor protect a part of the ground floor terrace.

This house type can be called the contemporary British Columbia house in its simplest form. Although representative above all of the 1940's, it is by no means restricted to that first phase. Its appropriateness is no doubt the reason for its continued popularity at least as late as the end of the next decade. Soon however, research made into structure and spatial organization allowed this architecture to renew itself, all the while remaining consistent with its fundamental principles. The structure of these early houses is the conventional stud framing construction, except for the living room where square posts separate sheets of plate glass and glass doors opening onto the terrace. Exterior walls are covered with natural unpainted cedar clapboard or vertical siding. The rustic appearances is also conveyed by the exposed joists under the second floor terrace and by the rafters. This tendency to reveal the structural members, which prepared the advent of the more skeletal post-and-beam system, had already been a distinctive characteristic of British Columbia houses for several decades. Constructors in that province had for a long time protected the wooden walls of their houses with wide overhangs supported (or looking as if they were) by all sorts of brackets, in the California bungalow style. It was also common simply to expose the rafters, as did post-war architects.

The first example of the post-and-beam is the house John C. H. Porter designed for himself in West Vancouver. It was built in the winter of 1948-49, and along with a few other houses of about the same years it initiates a new phase in the evolution of the post-war house in British Columbia. Its popularity was so great that less than a decade later it was estimated that some 2,000 houses in Greater Vancouver alone were of the post-and-beam type.[1] Apart from being cheaper to build, it allowed a more complete opening of the house onto the outside, and at the same time it permitted a more dramatic exploitation of the site. The Porter house already shows this double evolution from the rather tame appearance of the first houses which were built flatly on the ground. Its eastern and southern façades are entirely in glass on both levels except for one bedroom wall. The slope the house straddles is exploited to emphasize the continuity between inside and outside in a way that recalls certain houses by Richard Neutra. It is covered with the same sort of plants both inside the living room and outside the house. At the same time, the difference in levels helps to articulate the internal space by means of an open mezzanine for the sleeping quarters. This mezzanine expands outside into a cantilevered terrace, thus strengthening, right above the slope, the interplay between interior and exterior.

The post-and-beam structure also led to a more functional and dramatic rapport between the house and the site. By raising a part of the house on stilts and cantilevers, it became possible to locate the carport under the house. The little Arthur W. Way house in West Vancouver (fig. 13.1), designed by Robert R. McKee and built in 1950, is an early example of that treatment; but apart from that novelty, that house still carries on the compact planning of the earlier houses with the living-dining room overlooking the sea through an entirely open wall. The Botham house, built the same year by Semmens and Simpson, also has its carport tucked under the living room, but it introduces the partly enclosed courtyard

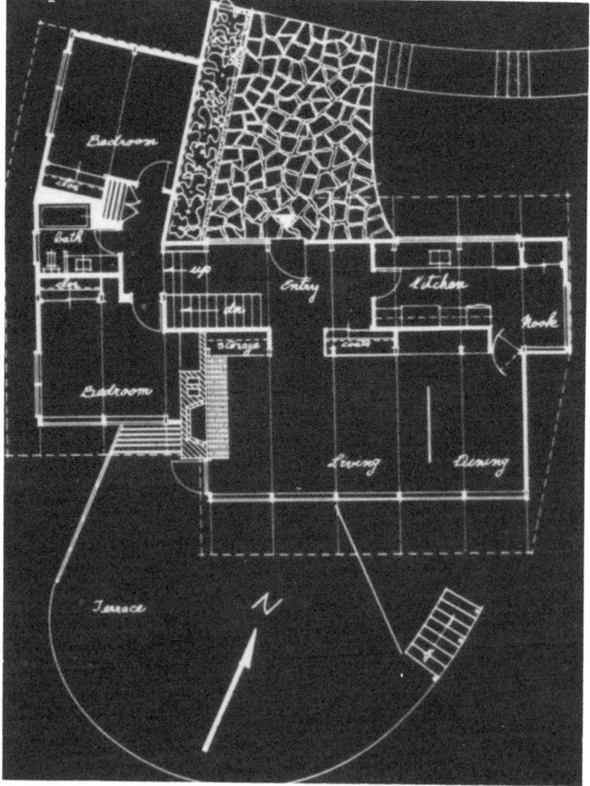

13.1. Robert R. McKee, architect. Arthur W. Way House. West Vancouver, 1950. (Photograph: Courtesy of *Journal of the Royal Architectural Institute of Canada*)

resulting from the parallel disposition of two main wings: the living areas in one wing and the bedrooms in the other. This functional division simply consists of bringing down to ground level what used to constitute the second story of earlier houses. From two exactly superposed stories as it was, the British Columbia house now tends to become more spread out and more articulated, even though the original type remained popular throughout the fifties. The various wings of the Botham house are on the same level; but soon architects such as Ronald J. Thom, Arthur Erickson, Geoffrey Massey, and also Wolfgang Gerson in his own house of 1958 will underline the articulation of the house into several wings to accentuate the slope of the ground and to increase the number of rooms that enjoy a far-reaching view.

Ron Thom's house for Dr. Copp built in 1951 in Vancouver is composed of two perpendicular wings on different levels. The bedroom wing sits half on the ground and half on top of the main wing facing north toward English Bay and the mountains of West Vancouver. From the bedrooms one glimpses the skyline of downtown Vancouver. In order to bring light from the south into the living room, the architect has designed a clerestory whose roof is halfway between those of the two overlapping wings. At the point where these three flat roofs meet, a huge chimney forming an L shape with a masonry wall crowns the entire composition. This grouping of horizontal planes around the chimney obviously recalls Frank Lloyd Wright's "Falling Water." The influence of the master of organic architecture is easily detected in several houses of the fifties and sixties, namely those attributed to the firm of Thompson, Berwick, and Pratt, with which Ron Thom was then connected.

The influence of Wright is also present in the work of Arthur Erickson and Geoffrey Massey. It is after he had read about Taliesin West that Arthur Erickson decided to become an architect; but when he graduated from McGill University in 1950, a travelling scholarship changed his plan of working under Wright, and instead he undertook an extensive tour of Mediterranean countries. Some of the houses he and his onetime associate Geoffrey Massey designed during the sixties provide the most articulate expression of the characteristics displayed by British Columbia houses since the war, especially the prime concern for the site and the emphasis on the structural members. Arthur Erickson acknowledges the site as being the "basic generator" of the forms he creates.[2] His houses are composed of several volumes arranged on various levels giving a cadence to the natural slope on which they are built. The Graham house of 1962 has no fewer than six different levels, all strongly emphasized by very deep beams all parallel like giant steps extending far beyond the volumes of the house. Each room opens onto a terrace built on the roof of a lower volume. Access to the house is made from the highest level down to the living room which is essentially a glass box. In this house, as in the Gordon Smith house of 1964, Erickson has developed the post-and-beam structure on a scale unprecedented in British Columbia houses, thus obtaining large unbroken surfaces of glass as well as giving a strong sculptural presence to the structure.

Erickson has also imagined a more subtle and calculated approach to the landscape, unveiling the views only gradually. The visitor arriving at the Smith house is offered his first glimpse of the sea right at the entrance. From here the house develops around a central courtyard, each wing a few steps higher than the preceding one to complete a square spiral that ends up on the roof of the lowest wing, that is right above the entrance. Like the Smith house, the Bayles house, also of 1964, is planned around a central courtyard; here, the breathtaking view of the sea is revealed in its immensity only after the visitor has walked through a totally enclosed court first and then a partially enclosed one that shows only a narrow slice of the view. Thus, the site and the view, which had been essential components of the British Columbia house since the war, reach their climactic effect in Arthur Erickson's houses.

The site, the view, and the structure have continued to characterize the British Columbia house up to this day. The obsession with the far-reaching view has led younger architects, like Ken Charow and Paul Merrick, to emphasize sometimes theatrically the skeletal wooden structures of their houses. In Merrick's own house of 1974 erected in a cleft, the elaborate criss-cross of posts and cantilevered beams seen against the sunlight suggests a complete dematerialization of the volume. The rustic treatment of wood, too, has remained a constant characteristic of these houses up to this time, so that when, in the late sixties, the Shed Style became popular, it fit into a trend which had been set three decades earlier, while at the same time confirming the continued affinity of domestic architecture in British Columbia with that of the rest of the North American West Coast.

Row Housing in Toronto and Mediterranean Picturesqueness

Single detached houses built in Canada since the war did not often reach as high a level of artistic expression as the British Columbia houses we have just seen. Had they, the resulting urban picture would certainly have been more satisfying that it is, although it is just as safe to hold that housing problems and the aspect of the townscape would not have found a proper solution either. The number of houses and their bad grouping were more destructive to the environment than their design. Of the more than 1,700,000 houses built between 1946 and 1961, around 70% were single detached houses. Already before the war the private house was the most popular form of dwelling in Canada, except in the Province of Quebec, and after 1945 that popularity increased in all parts of the country. The increase in earnings and the relatively low cost of the land, which in those years of plenty one was inclined to regard as unlimited, both helped the dreams of an individualistic people for a house standing on its own plot of grass to materialize. For those whose financial situation made that dream more remote, a national policy of low interest loans was set up to help as many Canadians as possible to become home owners. The National Housing Act of 1944 made possible the financing of 50,000 units for home owners from 1946 to 1949, and of only 8,500 rental units. Out of more than one million new dwellings completed during the decade following the war, only 25% were for rental. In those years, home ownership meant essentially the ownership of a single detached house. Cooperatives, condominiums and row houses were still unknown to Canadians.

Founded in 1945 by the federal government to administer the National Housing Act and coordinate the activities of that government in housing, the Central Mortgage and Housing Corporation immediately launched a competition for "a house of modest cost for a typical Canadian family, located in various regions of the country." The house had to be designed for a lot not exceeding a width of 40 feet. With this initiative, the CMHC started building up a repertoire of plans it made available to those who wanted to take advantage of special financial arrangements under the National Housing Act. The inevitable result was a repetitious monotony *a mari usque ad mare*, which the absence of an art of house grouping made even worse. The fad for the one-story bungalow, which appeared immediately after the war, grew rapidly so that at the end of the fifties eight out of every ten new single family houses were of this type. Over the years too, the Canadian house became larger, that is more spread out, and the width of the lot passed from 40 to 60 feet. Given the large expansion of the cities, one third of whose population lived in houses built since the Second World War, it was estimated, by 1960, that urbanization swallowed about 100 square miles of agricultural land every year, housing alone consuming 70 of them.

By 1960 however, when the Royal Architectural Institute of Canada published the results of its inquiry into problems associated with the country's residential growth and development, the housing situation was already experiencing a change. Private houses which, in 1948, made up more than 80% of all dwelling units built that year had progressively decreased to 63% by 1960. This decrease continued more drastically during the sixties to the point where single detached houses represented only 37% of all new dwelling units built in 1970. Out of necessity and also out of taste, Canadians were rapidly turning to collective housing, either in the form of apartment buildings or row houses. The cost of the land and the cost of servicing it made the private house more and more out of reach. On the other hand, the interest in home ownership was shared by fewer people who replaced it by a searching for mobility. The generation, who a decade earlier was dreaming of isolation in a suburb, was, as the sixties progressed, followed by one who preferred the pleasures and excitement of urban life. Nowhere in Canada was this reversal more pronounced than in Toronto. The population of Metropolitan Toronto increased from 910,000 in 1941 to 2,086,000 in 1971. Nearly all this influx was absorbed by the suburbs which extended as far as 20 miles from the city center. Land costs had become by far the highest of any urban area in Canada, amounting to over 31% of total housing costs in 1964. Under these circumstances, Torontonians, who until the 1950's had lived in detached or semi-detached houses, rapidly made the move to collective housing. In 1951, only 16% of all new housing units were apartments. During the first half of the sixties the proportion of apartment units increased to slightly over 50% and almost reached 80% during the second half of the decade.

During the sixties also, row housing gained remarkably in popularity in Toronto. While only 79 such units were started in 1960, their number grew to the point where nearly 6,000 units were started in 1973, representing one fifth of all new housing units in Toronto and slightly more than one third of all row houses started in Canada that year. Compared to high rise apartments, this might be considered a rather modest progress, but it is a progress of great importance for those of us who are concerned with the main developments in Canadian architecture since 1945. The row house is a more satisfactory solution, both aesthetically and socially, than the high rise apartment building. Row houses built in Canada from the late 1950's onward were the result of a concerted movement, involving architects, planners and agencies concerned with housing, whose objective was to provide a solution more socially and aesthetically adequate as well as more urban in character. This initial movement can also be circumscribed geographically. Row houses are now being constructed in every part of the country, and, not surprisingly, the most successful achievements have been accomplished in the cities where the cost of housing is the highest, that is Toronto, Calgary and Vancouver. However, Toronto deserves to be recognized for having played a pioneering role, and it has been by far the most active center. Among the architects who designed row houses in that city are those who contributed the most to promote this type of dwelling on a national scale, namely James A. Murray, Henry Fliess, Jack Klein, Henry Sears, and Irving Grossman. Finally, there is a great deal in common between most row housing projects built in Toronto since the late fifties, some of them clearly emerging as major influences and others as derivatives.

Toronto architects were fortunate in having a locally-based professional journal to promote this form of dwelling. James A. Murray and Irving Grossman were respectively editor and consultant for *The Canadian Architect*, while Fliess, Klein and Sears were frequent contributors. Founded in 1955, this journal was much concerned with housing right from the start, and as early as February 1957, it devoted an issue to row houses. The year before had seen the founding of the Canadian Housing Design Council, an independent organization largely composed of architects, planners and builders, whose objective was to encourage improvements in housing design. To that end the Council distributed awards, sponsored public lectures and published studies on housing. Although not committed to row housing alone, the Council, through its various activities, tried repeatedly to popularize that type of dwelling. Its first publication, *New Forms of Family Housing* (1960), was a study on multiple horizontal housing by James A. Murray and Henry Fliess. The authors analyzed the housing needs of different age groups, established design principles for livability at high density, such as identity, human scale and private outdoor space, and finally they considered various ways of grouping houses in rows or around a central courtyard. The Council's second publication, *Housing in Cities* (1964), was again a plea for row housing by the Montreal architect Norbert Schoenauer. Later, in 1971, a third publication appeared on the same subject, *The Row House*, by Jack Klein who had already designed several projects in Toronto.

These studies invariably stress, on the one hand, the economic advantages of row housing over the detached house and, on the other, the better living conditions it offers to families compared with apartment dwelling. The aesthetics peculiar to row housing is also always a major point of their argumentation. The promoters of row houses in the early sixties in Canada knew they had to face strong prejudices agains row houses due to their similarities with houses of XIXth-century industrial cities which were still to be found in the most rundown districts. Row houses had to be visually attractive, and it is fairly safe to hold that the picturesque grouping and landscaping of the first row houses built in Toronto contributed to their popularity in that city. James A. Murray, who designed the first influential row housing development in Toronto, concluded the first public lecture sponsored by the Canadian Housing Design Council by saying: "Finally, we cannot escape the most important questions of all those posed by the Architecture of Housing. Do not the real design problems of housing transcend the architecture of individual buildings? Is not the architecture of groups of buildings, of total townscapes, the real issue?"[3]

Those who promoted row houses never failed to emphasize that they contribute to the formation of well-defined urban spaces, as opposed to the loose tissue of colorless suburbs. Again Murray insisted: "It is time once more to build our cities and towns with compact positive form and to do so with the vitality, variety and beauty which has evoked the love and respect men feel for the urbanity of the streets of Florence, the crescents and circles of Bath, the terraces of London."[4] The origins and the rise of row housing in Toronto in the late fifties and even more so in the sixties correspond indeed to a growing interest in urban life, and this form of dwelling had an influence on architectural preservation. Immediately following the construction of the first row housing developments, modest contiguous houses of the turn of the century, especially those presenting a uniform façade, began to be completely modernized inside, while on the outside the brick was painted in a single color to make terraces. This fad for the townhouse has constantly gained momentum to the point where entire streets and districts considered slums (Yorkville, Cabbagetown) in the fifties have been rehabilitated for a more afluent class who deliberately chose that type of living out of taste more than out of necessity.

The first row houses built in Toronto after the Second World War are those of Regent Park North, the first project of public housing built in Canada under the National Housing Act. Started in 1947, it comprises 56 row houses and over 1,200 apartment units designed by J. E. Hoare Jr. Regent Park is in no way attractive. Its configuration is merely the result of a rational analysis in the CIAM style, where the apartment buildings are widely scattered in order to provide large open spaces for playgrounds and excellent natural lighting of the interiors. Row houses occupy the empty lots left on the corners of the superblocks, four houses facing on either of the meeting streets. This is much too short a row to define any space. Nonetheless, row housing proved its superiority over apartment buildings for families with children, and eight years later, in Regent Park South, the authorities decided to provide approximately one in every three dwellings in the form of a row house, and in a third major public housing complex, Alexandra Park, built according to a plan prepared in 1966, two thirds of all units were row houses, that is, enough for all families with children.

Picturesqueness is a characteristic shared by most row housing developments in Toronto, and as the theme evolved the projects became more and more picturesque. These projects are always on a fairly large scale, covering several acres. Separation of various types of traffic is also a common feature, cars being kept at the periphery or hidden underground, allowing greater freedom for landscaping and for the provision of narrow, enclosed spaces for pedestrians only. Southill Village, in the suburb of Don Mills, set the trend thanks to the wide publicity it received. Don Mills was planned in 1952 as a residential and light industry community built around a center of commercial services. Southill Village belongs to the second phase of the development plan, and it was built in 1955-56 according to the designs of James A. Murray and Henry Fliess.

In Southill, pedestrian and vehicular traffic are not yet completely separated, but the rows of houses front on dead ends and crescents that exclude all transit traffic, and collective parking lots are hidden behind the houses. This has made the narrowing of the streets possible as well as a narrowing of the front lawns. The integrated arrangement of the latter, the small scale of the houses, and the enclosure produced by the continuous façades all contribute to an ambiance of calm, and suggest a sense of communal living. Southill reminds one of a peaceful village comfortably tucked under its tall protective trees. The picturesque effect is also heightened by a variety of architectural treatment within an overall unity.

If Southill Village was the first influential project, the prize for the most influential one has to be awarded to Flemingdon Park which achieved international recognition. These row houses were conceived in 1959-64 by a young architect, Irving Grossman, who wanted to reproduce the kind of narrow enclosed spaces he admired in ancient cities, especially Mediterranean cities. A main novelty of Flemingdon Park is an underground parking garage where each tenant can park his car right under his own house which communicates directly with the garage. On this elevated ground, the houses turn their backs to the main streets. Instead, they front on narrow pedestrian streets with views limited by staggered façades on either side. The pavement, which in parts extends to the entire width of the pedestrian areas, certainly makes the maintenance of public spaces easier, but it also reinforces the resemblance to ancient towns. Planting and picturesque landscaping are mainly reserved for the larger play areas at the center of the blocks.

Flemingdon Park has had very successful offspring, often more successful than the model itself which went through a somber period right after its construction. Grossman himself designed Edgeley in the Village in 1964, an experiment in social mix which includes public and private rental housing, elderly persons' housing, and community services. It is more attractive than Flemingdon, due partly to the gently rolling landscape and partly to the pedestrian mall flanked by public buildings and acting as a spine through the entire development. The example of Flemingdon Park was also propagated by Rubin Corporation Limited, a building firm whose president, Alex J. Rubin, had been the president of Industrial Leaseholds when the latter decided to build Flemingdon Park. During the 1960's, the Rubin Corporation was engaged in the construction of Oakdale Manor, Yorkwoods Village, and Don Valley Woods, all three designed by Jack Klein and Henry Sears with the collaboration of Landscape architects Sasaki, Strong & Associates Limited.

"With row housing," wrote Jack Klein, "the designer can create and manipulate spaces, views and enclosures." These were fully exploited in the developments he designed with Henry Sears for the Rubin Corporation. The site was an influential factor in the design of Don Valley Woods and Yorkwoods Village. Both achieve a picturesque effect, but in different ways, due to their different sites. The 143 units of Phase I of Don Valley Woods are surrounded on the east and the south sides by a wooded ravine, and to offer this beautiful view to the largest number of tenants, the architects have superposed two rows of two-story houses. The roofs of the lower row houses form a continuous terrace in front of the houses of the higher row. (Klein and Sears have repeated this composition in Phase IV of Yorkwoods Village where the houses of the eastern row also face a ravine, and it has been adopted by other architects for several developments in similar locations.) On the east side, the houses of the top row open onto a paved pedestrian street built over the underground parking garage (fig. 13.2). Again this is reminiscent

13.2. Jack Klein and Henry Sears, architects. Don Valley Woods, Phase I. North York, 1963. (Photograph: Courtesy of the author)

of Flemingdon Park, but the trends initiated in the latter became more pronounced at Don Valley Woods. First, the irregular terrain as opposed to the flat open fields at Flemingdon has made possible a more jagged roofline and an attractive play of levels, stairs and footbridges. Second, the pedestrian street is entirely paved and articulated by flower boxes here and there. This solution still comes closer to ancient townscapes than the streets of Flemingdon which were largely grassed. At Don Valley Woods, the trees and the sinuous alleys along the ravine convey the feeling of isolation in a forest, while the narrow street bordering the opposite façades of the same houses reproduces the ambiance of a densely populated town.

When the land was flat, as in Phase II of Don Valley Woods and in the earlier parts of Yorkwoods Village, Klein and Sears have resorted to sloping roofs of various kinds and stuccoed fire walls contrasting with brick and wood façades, to make up for the lack of picturesqueness in the natural landscape. This treatment, reminiscent of Soholm Housing Estate in Denmark by Arne Jacobsen, largely contributes to the ambiance and to the scale of a village.

A growing tendency toward the picturesque characterizes the general development of row housing in Toronto during the late fifties and the sixties. At the beginning, this characteristic applied mainly to the grouping of the units and the formation of spaces. The effect sought was either that of an undisturbed landscape, even though mounds were often artifically made with the earth from excavations, or that of a thoroughly artificial milieu such as a Mediterranean town. With time, picturesqueness invaded architectural detailing. The simple, straightforward volumes of Flemingdon Park and their uniform height make the architecture of this early complex in no way picturesque. Even the grouping of the houses is less picturesque than the early photographs tend to show and also probably less than intended by the architect, who declared: "We have intentionally attempted to be as 'unarchitectural' as possible, if that is feasible. In my opinion, mass housing is not an 'art.' When it tries to be, I think it loses its contact with the vitality of the randomness in urban life."[5] In fact, Flemingdon Park never comes close to randomness, except perhaps in the colors which differentiate the houses of a same row. Some later developments, however, were clearly designed to create the effect of randomness, to the point that no two houses looked alike. But these developments are never as satisfying as those unified by a consistent architectural treatment, all the same leaving room for a limited range of variety which identifies the units with clarity and provides lively contrasts. Plasticity gives row housing a richer appearance. Understandably, architects and developers had to convince the public that row housing was not a solution only for those who could not afford a detached house. The squarish structures and flat façades of Flemingdon Park and Oakdale Manor still displayed an air of pauperism; but soon, bay windows, prominent chimney stacks, sloping roofs and recessed façades made up a vocabulary currently used to soften the architecture of row houses.

This evolution can be summed up in Phase III of Don Valley Woods, known as Citadel Village and built in 1966 according to the designs of Tampold & Wells (fig. 13.3). The ground slopes down on all sides

13.3. Tampold & Wells, architects. Citadel Village. North York, 1966. (Photograph: Courtesy of the author)

of the site and this has permitted the construction of two superposed rows of houses with ample terraces on the roofs of the lower row. The façades and the lines of the sloping roofs are constantly broken, but the design is consistent throughout and unity is reinforced by the use of white stucco which, together with the other characteristics, reveals once again the almost constant influence of Mediterranean townscapes.

That influence reaches a dramatic peak with

Habitat, presented as a housing exhibit at Expo 67 in Montreal, although it cannot be claimed that the conception of this spectacular structure proceeds from the row house development. Its designer, Haifa-born Moshe Safdie, in association with the firm of David, Barrott, Boulva, has piled up eleven stories of precast load-bearing units to make 176 houses of different shapes and sizes resulting from the combination of one, two or three units. They form apparently disordered groupings that look like stepped hills, at least on the north front which hides additional structural members of gigantic posts and beams which also carry the mechanical services as well as the horizontal and vertical circulations. Each housing unit is extended externally into an exceptionally large terrace, for Habitat was conceived as a solution to guarantee on the one hand the isolation and the external life a detached house offers, and on the other hand the excitement of a dense urban environment. The Central Mortgage and Housing Corporation, which had in the previous decades encouraged ownership of the small private house on its own plot of grass, became a strong supporter of Habitat. It was confident that this daring structure would "set housing in Canada fifteen to twenty years ahead."[6] That proved to be wrong, and fifteen years later Habitat is still without descendants in Canada. Its structural complexity and its building cost forced architects, engineers and promoters to have second thoughts before repeating the experience.

A more traditional conception of the apartment building has continued to prevail in our cities, especially the slab with apartments on either side of a central corridor. In the Jardins Mérici (1975) in Quebec City (fig. 13.4), the architects Gauthier, Guité, Roy have still resorted to that plan, although the silhouette and the grouping of their buidings at the top of a cliff emphasize the general contours of the ground. The terrace apartments on the first four stories of each building form an extension of the slope while, by placing the higher buildings away from the cliff, the architects have been able to allow an unhindered view of the St. Lawrence River from 75% of the units.

"The City Turned Inside Out" or the Heritage of the Shopping Center

This expression, "the city turned inside out," was coined by Raymond Affleck, the Montreal architect who at one time was a strong supporter of that type of architecture which consists of replacing traditional

13.4. Gauthier, Guité, Roy, architects. Les Jardins Mérici, Quebec City, 1975. (Photograph: Courtesy of the architects)

streets by a network of climate-controlled pedestrian lanes bordered with shops and offices opening exclusively—or almost—onto those lanes. Of all developments in Canadian architecture, this one is by far the best known abroad. In his book, *Megastructures: Urban Futures of the Recent Past*, Reyner Banham devotes some 35 pages to it, including an entire chapter on the city of Montreal alone. It has also received much attention in architectural journals. This is manifestly the architecture most identified with Canada, because of the protection it offers against a rigorous climate, although it is by no means exclusively Canadian. In almost all its manifestations this introverted architecture has in one way or another a foreign origin, mainly American. But many Canadian buildings in that category have received a great deal of attention because they are often on a much more ambitious scale than is found in other countries, like the four miles of underground shopping arcades in downtown Montreal, and a 950-foot long skylighted galleria at the University of Alberta. The Canadian contribution is no less original for that reason. On the contrary, bigness is an essential feature of this type of architecture, since one fundamental objective is to house in one structure a large number of urban functions including the means of communication, at least pedestrian and often vehicular traffic as well. In Canada, this architecture has evolved principally since the mid-fifties in commercial centers, either suburban or downtown, on university campuses, and in city centers of new towns built in the northern regions of the country.

Even though ancestors of this form of architecture can be traced back to such structures as the Ponte Vecchio in Florence and the Galleria in Milan, its post-war origin begins with the suburban shopping center. In spite of their importance in post-war architecture and cities, suburban and regional shopping centers have been almost totally ignored by architectural historians who have been more concerned with styles than with planning. Not only are they the earliest building type to include several city functions along with pedestrian traffic under one roof, but they also had a strong influence on other categories of buildings turned upon themselves. The shopping galleries of Alexis Nihon Plaza (1967) in downtown Montreal are basically an enlarged version of those at Place Laurier built in a suburb of Quebec City five years earlier. Likewise, the campus of Simon Fraser University (1965) is consciously or unconsciously planned like a shopping center, that is, all the services are strung out on either side of a glass-covered mall with the classrooms and laboratories at one end and the residences at the other end acting as two poles in the same manner as department stores at either end of a shopping center. Finally, town centers of northern settlements, like Faro in the Yukon (1970) and Leaf Rapids in Manitoba (1974), are basically shopping centers comprising in addition all the social and communal activities of the town.

A leading theme runs through the construction of these various building types: it is the creation of a colorful and picturesque urban milieu influenced somewhat by the character of ancient cities. The necessarily restricted size of these buildings as opposed to the real city, and their total dedication to pedestrians enabled their planners to achieve a dense, compact grouping and create spaces on a small scale, that the requirements of vehicular traffic were at the same time destroying in the city itself. This was first apparent in suburban shopping centers derived from Victor Gruen's Northland in Detroit (1954) with their limited perspectives and their arcades leading to an open square. Conscious that they were designing structures which, to be successful, had to have public appeal, the architects of the shopping centers did not hesitate to resort to picturesqueness in the treatment of spaces and the use of materials. Thus they produced buildings which were incongruous with the heritage of the International Style, and because of that, they did not find their place in the histories of twentieth-century architecture. It is significant that both suburban shopping centers and downtown shopping concourses, which came later, are called by the same appellation, plaza (or *place* in French). The appropriateness of these terms has already been questioned on the grounds that a complex like Place Ville-Marie or Place Bonaventure bears no resemblance to the physical form of a *place* and that a *place* has no roof. Nonetheless, they are gathering places of large crowds, and thus they perform functions of a lively town square. Universities built from the late fifties onward were equally considered as cities in miniature by those who designed them. All these new campuses are endowed with an "agora," a "forum," or a "meeting place" either sheltered or in the open, in front of the main library. The influence of the Mediterranean townscape, already noticed in contemporary row housing developments, is also evident in the shopping plazas and university campuses of the late fifties and the sixties, and it continues in the "gallerias" built for universities and shopping malls in the seventies.

The earliest suburban shopping centers in Canada date from the early fifties. They consist simply of one row or two perpendicular rows of shops facing a large parking lot with a sidewalk separating the latter from the shops. Although not enclosed, these early shopping centers already practised a rudimentary separation of pedestrians from vehicles, deliveries being made at the back. The 1953 preliminary study of John B. Parkin Associates for a shopping center with an adjoining office tower in Don Mills near Toronto made use of two new concepts, each one characterizing a distinct phase of its construction. While Phase I consisted of shops linked by arcades encircling two perpendicularly oriented gardens, in the manner of Northland to be inaugurated in Detroit a year later, for Phase II the architects envisaged the construction of two levels of shops around a covered, air-conditioned central mall. That novelty had just been intróduced by Victor Gruen at Southdale Center, in Edina, Minnesota, whose construction was started in 1953. Phase I of Don Mills Centre was built according to the original plan, but for Phase II, completed only in 1959, the architects Fisher, Tedman & Fisher dropped the idea of a covered court, returning to the concept of Phase I. That was indeed the most widespread solution for Canadian suburban shopping centers throughout the later fifties, that is, a complex of shops turned toward central open pedestrian courts or lanes.

Because these centers turn their backs to the exterior in order to create their own artificial environment, the view from the mall is always more attractive than the prospect from beyond the encircling parking lots. Actually the malls often produce the most agreeable arrangement of spaces. Don Mills Centre and the later Rockland Shopping Centre (1959) in Montreal, designed by Ian Martin and Victor Prus, are two remarkable examples. Traffic segregation is more pronounced than in the earlier centers since the parking lots are no longer visible from the pedestrian malls. A further step in the classification of traffic was taken at Oshawa Shopping Centre inaugurated in 1956 and designed by the New York shopping center specialists, John Graham & Company. Here a quarter-mile long truck concourse runs beneath the pedestrian mall to serve the stores for the delivery of goods.

Up to this point in its evolution the shopping center had been a suburban phenomenon. When later it made its debut in the city center, higher land costs imposed a more compact organization and a wider range of functions. Begun in 1957, Wellington Square in London, Ontario, Canada's first downtown shopping center, was designed by John Graham & Company for Webb & Knapp Canada Ltd. It is a totally enclosed mall of some forty stores at street level and covering an entire city block. In addition to an underground truck concourse for deliveries, the complex includes parking space on the roof and in an adjacent multi-story structure.

Had Wellington Square added to its services those of an office tower, as at Don Mills Center, it would have, although on a smaller scale, approached the complexity of Place Ville-Marie in Montreal, a building which has received a great deal of attention for the type of urban development it was considered to initiate. It is worth pointing out that Place Ville-Marie was commissioned by the owners of Wellington Square, and Ieoh Ming Pei's master plan for the Montreal project was submitted in 1957, the very year construction began on the London shopping center. Even though Wellington Square still reminds one of a suburban shopping center while Place Ville-Marie is definitely urban in character, the circumstances surrounding their construction tend to show the affiliation of these immense urban redevelopment schemes of the 1960's with suburban shopping centers. Given the tremendous success of the latter to the detriment of downtown business, it was natural to try to offset that harmful competition by offering in the city center the same type of accommodations that were available in the suburbs. That meant opening the city center to a greater invasion of cars and planning commercial premises for one-stop shopping. This view was substantiated by the president of Webb & Knapp, William Zeckendorf, who, when he submitted his plan for the development of two large lots on either side of Central Station, stressed that his proposal was for "a city within a city." Even though this assertion is clearly an exaggeration, it leaves no doubt as to the intention of the developer to build a self-sufficient complex of buildings.

Pei, who worked in association with the local firm of Affleck, Desbarats, Dimakopoulos, Lebensold, Michaud & Sise, developed the scheme for an underground shopping mall only after he had submitted his master plan. Various conditions suggested the placing of the mall below ground level. For almost half a century the site consisted of a deep hole with railroad tracks at the bottom. Not only had the hole to be filled without disturbing the train movements, but pedestrian connections between Place Ville-Marie on the north side of Dorchester Boulevard and the new Queen Elizabeth Hotel and Central Station—itself built in a hole as well—on the south side had to be made underground. These conditions led to the construction of approximately 150,000 square feet of shopping promenades under the podium of Place Ville-Marie, thus initiating in the center of Montreal a network of weather-protected pedestrian streets which was to expand to some four miles in the following decade.

Above the podium, acting as a terrace almost at the level of Dorchester Boulevard, Pei has carried out the arrangement of an office tower framed on two sides by lower wings reminiscent of the Mile High Center in Denver, Colorado, where the same architect and the same developer had worked together before undertaking the Montreal project. The latter is however on a much grander scale with its forty-story cruciform office tower providing almost one acre of floor space at each story. The ground floors of both the tower and the wings contain retail areas. These were meant to bring life to the plaza, but the fourteen-story wing on the south-west and the seven-story one on the north-west cast shadows over most of the plaza at any time, with the result that the underground shopping promenades have been infinitely more successful in attracting crowds than the wind-swept plaza.

Schemes like Place Ville-Marie were carried out in every large Canadian city throughout the sixties. They all include office towers, shopping promenades immediately below ground level and sometimes also at ground level, and several stories of underground parking. A further step was accompliished in 1964-67 with the construction of Place Bonaventure. It is the work of Affleck, Desbarats, Dimakopoulos, Lebensold and Sise who had been associated with I. M. Pei for the construction of Place Ville-Marie. Whereas the latter still maintained open façades along parts of the surrounding streets, Place Bonaventure turns its back brutally to all the streets. It is a building standing in almost complete isolation. Ray Affleck, the partner in charge of the project, likes to describe it as "the city turned inside out." It was the first time the inwardness that characterizes the suburban shopping center was so decisively transposed into a city center. This mammouth cube wrapped around with almost completely blind façades of corrugated cement contains 150,000 square feet of shops on two levels, underground parking for 1,000 cars, an exhibition hall, a merchandise mart and a hotel at the top with roof gardens. The square plan and the massive appearance of the exterior emphasize the idea of a container neatly separating what is inside from what is outside. Ray Affleck, who does not like the expression "underground city" that has been used to describe Montreal's weather-protected pedestrian network, has located the shopping concourses of Place Bonaventure on the first two floors above ground. But, as the architect himself remarks, in such buildings the notion of ground is artificial. Whether underground or above ground the interior shopping promenades have no relationship with the city streets, because such buildings deliberately disregard the street. Their access is from underground. In other words, emphasis is put on internal space to the detriment of exterior space.

In spite of the vast areas they cover, the shopping concourses of Place Ville-Marie and Place Bonaventure do not equal the spatial qualities some suburban shopping centers already displayed, such as Place Laurier in Quebec City. When it was first built in the early sixties, according to the design by Ian Martin and Victor Prus, this shopping center consisted of an extensive rectangular hall surrounded by shops on two levels, and lit by clerestory windows. This spacious treatment was resumed on a still grander scale in later shopping malls built in city centers, like Montreal's Alexis Nihon Plaza, inaugurated in 1967. It is the work of Harold Ship and his consultant Stanley King. The low horizontal structure, which acts as a podium for the apartment and office towers, is made up of three levels of shops (100 in all) around a large rectangular hall, surmounted by three levels of parking. All floors are reached by open galleries forming an impressive interior lit by a skylight. Although only one bank and one restaurant are directly entered from the streets which surround the building on three sides, Alexis Nihon Plaza has achieved a stronger link with the street than the previous shopping concourses, thanks to several show windows and especially to its well-located main entrance at the corner of two busy streets.

Alexis Nihon Plaza thus points to a new tendency in Montreal's downtown shopping malls. This greater emphasis on intercommunication distinguishes the large commercial complexes of the seventies, such as Place Desjardins and Les Terrasses both built in Montreal in 1976, and Eaton Centre (Phase I: 1977 and Phase II: 1979) in Toronto.[7] This trend began in Toronto with a building by Gerald Robinson called The Colonnade (1964). The interior mall of The Colonnade is relatively small, although remarkably crowded, and it communicates directly with Bloor Street not only by means of the deep exedra leading to the main entrance, but also through shops on the ground floor, and a restaurant on the second reached by an exterior staircase. The Colonnade also has the distinction of being the first large downtown reconstruction scheme to include a variety of functions which, in addition to shops, offices and a theater, comprises several floors of apartments.[8]

During the second half on the sixties, it is in universities and colleges that the most innovative experiments were made with the enclosing of large volumes of space to facilitate pedestrian movement. According to projections made in 1961, the number of students in Canadian universities was expected nearly to triple during the next ten years. In order to face these needs, the Banff Conference, sponsored annually by the Royal Architectural Institute of Canada and the Alberta Association of Architects, was in 1964 devoted to the planning of campuses. On that occasion several projects were displayed, among them revolutionary ones, still on the architects' drafting boards. Simon Fraser University and Scarborough College were two of them. They gave an inkling of the campuses of the sixties which were to mark a complete break with those of the previous decade. Campuses of the fifties, like Laval University in Quebec City and the University of Manitoba in Winnipeg, were built on an academic plan of wide axes with the pavilions far apart. This dispersed planning made the the campuses rather unhospitable places, considering that in most regions of Canada hard climatic conditions prevail the greater part of the academic year.

Simon Fraser University, whose plan dates from 1963, is generally considered to be breaking new ground for distributing all the functions around a weather-protected mall. Actually this concept of establishing weather-protected communications between the pavilions of a campus was initiated in a less theatrical manner in a project of 1962 for Laurentian University in Sudbury, Ontario. The architect-planner was Dr. Thomas Howarth who the year after served on the jury for the Simon Fraser University competition. In his master plan for Laurentian, six pavilions arranged in terraces on a rocky hill were interconnected by climate-controlled overpasses. At the upper end, a perpendicular wing (Arts and Humanities) linked that group of pavilions to the library and administrative building. Although certain details have altered the original plan, the academic quarters of Laurentian University more or less form three continuous sides of a courtyard open toward a lake. This courtyard is the "forum" or the "agora" featured in all Canadian universities planned during the sixties and generally situated in front of the main library.

The concept of the agora and that of weather protection for pedestrians are expressed much more convincingly in Arthur Erickson and Geoffrey Massey's master plan for Simon Fraser University. And these are not the only novelties of this campus sitting on top of a mountain outside the city of Vancouver. In order to favor interchange between the members of the community or, as Arthur Erickson puts it, in order to "suggest that education is an urban process involving everyone in a total mix as in the city," the facilities are distributed according to function rather than to discipline. For the architects of the post-CIAM generation, and largely due to the success of Jane Jacobs's *Death and Life of Great American Cities*, published in 1961, social interchange had replaced the emphasis on efficiency as the primordial function of urban life. Campuses had always been the realm of the pedestrian, but in the sixties they were planned to avoid the scattering of their users. The planners of Simon Fraser University have established precise architectural limits to the campus which cannot but recall ancient fortified hilltop towns. A more contemporary comparison is the shopping center again, a basic objective of which is to contain its consumers within confines and to guide them according to a precise pattern of movement. Whereas the shopping center makes the crowds move between two department stores, at Simon Fraser University the Academic Quadrangle (classrooms, laboratories, and professors' offices) terminates the mall at the east and the students' residences at the west. Halfway between these extremities stands the Transportation Centre, the arrival and departure point of those living off campus. Everybody traverses along the same route, moving along an open monumental mall covered with glass above the meeting place in front of the library to the north. This is situated between the Transportation Centre and the Academic Quadrangle, the unique point all members of the community have to go by.

The mild climate of the Pacific Coast made possible the happy mixture of open and covered public spaces along the central spine of Simon Fraser University. For the less congenial weather in other parts of the country total enclosure was more recommendable. As we know, the solution was first attempted at Laurentian University, but it is John Andrews who first translated it into expressive architectural forms in his 1963-65 project for Scarborough College near Toronto. Laurentian University was still made up of individual pavilions linked by narrow protected corridor-like passages, but at Scarborough the architecture expressed the continuity of the pedestrian movement as a basic planning principle. The horizontal pedestrian streets inside both the science and the humanities wings winding at the top of a ravine converge to a "meeting place" in an inverted truncated pyramid. It is a large skylit hall about 50 feet high, located near the main entrance to the college and surrounded by all the community services, such as library, bookstore, cafeterias, lounges, and administrative offices.

The influence of Scarborough College was immediate and widespread, but its followers soon tried to establish a closer link, at least visually, between interior and exterior, a good example of that being Lakehead University in Thunder Bay, Ontario (1970), designed by Fairfield and DuBois. At Scarborough, the brutalist fad for heavy, sculptural supports and stairtowers considerably reduces the view from the interior street, and as one approaches the "meeting place" one's impression is that of penetrating into underground galleries. This impression is not totally absent at Lakehead either, for here too the meeting place is a fairly secluded space. However, the street that leads to it offers unobstructed views of a lake and of the campus built around it. Furthermore, the wings are oriented in such a way that they form exterior spaces protected against cold winds.

The most straightforward and logical step to take in order to favor social interchange and strengthen the resemblance between city and campus is to imitate city streets, more specifically ancient streets generally considered more congenial to human interaction than modern ones, that is streets bordered with housing quarters above a ground floor of shops, banks, cafés and restaurants. This combination, which might be a transitional phase before universities cease to be isolated entities and become interwoven with the urban fabric again, was accomplished by the architects Diamond & Myers, in association with Richard L. Wilkin, for a students' residence at the University of Alberta in Edmonton, completed in 1974. The result is two parallel structures, 950 feet long and seven stories high, facing onto a pedestrian street covered with a glass roof. This pedestrian street was built above an existing street which now serves for deliveries. The glass frontage of the shops on the "ground" floor protrudes in the manner of sidewalk cafés. The breadth of space abundantly lit by natural light and the large surfaces of glass used on the façades along with the vivid colors of the window shutters all contribute to dissipate the oppressive sensation that is so often felt in a large enclosed space.

The concept of a totally enclosed building to house a shopping center had barely made its debut in Canada when it was exploited for entire town centers in remote northern regions. Since the war, these regions have been the theater of important activities based mainly on the exploitation of natural resources and on the construction of a system of defence for the continent. In spite of the needs for new and very special solutions, Canadians have shown very little imagination in the form of the human settlements they built there. They imported the techniques of construction and the type of planning from the south. As late as the second half of the 1950's, the Department of Northern Affairs built the new town of Inuvik, some 100 miles north of the Arctic Circle, on the loose plan of any North American suburb around a town center of widely scattered public and commercial buildings.

Construction had hardly begun at Inuvik when a group of young architects, including C. Ross Anderson, Frank Chapman, Peter Stokes, and the British architect Jacqueline Tyrwhitt, worked out a study for a mining town in Northern Saskatchewan. Prepared in the winter of 1955-56, it was presented at the 1956 CIAM meeting in Dubrovnik. The town square was a round, covered hall with a diameter of over 200 feet. It was linked by covered passages to a hotel, offices, a sports and recreation center, a theater, and a shopping mall. With only minor modifications this has become a standard solution for town centers in the Canadian North up to the present day, even though it took some time for the first one to be built.

Since practically all social life in those regions is meant to evolve indoors for the greater part of the year, it is important to pay particular attention to details in order to vary the interiors, making them at the same time lively and relaxing. This was achieved with success in the town center of Leaf Rapids, in Northern Manitoba (fig. 13.5). Instead of leaving the mining company to build its usual shacks, the provincial government undertook the construction of the town and in 1971 it commissioned the architect Leslie J. Stechesen for the design of the town center complex. The internal street is based on a cross-shaped plan with the town square at the intersection. This "crossroads" is emphasized by a much more airy space than in the rest of the mall. Actually, spatial interplays of galleries, stairs and bridges are the most important devices used by the architect to produce a lively and changing interior. On the other hand, the extensive use of unpainted wood gives warmth and unity, and very likely a certain feeling of nature.

13.5. Leslie J. Stechesen, architect. Leaf Rapids Town Centre. Leaf Rapids, Manitoba, 1974. (Photograph: Courtesy of *The Canadian Architect*)

In Leaf Rapids, year-round weather protection is secured only in the town center. The schools are located there and make use of the town's cultural and sports facilities. The residential areas, however, continue the suburban pattern, isolated and exposed to high-velocity winds and temperatures as low as −50° (C). In Northern Quebec, the new town of Fermont extends that protection to most of the town in a plan unveiled in 1971. Influenced by the Swedish town of Svappavaara designed by Ralph Erskine, who was a consultant at Fermont, the architects Norbert Schoenauer and Maurice Desnoyers & Associates have designed a 5½-story windscreen measuring 2,200 feet to protect most of the quarters of detached and semi-detached houses against the predominant winds from the north and the northwest. This protective "wall" itself houses over 300 apartments and, in contrast to Svappavaara, its ground floor contains the entire town center which comprises commercial, educational and recreational facilities all linked by a climate-controlled pedestrian mall.

The examples of enclosed public space seen so far have a basically practical purpose, which is to provide shelter against the rigors of the climate. It can be downright utilitarian, like attracting and keeping customers, or socially oriented as in university campuses, town centers for the North and also in some commercial galleries. Since the late sixties the builders of shopping malls have actually been more concerned with the construction of enclosed spaces that are not only walked through but that can also be enjoyed and lived in agreeably. From low and cavernous as they were, they have become more airy and more abundantly lit by direct sunlight. Some spaces are even of a purely hedonistic nature. The twin towers of the Toronto Dominion Square in Calgary (fig. 13.6), designed by J. H. Cook Architects in association with Skidmore, Owings & Merrill and completed in 1977, rise above a podium that covers an entire city block. Inside this podium, three stories of shopping arcades are crowned by an enclosed public park—a 2.5 acre conservatory—of exotic plants, cascades, ponds, a sculpture court, and a skating rink, for the enjoyment of the citizens, 46 feet above street level. Raymond Moriyama goes as far as to claim a purely symbolic meaning for the empty enclosed spaces he has designed for the Scarborough Civil Centre (1973) and for the Metropolitan Toronto Library (1977). An immense hole at the center of open galleries of either offices for civil servants or book stacks is meant to suggest respectively a collective identity and personal self-fulfillment. Whether the assumption that essentially the same form can extol both the collectivity and the individual may be disputed. Nonetheless, such buildings illustrate the progress made by the architecture of large enclosed spaces from the mid-fifties through the seventies in Canada.

13.6. J. H. Cook, architect and Skidmore, Owings & Merrill. Toronto Dominion Square. Calgary, 1977. (Photograph: Courtesy of the Oxford Development Group Ltd.)

Notes

1. V. Lyman, *A Survey of Residential Post-and-Beam Construction in Greater Vancouver 1957-58* (Ottawa, 1959), Preface by Robert F. Legget.

2. Arthur C. Erickson, *The Architecture of Arthur Erickson* (Montreal, 1975).

3. James A. Murray, *The Architecture of Housing* (Ottawa, n.d.), p. 23. This first Canadian Housing Design Council lecture was given in November 1962.

4. James A. Murray and Henry Fliess, *New Forms of Family Housing* (Ottawa, 1960), p. 2. Reprinted in 1970 under the title *Family Housing*.

5. "Pedestrian Streets, Flemingdon Park," *Progressive Architecture*, XLV (August 1964), p. 142.

6. Moshe Safdie, *Beyond Habitat* (Montreal, 1970), p. 75.

7. The architects of Place Desjardins are LaHaye-Ouellet; Longpré, Marchand, Goudreau; Blouin, Blouin; Gauthier, Guité, Roy; Ouellet and Reeves, while Les Terrasses were designed by Webb, Zerafa, Menkès, Housden. Eaton Centre is the work of Bregman & Hamann and Zeidler Partnership. It is a good illustration of the regional shopping center transposed into the heart of the city. To

make room for its construction, five blocks were demolished, including the Eaton department store. A new store was constructed at the north end of the new center, acting as one pole, while Eaton's competitor, Simpson's, remaining in its 1895 store, performs the same role at the opposite end. A 900-foot skylit galleria connects these giants with three levels of retail shops.

8. To trace the origins of this new trend back to the Colonnade, it is appropriate to mention that Alexis Ninon Plaza, the first complex in this trend in Montreal, was built by a Toronto developer and that it was originally to be called The Atwater Colonnade until the owner of the land required that his name be given to the entire complex.

CANADA

EDITH S. SANDERSON

Traditionally, Canada has been no melting pot but rather a mosaic of ethnically varied peoples, each with its own cultural heritage. Although Canada occupies a geographical area of 3.85 million square miles (9.98 million square kilometers) with a severe climate throughout most of the land her comparatively small population (about 24 million) lives mostly in the large cities along the southern border. While Canadians share common aspects of the nation's history, the historical and economic backgrounds of each of the ten provinces and two territories are different.

These facts led to the strong regionalism that is evident in Canadian architecture, even when the regional choices themselves were influenced by architecture outside her borders. Architectural sources were from England and France primarily. Areas of the United States, especially those directly to the south, have also been natural sources of local inspiration and influence.

Since World War II there has been a growing awareness of the Canadian identity. Coincidentally, this trend has created a reaction among those who desire the smaller scale, more familiar, and hence more comfortable regional patriotism. In architecture, within the expected diversity and variety, a growing number of adaptations to the specifically Canadian environment have been realized. Accommodation to Canadian circumstances is particularly in evidence in the more public buildings, while the regional sources have remained stronger, with some exceptions, in the smaller, more private personal buildings.

The carefully developed design philosophy of the Modern Movement that was expounded in schools of architecture in the early forties was especially traceable to people who had fled to Canada from Nazi Germany. Most Canadian architectural firms disregarded the new ideas. However, among the first to encourage the "new" internationalist architecture was C. E. (Ned) Pratt of Sharp and Thompson, Berwick, Pratt (now Thompson, Berwick and Pratt) in British Columbia. He gave younger architects an opportunity to realize their ideas in an area of the country where orientation of a structure's rooms to the individual site and view was of paramount importance, making each project unique. In the late 1940s through the 1960s the offices of John B. Parkin Associates in Don Mills, Toronto, Ontario, was a training ground for young graduates of Canada's schools of architecture. These schools now number eleven (*see* Appendix A, p. 535).

As editor of the journal of the Royal Architectural Institute of Canada (RAIC) for a number of years, Professor Eric Arthur of the University of Toronto advocated national competitions for larger works of architecture. In 1956 Vincent Massey established the Massey medal competition for architecture in which finished works are judged on the basis of photos. While photos may miss a great deal and taste may tend to become homogenized, the publishing of winning entries has given architects and clients the opportunity to see what is being done in all of Canada.[1] Today, there are many different competitions.

EDITOR'S NOTE: As Professor Bergeron has stated in the preceding section, his considerations ". . . cannot pretend to illustrate all of the major trends of post-war architecture in Canada"; they have been augmented by this second consideration.

In general, architectural problems are posed and attempts are made to solve them as influenced by time, technology, culture, politics, and economics. However, the fundamental needs of the family change comparatively little over the years and most homes reflect this, becoming more "modern" slowly and keeping ties to the traditional. Alan Gowans pointed out several such connections, illustrating his observations with three houses across the country, in Quebec, Ontario, and British Columbia.

The first two examples were designed for mass construction in the early 1960s, while the third was a private residence showing ties "with the strong arts-and-crafts movement on the West Coast in the earlier years of this century."[2] This house, designed by Thompson, Berwick, Pratt and Partners for Terry S. Forrest in West Vancouver, British Columbia, was built in a tradition continued from such residences as the house built in West Vancouver, British Columbia [1948-1949] by J. C. H. Porter for himself. Porter was one of the first to use modern cedar post-and-beam construction which allowed the dissolution of the traditional barrier between indoors and outdoors. Partitions were used only to indicate living areas, not to separate them. Glass-panel doors and even the abundant use of houseplants added to the illusion of continuity.[3] Very important for the development of these types of houses was the early home R. A. D. Berwick built for himself in 1939 (alterations 1948). Ned Pratt, Berwick's future partner in the firm of Sharp and Thompson, Berwick, Pratt, who also built his own house in 1948 and another for himself in 1951 using the post-and-beam system, was among the first to bring the ideas of the International Style to Vancouver, objectively adapting building solutions to local site and climatic conditions. The use of the post-and-beam system which provided the house structure with a feeling of lightness, was one important result of this design philosophy. Among the many other well-designed and well-built houses in the area are the D. H. Copp house by Ron Thom of Sharp and Thompson, Berwick, Pratt [1951], which translates Thom's "respect for Frank Lloyd Wright into something fresh . . . [and] . . . exploits the contours of the terrain";[4] the Bowker home [1968] by Barry V. Downs of Downs, Archambault Architects, which is the unique result of an architect trained in Bauhaus concepts, wanting a more organic approach, and following the ideas of Ron Thom and San Francisco Bay architects; and the Jerry S. Forrest home (Thompson, Berwick and Pratt, Partners) mentioned above, in which the use of steel beams allowed further reducing of the walls to sheets of glass with the roof line following the site's contour.

Vancouver houses have been exemplified here, though many other fine houses have been built in Canada, because in that region, despite its mild climate, outstanding ingenuity is required to fit houses to their beautiful, sometimes difficult sites, and each house is necessarily differentiated. Therefore, at its best, there is a poetic response in which a house becomes a "device to enhance the magic of the site,"[5] light, and view. The site dictates the house.

Arthur C. Erickson, an outstanding architect now acquiring the international reputation his work so well deserves,[6] has developed an interesting approach. In his book he writes that he learned "how inseparable style was from climate and place,"[7] and that design should be approached with an empty mind, trusting to the unconscious. Should one unfamiliar with his work become skeptical at this statement he continues, saying, ". . . that ignorance, or more accurately innocence, is important in design. One should not know too much. Experience is something else and one can never have enough."[8] The mission of architecture is "transforming human aspirations into habitable space."[9] Architecture is for reaffirming the human spirit.

One of his first private homes was the Filberg house of 1958.[10] For it the ground was bulldozed to try to make the site look as though nature had shaped it. In the Graham House [1962] he set a multistory house as a ladder against the cliff, and he provided a swimming pool and a reflecting pool to heighten the effects of water, sea, pines, and rock seen from a variety of points of view. Six different, loosely articulated, interlocked levels are strongly emphasized by parallel, wood railing-height walls that project successively far beyond the volumes of the house. The Hillborn House of 1974, unlike the others discussed which are all in British Columbia, is near Preston, Ontario. The approach to it is over a roof with gardens or through what the architect describes as long lateral tubes of space which terrace down the hillside. Whether dining room, kitchen, bedrooms, or living room, all spaces are laid out like a series of rectangular terraces, each sized to accommodate its functions and framed in glass with a support structure of careful brickwork and built-up wooden beams. Here is a home that exists with and is of nature's materials, in itself a pronounced Erickson characteristic.

Individual homes have always been the favored residences of Canadians. In 1970, 60 percent of the population of the average city owned their own homes. However, multiple housing is becoming increasingly important for social planners and developers and for architects. Slower economic growth, the high cost of energy, land, transportation, taxes, and building construction itself, as well as the continued preferences of a growing number of people for an urban life-style have made multiple dwellings either more desirable or at least more necessary.

James A. Murray and Henry Fleiss's booklet, *Family Housing* suggests that the environment in large, single-dwelling communities where sprawl predominates may be bad for people, and actually more unworkable than in low-rise multiple dwellings. In Toronto, as discussed in the previous section of this chapter, there was an especially vital interest in stacked row housing, garden court, and back-to-back row houses after World War II.

Multiple housing is of particularly great concern to a number of Quebecers. In 1970, while 60 percent of average urban Canadians were home owners, the situation was quite different in most Quebecois centers, with 80 percent or more of the population of Montreal being renters.[11] Yet Quebec has been slower than the Toronto area to build row houses and row-house developments; and high rises have proliferated. Perhaps there has been prejudice against row housing because so much poor urban housing in Quebec has consisted of miles of attached two- and three-story dwellings. One development of promise in public housing is Îlots Saint-Martin by Jean Ouellet. Started under the auspices of the Municipal Housing Bureau of the City of Montreal in 1968, it attempts to integrate its row houses and low-rise buildings into the existing area. Unfortunately a freeway was built nearby.[12] Quebecers have had perhaps more success with the restoration of older housing stock. The very typical, varied, well-built, creative, attached houses of an earlier period have become most attractive both because the government has introduced incentives to buy and to improve them and also because downtown living is becoming increasingly attractive to a great many people.

Nevertheless, Jean Ouellet speaks for many in seeing the aim of architectural judgment as " . . . selection of worthwhile achievement in housing rather than that of outstanding architectural performance. . . . Affordable housing does not (necessarily) entail low quality design."[13] Ilots Saint-Martin remains one of the better Canadian examples of government-assisted housing. An example of a fine late-1970s project [designed, 1977] is the Deseronto Senior Citizens' building in eastern Ontario by M. Paul Wiegand where thirty-five units are sited in a pleasantly relaxed and attractive way.[14]

No discussion of multiple housing is complete without mention of Moshe Safdie's exciting, though not practically replicable, Habitat (fig. 13.7). This eagerly visited housing display of Expo '67 in Montreal, seemed to have offered a distinct alternative to row-house design. Moshe Safdie, with the firm of David, Barrott, Boulva, created 176 residences in eleven stories of loosely articulated spaces from various combinations of one, two, or three precast load-bearing units. Different cubiform shapes and sizes of masses and volumes were piled up in apparently disordered Mediterranean hilltown fashion. Especially on the north front they partially conceal gigantic structural members and various circulation conduits. Comments about the dense, terraced complex have ranged from Reyner Banham's rather scathing assessment of Safdie's actually ". . . getting a fifth year student thesis built" to George Banz's that "the Habitat project is probably the closest a Canadian architect has come to designing a great housing complex—always assuming there is such a thing."[15] Perhaps the best recommendation of Habitat as a dwelling comes from the residents who chose it and have remained there.

13.7. Moshe Safdie with David, Barrott, Boulva, architects. Habitat, Montreal, 1965-1967. (Photograph: Courtesy of Edith Sanderson)

By 1978-1979 Canadian accomplishment in multiple housing had grown so that Toronto architect David Sisam and his associates were prizewinners for their town-house group in the 1978 Shinkenchiku residential design competition sponsored annually by

Japan Architect. For the 1978 Awards of Excellence competition of the journal *Canadian Architect*, 125 of the entrants presented housing projects and six of fourteen awards were in that area of design. Among the winners were Irving Grossman's Alvin Avenue Housing in Toronto, a mixed-use development with 108 dwelling units of no more than five stories and some "front-door" housing; the quiet although downtown Rosegarden Mews, thirty-five clustered condominium townhouses, again in Toronto by Ernest Annau; interesting projects in Vancouver, especially the Barclay Street Infill Townhouse project by Hassell and Griblin Associates; and the False Creek development (discussed below).[16]

People's concern with their places of worship is reflected in architectural trends, from the latest to the most conservative, from the most international to the most parochial, even within the same time period. This interest is very apparent in Quebec. With the typical church type—a small building with a steep gable and a tall sharp steeple, established since the eighteenth century (the Lacadie Parish church [1752-1816 and 1802-1812])[17]—there were many heated controversies about the shape and image of the church in the Quebec of the 1930s and 1940s. By the 1950s modern design began appearing in local church architecture. The Marial Chapel at Lac Bouchette, one of the best of these, was designed by Henri Tremblay in 1952 as the south transept for a pilgrimage church to be built 200 miles north of Quebec City. With its parabolic, concrete, five-inch-thick shell construction, contemporary techniques resulted in a quite contemporary appearance in this building. At the same time it has all the elements traditional to Quebecois architecture, such as a steep roof, high transept, open belfry on the exterior, vaults arching into side aisles, and a large table placed against the back wall of the apse on the interior.[18]

A later example is Notre-Dame-de-Fatima, Jonquière, Quebec [completed 1963] by Léonce Desgagné and Paul Marie Côté, with Louis Lemieux the engineer. The basic structure, a shell of precast-concrete Gunite, four-inches thick, is a cone separated vertically in its axis. Its two sides are offset, allowing indirect lighting of the nave and choir. Unusual and innovative plans were also carried out in other churches of the 1960s, including St. Gérard Majella at Saint Jean by Eva Vecsei of Affleck, Desbarats, Dimakopoulos, Lebensold, Sise.

In other parts of Canada experiments in church architecture led to some unusual interpretations. The Paroisse du Précieux Sang, at St. Boniface, Manitoba, by Etienne Gaboury and Associates [1967] has a spiral arrangement with a wraparound conical roof that flares out at the top reflecting a type of Indian teepee. A complexity of geometry applied to church design is successfully concealed here. St. Mary's Church at Red Deer, Alberta, by Douglas Cardinal [finished in 1968], seems an almost obvious reference to Henry Moore in its sculptural form with brickwork replacing bronze. Cardinal sees his church as an organism that ". . . should wrap around its function like a sea-shell around a sea urchin. . . ."[19] In 1970 Etienne Gaboury successfully solved the problem of incorporating an old church, also at St. Boniface, Manitoba, where a fire had destroyed most of the 1903 structure, into the new building. It was decided that the east-end apse would serve as enclosure and base and that the front part would remain as an atrium with the new, smaller, contemporary building of wood, glass, and weathering steel.[20]

By the late fifties some very interesting educational buildings were beginning to be seen in Canada. One of these was the J. A. Russell Building, Faculty of Architecture, at the University of Manitoba [1959] by Smith, Carter, Parkin Associates. The Parkin Associates could perhaps have been seen as Canada's Skidmore, Owings and Merrill, but the influences most readily seen are Walter Gropius and Ludwig Mies van der Rohe. Here are the curtain wall of glass and metal and the formally rectangular building. On the interior is a two-story courtyard surrounded by the library, offices, and lounges. Public School No. 2 in Thompson, Manitoba, is a balanced, symmetrical building by Waisman, Ross and Associates. At the same time it is an exciting example of contemporary technology and engineering because of the problems to be solved in building a structure portions of which would be on permafrost. Massey College, a graduate college of the University of Toronto [1961-1963] was built by R. J. Thom of Thompson, Berwick, Pratt and Partners, the winner of a design competition. Built on a small noisy site, it was designed as a quadrangle with an inner court on which all windows open. It is an arrangement very reminiscent of Adam Cram's Graduate College at Princeton [1909-1913].[21]

During the middle 1960s interesting and innovative solutions were being found to enclose large volumes of space and facilitate pedestrian traffic. In 1963 the government of British Columbia held an architectural competition for a master plan for a new university, Simon Fraser, to be placed in a dramatic site in the forest on Barnaby Mountain, overlooking Vancouver's harbor. Arthur Erickson and Geoffrey Massey won unanimously. Because the buildings were to be ready by 1965, the four runners-up were to build five buildings, under Erickson's general design supervision. Their linear plan took advantage of the mountain ridge with a string of low-rise buildings.

Since they believed in the "community of learning" and an urban complex in the "suburban west," they set up the university by function rather than by discipline, which proved to be practical as well since it prevented duplication of facilities. The plan thus called for classroom buildings and an academic quadrangle at the top (by Zoltan S. Kiss) which leads to the "social crossroads" of the university: the high and broad glass-covered central mall, with all "major common facilities around it" such as the library (by Robert F. Harrison), theater (by Duncan McNab and Associates), cafeterias, and lounges. The walkway continues to the quiet end of the university, the residences. Thus the walkway is a central spine and, in this mountain setting, it is also a 1,000 foot pedestrian bridge.

Simon Fraser was built for the mild climate of the Pacific Coast, using the glass-covered mall as a meeting place protected from rain. At Scarborough College [1964-1973] (fig. 13.8), Toronto, a basic planning principle of Australian architect John Andrews was used in the wide, vaulted, pedestrian streets for easy circulation in all kinds of weather. The streets course within the science-wing on one side and the humanities-wing on the other. The social crossroads takes the external form of an inverted, truncated, stepped pyramid. It is formed in fact of two such pyramids in parallel, between which is a broad and cavernous, single, ground-to-roofing expanse of space—the spacious central street that unifies this fortresslike, Brutalist complex.

A. J. Diamond and Barton Meyers served as planning consultants to the University of Alberta from 1969, when they presented their development plan and guidelines. At the time there were 18,000 students at the university with an enrollment of about 28,000 expected within the next ten years. Nearer the Arctic Circle than any other North American city (except the much smaller Anchorage, Alaska), Edmonton's climate can be severe. Thus, the general plan was for linear structures with enclosed pedestrian concourses (a concept in part inspired by the Medieval University of Bologna, Italy), and a large variety of academic, social, and residential functions. Their Students Housing Union Building (figs. 13.9, 13.10), in association with R. L. Wilkin [1969-1972] encloses two parallel hi-tech structures, 957-feet long and seven-stories high, that face one another across a high, broad, glass-roofed pedestrian street, beneath which a preexisting street serves for deliveries. The light steel trusswork and flexiglass roof spans the 28-foot-wide street and gives a great deal of natural light. Air ducts are suspended above the middle of the street and multicolored, glass-paneled surfaces adorn the student residential units flanking it. The thoroughfare idea used here was seminal to the connecting atrium building so well developed in Canada throughout the seventies.

Three other university complexes must be mentioned. The building of Lethbridge University at Lethbridge, Alberta [1972] by Erickson/Massey is mostly concrete. It fits into its site, bridging the top of the valley to reduce the effects of prairie climate and it has windows that are narrow to escape the harsh daylight. Lester B. Pearson College of the Pacific on Vancouver Island, by the Thom Partner-

13.8. John Andrews, architect. Science Wing, Scarborough College. Toronto, Scarborough, 1946-1966. (Photograph: David Harford, courtesy of Scarborough College University of Toronto)

ship, is very different, with shingled roofs, half-gabling and wood facings. Here is a vernacular complex that is sited to fit organically with nature. Again very different are the University of Quebec buildings at Montreal, by Dimakopoulos. The remaining south-transept windows and west tower of the old St. Jacques church have been built in, with the nave serving as part of a multifunctional atrium. Galleries open to view the ground level, which is a pedestrian concourse to the metro.

In the 1950s the Modern Movement in architecture became widespread in Canada. By the 1960s large projects and skyscrapers proliferated. For a variety of reasons during these years many of Canada's

13.9. A. J. Diamond and Barton Myers, with R. L. Wilkin, architects. Housing Union Building (HUB), University of Alberta. Edmonton, Alberta, 1969-1972. (Photograph: John Fulker, courtesy of the architects)

13.10. A. J. Diamond and Barton Myers with R. L. Wilkin, architects. Housing Union Building (HUB), University of Alberta, exterior view, Edmonton, Alberta, 1969-1972. (Photograph: Courtesy of the architects)

business and government leaders looked beyond her borders for the architects who would build some of the major buildings. The C.I.L. office building by Skidmore, Owings and Merrill [1962], the Westmount Square residential-commercial complex by Mies van der Rohe [1965], and Place Victoria by Luigi Moretti with Pier Luigi Nervi, D'Allemagne and Barbachi as structural engineers [1966] are all in Montreal. In each Greenspoon, Freedlander and partners were the affiliated local architects. Also in Montreal the Place Ville Marie Development Complex [1962-1966] is by I. M. Pei and Associates with the local firm of Affleck, Desbarats, Dimakopoulos, Lebensold, Michaud, Sise as associated architects. In Toronto, the design by Viljo Revell and Associates for the City Hall and the adjoining Nathan Phillips Square was chosen from among 520 entrants from 42 countries, and it was built with the John B. Parkin firm [1958-1965]. Although the open but protective design of its twin towers acts as a symbol of democratic government, resembling large and gentle hands, the same design may also be seen as turning its back on the rest of the city, rejecting its traditions and all the buildings nearby. Attractive and an unmistakable landmark, its plaza set a new urban trend in Canada.

In the late 1960s Montreal had a very rapid spurt of growth, in part because of Expo '67; Toronto was Canada's enlarged central city; and the cities of the prairies and far west were changing rapidly from rural to urban. During the same period Canada was gaining a growing number of well-trained and well-educated architects who had more opportunity to design and build than ever before. The plan of the International Airport at Toronto by John B. Parkin [1957-1964] solved the problem of the long walk to and from the airplane: from a parking ramp one takes an elevator to the proper area and then has but a short walk to the plane. Unfortunately when the capacity of the only one of the four projected aeroquays built was reached, additions were of the conventional linear sort. Another unusual project is the Sifto Salt Mill and Warehouse by the same architect. This is a no-nonsense industrial solution for a salt firm. The shape, rather attractively sculptural with an irregular tower and several low levels, is determined by the flow of operations within, and the whole is sheathed in ribbed cement and zinc paint-covered steel which prevents corrosion by salt.

Britannia House, Winnipeg, Manitoba, by Waisman, Ross, Blankstein Coop is, according to Gowans, a good small exemplification of Louis Sullivan's belief that "the tall building should be lofty . . . should soar. . . ." A landscaped strip crossed by a small bridge separates the building's platform from the street. Columbia Centre in Vancouver by Winnipeg architect R. C. Baxter of the Waisman Architectural Group contains four buildings built between 1965 and 1975. Especially interesting are the alternating square and circular colonettes of the thirteen-story Baxter building [1965] with the circular ones being ventilation ducts. This idea was used even more effectively in the twenty-seven-story Board of Trade Tower. By the mid-1970s many architects preferred a thoughtful intervention, a fitting-in with the urban landscape, rather than the often assertive intrusions of the International Style. A good example is Eng and Wright's 1975-1976 building at 815 West Hastings Street, Vancouver. The building reflects the design of its larger neighbor (built in 1912) and is lowered in height at one end to relate to another building giving the block a dignified yet relaxed appearance.[22]

One of the most important hospital projects of the sixties was the Health Sciences Centre at McMaster University, Hamilton, Ontario, by Eberhard H. Zeidler with Craig and Strong [designed 1967].[23] The architects had to be particularly concerned with cost-efficiency and wanted to design a building versatile enough to continue its usefulness through changing needs and concepts of patient care, while providing the best of patient facilities. They decided on primary buildings, permanent elements, and secondary buildings that would not be as costly and could be changed or discarded. Since most hospital buildings need changing at least every ten years, unlimited flexibility is impossible, and such principles are important. Using these concepts the Zeidler Partnership projected other hospitals, as at Fredericton and St. John in New Brunswick. With Groves, Hodgson, Palenstein and Wood and Gardner, E. H. Zeidler has another unusual hospital project at the Walter C. McKenzie Health Services Centre, Edmonton, where the linear atrium is to offer staff and patients a communal space for normal, everyday activities. Arthur Erickson with McCarter Nairne and Partners also has a long-range project for British Columbia Medical Centre in Vancouver, using repeatable building models in a totally integrated and flexible facility.

Shopping centers and complexes have become popular everywhere. They have had perhaps their most consistent realizations in Canada where, mainly because of the climate, enclosed multifunctional centers have great appeal for developers and users alike. At their best some have become new town squares affording a congenial place for people to meet, stroll, talk, and take part in whatever activities are offered. The ideas engendered by the shopping complex have dramatically changed such educational facilities as universities and libraries, as well as banks and government buildings, residences and hospitals all across Canada. Often it has proven economical to build enclosed areas, as many cost-efficiency studies have shown. Increased business is another economic factor. Even if this were not so, one could still humanely calculate that enclosing is a cost of living and building in a severe climate. At any rate these complexes have often been built on such a large scale that they have received worldwide attention.[24] Place Ville Marie [1962-1966] in downtown Montreal was built by I. M. Pei Associates with the Canadian firm of Affleck, Desbarats, Dimakopoulos, Lebensold, Michaud, and Sise (now, Arcop Associates). This seven-acre urban building-complex, envisioned as a city within a city, was not the only enclosed complex at that time in Canada, but it was certainly the largest.

Affleck, Desbarats, Dimakopoulos, Lebensold, Michaud and Sise's first project together was a concert hall which would form the central building of a multiblock civic center in Vancouver. In 1954 they won a competition there for the Queen Elizabeth Theatre built in 1950-1959 (and augmented in 1962)[25] with a design that influenced a large number of theater complexes. In Montreal, opposite Place Desjardins that same firm built the main building of the Places des Arts, the Wilfrid Pelletier Concert Hall. Affleck speaks of "the city turned inside out" and strongly advocates an architecture that replaces traditional streets with an indoor network of climate-controlled pedestrian lanes bordered by shops and offices as at his Place Bonaventure in Montreal [1967]. He has constructed a large, city-block, Brutalist, concrete building integrating a 400-room hotel in the upper-most stories with a merchandise mart, shopping center, and ample parking facilities beneath. This essentially closed-in massive building offers strength and the promise of warmth to any passerby who wants to quickly dart in from the cold through one of its many entrances.

Large, enclosed multifunctional complexes may invite one to remain indoors; with their pleasant environments, plantings, and feelings of spaciousness they have proven psychologically and pragmatically beneficial. Complex Desjardins (fig. 13.11), by Sociéte LaHaye and Ouellet [1976] in Montreal, within its tight-skinned concrete-and-glass exterior has an elegantly large inner atrium that allows a feeling of continuity between outside and inside through high, glazed entrance ways on either end. The podium of the complex which includes the central complex with its well-illuminated central atrium space, is surmounted by a hotel and three office towers at the corners ranging from twelve to forty stories. Diners in the many restaurants, shoppers and office workers can watch the activities and the strollers from various galleries and balconies. TV shows often take place and there is a changing kaleidoscope of plantings and decorations, depending on the season. The complex has an underground garage and connects by underground passageways with the metro and with the Place des Arts theater complex across the street.

Another large enclosed complex is the excitingly beautiful Citadel Theatre in Edmonton, Alberta [1973-1976] (fig. 13.12) by Barton Myers Associates with R. L. Wilkin. The construction and technology is apparent but restrained, stopping short of a hi-tech impression. The three-tiered transparent glass-and-

13.11. Jean Ouellet with Société LaHaye, architects. Place Desjardins Complex. Montreal, 1976. (Photograph: Courtesy of Edith Sanderson)

13.12. Barton Myers Associates with R. L. Wilkin, architects. Citadel Theatre. Edmonton, Alberta, 1973-1976. (Photograph: John Fulkner, courtesy of the architects)

glazed-roofed lobby area of the forward half of the theater is unified with the solidly walled part by a high, massive, transverse flyloft above their juncture There is a predominant rectilinearity softened by the slant of the hipped roof. In the glassed-in lobby the exposed steel structure and the diagonals of open, suspended, steel staircases are integrated skillfully into the design. Each of the three theaters within is different. The largest, the Shoctor, traditional in shape though innovatively planned throughout, is of reinforced-concrete columnar beam-and-slab construction and is totally panelled in very beautiful redwood. The whole building is a "well thought-out and jewel-like facility."[26]

Raymond Moriyama's Scarborough Civic Centre [1966-1973] (fig. 13.13), part of metropolitan Toronto, is a multifunctional project containing borough offices, the Board of Education, and the Board of Health. Reminiscent of Walter Gropius's 1931 Palace of the Soviet's project, it is circular in plan with alternating solid and void quadrants in a forcefully sculptural design. Direct access to a large, five-story, central, enclosed atrium (fig. 13.14) is from one of the two open quadrants of space. Within, varied floor levels (including one curved series of steps and a round meeting hall opposite the entry) and carefully distributed plantings, and stepped balconies bordering the central atrium help make it a lively enjoyable space. The various slightly wedge-shaped rooms radiating from the center are linked by a corridor within the periphery of the two built quadrants and are also linked by passages paralleling the straight walls leading toward the atrium. Before the entry a man-made lake reaches out from the building, while on the entrance facade the ideas of wedge shape and opaque solidity, contrasted with reflective fluidity, are echoed in the solid right triangles of aluminum siding joined with its glass counterpart. The Scarborough Civic Centre ". . . effectively and handsomely celebrates the drama and process of local government."[27]

In Toronto itself the Royal Bank Plaza by the Webb, Zerafa, Menkès and Housden Partnership [1973-1976] (fig. 13.15) has two bright, high, triangular towers (one forty-one stories, one twenty-six) of gold-tinted glass flanking a central, much lower, mass that is cornered by four solid pylons joined to the towers. All surfaces are broken by angulations and except for the four pylons all is glass. Inside is a 130-foot high, huge, opulent atrium with a substantial mezzanine called the "urban room" and a central well of space that is interrupted only by elegant, vertically hanging, white and yellow, variegated screenlike sculptures in perspex rod by Jesus Raphael Soto. The cavernous atrium has waterfalls, restaurants, and shopping areas. An underground pedestrian route from Union Station to the Dominion Plaza of Mies van der Rohe courses the lower levels.

The heavily trafficked Toronto Eaton Centre is a retail center that stretches nearly three city blocks, paralleling Yonge Street, one of Toronto's main

13.13. Raymond Moriyama, architect. Scarborough Civic Centre. Toronto, Scarborough, Ontario, 1966-1973. (Photo: Courtesy of the architect)

13.14. Raymond Moriyama, architect. Scarborough Civic Centre, interior central atrium. Toronto, Scarborough, Ontario, 1966-1973. (Photograph: Courtesy of the architect)

13.15. Webb, Zerafa, Menkès, and Housden Partnership, architects. Royal Bank Plaza. Toronto, 1973-1976. (Photograph: Duncan McDougall F.R.P.S., courtesy of the architects)

streets. it has parking for almost 2,000 cars and is also accessible from three subway entrances. Meant to be built in three phases by the Bregman, Hamann and Zeidler partnership with E. H. Zeidler the design architect, Phase One opened in February 1977; Phase Two in August 1979. This linear glass-covered arcade, similar in conception to Barton and Myers's enclosed street in their Students' Housing Building at the University of Edmonton, now courses almost 900 feet (274 meters). It has three levels of shops and restaurants (almost 300 in all), low-rise offices above, and four tiers of parking. Within the galleria, ventilation tubes are exposed, elevators open to the view, and there are numerous settings with plants and water. The facade on Yonge Street recalls an elongated, tamed Centre Pompidou structuralism and is interesting. Shops are not open directly to the street, though access to the galleria may be gained from some few streetside entrances. Parking, galleria, and Eaton's and Simpson's department stores are linked by sky-bridges and lower level pedestrian ways. Phase Three will include an office tower and residential development.

Not far from central Toronto, Ron Thom's Atria North, in North York, features huge interior central spaces. A multistage project, each part has a broad four-story office building, within the midst of which an atrium courses ground to ceiling, replete with trees and plantings and a variegated floor level. The glazed roof and plant room above are supported by concrete pylons. One of the sections planned has been completed in this arrangement, with office spaces limited only by the simple structural grid. The less-interesting exterior alternates strip windows horizontally with simple aluminum anodized panels whose color will become varied with time.

In Ottawa two glass-mirrored buildings face one another, reflecting the street traffic and each other. One is Adamson's C. D. Howe building. It has two atria, one on each side of the large structure. Across the street is the Bank of Canada Building, built by Erickson, Marani, Roundthwaite and Dick [planned 1970; finished 1979]. Two mirrored-glass office towers are symmetrically linked by the neo-Classical (preserved and still functional) concrete, 1930s Bank of Canada building and also on one side of this by a magnificent new ten-story atrium with a reflecting pool and sumptuous floral setting. Bridges form a single pedestrian network above the long atrium. Mirror facings cover bridges and columns, providing a myriad of reflecting changing images.

Part new development, part preservation of the old courthouse, Robson Square in Vancouver [opened in 1979] has a mixture of uses. Much more open than other complexes because of Vancouver's mild climate, this is a megastructure, a civic, cultural complex including a government building, the old courthouse to be recycled as a museum at one end and Erickson Architects' new Law Courts at the other. The multilevel, three-block expanse has several terraced levels that may be ascended by a monumental stairway toward a large rectangular reflecting pool at the top that cascades down two levels. The lowest level, lower than the street and partly covered, is an entertainment area, with a skating rink bordered on each side by shops and cafes. Man-made parks and plantings contrast happily with the rectilinear geometry of concrete terraces and stairs. The provincial Government Services Center is set back, stepping up three stories above and down three stories below street level. Erickson's Law Courts are of steel, glass, and concrete that turns a rosy hue in the rain. Its large hall is seven-stories high and covered by a huge glass roof. It has, among its many facilities, thirty-five very visible courtrooms. Many plants and the interior furnishing make the courthouse seem an inviting place. Moreover, it contains a major public space and walkway under its roof that links with the parks across a bridge past the reflecting pool. The buildings here are fuel-efficient and have a computerized climate-control system and an energy storage tank that is cooled in off-peak hours when natural-gas rates are lowest.[28]

Robson Square (fig. 13.16) has combined new development with restoration and recycling. In the False Creek area of Vancouver it is not restoration of architecture but development that recycled a whole once-decrepit industrial waterfront area. Thompson, Berwick, Pratt and Partners were chosen in a competition in 1974 to develop an overall plan with integrated housing. These "neighborhoods" have been developed since 1978 by a range of interested groups, from nonprofit organizations to housing cooperatives and even to some privately owned areas. All groups lease the land from the city. Mostly townhouse clusters, there are some apartment buildings in this variegated cityscape. Here "one can

13.16. Arthur C. Erickson, architect. Robson Square Complex. Vancouver, 1979. (Photograph: Simon Scott, courtesy of the architect).

appreciate the picturesqueness of False Creek's version of the New West Coast architecture—a studied irregularity that nevertheless holds together well."[29]

Restoration and recycling, as in many parts of the world, is becoming ever more important. This is especially true of inner cities. We have mentioned examples in Vancouver, Winnipeg (St. Boniface), Toronto, and Montreal. In Toronto, restoration of the Yorkville area started as early as the 1950s. The "Cabbage Town" area near downtown is being revived as well. Andrew S. Volgyesi's conversion of a house on Carlton Street there is outstanding, with its interior completely renewed. The living-dining room now is a large space with a single, straight wall over which a ceiling, bounded by the arabesque wall of the second story, seems to hover. Spaces are diversified. The key to the conversion are diagonally placed staircases with an exterior that preserves the traditional, gingerbread manner of the neighborhood. Winnipeg too, among many other towns and cities, has been restoring and recycling in her inner core, which is especially rich in warehouses and office buildings from the 1880s on.

In Montreal there has been the slow restoration of attached homes, a very few large homes, and "Vieux Montreal" with its buildings constructed since the seventeenth century. Eric McLean's restoration of the Louis-Joseph Papineau House was sensitive and gave the old home all the necessary close attention to detail. In beautiful old Quebec City houses are also being restored, including that of the Ursulines and one said to have been General Montcalm's.

At Brudenell River Provincial Park on Prince Edward Island (about twenty miles from Charlottetown) architect Victor Prus developed a plan [from 1971] for an area with a large number of leisure facilities. The main activity area was planned to preserve the character of the park by building and siting carefully to fit the natural, extant context. And in Halifax, Nova Scotia, there has been a beautiful restoration of the harborside. Shopping and restaurants have been included in the recycling of the old warehouse area. Architects Duffus, Romans, Kundzins, Roundsefell Ltd. and Cochrane and Forsyth, Architects Ltd. worked with careful attention to the existing buildings and to original construction methods. At Louisbourg, Cape Breton Island, also in Nova Scotia, there is an ongoing reconstruction [since 1961] with John Fortier as head of research and Yvon de Blanc as chief architect. The largest French military complex in North America, built in 1640 and destroyed in 1760, the town is being faithfully restored to its 1740s appearance.

In addition to the many kinds of building activity already mentioned, there have been such unusual structures as that landmark, John Andrews's 1,500-foot CN Communications Tower of 1974 with its revolving restaurant and Roger Taillibert's stadium for the 1976 Olympics at Montreal, a beautiful design plagued initially by problems and scandal. Erickson Architects' Canadian Pavilion [1967-1969] in Osaka, Japan, was highly unusual and fine, taking the best-pavilion award at Expo-1970. The design sensitively demonstrates the Erickson concern for site, light, and cadence (the rhythm of the building), with particular concern for the Japanese exhibition-visitors' psychology and traditions. For instance, the building was mirror-sheathed and "roofed" with five high "umbrellas" that rotated continually, giving a notion of change and impermanence that the Japanese could appreciate. The building, set on an almost square podium, was designed with wedges so monumental that they work with space to suggest a pyramid. The entryway cuts one corner of the "pyramid," forcing the existence of space upon us. Conceived as two large Canadian "mountains" of ice, the large mirror-clad prisms reflected all around them to such an extent that the "building itself could vanish."[30]

Almost directly opposite in purpose is Jerome Markson's recent addition to the Jewish Community Center in Toronto with its emphasis on lively changes in large and simple geometric forms. But the forms are laid out with a sense of permanence, in a manner that recalls such late Roman private palaces as that at Piazza Armerina [ca. 300 A.D.]. To the left of the triangular entrance court is the large theater section with its complex array of ancillary spaces. To the right, the smaller portion, the art and ceramics studios and lecture halls are built onto the eastern corner of the extant building. Finally, the breadth and scope of Canada's architects may be emphasized by mentioning Peter Rose, Peter Lankin, and James Righter's "Pavilion 70" St. Sauveur ski lodge [1976-1977] that serves in the summer as a swimming and tennis resort. It may be characterized as a reinterpretion and synthesis of vernacular design and sixteenth-century Italian Mannerism with a Pop-Art use of color—the irrational forcibly unified by design.

Avant-garde concepts and striking experiments are often seen first in private residences. Among recent projects have been the Shields residence in Toronto, Anthony Kemp's contemporary reinterpretation of Le Corbusier; the Wolf residence by Diamond and Myers with its hi-tech displayed; and Douglas J. Cardinal's unique and energy conscious design for his own house in Edmonton. Great-grandson of a Stony Indian woman, hi-tech man and concerned architect, Cardinal's home, recessed most unobtrusively into the side of a hill and following its contours, is sloped in glass to gain a greenhouse effect. It contains other energy related devices, including such nice aids to energy efficiency as an indoor pool and garden. The building accommodates well, not only to the landscape but, moreover, to the severe weather of Edmonton.

Most of Canada confronts a difficult climate and has developed internalized architecture as a way of accommodating. Another new example of this is William Grierson's, with R. G. Goodall, office building for Northwood Pulp and Timber in Prince George, British Columbia, near the company's pulp mill. Designed as "a kind of formal oasis in the omnipresent forest,"[31] it is isolated in an area that can be harshly cold. A long, low two-story building of mostly wood construction with an oblong glass-roofed central atrium that serves as a public space, there is, internally, a sense of open continuity of both structure and volume. Set in a site in the midst of a forest, energy-saving devices are not noticeable in or around this building.

Concepts of energy efficiency are among the facts of life for Canada's architects. Though fuel of various kinds, water, gas, oil, is relatively plentiful and inexpensive here, Canadians are aware of the economic facts of scarce and nonreplenishable resources. Articles concerning the problems and solutions for architects and architecture have been varied, numerous and often quite comprehensive.[32] Canadians necessarily have been concerned with the problem of heating for severe climates. There have been many designs and projects for constructing buildings in areas like Frobisher and Ungava Bay, 1,800 miles north of Montreal in the Northwest Territories.[33] In 1973 Ralph Erskine of Sweden designed a new arctic town for the government in Resolute Bay with Boris Culjat as collaborator.[34] This is located at 74°43′ latitude north, 94° 59′ longitude west. User participation, including Inuit peoples and immigrants, directly influenced the design. Perhaps surprisingly, detached houses were favored for a variety of social and other reasons rather than the more energy-efficient multidwellings and communal spaces. Erskine's design has been much altered.

A brief mention of other projects includes the Saskatchewan Conservation House in Regina, a cubically shaped two-story structure which uses heat-absorbent materials, solar collectors, a ventilation system with a heat exchanger to capture 50 to 70 percent of the heat in its vented air, a waste water heat-recovery unit, and various other technological and design advances. It cost sixty dollars for heating in 1979. A project for a total community of housing and business is planned by architect John Hix, to be built by Cadillac-Fairview Corporation as an energy-conserving complex in March Township, Ontario. The low-rise four-story buildings of the Thom Partnership's Atria North office complex in North York discussed above are expected to be 33 percent less costly in energy and ongoing maintenance than a nineteen-story building of the same total area and quality. The use of less exterior glass is one main reason for the lower figure because most office windows overlook the atria. Heat pumps will collect the heat generated by lights, people, and so forth. The new modular "task light" ceiling system consumes almost three-fourths less energy than conventional systems (see Hydro Place, below).

Webb, Zerafa, Menkès, Housden Partnership's Scarborough Courthouse, four stories high and of precast concrete, uses solar collectors and has a central supervisory data-monitoring and control panel, metering all energy-consuming systems. And a low-energy complex planned for Regina by R. E. Hulbert and Partners will also use solar heating for its 2,380 square meters of retail, office, and hotel space. This development uses modules surrounding glazed atria which function as buffers from the outdoors.

On 23 February 1977 the *Montreal Star* proclaimed "No-furnace building works" in an article about Hydro Place, Toronto. Ontario Hydro, one of Canada's energy suppliers, encouraged the building of this energy-economic building in 1975 by Canada Square Corporation with Kenneth R. Cooper, architect. The Encon energy system used was pioneered by Gerhard Moog and developed by him and others over fifteen years for their company, Canada Square. It does not use solar heat. Instead, using no furnaces for heating, the system collects and recycles the heat from electrical equipment and people through the air-conditioning system. Most of the energy consumed is for cooling the water stored in basement tanks for air-conditioning. Energy heating and cooling is used mostly in off-peak hours. In 1976 Canada Square Corporation and Ken Cooper, and Adamson Associates architects won the bid for Gulf Canada Square in Calgary, giving them an opportunity to further improve the system. Once again the same principles were used. The building's curtain wall uses double-glazed panels of silver-treated glass that reflect 85 percent of the sun's heat, insulate, and give a mirror-cladded appearance. The waterfall on the plaza conceals the tower through which heat is vented. The pollution-free incinerator's heat is also recycled. Claimed as the world's most energy-efficient building, it uses even less energy than Hydro Place and about one-fourth the amount used per square foot in conventional buildings in Calgary.[35]

Summarizing, we find a variety of buildings in regional and in international styles that demonstrate an acquaintance with works in other countries. Contemporary theories of architecture and their proponents, so much a part of the European architectural scene, for instance, have emerged in Canada only relatively recently. Montreal's Melvin Charney writes that architecture should not be a formal image, for it is the process of which the building is the image that is important. The process should be studied if one believes in architecture as involvement with human processes rather than with designed things. This is certainly an interesting concept but carries within it the destruction of that which it seeks to clarify. Anthony Jackson of Halifax (*The Future of Canadian Architecture*) has stated that Canadians have not made up their minds and have no sense of general direction. And Arthur Erickson sees no "solutions" since each answer creates further questions. He concludes that "the architect must understand that the essence of form is relationship."[36]

Seeing architectural form as resulting from relationships, we can appreciate the Canadian concern with internalized architecture. We can then better understand structures that ". . . relate their outside forms to their locational context and their inside spaces to their social use."[37] And, we can understand that the use of atria is "turning Canadian architecture not inside out, but outside in."[38]

During the last thirty years, after the slow introduction of modern architecture in the 1940s and 1950s, interest in and examples of advanced technology and design became more frequent. By the early 1960s, with economic optimism and with many more young and broadly educated architects, innovative programs were initiated. In the 1970s Canadian architects continued to prefer a great diversity of building types. While this country has a significant number of outstanding architectural talents, generally architects have been adapting, reinterpreting, and innovating widely to present a landscape of Canadian building uniquely suited to the country.

Notes

1. John Bland, *Three Centuries of Canadian Architecture* (Montreal: Georges le Pape, 1971), pp. 116-17.
2. Alan Gowans, *Building Canada: An Architectural History of Canadian Life*, rev. and enl. ed. (Toronto: Oxford University Press, 1966) (unpaginated, opposite plate 218).
3. Alan Gowans, *Looking at Architecture in Canada* (Toronto: Oxford University Press, 1958), p. 203.
4. Harold D. Kalman, *Exploring Vancouver 2* (Vancouver: University of British Columbia Press, 1978), p. 202.
5. Carol Moore Ede, *Canadian Architecture 1960/70* (Toronto: Burns and MacEachern, 1971), p. 7.
6. *See The New Yorker* 55 (4 June 1979): 42 ff.; *McLean's* 93 (10 September 1979): 46 ff.; *Time* 114 (1 October 1979): 72-73; and *Architectural Review*, June 1980.
7. Arthur C. Erickson, *The Architecture of Arthur Erickson* (Montreal: Tundra Books, 1975), p. 13.
8. Erickson, *Architecture*, p. 15.
9. Ibid., p. 13.
10. In fact, until Simon Fraser University (1963-1965) he had built only small projects.
11. Melvin Charney, "Pour une définition de l'architecture au Québec," *Architecture et Urbanisme au Québec* (Conférences J. A. de Sève 13-14), Montreal: Les Presses de L'Université de Montréal, 1971), p. 36.
12. Melvin Charney in "Towards a Definition of Quebec Architecture," *Progressive Architecture* 53 (September 1972): 107.
13. Jean Ouellet, *Canadian Architect* 24, no. 4 (1979): 42.
14. *Canadian Architect* 23, no. 9 (1978): 34-37.
15. Reyner Banham, in *Architectural Design* 37 (July 1967): 347 and George Banz, in *Canadian Architect* 24, no. 5 (1979): 40, 68.
16. *See* the *Canadian Architect* 24 (January 1979): 1-2, 18-41 for more about the award winners who include, in addition to those mentioned, William McCreery, Victoria, B.C.; DuBois and Associates, Toronto; and A. J. Diamond, Toronto.
17. Gowans, *Looking*, pp. 60-61.
18. Ibid., p. 223.
19. Ede, *Canadian Architecture*, p. 198.
20. William Paul Thompson, *Winnipeg Architecture 100 Years* (Winnipeg: Queenston House, 1975) (fig. 68).
21. Gowans, *Building*, fig. 231.
22. Kalman, *Vancouver*, p. 114.
23. Eberhard Zeidler, "Krankenhausbau auf neuen Wegen, McMaster und danach," *Bauen und Wohnen* 29, no. 5 (1975): 186-88.
24. More than a chapter in Reyner Banham, *Megastructure: Urban Futures of the Recent Past* (New York: Harper and Row, 1976), pp. 104-29. *See also* "Canada" (Special Issue), *Architectural Review* 167, no. 999 (May 1980): 273-85.
25. Kalman, *Vancouver*, p. 99.
26. "Canada," *Architectural Review*, May 1980, p. 319.
27. "Civic Center for Scarborough, Ontario, designed by Raymond Moriyama to celebrate the Drama of Local Government at work," *Architectural Record* 156 (July 1974): 1.
28. *Time*, 1 October 1979, p. 73.
29. Kalman, *Vancouver*, pp. 173-77.
30. Erickson, *Architecture*, p. 192.
31. "Design: Office Building for Northwood Pulp and Timber, Ltd., Prince George, B.C.," *Canadian Architect* 25 (March 1980): 36-42.

32. For energy conservation *see Canadian Architect:*
21 April 1978, pp. 27-38—for a discussion of Hydro Place, Toronto.
John Hix. "Dark Horizon: Energy Conservation and the Architect," 22 February 1977, pp. 20-38.
John Hix. "Energy Conservation and the Architect: Part 2," 22 March 1977, pp. 28-50—includes other articles on projects ranging from the single house to townhouses and office buildings.
23 October 1978, pp. 18-52—for a discussion including specific buildings such as the Thom Partnership's Atria North and the Webb, Zerafa, Mènkes and Housden Partnership's Scarborough Courthouses.
23 November 1978, pp. 28-52—for an issue mostly devoted to energy conservation and to particular examples.
25 January 1980, pp. 19-21—for a low energy complex in Regina.
25 May 1980, pp. 27-33—for an article entitled "Energy Management."

33. "Far North Solutions," *Progressive Architecture* 53 (September 1972): 120-25.

34. *Architectural Design* 47 (November-December 1977): 750-851 are devoted to a profile on Ralph Erskine. For Resolute Bay *see* pp. 846-51 of the same issue.

35. *Gulf Canada Square*, a pamphlet of Gulf Canada, Ltd., Calgary, Alberta.

36. Erickson, *Architecture*, p. 207.

37. Anthony Jackson in referring to B. Myers and A. J. Diamond's Housing Union Building at the University of Alberta in "The Democratisation of Canadian Architecture," *Architectural Review* 167, no. 999 (May 1980): 307.

38. Lance Wright, "Canadian conclusions," *Architectural Review* 167, no. 999 (May 1980): 329.

Bibliography

BOOKS

Architecture et Sculpture au Canada. Le Pavillon du Canada, Expo '67, Montreal. Ottawa: Roger Duhamel, 1967.

Banham, Reyner. *Megastructure: Urban Futures of the Recent Past.* New York: Harper and Row, 1976. *See* especially chap. 6, "Megacity Montreal," 104-29.

Beaulieu, Claude. *Architecture Contemporaine au Canada français.* Quebec: Ministère des Affaires Culturelles, 1969.

Bland, John and Mayrand, Pierre. *Three Centuries of Architecture in Canada.* Montreal: Federal Publications Service, Georges le Pape, 1971.

Charney, Melvin and Bélanger, Marcel. *Architecture et Urbanisme au Québec.* Conférences J. A. de Sève 13-14. Montreal: Les Presses de L'Université de Montréal, 1971.

Ede, Carol Moore. *Canadian Architecture 1960/70.* Toronto: Burns and MacEachern, 1971.

Erickson, Arthur C. *The Architecture of Arthur Erickson.* Montreal: Tundra Books, 1975.

Gowans, Alan. *Building Canada: An Architectural History of Canadian Life.* Rev. and enl. ed. Toronto: Oxford University Press, 1966.

Hailstone, Leslie, ed. *Architecture Canada Directory 74/75,* 11th ed. Toronto: The Royal Architectural Institute of Canada/L'Institut Royal d'Architecture du Canada, Greey de Pencier Publications, 1974.

Jackson, Anthony. *The Future of Canadian Architecture.* Halifax, Nova Scotia: Tech-Press, Nova Scotia Technical College, 1979.

Kalman, Harold D. *Exploring Vancouver 2.* Vancouver: University of British Columbia Press, 1978.

Safdie, Moshe. *Beyond Habitat.* Edited by John Kettle. Montreal: Tundra Books, 1970.

______. *For Everyone a Garden.* Edited by Judith Wallin. Cambridge, Mass.: MIT Press, 1975.

Schoenauer, Norbert. *Architecture Montreal.* Southam Business Publications, n.d.

Thompson, William Paul. *Winnipeg Architecture 100 Years.* Winnipeg: Queenston House, 1975.

JOURNALS

See all issues of *The Canadian Architect* and *Habitat*, quarterly of the Central Mortgage and Housing Corporation (CMHC).

"Scarborough College, Toronto." *Architectural Design* 37 (April 1967): 178-87.

"Bank of Canada." *Architectural Record* 160 (mid-August 1976): 72-75.

"Canada." *Architectural Review* 126, no. 752 (October 1959): 153-72.

"Metropolitan Toronto Library." *Architectural Review* 165 (May 1977): 286-89.

"John Andrews." *Architecture and Urbanism* 41 (May 1974): 25-137 (in Japanese). In English: Editor's note, 4; 25 by John Andrews; captions.

"La communauté dans la ville, centre d'accueil à Sainte-Foy, Québec." *L'Architecture d'Aujourd'hui* 168 (July 1973): 56.

"Cittadella trasparente." (Edmonton.) *L'Architettura* 25 (March 1979): 176-77.

"Eaton Centre, Toronto, Ontario." *Domus* 556 (March 1976): 1-4.

"Galleria in Canada: Pedestrian Urban Environment." (Toronto.) *Domus* 582 (May 1978): 17-21.

"Architecture and Allied Arts." (Special Issue.) *Arts Canada* 17 (November 1960): 323-71.

"Robson Square." *Landscape Architecture* 69 (July 1979): 377-79.

"Canada: A View from the South." *Progressive Architecture* 53 (September 1972): 88-139.

"Place Ville-Marie in Montreal." *Werk* 59 (January 1972): 24-25.

Blouin, André. "Architecture religieuse au Canada." *L'Architecture d'Aujourd'hui* 96 (June/July 1961): 68-72.

Brown, H. F. "Canada 1967." *Royal Institute of British Architects Journal* 74 (April 1967): 143-57.

Burchard, Marshall. "Canada . . . " *Architectural Forum* 117 (August 1962): 80-95.

Egelius, Mats. "AD Profile 9: Ralph Erskine, Humane Architect." *Architectural Design* 47 (November/December 1977): 750-851.

Freeman, A. "In Montreal, Promenades Weave MXD's into Integrated Core." *American Institute of Architects Journal* 66 (September 1977: 38-41.

Jackson, Anthony. "Canada." *Architectural Design* 34 (July 1964): 321-60.

Mahony, William. "Fermont, a design for Sub-Artic Living." *Habitat* 21, no. 3 (1978): 17-21.

Myers, Barton. "An Architecture of Accommodation." *Habitat* 20, nos. 3/4 (1977): 57-61.

Schmertz, Mildred F. "A Civic Center for Scarborough, Ontario—Designed by Raymond Moriyama to Celebrate the Drama of Local Government at Work." *Architectural Record* 156 (July 1974): 91-98.

______. "Spaces for Anthropological Art." *Architectural Record* 161 (May 1977): 103-10.

Smith, C. R. "Monochromatic Contextualism; Citadel Theatre." *Progressive Architecture* 58 (July 1977): 68-71.

Sykes, Meredith. "Imitation to Innovation." *Habitat* 20, nos. 3/4 (1977): 13-19.

Van Ginkel, Blanche, ed. "Montreal." *Architectural Design* 37 (July 1967): 305-47.

Wright, Lance and Collymore, Peter, eds. "Canada." *Architectural Review* 167 (Special Issue), no. 999 (May 1980): 262-330.

Zeidler, Eberhard. "Krankenhausbau auf neuen Wegen, McMaster und danach." *Bauen und Wohnen* 29, no. 5 (1975): 186-92. (French and English summaries and captions.)

______. "Kritik und Ausblick." *Bauen und Wohnen.* 29, no. 12 (1975): 506-8. (French and English summaries and captions.)

14
CHILE
RAMÓN ALFONSO MÉNDEZ

Modern architecture in Chile developed late in relation to Europe (fig. 14.1), though not in relation to Latin America, and received a surprising degree of public acceptance.

The beginning of the Second World War in Europe and the advent of the Popular Front government comprise the background of the consolidation of contemporary architecture in Chile. Chile's national economy based almost exclusively on copper production was seriously damaged by the low prices she accepted as her contribution to the Allied war effort. Moreover, a devastating earthquake in January 1939 left ruin and destruction in the central area of the country, with more than thirty thousand dead and practically all cities destroyed. With the difficulties imposed on commerce and imports in wartime, and with an urgent need to replace the housing stock of the damaged areas as well as to substantially raise living standards, the new government began an ambitious program of industrialization. One of the most important acts of the period was the creation of the *Corporación de Fomento de la Producción* (Production Development Corporation), the successful model of which would be repeated years later by the countries of the Andean Pact.

The Consolidation of Contemporary Architecture: 1945-1960

Architectural development profited soon after the end of the war from the appearance of new materials in the market, most of all from the iron of the blast furnaces of the Compañía de Acero del Pacífico (Pacific Iron Company), created in 1950 at Huachipato. Iron production led to a renewed interest in steel construction. But with the very limited pattern of production, for many years mostly ordinary round steel was fabricated for reinforced concrete. Despite limitations, architects managed to design imaginative structures in folded or laminated steel or stereometric netting.

14.1. Juan Martínez Gutiérrez, architect. School of Law Building, University of Chile, Santiago, designed c. 1934, erected 1936-1938. (Photograph: Courtesy of Photographic Laboratory, University of Chile)

The forties were important for the development of certain institutional and legal aspects of the architectural profession. In 1942 a special law (no. 7211) created the Colegio de Arquitectos de Chile (Institute of Chilean Architects) defining the profession in terms of design, building, and town planning, with careful consideration also to professional ethics. A new legal incentive in the so-called Pereira Law (1948) led the private sector to build medium-sized, economic housing. Unfortunately, the standards for the qualification "economic" were in overall surface area, surface area per room, height, and the use of

Translated by René Martínez Lemoine, Architect, Santiago.

cheap materials. In this law important tax deductions for builders were set forth and after a short trial period, the bulk of the housing industry was directed to the housing needs of the extensive Chilean middle class. For "architecture," however, the result was of little importance, since most architects' work consisted of a sort of puzzle of square meters and legal dispositions.

By the end of the war, in 1946, a definite change in program and methods was in force at the School of Architecture of the University of Chile. As early as 1933 there had been a desire to make changes. A number of faculty members, who had studied in Europe under Scharoun, Holzmeister, or Le Corbusier were brought in. But the roots of academic training and the Beaux-Arts tradition in Latin American schools of architecture in the thirties were too strong to disappear. The "Reform of 1945" was the first radical change in architectural education with a deep and lasting impact in other Latin American schools of architecture.

The theoretical basis of this reform is to be found in the early Bauhaus and its European followers, but the similarities were not as strong as was thought in Chile. Objectives for the Bauhaus were bolder and wider: architectural training there was only possible after full and extensive experience in the techniques of different crafts and arts. Some years later, schools of architecture in Santiago and Valparaíso followed a similar course.

Notwithstanding the value of some of the best architectural works of the decade, the new well-to-do garden suburbs towards the northern part of Santiago were still built in historically eclectic styles. For more than twenty years a formidable architectural competence appealed to ostentation and social status. Each home was a masterpiece of antiquity and style, though brand new and solidly built in reinforced concrete.

This is the framework in which contemporary architecture in Chile began its struggle for consolidation. By 1943, Mauricio Despouy built a very significant apartment building, the value of which lies both in its plastic vocabulary and in careful functional considerations. It is organized in duplex apartments for easier and more economical circulation and to take better advantage of the views of an adjoining park, a river, and distant hills. The unusual location of the elevator, isolated in the center of a glass lobby and opening away from the entrance is noteworthy. One is guided into the building by two curving walls sheathed in black mirrors reflecting and fragmenting the landscape at one's back. Once in front of the elevator, the user again faces the exterior landscape through which he entered.

There is a rich treatment of fenestration that avoids the monotony so frequent in early Rationalism. Covered balconies adjoining living areas are an early instance of a tendency which flowered later. They are reminiscent of the ancient Chilean tradition of corridors filled with plants and flowers serving as the suitable place for outdoor rest in the hot summer climate. Originally the color, from white to navy blue, fostered a better reading of the building. Today, the color has disappeared under successive whitewashes.

A year later, in 1944, Enrique Gebhard began the Instituto de Biología Marina (Institute of Maritime Biology) for the University of Chile at Viña del Mar, on an exclusive, rocky site of outstanding beauty. Its five different volumes accord with the different requirements of the program. There is a strong relationship with European post-Expressionism and a faithful, recognizable application of Le Corbusier's *principes d'architecture*, with extensive use of the *pilotis* supporting two and three stories, the use of the continuous window, flat roof, and so on. In spite of this ostensible dependency, Gebhard's work was noteworthy for his pioneering use of *béton brut* which antedates Le Corbusier's *Maison Jaoul* and any example of British Brutalism by eight years.

From 1946 to 1947, on a spectacular site facing Forestal Park and the Museum of Fine Arts, Sergio Larraín García-Moreno with the assistance of Walter Reis built a mixed-function structure of shops, flats, and offices. A truly remarkable piece of work, with originality it recreated earlier principles of modern architecture evident in the work of Louis Sullivan. Two important shops at street level are surmounted by six stories of flats and a penthouse which houses the architect's office. Covered balconies, again, form part of the living areas. Its elegance of proportion together with the serenity arising from a horizontal layout of the facade is to a certain extent reminiscent of the Carson, Pirie, Scott and Company building in Chicago. The building fits easily into its urban setting, without disturbing any norm of visual harmony; on the contrary it makes for a richer and fuller open space by continuity of form and function.

In the meantime, a slow but enduring change was taking place in the concepts of "use" and "space" within the average house. Up to the forties, rooms had been isolated, scarcely related, and their locations followed a preconceived pattern: living places facing the street, service areas to the back of the site, sleeping quarters in between or on the second floor. It must be remembered that for the average middle-class family, one or two domestic servants living in the house was a current practice. From the forties onward, a very slow change began to take place. Living and dining areas became closer, though still isolated by heavy glassed doors which tended in the end to disappear. Similarly, the pantry and kitchen were turned into a single room. Service was displaced to the front of the house for better, more immediate control of the entrance. Finally, the living areas slowly were opened into the garden for its privacy, view, and outdoor life. The number of bathrooms was increased and built-in fixtures began to appear.

These new ideas were cleverly abstracted by Emilio Duhart Harosteguy, a graduate of the Catholic University School of Architecture who, after his formative years in Chile, had studied at Harvard under Walter Gropius. In the United States for a short time he worked with I. M. Pei, his former fellow student at Harvard. Returning to Santiago, he built a set of two continuous two-story houses on Pocuro Avenue, breaking every tradition of enclosure in the placing of the buildings by eliminating exterior fences and thus integrating street and garden. With the continuous building, the architect also called attention to the possibility of much higher densities in the city. Inner space was worked out with absolute continuity, making for a unique overall space. Careful consideration was given to detailing and finish, with special attention to hues, textures, and color variations. The structure of the building consists of a concrete frame of pillars, beams, and slabs with brickwork acting as infilling, a formula Chilean architects were to use for thirty years.

The seismic danger to construction in Chile has led to strict regulations in methods of building with reinforced concrete. As a result, Chilean architecture has developed a sort of vernacular expression in which brickwork infilling is carefully stuccoed, making structural elements seem isolated from the whole. In a sense, this is a sort of early Brutalism, markedly different from the whitewashed, stuccoed volumes of Oud, Loos, Gropius, or Le Corbusier, though maintaining such features as the flat roof, free plan, and continuous window.

By the same period, a new partnership that was to have a brilliant effect upon architectural development in Chile was formed. Héctor Valdés Phillips, Fernando Castillo Velasco, and Carlos García Huidobro, all were destined to rise in academic and administrative circles. In 1953 they were joined by Carlos Bresciani. One of the boldest houses of the period was built by Fernando Castillo for himself in 1947. In it a bare horizontal concrete slab is supported by steel columns; partitions disappear with the exception of the service areas, and isolation is achieved by the placement of furniture, which provides for great flexibility of use. In external expression it is neat and simple, evidently anticipating and resembling the Glass Pavilion built in New Canaan, Connecticut in 1949 by Philip Johnson. A year after Castillo's home, Carlos García Huidobro built a very similar house on an adjoining site.

Juan Martínez Gutiérrez built an office building in 1948 for the Unión Española de Seguros (Spanish Insurance Union), a building curiously similar to the John F. Kennedy Center, planned by Walter Gropius many years later for construction in the heart of Boston. An interesting feature of the new building is the use of industrial molding: that is, the covering of the entire facade is of prefabricated cast marble, which takes the place of ordinary molding. In such a way the building process is, so to speak, reversed and the building begins with the setting up of the exterior covering. Occupying a corner on a narrow busy thoroughfare, the building breaks the traditional right angle in a plastically expressive curve, which provides for a better understanding of the unity of the building and the careful reticulation of its precast modular facade. At street level, the architect used copper as exterior finishing in an effort to introduce and to test a vernacular material. The experience, however, was not successful due to bad weathering of the material, and it has not been repeated. An interesting feature was the pioneering use of the free plan. There are no inner partitions, save those enclosing stairs and service areas. Thus the building was sold by square meters according to the particular needs of the customer, and divisions were put into place afterwards.

Years before, in 1943, Juan Martínez had been the winner of a national competition for design of the Military Academy, a project whose execution took too many years. (Even today it does not accord with its original design, as the tower of the facade was never built to balance its monumental horizontal portico.) Despite the variety of the program, specialized buildings and open spaces are treated as a corpus with enormous plastic possibilities upon a generous site but with a mechanical determination of the functions involved in a military school. The severity of the building, enhanced by the extensive use of exposed concrete not only throughout on exteriors but also in the interiors, makes this a most extensive and early use of *béton brut*. A very similar pattern was repeated in 1951 in the School of Medicine of the University of Chile, a national competition in which, once again, Juan Martínez won first prize.

By the end of the forties, the first phase of the Verbo Divino School was completed. The project, the result of a national competition won by Sergio Larraín García-Moreno, Emilio Duhart, Mario Pérez de Arce, and Alberto Piwonka, was conceived with extreme simplicity. Several sets of classrooms were arranged in a pattern of open corridors; and "inner space" resulted from the formal interaction of the different buildings. This plastic expression is, it seems, the result of principles of organization rather than the mere use of a successful traditional formula. Larraín García-Moreno and Duhart became associated and the partnership produced works of the highest value in the following years. By 1952 Emilio Duhart took up postgraduate studies in France and worked under Le Corbusier.

As a result of the new teaching approach in Chilean schools of architecture since 1946, by the beginning of the fifties a generation of young, socially minded architects with new ideas was coming into practice. And with them came the end of historical eclecticism in Chilean architecture. Public institutions became more open minded toward new architectural ideologies; a rather slow but continuous replacement of staff, together with the growing acceptance of new models from the cultural avant garde, began to displace worn-out architectural formulae.

In 1953, public housing bodies that had been formed first after the earthquakes in Talca (1928) and Chillán (1939) were integrated into the Corporación de la Vivienda (Housing Corporation) in an effort to concentrate public investment and encourage private participation in house building for low income groups. Housing programs, however, sought for quantity rather than quality, and there was a considerable cultural gap between architects and users. Social or mass housing became a reduced version of upper-middle-class housing, with no relation whatsoever to the values, cultural patterns, or needs of low-income groups. On the other hand, there had never been any creative approach to building methods and techniques for mass-construction needs, even with decades of valuable experience in this area including the work of Hassan Fathy in Gourna.

The industrial ironworks built at Huachipato in 1950 opened up the possibility of steel-frame construction. By the early fifties Sergio Larraín and Emilio Duhart proposed a fifteen-story steel tower for Santiago's main central square. Instead, a new project came about, a large unit facing on three main streets, with a double-decked commercial slab and a free-standing volume fourteen stories high. All told it resembled the volumetric disposition of the Lever House, built two years before by Skidmore, Owings and Merrill in New York. The commercial slab was integrated easily with surrounding built-up areas, improving on the traditional galleries that break through the inner core of the central blocks of the city, galleries that had provided sheltered shopping since the nineteenth century in Santiago. The free block breaks the classical formality of the old city, permitting greater airiness, sunshine, and uninterrupted views, while the roof of the commercial slab provides a generous garden-terrace.

Built entirely of reinforced concrete, a new structural concept was evident, unconventional and freer when compared with those of the previous decade. Strongly supporting elements placed into the bulk of the building left free facades on all four sides on which a lavish use of cantilevered balconies gives an impression of airiness and lightness. The only possible criticism for a building of such a clear conception is a sense of its being too economical. This is apparent not only in the use of cheap finishes but also in the restrictions of space. Both of these factors accounted for the rapid decay and the loss of image that conceal today the merits of the building. In the same way, the narrowness of the balconies or loggias worked against their full use. As a consequence, some have been closed in with windows while others have been turned into exterior waste-rooms, all of which destroyed the original plastic conception of the building.

Two years later, the same architects raised another building in the very heart of Alameda Avenue, Santiago's main thoroughfare. On the whole, the new building followed the same pattern: double-decked commercial slab, inner gallery, and isolated tower. The roof terrace was for some time intended as a museum of modern art, but in the end a row of cheaply constructed offices was built, spoiling the neat initial conception. In the same way, as in the previous case, the building has suffered from premature decay and loss of image, proceeding from a very low budget, an endemic situation for Chilean architecture!

In 1954, the Caja de Empleados Particulares (Private Employees Fund) bought a substantial part of the ancient Quinta Normal de Agricultura, to build a low-to-medium-income housing estate for some two thousand families. The project, entrusted to the firm of Bresciani, Valdés, Castillo and Huidobro and completed by 1960, is one of most imaginative pieces done in Chile in the housing field. Taking advantage of a privileged site and fine views, it opens to the northern sun and eastern views of the Andean ranges, purposely blocking the disadvantageous highway on the west by means of very long and rather high apartment blocks.

An interesting feature, a network of elevated pedestrian walks, was made possible by the clever use of the slight gradient of the site. This horizontal network running at roof level of the two-story housing blocks connects in the end with the third level of the large western blocks. From this level, the building ascends to the maximum height established by law for construction without mechanical vertical circulation. This ingenious design permits a total height of seven stories without elevators, which were then too expensive for Chilean economical housing. At the same time, the novel height is used to define a clear spatial border for the whole unit. The monotony of the average four-story scheme used in low-cost housing programs was thus broken. At both ends of the higher block, a car ramp provides limited vehicular access to the third-level gallery which was intended as an elevated street, for such services as ambulances, waste collecting, small service vans, and so on. In this way, a new sense of an external corridor emerged, with a rich and varied activity from service use to social gatherings, which is not comparable with the ordinary concept of a corridor or passage in a housing block. The elevated pattern of pathways gives great diversity to spaces and views, with unsuspected joints and meeting places, and cannot be compared with the various Unités d'Habitation or the Pruitt Igoe project in Saint Louis, Missouri.

The whole scheme of the Quinta Normal housing estate follows the Brutalist trend with exposed concrete as the main external feature. On the western facade this treatment is completed with delicate vertical louvers more in the form of shutters or blinds than strong tropical sun-breakers.

At the same time, the office of Bresciani, Valdés, Castillo and Huidobro was actively engaged in a housing project facing Cousiño Park. The site was a traditional block, upon which the new buildings were placed, following the line of the street and forming a grand central courtyard (as in fig. 14.2). The traditional continuity of the street was thus preserved and its functional relation to the rest of the area was maintained by means of shopping premises facing the main street.

This general layout, strongly related to the formal

14.2. Bresciani, Valdés, Castillo and Huidobro, architects. Unidad Vecinal Portales, Santiago, 1954-1960. (Photograph: Courtesy of architect Jorge Torrico M., 1980)

and traditional organization of Chilean urban space, was enhanced by a rich treatment of the facade that combined a concrete frame with red clay-brick infilling. The careful proportioning was further enhanced by means of an artful breaking of the facade to express the individuality of each housing unit. Such a disposition reflected the spirit of the Royal Crescent in Bath, in which John Wood, the architect, praised "the individuality of the single household in the unity of the whole."[1] By the end of the fifties, the Bresciani, Valdés, Castillo and Huidobro group was actively exploring possibilities of color in architecture in a bold new scheme on Providencia Avenue at the corner of Holanda Street.

From the middle of the nineteenth century in Chile, steel had been used intensively in the form of industrial infrastructures, bridges, railway stations, and commercial buildings. In the early twentieth century, some architectural attempts, such as the Gath and Chavez building [1909], San Alfonso Church [1919] or the Carmelita's Church [1920], had no direct followers because of the introduction of reinforced concrete by the early 1920s. Furthermore, in the last examples cited, the steel skeleton was hidden under heavy and elaborated plaster, unlike the approach of such excellent nineteenth century structures as the Edward's Building by Eugenio Joannon [1892] or the Paris Pavilion by Henry Picq [1889], both in the grand manner of Paxton, Bogardus, or Labrouste.

The influence of the new architecture of the forties proceeding from such spectacular projects as Mies van der Rohe's Lake Shore Drive apartments or the IIT buildings was reflected in two new projects of the fifties. Neither was built, but they were an index of Chilean creativity: the block of tower apartments by Emilio Duhart [1953] previously mentioned and a twenty-story tower building in Concepción, by Jorge Larraín and Hernán Riesco [1954]. During the mid-1950s the first double-curved spatial structure in Chile, the church of Los Angeles, was presented by Jorge Larraín and Hernán Riesco in 1954. By the mid-1950s too, Horacio Acevedo Davenport was charged with a project sponsored by COPEC (Chilean Petroleum Company) to build a series of dismountable or temporary service stations, most of which were to be erected on rented sites. Acevedo Davenport prepared two modular schemes corresponding to two different solutions of roof coverings: the first used a prefabricated asbestos-cement vaulting system while the second employed a stereometric, flat, steel frame. Both were supported by steel columns in which a variety of partitions was made possible by the careful detailing of structural joints.

Rationality, technical skill, and clever use of materials are the main features of these valuable experiences that exemplified the ingenuity with which the architects of the 1950s were overcoming shortages of materials. Acevedo Davenport's next step was to extend the use of stereometric steel frames to housing units. This occurred in 1956 with his steel exhibition tower for the Pacific Iron Company.

The Central Institute of Chemistry and the School of Engineering at the University of Concepción are the work of Emilio Duhart who, in 1958, also explored the possibilities of steel. His was notable work in which a Rationalist approach provided openness and transparency to the new buildings that overlooked the central agora of the university. At the same time, the single expedient of detaching the facade from the supporting structure gave the impression of depth and lightness. The experimental character of these buildings was emphasized when the earthquake of 1960 produced serious damage in areas where the more solid service nuclei were in contact with more flexible sections of the structure.

With fewer resources available, Ventura Galván began his School of Applied Arts for the University of Chile [1959], a building conceived as a low-cost structure to be erected in situ, by means of a series of folded pieces of laminated steel. Flexibility in the use of space, a human scale and proportion, permanent interaction between inner and outer spaces following the variety of its courtyards, together with the simplicity of its building system, make this structure the closest approximation of the ideas of Hassan Fathy in Chile.

By the end of the 1950s, Jorge Larraín, Hernán Riesco, Horacio Borgheresi, Jorge Penelló, Octavio Soto, and Jorge Prieto prepared the Chilean Pavilion at the Fair of the Pacific in Lima [1959] as a temporary dismountable structure with a light translucent covering suitable for the climatic conditions of Peru, the host country. Despite the limitations of the Chilean steel industry, in the following years there were several other attempts to build in steel including the Seminary for the Pallotine Fathers, by Ramón A. Méndez [1960] and the Church of Saint Xavier by Bresciani, Valdés, Castillo and Huidobro [1963], among others.

Looking back to the intensive period that ended in 1960, it is most evident that a main feature was a concern for problems of spatial organization employing the formal vocabulary of Rationalism. The vernacular expression of this concern extended the earliest trend of differentiating structure or frame from infilling by means of color, texture, and leveling. The resulting architecture of the period, therefore, was substantially different from the white boxes of the European thirties. For a time, the only "modern" feature seemed to be the omnipresent flat roof. In retrospect, a surprising feature of the fifties is a sort of natural integration of modern architecture with the structure of the city, even in its most traditional quarters, together with a thorough understanding of spatial determinants and different ways of life.

At the same time, the role of furniture as a mediator between space and man began to be considered. Built-in furniture and contemporary decoration were fostered by pioneering industries, such as Muzard, Muebles Sur, Cristián Valdés, and Montero y Cía. Most striking then was the high quality of work done in steel, in spite of the limited range of national production. According to Monserrat Palmer Trias, steel used with imagination, technical skill, and originality made the period from 1950-1960 one of the richest periods of Chile's architectural achievements.[2]

Neo-Expressionism: 1960-1969

In 1960 the end of Chile's period of consolidation of modern architecture and the beginning of neo-Expressionism was marked again by two earthquakes and the heavy task of reconstruction of the nearly one-third of the country that was in ruins. By the end of the fifties a growing concern with the urbanization process and housing problems moved the government to promulgate Decree Number 2 (July 1959), better known as the Housing Plan. The new decree was intended to provide incentive for private investment in the economic solution of the social-housing problem. A limit of 140 square meters per dwelling first was considered. A year later, a series of new aspects were added and by Decree Number 1,001 (18 July 1960), a definitive text existed for the housing plan.[3]

The plan represented a substantial advance compared to the previous Pereira Law of 1948 and in a short time a considerable amount of money from the private sector was invested in medium-priced housing. From the architectural point of view, the increase of building activity, however, had very little significance due to the restrictions of surface and materials in the law. The system was improved further by the creation of the National Savings and Loan Corporation, through which one could finance the building cost of an economical house. A certain amount of savings entitled the owner to get a loan up to the total cost of the dwelling. The loan was repaid according to the owner's income as a monthly rent over a period of from ten to twenty years.

From the formal point of view, the 1960s in Chile corresponded with the neo-Expressionist architecture of the previous decade in Europe and the United

14.3. Emilio Duhart, architect. ONU/CEPAL (Economic Commission for Latin America) Building. Santiago, 1960-1966. (Photograph: Courtesy of architect Jorge Torrico M., 1980)

States, replacing the more Classical forms of the consolidation period with more Baroque and dramatic forms.

In the Tajamar Towers [Bresciani, Valdés, Castillo and Huidobro; Bolton, Larraín and Prieto, 1960-1963] the central building rises twenty-six stories, practically twice the usual height of the 1950s and breaks the customary alignment of building with street with an unusual diagonal. A great "urban window" that perforates either side of one of its towers, opening up a spectacular view of the city and the distant mountains, is particularly dramatic.

In 1960 an international competition for the Headquarters of the Economic Commission for Latin America was won by Emilio Duhart. His design consists of a two-story structure in which the upper level practically floats over a non-existing first floor, bounding an open yard that is square in plan (figs. 14.3 and 14.4). With the floor level entirely open, there is easy access to the glassed reception lobby, the conference hall, and various other spaces, all of a very high plastic quality. The huge pyramidal columns supporting the upper quadrangle, the slender translucent bridges relating the central lobby to an outer ring, the vast overhang dominating the entrance, the use of an artificial lake as an enormous mirror that reflects the image of the main facade, and many other features closely relate this "period piece" to the neo-Expressionist movement nurtured in the last works of Le Corbusier and Saarinen, and in Brazilian and Japanese architecture. At the same time, Emilio Duhart built two hotels on the southern island of Chiloé in Ancud and Castro. The second, very interesting spatially, is conceived in a rectangular plan, covered by a great triangular roof that accords with the climatic conditions of the region, and that served at the same time as a symbol and as a necessity.

A particular contribution to the reconstruction of

14.4. Emilio Duhart, architect. ONU/CEPAL Building, detail. Santiago, 1960-1966 (Photograph: Courtesy of Photographic Laboratory, University of Chile)

Chile's south was made by the School of Architecture of the Catholic University at Valparaíso in certain church plans. The Bío Bío Chapel, at the mouth of a large river, is by far the most interesting. Local materials and traditional techniques were used to create a square, plain, wooden structure, in which the altar is located at one of the vertices. Walls and roof constitute a single unit built in the form of four inverted ship prows; and huge lifting doors are used to integrate the building with its outer space for massive religious celebrations.

In the same neo-Expressionist trend, Mauricio Despouy built [1965] a one-story house, known as *La Teja* (The Tile), at the foot of Manquehue Hill, resembling in the shape of the roof a single, huge, inverted tile. The Tile is an example of the frequent use of metaphoric vocabulary in Chilean architecture, even when not intentional, such as the "Roof" (in

Castro), the "Boat" (in Bío Bío), the "Patio" (in shopping centers), and the "Portal" (in Vitacura). Earlier examples seen in Chile are the brilliant work of Roberto Dávila Carson known as *Cap Ducal*, a "grounded" ship on the coastal rocks at Viña del Mar and the great "Portal" at the University of Concepción.

In the development of international neo-Expressionism an important factor was the nationalistic search for vernacular forms. Chile is no exception to this rule. Initial interest in vernacular architecture came from Julio Bertrand, Pedro Prado, and the "Group of Ten" at the beginning of the century. This interest, a kind of romantic revival, was taken up by Roberto Dávila Carson in *La Portada*, published in 1927, with the subtitle: *On the Architecture of Our Past*, a subject which was the central concern of his professional and academic life.

The 1960s are marked by a vigorous growth of the same concerns, the study of traditional forms of architecture, patterns of settlements of the central valley, and the characteristics of Chile's urban layouts. Pioneering works in this field were Manuel Eduardo Secchi's *Architecture in Santiago, XVIIth to XIXth Century* (1914) and Alfred Benavides Rodríguez's *Architecture in the Vice Royalty of Peru and Captaincy General of Chile* (1941). Differently oriented was Guillermo Ulrikssen's book, *La Serena Plan*, an ambitious project to remodel the city of La Serena while preserving its traditional values. Roberto Montandón Paillard initiated archeological research and reconstruction in the Pukara at Lasana. Raúl Irarrázaval Covarrubias centered his attention on the traditional rural manor (*The Landlord's House*, 1967; *An Order in the Valley*, 1967; and *Land of Light*, 1971). José Ricardo Morales, a native of Málaga, Spain, poet, dramatist, and historian, published an essay on theory and criticism of architecture, *Architectónica* (1966), in two volumes. At about the same time Juan Borchers presented some of his writings and lectures in *Architectonic Institution*; and finally, Gabriel Guarda, O.S.R., published *The Chilean City of the Eighteenth Century* (1968) in Buenos Aires.

Academic cloisters were not alien to concerns with the vernacular idioms. The Institute of History of Architecture of the Faculty of Architecture at the University of Chile has been active in the analysis and interpretation of traditional values, in a series of important studies that include the surveying of ancient monuments. Patricio Gross, Gustavo Munizaga, Roberto San Martín, Myriam Waisberg, and others are currently contributing to the subject in diverse periodical publications.

The search for regional expression is well represented by the Salar del Carmen housing project in Antofagasta, the work of Mario Pérez de Arce Lavín and Jaime Besa Zañartu. An absolute unity of whitewashed volumes, the horizontality of its roofs and the organization of dwellings around an open courtyard all proceed from a sensitive recognition of the particularities of the subtropical climate.

Bresciani, Valdés, Castillo and Huidobro fulfill the same intention in their stadium and their casino for the northern city of Arica. The casino is particularly interesting by "the absolute absence of overhangs or canopies . . . unnecessary . . . where it never rains, the scarcity of fenestration in accordance with the extreme luminosity of the air and the nature of its interior functions, the free setting of volumes in the gentle slope of the beach, all of which contributes to an unmistakable image of locality."[4] The same city of Arica is the seat of a regional branch of the University of Chile, designed by Mauricio Despouy, in which an extensive use of heavy vertical sun-breakers dramatizes the climatic condition of the place.

In Vicuña, a small city in the so-called Little North and the birthplace of Gabriela Mistral, Nobel Prize winner in 1945, the Gabriela Mistral Museum created by Oscar McClure Alamos [1969], is a remarkable, vigorous structure in concrete and stone with a continuity between inner and outer spaces and a clever modulation of light. Oscar McClure is also responsible for the Normal School at Viña del Mar, a building impeccably sited in the existing, traditional, urban structure, by means of the careful consideration of mass, light, and formal continuity and an organization into courtyards.

Two more ambitious housing projects of the 1960s were the San Borja and Villa Frei. Both reflected a new tendency towards concentration of efforts in vast high-rise housing schemes. San Borja is located on the former site of an old hospital that has been engulfed by the growth of the city. Its 22 hectares provided space enough for an entire neighborhood unit to be built within walking distance of the central urban core. The project, sponsored by the National Corporation of Urban Renewal (CORMU), consists of twenty-eight towers, each of twenty-two stories. The official policy of the Ministry of Housing then was to increase densities in order to control urban growth. This sort of scheme, however, is obviously destructive to the former social character or community organization of an area.

Villa Frei, on the contrary, situated in the outskirts of the city on the site of a small farm, did not interfere with previous life-styles. It consists of a variety of solutions, from isolated dwellings to medium-height blocks and high-rise apartment towers in a complex of humanly scaled ambiences that invite social gatherings and interaction. In spite of its many merits, the very controversial location of servicing and commercial units and the lack of a clear overall image and identity for its various parts is demonstrative of the difficulties architects face in urban renewal.

Architecture in steel during the 1960s was not as imaginative as it had been in the 1950s. The most extensive and significant work of the period was the development of a prefabricated system by the National School Building Society. As a result, by the end of the 1960s more than 250,000 square meters of school buildings were built, substantially changing the image of the Chilean school. The housing corporation invited submission of models in 1965 for community facilities buildings in prefabricated steel structures. Some of the first and best are by Juan Cárdenas, José Covacevic, and Raúl Farrú. Some years later this group was responsible for the Cyclotron building, a totally steel structure for the Faculty of Science of the University of Chile. In 1967 Sergio Larraín, G. M., Ignacio Covarrubias, and Jorge Swinburn designed the INACAP building in Antofagasta, an example of the only lasting use for steel in Chilean architecture, the covering of vast industrial spans. The last two examples of Chilean architecture in steel are the DISTRA building, a completely exposed steel structure by Mario Recordón and Alberto Sartori and the office building for the Pacific Iron Company (CAP) by Héctor Valdés Phillips and Carlos García Huidobro, a seven-story structure. Both were built in 1968.

Since then the city of Santiago has outgrown all demographic forecasts, with a consequent serious deterioration of the quality of its urban life. Persistent migration into the city, increasing numbers of vehicles, environmental pollution, marginal and spontaneous settlements, lack of accessibility—all constitute the fundamental problems of its "metropolization." This phenomenon of the concentration of population in one major city is common to all Latin American countries and Chile is no exception, with one-third of her total population living in Santiago.

To cope with the situation, the government set a vast plan into motion, including the construction of a metropolitan subway system (metro), rigid control over the city limits, comprehensive development of a highway system, and the creation of the Ministry of Housing and Urban Planning. The serious housing problem led to the adoption of new construction programs. All of these introduced serious changes into the structure of the city and its functioning which as yet are not fully recognized. Despite heavy investment in the reconstruction of the southern provinces, there was also a high level of investment in workers' housing. On the other hand, the new legislation increased private investment in middle-class housing and for the first time in many years there was a real improvement in housing conditions.

Towards the end of the decade neo-Expressionism tended to decline, leaving an image of vigorous architecture, mostly of large-scale buildings (fig. 14.5) and expansive estates. Formally, Chilean neo-Expressionism emphasized structure in a melodramatic manner, as with the pyramidal columns by Emilio Duhart (fig. 14.4) in the CEPAL building or the Ostornol House by Cristián de Groote, which shows a delicate balance between supporting and supported elements in a modular system of vaulted slabs. In the Ministry of Labor building, the last work in Chile by Emilio Duhart done in partnership with Alberto Montealegre K., the disposition of windows follows a diagonal pattern. The tower of this building, its four corners broken to produce an eight-sided image, is supported by freestanding columns whose sculptured forms proceed from the recognition of the inner forces of the material. This recalls a similar treatment in James Stirling's engineering building for the University of Leicester [1959-1963].

14.5. Mauricio Despouy, architect. Worker's Hospital. Santiago, 1969. (Photograph: Courtesy of architect Jorge Torrico M., 1980)

There are other examples in which the overall pattern is broken into minor elements which, in turn, organize the whole in an original manner and change the image of an established type. Such is the case in the Saint George's School, by Manuel Atria, José Antonio Gómez, Francisco Lira, and Gustavo

Munizaga, conceived as a system of classrooms with pyramidal decks organized in a nonlinear sequence. Similarly, in the housing block Remodelación República by Vicente Bruna, Víctor Calvo, Jorge Perelman, and Orlando Sepúlveda [1963-1965] a combination of five different continuous horizontal frames is used to express the variety of activities taking place in the buildings. One thinks particularly of the continuous curving window by Stanley Tigerman for the Chicago Library for the Handicapped, fifteen years later, in relation to this approach.

A very keen sense of processional sequence is also characteristic of the 1960s. Apart from the example of the CEPAL building, previously mentioned, Gabriel Guarda produces a most remarkable use of light in the transition from the entrance to the altar of the chapel for his Benedictine Monastery.

All of these formal inventions are almost always embodied within a wider spatial play, in which the unity of the parts is the central concern. This is clearly noticeable in the commercial courtyards accompanying nearly all offices and apartment blocks of the period. Usually designed as two-storied, they frame an open yard in which a play of double heights permits an integration between interior and exterior landscape. The same effect is found in such buildings as the hotel by Duhart in Castro; the hotel of San Felipe; the social security building in Antofagasta; the group of flats on Manuel Montt Avenue in Santiago, by Bresciani, Valdés, Castillo and Huidobro; and the University of Chile in Arica by Despouy.

A new freedom in the management of formal relations led to a more varied and enriched approach reflecting an Organicist influence, despite tendencies towards vernacular expression. This last remained then mostly theoretical. Formal richness extended beyond architecture to urban design. In the Jardín del Este residential district, Emilio Duhart broke with the classical Spanish layout to plan an undulating play of streets, while in the Villa Frei and the Remodelación San Borja traditional blocks disappeared to be replaced by superblocks with a new manner of road distribution.

Overcoming Crisis: Towards New Architectural Trends, 1969-1980

By the end of the 1960s, the country faced a presidential election in which three political currents, right, center, and left, were almost equally strong. The uncertainty over the political destiny of the country became a major factor in a building recession.

During the 1970s, a most radical change took place in Chile's political, economic, and social structure. Two contrasting political systems made substantial changes, modifying the democratic tradition of the country. From 1970 a Marxist experiment took control of agricultural land and the means of production, with a complete disruption of the economic system. By the end of 1973 a military coup d'etat led to a complete turnabout in economic policy. As President Allende had seen it, the country had all the disadvantages of capitalism and none of the advantages of socialism; and, therefore, it was not difficult to understand the reasons for one of the highest monetary inflations in the world.

Naturally architecture was affected by political circumstances and the critical situation was aggravated still more by the 1971 earthquake.

The so-called Popular Unity government began in 1970 with the announcement of a most ambitious housing program, amounting to some 85,000 units per year. The real capacity of the building industry, however, was insufficient for such massive construction and so in the end the entire program came to a standstill.[5] By 1973 the building industry was practically paralyzed and its subsequent recovery has been long and difficult. The housing deficit reached a most alarming level, rising according to later figures to 600,000 units. Taking into account the overall existing housing stock, this amounted to a third of the population lacking a decent dwelling. Since 1978 a "housing subsidy" has been provided to enable low-income families to live in proper dwellings.

Within this problematic background there was nevertheless room for concern with the vernacular, though at this time its origins were to be found first in "socialist realism" and later in the works of the Italian architect Aldo Rossi. Redevelopment of the Cousiño Park area (renamed O'Higgins Park) gave way to the erection of a small "Chilean" village for recreational purposes. This village became a mere decorative imitation of traditional architecture, with no consideration of the formal, structural, or volumetric dispositions of buildings that formerly were imbued with vernacular intents. Only by the end of the decade did Raúl Irarrázaval succeed in bringing some of the formal principles of a Chilean vernacular into the Vitacura Park [1979] project. In such projects, from first to last, a certain number of common elements is always present: the yard or patio organizing space and buildings; and those formal characteristics of Mediterranean architecture most typical of Spanish-American colonial styles.

Interest in traditional architecture seems to have diminished early in the 1970s, though a small group held to it in theory. Montserrat Palmer Trias published a study (1970 and 1971) on *Architecture in Steel*, covering the years from 1863 to 1970. Carlos Martner and Alfonso Raposo explored the possibility of expandable housing in *Dynamic Dwellings* (1972) in which the central yard plays a dominant part. Myriam Waisberg considered the life and works of an eighteenth-century master, in *Joaquín Toesca, Architect and Master-Builder* (1975) and a year later, a *Guide to the Architecture of Santiago* by Magda Anduaga, Carlos Miranda, Oscar Ortega, Silvia Pirotte, Fernando Riquelme, and Antonio Sahady, put together some of the most valuable examples of Chilean architecture, from national monuments to other buildings of architectonic or cultural value.[6]

Villages, chapels and Spanish architectural remains became the subject of Juan Benavides, León Rodríguez, and Rodrigo Márquez de la Plata in their *Architecture in Northern Chile*. Later, Juan Benavides published *Fundamentals of Modern Architecture*, an essay on the ideas behind today's architecture. The drawings and sayings of Roberto Dávila Carson were gathered together by Oscar Ortega and Silvia Pirotte, in *Sketches of Colonial Architecture by R. Dávila*, a book that is a tribute to the late master. Enrique Brown turned his attention to the problems of space and culture in *The Use of the House and City*, published in Buenos Aires (1978); and Raúl Irarrázaval concentrated again on Chilean traditions in his *Architecture in Chile, a Search for Order in Space* (1979).[7]

Very important in the 1970s has been the preservation and restoration of historical buildings. The present day approach is quite different from the practices of the beginning of the century. New principles in use are the *mise en valeur* of formal values and functional motivation. From 1960 on and considering the earthquake-prone nature of the country, there has been a growing concern for the restoration of historic churches such as the convent of Curimón, the Dominicans' chapel in Apoquindo, the Saint Dominique church, and the San Francisco church in Santiago.[8] By mid-century the Cousiño Palace of 1871, the work of French architect Paul Lathoud, was destroyed by fire. For three years (1977-1980), architect Rodrigo Márquez de la Plata has been engaged in its "archeological" restoration. The same architect had been in charge of the initial works of reconstruction of the Palace of La Moneda, destroyed during the coup d'etat in 1973.[9] The Faculty of Architecture of the University of Chile, through the Department of Architectural Restoration has been in charge of work on two very different buildings, the Edwards Palace [1887-1899], housing the Diplomatic Academy, and the Manor House of Lo Matta [c. 1650].

In Fernando Riquelme Sepúlveda's restoration of the old Customs House [1808] in Santiago, the opening of an interesting pedestrian arcade solved the problem of a building that had expanded beyond the usual building line of the city's streets. The restoration of the Casa Colorada [mid-eighteenth century] in Santiago and the Church of La Matriz [1830] in Valparaíso posed both difficult and interesting problems. The former had been seriously damaged in its fabric and ornamentation, and in the latter structural problems of the tower and presbytery were overcome by employing original materials such as wood and adobe. In an interesting effort Gonzalo Mardónes Restat recycled two Art Nouveau houses to become the central premises of the Chilean Architects' Association. Finally, during the rehabilitation of the old El Mercurio newspaper building in Valparaíso, Cristián de Groote and Associates carefully removed plaster ornamentation and inner partitions to uncover a most interesting structural system of steel and brickwork, and cleverly adapted this into new and original spaces.

The decade of the 1970s was poor in urban design and city planning, apart from the works of the metro and public roads. It is only very recently that an ambitious plan of rehabilitation of the central area in Santiago has been implemented by the city under Major Patricio Mekis. Two main central thoroughfares were closed to vehicular traffic and turned into pedestrian precincts. As a result there has been a revival of activity in areas that were decaying and a rapid renovation that has made the environment more human. A project for the renovation of the central area, the work of students of the School of Architecture of the Catholic University of Chile, under Professors Hernán Riesco, Renato, Parada, and Sergio del Fierro, was conceived with the collaboration of Imre Halasz and Michel Underhill, both from the Massachusetts Institute of Technology. For now it remains only a theoretical exercise.

The School of Architecture at Catholic University in Valparaíso has been active in projects of regional importance such as the Coastal Avenue, the rehabilitation of the Marga-Marga river, as well as one plan that would have provided new access to the city.

One of the most significant steps of the 1970s in this area is due to architect Fernando Larraguibel: the creation of the Urban Ecology Group, an interdisciplinary team from the faculty of architecture of the University of Chile. For the last ten years, the group has worked with low-income groups and has been concerned with the uses of street space as well as with cultural values. In 1980 the program completely transformed a street into a recreational and cultural area.

Urban concern has not been alien to theoretical studies. Jaime Garretón presented his *Cybernetic Theory of the City System* in 1975, interpreting the laws governing urbanization process and suggesting an operative method for effective control of its development.[10] *Santiago in the Third Quarter of the XXth Century*, the work of Juan Parrochia B., accounts for twenty-five years of metropolitan transport planning and advocates solutions to the increasing traffic and transportation problems of the capital of Chile (1980). The historical point of view is represented by René Martínez Lemoine in *The Classical Model of the Colonial Spanish-American City*. The traditional grid or checkerboard is analyzed as "the spontaneous growing of a model developed after the city of Santo Domingo as the idealized image of the new American city . . . with absolute independence of any legal disposition" such as the Leyes de Indias.[11] And Gabriel Guarda authored a monumental *Urban History of the Kingdom of Chile, 1540-1826*, to date the most complete and documented relation of the origins and development of Chilean villages and cities.

Our presentation of written works on architecture and city planning hardly hints at the lack of discussion in these fields: there is little interest in theory, whether in professional or academic circles. Two architectural magazines give us useful information on the profession: the *Revista AUCA*, directed by Raúl Farrú, has reviewed architectural activity since 1966; and the *Revista C. A.*, directed by Jaime Márquez, is the official organ of the Association of Chilean Architects. An important occurrence was the institution of Chile's Biennial of Architecture in 1977, from the beginning organized as an international event. With this, Chilean architects were able to break out of their professional isolation and make contact with some of the most prominent personalities in the field.

By 1977 a Center for Architectural Studies (CEDLA) came into existence under the direction of Cristián Boza. Until its demise in 1979 it was a center of encounter and debate for a new generation of architects; and the philosophy of the new group remains in three numbers of its controversial magazine *ARS*.

Architectural activity in the 1970s began with the Third UNCTAD Conference building (fig. 14.6), which President Allende asked Chilean architects to design on extremely short notice. Architects José Covacevich, Juan Echeñique, Hugo Gaggero, Sergio González, and José Medina faced two serious problems—first, the transformation of a twenty-two story apartment building then under construction into the Secretariat of the Conference and, second, the very short time limit in which to finish their work. Thus, the final result lacks space and perspective for so monumental a structure.

The economic policy originated anew in 1973 by the military government provided the necessary bases for the expansion of commercial activities. Conversion of houses into shops became common practice, with many imaginative solutions that may be considered as original architecture in themselves. The Bank of Concepción in Providencia Avenue became a fine example of careful and sensible recycling, when Sergio Miranda Rodríguez turned a simple two-storied house into an airy, transparent, and dynamic volume.

14.6. José Covacevich, Juan Echeñique, Hugo Gaggero, Sergio González and José Medina, architects. Building for the Third United Nations Conference on Trade and Development (UNCTAD). Santiago, 1972. (Photograph: Courtesy of Photographic Laboratory, University of Chile)

The expansion of commercial activities proceeding from the new free-import policy led to a second generation of high-rise commercial buildings. The better known form of these buildings is the so-called snail, consisting of a spiral ramp rising to four or more stories and giving access to rather small, commercial cubicles that face inwards to an open space. The first ramps were isolated helicoids; but fashion and mannerism turned them quickly into double-snail, square-snail, twin-snails, and so on. In their present form, these are nothing more than aerial shopping corridors with no possibilities for human encounters. Closed to the urban scene and the distant landscape, they are merely the plastic expression of a consumer society,[12] although the origin of the Chilean commercial snail block was supposedly in New York's Guggenheim Museum (1958) by Frank Lloyd Wright.

A very different approach to commercial activity is seen in Plaza Shopping at Vitacura. Jaime Bendersky and Juan Luis Brunetti gave a new and human interpretation to the traditional plaza or central square of the Chilean city by combining shops in different levels, promenades, encounter spaces, outdoor recreation, and cultural activity areas, with the whole organized around an open space as a center of activity.

In spite of its suburban location, Plaza Shopping attracts people from far and near, be it for window-shopping, skating in the open, film viewing, or just to see and be seen.

The Ralún Hostelry, near Puerto Montt in the far south, marks the beginning of a new architecture in harmony with land and climate, rich in inner spaces, and making sensible use of local materials such as stone and wood. With much technical skill Cristián de Groote (Molina, Barros, Pertuiset, collaborators) has created an admirable piece of work there in a severe plastic vocabulary, full of local character.

In high-rise buildings, offices, and flats, there has been, since the previous decade, at best a lack of inventiveness, a mechanical repetition of typical solutions, and a decorative, mundane play of almost useless little balconies. The fundamental change that took place with the incorporation of generous intermediate (linking) spaces into high-rise building was not entirely new in the 1970s, for Germán Lamarca and Eduardo Valdés Freire had used the open loggia running the length of the facade as early as 1956 at 330 Santa Lucia Street in Santiago. Ten years later, Gustavo Krefft encircled the four sides of a block of flats with broadly spacious corridors at Vitacura and Kennedy (fig. 14.7), to make ample use of one of the most spectacular views of the city.

Sensibility towards traditional spaces, corridors, loggias, and pergolas is slowly coming back to residential architecture. It is a deep-rooted tradition that these spaces have always been lavishly covered with plants "for color and scent," with herbs and spices which are "good for health," and with flowers of the season. From 1962 to 1967 Jaime Sanfuentes Irarrázaval had built a series of one-storied mansions, vast horizontal structures with very generous intermediate spaces, which seemed to unite the house with the landscape; then built-in flower stands came to replace the railings of balconies; by the end of the 1960s, Mauricio Despouy used them in his Worker's Hospital (fig. 14.5), and ten years later they were the most characteristic feature of new apartment blocks in the upper-set quarters of Santiago. Deep loggias hid recessed facades, with a profusion of plants and flowers hanging and climbing from within. It is as if after fifty years *le ville superposée* had come to life in Santiago, though more heavily loaded with flowers and vines than the neat and graceful drawings of 1922 by Le Corbusier.

14.7. Gustavo Krefft, architect. High-rise flats. Santiago-Kennedy, 1975. (Photograph: Courtesy of architect Jorge Torrico M., 1980).

Turning back to the problematic 1970s, it is difficult to overlook the dramatic background of the housing shortage or the loss in quality of the natural environment and urban life. In this context the Third Generation appeared,[13] but without significant external influences such as Brutalism, Archigram, or the Metabolism of the 1960s.

There were apparently two distinctive conceptions of the urban scene in the 1970s. One came from a rediscovery of urban values, a search for a vital urban environment in which street and place are natural extensions of the dwellings, and land, climate, and cultural values are the distinctive elements of each particular human society. The other was the opposite: the expansion of towns into endless suburbs and the internationalization of culture.[14]

Though for more than a decade it has not been easy to discern tendencies or currents in architectural thought and design, we may recognize two trends of major proportions. On the one hand, the International Style has been adopted and adapted in such a way that one may, so to speak, see Barcelona, Milan, or Paris in parts of many of our cities. Such architecture is being built to a very high standard, with ceramics from Italy, British carpets, crystal from Belgium, and American aluminum, most of which come from cultural traditions with which the Chilean user is not always acquainted. On the other hand, a search for identity based on building traditions of four centuries continues. Brick and wood, wooden and clay tiles, are still used following principles, more than forms, which have always been present in Chilean architecture. In the end, these two trends are no more nor less than Rationalist and Organic.

Oversimplification is perhaps not fair to the above-mentioned tendencies and possibly it would be better to recognize schemes of opposites as devised for instance by Jencks: "A structural analysis may well be made with a greater number of categories, but the . . . pairs considered here, represent the principal architectural tendencies since 1920, and a greater number would certainly obscure some issues."[15] Whatever the number of variables, the period is rich in experiences, and its variety marks a spirit of search and definition.

A new phase is slowly coming upon the Chilean architectural scene (fig. 14.8). New names replace first- and second-generation architects. A new approach to formal aspects seems the result of a fusion of offshoots of Rationalism and Organicism that are compatible. A degree of semiological exploration is present, whether in a methodological approach or in possibilities of language as metaphor. Direct formal affiliations and historical reminiscences are the characteristic features of present-day architecture, as much in Chile as elsewhere. "We look for significance rather than for reasons, places instead of spaces, communities instead of areas, images but not schemes. . . . "[16] The new generation is keenly interested in metabolic considerations, relations between location, site, and building, in the use of solar energy, rational use of resources, use of waste, recycling, and so forth. In this search, a strong relation with the past, within or outside the country's boundaries, is to be noticed. Giedion has pointed out that this is not a matter of mere forms but a profound longing for "continuity" and an "inner relation" with the past,[17] and this is particularly true in the case of Chile.

Architecture in Chile is restricted and sober in comparison with the more elaborate forms of Latin American vernaculars. But the principles on which Chilean architecture is based are so deeply rooted in national characteristics and values (physical, seismological, economic, social, and cultural) that they exist as vitally as ever within many a form and offer possibilities for cultural development. These principles are not formal *per se*, but reflect deeply rooted attitudes related to modes of installation in space. That is why it is possible to speak of a potential ever present continuity that awaits development. In this case, the dilemma presented by so many formal continuities is avoided: tradition can be generously interpreted in many ways—in the immensity of the desert north, in the greenery of the central valley, and in the labyrinth of the southern islands and channels. Man in Chile is one of the most isolated of beings. Therefore, he is one of the most "outside"-minded. This is his real value and also his real peril.

Deeply rooted in the past, Chilean architecture may project itself towards the future in many different ways. In Pascal's words, diversity which does not merge into unity is negation; unity which does not derive from diversity is tyranny.

14.8. San Martín, Browne, Wenborne, architects. Shopping Center, Santiago, 1979. (Photograph: Courtesy of architect Jorge Torrico M., 1980)

16. Humberto Eliash, Letter to *Revista C. A.* in *Revista ARS*, no. 3 (August 1979).

17. Sigfried Giedion, *Space, Time and Architecture*, 5th ed. (Cambridge, Mass.: Harvard University Press, 1967), p. 668.

Notes

1. Charles Jencks, *The Language of Post-Modern Architecture* (New York: Rizzoli International Publications, 1977), p. 23.

2. Montserrat Palmer Trias, *50 Años de arquitectura Metalica en Chile, 1920-1970* (Santiago: Facultad de Arquitectura y Urbanismo de la Universidad de Chile, 1971).

3. *Plan Habitacional* (DFL no. 2, 1959) (Santiago: Ediciones Gutemberg, 1967), p. 7.

4. Ramón A. Méndez Br., "La Arquitectura Chilena Contemporanea," *Hogar y Arquitectura* [Madrid], March-April 1970, p. 20.

5. Alberto Arenas, "Hitos Singulares en el Desarrollo Technologico," *Revista C. A.*, no. 24 (August 1979): 5.

6. O. Ortega, M. Anduaga, C. Miranda, S. Pirotte, F. Riquelme, and A. Sahady; *Guia de la Arquitectura en Santiago* (Santiago: Facultad de Arquitectura y Urbanismo de la Universidad de Chile, 1976), p. 10.

7. *Revista C. A.*, no. 25 (December 1979): 30.

8. Eugenio Pereiras Salas, *La Arquitectura Chilena en El Siglo XIX* (Santiago: Anales de la Universidad de Chile, ca. 1958); *Revista C. A.*, no. 22 (December 1978): 11.

9. *Revista C. A.*, no. 25 (December 1979): 26.

10. Jaime Garretón, Introduction to *Una Teoria Cibernetica de la Ciudad y su Sistema* (Buenos Aires: Ediciones Nueva Visión, 1975).

11. René Martínez Lemoine, *El Modelo Clasico de la Ciudad Colonial Hispanomericana* (Santiago: Facultad de Arquitectura y Urbanismo de la Universidad de Chile, 1977), p. 54.

12. Jorge and Sergio Gonzalez E., "Algunas Ideas en Torno al Concurso Bienal," *Revista C. A.*, no. 25 (December 1979).

13. Philip Drew, *Tercera Generacion, La Significacion Cambiante de la Arquitectura* (Barcelona: Editorial Gili, 1973).

14. Oriol Bohigas, A 1969 interview cited by architect Humberto Eliash in, *Revista ARS*, no. 3 (August 1979).

15. Charles Jencks, *Arquitectura 2000, Predicciones y Metodos* (Barcelona: Editorial Blume).

Bibliography

BOOKS

Benavides C., Juan. *Fundamentos de la Nueva Arquitectura.*

Borchers, Juan. Institución *Arquitectónica.* 1968.

Brown, Enrique. *El Uso de la Vivienda y la Ciudad.* Buenos Aires, 1978.

Garretón, Jaime. *Una Teoria Cibernetica de la Ciudad y su Sistema.* Buenos Aires: Ediciones Nueva Visión, 1975.

Irarrázaval Covarrubias, Raúl. *Arquitectura Chilena, la Busqueda de un Orden Espacial.* 1979.

Martner, G., Carlos and Raposo M., Alfonso. *La Vivienda Dinámica.* 1972.

Morales, José Ricardo. *Architectónica.* 2 vols. 1966.

Ortega, Oscar; Anduaga, Madga; Miranda, Carlos; Pirotte, Silvia; Riquelme, Fernando; and Sahady, Antonio. *Guia de la Arquitectura en Santiago.* (Santiago: Facultad de Arquitectura y Urbanismo de la Universidad de Chile, 1976).

Palmer Trias, Montserrat. *50 Años de arquitectura Metalica en Chile, 1920-1970.* Santiago: Facultad de Arquitectura y Urbanismo de la Universidad de Chile, 1971.

Parrochia B., Juan. *Santiago en el Tercer Cuarto del Siglo XX.* 1980.

JOURNALS

Arenas, Alberto. "Hitos Singulares en el Desarrollo Tecnologico." *Revista C. A.*, no. 24 (August 1979): 5.

Méndez Br., Ramón A. "La Arquitectura Chilena Contemporanea." *Hogar y Arquitectura*, Madrid (March-April 1970: 20.

USEFUL JOURNALS

AUCA (Arquitectura, Urbanismo, Construccion, Arte), Sociedad Cooperativa A.U.C.A., Santiago, Chile.

Revista C. A. (Colegio de Arquitectos de Chile).

15

PEOPLE'S REPUBLIC OF CHINA

FENG CHI-CHUNG

China is prominent in her architectural tradition, the art and technique of architecture having once reached a very distinguished level. The concept of city planning and city plans was discussed in documents as early as the fifth century B.C. The building of Chang An, the capital of both Sui and Tang dynasties [A.D. 581-907], began at the end of the sixth century A.D. and by the eighth century it had developed into a city covering 87 square kilometers with a population of one million. It comprised a well-coordinated city pattern of a size then that was unprecedented in the history of city building in the world. And the *Ying Zao Fa Shi* [*Treatise on Construction Methods*], a large volume published in the Sung dynasty [960-1279], systematically summed up previous experience with the standardization of building elements. When the Industrial Revolution flourished in Europe, however, together with the building techniques that resulted from it, China was still in the seclusion of feudalism. After the mid-nineteenth century, China gradually declined into a semifeudal and semicolonial country. The development of her production was extremely slow, and the country was utterly backward in science and technology. In the vast inland, buildings and houses were still constructed using native forms and techniques, while new approaches appeared in only a few new buildings in some coastal cities and in those along large rivers. Not until the establishment of the People's Republic of China did the cause of architecture begin to prosper again.

China, still a developing country, poor and backward, requires a considerably long term of hard work before it will be built into a modernized nation. Hence, "to build industriously and thriftily" is always our persistent and fundamental policy.[1] Buildings essential to industrial production have priority over those for other purposes, which, though indispensable to the needs of the people, are being provided only gradually. The principle proclaimed by the government concerning architectural design, "commodity, economy, and where possible attention paid to aesthetics,"[2] is based upon such particular considerations.

The development of architecture in China during the 1950s was rather significant. China had suffered severely from long years of wars. But in spite of a shortage in raw materials and construction force, difficulties were soon overcome, and production resumed within a short period. New factories were built, as well as the most needed housing projects and public facilities. With the initiation of the national economic plan in 1953,[3] cities were planned and industrial buildings put up. The scale of city building and housing was gradually increased. Prefabrication, prestressed concrete, and concrete shells appeared at various building sites. In the later 1950s, the personnel concerned with design and construction was increased further. To keep pace with "large, medium-sized and small industries developing simultaneously,"[4] large-scale city planning and design of all sorts of industrial and civil buildings took place. Industrialization in construction work and prefabrication systems of single-story factory buildings began to appear. There was extensive research on the construction of multistoried factory buildings and buildings with large block and large slab construction, and the findings were soon put into practice. However, there was such an enormous demand for houses and such limited means that, in vast urban areas and countrysides as well as in some newly developed industrial bases, conventional masonry construction and sometimes, where possible, rammed earth walls were still employed.

Not long after the national economy had been recoordinated following the depression caused by natural calamities and other factors in the late fifties and early sixties, the state of peace and unity in the nation was again severely interrupted. In the late sixties and the years thereafter, the national economy was almost at the brink of collapse. Thus the state of architecture remained at the level of the fifties, and the standard of housing facilities was even lowered.

The People's Republic of China is now endeavoring to modernize in industry, agriculture, national defense, science, and technology. New China's achievement in architecture during the first thirty years was but the first stride upon a long road of progress.

Urban Planning

In the fifties most of the large cities began to be planned in accordance with the policy of "taking agriculture as foundation, and industry as leading factor."[5] Cities were classified, and urban and regional plans were established for some ten economic regions including Beijing (Peking), Baotou, Xian, and Lanzhou. By the end of the fifties more than 1,300 cities of different sizes had been planned. With cities being developed for new industries and the reconstruction of old cities, the irrational and unbalanced state of the industrial development of old China began to change. Consumer cities were transformed into productive ones. New industrial cities and towns sprouted in the inland, along borders, and even in the prairies. Socialism's public ownership of land provided an excellent prerequisite for city planning, thus facilitating the utilization of land and comprehensive planning.

In the reconstruction plan of Shanghai during the earliest years of the People's Republic the original distribution of industries was reconsidered and modified. The zoning of the city was restudied, and a new plan was projected to establish an organic pattern of functions.

In Beijing Tienanmen Square and the east-west Chang-an Boulevard were rebuilt in 1959 on a vast scale, numerous green areas were planned, and the outskirts were developed into various industrial bases, and cultural and administrative divisions. In the late fifties, attention was paid to avoiding the sprawl of large built-up urban areas; and satellite towns and new towns were built in the surrounding districts of major cities. In recent years, the plans for many cities have been modified in order to keep pace with contemporary social development.

He-fei, the capital city of An-hui province, is a city with over two thousand years of history. It was a consumer city with only about 50,000 inhabitants thirty years ago. The city walls enclosed an area of 5.2 square kilometers, and the built-up area was scarcely 2 square kilometers. Now the population has increased to 450,000, and the city is industrialized with more than 50 square kilometers of built-up area.

According to the initial plan, the city was to be developed further to the east, the north, and the southwest outskirts, with the existing city remaining as its core. In the newly developed areas, residential quarters were laid out parallel with industrial districts. To the southeast of the city core, there was a wedge of open space where vegetable farms for the city were planned, since the land was fertile and the condition of soil poor for buildings. This wedge is arranged in the direction of the prevailing wind so as to bring fresh air from Chiaohu Lake into the city. In the northwestern part of the city, situated below the dam, is an undulating terrain used for nurseries and fruit farms, with a number of resort buildings scattered among them. In the northeastern suburb are railroad stations and yards. Along the railroad is a green belt. Thus, a windmill plan was envisaged for the city with three wings extending from the old city with green wedges between them. A ring-and-radial road system connects the three industrial districts and the suburban areas. There is a green belt, 200 meters wide, along the city moat where the original city wall has been demolished.

With its recently revised city plan, He-fei (fig. 15.1) will become a city of industry, a railroad junction, and a science center. In order to control the size of the city, a part of its industrial establishments will be set up in small towns nearby. The road system in the original plan has been modified into one with express highways, city arteries, bicycle paths, and pedestrian ways functionally separated.

In 1958 several satellite towns were planned and built around Shanghai. The plan was designed to control the sprawl of the city, to limit the population in the central urban area of the city, and to distribute new industries. In the planning of the satellite towns themselves, the following guidelines were established: each should have its own specific industries; the satellites should be kept at a distance of 10 to 50 kilometers from the city center; and their town plans should be compact, with the average distance from home to work being the determining factor in their size. Compact plans mean a saving of the rich soil in the vicinity and an economy in power lines and water and sewage lines.

Min-hang was the first satellite town built for Shanghai. Situated at the upper Huangpu River,

15.1. General Plan of He-fei (toward 1978). (Photograph: Courtesy of the School of Architecture, University of Tongji)

about 30 kilometers from the heart of Shanghai, it was built on flat terrain located high above the highest flood level. Thus very little earthwork was required. Min-hang's docks can accommodate 10,000-ton ships and are conveniently connected with Shanghai by railroad and highway. The core industry in Min-hang is power generating equipment. Light industries are also provided to balance the working population between men and women. Residential quarters were built and developed in parallel with the industrial areas.

In the fifties the satellite towns were planned according to the static conception emphasizing dependence upon the mother city, and the towns lacked the magnetic force they should have possessed in themselves. In my view, an interdependence between the satellites and the mother city and among the satellite towns themselves should be furthered. Besides its own industries, each town should be given an indispensable role in the region while its facilities also serve the whole region of the core city. A satellite town's vitality can only be achieved where the statellite and the core city are closely related to and reliant upon each other, a rather kinetic relationship instead of only a static one. The term "satellite" is therefore inaccurate since a town so described should be one in a comprehensive network of cities and towns of various sizes in a tightly woven pattern.

Housing and Residential Districts

Some 400,000,000 square meters of housing have been built in China since 1949. Though this figure is unprecedented in the country's history, it is still hard to meet the growing needs of the urban population. An intensive, painstaking effort must be undertaken to solve the housing problems of China.

New housing has generally been built in accordance with the planning of residential districts and accompanied by necessary public facilities. The standard is not high. Most of the dwellings are of one or two rooms and are allocated according to family size. Those houses built in the fifties were provided only with shared kitchens and communal lavatories; and suites of three or four rooms together with kitchen and toilets designed for one family were temporarily used by two or three families. Later, self-contained, small-area, single-family types of dwellings were designed and provided. The layout of residential buildings is usually in rows, mostly facing the best orientation, with the exception of those built in the earlier years in perimetrical forms. In many residential districts simple, practical, yet pleasing environments were achieved through a well-considered organization of traffic, open spaces, and public facilities. But unfortunately most of them seem to have an overly monotonous appearance.

Vast-scale construction was achieved by means of standardization and modular design. During the fifties many provinces and cities stipulated a series of standardized designs for differing local conditions. At the end of the fifties, experimental housing projects with prefabricated blocks or large panel construction were built in Beijing. In the seventies research upon industrialized construction of housing has stressed innovation in wall systems, and work has been spread all over the country. Many of the numerous recently built multistoried houses and high rises have used industrialized or semi-industrialized construction methods.

Cao-yang New Village is the first residential district built in Shanghai according to a prescribed plan on a large scale. Planning and construction began in 1951 in an area of 95 hectares. The New Village plan was influenced by the neighborhood-unit idea. Its structure consists of housing districts, each of which is a basic living unit, covering 3 to 4 hectares, with kindergartens, nursery schools, and a primary school. The distance to school from home is less than a ten-minute walk and the children are free from auto traffic. The whole New Village area is divided by a T-shaped road system into three housing districts. Public facilities are located in the district center, with a service radius of about 600 meters; and groceries, markets, and small shops at the borders of the districts serve contiguous housing groups. The houses, which have two or three stories and timber-and-masonry construction, are arranged in rows, and there are green areas between them as well as along the river banks. Later, additional stories were added to some of the houses, and various open spaces were provided with new houses. The residential district's center was developed in stages with different styles of architecture on different standards. Since the whole is not consistent architecturally, it does not seem to be very well conceived.

Planned in 1964, the Fan Gua Long housing group in Shanghai is the first reconstruction of a slum area on a mass scale in urban China. Owing to the shortage of building land, high-density construction was recommended, but sufficient daylight and ventilation was to be ensured. A railroad line runs along the north of the site, and roads to the east and south have heavy traffic. Buildings were set back from the road as far as possible in order to keep them away from the traffic noise, while also accommodating the original population. Groups of C- and E-shaped buildings are

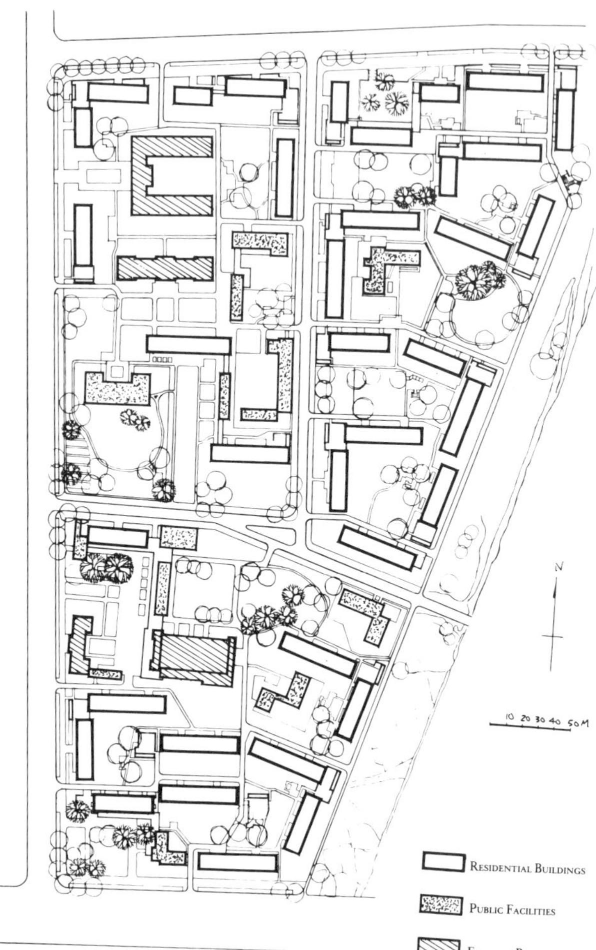

15.2. Plan of the Xing Fu Cun residential quarter in Beijing, 1975. (Photography: Courtesy of the School of Architecture, University of Tongji)

arranged with openings oriented towards the direction of the prevailing breeze. Point blocks of considerable dimensions are positioned at the middle of the group. Though spacings between buildings are relatively small, adequate sunlight and ventilation can be obtained, since most buildings are relatively low. The depth of the buildings was increased by introducing an inner court amidst the floor plan. Thus, the floor area ratio was increased up to 17,600 square meters per hectare.

Xing Fu Cun, a residential quarter in Beijing, was built in 1957 and covers an area of 11 hectares. The entire quarter was well planned (fig. 15.2) in relation to the topography and other existing conditions. It was divided by existing roads into three parts. In the southern sector, an open space in the center is partially enclosed by an existing clubhouse and other buildings, and three large nearby locust trees have been preserved. In the south and east ends, there are two small open spaces surrounded by residential buildings.

Three- or four-storied residential buildings with open exterior passageways mostly facing south, cluster around courtyards of different sizes. Various activities take place in these courtyards, where there are playgrounds for children, gardens with flower beds, trellises, and embankments, as well as service yards with refuse boxes, bicycle sheds, and spaces for laundry drying.

The service radii for daily supplies in the district are within 150 meters. In addition to the three- and four- storied residential buildings, there are some low one-or-two-storied buildings used as schools, kindergartens, and shops and one six-storied apartment house. Buildings of different heights constructed with strongly projecting eaves and provided with greeneries give the whole district a sense of lively and properly scaled architectural space and form.

Long before this project was entirely realized, however, additional structures were placed between the houses surrounding the courts, marring the more open original concept.

The Mei San Residential District is situated in hilly country, 20 kilometers southwest of Nanjing. Covering an area of about 20 hectares, it was planned in 1969 and built in 1971. The hillside site, slanted from north to south with a difference in elevation of about 15 meters, was divided into different zones in accordance with its terrain, and the building arrangements followed the natural contour, reducing any sense of monotony. In some of the residential buildings staggered floor levels are arranged by half-floor heights with the stairwell at the center. The district's center consists of shops, a post office, a bank, a restaurant, a cinema, and other facilities. It is located near the highway, making it easily accessible to the residents of the district as well as to the people from the surrounding countryside.

Industrial Architecture

"To be sturdy and practical, economical and rational, and advanced in technique"[6]—that is the principle upon which the design of industrial architecture in China is based. It is generally in industrial architecture, rather than in other types of building, that new building techniques have been developed. Concrete-shell structures first appeared in factory buildings in 1951, and prestressed reinforced concrete, now widely used, made its debut in 1956 also in industrial buildings. At that time prestressed-concrete roof trusses spanned as much as 60 meters. Due attention has been paid to standardization ever since, and prefabrication systems have been quite widely used. By the end of the fifties they were used in as much as 50 percent of all industrial construction. Codifications, such as "The Unified Modular System" and "The Fundamental Regulations on the Unification of Factory Building Structures" formulated the optimal areas between supports, the heights to which buildings were to be designed, and their dominating axes. "Standardized Structural Elements Used for Single-Story Factory Buildings," "Detailing of Architectural Fittings," and "Standardized Designs for Medium and Small Factory Buildings of Various Types" were also formulated. Since the early sixties larger prefabricated building elements have been introduced in order to reduce the dead-load of the building and save materials, and rapid progress has been made in this field.

The Yanshan Petrochemical plant in Beijing, begun in 1969 (fig. 15.3) provides an important example of industrial architecture. The whole complex consists of eight divisional factories arranged around a range of hills and linked by roads and pipelines. Special railroad lines were laid for plants that required a large amount of transportation. Divisional factories were planned according to their processing sequences, and their buildings were closely related to the topography of the landscape. In the oil refinery, buildings, structures, tanks, and pipelines were grouped compactly within an elongated belt area between two valleys in an arrangement that met functional requirements. In the main factory large-sized, high-precision equipment, such as blowers, air-compressors and vacuum-filtering machines, stands along the main road; towering equipment, such as distillers and multistoried frame structures, has been erected in the central area; and on strips of borderland very tall boilers are situated far away from their instrument rooms, thus keeping the instrument rooms free from noise or hazard of fire and facilitating servicing and inspection. The pipelines are all laid along the side of the main road by one of

15.3. Section of the Yanshan Petrochemical Plant, Beijing, from 1969. (Photograph: Courtesy of the Yanshan Petrochemical Plant, Beijing)

the hills. Thus, there are no pipe structures around the plant; nor are there any obstacles to traffic or views. Oil tanks are set up on leveled terraces on the slopes of hills, making gravity flow possible. The administrative center of the complex is near the main road of the factory district, but separated from the factories by a well-landscaped open space. The roofs of most factory buildings are of stressed-concrete slabs in the form of accordion folds; the cooling towers are also in prestressed, reinforced concrete. The structure for the solvent-reclaiming processing was built with a lift-slab construction method in which large flat elements (floors, walls, roof portions) cast of reinforced concrete at ground level were jacked up to their desired levels and positioned according to plan.

Public Architecture

Along with housing, other types of buildings have been provided for public use in cities and mining districts. Those buildings that were most needed and extensively used were often erected according to lower standards and were usually modest in appearance. However, municipal and national edifices, memorial architecture, and many other important buildings were considered in detail and elaborately developed, often with different architectural concepts converging in their designs. During the reconstruction of Beijing's Tien An Men Square, the Great Hall of the People (fig. 15.4), the Museum of Chinese History, and other major buildings were completed within a single year. They reflected, to some extent, a search for a new expression in architecture. Generally, innovation in architecture has not satisfactorily promoted a Chinese architectural tradition. The creation of a contemporary Chinese vernacular architecture still requires tremendous effort. Nevertheless in new buildings recently constructed in southern China, for instance in some hotels in Guangzhou, favorable attempts have been made to interrelate the landscape organically with architecture and to create architectural space within a Chinese tradition.

New structural forms were introduced in assembly halls, gymnasiums and stadiums, and other buildings requiring large, unobstructed spaces. In Beijing Railroad station, built in 1959, the central concourse is roofed with a 35 meter x 35 meter bilaterally curved concrete shell. Over the Beijing Workers' Gymnasium is a double-layered, radially tensioned structure 94 meters in diameter. In 1960 China's first lamella-arch system of prefabricated reinforced concrete, forming a network of interlocking diamond shapes, spanned the assembly hall at Tongji University,

15.4. Great Hall of the People, entrance façade, reconstructed 1959. (Photograph: Courtesy of the Beijing Institute of Architectural Design)

Shanghai. In all the gymnasiums built in the later period, such as the Capital Gymnasium in the seventies and those in Nanjing and Shanghai, steel spaceframes have been used.

A resort building, the Kuan Quan Hotel in Guangzhou, was designed in a traditional garden-architecture style. Construction began in 1964. The focal point of the hotel's courtyard is a shallow pool of water which appears between two three-storied guest-room wings and extends into the ground-floor space of the south wing, a wing used for relaxation and recreation. In the planning and molding of space inside and outside the buildings, the pool and the open space were supplemented by flat bridges, zigzag, open pavilions, a hanging stairway, stones at occasional intervals, and flowers and trees. Through the interpenetration of interior and exterior spaces and the juxtaposition of curved and straight forms, a dynamic though not overwhelming spatial effect was obtained.

The Wu Tai Shan Gymnasium in Nanjing, inaugurated in 1975, is octagonal with a floor area of 18,000 square meters and a seating capacity of 10,000 (fig. 15.5). The rate of the rise in the line of sight used in determining head clearance is 6 centimeters, the longest sight distance along the central axis is 51 meters, and the maximum vertical angle of sight from the seats is 20 degrees. About 57 percent of all seats are within a maximally satisfactory viewing area. The design is such that no more than three minutes is required to clear the whole gymnasium of all spectators.

The roof structure is a steel space-frame: the ceiling over the seating area was made with perforated steel, hung on the lower members of the frame, while that over the arena was covered with perforated fiberglass, suspended from the frame structure. With sound-absorbing materials used on walls and ceilings over a balcony, reverberation time in full assembly is

15.5. Wu Tai Shan Gymnasium. Nanjing, 1975. (Photograph: Courtesy of the School of Architecture, Tongji)

recorded at 1.68 seconds. This gymnasium design has proven to be highly efficient in practice.

Preservation of Historical Buildings

The preservation and restoration of buildings with historic and cultural value has received persistent and particular attention since regulations for this were proclaimed shortly after the founding of the People's Republic. Many historic buildings were renovated, restored, and opened to the public or used as museums. Most notable among these are the Nan Chan Temple in Wu Tai Mountain, Shanxi Province, the oldest timber structure [A.D. 784] that has survived in China, and Fo Guang Temple, another building dating back to the Tang dynasty, a little later than the former temple. The Palace Museum in Beijing, formerly the Imperial Palace of Ming and Qing Dynasties [1368-1911], is highly esteemed for its invaluable collections as well as its architecture. Since a unique garden-culture is also China's pride, old gardens of different styles, imperial gardens in the north and private gardens in the south, have been preserved and turned into public gardens. This tradition continues to influence architectural design as we have seen, for instance, in the Kuan Quan Hotel in Guangzhou.

In 1954 when a factory was being constructed at Banpo Village in the eastern suburb of Xian, Shenxi Province, an ancient village of the New Stone Age was discovered. Construction work was halted immediately, and the factory being built was soon transferred to another site. Quick action was taken. Excavation was done, soil silicified, and then a museum was inaugurated. In Yongji County in Shanxi Province, Yong Le Palace, a fine example of Yuan dynasty architecture, built in 1262, was situated on the site of a reservoir to be constructed for the Yellow River conservation project. To save this historic relic, the entire architectural complex was transplanted to Rui Cheng city and reconstructed.

In Yangzhou on the Yangtze River, the Memorial Hall of Jian Zhen Fashi,[7] a court of halls in Tang style, was built (fig. 15.6) in commemoration of the famous honorable Jian Zhen, the saintly Buddhist priest who sailed to Japan in the eighth century to preach Buddhism. It was erected for the 1200th anniversary of his death (1963). The hall was designed after the architecture of Kindo, Toshadai-ji in Nara, Japan, which was build in A.D. 759 by Chinese workmen under the direction of Jian Zhen himself.

In the middle of the compound is a paved courtyard, and on the north of the courtyard is the main hall, which is single-eaved and hip-ridged with a timber frame construction. A single-eaved pavilion, in which a stone tablet bearing the memorial epitaph was laid, is on the south side of the courtyard. Both the main hall and the pavilion are parallel to the central axis of the complex, and the other two sides of the courtyard are lined with covered passageways which link the two buildings. The courtyard so enclosed offers, within, the typically tranquil atmosphere of a Buddhist temple.

During the last thirty years, the new China's considerable architectural achievements have been made possible by a well-planned socialist national economy in which construction has served the manifold needs of production and the people. A wide variety of industrial buildings has been erected, living conditions initially improved, cities favorably transformed, and

15.6. Memorial Hall of Jain Zhen Fashi in the manner of eighth century Japan, Yangzhou, 1963. (Photograph: Courtesy of the Architecture Department of Quinghua University)

advanced techniques of construction have been adopted in certain major projects. These achievements have been inadequate, however, since production of housing is still being outstripped by the needs of the population, and limitations of materials and design often result in too crude or monotonous an architecture.

In the course of building China into an up-to-date nation, the tasks of the architectural profession are to carefully modernize the building industry and to advance the philosophy and design of architecture to a new level of understanding.

Notes (All references are to works published in Chinese.)

1. *Selected Works of Mao Tsetung*, vol. 5, 1st ed. (Beijing: Foreign Languages Press, 1977), p. 419.
2. *Architectural Journal* no. 1 (August 1955): 32.
3. *The First Five-Year Plan for Development of the National Economy of the People's Republic of China, 1953-1957* (Beijing: People's Publishing House, 1955).
4. *Architectural Journal* no. 12 (December 1958): 1.
5. *Architectural Journal* no. 9 (September 1962): 3.
6. Foreword to *A Decade of Chinese Architecture, 1949-1959: In Celebration of the 10th Anniversary of the People's Republic of China*, edited and published by the Academy of Building Research, the Ministry of Building, 1959.
7. Fashi is a title of respect for a master Buddhist priest.

Bibliography (All publications listed, except the first, are in Chinese.)

Architectural Design no. 1 (July 1958) - no. 9 (September 1965).

Architectural Journal. Edited by The Architectural Society of China, Beijing, no. 1 (June 1954) - no. 2 (March 1979).

Bozhi, Mo et al. "Architecture and Landscaping in Guangzhou." *Architectural Journal* no. 3 (September 1977).

A Decade of Chinese Architecture, 1949-1959: In Celebration of the 10th Anniversary of the People's Republic of China. Edited and published by the Academy of Building Research, the Ministry of Building, December 1959.

Lanhong, Hua. "Planning of the Residential Quarter, Xian Fu Cun in Beijing." *Architectural Journal* no. 3 (March 1957).

Shanghai Design Institute of Industrial Buildings. "Planning of the Living Quarters of Mei San Iron Plant in Nanking." *Architectural Journal* no. 1 (October 1973).

Sicheng, Lian. "Design for the Memorial Hall of Monk Jian Zhen." *Treatises on History of Architecture* no. 2. Edited by the Architectural Engineering Department, Qinghua University, 1979.

16

COLOMBIA

JAIME SALCEDO SALCEDO

Modern architecture was introduced into Colombia by a few foreign architects and Colombians who knew their work directly or had studied in European or American universities.[1] In 1934 the Sociedad Colombiana de Arquitectos (SCA) was founded to stimulate the development of architecture and its modern principles in Colombia. By 1936 the first School of Architecture was established at the Universidad Nacional in Bogotá, and brought together an excellent faculty. Soon it started to publish a magazine, *Ingeniería y Arquitectura*, in which modern architectural projects, new urban planning ideas, and new data on the use of concrete were shown. The role of this school has been most important especially because of the activities of its graduates, some of whom became Colombia's most outstanding architects; and because it has served as a model for the creation of schools of architecture at other Colombian universities.

Since the end of World War II circumstances have favored the development of Colombian architecture. The power struggle between Colombia's two principal political parties, Conservative and Liberal, generally known as the "Undeclared Civil War," resulted in an extremely violent situation in the country's rural areas. A strong migration of the rural population to the large cities, a direct consequence of the war, created a new situation. Housing problems were intensified, new consumer markets were created, and a large amount of eager inexpensive hand labor was concentrated in the cities. The process of industrialization was begun and banking developed to a new level to accommodate the country's new consumer society.[2] Publicity, with slogans such as "today's goods are better than yesterday's" created a need for the new, especially among the more highly educated classes. Modern architecture too came to be viewed as a symbol of progress.[3] In 1948 a most violent revolt took place, destroying almost all of Bogotá's downtown. As a result many activities moved out to other areas of the city, making it necessary to regulate growth and reorder the urban structure.

In 1949 Le Corbusier was invited to elaborate the "Plan Piloto de Bogotá," the city's master plan. Completed in 1951, it proved inappropriate for local conditions since it proposed a linear growth structure while the city actually grew in a radial, semicircular pattern.[4] Applied in part during the 1950s nevertheless, the plan heavily influenced Colombian architects, and many cities established regulating plan offices, with varied success. These offices were later broadened to become district planning offices and for the past twenty years, with comparative political and administrative stability, there has been a rich evolution of architecture and urban planning.

Some foreign architects, such as Leopoldo Rother (1894-1978), born in Germany, and the Italian-born Bruno Violi (1909-1973) have had outstanding influence. Their importance is due not only to their professional work but also to their rich involvement in Bogotá's universities and their work with young Colombian architects. In 1936-1938 Rother planned the Ciudad Universitaria, the campus of the Universidad Nacional in Bogotá, and designed several of its main buildings such as one for the Instituto Químico Nacional in Bogotá [1942-1945]. In the building for Universidad Nacional's press [1946], with Guillermo

Spanish text translated by Rafael Rojas, architect.

González Zuleta as engineer, he used concrete vaults. All this architecture by Rother is very rationalistic. Violi, who collaborated wtih Rother in the building for the School of Engineering [1941-1942], developed his elegant designs of the 1950s following the aesthetic ideas of Auguste Perret. One of his most interesting works in this line is, undoubtedly, the building for the *El Tiempo* newspaper [1957] in Bogotá, with concrete as the finishing material and with fine casting details in which the influence of the later works of the Belgian-born Perret for Le Havre [1944-1954] can be recognized. In Girardot, a city 90 miles south of Bogotá, Leopoldo Rother designed a large and spectacular concrete structure [1947-1949] for the marketplace in association with José Antonio Parra, an engineer. It was formed by vaults suspended from beams which were supported on V-shaped columns. The vaults, according to his highly innovative plans, were to be permanently filled with water. His ingenious idea was an effective and unusual response to the year-round tropical heat of the city, combining free ventilation with the cooling effects of evaporation of the water deposited on the vaulted roof.[5] Such collaboration between architects and engineers has often been fruitful in Colombia. We will later consider the achievements of these two complementary professions in the art of building.

Colombia's architecture traditionally has been sober in its formal expressions, despite a wide range of architectural influences that have been brought to bear, usually briefly, upon this land's architects. Conceptual, formal, and technological innovations from abroad have left few deep traces, with results almost extraneous to the Colombian environment, although they are reflected in some important works from time to time. For this reason, works of architecture such as Skidmore, Owings and Merrill's (SOM) National Administrative Center [1955] and Banco de Bogotá buildings or the Banco de la República building [1958] of the Spanish architect, Alfredo Rodríguez Orgaz, had no lasting influence.[6] Nor did Niemeyer's and Costa's works in Brasilia influence the development of Colombian architecture. On the other hand, Gropius's Rationalism as well as Le Corbusier's Brutalism in past decades, and, more recently, the spatial and aesthetic concepts of Aalto, Rudolph, and even Mies and others, have had followers among our architects. An influence takes root only when it is deliberated upon, accepted fully, and is adaptable to the economic, technological, and aesthetic conditions of the country.

As we have already seen, Le Corbusier's plan for Bogotá was relatively unsuccessful. His influence as an architect, rather than as a city planner, however, was important. On the other hand, the appearance in this country of so many buildings of reinforced concrete brought about the acceptance of *béton brut* and the international ideas of the architecture of Brutalism. Especially because it could be manufactured by labor-intensive means, reinforced concrete has been the forming material of a great many structures here since the beginning of this century and has been developed most inventively by Colombian engineering.

Good architectural design in modern Colombia has been characterized for decades by discretion in the use of materials, an intuitive dislike of monumentality, and a most skillful handling of space.

Since the 1940s, a broad range of building types has been constructed, including office and commercial structures, sports arenas, civic and cultural buildings, educational plants, and housing. Some are derived from internationally employed designs while, in those that show originality of design, the innovative aspects are usually a function of their technological sophistication, which has varied greatly. Though particular functional requirements have been satisfied for the most part, the manner in which new structures have been set into their neighborhoods has resulted until recently in frequent and distressing environmental disharmonies. As in most countries, the level of design in too much of the recent urban building stock has led to a relatively anonymous, blanket of uniformity in the larger cities.

Late in the 1930s Leopoldo Rother had taken the lead in university campus planning, but the admirable unity of the Universidad Nacional at Bogotá gradually was upset by the introduction of diverse, uninteresting buildings. A notable exception to this process was the fine design for the auditorium [1971-1974] at this university by architect Eugenia de Cardozo.[7] With the increasing student population more universities were required: in 1945-1947, the campus of the Universidad Industrial de Santander in Bucaramanga was planned;[8] in 1969-1973, the Francisco de Paula Santander University in Cúcuta was built;[9] and in 1965-1972, in Cali, the Universidad del Valle's master plan was put into effect.[10] With each building of the university well designed by a different group of architects and well built, an effect in which the parts are superior to the whole was produced.

So many architects, such as Guillermo Bermúdez, Hernán Vieco, Arturo Robledo, Hernán Herrera, Francisco Pizano de Brigard, and many others, have had excellent results in designing multifamily buildings that to discuss their work here would be impractical. The bibliography at the end of this chapter, especially the journals mentioned, provides sufficient information. It is important, however, to mention some of the outstanding housing projects designed under the aegis of the Instituto de Crédito Territorial (ICT), the state organization charged with building low-cost housing. In ICT construction in the 1950s and 1960s for instance, new structural systems and concepts such as community centers and new forms to subdivide blocks were introduced in one- and two-story residential areas. In 1950 the "vertical city" theories then in style were applied in the Centro Urbano Antonio Nariño at Bogotá with good results.[11] In 1961 superblocks of four-story apartment buildings that incorporated commercial and community centers and safeguarded pedestrian traffic were designed in the Techo housing project, later called Ciudad Kennedy.[12] More than one-half million people live here. In 1970 in the same project, ICT's Design Department developed an experimental plan for 276 modular homes grouped in one- to four-story blocks with service modules and easily divisible space for each family. Of considerable interest is an ICT project in Manizales [1972][13] in which a group of houses was built in *bahareque*, a native Indian construction system consisting of mudfill and covered walls of *guadua* (*Bambusa guadua angustifolia*, a gigantic Colombian bamboo). *Guadua* construction systems have been the object of many studies, one of which, by Dicken Castro, was presented at the 1964 Colombian Architectural Biennial Exhibition.

At a different social level, the Banco Central Hipotecario has sponsored construction of several multifamily buildings for medium-income families, such as the Residencias Sabana [1960],[14] the Hans Drews Arango housing unit [1960],[15] and the El Parque housing group [1965-1972].[16]

During the last ten years the building of educational centers such as the Cafam School in Bogotá [1968-1971][17] and the INEM's (Instituto Nacional de Ensenañza Media) at Cúcuta [1973][18] and Manizales [1973][19] has responded particularly well to special programmatic and didactic needs, using common, easily accessible materials (brick walls, fiber-cement roofs) and including extensive sports areas. Groups of buildings erected to house public and administrative offices have been located increasingly in large green areas, complemented with large civic squares. The Centro Administrativo Municipal at Cali [1967], by Germán Samper and José Prieto,[20] organizes the mayor's offices, City Hall, and the public service offices around a beautiful civic square facing the city's river and park, while Bogotá's two well-articulated administration center buildings [1967], by Cuéllar, Serrano, Gómez,[21] are lodged in a very open area and surrounded by a park.

The firm of Cuéllar, Serrano, Gómez, formed by Gabriel Serrano, Camilo Cuéllar, José Gómez, and Gabriel Largacha, has been important in construction and design in Colombia for some forty-five years. Cuéllar, an architect graduated from London's Architectural Association School in 1934, and Serrano with his engineering degree from the Universidad Nacional, Bogotá, in 1933 joined forces with the engineer Gómez to begin their successful enterprise. Some years later the architect Gabriel Largacha became associated with the firm. Serrano's personal interest led him back to the Universidad Nacional where in 1950 he added to his knowlege of engineering to become an architect. In Gabriel Serrano's architecture rational volumetric organization combines with a rejection of unnecessary aspects of formal vocabulary to attain a high level of aesthetic purity. All of his work has about it a sense of the permanent and a dignified character that may be seen, for instance, in the three Bogotá buildings that follow. The David Restrepo Maternity Hospital [1948-1951], an important early design, is an unpretentious brick building with continuous metallic windows. The Ecopetrol building [1957-1959], accomplished in collaboration with Gabriel Largacha, won the prize as the best Colombian building in the first Biennial of Colombian Architecture at Bogotá in 1962. The mass of this eleven-story cubiform structure (fig. 16.1) is lightened in three ways: by the vertical articulation of its exterior walls in continuous mullion strips that frame regular rows of windows; by the sculptural variety in which the top floor is treated, providing dramatically shadowed sections; and by setting the building upon rectangular *pilotis*, creating an open spacious portico. In the whole one sees admirable wit and yet sobriety. The Flota Mercante Grancolombiana building [1961-1964], in association with Hans Drews, is discussed below. All of these are masterpieces of Colombian architecture.[22]

In our review of individual achievements by Colombia's architects beginning with the 1940s, it is important to mention the influence of Le Corbusier. His work on the *Plan Piloto de Bogotá*, his visits to Colombia, and the fact that some Colombian architects who worked in his studio went on to brilliant accomplishments have led to the long-lasting high esteem in which Colombian architects have held this great master of architecture. Germán Samper and Rogelio Salmona are two outstanding examples of architects who returned to our country after assimilating his influences, developing their own personal styles and architectural theories later.

Germán Samper took his architecture degree at the Universidad Nacional in 1948 and has done most of his work within the firm of Esguerra, Sáenz, Urdaneta, Samper. His vigorous architecture successfully communicates as a symbol of the institu-

16.1. Gabriel Serrano and Gabriel Largacha (Cuéllar, Serrano, Gómez), architects. Ecopetrol Headquarters building. Bogotá, 1957-1959. (Photograph: Courtesy of Rafael Ibarra)

16.2. Germán Samper (Esguerra, Sáenz, Urdaneta, Samper). Interior view, Concert Hall, Luis Angel Arango Library. Bogotá, 1963-1966. (Photograph: Courtesy of Rafael Ibarra)

tions contained within the urban environment. In Bogotá, at his SENA's (Servicio Nacional de Aprendizaje) building [1958-1962] concrete supports emerge from the ground like two pairs of hands whose fingers sustain the building. The narrow forty-story Avianca tower [1963-1969], on the corner of Santander Square and the city's main avenue, is firmly implanted as an urban landmark.[23] His Coltejer tower in Medellín [1968] achieves the same character, so much so that the textile corporation that owns the building adopted its silhouette as its commercial symbol. The Exposition Center and Concert Hall of the Luis Angel Arango Library [1963-1966] in downtown Bogotá's historic center embraces, visually, the old Casa de Moneda and the towers of the cathedral with its generous porticos. Samper's admirable control of space is specifically evident in the concert hall of the Luis Angel Arango Library, in which a spectacularly beautiful wooden ceiling (fig. 16.2) gathers into its designs the tubes of an organ and, with a sense of sheer elegance, serves as a part of the combination that results in excellent acoustic characteristics. In the Gold Museum (fig. 16.3) [1961-1963][24] he solved all problems of circulation, imparting a fluent, easy sense of space to a neutral atmosphere that is most suitable for the exhibition of small objects. Samper's most recent project, the Convention Center in Cartagena (designed in 1979 and currently under construction) achieved well his aim of resolving the difficult problem of integrating modern architecture into a valuable historic center.

The architectural design of Rogelio Salmona also has evolved in an interesting manner. Taking advantage of able local craftsmanship in bricklaying he adopted bricks to produce strongly sculptural effects, for instance in the apartment buildings of El Polo housing project [1965] in collaboration with the architect Guillermo Bermúdez. The influence of the vigorous lyricism of Le Corbusier's later work can still be seen; but, at the same time, there is the organic dynamism of volume and spatial organization which Salmona developed later in several houses, in the stepped buildings of large housing projects such as San Cristóbal's at Bogotá [1963-1976], in the residential El Parque group, and in the Sociedad Colombiana de Arquitectos headquarters

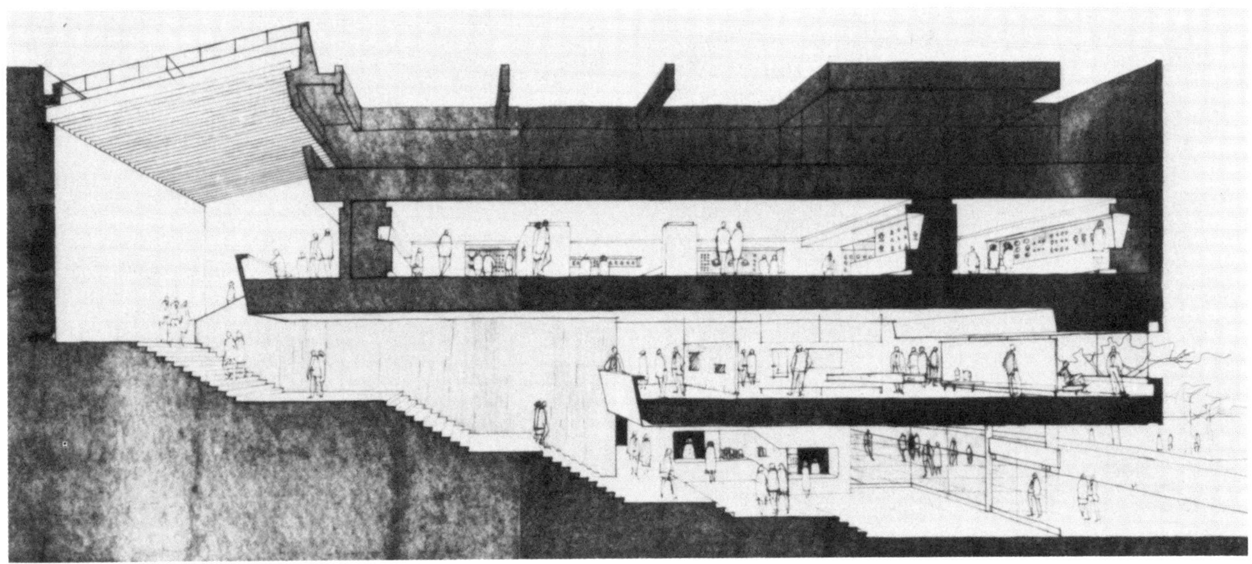

16.3. Germán Samper in collaboration with Fernando Jiménez (Esguerra, Sáenz, Urdaneta, Samper), architects. Section-perspective drawing, Gold Museum. Bogotá, 1961-1963. (Drawing by Germán Samper, courtesy of the architect)

building [1963-1976]. Gradually, as his latest buildings demonstrate, he also interpreted in brick, and very successfully, some architectural themes of Frank Lloyd Wright, with a nod as well in the direction of Aalto's Säynätsalo work of 1950-1952. In his El Parque group [1965-1972], in which Salmona develops a theme based on Hans Scharoun's "Romeo and Juliet" Stuttgart apartment towers [1954-1959],[25] he freely achieves a dynamic baroque quality (fig. 16.4) with massive brickwork forms that

16.4. Rogelio Salmona, architect. El Parque housing. Bogotá, 1965-1972. (Photograph: Courtesy of Jaime Salcedo Salcedo)

admit ample light despite the urban surroundings. Seen against the background of impressive mountains that are not far off, Salmona's plastic synthesis of his past influences in this project produced spectacular results. Of his most recent works, in Bogotá, a standout is the Museum of Modern Art [designed in 1975], of which the first stage has been built and in which the walls become unusually dynamic.[26]

Architect Fernando Martínez's first works between 1950 and 1960 are in the Rationalist manner of Le Corbusier, with a clear, cubicular organization, walls in white or primary colors but also with exposed brick masonry introducing round and oblique walls. After a critical period, 1961 to 1965, during which he produced some excellent buildings including the Santos, Wilkie, and Calderón house grouping [1962-1963] and some works with Rogelio Salmona, he adopted principles of Organic architecture. His project for the Emilio Cifuentes School in Facatativá [1959], in collaboration with Guillermo Avendaño, has been considered as the first work of Organic architecture in Colombia and won the prize for best design at the first Biennial of Colombian Architecture in 1962. Since 1965 his work has been characterized by a visual and formal continuity with the site, a fluent spatial organization, and a use of the materials of the region, frequently brick and Arabian roof slate. In later projects, such as his Hostería in Garzón [1968] and an apartment building in Bogotá [1969] he has experimented with (fig. 16.5) geometrical combinations of triangles, pyramids, pointed arches, and vaults, and with long lines of windows and panelling that contrast with continuous wall surfaces. In his 1974 Bavaria Offices Building, in Bogotá, Martínez returns to cubicular shapes, the slab form, some symmetry effects, and introduces patios.[27]

Technological advances in the use of materials and devising of systems in industrial, commercial, and residential buildings have been primarily the province of architectural engineers. Guillermo González

16.5. Fernando Martínez, architect. Apartment building. Bogotá, 1969. (Photograph: Courtesy of Rafael Ibarra)

Zuleta for instance, who had worked as engineer with Leopoldo Rother in the building for Universidad Nacional's press [1946] at Bogotá, has contributed greatly to developments in the technology of concrete in Colombia. For the Baseball Stadium [1947] at Cartagena he designed, with the collaboration of architects Gabriel Solano, Jorge Gaitán Cortés, Alvaro Ortega, and Edgar Burbano, a flying parabolic supporting structure united by the grandstands and a concrete, membrane-thin roof, thus doing away with the need for columns which would have obstructed the view of some spectators.[28] In the 1950s, again aiming to avoid visual obstacles, he created other structural designs which were just as successful. In the grandstands for Bogotá's Techo Racetrack,[29] the daring overhangs support transversal concrete vaults. In Cartagena's Football Stadium[30] the structural nerving of the roof spreads in a very geometric, rhomboidal pattern. In the 1960s for the Bullfight Arena at Cali[31] in order to accommodate 20,000 spectators, he designed a gigantic bottomless concrete bowl with a circular supporting foundation, an impressive technical feat of no less than 950 feet upper diameter and 500 feet diameter at the middle of the base, as the grandstand of post-tensed construction.

For Cuéllar, Serrano, Gómez, the engineer Doménico Parma designed a lightweight floor-slab system of constant thickness called *Reticular Celulado*, in which support is given directly by the structural columns rather than by the intermediate beams. A combination of a reticular-shaped pattern of narrow beams and simple precast-concrete "boxes" acts like WF beams (double T section) in its structural principles. It has been widely applied in many Colombian constructions, from houses and office buildings to hospitals and airports since the first years of the 1950s. Parma has worked upon many major structures of superior architectural quality, such as the floating foundation and structure for Samper's forty-story Avianca tower building [1963-1969], the passenger terminal for Eldorado Airport [1958],[32] and the chapel[33] for the 39th International Eucharistic Congress, held in Bogotá in 1968.

The pre-tensing and post-tensing of concrete has allowed the building of some complex structures. In the Flota Mercante Grancolombiana building [1961-1964] (fig. 16.6), already mentioned, pretensed eight-meter overhangs, with supporting porticos set back, yield a very free ground-floor plan and take the vectors of forces from external columns which support the first half of the floors by compression and the remainder by tension, thus making possible the delicate lightness of the facade. In Samper's Banco Central Hipotecario headquarters building [1963-1967] post-tensed floor slabs supported on one central structural nucleus were used. Cali's Coliseo Cubierto [1968][34] has a double-curved roof, supported by two central parabolic arches 97 meters long and 19 meters high, held together by a perimetral structural ring, which is formed by a network of pre-tensed steel cables. And, the Barranquilla International Airport [1972-1980][35] is done with ingenious and daring pre-tensed structures. These achievements made possible the appearance of many buildings taller than thirty stories in Bogotá, such as the thirty-four-story tower in the Centro Colseguros [1964-1973],[36] with the highest being the forty-seven-story Seguros Colpatria building [1971-1975].[37] This type of architecture has been used as well in other Colombian cities such as Cali and Medellín.

For Hernando Vargas's firm, Guillermo González Zuleta, who had worked as engineer in the innovative Baseball Stadium [1947] at Cartagena, introduced a system already used in other countries for the construction of the twenty-one-story Ugi building in Bogotá [1973-1975]. Once a square, hollow, concrete

16.6. Gabriel Serrano in collaboration with Hans Drews (Cuéllar, Serrano, Gómez), architects. Flota Mercante Grancolombiana building. Bogotá, 1961-1964. (Photograph: Courtesy of Rafael Ibarra)

service structure was built, the twenty-one floors were cast, starting with the topmost and hung around the central element from top to bottom. With this method the time required for construction was significantly reduced.

For problems such as massive government-sponsored housing projects, where deficits increase year after year, technical advances are seldom applied and abundant hand labor is usually employed. Yet some experiments have been made in this field. In the late 1940s and early 1950s, architects Alvaro Ortega and Gabriel Solano used the vacuum concrete system to an economic advantage derived from the speed of execution in housing projects, such as Barrio Quiroga in Bogotá. At this low-cost housing district, houses were built by casting the walls and the roof vaults on the site, with vacuum concrete, which accelerated the construction and thus lowered the costs. Architect Jorge Gaitán Cortés (d. 1968) developed some interesting designs in 1949 in which precast-concrete elements such as beams and window frames were used in the employees' homes for the Los Alcázares housing district of Bogotá, built under the auspices of the Instituto de Crédito Territorial. The ICT has often used undulating vaults of fiber-cement in the roofing of housing projects, but the same material when tried in walls as well proved to be not very pleasant in appearance. ICT recently sponsored a very ambitious project in Bogotá, the Ciudad Bachué [from 1977][38] of 18,000 production-line houses with precast columns, beams, window frames, and wall panels with incorporated electrical and sanitary installations. The panels, whether small and lightweight or large and heavy were installed with cranes, a method that, as planned, will allow the housing units of this group to have future vertical additions, rather than horizontal ones that would use up open areas.

CINVA (Centro Interamericano de Vivienda), a now-defunct agency of the Organization of American States, sponsored important research on traditional and modern construction methods that could be applied economically to urban and rural constructions, developed new construction materials, such as dirt-cement blocks, and published some useful handbooks intended for the use of peasants and laborers, not only of Colombia, but in all other American countries.

Nevertheless, construction of economic housing continued to be generally very traditional, with brick walls, metallic window frames and fiber-cement roofs on wooden or concrete beaming. Such construction is also inexpensive and very often houses are sold unfinished, with the buyers responsible for their completion.

Since World War II the achievements of Colombian architects have been aided increasingly by a broadening basis of professional training. In the education of architects there are no fundamental differences between the various schools since the curriculum and teaching methods of the Universidad Nacional at Bogotá, organized mainly by architects who had studied abroad, have served as the models for Colombia's seventeen schools of architecture. Emphasis is given to the humanities as a complement to studio-training in design and students are encouraged to search out the information needed for their academic work. Though there are great advantages for the student in this system, there are drawbacks, especially in the social and technical fields that have expanded so rapidly in recent years. Recently, in a new departure, graduate courses have been organized in cognate fields such as regional and urban planning and, in some cases, interdisciplinary studies.[40]

Furthermore, the national professional society, Sociedad Colombiana de Arquitectos, serves as a forum for architectural and urban problems. It also organizes nationwide architectural contests, has sponsored the Biennial since 1962, and has offered the Premio Nacional de Arquitectura since 1971 for the best work of Colombian builders. Since 1971, also, SCA publishes the *Colombian Architectural Annual*, supposedly containing Colombia's best architecture each year, though, unfortunately, its criteria of selection are not always rigorously applied.

Discussion of theories of architecture seldom occurs beyond university campuses. Still there are some few specialized journals that deal with architectural, urban, and structural themes. For instance, *Proa*, founded in 1946 by Architects Carlos Martínez and Jorge Arango, publishes many of our architects' projects, plans, and theories and has encouraged discussion of these. In 1951 and again in 1963, Carlos Martínez published a compilation of Colombian works of architecture. A more recent publication, *Escala*, has been oriented toward a concern with one specific theme in each issue, and this has been most useful in architectural circles.

Among Colombian critics of modern architecture four stand out: Carlos Arbeláez, Dicken Castro, Germán Samper, and Germán Téllez. Arbeláez, the first director of the Regulating Plan Office in Bogotá (1950-1952), had his own independent studio and was important as a lecturer and scholar in the history of Colombian architecture. Castro is not only an architect but an excellent graphic designer and writer. Germán Samper, an especially highly respected architect, has published some very interesting perceptions of modern architecture and the social role of the architect. Perhaps the only architect who has been constantly dedicated to the rational criticism of Colombian architecture is Germán Téllez. His essays, generally characterized by a thoughtful originality and a fine sense of irony, have sparked important national debates over the years. It is perhaps to him and others like him that we must look to provide the necessary stimulus to overcome the architectural crisis suffered today, not only in Colombia, but throughout the world.

Notes

1. Carlos Arbeláez, "Ensayo Histórico sobre la Arquitectura Colombiana," *Apuntes del Instituto de Investigaciones Estéticas*, no. 1 (November 1967). Germán Téllez, "Notas para una Historia de la Arquitectura Contemporánea en Colombia," *Crítica y Imagen* (Bogotá: Escala Fondo Editorial, 1977).

2. For a comprehensive and detailed view of social problems, migration, and urban development in Colombia, consult: Ramiro Cardona, ed., "Migración y Desarrollo Urbano en Colombia" (Bogotá 1970).

3. However, during these years, Colombian architects felt some uncertainty about modern architecture, as reflected in the justification of the interesting project for the new railroad station (1947) in Cali, by architect Alfonso Caycedo Herrera: It is "of a modern style—says the report—because this style is the one that adapts better to big constructions."

4. Le Corbusier's plan was supposed to solve Bogotá's problems for forty years. In 1950, Bogotá had 500,000 inhabitants and was supposed to grow to a maximum of 1,600,000 inhabitants by 1990. In 1980, however, the city already had a population of 5,000,000 and a projected population of 8,500,000 for 1990. Nevertheless, Le Corbusier's ideas about zoning have prevailed and only now are being reevaluated. The plan is published in *Le Corbusier: Oeuvre Complète 1946-1952* (Zurich: Editions Girsberger, 1953), pp. 42-47. Le Corbusier's master plan was complemented by José-Luis Sert and Paul Lester Wiener, who were responsible not only for Bogotá's city planning but also for the planning of other Colombian cities.

5. A book on the life and work of architect Leopoldo Rother, written by his son Hans, architect as well, is to be published by Escala Fondo Editorial.

6. For example, Skidmore, Owings and Merrill's Banco de Bogotá building has a structure of imported steel. Steel-beamed structures have been used only occasionally in Colombia due to their high cost and their need for sophisticated technology. We find only one other building in Bogotá that used a steel structure: the Caja Colombiana de Ahorros building [1947] by Cuéllar, Serrano, Gómez. There might be, at the most, two or three other cases of this type of structure in the country.

7. The chamber of this auditorium is fully covered by wood and, with a capacity of 1,630 spectators and 100 musicians or 300 singers, has optimum acoustic and visibility conditions. It reminds one somewhat of Scharoun's concert hall, the Berlin Philharmonic. The Sociedad Colombiana de Arquitectors awarded this project the National Prize of Architecture in 1973.

8. Architects: Jorge Gaitán Cortés (d. 1968), Alvaro Ortega, and Gabriel Solano. These architects will be considered again.

9. Architects: Aníbal Moreno and Jaime Cruz. Aníbal Moreno designs with remarkable skill in the formal manner of Paul Rudolph. Perhaps his most notable work of this kind is the building for the School of Nursing of the Universidad Javeriana in Bogotá [1965-1967]. Moreno is also responsible for planning and architectural projects in Venezuela such as the nuclei for the Universidad de Oriente [1972-1975] in Carúpano, Cumaná, Ciudad Bolívar, etc., the Universidad de San Cristóbal del Táchira [1976], and others. Later, other works in which Moreno and Cruz have participated will be mentioned.

10. The Sociedad Colombiana de Arquitectos awarded it the National Prize of Architecture in 1972. The architects of the master plan were Jaime Cruz, Diego Peñalosa, Javier Naranjo, and Armando Velasco, with Bruno Violi (d. 1973)

as advisor. Among the designers were, besides those already mentioned, Fernando Martínez, Aníbal Moreno, Lyda Caldas de Borrero, Rafael Esquerra, Germán Samper, Manuel Lago, Jaime Camacho, Julián Guerrero, Rodrigo Bonilla, Harold Borrero, Alvaro Rivera, and so many others that it is impossible to mention them all here.

11. Architects: Rafael Esquerra, Néstor Gutiérrez, Juan Menéndez, and Alberto Herrera.

12. The original plan for Techo, or Ciudad Kennedy, was designed by architect Arturo Robledo. In its different developmental stages many other architects were involved.

13. Architect: Marco Aurelio Montes.

14. Architect: Roberto Rodríguez Silva. This building is an interesting application of the system proposed by Le Corbusier in his *L'Unité.*

15. Architects: Carlos Arbeláez (d. 1969), Eduardo Pombo, and Hans Drews (d. 1961).

16. Architect: Rogelio Salmona. Later in this chapter there is more information about this architect and this project.

17. Architect: Mario Pinilla with Hernán Herrera and Fernando Medina of the firm Rubio, Medina y Herrera. This project was awarded the National Prize of Architecture by the Sociedad Colombiana de Arquitectos in 1971.

18. By the same team of architects.

19. Architects: Jaime Camacho and Julián Guerrero (Camacho y Guerrero). Another remarkable building by these architects in collaboration with Manuel Lago and Jaime Sáenz (Lago y Sáenz) is the Carvajal building in Cali [1970] designed, due to the hot climate of that city, in a wedge form, and sheathed in white limestone that completely closes two facades while the two others open in narrow strips that act as a *brise-soleil.*

20. With firms Esquerra, Sáenz, Urdaneta, Samper (Rafael Esquerrra, Alvaro Sáenz, Urdaneta, and Germán Samper) and Ricaurte, Carrizosa y Prieto (Santiago Ricaurte, Manuel Carrizosa and José Prieto).

21. The building for district services, the first built of the two, consisting of a low square block, very versatile in distribution of spaces, was given the maximum distinction award in the first International Biennial of São Paulo, Brazil, in 1973. Architects: Gabriel Largacha, Gabriel Serrano, Jaime de la Torre and Inés Vásquez.

22. The firm of Cuéllar, Serrano, Gómez has published illustrated booklets describing their works. The first, in 1954, contains works of the period 1933-1954 (525,000 square meters constructed in 21 years); another, in 1958, in celebration of 25 years of existence, includes their contributions to Colombian engineering (bridges, reservoirs, foundations, the Reticular Celulado system, etc.). In 1947 Gabriel Serrano received the National Engineering Prize. Another field in which Cuéllar, Serrano, Gómez has excelled is the design and construction of hospitals with Serrano's hospital architecture characterized by its rationality and efficiency.

23. The project was developed jointly by firms Esquerra, Sáenz, Urdaneta, Samper and Ricaurte, Carrizosa y Prieto.

24. The Sociedad Colombiana de Arquitectos awarded the Gold Museum first prize in the Colombian Architectural Biennial of 1970. It was designed jointly with Fernando Jiménez.

25. A good analysis of Salmona's sources, such as Scharoun in El Parque, is that by Marina Waisman, "De Tipos y Contratipos," *Cuadernos Summa—Nueva Visión,* no. 3 (June 1975).

26. Salmona's work has aroused great interest internationally and his projects have been published very often in architecture books and magazines throughout the whole world.

An interview with Salmona about urbanization and Colombian architecture was published in Damián Bayón and Paolo Gasparini, *Panorámica de la Arquitectura Latinoamericana,* copyrighted by UNESCO (Barcelona: Editorial Blume, 1977), pp. 65-85. Commentaries and photographs of Salmona's works are to be found in: Francisco Bullrich, *Nuevos Caminos de la Arquitectura Latinoamericana* (Barcelona: Editorial Blume, 1969), pp. 93-97 (original title in English: *New Directions in Latin American Architecture*); Germán Téllez, "Notas," *Crítica y Imagen*; and Cuadernos Summa—Nueva Visión, nos. 2 and 3 (April, June 1975).

27. Fernando Martínez's architectural work until 1978 was published by Fernando Montenegro in a profusely illustrated volume titled *Fernando Martínez Sanabria: Trabajos de Arquitectura* (Bogotá: Escala Fondo Editorial, 1978).

28. This structure was at that time so innovative that, according to Germán Téllez ("Notas," p. 87), virtual replicas of it—such as the baseball and olympic stadia at Universidad Central of Venezuela in Caracas by Carlos Raúl Villanueva [1950]—were constructed very soon thereafter in many countries, including the United States. A section on Cartagena's Stadium, in comparison with other covered grandstands, is published in Rudolf Ortner's *Sportbauten* (Munich, 1956), p. 28.

29. Architect: Alvaro Hermida.

30. Architects: Germán Samper, Eduardo Pombo, with Ricaurte, Carrizosa y Prieto, and Obregón y Valenzuela.

31. Architects: Camacho y Guerrero.

32. Architects: Cuéllar, Serrano, Gómez.

33. Architects: Cuéllar, Serrano, Gómez.

34. Architects: Enrique Richardson and Libia Yusti de Chatain (Richardson y Yusti).

35. Architects: Aníbal Moreno and Ricardo González Ripoll.

36. Architects: Rafael Obregón (d. 1975), José María Obregón, Hernando Tapia, Edgar Bueno, and Manuel Forero of the firm Obregón y Valenzuela.

37. By Obregón y Valenzuela and Pizano, Pradilla, Caro, Restrepo (Juan Pizano de Brigard, Alvaro Pradilla, Luis Caro, and Manuel Restrepo).

38. Architects: Patricio Samper, Luis F. Tapias, César Moreno, and Gregorio Marín.

39. CINVA was established in 1951 as a Technical Cooperation Program of the Organization of American States. In 1972 it became an organism of the OAS: the Inter-American Information Service on Urban Development (SINDU) that existed as such until December 1977

when the OAS gave it to Colombia, under the auspices of the Universidad Nacional at Bogotá, where it operates as SINDU—NAL. The program objectives of CINVA were the in-depth study of Latin American housing problems; the identification of techniques and solutions related to those problems; the training of professionals of the member countries of the OAS so that they could act as disseminators of techniques in their countries of origin; the development of models of solutions; and the edition and distribution of technical and social publications in this field.

40. Many architects have distinguished themselves in education. Standouts are Rother and Violi whose work in this field has already been mentioned, Fernando Martínez, Edgar Burbano, Guillermo Bermúdez, Carlos Arbeláez, Germán Samper, Rogelio Salmona, Roberto Rodríguez, Jaime Cruz, Arturo Robledo, Hernán Vieco, Francisco Pizano de Brigard, Juan Ferroni, Manuel Carrizosa, and so many others that it is impossible to list them here.

Bibliography

BOOKS

Martínez, Carlos, and Arango, Jorge. Arquitectura en *Colombia 1946-1951.* Bogotá: Ediciones Proa, 1951.

Martínez, Carlos and Burbano, Edgar. *Arquitectura en Colombia 1952-1962.* Bogotá: Litografía Colombia, 1963.

Montenegro, Fernando et al. ''Fernando Martínez Sanabria,'' *Escala.* Fondo Editorial, Colección Arquitectura, 1978.

Téllez, Germán. "Arquitectura en Colombia (1930-1952)" and "Arquitectura en Colombia (1952-1976)." *Historia del Arte Colombiano.* Vol. 7. Bogotá: Salvat Editores Colombiana, 1977.

Téllez, Germán. *Crítica y Imagen.* Bogotá: Escala Fondo Editorial, Colección Arquitectura, 1977.

JOURNALS

"40 Años de Arquitectura," *Revista de la Asociación de Arquitectura Egresados de la Universidad Nacional* no. 5 (1976).

Arbeláez, Carlos. "Ensayo Histórico sobre la Arquitectura Colombiana." *Apuntes del Instituto de Investigaciones Estéticas* no. 1 (November 1967).

Sociedád Colombiana de Arquitectos, *Anuario de la Arquitectura en Colombia,* since 1971.

USEFUL JOURNALS

Escala (monthly architectural magazine) 1962-1981.

Proa (monthly architectural, urbanistic, and construction magazine) 1946-1981.

17

CUBA

JAMES B. LYNCH, JR.

By the end of World War II demographic, socioeconomic, and cultural patterns in Cuba had become firmly established.[1] The population of Havana was approximately five times that of the second largest city, Santiago de Cuba. Moreover, the magnetic pull of financial, medical, and educational resources into the capital—the Havana "brain drain" away from rival centers—had resulted in an urban imbalance that was equally lopsided.[2]

In addition to these problems it is important to note two extraordinary inequities, the resolution of which under socialism was to have enormous consequences in all areas of Cuban society including the arts. We refer, on the one hand, to the economic subjugation of Cuba by the United States, which accelerated after 1945. On the other hand, we have in mind the malign neglect, harshly disadvantageous to the peasantry, of rural Cuba by urban Cuba except as a zone of exploitation.

From the turn of the century, soon after the island dissolved its Colonial ties with Spain, such disparities had festered and swelled decade after decade. Thus, as the tides of internal and external immigration poured into Havana soon after 1900, the moneyed classes began to move from the heart of the city into mansions, villas, and eventually apartment houses in such coastal suburbs as Vedado and Miramar. A melange of traditional and conventional styles accommodated their housing needs.

Certain architectural constants continued to prevail, however, just as they had during Colonial times and as they would, by and large, under Castro. Almost since the Conquest this tropical island had learned to adjust to a hot humid climate, occasionally freshened through offshore breezes, by means of high-ceilinged rooms, plenty of cross-ventilation, and latticed openings designed to exclude heat and promote circulation of cooling air.

During the decade before World War II "Modernism" arrived in the architectural circles of Havana and other large centers. Concepts of *Neue Sachlichkeit, De Stijl*, and Art Deco were expressed in a considerable number of structures, particularly in wealthy suburbs where bellwethers of new fashions proliferated. Thus, many of the homes of the well-to-do began to reflect an International Style, highly functional in character, inspired by and large by such European architects as Le Corbusier, Gropius, and Mies van der Rohe. The heavy bearing walls of the old-style houses were replaced by sleek porous membranelike walls, enlivened only by sharp contrasts of light and shadow. Inside such houses there was a rational and often flexible distribution of spatial units, with perhaps here and there an American-style kitchen.

Nevertheless, large single buildings and apartments were virtually a monopoly of the upper and middle classes. Tenements housed the poor. And in the countryside there was, as from time beyond memory, the ubiquitous *bohío*—the peasant's hut.

As for public architecture, presidents and dictators in twentieth-century Cuba, like their counterparts in Europe, turned eagerly to it as an exemplary expression of cultural and political ambition, creating out of marble, mortar, and brick monumental symbols of power. José Miguel Gómez (president, 1909-1912) borrowed his notion of a grand Presidential Palace (completed 1920) from such middle-European prototypes as the Berlin Reichstag. From federal Washington came the inspiration of Machado's Capitol [1929]. The pseudo-Classicism of public buildings in Hitler's Germany and Mussolini's Italy suited well the architectural tastes of Castro's, predecessor, Fulgencio Batista.[3]

During much of World War II, as one might have expected, building activities waned or remained in check. Soon after the conflict ended, however, unleasing trammeled energies, a seemingly roseate new future opened for the island. Prodigious amounts of construction became necessary to satisfy rising demands for office buildings, hotels, casinos, and other structures in the capital as it became a tourists' paradise. The skyline of Havana was elevated by scores of high-rise edifices, many with curtain walls of aluminum and glass like those of North American skyscrapers. No matter that air-conditioning, at least during these first few years, scarcely existed!

A number of distinctive—and even several distinguished—structures were built during the decade before the Revolution. Among the latter we may cite Aquilo Capablanca's Office of the Comptroller [1952-1954] (fig. 17.1) and Max Borges's Cabaret Tropicana [1952] (fig. 17.2), both in Havana. As Henry-Russell Hitchcock observed many years ago, the Office of the Comptroller followed in general ". . . the Corbusian formula introduced at the Ministry of Education fifteen years earlier in Rio."[4] On the sun side of this striking edifice each *brise-soleil* helps form a richly textured honeycomb pattern. On this same side, incidentally, a projecting block appears from a distance to be concave. Actually it forms an obtuse angle, and in context it seems a quirky gambol. This vagary, incidentally, will reappear a decade later among the National Schools of the Arts in Castro's Havana. On the shade side the warm beige limestone gives way to a glass facade.

17.1. Aquilo Capablanca, architect. Office of Comptroller Building, Havana, 1952-1954. (Photograph: Courtesy of *The Art Journal*)

As for the Cabaret Tropicana, consider its plan and elevation. Along a gently curving axis five vaulted shells of concrete, alternating with glass arches, create the effect of a fantastic tunnel. Stunningly novel, it nevertheless evokes vague memories of other, older buildings, such as the Bibliothèque Nationale and the Gare d'Orsay of Paris. Vegetation inside, including trees, dissolves the conventional barriers between interior and exterior space as architecture and environment fuse. The architect, U.S.-trained Max Borges, had this to say of his building: "I thought of the vault device because one cannot say where the wall ends and the ceiling begins. Besides it proved to be the cheapest enclosure, and provided an area uninterrupted by columns."[5] Cabaret Tropicana continues today to attract packed audiences including Cuban bureaucrats and Soviet technicians, who are titillated nightly by the sight of scantily clad chorus girls dancing and singing in this air-conditioned symbol now of socialist decadence.

17.2. Max Borges, architect. Cabaret Tropicana Interior, Havana, 1952. (Photograph: Courtesy of *The Art Journal*)

By the late 1950s the vogue of Modernism in Cuban architecture had deteriorated into an often shallow and vulgar eclecticism. For instance, as described in the *New York Times* on the eve of the Revolution, the new house of Emilio del Junco in Havana consisted of prefabricated materials, including pillars and ceiling beams in a vaulted design. Pierced wooden panels replaced windows, and the overhanging roof protected against sun and rain. Old iron grillwork and floors of ceramic tile further enhanced a Colonial flavor. Antique stained glass, fan-shaped, was used for an over-door. Nineteenth-century and modern Cuban furniture coexisted with contemporary Scandinavian. Such was the state of Cuban architecture in the years just before the Revolution.

Of all the arts, architecture since the Revolution has been subjected to the most insistent and prolonged pressures through government planning. Under Castro the development of architecture has been shaped largely by three events which occurred in the early 1960s: 1) the U.S. embargo, 2) Castro's proclamation of the socialist character of the Revolution, and 3) the Seventh Congress of the International Union of Architects in Havana. Let us consider each of these.

First, as early as 15 October 1960 the United States declared a partial embargo on trade with Cuba in retaliation for the nationalization by Cuba, four days earlier, of nearly 400 major enterprises and banks. On 25 April 1961 the United States declared a total embargo. This economic squeeze of Cuba, which had been virtually an economic colony of its northern neighbor, produced shortages in vital industries, rationing of many goods, and a search for markets within the Communist bloc. During the early 1960s housing projects were often delayed by lack of elevator machinery or other equipment such as plumbing fixtures and kitchenware—all of which had to be imported. Timber as well as steel was scarce.

Second, Castro's proclamation of socialism ensured that the urban-bourgeois, rural-feudal basis of Cuban society would undergo a momentous transformation. Thus, the collectivizing spirit of the Revolution found appropriate architectural expressions in new urban complexes for workers and peasants with extensive cultural, recreational, and service facilities—often including communal dining rooms; boarding institutions for secondary students; hospitals, and schools in remote mountain regions; cooperative farms, and so on. Some examples are the secondary school, Ciudad Escolar, *Camilo Cienfuegos* [1964-1965] by the architect Emilio Escobar, which is in a remote mountain district (Oriente Province); the state farm Ciudad Sandino (*see* below); and the V. I. Lenin Hospital at Holguín (Oriente Province) [1965, by architects M. Mesa, A. Menendez, L. R. Columbre, and others]. On the other hand, office buildings, casinos, large private homes—and other architectural manifestations of so-called capitalist culture—were eliminated, curtailed, or converted.

For example, during the 1960s an estimated 100,000 scholarship students took over the abandoned, confiscated mansions of Miramar, once a wealthy suburb of northwest Havana.[6] Former citadels of finance and bastions of luxury began to house workers' clubs, associations, government agencies, and so forth. During the so-called Great Revolutionary Offensive, launched by Castro in March 1968, over 16,000 private enterprises were closed in Havana alone, while throughout the island nearly 60,000 "stalls," shops, and private service establishments were nationalized.[7]

Such actions, however, were in vivid contrast to government policy in the first years of the Revolution. For instance, private enterprise in the field of architecture was not suppressed, nor even discouraged, until after 1963. In that year the state planned the construction of 55,447 dwellings; private enterprise planned 30,000.[8] After 1963, however, came a strong thrust toward collective work, elimination of private practice, diminution of single-unit homes, and a rapid increase of state investment in the architectural sector.

A side effect of the Revolution was a depletion of architects, 30 percent of whom left Cuba in the first few years. This large-scale defection can be explained more or less by the fact that before the advent of socialism Cuban architects never enjoyed the professional independence belonging to their European counterparts. Instead, according to the arguments of partisans of the regime, they were tightly bound to the contracting industry, itself closely identified with North American financial interests. To compensate for the shortage, young architects were trained as swiftly as possible. By 1964, five years after the Revolution began, the School of Architecture of the University of Havana had 400 students. Nevertheless, in the first years of the new regime it was no great exaggeration to speak of "an architecture without architects."

As for the third factor, the Seventh Congress of the International Union of Architects (IUA) was held at Havana in September-October 1963. The first convention of the IUA ever staged in the Americas, the Seventh Congress was attended by more than 2,000 architects, representing 80 countries.[9] They attended sessions dedicated to the general theme of "Architecture in Emerging Countries." Specific topics in the agenda of these sessions included national planning, construction techniques (especially prefabrication), and the neighborhood unit. Since the latter concept, which derives from Soviet architectural theory, has been adopted in most schemes of urban and rural planning in Cuba, it needs to be explained. Soviet planners developed a microsector in which 10,000-12,000 persons are concentrated within a radius of about 1200 feet from public transportation, thanks to high-density housing.[10] Each microsector contains two schools in addition to primary public services (that is, those which provide the inhabitants with articles of daily use) and secondary public services (cinemas, pharmacies, swimming pools, and so on), for every 1,000 to 4,000 persons within a radius of 300 to 500 feet. Within the microsector it is this latter small unit that constitutes the neighborhood unit. Both the microsector and the neighborhood unit, with certain modifications, have been incorporated into Castroist architecture.

Fundamental to the adoption of such planning, along with prefabrication techniques, is the central fact that Cuba, under Castro, is emerging from underdevelopment along Marxist lines. As a result, the old, specifically bourgeois, forms of architecture can no longer serve her ideological needs. To writers like Roberto Segre, the most articulate and authoritative spokesman for Castroist architecture, the dynamic, often innovative, structures of Brazil's Oscar Niemeyer and Venezuela's Carlos Raúl Villanueva are merely symbols of a sterile elitism rather than monuments of a truly revolutionary architecture.

To create an ideologically sound architecture to fulfill the goals of the Revolution, Cuban structures must, then, be wholly responsive to constantly evolving technological and social needs. Prefabrication, as we shall see, has become the key to the kind of quality of new structural requirements. Modular interchangeable units, plugged into standardized frames, have risen from the José Martí microcity, bordering Santiago de Cuba, to the University City outside Havana.

As these urban complexes extrude into the countryside, Castro and his architects would have us believe that the old pre-Revolution physical, economic, and psychological barriers between urban and rural areas are in the process of dissolving. Whether or not they are correct is a question we shall later examine more closely. At any rate, from the vantage point of Havana they cite proudly, as justification of the success of their policies, *Cordón de la Habana*. Inaugurated in April 1967, it is a greenbelt 8 kilometers in depth and 30,000 hectares in area, melding the capital with its rural environs and providing food, employment, and recreation.

From this general survey let us turn now to specific buildings of the Revolution, beginning with Havana and moving on to towns and rural areas outside the capital.

Two of the most impressive structures in socialist Havana are the National Schools of the Arts (fig. 17.3) and the East Havana Housing Project, both of

17.3. Ricardo Porro with Roberto Gottardi and Vittorio Garatti, architect. National Schools of the Arts. Havana-Cubanacán, 1961-1963. (Photograph: Courtesy of *The Art Journal*)

the early 1960s. The National Schools of the Arts are the more distinguished and, at the same time, the more unorthodox of the two. Comprising ballet, dramatic arts, modern dance, plastic arts, and music, the schools are located on the expropriated grounds of a former country club in Cubanacán, a southwestern suburb of Havana. Due to the scarcity of steel, timber, and other imported materials, the buildings were constructed almost entirely of brick and tile at a cost of more than 13 million pesos. Designed by two Italian architects, Roberto Gottardi (dramatic arts) and Vittorio Garatti (music, ballet) and a Cuban, Ricardo Porro (modern dance, plastic arts), Islamic-style cupolas, brick vaulting reminiscent of seventeeth-century Catalonian techniques, and fan-shaped woodwork derived from colonial mansions coexist with more modern elements to give the buildings a motley character. Each school has its own autonomous space, its own library, cafeteria, and so on; yet a kind of gravitational force seems to pull the five complexes together into a unity of form and space. A lava of tile and brick, they appear to flow toward one another in the midst of a rich tropical vegetation.

Labeled Baroque, even Mannerist, the schools exalt an irrational, sensuous, undisciplined spirit profoundly disturbing to their critics. Space and form are mischievously, perhaps maliciously, warped, violated, and subverted. With a chilling finesse, the itinerant viewer is subjected to numerous visual and psychic shocks. As Alberto Ferrari has observed, "The corridor, from a service center, becomes a building in its own right."[11] Nonrectangular intersections—the Office of the Comptroller (see fig. 17.1) comes to mind—take place between component units. One wanders uneasily through a labyrinthine sprawl of seemingly discrete spaces, segmented walls, gaping voids between cupolas and walls, shifting roof levels, flowing stairs. The effect is vertiginous. At ground level, "[Each] school at first appears to be the result of a sweeping impulse, but . . . no form is completed, no formal succession is accepted, no order seems to have been desired. In short it appears to express clearly revolutionary Cuba's mood in the early sixties."[12] On the other hand, from an aerial view, seldom possible for a viewer, it appears that an organic, cellular unity, never apprehended at ground level, has been imposed bringing order out of chaos.

In Porro's School of Plastic Arts structural forms take on a quasibiological character. Drawn into an esophageal corridor by the beckoning central entrance, one seeks axial clarity and communicative significance in vain along this passage—it ends in a veritable cul-de-sac, whereas its flanking corridors become galleries. Breasts, tracheae, viscera, such are the images which the architectural forms evoke.

Whence the inspiration for the undulating planes, swelling volumes, and ambiguous spaces of these schools? The serpentine forms recall the *Carioca* style of Brazil's Oscar Niemeyer, Eduardo Affonso Reidy, and Roberto Burle Marx. At the same time they suggest the floor plan of Borges's Cabaret Tropicana. Regardless, however, of the eclecticism involved in design and technique, all components are merged together into a fresh synthesis.

These schools drew sharp criticism from Castro himself. In his 1969 address to the First Congress of Builders *el Jefe Máximo* criticized architects like Ricardo Porro for using excessively egocentric criteria and for pretending to make a particular case out of every building. In the Soviet Union such charges of bourgeois individualism would have been made less euphemistically. Discouraged and inhibited, Porro left Cuba for Paris in 1965. Writing almost a dozen years later in the Italian journal *Casabella*, Alberto Ferrari said about the schools: "Later, owing to economic difficulties, the Art Schools' program was abandoned. The buildings planned by Porro—the Modern Dance School and the School of Plastic Art—were the only ones to be completed and utilized."[13]

Notwithstanding, in 1966 the National Center of Scientific Research of the University of Havana, was constructed in the capital. Indeed, it rose in the same suburb where the schools were built, Cubanacán. What a striking example of Expressionism! The canopy beyond the entrance juts out aggressively like the prow of a ship. The concave roof dances on its walls. And the flanking concrete stanchions resemble the fingers of gigantic hands drumming on the ground.

Another showpiece of early socialist architecture was built across the bay in East Havana. Designed by a twenty-member team at the Ministry of Construction from the master plan [1959-1960] by architects Fernando Salinas and Raul Gonzalez Romero, the East Havana Housing Project [1960-1963] was intended to mark the eastern terminus of an axis extending through Calle 23—*La Rampa*, one of the most prominent of Habanera thoroughfares—to the National Schools of the Arts in southwest Havana. Just before the Revolution East Havana, until then the slowest growing sector of the metropolitan area, suddenly became the object of intense activity in land speculation. Buyers began to gobble up undeveloped land along the new roads which were built to connect the capital with a whole network of beach resorts for the wealthy. Ironically—and symbolically, like the Spanish monuments raised on pagan ruins in the New World—the acres on which the East Havana Project is now located had been acquired on the eve of the Revolution for a luxurious residential center that had been planned by Skidmore, Owings and Merrill.

According to the master plan, the project was designed to shelter a population of 100,000 in its ultimate stage of development. For the initial phase, on the other hand, the number of dwellers was limited to 8,000 and the units to 1,500—a ratio of slightly more than 5:1. Such utopian concepts of high-density housing were soon to evaporate before sociological and technological realities. With its full provision of social and cultural facilities the complex provides two shopping centers, several schools, a sports center, a community center, and so forth. Peripheral circulation is maintained through a broad avenue encircling the project, while inside there is a hierarchy of roads and footways.

That the skyline of the project varies between four- and ten-story blocks can be attributed indirectly to the United States's boycott against Cuba, which included elevators. After the first few blocks had been constructed, it became unfeasible to import elevators from Eastern Europe—the new source of supply. Instead, they had to give way to more desperately needed industrial imports. Without elevators, of course, ten-story blocks became impractical.

In later housing projects Cuban builders have continued to avoid such high-rise blocks. What was structural common sense turned out to be sociological wisdom. For many years urban studies have fixed attention on psychological problems fostered by large-scale high-rise housing projects. As distant neighbors of Venezuela, Cuban planners must have been aware of the sociological chaos produced in the mammoth projects of Caracas during the 1950s.

Whatever its future population (its population is about 10,000 at present), the East Havana Housing Project will probably not become the cause of the sort of urban sprawl that blights Europe, the United States, and Latin America. The need to thrust out beyond the project toward more or less distant service and cultural facilities—a need which is a primary force in urban sprawl—does not appear to exist at East Havana. In short, such pioneer projects of Castro's long-range plan to redress the demographic imbalance between East and West Havana are apparently self-sufficient.

Finally, it must be acknowledged that the East Havana Housing Project is exceptional. Cubans were warned by Castro himself that the high standards set by the complex were more than the island could afford.[14] The excessive cost of the project, incidentally, had resulted from the retention of traditional, "crafted" techniques of building. Later housing projects, on the other hand, shaved costs by utilizing instead prefabrication and modular construction.

Construction techniques, especially prefabrication, had been a major item on the agenda of the Seventh Congress of the IUA at Havana in 1963. By 1967 prefabrication had become an architectural dogma enforced nationwide by Castro's planning boards. A varied repertory of building techniques, materials, machines, and labor practices contributed richly to its implementation. For instance, "NOVOA" (trade name based on manual prefabrication) was introduced into rural areas where unskilled labor had predominated, such as in the state farm founded under the auspices of INRA (National Institute for Agrarian Reform) at Sandino in Pinar del Rio province.

Begun July 1964 with a nucleus of 500 families, Sandino was planned by architects Josefina Rebellón and Javier Gutiérrez for an eventual population of 15,000, occupying some 96 hectares astride the central highway (the Carretera Central) linking the eastern and western extremities of Cuba. Stark, impersonal, shedlike blocks of flats, divided into neighborhood units, from one- to four-stories high, constitute this dispersed, low-density, rural community. Traditional patterns of peasant life have been disrupted in Sandino. Communal living at various levels has replaced the one-family *bohío* . Refectories and central kitchens have altered age-old cooking and eating habits. Wherever feasible, human activities have been converted from private to public. One begins to wonder if the bleak uniformity of architecture at Sandino was conceived as a means to condition human behavior toward such a state of collectivity.

More than 600 miles to the east, on the outskirts of Santiago de Cuba (Oriente province), lies the new town of José Martí. Like Sandino, it was founded in 1964 but for a larger population of 50,000. José Martí consists of two microsectors—one with five neighborhood units, the other with two. Soon after Hurricane Flora devastated Oriente province in 1963, the Soviet Union as a gift gave Santiago a prefabrication plant specializing in *Gran Panel* construction.[15] "Big Panel" construction consists of huge modular components which, when boxed together, quickly and efficiently provide standardized units for apartment complexes. Giant cranes helped lift *Gran Panel* sections into place. Other methods of elevating heavy framing and insulating components have been ingeniously employed. For example, in the early stages of construction at University City, Havana (ground was broken in March 1961), floors in low-rise units were raised by the lift-slab technique of construction, involving hydraulic jacks and other equipment already in use on the island. Moreover, the architects sensibly opted for light materials such as Siporex (a porous cement) and aluminum as concomitants of this bold system.

Monoblocks at José Martí, while a standard four stories in height, vary between 16, 32, and 48 units per building. Floor plans indicate a rational distribution of space, comfort, and convenience in living,[16] and good cross-ventilation. Private loggias provide transitions between indoor and outdoor spaces. Above all, the molded *brise-soleil* produces an effect of filigree, delicate and light, and heretofore absent in systems of heavy prefabrication.

So much for Cuban architecture in the early stages of socialism. During the late 1960s and early 1970s extraordinary drives took place, involving labor-intensive activity, to flood the Cuban countryside with schools, homes, hospitals, recreational facilities, and even new towns. One of the innovations which contributed markedly to these efforts was the formation of so-called microbrigades. Each unit consisted of thirty-three workers, who took leave of their regular jobs to learn building skills on site under the guidance of experts. These microbrigades in turn released professional construction forces for building schools, highest in priority as the result of nationwide literacy campaigns.

A classic example of this makeshift policy of massive construction with unseasoned labor is to be found in the creation of Alamar, a new town (now populated by 30,000) on the Atlantic coast a few miles from Havana. According to reports: "The buildings are pre-fabricated concrete, the latest made with Yugoslav technology. There are factories, schools, health centers—even a nurse who makes daily home visits—recreation and day-care centers."[17]

As one might have expected, aesthetic values began to languish in this second decade of Cuban architecture under socialism. Prefabrication had been predicated on standardization and that meant sameness—the repetition of components, units, blocks, complexes, and even towns according to basic modular norms. Architectural theorists spoke bravely of differentiating units by function, use, or lifestyle, but nevertheless sameness ruled. As early as 1966, for example, José Antonio Portuondo, a distinguished critic, admitted that: "The pressing need to build houses, factories, schools, hospitals, etc., in the shortest possible time and at minimum cost was solved through increased use of prefabricated elements with consequent uniformity, monotony, and aesthetic mediocrity."[18]

The huge secondary schools which have spread throughout the island are stultifying examples of this aesthetic mediocrity. Take, for instance, the vocational school at Holguín, built in the late 1970s to train some 4,500 elite students for university careers in technology and science. It is aesthetically a kind of tropical Stonehenge with block after block of identical, stark, narrow (for air circulation), low-rise slabs. In the latest units color has been mercifully added to relieve the general dreariness of design. Notwithstanding, the whole is enough to induce Le Corbusier, unwilling progenitor of this complex, to roll in his grave.

Perhaps we are too harsh. It is only fair to point out that while quality has suffered, it has by no means been eliminated. Two striking examples of good, simple architecture come to mind: both from the middle 1970s, both in Havana. They are the Salvador Allende School and a late addition to the Lenin Vocational School, the earliest of its kind, incidentally, to be constructed in Cuba. What do they have in common? A likeness to abstract paintings. Planes seem to drift lightly upon the surfaces of volumes; voids have functional as well as aesthetic significance; and pastels burnish the forms. Summon the muses!

There have been of course vast changes in socialist Cuba. Nevertheless, traditional and long-lived factors persist. Although downgraded by the urban planners of Castro's regime, Havana is still very much *primus inter pares*. Recent graphs appearing in *Arquitectura Cuba*—the most reliable and informative guide among Cuban periodicals in the field of architecture—reveal that the age-long imbalance between Havana and the hinterland still exists.[19] The capital remains overextended; conceivably only some dreadful catastrophe could reduce it to parity with the rest of the island: "Traveling west from Alamar, the landscape becomes more rural—except for a middle-class resort built in the 1940s and still flourishing with rows and rows of small pink stucco cottages. There are pastures dotted with black and white cows and an occasional cowboy on a pinto horse, his straw hat turned up on both sides."[20]

Other factors continue to prevail. Right-wing predecessors of Castro, as we have seen, turned to architecture as symbols. So, too, has he. For instance, the Moncado Barracks at Santiago, where the Revolution began on 26 July 1953, have been converted into a school. The Plaza de la Revolución in downtown Havana has been turned into a staging area for the actors of the revolutionary dramas.

In terms of architectural symbol, however, no monument is more eloquent than the Mausoleum of the Artemisa martyrs.[21] It is the Calvary and the catacombs of Cuba. In front of each crypt is a portrait of a hero, reminding present and future generations of the need for struggle and the price to be paid.

At times in architecture, as in economics, Revolutionary Cuba has—with the best or worst intentions—made profound mistakes and ignored compelling realities. One can, for instance, leaf through countless pages in architectural periodicals, technical journals, and books without encountering a deep awareness of ecological problems. In Cuba, a small country with a long, lean configuration, a system of linear cities paralleling the Carretera Central appears to be a rational solution for national urban planning. Architects of the Revolution, however, seem indifferent to such a concept. Above all, these same architects, for all their goodwill, seemingly blink at important sociological factors in urban planning. Do Cuban peasants really *want* kitchenless apartments, communal dining halls? Do their children *want* to be separated for months, even days, from parents and home while attending obligatory boarding schools?

Is this bureaucratic paternalism necessary to create the "new Cuban"?

On the other side of the balance sheet, however, there are rich assets. Consider, for example, the idealism of architects—many of them women—who lend their talents for so little remuneration to the noble task of housing in comfort and dignity masses of people who, for generations, have lived in hopeless poverty and squalor. Imagination and ingenuity bordering on brilliance have marked the desperate efforts of builders to surmount deficiencies caused by the boycott and by unwise economic policies. Not least among these assets is the buoyant enthusiasm of men and women who consider themselves not simply builders of monuments, but also architects of a new and better society.

In time, no doubt, as the quantitative goals of Cuban architecture are fulfilled, aesthetic levels will rise. In recent years, as we have indicated, edifices of simple but striking beauty have risen. Perhaps a balance has been achieved between form and function. The next generation of Cuban architects presumably will be better-trained and more sensitive to harmonious relationships between these criteria of modern architecture.

Notes

1. Slightly revised, portions of this essay appeared originally in "Cuban Architecture since the Revolution," *Art Journal* 39, no. 2 (Winter 1979/80): 100-106. I am grateful to the publisher of *Art Journal* for permission to reprint them.

2. Susana Torre, "Architecture and Revolution," *Progressive Architecture* 55 (October 1974): 86.

3. Editorial CENTSCO (*Arquitectura Cuba*), *La Habana* (Barcelona, 1974), pp. 53-54.

4. Henry-Russell Hitchcock, *Latin American Architecture since 1945* (New York: Museum of Modern Art, 1955), p. 73.

5. Gilbert Chase, *Contemporary Art in Latin America* (New York, 1970), p. 246.

6. R. Dumont, *Cuba: Socialism and Development* (New York, 1970), p. 126.

7. K. S. Karol, *Guerillas in Power: The Course of the Cuban Revolution* (New York, 1970), p. 442.

8. Roberto Segre, *Cuba: L'Architettura della Rivoluzione* (Padua, 1970), p. 62.

9. *Arquitectura Cuba*, no. 331 (January-March 1964): 3-23.

10. A. Gutnov et al., *The Ideal Communist City* (New York), p. 76. *See also* below, chapter 36 by Igor Golomstock.

11. Alberto Ferrari, "Ricardo Porro: Fancy in Power," *Casabella*, no. 386 (1974): 31.

12. Francisco Bullrich, *New Directions in Latin American Architecture* (New York: George Braziller, 1969), p. 62.

13. Ferrari, "Ricardo Porro," p. 30.

14. Bullrich, *New Directions*, p. 62.

15. "Ensemble d'Habitation 'José Martí,' Santiago de Cuba," *L'Architecture d'Aujourd'hui* (October-November 1968): 83.

16. The juxtaposition of kitchens and toilets, however, might vex tenants elsewhere.

17. *Baltimore Sun*, 22 March 1978, p. 2.

18. J. A. Portuondo, "Por una Arquitectura Cubana y Socialista," *Arquitectura Cuba*, no. 336, p. 60.

19. *Arquitectura Cuba*, nos. 347-348 (1978).

20. *Baltimore Sun*, 22 March 1978, p. 2.

21. It commemorates and holds the remains of the seventeen martyrs from Artemisa (Pinar del Rio) who died in the attack on the Moncado Barracks.

Bibliography

BOOKS

Bullrich, Francisco. *New Directions in Latin American Architecture*. New York: George Braziller, 1969.

Editorial CENTSCO (*Arquitectura Cuba*). *La Habana*. Barcelona, 1974.

Hitchcock, Henry-Russell. *Latin American Architecture since 1945*. New York: Museum of Modern Art, 1955.

Segre, Roberto. *Cuba: L'Architettura della Rivoluzione*. Padua, 1970.

______. *Cuba: L'Architettura della Rivoluzione*. 2d ed. Venice, 1977.

______. *Diez Años de Arquitectura en Cuba Revolucionaria*. Havana, 1970.

Weiss, Joaquin E. *Arquitectura Cubana Contemporanea*. Havana, 1947.

JOURNALS

Consuegra, Hugo. "Las Escuelas Nacionales de Arte." *Arquitectura Cuba*, no. 334 (1965).

Ferrari, Alberto. "Ricardo Porro: Fancy in Power." *Casabella*, no. 386 (1974).

Lynch, James B., Jr. "Cuban Architecture since the Revolution." *Art Journal* 39, no. 2 (Winter 1979/80).

Portuonodo, J. A. "Por una Arquitectura Cubana y Socialista." *Arquitectura Cuba*, no. 336 (1966).

Richards, J. M. "Report from Cuba." *Architectural Review*, March 1964.

Segre, Roberto, "Architecture, sous-Developpement, et Revolution." *L'Architecture d'Aujourd'hui*, no. 140 (October-November 1968).

Torre, Susana. "Architecture and Revolution." *Progressive Architecture* 55 (October 1974).

18

CZECHOSLOVAKIA

JOSEF PECHAR

Introduction

Architecture after the Second World War was developed in Czechoslovakia in concert with the realization of new social programs. Extensive reconstruction of towns, settlements, and villages that had developed over the span of a thousand years of changing social conditions resulted in their losing features of a previously uneven economic and cultural growth. Undesirable differences in economic character and living standards between the Czech lands and Slovakia now have been alleviated and contradictions apparent in the towns and villages have gradually disappeared. Thus, architecture and town planning have formed environments for all of the people of the Republic, environments without class imbalances and without essential differences in functional and aesthetic qualtities.

The territory of Czechoslovakia, almost 60 percent of which is forest, comprises some 128,000 square kilometers in the center of Europe and is relatively densely inhabited (116 inhabitants per square kilometer). Notable for the great variety of natural features in its landscape, it is utilized intensively for agriculture and recreation. Collectivization of agriculture began in the 1950s, and the transition to large-scale agricultural production helped abolish basic differences between modes of working and the standards of life of our rural population. This process not only has led to the building up of quite new production complexes for cooperative and state organizations but it also has resulted in changing the character of the landscape, with new groupings of agricultural areas and new utilizations and functional transformations of countryside localities. Changes in the appearance of the landscape and urbanization were in part furthered by the construction of about a hundred large water reservoirs and dam systems, especially on the Vltava and the Váh rivers; and in part by the construction of new power lines and motorways.

Among the network of settlements across the country, no more than some 3 kilometers apart from one another on the average, are many historical towns and villages that have preserved much of their physical structure for over 500 years. This historical heritage was unaffected by the Second World War and continues to determine the architectural character of the countryside.

The preservation of architectural monuments in many historical localities was undertaken by the state after the war. Regulations and acts concerning the preservation of cultural monuments and natural features were effected to control all interventions into the historical environment. As early as the end of the 1940s the government proclaimed the task of reconstructing the historical cores of towns. Today this has been accomplished for thirty-five towns in Czech lands and ten in Slovakia. Almost 40,000 historical buildings and complexes have been included in the list of protected architecture, and the most important of these have been designated as national cultural monuments. In addition to historic restoration and preservation there has been a careful and necessary adaptation of historical towns and buildings to contemporary needs.

Czechoslovakia ranks among the world's leaders in mass housing construction. Over half the population lives in dwellings built after 1945, with the majority in fully furnished flats that average 12 square meters of area per person. Thousands of old flats have been modernized as well; and especially since the beginning of the 1960s a good amount of reconstruction planned for the centers of historical towns has been carried out.

Postwar Nationalized Planning and Industrialization

The development of architecture after 1945 was determined decisively after February 1948 in the new Košice government's program of socialist development for the Republic. This led to fundamental changes in the building industry, particularly in its organization and methods of design. The thousands of private firms with not more than ten employees that comprised the prewar building industry were transformed by nationalization into state organizations, each with several thousand employees. Since the demands for architectural and town planning projects required preparation that exceeded the practical possibilities of individual architects and private offices, larger organizations in which there is extensive cooperation between architects and other specialized building experts were formed. Architecture has become the product of the nationalized planning sector and the large-scale industrialized building industry, and this has led to a tripling of the productive potential of the industry.

Extensive industrial investments after 1945 led to the abolition of both the uneven distribution of economic potential and differences in the living standards between the regions of the Republic. The postwar industrialization of Czechoslovakia is illustrated especially by the development of Slovakia, where industrial potential has increased thirty times. Czechoslovakia belongs to the ten most industrialized countries of the world, whereas its population is less than 0.5 percent of the total world's population.

Postwar industrialization not only followed the structure of historical settlements, but included newly founded towns, localities, production facilities, and transport and power systems all of which reflect the new administrative and economic organization of the territory of the Republic and have led to a balance in the living standards of all inhabitants. The most extensive urbanization took place in Slovakia where the number of inhabitants increased by over one-third. About one-half of some 15 million people reside permanently in towns of about 5,000 inhabitants while the other half resides in villages and small towns. Settlement is being concentrated in urbanized localities of more than 5,000 inhabitants and in so-called center localities of between 1,500 and 2,000 which at the beginning of the 1960s made up the developmental basis of rural localities. A new distribution of working activities in main towns and industrial and mining centers led to reasonable growth trends that, however, have changed the character and structure of Czechoslovakian towns and cities. From these and other historical events since the Second World War, new social motivations for architecture have arisen.

Through understanding, some theoretical concepts underlying the architecture of the 1920s and 1930s have been useful in large-scale practical application and ultimately in syntheses. Functionalism, as exemplified so well in Bohuslav Fuchs's Women's Professional School and Students' Home at Brno of 1931 and Mies van der Rohe's Tugendhat house in the same city the previous year, had been more fully accepted in Czechoslovakia than in many other European countries before the war; and continued to be applied after, but with Functionalism's precepts adapted to the aims of a socialist society. The prewar architectural and town-planning avant-garde had postulated programs which were to be successfully realized only after 1948. Among the fundamental features set forth as early as about 1930 were a fair social solution of the housing problem, the industrialization of the building industry, the introduction of scientific methods into architectural designing, the creation of a scientific and research-oriented basis for architecture and town planning, the establishment of a unified educational system, and an organization that unified the architects of Czechoslovakia. The prewar architectural avant-garde anticipated changes in the social order that led eventually to the transition from a private to a social contract and to new ways of organizing both the building industry and architectural planning.

Since 1929 this orientation was evident in the architects' section of the Left Front (*Levá fronta*). In 1933 the same architects founded the Union of Socialist Architects and, one year later, the Block of Architectural Progressive Unions (BAPS). Comprised of the majority of architects' unions in Czechoslovakia, the continuity of this group provided an impetus for the revival of their programs and indeed their organization immediately after the war. In all of this an important role was played by the Architects' Club and its respected journal *Builder* (*Stavitel*) which ever since the beginning of the 1920s had supported Functionalism and had spread functionalist concepts internationally.

The uniting of Czechoslovakia's progressive-front architects came about at a time when in neighboring countries the most progressive forces of the prewar avant-garde were declining and weakened. The German Bauhaus was dissolved at the beginning of the 1930s, and a majority of modern architects was forced to leave after the ascent of Fascism, when the most progressive social ideas of the avant-garde were consistently suppressed. After the occupation of Czechoslovakia in 1939 it became impossible to develop publicly and fully the efforts of the prewar architectural avant-garde, particularly its left-wing groups. An illegal Club of Architects was formed to discuss the survival of Functionalist principles and to consider new organizational forms of building and designing for a new social system in Czechoslovakia. This ensured a continuation of program efforts and helped prepare for practical applications in postwar Czechoslovakia's architecture.

Postwar Renewal, 1945-1948

The first phase of postwar development was characterized by attempts to renew continuity with prewar functionalist approaches in parallel with the International Style in world architecture. Among the many representatives of the prewar avant-garde who held leading positions in professional and political life after the liberation of Czechoslovakia were Emil Belluš, A. Benš, A. Černý, F. Cubr, J. Fragner, Bedrich Fuchs, J. Havlíćek, V. Hilský, Karol Honzík, Karol Janů, P. Janák, Vladimir Karfík, J. E. Koula, Juraj Kroha, Oldrich Starý, J. Štursa, J. Vaněk, L. Žák. For the most part they designed the most important architectural works, were prominently engaged in theoretical work, and were appointed professors at colleges of architecture in Prague, Brno, and Bratislava.

A close connection with the principal ideas of the prewar period may be traced particularly in architectural programs by the Block of Progressive Unions of Architects (BAPS) and also in the review *Architecture in Czechoslovakia* which had been established by uniting the three most significant prewar reviews *Structure* (*Stavba*), *Style* (*Styl*) and *Builder* (*Stavitel*). BAPS had elaborated functional and master plans for housing which later became fundamental. In the first program of 1945, the BAPS architects asked for the fulfillment of basic demands set down earlier, including the solution of problems connected with the pressing need for new housing, industrialization of mass production, application of modern town-planning principles in building new towns, linkage of town planning with the planning of the national economy, and a further uniting of architects' organizations within the whole Republic.

Immediately after the war, Czech theory of architecture based on the functionalist approach was criticized for its mechanical conception. In addition, new trends concerned with detailing a theory of psychical and aesthetic factors in architecture were becoming more firmly established, especially because of the work of K. Honzík in such books as *Architecture as Physioplastic Creation* (1938), *Introduction into the Study of Psychical Functions in Architecture* (1945), and *Creation of Living Style* (1945). Functionalism was not taken as a doctrine of style but as a way of thinking and creating. Theoretical and conceptual problems of landscaping were treated by L. Žák and E. Hruška. Industrialization of building, the rationalization of design-work and the most efficient ways of carrying out building construction were elaborated theoretically by J. Štursa, but more so by K. Janů in his book *Socialist Building* (1946).

From the continuity established immediately after the war with the thinking and creative experience of the 1930s, there emerged a creative confidence in the possibilities of effecting a great number of well-conceived structures. Among housing complexes we may mention collective housing at Litvínov (figs. 18.1 and 18.2) and Gottwaldov (formerly named Zlín), designed by V. Hilský, E. Linhart, and others between 1945 and 1947. Following functionalist principles of style, these may be linked with collective housing of 1938 in Czechoslovakia. The building of Gottwaldov in a uniform architectural form was attained by systematic standardization of reinforced-concrete construction augmented by unplastered brick walls. Between 1945 and 1948 the new village of Lidice was founded, along with experimental housing estates that were situated in the most industrial areas of the country, such as Most, Rozdělov near Kladno, and Bělský-les near Ostrava. Partial industrialization was involved in the construction of the Solidarity neighborhood unit in Prague [1947-1949].

In addition to prewar Functionalism, the design and building of neighborhoods in the postwar years were based on collectively worked out plans. Besides actual housing-estate designs, model studies of industrial towns and neighborhood units, especially so-called pedestrian communities, were prepared immediately after 1945. In composition, materials, and architectural expression, functionalist principles continued to prevail not only in town planning, but also in certain individual buildings, such as the children's hospital in Brno, the former post office building in Bratislava, and many others. Within the framework of nationwide reconstruction and restoration the architects united in the BAPS collectively worked out master plans for areas in Bohemia which had been destroyed during the Second World War. Simultaneously, the restoration of localities in Moravia and Slovakia, centrally controlled by state authorities, was in full swing.

18.1. V. Hilsky, E. Linhart et al., architects. Collective housing group at Litvínov, 1946-1958. (Photograph: Courtesy of Technical University of Prague)

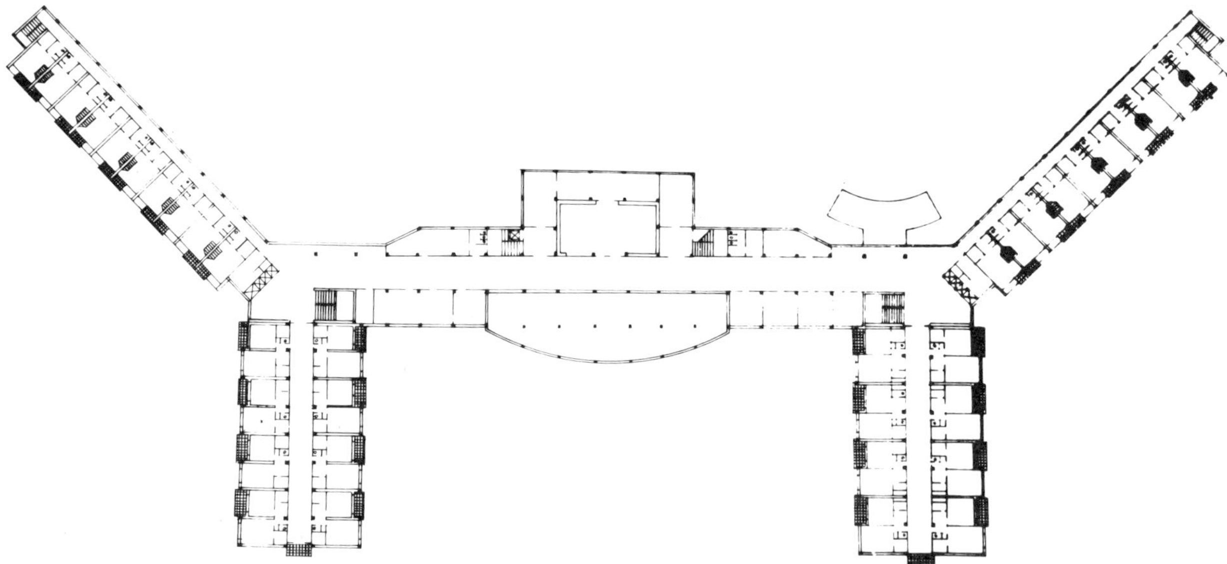

18.2. V. Hilsky, E. Linhart, et al., architects. Plans of collective housing group at Litvínov, 1946-1958. (Photograph: Courtesy of the Technical University of Prague)

Socialist Beginnings: 1948 into the 1950s

The next phase of architectural development in Czechoslovakia was connected with the beginnings of socialist building after February 1948. The change of the social system resulted in nationalization of building which previously had been 90 percent or more privately owned. Conditions were set forth for founding a unified state-controlled design institution, and were included in the Act of Nationalization of the Building Trade in 1948. In the course of that year the first such design institutes, called Stavoprojekt, were established. Among their founders and leading personalities were such significant left-wing representatives of the prewar avant-garde as J. Havlíček, K. Janů, M. Kusý, O. Nový, and J. Voženílek. When the nationalizing of the building trade and the establishing of Stavoprojekt were completed in the late forties to the early fifties, Stavoprojekt with over 11,000 employees and with its great number of architects became one of the largest architectural design-institutes in the world.

During the fifties a great number of other state

design-institutes were established in specialized fields and to facilitate building in particular regions of the republic. Within Stavoprojekt were departments and studios for developing master designs for housing estates, for the reconstruction and protection of historical towns and monuments, and for standardization of architecture. These departments became the bases for later research-and-development institutes in architecture, town planning, and building. A higher degree of scientific management of organization and methods of design ensued that accorded not only with the intentions of Czechoslovak architects, but with the 1948 resolution of the Lausanne Congress of the International Union of Architects (UIA). In 1949 the Institute of Architectural Studies and Standardization was established in Prague and in Bratislava. Here the first standards of capacity, construction, and economic design for blocks of flats and civic buildings were worked out and accepted by all design-institutes. The basis for these standards was incorporated in the so-called Standardization Code of 1951-1952, written by E. Kohn and fellow workers. The first sets of standardized blocks of flats and cinemas were built in Prague, Adamov, and in the Ore Mountains from 1949. From these came also general standards for the production of furniture. For functional town planning to be directly related to national economic planning the first Town and Country Planning Act [1949] and the Institute of Town and Country Planning [1954] were created. By the second half of the 1940s a great number of programs formulated between the two world wars and immediately after the May 1945 revolution were brought into effect. Today Czechoslovakia ranks among the few countries in the world where economic and building changes are controlled by law on a national scale.

At the beginning of the 1950s, with increasing criticism of the technological aspects of society and the one-sidedly Rationalistic sources of the so-called International Style, the Functionalism of the first postwar years was set aside. Czechoslovakia's social-realist cultural basis required increased ideological communication, and simultaneously emphasis was placed upon connections with domestic architectural traditions. The orientation towards social realism was anticipated by the Congress of National Culture in 1948, the principles of which were embraced by the Central Action Committee of Architects in the Czech Socialist Republic and by the first Conference of Czech and Slovak Architects in 1953, at which the foundation of the Union of Czechoslovak Architects was established. The new ideological orientation, however, resulted temporarily in historicism's being erroneously identified with social realism, as in the pristine reconstruction of the historic central square of Telč between 1950 and 1955 by A. Kudrnač, V. Pelzbauer, and their collective group. The use of historical forms and principles, accompanied by the notion that tradition was of great sociopsychic importance led in architecture to a reliance upon traditional structural materials and techniques. Sources of inspiration were sought in the specific features of historical building in Bohemia and Slovakia as well as in ancient Greece. In this spirit houses of culture in Ostrava and Příbram, the monuments on Slavín in Bratislava, and new theaters and schools were built. The architecture of large housing complexes in the district of Ostrava, in Most, Dubnica, and other towns built at the beginning of the 1950s was also affected. The master plan of Ostrava of 1951 by V. Meduna (and collective) was among the first to include broad territorial and functional factors.

The Institute of Building and Architecture of the Slovak Academy of Sciences was founded in 1953. The Research Institute of Construction and Architecture was established in 1954, and historical research was supported at the theoretical institutes of the Faculties of Architecture in Prague, Brno, and Bratislava. With this and an increased interest in historical monuments, buildings were protected by legislation and vast reconstruction and restoration programs were developed. The State Institute for the Reconstruction of Historical Towns and Buildings was founded in Prague in 1954 and the Cultural Monuments Act was passed in 1958. In historical towns selected for historical preservation gradual reconstruction was started. Today the results of this program are evident not only in Prague and Bratislava but also in Český Krumlov, Olomouc, Litoměřice, Nové Město and Metují, Slavonice Tábor, Telč, Znojmo, among others. In the towns of Bardějov in Slovakia and Cheb in West Bohemia particularly complex reconstructions of historical centers were accomplished. Important and vast historical reconstruction occurred at the Prague Castle led by J. Fragner and O. Döbert [1969] and at the Carolinum in Prague, while the restoration of Prague's gardens was accomplished under the leadership of P. Janák and J. Fragner. Much attention was given to the preservation of rural architecture and protection of the folk-architectural-style countryside through the fifties, and in the sixties many country homes were erected.

By the end of the fifties increased claims of the importance of speed and economy in mass building resulted in a decline of interest in historicism and a concentration upon augmenting technological building development. Architectural forms, town-planning programs, and the design of individual buildings started to be affected consistently by industrialization. The continuity and development of building types became an important tool of national construction management. At the same time, Czechoslovakia began to take part in a permanent committee set up in 1956 in the Council of Mutual Economic Assistance (RVHP) for solving questions of standardization in design and for industrializing building.

The idea of standardization in prefabrication was certainly not new to postwar Czechoslovakia. As early as the 1920s architect J. Vaněk mass-produced sectionalized furniture in the UP factories at Brno; and in the 1930s complete bathrooms came off the production line for use in the mass construction of apartment buildings. From 1953 prefabricated mass housing construction began, and from the end of the 1950s construction with reinforced-concrete panels and assembled reinforced-concrete frameworks became widespread.

Developments in the 1960s and After

With the onset of the 1960s Czechoslovak architecture returned to closer connections with prewar traditions, employing new expressive means and stressing functional spatial composition, new constructional forms, and the materials of structure. These concerns have been demonstrated in such public buildings as D. Kuzma's monument to the Slovak National Uprising in Banská Bystrica [1969]; the Crematorium in Bratislava by Milučký [1968]; and K. Hubáček's television tower and hotel on Ještěd [1969], with the latter having been awarded the A. Perret Prize. For its expressive quality Kuzma's remarkable monument (fig. 18.3) deserves particular attention. Set upon an embankment and accessible from the field below by a great stairway, it consists of a long concrete structure upon which a massive saucerlike form is placed, a form broken however into halves. The break, darkened by cast shadow, is aligned with the entrance at the top of the monumental staircase. The narrow chasm on an axis with the entrance, because of the two great concrete hulks flanking it, takes on an unusual volumetric density consistent with the expressive force of the monument as a whole. In Prague the completion of the National Assembly building and the main railway station [J. Danda, J. Bočan, 1978] as well as the subway stations [1969-1979] must also be mentioned. The Czechoslovak pavilion of the 1958 Brussels World's Fair by F. Cubr, J. Hrubý, and Z. Pokorný, confirmed the initiative of our architects by suggesting new elements of architectural style. Following this, Czechoslovak Pavilion of the 1958 Brussels World's expositions at the world exhibitions in Montreal [1967], Osaka [1970], and elsewhere.

A series of experimental housing estates in Prague,

18.3. D. Kuzma, architect. Slovak National Uprising Memorial in Banská Bystrica, 1964-1969. (Photograph: Rajmund Müller, courtesy of the Technical University of Prague)

Plzeň, Brno, and Bratislava around 1960 continued the emphasis upon industrialized techniques and led to an important national discussion concerning housing. The rational distribution of high rises, low rises, and shopping areas is clearly exemplified at Lesná in Brno (fig. 18.4), constructed over nearly a decade [1961-1970] by M. Dufek, V. Rudiš, L. Volák, and F. Zounek. This became a starting point for new types of housing blocks erected throughout the Republic in the 1960s and the 1970s. By the first half of the 1970s for every thousand inhabitants 9.5 flats averaging 70 square meters living area, each with 3.5 rooms, were built. The call for industrialization of construction by the prewar avant-garde became a concrete program after 1945, with its most consistent realization occurring in the 1960s and 1970s. Such success was furthered also by the integration of construction, especially with mechanical engineering and the chemical industry. Ninety percent of the flats built employed industrial methods in standardized projects, and the same may be said for industrial, agricultural, and transport structures. Because of the speed of mass construction and its broad use, architecture has helped effectively to reduce a wide variety of social problems in Czechoslovakia.

Since the 1960s town planning, building, and landscaping have developed further. With the Town and Country Planning and Building Code Act of 1976 the legal bases of construction were clarified and unified more than at any time since the Second World War. Present concepts of town planning have their basis in overall regional plans originally worked out for the major industrial and recreational regions of the nation and furthered in the master plans for the development of Prague [1976], Bratislava, and various regional centers. The centers of towns of all sizes whose plans, architecture, and fundamental functions developed at the turn of the century were reconstructed; and on the periphery of urban areas vast new systems of housing estates that exceeded the sizes of the existing neighborhoods were planned. Among early examples at the beginning of the 1960s are the towns of Mladá Boleslav (O. Döbert) and Nitra (M. Scheer). In larger cities reconstruction has penetrated the historical center of Bratislava under I. Matušík [between 1971 and 1977] while the extensive program at Prague was connected with the building of a north-south trunk road, the underground, and the reconstruction of the Žižkov residential district. Present town-planning theory and practice differs from rather unambiguous functionalist conceptions with segregation of basic urban functions. The transformation of free spatial patterns into systems which are more compact in space and function may

18.4. M. Dufek, V. Rudiš, L. Volák, F. Zounek, architects. Housing Estate of Lesná in Brno, 1961-1970. (Photograph: Courtesy of the Technical University of Prague)

be demonstrated as early as 1963 in experimental new town-planning forms such as K. Honzík's "Domurbia" (fig. 18.5), and four years later in G. Čelechovsky's "Etarea," as well as in designs actually realized in Prague's Southwest Town and in Karlova Ves (fig. 18.6) near Bratislava, the latter built under S. Talaš, J. Fabianek, K. Ružek, and their collective, between 1967 and 1975.

18.5. K. Honzík, architect. Study of "Domurbia" (model), 1963-1965. (Photograph: Courtesy of Technical University, Prague)

Czechoslovak architects are trying to solve problems of contemporary architecture and town planning with a view to the reshaping of the living environment. In Czechoslovakia the ideological roots of this conception go back to the end of the 1930s.

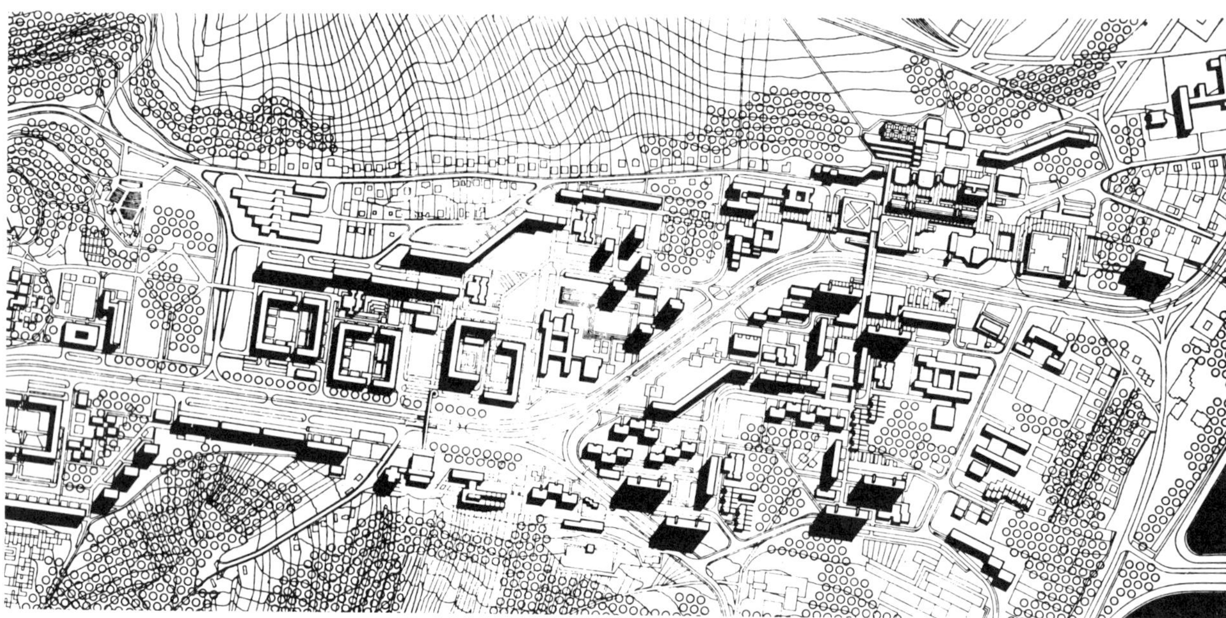

18.6. S. Talaš, J. Fabianek, K. Ružek, architects. Plan of the new Karlova Ves housing estate in Bratislava, 1967-1975. (Photograph: Courtesy of Technical University, Prague)

Since the war the problems of creation and protection of man's environment have been dealt with from the 1950s mainly by Z. Lakomý (*see* his book, *Man Is Changing The World*, 1967). Viable solutions have been offered, thanks to the state plan for scientific research, by a great number of institutions such as the Czechoslovak Academy of Sciences, the Slovac Academy of Sciences, and various colleges of architecture. Theories of architecture and town planning, meanwhile, have become closely connected with the natural (ecology) and social sciences (economics, sociology, social psychology, aesthetics, and semiotics), and a variety of other fields of human endeavor. Architecture and the environment were the main subjects discussed at the Ninth Congress of the International Union of Architects (UIA) held at Prague in 1967; and in 1971 Czechoslovakia took the initiative in organizing a symposium of the European Economic Committee on the protection, reshaping, and development of the living environment. The Union of Architects of the Czechoslovak Socialist Republic, established federally only at the beginning of the 1970s, continues to work well in these directions under the guiding provisions of the social and economic development plan of Czechoslovakia (fig. 18.7). Thus, individual architectural creation and town-planning schemes have moved toward creative designs that meet the needs of Czechoslovakia's society as a whole.

18.7. J. Kulišták, architect. Point block of flats in Prague-Ďáblice, 1975. (Photograph: Courtesy of Zdeněk Voženílek)

Bibliography

BOOKS

Benešová, M.; Pechar, J.; Foltýn, L.; and Procházka, V. *Czechoslovak Architecture of the 20th Century*. Prague, 1967. (Exhibition held in Prague, Havana, Charleroi, London, Moscow, Graz, Vienna, and Geneva.)

Dostál, O; Pechar, J.; and Procházka, V. *Moderní architektura v Československu*. Prague, 1970.

Kusý, M. *Architektúra na Slovensku, 1945-1975*. Bratislava, 1976.

Nový, O.; Pechar, J.; Růžička, V.; Steiss, R.; Titl, L.; Zalčík, T. *Catalogue: 25 Years of Socialist Design in Czechoslovakia*. Prague, 1973. (Exhibition held in Prague, Bratislava, and Warsaw.)

Pechar, J. *Československá architektura, 1945-1977*. Prague, 1979.

Starý, O, a kol. *Československá architectura*. Prague: 1965.

JOURNAL

Kibic, Karel. "Neue Bauten in Prag." *Architektur der D.D.R.* 28, no. 3 (March 1979): 174-76.

19
DENMARK
EDITH S. SANDERSON

Modern architecture has often been seen as the result of efforts to come to terms with, indeed, to effectively use, the tools of industrialization and the resultant strides in technology. Thus the Bauhaus broke with the formal expressions of the past and even with the materials used. In Denmark, however, the development continues, as it has always, to be evolutionary, not revolutionary. Different stylistic periods follow each other in easy transitions. International trends are interpreted with moderation, resulting in neither great excesses nor in monumental landmarks.

In the early 1920s the simplified formal expression of neo-Classicialism that was preferred was questioned, particularly by Poul Henningsen in his journal, *Kritisk Revy*. It was not till the early thirties, however, that the International Style took hold in Denmark, inspired by the Stockholm Exhibition of 1930 (where Sweden's Erik Gunnar Asplund had been responsible for the overall plan and some of the buildings) as well as by the work of Le Corbusier. The modern development, perhaps as a revaluation of moral values, was well suited to the social ideals and programs of the times. Optimistic, rational, and international, it was well adapted to the goals of the welfare state. As practiced in Denmark, functional architecture, though it seemed a clear break with tradition, nevertheless kept its close relation to the crafts movement of the beginning of the century, to common materials such as brick and timber, and to a paramount concern with human needs. Architect Poul Henningsen's PH-lamp, designed in the 1920s, became an avant-garde symbol as proof that function and form were rational, human, and nonconflicting. And architect Kaare Klint's carefully produced furniture that was the result of serious studies of the furniture of other countries and of human needs used highly refined modular systems. As Nils-Ole Lund of the University of Aarhus has mentioned, the cooperation between craftsman and architect became known as "Danish Design" of the 1950s and resulted in another generation of well-known furniture-designing architects such as Ole Wanscher, Mogens Koch, Nanna and Jørgen Ditzel, Børge Møgensen, Hans Wegener, and Finn Juhl.

In Danish buildings Functionalism was combined with a high degree of workmanship that avoided the technical shortcomings so often seen in other functionalist architecture. A most important example of what Kay Fisker named the "Danish Functional tradition" can be seen in the buildings of the University of Aarhus, Jutland. In 1931 Kay Fisker, perhaps too simply described as a historical Classicist, C. F. Møller, and Povl Stegmann were awarded first prize for their plan to place the many different functions of a university in self-contained buildings scattered about a small park that lay near a brook. The first of the buildings, the Chemico-Physical Institute [1933], shows concerns with the effects of materials, with the many modes of expression possible with brick, with a cubic clarity in building volumes, and with a strong relationship with the site. This prototype for later buildings is of yellow brick with white, steel-framed windows and a yellow tiled roof with a 30° pitch. The landscape architect was C. Th. Sørensen. Though substantially finished by 1965, some construction at the university still continues.

The war years were a period of stagnation. Materials were in short supply. The building industry was brought almost to a complete standstill. Those few major buildings finished then had been designed earlier, such as the main building at the University of Aarhus, built under C. F. Møller [1942-1946] (fig. 19.1) or the Aarhus Town Hall (1939-1942] by Arne Jacobsen in collaboration with Erik Møller [1949].

19.1. C. F. Møller. Aarhus University, main building, 1942-1946. (Photograph: Courtesy of Thomas Pedersen)

Most of the best building was of small, semidetached, and terrace houses that could be built with local materials and less advanced technology. Furthermore, there was an isolation from trends in other countries and a psychological desire for a Danish nationalist tradition. Especially noteworthy in this context are Viggo Møller-Jensen's artists' homes at Utterslev Moor. Constructed privately by the cooperative Socialt Boligbyggeri, the small development has twenty-one modest, semidetached houses attractively sited in a former garden.

After the war Denmark faced a housing crisis caused by the years of stagnation during the war, the accelerating birthrate, and the increased migration from countryside to city. The strong solidarity created during the war became the political basis for reforms concentrated on low-income housing and on raising housing standards in general. Government-supported bonds were introduced at low interest to promote building, and regulations were set forth that included criteria for how much should be constructed, the rents, and which people should have first access to the new housing. Bylaws were enacted to regulate building, reduce costs, and improve the use of the available labor force. Since no large-scale construction firms using newer technologies existed, a government center was established for building research. Here were studied assembly-line methods, improved building techniques against cold and humidity, the production process, and the layout of the building site. By the late sixties there was emphasis on advanced management systems, standardization, and modular coordination as well as on urban and regional studies. By the seventies priorities became participation, rehabilitation, energy-conservation, and low-rise, high-density housing. Copenhagen developed a comprehensive approach, the five-finger plan, during the late forties. The hand is old Copenhagen; the fingers are new districts with intact green areas between. Leaving the old center intact was unusual and farsighted in the decades when so many old towns were being razed to make room for the new. Some of the fifty communes that are the fingers are discussed with housing estates below.

By the early fifties the economy had improved and housing built with government help increased. Endless repetition with mass-production housing units led to monotony and urban sprawl. By the seventies 70 percent of all dwellings were single-family units; the building industry had expanded threefold. The output of dwellings had multiplied fourfold, public buildings threefold, and buildings for trade and industry had doubled. Denmark had been changed from an agricultural to an industrial country.

In the midst of monotony many fine estates and projects nevertheless were erected. One of the first was the Søndergårdsparken Estate at Bagsværd [1950] built by Poul Ernst Hoff and Bennet Windinge (architects under the *Dansk Almennyttigt Boligbyggeri*), which remains a most attractive residential area today. Kay Fisker's large Voldparken housing at Utterslev Moor, Copenhagen [1952] has tall and semitall buildings with balconies that provide a strong relief effect. Other developments of this period include the Bellahøj estate with its twenty-eight high rises by Mogens Irming, Tage Nielsen (the master plan), F. C. Lund (Copenhagen's city architect), and others; and Søllerød Park [1953-1955] by Eva and Nils Koppel.[1] Arne Jacobsen also built some housing projects such as the early, youth housing project at Gentofte [1947], the Bellevue Bay project at Klampenborg [1961], and a small and lovely development of individual, linked and terraced houses at Søholm [1950-1955], Klampenborg.

The break from a "nationalistically colored wartime romanticism"[2] can be seen most easily in Jørn Utzon's own house of 1952 at Hellebæk, North Zealand. His is an interest in design with rustic materials akin to the ideals of Wright and Aalto at a time when the influences of America (especially the San Francisco Bay area) and of far-away Japan were beginning. Closed on the north, it opens to sun and woods on the south so that the break between interior and exterior begins to disappear. Here light, topography, and nature are architectural elements. Like Utzon, Erik Christian Sørensen, Halldor Gunnløgsson, Arne Jacobsen, Knud Peter Harboe, Jørgen Bo and Vilhelm Wohlert, Gunnar Jensen, Finn Monies, Harold Plum and Mogens Lassen, Knud Friis and Elmar Moltke Nielsen, and others all built distinguished houses, each different from the others, but almost all showing international influences and exhibiting the beauty of common materials used in a structurally straightforward way that can best be described as the Danish building tradition.

Jørn Utzon's work, however, often showed too bold and dramatic a creative imagination for Danes more comfortable with a simple expression. His much admired project for the Silkeborg Art Museum [1963] was not realized. Among the projects that were built in Denmark are the Kingohusene Court development at Elsinore (Helsingør) [designed 1953, built 1958-1960] and the housing estates at Fredensborg [1962-1963]. At Fredensborg the siting is sculpturally monumental, while the scale of the individual houses is small and comfortable. As with Fredensborg, the estate at Elsinore shows an analogy to Mediterranean towns, but remains strongly Danish. One of the least-expensive projects of its time, its sixty-three court houses undulate across the site to maximize sun and view. But Utzon is best known for his Sydney Opera House [1960-1973] (*see* Chapter 8 concerning Australia). So bold and luxurious in its ideas and forms, it is a statement that requires an enthusiasm and exuberance on the part of the user that seems out of place in the Danish temperament.

Clear individualist statements have long been particularly appreciated in Danish school design. Unlike the standardization preferred or necessary in other countries, Danes have, through architectural competitions, encouraged pedagogical and architectural experiments. The bungalow-type which has been preferred is well exemplified in the Munkegårds School for children aged seven to fifteen at Gentofte [1952-1956] by Arne Jacobsen (fig. 19.2). Its twenty-four standard, single-storied classrooms are arranged

19.2. Arne Jacobsen, architect. Munkegårds Elementary School. Gentofte, 1952-1956. (Photograph: Strüwing-Reklamefoto, courtesy of Royal Danish Ministry for Foreign Affairs)

in a grid system so sited that for each pair there is an ample enclosed adjacent courtyard. Each standard classroom is well illuminated by large windows that look into the courts and with setback clerestory windows. Crossing the classroom pavilions are enclosed corridors, completing the grid and linking with a two-storied pavilion of special classrooms. Landscaping and furnishings, including tables, chairs, lamps, curtains, and even the auditorium stage curtains were designed by the architect. The school, though still functionalist, is brightly rather than coldly formal. Another excellent example of a large one-story complex that exhibits a necessary tidiness and orderliness, simplicity without monotony, is Eva and Nils Koppel's Buddinge School. There form and color are effectively used in a complex that contains a community center, primary grades through high school, a cinema, library, gymnasium, and so forth. Max Brüel, Gehrdt Bornebusch, Jørgen Selchau, and Henning Larsen's Vangebo School at Søllerød [1957-1960] is more robust with unplastered walls, tarred timber, and unplaned wood. Here, contrary to the cool industrialization evident in so much architecture, a natural romanticism shows itself in the individual classrooms, each of which is a self-contained unit with its own garden. The classrooms are linked by low corridors. Jacobsen used a center corridor and large windows and clerestories looking from the classrooms into large oblong courts in his Nyager School, Rødovre [1965]. Among other noteworthy school buildings are: the Hanssted School [1954-1958] by Copenhagen city architect F. C. Lund and Hans Christian Hansen; Fisker's Voldparken School [1951-1957]; Henning Larsen's Klostermarken School at Roskilde [1965]; a grammar school at Grenå [1964] by Johan Richter and Arne Gravers; Worker's High School near Elsinore designed (never built) by Utzon; and Herning High School by Viggo Møller-Jensen and Tyge Arnfred [1962].

Arne Jacobsen was the best internationally known Danish architect, a man who was open to new ideas that he incorporated into his appreciation for the Danish tradition. In his work he combined warmth and humanity, a native sense for order, modular rhythms and proportions, and mathematical precision and refinement. To the few of his buildings already mentioned we need to add a series of office and administrative buildings in which he used internal supporting members and curtain-wall facades, derived mostly from new American techniques. He designed his "simple" buildings with highly sensitive concerns for proportion and detail. The Jespersen and Søn Building [1955] in Copenhagen with its cantilevered reinforced-concrete framework and light curtain-wall facade is a masterpiece of clarity and rationality within and without. Two massive single-story piers, that permit free passage to a courtyard, and in situ cast end-walls with their wooden panelling are continuous with a very narrow strip of wood along the top to frame an exterior grid that is clearly and elegantly defined by aluminum clad bars. Oblong wooden panels and green glass windows alternate in parallel vertical sequences to complete the delicate rectangular design of the curtain walls. Within, each of the two massive, supporting piers is split into two slender columns upon either side of a central corridor. The corridor courses the length of the building to the service facilities, and the remaining spaces of each floor are left free of structural encumbrances, to be arranged as usefully as possible. The Town Hall at Rødovre [1955], using the same structural principle for a three-story office block and a single-story council chamber and committee room annex, is another masterpiece in its handling of seemingly simple masses and in its attention to detail. The outstanding SAS building, Copenhagen [1960] (fig. 19.3) is a two-part unit with a twenty-two story block

19.3. Arne Jacobsen, architect. SAS Hotel Royal with restaurant and air terminal. Copenhagen, 1958-1960. (Photograph: Strüwing Reklamefoto, courtesy of Royal Danish Embassy, Canada)

of hotel facilities set upon a long, low, two-story air terminal and hotel foyer in an almost classical equipoise. The first of Copenhagen's skyscrapers, this mirrors the sun, the sky, and its surroundings near the Central Railway Station. The interior with its delicate, open spiral staircase between foyer and restaurant and its splendid appointments are also Jacobsen's designs. Among his best industrial structures are the Carl Christensen factory, Aalborg [1956], and the Tom Chocolate factory, Ballerup [1961]. Very different is his fortresslike National Bank in the center of Copenhagen [1965-1971], finished after his death (1972). Among his latest realizations were an interior renovation in the American Express Bank, Copenhagen, and a major project, St. Catherine's College, Oxford [1964-1966].

The fifties and sixties brought a marvelous variety of building. The fine design by Kaare Klimt in 1944 for F. A. Thiele A/S optician's shop in Copenhagen was finally realized in 1956 by Vilhelm Wohlert. The Danish master of Functionalism, Vilhelm Lauritzen [airport building, 1937, and Broadcasting House, 1937-1945] built Kastrup Airport, Copenhagen [1957-1960] with Mogens Boertmann, Jørgen Anker Heegaard, and Helge H. Hoppe. A younger architect in the late fifties, Halldor Gunnløgsson, with interest in Japanese ideas and the work of Mies van der Rohe, was designing a severe, classical architecture. An outstanding example is his and Jørn Nielsen's Town Hall at Tårnby near Kastrup [1959].

The Louisiana Museum of Modern Art by Jørgen Bo and Vilhelm Wohlert [1958] is set in a park near the sound. An old villa has been preserved and the new buildings connecting with it by corridors are placed so that one may enjoy the park and the sea through their large windows. Walls are whitewashed brick, roof beams are laminated steel, eaves are teak. Walls inside are white with brownish red tile floors. Here is a contemporary building that has been greatly appreciated, deservedly, by architects and the public, since it is well designed and shows sensitivity as well as modesty in its external effects. Other museums include Erik Christian Sørensen's for Viking boats at Roskilde, Zealand [1963], which projects into the fjord and has three levels for walking and viewing; and Utzon's already noted Silkeborg design.

While craftsmanship remains important to Danish work, technical and economic developments have been changing building. A most important project has been the Herlev District Hospital [1965—] by Jørgen Selchau of Bornebusch, Brüel and Selchau (fig. 19.4). The complex has several buildings including a restaurant and auditoriums, a technical-services area, a religious-services building, a school, an in-patient tower, and a huge building for patient diagnosis and treatment. The long low volume of the diagnosis and treatment building is joined on its longest facade by the tall, asymmetrically located, in-patient tower. Diagonally placed in relation to and linked with the tower is the two-story restaurant structure. On the long side of this, away from the tower and the diagnostic building, two unequal auditoriums, each a one-quarter pie-shape, rise elegantly with their structural supporting elements fanning out from their foci. This is the only activating aspect of the entire group and seems a sudden, small but lovely flourish within the otherwise quite sober complex. The disjointing of the two unequal auditorums signals the sectional, indeed modular, concept of both ground plan and elevations evident throughout. A careful and studied formal Rationalism prevails here, enlivened by boldly colorful treatments of the interiors, treatments that simulate the pop and op art of the sixties. The latest technologies are used here (15 meter by 15 meter module units for maximum flexibility, for example) with great emphasis on quality and cost and with concern for details. The landscape architect is Sven Hansen and consulting engineers for the structure are Johs. Jorgensens A/S.

An interesting new technology of the seventies is a Danish modular system for single-story buildings, especially schools, that allows extensions to 900 square meters in two months construction time. Another is an office furnishings system, easily assembled and variable with four basic components consisting of a sound-absorbing wall panel, a shelf, desk, and chair. And the zero-energy house at Lingby that has been used as an experimental lab by several families is concerned with energy conservation and efficiency. It was constructed by the Technical University of Denmark from Knud Peter Harboe's plan in 1976.

Economic growth slowed in the 1970s. The optimism of the 1960s was tempered by the economic, social, and political realities of the 1970s. The change was reflected in architecture by a tendency of architects to refute the International Style, returning to an interest in Danish history and more concern with the human scale, participation, the existing urban landscape, energy considerations, and rehabilitation, recycling, and renewal of older buildings.

Indicative of the change, Algren, Arnfred, Johnsen and Kragh's (Bureau Vandkunsten) Tinggården Housing Estate in Herfolge [architectural design competition winner, 1971], is unlike the too cold Høje Gladsaxe development near Copenhagen [1964-1968]. These buildings, five sixteen-story

19.4. Jøgen Selchau of Bornebusch, Brüel and Selchau, architects. County Hospital, Herlev; planned 1965, built 1970s. (Photograph: Jørgen Jørgensen, courtesy of Royal Danish Ministry of Foreign Affairs)

blocks with about 1800 dwelling units, built by P. E. Hoff, B. Windinge, J. J. Møller, K. Agertoft, and A. Poulsen (all of whom are more appreciated for other buildings), were most likely a turning point, the last of their type. Tinggården, more human in scale, has six small groups of twelve to fifteen small flats each, with courts and a community building. Using prefabricated elements the estate nevertheless avoids houses built row on row. Another new example, a small group of detached one-family houses in Klampenborg by Finn Groes-Petersen, is grouped around three sides of a court whose fourth side faces the street. The architectural masses are enlivened by the contrasting directions of strips of wooden sheathing applied in sections and by brightly tiled sequences of pitched roofs. Human scale also is characteristic of the student housing for the Viggo Jarl foundation about ten miles from Copenhagen, by architect Jørgen Hersaa, built in the late 1970s. Four low wings built of brick and wood and with large windows face a common court. The standard of building craft is high and the ambience both warm and simple.

Uglegårds School at Solrød, by Halldor Gunnløgsson and Jørn Nielson in the late 1970s, was

19.5. Knud Friis and Elmar Moltke Nielson, architects. Grammar School. Viborg, 1973. (Photograph: Courtesy of Thomas Pedersen)

designed for 900 primary school students. It has eight distinct buildings in two parallel rows separated by a canal. On the side near the sports ground and the playground one row, containing standard classrooms, has flat roofs and module-designed fittings (that is, aluminum light-fixtures, cupboards, shelves, and blackboards). The other row has specialized classrooms (such as the gymnasium, reading room, auditorium) and, for the larger units, vaulted ceilings with skylights. The vaults are mainly of laminated-wood beams. The school is notable for its superb attention to detail. Seemingly different is a school built in 1973 by Knud Friis and Elmar Moltke Nielsen in Viborg (fig. 19.5), a school of which we were made aware by Nils-Ole Lund (Aarhus). From the outside the school presents a rusty steel and concrete facade. However, one enters through a bright yellow porch and finds oneself under a large roof which overhangs the classroom wing and creates a continuous space running the length of the building. Streets, such as in an earlier school outside Aarhus by the same architects, and whose principle can be traced to the parallel corridors of Jacobsen's Munkegårds School, have disappeared. Instead, there is a public meeting place, a square with balconies and steps, a place for people to eat and to read. The materials are crude, the architecture is rather dramatic, yet simple, and the space is elaborate.

Under construction in 1979-1980 near Aalborg in Northern Jutland, Denmark's newest university contains architectural ideas from the past thirty years. The ideology is familiar from the townscape ideas of the 1950s, with architectural drama created by streets, squares, street furniture, trees, and a canal system. Far from any city center, its location accords with a typical solution of the 1960s when one planned for unlimited expansion. The architecture is sturdy and Brutalistic but the scale of buildings is rather small, with all being variations of the same prototype and partly prefabricated. The low, red brick blocks give the university town some of the atmosphere of an anonymous Mediterranean village. Designed by Hans Dall and Torben Lindhartsen, who won first prize in competition for the Aalborg University center, construction was started in 1976 (fig. 19.6 and 19.7). Aalborg University invites comparison with that at Aarhus. The latter is a campus university with buildings scattered in a park; the former is situated in a town in the open countryside and compactly organized where planners expect the future suburbs to be. Both are examples of the best in Danish architecture, products of a tradition of carefully designed, middle-of-the-road architecture.

At Aalborg, too, is the North Jutland Museum of Arts [1958] built by the Finnish architect Alvar Aalto with Elissa Aalto and Jean-Jacques Baruel [1972], where controlled daylight gives the central gallery a unique luminosity. In Odense the Hans Christian Andersen Museum has been renovated, and four new building additions have been lovingly added. This is part of a conservation area in the middle of Odense where the architectural firm of Knud, Erik and Ebbe Lehn Petersen tore down and rebuilt dilapidated housing stock which then proved very saleable. The museum, also by E. L. Petersen, is so carefully done that it blends almost too well into its surroundings. Another recycled building is Copenhagen's Cado Center, designed in 1910 by Ulrik Plesner from the inside out. Though the exterior appears to have five levels, the interior actually has eleven with a variety of ceiling heights and room sizes. In 1972 the young architect, Jørgen Raaschow-Nielsen, won a competition that included 140 architects. In his restoration whatever could be saved was, but what has been added is obviously new. Old and new in effect nod to each other, though they do not mix in this new town square headquarters.

An entirely different appeal is evident at Copenhagen's new Bella Center, by architect Ole Meyer and project manager Erik Jorgensen. While construction is similar to the old Bella Center, the large size and spaciousness and the soaring glass roof give a protected great greenhouse of tomorrow effect. Inside are crossing bridges with the central crossover giving a feeling of weightlessness. New visual relationships are discovered constantly. Though construction costs were low, the amenities were considered, making this a marvelous showplace for Danish design.

In two houses, one by Børge Møgensen with Arne Karlsen at Limfjord [1971], the other by Frank Vestergaard at Herning [1973], a general preference for the more traditional seems now to have been followed. Although one can see fundamental avant-garde ideas in these houses, they also have been pragmatically adapted to their local contexts. Evident is their unpretentiousness, economy of means, respect for materials and for construction techniques. In the Møgensen house quite diverse elements such as odd ceiling heights, varying window sizes, and obviously offset columns, for example, make up a simple harmonious whole that is totally contemporary. At the same time, the architects have chosen traditional elements such as unfinished wood for the ceilings and slightly irregular floor tiles.

Finally, we return to Jørn Utzon. In the 1970s he completed a church at Bagsværd near Copenhagen

19.6. Hans Dall and Torben Lindhartsen, architects. Aalborg University, 1976. (Photograph: Courtesy of Nils-Ole Lund)

(figs. 19.8 and 19.9). The materials are simple: on the exterior, glass roofing, aluminum cladding, bright concrete; on the interior, concrete and some open brickwork, relieved by bright textiles designed by the architect's daughter. Extreme care has been taken in the making of the concrete, and even altar and furnishings are of the superbly finished concrete. The site is uninteresting, and so the architect has concentrated his dynamic, organic creativeness on the interior and its courtyards. The outside may perhaps remind one of an industrial structure in its cool formality. On the inside the softly curved vaulting and the light filtering from between the vaults and from the sides above provide an unforgettable, exciting space. The building is oblong and consists of a four-part complex of church block with its sacristy, office block around an atrium garden, parish hall, and a meeting-room block that encloses a much smaller atrium garden. Each of these four spatial blocks is separated by transverse corridors that join the building's long southern corridor on one side and segments of a corridor on the opposite, more open, long side. All of the corridors are skylighted to permit natural illumination. Thus, the discrete areas of activity behind the church block seem to float in planned regular relation to one another, in the light and space continuum of the corridors.

In the church, itself, the presence of an essentially square plan hardly enters our consciousness, for above us the marvelously turning variations on barrel vaults, waves of light concrete moving in and out from above the altar to high over the main space and down again toward the entry facade, take our attention. They are naturally illuminated by glass panels between them, unseen from within, and on either side light also enters from the corridors. Less dramatic vaulting comprises the roofing system of the office block behind the church space proper. Access to this and the remaining blocks is from the corridors. Details such as the friendly angling of the pews, rows

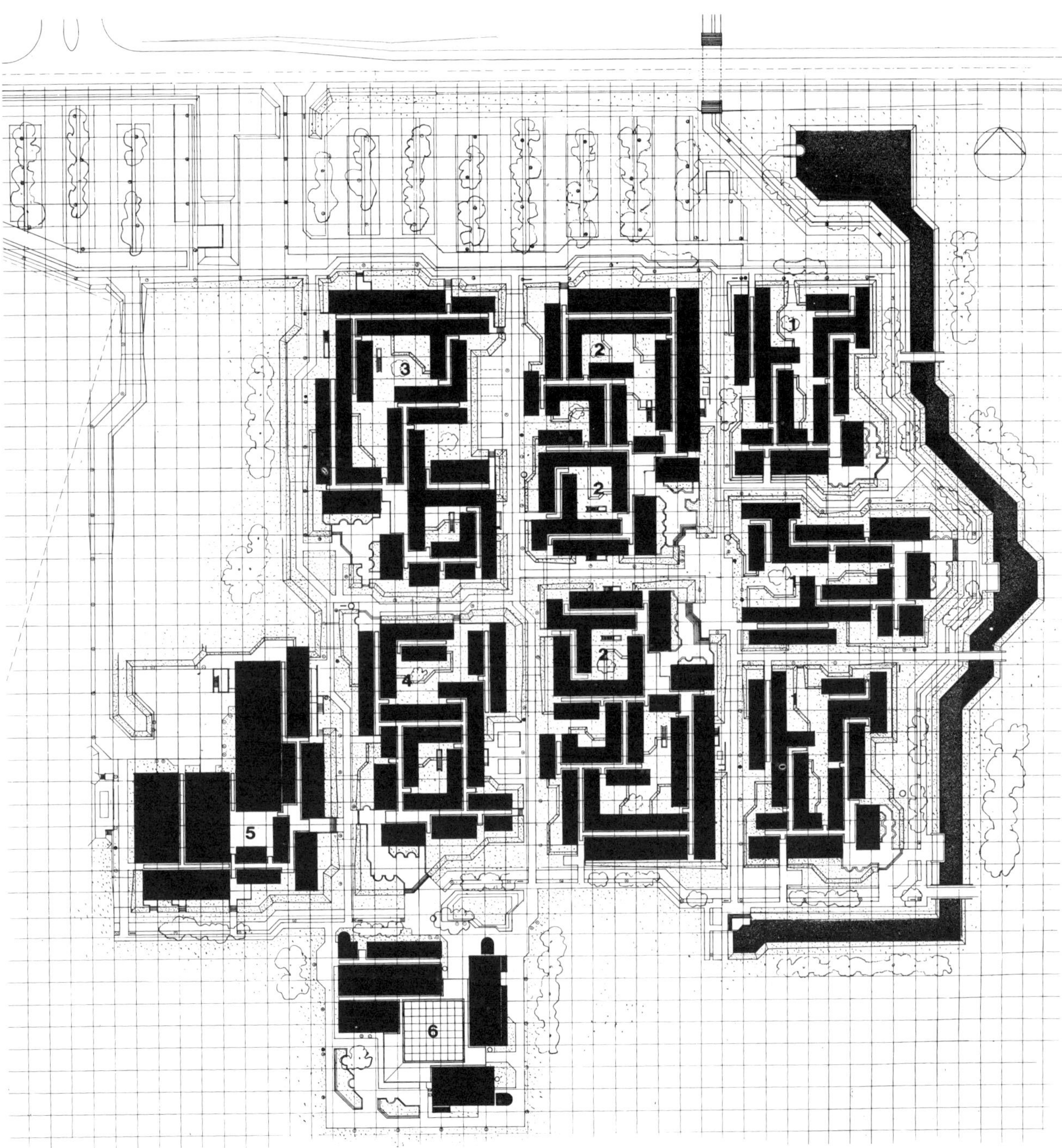

19.7. Hans Dall and Torben Lindhartsen, architects. Site plan, Aalborg, University, 1976. (Photograph: Courtesy of Nils-Ole Lund)

of glowing filaments, and brightly colored textiles add warmth, friendliness, peace. Sigfried Giedion said of Utzon: ". . . he is able to have direct contact with the cosmic elements of nature and the past and also complete control of contemporary methods of industrialized production—especially prefabrication. As a result he is able to detach prefabrication from its purely mechanistic attributes and bring it nearer to the organic."[3]

Danish architecture has come from the neo-Classicism of the 1920s through Functionalism in the 1930s; a nationalistically colored romanticism in the 1940s, through the optimistic Internationalism of the 1950s and 1960s. In the 1970s there were tendencies to return to the national, the historic, the more traditional—the Danish house and Danish functional tradition. Danish architecture has always been best known for its high standards, its conscientious and

19.8. Jørn Utzon, architect. Church at Bagsværd, interior, 1970s. (Photograph: Courtesy of the architect)

workmanlike character, direct expressions with boldness limited by bourgeois solidity. The harmonious relationship between landscape and buildings striven for and achieved by the best of Danish work is the result, said Thomas Paulsson, of integration, not tension. The scale between building and nature is less, therefore the contrast is less apparent. Denmark in the 1980s cannot turn in upon itself. Paul Erik Skriver has explained that a national art will always lead to stagnation or reaction. He sees Danish architecture as an example of a fertility that results from open access to international influence.

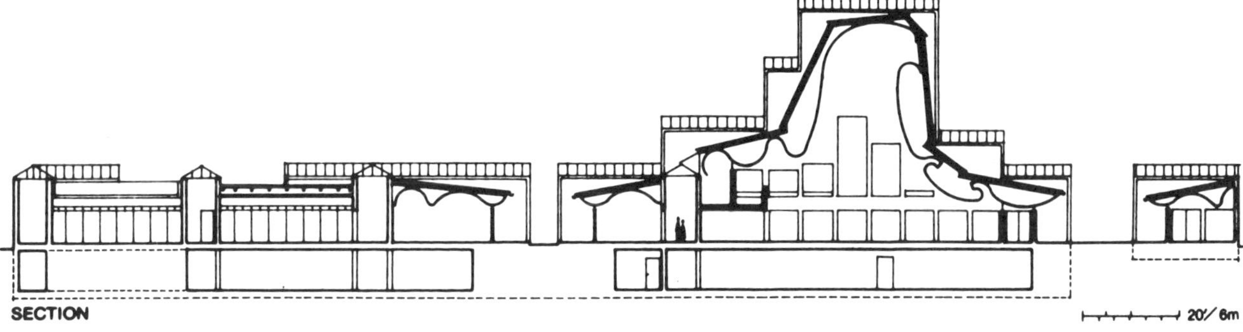

19.9. Jørn Utzon, architect. Longitudinal section, Church at Bagsværd, 1970s. (Photograph: Courtesy of the architect)

The end result, though on rare occasion breathtaking, is most often a moderate and well-done professional architectural solution.

Notes

1. See Tobias Faber, *New Danish Architecture* (New York: Praeger, 1968), pp. 14-18 and M. Jolivel, ed., "L'Architecture au Danemark," *L'Architecture d'Aujourd'hui* (special issue) 24 (June 1949): 40-45.

2. Paul Erik Skriver, "Recent Danish Architecture," *Architect's Yearbook 10*, ed. Trevor Dannatt (London: Elek Books, 1962), p. 104.

3. Sigfried Giedion, *Space, Time and Architecture*, 5th ed. (Cambridge, Mass.: Harvard University Press, 1967), p. 678.

Bibliography

BOOKS

Dyssegaard, Søren, ed. *Arne Jacobsen, A Danish Architect*. Copenhagen: Ministry of Foreign Affairs, 1971/1972.

Faber, Tobias. *New Danish Architecture*. New York: Praeger, 1968.

Fisker, Kay and Millech, Knud. *Danske Arkitekturstrømninger 1850-1950*. Copenhagen, 1951.

Habegger, Jerryll. *Europe Architectural Guide 1860-Today*. Chicago: Habegger, 1974.

Langkilde, Hans Erling. *Arkitekten Kay Fisker*. Copenhagen: Arkitektens Forlag, 1960.

Monies, Finn. *Wood in Architecture*. New York: F. W. Dodge, 1961.

Monies, Hjort Røgind. *Contemporary Danish Architecture*. Copenhagen, 1956.

Paulsson, Thomas. *Scandinavian Architecture*. London: Leonard Hill, 1958.

Richards, J. M., ed. *Who's Who in Architecture*. London: Weidenfeld and Nicolson, 1977.

Skriver, Paul Erik. "Recent Danish Architecture." *Architects' Yearbook 10*. Edited by Trevor Dannatt. London: Elek Books, 1962, pp. 104-23.

JOURNALS

"Aarhus' School of Architecture 'Den Jyske Arkitektakole'." *Arkitekten* Copenhagen 78, no. 9 (11 May 1976): 165-93.

Addington, Peter. "Housing in Denmark." *Royal Institute of British Architects Journal*, February 1977, pp. 62-67.

"L'Anti-design est un art de vivre." *L'Architecture d'Aujourd'hui* 178 (March 1975): 69-77.

"Casa dello studente per le fondazione Viggo Jarl, Copenhagen, Architetto Joergen Hersaa." *L'Architettura* 12 (April 1977): 702-8.

"Copenhagen's Recycled Cado Center." *Interiors* 134 (September 1974): 102-11.

Diamant-Berger, Renée, ed. "Architectures Nordiques: Danemark." *L'Architecture d'Aujourd'hui* 134 October 1967): 46-69.

______. "Pays Nordiques: Danemark." *L'Architecture d'Aujourd'hui* 93 (December 1960): 42-55.

"15 M. System by René Block for single story buildings." *Domus* 546 (May 1975): 14-15.

Giedion, Sigfried. "Blick auf die nordische Architektur." *Zodiac*, no. 12 (1963), pp. 66-81.

"The 'Great Greenhouse' of Design—The New Bella Centre." *Interiors* 136 (September 1976): 16.

"Hans Christian Andersen Museum in Odense." *Architectural Journal* 169 (25 April 1979): 847-52.

Heide, Erik. "Kunst und Bau, Ravnsbjergkirken, Viby, C. F. Møller's Tegnestue, Aarhus, Dänemark." *Bauen und Wohnen* 32, no. 3 (1978): 121-24.

Jolivel, M., ed. "L'Architecture au Danemark." *L'Architecture d'Aujourd'hui* (special issue) 24 (June 1949): 1-57.

"North Jutland Museum of Arts, Aalborg, Denmark." *Architectural Review* 153 (March 1973): 155-67.

"Open space at Ballerup, DK." *Domus* 549 (August 1975): 44-45.

Palumbo, Roberto; Pennestri, Giancarlo; and Crespi, Giulio Rossi. "L'Ospedale di Herlev presso Copenhagen, progetto di Jørgen Selchau." *Casabella* 38, nos. 392-93 (August, September 1974): 17-32.

Schneidratus, Werner. "Architecture and Housing in Denmark." *Architektur der DDR* 28, no. 1 (January 1979): 34-40.

"Siedlung 'Tinggården' in Herfølge." *Baumeister* 77, no. 2 (1980): 180-81.

Tintori, S. "Kay Fisker, architetto danese." *Casabella* 239 (May 1960): 4-21.

"Uglegårds School." *Architectural Review* 159 (March 1976): 190.

"Wohnquartiere." *Baumeister* 77, no. 5 (1980): 462-66, 486-89, 500-501.

"The Zero Energy House: Lingby." *L'Architecture d'Aujourd'hui* 192 (September 1977): 57.

20

FINLAND

ROSALIE STALEY and SARAH McCUTCHEON

Cultural Heritage and Nationalist Romanticism

In Finland where man and nature exist in delicate balance, a modern architecture of imagination and integrity has developed. Adapting itself to the rugged land through the scientific-aesthetic genius of architects such as Alvar Aalto, Aarne Ervi, and Aarno Ruusuvuori, it is an architecture that reflects love of place in the midst of harsh winters, and that communicates social responsibility while surmounting environmental odds. Thoughts of Finland conjure up images of vast birch and pine forests, green in summer, intensely dark in winter amid the changing northern lights. Ice plays upon the rugged, island-dotted coastline in winter, sculpting glasslike designs on land and rock. The feeling of space in Finland has inspired Hudson Street's poetic comment: "Everywhere there is a feeling of infinite space beneath the sky. Space for a grown man's breathing. . . . It is not the same sort of space one finds in the monotonous pampas of Argentina, where one may suffer acute agoraphobia. It is a companionable space where man can speak to the earth and where nature knows the code that reaches mankind's heart."[1]

The affection of the Finnish people for their forested spaces is evident in an age-old preference for wood in both furniture design and architecture. From early Finnish history, not only farms and barns were built of wood, but also churches, country houses, and entire towns. Due to frequent fires, old wooden architecture is disappearing. Yet its charm remains: "For the connoisseur of the vernacular styles of building, Finnish towns are fascinating places, full of unrecorded treasures and unexpected variations on a common theme."[2] Imaginative contemporary uses of wood are readily seen in balconies, stairs, and exterior sculptural designs for buildings as well as in the paneled ceilings of Aalto, among others.

Climate and topography have been important in forging a unique modern architecture in Finland. A careful choice of sites and appropriate landscaping of buildings are distinctive features of Finnish architecture. In the design sketches of the outstanding Finnish architect Alvar Aalto, surrounding landscape features are often depicted with as much emphasis as the building forms. Indeed, it is virtually axiomatic that a Finn would rather build around a tree than take it down. Tall trees afford both important building materials and also pleasant views. Rocky surfaces, the surrounding sea, and lakes, hills, and terraces are integral to Finnish design. Conceived on a human scale, contemporary buildings in Finland do not dominate the land but become part of their sites. There are few skyscrapers; most high buildings are only six or eight stories, and are juxtaposed harmoniously among the older buildings around them.

Within the original plan of Helsinki, the capital largely rebuilt acording to the plans of C. L. Engel [1778-1840] during the first half of the nineteenth century, outstanding modern buildings by such architects as Alvar Aalto, Aulis Blomstedt, and Kaija and Heikki Siren coexist graciously with the monumental styles of the early part of this century by Eliel Saarinen, Selim Lindqvist, and Lars Sonck. Finnish towns, many of which were spawned by twentieth-century industrialization are characterized by an air of modernity. Often, new satellite towns with their civic centers, schools, universities, hospitals, and sports complexes have been totally planned and designed by outstanding contemporary architects. Throughout Finland there is an almost uniform type of housing complex, usually with two or three levels and large balconies or terraces surrounded by trees. Here good design and quality craftsmanship often become part of daily Finnish life.

Despite its proximity to the cultural and political pulls of both Sweden and Russia, Finland has maintained its own strong identity. Annexed at different times to both countries, the Finnish people have managed to avoid assimilation and have asserted an independent character which finds a vital outlet in their architecture. Yet, as J. M. Richards asks, just how has Finland, a small country with a population of less than five million, and a brief national history, been able to continue to make major contributions to contemporary architecture internationally?[3] The answers he has suggested are that: (1) architects and architecture enjoy considerable prestige in Finland; (2) Alvar Aalto's international reputation invites further building; (3) the country's competitive system offers opportunities to young architects and thus allows an expansion of new ideas; (4) industrialization has rapidly brought technology into Finnish resources; (5) the climate's severity offers the discipline of challenge; and (6) a consciousness of national identity finds its expression in architecture.[4] In omitting considerations of the aesthetic beauty of Finnish architecture Richards has left out a major source of appeal for the visiting architect or writer. In order to understand more fully the special qualities of Finnish buildings and Finland's contemporary international prominence in architecture, one must consider other factors as well. An examination of the evolution of styles and design during Finland's short national history (since 1917) will help explain how Finnish architecture has so quickly achieved the prominent position it has held in the contemporary scene.

The first half of the twentieth century had produced a number of outstanding "national" architects, so that by 1945 conditions were favorable for the development of a mature, modern Finnish architecture. At the turn of the century a national romantic movement in the arts and literature revived folk legends, motifs, and forms, such as the original Karelian log cabin, and found new expression in the creative architecture and interior design of that time. Three architects, Eliel Saarinen (1873-1950), Armas Lindgren (1874-1929), and Herman Gesellius (1874-1916) were responsible for several exceptional buildings which very consciously reflected the stylistic ideals of a national identity. The nationalistic style of the National Museum of Helsinki [1905-1912] featured indigenous rough-cut granite with a life-sized stone bear at the entrance and other cultural forms carved in sandstone. Offices and lodgings built by Saarinen, Lindgren, and Gesellius [1902-1904] as a retreat at Hvitträsk outside Helsinki reflect the same qualities with much of the interior displaying rough wooden beams to resemble the traditional log cabin. The furnishings as well as the design are a Finnish development of the Arts and Crafts movement of this period. The romantic nationalist school of architecture culminated in Saarinen's design for the Helsinki Railway Station [1907-1914] which, despite its reinforced-concrete structure, marked the end of a nostalgic architectural concern for the past. Already by this time there were signs of a new internationalist aesthetic developing in Finnish architecture as ideas were exchanged with the outside world. While for many the years before 1927 were of no importance for the spread of the new architecture, during the teens and the twenties "functionalism actually put into practice what the preceding decades had prepared."[5] Certain new aspects of architecture such as the absence of ornamentation, the free floor plan, and the prominence of structure had already evolved in Finland in the twenties. Late in the 1920s leading Finnish architects such as Aalto, Erik Bryggman, Hilding Ekelund, and Pauli Blomstedt developed functionalist styles with simplicity and a sense of social meaning. From then on the very personal and innovative architecture of Alvar Aalto [1898-1976] loomed in the forefront of developments.

Architectural Solutions, 1928-1940

Finland adopted the bold new architecture of the International Style only in the thirties, though earlier efforts to introduce it had been made. At the height of the previous national romanticism when embellishment and neo-Classic facades were favored, Sigurd Frosterus's design for the Helsinki railway station won second prize to Saarinen's. The former's international rational design, in the style of Mies Van der Rohe, was criticized as an architecture brought from abroad and not part of the Finnish establishment's tradition.[6] Sigurd Frosterus, architect and theorist, went his own way in the twenties and thirties advocating international Rationalism with Gustaf Strengell and setting the pace for the international Functionalism of the thirties. For Frosterus the architecture of the future required an economical use of materials, a minimum of decorative display, and confinement to structural needs.[7] His largest building, the Stockman department store [Helsinki, 1924-1930], reveals an emphasis upon vertical construction typical of the second decade of the century, with its interior representing an intelligent, functionalist solution to problems of lighting (including a skylight) and with expansive open space at each store level.

Alvar Aalto's influence emerged during the late twenties and thirties when he began to articulate his own, unique style and laid the foundations for the development of an internationalism in Finland. Despite its modernism and dependence on technology and innovation, Aalto's architecture was very much rooted in the history of Finnish building, as he himself made clear in 1922:

> The serious and esteemed study of our old local architecture and its enduring values is already so important for us as professional architects that it has become a basis for our work. . . . Architects . . . should draw the public's attention to our architectural heritage and emphasize its ideas and their artistic value in order to prepare a favourable reception for modern architecture.[8]

An interest in asymmetry and in the dividing of a building into effective spaces that evolved in the work of Aalto and others in the twenties led to the more loosely defined, open-plan design which was a hallmark of Functionalism. Le Corbusier's works, known in the late twenties in Finland, had influenced both Blomstedt and Aalto, as well as Bryggman, and it was the clear vision of these Finnish architects that was largely responsible for the adoption of the new style. In turn, emphasis upon the structural nature of reinforced concrete, so prominent in Aalto's commission for the standard block of flats in Turku [1927-1929], helped achieve an early modernization of this building type.

Two functionalist works in the thirties by Aalto brought prominence to Finland and to their architect, the Tuberculosis Sanitorium at Paimio [1929-1933] and the Viipuri Municipal Library with Aino Aalto [1927-1935, destroyed 1940]. At Paimio, Aalto also developed the first mass-produced, shaped plywood chairs which came to have international impact. The undulating wood strip ceilings of the auditorium at Viipuri reflect the beginning of a warm romantic style which he would continue in other works.[9] At Viipuri Aalto developed a new approach to architecture, softening the functionalist lines of the International Style with romantic and textural elements. In his concerns for such details as the acoustics of these buildings, as well as all of their spatial and programmatic elements, Aalto personified a new humanism in architecture.

In his Sunila housing estate and cellulose factory [designed in 1936-1939; extended 1951-1954] Aalto set forth architectural and social concerns which would be emphasized on a broader scale by other architects after the war to meet new housing and industrial needs. The Sunila factory was imaginatively planned to harmonize its successive levels dramatically with the rugged land on the steep edge of an arm of the sea and to allow for close docking of ships.[10] The Sunila employees housing estate consists of parallel blocks on the southern slopes of an undulating site. Viipuri and Sunila show us Aalto's architectural maturity with his loosening of traditional forms, a confident handling of materials, sculptural modeling of masses, and a consciousness of the social responsibility that was shared by Bryggman and others.

Erik Bryggman (1891-1955) worked in Turku with Aalto to 1933, remaining there after Aalto's move to Helsinki. He designed a number of buildings at Turku, including a hotel [1929], a library [1936] for the Abô Akademic Swedish-language university, an insurance company [1938], and a chapel [1939]. This Chapel of the Resurrection (fig. 20.1) with its powerful concrete form and its delicate window lighting seems almost a prefiguration of Le Corbusier's Ronchamp on a smaller, perhaps more human scale.

20.1. Erik Bryggman, architect. Funeral Chapel. Turku, 1939. (Photograph: Courtesy of the Embassy of Finland)

There were, by the beginning of the Second World War, many notable examples of functionalist architecture in Finland including the work of such architects as Hilding Ekelund [the church at Töölö, Helsinki, 1929], O. Flodin and E. Seppälä [Tampere railway station, 1936], J. S. Sirén [the office building of Lassila, Tikansja, Helsinki, 1935], Lindegren and Jäntte [inventive Olympic Stadium, Helsinki, 1934], and Erkki Huttunen [cubistic church at Nakkila, 1937, and industrial building at Oulu, 1938]. Huttunen also made several designs for wooden houses with standardized parts, thus anticipating prefabricated houses.[11] Architect Pauli Blomstedt (1900-1935) designed such outstanding works as the Finnish Savings Bank in Helsinki [1939], a hotel at Rovaniemi [1936], a church at Kannonkoski [1938], and the distinguished Aulanko Hotel [1938]; all were built posthumously.

Finnish Architecture After 1945

Functionalism still had its opponents in Finland who felt it had overrun their land as a packing-case architecture. Perhaps, from the form of white stuccoed houses with stone or board walls and a shed roof seen as a flat roof, it deserved this name. The Second World War had interrupted the functional tradition of modern architecture but the disruption became a creative one,[12] forcing Finnish architects to design with ever-limited materials, counterbalancing monumental aspects of their Functionalism. From Sweden a type of romanticism appeared which, while still using modern techniques and materials, spiritually countered the hard line of Functionalism.

Following the Second World War, 2 percent of the Finnish population had been lost, another half-million people were displaced from the province of Karelia which was occupied by the USSR, many areas had been very badly damaged, and the country's most impelling need was to resettle 15 percent of the Finnish population in new housing.

In 1941, Aalto wrote a proposal for mass-produced housing which he hoped would avoid the building of inhuman, barrackslike villages. He emphasized that standardization must occur in a way that allowed for variation and flexibility, in consideration of man's complex and changing needs.[13] In 1942 the Finnish Association of Architects set up a standardization institute headed by architect Viljo Revell to develop houses suitable for the reconstruction project. But critic Aslo Salokorpi among others, had a dim view of this organization: "The activity of the group may indirectly have been responsible for spreading the stereotyped, ridge-roofed, single family house throughout Finland, regarded as the worst step backwards in modern Finnish architecture."[14] The need for housing had an effect on the development of established Finnish architects and gave new opportunities to younger architects. Meanwhile Alvar Aalto, in his own work, began to pay increasing attention to problems of regional and urban planning.

Aalto's affinity to Frank Lloyd Wright in the late forties became evident in his freer, more organic mode of design. Aalto, moreover, was a leader who especially encouraged younger architects. During the rebirth of creative building in Finland in the fifties Aalto's use of brick and wood, as well as his organic sculptural approach to architectural design complemented his rational and humanistic philosophy. In the beautifully sited Säynätsalo Town Hall complex [1950-1952] (fig. 20.2) his originality shone forth. The organization of its widely variegated spatial elements and the juxtaposition of its masses around a compact inner court posed atop a not-too-monumental staircase, as well as its somber brickwork, results in a generally monumental but not monolithic impression. The natural wood ceilings in its red birch interiors and their lighting add to Säynätsalo's warmth. Both scale and form subtly express genuinely human qualities. Aalto never forgot that a monumental building can be remarkably human in its scale, as one of his last buildings, Finlandia Hall in Helsinki [1967-1971] again demonstrates (fig. 20.3). Finlandia Hall is located at the focal point of the plan for the center city, opposite the National Museum by Gesellius, Lindgren, and Saarinen [1910]. The first stage of the hall, involving two concert halls (with 1750 and 350 seats) was constructed in 1967-1971; the second stage, with a conference center, was constructed in 1973-1975. Finlandia Hall, with black granite and white marble on the exterior and containing his most elegant auditorium, has been termed Aalto's finest large building.[15]

Until Finlandia Hall was completed the largest civic building constructed in Helsinki since the Second World War had been Timo Penttilä's Civic Theater [1964-1967] (fig. 20.4). While Finlandia Hall intervenes in the city's center, the Helsinki Civic Theatre, a tactile, expressionist building, is skillfully sited in parkland. Though particularly reminiscent of Aalto's mode, blending the monumental with the organic and yet relating to human scale, Penttilä's building presents "a tough-minded clarity of detail"[16] that places him in the architectural milieu not only of Aalto but also of Ervi and Pietilä. Indeed, with this building Penttilä took his place in the forefront of Finnish architecture.

Viljo Revell (1910-1964) and Aarne Ervi (1910-1977) both of whom were Aalto's students in the thirties, established and developed their own reputations during the fifties. Revell became one of

20.2. Alvar Aalto, architect. Town Hall Complex. Säynätsalo, 1950-1952. (Photograph: Courtesy of Museum of Finnish Architecture)

20.3. Alvar Aalto, architect. Finlandia Hall, Helsinki, 1967-1971. (Photograph: Courtesy of the Embassy of Finland, Ottawa, Canada)

20.4. Timo Penttilä, architect. Civic Theater. Helsinki, 1964-1967. (Photograph: Courtesy of the Embassy of Finland, Ottawa, Canada)

the most influential of architects in Finland, taking up new industrialized techniques and encouraging younger architects as had Aalto. He is most widely known for the Palace Hotel in Helsinki [1952] designed with Keijo Petäjä and for the City Hall of Toronto [completed 1965] (fig. 20.5) with Heikki Castren, Bengt Lundsten, and Seppo Valjus and built with John B. Parkin Associates. Inclined more toward a rationalist than a sculptural approach to monumental building projects such as Toronto's City Hall or Buenos Aires's Peugeot Building [1962], Revell shared with other architects in the use of reinforced concrete, as seen in his 1954 flats at Tapiola. He could also be quite sensitive and refined, as in his apartment buildings at Helsinki. Revell designed each of his buildings in partnership with one or another of the architects in his office, thus facilitating the continuation of his methods and craftsmanship.[17]

20.5. Viljo Revell, with Heikki Castren, Bengt Lundsten, Seppo Valjus and with John B. Parkin Associates, architects. Model of City Hall. Toronto, Canada, 1965. (Courtesy of the Embassy of Finland, Ottawa, Canada)

Aarne Ervi's interests included investigation into prefabricated structures. He employed them in his Institute Building of the University of Helsinki [1951]. The "Portania" building [1957] marked the first use of prestressed- and precast-concrete construction in Finland. His Turku University Library in 1954 shows a more classic simplicity and a somewhat less adventurous design than in Aalto's work. Perhaps one of Ervi's best works is the Administrative Center [1961] (fig. 20.6) for the satellite

20.6. Aarne Ervi, architect. Administrative Center, Tapiola, 1961. (Photograph: Courtesy of the Embassy of Finland, Ottawa, Canada)

town of Tapiola, suburb of Helsinki that was begun in 1952 and planned for expansion to 1966. Ervi won the competition for the layout of the town with a design consisting of three residential neighborhoods of equal size, each with a mixture of terrace houses and apartment dwellings built to a low density among trees and roads. The main administrative center of Tapiola is a thirteen-story white concrete office-tower block with a restaurant on the top floor. The winner of a competition of 1954,[18] this administrative center is most effectively characterized by night illumination.

Some dozen different architects have designed houses and apartments at Tapiola over the years. The overall effect is aesthetically pleasing as well, with large buildings and smaller houses virtually sculpted into the rolling, pine-forested land, each structure expressing a pure geometric harmony with nature and with the buildings around it. Only enough forest is cleared for the three widely spaced neighborhoods and the administrative center; the human scale of building seems gentle and friendly in its natural setting. Among the exceptional buildings at Tapiola are a group of studio houses by Aulis Blomstedt [1956], each with a terrace and balcony; a block of apartments by Viljo Revell [1954] raised on *pilotis* and constructed of prefabricated, reinforced-concrete units; a quadrangle enclosed by apartments, again by Viljo Revell [1958]; and a row of luxurious yet understated houses by Kaija and Heikki Siren [1959]. The latter houses make use of a sloping site above road level with the living rooms, posed over double garages, extending into balconies facing south. The Sirens' work is striking in its harmonious blend of dark woods with lighter brick, so appropriate for the natural setting. Tapiola was, unfortunately, the exception in housing plans, a very large-scale project that made full use of the talents of outstanding architects. Although criticized by some for its free-form planning and luxurious land use, its buildings have been almost unanimously highly praised.

Since the early sixties, many housing projects in Finland have incorporated prefabricated parts and industrial structures, accounting for some of the similarity of housing units in different parts of the country. Nevertheless, many of the developments reflect a concern for careful planning and a respect for the environment that have come to be embodied in strict environmental laws and housing policies. Building permits are issued only after careful consideration by municipalities of the designs and even the colors to be used; the sizes of building lots are regulated and only a certain number of trees at a building site may be taken down. All of these considerations have contributed to a high level of building so that there are now far fewer poor new buildings in Finland than in other countries.[19]

Kaija (b. 1920) and Heikki (b. 1928) Siren, while influenced by Aalto's use of brick, have developed a style of their own, often showing a particular virtuosity in handling wood. The interior of the restaurant for students of the technical university at Otaniemi is a good example of a scientific and aesthetically pleasing approach to a wood ceiling carried by wood frame supports. Wooden struts and ties, held together with iron straps and bolts, create a work at once very well engineered and sculptural. The Sirens's Otaniemi Chapel [1956-1959, destroyed by fire, 1975] exemplifies their architectural philosophy that a building should be unobtrusive and very much part of its surroundings. Inside, an altar is simply and elegantly designed to harmonize with a view of the forest outside and, carefully planned to help integrate building with environment. An austere white cross located outside the chapel is visible through the glass behind the altar. The architects related the basic features of this chapel to the traditions of old Finnish church-building:

> Our old stone churches have always been stark and ascetic in character. . . . Even very early on, our wooden churches used the roof structures as features of the interior. This method also fits in with modern trends. The only decorative motif in the restrained Lutheran church is the altarpiece, marked by the various styles of each era.[20]

On their vacation island, Lingonso, the Sirens have built their own chapel [1966-1969], a rectangular structure of wood frames for glass walls with a view to the sea across the granite ridges upon which it rests. They have also designed a prefabricated housing unit of wood paneling for use in northern regions [1968] as well as several individual private houses, apartments, and public buildings which are especially characterized by simplicity of form and the use of natural building materials.

Another outstanding architect is Aarno Ruusuvuori (b. 1928) who realizes his excellent sense of form in reinforced concrete, steel, and glass. Le Corbusier's influence may be seen in Ruusuvuori's church at Huutoniemi [1964], where a masterly combination of a tough and functional approach to building materials is combined with a well-lighted interior. Ruusuvuori's Weilin and Göös's printing works [1963-1964] at Tapiola expresses the somewhat primitive, yet abstractly rational qualities of his style; a style reflecting the poetic-scientific accomplishments of Le Corbusier.

If there is a new Romanticism present in Finnish architecture of the 1960s, Reima Pietilä (b.1925) must be cited as one who shuns Rationalism and affirms a greater freedom in creating architectural forms.[21] While Aalto sought to bring a warm humanity to international Rationalism through his technological and aesthetic approach, Pietilä wished to avoid architectural norms and the fetters of geometry. His Kaleva church at Tampere [1964-1966] (fig. 20.7), a freely formed spatial design enclosed by a series of vertical concrete chutes rising on a low hill at the end of the town's main street, won first prize in a competition in 1959. Here attention is paid to function amid intersecting spaces, and a feeling of unity and quiet space predominates in the sanctuary. Detail is rendered as carefully as the larger forms. Pietilä's design of the Dipoli Center at the Finnish Institute of Technology at Otaniemi [1961] with Raili Paatelainen (fig. 20.8) takes as its starting point the established cavernous spaces of the Student Union [1903][22] and, with a freer sculptural form, imparts to its original romanticism a modern conception of sheltered spaces. Dipoli contains occasional, disconcertingly nonfunctional aspects, such as the contrast between outer free-form designs and its more rectangular nature. On balance it is a fine building with a roof that is lively, weaving and twisting above the large and smaller meeting rooms; and with stairs that are elegantly designed to benefit from a play of light upon their surfaces. Dipoli is entirely wrapped in copper, which as Pietilä anticipated, gradually has mellowed toward the color of the pine grove in which it was built. Pietilä's Student Union building contrasts with Aalto's work (fig. 20.9) at the same institution. They each justify the considerable attention school architecture has received in Finland.

20.7. Reima Pietilä with Raili Paatelainen, architects. Kaleva Chapel, Tampere, 1966. (Photograph: Martii I. Jaatinen, courtesy of the Embassy of Finland, Ottawa, Canada)

20.8. Reima Pietilä with Raili Paatelainen, architects. Dipoli Students' Union Building. Otaniemi, 1964-1966. (Photograph: Courtesy of the Embassy of Finland, Ottawa, Canada)

The innovative secondary school at Kulossari [1955] by Jorma Järvi (1908-1962), the pioneer of modern Finnish school building,[23] has a spectacular brick and wood paneled assembly hall with stairs dramatically bracketed along the wall leading to

20.9. Alvar Aalto. Finnish Institute of Technology. Otaniemi, 1955-1965. (Photograph: Ingervo, courtesy of Museum of Finnish Architecture)

classrooms on the floors above. Kaija and Heikki Siren's Pappitansalmi secondary school at Hamina [1962] is a more functionalist school design, based on a central plan: its two levels of classrooms, administrative offices, and various other rooms are organized around a large two-story gymnasium-assembly hall. The open spacious quality in its many rooms may be modified as required by means of elegant wooden folding doors; and paneled wood-strip ceilings soften the effect of overhead lighting. A multifunctional secondary school in Helsinki, designed by Erik Kråkström, Kirom Mikkola, and Juhani Pallasmaa in the 1960s, is constructed as two adjacent buildings in brick and wood: one, central in plan, houses a large meeting hall and classrooms; the other, with sports facilities and kitchen, is designed to serve the public in the evenings and on weekends. Both were built in two levels with large areas of fenestration throughout and with several large skylights providing natural light for the central meeting hall.

The exciting design of the new Oulu University [1971-1981] by Kari Virta Associates (Erkki Viennen and Perkki Ahtianen, engineers) is central in plan and on a much larger scale. A focal auditorium is accessible from the various campus buildings by means of a system of glassed-in pedestrian channels. Brushed concrete and brightly painted, stove-enamelled aluminum sheeting on the exterior together with a sleek industrial interior, in bright primary colors, make this a visually stimulating, innovative complex that is equally appealing against the white snow of winter and the green trees of spring. Although its brightly colored industrial forms may seem to have more in common with the Centre National d'Art et de Culture Georges Pompidou in Paris than with the natural Functionalism of Alvar Aalto, Oulu University reflects a very different social attitude and sense of history. Unlike the Centre Pompidou, which was built in the midst of the former Les Halles marketplace as an intervention in the city, the new Oulu University campus was designed outside of the town of Oulu in a new urban area planned at the same time and by the same planners.[24]

Respect for the surroundings of a building and a sense of social responsibility are recurrent in Finnish architecture. One of Alvar Aalto's later buildings, the Akedemic Bookstore in Helsinki [1969], stands next to Sigurd Frosterus's Stockmann department store [1924-1930] to which it belongs. The bookstore space consists of low, booklined galleries (accessible by escalators) contrasting with and enclosing an airy open central hall that employs sculpturesque skylights to maximize natural illumination.

A recent project commissioned by the Tammisaari Town Council, a new library and adult education institute, was built by architects Ola Hansson and Pekka Manner in 1977, alongside a group of old Empire-style houses constructed in wood during the 1870s and 1880s. Three of these original buildings had already been converted into a library, school, and kindergarten when the new complex, which occupies an area roughly equal to that of the older buildings, was integrated so naturally into the site that it now is difficult to recognize where the old ends and the new begins. In the new Tammisaari Center a remarkable virtuosity is evident in the combining of features of the past with functional, new designs, as for instance in its hipped roof, with wood strips and beams visible on the interior.

Although there has been ample criticism by Finnish architects of the excessive bureaucracy and planning affecting architecture during the seventies, there seems to be evidence of a renewed humanizing attitude in the work of individual architects such as Juha Leiviska [Cultural and Religious Center of St. Thomas, Oulu, 1976], Virta Associates [University of Oulu, 1971-1981], and Osmo Mikkonen [the architect of an outstanding suburban Helsinki elementary school and of a sausage factory in Riihimaki, 1977].

From their efforts and others we may look forward to Finnish architects continuing their expressions of influential ideas in both the international and regional arenas.

Notes

1. Matti Saanio and M. Jäätyy, *Where the Gulf Stream Freezes* (Helsinki: Kustannusosakeykitiö Otavana Syvätaino Publishers, 1972), p. 36.
2. J. M. Richards, *A Guide to Finnish Architecture* (London: Hugh Evelyn, 1966), p. 57.
3. Ibid., p. 84.
4. Ibid., pp. 84-85.
5. Aslo Salokorpi, *Modern Architecture in Finland* (London: Weidenfeld and Nicholson, 1970), p. 14.
6. Egon Tempel, *New Finnish Architecture.* (New York: Praeger, 1968).
7. Ibid.
8. "Alvar Aalto," *L'Architecture d'Aujourd'hui* 191 (1977): 122.
9. Salokorpi, *Modern Architecture*, p. 26.
10. Richards, *A Guide to Finnish Architecture*, p. 79.
11. Ibid., p. 77.
12. Salokorpi, *Modern Architecture*, p. 35.
13. Alvar Aalto, *Post-War Reconstruction, Rehousing Research in Finland* (New York, 1941).
14. Salokorpi, *Modern Architecture*, p. 37.
15. Steven Groak, "Finlandia Hall 1967-1971," *Architectural Design* 49, no. 12 (1979): 18-21.
16. Malcolm Quantrill, "Après Aalto, une Nouvelle Vogue?" *Architectural Design* 49 (December 1979): 22.
17. Salokorpi, *Modern Architecture*, pp. 40, 41.
18. Richards, *A Guide to Finnish Architecture*, pp. 90, 91.
19. J. M. Richards, *800 Years of Finnish Architecture* (London: David and Charles, 1978), p. 154.
20. Erik Bruun and Sara Popovits, eds., *Kaija and Heikki Siren, Architects*, 2d ed. (Helsinki: Otava Publishing Co., 1978), p. 33.
21. Edward Marc Treib, "Pietilä: Rebel in Finland," *Architectural Forum*, December 1967, p. 75.
22. Salokorpi, *Modern Architecture*, p. 43.
23. Richards, *800 Years*, p. 160.
24. "Università Quasi Polare," *Domus* 574 (September 1977): 24.

Bibliography

BOOKS

Alander, Jyosti, ed. *Viljo Revell.* New York: Praeger, 1966.

Bernier, George and Bernier, Rosamond, eds. *The Best in Twentieth-Century Architecture.* New York: Reynal and Co., 1970.

Brunn, Erik and Popovits, Sara, eds. *Kaija and Heikki Siren, Architects.* 2d ed. Helsinki: Otava Publishing Co., 1978.

De Biasi, Mario. *Finlandia: Profile of a Country.* Helsinki: Tammi Publishers. (Printed in Zurich, Switzerland by Konjet and Huber.)

Dunster, D., ed. *Alvar Aalto.* (Architectural Monographs No. 4.) New York: Rizzoli, 1979.

Fleig, Karl. *Alvar Aalto.* New York: Praeger, 1975.

Fleig, Karl, ed. *Alvar Aalto, 1963-1970.* London: Pall Mall Press, 1971.

Joedicke, Jurgen. *Architecture Since 1945.* London: Pall Mall Press, 1969.

Kallas, Hillar and Nichels, Sylvie, eds. *Finland: Creation and Construction.* London: George Allen and Unwin, 1968.

Leskinen, Jyrky, ed. *Facts about Finland.* 16th rev. ed. Helsinki: Otava Publishing Co., 1979.

Petaya, Keyo; Hansson, Olof; Ruusuvuori, Aarno; Alander, Kyosti; and Helenius, Pentti. *Helsinki Architectural Guide.* Helsinki: Otava, 1965.

Richards, J. M. *800 Years of Finnish Architecture.* London: David and Charles, 1978.

———. *A Guide to Finnish Architecture.* London: Hugh Evelyn, 1966.

Saanio, Matti and Jäätyy, Missä Golfvirta. *Hvor Golfstrommen Fryser* [*Where the Gulf Stream Freezes*]. Helsinki: Kustannusosakeykitiö Otavana Syvätaino Publishers, 1972.

Salokorpi, Aslo. *Modern Architecture in Finland.* London: Weidenfeld and Nicholson, 1970.

Seminar on Architecture and Urban Planning: Towards Democratic Planning. (Finland 1971, Government Bulletin.) Helsinki: Government Printing Center, 1972.

Sharp, Dennis. *A Visual History of Twentieth-Century Architecture*. Greenwich, Conn.: New York Graphic Society, 1972.

Tempel, Egon. *New Finnish Architecture*. New York: Praeger, 1968.

JOURNALS

"Abbey Library." *Architectural Review*, June 1972, p. 344.

"Actualités Finlandaises." *L'Architecture d'Aujourd'hui* 199 (October 1978): vii-xv.

"Alvar Aalto." *L'Architecture d'Aujourd'hui* 191 (1977): 57-125.

"Alvar Aalto." *Progressive Architecture* 58 (April 1977): 53-77.

"Centre culturel et religieux St. Thomas, Oulu, Finlande." *L'Architecture d'Aujourd'hui* 198 (February 1977): 24.

"English Summary." *L'Architecture d'Aujourd'hui* 134 (October/November 1967): clxxxiii-clxxxiv.

"Finland: Export Design." *Progressive Architecture* 51 (March 1970): 74-79.

"Finnish Vernacular." *Architectural Review*, March 1968, 229-32.

"Helsinki." *L'Architecture d'Aujourd'hui* 156 (June 1971): 40-42.

"Identité et différence." *L'Architecture d'Aujourd'hui* 178 (March 1975): 78-79.

"L'église à Kannelmaki, Helsinki, Finlande." *L'Architecture d'Aujourd'hui* 152 (October 1972): lix.

"Per Studenti in Finlandia." *Domus* 576 (November 1977): 9-13.

"Profile 25: Aalto and After." *Architectural Design* 49, (December 1979): 1-38.

"Salisicoce a Catena." *Domus* 568 (March 1977): 9-11.

"Università Quasi Polare." *Domus* 574 (September 1977): 22-29.

Pearson, Paul David. *Alvar Aalto and the International Style*. New York: Watson-Guptill, 1978.

Quantrill, Malcolm. "An Architect of Genius." *London Sunday Times*. 3 September 1978.

______. "Après Aalto, une Nouvelle Vogue?" *Architectural Design* 49 (December 1979): 22.

Treib, Edward Marc. "Pietilä: Rebel in Finland." *Architectural Forum*, December 1967, pp. 74-79.

Whittick, Arnold. "A Guide to Finnish Architecture." *British Journal of Aesthetics*, April 1969, pp. 202-20.

21
FRANCE
YVES BRUAND

The Historical Situation

THEORY AND PRACTICE: 1920–1950

During the years between 1920 and 1940 France contributed effectively to the birth and development of international Rationalism, but her contribution, major in making and refining doctrine, proved limited in turning doctrine into architecture. Though some few buildings played an exemplary role, modern architecture remained a very minor part of French construction. Since 1945 it has been quite different as political, social, and economic conditions evolved rapidly. Government authorities, very conservative during the Third Republic, became more open to the Modern Movement in the Fourth (1945-1958): first-rate architects were offered official commissions thanks to the understanding and the action of a few dynamic personalities. The evolution accelerated from 1958 under the Fifth Republic which made Rationalism an official style and launched a number of prestigious operations made possible by economic expansion. Even more important is the fact that the construction market found it had to respond to new and immense needs. While between the two wars France had experienced a deep despondency because of population stagnation, economic crisis, and the consequences of the rent-control law, the situation was very different during the postwar period. First, the cities destroyed in battle or by bombing had to be rebuilt, a task actively undertaken in the years following the liberation and finished only during the following decade. Then, from 1950, real estate promoters gradually took over, encouraged by new legislation favorable to the rise of private construction. The enormous need for living accommodations in large or medium-sized areas was caused by the aging of available housing stock, insufficient renovation during the past thirty years, demographic growth coupled with rural exodus, and a continuing acceleration of urban concentrations. These factors gave architects and developers a huge market which was rapidly augmented by the demand for office buildings and public edifices. The building explosion was the result, as well, of the growth of old cities and the birth of new ones. The accelerated industrialization of areas and the renovation of outdated factories, as well as the setting up of large sectors for leisure activity, completed the panoply of construction sites all over the country. The volume of the demand and the need to work fast encouraged the use of modern artificial materials (reinforced concrete, steel, glass). It also encouraged mechanical standardization and simple forms, large complexes of boxlike buildings, and contributed to the triumph of mass construction. Though mediocre, the new buildings led to a break with the past and to the creation of a different urban panorama in which there were applied, well or badly, the principles elaborated by the pioneers of modern architecture during the first half of the twentieth century. One cannot stress too strongly the importance of phenomena which, in France, constituted a real revolution in professional methods and in the public mind. There were, of course, a certain number of failures, as many sociologically as aesthetically, because of the absolute priority given to extreme economy. These failures, moreover, were at the root of a dispute during recent years concerning the partial reevaluation

Translated from the French by Elise Bernatchez and Priscilla Veitch, Montreal.

of the principles of the pioneers. Generally, architects did not lack work and the most qualified were able to express themselves in first-rate programs so that this period was also characterized by intense activity on construction of very rich quality.

On a theoretical level, the postwar years were not marked by intense reflection in French professional circles. While in the United States and in Italy a passionate debate developed with the partisans of Organic (Rationalist) Style, this quarrel had no repercussions in France. The strong personality of Le Corbusier, paladin of the latter movement and polemicist without peer, had monopolized the attention of the adversaries of a still very strong traditional current in the immediate postwar period. Thus, it was that the theories elaborated in the twenties came to be applied without much rethinking. The efforts of French architects were directed more toward building and methods of construction than toward architectural thought itself. No doubt educational establishments played a role in this.

THE EDUCATIONAL STRUCTURE

Architecture was taught in two Parisian schools, l'Ecole National des Beaux-Arts and l-Ecole'Speciale d'Architecture, and in thirteen regional schools founded in 1904. Priority was given to the first school, which was dependent upon the Institut de France and ensured academic tradition, for it was the only school that opened the royal way to the Prix de Rome and to important state commissions. The anachronistic character of its training has often been pointed out. Preference was given on the one hand to drawing and classical forms at the expense of research in technical and aesthetic usage of contemporary materials (metal, glass, and reinforced concrete), and on the other hand to the study of arbitrary programs which did not correspond to twentieth-century priorities. While the tests for the Prix de Rome fell justly under a great deal of criticism, the preparation for the competition was only the final part and not the whole of the curriculum. Graduates of the Ecole des Beaux-Arts were well aware of functionalist theories and the writings of the great masters of international Rationalism beginning with Le Corbusier, and there are many who applied these ideas in their work.

Though the holders of the Prix de Rome had to submit to a discipline which was somewhat archaic, they did not lose their creative imagination nor did they lack necessary technical knowledge, as seen in the works of Henry Bernard, Bernard Zehrfuss, Jean de Mailly, and Guillaume Gillet, the leaders of an original architecture based on plays of volume and on concrete structures. Selection was no doubt far from perfect as with any competition. Strict rules for the presentation of drawings were in any case excellent training; and it is not by chance that, after a period of laxity, there is interest again in old projects as a subject of study. The events of 1968 upset teaching structures completely. The student revolt and the action of André Malraux, the minister of culture responsible for this sector, caused the breakup of the old schools into pedagogical units of architecture which then were multiplied in Paris and in the provinces. The new system of open admissions added enormously to the number of applicants for a degree, now given very liberally, and created enormous problems of organization and problems for the professional marketplace. The curriculum, previously oriented toward the technical and toward architectural design, was enlarged by adding cultural subjects with sociological emphases. Theory then tended to dominate practice, which was sometimes completely neglected. Thus, the return to preoccupation with architectural theory was not always beneficial. The reform of architectural studies today is concerned with the laxity in structure and discipline at certain institutions and the reestablishment of a better equilibrium between theory and practice. It also has as its aim limiting the large surplus of future architects who will have little chance for qualified employment under existing market conditions, especially since the economic crisis which has hurt the construction industry.

ARCHITECTURE AS A PROFESSION

The architect's career is a liberal profession demanding large financial means. An architect must have a large administrative and technical staff not only for the project itself, but also in order to coordinate programs, do market studies and act in close collaboration with real estate promoters. The present tendency is toward agencies directed collectively and with a preeminent, dominant personality. In current programs there is constant collaboration with industry, and the use of systematically standardized materials for costing purposes at times permits the engineer to take the place of the architect. The need for a qualified engineer or architect was in fact not obligatory until the passing in 1978 of a law on architecture. That gives the profession guarantees in the name of architectural quality for the fight against the proliferation of tacky construction found pretty much everywhere. This same law envisages the installation in all French Departments of architectural councils directed by state architects to guard quality and to advise individuals on the construction of their residences. Launched several years ago in the Lot

Department in an experiment to protect the region's urban and, above all, rural landscape, this effort paid off with excellent results and fits into the ever more salient concern with the renewal and protection of the ecology.

Postwar Reconstruction and Urbanism

REBUILDING CITIES

In 1945 some important cities which had come under heavy attack and most of the large ports were totally in ruins, while in others entire districts had been razed. The Ministry of Reconstruction and City Planning had studies made by its architectural services of types of general plans and developments conceived on the scale of the destroyed cities and districts, in which the notion of reestablishing the urban fabric as it had been was discarded and new groupings were planned wherever the magnitude of the ruins justified them. They were in fact only repeating on a larger scale experiments which had been carried out during the war for towns damaged during the French campaign of 1940. In many cases the classic style of a street lined with houses was maintained. In Caen the architecture chosen for such houses was deliberately traditional, with stone facades and slate roofs to conserve local color. In other cases, as in Maubeuge, where André Lurçat worked, and in Dunkerque, Calais, Boulogne-sur-Mer, Brest, and Toulon, buildings were grouped in an uneven fashion to make very airy islands, applying some of the principles of the Charter of Athens (1933). In the Old Port of Marseille a synthesis was attempted between a Rationalist architecture composed of quadrilateral blocks and a Mediterranean style incorporating porticos and loggias. Planned 1945-1956, the results were not always very happy, for buildings considered individually were often austere, without character, and built with an eye to economy; but, in all, coherent groups of buildings were formed under the direction of the chief architects in authority.

A prestigious operation was undertaken in 1945 at Le Havre, a totally flattened town, for which Raoul Dautry, Minister of Urbanism and Reconstruction, called upon seventy-one-year-old Auguste Perret, who had become one of the official eminences of French architecture after having been long unappreciated by the authorities. A pioneer in reinforced concrete and one of the first to use its technical possibilities for practical and aesthetic purposes, Perret had created, since the beginning of the century, an original, strong, and severe style which had evolved toward a classical Formalism based on the use of the new material. For him, the reconstruction of Le Havre (fig. 21.1) was a windfall and a crowning reward. There, he was able to affirm his conception of a monumental urbanism: broad axes and open or closed perspectives emphasizing particular buildings; a concern for geometric regularity and a use of squared orthogonal frames; and the adoption of a module applicable to the buildings as well as to the spaces they delimit. There was an affirmation of a rigorous architecture with well-defined proportions indelibly marked by its creator in exposed

21.1. Auguste Perret et al., architects. View of the reconstructed Harbor area of Le Havre, 1947-1954. (Photograph: M.R.L., courtesy Photothèque of the Documentation Française, Paris)

concrete, a facade structure with bearing elements evident, a cornice, high windows, and discretely colored filler walls. Though Perret had surrounded himself with a team of young collaborators, reserving for his own efforts only the city hall, its neighboring buildings, and the Saint Joseph church, the whole of the city reconstructed from 1947 to his death in 1954 was clearly determined by him. Its unity is indisputable but its success is less certain. The urbanistic conception, striving to be revolutionary on the technical level, remained very much attached to classical tradition as much in its layout as in its formal basis. As for the architecture, it clearly derived from models established by its author between 1920 and 1940 and maintained a severe and slightly gloomy harmony. The reconstruction of Le Havre, as all of Perret's work in the immediate postwar period, seems therefore more of a prolongation of the past than an opening into the future. This attitude moreover was typical during the years 1945-1950, when no proposal that advocated the CIAM's urbanism and the Charter of Athens was accepted. Le Corbusier himself, in spite of the reputation he enjoyed abroad, saw himself excluded by the authorities and his project for the erection of a new city core in Saint-Dié was swiftly abandoned.

SUBURBAN AND URBAN CONSTRUCTION

After 1950 the very great need for new housing led to the construction of large complexes on the periphery of cities in suburban agglomerations. The principle of groups of houses distributed more or less uniformly upon vacant lots or formerly agricultural terrain taken over for this purpose prevailed systematically. Low and elongated slabs were more evident than high rises, though there often was a mixture of both building types. The same held true for urban planning in isolated blocks which was generally preferred to organization in continuous series. Necessary services for apartment buildings were housed either on the ground floor or more often in low buildings specifically in the center of a complex. This new conception, giving preference to dense, community-oriented living in the midst of green spaces (or spaces that would become green) and with a renunciation of the classical shopping street, resulted in a profound break with the past. Consequences in the life-styles of tenants and apartment owners were quickly perceptible, as the Rationalist theoreticians of the CIAM had predicted, but the inconveniences outweighed the advantages. Programs were in fact dominated most of the time by economic considerations, which took precedence over all others and produced a monotonous and mediocre architecture. Moreover, one of the main points of the Athens Charter was not respected: with the advent of dormitory cities workers were forced to make long daily journeys. This phenomenon was particularly obvious in the Paris area where the town of Sarcelles [1956-1972] on the outskirts north of the capital was the typical example of mass housing conceived between 1950-1960. A reaction appeared, however, when Emile Aillaud tried to counter the stereotyped orthogonality of large complexes by giving a flexible layout to his buildings, making them wind across the terrain [*Les courtilières* at Pantin, 1959-1961], then completing the curves with a colorful liveliness and a very studied treatment of the surrounding space [*La Grande Borne* at Grigny, 1967-1972]. This return to plastic preoccupations in inexpensive constructions certainly did not solve the fundamental problems but tended to diminish them by providing a more hospitable setting.

From 1960 large complexes little by little penetrated the cities themselves. Numerous renovation projects took place in the peripheral areas of Paris and in the provincial metropolises, even in the medium-sized cities, in certain cases reaching into the heart of built-up areas. It was no longer a question, however, of residential programs but of the creation of business zones dominated by enormous office buildings, possibly associated with residential accommodations. The first project of this kind was the development of the Défense area in the west of Paris, outside the administrative limits of the capital but along the axis of the broad perspective of the Tuileries-Etoile. The master plan of Raymond Lopez, evolved since 1951, imposed an ordered architecture consisting of a series of high rises placed in a quincunx of identical molds, connected by a flagstone covering (over infrastructures) used for pedestrian traffic. The principles expressed by Le Corbusier (placement of buildings, strict zoning, differentiated circulation) thus found specific application in the Défense district. The choice of site permitted an autonomous development and avoided a break in scale with the town planning and historic architecture of Paris. Unhappily, the modification of the original plans and inordinate height of some of the towers broke the expected unity and stupidly altered the purity of the Champs-Elyssés perspective. Raymond Lopez's team, responsible for working out the master plan for the city planning of Paris applied the same principles in other major renewal projects: Maine-Montparnasse, the Front de Seine, the Italie quarter, all carried out from 1960 to today with complete contempt for the environment. The brutality of these badly implanted grafting operations and their tendency to be colossal, coupled in many cases with remarkable plastic mediocrity, led to a setback for Rationalist urbanization which was denounced as inhuman. The year 1974, which saw the death of Georges Pompidou, an unconditional partisan of Modernism, and his replacement as President of the Republic by M. Giscard d'Estaing, much more cautious in this field, marked a turning point in official policy concerning these matters. The delay of the program forecast for the renovation of Les Halles quarter was no doubt a sign of this. We won't dwell on the modernization of provincial cities which used the same criteria and which was pursued with the same vigor almost everywhere. The transformation of Grenoble for the Winter Olympic Games in 1968 was particularly extensive. Lyon, Marseille, and Montpellier can be cited as examples of the creation of new business centers near the old heart of the city. In Toulouse and in the urban community of Lille, with the Mirail and Villeneuve d'Asq sections, actual parallel cities sprang up which were destined to live in symbiosis with their larger neighbors as well as being new cities in themselves.

NEW TOWN DEVELOPMENT

The idea of new towns, conceived from the beginning as poles of development incorporating all urban functions in the image of their English homonyms which were born after the Second World War, did not take hold until 1965, though Candilis's projects for Toulouse-Le Mirail date from 1961. Determined to avoid the spotty and haphazard expansion of the large metropolis, these new French cities are especially numerous in the Parisian area. The conditions of their implantation were quite varied. Some were created on vacant, fairly isolated sites such as Evry, the new prefecture of the Essonne, the Vaudreuil near Rouen, and Isle d'Abeau near Lyon. Cergy, a new prefecture of the Val d'Oise, is juxtaposed with the old town of Pontoise. Créteil, new prefecture of the Val-de-Marne, is a complete remodeling of an already existing small built-up area. Saint-Quentin-en-Yvelines and Marne-La-Vallée is a regrouping of scattered communities. Development plans anticipated a large population expected to rapidly surpass 100,000, with numerous jobs in secondary and tertiary sectors and first-class community equipment. Priority was given to the latter and to construction of monumental centers, regrouping them so as to have, from the beginning, real cities with an active core. Again the principles of Rationalist urbanism were systematically applied, at least in the first developments. A return toward more traditional conception, however, has recently appeared in the organization of dwellings. Thus, the plans for the future residential districts of Cergy show the reappearance of the street as an essential element of articulation and animation without, however, renouncing the principles of contemporary architecture in terms of functional requirements.

Finally, it is necessary to mention the appearance of a last category of new towns that has the very particular function of leisure cities at mountain resorts or along the coast. The first were in response to the needs created by the vogue for skiing. Situated in high mountainous areas on virgin and precipitous sites, they multiplied between 1960 and 1975. Though at Flaine (Haute-Savoie) Marcel Breuer, as a good disciple of Gropius, wanted to organize the space and the totality of the landscape in a pure and austere architecture of a Bauhaus lineage, at other locales there was an attempt instead to effect integration with the environment by designing continuous buildings that followed the lines of relief of the mountains and were animated by multiple horizontal and vertical breaks. The use of natural materials such as the red cedar tiles at Avoriaz (Haute-Savoie) by Charles Labro, Jean-Jacques Orzoni, and Jean Pierre Rogues did contribute to the desired effect in certain cases, but Jean-Claude Bernard showed similar concerns at Tignes and at La Daille (Savoie) while restricting himself to industrial products. From 1962 the development of the Languedoc and Roussillon coastline into tourist areas with a distinctive character, to avoid the wild and continuous urbanization which disfigured the Côte d'Azur, gave rise to coherent complexes with very separate personalities. This program was made possible thanks to the massive intervention of official authorities who furnished the necessary credit for the cleaning up of an unsanitary shore line, for the planning of the units in question, and for beginning the work. Very diverse solutions were adopted. At La Grand-Motte (Hérault) Jean Balladur opted for a marvelous work of pyramidal buildings that stressed decorative structures on the flat and characterless landscape. At the Cap d'Agde (Hérault) Jean Le Couteur sought, on the contrary, to recover the spirit of a Mediterranean village without succumbing to pastiche. At Port-Leucate (Aude) and Port-Barcarès (Pyrénées-Orientales), Georges Candilis adopted a Brutalist conception in which, on the exterior, the concrete blocks making up large blind walls with successive breaks remind one of construction games while on the interiors there was an attempt at intimate solutions organized around patios.

French city planning since 1945 has, therefore, been closely controlled insofar as all large operations were conducted under the aegis of and with credit from the state or local communities. The role of the architects-in-chief charged with carrying out projects was essential and their personalities played a large part in the directions which were taken. After a fairly timorous first period, corresponding to the immediate postwar period and the reconstruction, the Rationalist vogue, directly inspired by the theories Le Corbusier expressed as early as the decade of the twenties, prevailed with an often excessive brutality. Only in particular limited programs, such as certain Alpine winter sports resorts, was this more or less eluded and an effort made (1965-1970) to take the environment into consideration. The contempt for natural and historic contexts led to a reaction in public opinion and among concerned authorities, which was translated, from 1974, into a condemnation of gigantism and notably of high rises in medium-sized cities and in the center of important built-up areas. The forming of tracts grouping single-family houses has taken precedence over large developments, but this evolution which has moreover coincided with the slowing down of economic activity since the oil crisis of 1973 has posed a number of problems (availability of land, extension of widely spread communities, distance). The search for more human and less technical solutions, better suited to the aspirations of a population conscious of ecological problems, is now clearly discernible.

Major Architectural Tendencies and Principal Projects

PERRET AND HIS SCHOOL

Having become one of the stars of official architecture at the age of seventy, Perret was entrusted with many tasks immediately after the liberation. First, naturally, there was the reconstruction of Le Havre (fig. 21.1), where he reserved the main buildings for himself: the city hall, its neighboring buildings [1947-1954] and the Saint Joseph church [1949-1956]; but he also planned Marignane airport near Marseille [1947-1952], the development of the square at the railroad station of Amiens [1947-1948], dominated by a high-rise building more than 100 meters high; and, finally, established the overall plan for the Nuclear Studies Center [1948-1953] of Saclay in the suburbs south of Paris. These monumental works confirm the extraordinary stability of Perret's work. He remained faithful to his first principles: the use of reinforced concrete, an externally visible framework, terraces, cornice moldings, windows the height of a man so that air and light could penetrate right to the floor, church walls treated in *claustre* (perforated concrete), the plays of decreasing and varied volumes of steeples, belfries, and towers, and an eggshell-thin vaulting cleverly buttressed in his industrial buildings. Each building, besides, derives directly from previous works by Perret in which its theme had been developed. Formal Classicism had been adapted to a new material.

Perret trained many disciples who followed the line traced by the master, ridding their architecture of reminders of the past and simplifying it to the point of austerity. This was notable in the case of Urbain Cassan who had collaborated with him on the Nuclear Studies Center at Saclay and was one of the architects for the Maine-Montparnasse project. Linked with this current also was Fernando Pouillon who became known for the building complex erected after 1945 on one of the hills dominating the Old Port of Marseille. A vigorous return to the principles and the style of Perret, with a marked historicist accent, is perceptible in recent projects of Ricardo Bofill and his Barcelona atelier, Taller de Arquitectura. Called upon in 1975 by the president of the Republic to participate in the renovation of Les Halles district of Paris, Bofill's proposals were, in the end, not retained. By contrast his ensemble of the Lac quarter in the new town of Saint Quentin in Yvelines, in the process of realization in 1980, is an example of classic monumental concrete architecture that its creator has not hesitated to qualify as a "Versailles for the people."

LE CORBUSIER

Paladin of the new architecture between the two world wars but not well regarded by the authorities, Le Corbusier finally received an official commission thanks to the Minister of Reconstruction, Claudius-Petit. At the Marseille Unité d'Habitation [1947-1952] (fig. 21.2) he was given total freedom to express his conceptions of modern dwellings for the middle class. For him it was an opportunity to put into practice theoretical ideas elaborated twenty years previously: the determination of diverse types of apartments to accord with their functionings as homes; the prefabrication of housing elements; an independent structure; a great deal of light and sun that enters through large windows; the extension of the dwelling's space in loggias; and inclusion of communal services to make the building an autonomous ensemble. An emphasis on the plasticity of the building with *pilotis* forming porticos, facades animated by the play of alternating loggias, a use of the modulor in determining proportions, and the employment of boldly sculptural superstructures as well as the use of rough concrete with its woodlike

21.2. Le Corbusier, architect. Unité d'Habitation, Marseille, 1947-1952. (Photograph: Courtesy of Photothèque of the Documentation Française, Paris)

grain evident were new elements that evolved from his prewar realizations of the thirties. Criticized by some, admired by others, the Marseille Unité d'Habitation achieved considerable renown. Le Corbusier received similar commissions at Rézé near Nantes [1952-1953], at Briey-la-Forêt [1957-1959], at Meaux [1956-1961], not to mention the Firminy commission [1960-1968], a work of his student and successor André Wogenscky. All of these are based on the same principles but varied somewhat in their execution to take into account programs and means of financing.

In the field of individual housing the most original work of Le Corbusier in France was the ensemble of the Jaoul houses at Neuilly [1954-1956] where, on a site plagued by contradictory regulations, the architect didn't hesitate to use elementary traditional materials such as bricks and flat tiles, forming light Catalonian vaults built without centering, as he had in fact before the war for economical construction. But this time he used a clearly brutalist style. Many of Le Corbusier's major works were built outside France, notably in India and in Japan after 1950. The Brazil pavilion at the Cité Universitaire [1957-1959] in Paris was a foreign commission in which the architect carrying out the work developed a project initially planned by Lucio Costa. Let us note as well among his cultural buildings the Maison de la Culture of Firminy [1965], the last project he accomplished.

There is a field in which Le Corbusier was particularly brilliant, that of religious architecture. The chapel of Ronchamp [1950-1954] broke radically with the theories expounded by its author in the twenties, with its unprecedented curvilinear forms, adopted as much for the walls as for the concrete roof. The power of the composition comes from the apparent weight of the roof, although in reality it is composed of a double shell, two membranes separated by an empty space of more than 2 meters. The formal consideration almost touching the informal and the accent put on symbolism break completely with Functionalism, even though the technological solutions adopted are far from being antifunctional. The Convent of La Tourette [1957-1960] at Eveux-sur-Arbresle near Lyon, built for the Dominicans, is a powerful and original creation, with its massive church with blind concrete walls, and its monastic buildings on *pilotis* in which corridors replace the traditional cloister made impossible by the slope of the land. Here the functional is closely connected to symbolic considerations and to a monumentality which is expressed by a power based on the extremely careful use of the raw material, on the bold and clever oppositions of structures, volumes, and spaces, and on the sense of proportion. Le Corbusier's work has therefore evolved toward a more and more evident plasticity and a freedom from the constraints that the apostle of modern architecture had imposed on himself from the start without, however, renouncing his major principles and while maintaining an undeniable continuity.

RATIONALIST CONTINUITY, GEOMETRIC VOLUMES, AND BRUTALISM

It is with the Rationalist stream that the largest part of postwar French architectural production is connected, but in many cases it is a matter of mediocre work using simple prismatic volumes (high rises or horizontal slabs) treated mechanically. The spirit of the Bauhaus can be found in the architecture of Marcel Breuer, a collaborator of Gropius, notably in the Alpine resort of Flaine (Haute-Savoie), a dry and heavy complex constructed of prefabricated concrete elements [1963-1972]. Breuer was less unfortunate at the UNESCO palace in Paris [1955-1958 and 1963-1965], jointly designed with Pier Luigi Nervi and Bernard Zehrfuss, at the IBM Study and Research Center at La Gaude near Nice [1963] and at the Sarget pharmaceutical laboratories in Mérignac near Bordeaux [1972], where he played on the themes of the *pilotis* and the concave facade.

The example set by Mies van der Rohe inspired most of the metallic framework constructions and curtain walls which have multiplied since 1950, though reinforced concrete has on the whole remained the most popular framework material for French and foreign architects working in France. However, realizations which can rival the creations of the great German-American master are rare, especially as financial constraints were often draconian. We may single out as works of quality the Savings Bank for Family Allowances of Paris by Raymond Lopez [1959], Orly airport by Henri Vicariot (fig. 21.3) [Orly-Sud, 1960, Orly-Ouest, 1971], the Museum for Art and Popular Traditions [1959-1969] in the Bois de Boulogne in Paris by Jean Dubuisson, the Faculty of Medicine of Angers [1972] by Michel Andrault, Pierre Parat, and Philippe Mornet, and the Havas Agency building at Neuilly [1973] by Michel Andrault, Pierre Parat, and Jean-Philippe Sarrazin. Interesting studies in the field of metallic structures have been carried out by the engineer Jean Prouvé: the Exhibition Palace of Grenoble [1967], the refreshment bar of the Cachat Spring [1957] and the Nautical Center of Evian-les-Bains, designed by Maurice Novarina. But the best-known building with a metallic structure built in France is the Georges Pompidou National Center of Arts and Culture [1969-1976] by the Italian-English team Renzo Piano, Richard Rogers, and the engineer Edmund Happold of Arup and Partners. Typical of English Brutalism, its enormous conduits are exposed on the facade, giving the building the look of a factory or a steamship.

The architectural current which sprang from Le Corbusier is represented by the Catalan José Luis Sert, architect for the Maeght Foundation [1964] at Vence (Alpes-Maritimes); and by the collaborator and successor of the French-Swiss master as the head of his firm, Wogenscky, architect of the Prefecture of Nanterre [1972] and the House of Culture of Grenoble [1967], among others. In this last building, deliberately massive, Wogenscky played on the effects of simple prismatic and semicircular volumes, and oppositions of color and materials.

A play of simple volumes was used by Henry Bernard at the University of Caen [1953-1955]; at the House of Radiotelevision of Paris [1959-1963], a circular building, somewhat cold in spite of partial breaks in spiral form; and at the Prefecture of Cergy-Pontoise [1965-1970], which looks like an inverted pyramid with its projecting cantilevered stories and its oblique balustrades flared towards the bottom in alternation with vertical glass walls. The inverted pyramidal form was used again by Willerval for the Headquarters of the Pernod factory at Créteil in the Val-de-Marne [1972], while the hollow cylinder served as the theme at the Faculty of Sciences of Nancy [1971] by Georges Tourry and Claude Goclowsky and at the Roissy airport by Paul Andreu [1974]. More complex in its expressive determination, inspired by the symbolic attributes of the hammer and sickle, the Headquarters of the Communist Party [1971] in the Xth arrondissement of Paris, by Oscar Niemeyer, is also the product of a clear combination of volumes. A clear combination of volume is found again in the Forum des Halles, the deluxe commercial center introduced into the heart of the capital and opened in 1979. Claude Vasconi and Georges Pencreac'h conceived a subterranean architecture arranged around an immense central shaft constituting an inverse pyramid open to the sky and bordered by metal and glass galleries with curved armatures. The sober monumentality which it emits is not devoid of brilliance.

A very clear tendency to make use of the hexagon has become evident since 1960. Pierre Dufétel and René Sarger used this geometric form for the Franciscan church of the Convent of the Sea at Boulogne-sur-Mer [1962]. But it is especially as a compositional unit within complex buildings that the qualities of functional and plastic suppleness of this form are demonstrated. This is evident in the House of Art and Leisure at Thonon-les-Bains [1966] by Maurice Novarina; the university restaurant at Montpellier [1969] by René Egger; the primary and nursery school of Cergy-Pontoise [1972] by Jean Renaudie; the Toulouse School of Architecture [1970] by Georges Candilis, who had already used the hexagon

21.3. Henri Vicariot, archiect. Orly Airport South Terminal, near Paris, 1960, before construction of underground parking facilities. (Photograph: Aeroport of Paris, courtesy Photothèque of the Documentation Française, Paris)

as a basic element for the urbanization of the Mirail quarter of the same city; the Vasarely Foundation at Aix-en-Provence [1973-1975] by Jean Sonnier; and the Toulouse-Lautrec Lyceum [1975-1976] and Collège Jolimont [1978-1980] at Toulouse by Roger Taillibert.

Georges Candilis and his associates, Alexis Josic and Shadrach Woods, have been declared partisans of a functional Brutalism founded on the articulation of volumes and spaces. However, in their French projects they have not recaptured the originality which characterized their buildings in Morocco. The large complexes [1958] at Bobigny and Gagny in the Parisian suburbs, and at Nîmes, Lyon, Marseille, Aix-en-Provence, Bagnols-sur-Cèze, and Manosque [all built between 1956 and 1961] remain too much the result of an architecture of economy, despite their praiseworthy efforts to enliven blocks of high rises and break up boring alignments. The same goes for the Marseille-La Viste (1961] and Toulouse-Le Mirail [1963-1970] commercial centers where staggered roofs, that admit light from narrow strips at the top, are inserted in a kind of game of mechanical construction. At the Toulouse-Le Mirail university this same repetitive system is extended over such a wide area that it ends up creating a sense of monotony.

STRUCTURAL RESEARCH

French architecture has been particularly distinguished in the field of structural innovations. Guillaume Gillet, for instance, played with awkward surfaces and light vaults with saddlelike double curves. At the Church of Royan [1954-1959], designed with engineers Bernard Lafaille and René Sarger (fig. 21.4), this type of roof rested on V-shaped concrete "sails" that alternated with glass bands to create a remarkable plastic composition. Similar efforts, combined with a metallic framework, led to the French Pavilion at the Brussels International Exhibition [destroyed 1958], to the service stations at Villefranche-sur-Saône [1970] and on Autoroute A13 in the Morainvilliers area, with less success, however, from an aesthetic point of view.

The Palais of the CNIT (Centre National des Industries et Techniques) in the Défense district at Puteaux [1958] by Robert Camelot, Jean de Mailly, and Bernard Zehrfuss, consists of an immense self-supporting concrete vault covering a triangular surface of 22,000 square meters and resting on only three points. The subterranean Basilica of Lourdes [1959] by Pierre Vago, André Le Donné, and Pierre Pinsard is also a good example of the covering of a large open space destined to shelter crowds of pilgrims. The works of Pierre Dufétel and René Sarger at Boulogne-sur-Mer [Elf service station, 1959; the Jean Bart Technical Lyceum, 1965] make masterful use of the possibilities of thin concrete sheets with the parabolic ellipsoid shell form, and V-shaped porticos. Roger Taillibert distinguished himself in the area of sports facilities with the swimming pools at Deauville [1965-1966], the Carnot Boulevard in the XIIth arrondissement of Paris [1968], Lyon-Vénissieux [1971], the complex of

21.4. Guillaume Gillet, architect, with Bernard Lafaille and René Sarger, engineers. Church at Royan, 1954-1959. (Photograph: Municipality of Royan, courtesy Photothèque of the Documentation Française, Paris)

21.5. Roger Taillibert, architect. Stadium of the Parc des Princes. Paris, 1972. (Photograph: Courtesy Photothèque of the Documentation Française, Paris)

Chamonix, the pre-Olympic center of Font-Romeu [1967] in the Pyrénées, and the stadium of the Parc des Princes (fig. 21.5) at Paris [1972]. With great technical and plastic mastery he played with porticos supporting tiers and cantilevered vaults and with mobile roofs resting on prestressed cables, moved with the aid of automotive trolleys. He had anticipated the synthesis of these two types of experiments in his Montreal Olympic Stadium [1976].

Reinforced concrete shells without framework, placed directly on the ground, were used by Pascal Hausermann to create an extremely curious, explosive architecture. Le Balcon de Belledonne [1966] at Sainte-Marie-du-Mont in Savoie is a house of multiple elements hooked onto a steep slope in an unstable equilibrium, a mixture of flying saucer, of amphoras, and other strange forms. His Raon-l'Etape Motel and the Saint-Dié Hotel in the Vosges are made up of a succession of ovoid shells freely implanted around a central building. These shells are of concrete on a metallic armature in the first case and of plastic material in the second.

Plywood has once again become a much used structural material in recent years because of its flexibility and its lightness. Examples include a skeletal framework at the Church of Stella Matutina in Saint-Cloud by Alain Bourbonnais [1965] and the Berck swimming pool in the Pas-de-Calais by Henri Maillard and Paul Ducamp, as well as shells for the amphitheaters of the Faculties of Law and Letters of Reims by André Dubard de Gaillarbois [1972] which dominate the campus with their surprising and elegant corollas.

THE DENIAL OF FUNCTIONALISM

The mediocre and unimaginative architecture which invaded France after 1950 in the name of the primacy of Functionalism and economy led to various reactions putting the principles of the functionalist movement and the lack of variety of the Rationalist esthetic into question. Certain people adopted an attitude of total rejection and turned towards the past, especially in the field of individual housing, isolated or grouped, where an important favorable clientele existed. Multiple-dwelling estates, imitating regional styles with more or less happy results, bear striking testimony to this. The most characteristic example of this state of mind is the Port Grimaud development by François Spoerry, a group of dwellings situated on the Provenąl coast. Started in 1966 it was much criticized at the beginning in professional milieux but seems today to have regained a certain vogue. L'Unité d'Habitation of Cap d'Agde [1962-1980] on the Languedoc coast by Jean Le Couteur also attempts to arrive at a synthesis between the present and the traditional, while trying at the same time to avoid a pastiche effect.

Another form of denial has been to create sculptural architecture rejecting all rational finality and the use of orthogonal projection. This is the case with Jacques Couelle in his village of Castelleras-le-Neuf (Alpes-Maritimes), dating from 1964. Here traditional techniques are used to create the appearance of unexpected plastic constructions with supple forms, the romantic strangeness of which makes one think of Antonio Gaudí. The drawbacks to this formula are in the finishing that resembles bricolage and in the high cost which limits this type of realization to exceptional experiments.

The painter, Georges Mathieu, known as an apologist for the intuitive-action movement, designed the forms and the green spaces of a factory in the Fortenay-le-Comte region in Vendée. The refining of the design and its execution were done by the architect Raymond Epardaud [1971]. The extraordinary composition, bursting into a free star with branches ending in very sharp angles, led to a building of remarkable plastic beauty. This solution, which completely satisfied the proprietor and the people who used the factory in spite of the multiplication of nonfunctional interior spaces, cannot be anything but exceptional. Only the protection of financiers and the impressive public image it offered made possible the adoption of such a resolutely antieconomic choice.

It is curious to note a formal similarity between the factory designed by Mathieu and the star-shaped building clusters by Jean Renaudie at Ivry [1969-1976] in the Paris outskirts (fig. 21.6), for the two first portions of the program which have actually been carried out, or at Givors in the vicinity of Lyon (work in progress, begun in 1974). The resemblance stops there, however, for the motivations are different. Confronted with a moderate-rental housing development, Renaudie could not ignore costs nor waste space. The multiplication of breaks in height, with the formation of private terraces establishing the natural extensions of the apartments, permitted him to achieve maximal possibilities from the design plan he had adopted. Thus, future tenants were offered the pleasant framework for living preached by all the theoreticians of modern architecture by Renaudie, who called for a formal geometry that would make possible a completely new spatial conception (fig. 21.7).

21.6. Jean Renaudie, architect. Urban renewal housing development at Ivry-sur-Seine, near Paris, 1969-1976. (Photograph: Courtesy Photothèque of the Documentation Française, Paris)

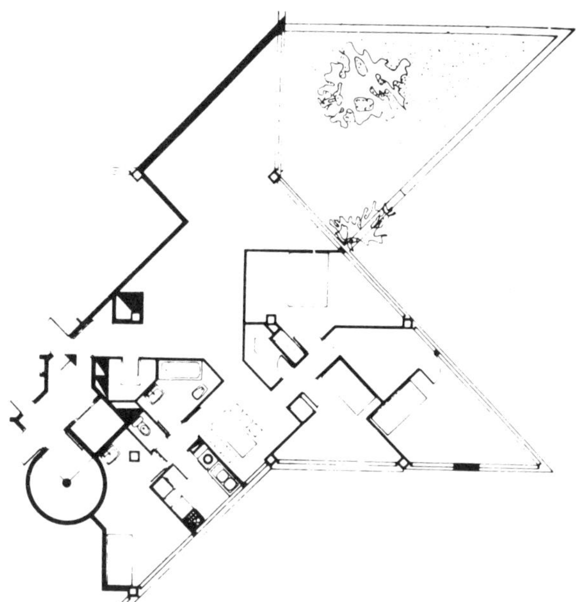

21.7. Jean Renaudie, architect. Urban renewal housing at Ivry-sur-Seine, plan of typical apartment, 1969-1976. (Photograph: Courtesy of the architect

The wish to go beyond Rationalist severity without denying certain acquired experience was the origin of the priority given to oblique form by Claude Parent. Massive, inclined planes in raw concrete determine the external volumes and the internal spaces, even in some cases the grounds of his buildings: the Church of Saint Bernadette of Nevers [1963-1966], the House of Youth and Culture at Troyes [1964], and especially the commercial centers and supermarkets of Sens, Reims, Epernay in Champagne, and Ris-Organis in the Paris suburbs are all programs that lent themselves to the windowless architecture favored by the leader of the *Architecture-Principe* group. Jean Balladur's work is the product of a completely different inspiration, although he also dealt with the effects of forms determined by oblique lines in his pyramids of La Grande-Motte (Hérault) [1962-1980]. He did not hesitate to affirm the priority of form over function, though the former was partly inspired by climatic conditions favorable to the multiplication of covered terraces attached to inclined planes. His concern with rehabilitating decoration led him to play with the effects of reinforced-concrete sheets with cutout forms to animate his facades, reviving, not without a certain excess, the discoveries of Niemeyer in his palace at Brasilia.

Some Conclusions

Any rapid, panoramic view is naturally subject to caution but there are nevertheless some conclusions which become evident. Since 1945 France has developed a new appearance because of construction on a large scale of buildings answering intensive immediate needs. Modern architecture, which had a great deal of difficulty achieving a significant breakthrough between the two world wars, asserted itself quantitatively starting from the 1950-1960 decade. The triumph of Rationalism was unfortunately not always accompanied by a similar qualitative effort; the latter being generally restricted to a few remarkable buildings. The striving for plasticity was directed toward research in volumes and especially in structures with reinforced concrete, which remained by far the material most often used and the most appreciated by the major creative minds for its malleability. This concern for suppleness in the frameworks also explains the recent strong return to wood, graced by the technology of plywood. Moreover, glass and metal architecture has carved out an important part of the market for itself. The abuses of mediocre and stereotyped mass production have led architects to react against repetitive models by a diversification of tendencies and pursuits, notably starting from the years 1965-1970. We are now seeing a partial requestioning of principles accepted for twenty years in city planning as in architecture. Demands for quality are increasingly replacing those for quantity.

Bibliography

BOOKS

Amouroux, D.; Crettol, M.; and Monnet, J.-P. *Guide d'architecture contemporaine en France*. Paris: Technic Union, 1972.

Besset, Maurice. *La nouvelle architecture française*. Teufen: Editiones Arthur Niggli, 1967.

______. *Qui était Le Corbusier?* Geneva: Skira, 1969.

Candilis, Josic, Woods, Une décennie d'architecture et d'urbanisme. Paris: Eyrolles, 1963.

Champigneulle, Bernard. *Perret*. Paris: Arts et Métiers graphiques, 1959.

Le Corbusier 1910-1965. Zurich: Girsberger, 1965.

Prouvé, Jean. *Une architecture par l'industrie*. Zurich: Artemis, 1971.

Taillibert, Roger. *Construire l'avenir*. Paris: Presses de la Cité, 1977.

______. *Oeuvres récentes*. Paris: Metropolis, 1977.

Zahar, Marcel. *Auguste Perret*. Paris: Vincent et Fréal, 1959.

JOURNALS

L'Architettura 208 (February 1973) (issue on Claude Parent).

Chabot, Anne. "André Wogenscky et l'architecture active." *L'Information d'histoire de l'art* (November-December 1972): 237-40.

Loyer, François. "Dix ans de renovation." *Revue de l-art* (special issue "Paris?") 29 (1975): 57-82.

Parinaud, André. "Dix ans d'architecture et d'urbanisme en France." *Galerie-Jardin des Arts* 129 (September 1973): 39-62; 130 (October 1973): 58-79; 131 (November 1973): 87-89.

Ragon, Michel. "Jacques Couëlle." *Cimaises* 103 (October 1971.

"Réalisations de Jean Renaudie." *Architecture, Mouvement continuité* 45 (May 1978): 44-70.

USEFUL JOURNALS

L'Architecture d'Aujourd'hui (Boulogne-sur-Seine, from 1929).

Architecture, Forme, Fonctions (Lausanne).

Architecture française (Paris, from 1940; became *Architecture* in 1976 and was incorporated into *L'Architecture d'Aujourd'hui* in 1978, from no. 403).

Architecture, Mouvement, Continuité (Paris, la Société des Architectes Diplômes par le Gouvernement, from 1967).

Architecture Principe, edited by Claude Parent (9 issues, from February to December 1966).

Cahiers de la Recherche architecturale (Paris, from 1967).

Paris-Projet, revue mensuella (l'APUR, Préfecture de Paris, from 1970).

Techniques et Architecture (Paris, from 1941).

Urbanisme (Paris, from 1950).

22

FEDERAL REPUBLIC OF GERMANY

WINFRIED NERDINGER

Determinants and Problems of Postwar Architecture

As with all other aspects of life after 1945 in the Federal Republic, the course of architecture was at first conditioned by the preceding twelve years under National Socialism. The destruction of the cities had been preceded by the driving out of the creative imagination. Most of the important architects of the 1920s, except for those few who found their way into industrial building or whose work remained very much limited, had left Germany by the beginning of the war. Avant-garde architects, however, had been responsible for only a small part of the building activities carried on during the years of the Weimar Republic. A broad current of conservative building had continued into the 1930s, unrestrainedly mixing starchy suburban Classicism (*Vorstadt-Klassizismus* as Hans Poelzig put it) with megalomaniacal outbursts and vernacular architecture. Only some few city blocks here and there, a few important architectural breakthroughs, and two new towns, Wolfsburg and Salzgitter, remain from that period. Very controversial modern buildings constructed during the 1920s were reworked and often provided with saddle roofs—that is, they were "Germanicized" (*eingedeutscht*). Before the difficulties inevitable in effecting innovations could be overcome and its advantages realized, the development of modern architecture in Germany was abruptly halted.

The architects of the reconstruction after 1948 were part of a bewildered generation, without teachers, recently denazified, and educated in rapid, short courses. These architects sought to establish connections—in part because it was necessary to do so—with forms of architecture that had been developing in other western countries for fifteen years, though such forms had become an organic part of the architecture of only a few countries. The style of architecture, which had become "International," was adopted, like the new form of government, as if it were a natural obligation. Thus, one can speak only qualifiedly of a German architecture during those first postwar years. Although conservative architects continued to build in a traditional manner, any connection with regional, folk, or historical architectural thought after the many years of their perversion remained impossible. Difficulties in establishing links, confusions of identity and lack of orientation were exacerbated by the total situation of postwar Germany. The trauma of National Socialism, war and destruction, led to attitudes and ways of thought which, though quite understandable, were nevertheless disadvantageous. Throughout the country there was no comprehensive planning; freedom newly obtained frequently led to individualistic high-handedness; gratification of private needs came first; theoretical discussions of architecture and urbanism, even of ideal designs, were seldom heard and were often considered disturbing and obstructive. It was a stifling, gloomy, and repressive time, a time to work and to fulfill a huge backlog of consumer needs. With the establishment of the Federal Republic and the beginning of building activity there were basically only two pursuits for architecture in 1948—reconstruction and the creation of new residences, both of which were measured only in terms of quantitative accomplishment.

Translated from the German by Edith and Warren Sanderson.

Rebuilding and Residential Construction, 1948 to 1955

Among German architects particularly from 1948 to 1955 the form that the rebuilding of destroyed cities would take engendered the most lively discussion of the entire postwar period; and since the 1970s, it has been taken up again in a reconsideration of historical and urbanistic ideas. During those first postwar years, the suggestion of Rudolf Hillebrecht that systematic, orderly provisional arrangements should be enacted remained unheard. For the most part advocates of the architecture of the 1920s were installed by the occupying powers as heads of municipal reconstruction bureaus. These so-called utopianists planned radical new constructions which involved setting aside the historical character of the inner city with retention, at best, of broadened main streets as well as construction, according to the CIAM program, of the low-density, functionally loosely integrated city in the manner of Le Corbusier's Ville Radieuse or Ludwig Hilberseimer's futuristic ''city of tomorrow.''

The great plans of Hans Scharoun for Berlin, Werner Hebebrand for Frankfurt, Richard Doecker for Stuttgart, Rudolf Schwarz for Cologne, Hubert Hoffman for Hamburg, Walter Schwagenscheidt for Emden, and Gustav Hassenpflug for Nürnberg between 1945 and 1952 were frustrated and undone, apart from questions of financing, by the difficulty of overcoming problems of individual land ownership, about which the laws of the Federal Republic were hardly concerned. Only in inner-city areas, as in Stuttgart, Kassel, and Kiel, were large programs of restructuring undertaken. A new provincial property law led in Frankfurt to well-planned, low-density new housing in the old city center. The greatest changes resulted from Hillebrecht's new planning in Hannover which rerouted major traffic arteries through the inner city. In Hannover, too, Hillebrecht organized the first architectural exhibition in which he demonstrated his program of renovation in the "Constructa" housing developments. For a short time the idealistic pathos of the 1920s was once more ignited. New buildings were to create new cities, and in the process the new mankind of the Republic was to be reared (Rudolf Schwarz, *Das neue Köln*, 1950). From the destruction that had been wrought, a great opportunity was seen for the contemporary cleaning up and renewal of the cities and their architecture. Reconstruction was understood as being formative and expressive of a new era.

Quite the opposite of these utopian programs were historically precise, individual architectural reproductions, the first of which, the Goethe House in Frankfurt, is still considered by many architects as an example of an uncreative and dead, mock architecture. The Goethe House was followed by the principal marketplace in Münster, the rebuilding near the church of St. Martin in Cologne along the banks of the Rhine River and many other historical works of architecture that, for the most part, were reproduced in simplified forms. The idea of reducing a building to its basic structural elements with extensive sacrifices of decorative motifs formed the basis for countless mock buildings with false facades and for stock blocks with decorative incisions upon their exteriors where once there had been a plastic architectural articulation.

The battle to save historically important ruins extended into the 1960s. Even distinguished palaces in Stuttgart and Hannover were slated for destruction to make room for new buildings; and the palace at Braunschweig was razed as late as 1962. Between the contrasts of so-called modern building and exact reproduction, an entire spectrum of solutions was developed in the various cities of Germany. The retention of the old system of city blocks usually led to buildings that were of accommodating scale and proportions, while changes in the sizes of city blocks to make larger buildings possible led to drastic physical encroachments. The civic construction offices often regulated these processes by changes of alignments or increases in taxation rates. For historically important works of architecture many architects developed a kind of reconstruction aesthetic which consisted in either a deliberate exhibiting of the destruction (the Alte Pinakotek [1951-1957] and the cemeterial precincts in Munich by Hans Döllgast), the reworking of old building materials and remains (forty-eight rubble churches by Otto Bartning [1946-1949], the building of old parts unchanged into the construction (the theatre in Münster [1954-1956] by Harald Deilmann, Ortwin Rave, and Werner Ruhnau, and the Kestner museum in Hannover, 1961 by Werner Dierscke), or the confrontation of ruin with new building as a monument commemorating destruction and reconstruction (the Memorial Church in Berlin by Egon Eiermann [1956-1963] (fig. 4.1) and the Christ Church in Bochum [1957-1959] by Dieter Oesterlen).

Well into the 1970s, buildings of the unloved nineteenth century had almost no chance of survival since almost all were considered as architectural sins by architects and architectural bureaucrats alike. Even Erich Mendelsohn's Schocken Department Store of the twenties in Stuttgart was sacrificed to cost efficiency. With arguments against sentimentality in the forefront, the architectural profession concealed its lack of historical consciousness. Calculations of profit and concern with controlling traffic outweighed the primacy of architecture and city building. The thought of lively, profit-creating traffic opened the cities up, and gradually a self-imposed noose, consisting of the belief in the *Wirtschaftswunder* of German recovery and the shortsightedness of reconstruction, was slowly tightened. Residential architecture developed in the same way.

By the end of the war approximately one-fifth of all dwellings had been destroyed. In addition some eight million refugees from East Germany had sought living quarters in the West so that a deficit of six million units existed. In view of this urgent situation, architectural efforts were measured only quantitatively. Building on such a huge scale became an imperative that practitioners could not fulfill well. This was all the more a problem because Germany was confronted with a creative vacuum, an economy still in disarray, and lacked links with the tradition, teaching, and ideas of architecture. The sheer need of ensuring existence alone permitted, in practice, neither ideas nor experiments. From 1945 to 1948, because of the regulations of the occupying powers as well as a dearth of money and materials, almost nothing was built. Then, in 1948-1949, 100,000 dwellings were started with American assistance through the ECA free competition. From 1945 to 1954, 2,500,000 habitations were erected. Thus, by 1954 approximately every fifth German resided in a newly constructed building. Annual construction of some 500,000 abodes continued into the seventies and constituted a kind of rebirth of the nation, overshadowing every earlier period of intense architectural activity in Germany's history and forming the backbone of the so-called German economic miracle. The basis of the free market economy announced in 1948 was publicly assisted housing construction, which was valuable politically as well since it offered employment. Seen broadly, however, the provisions for allocating public means severely reduced the possibilities for creating new forms. Moreover, the image of the single-family home each with its own garden was introduced for its political value, reflecting the cold war doctrine that the best bulwark against communism was private home ownership. The encouragement of all sorts of investment initiatives by the government led to a mushrooming of residential developments and mass-produced buildings of the greatest ugliness, since in the aesthetics of the free market beauty consisted in the economic and the prosaic, and everything existed to fulfill the wishes of the purchaser.

An endless wasteland of row houses and scanty cottages, usually following stereotyped models and without the involvement of an architect, stretched out over the countryside. As early as 1952 urban construction had so degenerated into the building of housing complexes that it was considered architecturally bankrupt. A questionable result of this development was an ever-increasing concentration of architectural construction companies, of which Neue Heimat with its own company union is today the foremost in Europe. Quality of architecture is usually in inverse proportion to the size of these companies. Emerging from the uniformity of these architectural complexes and expressing new conceptions were the first residential skyscrapers at Hamburg-Grindelberg [1950-1956, by Hermkes, Jäger, and others], the stepped-slab buildings in Rheinhausen [1954, by Otto Ernst Schweitzer] and the garden-city community of Bogenhausen at Munich [1954-1956, by Johannes Ludwig and Franz Ruf].

Simultaneously with the progress of residential building there was a good deal of effort given to another kind of construction: developments with large administrative and office buildings in which a shallow creative quality of architectural forms was concealed by natural stone and similarly unusual materials placed upon ultimately nondescript buildings. First Swiss and then American architecture furnished the primary orientation here, though only a few buildings still extant today, such as the handkerchief factory in Blumfeld by Egon Eiermann [1951], administrative buildings by Friedrich Wilhelm Kraemer in Braunschweig, or the Westfalia Hall in Dortmund by Walter Hoeltje [1951-1952], stood out against the anonymity of the then mass-produced buildings. In all, Theodore Adorno's verdict is valid: "There is nothing more dreary than the mediocre modernity of German reconstruction architecture" (*see, Ohne Leitbild, Parva Aesthetica; Funktionalismus Heute*, Frankfurt, 1967). Even buildings by formerly avant-garde architects were products of a pennypinching, half-hearted modernity, with surfaces reserved for representations in fresco, mosaic, or the graffiti of a 2 percent art-on-the-building law, indicative of perverted conceptions of Functionalism. Here it is clear that the quality of buildings developed under economic conditions as unfavorable as in the twenties resided in the artificial overemphasis upon and utilization of the same basic elements and materials. Gropius expressed the highly biased judgement of architects concerning this falling off in quality very well when he declared that it was the public as a whole that gave up thinking about how a better setting for life could be created, and instead learned to sell itself a system for the quick turnover and the appreciation of substitutes.

The creative beginnings of German architecture crystallized around Egon Eiermann (1904-1968) in Karlsruhe, Hans Scharoun (1893-1972) in Berlin, and

Rudolf Schwarz (1897-1961) in Cologne and Aachen. With his efforts to "make the order or urban planning visible down to its smallest details," Eiermann, a student of Hans Poelzig, became an exponent of the Rational, material pole of architecture in the great lineage of Mies van der Rohe and Walter Gropius. Opposed to this was Scharoun who developed the expressive German architecture of the twenties farther and entered the realm of Hugh Häring's Organic architectural theories. Scharoun certainly could convey theoretically the perception of space as the organ of its function, but his highly individualistic manner of form was resisted by a market for architecture that favored mass construction and conformity. Thus many of his designs, such as a school building in Darmstadt or a theater for Kassel, were unfortunately never carried out. His later buildings indicate the limits of organic architecture when used on a large scale.

Another student of Poelzig, Rudolf Schwarz, represents a third position, the perception of architecture as image. In lively discussions that developed into polemics, this master of church construction rejected the stereotyped application of the dogma of form-follows-function that had served as a crutch for an entire generation of German architects and called for a technology that would assist rather than lead architecture.

Although Schwarz, who died early, in 1961, set strong creative impulses into motion, like Scharoun in the fifties he had no far-reaching effect. He differentiated between "effective form" (technology, material, and so on) and "significant form" (content, intellectual substance). Against the generally predominant sense of truth to materials, he posed the designing of an image for mankind in a time of imageless abstraction. He demonstrated applications of his ideas in church architecture, for instance, in the "protective mantle" at St. Anna in Düren [1951-1956], with the "chalice" at St. Michael in Frankfurt [1953-1955], and in the Church of Mary Queen of Heaven (fig. 22.1) in Saarbrücken [1956-1959]. Besides Rudolf Schwarz, whose ideas are gaining importance once again, one should also mention Emil Steffan (Parish Church of St. Mary, Düsseldorf-Wersten, 1958). Otherwise, church architecture became for German architects only a field for idiosyncratic games. With monies from income taxes and tithes, from as early as two decades after the war, more churches were built in Germany than had been built there altogether since the time of the Reformation. While in residential construction, strict attention had to be paid to costs, and in governmental or private firm construction careful attention had to be focused on what the buildings were to represent, the architects of churches believed themselves to be relatively free from restraints. Thus, there came into existence hundreds of unfortunate efforts toward a glass-and-stone mystique and an aestheticism of concrete.

22.1. Rudolf Schwarz, architect. Church of Mary Queen of Heaven. Saarbrücken, 1956-1959. (Photograph: *Neue deutsche Architektur 2,* Conrads/Marschall, Verlag Gerd Hatje, Stuttgart)

Adaption, Linkages and New Impulses, 1955-1960

The five years between the recognition of the Federal Republic as a sovereign state and the legislation of a federal building law, the first measure that took some steam out of the construction market, were characterized by a renewal of links with international developments on the part of industry and architectural technology. The dominant images of architecture began to be clearly differentiated. Industry became more strongly oriented towards the United States, and the architectural forms of Mies van der Rohe became effective representational symbols through the agency of Skidmore, Owings and Merrill. The Institute for Design at Ulm, considered as a new edition of the Bauhaus, opened in 1955 and transmitted strong impulses of a new sense of form, of industrializaton, standardization, and prefabrication of buildings, even though in American terms German architectural technology remained comparable only to handicraft. Konrad Wachsmann's single year at Ulm was especially effective for his teaching that the crux of building was in design *as* structural engineering.

The so-called triple-slab skyscraper (*Dreischeiben-Hochhaus*) in Düsseldorf by Helmut Hentrich and Hubert Petschnigg (1957-1960] demonstrated the connection with the American development. With its curtain wall of Nirosta steel, aluminum, and glass, and with its three-part ground plan developed from the architecture of Skidmore, Owings and Merrill, it became a symbol of the newly strengthened German building industry. Furthermore, this skyscraper became a landmark of the Ruhr region and, indirectly, a signal of Germany's growing orientation toward American models in all aspects of life. If at that time a Russian architectural critic was able to say of the architecture of the German Democratic Republic that German architecture means Russian construction, then for the Federal Republic of Germany one can replace the word *Russian* with *American*. Dominated for centuries by churches, palaces, and city halls, and more recently by parliaments and courthouses, the image of the German city was changed by symbols of the power of the new anonymous rulers. Administrative buildings, usually skyscrapers, invaded the city, in part welcomed during the sixties by the "skyscraper policy" of some metropolises. Marveled at and admired as an expression of a new era in the sixties, after the destruction of entire quarters of cities, they are viewed by most citizens today with irritation and anger. The use of a principle of design that imitated Mies van der Rohe was seized upon subsequently in buildings that represented industry and government and from there triumphed over almost all types of architecture. For this direction, which was still important in the sixties and which, though most strikingly transparent, was confused with Mies's ascetic space and transcendent construction, we need only be reminded of the Provincial Assembly building [1959-1960] in Stuttgart by Horst Linde, Erwin Heinle and others, of the Landeshaus in Cologne [1956-1959] by Eckhardt Schulze-Fielitz and Ernst von Rudloff, and of the industrial administration buildings of Walter Henn [Osram, Munich, 1962-1966] and Hans Maurer [Munich, 1964]. Often further developments occurred, as with the Unilever-Haus [1962] in Hamburg with its triangular plan of three wings by Hentrich and Petschnigg.

Besides this dominant American image, a Scandinavian style was introduced. At first, however, this consisted in little more than a new delight in buildings that displayed the raw materials of nature. A change in taste was underscored in design and interior decoration with a gradual discarding of kidney-shaped tables and rubber trees. From this mode of living, gradually and without our being able to say just when, refinements occurred in the more careful design of details of buildings, in a better and more tasteful selection of materials, and in designing for experimental spatial values that brought in nature.

Plastic, pace-setting solutions for two new types of marginally architectural projects were developed in those years. The Stuttgart television tower by Fritz Leonhardt [1956] became the prototype for a building genre that has been very much improvised upon throughout the world and still is effective as a symbol of the media age. Gerhard Weber's research reactor in Garching near Munich [1957-1960], called the "Atom-Egg," not only symbolized convincingly the basic forces at work inside it but also became a universal symbol of science and research for postwar Germany. These two architectural symbols, developed from their functions, may be counted among the few instances of pictorial readability in German architecture of the twentieth century.

International attention was drawn to German postwar architecture for the first time at the 1958 Brussels World's Fair in the pavilion group by Egon Eiermann and Sep Ruf. The elegant proportioning of its masses, the sensitive profiling and broad, delicate grid of its facades, next to which the interior arrangements were of no notice, gave this architecture a unique quality. After nearly thirty years, here was a thoroughly unique continuation of the legendary Barcelona Pavilion of Mies van der Rohe. In Eiermann's next building, the central offices of a mail-order house in Frankfurt [1958-1960], he reconciled a staircase that coursed across the entire facade as a freely plastic element with his basic orthogonal system. This new plasticity showed an architectural freedom and stronger spatial and volumetric refinement, that, with the growing influence of Le Corbusier and Brutalism, came to determine the shape of the sixties.

One more important step toward reestablishing connections with international architectural developments was the "Interbau Exhibition" of 1957 in Berlin. The framework for the reconstruction of the destroyed Hansa quarter was provided by a competition under the direction of Otto Bartning in which fifty-three German and foreign architects were to show the present state of architecture in all of its multiplicity. All kinds of dwellings were presented, from the single-family home upon a cement-slab foundation to the cottage with pitched roof, but the basic idea of organizing individual works of architecture as free sculpture on broad green tracts resulted only in an accumulation of architectonic objects for demonstration. This lack of overall principles of order and internal relationships also characterized another architectural display piece the same year, the large housing development at Bremen-Vahr by Ernst May, among others. The addition of functions in the interior corresponded to the pure adding-on of slabs: dwellings came to be prescribed by architects.

Besides the presentation of an urban landscape and its architecture as freestanding sculpture, there were other themes. Walter Schwagenscheidt publicized his "spatial city" (*Raumstadt*) in which, by grouping high and low buildings, a renunciation of closed city spaces was to be achieved. In the Northwest City at Frankfurt planned by Schwagenscheidt and Tassilo Sittmann, residential buildings were organized in the form of neighborhood units around green spaces. The missing urbanity was to be supplied in a large center [Apel, Becker and Beckert, 1961-1965]. The unraveling of urban functions, the existence of social monocultures, as well as the unsuitability for mass transportation of such cities created in them the well-known sense of isolation found in the bedroom suburbs of other countries.

Hans B. Reichow sought to bring into being his teachings of the "organic formation of cities" (*Organische Stadtgestaltung*) at Senne-Stadt near Bielefeld [1954-1957]. Besides the ideas of the urban landscape and division of functions which he considered most valid, he used sharp turns and offset street intersections to develop a network of streets without real crossings in accord with the principle of internal branchings. Then, a network of ring-roads was supposed to relieve any constriction of traffic. Just this kind of planning, that Reichow characterized as fair to the automobile (that is, the auto should be kept in its place), was soon so very much perverted that, quite to the contrary, the city was arranged for the automobile.

Scharoun's residential courts (*Wohngehöfte*) in the Charlottenburg-Nord development [1955-1961] at Berlin are another effort in which he brought stepped groupings of buildings together to create an overall spatial unity. In their sizes and their differences of refinements these dwellings were to correspond to the various biological, social, and professional requirements of their inhabitants. As with his contemporaneous Stuttgart residential skyscrapers (Romeo and Juliet), whose living units were oriented toward the sun like "buds on the branches of a plant," he designed spaces that were most appropriate for human-scale living. However, as comparison with his own residential buildings of the twenties shows, in this project the more limited quantity of living space that he had to deal with detracted greatly from the architectonic quality and originality of the design. In the fifties only the residential buildings of Oswald Matthias Ungers in Cologne-Nippes and Cologne-Chorweiler attained the approximate architectonic *niveau* of the Siemens development in Berlin or of Dammerstock at Karlsruhe.

While the significance of the architecture of the twenties in Germany rests directly in architects' concentrating on the Rational objective pole and on the Expressive Organic pole, the fifties as well as the sixties were characterized by a thinning out of these positions. The predominant direction of architectural creativity—a new positivism in the sense of individual elements of the whole being independent and absolute (Arnold Gehlen) and a pragmatic concentration on individual tasks for the fulfillment of obligations to construction and functions—was a direct obstacle to the overwhelmingly organic unities of the coordinated forms of Scharoun and his school. Scharoun could only rarely effect his projects, as for example the Geschwister Scholl Gymnasium in Lünen [1955-1962], where he conceived a system of pavilions for classrooms as living areas that would fit with the idea of educational divisions. Here he grouped the architectural masses to accord with stages of development of the students and planned a particular kind of illumination for each space. His works remained unique in the architectural landscape through the sixties. They opened no new pathways, and few buildings inspired by him were constructed, with some exceptions, such as the Beethoven Hall in Bonn by Siegfried Wolske [1959] and the school of Sargius Rügenberg (Grammar School, Berlin Reinickendorf, 1966).

Intensive Planning and Construction, 1960-1970

A virtual euphoria of planning and construction reached from the early sixties to approximately the beginning of the economic recession of the seventies. The completion of some very large-scale projects begun then, such as the ICC Congress Center in Berlin to accommodate twenty thousand people daily [Rolf and Ursulina Schüler, 1973-1979], would extend far into the next decade. Besides the undiminished and ever-increasing production of residential architecture which reached its high point and collapse simultaneously in 1973 with the building of 714,000 living units, the belief of unlimited growth and an unshakable euphoria of planning led to a powerful building boom in which an extraordinary number of famous buildings were developed. Municipal governments especially seem to have wanted to overstep their limits in their desire to have the most modern and the largest city halls, civic centers, baths, schools, hospitals, museums, theaters, and sports complexes. The allocation of all of these projects, mostly through competitions, led these local authorities to a kind of particular dynamics in which, on the one hand, fashionable trends were sought out that in part led very directly to the development of competition sharks who would produce such novelties and whose works therefore seemed old-fashioned within a very short time. On the other hand German architecture was opened to international architects, leading to a most fruitful exchange of ideas. In no other country in the world was so great a number of important projects permitted to be carried out by foreign architects (Alvar Aalto in Wolfsburg and Bremen; Arne Jacobsen in Mainz and Hamburg; Jacob B. Bakema in Marl; Georges Candilis, Alexis Josic, Shadrach Woods in Berlin; Philip Johnson in Bielefeld; James Stirling in Stuttgart; Aldo van Eyck in Düsseldorf; not to speak of the Austrians: Karl Schwanzer in Munich; Roland Rainer in Ludwigshafen and Bremen; Hans Hollein in Mönchen-Gladbach).

The search for the exceptional and the great names in the field went so far that Hans Scharoun was finally awarded a most important project and German emigrants were called back as, for example, Walter Gropius for the factories in Selb [1967] and Amberg [1969-1970] and Mies van der Rohe for the new National Gallery in Berlin. The two most beautiful spaces of postwar architecture in Germany, the Philharmonic Hall [Scharoun, 1960-1963] and the National Gallery [Mies, 1963-1968], both in Berlin, indicated by their antagonisms and their incompatibility two particular end points of the architectural development of the twenties. They were completions, however, also in the sense that they were each, architecturally, the ends of a road. While Mies designed an absolutely ideal space that was open to an infinite variety of functions, the basic thought behind the Berlin Philharmonic Hall (fig. 22.2) was "music is central." Admittedly both the Philharmonic Hall and the National Gallery remained problematic because the Philharmonic concentrated on bringing exterior form towards the interior, while the complete freedom of utilization of the National Gallery placed a high moral demand on its users. However it is precisely in this absolutism that the greatness of these buildings resides.

Design and Functionalism made solely to the measure of and for man were lacking in the other large projects of the sixties which were concerned almost completely with the standardization of values, systematization of schemata, and maximization of utility, that crushed every architectural design in toilsome efforts to achieve functional fulfillment. This is especially clear in provincial and municipal showpieces such as the hospital complexes in Munich

22.2. Hans Scharoun, architect. Philharmonic Hall. Berlin, 1960-1963. (Photograph: *Deutsche Architektur 1969-70,* Wolfgang Pehnt, Verlag Gerd Hatje Stuttgart)

[Grosshadern, Eichberg, and so forth, 1968-1976], Berlin [Curtis, Daivis, Morken, 1965-1970], and Aachen; the large international airports at Frankfurt [Alois Giefer, Hermann Mäckler, Heinrich Kosina, 1972], Cologne [Paul Schneider-Esteben, 1970], and Berlin [Gerkan, Marg, 1974], and some newly founded universities. The enormously concentrated teaching factory for eighteen thousand students in Bochum by Hentrich and Petschnigg is the result of optimistically high projections made on the basis of statistical studies. However, besides the degradation of the ideal of university studies, any change of such parameters as spatial needs, continuity of education, or teaching plan puts into question the total concept realized. The system of open planning used at the University of Marburg [Kurt Schneider, Gottfried Bondzio, and so forth, 1964-1970], the addition of basic elements to form a loose mosaic, certainly works against the obligation for a single stipulated overall sense of form there. It is devoid therefore of inner cohesion. However, the limited boundaries of the University of Konstanz (University Planning Bureau, 1965-1975) resulted in what is still the best solution, since the separate areas there are individually, carefully, and thoroughly worked out on the basis of an established overall pattern and a dense interlocking of functions. Nevertheless one gets a sense of a well-proportioned total design that fits into the landscape.

The belief in growth and unlimited production reached its high point toward the end of the sixties in a series of systematic building projects and megastructural dreams. Among the former are the huge structural systems so sensitively interpreted by E. Schulze-Fielitz following the work of Yona Friedman and the "house of houses" (*Haüyserhaus*) by Roland Frey. Among the latter are the Meta City (*Metastadt*) of Wolfgang Dietrich (partly built in the new town, Wulfen, 1968-1970); the Wohnberg of Erich Schneider-Wessling and the sculptural tower-houses by Wolfgang Döring (1966]. Apart from the compulsory monotony of this architecture, despite the twisting and turning of its building blocks, the quick obsolescence of purely technical elements and the reptilian appearance of the established structures put the architectonic validity of these enormous buildings into question.

The harsh reality of this architecture is bad enough, since, though the new "monumentality" around which a very lively discussion has developed may still be applied for individual building, sometimes even being unavoidable, in the case of residential building it leads to catastrophe. With the construction of new city districts, of new subdivisions and satellite cities, "the wandering socks of the planner" (*Ringelsocken der Planer*) as Hillebrecht had already gibed in the 1950s, demonstrated at last the bankruptcy of unidimensional urban images and purely functional realizations. From the so-called Gropius-city of Brits-Buckow-Rudow [from 1965 on] in Berlin the ever more desolate errant pathway courses to the new city of Wulfen [Fritz Eggeling, 1964-1970] through the Märkische quarter [Düttman, Henrich, Müller, 1963-1972] as far as Düsseldorf-Garath [Max Guther, 1966-1973] and Munich-Perlach [Neue Heimat after Bernard Lauter's design, 1967-1976]. Finally, even qualified architects could design only with the use of pails of paint and writing boards. Whatever else was planned is best forgotten. The damage done by the infamous "area rehabilitations"(*Flächensanierungen*), because of which whole city districts were destroyed, is indeed irreparable. In the final analysis, nevertheless, architecture here was no more than the expression of the entire society's belief in growth.

A pseudo-Functionalism dominated German architectural theory of the 1950s and 1960s. The "crutch of Functionalism" (Philip Johnson), so seemingly helpful and all too eagerly grasped, especially by less qualified architects, proved itself to be extremely dangerous. Its favorite motto, "That which functions is beautiful," revealed itself to be a false aesthetic, since what functions best must be at the same time also the most economical. This key concept of the time which however leads to nothing more was joined to a fetish for the material, a kind of minimal architecture. In place of banished ornamentation and decoration bare material was preferred: the empty brick wall or the visible concrete. It was altogether overlooked that concentration on the material alone would result, in the final analysis, only in a kind of amateurish construction. The strict fire statutes of the Federal Republic also added to this effect, so that the steel building remains totally underdeveloped and has seldom been fully mastered by German architects. After the collapse of the residential building market and of the ideal of Functionalism, an ever increasing criticism was heard from the mid-1960s on which led to a kind of formal silence but also to some rethinking of new statements.

Criticism of Architects and New Statements, 1965-1975

German postwar architecture was accompanied from the beginning by rather sharp criticism, which remained almost unnoticed, however, until the enormous need to catch up was satisfied. Only after homesteads and prosperity were secured did one look up to see where one was. Hans Paul Bahrdt's urban sociological investigations (*Die Moderne Grosstadt*, Reinbek, 1961) were followed by Alexander Mitscherlich's provocative writing on *The Inhospitableness of Our Cities* (*Die Unwirtlichkeit unserer Städte*, Frankfurt/Main 1965) and Theordore Adorno's "Functionalism Today" ("Funktionalismus Heute," *Neue Rundschau*, 1966). The critics followed hot on each other's heels. It became almost a matter of course to hold the architectural profession responsible for everything. The reaction took an enormous variety of forms.

In place of the previous shortage of theories there followed overtheorizing; planning occurred in ever more complex forms; economics and especially sociology became the protective shields of architects. In an environment which only pointed its finger at the architect, the sociologist became his psychiatrist and without the sociologist he could draw not so much as a line: the sociologist supplied the architect with justification and legitimization. It was only after the economic recession that a rational balance between theory and practice was struck.

A second answer to the critics was an overaestheticizing of Functionalism. The chief spokesmen for this direction were Wolfgang Döring [the Mayer-Kuckuk house in Bad Honneff, 1967] and especially Ludwig Leo. In the case of his DLRG (Deutsche Lebensrettungs Gesellschaft)-Station in Pichelsdorf-Berlin [1969-1972] and even more so in the water research installation of the Technical University of Berlin [1976], he approximated industrial design, despite his greater architectonic quality. His functional styling reminds us of the streamlining of the automobile chassis.

German architecture of this decade is characterized by a strong broadening and variety of forms in which developments that reflected the influences of the Brutalists or Louis Kahn also answered the criticisms of monotony, lack of inspiration, and poverty of experience. These criticisms were most quickly countered by means of livelier masses, contrasts of materials, and individual appeals. The polygonal ground plan and elevation, alternation of closed and open wall sections, multiple movements by means of stairways, courtyards, or offset floor levels, and ingenious illumination and viewpoints soon belonged to the new repertoire. From among a multiplicity of examples we need refer only to the works of Harold Deilmann [the West German National Bank in Düsseldorf (1974-1976) and the Municipal Savings Bank in Schwelm (1976-1978)], Friedrich Spengelin and others [Hamburg-Mannheimer Insurance Co., Hamburg, 1975], and Georg Heinrichs and Hans C. Müller [Leitz Factory in Stuttgart, 1966-1967]. The inner logic and purposive invention of forms of a Louis Kahn is lacking in Germany, and despite a broadening of formal vocabulary in response to earlier deficiencies, it is usually overlooked that too much movement and a superficial overabundance of charm also result in monotony.

Buildings that seem to be almost architectural sculptures belong in the realm of highly variegated forms and novel spatial effects. The best known proponent of this tendency, Gottfried Böhm, son of the specialist in church architecture, Dominikus Böhm, was associated in his draftsmanship with German Expressionism of the twenties. His buildings are characterized by a freely plastic conception of architecture rather than the organic approach of Scharoun or Häring. He attains richly experimental but at the same time highly subjective and in part outspokenly arbitrary architectural formulations that are often seen as autonomous, totally self-sufficient sculptures. What appears in the City Hall of Bensberg [1965-1967] (fig. 22.3) as a happy accommodation of a contrasting building structure to an old neighborhood (a building in which even the city hall tower, though nonfunctional, seems sensible) becomes a subjective prismatic concretion of an almost anxiety-producing strength in the Church of the Home for the Aged at Düsseldorf-Garath and more so in the Pilgrimmage Church at Neviges [1967].

22.3. Gottfried Böhm, architect. City Hall at Bensberg, 1965-1967. (Photograph: Courtesy of Winfried Nerdinger)

The breadth of these sculpturesque architectural efforts extends from the relatively gentle convex-concave swinging movements in the Düsseldorf theatre [1970] by Bernard Pfau through the Berlin educational center [1974] of Hermann Fehling and Daniel Gogel (an interpretation of Scharoun, in which the entire spatial richness unfolds not altogether reasonably in the stairwell) to the brutalist concrete castle of the theater at Ingolstadt [1966] by Hardt-Waltherr Hämer. These plastic interpretations border upon a mania for originality and pseudo-artistic self-indulgence. The claim of affecting the fantastic, emotional, and irrational side of mankind by means of a sculptural architecture appears to have been very well justified in the Mensa [1970] of the University of Saarbrücken, a collaborative work of the architect Walter Schrempf and the sculptor Otto Herbert Hajek. Nevertheless, no new direction is suggested here since basically it is a building developed functionally by means of a clear modulus in its ground plan upon which there was built a thoroughly plastic modeling of upper surfaces and spaces.

Only formal aspects have been described in our discussion of an increased and more differentiated architectural vocabulary. In terms of content new thematic concepts such as flexibility, multifunctionalism, mobility, variability, complexity, and concentration have become magic words of enchantment and panaceas for architecture and town planning. Their employment leads to the most standardized large-scale buildings with the most varied architectural functioning. In office buildings, one of the best of which is Egon Eiermann's last work, the Olivetti Administrative and Technical Center (fig. 22.4) in Frankfurt [1967-1970], the monumental, American-style, uninterrupted office space becomes a veritable landscape of offices flowing into one another. Religious buildings become church centers. And convention centers become multifunctional municipal halls and sports arenas, multipurpose spaces with sliding walls, movable partitions, variable floor levels, and so on, to express an evidently unlimited demand for openness for multiple uses. These are in reality an index of a total exploitation of every sector of human life (*Vernützung*, after Martin Heidegger). A zenith was attained in the development of school construction. There, a multiplicity of types was created in response to divergent and constantly changing notions of pedagogic goals and experiments in culturally and politically independent federal provinces. The school in Osterburken (Baden-Württemberg) by Bassenge, Puhan-Schulz and Schreck [1968] marks a breakthrough to building with concentrated, well-integrated functions. Community schools, elementary-junior high schools (*Gesamtschulen*) and central schools, as well as the experimental University of Bielefeld, were developed into appalling factories for schooling and show that only a certain measure of flexibility is sensible. A looser type, of which the Progymnasium in Lorch [1968-1970] by Behnisch and Partners is a perfect example, indicated the direction the seventies would take.

22.4. Egon Eiermann, architect. Olivetti Administration and Training Building. Frankfurt/M, 1967-1970. (Photograph: Courtesy of Winfried Nerdinger)

In residential construction the new motto is "concentration"; in town planning, "urbanity." Opposed to dispersed communities is the idea of concentration; against loosening up, density; against healthy greenery, metropolitan atmosphere. The dense siting of buildings in accord with the Anglo-Saxon ideal of "low rise, high density" led to no particularly noteworthy solutions in West Germany. The "Hill House" ("Hügelhaus") of Roland Frey, Hermann Schröder and Peter Faller [1964-1966] in Marl was a kind of fly-by-night design. The combination of skyscraper with low outer buildings as in Buxtehude and Göttengen by Friedrich Spengelin and others [1970-1973] or the residential precinct for the 1972 Olympic Games in Munich by Irwin Heinle and Robert Wischer are insensitive and lacking in inspiration when compared with English and Dutch solutions.

The passion for flexible spatial frames and construction resulted nevertheless in the rise of a seemingly related field that had remained unnoticed for quite some time. The investigation of Frei Otto in light load-bearing building and especially his research in lightweight construction for structures of great breadth have been the most important German postwar contributions to architecture and have become international in scope. Frei Otto's work began in the fifties with systematic research into the characteristics of membranes. Knowledge of the age-old practices of pitching tents afforded him important bases for techniques of light-load construction, such as the minimalizing of weight and surfaces, natural flexibility, and optimization of tensile constructions. Lightness of weight as a measure of constructional efficiency led to the study of biological processes, since the procedures of creating and optimizing forms in lightweight buildings are analogous to the biological laws of mutation and selection. Thus, the principles of the light load-bearing building with minimalization of material and optimization of construction impressed themselves upon the world of living, natural forms. Frei Otto works with models especially. His developmental models are no longer discoveries of form, but rather inventions of form based upon a recognition of active forces and the realization of relationships between form, force, and mass that provide essential answers to problems of architectural form and structure.

After such tent structures as the pavilions for the flower shows in Cologne [1957] and Hamburg [1963], Frei Otto turned in the sixties towards cable-net systems, the research for which culminated in his and Rolf Gutbrod's German Pavilion at the Montreal World's Fair of 1967. The structures erected by Günther Behnisch and Partner in consultation with Frei Otto for the 1972 Olympics (fig. 22.5) in Munich were the high point in the construction of tensile surface structures. Necessarily many compromises and modifications were made, but, taken altogether, the outstretched tensile cable networks of the roof constructions and the harmonic combination of architecture and landscape at the Munich Olympics are undoubtedly the most spectacular events in postwar German architecture up to now. Whether, of course, the supposition by architectural critics of the symbolic content of a light, "free architecture" is transferable to other realms, as the architectural team planning the new governmental quarter in Bonn would like to demonstrate, or whether any further development or effect is indeed possible, is still an open question.

In any case, Frei Otto has opened up a series of further possibilities for architecture. In the hotel and convention center at Mecca [1968-1969], working again with Rolf Gutbrod, a freely suspended system of load-bearing tensile surfaces is employed as the main roofing. Thereby, a central concern of Frei Otto is satisfied, the accommodation of architecture to its climatic environment and the creation of spacious coverings, each with its own comfortable microclimate, by means of broad spans of thin, shading roofs. The new spatial possibilities tested in the Montreal pavilion's grid shell, the return to a hanging chain network, is demonstrated in the multipurpose hall erected in Mannheim in 1975 (fig. 22.6) in cooperation with Carlfried Mutschler and Partners. Here a grid shell, a spatially curved, highly compressed, strut system with a protective, membranelike film drawn over it, is constructed upon a free-form ground plan. Beyond this, Frei Otto has experimented with variable shifting roofs in theaters at Cannes [1965] and Hersfeld [1967] and at a year-round swimming pool at Regensburg [1970] as well as with pneumatic constructions. The special, still far from fully understood meaning of Frei Otto's work resides also in his having opened a pathway toward an architecture adaptable to all sorts of problems and landscapes, an architecture in accord with its total environment.

Contemporary Trends

At the end of the 1970s and in the 1980s we are still unable to speak of a specifically German contemporary architecture. International diversity and an insecurity of form with which, nevertheless, architects experiment indiscriminately—form that is

22.5. Günther Behnisch and Partner, architects, with Frei Otto, consultant. Olympic Grounds. Munich, 1969-1972. (Photograph: Courtesy of the Institute für leichte Flächentragwerke)

totally, inadequately, and forcibly classified with the pseudoepochal ideas of neo-Mannerism, Post-Modern and Second Modern, among others—may be found with necessary modifications throughout Germany. Only in the case of some architectural teams such as Frei Otto and Günther Behnisch are there relatively independent architectural aims without, however, special national significance. For this one might cite the efforts of Otto Steidle and Doris and Ralph Thut in Munich with a new type of residential building consisting of industrial, prefabricated parts.

From the beginning of the 1970s an intensified reflection upon our historical heritage found expression in far-reaching laws for the protection of monuments, in the reconstruction of older sections of cities, in the creation of pedestrian zones, in a new trend favoring the inner city as well as in criticisms of growth and Rationalism. Architectural discussion has become concerned with historical buildings, the new building within the older neighborhood, and the search for ties and identity with the history of what has been built as a central area of interest.

The organic and continuous processing of regional and historic architecture in other countries provoked a sense of neohistoricism in Germany, after years of abstinence because of its misuse in the 1930s. A new Biedermeier is marketed, for instance, as showing a new German quality of life, just as had occurred

22.6. Carlfried Mutschler and Partners, Frei Otto, architects. Multiple Purpose Hall of the National Garden Show. Mannheim, 1975. (Photograph: Courtesy of the Institute für leichte Flächentragwerke)

previously with the bleakness of the so-called International Style of architecture. This waxworkslike architecture of accommodation, a kind of paraphrased historicism that found its climax in the building of the Neue Pinakothek in Munich by Alexander von Branca [1975-1980], in the last analysis signals nothing more than a fad. The historical environment destroyed during the Second World War is not to be reconstructed motivated by a search for national identity as in Poland, but rather, after some thirty years' delay, it is to be reconstructed artifically with renowned buildings and architectural investments that are financially profitable.

Besides these imitative abuses, there are also, however, statements resulting from highly sophisticated analyses of architectonic linkages and of the historical language of architecture. Thus, from a sketch by Scharoun, Werner Düttmann enclosed the destroyed Mehringplatz in Berlin-Kreutzberg with a new, circular development [1970-1975], that transposed the old Belle-Alliance-Platz effortlessly into the present. Similarly, in Hannover, Dieter Oesterlen fit the neighboring city fortress to the Historical Museum and with Heinrich Moldenschardt dovetailed the Home for the Elderly in Berlin-Charlottenburg [1969] with an historical quarter of the city. For the development of the district at the Rotebühlplatz in Stuttgart [1975-1978] Hans Kammerer and Walter Belz understood how to link the old passages and arcade motifs with a new architectonic context. Johannes Uhl integrated an historic frieze by the neoclassicist architect Friedrich Gilly with the Home for the Aged at the Charlottenburg Palace in Berlin [1975-1977], and in the process developed an architectural vocabulary based upon the formal assumptions of the palace. The breaking up of space into small sections and the great variety of spatial forms in these examples are no chance kinks and twists of similarly oriented little boxes, but rather constitute a sensitively felt ordering of complex requirements and relationships.

Oswald Mathias Ungers's "humanistic architecture'' provides the most profound start toward an integration of historical elements with contemporary demands. Knowledge gained from history, the acceptance and assimilation of historical precedents, the analysis of a mature and multilayered, imprinted environment represent the same humanistic beginnings. An integration with the present, an accentuation and distinguishing of the site, a creative realization of various tasks in accord with the employment of basic architectonic precepts and archetypes all characterize Ungers's endeavors. For him the history of architecture is the living reservoir of fundamental ideas upon which his projects are built in a totally new manner. This is particularly clear in his competition designs for the Berlin Museums [1965], the Wallraf-Richartz Museum at Cologne [1975] and the Hotel Berlin [1977]. Perhaps it is significant that Ungers as yet has been unable to build any of his projects in Germany. Perhaps one day a new German architecture will grow out of inquiry into the reinterpretation and new interpretation of the vast repertoire of architectonic forms and out of the harmonizing of history with the present, toward which many architects today are striving.

Bibliography

BOOKS

Behnisch und Partner. *Bauten und Entwürfe*. Stuttgart, 1975.

Burchard, John. *The Voice of the Phoenix: Postwar Architecture in Germany*. Cambridge, Mass., 1966.

Conrads, Ulrich, and Marschall, Werner. *Neue deutsche Architektur 2*. Stuttgart, 1962.

Drew, Philip. *Frei Otto: Form und Konstruktion*. Stuttgart, 1976.

Feuerstein, Günther. *New Directions in German Architecture*. New York: Studio Vista, 1968.

Hatje, Gerd; Hoffman, Hubert; and Kaspar, Karl. *Neue deutsche Architektur*. Stuttgart, 1956.

Hitchcock, Henry-Russell. *Hentrich-Petschnigg und Partner, Bauten und Entwürfe*. Düsseldorf, 1973.

Klotz, Henrich. *Architektur in der Bundesrepublik*. Frankfurt/M, 1977.

König, Giovanni Klaus. *Architettura Tedesca dei Secondo Dopoguerra*. Bologna, 1965.

Nestler, Paolo, and Bode, Peter M. *Deutsche Kunst seit 1960, Architektur*. Munich, 1976.

Pehnt, Wolfgang. *Neue deutsche Architektur 3*. Stuttgart, 1970.

Reichow, Hans Bernhard. *Die autogerechte Stadt*. Ravensburg, 1959.

Scharoun, Hans. *Austellungskatalog*. Berlin, 1967.
Schwagenscheidt, Walter. *Die Raumstadt*. Heidelberg, 1949.
Schwarz, Rudolf. *Wegweisung der Technik und andere Schriften*. Braunschweig, 1979.
Simon, Alfred. *Architecture in Germany*. Essen, 1969.
______. *Bauen in Deutschland 1945-1962*. Hamburg, 1963.
Werner, Bruno E. *Neues Bauen in Deutschland*. Munich, 1952.

JOURNALS

Bofinger, Helge, and Bofinger, Margret, eds. "Architektur in Deutschland." *Das Kunstwerk* 2, 3 (1979).
Goulet, Patrice, and Lacombe, Pierre, eds. "Allemagne." *L'Architecture d'Aujourd'hui* 57, 58 (October 1967).

USEFUL JOURNALS

Arch +, Aachen
Architektur und Wohnwelt, Stuttgart
Bauen und Wohnen, Stuttgart
Baukunst und Werkform (since 1972: *Deutsche Bauzeitung*), Stuttgart
Baumeister, Munich
Bauwelt, Berlin
Bundesbaublatt, Bonn
Detail, Munich
Der Architekt, Bonn
Deutsche Bauzeitung, Gütersloh
Deutsches Architektenblatt, Bonn
Wettbewerbe Aktuell, Munich

23
GREAT BRITAIN
MALCOLM QUANTRILL

In order to appreciate the evolution of British architecture since the Second World War it is helpful to recall its main developments from the beginning of the century and more particularly those of the between-the-wars period. In a perspective of this background the work of Mackintosh, Voysey, Baillie Scott, and Lutyens stands out against a backdrop of eclecticism that characterized the period from 1875 to the outbreak of the First World War. But much of the vitality of British architecture, especially as evidenced by the late flowering at the turn of the century, had disappeared by 1910. The focus of new developments, already rooted on the Continent in the 1890s, therefore shifted away from Britain. Mackintosh did little work after 1907, Baillie Scott became a neo-Georgian reactionary, and it is difficult to believe that Voysey lived until the 1940s. Lutyens, too, became conservative, although retaining that essential wit which Pevsner praises, while his mastery of monumental scale was evidenced by his planning of New Delhi in 1920-1921.

Adams, Holden, and Pearson's Morden Station for the London Underground of 1926 is a milestone in British work, beginning a decade of clear-cut geometric forms with fine brickwork and little apparent Continental influence. In 1927 Frederick Etchell's English translation of Le Corbusier's *Vers une architecture* and Bennett's *Architectural Design in Concrete* were published. This new building material became closely associated with developments in Britain and on the Continent. In this connection the influence of Sir Owen Williams, an engineer rather than an architect, became paramount in British work, and the significance of his warehouse for Boots at Beeston, Birmingham [1931-1932] remains: it was a most daring example of cantilever construction from mushroom columns.

At that point the influence of two schools of architecture became important: the Architectural Association in London and Liverpool University. But the native products schooled in the rather free atmosphere of the Architectural Association in London and at Liverpool University under Sir Charles Reilly were balanced by the influx of a large group of Continental architects in the 1930s, including Gropius and Mendelsohn and the Swiss-born Lescaze who was working on Dartington Hall from 1931 for an American client. All three went on to America but the Russian, Berthold Lubetkin, stayed and became a leader of the new generation. His Gorilla House for Regents Park Zoo of 1931 brought the International Style to Britain, while his Penguin Pool of 1933 put Britain back into the international league. His collaborator in these works was none other than the Danish-born engineer, Ove Arup, who has been so influential in British architecture since 1950. Also in 1933 Lubetkin and his associates (grouped together as the firm Tecton) constructed the first English "point-block" of flats known as High Point I, in Highgate, North London. A ten-story block of flats, it combined Lubetkin's idiosyncratic use of Corbusian curves with his acknowledgement of Perret's concrete techniques. It was followed in 1937 by a second block, Highpoint II.

The year 1935 saw the arrival in England of Erich Mendelsohn, who with Chermayeff produced some interesting private houses and the Bexhill Pavilion, which recalled in its curved glass stairwells Mendelsohn's earlier Schocken department store in Stuttgart. By that time, too, Maxwell Fry (who was briefly in partnership with Gropius) and F. R. S. Yorke (who worked with Breuer) and Wells Coates had established themselves in practice. Both Breuer and Gropius arrived in England in 1936, providing more Continental influence before they moved on to the United States. Breuer and Yorke produced the Gane Pavilion for the Royal Show in Bristol [1936] and Gropius and Fry set the pace for postwar school design with the Impington Village College, Cambridgeshire [1937-1938]. But even given the stimulation of Continental architects passing through, and Lubetkin's leadership, modern architecture of quality occurred only sporadically, with Owen Williams's Peckham Health Centre and William Crabtree's Peter Jones's department store (with Charles Reilly) as significant as the work involving Continental partners. Certainly, between the wars there had been no large-scale conversion of British architecture to the Corbusian or Bauhaus ethic to which Lubetkin devoted himself.

There was virtually no continuity of personnel from the pre-1939 to the post-1945 period. The notable exceptions were F. R. S. Yorke (who died in 1962), Maxwell Fry, and Frederick Gibberd. But all the architects in the forefront of developments in the 1950s and 1960s, the Smithsons, Leslie Martin, James Stirling, Denys Lasdun (a late partner in Tecton but not active in the mid-1930s), and Richard Sheppard, constitute a distinct postwar generation.

Already in 1945 Frederick Gibberd got off to a promising start with his steel-framed semidetached houses for Northolt. Experimental in both plan and construction, they reflected Britain's preoccupation at the time with industrialization and industrial education, and as Cyril Mardall described them in 1948 they were probably the most important contribution to permanent prefabricated housing. After the claustrophobic war years, we looked again to the outside world, and there were many reviews of Continental work in our journals, dominated at first by attention to neutral Switzerland. By 1947-1948 we had begun to focus also on Scandinavian work, particularly that of Denmark and Sweden. In 1948 there was a renewed interest in Dutch architecture (Dudok had been a great favorite with British architects in the 1930s), particularly in the new buildings of Brinkman and Van den Broek and the rebuilding of Rotterdam.

The year 1947 saw the publication in the March issue of the *Architectural Review* of Colin Rowe's article "The Mathematics of the Ideal Villa: Palladio and Le Corbusier Compared." It also brought the Royal Fine Art Commission's expression of dissatisfaction with Sir Giles Gilbert Scott's design for the rebuilding of Coventry Cathedral and the exciting concrete design for the rubber factory at Bryn Maur by the Architects Cooperative Partnership with Ove Arup, with its wide spans and rectangular domes over the production area. The schools at Ruislip and Eastcote by Howard Lobb completed in 1948 reflected the Adams, Holden, and Pearson Underground Stations of the thirties. The February 1949 *Architectural Review* editorial "Towards a Philosophy of Architecture" was followed by Eric de Mare's "CANON—Towards a Consistent Theory of Modern Architecture." By 1950 *Architectural Review* included its first serious study of traditional (vernacular) surfaces and textures; J. M. Richards's article "The Next Step" raised the question "what are the alternatives to functionalism itself becoming a style?" and suggested that architects need a human as well as a scientific ideal, while defining the routes by which contemporary architects could lead themselves out of their difficulties by: (1) the maximum exploitation of mechanization; (2) conscious humanization; and (3) a social-realist approach. By 1950 also, there was a preview of the South Bank Festival of Britain Exhibition and the first appearance of the work of Arne Jacobsen in British journals, while Colin Rowe, always ahead with his historical comparisons, published his article "Mannerism and Modern Architecture" in the May issue of *Architectural Review*.

In 1951 the conversion of No. 70 Piccadilly by James Cubitt and Partners, for the South African Tourist Corporation, completely broke down the barrier between street and interior. But British architecture, the Bryn Maur factory aside, was still in the grip of austerity and restrictive building legislation and largely preoccupied with small-scale gestures, more utilitarian than functional: there was certainly nothing to compare with the new railway terminal in Rome. The Festival of Britain Exhibition drew together Hugh Casson (Director of Architecture), Misha Black, H. D. Cadbury-Brown, Ralph Tubbs, Edward Mills, Powell and Moya, Basil Spence, Leonard Manasseh, Maxwell Fry, and Jane Drew. The Royal Festival Hall by Robert Matthew and Leslie Martin translated Functionalism into a festival decorative style, a celebration of peace. Its interior spatial concepts owed something to the work of Martin's friend, Naum Gabo, and managed to absorb many Continental influences while remaining English in its sense of heraldic clutter, with more style than substance. Emberton's flats in Killick Street, Finsbury, of this period, owe more to Wells Coates's Lawn Road flats than to his own work of the 1930s. But in 1951 we also saw completed the Churchill Gardens housing estate in Pimlico (first phase) by Powell and Moya, which was the most distinguished piece of modern housing in Britain since High Point [1933-1937].

Peter and Alison Smithson first came into prominence in 1949 when they won the competition for a new school at Hunstanton, Norfolk (*Architectural Review*, April, 1954). Their work provided a stark contrast to the sentimental gestures of the Festival of Britain team, which had been concerned more with a chauvinistic celebration than architectural exploration. The Smithsons wanted to create what they described as "an architecture of reality"; they thought "our generation must try and produce evidence that men are at work." They wanted "an art concerned with natural order, the poetic relationship between living things and environment." In the tradition of Fabianism they desired "towns and buildings that do not make us feel ashamed." "We live," they wrote, "in moron-made cities" with architecture "reduced to a mindless routine." (For a selection of their ideas see, for example, "English Brutalism, Selection of Writings," *Zodiac* 18 [1968]: 43-50). Their importance has been not only as architects but also as pamphleteers, creating their own scenarios, propagating theory in tandem with practice. They moved on from their opening position, what Robert Maxwell calls the New Empiricism—a blend of realism and sentimentality—to Brutalism. This new expression was less concerned with quality for its own sake and more devoted to the intrinsic interest of materials, junctions, and connections. Nothing was hidden beneath cunning detail: almost all was revealed. The quasi-elegance of the Festival of Britain was "out," and with it went parochialism, as a new urban formality was proposed and worked out by the Smithsons.

Beginning with Hunstanton School [completed 1954], they went on to consolidate their position with the Economist Group and St. Hilda's College, Oxford (fig. 23.1), with their attachment to Brutalism as such traceable to a project for a Soho town house of 1952. Banham fixes the new and long overdue explosion in architectural theory—"New Brutalism"—as taking place in 1954. Its development in Britain once again linked British architecture with Le Corbusier. Briefly, through the design of the flats at Langdon House Close, Ham Common [1958], James Stirling and James Gowan were associated with Brutalism. Stirling's article "Garches to Jaoul" appeared in the *Architectural Review* in 1955, following on the publication of the Smithsons' manifesto in *Architectural Design* (January, 1955).

23.1. Alison and Peter Smithson, architects. Gorden Building, St. Hilda's College, part-cellular structure, "interpretable" façade, 1967-1970. (Photograph: Courtesy of the architects)

New Brutalism combined vernacular elements, particularly those observed in Le Corbusier's Mediterranean sketches, with the clarity of expressive detailing in the Japanese tradition. Its translation into a British statement, the conversion of a Mediterranean peasant tradition with small windows and affinity with the landscape, came not from the Smithsons but Richard Llewelyn-Davies and John Weeks in the village rebuilding of Rushbrooke, Suffolk. The Smithsons' contribution belonged more to the *béton brut* and the Japanese tradition, and their work had profound echoes in the interpretations of Colin St. John Wilson and Alex Hardy's 1959 extensions to the Cambridge School of Architecture, Sir Leslie Martin and Colin St. John Wilson's 1962 Harvey Court at Caius College, Cambridge, and Richard Sheppard, Robson and Partners' 1964 Churchill College (fig. 23.2).

23.2. Richard Sheppard, Robson and Partners, architects. Churchill College, 1964. (Photograph: Courtesy of Sam Lambert, London)

Thus, if they were not in the forefront of built work, the Smithsons dominated a substantial area of the theoretical field. The competition for Coventry Cathedral was won in 1951 by Basil Spence, but the failed designs were more instructive, especially the Smithsons'. It was also something of an irony to see their "style" rather than their entry win the Churchill College competition. Their influence, through their writings, has remained paramount, although their own practice has dwindled.

The year 1952 saw not only the first tentative beginnings of New Brutalism in Britain but also the completion of the Bryn Maur factory and, of equal importance, the real beginnings of the Hertfordshire School Programme under C. H. Aslin. All the schools were prefabricated and of the first three Croxley Green Junior Day Nursery School at Garston was the most advanced, being the first to adopt the 40-inch grid, the imperial equivalent to the meter. These Hertfordshire developments led to the establishment of a substantial prefabrication program for British schools under the aegis of the Consortium of Local Authorities Special Programme (CLASP).

In addition to Brutalism and the development of industrialized building programs, particularly in relation to the design of new schools, the fifties also saw the expansion of the British universities system, the results of which were to be realized in the sixties. It was a decade of substantial developments in the work of the London County Council, beginning with the completion of the Royal Festival Hall on the South Bank (Robert Matthew and others) and ending with another high point in housing at the Alton Estate, Roehampton, completed in 1959. In the private sector a number of architects consolidated their reputations. Basil Spence, whose Coventry Cathedral had been criticized for "the uncertainty of its structural character," went on to become the establishment architect. He was able to turn his hand to almost any form of expression, as the neo-Brutalist Falmer House, University of Sussex [completed 1960] showed. Spence's British Embassy in Rome (with Anthony Blee) begun in 1960 and completed in 1971 exhibits a mannerism which "fitted perfectly into the general panorama of world architecture" (Bruno Zevi). Richard Siefert emerged as the master of plot-ratio, giving him an edge on all other architects in the design of commercial office buildings, which were to dominate London building activity in the late fifties and throughout the sixties.

Denys Lasdun produced work of distinction in the fifties, providing in the relative purity of his forms and detailing a marked contrast to the Brutalists. Both his Hallfield School [1955] and the so-called cluster blocks of flats [1955-1959] continue the highly articulated expression associated with Tecton. His luxury block of flats, Green Park [1958-1960], saw further refinement which was maintained in the prestigious commission for the Royal College of Physicians in Regents Park [1960-1964]. He went on to provide the plan and design the main buildings of the University of East Anglia, before realizing the long-standing ambition of the country in his National Theatre building on London's South Bank [1976]. Throughout his postwar work he has maintained a hard-line attachment to working out the Formalism rather than the Functionalism of the Modern Movement. Lasdun's buildings are always distinctive in form, sometimes elegant as the Green Park flats and the Royal College of Physicians, often controversial as the National Theatre and the new University of London buildings in Russell Square: his architecture has a forceful determinism, a no-nonsense take-it-or-leave-it approach to both site and building. In Colin Rowe's terms, Lasdun's buildings are very definitely objects, containers styled to have impact rather than to be in keeping. Lasdun is no apologist for the Modern Movement; rather his work asserts, often aggressively, the necessity for it to be taken on its own terms. This is particularly the case with the hostile, bunkerlike exterior of the National Theatre, which offers an austere, even drab image of grey concrete for this important national monument. Lasdun provides a sharp contrast to Basil Spence, whom he succeeded as the establishment architect in the 1970s since it is clearly his aim to express rather than to please.

Soon after the end of the Second World War F. R. S. Yorke created a partnership with Eugene Rosenberg and Cyril Mardall. This collaboration preceded by a few months the establishment of both the Architects' Co-Partnership (Great Britain) and the Architects' Collaborative (United States) and it was of international calibre both in origin and impact. Yorke, the Englishman, joined forces with Rosenberg, the Czech, and Mardall, the Finn. It was not a formalized partnership in the legal sense until shortly before Yorke's death in 1962, but instead what Banham describes as a "friendly cohabitation" of three separate but equal practices. We have come to think of the 1970s as the decade of survival for the profession, yet the 1950s had already provided a major time of trial in Britain. There had been an extremely tight control on private construction from the end of the war until the mid-1950s, with the building permit system in operation until 1954. Thus, from the mid-1940s until the mid-1950s the vast majority of York, Rosenberg, and Mardall's (YRM) work was for public-sector clients. During this period also, because of the loose nature of the partnership there was no single corporate image. This was changed not so much by the formalization of the partnership as by changes in its structure: Randall Evans (a member of Yorke's earlier partnership with Breuer) and Sheffield-trained David Allford were made full partners in 1958, while Edinburgh-trained Brian Henderson was created a partner in 1961. Both Allford and Henderson were in their thirties when made partners and they have contributed substantially to the deliberate policy that has created the image of YRM as the British equivalent to SOM (Skidmore, Owings and Merrill) in terms of standardization, clarity of thinking, and uniformity of quality.

The new tough-mindedness towards unified design standards was not aimed at the achievement of a style as such. But there was one clear influence upon the new thinking at YRM, the Smithsons' Hunstanton School, completed in 1954, and this was evident in their design of the steel and glass terminal for London's second airport at Gatwick, the first phase of which was opened in 1958. Of course the origin of the Hunstanton idiom is to be found in the work of Mies van der Rohe but it is important to realize that Gatwick airport predates all other airports in the Miesian style and thus secured renewed international standing for YRM. The design attitude which molded the policy of professional service offered by YRM was certainly not one of compromise. The firm believed in the Mies maxim that "God is in the details" and it set itself against the indifferent and arbitrary detailing that characterized so much British work of the fifties. Gatwick Airport was readily recognized as a high quality product but the partners were not content to mark time and allow this experiment to become a fixed style. They wanted a developing architectural mainstream, originating from the modern international movement of the 1920 and 1930s, but importantly they saw the creation of architecture not as a prima donna activity but as one of collaborative teamwork. Thus, their buildings while recognizable as the products of thoughtful minds have a quiet, low-key quality that reflects the anonymity of an established tradition, reflecting their belief that architecture is an art requiring the maximum application of a person's intellect, and this in turn demands an understanding for the need to develop a rational and visual sense of order.

The corporate image of YRM is probably most closely identified with their white-tile period, which began in the late 1950s and combined with the hard-edged, International Style motifs of stripwindows (some of which turned corners) with a quality reminiscent of good Georgian brickwork. But unlike its eighteenth-century precedent the white-tile style was so refined and had such a complete set of "specials" to deal with the detailing of junctions that on tiled surfaces no tile ever needed to be cut. YRM did not design to a tile-module: conversely the titles fitted a rigorous modular system, so that dimensioning of production drawings became almost superfluous because that "rational and visual sense of order" was built into the total design. Thus Warwick University and their own office at Greystoke Place in London became symbols of an oppressive uniformity. The fact that some tiles fell off the Warwick buildings did not improve their corporate image.

In spite of adverse criticism, YRM has achieved a variety of formats and expressions within a unity of means. Their work has ranged from airports to hospitals, and includes a collaboration with SOM on the new office block for the Boots Pure Drug Company at Beeston, Nottingham [1968]. They have designed housing for the Greater London Council (GLC) at King Edward's Road, Hackney [1971] and the London Borough of Tower Hamlets [1967], as well as the Manchester Magistrates' Court. In addition to Gatwick Airport [1974], there are those at Newcastle [1967, 1972], Stansted [1969], and Luton [1966]. Their most ambitious hospital is undoubtedly St. Thomas's, London [1975], while the extension in the courtyard of the Ashmolean Museum at Oxford has provided an unusual challenge of integration.

In terms of influence, the individual expression of Lasdun and the corporate statements of YRM have had less effect than the work and theories of the Smithsons. Indeed, among all the individual contributions to the British architectural scene only that of James Stirling has continued to have an equivalent impact at home and abroad. Stirling is a product of the Liverpool University School and his career began in 1950, the year of his graduation: the promise of his thesis design for a community center was soon developed in the following year with his "core and crosswall" house project which, contrary to current practice of that time, was based on a wide frontage. His early housing experiments range from the "stiff" domino housing of 1951 (precast reinforced-concrete post, beam, and slab) through the load-bearing brick and timber suburban house for North London [1953]—a single unit with terrace possibilities—to the Isle of Wight house designed with James Gowan [1956], with its two wings and core, and the House in the Chilterns [1956]: all possess an "essential homage to the square," as does the entry for the Churchill College Competition of 1958. This last project was described by Colin Rowe in the *Cambridge Review*, October 1959 as "the Blenheim of the Welfare State."

The Leicester University Engineering Building [1959] established the reputation of Stirling and Gowan, but the end of their partnership came soon afterwards. By 1964 Stirling was already assisted by Michael Wilford and their work together includes the unrealized Dorman Long Headquarters project [1965], the housing for Runcorn New Town [1967], the Olivetti Headquarters project for Milton Keynes [1971], and the Arts Center for St. Andrew's University [1971]. Roy Cameron partnered him on the flats in Camden Town [1964] and the Queens College Oxford extension [1966]. The competition project for Derby Civic Centre (fig. 4.2) he undertook with Leon Krier [1970].

Stirling has been much influenced by Colin Rowe, who was his thesis tutor, particularly by Rowe's pioneering work in exploring analogies between the villas of Le Corbusier and those of the Italian Renaissance. His work avoids cubic compression, expanding instead within a "free assemblage of varying accommodations" (Jacobus). Stirling could be said to be an impressionable designer. Already before his Liverpool thesis he had visited the East Coast of the United States for his five months "office practice" and seen all the New York buildings, plus George Howe and William Lescaze's Philadelphia Savings Fund Society building [1931-1932] in Philadelphia and Wright's sun-trap houses at Ardmore.

Stirling's buildings are projects; indeed they are "manifestoes" in themselves. His view that it might be more realistic for the architect to provide a completely negative interior led to emphasizing the wall, the skin, the enclosing membrane. His architecture is expressive (fig. 23.3) rather than expressionistic. As he

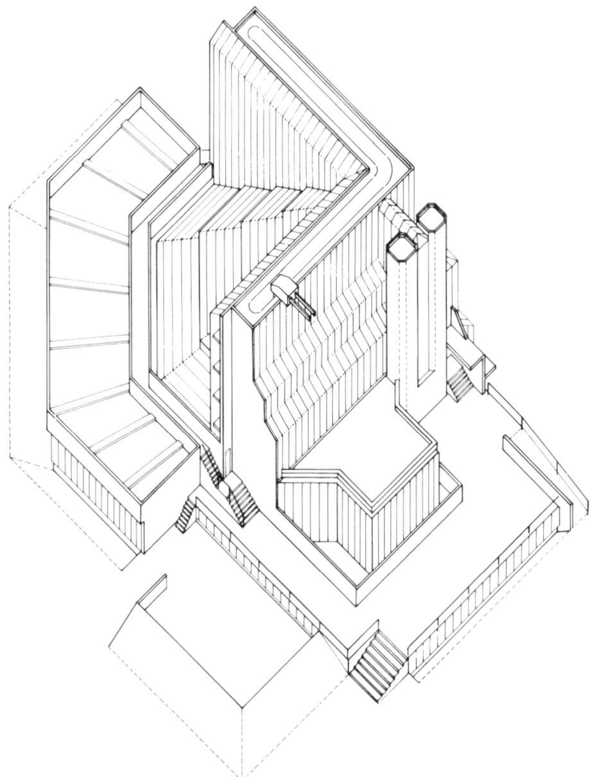

23.3. James Stirling, architect. History Faculty Library Building, Cambridge University, axonometric drawing, 1946-1967. (Photograph: Courtesy of the architect)

put it, "It is not assumed that every element should be expressive, but it is important that a hierarchy of the most significant volumes is recognizable in the ultimate composition" (from a lecture entitled "Anti-Structure," at a symposium held at Bologna University, November, 1966 and then published in, *Zodiac* 18 [1968]: 51-60). When, in the early fifties, he visited the Maison Verre in Paris by Pierre Chareau and Bernard Bijvoet [1932] with Colin Rowe and David Crowe, Stirling was reconsidering the use of glass and concluded that there were economic and design advantages to using industrial glazing bars capable of being cut and fitted on site, like carpentry.

The History Faculty Library (fig. 23.4) for Cambridge University [1964-1967] appears, superficially, to be a continuation of the "style" of the Leicester Engineering Building in its play between brick and tile, glass and plyglass, but it is as fresh and uncompromising as its predecessor. Circulation is the primary organizing element in the library, the L-shaped plan gripping the reading room which, as the raison d'être, is the inescapable focus. Also, the complete cross section of the building is experienced as one moves along the tier of galleries that form the corridors of the upper floors. Thus, Stirling replaces prewar modern architecture's free plan with a partially enclosed one. His design for Churchill College is an example of creating a sense of enclosure that was particularly significant to that site, isolated as it is from the sheltering form of the town, the urban enclosure.

In Stirling's view: "A great deal of modern architecture is banal, partly through the easy acceptance of compressing room accommodation into simple overall forms. We usually try to keep the ideal specific shape of a room and avoid distorting it to fit a structural module or a preconceived overall shape" (*Zodiac* 18 [1968]: 51-60). Thus, the History Faculty Library building is a stack of ideal room shapes, with the largest rooms at the lower levels and the smaller ones at the top. Stirling's adherence to a "hierarchy of the most significant volumes" expressed in the composition means that both Leicester and Cambridge are suggestive of 1920s construction.

Stirling's St. Andrew's University building, a hall of residence [1964-1967], is sited on an amphitheaterlike hillside that overlooks a flat shoreline, with the North Sea stretching beyond the horizon. The architect wanted each student to have this panorama. For this reason the building is backed against the deepest part of the slope, with the roofs stepping down from the plateau behind, matching the descending slope of the ground. Selection of materials was a fundamental problem as there was nothing local. Stirling decided on a kit of precast-concrete elements, employing considerable innovation. The external wall units have an incised diagonal pattern, similar in effect to herringbone, stressing the fact that although it is concrete it is a concrete "skin" and must therefore express tautness.

In the Dorman Long Headquarters project [1965] within its large-scale external steel framing the skin is pushed back behind the skeleton. It is basically a high office slab but splayed at the bottom to accommodate large space elements such as the canteen, library, and so forth, with the upper floors filled by the smaller offices. The externalized structure frees the internal plan. As Stirling has revealed:

> It transpired that there was a choice of about six alternatives for this structural grid, all using approximately the same weight of steel—it could be all diagonally braced or it could have horizontal stiffener beams at each floor. . . . The particular choice was therefore arbitrary. . . . A design which is primarily dependent on expression of structure is really superficial. . . . We made an architectural decision . . . horizontal wind stiffener beams adjacent to every floor on the upper part of the building but on the splayed front we omitted them at every other level, replacing them with diagonal struts. . . . The scale of structural grid therefore relates to the building section. (*Zodiac* 18 [1968]: 51-60.)

Stirling has argued that in England one must never talk about aesthetics and that all design explanations must always be in terms of common sense, function, and logic. He concluded that this probably means a design can never be far removed from common sense and logic. But the fact is that he favors the complex, articulated volumes which depend upon junctions other than right angles. From this point of view the Florey Building at Queens College, Oxford [1966] probably represents more of a composite of his own previous ideas than any other work. The plan, a five-sided, bent slab that forms an area opening onto the Cherwell, with struts on the rear to support the off-center weight of the upper stories, refers certainly to the Selwyn College project of 1959, although the wall of Selwyn was canted forward whereas Queens College is stepped back as in the 1965 Dorman Long project.

Stirling's position in British architecture is unique and personal. He is one of the new generation of practitioner critics, constructively critical of the International Style. His work shows us possible scenarios for the future, whilst giving us a better understanding of the recent architectural past. Nowhere is this more apparent than in the Derby Civic Centre (fig. 4.2) (with the facade of the old Assembly Hall preserved on a raked dais) and the St. Andrew's Art Centre projects. The "skins" on Stirling buildings come in different weights, indicating different architectural climates. Runcorn Town housing [1967] has probably the heaviest elemental form, contrasted by the light and mechanically industrial character of the Olivetti Training School at Haslemere [1969]. The mechanical quality of drawings from Stirling's office is a reflection of and reflected in the precision and clarity of his buildings. They are projected concepts, perfectly drawn so that they may be perfectly made. Although Pevsner reacted to Leicester by feeling that the Modern Movement of the Bauhaus had given way to Expressionist excess, it is clear that without the antistructural Rationalism of Stirling the renaissance of the Modern Movement in Britain would have been a rather tame affair. He has given it instead the benefit of a boldness which recalls that of Vanbrugh and Hawksmoor. Without him the postwar architectural scene in Britain would have been much impoverished. His work has brilliance, variety, and toughmindedness that sets it apart. His appointment to build the new Tate Gallery represents official recognition of his talents at home long after they have been rewarded in Germany.

In contrast to the "free assemblage of varying accommodations" that characterizes much of Stirling's work, that of his former partner James Gowan speaks of a tightness of plan, form, and order that reflects his interest in Palladio and Palladianism. This is particularly evident in his domestic work. His Schreiber House, Hampstead [1964], is probably the most finite example of this sense of order at work. The original house was modified by the addition of a glass-domed, circular swimming pool in 1967 and modular plywood built-in storage units and furniture in 1968. Thus, the Schreiber House remains his most complete expression of overall design control and attention to detail.

Its exterior vertical expression, with vertical window slots deeply recessed between wide, blue-rustic Staffordshire engineering brick piers, conceals the basic, horizontal organization of the house, with its service rooms and garage in the basement, living rooms on the ground floor, master suite on the first floor, and bedrooms and studio above. At ground level the plan form is marshalled into three distinct "pavilions," but the longer east one stops at the ground, with the exception of the staircase tower which rises to feed the other two pavilions on the upper floors. Points of access, circulation, and bathrooms are gripped tightly between the pavilions.

The glass dome over the swimming pool, rising out of a carefully manicured grass mound, stands in relation to the three brick towers as a conservatory or palm house to a Palladian villa. Detached from the house, with no covered access, the pool is thrust out on the circulation axis that provides the east-west spine of the plan, so that the order if not the plan is determinedly classical. The northern view (of Hampstead Heath) and the southern (sun) orientation of the rooms in the two towers explore the limitations of the site and that of the neighboring Victorian house to the west. In its geometry, with the three-foot-square planning grid and the circular, spherical forms of the swimming pool, the Schreiber House contains all the basic elements of Gowan's vocabulary. What links the Schreiber House to the Leicester University Engineering Building is the prevalence of technological perfection, as evidenced by the Georgian, wired and polished one-quarter-inch plate-glass bent to a hemisphere over the pool, the laminated-plywood furniture constructed on the Schreiber system shell-forming presses, and the handrails to the main staircase (reminiscent of William Pye sculpture).

The geometry of the Schreiber House also suggests that Gowan was the dominant influence in the Stirling and Gowan Churchill College Competition entry of 1958 as well as the dining hall for the Brunswick Park Primary School, Camberwell [1958-1960]. Its clarity and, in a sense, rigidity is found also in his conversion of a mansion flat, Mayfair [1969, demolished 1973] and the housing at East Hanningfield, Essex [begun in 1975]. The latter in particular, with its split gable-ends and rounded windows has the effect of dignifying this mixture of old people's dwellings and five-to-seven-person houses, raising them to a series of collective villas rather than the echelons of Radburn housing which in fact they are. The curious circular house at St. David's, Wales [1967] which, with its horizontal, metal, glazing bars looked back to the thirties, also anticipated the Schreiber swimming pool's form. It is, of course, difficult having achieved the masterpiece that the Schreiber House undoubtedly is to continue to reflect its standards in lower-budget domestic work. Although Gowan's sense of perfectionism is clearly attuned to the small scale of the private house, his work in this field has been mostly limited to projects. Housing does not, unfortunately, give him the same scope for his considerable talents, and he has been deprived of the opportunities of more expansive commissions. The seriousness of his intentions, his architectural intelligence, and the quality of his work have never been in doubt. Yet he remains an enigmatic figure as though living out of his time and place, while clearly attached to it by the depth of his thinking.

Although exhibiting a marked contrast of style, not merely in the architectural sense but in the wider meanings of personality and attachment, Stirling and Gowan clearly engaged in a common architectural battle. The thinking and work of Cedric Price is concerned with an entirely different mode of reference, being centered on invention rather than historic example and a flexibility of approach rather than the conservation of formal attitudes, whether aesthetic or professional. Robert Maxwell has said that Price "denies a rhetorical intention," seeing a building as a functional mechanism that accommodates those things that he wants to make happen. Perhaps his proposal for a Fun Palace is the best example of this lack of rhetorical intention, yet this large-scale structure, complete with cranes to permit the desired transformation of scene, seems to suggest building as performance as much as any cathedral, the changes being mechanical rather than liturgical. While his Aviary at London Zoo [1962] with Lord Snowdon and the engineer Frank Newby is a building absolutely determined by the need to view the birds and to demonstrate their different habitats, the suspended tensegrity structure (that is, the triangulated structure with its cables in a state of pure tension, its rods in pure compression) is the mechanism that accommodates scene and performance. The computer building at London Airport is equally a determinedly anonymous container, the Price maxim being "well-serviced anonymity." Yet there is no less anonymous figure on the British architectural scene. For Price combines the earnestness of a Welsh preacher with the knock-about debating style of a stand-up comic. A great deflator of the pompous intention, he is still the well-trained architect, with an eye for the saucy or provocative detail, such as the angled rainwater pipes on the London Airport computer building, a device that removes them from their proper function so that, no longer to be confused with structure, they resemble handles.

While between the wars the Architectural Association and Liverpool University were the training grounds of the architects of the Modern Movement in Britain, as the Architectural Association has remained (and Liverpool to a lesser extent) since 1945, we must add a third "school" to the postwar educational framework. That is the real-life studio provided by the Architects' Department of the London County Council (LCC) and later the Greater London Council (GLC). In the first fifteen years after 1945, while the return to private work of healthy peacetime conditions proceeded slowly, the Architects' Department at County Hall on the South Bank provided a focus for the talents and energies of many architects who were to flourish on their own account in the sixties. Robert Matthew, formerly of the Department of Health for Scotland, was appointed Chief Architect to the LCC in 1946. In 1948 Leslie Martin, the prewar head of the school of architecture at Hull, was appointed as Matthew's deputy with special responsibility for the design of the Royal Festival Hall. Associated with Martin in the design of the concert hall was Peter Moro, who has since made his mark with delicate and elegant buildings such as the Hille International headquarters in Albemarle Street, London, and the Gulbenkian Centre, Hull [1967]. Whitfield Lewis became head of the newly created housing division of the Architects' Department in 1950, and Colin Lucas (of the distinguished prewar practice Connell, Ward and Lucas) joined the division in the same year.

The LCC housing division, with a staff of three hundred architects and an annual building program of twenty million pounds, was to have a tremendous impact on the changing face of London during the next two decades. Its first project was the Ackroydon Estate, Wimbledon, an arrangement of eleven-story towers and lower terraces which set the pattern for future mixed developments. Both Ackroydon and the contemporaneous Alton East Estate at Roehampton were influenced by the Scandinavian models, particularly Swedish ones, favored by Whitfield Lewis, while at the new Alton West Estate the influence of Le Corbusier's Unité at Marseille was evident, with a team of recent graduates reinterpreting the Ville Radieuse. Alton West reflected a wing towards the Unité d'Habitation as a comprehensive source of structure, components, and spaces all related by dimensional and proportional coordination. Designed 1952-1953 and built 1955-1959, Alton West is sited on and between parkland. Housing a population of over sixty-five hundred, with shops, schools, and community facilities, it is another landmark in the evolution of British housing. It consists of two clusters of twelve-story point-blocks and a series of five ten-story slabs, raised on columns stepping down the grass slopes, achieving an environment of urban living in a country landscape that had long been the ideal of modern architects. But, and this is an important reservation, its success was more aesthetic than environmental and the supposed success of the point-blocks led to further unsatisfactory experiments in high-rise living that culminated with Ërno Goldfinger's twenty-seven-story interpretations of Marseille in London's East End.

During Kenneth Campbell's long innings as Housing Architect to the GLC (he retired in 1974 to be succeeded by Gordon Wigglesworth), policy changed radically from that exhibited at Alton West. Although high point-block development continued throughout the sixties, medium rise began to be favored by the end of the decade. Nevertheless, the major developments like the Kidbrooke Estate, Greenwich, the Pepys Estate, Lewisham, and the new town of Thamesmead were all mixed developments, and much of the best work from the GLC in the late sixties was designed for the smaller-scale Town Expansion Programme, aimed at removing population and jobs from London. The terraced units produced by the GLC for Andover, Hampshire, and Thetford, Norfolk, set new standards for this pattern of housing. Thamesmead certainly had the most experimental work to emerge from the GLC in the second half of the sixties. Intended to house sixty thousand Londoners ultimately, this riverside development on the South Bank of the Thames had to cope with the problems generated by the Ringway 2 Motorway that crosses the site. The design of linear blocks to contain vehicular noise produced a distinguished solution which uses an industrialized system (Balency) to combine maisonettes and old people's flats with spacious terraces and internal first-floor pedestrian access built over a ground-floor deck containing garages.

Housing is only one of the many divisions within the GLC Architects' Department which provides the most comprehensive design service in the world to what is the largest client body. Under Michael Powell the Schools Division provided many distinguished buildings, of which the Bromley Hall School for Physically Handicapped Children is one of the most human and the Pimlico Comprehensive School perhaps the most daring. In addition to housing, town expansion, and schools, the department undertakes special building projects. Probably the most comprehensive of these special tasks has been the further development of the South Bank, adding to the Royal Festival Hall the Queen Elizabeth Hall and the Purcell Room (both concert halls), the Hayward Gallery and the National Film Theatre. There is, of course, an inherent danger in retaining so large and comprehensive a brief within a single corporate office: the result of the GLC's development of the South Bank's cultural complex is one of monotony, lack of scale, and detachment from the river. Like so many good schools and design teams, the GLC Architects' Department has been overtaken by the change which it helped to create. The South Bank required variety, interest, intimacy, and association with the Thames. It is an irony that a design team based only a hundred yards from the site did not have the detachment necessary to realize this.

Leslie Martin left the GLC in 1958 to become Professor of Architecture at Cambridge and exerted a substantial influence on the development of British architecture not only through his practice but by teaching and research. During the sixties he made the Cambridge School a focus for intellectual and research activity providing a genuine counterweight for the London center of the Architectural Association. Evidence of this is to be found in the Harvey Court extension to Caius College, Cambridge [1960] and the original proposals for the extension of the British Museum in Bloomsbury (both with Colin St. John Wilson); the Brunswick Centre housing project on the Foundling Estate [with Patrick Hodgkinson, 1960-1970]; and the creation of the Land Use and Built Form Centre at Cambridge. Colin St. John Wilson, now himself the Professor of Architecture at Cambridge, has developed into one of the major architects of the new generation with his exquisite Cornford House, Cambridge [1966] and the revised British Museum extension, now the British Library next to St. Pancras Station due to be commenced in 1980. Among the other architects associated with the Cambridge School, Michael Brawne, now Professor at Bath, deserves special mention. His house at Fisher's Pond, Hampstead [1964] reflects with Boston (England) City Hall and Southampton University Building by Spence, Bonnington and Collins (1964) the model of recessed *pilotis* and oversailing upper story provided by Le Corbusier in the monastery of La Tourette.

The influence of Le Corbusier continued to have an impact on British work in the sixties; this is particularly evident in the Linstead Hall of Residence for Imperial College by Sheppard, Robson and Partners [1960] and to a lesser extent in the massive Park Hall housing project in Sheffield by J. L. Womersly (with Ivor Smith). There was also a substantial reflection of the Miesian model of the all-round facade always evident in the work of Yorke, Rosenberg and Mardall, as well as that of John Winter who remains Britain's most dedicated disciple of Mies. The brutalist mode has continued to be interpreted by Howell, Killick, Partridge and Amis, who have suppressed its more brutal aspects by the sophistication of their present concrete detailing: qualities that are evident in their St. Anne's College, Oxford [1962] and in the Acland Burghley School [1962], the University Centre, Cambridge [1964] and the Weston Rise housing estate, Islington [1965] with their St. Anthony's College, Oxford postgraduate extension [1970] being their coolest university building.

Ahrends, Burton and Koralek began their professional career by winning the competition for the extension of the Trinity College Library, Dublin, in 1961 [completed 1967], an exercise with distinctly Corbusian overtones. Their work has continued to reflect a personal interpretation of a number of mainstream influences: in the case of their Theological College, Chichester [1963] that of the brutalist school, while the Catholic Chaplaincy at

Oxford [1972] is a sensitive infill within the conservationist framework (fig. 23.4), and the Oxford Management Centre [1969] is a delightfully underplayed statement of order and coherence.

23.4. Ahrends, Burton and Koralek, architects. Glazed walkway of residential building at Keble College, Oxford, completed 1972. (Photograph: Courtesy of Antoine Raffoul)

Arup Associates has been one of the consistently interesting practices in the sixties and seventies, with a wide range of university and commercial work. Notable among their university achievements have been the George Thompson Building for Corpus Christi College, Cambridge [1963], the Wolfson Building for Somerville College, Oxford [1966], and the extension to Trinity Hall, Cambridge [1969]: this latter building has carefully modulated oriel-type windows with turned-up sills, precast-concrete frame and wall elements, presenting a highly articulated post-"Economist" statement. Their IBM Building, Havant [1972] is a simple and elegant industrial exercise, while they are to be seen at their most sophisticated in the new tobacco factory for John Player and Son at Nottingham [1972] and the Bush Lane House office building in the City of London [1973]. The Player's factory presented a difficult program of technological and environmental problems associated with tobacco production, with the aim of providing "the best working conditions and surroundings for people." Bush Lane House incorporates a unique diagonal, water-filled, stainless-steel tubed, external structural frame, supporting the black glass box of the office accommodation.

Team 4 consisted of Norman and Wendy Foster and Richard and Sue Rogers; their distinctive and brilliantly clear detailing, evidenced by the Reliance Controls Electronic Factory at Swindon [1967], won the *Financial Times's* Industrial Architecture Award for 1968. In the development of British architecture it did for the steel frame what Brutalism did for brick and concrete. Another Team 4 building, a seaside house in Cornwall [1967] is planned along two axes: one is external and splits the building with a flight of approach steps, while the other is internal and provides a top-lit picture gallery. This house, with its sharply angled plan forms, is built of cream-colored concrete blocks and is elegant rather than brutal.

Team 4 split up, Richard Rogers going into partnership with Renzo Piano while Norman Foster formed Foster Associates. Piano and Rogers are probably best known for the Centre Pompidou, Place Beaubourg, Paris, while Foster Associates have become one of the most successful firms of the seventies. The clarity of thinking and detailing that has established their reputation may be seen in the Operations Amenity Centre for the Fred Olsen Shipping Line and the Pilot Head office for IBM. Foster believes that the IBM building is a synthesis of systems with the integration of structure, environmental control, and movement and location. The organization of the building is a direct response to a program typical of a company with a high growth rate. Foster Associates are the leaders of a new Rationalism which is admirably demonstrated by their island office block for Willis, Faber and Dumas at Ipswich [1973-1975], an elegantly curved, bronze glass box with its curtain wall designed in consultation with Jean Prouvé (fig. 23.5).

Of the older generation, the office of Leonard Manasseh continued to hold its own in the sixties and seventies, specializing in building with interesting structural solutions. These include the Rotork Engineering factory at Bath [1968] with its triodetic space-frame on perimeter columns and the outstanding, exquisitely sited and detailed National Motor Museum at Beaulieu, Hampshire [1972].

Other established practices continued to design distinguished buildings during the same period. For example, the Cripps Building at St. John's College,

23.5. Norman Foster Associates, architects. The Willis, Faber and Dumas Building at Ipswich, Suffolk, 1973-1975. (Photograph: Courtesy of John Donat Photography)

Cambridge [1964] by Powell and Moya is arguably the most successful of the new "Oxbridge" buildings in the way it fits so precisely into its surroundings without in any way compromising its modernity. Ralph Erskine (although domiciled in Sweden since the 1940s) has increasingly built in England during the 1960s and 1970s, achieving a unique brand of loose-fit Vernacularism: both his combined residential-social workplace for scholars of all ages at Clare Hall, Cambridge [1966] and his Byker Wall housing at Newcastle [1977] demonstrate his special contribution. And in the City of London, Gollins, Melvin, Ward and Partners broke with the tight street pattern in their development at St. Mary Axe, where the finely detailed, glass Commercial Union Tower and the low, adjacent P. & O. office block provide the internal frame for a corner piazza. (Richard Rogers has argued against this breaking of the City framework and maintained the tight street boundaries in his 1979 proposal for Lloyds new Underwriters' Room, with the vast Room itself occupying the central space of his "doughnut" plan for the lower floors.)

The sixties saw the emergence of other talents who went on to consolidate their reputations in the seventies. In the housing field the most outstanding new contribution came from Darbourne and Darke, who won the competition for the Lillington Street Estate, Pimlico (not far from Powell and Moya's Churchill Gardens) in 1961 and have gone on to provide other original solutions, as at Lower Holloway in North London. Lillington Street offered one of the most humane high-density designs since the war, while the Raportan Road scheme at Hammersmith by Higgins and Ney brought with it the restoration of the street to public housing, providing an internalized deck-access with two sets of maisonettes interlocking to give four-story stepped terraces arranged back-to-back with the deck spanning as the "street" between, and servicing and parking hidden underneath.

In common with their counterparts in continental Europe and North America, British architects in the seventies concentrated on the problems of the inner city, with an increasing emphasis on pedestrianization in central-area shopping precincts. An outstanding example of this precinct treatment is provided by the Brunel Centre at Swindon by Douglas Stephens and Partners, which combines a galleria-type shopping arcade as the main feature of the center, with a canal-side walkway. The other feature of the center is the David Murray John Tower, the result of collaboration between Stephens and Partners and another internationally known practice, the Building Design Partnership.

Perhaps in the seventies the most marked characteristic in British work has been a move, at home at least, against pure Formalism toward the new Rationalism of Norman Foster on the one hand

and vernacular adaptation and ad hoc assemblage on the other. Foster Associates' Sainsbury Centre for the Visual Arts at the University of East Anglia, Norwich [completed 1978] converts the architectural program of this cultural symbol (fig. 23.6) into a solution which is an elegant "shed," a universal envelope that offers uninterrupted continuity of internal space. The Sainsbury Centre provides a marked contrast to such projects of James Stirling and Partner as their North Rhine Westphalia Museum, Düsseldorf [1975], the Wallraf-Richartz Museum, Cologne [1975], and the Meineke Strasse, Berlin [1976]. This last Stirling project generates a new complexity of geometry, actually carving out the space in the city, with the architectural forms becoming sculptural in the Baroque sense but within the historical context of the Modern Movement. This context is again played upon in the street treatment of his Marburg project, which incorporates a joke "hinge" as the corner feature. A complex interplay of forms and spaces within the city site is also the theme of the project for the extension of the Staatsgalerie with a new Kammertheater for Stuttgart (1977). The award of the 1980 RIBA Gold Medal to Stirling two years after he received the Aalto finally gave him the recognition at home that he has long enjoyed abroad.

In the area of vernacular adaptation the work of Aldington and Craig deserves mention, as it expresses an almost anonymous quality that has all the comfortable and reassuring attributes of the English tradition. The Glasgow firm of Gillespie, Kidd and Coia has in its St. Bride's Church, East Kilbride [1960] and The Lawns hall of residence for Hull University, contributed to that revival of brickwork quality already noted at Harvey Court, Cambridge. Also, in Norfolk, the vernacular brickwork tradition has been particularly well adapted by the Norwich firm of Feilden and Mawson, especially in the new housing they have so deftly fitted into the Norwich Cathedral Close.

Another rationalization, more modest in means and expression, also came into being in the seventies. With that approach the names of Farrell and Grimshaw, and Edward Cullinan are inseparably linked. Farrell and Grimshaw developed an expression that derived directly from economy of means, which was already evidenced in their bathroom tower addition at the rear of a hostel conversion in the monumental Westbourne Terrace, Bayswater, London [1967] and their cooperative housing tower that overlooks London's Regent's Park [1968]. Edward Cullinan's contribution derived from an equal simplicity of approach, harnessing a full range of technology to create unpretentious but poetic envelopes. His series of Olivetti branch premises [1969-1971], which gives flexibility of planning to meet different site conditions within a clearly recognizable design envelope, is typical of the elegance of his thinking, while his back-to-back semidetached housing at Highgrove, Ruislip [1972-1977] gave new life to this traditional form of popular British housing.

Again in the field of housing, the work of Martin Richardson has remained remarkably consistent in his search for an expression of freedom, often with distinct vernacular references, within a recognizable overall architectural coherence. Richardson first made his mark with the Yorkshire Development Group [1962-1968] and has produced some of the

23.6. Norman Foster Associates, architects. The Sainsbury Centre for the Visual Arts, University of East Anglia, Norwich, completed 1978. (Photograph: Courtesy of Malcolm Quantrill)

more interesting housing at Milton Keynes new town in his Great Linford estate [1973-1976], which is characterized by the emphasis of the roof as the dominant and ordering element.

Of all the private architects working in the field of housing Eric Lyons remained the most energetic, persistently removing himself from mainstreams of style yet always finding new solutions to the very different problems he tackled throughout his career. His celebrated SPAN developments, which date back to the Ham Common one of 1954, where his real partner was the contractor Leslie Bilsby, represent a milestone in postwar speculative housing. And his fine group of towers at World's End, Chelsea, is widely regarded as the best high-rise housing in Britain. Although Lyons worked for Gropius and Fry just before the war, he was a highly intuitive architect rather than an intellectual modernist. He died early in 1980 but was able right up to the end of his life to be inventive, even playful, in his designs, as in his apartment blocks for the Portuguese resort of Vila Moura. Seen as a whole his work offers a yardstick of British housing since the war.

It is simply not possible to summarize adequately the immense complexity and variety of British architectural contributions since the war in so brief a space. But even from this selective evidence it will be seen that a period that began with provincialism and tentativeness flowered into one of confidence, maturity, vitality, and invention. In the process it has witnessed the excitement of attachments to various international trends, seeing the evolution of new home-bred attitudes and manifestoes, achieving leadership through the work of the Smithsons, Foster, Rogers, particularly Stirling, and others, producing formal masterpieces that have kept British architecture in the forefront of world design. There are now two strong and important counterblasts to this Formalism. The first seeks to humanize through reference either to past styles or the vernacular, while the second replaces the concept of a stylistic language with a concern for the logic of assembly and the interpretive freedom this brings to the design process. It was, after all, variety which was sought by Hugh Casson's team when in 1951 they produced the curious funfare of British architecture that housed the Festival of Britain. Now variety has taken root as a natural expression of the British modern tradition.

Bibliography

BOOKS

Banham, Reyner. *The Age of the Masters*. London: Architectural Press, 1975. (Published formerly as *Guide to Modern Architecture*. London: Architectural Press, 1962.)

______. *The New Brutalism*. New York: Reinhold, 1966.

______. Introduction to *The Architecture of Yorke, Rosenberg and Mardall 1944-72*. London, 1973.

Cook, Peter, ed. *Archigram*. London: Studio Vista, 1972.

______. *Experimental Architecture*. New York: Universe Books, 1970.

Curtis, William. Introduction to *A Language and a Theme: The Architecture of Denys Lasdun and Partners*. London, 1976.

Dannatt, Trevor. *Modern Architecture in Britain*. London, 1959.

Donat, John, ed. *World Architecture* , Vols. 1, 2, 3. London Studio Vista.

GLC Architecture 1965-70. London: GLC Publications, 1971.

Hitchcock, Henry-Russell. *Modern Architecture in England*. New York, 1937.

Jackson, Anthony. *The Politics of Architecture*. Toronto: University of Toronto Press, 1970.

Jacobus, John. Introduction to *James Stirling: Buildings and Projects 1950-1974*. London, 1975.

Jencks, Charles. *The Language of Post-Modern Architecture*. New York: Rizzoli, 1977.

Landau, Royston. *New Directions in British Architecture*. London, 1968.

Maxwell, Robert. *New British Architecture*. London: Thames and Hudson, 1972.

Quantrill, Malcolm. *Ritual and Response in Architecture*. London: Lund Humphries, 1974.

Reilly, C. H. *Scaffolding in the Sky*. London, 1938.

Stephens, Douglas, with Frampton, Kenneth and Carapetian, Michael. *British Buildings 1962-1964*. London, 1965.

Teodori, Massimo. *Architettura e Città in Gran Bretagna*. Milan, 1967.

JOURNALS

Amery, Colin, Bayley, Stephen, et al. "British Architecture 1952-1977—Living in Britain." *Architectural Review*, November 1977.

"British Architecture 1954-1964." *Architects' Journal*, 15 January 1964.

"British Architecture 1940-1970." *Design*, January 1970.

Crawford, David. "Modern Building in the City (London)." *Building*, 25 July 1975.

Hitchcock, Henry-Russell. "English Architecture in the Early 1960s." *Zodiac*, no. 12 (Milan), 1964.

Jencks, Charles. "Pop, non-Pop—The Scene of Recent British Architecture." *Architectural Association Quarterly*, Winter 1968/69.

Joedicke, Jürgen. "British Architecture—The Best in the World." *Royal Institute of British Architects Journal*, August 1979.

______. "British Architecture Viewed from the Continent." *Bauen and Wohnen*, 12/1967.

"Re: Alison and Peter Smithson." *Architectural Review*, April 1954.

"Review of British Architecture." *Zodiac*, no. 18 (Milan), 1968, pp. 5-295.

Richards, J. M. "Architecture Today Exhibition" (Extracts from Exhibition Catalogue). *Royal Institute of British Architects Journal*, June 1961.

Scully, Vincent. "New British Buildings." *Architectural Design*, June 1964.

Stevens, T. "Observations on Contemporary British Architecture." *Bauen und Wohnen*, 12/1967.

"Theory into Practice—British Architecture 1955-1977." *Architectural Design*, nos. 9/10, 1977.

"A Tour of British Architecture 1945-1970." *Architects' Journal*, 21 January 1970.

"25 Years of British Architecture 1952-1977." *Royal Institute of British Architects Journal*, May 1977.

USEFUL JOURNALS

Architects' Journal (weekly)
Architectural Association Quarterly
Architectural Design (monthly)
Architectural Review (monthly)
Building (weekly)
Building Design (weekly)
International Architect
Journal of Architectural Research
Royal Institute of British Architects Journal (monthly)
The Town Planning Review

24

GREECE

DIMITRI PHILIPPIDES

The development of Greek architecture since 1945 may be seen as a clash between two opposing, sometimes supplementary directions. The first has pointed to the future with an implicit recognition of Greece as a modern Western state. The second has been oriented to Greece's past, to the recognition of Greece as a backward country attached to Balkan and Near Eastern heritages that serve as sources of inspiration and identification. The first direction is expressed in architectural terms that are allied with developments in the Western world, while the second partakes of a more indigenous tradition. In their evolution since 1945, one can grasp the entire spectrum of architectural activity in Greece and trace the effects on building that the interplay between these main trends has had.

A brief analysis of major socioeconomic characteristics directly associated with construction in Greece will provide an appropriate setting against which one may appraise individual architects and their works in the postwar period.

In the years immediately after the Second World War, the situation in Greece was difficult. Having suffered a severe economic collapse under the German occupation, Greece experienced a particularly destructive civil war which lasted till 1949. The countryside was extensively ravaged while most of the urban centers underwent lighter losses.[1] As a result, the country was sorely in need of reconstruction. An effort was initially undertaken by a team led by the architect-planner Constantine Doxiadis (1913-1976), who served as Minister of Reconstruction between 1946 and 1948. A number of programs for the countryside were forwarded and then implemented with heavy American aid. These included the relocation of 150 rural settlements and the construction of around 200,000 new housing units in rural areas.[2]

To make things worse, a number of earthquakes hampered the reconstruction program of Greece.[3] In 1953 in the Ionian islands alone a total of 20,000 units had to be completely rebuilt. Meanwhile the population was steadily shifting toward the larger urban centers. For the first time, in 1971, a census registered a numerical superiority of urban population against rural.[4] This census also revealed an ever-increasing gap between the supply and demand of housing: there was a total need for 600,000 new housing units.[5] To cope with such a state of prolonged emergency, the state tried to organize the planning, financing, and implementing of badly needed programs. These efforts, however, were thwarted by a proliferation of uncoordinated public agencies;[6] and, as a result, it was very difficult for such agencies to perform efficiently. Moreover, allocations of funds were drained by relatively high land values and a lack of industrialized methods of construction. It was thus almost impossible to provide low-cost housing well within the reach of economically weak classes in Greece.

This failure of the public sector of construction in Greece had two immediate consequences: first, the uncontrolled spread of illegal housing on the periphery of the major urban centers; and second, the dominance in the housing market of privately financed companies. The former effect has been a continuous burden on the national economy and consecutive governments have been unable to arrive at any coherent approach toward the problem of squatters. On the other hand, the overwhelming presence of the private sector in construction,[7] coupled with the chronic economic instability and the lack of other forms of investment in Greece, resulted in a disproportionately large role played by construction in the Greek economy and an unprecedented expansion of land speculation. Urbanization and the draining of the rural population helped further accentuate the catastrophic effects of the absence of a land policy. A number of regional and master plans commissioned during the 1960s were never put into practice for the lack of proper legislation, proper administrative organization, and the lack of sufficient funds. The creation of the Doxiadis Associates office in 1954 and its subsequent phenomenal expansion was mainly due to large-scale projects undertaken in foreign, mostly underdeveloped, countries. Despite the fame that Constantine Doxiadis acquired outside of Greece, he was unable to contribute significantly to the amelioration of conditions in the built environment of his country.[8]

At first, in the years immediately after the war to the mid-1950s architects played an unimportant role;[9] and a real architectural setback occurred when the prewar effort to transplant the International Style to Greece was completely abandoned. Constantine Kapsambelis, Emmanuel Vourekas, Rennos Koutsouris, Panos Tsolakis and Spyros Staikos, and particularly Constantine Kitsikis, who had distinguished himself before the war, reversed the direction of architecture. Buildings came to imitate a neo-Classical architecture that had flourished in Greece prior to the 1920s. Their work, now severely criticized,[10] sought to tie Greek architecture to a local idiom, to the neo-Classical style brought to Greece largely from Germany by its first monarch in the early nineteenth century.[11]

A simplified version of neo-Classicism became the rage of the postwar period, complete with free-standing Greek order columns, while at times the influence of the freely curved lines of prewar eclecticism in France and elsewhere also became evident. This eagerly sought neo-Classical "style" was adopted particularly by the newly rich who had quickly risen to prominence. This group evidently wished to secure its position by referring to architectural elements that held particular significance for Greeks, such as antique columns, pediments, and moldings. Thus, the architecture of the late 1940s expressed the prevalence of the conservative faction in Greek politics by reaching backwards to a respectability literally dressed in a traditional garment.

Constantine Kitsikis (1893-1969), an extremely versatile businessman rather than a professional architect, was appointed as Professor at the School of Architecture in Athens in 1940. Among his major works, aside from those designed before the war, are the Telecommunications Organization Headquarters in Athens [1966] and the Commercial Bank of Greece [1957]. Kitsikis's main architectural concern was the creation of a monumental style suitable for the demands of various banking and public agencies. His pragmatic approach to the problems of Greek architecture was quite the opposite of Pikionis's, also a professor at the Technical University of Athens, whose work we shall examine later. Both Kitsikis and Pikionis, by their contrasting natures, influenced the development of architecture in Greece extensively.

Constantine Kapsambelis (b. 1909)[12] was perhaps the most productive representative of this group. He built a number of apartment houses inside Athens and innumerable private residences in the suburbs around the capital. In the latter he used mixtures of rustic style, with some effects borrowed from Greek vernacular architecture, thus following similar currents in other countries, particularly the architecture of villas in southern France. The architecture of Kapsambelis could be called "neovernacular" since it sought to reinterpret traditional architecture by utilizing modern means. His example was followed by a large number of designers who finally created a fashion out of the imitation of the local vernacular idioms. Perhaps the most extensive project to be undertaken by Kapsambelis has been the unfinished (as of 1980) Porto-Carras "village," a tourist development on Chalkidiki in northern Greece, designed entirely in imitation of the traditional northern Greek house type. The clientele of Kapsambelis, as well as of the other established architects of his time, has left its mark on their work. It is apparent that none of those "neovernacular" buildings has retained the simplicity and sincerity of the genuine vernacular architecture. On the contrary, Kapsambelis's projects reflect instead the dubious status of those who commissioned them. Since architecture has almost always catered to an affluent minority in Greece,[13] this has been the rule rather than the exception.

The adherents of Dimitri Pikionis (1887-1968), the most revered architect to have emerged in the postwar period, however, clung to a diametrically different ideology. To them the neovernacular idiom was not another formalist alternative but a genuine means of conveying a certain way of life. The teaching of Pikionis at the School of Architecture of the Athens Technical University (1925-1956) was essentially based on a prominent "return to national roots" cultural movement that had been initiated in the 1920s.[14] Pikionis himself alluded to that movement when he wrote in 1924:

> Some among us believe that it is our duty to choose, from our national heritage, our immediate past, our folk art. . . . Why should not the simplicity of that folk be our own. Nevertheless no one of us can attain that simplicity,

that purity. In reality we remain all the same, empty, that is, without a world of our own. We never realize that the purity and truth which we recognize in the art of the folk presupposes a complete human being, a complete setting of life, pure and natural.[15]

Believing that man should follow nature in his life, he points to the peasant as one who embodies the virtues of living by nature: "The necessary, the useful are so much a part of his life that no space is left for the arbitrary, the useless."[16] Hence, the way a peasant builds his house could serve as an appropriate example for all architects to follow. This movement was translated into a search for an ethnic identity through the application of traditional forms and motifs.

Pikionis had been a practicing architect since 1923. In 1933 he experienced his first doubts about the International Style and concluded that "the ecumenical spirit should be combined with the ethnic one."[17] From that date onwards he took a decisive step toward the application of the vernacular architecture of which he was so fond. In his autobiographical notes he states that "the East and Byzantium have demonstrated to me that the only valid way to express our ideas and emotions is through the creation of a symbolic language derived from nature and the substance of imitation."[18]

It was during the 1950s that Pikionis finally put into practice some of his lofty ideas, such as the design of an exceptionally landscaped approach (fig. 24.1)

24.1. Dimitri Pikionis, architect. Landscaped approach to the Acropolis, and Philopappou Hill, Athens; view from the top of Philopappou Hill, 1951-1957. (Photograph: Courtesy of Dimitri Philippidis)

to the Acropolis [1951-1957],[19] the Potamianos residence in Philothei [1954] and the Xenia hotel at Delphi [1955]. Pikionis, a mystic at heart, remained aloof from the pressing problems that plagued Greek architecture and instead seemed to favor a certain escapism as an essential ingredient of keeping one's integrity. His influence has had equivocal side effects. Some of his disciples took his message too literally and ended up imitating Kapsambelis; others vainly tried to compromise with the demands of contemporary construction methods.

Meanwhile a steady flow of external influences was inundating Greek architecture, resulting in a deep chasm that separated architects. One group espoused the architecture designed in the industrialized Western countries, while the other followed that practiced in developing countries around the world. This situation in the profession was exacerbated by the fact that Greece in the 1950s simultaneously demonstrated signs of approaching the level of the developed economies of the Western nations while it still offered ample proof of its underdevelopment. One need only have compared the declining, primitive character of the countryside, which was losing its population through emigration, and the booming metropolis of Athens.[20] Regardless of the speed with which per capita income was increasing in Greece as a whole, it could not yet be considered fully among developed countries simply because it lacked the industrial means and technological know-how to produce badly needed construction materials. By necessity, the lack of appropriate materials and skilled labor was translated into an architecture which could only superficially imitate foreign prototypes, while in reality it was based on the old, almost preindustrial methods of construction. Such an inconsistency seemed not in the least to bother those who eagerly sought to identify with certain American or European prototypes.[21] Such architects may be collectively termed Modernists, and we shall analyze their development after our consideration of the neovernacular movement.

Adherents of the neovernacular architecture felt themselves compelled to take into account the message of Le Corbusier, especially that conveyed by his postwar Chandigarh project (fig. 1.1). There, a number of primitive techniques had been utilized for the creation of dazzling effects. It became clear that industrialization and high technological competence was not a prerequisite of fine architecture. For those who readily followed Le Corbusier's example, Greece could benefit by resorting similarly to almost paleotechnic construction techniques. Moreover, the relationship of Le Corbusier's sculptural work to vernacular architecture in Greece was too apparent to be ignored; in other words, Greek architects were learning to appreciate Greek folk architecture through the eyes of a foreign master. For the second time since 1933,[22] Greek architecture was directed toward a reevaluation of its traditional built environment in order to employ foreign developments in architecture.

Prominent among those who attempted to fuse local and international idioms without resorting to Pikionis's eclecticism was Aris Konstandinides, doubtlessly the most gifted architect to emerge in postwar Greece. Konstandinides briefly served as an aide to Pikionis at the university after the war, and then joined the Workers Housing Agency (1955-1957) where he put his stamp on a number of projects throughout Greece. Some of his trademarks were incorporated in these projects; exposed post-and-beam frame, a four-by-four-meters grid, an overall simplicity and plainness of volumes, and the use of primary colors on panels. Konstandinides was subsequently hired by the new Greek Tourist Organization (EOT) where he remained till 1977. During his first involvement with EOT (1957-1967), he designed a number of exceptional hotels for both mainland and insular tourist centers, including Andros [1958], Igoumenitsa [1959], Larisa [1959], Mykonos [1959], Kalambaka [1960], Olympia [1960], and Poros [1961]. In his second period of stay with EOT, Konstandinides was involved in an ambitious program of salvaging a series of traditional settlements in the countryside by recycling existing vernacular structures and renting them, instead of adding a new crop of monstrous hotel developments for mass tourism.[23]

Being not only an accomplished designer, Konstandinides has been also a fervent proponent of the value of vernacular architecture. Eager to publicize his ideas, he has written a number of books and articles and has exhibited his outstanding photographs of the Greek countryside.[24] No less a romantic than Pikionis, he nevertheless restrained himself and avoided the excesses of Pikionis's school. His essentially ascetic temperament has been amply demonstrated by a carefully limited architectural vocabulary.

In his first published text, Konstandinides defined his interests as being outside of the cities where,

> a more lively vibration moves body and mind with a mature and genuine language. In this case now, a folk moves. It is man-in-folk who utters words and speaks the language of nature; he is part of nature, having grown on its soil as the bush, the tree, the flower. Who, when time comes to build his house—which is an extension of body, soul and property—will recreate in it the curves of mountains and the lines of the same landscape. So that he may too become a landscape in his land—man is landscape provided he remains folklike, not estranged from nature.[25]

A few years later he wrote of the steps that an architect should take:

> We should bare ourselves from any unnecessary garment and be satisfied with the truth of substance and structure, working for the ephemeral and not for turning life's functions into a monument; these functions are fluid and passing, hence full of beauty and grace. Do we also want to buttress our action through the vision of memory? Then we should open our emotions and intellect toward the *beginning* of our country, therefore to those old forms which always stood as genuine manifestations of an architectural initiative.[26]

The work of Konstandinides has been the first rational synthesis of the old with the new (fig. 24.2), that did not bow to any of the architectural fads that raged in the 1950s and the 1960s.[27] This had been

24.2. Aris Konstandinides, architect. Residence at 18 Archimedes Street, Pangrati, Athens, 1961. (Photograph: Courtesy of Dimitri Philippides)

heralded by the most important theoretician of architecture, Professor Panayotis Michelis (1903-1969) who untiringly cautioned his audiences against the pitfalls of neovernacular architecture as practiced by the Kapsambelis school or even by Pikionis. In a well-known text published in 1951, he stated that the International Style relieved Greek architecture from a pathogenic adoration of folk art.[28] Considering that the essence of vernacular art was its simplicity, its measure, and its economy of synthesis,[29] he proclaimed later that the Greek character in architecture could be accomplished only by digesting in a creative way the new architectural principles, adding that "every Greek inherently possesses the 'Greek spirit'."[30]

Konstandinides thus proved, at least in his own case, that Greek architects need not imitate foreign prototypes but instead may fruitfully search inside themselves for the solutions appropriate to the Greek climate and socioeconomic conditions. By stressing the moral obligations of architects toward the environment and society in general, he was actually pursuing a line familiar from the prewar era, when the formal purism of the International Style was contrasted with a purportedly decadent eclecticism.

The architecture of Konstandinides was deceptively easy to copy and a whole generation of younger architects followed his example. In their case, however, the message of Konstandinides was transformed to fit a more flexible vocabulary. Among the major representatives of this direction in Greek architecture one may mention Constantine Decavallas, Dimitri Fatouros, and Susanne and Dimitri Antonakakis. Constantine Decavallas (b. 1925), as head of a governmental team, was chiefly responsible for a very imaginative scheme for housing of earthquake victims on the island of Santorini in 1956. He conceived a set of standardized housing units which blended ideally with the exceptional character of the vernacular environment of that volcanic island.[31] Decavallas also designed a quite influential apartment block on Lycabettus Hill, Athens [1964], in collaboration with Thales Argyrcopoulos.[32]

Dimitri Fatouros (b. 1928) has influenced the development of Greek architecture mostly through his teaching position at the Technical University of Salonica since 1959. Aside from a number of private and public projects,[33] he has attempted to break the barrier between architects and the general public by popularizing his views through the mass media. Susanne and Dimitri Antonakakis (b. 1935, both) perhaps are the leading figures in a group called Lab 66. Their work, which is heavily influenced by that of Konstandinides, is extensive, both in the private and the public sector. Some representative projects of Lab 66 are a house at Ilissia, Athens [1965, in collaboration with K. and K. Gartzos], a hotel complex at Hermionis [1965-1973], a museum on Chios island [1972] and a house at Oxylithos [1975].[34] With the consideration above of the inheritors of the neovernacular movement the development of one major direction in Greek architecture has been fully followed.

The modernists seemed to make few concessions to local conditions; their major aim has been to be on a level with contemporary currents in architecture at any cost. Nikos Valsamakis (b. 1925) was the first to break away from the impasse of Greek architecture in the postwar period. He designed a number of exemplary apartment houses with his first on Semitelou Street [in 1953], where he showed a skillful use of various textures and contrasting materials. Another daring project of his, an office block in downtown Athens [1958], used a post-Byzantine church as a setting against which a curtain wall sheathed in marble and interspaced with glass panes was developed.[35] As with all his projects, the detailing was sparse, almost austere, and contrasted successfully with the picturesque old church in the foreground.

In the wake of his newly acquired fame, Valsamakis built a number of villas in Anavyssos (fig. 24.3), on the coastline of Athens [1961] and elsewhere, most notably at Rio and Porto Rafti [1968]. His private residences demonstrated his wish to transplant to Greece a mixture of Miesan clarity with the particular way it had been applied by Arne Jacobsen. Thus he utilized more than once an elegant

24.3. Nikos Valsamakis, architect. Residence at Anavyssos, on the coastline of Athens, 1961. (Photograph: Courtesy of Dimitri Philippides)

slab with metal supports covering a sequence of open-ended, overlapping spaces, enclosed by a continuous band of glass panes. The overall impression of the unusually long cantilever, which seemed to float above ground, was that of precision and lightness; for the first time in the 1960s the principle of Mies van der Rohe's Barcelona pavilion was applied in Greece. Although Valsamakis has since designed a substantial number of residences, hotels, and other public buildings, his first purist statements in the early 1960s have become veritable landmarks of modern Greek architecture. Some of his more important buildings following this were the hotels at Delphi [1967] and Voula, Athens [1974], and the National Television and Broadcasting Building at Agia Paraskevi, Athens [1974, in collaboration with Thymios Papayannis and Sthenis Molphesis]. Regardless of his eventual shift toward more solid or sculptural schemes, Valsamakis has always been distinguished for his thoroughness in organizing layouts and studying details meticulously.

Takis Zenetos (1926-1977) was educated in France and took Greek architecture by storm upon his return. An extremely gifted designer, who could not accept the shortcomings of architecture in Greece, Zenetos in theory and in practice proved an untiring proponent of the modernistic ideal.[36] Time and again one can discern in his projects, especially in his highly virtuoso sketches, an effort to do away with minute details of the site, the program and the materials; instead, the entire project is conceived as a materialization of an abstract concept. Aside from etherializing space—a concept which seems to have permeated his life—Zenetos usually referred to his buildings as a void between a series of concave lines [house in Glyphada, 1967], as a supplement to a sweeping cantilevered balcony [villa at Cavouri, 1964], or as a rectangle sitting on a molded site [house in Psychico, 1964).[37]

In fact, Zenetos's disregard for conventional construction methods did not merely affect the detailing of his buildings, but also their fundamental conceptualization. For example, in his block of flats on Amalias Avenue, Athens [1963, in collaboration with M. Apostolides] (fig. 24.4), Zenetos dismissed then-current views (including the need to limit large expanses of glass in a warm climate to provide flexibility and avoid monotony) by proposing an original scheme based on interlaced vertical and horizontal grids which are fitted with various partition types, "opaque, semi-transparent for lighting or heating, etc."[38] This ability of Zenetos to design an office block in the image of a utopian model of urban space has been unique among Greek architects and has re-

24.4. Takis Zenetos with M. Apostolides, architects. Block of flats on Amalias Avenue. Athens, 1963. (Photograph: Courtesy of Dimitri Philippides)

mained virtually unchallenged. In this respect, Zenetos's work was prophetic, not so much for the actual development of Greek architecture, but rather for the eventual progress of architecture in general, in which he fervently believed. Few would imitate his daring feats; most preferred to copy the continuous, narrow strips of windows that he applied on the Fix Brewery on Syngrou Avenue [1961] or his popular tricks with balconies for apartment buildings.

An extreme case of the application of modern architecture in Greece has been the office block designed by Dimitri Papazisis on Constitution Square, Athens [1962]. For the first time, the government itself intervened and attempted to quench a public outcry against the "un-Greek" character of that building. A committee was appointed to solve the problem; fortunately, its recommendation was relatively harmless: the addition of a railing on top as a visual termination of an endless curtain-wall facade.

It has become apparent that some vague sensitivity concerning architecture existed among various segments of the Greek public. The issue, however, was never fully brought into the open. Occasionally, an outburst of public indignation would be registered against the replacement of yet another old building by a modern "monster." This reaction was only natural in view of the extensive replacement of older, neo-Classical buildings, mostly two to three stories high, by ten-story structures without any change in their setbacks. Athens and Salonica had experienced an unparalleled redevelopment rate; entire neighborhoods had been indiscriminately razed and a continuous wall of high apartment blocks arose in their place. The increase of vehicular circulation, the concentration of the population in high-density apartment buildings, the failure to control the expansion of industry in the major urban centers by zoning regulations, and the lack of any realistic antipollution controls have made these cities seem almost uninhabitable in the last decades.

This situation has been inherited by the younger generation of Greek architects. To make things even worse, a disproportionate number of graduates of both our schools of architecture[39] have been entering an already saturated local market every year. If one were to add to these those Greek students who attend foreign universities—at least as many as those studying in Greece—it is apparent that an overwhelming number of architects have remained unemployed in the last decade, when the market was tight and plagued by inflation.[40] Meanwhile, a number of architects have become more sensitive toward the major socioeconomic issues in Greece. The social consciousness of architects was further stimulated by recent political and economic developments in Greece, notably the seven-year dictatorship (1967-1974), the severe recession suffered in 1973, and the Cyprus invasion (1974). Economic instability and political upheaval were thus responsible for the growth of a radical student movement, in which students of architecture played a prominent role.[41] It was acknowledged that an architect's place should be not only at the drafting table but also where the action is. The deterioration of the built environment, the unchecked operation of heavily polluting industries in urbanized areas, and the never resolved problem of illegal housing became areas of activity for architects. Opportunities did not fail to appear; Saronic Bay, facing Athens, was declared a dead sea; the allocation of shipyards at the historical site of Pylos in 1976 and the forceful eviction of squatters at Perama (Piraeus) in 1974 were events heavily attended by architects. In the wake of such an approach some became disillustioned concerning their traditional role as designers. It is perhaps too early to judge the outcome of this radical attitude: for the time being at least, no changes have been made in architectural practice per se.[42]

Concurrently, some relatively older architects have remained active. Emmanuel Vourekas, whose career had started in the late 1940s, is a striking example. In collaboration with Prokopis Vasiliades (d. 1976) and Spyros Staikos, he was responsible for the Athens Hilton Hotel [1958-1963], an important building not so much for its imposing size but for the influence it has had on the development of Greek architecture. Coming a few years after the construction of the American Embassy in Athens by Walter Gropius [plans published in Greece in 1959; project completed in 1961], the Athens Hilton similarly attempted a reinterpretation of classical Greek architecture. This was accomplished with a recessed fenestration emphasized by heavy vertical fins made of white marble, which from a distance would remind one of a classical colonnade.[43] The Athens Hilton was a veritable paradigm of academic design in Greece; most of the work produced afterwards made unmistaken allusions to its design and underlying concepts.[44] Vourekas himself, in his most recent project, the Building for the Friends of Music, which is being erected next to the American Embassy in Athens, has proved consistent with his older concepts. More direct nods toward a classical past were made by Yannis Despotopoulos (also known as Jan Despo during his stay in northern Europe). In his Athens School of Music, part of the Cultural Center [1977] (fig. 24.5), the principle of the ancient stoa was applied to a two-story elongated building, sheathed in white marble. Perhaps this scheme, more than any other, personifies the major characteristics of "official" Greek architecture: namely, the expression of a classic serenity and clarity. Such an impression is accentuated by an abundant use of marble, an overemphasis placed on the vertical axis, and by a preference for tinted glass and an anodized aluminum frame. This standardized architecture, fit for public and monumental buildings, presumably alludes to an implicit luxury and respectability.

24.5. Yannis Despotopoulos, architect. Athens School of Music, front elevation. Athens, 1977. (Photograph: Courtesy of Dimitri Philippides.

By contrast, in the work of another group of architects, where adherents to traditionalism may be found, the use of such presumptuous materials is avoided; and instead we find exposed concrete, sparse detailing, and low-cost furnishings. The Brutalist origins of such preferences are clearly obvious not only in the use of certain materials but more significantly in the underlying ideology which coincided with that of the traditionalists. Some examples in this category would be the National Gallery in Athens [completed 1974] by Dimitri Fatouros and Paul Mylonas and a group of buildings at the campus of the Salonica University erected between 1961 and 1978 by Constantine Fines and Constantine Papaionnou (both b. 1934).[45] Such preference for exposed concrete continues to be abhorred by the majority of established proponents of the official architecture. Nonetheless, its acceptance by the old guard may not be too far off, possibly in the guise of a toned down Brutalism. This is suggested by the Passenger Terminal at the port of Piraeus by Yannis Liapis and Ilias Scroumbelos [1971], the Hoechst factory [1972] and the Texaco Company building in Athens (under construction, 1980) by Thymios Papayannis, and the French Institutes in Athens and Salonica [1974 and 1972 respectively] by Sthenis Molphesis.

A notable escape from classicist academicism may be seen in the work of Alexander Tombazis (b. 1939), who has demonstrated a strong preference for modern Japanese architecture in all of its neo-Baroque splendor. His most representative works are the headquarters for the Bothosakis Group of Companies in Athens [1976], two residential towers [1976 in Kifissia and 1977 in Chalandri (fig. 24.6)], a summer house at Kineta [1972] and another at Philothei [1975]. The two residential towers in particular represent a novel formal treatment of the conventional boxlike residential block in Greece. In these projects different types and shapes of apartments were stacked between a series of evenly spaced, massive, concrete walls, thus signaling Tombazis's indebtedness to both the Metabolists and the Brutalists.

In conclusion, we may assert that for the most part in Greek architecture, the old dichotomy between traditionalists and modernists has been replaced by a newly formulated one: an official academicism on the one hand and an unconventional robustness on the other. Academicism operates by directly invoking ancient Greek architectural forms and by imitating evolutions of these in Western countries, as in the Beaux-Arts academicism of Edward Durell Stone, Philip Johnson, Louis Kahn, and the Skidmore, Owings and Merrill firm, or the "historicism" of Minoru Yamasaki. The more unconventional current adheres to the Formalism of Le Corbusier's late work while reaching out toward the traditionalists of the previous generation by identifying with the Greek vernacular idiom in materials, construction methods, and climatic solutions. In other words, those in the academic camp of architecture may easily be grouped with the prewar "Modernists," for in both cases their work reflected a heavy dependence upon international currents. Similarly those in the "Formalist" camp are directly related to the older "traditionalists" by virtue of their adherence to traditional architectural values. In essence, a vital dichotomy has been retained in Greek architecture throughout the postwar period.

24.6. Alexandros Tombazis, architect. Residential tower at Chalandri. Athens, 1977. (Photograph: Courtesy of Dimitri Philippides)

Notes

1. *Housing in Greece: Government Activity* (Athens: Technical Chamber of Greece, 1975), p. 24. Out of a total 1,740,000 housing units, 450,000 or 25 percent were completely destroyed.

2. Ibid.

3. Areas affected by earthquakes included the Ionian islands (1953), and Thessaly and Santorini island (1956).

4. According to the 1971 census, 53.2 percent of the total population resided in urban centers (of 10,000 or more inhabitants) while 11.7 percent were in semiurban centers (of 2,000 to 9,999 inhabitants).

5. The above figure includes 235,000 units required in the metropolitan Athens area, 60,000 units in Salonica, and another 105,000 in lesser centers. *Housing: Government Activity*, p. 46.

6. Ibid., pp. 47-48. Under the auspices of the Ministry of Coordination and Planning, four major agencies concern themselves with housing: the Ministry of Public Works, the Ministry of Social Services, the Organization for Workers' Housing, and the Independent Construction Organization for Army Officers. Financing is controlled by four distinct sources: the National Mortgage Bank, the Loan and Consignations Bank, the Postal Savings Bank, and the Agricultural Bank.

7. The majority of landowners in Greece hold relatively small plots and operate with minimal financial means. Such a predominance of low-middle-class owners-investors has played a crucial role in the development of urban centers and has significantly hampered the implementation of a land policy by the state. On a yearly average during the period 1960-1972, the state's participation in construction never rose above 5 percent. *Housing in Greece: The Private Sector* (Athens: Ministry of Public Works, 1975), p. 62.

8. The Regional Plan of Greece project, commissioned of Doxiadis Associates during the dictatorship period and submitted in 1976, has been violently attacked by various groups, such as the Technical Chamber of Greece and political parties of the opposition and faces almost insurmountable difficulties in being implemented.

9. In Greece civil engineers and land surveyors are permitted by law to undertake the design and construction of almost any type of building. As a result, they easily gained a virtual monopoly of all low-budget construction, which constituted the bulk of the building activity in Greece. Due to such practices, in periods of economic deprivation, such as during the late 1950s, architects were almost altogether eliminated from the scene.

10. François Loyer, "Architecture de la Grèce Contemporaine" (doctorat de troisième cycle, University of Paris, 1966), pp. 721-32.

11. Otto I, formerly a Bavarian prince, was the first king to reign in modern Greece. He commissioned a number of distinguished German architects (e.g., Schinkel, Weiler, Gartner, Klenze) to design various public buildings for his new capital, Athens.

12. C. Kapsambelis was an instructor under C. Kitsikis at the School of Architecture in Athens, a fact which explains his affinity for his master's style.

13. Since the state failed to sponsor a sizable portion of the construction activity in Greece, it was natural that private enterprise would turn virtually exclusively toward luxury construction, the most profitable sector of the market. The use of architects seemed a guarantee of high-quality design and helped further boost the price of the finished product.

14. Its message was an appreciation of the cultural heritage of the post-Byzantine period, and, in some respects, a reaction to the westernization of Greece which had devastating effects on local cultural traditions.

15. "We and Our Folk Art," trans. Dimitri Philippides, *Philiki Etairia* (periodical) 4 (1924): 145-58. Reprinted in *Oikonomikos Tachydromos* 1054 (4 July 1974): 5-8.

16. Pikionis, *Oikonomikos*, p. 6.

17. "Autobiographical Notes of Dimitri Pikionis" (in Greek), *Zygos* (periodical) nos. 27-28 (January-February 1958): 7.

18. Ibid.

19. Cf. Anthony Antoniades, "Poems with Stones: The Enduring Spirit of Dimitrius Pikionis," *Architecture and Urbanism*, no. 72 (1976): 17-22; *see also*, N. Kurokawa, "Architecture of the Road," *Kenchiku Bunka*, January 1963.

20. Reconstruction was almost completed and the period of peace that ensued allowed Greece to develop at a fast rate. The per capita income (corrected to 1978 values) rose from $473 in 1963 to $908 in 1970.

21. The local lack of technological means was bypassed by Greek architects for a second time as it had been in the 1930s, when architects enthusiastically had introduced the International Style to Greece.

22. During the fourth CIAM conference which took place in Athens in 1933, Greek architects proudly showed the foreign participants around in an effort to prove that Greece too could boast of an avant-garde architecture. Cf. *Technika Chronika* (official publication of the Technical Chamber of Greece) 4, nos. 44-46 (1933).

23. The main drive of EOT initially concerned five representative traditional settlements (Vathis, Oia, Makrinitsa, Mesta, Fiskartho), where such a recycling would be attempted experimentally. The first efforts toward the recycling of old structures to serve tourists, however, were undertaken by Basil Giannakis, an EOT employee, who restored the Mouslis mansion in Makrinitas [1975] and converted it into a hotel. Working independently in Crete, Voula, and Takis Zervas restored for the same purpose a small cluster of rural houses [1976]. Charis and Alexandros Calligas were first involved in 1967 in the rehabilitation of privately owned vernacular houses in Monemvasia, a Medieval town in the Peloponnesus. Ever since, their numerous works in the same area have been justifiably acclaimed [cf. *Architectural Review*, no. 906 (August 1972): 100-104].

24. His most prominent publications are: *Old Athenean Houses* (1960); *Elements for Self-Identity for a Truthful Architecture* (1975); "Life Vessels or the Problem of a 'Genuine' Greek Architecture," *Architecture in Greece*, no. 6 (1972): 27-49.

25. *Two Houses from Myconos*, trans. Dimitri Philippides, 1947, pp. 14-15.

26. *Old Athenaean Houses*, trans. Dimitri Philippides, 1950, p. 20.

27. One possible influence on Konstandinides has been Egon Eiermann, whose German Pavilion at the Brussels Fair [1957-1958] and German Embassy in the United States [1958-1964] show certain similarities with Konstandinides's work.

28. *Architecture as Art* (in Greek), 2d ed. (Athens, 1951), p. 355.

29. Ibid., p. 351.

30. Panayotis Michelis, "Modern Greek Architecture and Contemporary Trends," *Architecture in Greece*, no. 2 (1968): 20.

31. Local houses are either dug into the soft pumice layer or built by a mixture of low-weight volcanic stone and porcelain in the form of various types of vaults. Cf. A. Radford and G. Clark, "Cyclades, Studies of a Building Vernacular," in P. Oliver and O. Doumanis, eds., *Settlements in Greece* (Athens, 1974), pp. 64-82.

32. Since C. Decavallas, on the other hand, was in part influenced by N. Valsamakis, a prominent modernist, he should not be thought to be exclusively in one or the other of the two camps.

33. Such as the archaeological museums at Philippi, Cavalla and Polygyros [1961-1963 in collaboration with I. Triantaphyllides].

34. The museum on Chios clearly shows the influence of A. Konstandinides's own museums at Yannina [1967] and at Komotini [1972].

35. This constituted an adaptation of the formal but not the structural characteristics of the curtain wall to then current Greek construction technology.

36. Cf. his articles in Greek periodicals, such as "Town and Dwelling in the Future," *Architektoniki*, no. 42 (1963): 48-55; "City Planning and Electronics," *Architecture in Greece, 1969-1970* and *1973-1974* (later published as a separate text).

37. "It is possible to manipulate the natural environment, to sculpt the earth and construct it in the same way we construct the architectural project it will receive," *Architektoniki*, no. 56 (1966): 49.

38. *Architektoniki*, no. 39 (1963): 50.

39. The School of Architecture at the Athens Technical University was founded in 1917 while the one at the Salonica Technical University was established in 1959.

40. Foolishly, the building industry was manipulated by the dictatorship as a means of accelerating the rate of economic growth. When the international economic slump finally reached Greece in 1973 in full force, construction was almost completely halted forcibly by imposing heavy economic penalties in a vain effort to control the recession.

41. The most prominent event in this movement was the student uprising at the Athens Technical University in November 1973, which helped topple the military regime a few months later.

42. A notable exception to this is exemplified in the books of Manolis Papadolambakis, who argues strongly for a populist takeover of the means of production of the built environment, in the interest of the people rather than of any powerful minority. In this he is obviously influenced by the work of R. Goodman (*After the Planners*, 1972), Chr. Alexander (Lima Housing Project, Peru) and, strictly on a theoretical level, by the sociologist Henri Lefebvre. Out of this kind of thinking four attitudes toward action—the pragmatic, the cynical, the escapist, and the radical—are possible for Greek architects as seen by A. Romanos in his "The Role of the Architect in Society" (in Greek), *Bulletin of the Greek Architects' Association* (1972): 102-106.

43. The American Embassy in Athens had a similar peripheral colonnade.

44. For example, both the "Athens Tower" [1971] and the Foreign Ministry Annex [1978] by Yannis Vikelas, one of the top, established Greek architects, show an identical treatment of the elevations. In this, however, there may also be the influence of the work of E. D. Stone.

45. I refer to the following buildings at Salonica University: Administration, Library, Main Assembly, Law School, and Divinity School.

Bibliography

BOOKS

Antoniades, Anthony C. *Contemporary Greek Architecture*. Athens: Man and Space Editions, 1979.

Kidder-Smith, G. E. *The New Architecture of Europe*. Penguin Books, 1962, pp. 146-52.

Konstandinides, Aris. *Ferienhäuser in Europa*. Munich: Callwey, 1968, 144-49.

Loyer, François. *Architecture de la Grèce Contemporaine*. Doctorat de troisiéme cycle, University of Paris, 1966.

JOURNALS

Antoniades, Anthony C. "Poems with Stones: The Enduring Spirit of Dimitrius Pikionis." *Architecture and Urbanism*, no. 72 (1976): 17-22.

Doumanis, Orestis. "Introduction to Post-War Greek Architecture." *World Architecture* 1 (1964): 116-23.

Fatouros, Dimitris. "Greek Art and Architecture 1945-1967." *Balkan Studies*, no. 8 (1967): 430-35.

Konstandinides, Aris. *Architectural Design*, no. 5 (1964): 212-35.

Loyer, François. "A Critique of Contemporary Greek Architecture" (with English summary). *Architecture in Greece*, no. 2 (1968): 22-35.

Michelis, Panayotis. "Modern Greek Architecture and Contemporary Trends" (with English summary). *Architecture in Greece*, no. 2 (1968): 18-21.

Porphyrios, Dimitri. "Modern Architecture in Greece" (with English summary). *Design in Greece*, no. 10 (1979): 14-33.

Simeon, Andreas. "The State of Contemporary Greek Architecture" (with English summary). *Architecture in Greece*, no. 2 (1968): 36-40.

25

HUNGARY

JÁNOS BONTA

Located in central Europe, at the intersection of many routes of cultural interchange, Hungary embodies in architecture a variety of influences that have acted upon her own ancient popular traditions to create peculiar syntheses. With a slow social development, bourgeois civilization never was fulfilled and technological development was considerably delayed. Thus, ancient Hungarian folk art along with that of other Central and Eastern European nations remained vital until the recent past. This meeting of modern life-styles with older popular tradition, perhaps best known internationally in the music of Bartok, has also been expressed in other endeavors including the art of architecture.

Architecture in Hungary between the two world wars was characterized by three main trends: eclecticism, the reassertion of a vernacular architecture, and the introduction of the International Style.

Neoeclecticism, particularly in its neo-Baroque version, was the official style of the "gentry" in Hungary when the feudal system of giant landed estates was maintained. The real problems of the age were bypassed through a superficial ornamentation.[1]

Those interested in folklore sought inspiration and solutions in the peasant art of the country, with its deeply rooted traditions. During and after the Art Nouveau period, Ödön Lechner and Béla Lajta, mainly, created a rather modern metropolitan architecture by making use of peasant motives.[2] Popular or folk art efforts in architecture between the two world wars were no more than faint echoes of the great traditions.[3] The problems of the age could not be approached merely by the utilization or modernization of peasant forms and building types.

International modern architecture became the most salient representative of the age and its future, but backward conditions at home compelled the best of our intelligentsia to emigrate. Among Hungarian architects studying and working abroad, the Bauhaus exerted the strongest influence upon the development of architects such as Laszló Moholy-Nagy, Marcel Breuer, Alfred Forbát and Ernö Kállai. Among the Bauhaus architects Farkas Molnár (1897-1945) was particularly distinguished with such outstanding works as a single-family cottage on Lejtó Street, Budapest [1932]; a block of freehold flats on Lotz Károly Street, Budapest [1934]; and with his coworker József Fischer (b. 1901), the hospital pavilion at Pestujhely [1935]; a block of freehold flats on Pasaréti Road in Budapest [1937]; and a villa on Mese Street, Budapest [1937]. József Fischer's own significant works were single-family residences on Zenta Street [1934] and Bajza Street, Budapest [1936].[4] Toward the end of this period, contemporary forms became more widespread in public and office buildings, not necessarily according with Bauhaus principles, but rather in a more decorative expression of that manner as for instance in the post office building on Dob Street, Budapest [1937] and the sports hall at Budapest [1941] by Rimanóczy and his coworkers. With the direct and indirect participation of such architects, modern Hungarian architecture between the world wars reached the level of the most outstanding of European achievements.

In the first years after the Second World War ruins had to be cleared and everything that could be at all restored was most urgently reconstructed or replaced, and then often supplemented. The magnitude of this task was enormous. About 26 percent of the residential buildings of Budapest, some twenty-nine thousand, and 90 percent of its industrial buildings were completely destroyed or seriously damaged. All of what once had been the pride of the capital, including the Danube River bridges, was in ruins. Under these conditions architects had to concentrate upon solving practical problems to ensure a rapid rate of construction and there was little inclination to engage in theoretical questions concerning styles.

The first new construction between 1948 and 1950 was, typically, residential building of miners' colonies and workers' districts, outpatients' facilities, and some typical public buildings.[5] The conservative, neoeclectic, and popular trends seemed to disappear, new constructions represented unequivocally the effects of the "new architecture." New horizons opened for all who for decades had been unable to participate in creative architecture, or whose architectural activity had been restricted mainly to the design of relatively small-scale private family houses. The advocates of the new architecture soon mastered all the methods developed in modern architecture throughout the world. Since industrialization had not been introduced into Hungary, relatively unusual individual buildings were erected, for example in the Budapest headquarters of the Building Industry Workers' Trade Union [1947-1950] by Lajos Gádoros, Imre Perényi, Gábor Preisich, and György Szrogh (fig. 25.1), where enormous columns five

25.1. Lajos Gádoros, Imre Perényi, Gábor Preisich, György Szrogh, architects. Headquarters of the Building Industry Workers' Trade Union. Budapest, 1947-1950. (Photograph: Courtesy of Artisjus)

stories high, a variation upon Le Corbusier's *pilotis*, create an open ground-floor pavilion and are connected to the floor constructions through small beam studs. The visible construction is in contrast to the reality.

From 1949 on the building industry encountered significant tasks when the industrialization of the country was finally begun. These involved the construction of new industrial plants and the establishment of new residential areas including such entirely new towns as Almásfüzitö, Komló, Várpalota, Dunaujváros, and Kazincbarcika.[6] During the 1950s, problems of completely new dimensions revealed the contradiction between the exclusive character of architecture in the first postwar years and the actual situation of the country's building industry. The basic material of mass housing remained invariably brick; and there were no up-to-date designs for floors, doors and windows, and so on, suitable for mass-construction purposes. Thus, whether desirable or not, we had to return to a more provincial brick-and-plaster architecture. Other circumstances reinforced this decision. For the people and their leaders, the world of modern forms was then still very much alien. Reacting to the politics of cold-war propaganda, a greater development of indigenous building traditions was urged to combat modern trends regarded as "cosmopolitan." Conservatives formerly in temporary retreat entered the scene once again with an ideological support of socialist colors. Those who favored peasant art promoted the resurrection of the awkward classicism of county halls and the provincial mansions of country squires as well as the traditional plaster architecture of Hungarian small towns. This is exemplified in Zoltán Farkasdy's Applied Arts School, Budapest [1953]; Béla Pintér's Cultural Center, Tolna [1952]; and Lóránt Radnay's apartment buildings, Várpalota [1951-1953]. Others abhorring archaizing, experimented with the refined and modernized classicism of Gunnar Asplund of Sweden or, more precisely, with its much more decorative version, somewhat towards Art Nouveau as in András Ivánka's Outpatient Clinic at Dunaujváros [1951], György Szrogh's new buildings for the Technical University of Budapest [1954], and Tibor Weiner's Vasmü Road at Dunaujváros [1952]. A few attempted to transplant the large scale of classicistic Soviet architecture to conditions prevailing in Hungary, for instance at Steel Works Road in the town of Dunaujváros.

Plaster architecture, whatever it may have represented, masked brick-walled buildings of usually modest load-bearing capacity. Their facades were articulated in a uniform rhythm by standardized small-sized windows that concealed similarly standardized rather humble apartments. Despite their traditional "artistic" forms of facades, these new residential districts exhibited a rather schematic pattern. To counteract this effect in modern settlements of row and cube houses, another device of design slowly gained considerable ground between 1951 and 1955. Corners of buildings were offset in sequences at Dunaujváros, Kazincbarcika, Tatabánya, as well as at the housing estate planned by Zoltán Legány and Lajos Schmidt and constructed along the Kerepesi Road, Budapest [1951-1952], in order to create theatrical, symmetrical compositions of meandering forms.

This architecture satisfied neither the economic requirements of constructional engineering nor the social and aesthetic strivings of that period. Precast flooring elements and brick-wall building methods solved the problems of mass housing only temporarily, while schematic formal systems of built-ins and archaistic plaster architecture were combined to create an environment which, from the very beginning, worked against an accommodation of modern technology to the social structure of what was then a backward peasant country.

The failure of archaism to solve the pressing problems of that period is well exemplified in industrial architecture. During the first years following reconstruction, a number of large-sized power stations and factory halls were erected including Ferenc Székely Kovács's Ganz Carriage and Wagon Works, Workshop Hall A, Budapest [1950]; Miklós Gnädig's Borsod Chemical Works, storehouse for chemical fertilizer, Kazincbarcika [1951]; Gyula Mátrai's and co-workers' Ganz Shipyard and Crane Works' assembly hall, Budapest [1951-1952]; Gyula Mátrai's and co-workers' Borsod Power Plant [1952] and the Inota Power Plant [1953]. The character and great dimensions of the problems involved in planning these buildings led talented engineers and architects away from the usual approaches and toward on-site prefabrication of reinforced concrete. As a result, elements as much as twelve to twenty-five tons in weight were produced, hoisted into position, and assembled. Such bold buildings without traditionally archaistic surface treatment brought Hungarian industrial architecture a high level of appreciation in professional circles.

The intermezzo of archaistic experimentation that lasted for four or five years left deep traces in only a few towns established at that time. Dunaujváros, a typical example, built primarily as a residential precinct for the iron works, has grown to be a center of fifty thousand inhabitants, with a significant amount of light industry.[7] However, archaistic experimentation exerted other permanent effects on the subsequent development of Hungarian architecture. It brought about an appreciation of imposed conditions of place and time, of the *genius loci*; it thrust into prominence a noble common cause, the task of safeguarding, improving, and accommodating our building traditions, town structures, monuments, and monumental ensembles to the processes of contemporary life. Still appreciable in 1955, however, was a neglect of sociophyscial and artistic idealizing aspects in favor of practical, economic, and technological interests in the narrowest sense.

Mass demand soon brought about changes in the methods of construction of residential building settlements. Not only floor beams but also floor and balcony slabs were precast. Then, lightweight concrete blocks were introduced, a characteristic element in the transition to industrialized large-scale building systems. The opposition between archaistic forms and industrialized mass construction intensified, and led to another turning point. At the 1954 General Assembly of the Union of Hungarian Architects, speakers clearly expressed criticisms of the excesses of archaism—criticisms strongly supported, not long after our General Assembly, by similar attacks in the Soviet Union where archaizing had been even stronger.

In the next years architects abandoned their earlier creative approaches only with considerable difficulties. They employed modern forms and methods almost uncritically, as novelties; and, despite their eclectic schematic uses of clichés of design, won full acknowledgement for their efforts. As a result, residential and public buildings took on virtually identical, undistinguished facades during the second half of the 1950s.

After the political upheavals and shock of 1956, in which downtown Budapest suffered heavy damage, the reconstruction was combined fortunately with modernization in initiatives that improved the appearance of many sections of the city. Shop windows along main streets were renewed, the public illumination system updated, and Rákóczi street, the main axis of Budapest, was lined with arcades to increase its capacity as a thoroughfare, while sites vacant ever since the Second World War were gradually occupied by new buildings. Some examples are Miklós Csics's apartments on József Boulevard, Budapest [1958]; Lajos Schmidt's apartments on Gellérthegy Street, Budapest [1964]; and Lajos Földesi's multiple dwelling building on József Nádor Square, Budapest [1966].

The renaissance of Hungarian architecture began in the early 1960s following the restoration of legal order, after the leaders of the country introduced much more flexible and better-balanced economic and cultural policies than before to suit existing conditions. This opened up new possibilities that led to the establishment of the infrastructure required for up-to-date production. The renaissance of the 1960s saw the creation of an architectural environment that encouraged a modern way of life. By the application of large-scale industrial technology our industrial communities established before 1956 grew and developed from residential settlements into organic towns as at Dunaujváros, Kazincbarcika, and Komló, for example, as well as at the somewhat later new towns of Leninváros and Százhalombatta.

The period from 1960 to today may be characterized, fortunately, not so much by abrupt changes but rather by continuous development.

The number of apartments constructed in the last fifteen years has amounted annually on average to about ninety thousand, enough to house 9 percent of the total population. About 25 to 33 percent of apartments were built by large-scale industrial methods, involving in most cases wall-sized room elements produced by permanent plants, "housing factories." Typically, apartments are rather small with some 54 square meters, but with a high level of technical services such as area heating, hot water, built-in cabinets and kitchen furniture. Central parts of Budapest and some of our major country towns are encircled now by such new residential settlements, as for instance at Pécs, Debrecen, and Szeged. Significant among the housing estates built with large-scale industrial techniques in Budapest, are those in the Kelenföld section (fig. 25.2) at the abutment of the Árpád Bridge; in Óbuda, on the Örs-vezér Square; and others in the Ujpalota and Békásmegyer districts, for most of which construction was begun in 1964.[8]

A number of sociological, psychological, aesthetic, and, of course, architectural problems have arisen from new residential settlements, as occurs in other countries. To facilitate the concentration of resources and efforts and to demolish relatively few older buildings, new residential construction was carried out mainly on the outskirts of existing towns. Downtown areas have hardly been affected, with some few exceptions, as in Salgótarján (fig. 25.3). With the establishment of new settlements, some older areas, such as the VIIth, VIIIth, and IXth districts of Budapest, started to deteriorate rapidly into slums. It is axiomatic that the younger generation always moves into newer apartment buildings while older generations remain in depreciated dwellings of the city core. Many small, older villages, for instance in Zala county, and farms on the great Hungarian Plain, came to be almost totally depopulated.

Before the 1960s a rather strictly limited technology, the factory system of prefabricating housing, and the special interests of overloaded manufacturing and assembly enterprises necessarily influenced architects. As a result, new residential districts assumed a schematic, uniform character that insufficiently accommodated to particular social requirements. Ignoring regional conditions, the size and historical development of particular settlements, their terrain whether plain or hilly, whether in the capital or in small rural towns, the same ten-story apartment blocks were constructed.

Size and layout of individual apartments failed to accommodate different life-styles, economic levels, and the familial compositions of their inhabitants. Most flats were produced to meet requirements set by small, single-generation families, and this worked against our demographic policy.

There were neither promenades nor small, humanizing squares between individual buildings. Since buildings for community use were completed

25.2. Town Planning Institute. Dwelling estate, Budapest-Kelenföld. Budapest, 1967-1968. (Photograph: Courtesy of Artisjus)

generally only with much delay, there was no place where the generations could meet and interact easily. Centers around which activities of the entire settlement could be organized were lacking or at best were completed long after residential facilities. People are relatively satisfied with their attractive new apartments but regard the settlements themselves as rather dull and monotonous and care not at all about the planned public areas.

Experimentation to eliminate these faults in design was started only in the most recent years. In the newest residential districts rooms are somewhat larger; more larger apartments have been built; different colors enliven the environment; and increased efforts have been exerted to overcome deficiencies recognized particularly in buildings for children's welfare and education. The limitations imposed by large-scale industrial technology have been set aside by an alliance of enthusiastic local patriotism and talented architects, as exemplified by the renewed central cities at Salgótarján, Szekszárd, Zalaegerszeg, Kecskemét, and other provincial towns. The most successful was Salgótarján whose town center has apartment houses (fig. 25.3) designed by Géza Magyar [1965]; the Hotel Karancs, the work of György Jánossy [1963]; the community social center by György Szrogh [1962-1965]; and the department store by József Finta [1967-1968]. Notable also in this new town is Imre Vargha's statue of the great Hungarian poet Miklós Radnóti who was murdered during the Second World War. The buildings in Szekszárd's town center were planned by Károly Jurcsik and Levente Varga [1966-1972]; the richly shaped apartment houses of Zalaegerszeg's city center, meant to remind the observer of the secession period, were designed by György Vadász [1976]; and the hotel in the city center of Kecskemét was by István Janáky [1962].

The greater part of residential construction is now from private resources with governmental subsidies; the majority is in small family houses with only a small fraction being apartment house flats owned by tenants in rural towns. Particularly in the developing rural communities small, urban-type bourgeois houses built by handcraftsmen or families themselves are replacing the homes of the former peasantry. This phenomenon involves serious cultural losses. As with other aspects of the former peasant life-style, owners of older peasant homes see nothing in them but the memories of poverty and reject modernized

25.3. Géza Magyar, József Finta, architects. Dwelling houses and shopping center. Salgótarján, 1965-1968. (Photograph: Courtesy of Artisjus)

ideas of renovation. The remaining traditional architecture of Hungary will be preserved it seems as museums of a former peasant mode of life, and in many instances as restored old peasant houses and farm buildings that serve some few as summer cottages. But some few single-family cottages are still being designed by architects. Among these we may mention one on Tanács Street, Budapest [1962], by Béla Pintér; a weekend houe [1966] and summer residences at Ábrahámhegy [1967] and Tahi [1970] by György Vadász; as well as a summer residence on Normafa Road, Budapest [1971], by Sára Cs. Juhász and László Csaba.

In 1976 the complex restorations of our early fortresses, castles, village churches, particularly ensembles of monuments in the Buda Castle district of Budapest and in towns such as Sopron, Eger, and Györ, were very much admired by members of the International Commission on Museums. In an exemplary manner Hungarian architects have solved the problems of accommodating modern buildings to old environments,[9] and of displaying antiques and fragments of earlier architecture. The coexistence of old and new is particularly evident in Zoltán Farkasdy's work in the Bourg-quarter of Buda, Uri Street, Budapest [1957-1959]; György Jánossy's promenade Tóth Árpád [1962-1963], also in the Bourg-quarter of Buda; and Szentháromság Street [1965-1968] by Csaba Virág in the same part of Buda.

Relatively few exclusively public buildings have been constructed recently. The architecture of office buildings, department stores, hospitals, residential and communal buildings has been largely dictated by an urgent need to remedy existing shortages of these, by economic requirements, and by the technology of mass production. In those few exceptional cases when architects could make use of more widely varied and more expensive materials and structures, they moved toward the extreme richness of the Hotel Duna Intercontinental [1966-1969] by József Finta (fig. 25.4), and the overdesign and overdecoration both in interiors and upon exteriors at the Hilton Hotel [1976-1978] Budapest, by Béla Pintér.[10]

Industrial architecture, extremely successful from the outset, has continued to improve, following a well-balanced course. Transforming necessity into merit, industrial architects have developed on-site prefabrication systems of quite a gigantic scale, spurred on in 1961 by the Perret award to our Industrial Building Design Institute. The Perret award cited the remarkable results achieved since 1948-1949 by the institute in the fields of large panel prefabrication and the systematic development of large-scale building construction manufacture to serve industrial and agricultural requirements. The institute carried out pioneering research into economic and purposive building construction, always aiming, however, for the highest conditions of architectural quality. Certain changes introduced after 1960 in a more sophisticated policy of industrial development brought about less spectacular but more economic and more flexible building systems. Buildings that could be modified were prefabricated for use at sites that could be designated later; and the integration of factories with their surroundings became an important aspect of design, as in the Dunaujváros paper mill and canneries. The architecture of contemporary Hungarian industrial buildings shows amply that even with the strictest of technological requirements a civilized, humane environment may be built.[11]

25.4. The reconstructed Elizabeth Bridge (foreground), Budapest, 1964. József Finta, architect, Pál Sávoly, structural engineer. Hotel Duna Intercontinental. Budapest, 1966-1969. (Photograph: Courtesy of Artisjus)

Among the more organic structures of the Hungarian architectural environment that have been rapidly transformed are major traffic junctions, the reconstructed Budapest bridges and their elevated approach routes, motorways and their graceful viaducts, and many stations and tunnels of the subway system. Of these, though progress has been made that is comparable to our industrial buildings' architectural development, I cite only two examples:

György Kőváry's Southern Railway Station in Budapest, begun in 1976, and Tibor Bakonyi's water tower of 1977 at Szeged.

We have seen that most Hungarian architecture since the Second World War has been aimed at radically transforming the formerly feudal and peasant environment of a poor, backward country to accord with the modern requirements of industrialization. Accomplished with very modest and practical economic means, this has led, unfortunately, in many cases to somewhat monotonous results. All in all, modern Hungarian architecture began to develop freely only after 1960 and is still rather immature. Though Hungarian architects successfully employ many features of international modern architecture, since they do not coordinate them with the atmosphere of the nation's landscape and culture, Hungarian architecture now appears colorless and without especially innovative characteristics.

Our architectural deficiencies are particularly painfully felt by our most sensitive generation, the young. Dissatisfied with an atmosphere of technological priorities, the younger generation's efforts are clearly reflected in the organic decorative forms of dwellings built, for instance, for the employees of the nuclear power station at Paks, in which motifs definitely related to the folkways of the past may be seen. Architect György Csete has been especially active in this mode of design with his so-called Tulip Houses at Paks, begun in 1976, and the house of a speleologist at Orfü, built in 1976-1977. Similar concerns are revealed by some small-scale restaurant architecture that was accomplished with materials and the structural design of Hungarian folk art. Typical here are two restaurants by Imre Makovecz: Csárda Sió at Szekszárd [1964] and the Csárda near the Tatabánya highway [1969]; as well as a church by Zoltán Bachman at Szamoskér [1978]. And these concerns are equally evident in the reappearance of rich combinations of form that seem to synthesize Art Nouveau or Art Deco and the International Style, as in Péter Fazekas's and Gábor Sellyei's Hotel Claudius at Szombathely [1972], György Vadász's apartment house (fig. 25.5) on Árnyas Street in Budapest [1970-1974], and István Szabó's Roman Catholic church in Budapest-Farkasrét [1977]. Though isolated and as yet immature these efforts may signal a new national trend. Surely soon, talented Hungarian architects will find the ways and means to fulfill the complex cultural and intellectual expectations of our society and to create an up-to-date mature architectural environment that will conform with the material, social, and cultural conditions of our country and our times.

25.5. György Vadász, architect. Apartment House on Árnyas Street, Budapest, 1970-1974. (Photograph: Courtesy of Artisjus)

Notes

1. The greatest Hungarian master of the neo-Baroque style, Gyula Wälder (1884-1944), was well represented by a former grammar school and a Cistercian church in Budapest [1930]. Typical of neo-Romanticism is the ensemble of the Cathedral Square at Szeged [1930] by Béla Rerrich, architect (1881-1932), and the church of the order of St. Paul at Pécs [1935] by Károly Weichinger, architect (b.1893). The most distinguished neo-Classical architect was Dezsö Hütl (1870-1945) as seen in his apartment house at the corner of the avenue Rákóczi and boulevard Tanács, Budapest [1936].

2. Among the masterpieces in this manner were the Museum of Applied Arts, Budapest [1891-1896], the Institute of Geology, Budapest [1898-1899], and the Post Office Savings Bank, Budapest [1899-1901], all by Ödön Lechner. Béla Lajta (1873-1920) followed with his early buildings in the style of Ö. Lechner such as the Asylum for the Blind, Budapest [1905-1907]; the Alms House, Budapest [1908-1911]; and his mature works that included the School of Commerce, Budapest [1910-1912] and apartment and office buildings on Martinelli Square, Budapest [1911-1912].

3. This is evident in the Roman Catholic church at Budapest [1920] by Aladár Árkay (1868-1932); the agricultural school at Ráckeve [1941] by János Wanner; and the dressing room building for a sports facility in Budapest [1942] by Gyula Rimanóczy (1903-1958).

4. Other important architects of the Modern Movement in the interval between the wars were Máté Major (b.1904) who is best represented by a four-family villa at Sashegy, Budapest [1934]; Zoltán Kósa (1902-1979), a cottage on Széher Street, Budapest [1934], Virgil Borbiró (1893-1956) with his airport traffic control building, in collaboration with László Králik, at Budaörs [1936]; Lajos Kozma (1884-1948) especially with his gem of a weekend-house on the Isle Lupa, Budapest [1934]; two co-workers of Le Corbusier, Károly Dávid, Jr. (1903-1974) with a family cottage at Mount Gellért, Budapest [1934] and János Wanner (b.1906) with the headquarters of the former Chamber of Engineers, Budapest [1940]; and also László Lauber (1902-1953) and István Nyiri (1902-1955) in an apartment house on Kékgolyó Street, Budapest [1935] and the headquarters of the former Central Corporation of Banking Companies, Szabadság Square, Budapest [1940].

5. We may mention Lajos Gádoros's standard apartment house with outside balcony leading to the flats [1948], constructed in Salgótarján and Csepel; József Schall's miners' dwellings at Petöfibánya [1949-1950]; Jenó Szendröi's and Andor Lévai's outpatient clinic, Budapest [1949]; Ferenc Kiss's outpatient clinic, Ujpest [1949]; István Nyiri's bus terminal, Budapest [1949]; Lajos Gádoros, Imre Perényi, Gábor Preisich, and György Szrogh's center for the Trade Union of the Building Industry Workers, Budapest [1947-1950]; and Károly Dávid and co-workers' People's Stadium, Budapest [1947-1953].

6. Plans were projected by the Institute for Planning Residential Buildings, the Institute for Town and Regional Planning, and the Institute for Town Planning of Budapest. The head architects for these new towns were as follows: Almásfüzitö [1949-1950], architect and town planner, Ipoly Farkas; Komló [1949-], architects, József Schall and László Zoltán; Várpalota [1951-], architects, Lóránt Radnay and Antal Károlyi; Dunaujváros (formerly Sztálinváros) [1950-], architect and town planner, Tibor Weiner; Kazincbarcika [1951], town planners, Károly Valentiny and co-workers.

7. All phases of postwar architecture may be observed in the Dunaujváros townscape, from the monumental Vasmü Road and its vicinity marking the archaizing period, and apartment housing estates placed in a green environment mirroring the attitude of the Athens Charter, to the past two decades of building by means of industrialized methods.

8. The town plans were developed for the most part at the Institute for Town Planning and Construction of Budapest or at the Institute for Planning Residential Buildings by architects such as Tibor Csordás, Tibor Gáspár, Zoltán Farkasdy, and János Pomsár. In Pécs, town plans were accomplished at the Institute for Planning of Pécs under architect Ernö Tillai; in Debrecen and environs by Tibor Mikolás and Bernát Beruzs; in Szeged by Béla Borvendég, Máté Takács, and István Tarnai. In designing small public buildings and communal centers Károly Jurcsik and his co-workers have achieved considerable success since 1974 using industrialized systems (of frame panels and small panels).

9. The blocks of freehold flats by László Iványi on Tulipán Street in Budapest [1963-1966] and by György Kévés, Sashegy, Budapest [1966-1969] exemplify well a terracelike modern adaptation to the hilly terrain of the Buda section of Budapest.

10. A fuller discussion of Hungary's architecture since 1960 would include the construction of numerous office buildings, schools, cultural and related centers, hotels, and hospitals. Significant among each of these functional types are the following: *office blocks*—the foreign trade company, Chemolimpex's center in district V, Budapest [1962-1964] by István Gulyás; the headquarters of the Hungarian Aluminum Trust, Budapest [1964-1967] by Olga Mináry; and the center of the Hungarian-Bulgarian Company Intranszmasz [1966-1969] in Budapest, by Elemér Nagy. *University and High School buildings*—the main building of the Technical University at Miskolc [1966] by István Janáky; the university library building at Miskolc [1966-1969] by Lajos Tolnay; the High School for Agricultural Sciences at Debrecen [1960-1963] by Tibor Mikolás; the central building of the Semmelweis Medical School in Budapest [1978] by Ernö Südi and László Wagner; and the High School for Telecommunication at Györ [1978] by Miklós Hófer. *Buildings for cultural purposes*—cinema-theaters at Köbánya, Budapest [1964] by Péter Molnár; Eger [1960-1964] by László Mányoki; and Györ [1978] by Kálmán Vince; the House of Culture at Orgovany [1968-1969] by Károly Jurcsik and Levente Varga; and the Young People's House at Salgótarján [1977-1978] by Géza Magyar. *Hotels*—a motel for the Lake Balaton shore at Tihany [1954-1961] by Károly Polónyi; the Hotel Annabella, Balatonfüred [1966-1967] by Margit Pázmándi; another hotel at Lake Balaton, Siófok [1960-1961] by Lajos Földessy; the Hotel Budapest in Budapest [1965-1967] by György Szrogh; and the Hotel Volga, Budapest [1971] by József Finta. *Hospitals*—at Dunaujváros [1960-1966] by Zoltán Farkasdy; Salgótarján (1961-1967] by Ferenc Ulrich; the Medical School Clinic at Pécs [1958-1966] by Lajos Gádoros; and hospitals at Kazincbarcika [1964-1967] by György Jánossy and his co-workers and in Kisvárda [1975] by Tibor Mikolás.

11. Examples of distinguished industrial architecture after 1960 are numerous. In the following list only the names of the head architects or construction engineers are given: Viktor Pásztor, cold rolling mill at Danaujváros [1963-1967]; Ipoly Farkas, light metal works at Székesférvár [1960-1968]; József Orbán, "Icarus" tool shop, Budapest (1967-1969]; László Bajnay and Miklós Gnädig, chemical fertilizer works at Leninváros [1960-1963]; András Mészöly, Institute for Planning, chemical works and PVC polymer works of the firm UHDE (GFR) at Berente [1966-1968]; György Balázs, the kiln and kiln building of a lime burning works at Hejöcsaba [1962-1965]; Imre Fülöpza, a housing factory at Dunakeszi [1967-1970]; Lajos Arnóth and Jenó Szendröi, factory for telecommunication equipment, Budapest [1961-1964]; Lajos Földesi and Jenö Szendröi, canning factory at Nyiregyháza [1962-1966]; Lajos Földesi, canning factory at Debrecen [1965-1969]; and finally, István Bakos and Tibor Karsay, the Atheneum printing office in Budapest [1957-1962].

Bibliography

BOOKS

Kubinszky, Mihály, ed. *New Encyclopedia of Architecture.* Budapest: Müszaki Kiadó, 1978. (In Hungarian)

Merényi, Ferenc. *The Hungarian Architecture 1867-1967.* Budapest: Müszaki Konyvkiodó, 1969. (In Hungarian)

______. "1867-1965 Centro Anni Architettura Ungherese" (Accademia d'Ungheria in Roma, Anno Accademico 38). *Quaderni di Documenta,* 7th year, 1 (September 1965).

Szendröi, Jenö; Arnóth, Lajos; Finta, József; Merényi, Ferenc; Nagy, Elemér. *Hungarian Architecture 1945-1970.* Budapest: Corvino Kiadó, 1972. (In Hungarian)

Szendröi, Jenö; Arnóth, Lajos; Finta, József; Merényi, Ferenc; Nagy, Elemér. *Ungarische Architektur 1956-1970.* Budapest: Corvina Verlag, 1977.

Szendröi, Jenö; Bajnay, László; Bonta, János; Gyöngyösi, István; Kürthy, László. *Hungarian Architecture 1945-1955.* Budapest: Képzömüvészeti Alap Kiadóvállata, 1955. (In Hungarian)

26

ISRAEL

GILBERT HERBERT

The state of Israel, at the time of writing, is slightly more than thirty years old; the roots of the Jewish people in the land of Israel, however, extend millennia deep into history. I write here not only of a spiritual and cultural attachment to the promised land, not only of symbolic roots, but of the fact of an almost continuous physical presence, despite enforced exile and the ongoing deterrence of heavy-handed foreign dominance. This Jewish presence in the land of Israel had always been significant in the ancient centers of learning, in Tiberias, in Safed, and, of course, in Jerusalem. But in more recent times, in the past hundred years or so, it became more manifest with the establishment of the first Jewish settlements of the Zionist era: the urban neighborhoods beyond the walls of old Jerusalem, the villages and the agricultural settlements, the founding of Tel Aviv. In constitutional terms the state of Israel may be said to result from the United Nations decision of 1947, and the subsequent Declaration of Independence, but the reality of Israel *de facto* had long before been fashioned by internal forces and external pressures, shaped and tempered by idealism and stern necessity, by dreams and pioneering labor, by purchase, reclamation, and settlement, by physical construction and the building of institutional frameworks, and—not least, but certainly not only—by determined and courageous defense in the face of incessant violence and unremitting hostility.

The land of Israel—wherever its final borders will be—is physically tiny, its breadth from desert to sea only a few minutes jet-time. Within this meager compass of space a wide variety of geographic regions is embraced: the lovely, once stone-covered but now afforested mountains of Galilee; the fertile, intensely cultivated northern valleys; the Sharon plain flanking the long Mediterranean coastline, with its heavy concentrations of urban population; the green forest-covered foothills leading to Jerusalem-the-golden and, abruptly, to the Judean wilderness beyond; the long declivity of the Great Rift from the Kinneret in the north through the Jordan valley to the aridity of the Dead Sea; and the desert, stretching from Beersheva southwards to the Red Sea.

The Jewish population of this minuscule state, a mere six hundred thousand at its founding, now grown fivefold, comes from every corner of the earth; it is, indeed, an "ingathering of the exiles." To join the seventh-generation *Yerushalmis* there have come the pioneer Zionists and Socialists of Russia and Poland; the remnants of European Jewry—victims of the Nazi terror forty years ago, of Communist harassment today; western Jews from the developed industrial societies of the English-speaking world and from Latin America; oriental Jews from the Arabian peninsula and North Africa, from India and Persia. These three million people, so diverse in culture, background, language, even ethnic appearance, are tenuously but indissolubly united by a common thread of Jewishness, a multiple thread whose many strands comprise a shared history of spiritual grandeur and of persecution, and a religious tradition ranging from the eternal truths of the Torah on the one hand to the rewarding folk and family rituals of Judaism on the other. Side by side with this anthropological mélange, as it were, and compounding its complexity, are Israel's non-Jewish minority groups: Moslem and Druse, Christian and Circassian, who today number some six hundred thousand souls.

These well-known facts of history, geography, and

demography are a prerequisite to any understanding of Israel's architecture. It was former Israeli Foreign Minister Abba Eban who once remarked: "He who does not know our history cannot understand our policy." We may legitimately appropriate that aphorism to our present purpose—to attain an insight into the achievements and problems of Israel's architects in this the fourth decade of the state. What a mixed bag of architectural styles existed as the physical heritage of the new state—what a stratification and compression of architectural history. Upon the bedrock of the ancient biblical civilizations (not always immediately visible to the eye, but always present in the national subconscious) lay strata upon strata of architectural achievement, an environmental fabric woven on the loom of time. Each age has left its monuments, each dominant power its impressive relics: Greece and Rome, Byzantium and the Crusader Kingdom, Ommiad and Ottoman. The imported styles lie in the enduring matrix of a more vernacular architecture: picturesque Arab villages, cubist exercises on terraced hills, dignified stone houses with flat roofs and vine-pergolas. When, towards the end of the nineteenth century, the first Jewish neighborhoods were built beyond the walls of the Old City of Jerusalem—Yemin Moshe, the Bukharim quarter, Batei Hungarim, Mea Shearim—they constituted urbane groupings of simple dwellings around communal places, in a style unmistakably that of Jerusalem but with central European overtones. At Rishon LeZion and Zichron Yaakov there are hints of Gallic charm in the houses clustered around the wineries, vigorous examples of nineteenth-century industrial vernacular, which were established with typical Rothschildian initiative by "Le Baron."

A new strain was introduced into the pattern of architectural development with the liberation of the Holy Land from Turkish domination by Allenby towards the end of the Great War. During the period of the British Mandate which followed, the infrastructure was laid for sound urban development and sensible planning control. The architecture of such talented designers as Austin St. Barbe Harrison, the architect of Government House in Jerusalem and the Law Courts in Haifa, and C. Holliday, designer of Jerusalem's Scottish Church and winner of the competition for the development of Kingsway in Haifa, set an example of distinction and civic propriety. In the 1930s a strange phenomenon erupted in this architecturally tranquil but politically troubled British outpost in the Middle East. With the influx of immigrants fleeing Hitler's Germany, a new architecture began to appear in Tel Aviv and Haifa, an architecture whose functional design found expression in crisp, white, cubic structures, set free of the ground on *pilotis*. This architecture, at first a tentative emergent, soon become dominant in the coastal cities. At one level this architecture formed a high-style transplant of the International Style, carried out under the influence of the newly arriving architects, some of them, like Arieh Sharon, the grand old man of modern architecture in Israel, or Munio Weinraub-Gitai, graduates of the Bauhaus itself. Many first-class buildings were built, some, such as Zeev Rechter's Bet Engel in Tel Aviv [1933], of a quality which would ensure them a place in any comprehensive catalogue of the pioneers of the Modern Movement. However, at another and perhaps as significant a level, an overall standard of modern design was achieved, of wide generality, a kind of "Bauhaus vernacular" which was unique in its time for its scope, extent, and quality. By means of this transfer of architectural strength from Europe to Israel, at a time when the development of Eretz Yisrael posed a challenge both idealistic and practical, parts of Tel Aviv and Haifa were transformed into perhaps the most extensive and consistent environment of wholly modern architecture to be seen outside the pioneer *Siedlungen* of Stuttgart, Frankfurt, and Berlin.

At the time of the proclamation of the state (1948), not only did the coastal cities constitute a veritable museum of modern architecture but this most urbane of styles had penetrated the rural areas where, side by side with the utilitarian structures of kibbutz and moshav (heirs of the stockade-and-watchtower tradition of the early agricultural settlements), were now to be found dining halls and other communal buildings of no little sophistication. In the hands of capable architects like Richard Kauffman, permutations were made of the universal forms of the Modern Movement in order to adapt them to local climatic conditions. His Dead Sea Works houses of 1929 with their parasol roofs is a typical example. But it is the genius of Erich Mendelsohn that had, in the years immediately prior to the Second World War, transmuted the International Style into a valid and viable regional expression, responsive to climate, local building techniques, and the landscape and townscapes of Eretz Yisrael, in such serene examples as the Schocken House and Library [Jerusalem, 1936], the house for Professor Chaim Weizmann [Rehovoth, 1935-1936], and the dramatic Hebrew University medical center on Mount Scopus, Jerusalem [1936-1939]. In these buildings, Mendelsohn consummates those experiments initiated decades before by such architects as Alexander Baerwald, designer of the first Technion building in Haifa [1912-1924], who sought to generate a new synthesis between the architecture of East and West.

After independence, with the doors at long last open, immigrants flooded in, from the displaced persons camps of Europe and the ghettos of the Arab world, by boat from Cyprus, by "operation flying carpet" from the Yemen. The main priority, naturally, was housing—and, on the whole, it has so remained. Since 1948 Israel has witnessed an almost convulsive outpouring of public housing. With only occasional fluctuations of tempo, resulting from periodic economic recessions, the provision of shelter has been a continuously expanding, almost frenetic process. Two factors dominated: speed and quantity. A long tradition of socialized housing already existed by the late 1940s not only in the rural settlements but in the cooperative housing experiments of the urban workers. This housing, and that which ensued in the following decades, was modest in size and austere in architectural expression, a natural extension of the habitation-minimum movement of the twenties and early thirties, in which architects now resident in Israel, notably Alexander Klein, had provided the theoretical, functionalist framework. We look back today at these early *shikunim*, or housing estates, with a critical eye, rejecting their mechanistic repetitive forms and their minimalistic standards, their often hasty construction and poor standards of workmanship. But our criticism is tinged with nostalgia, as we see in them, or read into them, something of the dimensions of an heroic age now past, whose architectural innocence was an expression of the pioneering spirit, conscious denial of the self for the communal good, and the willing acceptance of material restraint and a regime of austerity.

In housing there has been a rising graph of constantly improving standards: larger apartments, sounder construction, increased numbers of dwellings. At the same time, neighborhood planning has become more comprehensive. It has begun, still inadequately, to deal with the space between buildings and has slowly begun to make provision for (some would argue overprovision, in the sense that it has begun to be dominated by) the motorcar, a phenomenon rare indeed in 1948. That there are inadequacies in the detailed design of dwellings and the overall design of community space must be acknowledged. But, despite intensive self-criticism on the part of Israeli architects and general public dissatisfaction (which somehow is always generated when social housing goes beyond the crisis stage of providing basic shelter and seeks to offer a higher level of amenity), the housing story in Israel must be regarded as no mean achievement. Among many examples, we may cite the East Talpiot development in Jerusalem, by a team headed by architect David Best, and the Shaar Ha'aliyah neighborhood of Haifa, the realization in 1976 of a housing competition [1973] won by Al Mansfeld and Dani Havkin (fig. 26.1). To attain this satisfactory level of performance, in quantitative and qualitative terms, has of necessity demanded a high level of centralization and standardization from an administrative, design, and construction point of view. This standardization, however, inhibited diversity in the public housing sector, and it is the comparative uniformity of the housing product, in the face of Israel's geographic and demographic diversity, which lies at the heart of the most pertinent criticisms which may legitimately be leveled at Israeli housing. Despite some experimentation with other housing forms, such as high-rise

26.1. Al Mansfield and Dani Havkin, architects. Shaar Ha'aliyah Residential Quarter. Haifa (design competition, 1973; implementation, 1976). (Photgraph: Courtesy of the architects)

buildings (introduced relatively late and largely rejected for social, psychological, and technical reasons); patio-houses and carpet development (designed, I believe, at too high a density to ensure privacy and adequate, private, open space); pyramidal and other complex vertical clusters (very photogenic but a trifle too much akin to a beehive for this observer's taste); and stepped houses (potentially of great promise on the hills of Jerusalem and Haifa but often planned unskillfully), the predominant housing form is the four-story walk-up building, with two, four, or six apartments per staircase. Bland in silhouette and surface treatment, these plastered cubic forms with their plastic shutters are the universal paradigm, from Metulla to Eilat, in the spreading suburbs of the major metropolitan centers and in every new development town. Israel's new-towns program, which has been vigorously implemented over the past decades, resulted from a desire to decentralize population. This program, which has been thoroughly documented, has been questioned on social grounds, as many of the towns have failed to achieve the critical mass essential to healthy social development. But in urban planning and design terms many of them, Arad in the Negev, for instance, are bold and innovative achievements.

Apart from housing, perhaps the most significant architecture in the building of a new country is that of its institutions, which are the nodal points of that intense political and cultural activity which follows independence. These institutions are more than mere buildings. Their importance is more symbolic than pragmatic, for they are potent signifiers of emergent nationhood. They are an expression in vivid physical terms of that longing for instant maturity, symbols of a search for stability and prestige which older countries acquire more gradually and perhaps more gracefully. In Israel, of course, the term *statehood,* or *independence*, is somewhat ambiguous. This old-new nation has several fine institutions predating the formal declaration of independence. After 1948, however, the fleshing out of the institutional framework of the country in appropriate architectural terms began in earnest—and in haste. If some of the results are perhaps brash or self-consciously pompous, this is understandable, for the period of independence has been very short indeed for a task which can only be termed monumental. The wonder is that so much has been done so well.

Naturally, for the people of the book, universities take pride of place. Two of the oldest, the Technion in Haifa and the Hebrew University in Jerusalem, have already celebrated their golden jubilees; but there are several newer campuses that are noteworthy. The new Hebrew University campus on Mount Scopus (on the site of Mendelsohn's original buildings, which were cut off from Jerusalem from 1948 until the reunification of the city in 1967) is a massive remodeling of an entire hilltop, in a complex, unified, intricate megastructure,* a far cry indeed from the ordered tranquility and dignity of the university's other campus at Givat Ram begun in 1954 with its official opening in 1958. The Ben Gurion University (begun in 1965 with construction continuing), with important contributions by Abraham Yaski (fig. 26.2), Ram Karmi, and others, is a striking, compact organization of bravura concrete forms, richly modeled and highlighted by accents of primary color, whose strength and vigor proudly proclaim man's dominance over the surrounding Negev desert. Haifa University by architect Oscar Niemeyer, in association with Israeli architect Shlomo Gilead, deserves comment but not praise for its pristine tower located, typically but incongruously by Niemeyer, on the ridge of Mount Carmel. Other campuses—Tel Aviv University [master plan 1953-1955, first building 1960], the Technion in Haifa [city campus's first building from 1953; main complex 1956-1960; Churchill Auditorium, Senate, Library, construction continuing], the Weizmann Institute [early buildings in the 1930s; modern campus from 1953], the Bar Ilan University [opened 1955 with construction continuing]—all contain fine individual buildings, or even groups of buildings, but the campuses as a whole lack integration, with no unifying concept or central theme.

Both the Hebrew University and the Technion have small, effectively designed synagogues, the former by Rau and Reznik [1957], the latter by Aharon Kashtan [1969]; but, generally speaking, the Israeli architect has not responded to the challenge of the modern spiritual center. And outside of the universities there is no new synagogue that can match the character of the recently reconstructed synagogues of the old Jewish quarter of Jerusalem. Louis Kahn's monumental project of 1960 for the Hurva Synagogue, Jerusalem, was controversial, but it remains a paper project only, whose concept is unlikely to be concretized. An alternative proposal has been prepared by Sir Denys Lasdun.

In the late 1930s Erich Mendelsohn built two great hospitals. The Hadassah Hospital in Jerusalem was

*Foundation stones laid 1918, university opened 1925, construction continued into the 1930s. Campus inaccessible 1948-1967; rebuilding and extension of campus begun immediately thereafter and still continuing.

26.2. Abraham Yaski and Partners, architects. Ben Gurion University, Lecture Hall Building, Engineering School. Beersheva, 1965. (Photograph: Courtesy of Ran Erde)

badly damaged by enemy action and was cut off from Israel for nineteen years; today it has been widely and sensitively remodeled and extended by architects Yacov Rechter and Moshe Zarhi. The Rambam Hospital in Haifa, Mendelsohn's other hospital (originally the Government Hospital, 1937), has also suffered grievously, but from neglect, and the addition of a large tower block shows little respect for the tarnished architectural quality of the original. Also in Haifa, a hospital, the Carmel Hospital, by Rechter and Zarhi [1969-1975], has appeared which dominates the Carmel skyline—a sculptured, slope-walled, Crusader-fortresslike structure whose pink-clad massive buttresses glow in the setting sun, a rose-red edifice seemingly half as old as time. These, and other new hospitals, are impressive in their handling of architectural space for the technical intricacies of modern medical care; but the architectural expression is overemphatic, perhaps overdemonstrative compared with the Mendelsohn prototypes or with the simple but impressive regional hospital in Beersheva built more than twenty years ago.

Museums are repositories of history, galleries of art past and present, and multifaceted cultural centers in the positive sense of the word, that is, as generators of cultural activity. Two fine Israeli examples, very different in their concept and architectural expression, are the Israel Museum in Jerusalem, by Al Mansfeld and Dora Gat [1959], whose elegant pavilions predicated a flexible, growing plan; and the Tel Aviv Museum, designed by architects Yashar and Eitan in 1971, an exciting spatial exercise but in much more finite terms. Both museums achieve that delicate balance where the architectural container, interesting in its own right, does not detract from the contents displayed. There are many smaller, specialized museums of considerable architectural merit: the illegal-immigrant museum in Haifa, which makes skillful use of an actual ship to evoke powerful images of the dark days of the White Paper which sought to limit Jewish immigration to Palestine in the hours of most pressing need; or Abba Elhanani's Yad Vashem [1959-1964], whose poignant simplicity of design conveys a brooding sense of the tragedy of the Holocaust, with an intensity of atmosphere I have felt before only at the Fosse Ardeatine outside Rome. These museums are shrines to the past and Israel is rich in them, for rarely has a new country been so burdened by a sense of its so often tragic past. In Israel memory is a human and national resource, appropriately institutionalized in its museums and memorials. These latter are numerous, but in my view there has in recent times been a sad regression in their design quality. A simple incised slab, a cairn of stones, bespeaks an abiding sense of loss for the fallen, whereas the inflated steel and concrete abstractions recently erected seem to me to be monuments only to the artist's ego: instead of eloquent evocations of past tragedy and achievement, we are offered only empty rhetoric and blatant gesturings.

An urban development which tries to capture something of the ambience of the past, but paraphrased in contemporary terms, is the exercise in the renewal of historial areas in several Israeli cities. While attempting to maintain the urban grain, material texture, scale, and spatial continuities of

Jaffa, that ancient seaport has been converted by Yaar, Mandel, and Frenkel [1961] into a picturesque—almost film-set—precinct of elegant townhouses, art galleries, boutiques, and nightclubs. Part of the old town of Safed has undergone a similar translation into an artists' quarter but much remains to be done in this venerable center of cabalistic learning. Hopefully, by means of the development plan of the old Jewish quarter by Yaakov and Ora Yaar [1970], it can safely be steered between the kitsch of the picturesque revival and the bulldozers of prospective "developers" seeking a *tabula rasa*. Most important of all these renewal schemes of historic areas is the one for Jerusalem. The regeneration of the destroyed Jewish quarter of the Old City has been undertaken with great sensitivity and imagination by the Company for the Reconstruction and Development of the Jewish Quarter of the Old City of Jerusalem (chief architect: S. Gardi) (fig. 26.3). Moshe Safdie's proposal of 1970 for the development of the area fronting the Western Wall is equally imaginative, and much bolder, but the strength of its central concept has provoked bitter controversy, for there are those who fear that it will compete with, rather than enhance, the ancient treasured fragment of the Second Temple. The ultimate question is whether the Western Wall (the ancient Wailing Wall) is to be the locus of personal, intimate recollection, introspection, and devotion, or an arena in which are played out the meaningful rituals and pageantry of the nation, a theatrical space which is the natural gathering spot in times of crisis and of joy. There are few such places in Israel where the drama of great events can be performed with spontaneous or planned public participation. Niemeyer's Kikar Malchei Israel, the great open space in front of the bland buildings of the Tel Aviv Municipality is one such space, which as an urban place (realized by Israeli architects Lotan and Elhanani) is weather-exposed and sterile; but how it comes alive when filled with a hundred thousand Israelis rejoicing at the remote prospect of peace. Other national meeting places are the Convention Hall in Jerusalem, by Rechter, Zarhi and Rechter [designed 1949, completed about 1960], the new Jerusalem Theatre, a pleasing work of architecture by Nadler, Nadler and Bixon, and of course the older, but still very impressive Mann Auditorium in Tel Aviv, by two of the father figures of modern architecture in Israel, Zeev Rechter and Dov Karmi [1953-1957]. If rescued from its marooning seas of parked automobiles, the Mann Auditorium has a civic presence which would match its splendid interior.

26.3. Ahrends, Burton and Koralek in association with J. Schonberger, architects (supervising architect: Reuven Druckmann). The Jewish Quarter of the Old City, private residence, Jerusalem, 1973. (Photograph: Courtesy of Gilbert Herbert)

Today the most prominent works of architecture on the skylines of Jerusalem and Tel Aviv are those commercial buildings which are the heart of every major metropolis, at least in the Western world: the tall office towers, the multipurpose commercial and shopping centers, and the international-standard hotels, posturing and competing for the tourist trade. These buildings sit comfortably in Tel Aviv, which is by nature international and representative of the universal, homogenized, postindustrial culture. In Jerusalem, however, with its brooding sense of place and time, a far more difficult problem confronts the architect, and there are few topics more likely to provoke public debate than the height, location, and character of each proposed new comprehensive commercial development. In Tel Aviv one may or may not like the architecture, or one may question the economic viability of such grand (or grandiose) developments as the new but far from completed Central Bus Station complex by architect Ram Karmi, which promises to be one of the most exciting spatial experiences in Israeli architecture; or the Dizengoff Center (original concept of Niemeyer, much altered: completed by a design team under architect Ms. Toledo), or architect Yacov Rechter's Kikar Atarim on the seashore; but the essence of the proposals is accepted gladly, as adding amenity, sophistication, and vitality to the city. In Jerusalem, however, Moshe Safdie's Mamilla proposal, and every new hotel, is the occasion of much heartburning, even when the specific designs are of a very high standard: the central question is their very appropriateness in an urban townscape which inevitably invites confrontation with the historic core of the old city. It is ironic, incidentally, that the only large international hotel which retains a sense of place, a local specific identity, is the old and old-fashioned King David Hotel in Jerusalem. In the other luxury hotels in the major cities, it is the view from the window (if the drapes are open) or the Israeli buffet breakfast, but, alas, not the architectural character, which will identify to the traveller where, that day, he is. Smaller places are more successful in capturing the *genius loci*: the charming Rimon Inn at Safed or the really beautiful recreation home in Zichron Yaakov by Rechter and Zarhi [1969] (fig. 26.4), which undulates gently on the escarpment of Mount Carmel, south of Haifa, overlooking the coastal plain below, in one of the happiest marriages of architecture and nature in Israel.

I have written of the wide range and considerable extent of "architecture in Israel," and not of "Israeli architecture." This question of architectural character and identity needs to be addressed. Despite the disintegrative tendencies of modern culture everywhere and the intense (almost notorious) sense of individuality claimed (but not always practiced) by the creative Israeli, there is a remarkable consistency and coherence of character in the architecture of Israel today, just as there was some thirty years ago. However, Israel has moved from an earlier consensus to a new, different, and visually much richer one. More precisely, we have moved from the simplicity and austerity of the 1940s and 1950s to the complexity and bravado of gesture of the late 1970s. Neither the architecture of the immediate postwar and postindependence era nor that of today is unique to Israel, in the sense that its architectural forms were invented here *de nova*. While not tamely derivative, it is apparent that our architecture benefits from prototypes and precedents from the wider architectural scene. But, considered as an overall statement, considered as a consistent national architectural stance, I believe that Israel has few parallels in the world. This striking coherence and unity does not derive from a unified architectural philosophy or viewpoint but rather from the forces and characteristics inherent in the Israeli situation. In this sense we may legitimately talk of an Israeli architecture.

The restrained architecture of the new state was compounded of three factors: first, a functionalist, purist aesthetic whose inspiration was the International Style in general and the Bauhaus in particular—that is, an aesthetic that was central-European and prewar in its origins although modified locally; secondly, an economy of means resulting from material causes, that is, from a critical paucity of resources of money, materials, techniques, and skills; and, thirdly, an austerity of expression ideological in intent, symbolizing a puritan, egalitarian society. Today, the architecture is far from austere, but as against this it is neither luxurious nor effete. It is strong, vigorous, and bold; its textures are coarse and abrasive; its forms are hard-edged, sculptured, and self-assertive; it is a complex architecture, formally and spatially intricate; it is highly imaginative, sometimes to the point of extravagance, in both the economic and artistic sense of the term. As with many strong personalities, its defects are the obverse of its virtues. Despite the very high proportion of women architects who graduate in Israel, it is a demonstratively masculine architecture, at its worst tending towards machismo, at its best cast in a heroic mold; but gentleness and humility are rare, elusive qualities. While the Israeli architect is humane in his analysis of environmental problems in

26.4. Yacov Rechter and Moshe Zarchi, architects. Recreation Home, Zichron Yaakov, 1969. (Photograph: Courtesy of Keren-or)

their psychological and social dimensions, he has not always succeeded in casting his solutions in humanistic forms. These are all dangerously sweeping statements, but it is nevertheless valid to generalize about Israel's architecture for it represents a fundamentally monolithic body of work. Israel may be culturally polyglot, but it is architecturally monolingual—and the diverse tongues of post-modern architecture for good or for evil are yet to be heard in the land of Israel.

It seems clear that the characteristics of Israeli architecture are both a reflection of international tendencies and a response to the Israeli personality and the Israeli situation. The international tendency most apparent in Israel, even at this late date, may be summed up in the term New Brutalism. Its prophets were Le Corbusier and Louis Kahn, and its paradigms the Unité d'Habitation, Chandigarh, the Richards Medical Center, and the neomonumental architecture of Dacca. If we add some overtones of Kenzo Tange, a touch of I. M. Pei's Formalism, some textural reminiscences of Paul Rudolf, and an echo of John Andrews at Scarborough, the source book of imported formal inspiration is just about complete. These sources have been assimilated and new syntheses generated in Israel with great virtuosity and architectural skill. But the range is limited. What is striking here are the omissions: there is no reference to Mies van der Rohe's polished and simplistic elegance; to Latin America's tropical mutations of the International Style or its colorful exuberance; to the structural virtuosity of Pier Luigi Nervi or Félix Candela; or to the nostalgic romanticism, the new empiricism of postwar Britain and Scandinavia. Nor in more recent years is there any tangible evidence of that spectrum of post-modern architecture which stretches from Venturi and Moore, through such Formalists as Aldo Rossi or the Krier brothers to Arata Isozaki. There would seem to be no reflection in Israel of those turbulent crosscurrents, the intellectual probings, the doubts and polemics, which have so characterized creative architectural development elsewhere. It is as if all the passion and tension in Israel has been directed in political rather than architectural channels.

New Brutalism in both its original forms and its Israeli mutations is an architecture highly apposite to the prototypical Israeli personality: youthful and assertive, outwardly tough, essentially honest and direct, but blunt and with little finesse. Both in manners and in architecture it demonstratively rejects the polish, refinement, and restraint of the cultivated European style of the prewar era and is eager to substitute direct action for contemplation. To a nation with character traits such as these, to a young nation intent on establishing itself and making its mark in an environment both politically and climatically hostile, it is inevitable that the emphatic, noncompromising forms of New Brutalism would appeal. The massive geometry of the architecture, the material durability of *béton brut*, seems to speak in an unequivocal tongue, both to threatening neighbor and to intimidating desert: "Make no mistake, we are no ephemeral illusion, we are here to stay." All the realities of the Israeli situation reinforce the predilections of the Israeli temperament: first, the rigors of the climate, for it is the desert which is the symbolic climate that sets the tone, notwithstanding the fact that most of the population live in the humid coastal plain; second, the universality of reinforced concrete as a building material, both cast *in situ* and in prefabricated form—the raw materials are available locally, and there are considerable skills in its use; and third, the insistent cubist quality of the prevailing vernacular architecture, which somehow gives historical depth and regional validity to the analogous modern forms. In general, Israeli architecture may be characterized by its attitudes to external forms rather than by an emphasis on space. These formal attributes, deriving from a repetitive geometry, a complex reiteration of prismatic units, are partly the result of a rationalized, industrialized building process and partly the fruit of an emphasis on the teaching of morphology in the Technion, Israel's only school of architecture. This morphology, which is such a creative discipline for design when used intelligently, can degenerate to a compulsion in less sensitive hands.

There is an inherent paradox in the architecture of Israel. A small country with an intense sense of national unity and historic purpose, it is nevertheless diverse in its peoples and its regions. There are many forces which direct the architecture of Israel into a unified if not conformist mold: the imperatives of creative nationalism and the need for identity; the centralization of building initiative in the public sector, the most significant sector, in bureaucratic hands; the internal, financial, and technical logic of standardization in a rationalized building process; a very restricted range of building materials and methods; and a tendency to homogeneity in architectural training, where the education of the architect is ingrown and restricted to one institution. As against this, with a multiplicity of component cultures and a variety of regions, diversity is demanded if a sense of individual identity and a sense of place are to be achieved. A housing environment suitable for an immigrant from Miami Beach is not necessarily relevant to a Russian from Georgia—at least not in the first generation; an architecture which is magnificently appropriate in the desert may be obtrusive in the green hills of the Galilee or a trifle absurd when faced, skin-deep, in stone and decorated with arches in Jerusalem. While the pluralism which marks world architecture would be disruptive in Israel, somehow a balance must be struck, and a richness of diversity must be created within the overall framework.

The natural and deserved pride in the tremendous achievements of the years of statehood—in the building of a new country which in many senses must be taken literally, from the building of the soil to the making of new cities—must not lead to a new monumentalism, a present danger in what Israel laughingly calls its "edifice complex," but rather to a new humanism, to an architecture of restraint and an environment that is kind to man and to nature. This is the hallmark of a civilized society. In many small ways encouraging signs of such an approach are emerging: sensitivity to human values and the legitimate nuances of human behavior in the design of the dwelling and the neighborhood; concern with social values in housing; a greater appreciation of landscape as a mediator between man and the man-made object; the beginning of a greater diversity of building form and a richer palette of building materials; and a new dimension of choice and diversity, with the involvement of the user in the responsive environment. These are not the dominant characteristics of Israeli architecture at the moment but tentative new emergent strains. When they come into greater prominence, and more intellectual ferment is generated in Israel's architectural climate, we may expect an architecture which may be not only representative of Israel's small and unique reality but of its potential, symbolic world role. Only then will the architectural light go forth from Zion.

Bibliography

BOOKS

Bickels, S. *Theory and Planning of the Kibbutz Settlement* (International Seminar on Rural Planning, October-November 1961). Tel Aviv: Ministry of Foreign Affairs (in collaboration with Ministries of Labour and Agriculture), 1961.

Canaan, Gershon. *Rebuilding the Land of Israel.* New York: Architectural Book Publishing Co., 1954.

Golani, Y. and von Schwartze, D. G., eds. *Israel Builds 1970.* Jerusalem: Ministry of Housing, 1970 (text in English).

Harlap, Amiram, ed. *Israel Builds 1973.* Jerusalem: Ministry of Housing, 1973 (text in Hebrew and English).

Harlap, Admiram, ed. *Israel Builds 1977.* Jerusalem: Ministry of Housing, 1977 (text in Hebrew and English).

Kaufmann, Richard. *Planning Jewish Settlements in Palestine: A Brief Survey of Facts and Conditions.* London, 1926.

Rivolta, M. Bassa and Rossari, A. *Alexander Klein, Lo studio delle piante e la progettazione degli spazi negli allogi minimi; scritti e progetti dal 1906 al 1957.* Milan: G. Mazotta, 1975.

Sharon, Arieh. *Kibbutz and Bauhaus: An Architect's View in a New Land.* Stuttgart: Kramer; Tel Aviv: Massada, 1976 (text in English, German, and French).

Spiegel, Erika. *New Towns in Israel: Urban and Regional Planning and Development.* Stuttgart: Kramer, 1966 (text in German and English).

Zevi, Bruno. *Erich Mendelsohn: opera completa. Architettore e imagini architettoniche.* Milan: Etta Kompass, 1970.

JOURNALS

"Architecture en Palestine," *l'Architecture d'Aujourd'hui* (special issue, fully illustrated), no. 9 (September 1937).

"Architektur, Planung und Kunst in Israel," *Werk* (special issue, fully illustrated), January 1973.

"Educational Buildings," *Tvai* (quarterly for architecture, town planning, industrial design, and the plastic arts; special issue, fully illustrated; text in Hebrew and English), nos. 13/14, 1974.

Habinyan (special issue: villas and gardens; text in Hebrew with English table of contents and summaries; fully illustrated), November 1937.

"Hospital Buildings," *Tvai* (special issue, fully illustrated; text in Hebrew and English), no. 15, 1975.

Palestine and Middle East Economic Magazine, nos. 7/8, 1933 (survey of building architecture, town and country planning in Palestine).

"Planen and Bauen in Israel," *Baumeister* (special issue, fully illustrated), January 1962.

27

ITALY

MARIO F. ROGGERO

Postwar Problems of Reconstruction

At the end of the Second World War, Italy was so weakened that political, economic, and social choices for her were made elsewhere. With the Marshall Plan, the European Reconstruction Project (ERP), and the United Nations Relief and Rehabilitation Administration (UNRRA), came plans favored by the United States. These led towards a policy of economic consumption and made it possible for the governments of De Gasperi and La Malfa to dismantle the former Fascist government's protectionist system. A policy that promoted a free market economy related to the European Common Market (ECM) was put into action. By around 1950 the average Italian's income was equivalent to that of 1938, and the so-called period of reconstruction came to an end.

UNREGULATED REBUILDING

In 1945 there was physical destruction everywhere and society's institutions were either in total disarray or completely broken down. Even the new Constitutional Charter, promulgated in 1948 following a serious debate by the country's political forces, came to be considered by far too many merely as an abstract assertion of principles, rather than as the authentic juridical foundation of the new state. Thus, in practice, its aims remained frequently unfilled.

The processes of reconstruction unleashed some dangerous forces. Realistic planning shared the field with utopian evasions but concrete programs were totally lacking. So were laws and regulations designed to curb the ambitions of unscrupulous real estate operators. In the restructuring of the economy and the country's productive capacities, the building industry assumed a prominent position. Financial resources were mobilized to help create new social aggregations that were centered around home ownership and that had important demographic effects. In such a context the participation of architects in the concrete processes of rebuilding was at best sporadic and marginally limited. The ravages of war brought ruin to Italy's monumental heritage as well as to her architectural infrastructure. The architectural panorama of Italy suffered after 1945.

Architectural problems were augmented by social problems. Entrepreneurial initiative, in keeping with the policy of rebuilding the country's productive systems as quickly as possible, led to uncontrolled migration towards northern Italy that inevitably had destructive effects on traditional, rural and urban territorial structures. The more solidly based urban centers witnessed a growth of their populations despite the lack of any appropriate provisions for their needs. Imbalances between north and south, between marginal areas and larger centers of growth, brought increased pressures, changed all previous modes of behavior, and led to new urban configurations. The abrupt installation of new industrial plants in areas that had once been agricultural and were economically underdeveloped became a dangerous practice. Then, between the end of the 1950s and the beginning of the 1960s, the nation witnessed a building boom dictated primarily by a growing desire for new dwellings and by accumulations of wealth in proportions seldom seen before.

The editor is indebted to M. D'Allessio, Montreal, for his invaluable assistance in translating this chapter.

HOUSING AND LAND-USE POLICY

Faced with a building boom, the government neither proved itself capable of controlling dangerous land exploitations by private enterprises nor was it able to launch well-planned, carefully interrelated public building initiatives. Politically, the most significant moment came in 1949 with the introduction of the Fanfani Plan to increase the number of jobs for workers. This envisaged massive financing of homes for workmen with the partial use of industrial profits and with a portion of the income of the self-employed. Such action would have instilled new life into the building industry and set into motion building programs throughout the country. Construction would have varied, since it was to have been based on the ideologies of growth of individual districts. Such a formula could have led to new forms of architectural experimentation, planning, and production, had it been accompanied by efforts to move into more advanced forms of economic development. In the Vanoni Plan the latter was proposed. It was, however, quickly turned down.

In 1960 the reactivated, reformed National Institute of Town Planning (INU) that had been founded in 1932 presented a Town and Country Planning Code that formulated alternatives to the political handling of land use. A broad debate began that culminated in 1962 with a bill introduced by Fiorentino Sullo, the responsible minister. The bill, however, was immediately disowned by the government itself. Indeed, the government went on to very substantially reduce subsidized building projects and granted more room for entrepreneurial speculative initiatives.

Public works designed to safeguard the land and provide protection against the destructive phenomena of nature, never the expression of a planned policy, became even more rare. The result was a decline of frightening proportions in hydrogeological conditions throughout the nation. From Agrigento to the Polesine, landslides, geological slippages, and floods struck within Italy's historically richest areas. In the face of this failure of policy and because of international public opinion, the government was forced to take drastic steps to safeguard Italy's artistic and environmental heritage.

At this time the so-called stop-gap law was promulgated (1967), imposing upon the individual municipalities the adoption of building and land-use plans based on town planning standards that were aimed, at last, at governing the ratio between residences and services, between the established population of an area and its built utilities. Workers' claims shifted from wages to demands for reforms, with those relating to housing soon becoming the most significant. In the wake of general strikes during 1970 and 1971, Bill 865 was passed, bringing new impetus to public spending in the building sector and vesting in local authorities the power to acquire land by purchase or expropriation.

Not until January 1977 and Bill 10, however, was there to be regional legislation on the protection and use of land. Rules for the suitability of land for building purposes were sanctioned with precise provisions for planning tightly, relating every activity that involved town planning and building changes to their financial costs. Civic authorities were finally released from these responsibilities, which were transferred to the regional authorities. Thus town planning and building could be better geared to particular local requirements. Much more timely action became possible, though bureaucratic mechanisms continued to hamper funding efforts. Currently, faced with contrasting and ill-defined experiences, it would, nevertheless, appear that the forces that monopolized the building market for so many years to their own advantage are in profound decline.

URBANISM AND THE ENVIRONMENT

During the entire period with which we are concerned, the absence of an active land-use policy opened the way to systematic and disastrous assault on the nation's great heritage, its countryside and its monuments. First came the cry of "reconstruction at any price," with the corresponding preference for the easiest and apparently least burdensome solutions. Then, in the wake of the boom years—and their deceptive lack of substance is now so clearly evident—came architectural exercises in showy private ownership. The result has been an indiscriminate multiplication of eyesores from one end of the country to the other. Along with the nation's most important panoramas, cities renowned as architectural treasure houses from Florence to Venice, and from Naples to Rome, have all been subjected to savage, indiscriminate attack by the ever more aggressive interests of speculation which, by aiming at the appropriation of a great common heritage for the benefit of a few, destroyed the fundamental role of the environmental background.

Groups like Italia Nostra sprang to the defense of the environment with the same old selective tactics, sterilely preserving single monuments in isolation from their surroundings and thus depriving them of value as dynamic sources of discussion and inspiration.

Perhaps the only fortunate exception to this is the city of Urbino which from the 1950s was reconstructed and restored by the energetic, wise, and intelligent Giancarlo de Carlo. He was inspired by a deep concern that those who would benefit the most, the users, should participate in every aspect of planning; and carefully looked after every architectural expression that originated from such participation. De Carlo faced administrative and methodological problems at Urbino in an exemplary way, involved the inhabitants in a process of acculturation, and addressed himself to the intricacies of specific building solutions with a rigorous coherence. His stated goal was nothing less than the retention of everything that could assist in the understanding of an area that was dominated by an extraordinary historical and environmental landscape; and this he achieved admirably, as for instance in his accommodation of the college at Urbino to its landscape.[1]

We have elsewhere witnessed the spawning of heavily polluting industries from Venice, for instance with the Montedison petrochemical facilities at Porto Marghera, to Naples with the Italsider ironworks at Pozzuoli, to cite just two important examples. And we have seen disorderly heapings of dwellings in the Alps and along the coast, while the name of tourism has been misguidedly invoked to justify inroads on the country's most attractive, unspoiled, and environmentally valuable areas. And romantic whims, calling for the preservation of this or that poetic view rather than a celebrated monument, have led to absurd compromises that have quickly torn holes in the entire historical fabric with which Italy was so richly cloaked.

ARCHITECTURAL BEGINNINGS

Architects played little more than a casual, occasional part. Most, indeed, were isolated, thoughtful, but weaponless craftsmen, in an unequal struggle dominated by culturally and professionally unqualified forces. Italy's heritage, therefore, was almost frittered away in but a few decades; and only the voices of small, intellectual groups, with the sometimes incompletely digested thoughts of a few, solitary, courageous souls, have been raised in protest.

The few concrete architectural works that emerged were either the fruit of isolated efforts, or struggled painfully forth from the shoals of bureaucratic control. In spite of the universal lip service paid to it, the notion of accommodating to the environment offered by the new architecture found but scant and episodic expression. The plain spontaneity of Giovanni Michelucci's Borsa Merci [1950] at Pistoia and his church [1954] at Collina; the intimate inflections of Mario Ridolfi in the rebuilding of Rome's Tiburtino quarter [1950] (Fig. 27.1) and in the Cerignola district [1950], with their blends of refinement and the common touch; and the lucid, contrasting town planning of Ludovico Quaroni, derived from Scandinavian approaches as evident in the village of La Martella [1949] near Matera in southern Italy; Ignazio Gardella's buildings of the 1950s at Alessandria that are essentially Rationalist with a neo-Classical sobriety; as well as the collaboration of Gardella with the BBPR group (Lodovico Belgioioso, Enrico Peressutti, and Ernesto Nathan Rogers; the other "B" is for Gianluigi Banfi, who was killed in the war against the Nazis) and with Franco Albini in the Cesate district [1950-1954]—all of these were isolated, explicit expressions of ideas of environmental accommodation generally shared by architects in the decade following the conclusion of the war.

In that same decade, Alvar Aalto, well known in Italy almost exclusively for his Tuberculosis Sanatorium [1929-1933] at Paimio, Finland, and Frank Lloyd Wright, better known, particularly because of his Kaufmann House [1936-1937] and from Bruno Zevi's *Towards an Organic Architecture* (1945); both received a good deal of attention for their individualism and their attitudes towards an architecture that respected the environment. Many were the debates among Italian architects then. In the architecture of Aalto and Wright they recognized the possibility of an alternative to the rationalist movement, an alternative expressed essentially, if briefly, first in the beautifully sited works of a few architects such as Marcello d'Olivo [Children's Village at Opicina, Trieste, 1949-1958, and the village Manacore, Gargano, 1962] and of Luigi Pellegrin. The appearance of images inspired largely by Wright and Aalto on the Italian horizon signaled in fact, more often than not, the establishment of a provincial fashion during the supposed twilight of Rationalism, rather than the materializaton of a genuine alternative with an inner meaning known among a limited vanguard.

The introduction of these new images nevertheless had a wider influence. A "reduced reading of Functionalism," as defined by Agnoldomenico Pica came about, spreading its worst interpretations in the most vulgar of building productions in a seemingly irreversible trend. The most active Italian architects, however, adapted the new, formal vocabulary to the old, though sometimes with questionable results. There ensued a critical reformulation of architectural design that salvaged at once the innovations of Wright and Aalto and the Rationalism of Le Cor-

27.1. Mario Ridolfi, Ludovico Quaroni, Mario Fiorentino, architects. Tiburtino district. Rome, 1950. (Photograph: Courtesy of Mario F. Roggero)

busier, Walter Gropius, and Mies van der Rohe. However, this expressed an attitude that was more intellectual than creative, an attitude that led finally to modest results which did not fulfill architects' intentions. At length a convergence of politico-cultural intentions of broad scope and concrete answers concerning historical centers, and their business areas, designed to relieve urban congestion began to take shape. At that point the fundamental political question of the proper use of what remained of the nation's heritage rekindled bitter conflicts over correct aims and methods with picayune attention to detail at every stage. Thus there was a long delay between the discussion of ideas and their concrete implementation. In this respect, the experiment at Bologna remains both typical and illustrative. Between its conception in 1964 and its completion in 1977, renovated and rebuilt sections were inserted into the old city center under municipal auspices as part of a generally economic home-building plan that had a clearly political frame of reference. Rebuilding in Italian cities as well as planning and construction of new towns have ultimately drawn attention to the "substantial change that has taken place in the role of architects, members of a profession that has been further recast and delineated by the gradual transformation of its traditional clientele."[2]

The continually surfacing conflict between ideological tension and practical building is a fundamental characteristic of Italian postwar architecture. Much more than can be seen in other countries such as France (where inquiries into formal design have led to a degree of nationalistic chauvinism) or in the Anglo-Saxon countries (where a certain pragmatic acceptance of the supposed stability of society has been directed to the drawing of rigid distinctions between tasks and objectives), the travails through which Italian architecture has passed have brought home an important lesson: the essential problems of our time within a given environment cannot be solved by isolated, specially tailored, architectural interventions, however apt these may be formally, or by the simple repetition of obsolete cultural patterns of architecture. Only by continuous and critically controlled direction may the environment be transformed without depriving it of its deeply rooted, basic features.

The Arena of Architectural Debate

The architectural debate that has taken place in Italy during the last thirty-five or more years has been extremely lively, often with a strong dose of contentiousness, and conducted in highly ideological terms. Within the major arena of architectural debate are a few organizations of like-minded architects, critical journals, book-publishing houses, certain major critics, and the architectural faculties of the universities. Architecture has been seen as a reflection of cultural, technical, and political aims, and has been judged in part by the degree of its adherence to particular programmatic premises. But discussion concerning architecture is not limited to a broad review of architectural works and their meanings, in which factors such as the intentionality of the expression and its relationship to social and political realities may be emphasized. Discussion may also be oriented towards offering innovative critical foundations that will help to enhance the architect's work, making it more complex and richer in interest.

Debate concerning contemporary issues and investigations in architecture was taken up in 1945 with the formation of the Associazione per l'Architettura Organica (APAO) in Rome and the essentially Rationalist Movimento Studi per l'Architettura (MSA) in Milan. Bruno Zevi in Rome vigorously forwarded the most outstanding expressions of Frank Lloyd Wright's Organic architecture, while in Milan, among the most sensitive and involved architects, BBPR took up the cause of Rationalist architecture just as this doctrine began to undergo a critical reformulation.

Since the twenties, the Modern Movement had tried to end the cultural isolation of architecture by publishing journals that became, in effect, permanent infrastructures for discussion and confrontation. The vehicles for Italy's postwar national discussion of architectural issues, more often than not, have been those critical publications that began to proliferate immediately after 1945. At times, critics forcibly charged architectural works with emblematic meanings that tended to establish them as the only alternatives to current norms. In addition, the new architecture was looked upon as concrete evidence of views supported and defended in one or another journal. The short life spans of certain architectural journals and the involuted growth parabolas of others (often markedly changed by a turnover in the editorial staff with consequent changes in the journal's architectural advocacies) may best be understood, it seems to me, by recognizing that often the cumulative effect of changing architectural works too frequently, with perhaps overly brilliant intentions and critical meanings, gradually destroys the ability of a journal to systematically influence the formation of cultural attitudes. Then too, the provocative way in which viewpoints are expressed and the contradictory tones of individual contributors, with one contention heaped upon another, makes it difficult for the uninitiated to make out arguments and trends with any genuine clarity. And, usually, paralleling the loss of credibility and clarity is a loss of readership.

Of the eighteen outstanding Italian architectural journals published between 1945 and 1978 some continue to flourish; others do not.[3] Typical perhaps of more than the Italian scene, most have been edited and directed by architects. In Rome between 1945 and 1954 Luigi Piccinato, Silvio Radiconcini, Mario Ridolfi, and Bruno Zevi published *Metron* which, with its wealth of social and cultural references, was fundamental in reframing the architectural questions of the time. *Metron* was followed by *L'Architettura. Cronache e Storia* under the editorship of Zevi, which continues today to pose often complex critical requalifications of architectural experiences. In Milan two famous prewar journals reappeared: in 1946 *Domus* was founded by Gio Ponti, and *Casabella* by Giuseppe Pagano and Edoardo Persico, both of whom unfortunately died young. *Domus*, published under the editorial direction of Ponti (except for a short period in the years 1946-1947 when E. N. Rogers was editor), dealt with interior decoration and design. *Casabella*, under the direction first of Franco Albini, then from 1954 of E. N. Rogers, and from 1965 of Giannino Bernasconi, Giovanni Koenig, Alessandro Mendini, and Tomas Maldonado, spurred a dialogue between architecture and historical criticism from the mid-1950s and today is still highly regarded for its critical presentations of some of the most stimulating tendencies in Italian architecture. *Controspazio*, edited by Paolo Portoghesi, though less regular in appearance, also tends toward relating architecture and history. It set forth the most interesting ideas explored in Milan's Faculty of Architecture between 1968 and 1975 and continues today as an active, vital publication. *Edilizia Moderna*, in Milan, ceased publication after a period of great influence between 1963 and 1965 under the direction of Vittorio Gregotti, when it brought out significant monographic numbers. *Spazio*, edited by Luigi Moretti, though published in only six issues between 1950 and 1953, displayed so high a degree of critical insight that it deserves mention here. In the field of analysis and of land-use planning *Urbanistica*, the official publication of the National Institute of Town Planning (INU), commenced republication at Turin from 1949 with Adriano Olivetti as editor and from late 1953 was under the direction of Giovanni Astengo; while in Milan both *Zodiac* until 1973 and *Comunità* until 1975 completed the impressive trio of journals of the Edizione di Comunità supported by Olivetti. Adriano Olivetti, industrialist, urbanist, politician, sociologist, and mainspring for many initiatives, was a remarkable embodiment of the aspirations of postwar Italy. Thanks in large part to his efforts, particularly, the journal *Comunità* (in which political, social technical, and cultural aspects of urban problems were brought together in relation to various concerns) remained most helpful to those who wished to maintain an up-to-date awareness of the changing relationships between objectives and results of urban projects.

In the last decade, book publishing seems to have overtaken the journals, presenting basic discussions of ongoing problems affecting architecture and encouraging contributions from other disciplines. While the necessity of exhaustively considering the complex theoretical problems of architecture would seem to demand ever more space, significant architectural criticism in contemporary Italy has dwindled to a very low volume. Architectural journals seem to be oriented toward the specialist. As they return to reporting more narrowly upon the various architectural currents of the day, the era during which they were among the major leaders of cultural thought appears to be closing.

The various book-publishing initiatives undertaken in recent decades today form the framework within which the most vital and conflicting architectural experiments are being developed, whether they are ideologically based or follow trends in the interpretation of historical situations. Two virtual dictionaries of the language of criticism that provide backgrounds for communication between various specialists and the codifiers of the most disparate, theoretical, and practical architectural experiments are the *Enciclopedia Universale dell'Arte* edited by Massimo Pallottino,[4] and the *Dizionario Enciclopedico di Architettura e Urbanistica* edited by Paolo Portoghesi.[5] Two manuals seem equally important: the *Manuale dell'Architetto* edited by Mario Ridolfi, Cino Calcaprina, Aldo Cardelli and Mario Fiorentino[6] and the *Architettura Pratica* prepared by Pasquale Carbonara.[7] These four outstanding contributions articulate with singular methodological clarity a broad range of critical assessments of architectural urbanistic phenomena.

Singular contributions have been made to the history of contemporary architecture by Bruno Zevi, Leonardo Benevolo, and Manfredo Tafuri. A forceful proponent of Frank Lloyd Wright and Organic architecture, Zevi's almost polemical writings and his broad range of historical and critical activities represent one of the vital points of reference for architectural criticism not only within Italy but internationally. With constant engagement and in dynamic language he has encouraged architects toward a renewal of the motivations underlying their work. Leonardo Benevolo, ever more conscious of political pressures expressed in the country, forcefully "developed a determining position in the Italian architectural milieu of the 1950s. In new and rigorous terms he counterposed the pluralistic researches of reintegrating [architecture] and historic tradition with a reliance upon Rationalist method that sought simplified schemes theoretically based on connections with social solutions. . . . [while Manfredo Tafuri] has moved progressively nearer to a conception of history as the foundation for a radical criticism of architectural ideologies on the basis of rigorous use of Marxist thought."[8]

Having considered professional associations in Milan and Rome and Italy's publishing industry as loci of architectural ferment, one more factor in the arena of architectural influence in Italy must be recognized: the faculty of architecture. For the presence of its diverse viewpoints, for its intense and systematic contributions, for the level of its confrontations, no less than for its influence upon the formation of architects, the faculties of architecture are coming to be almost archetypically the natural seats of debate, the sources of every nascent cultural movement, the laboratory for thousands of sharply different experiments, and the sounding board of emerging conflicts. Ten architectural faculties are scattered across the country today in major sociopolitical centers, constituting a grid of reference and the fulcrums for all sorts of fresh proposals of architectural themes. The story of their formation from the first at Rome in 1926, their multiplication and vast increase to some 46,460 enrolled students in 1977, amidst crises, oppositions, and contradictions, would provide us with a detailed account of the Italian architectural panorama. It must suffice here to mention how they have changed from platforms of the elite with few practical echoes to bastions of consistency and of critical outlook that have had and continue to have their effects.

With the strengthening and growth of the jurisdiction granted by the state to local authorities, and with a much more attentive, responsible, and timely presence in matters concerning land use and construction, the faculties of architecture are tending to assume greater vigor and to earn a wider recognition of the competency of their contributions. They are genuine meeting places where diversified, often contradictory experiences may be discussed. It is no small thing that the most lively publications and the most stimulating realizations come from a university world whose members at least in one of its most conspicuous parts, the faculties of architecture, for the most part no longer seek almost any sort of commissions but instead address themselves to the definition of the most generally interesting and engaging problems.

The Architectural Panorama

While no single key may be offered for the understanding of Italian architecture, the buildings that have been erected throughout the country are much more subtly linked to each other than it might appear because of the intermingling in them of many different matrices. Because of this, it has been of the utmost importance to point out how the different universities, thanks to their provocative cultural discussion, represent the places where particular motivations and developments have been revealed.

Many of the most representative postwar figures had made their own, original contributions in prewar years. A partial list would range from Pier Luigi Nervi to Adalberto Libera; from Franco Albini, BBPR, and Ignazio Gardella to Ludovico Quaroni, Luigi Moretti, and Giuseppe Samonà; from Giovanni Michelucci and Carlo Mollino to Giuseppe Vaccaro and Luigi Carlo Daneri, to mention only a few. The working continuity thus established cannot be artificially broken down. Yet the immediate postwar period had its particular importance.

THE IMMEDIATE POSTWAR YEARS: 1945-1960

Rome and Milan represented the most active centers for architecture. Milan turned its attention toward the reconstruction of the productive apparatus of its own region. Here a rapid succession of concrete proposals showed the capability of Milan's architects to elaborate the Rationalist themes of the Modern Movement with rigorous continuity. In a sociopolitical context which was assuming new distinguishing features the works of Franco Albini, BBPR, Ignazio Gardella, Luigi Figini and Gino Pollini, Pietro Bottoni, Marco Zanuso, and of their younger colleagues took on new importance. Rome, which was almost devoid of industrial structures like all capital cities, directed its energies toward large urban expressions in its outskirts. Looking more toward empirical methods rather than examining problems with critical rigor, new forms of avenues were planned that broke away from traditional, classicizing, essentially ecletic traditions. The person who, with Adalberto Libera and Mario Ridolfi, fashioned this experimental attitude was Ludovico Quaroni.

At the same time, in the Piedmont there was concentration on town planning in keeping with the ideas of Olivetti and the *Comunità* movement. Here major fermenting forces and the most outstanding of urbanistic experiments came together. These contributed as much to the spreading of ideas and the affirmation of opposing trends as to the stimulation of new forces in centers which had been traditionally less inclined until then toward cultural exchange.

Under these conditions the cultural milieu established in Venice became archetypical. In its School of Architecture the many protagonists of architectural renewal from Rome and Milan included Bruno Zevi, Luigi Piccinato, Giovanni Astengo, Lodovico Belgioioso, Ignazio Gardella, Franco Albini, and Carlo Aymonino. Under the leadership of Giuseppe Samonà they proposed a systematic revision in the linkage between formal themes and scale of construction, especially in the relationship between architectural and urban planning. In this ambience, the most original of local contributions was rapidly revealed. The first among these was the work of Carlo Scarpa who took heed of the lessons of neoplasticity and of that which was organic in the environment. His sensitive restoration of the main hall of the Ca' Foscari at Venice exemplifies an elegant use of wood and glass, while for other examples one may mention the Olivetti Shop in Piazza San Marco, Venice [1958], and the later Soc. P. A. Gemini (formerly the Gavina Athos store) in Bologna [1968]. Scarpa brought out the expressive capacities of materials, propounding some of the most poetic and rigorous testimonies of the period.

In the meantime, in almost every section of the peninsula, the first major projects to try to solve the problems of low-cost dwellings were taking form. Programs of subsidized residential building led to a convergence of architects' efforts and to an embryonic formulation of planning teams throughout the country. By comparisons of the different works of the same group or of the solutions of different groups working on the same theme (that is, low-cost residences with standard equipment) a detailed picture of Italian architecture up to the threshold of the 1960s may be obtained. Emphasized here should be the function of Naples, then as now, as the coordinating center for the development of southern Italy.

Giving evidence of the breadth and the potential results achievable, one may recall, for Rome, the "horizontal unity" of Tuscolano [1949-1951], the clarity or Rationalist expression of Adalberto Libera, and the Tiburtino quarter [1949-1950] (fig. 27.1) by Mario Ridolfi, Ludovico Quaroni, and Mario Fiorentino, which has become the neorealistic symbol of an architecture understood as a vernacular product. One may add to this the village of La Martella near Matera by Quaroni [1951] because of its ideological matrix and the excellence resulting from its dialectic inspiration. In Sicily, architecturally opposed to La Martella, the informally sited village of Riesi [ca. 1964-1966] by the Florentine Leonardo Ricci, is pervaded by a metaphysical tension which brings him closer to the "habitable structures" of André Bloc. In Milan the QT8 [1948-1950], a pilot district proposed by Piero Bottoni for the Seventh Triennial, though dependent upon a previous hypothesis by Giuseppe Pagano, represents the prototype of satellite centers which later were realized, with some changes, in the outskirts of Milan. For instance, there are the early Cesate quarter [1950-1952] embodying the works of Franco Albini, BBPR, and Ignazio Gardella, and, much more recently, the Gallaratese apartments (fig. 27.2 and 1.8) of Carlo Aymonino and Aldo Rossi, two architects differing stylistically.

Outstanding individual efforts in the years between 1945 and 1960 are far too numerous, and often

27.2. Carlo Aymonino, architect. Residential condominium, Gallaratese district. Milan, 1967-1974. (Photograph: Courtesy of Alessandro Carlotto)

isolated, to be discussed here in any representative fashion. We have already mentioned (in Urbanism and the Environment above) reflections of the influence of Organic architecture as espoused by Zevi in the work of Marcello d'Olivo and Luigi Pellegrin.[9] To this we may add Luigi Moretti who continued his prewar successes with his remarkable, sculpturally bold house [1956-1957] at Santa Marinella on the Tyrrhenian Sea. More compact in its composition and more abstract in its powerfully curved masses, it evokes as much of the expressive spirit of Erich Mendelsohn as of Frank Lloyd Wright.

To fully grasp the evolution of Ignazio Gardella and of Franco Albini from the postwar period to about 1960 one must follow the changes in form evident for both. Gardella's Borsalino employees' house in Alessandria [1951-1953] reflects a neoclassic simplicity, while the house on the Zattere in Venice [1957] presents a somewhat rationalistic compromise with that city's vernacular. Albini's Youth Hostel in Alpine Cervinia [1959-1960] effectively synthesized traditional local construction with a sequence of stately round piers while posing a simple wooden chalet atop a sophisticated three-story wooden structure. His important Rinascente department store in Rome [1959-1961] is very different with its exposed steel frame and nearly windowless, pleated concrete walls. The maturity of BBPR is programmatically centered on the Velasca tower [1956-1958], a really brilliant departure to restructure (fig. 27.3) the old urban fabric of Milan that had been ruined, by inserting a building that was newly objective in its technical complexity yet deliberately reminiscent of a substantial Medieval tower. In Milan, too, Gio Ponti's masterpiece, the Pirelli Building (fig. 27.4), was erected between 1956 and 1959 in collaboration with Pier Luigi Nervi as structural engineer. The contrast between two essentially rationalist skyscrapers, built at almost the same time in the same city, could hardly be greater than that between the openly historicist Velasca tower and the sleekly and elegantly modern Pirelli building.

In the meanwhile Luigi Figini and Gino Pollini were completing a series of experiments, some subsidized housing in various parts of Milan and surroundings, and the Olivetti Social Services Center in Ivrea [1954-1957]. All were characterized by a clear structural rationality and refined unity together with a rigorous attention to the environmental setting. In Genoa, two masterpieces of low-rise residential buildings, the Villa Bernabo Brea apartments [1951-1954] and the Forte Quezzi Quarter [1958] on the hill, were designed by a group under the leadership of Luigi Carlo Daneri. Both departed from the functionalist tradition in its narrowest sense and were tempered in addition by the recent experiences of organic architecture, as one can see from their easy integration into the landscape. On this same line of development, but with more accentuated forms, Giovanni Astengo, Sandro Molli Boffa, Mario Passanti, Nello Renacco, and Aldo Rizzotti carried out the building of La Falchera district [1949-1952] in Turin. One of the first Italian examples of coordinated town planning, construction here tends to articulate a complex connection with the natural and social environments of the inhabitants. The theme of connections between workers' residences and working environments found an interesting expression in the work of Luigi Cosenza at the Olivetti plant and its annexed quarter at Pozzuoli [1955]. At the same time, Giovanni Michelucci in Florence, thanks to his very acute sensitivity to urban spaces, carried out one of the rare, exemplary interventions of reconstruction in the historic center of that city, the houses of Guicciardini Street [1955-1957]. He also coordinated the overall urban plan of Florence [1955-1958] and, again in these same years, he directed the low-cost dwelling projects for Florence's Sorgane district in which almost all of the most prominent architects of Tuscany participated.

Given the fervor of architectural creation then, and the newly found power to compose widely diverse projects, there was a tendency for some architects to become ever more brilliant. For example we may cite not only the neo-Liberty of Roberto Gabetti and Aimaro Isola in the Erasmus Shop at Turin [1953-1956] or of Vittorio Gregotti's apartment houses of the 1950s at Novara and at Milan, but also, a decade or more later, the neo-Rationalism of Aldo Rossi, both of which were revivals of sorts and tended toward a recovery and historical revision of the sources of modern architecture.

During this same period a few impressive architectural works were erected that are difficult to classify outside of the contexts in which they originated. We may mention, in Rome, for instance, the mausoleum by Mario Fiorentino, Gino Calcaprina, Giuseppe Perugini, and others for the Martyrs of the Ardeatine Caves [1945-1950], and the concourse of the Termini railway station begun in 1931 and completed 1949-1951 by Eugenio Montuori, Leo Calini, and a group of colleagues; in Turin the Memorial of the War for Freedom, by Carlo Mollino in collaboration with sculptor Umberto Mastroianni [1946] and the RAI (Radio Audizioni Italiane) Auditorium also by Carlo Mollino [1950-1951]; and in Pescia the Flower Market by Leonardo Ricci, Giuseppe Gori, and Leonardo Savioli [1951].

27.3. Lodovico Belgioioso, Enrico Peressutti, Ernesto N. Rogers (BBPR), architects. Torre Velasca. Milan, 1958. (Photograph: Courtesy of the architects)

To complete our picture of Italian architecture between 1945 and 1960, we must return to the singular figure of Pier Luigi Nervi whose exceptionally fascinating, poetic structures are manifestly efforts to interpret structural calculations in other than a purely Rationalist key. The extraordinary roof of the principal exhibition area of the Turin Exhibition Hall [1947-1950] (fig. 27.5) and the hall which flanks it repeats the prewar experience of his hangars at Orbetello. The so-called small Sports Palace [Palazzetto] in Rome [1956-1957], and the previously mentioned, imposing structural engineering worked out by Nervi for Gio Ponti's Pirelli skyscraper [1956-1959] in Milan remain unquestionably, and not only for Italy, among the most significant of testimonies to the congruence of the technical and the formal.

Finally, we must consider that particularly Italian peculiarity represented by the designing of museums that began in the immediate postwar period. The competition for the Gallery of Modern Art at Turin had already lent emphasis to some interesting prospects beyond the disputable choice made. In addition, there are the architectural accomplishments by BBPR for the Castello Sforzesco [1952-1956] and by Ignazio Gardella for the Gallery of Modern Art, both at Milan; by Franco Albini in Genoa for the Palazzo Bianco [1951] and for his masterpiece there (fig. 27.6), the Treasury of San Lorenzo [1954-1957]; as

27.4. Gio Ponti, architect, with Pier Luigi Nervi, engineer. Pirelli Building (foreground), 1956-1958. Melchiorre Bega, architect. Galfa Tower (background), 1957-1959, Milan. (Photograph: Courtesy of Italian National Tourist Office, ENIT)

27.5. Pier Luigi Nervi, architect. Turin Exhibitions Hall. Turin, 1947-1950. (Photograph: Courtesy of Mario F. Roggero)

well as by Carlo Scarpa for the Museo di Palazzo Abatellis in Palermo [1953-1954] and later for his recycling of the Castelvecchio in Verona [1964]. All exemplify an incomparable cultural tradition of interest in museum planning and design.

We have considered the period of the first fifteen postwar years (1945-1959) precisely because it represents a central moment for the incubation of dynamic ideas and their initial results. Furthermore, it was then that the bases for the theoretical evolution of successive experiments of the next two stages (1959-1970 and 1970-1980) developed in different and contradictory directions.

THE MIDDLE PERIOD: THE 1960s

The decade of the 1960s seems to be marked by reflection and rethinking. On the one hand, architectural quests moved in isolation upon a formal plane, reelaborating the specific themes of each personality. Such are the displays of high formal and technological sophistication by Franco Albini in his Baths at Salsomaggiore [1967] and in his office

27.6. Franco Albini, architect. Treasury of San Lorenzo. Genoa, 1957. (Photograph: Courtesy of Paolomonti)

buildings for the SNAM at San Donato Milanese [1968-1971]; by Ignazio Gardella in the low, beautifully sited, polygonal Olivetti cafeteria building [1960] at Ivrea and in his project for the Vicenza Theater competition [1969]; by BBPR in their Hall of Honor for the Twelfth Triennial of Milan [1960]; and, at Rome, in the work of Adalberto Libera and Luigi Moretti in the Olympic Village [1960]; and in Ludovico Quaroni and Giuseppe Samonà's outstanding Parliament Office Building [1967]. On the other hand, the growing debate concerning the postwar city, toward which legislative silence had contributed, led many architects to become deeply engaged in more congruent universal planning programs so as to be in a position to renew the institutional framework. Giovanni Astengo, Luigi Piccinato, Ludovico Quaroni, and Giuseppe Samonà, with an antibureaucratic attitude that was widespread in all of Europe, led polemical battles for the reform of legislation in matters of urban planning and for the revival of forms of low-cost building.

Two features common to architectural culture led in diverse directions: one was signaled by formal evasions that tended towards a veritable utopia of uncontrollable images; the other towards ever more scientifically exacting structures, towards complexes of mathematical definitions of engineering. The most interesting Italian contributions of the epoch are those which tried to mediate a course between these two tendencies, not in the compromising of theory and practice but in their methodological characterization as intermediate-level projects: for example, a town design which takes up the hypotheses of Kenzo Tange, with flexible open systems which can be gradually effected and freed of models, standards, and rigid zoning. The competition for the urbanization of the Barene at San Giuliano di Mestre, on the lagoon facing Venice [1959], represents the prototype of these interventions. In the winning project by Ludovico Quaroni and a group of designers, among whom Carlo Aymonino is the outstanding figure, the theme of the "quarter" promoted during the first years of the postwar period was definitely surpassed in favor of a system of substitution by successive interventions. Quaroni along with Luigi Piccinato and others reformulated this in the communication axis (transportation axis) for Rome's traffic master plan [1962] as a solution intended to rid Rome's historic center of congestion and to create gradual insertions in the outskirts to accommodate new areas of the city's expansion. Almost at the same time, Milan's intercommunity plan was presented with a remarkably worthwhile contribution by Giancarlo de Carlo, in response to analogous problems. It imposed solutions that foresaw transportation nodes with a design of spiral approach roads differing from a communication axis. Also in 1962, the results of the competition for the traffic center of Turin were made known. In it one can see, in particular, the contrasts between the brilliant solutions of the group of Quaroni, with a series of high buildings imposed on a multilevel defined plan and the solution of Giuseppe Samonà's group, with a monoblock of huge dimensions in which different functions are established, and, above all, the solution of the group under the leadership of Carlo Aymonino, who hypothesized an axially articulated ribbon based on the districts from which the feeder lines of the different sectors of urban services branch off. Between 1963 and 1966, Giancarlo de Carlo, in an organic and congruent urbanistic study, accomplished the central nucleus of the University College at Urbino, with common services and modular cells for the residence building.

Subsequently, throughout Italy there were some interesting examples of low-cost residential building, among which there are those of Carlo Cocchia and of Giulio De Luca in Naples, of Italo Gamberini in Florence, and (figs. 27.7 and 27.8) those of Roberto Gabetti and Aimaro Isola at Ivrea [1968]. The latter is of particular interest because of its respect for the environment, with its very pure structure emerging from and yet remaining within an embankment. The Gallaratese district buildings at Milan [1967-1974] with their remarkably conflicting confluence were accomplished by Carlo Aymonino and Aldo Rossi. Meanwhile Pier Luigi Nervi moved ahead to create a new and surprising structure made of reinforced concrete and steel for the Palazzo del Lavoro of Turin [1961]. And the architecture of Giovanni Michelucci took a surprising turn during the first years of the 1960s with his Autostrada Church [1960-1964] on the major approach road to Florence. From the cubic masses of his Collina church [1954] to the polygonal church at Larderello [1956] to the lighter, Ra-

27.7. Roberto Gabetti and Aimaro Isola, architects. Residential flats west, aerial view, Ivrea, 1968. (Photograph: Courtesy of the architects)

27.8. Roberto Gabetti and Aimaro Isola, architects. Residential flats west, view from court level. 1968. (Photograph: Courtesy of the architects)

tionalist, rectilinearity of his Pistoia Savings Bank [1959-1962] we are at best poorly prepared for the expressionist leap of the Autostrada church at Florence.

Other important examples may be found during the 1960s in industrial architecture and in works entered in competitions. An industrial complex at Beinasco by Corrado and Laura Levi [1962-1963] breaks the large low area of the factory with a three-story office building of reinforced concrete in an organic adaptation of structural reality. The openness of a load-bearing structure so evident at the Levis' Beinasco complex had been carried to dramatic extremes previously in Nervi's Burgo Paper Factory [1960-1962] at Mantua. There, steel cables suspended from two reinforced concrete pylons that rise far above the building provide the essential supporting elements of the roofing for an area of some eighty thousand square feet. Among works that have been entered in competitions, there are the proposals of Maurizio Sacripanti and Carlo Mollino for the Theater of Cagliari [1965]; the winning solutions of Luigi Pellegrin, as well as the proposals of Roberto Gabetti and Aimaro Isola, of Paolo Portoghesi, and of Carlo Aymonino for the Paganini Theater of Parma [1967]; or, for the Teatro Regio di Torino, again by Carlo Mollino [1968], and for the Congress auditorium in Florence by Pierluigi Spadolini [1965-1968]. Theater competitions, however, constitute an exceptional theme which has little bearing on the uncertain climate of Italian architectural culture and on the sometimes questionable architectural research of the younger generation.

Unfortunately in August 1967 came Bill 765, "Modifications and Integrations to the Urbanistic Law of 1942" nicknamed *Legge-ponte* (bridge-law). Although its intent was to regulate construction in the entire nation by restraining some of the new building activities, it consented, through transitional norms, to the savage exploitation of building spaces that remained unregulated for a year. Thus, there was an indiscriminate proliferation of innumerable low-quality buildings without any coordinated plan, in the midst of which the few examples of high-quality building were lost. The bill's full implementation came into force in 1968 with, as a consequence, an almost complete standstill of all planning activities and a contemporaneous explosion of university disputes that found most fertile ground in the different faculties of architecture, especially at Milan, Venice, Rome, Turin, Florence, and Naples. Altogether this brought an abrupt halt to architectural production for a time.

THE RECENT PAST: THE 1970s

In our third stage, the various evolving trends have so closed in on our perspective that they are most difficult to understand fully. Italian architecture of the 1970s has been regarded by Manfredo Tafuri as encompassing "not the history of one ideology, but of many ideologies, born from the work of some few architects, from the interaction of the real with the utopian, speaking not of forms but of what is concealed."[10]

The many pathways open in the 1970s have led intellectuals rapidly to many architectural investigations outside of normal professional practice. Most inquiries tend to be much more intensely directed towards totally reformulating the discipline to include an active user-involvement; and thus they have been identified as radical architecture. This participatory type of architecture proved particularly lively during the first years of the 1970s, reflects positions strongly critical of the architect's traditional role, of his narrow specialization within his discipline, and of his relationships with established institutions. A questioning of the architect's means of expression and new technological instruments ensued that quite rightly provoked a break between theory and practice. At the same time there occurred a total revision of the social ambiences of architecture that was beyond any comfortable, preconceived schema.

It was within this frame of reference that Giancarlo de Carlo stated his methodological theory of "destructuration" which must necessarily precede every restructuring of the language of architecture, a theory practiced in his exacting interventions at Urbino. Immersed in this theoretical nexus, he offered a plan for the village of Matteotti di Terni [1970-1975], where he proposed an innovative, concrete confirmation of his participatory ideology. At the same time Vittorio Gregotti proved himself a planner with similar ideas, but also with a more animated critical ability and rather more efficient, conceptional means. This is apparent in his collaborative project for the Zen section of Palermo [1970-1976] with its tightly organized network of oblong urban blocks and facilities including even a stadium and still more strikingly in the University of Calabria at Cosenza [1978], accomplished with Emilio Battisti and others. Both of these projects suggest the reevaluation of urban planning criteria, the sewing up of the sorely wounded environment, and a healing of lacerations (that had become apparent from critical analyses and operating proposals) by means of architectural realizations of the highest quality.

In the 1970s Giovanni Michelucci found yet another interesting manner in which to build, as exemplified in his church at Longarone [1976] so different from the Autostrada church [1964] at Florence. In the meantime the independent and laborious evolution of Aldo Rossi continued with various experiments, from the Scandicci town hall project at Florence [1969-1970] to the cemetery project for Modena [1971] to the student residence of Chieti [1965]. In each he employed an original linguistic analysis which returned to a few carefully selected rarefied elements, used as "pure signs" for their "original semantic value, in a communicative effort that does not confuse the heritage of personal and collective memories and that strongly restores its apparent simplicity."[11]

On the one hand, during the 1970s aspirations toward the unity of urban planning and architecture were revealed, while on the other hand, various efforts emerged to resolve the conflict between theoretical positions and differing proposals. Evident among these proposals and also very different from one another are, for example, Costantino Dardi's participation in the collagelike Rome-East project presented at Milan's Fifteenth Triennial (1973); Michele Capobianco's "micro-city" laid out on a gridwork adapted to the landscape [Hospital in Calabria, 1972]; and Marco Zanuso's outlook exemplified in his rationalization of the productive process at his IBM headquarters complex of the 1970s at Segrate. But ever typical of this difficulty in resolving theoretical differences is the figure of Carlo Aymonino. In his most recent works, from the Gallaratese dwellings at Milan [1967-1976] to the Marconi Lyceum at Pesaro [1971-1976], purely by means of some formal excitement, by his denunciation of his own theses, he seeks to assemble every possible contradiction in the complexity of an open context, yet without claiming either to compose artfully or with distortion. "Whenever the architectural language is presented as ripped, Carlo Aymonino repairs its woof [and he does so] almost by declaring an impelling need to understand the opposite."[12] Exemplifying these ideas, and with a profound sense of internal coherence, he inserted a totally antithetical building by Aldo Rossi [1969-1973] in his Gallaratese apartment complex [1967-1974].

To conclude this brief and necessarily incomplete panorama, we may mention interesting industrial-commercial buildings that have been erected in Italy since the Second World War, in addition to those of the 1960s. Two such works of the 1970s are by architects already discussed. In both the Alfa Romeo office building at Arese by Ignazio Gardella [1973] and the Palazzo per Uffici in the Piazza Meda in Milan by BBPR [1975], Rationalism has reached almost to the edges of Structuralism with a clarifying of the means of construction that provides an ever lighter, ever more elegant framework. Finally we may call attention to the Cemetery of Saint Vito in Treviso [1970-1972] by Carlo Scarpa and the exemplary museums that this major architect accomplished late in his life.

Notes

1. Compare A. S. Smithson, ed., *Team Ten Primer* (Cambridge, Mass.: M.I.T. Press, 1968), pp. 4, 12, 13.
2. Manfredo Tafuri and Francesco Dal Co, *Architettura Contemporanea* (Venice: Electa Ed., 1976).
3. *See* Bibliography, below.
4. Published by the Istituto per la Collaborazione culturale, Rome and Venice, 1958.
5. Published by the Istituto Editoriale Romano, Rome, 1969.
6. Published by the Italian National Research Council and the United States Information Service (U.S.I.S.), 1946; expanded edition, 1962.
7. Published by UTIT, Turin, 1954.
8. Leonardo Benevolo and Manfredo Tafuri, eds., *Dizionario Enciclopedico di Architettura e Urbanistica* (Rome: Istituto Editoriale Romano, 1969).
9. For Luigi Pellegrin's work to 1960, see also L-Architettura, Cronache e Storia 6 (1960-1961): 295-315.
10. Tafuri and Dal Co, *Architettura Contemporanea.*
11. Ibid.
12. Ibid.

Bibliography

GENERAL REFERENCES

Benevolo, Leonardo. *Storia dell'Architettura Moderna.* Bari: Ed. Laterza, 1960. An organic study of modern architecture. The Italian building field is studied on a wider range and compared with international building.

Conforto, Cina; De Giorgi, Gabriele; Muntoni, Alessandra; Pazzaglini, Marcello. *Il Dibattito Architettonico in Italia—1945-1975.* Rome: Bulzoni Ed., 1977. Complete and up-to-date papers, including bibliography, about the Italian building production together with cultural and critical premises and ideological matters.

Portoghesi, Paolo, ed. *Dizionario Enciclopedico di Architettura e Urbanistica.* Rome: Istituto Editoriale Romano Ed., 1968. Widest inventory of original critical essays related to the architectural world in all its aspects.

Smith, G. E. Kidder. *L'Italia Costruisce*. Milan: Ed. Comunità, 1955. General critical analysis of the development of Italian architecture after the Second World War as a careful examiner would see it.

Tafuri, Manfredo and Dal Co, Francesco. *Architettura Contemporanea*. Venice: Electa Ed., 1976. Available in English, Robert Erich Wolf, trans. *Modern Architecture*. New York: Harry N. Abrams, 1979. Accurate and learned critical essay well supported by documents about the architecture of the last century. The Italian architectural output, to a greater extent and in its own scale, is compared with those of different countries.

______. *28/78 Architettura—Cinquant'Anni di Architettura Italiana dal 1928 al 1978*. Milan: Ed. *Domus*, 1979. Catalog of the exhibition by *Domus* magazine together with the municipality of Milan. Comprehensive list of major architects, containing a wide bibliography of books and magazines.

ADDITIONAL SELECTED REFERENCES*

BOOKS

Argan, G. C. *Ignacio Gardella*. Milan, 1959.

Conforto, C.; de Giorgi, G.; Muntoni, A.; and Pazzaglini, M. *Il dibattito architettonico in Italia 1945-1975*. Rome, 1977.

ture. London: Studio Vista, 1968.

Galardi, Alberto. *New Italian Architecture*. New York: Praeger, 1967.

Gregotti, Vittorio. *New Directions in Italian Architecture*. London: Studio Vista, 1968.

Tafuni, Manfredo. *Theories and History of Architecture*. New York: Granada, 1980.

JOURNALS

Aymonino, Carlo et al. "Carlo Aymonino." *Architecture and Urbanism* 88 (February 1978): 3-44. (In Japanese and English.)

Bardeschi, M. D.; Nervi, P. L.; and Michelucci, G. "Italie . . ." *L'Architecture d'Aujourd'hui* 113/114 (April/May 1964): 158-71.

"Casabella, 1928-1978." *Casabella* 440/441 (October 1978): 11-111. (English translations and digests: I-VIII, after p. 112).

Ciucci, Giorgio; Huet, Bernard; Restucci, Amerigo; and Teyssot, Georges. "Politique Industrielle et Architecture, le Cas Olivetti." *L'Architecture d'Aujourd'hui* 188 (December 1976): 1-104 (English summary: LXI-LXIV).

Futagawa, Yukio, ed., and Paolo Portoghesi. "Carlo Scarpa, Cemetery, S. Vito, Treviso, Italy, 1970-1972." *Global Architecture*, no. 50, 1979.

______ ed., and Carlo Santini. "Carlo Scarpa, Olivetti Showroom, Querini Stampalia and Castelvecchio Museum." *Global Architecture*, no. 51, 1979.

La Pietra, Ugo. "Architettura Radicale in Italia." *Domus* 580 (March 1978): 2-7.

Rossi, Aldo et al. "Conception and Reality of Aldo Rossi." *Architecture and Urbanism* 65 (May 1976): 55-120. (In Japanese and English.)

Schmertz, Mildred F. "The New Architecture of Florence." *Architectural Record* 2 (February 1974): 95-108.

Teyssot, Georges and L'Institut d'Histoire de la Faculté d'Architecture de Venise, eds. "Italie 75." *L'Architecture d'Aujourd'hui* 181 (September-October 1975): 1-113 (English summary: LXIII-LXVI).

Vigano, Vittoriano, ed. "Italie." *L'Architecture d'Aujourd'hui* 48 (July 1953): 1-97.

______, and Diamant-Berger, Renée, eds. "Italie Habitation." *L'Architecture d'Aujourd'hui* 41 (June 1952): 1-93.

OUTSTANDING ITALIAN ARCHITECTURAL JOURNALS, 1945-1978

Architetti. Florence, 1950-1953.
Architettura (L'), Cronache e Storia. Milan, 1955-to-date.
Casa (La), Rome, 1955-to date.
Casabella, Milan, 1946-to date.
Chiesa e Quartiere, Bologna, 1956-1960s.
Comunità, Milan, 1946-1975.
Contropiano, Rome, 1968-1971.
Controspazio, Milan, 1969-to date.
Domus, Milan, 1946-to date.
Edilizia Moderna, Milan, 1948-1967.
Marcatré, Rome, 1963-1970.
Metron, Rome-Milan, 1945-1954.
Parametro, Bologna, 1970-to date.
Prospettive, Milan, 1950-1972.
Spazio, Rome, 1950-1953.
Stile, Milan, 1945-1947.
Urbanistica, Turin, 1947-to date.
Zodiac, Milan, 1957-1973.

*Compiled by the Montreal Staff.

28

JAPAN

EIZO INAGAKI

Background

The drastic changes which have taken place in Japanese architecture since the 1940s are paralleled only by those experienced in the second half of the nineteenth century, when the industrialized culture of the West was introduced into Japan for the first time. With it came various methods of stone and brick construction, the somewhat inorganic style of the Revivalist movement, and the highly esteemed concept of the architect as professional. That initial excitement of a century ago engendered by the impact of a culture very different from its own has been succeeded by a development of architecture that is based upon economics, industry, and technology and that is distinctive in its rapid growth, its systematic approach, and the degree to which it pervades daily life.

Before the Second World War most Japanese lived in wooden houses of traditional construction and sat on the tatami—resilient straw mats. By 1980 the greater number of city dwellers lived in small apartment houses, surrounded by electrical appliances. The landscape which once existed in the present suburban areas has already disappeared. It is no exaggeration to say that buildings of similar materials and styles are being constructed now throughout the country. The development of architecture has seen the International Style become so deeply rooted in Japan that it has replaced all previous styles. This environmental mutation has been caused primarily by the development of industry, but the extent to which architects have contributed new ideas is significant. Regardless of result, architects in Japan have generally been ready to accept any architectural form produced by industry and technology without opposition. No doubt the development of Japanese architecture after the war was influenced basically both by industry and by the attitudes of Japanese architects, which allowed a building to follow any form almost indiscriminately.

As new buildings superseded older ones, the path leading to the diffusion of modern architecture was full of vicissitudes not unlike those experienced by architects of other countries. There was a variety of experimental attempts, ideological conversions, dissents against tradition, and stimuli from abroad. Japanese architecture mirrors the actual problems imposed by social and economic conditions as well as the ingenuity and the ideals of the architects directed to answer them. Therefore, the following discussion is centered around important architects and their works as the foci of change.

Architectural Developments: 1940-1980

The forties were a decade of war and postwar recovery. The fifties became a time of departure, when postwar economic developments were motivated by circumstances resulting from the Korean War. Modern architecture took root in Japan during this period, while at the same time a warning of its transmutation and decay appeared. The sixties were colored by both prosperity and turmoil. Driven by economic and industrial development, diversification continued along with a pervasion of technological innovation within the whole sphere of architecture. At the same time, however, the strains of both industrialization and high economic growth emerged, and people became aware of the impending energy crisis. What followed in the seventies? For the majority of architects of the third generation, polarizations and diversifications of values grew swiftly. Though hope for Post-Modernism has been expressed, no one believes in the myth that Modernism itself has come to an end. The only sure fact is that the advent of the 1980s has occurred amidst continuing fundamental changes in attitudes and approaches toward Japan's architecture.

THE FORTIES: A TIME OF WAR AND POSTWAR RECOVERY

With the war in the first half of the 1940s and postwar recovery in the second, this was a decade of bitter trial for Japanese architects as well as for the entire population. Without any particular work to do, they were forced to reflect upon their aims and responsibilities amid the stirring currents of the time. The International Style had exerted a variety of influences, especially discernible in Japanese architecture well before the war. Architects in Japan, however, had scarcely been ready to face new ideas and methods of modern architecture when war became imminent. Thus, it is necessary to retrace briefly the germination of modern architecture in Japan as a premise for understanding its development in the forties.

After the enormous damage caused by the earthquake that devastated Tokyo and Yokohama in 1923, there was a greater interest in acquiring technical expertise from foreign lands to develop earthquake-resistant building techniques so that reconstruction so urgently needed in both cities would ultimately be more permanent. From then on, through the early thirties, modern style in Japanese architecture was gradually established. But it was not until the economic depression abated in the second half of the thirties that the earliest buildings worthy of the name of modern architecture appeared. Almost all the buildings of this period in Japan required a strictly rigid frame construction, primarily because of seismic conditions. Architects, therefore, devoted themselves to building structural masses composed of simple planes, a new tendency in Japanese architecture. Although they may have lagged behind international standards of design, the Morigo Building [Tokyo, 1931] by Togo Murano (b. 1891), the Nihon Dental College Hospital [Tokyo, 1934] by Bunzo Yamaguchi (1902-1978), the dormitory of Keio University [Yokohama, 1938] by Yoshiro Taniguchi (1904-1979), the Wakasa House [Tokyo, 1939] by Sutemi Horiguchi (b. 1895), and the Osaka Central Post Office [Osaka, 1939] by Tetsuro Yoshida (1894-1956) are among the guideposts that indicate the establishment of Japanese modern architecture.

The imminence of war threatened architects just as they were moving toward modern design methods. Apart from practical problems such as in the shortage of building materials and the decrease of professional commissions, there arose a militarist-nationalism that brought about the revival of traditional Japanese building principles and a suppressive atmosphere for architects. Various competitions held in the thirties continued trends of the last years of the nineteenth century with such prerequisites as "Japanese taste" or "Oriental style" and winning projects were commonly eclectic in style, adorned, for instance, with tiled roofs in the guise of Buddhist temples. This "Japanese style" was symptomatic of an intractability concerning the problems of inheritance and mastery of Japanese traditional building—problems that had remained unsolved, had been consciously avoided by the architectural movements of the twenties, and had emerged with renewed vigor alongside of a nationalistic trend that blocked the way for further development in the modern architecture in Japan.

Although anticipating rejection of their designs, a few architects in the thirties remained fervent in their confidence in the eventual establishment of modern architecture and forced their way into competitions with works embodying their views. One of the most liberal was Kunio Maekawa (b. 1905). He studied under Le Corbusier in Paris from 1928 to 1930, then worked at the Tokyo office of Antonin Raymond and in 1935 started his own office in Tokyo. It was in the competitions of the thirties that he made his challenging debut as an architect. It was he, too, who almost singlehandedly struggled against the hostility of militaristic nationalism to keep modern architecture alive through the wartime years. Despite the war, two competitions were announced: the first in 1942 for a "Monument Commemorating the Establishment of the Greater East Asia Co-Prosperity Sphere"; and the second in 1943 for the "Japan Cultural Institute at Bangkok." Although both required designs reflecting the idea of the Greater East Asia Co-Prosperity Sphere for the Japanese military authorities, architects advocating modern architecture willingly entered. Kenzo Tange (b. 1913), at that time a graduate student at the University of Tokyo, won first prize in both competitions. Are we to suppose that modern architecture had thus submitted to the authority of militarism? Tange's projects, especially the second, were furnished with traditional Japanese motifs in every possible part. But instead of demonstrating a real preference for traditional forms, they constituted a modern revaluation of traditional motifs imbued with a sensibility found in none of his competitors. Both were characterized by functional divisions clearly accomplished in the floor plan as well as by a formal coordination of the whole. The ideas and methods of modern architecture had been developing steadily, even during wartime.

The grand-prize-winning Japan Pavilion, built by Junzo Sakakura (1904-1968) for the Paris International Exposition of 1937, after his years of working at the office of Le Corbusier (1929-1936), showed what could be attained by an architect of the prewar generation. A light and open steel construction with ample use of glass, and asbestos and slate tiles, it nevertheless had an air of Japanese aesthetic throughout. Many Japanese architects of the time dreamt of an opportunity to revive in Japan itself what Sakakura had realized in Paris, that is, a free plan with form removed from structural restraints.

Through the thirties into the early years of the forties, the methods of the International Style became more and more deeply appreciated by enlightened architects, though opportunities to build were relatively few. The concerns of Tange and Sakakura were not to compose simple squares of white walls and oblong windows in the outer faces of a building, but rather to secure a unity of the whole through spatial articulation and explicit regularity. Their competence, nurtured in the forties, would bloom in the next decade when architectural activities would begin on a greater scale.

The outcome of the war was nothing but incalculable ruin for Japan with 115 cities damaged, 630 square kilometers of areas hit and 2,350,000 houses destroyed. The housing shortage totaled about 4,200,000 units throughout the country in April 1946. Little progress was made at first in the reconstruction of demolished houses because of extreme inflation and shortage of materials, and people were forced to live in even smaller and poorer housing than they had during wartime.

It was Uzo Nishiyama (b. 1911), then Associate Professor of Architecture at the University of Kyoto, who played a leading part among the architects of this postwar period. As a former official of the Housing Corporation, a house-building agency during wartime, he had already established his views on residential planning. Based upon an empirical method, his new theory consisted of a system that included the scale, type, and location of dwellings as well as their form and structure. Nishiyama's theoretical system, derived from a house-to-house survey of living conditions in small wartime housing blocks, was approved for practical implementation in the immediate postwar situation. Moreover, it would provide a theoretical scheme of house planning once again in the fifties when housing policy was vigorously furthered by the government.

The problems and concerns of architects in the latter half of the forties can be well summarized by the activities of the New Architect's Union (NAU). The largest postwar architectural movement, the NAU was organized in 1947 and immediately grew to a membership of eight hundred. Surrounded by burned-out ruins, the major topic of discussion became the architect's response to Japan's urgent needs. Discussion proceeded along two lines. First, in response to the establishment of democracy and to their country's recent defeat, they promoted new criteria: anything considered nondemocratic surviving in Japan's civilian world at the time was immediately subjected to severe criticism—the indigenous and the traditional in housing, traditional conventions of human relations, customs characteristic of the community of building traders, and eventually the hierarchical Japanese society as a whole. Impetuous judgements were applied negatively to these conventions and traditions. Never again were Japanese traditions judged from a single point of view under the name of democracy as they were in this postwar decade. Second, Functionalism became one of the distinctive characteristics of the NAU Movement for its members insisted that only through Functionalism actual problems could be solved and their future activities would be guided. The NAU may be traced back directly to the movements of the twenties, rather than to the architectural achievements of the thirties through the forties. Function, technology, class—these terms were repeated in their discussions without clear definitions, hence resulting in nothing of practical importance. Consequently, the NAU movement came to an end when architects became engaged more in practical work than in the movement itself. With the so-called business building boom caused by the Korean War of 1950 new opportunities arose, and in 1951 the NAU virtually disappeared.

THE FIFTIES: A TIME OF DEPARTURE

The year 1950 was a turning point in Japan's economic recovery. In only a few years it not only regained the same level of materials production as that of the thirties but soon matched the national purchasing power at that time. While the first half of the fifties saw a rise to prewar industrial capacities, during the second half institutions and organizations gained momentum for future developments. Furthermore, the first half of the fifties saw the production of principal building materials such as steel and cement exceed even the highest levels attained before the war. The Building Standards Law, a general building statute, and the Architects Law, a statute on the qualifications of architects, were both enacted in 1950. A system of statutory laws relating to the reconstruction of cities and territories was being codified toward the close of the decade.

The building rush caused by the Korean War started with the construction of office buildings in cities. With the majority of buildings which survived the war requisitioned by the occupation army, a need for business buildings led to new projects by the design sections of large construction companies and large architectural offices. Among the earlier examples in the center of Tokyo are the Nikkatsu Kokusai Kaikan Building [Takenaka Komuten Company, Ltd., 1951], the Tekko Building [Ikeda Architect and Associates, 1951], and the Bridgestone Building [Matsuda Hirata Architects and Associates, 1951].

Any discussion of postwar architecture should begin, however, with Antonin Raymond's (1888-1976) Reader's Digest Office Building [Tokyo, 1951]. The architect had visited Japan with Frank Lloyd Wright in 1919 for the Imperial Hotel project and returned later to continue to work in Japan, designing such fine buildings as the Chapel of Tokyo Woman's Christian College [1937]. He returned to the United States during the war, but in 1948 came back to Japan to resume his work, starting with the Reader's Digest Office Building. Japanese architects were astonished at the design and construction of the two-storied office building, for its standard of building technology was far beyond Japan's at that time. Every detail such as the exposed concrete walls, deep eaves, *brise-soleil* of steel, and the leitmotif as conveyed by the large sliding partitions and curtain walls revealed Raymond's mature quality of design. In addition, he brought with him an extensive knowledge of reinforced-concrete structures, with much data based upon experiments carried out in the United States. The Japanese construction industry responded well to his demands for great skill and accuracy in the execution of concrete work. Indeed, the building techniques used in the exposed concrete walls of the Reader's Digest building constituted the basis for walls of future buildings with the same finish. Other important aspects of this building are the homogeneity of its design and the use of beams projecting nine meters on either side from rows of central pillars, supported at their ends only by pin joints. Though applied once before in the Imperial Hotel by Frank Lloyd Wright, such a cantilevered structure had remained unfamiliar to Japanese technical experts. (Despite a good deal of protest, in 1964 this outstanding monument of modern architecture was razed to be replaced by an undistinguished high rise that made more efficient, more economic use of the site.) Raymond later designed two six-storied buildings with apartments of three types for the staff of the U.S. embassy. As had the Reader's Digest building until its destruction [1964], these afforded architects in the postwar period exemplary models for construction, finish, and detail.

The architecture of the fifties was of such variety that we must limit our description to the principal works of a few architects. Junzo Sakakura and Kunio Maekawa were once again able to design freely in the style they had been practicing since before the war. Sakakura's Kanagawa Prefectural Modern Art Museum [Kamakura, 1951] was a faithful reflection of his pavilion in the Paris International Exposition [1937]. Due to a material shortage during the fifties, the two-storied steel-frame building was finished with Ohya-stone on the ground floor and with asbestos boards on the upper floor. The white outer walls, as well as the clarity and openness of the plan developed around the central court, exemplify his complete understanding of the International Style. On the other hand, the Kanagawa Prefectural Library and Auditorium [Yokohama, 1954] designed by Kunio Maekawa is characterized as a building composed of two masses with an approachway between them. Maekawa who had worked before the war in the ateliers of Raymond and Le Corbusier, expressed what he thought to be modern style in various projects, with his facade treatments consisting of decorative precast-concrete blocks, large openings of glass, and very slender pillars of reinforced concrete. His works always displayed the results of very careful consideration and his spaces and architectural details were the products of minute and elaborate design. Among the architects of this decade, it was Kunio Maekawa who most fervently retained his method of design and emphasized more than anyone else the modern architecture of Japan. After the fifties he designed many community centers, all of which were highly regarded.

Of the architects who advanced the architecture of the International Style in the thirties and also distinguished themselves in the fifties, Sutemi Horiguchi [Wakasa House, 1939] is of particular interest, for he has also held an active interest in the traditional Japanese architectural style. No other architect surpassed him in his knowledge of the tea ceremony and teahouse architecture. His first major work after the war was an annex to the Hasshokan Inn, which was to be used by the imperial family. Basically designed in a traditional manner, and consisting of a mere two rooms, it nevertheless defined his entire sphere of knowledge and experience. Furthermore, it expressed his devotion to the traditional teahouse and garden, his aesthetic appreciation of paper and textiles as panels which enhanced the interior, and also his enthusiasm for modern architecture. The "modern" meaning of the annex can be found in the fact that the architect sought modern design while continuing the legacy of traditional architectural design.

The work of Yoshiro Taniguchi in the postwar period expressed his profound knowledge of Japanese tradition in the design of excellent wooden residences and also in stone memorial monuments of deliberate intention and exquisite sensibility. Typical of his style were two small wooden structures [Nagano Prefecture, 1947, 1951] commemorating Toson Shimazaki, a great man of letters. But his design method was consistently expressed, even in his industrial architecture, as for example in the second factory of Chichibu Cement Co., Ltd. [Chichibu, 1956] where he unified buildings of different size and height by using a rhythmic pattern created by vertical lines and gently curved roofs.

Togo Murano, another architect who contributed greatly to modern Japanese architecture of the postwar period, seems to have had no single theory on artistic form. Instead he derived the most appropriate solutions for the particular conditions determined by each project. In his wide range of works, his style was most characterized by a keen sense for details and a generous use of decorative elements. The World Peace Memorial Cathedral at Hiroshima [1953], a simple structure of exposed pillars and reinforced-concrete beams with walls of tinted terra-cotta, conveys a sense of crystalline tranquility which is a product of his many years of experience.

In the fifties young architects gradually had an opportunity to design buildings. At first, their primary works consisted of residential buildings, a field in which architects had long been active. Several architects of the new generation selected a particular theme of residential architecture and followed it systematically, creating many excellent works. Kiyoshi Ikebe (1920-1970), for example, made a complete functional analysis of housing. He introduced a series of experimental houses including a wooden minimal house [1950] completely lacking in superfluous spaces. Besides his research on functionalism in housing, he also investigated the prefabrication of housing, he also investigated the earliest stages of its use. Above all, he was concerned with the modular coordination in housing that was to play so important a role later.

Kiyoshi Seike (b. 1918) was another residential architect who led in the epoch of residential architecture with creative examples like the Mori House [Tokyo, 1951], the Saito House [Tokyo, 1952], and the Miyagi House [Tokyo, 1953]. He strove for a homogeneous space in conformance with the structural scheme and achieved this by adapting traditional Japanese timber construction to modern architectural design. The use of such traditional elements of Japanese architecture as shoji (a paper screen), fusuma (sliding, paper partitions), and tatami (straw matting) was reevaluated for and redesigned in his houses. Seike was also professor at the Tokyo Institute of Technology that subsequently produced a future generation of architects, including Masako Hayashi and Kazuo Shinohara.

Makoto Masuzawa (b. 1925), an architect from Raymond's office, also studied the details of wooden structures intensively in order to find a new way to create houses of reduced scale. He was especially interested in the possibility of a one-room living space with a service core in the center, a problem that would later occupy many, such as Kisho Kurokawa [Karuizawa House, 1974]. Other architects made similar proposals regarding methods of spatial composition, architectural details, and small-scale housing early in the fifties, attempting to design houses of less than 100 square meters according to a new Western design logic derived essentially from Mies van der Rohe and Philip Johnson. Kenji Hirose (b. 1922) made his appearance with an exceptional project [1953] composed of a framework of light-gauge steel and brick walls with large openings. The principal structure utilized steel angles and bars to create a new and lively expression through their slender dimensions and the essential quality of the material. Utilizing these materials in this way was something never done before in Japan. He was also very much concerned with the promoting of prefabrication and standardization of building materials.

The postwar architecture of Kenzo Tange started in Hiroshima city with his first large project, the Peace Center designed as early as 1946 in commemoration of the victims of the atomic bomb. During the ten years it took to complete this building Tange designed many others, including the Ehime Prefectural Hall [Matsuyama, 1954], the Shimizu City Hall [Shimizu, 1954], the factory of the Tosho Insatsu Company in Haramachi [Haramachi, 1957], the library of Tsuda College [Tokyo, 1955], Kurayoshi City Hall [Kurayoshi, 1957], the Shizuoka Convention Hall [Shizuoka, 1957], the Tokyo Metropolitan

Government Office [Tokyo, 1958], the Sogetsu School and Office [Tokyo, 1958; demolished and rebuilt by the same architect in 1977], and the Kagawa Prefectural Office [Takamatsu, 1958].

Tange's prolific building production may be divided into two groups, one using a shell structure and the other a rigid frame construction. Shell structures, often done in cooperation with Yoshikatsu Tsuboi (b. 1907), a structural engineer, were characterized by large spans and simple functions and were used for such buildings as factories and gymnasiums. This group comprises a series of buildings in which the Yoyogi Olympic Stadium and Saint Mary's Cathedral [Tokyo, 1964] are prominent. The shell as used by Tange, however, was not chosen exclusively because of practical necessities of span and volume. He began by relating his project to the major functions of the building; then he designed a shell with a structural form that might represent them best. The shell, generally speaking, constitutes the form of the structure without ambiguity. Its structural clarity expresses the functional clarity of the building. As applied by Tange the shell structure thus signified much more than a mere enclosure.

Rigid frame buildings assumed another meaning in his structural scheme. The architectural composition of a horizontal structure supported on *pilotis* in the Hiroshima project's Central Hall, Exhibition Gallery, and Public Hall seems at first to replicate the International Style in Japan. However, the concrete beams and pillars of these buildings may be best understood when compared with corresponding elements in Japanese wooden structures. Throughout the fifties Tange adhered to this analogy, which gave his rigid frame structures a significance associated with traditional Japanese architectural spaces. Earthquake-resistant walls were eliminated in these buildings in order to afford greater flexibility for partition walls in the interior.

In the Tokyo Metropolitan Government Offices and the Kagawa Prefectural Offices, shear walls in the center formed a structural core that allowed a distinctive openness and flexibility for the surrounding space. These buildings basically resembled the Hiroshima Memorial Hall in that their structural form was composed mainly of pillars and beams. Thus, Tange sought to retain the spatial integrity of the building while trying also to keep the fundamental structural pillar-and-beam frame. The Kagawa Prefectural Office project had marked the start as well as the culmination of this design-process. The appearance of the office building, resembling traditional wooden structures, was no mere imitation but instead required a series of intense studies regarding the space and construction of reinforced-concrete structures built after his Hiroshima Memorial Hall. From these studies Tange solved problems of form and function for the public spaces demanded in government buildings, developing a system of core-shafts and *pilotis* utilized in a manner very different from Le Corbusier. His concrete core-shafts served two functions essentially, containing service elements for the building while also serving in a basic, structural-supporting capacity. A third function was more fully realized in the sixties: the combination of core-shafts and horizontal elements in a gridlike plan made possible, theoretically, an infinitely expandable structure, a megastructure.

Generally reviewing the 1950s, a controversy was provoked around 1955, when heated discussions about the role of Japanese tradition in architecture abounded. What resulted was not a return to the stylistic patterns and traditional structures of Japan, such as a housing tradition based upon the post-and-lintel system which was, incidentally, intrinsically akin to the International Style. It was, rather, a rediscovery of a kind of robust primitivism in opposition to the refined traditions of Japanese architecture. Broadly speaking, it may have been a kind of reconsideration of the very remote Japanese past which had not previously been considered by modern architects. The apparent turning point in the mid-1950s involved a change in attitudes toward foreign architectural design as well, caused chiefly by Le Corbusier. The impact on Japanese architects of Le Corbusier's works, in particular Notre-Dame-du-Haut at Ronchamp [1954], the Palace of Justice at Chandigarh [1956], and the Monastery of Sainte-Marie-de-la-Tourette [1957], was significant. The change may have foreshadowed the future crisis in European Rationalist architecture, since issues concerning the New Brutalism advocated earlier by Reyner Banham among others constantly pervaded the thought of Japanese architects.

THE SIXTIES: A TIME OF PROSPERITY AND TURMOIL

The decade of the sixties was one of phenomenal upheaval caused by radical changes in the living environment and the landscape. Cities, rural areas, and family life were affected. The driving forces behind this change were economic growth and technological innovation. The sixties began with the National Income-Doubling Program established by the government in 1960; in 1961 the gross national product grew to more than fifty billion dollars and the real growth rate of the economy reached 14.4 percent. The government promoted land development. The creation of coastal industrial zones and the establishment of new industrial cities gave impetus to the development of backward regions and the growth of huge, planned, housing tracts. Along with this, urban redevelopment and the organization of the main traffic network caused sudden and radical changes in both urban and rural areas.

The economic growth of Japan in the early sixties allowed Japanese architects to practice fully the views and opinions that they had developed during the fifties, modified in part by influences of the third generation of Western modern architects. During this decade Japanese architecture achieved international stature. Japan shared in the same design problems that confronted other economically advanced nations and her architects presented highly innovative solutions. With the CIAM having been essentially dissolved in 1956, Japanese architects gradually began to feel that they could and should become leaders in establishing advanced architectural design-concepts.

The Urban Plan for Tokyo Bay-1960 by Kenzo Tange (fig. 28.1) was an imaginative, monumental

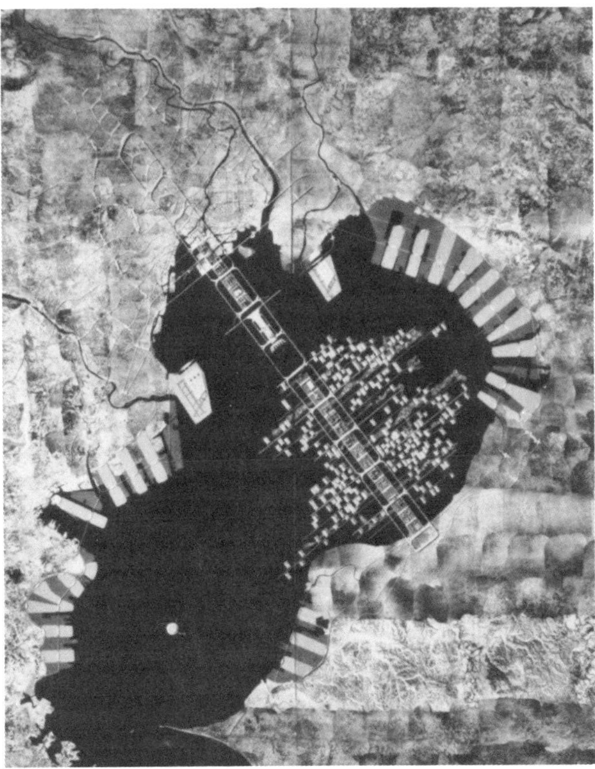

28.1. Kenzo Tange, architect. Tokyo Bay Plan. 1960. (Photograph: Courtesy of Akio Kawasumi)

project based upon the recognition of existing urban conditions. Tokyo was then already a city of ten million inhabitants. Its influx of population could not be effectively controlled; thus the very gravitation of people toward the city was a driving force in urban development. A second primary factor in the state of urban confusion lay in the traffic problem. Neither problem could be solved by applying such older methods and concepts of urbanism as redistribution of factories and functional decentralization of the city, nor by the satellite city and metropolitan subcenter plans. To save the megalopolis from urban confusion, Tange introduced the concept of a civic-axis, a multiple-road network called a "cycle transportation system," into his Tokyo plan. From the center of the city the axis was extended across Tokyo Bay as far as Kisarazu on the opposite coast. Along this axis major governmental and commercial office buildings were planned in addition to housing structures. Vertical circulation paths and large core-shafts for piping were envisioned for the intersecting points of the road network that would be in the form of a grid. The main concept of this project was unlike the traditional centripetal cities: it offered the possibility of an open system of spatial organization in which urban functions were linked by means of the traffic network axis. The transportation system would become the trunk and branches of the tree that was the city. The structural framing of individual buildings in this project was an elaboration of what had been proposed in the fifties by Tange. Here the wall girder and the slab were incorporated into a box girder which formed the living space. The concept Tange had been forming since the fifties may have reached its goal with this multiplex frame created by the unification of spatial and structural components. In fact, the architectural design of Tange changed drastically after this project.

While Tange was preparing his project for Tokyo Bay-1960, Arata Isozaki (b. 1931) and Kisho Kurokawa (b. 1934) were among his staff members. Undoubtedly their concepts and theories of design were developed under Tange's guidance. Isozaki presented "A Project for a City in the Air" [1962] and Kurokawa developed the "Helix Plan" [1961]. A contemporary, Kiyonori Kikutake, was pondering the "Marine City" [1961] which would later evolve into the "City on the Sea" [1963] along with a series of other works. All of these projects, including Tange's, may be characterized as megastructural systems to reorganize space. Thus, the 1960s began with a variety of theories about the city of the future.

In May 1960 over two hundred architects, designers, and critics from twenty-seven different countries met at the World Design Conference held in Tokyo. During that conference, the Metabolism group was organized under the direction of Noboru Kawazoe, with Kisho Kurokawa, Kiyonori Kikutake, Fumihiko Maki (b. 1928) and Masato Otaka (b. 1923) as members. Metabolism, with overall views on world conditions, epistemology, and design methodology can be regarded as a leading ideology of the 1960s. The very name *Metabolism* as well as the substance of its theory were derived from research on the city and its architecture developed by analogy with organic systems of life. The major themes of Metabolism, growth and change, overrode the static and limited systems of older planning theories that were based on the idea of the city as a mechanized entity. To conceive of the city as being analogous to the ecosystem was not a completely new idea. The historical meaning of Metabolism in Japan was derived from an optimistic anticipation of unlimited development in industrial production and technological innovation. The growing urbanization and the industrialization of the time seemed to justify this general view. At the same time, the technical basis that gave promise of acceptable growth and change was thought to be found in theories of fragmentation, standardization, unit coordination, mass production, and equipment fabrication, all of which later formed the theoretical bases of Metabolism.

Common to the projects proposed by Metabolism was a combination of the megastructure and substitutive functional spaces. This fundamental concept was held not only by Metabolists in Japan but also by their generation of architects internationally. The Japanese Metabolism group seemed to have been eagerly concerned with the means by which they could realize their theories in actual projects. Therein lies the very point of difference that distinguished Metabolism in Japan from its nearest rival, the Archigram of England. From its inception, a multitude of provocative propositions by Archigram were totally unrelated to practical solutions for actual problems. Archigram denied the entire system of established orders and attempted to construct a new environment by using a variety of visual metaphors. In the case of Metabolism, the revolt against existing values and orders was not necessarily total. Later, Kurokawa summarized the idea of Metabolism in an article in which he stated that its members had not intended to deny the movement of CIAM as a whole but that they had aimed at a new order of spatial quality created through coexistence between and overlapping of the established orders and new values.

Third-generation Japanese architects including the Metabolists did not start by criticizing their predecessors. The early leaders of modern architecture in Japan, such as Maekawa, Taniguchi, Murano, Horiguchi, and Tange, a second-generation architect, were never really ready to accept the entire strict doctrine of Functionalism. They preferred instead to develop modern architecture by interpreting it freely within the realities of life in Japan. Though Maekawa and Sakakura had both practiced under Le Corbusier, the culmination of their study was not a rigid set of design doctrines. Rather, it involved the process of finishing a building as an object of art and the belief that architecture should induce something pleasant in response to it. Tange also made frequent and fervent reference to art in architecture. Such an idea was inherited by the third-generation architects, who quite naturally expected not to abolish altogether, but to compromise with, existing established architectural values.

Principal works of the sixties must now be mentioned. In 1964 Tange completed two huge monumental buildings: the Yoyogi National Stadium which housed the Tokyo Olympic Pool and an attached gymnasium; and Saint Mary's Cathedral in Tokyo. The stadium consisted of a suspended roof structure made up of high-strength steel cables and an outer steel membrane. The gentle slope of the catenary roof covers 150,000 seats arranged in a circular fashion. Beyond a doubt, this stadium is the most perfect and creative example in the series of buildings in which Tange pursued a unity of building structure and functionality. The building well deserves to be called a hallmark among monuments of the first half of the sixties since its structure was made possible only through great achievements of the steel industry and systems engineering. The structure of the cathedral, on the other hand, is a shell molded with stainless steel and formed in the shape of a cross by hyperbolic paraboloids. The clear and simple structural framing itself produces a dynamic ascent of the circumscribed space. The Yamanashi Press and Broadcasting Center [Kofu, 1966] and the Shizuoka Press and Broadcasting Building [Tokyo, 1967] were further experiments by Tange. The former (fig. 28.2) is a megastructure formed by the conjunction of flat slabs with cylindrical core-shafts arranged on a grid. The latter consists of office units inserted into a single core-shaft. Both these buildings were models depicting the city-in-the-air concept which was derived from the Tokyo Bay Project-1960 and both buildings were designed as infinitely expandable systems.

Few buildings which manifested the intentions of the third-generation architects including members of the Metabolism group were actually built in the 1960s. Not until the 1970s did these architects acquire their own characteristic design traits. The architecture of the 1960s thus consisted of buildings designed mainly by highly recognized second-generation architects. In fact, the architects who had been practicing since before the war continued to

28.2. Kenzo Tange, architect. Yamanashi Communications Center. Kufu, 1966. (Photograph: Courtesy of Shokokusha Publishing Co., Inc.)

develop architectural designs and create fine buildings. A marked stylistic change in Kunio Maekawa's works occurred in the Kyoto Cultural Center [Kyoto, 1960] and the Tokyo Metropolitan Festival Hall [Tokyo, 1961], both of which are public halls consisting of multiple auditoriums. The major feature of these buildings is the massiveness of their concrete structure in which no vestige of his previous delicate style survives. The latter building, in particular, distinctively conveys Le Corbusier's latest style, using long enormous eaves of smooth reinforced-concrete and panelled walls finished with crushed marble. Although Maekawa quickly adopted such a new architectural style, he was not willing to accept Brutalism. In fact he persistently strove for a lively and vigorous space foreign to Brutalism. Several of his buildings, therefore, have been admirably integrated into their environments to afford a sense of liveliness, harmony, and contentment for the citizens.

The major works of Togo Murano in this period consisted of the new Literature Department at Waseda University [Tokyo, 1962], the Hibiya Building of the Nihon Life Insurance Company [Tokyo, 1963], and the head office of Chiyoda Life Insurance Company [Tokyo, 1966]. The three buildings drastically differ from each other, a characteristic typical of his design tendencies. The first building has a pleasant atmosphere created by a well-lit inner court surrounded by campus buildings. The second has an auditorium decorated on its interior with a Gaudí-like treatment of walls and ceilings and modified classical motifs on the balconies. The third has a distinctive appearance because of the cast aluminum panels that cover the entire facade of the building. Prominent in Murano's work, besides a thorough understanding of the relationship between the design-composition of the whole and its perfectly deliberated details, is his manipulation of dramatic spatial relationships in the design of the approach to his buildings.

Isoya Yoshida (1894-1974) was an architect who never quite forgot Japanese traditional design. His practice of disassociating traditional styles and techniques and then reconstructing them in entirely different contexts sets him apart from the creative method of Sutemi Horiguchi which stemmed directly from traditional design. In the 1960s Yoshida designed a series of fine houses done in the Japanese style but completely modified by modern architectural concepts. Yoshida, in this period, also designed some excellent, one-storied, small, art museums of reinforced concrete. The Goto Art Museum [Tokyo, 1960], the Yamato Art Museum [Nara, 1960], and the Gyokudo Art Museum [Ohme, 1961] are all beautiful spaces, with very tranquil interiors, enclosed by the traditional Japanese design of their exterior. Shizutaro Urabe (b. 1909), working in Kurashiki, a place where the traditional Japanese townscape is still preserved, was particularly interested in the concept of architectural localism. The Kurashiki International Hotel [1963] was his first solution relating modern design to a historical environment. With its leaning eaves using beams of reinforced concrete and its facades of white mortar plastering decorated with tiles characteristic of this prefecture, Urabe put forth a new theme of harmony between the universality of modern architecture and the oneness of a particular locality's traditional history.

Two distinctive and creative works mark the generally elevated design-trend of the 1960s. The first, designed by Kenji Imai (b. 1895) to commemorate the martyrdom of twenty-six Japanese saints [Nagasaki, 1962], is a group of memorial buildings consisting of the monument itself, the data library, the chapel of Saint Philip, and the rectory. Imai thought about the theme at great length until he arrived at a final design for these monumental buildings that was the expression of his own religious faith. Since the 1920s he had been interested in works of the Expressionists, Antonio Gaudí (Spain) and

Rudolf Steiner (Germany), and was the first to introduce their styles into Japan. So attracted was he to Gaudí's works that he even completed a part of the twin towers of the chapel and the mosaic phoenix on the side wall of the data library with his own hands. The second work is the head office of Shinwa Bank [Saseho, 1967-1969] by Seiichi Shirai (b. 1905). After graduating from the Kyoto College of Technology, unlike other Japanese architects, Shirai went to Germany to study philosophy under Karl Jaspers and Edward Spranger. Though his career as an architect can be traced from approximately 1935, his most significant architectural work appeared after the war. The Shinwa Bank clearly shows how Shirai's style had been shaped independently of contemporary styles in Japan. The first [1967] and the second phase [1969] of the building's construction were planned separately, yet the result was harmonious. The building itself has an exceptional appearance with its interior and exterior resembling travertine marble sculpture with bronze tiles. Although he conceived the exterior of the building as a box, he molded individual spatial elements such as walls, ceilings, openings, and staircases on the interior with great care. Thus, his building was an accumulation of spatial details that were free from any restriction but related to the totality of the whole. Since each compact detail of the building was expressive enough to make one feel tension, the design of the bank, as a whole, has a strong impact.

Among the comparatively younger architects influenced by Metabolism, Sachio Otani (b. 1924) marked a new point of departure in his Kyoto International Conference Hall [1966] (fig. 28.3)—with its four precast-concrete conference halls of different sizes. Otani won first prize in an open competition for a design that was based on a logical thought process and that resembled ancient Japanese shrines with their slanted, interlocked elements. The major spaces, such as the conference halls and lounge, were elevated in a trapezoidal form, while annexed spaces and offices surmounting them were characteristically raised in a V-shape. Through the use of coherent structural frames these two types of spaces were organically associated and unified in a complete design. Free and imaginative variations of interior spaces were created by a combination of piers and walls with equiangular inclines in contrast with the horizontal arrangement of beams. The novelty of this building lay partially in the architect's new approach to organizing spatial functions. He united individual spaces by adding and associating them within a coherent structural system. Otani consciously aimed at a new method of creating a strong coordination between function and structure. His Kyoto conference hall was no less than a realization of a method that would become established in the forthcoming decade.

28.3. Sachio Otani, architect. Kyoto International Conference Hall, partial view, 1966. (Photograph: Courtesy of Jennifer Taylor)

Masato Otaka, a member of the Metabolism group, proposed a housing project for the town of Sakaide [1968] which seems to have grown out of his Metabolistic views. Some 130 apartments and shops were projected above a reinforced-concrete platform 130,000 square meters in area. The platform was to have been elevated 607 meters to provide space for storage and parking. Otaka intended this project as a model for urban redevelopment, but unfortunately it never was built. The Prefectural Library at Chiba [1968] which, on the other hand, was built, was an attempt to invent a "free space" by combining prefabrication of housing components from the ture was made of precast pillars of cross-shaped section and tieplate beams of high-tensioned prestressed concrete, arranged in a certain formalistic rhythm that expressed the architect's intention.

Kiyonori Kikutake is the architect of many well known, dynamic works, including his own Tokyo home [Sky House, 1958], the office building of the Izumo Grand Shrine at Taisha [1963], the Tokoen Hotel [Kaike Spa, 1963-1965], the Civic Center of Miyakonojo City [Miyakonojo, 1966], and the Civic Center of Hagi City [Hagi, 1968]. Set in a very beautiful garden, the Tokoen Hotel is a clearly modern, dramatic structure in its larger, interlocking masses and volumes. It is also richly articulated in a variety of broad windows and screens that recall remarkably well the proportions and organization of traditional Japanese architecture. While each of Kikutake's buildings is highly interesting, as yet no single, unified architectural motif or style can be easily seen in his succession of works. Quite the contrary, the harmony of his architecture was determined by a functional articulation of a wide variety of traditional and modern modes, as in his Tokoen Hotel and also his two civic center auditoriums. But the architectural perfection of the Izumo Grand Shrine office building in particular seems to have surpassed that of his other buildings. Although it was a simple, small office building constructed with precast and prestressed concrete, its triangular sections and parallel rows of horizontal transverse beams were arranged with a delicate sense of proportion.

During the 1960s Arata Isozaki designed the Oita Prefectural Central Library [Oita, 1966], Fumihiko Maki built the Kumagaya Campus of the Rissho University [Kumagaya, 1967] and Kisho Kurokawa erected the Yamagata Hawaii Dreamland Park [Yamagata, 1967]. It will be more convenient, however, to consider these architects in the context of the architecture of the seventies.

In the sixties, a series of gigantic office buildings, constructed by large architectural design or construction firms in the central zones of metropolises, cannot be overlooked. They include the Kansai Denryoku Building [Osaka, 1960] by Takenaka Komuten Company Ltd.; the Hibiya Denden Building [Tokyo, 1961] by the design section of Nihon Telegraph and Telephone Company; the Palace Side Building [Tokyo, 1966] by Nikken Sekkei, Planners, Architects and Engineers; and the Kajima Construction Company Head Office [Tokyo, 1968] by Kajima Corporation Architects, Engineers and Contractors. Projects by large architectural firms were effected by superlative team coordination and planning, usually directed by an architect of great caliber. Perhaps most outstanding among directing architects are Hideo Kunikata in the design-section of Nihon Telegraph and Telephone Company, Shoji Hayashi in the Nikken Sekkei, Planners, Architects and Engineers, and Shin-ichi Okada in the Kajima Corporation, Architects, Engineers and Contractors, all of whom were concerned with the functional and economic aspects and artistic appeal of their projects. Nevertheless, from this manner of design, a sense of impersonality and anonymity was inevitably intensified in large modern buildings that became distinguishing features forming urban centers.

In Japan, there are huge architectural sections in the largest construction companies such as Takenaka Komuten Company, Ltd., Kajima Architects, Engineers and Contractors Corporation, and Shimizu Construction Company Ltd. These huge construction companies only occasionally engaged in architectural design before the war, but afterwards their efforts intensified enormously. In the sixties the design sections of the huge construction conglomerates had to be considered as organizations in themselves, proud of their quality of design and accomplishment. The greatest advantage for architects in these large construction companies is in the many fellow workers at their disposal, who are engaged in every phase of design and construction from the drawing board to completion of the project. Architects can check aspects of a project through each stage against the latest technical data on architectural design more easily within gigantic cooperations than as independent architects. Thus the design sections of the construction industry, while a problem for the smaller architectural offices, gradually became well established and capable of almost any project.

In the second half of the sixties, effective technological innovation entered not only the processes of construction work but also the design aspects of architecture and planning. The study of modular coordination of building components began by adapting architectural design to the viewpoint of building construction. At the same time, design research through computerization was introduced into building design and planning, and developed into systems engineering. One of the results of this technological development has been the construction of super high-rise buildings. In 1959 the president of the National Railway proposed the rebuilding of the Tokyo Station Offices as a twenty-four-storied high-rise building. In 1964 a law was revised to regulate the ratio of building volume to lot size instead of just regulating the height of buildings. This allowed enough leeway for super high-rise buildings, the first of which, the thirty-six-storied Kasumigaseki Building (Tokyo), was finished in 1968. Ultimately, super high-rise structures were made technologically possible in Japan through the contributions of structural engineers such as Kiyoshi Muto (b. 1903) who had developed new flexible structures and dynamic earthquake-proof designs.

It would be wrong to assume that the architecture of the sixties can be comprehended exclusively through an examination of buildings by architects who were ahead of their time. In this decade, the older traditional aspects of Japan's cities and countryside were almost completely forgotten and replaced by a new view. The driving forces behind this change took the form of large-scale projects sponsored by the government and very large enterprises that included the national traffic network, the construction of new towns in suburban areas within Tokyo, the expansion of industrial cities, and the urban development of huge office buildings. As a consequence of these overwhelming construction projects, the entire country was transformed into a homogeneous space with a new system of order. Individual values of locality, cultural climate, history, tradition, and custom were eradicated and the country was covered with a standardized culture. This great change characterized the sixties in the deepest sense.

Thus, it was not by mere chance that an active concern for vernacular architecture arose in the latter half of the sixties among the younger architects and students. They discerned that certain inherent values abandoned by modern architecture still existed in bypassed towns and villages. Though not immediately reflected in their architecture, this discovery was significant enough to have generated architectural changes in the seventies and perhaps beyond.

THE SEVENTIES: A TIME OF POLARIZATION AND DIVERSIFICATION

Expo '70, the World Exposition held at Osaka in 1970, was intended to sum up the sixties and to predict the progress to come in the seventies. The technology concentrated at the exposition was to promise a hopeful future. Several architects' projects for Future City were exhibited. Those by Kenzo Tange and the Metabolism Group, most of which had been formulated at the beginning of the sixties, at last could be built instead of remaining just plans on paper. The site-planning for the exposition was by Kenzo Tange. Kisho Kurokawa showed his inventive talent by designing two space-frame constructions. One covered the central festival plaza, and the other was a pavilion in the form of a type of capsule architecture which was based on his Metabolic theory and was the first application of its kind. Later in the course of the seventies, he was to realize a number of capsule buildings for practical use. As Futureland, however, Expo '70 was a failure for many Japanese visitors. During the time from the formation of Metabolism in 1960 to Expo '70, technology had progressed and projects of the early sixties had been realized little by little in various cities. Presented at the site of Expo '70 was an enlarged and emphasized aspect of what had already become reality itself. In short, Expo '70 showed vividly that the progress of technology had permeated the lives of the people more rapidly than architects could possibly have imagined.

Kisho Kurokawa's first capsule building construction was the Nakagin Capsule Tower [Tokyo, 1972] (fig. 28.4) which has a fixed central shaft containing elevators, staircases, and the plumbing systems units. Capsules that are mass-produced by the same processes as containers for transportion are fixed to the

28.4. Kisho Kurokawa architect. Nakagin Capsule Tower. Tokyo, 1972. (Photograph: Courtesy of the architect)

shaft with high-tension bolts and are connected to the plumbing system with flexible joints. Each capsule has only a space of 2.5 meters x 3.7 meters in which all the necessary equipment for living is installed. This building seems to have been intended for second apartments or as a hotel in the center of the city, but it has a greater significance as a symbol of the metabolic theory. Following this, Kurokawa built a model house made of capsulized units including bedrooms, kitchen, and a small tea-ceremony room, at Karuizawa in Nagano Prefecture [1973]. Technically speaking, this house has the same details as the Nakagin Capsule Tower, but surprisingly the interior space of the tea-ceremony room capsule of this model house is entirely traditional in design and detail. Referring to the design of this house, Kurokawa says that free combinations of various functions will create new figurative groups and will bring about an image of growth and change. In fact, however, his capsules are nothing but packed-in, narrow spaces loaded with the complicated contents of life. Although Kurokawa has shown genius in utilizing industrial technology in the form of architectural patterns, it seems that from the very beginning he abandoned the effort to reorganize the complicated elements of life into new patterns. Therefore, his capsules have been less successful in residential houses than in buildings such as the Sony Tower [Osaka, 1976] which aimed at visualizing "communication" as the firm's major image.

Kurokawa seeks a theoretical approach in his work, planning structure and space according to technological concepts. He does not refuse traditional approaches out-of-hand either, hoping to achieve a figurative perfection aligned with traditional forms. These two aspects have nothing to do with each other; neither one's logic supports the other's, nor does the one's purpose subsume the other's. In recalling the essence of Metabolism, Kurokawa says that these two points of view were introduced in order to control technological civilization by means of an ecological system and to seek for contact points between modern architecture and Japanese culture. It is doubtful that Japanese culture should have been a starting point of Metabolism. But Kurokawa probably had this in mind for his idea of artistic perfection in the seventies. Rather abruptly, he began to be inclined then toward Japanese Buddhist thought, pluralism, and Japanese ambiguity.

Several of the representative works that Kurokawa built in the seventies with their clarity of motifs and their near perfection of formal arrangement make us almost forget that he is considered avant-garde. In the Headquarters of the Bank of Fukuoka [Fukuoka, 1975] a focal point of his design is located in the space covered by the imposing roof. The Headquarters of the Japan Red Cross [Tokyo, 1977] is a unified building of two distinct blocks that contain, respectively, the Red Cross offices and offices for rental. In the National Ethnological Museum [Suita, 1977] the various levels separate complicated functions but are in fact linked by a core-shaft. Technological figuration is either very much restrained or entirely neglected. Instead, the architect's interest is concentrated on the treatment of the architectural skin formed of stone, metallic tile, glass, and so on. His natural sense of color and his taste for architectural unity and conformity make his works familiar and easy to understand, but these fine characteristics make it difficult to maintain originality and may lead toward the vulgarity of commercialism. In the seventies Kurokawa, stimulated by his deep interest in tradition, participated in the tendency among some architects to reevaluate ornament and architectural eclecticism.

Among the avant-garde of the seventies, the most outstanding and influential architect has been Arata Isozaki. Energetically, through his design and critical activities, he pushed forward with contemporary views for dissolving modern architecture. Based upon a wide review of past architecture, he is especially critical of the architecture of the sixties, and has developed his own methodology with his *Mannerism* as its main axis. It is difficult to summarize his thought, but the following explanation will clarify its essential aspects. Architecture does not merely evolve from an architectural heritage. It can be assumed that by the sixties various concepts formed in unrelated fields permeated achitecture and broke down preconceived ideas. For example, such concepts as Pop Art, computerization, space technology, ecology, epistemology, and so forth, are visualized and then invade architecture's own realm to control it. A classical way of thinking, which always aims at realizing a total entity, has no meaning today because the total entity itself cannot be visualized. Thus, nothing is left but details to give today's architects a key to solid thinking. The details here are not parts organized hierarchically within the whole; on the contrary they are independent; therefore, the outline of architecture is, as it were, nothing more than a sum total of these parts.

Isozaki develops his thoughts based on the relation of the whole and the parts as well as on the process of design according to what he calls "methodology deduced from philology." A metaphor is inserted in each form or part constituting a design unit, and its architecture is expected to be the sole generator of the metaphor. In some cases, his intention was to neutralize the whole space by the presence of many miscellaneous meanings which are complicated and overlapping. In other cases, the space was supposed to be a rhetoric in which the meaning could be clearly read. In short, his architecture has been an experimental essay to see what meaning architecture could add to the cultural context of society by manipulating details semantically.

He prefers a square or a cubic frame as a unit form. After having made experimental attempts in the early seventies in some of the branch offices of the Fukuoka Sogo Bank [Tokyo, 1971; Saga, 1973], he completed the Gunma Prefectural Modern Art Museum [Takasaki, 1974] (fig. 28.5). The exterior skin of this museum is covered with aluminum and glass panes, both in the same pattern of 1.2 meter squares. According to Isozaki, because the project started with the premise that a museum is only a place in which a flow of works of art is temporarily gathered, these square frames themselves form a meaningful metaphor. Thus, the basic structure of this museum, made of cubic space-frames resembling a box-frame lying casually on the lawn, represents the symbolic meaning. The Kita-Kyushu Municipal Museum [Tobata, 1975] also has a clear composition with two long parallel rectangular volumes covered by square panels. These long linear volumes suspended in midair dominate the central axis and emphasize its monumental character. Another of Isozaki's preferred motifs is the vault. The Kita-Kyushu Municipal Central Library [Kokura, 1975] consists of two long curving vaulted tunnellike spaces and blocks adjacent to them. The choice of square or barrel vault indicates that pure geometrical patterns are the starting point of his design. Nevertheless, he is interested in more than the spatial richness a vaulted space alone can create. He curves it, cuts it, or connects it with a dissimilar space; in short, he adopts it as an element with which to compose a discontinuous context. Since he is seeking for various appearances of fragmentary and separate spaces, such qualities as solidity or regularity of the whole space can never be found in his architecture. This is just what he intended from the beginning.

A remarkable tendency in the seventies is found in the attempts to deal with residential housing developments. The interest of the late sixties in the vernacular induced many design surveys of traditional towns. Architects found a new principle of settlement design created by people's life-styles rather

28.5. Arata Isozaki, architect. Gunma Prefectural Museum of Modern Art, Takazaki, 1974. (Photograph: Courtesy of Jennifer Taylor)

than based on monumental architecture, and at last in the seventies they had a chance to see it realized. The low terrace houses of Sakuradai Court Village [Yokohama, 1970] by Shozo Uchii is a pioneer work in this field. For the first time the architect has carefully considered a variety of designs for individual houses with attention to the problems of privacy and openness, systems of approach, and so on. Daikanyama Hillside Terrace [Tokyo] by Fumihiko Maki is regarded as a work that shows the most skillful treatment in the field of settlement design (fig. 28.6) as well as the architect's thoughtful insights into residential structures. Here the houses were built in three stages of construction, 1969, 1973, and 1977; and on a site of only 7,300 square meters three separate units, each containing houses of three stories, continue simply in a line. Most characteristic of this group of houses is that the whole was built according to a minutely detailed plan with the aim of securing the unification of the group and its continuity with the street. While making the most of the long and narrow site (fig. 28.7) along the existing street, Maki tried to keep as much privacy as possible for each house. In this work there is found not only a careful concern for human life but also a delicate reaction to the small natural variations of terrain and to the shape of the site. Both interior and exterior spaces are given a charm of variety by the arrangement of terraces and inner gardens and by the introduction of different floor levels, However, no surprising or extraordinary architectural concepts are used here. The Japanese traditional sense of design in the delicate treatment of uniting interior and exterior and yet keeping them separated is reintroduced here in an entirely new mode creating a new relationship between architecture and environment. Fumihiko Maki studied urban design at Harvard University, and after several years of teaching at Washington University and at Harvard he opened an architectural office in Tokyo in 1965. His design excellence cannot be separated from his profound concern for urban design in general.

He once belonged to the Metabolism group; but what sets him apart from other architects of his generation is that he never tries to extract an architectural design directly from theoretical thinking. Although he has an intense interest in various architectural concepts and technical possibilities, he never loses a sense of balance that controls everything in relation to the whole. Indeed, this defines his works. In some of his works of the seventies, for example, the Kato Gakuen Elementary School [Mishima, 1972], the Marine Life Aquarium built at the site of the Okinawa Marine Exposition [1975], and the Iwasaki Museum [Ibusuki, 1979], it is clear his design principle did not grow out of any preconceived theory or architectural concept. Instead, it was based upon his intense will and delicate innate sense of achieving an assimilation of the whole—architecture and environment.

Next, let us mention the work of Kazuo Shinohara (b. 1925) who exploited a new realm, making the design of single dwellings his main forte. In the sixties, by the time he left the laboratory of professor-architect Kiyoshi Seike, Shinohara had already begun to seek a new kind of space in the design of residences. His interest was concentrated principally on the problem of interior space. With Japanese traditional houses as a starting point, he moved forward unceasingly toward his aim of abstracting space. The process consists of eliminating various common elements composing a house until finally the area is reorganized into a minimum number of spatial components which assume an excessive symbolism. This concern of Shinohara may be considered as an expected outcome of the process of modernizing Japanese traditional space. He has accomplished his objectives with rich imagination, and his works have aroused much interest.

Reviewing the works of the seventies, we note that several old masters were still working vigorously. Kunio Maekawa, with his Saitama Prefectural Museum [Urawa, 1971] and Kumamoto Prefectural Museum [Kumamoto, 1977], has enthusiastically wrestled with the problem of the unification of architecture and plaza. Togo Murano, in his Japan Lutheran Theological College [Mitaka, 1970], has shown that shadows made by folded walls or some other particular devices of lighting could make for an unexpectedly intimate space. Shizutaro Urabe has succeeded in turning the old spinning company (1899) in Kurashiki into a hotel and plaza for young people [Ivy Square, Kurashiki, 1974] while still preserving the old structural body made of red bricks. This was a pioneering work that responded to the new problem of recycling old architecture.

Kenzo Tange, too, continues to work energetically, but his chief arena of activity seems to have moved to foreign countries. Since the Skopie Urban Center Rebuilding Project in 1965, he has continuously been involved with similar large development or redevelopment projects abroad. In general, his design concept seems to be an altered and refined version of the Tokyo Bay Project-60. However, some of his works in the seventies suggest a change of interest: for example, the main theme for the residential area for Catania City in Sicily lies no longer in the megastructure but in urban design that seeks a rela-

28.6. Fumihiko Maki, architect. Daikanyama Hillside Terrace Apartments, general overview. Tokyo, 1966-1977. (Photograph: Courtesy of Shokokusha Publishing Co., Inc.)

tion between architecture and environment.

In retrospect, the changes in the 1970s revealed that the trends were not only those promoted by our third generation of architects but included the ideals of a wider range of architects. Architects continued to work with large construction firms using innovative technological approaches, as for example in the Aquapolis, Expo '75, Okinawa, a high-tech model of an offshore city (fig. 28.8) by Kiyonari Kikutake and Mitsubishi Heavy Industries, 1975. It was also characteristic of the seventies that large architectural offices contributed to the development of skyscrapers, such as the IBM Headquarters Building [Tokyo, 1972] and the Sumitomo 3M Ltd. Building [Tokyo, 1974], both by Nikken Sekkei, Planners, Architects, and Engineers, and the Shinjuku Mitsui Building [Tokyo, 1975] by Nihon Architects, Engineers, and Consultants. It may be that the architects of these big firms as well as architects working for general construction companies can make the most of the technology acquired through the experience of Expo '70. Their capabilities have proven to be especially strong in urban redevelopment.

The Ashiyahama high-rise housing clusters [Ashiya, 1979] can be cited as an example of vanguard technology as reflected in a large project. It was planned in cooperation with the government, the community, and the Nihon Jutaku Kodan (the Japan Housing Corporation). In 1972 a combine of firms including Nippon Steel Corporation, Takenaka Komuten Company Ltd., and Matsushita Electric Works Ltd. won the competition for this project and it was completed in 1979 using a variety of remarkable new construction processes. Among them were standardization in the production system; complete prefabrication; product and quality controls throughout by manufacturers and builders; and systematization of fire prevention, regional air conditioning, water supply, trash collection, and so on. Certainly such technological systems could not have been realized without the cooperation of large and public groups.

The basic body of the high-rise building forms a gridlike megastructure made of core-shafts and beams crossing the common floors, in which dwelling-capsule units made of PC plates are inserted. In the final analysis, this project proved to be a magnificent experiment that brought to realization plans once considered only as a futuristic city. Its accomplishment has shown that the Japanese construction industry had the power to realize an idealized structure. Even if the appearance of the housing clusters lacks a poetic mood, the intended aim of pro-

28.7. Fumihiko Maki, architect. Daikanyama Hillside Terrace Apartments, view from street. Tokyo, 1966-1977. (Photograph: Courtesy of Kaneaki Monma)

moting industrial methods in building has been achieved.

Looking back over the seventies, perhaps we cannot draw the architecture of the whole decade into a unified image, for it was a period dominated by variety. The energy of the sixties continued in modified form into the seventies and the tendency to promote industrialization and commercialization of space according to a uniform sense of value judgements has never declined. But, on the other hand, with the coming of the oil crisis and widespread pollution, the glorious future predicted in the sixties has completely faded away.

A subtle change is beginning to appear in architecture. Instead of spatial concepts with magnificent megastructures, more delicate and softer aspects relating to human life now attract architects' attention as their new subject in common. Each architect

28.8. Kyonori Kikutake, architect, with Mitsubishi Heavy Industries. Aquapolis, Expo '75, Okinawa. (Photograph: Courtesy of Toru Waki)

is preparing solutions to the new situation according to his own design policy, but essentially no one is certain of the directions that the architecture of Japan will take in the future.

Bibliography

BOOKS

Drew, Philip. *Third Generation—The Changing Meaning of Architecture.* Stuttgart: Verlag Gerd Hatje, 1972.

Horiguchi, Sutemi. *Horiguchi Sutemi Sakuhin—Ie to Niwa no Kukan Kosei* [The works of Sutemi Horiguchi—space construction of his houses and gardens. Tokyo: Kajima-Shuppankai, 1974.

Jencks, Charles. *Modern Movements in Architecture.* Harmondworth: Penguin Books, 1973.

Kikutake, Kiyonori, ed. *Kiyonori Kikutake: Works and Methods 1956-1970* (in Japanese) Tokyo: Bijutsu-Shuppansha, 1973.

______. *Kiyonori Kikutake: Concepts and Planning* (in Japanese). Tokyo: Bijutsu-Shuppansha, 1978.

Kultermann, Udo, ed. *New Japanese Architecture.* New York: Praeger, 1960.

______., ed. *Kenzo Tange: Architecture and Urban Design, 1946-1969,* New York: Praeger, 1970.

Kurita, Isamu, ed. *Gendai Nihon Kenchikuka Zenshu* [The Complete Works of Contemporary Architects in Japan]. 24 vols. Tokyo: San-ichi-shobo, 1970-1975. Vols.: 1. *Antonin Raymond*; 2. *Togo Murano*; 3. *Isoya Yoshida*; 4. *Sutemi Horiguchi*; 5. *Motoo Take, Kenji Imai*; 6. *Yoshio Taniguchi*; 7. *Takeo Sato*; 8. *Junzo Yoshimura*; 9. *Seiichi Shirai*; 10. *Kenzo Tange*; 11. *Junzo Sakakura, Bunzo Yamaguchi*; 12. *Hiroshi Ohe, Shizutaro Urabe*; 13. *Makoto Masuzawa, Taro Amano, Tsutomu Ikuta*; 14. *Yoshichika Uchida, Teiichi Takahashi, Yasumi Yoshitake, Tomoya Masuda*; 15. *Yoshinobu Ashihara, Takamasa Yoshizaka*; 16. *Kiyoshi Seike*; 17. *Kenji Hirose, Kiyoshi Ikebe*; 18. *Masato Ohtaka, Sachio Ohtani*; 19. *Fumihiko Maki, Kiyonori Kikutake*; 30. *Shin-ichi Okada, Taneo Oki, Kimio Yogoyama*; 21. *Arata Isozaki, Kisho Kurokawa, Hiroshi Hara*; 22. *Kiyoshi Kawasaki, Masako Hayashi*; 23-24. *Other Architects.*

Kurokawa, Kisho, ed. *Architecture of Metabolism—Kisho Kurokawa* (in Japanese). Tokyo: Nobel-shobo, 1969.

______, ed. *Kurokawa Kisho no Sekai* [The works of Kisho Kurokawa]. Tokyo: Mainichi-shinbunsha, 1975.

Kurokawa, Noriaki (Kisho). *Metabolism in Architecture.* London: Studio Vista, 1977.

Maki, Fumihiko. *Metabolism 1960.* Tokyo: Bijutsu-shuppansha, 1960.

______. *Investigations in Collective Form*. St. Louis: Washington University Press, 1964.

Murano, Togo, ed. *Murano Togo wafu Kenchiku Shu* [Works in Japanese *Style Architecture* by Togo Murano]. Tokyo: Shinkenchiku-sha, 1978.

Raymond, Antonin. *Antonin Raymond—An Autobiography*. Tokyo: Kajima-shuppankai, 1970.

Ross, Michael Franklin. *Beyond Metabolism: The New Japanese Architecture*. New York: McGraw-Hill, 1978.

Shinohara, Kazuo, ed. *16 Houses by Kazuo Shinohara and His Architectural Theory* (in Japanese). Tokyo: Bijutsu-shuppansha, 1971.

______, ed. *11 Houses by Kazuo Shinohara and His Architectural Theory* (in Japanese). Tokyo: Bijutsu-shuppansha, 1976.

Shirai, Seiichi. *The Works of Seiichi Shirai* (in Japanese). Tokyo: Chuokoronsha, 1974.

______, ed. *Seiichi Shirai: Works and Essays* (in Japanese). Tokyo: Sekaibunkasha, 1978.

Tange, Kenzo, ed. *Kenzo Tange 1946-1958: Actuality and Creation* (in Japanese). Tokyo: Bijutsu-shuppansha, 1966.

______, ed. *Kenzo Tange 1955-1964: Technology and Man* (in Japanese). Tokyo: Bijutsu-shuppansha, 1968.

______, ed. *Kenzo Tange: Architecture and Cities* (in Japanese). Tokyo: Sekaibunkasha, 1975.

Yoshida, Isoya, ed. *Yoshida Isoya Sakuhin Shu* [The works of Isoya Yoshida]. Tokyo: Shinkenchikusha, 1976.

JOURNALS

Ishii, Kazuhiro and Suzuki, Hiroyuki, eds. "Post-Metabolism: The New Wave in Japanese Architecture." *Japan Architect*, October-November 1977.

Isozaki, Arata. "About My Method." *Japan Architect*, August 1972.

______. "The Metaphor of the Cube." *Japan Architect*, March 1976.

______. "Rhetoric of the Cylinder." *Japan Architect*, April 1976.

Jencks, Charles. "Arata Isozaki and Radical Eclecticism." *Architectural Design*, January 1977.

Kurokawa, Kisho. "Two Systems of Metabolism." *Japan Architect*, December 1967.

______. "Architecture of Grays." *Japan Architect*, June 1979.

Maki, Fumihiko. "At the Beginning of the Last Quarter of the Century." *Japan Architect*, April 1975.

______. "Japanese City Spaces and the Concept of Oky." *Japan Architect*, May 1979.

Nitschke, Günter. "The Metabolists of Japan." *Architectural Design*, October 1964.

______. "Japan's Second Heroic Age—The Age of Barbarism." *Architectural Design*, May 1965.

Okada, Shin'ichi. "Architectural Language for a Design Method." *Japan Architect*, January 1973.

Shinohara, Kazuo. "The Savage Machine as an Exercise." *Japan Architect*, March 1979.

Smithson, A. and Smithson, P., guest eds. "The Rebirth of Japanese Architecture." *Architectural Design*, February 1961.

29

MEXICO

EDITH S. SANDERSON
and WARREN SANDERSON

In Mexico, a land of exceptionally strong beauty and extraordinary contrasts, indigenous civilizations and a replanted Spanish culture have shaped a uniquely American people—the Mexicans of today. For more than three thousand to four thousand years of the architecture that is Mexico's heritage various pre-Hispanic cultures constructed works which ranged from the severity of Teotihuacán buildings in their dry topographical environment to the "plastic and ornamental lushness of the Mayan buildings" in the jungle.[1] The Spanish impressed their image on architecture for three hundred years. New towns were planned following Spanish rules, modified by local conditions; and many colonial churches remain as notable examples of Spanish styles.

Though Spanish prototypes were used, buildings retained a local character, built with local materials by local artisans. A most important early innovation in church architecture was the concept of the chapel open to the sky. This suited the climate, the indigenous population which had not conceived of a public building as enclosed interior space, and the Spanish who found it practical. By the eighteenth century we can recognize a formal language of decoration which developed into a distinguishably national idiom. Late in the eighteenth century a neoclassical style became popular though no particularly distinguished buildings were erected, perhaps because such buildings were usually intellectual exercises superimposed on the local scene. Independent Mexico, after 1869, favored a diversity of styles from different parts of the world, while the desire for an architecture that demonstrated national characteristics became pronounced after the 1910 Revolution. By the 1920s architects made their choices from among the favored styles, colonial eighteenth-century or pre-Hispanic, with some looking for inspiration to the salons of the Decorative Arts Exhibition of Paris in 1925.[2]

In the 1920s also, the International Style came to Mexico. A very few people, such as José Villagrán García, saw the importance of the new ideas of Functionalism as expounded by people like Gropius, but especially by Le Corbusier in *Vers une Architecture*. Not only was the new architecture with its lack of decoration theoretically and formally exciting but also it could be built with an economy that made it very exciting in its potential for finding solutions to the urgent health, social, educational, and housing needs of the nation. José Villagrán García's Institute of Hygiene and Sanatorium at Huipulco, D.F.[3] [1925] became the teaching example of modern Functionalism. His students at the National Academy then included Juan Legorreta, Juan O'Gorman, Enrique de la Mora y Palomar, and Enrique Yáñez de la Fuenta. Most of the architects of Mexico today have studied under him or with his students. Among the outstanding buildings of this time are O'Gorman's[4] house and studio for the eminent artist Diego Rivera in San Angel [1929-1930]; his Vocational School [1933] and a series of schools constructed for the Ministry of Public Education [1932-1936]. Juan Legorreta built the first workers' housing development in the Balbuena section of Mexico City in 1934. Many modern buildings were erected in the 1930s because they were theoretically interesting and economically satisfying. Moreover, the government recognized them as symbols of progress in themselves and as important for its social programs. This trend, especially the building of schools, hospitals, and public buildings, was continued vigorously in the early forties, though slowed during the war years.

The 1940s and early 1950s were a time of especially great enthusiasm. Architectural ideas and realizations were numerous. Privately financed buildings abounded; but beyond that, social programs seen as of the greatest importance for Mexico were reconsidered and enlarged with more and more effort put to their implementation.

The first large-scale housing development in Mexico was built as low-cost housing for civil employees under the auspices of the Pensiones Civiles by Mario Pani and a team that included Salvador Ortega Flores, the young architects González de León, Armando Franco, Guillermo Rossell de la Lama, Castro Montiel, and the engineer Bernardo Quintana. Built in 1947-1949, the complex Presidente Miguel Alemán contains 1080 apartments in a series of zigzagging thirteen-story buildings along with three-story buildings, post office, playgrounds, nursery centers, school, social center, shops, and swimming pools. In the 1980s the *Multifamiliar Alemán* has remained one viable answer to the problem of housing in Mexico. The complex has been described as born from the language of the Bauhaus and influenced by Le Corbusier in its play of light and volumes;[5] but especially its use of color, texture, and materials makes it a part of Mexico's architectonic language. While it reflects a major problem of our time, in which structures are built to last only fifteen to twenty years, its concepts and design have withstood time with dignity. The multifamily complex's continuing vitality is based on several factors. Among them are urbanistic-architectonic solutions that require a density of no more than one thousand people per hectare, leaving 80 percent of the terrain for gardens; the type of construction, and the use of materials such as the familiar tile and twentieth-century concrete. Rough-treated (*martelinado*) concrete was used in Mexico for the first time at the complex and the quality of these structures was significantly tested when they withstood the 1947 and 1957 earthquakes without damage.

This *Multifamiliar* was quickly followed by others. At the President Juárez Housing Development [Mexico, D.F., 1952] Pani and Salvador Ortega Flores continued to improve and develop the ideas demonstrated at the Alemán. Through traffic was eliminated and numerous dwellings that range from a thirteen-story slab to single-story buildings were spaciously arranged. Some were decorated by Carlos Mérida, while the openwork wall of cement blocks provides a practical decoration that allows ventilation and, at the same time, reminds one of native tilework.[6] Balbuena Gardens [Mexico, D.F., 1956] by Félix Sánchez, chief architect, is a huge complex for fifty-thousand people housed in a variety of buildings from ten-story-slab high rises to detached houses. A self-contained subdivison built chiefly by financing from the Bank for Mortgages and Public Works, Balbuena was planned to represent a variety of income groups in a complicated, thoughtful plan.

An organized program for the building of hospitals had begun in the late thirties. In the early forties the hospitals built, for example, by José Villagrán García—the Hospital of Jesus and the Matérnidad Arturo Mundet in 1943—were two among an increasing number. Under the Mexican Institute of Social Security (IMSS), formed in 1944, an increasing number of facilities were and are being added.[7] The highly respected architect Enrique Yáñez de la Fuente has become perhaps best known for his hospital construction. The Hospital de la Raza, D.F., was built in 1945. In 1952 the Main Social Insurance Hospital (Zone No. 1) complex was completed including facilities for 800 beds, a large outpatient clinic and a school for nurses. The buildings rest on wooden piles. Facilities depended upon the best theories for patient care of the time and include sculptured decoration as well as murals by David Alfaro Siqueiros (in the vestibule of the nurses' auditorium) and by Diego Rivera (in the main entrance hall). While hospital care was being extended in Mexico City, facilities in the rest of the country were not being built with the same speed.

In school building the situation was different. A concerted regard for education has been a constant factor in Mexican planning. The functional schools built so economically by O'Gorman in the 1930s were followed by major programs through the early 1940s. The Committee for School Planning, created in 1944, commissioned the building of thousands of schools throughout Mexico to be "free of extravagance in design, correspond to the economic and social realities of the school region and satisfy pedagogical requirements."[8] The effectiveness of the school building programs was hampered most by Mexico's population explosion. Moreover, very real difficulties were encountered because of lack of skilled labor. The transportation of materials was a difficulty with only 9,940 kilometers of roads in the country in 1940; and there were serious problems because of the large variety of environmental and climatic differences in Mexico. The *El Pipila* Elementary School [Mexico, D.F., 1950] by Pedro Ramírez Vázquez, Alfonso Garduño, and Horacio Boy, uses open corridors, has an open auditorium with brightly colored walls, and is carefully sited on the sloping land. A school by Luis G. Rivadeneyra, who built many in the state of Veracruz, uses traditional building methods in a three-story building of reinforced concrete with brick infilling that was stuccoed. Here, even play areas are sheltered because of the rain. Regional traditions and practical economics led Enrique del Moral to build a village school using local brick and tile, and peeled logs as columns. A variety of constructions and construction trends arose from respect for regional differences, the use of traditional building methods and materials, an awareness of geographical and climatic variation, and from the new uses of modules and prefabrication. These elements were considered and incorporated into clearer formulations of programs in the late fifties under the leadership of Ramírez Vázquez.

Technical schools were also built in many states increasing in number in the late forties. The Normal School Ribera de San Cosme [Mexico, D.F., built by Enrique Yáñez, 1946] is a functional concrete and brick campus on a tree-lined terrain. The 1945 Normal School by Mario Pani on the Tacuba Highway in Mexico, D.F., on a wedge-shaped tract, has a highly abstract plan that radiates from an apex and is crossed by a broadly arching, sectioned, slab building. A mural by José Clemente Orozco enhances the large, open auditorium that expands in front of this crossing element.

Architecturally interesting and exciting structures were being raised in every area of building. The Purisima Church at Monterrey [1947] by Enrique de la Mora was Mexico's first modern-style building using parabolic concrete shells. In 1952 Félix Candela and Raúl Fernández built a warehouse using economic and light, but strong, reinforced-concrete roofing. Employed in the shape of a series of gently curved elegantly lyrical vaults, this scheme was to be applied in a variety of ways and a variety of buildings in the years to come.

Juan Sordo Madaleno's movie theatre of 1950-1951 in Mexico City is a large volume, simple in its wedge-shaped lateral elevation and covering most of a city block. The Insurgentes Theater, Mexico, D.F., was built in 1952 by Alejandro Prieto with his brother Julio Prieto, the well-known set designer, as technical advisor. The structure's simplicity of volumetric buildup expresses its clear Functionalism; and upon its convex facade is a mural by Diego Rivera depicting the history of theater in Mexico. One of the most unusual works of architecture was the short-lived experimental theater, El Eco (the echo) [Mexico, D.F., 1952] by Mathias Goeritz with Luis Barragán as architectural advisor. Its design was developed more in the manner of an expressive sculptural discovery than as a carefully worked-out building. The effects of space were a primary concern, with diagonal accents and perspectival surprises serving to disorient the viewer.

The office space needed by Mexico's growing business sector was built using some of the best of contemporary Mexican thinking. One of the finest examples of such work is the Ministry of Hydraulic Resources Building [Mexico, D.F., 1946-1950] by Mario Pani and Enrique del Moral (fig. 29.1). The

29.1. Mario Pani and Enrique del Moral, architects. Ministry of Hydraulic Resources Building. Mexico City, 1946-1950. (Photograph: Courtesy of Edith S. Sanderson)

twenty-two-story reinforced-concrete building on the Paseo de la Reforma is built on the flotation principle to withstand earthquakes. A nearby building, also by Pani, in collaboration with Jesús García Collantes in 1951 on the same boulevard has a welded steel frame on a floating foundation that reaches thirty-one feet down. Originally the American Embassy occupied several floors, and now Sanborn's department store is located there.

The two buildings, located upon one side of the Paseo de la Reforma, are separated by a similar tall office slab erected by Juan Sordo Madaleno in 1958. There are many similarities between them, since they were begun only a few years apart, and their interrelationships are compelling. Both are on triangular lots, thanks to Mexico City's numerous diagonal crossing streets, and, in each, three elevators are prominently located opposite the apex of their triangular plan. Upon their facades narrow continuous bands of reinforced concrete alternate with broad, slightly recessed, continuous strips of windows; each building steps back to form a terrace at about two-thirds of its height. The most important difference between them is in the treatment of their most prominent corners, both of which face south: the south corner of the ministry building is flattened and broadly curved inward, while for the equivalent surface of the later building the lower two-thirds simply curves the corner, but from the terrace up the curve is reversed as in the ministry building. The two seem like members of a close family of high rises responding in a relatively Baroque fashion to the problems of corner siting and the expression of subtle interrelationships.

Apartment house design in the hands of Mexico's modern architects during the late forties and early fifties tended also to utilization of the functionalist theories of the International Style, as in Augusto H. Alvarez's three-story building in Mexico, D.F. Two other apartment buildings of special interest are both near Chapultepec park. A six-unit three-story apartment house by Abraham Zabludovsky has two units per floor and is sited to allow each apartment a maximum of light and view. One of the first of its kind, Augusto H. Alvarez and Juan Sordo Madaleno's nine-story building has sixteen units, with a large store at the ground level, and garages beneath. Long, broad balconies adjoin the living rooms, as in Zabludovsky's smaller building, and offer shade and a view, while giving the whole a sense of a decorative though solid rhythm.

Some of the most advanced concepts, as is so often the case, were being realized by architects not in the larger commercial buildings but in private homes. In Mario Pani's house in Cuernavaca, Morelos [1950], for example, straight, clean lines of the International Style and large walls of glass panels take advantage of the excellent climate and beautiful mountainous view. For this house the architect devised a plan of interlocking, stepped rooms in the sleeping area and a broad, open space in most of the living portion. In this fine design he has used materials from various regions—Puebla marble, Oaxaca stone, and Yucatán wood. Many other architects found interesting solutions for residences, the best integrating functional concepts and modern construction techniques with local requirements of topography and climate, traditional building methods and materials. Prominent among the architects of such residential buildings were Jorge González Reyna and Rafael Arozarena, Jorge Rubio, Nicholas Mariscal, Jorge Osorio and Mario Schetjnan Garduño, Luis G. Rivadeneyra, Max Cetto, Juan Sordo Madeleno, Guillermo Rossell, and Lorenzo Carrasco.

In the mid-1940s Luis Barragán acquired 865 acres of El Pedregal, San Angel, on the south of Mexico City. Created 2500 years ago by volcanic eruption, the area consists of solidified, purplish gray, lava rock in strange shapes and a variety of wild vegetation. Barragán envisioned here a new area of the city where architects would build simple, modern homes (no "colonial" homes here), as "retreats" with the "garden as the soul of the house,"[9] all placed behind the front walls so preferred for privacy. He built three wild and beautiful gardens to illustrate his beliefs that an economy of man's efforts in a natural environment allows for a maximum of visual effect. While the building codes he devised were often sadly ignored, many architects did build with respect for the almost surrealistic, natural setting. The first house built in the Pedregal was that of architect Max Cetto [1949]. Planned to fit into the rocky land and built mostly of a lava-rubble masonry with pin planks and exposed concrete, the rustic exterior of this L-shaped house encloses rooms that are both quadratic and irregular in shape but always finely functional. The garden planned by Mrs. Cetto is full-grown now, after thirty years, and unites with the architecture to make the house an organic part of its environment. Civilized man and thick lush nature live here in mutual and full harmony.

Santiago Greenham and Francisco Artigas placed a single-storied house on a concrete vault [compare Amancio Williams's house, Argentina, 1945] that bridged a natural break in the rocks which now forms a swimming pool. Oblong in plan with half its space for sleeping quarters and half for the living areas, it is connected by a ramp with the breakfast room and servants' quarters in a geometrically perfected functional design. Enrique del Moral and Manuel Rosen are among many other architects who built in the Pedregal during the fifties.

The progressive social concerns of the leaders of Mexico were demonstrated in the housing projects, hospitals, and schools we have described. What better method to lead the way to a better future, though, than in building a new university center as a perfect expression of contemporary policy? The university, founded in 1551 and the oldest in America, had been housed in old, inadequate structures throughout the city. Land in the Pedregal was acquired. Mario Pani and Enrique del Moral were asked to implement their master plan and to coordinate the works of all the architects involved. A young architect, Carlos Lazo, became executive director of about 150 architects, engineers, technical staff, and consultants and about 6000 workmen. The National Autonomous University of Mexico (UNAM) [1950-1953], intended to serve an expected student body of 25,000, now has about 50,000 on the University City campus alone, according to Mario Pani. Many architects, spanning several generations, built here, including in addition to those mentioned, Francisco J. Serrano, Juan Sordo Madaleno, Enrique Yáñez, Félix Candela, Enrique Guerrero, Guillermo Rossell, Roberto Álvarez Espinosa, Pedro Ramírez Vázquez, Ramón Torres, Vladimir Kaspé, and Alonso Mariscal. Here the words of José Villagrán García, the teacher of many of the architects and, with Alfonso Liceaga and Xavier Lascurain, designer of the school of architecture and art museum, were to be realized. Youth endowed with such promising artistic talent "should create authentically out of its own time."[10]

On the irregular terrain of the Pedregal, the huge University City was organized originally into four, very large sections; and by the seventies a fifth was added to it, greatly increasing its area. The academic campus and sports recreation sectors are separated from the enormous Olympic Stadium and nearby university residential area by a major north-south highway, while peripheral roadways bound each of these four sectors in an eminently functional approach to planning. The academic buildings are organized around a great grass quadrangle that is open in a series of smaller plazas to the west, bounded by rectangular clusters of cubiform and slab-like buildings to the south and east and by an extraordinarily long alignment to the north of three very much alike, oblong humanities buildings on *pilotis*. Set upon the western plaza confronting the entrance into the academic sector, the central administration building by Mario Pani, Enrique del Moral, and Salvador Ortega Flores consists of a fourteen-story tower on *pilotis* adjoined by a broad, low wing on the south. The tower is articulated in tall, interlocking, massive, rectangular shafts. At the fifth floor there is a dramatic spatial intervention: along the full length of north and south sides a bay is opened revealing three free-standing *pilotis*; and on the north side at the thirteenth floor there is another less dramatic void. Here is a high rise that refers in its daring design to the efforts of the European pioneers of modern architecture. At the northwest corner of the quadrangle Juan O'Gorman's library building provides a lesser accent behind the administrative structures, and far to the east on the quadrangle a second major accent of elevation exists in the fifteen-story research tower of the faculty of sciences by Raúl Cacho, Eugenio Peschard, and Félix Sánchez, a high-rise slab of reinforced concrete and glass. In the recreation area diagonally aligned fronton courts lend a peculiarly Mexican quality, while across the highway the Olympic Stadium, huge as it is and with its gentle contours, seems to nestle into the land.

At the university Félix Candela worked with architect Jorge González Reyna in the construction of the very small pavilion for cosmic ray research (fig. 29.2) to create a structure which is mostly a barrel-

29.2. Félix Candela and Jorge González Reyna, architects. Pavilion for Cosmic Ray Research. University City (UNAM), Mexico, D.F., 1952. (Photograph: Courtesy of Edith S. Sanderson)

vaulted roof—a roof whose concrete shell was then the thinnest (five-eighths of an inch thick) ever made. Candela's work is most remarkable. Spanish-born, he was no doubt familiar with the outstanding structures of the engineer Eduardo Torroja. Candela's construction methods, his knowledge and ability, and his innate sense of beauty allowed him to be able to cover all types of buildings, all sizes of buildings, with a seemingly infinite variety of concrete shapes which are economical to construct. Candela built many more structures in Mexico (and elsewhere) featuring the distinctive, seemingly free-form, hyperbolic paraboloid, shell-thin roofs—for churches, homes, factories, restaurants, gas stations, and markets.

The Modern Movement in architecture had been vital in Mexico for almost twenty-five years. At the same time there had been a continuing searching or questioning of what was an especially Mexican architecture. This often led to unimaginative copies and pastiches of colonial houses and to very self-conscious efforts. No one, it seems, realized that a peculiarly Mexican contemporary architecture could be seen in the already extant work of Luis Barragán. For many years the best of Mexico's painters had been less concerned with contemporary problems in painting than with social and political ones. They saw their work much as the Medieval and early Renaissance church muralists had seen theirs—as visual narratives for the edification of the masses. Many of the vast murals and frescoes of Diego Rivera, David Alfaro Siqueiros, and José Clemente Orozco were executed superbly in what might be called a genuine socialist realist style. A number of architects wished to integrate an architecture based on the International Style and theories of Functionalism with art, in order to create uniquely Mexican work, as had been achieved for instance in precolonial times when, for example, the nose of a figure on the exterior of a pyramid functioned as the pyramid's step.

At University City the effort to integrate architecture and art usually took the form of applying large works of art to functionalist buildings or of facing their rectangular surfaces with tiles, glass, and so on, as well as using works of art within. There are three murals by José Chávez Morado on the exterior of the Faculty of Sciences building and three murals by Siqueiros on the Central Administration Building, including his huge, polychromed wall sculpture covering the low wing. Sculptors such as Rodrigo Arenas Betancourt and Francisco Zuñiga have large works of sculpture on campus.

The best-known effort at integration, however, was to be the main library (fig. 29.3), built to house more than two million items, by Juan O'Gorman, Gustavo Saavedra, and Juan Martínez de Velasco. Basically the building is a ten-story, simple, mostly windowless rectangle posited on a much lower, wider base. The large cubiform library presented a perfect opportunity to decorate four sides with multicolored mosaics of stone from all over Mexico. Each side graphically or symbolically tells a different story—the pre-Hispanic past, the Hispanic period, Mexico today, and the directions of the university and Mexico for the future. The pedestal is covered with a variety of designs and reliefs.

The university's *frontons*, the ball courts for a sport with roots in pre-Hispanic times, were designed by Alberto T. Arai. The three perpendicular concrete walls of each court have been faced externally with sloping walls of native stone. The area between is sufficient for the necessary dressing and shower facilities. The slope of these walls gives an appearance to the whole of a series of small mountains

29.3. Juan O'Gorman, Gustavo Saavedra and Juan Martínez de Velasco, architects. Library. University City (UNAM), Mexico, D.F., 1950. (Photograph: Courtesy of Edith S. Sanderson)

or cut-off pre-Hispanic pyramids that echo the nearby mountain landscape. These courts are beautifully and uniquely Mexican.

At the large eighty-thousand seat Olympic Stadium the unexpected happened. A team of architects was forced to change plans because modern technology using steel or reinforced cement was too costly. Instead, the earth and the lava stone taken from the center was piled up around the sides to form the stands. Concrete was used only for the access tunnels. The resulting stadium by Augusto Pérez Palacios, Raúl Salinas Moro, and Jorge Bravo Jiménez is a gently curved and sloped construction which is so organically sited that it seems to have grown from its setting, as, in a way, it did. Even the polychrome stone mosaic in medium-high relief by Diego Rivera, curving over the main entrances, seems an integral part of the whole.

By the early 1950s, a few avant-garde architects realized that applying a rather traditional, sometimes Baroque, populist style of sculpture and art to the stripped-down, coolly intellectual, formally simple architecture of the International Style was not the way to integrate art and architecture to produce a Mexican mode. Furthermore, the unadulterated International Style seemed no better suited to Mexico than was the consciously intellectual neo-Classicism of the nineteenth century. Juan O'Gorman was most concerned that, while architects had been learning the theories of Le Corbusier and Mies van der Rohe, they had sadly neglected the work of Frank Lloyd Wright.

An Organic approach was often better suited to considerations of the total Mexican environment. O'Gorman's ideas, often prophetically intense intuitions that brooked no compromise, led him to consider his earlier work totally as social romanticism and to build a new house in the Pedregal in 1956. The living room was a grotto of lava rock; the whole house was encrusted with polychrome mosaics on the interior and the exterior. In all, it was a mannered, if not antirational, expression with influences of Gaudí, the "Holy Wood" at Bomarzo near Viterbo, Italy [1560], and somewhat reminiscent of Ferdinand Cheval's [1879-1912] dream palace at Hauterives, Drôme, France. O'Gorman sold this masterpiece of individualism with its land in 1959. The new owner, for whatever perverse reasons of her own, had the house destroyed—a loss to us all. We can tell at what location it once stood by the tile decoration still extant on the outside property wall facing on the street.

It was rarely recognized that the Olympic Stadium at University City had achieved the real integration of arts in architecture that occurs when a work succeeds so well it can be called art. Moreover, it was so appropriate for its purpose and its particular setting that it became a peculiarly Mexican example of architecture. And the fronton courts for the same reasons are uniquely Mexican architectural solutions.

Max Cetto wrote that "Mexican architecture can be good only when it harmonizes with its environment, and it will be Mexican of its own accord when it is good."[11] How fitting a statement that is when applied to the work of Luis Barragán. In describing Barragán's three-level house of 1947 in Tacubaya, set in a now wild garden, Emilio Ambasz said, "The house's architectural vocabulary owes little to the International Style of modern architecture. It represents a most subtle elaboration of that part of Mexico's provincial architecture Barragán loves so much: its ranches, villages, and convents."[12]

Luis Barragán is a native of Guadalajara, a city whose residents are often most comfortable with the colonial house. The plans for this type arrived in Mexico by way of southern Spain, where the concept of the home as walled enclosure came originally from Islamic notions of compartmentalized and successive garden spaces. His appreciation of the close relation between house and garden was reinforced by his trip to Spain and the gardens of the Alhambra in 1924.

Instead of merely opening a building to nature, Barragán creates in such a way that walls often seemed individual parts of nature. These act with their surroundings, earth, rock, shrubbery, water, or sky, to help form the sense of an enclosure, a work of architecture. No passive part, the wall takes on the role of an almost heroic, yet symbiotic, element in design. In this respect, Barragán seems not so much to have paralleled but, instead, independently to have enriched the vocabulary of De Stijl and Cubist architecture. His rental houses for Mr. Robles León and a house for Mrs. Harper de Garibi, all in Guadalajara, Jalisco [1928], may be described as having a formal simplicity that has been distilled and refined to take greatest advantage of natural conditions of climate and light. These earlier houses were white. Later he used vivid color for greater effect, even theatrical effect, as in the chapel for the Capuchinas Sacramentarias del Purísimo Corazón de Maria in Tlalpan, Mexico, D.F. [1952-1955].

In 1957-1958 Barragán and Mathias Goeritz built the five abstract towers of Satellite City, Queretaro Highway, Mexico City. From 100 to 165 feet high, the towers are brightly painted, seem to change shape when viewed from different angles and can be seen at a great distance. Whether they should be considered as an advertisement for the new subdivision or as aesthetically pleasing, rather Mannerist, abstract sculptures may depend on the sophistication of the viewer. I do believe, however, that one cannot consider them as architecture since architecture does serve a function as an enclosure for human activities. While I am quite aware that Barragán's walls may sometimes be little more than freestanding or almost freestanding expanses, they still are parts of a total architectural enclosure.

Where the beauty of Barragán's architecture resides in his carefully attuned personal arrangements of walls and spaces, the poetry of Félix Candela resides in his elegant, concrete, geometric forms that are applicable to a variety of architectural purposes. During the fifties Candela's work came to be much in demand and changed Mexico's landscape. He insisted that he used a sense of balance and understanding of physical forces much more than differential calculus in devising his ever more varied concrete shells. Included among his projects have been churches [the Church of the Miraculous Virgin, Mexico, D.F., 1954], factories [Bacardi Plant, Cuatitlan, 1963], the romantic, floating restaurant in Xochimilico [D.F., 1958] with Joaquin Alvarez Ordoñez, and markets. Instead of the tents and awnings of the traditional marketplace, Candela has created similar visual effects with sequences of delicate, inverted umbrellas of reinforced concrete that shelter people from the sun and rain, as at the "Jamaica" market, Mexico City. The same principle, in which each quadrant of each "umbrella" is a perfect hyperbolic paraboloid, is evident in the roofing of the market hall at Coyocoán, Mexico City, built with Pedro Ramírez-Vázquez and Rafael Mijares, where rows of roofs are at different heights and glass clerestories course between them. The pillars supporting these reversed vaults take very little space and serve simultaneously as drainage channels from the roofs.

Variations on the vocabulary of the International Style remained intellectually exciting and commercially and economically viable. In the private sector some very interesting structures reflect the thoughtfulness, diversity, breadth of ideas, even daring experiments of the times. The capital city's imposing Latin American Tower was erected in 1957: an evocation of the Empire State building and the Chrysler building, with curves translated into a straightened and smoothed International Style. Of special interest, the building was so well engineered and constructed by Dr. Adolfo Zeevaert (consulting architect, Augusto Alvarez) that the new forty-two-story structure easily withstood the severe 1957 earthquake and thus, soon after, its office spaces were fully rented. About the same time the first housing cooperative in Mexico was built on the Paseo de la Reforma by Mario Pani and Salvador Ortega Flores. Two broad towers, twelve and eight stories high, rising upon a common base of two stories, are separated by a common court, and are placed perpendicular to one another, creating an L-shaped spatial complex in the heart of the city. Condominiums, now so popular, were then such a novelty that, as Mr. Pani recalled, even the law allowing them had to be written.[13]

Enrique de la Mora y Palomar and Alberto González Pozo used the curtain wall in a building for the Compañia de Seguros Monterrey (Monterrey Insurance Company), Mexico, D.F., in 1960. They constructed two huge, hollow, concrete shafts seven stories high that support two long concrete beams from which transverse armatures project to raking rooflines. From these the whole building is hung. In the 1962 Edificio Monterrey (Monterrey Building) in the city of Monterrey, Nuevo León, Enrique de la Mora, González Pozo, and Leonardo Zeevaert suspended 6,000 square meters of offices from the roof. Hector Mestre's Companía de Seguros la Comercial (Commercial Insurance) building on the Paseo de la Reforma in Mexico, D.F. [1964] is a good example of a commercial building. Using a glass principal facade and an almost woven-looking pattern of windows on the narrower facades, the whole is separated by short pillars from a two-storied, textured, stone base in which are commercial shops.

Other and widely varied types of buildings include Enrique Carral's La Sagrada Familia (Holy Family) church [Col. Portales, Mexico, D.F., 1960-1965], Juan Sordo Madaleno's Palace of Justice [Niños Héroes, D.F., 1964] and, with José Villagrán García, the Hotel María Isabel Sheraton [1962] in Mexico City. Social concerns continued to receive a great deal of necessary attention. Manuel Rosen's Psychiatric Hospital for Children is one example. Enrique Yáñez furthered his work, especially in the field of hospital design,[14] and was the architect in charge of constructing the large Medical Center complex of the Federal District of Mexico [1954-1961] for the Mexican Institute of Social Security (IMSS). The overall plan contained fourteen buildings, each put up as a single block for equal stress on the poor terrain.

Architect Pedro Ramírez Vázquez had learned to understand the problems of school construction at first hand when he was responsible for school construction for CAPFCE (Committee for the Administration of the Federal Program of School Construction) in the State of Tabasco in 1944. There circumstances led to novel approaches and the beginning of the prefabricated school. Many of his ideas on the importance of the industrialization of architecture were actualized when he became director of CAPFCE in 1958.[15] Given such problems as differences in climate, geography, poverty, and transportation, Ramírez Vázquez advocated a system of prefabricated modules and parts that were simple to produce, to transport, and to put up. Though such a system requires little technical know-how and few skills for the raising of the building, it must be extremely flexible in order to allow for additions of local materials by local artisans so that the building may be completed to accord with its local setting. In 1960 he was awarded the grand prize of the Twelfth Triennial of Milan for this work. In six years as head of CAPFCE Ramírez Vázquez saw 23,284 schools built, of which 18,000 were raised according to his prefabrication system for rural schools. The system, as planned, was used in diverse ways: the three-story school of yellow brick in Ciudad Guzmán by Salvador de Alba appears totally functional and contemporary despite its use of many local materials by local workers, while other schools seem more traditional, especially when they are small, single-story buildings faced with local stone.

In Mexico City the urgent need for housing and for urban renewal led to Mario Pani's Unidad Nonoalco-Tlatelolco [1960-1964] (fig. 29.4). The program, under the Banco Nacional Hipotecario Urbano y de Obras Públicas, S.A. (National Urban Mortgage and Public Works Bank), was the result of the study of 100,000 families in the area. A neighborhood of low-rise and high-rise accommodations ranging from low rentals to condominiums, Tlatelolco has about 12,000 units with about 700 people per hectare. There is a park, three medical/dental clinics, three sports and social clubs, a movie, shops, subterranean and surface parking, and thirteen schools (nine grade schools, one high school and four other school buildings).

The new section has been a most important urban renewal project. It required a coordination among several federal authorities, banking institutions, and private firms that often had been difficult to achieve. As an added point of importance, research on types

29.4. Mario Pani, architect. Unidad Nonoalco-Tlatelolco. Mexico City, 1960-1974. (Photograph: Courtesy of the architect)

of concrete piles was carried out. It was found also that earthquakes, which react differently in Mexico City than in other places, react again differently in Nonoalco-Tlatelolco where the subsoil is unlike that of the center of the city. The new area has proved helpful as well in studying the variance in movement between the base of a tall building and the land at a distance from it. Pani has shown his thoughtfulness here, as in his other developments, for he has planned a balance between density and green spaces and kept traffic, especially cross streets, at a minimum. According to Juan O'Gorman, Pani has notably improved living conditions for Mexicans and his works have had great social impact. Therefore, in O'Gorman's view Pani was the modern architect who served Mexico best.[16]

The 423-foot-high Pyramidal Tower of the National Mortgage Bank by Pani may be seen, like the Satellite City towers, from a great distance. It should signal that here is a new mini-city, and one in which Mexicans have proudly kept their heritage in the Plaza de las Tres Culturas. The 590 foot by 722 foot space of the Plaza of the Three Cultures is bounded by apartment buildings, a secondary school, the Ministry of Foreign Affairs building; and on the east the preserved excavation of the ceremonial center of Aztec Tlatelolco. There also is the early sixteenth-century church of Santiago Tlatelolco with its adjoining Imperial School of the Holy Cross [1536].

By the middle sixties the sociopolitical climate was shifting. In Mexico as in other countries frustration fueled student activism that ultimately took complicated ideas and ideals and distilled them into simpler slogans. Architectural students were in the midst of the arguments as Mexicans saw the importance of finding architectural solutions to social problems. Teaching methods were changed to allow the introduction of various theories of architectural education. The number of architects grew, and it was hoped that the number practicing in the smaller cities and towns of Mexico would also increase, in quality as well as in quantity.

Many new hospitals and clinics were being constructed. During the years 1965 to 1970 IMSS alone put up forty-eight new units throughout Mexico. The Clínica Cuautla, Morelos, is a thirty-four bed facility built in 1967 by Enrique del Moral and José Manuel Echávarri that contains a very wide variety of clinical and medical services. The Clínica Hospital in San Juan de Aragón, Mexico, D.F., built in 1969 by the young Agustín Hernández Navarro is a seventy-seven bed clinic with teaching facilities. Where del Moral's hospital is arranged in rectangular plan, with many stilted, tunnel-vaulted rooms interspersed with garden courts open to the sky, Hernández's is organized in forceful diagonal forms upon a rectangular site.

At the same time, Luis Barragán went his own meditative way. With Andrés Casillas he built the San Cristobal stable, horse pool, swimming pool, and house for Folke Egerstrom [1967-1968] (fig. 29.5) in his (Barragán's) new subdivision of Mexico,

29.5. Luis Barragán and Andrés Casillas, architects. San Cristobal stable and horse pool, for Folke Egerstrom. Los Clubes, Mexico, 1967-1968. (Photograph: Courtesy of Luis Barragán and P. Ramírez Vázquez)

D.F., Los Clubes. The complex is a quiet testimony to Barragán's indefatigable inventiveness in his considerations of the textured, stuccoed wall, whether continuous or with a few, usually large, openings, whether pink, rust red, purple, orange, or white. The subtle sensibilities of proportional interrelationships that inform his creations here are compellingly engaging.

Thus, the world being as full of dichotomies as it is, the mid to late sixties were a time of troubled reevaluation and a time of pride and growth as tourism increased and Mexico looked forward to the 1968 Olympics. Mexicans had the foresight to choose the architect Pedro Ramírez Vázquez as president of the Committee for Organization of the Nineteenth Olympiad.

In 1962 he and Rafael Mijares had built a small but elegant museum, shaped like an open truncated cone, for the city of Juarez in the state of Chihuahua. As early as 1960 he had completed the Gallery of History in Mexico City's Chapultepec Park, with the sculptor José Chávez and Julio Prieto as interior designer. In 1964, with Rafael Mijares and Carlos Cásares, he designed the Museum of Modern Art with its undulating, continuous glass wall. In 1964 as well, a third museum by Ramírez Vázquez and Associates opened in Chapultepec Park. The National Museum of Anthropology (fig. 29.6) was

29.6. P. Ramírez Vázquez, Jorge Campuzano and Rafael Mijares, architects. National Museum of Anthropology. Mexico City, 1964. (Photograph: Courtesy of the architects)

designed with Jorge Campuzano and Rafael Mijares and became the joy of Mexican and foreign visitors for the treasures contained and for the architectural setting itself. The building complex basically consists of a series of compartmentalized rooms that course around a large rectangular court open to the sky, except for the umbrella of its monumental fountain.

Many of the major streets of Mexico were laid out during the nineteenth century under the influence of French ideas. The Paseo de la Reforma, for example, was to be Latin America's Champs Elysées. What that means for the modern Mexico City, D.F., with its population of fourteen million and still growing is one horrible and magnificent traffic jam, especially in squares where major diagonal streets cross. One solution was the Metro. Opened in 1968, it is fitting that French engineers and French-trained engineers were called in to assist engineer Bernardo Quintana in building twenty-two miles of subway lines in the wet subsoil. Each concrete and marble station is a unique work. Pino Suárez station, for instance, is built around an Aztec pyramid, while Insurgentes is faced with bas reliefs from Aztec designs and has a large glass dome that makes it a landmark.

Sports stadia erected in the Federal District include the Aztec Football Stadium [1965-1968] by Ramírez-Váquez, Rafael Mijares, and Luis Martínez del Campo and the Palace of Sports [1968] by Félix Candela with Enrique Castañeda Tamborrell and Antonio Peyrí. The dome of the Palace of Sports, its copper cells suspended from a frame of steel and wood, rests at four points upon a podium that serves as a great encircling terrace. Broad arches on its four sides are faced with zigzagging series of piers that continue the contours of the huge domical covering.

Another interesting solution for a sports facility is the Presidente Gustavo Díaz Ordaz Gymnasium constructed for the National Institute of Mexican Youth, Magdelena Mixhuca, Mexico, D.F., by Manuel González Rul in the early 1970s. Built exclusively for basketball, it was designed with a steel trusswork roofing system to form the letter *M* in transverse section while providing a long uninterrupted space.

The building activity of the late sixties continued into the seventies. Ramón Torres Martínez, with David Muñoz Suárez and Sergio Santacruz, built the new National Lottery building across the square from the 1930s Art Deco style Lottery building. Sleek, glass enclosed, copper colored, it is a steel structure triangular in plan. On a corner site, this elegant tower rises twenty-eight stories above a three-story base that is set back and framed with *pilotis.* About 1974 Eichelman and Gomez Palacio built the La Esmeralda development in the northeast part of Mexico, D.F. This group of triplexes and individual houses is laid out along the axis of a footpath and is bordered with green spaces. Its structures reflect a modernization of vernacular row houses ordered by a neo-Rationalist reduction of a few repeated forms and shapes. In 1975 a new Japanese embassy was opened. The weight of the floors of this building is carried by the four, corner, service pillars in which stairs and elevators are housed. The architects, Kenzo Tange, Manuel Rosen Morrison, and Pedro Ramírez Vázquez have succeeded in planting a building on the Paseo de la Reforma that has been described as a "Japanese born in Mexico."

New hotels abounded and continue to be needed and built. The Hotel de México by Guillermo Rossell de la Lama is an imposingly, almost menacingly huge forty-nine-floor corrugated slab, housing up to 2,700 clients. It is topped by a multistoried cylindrical structure that is illuminated in the evenings with multicolored lights that can be seen for miles. The design, interestingly, is based on hexagonal units. Just to the side of the hotel is the Poliforum Cultural Siqueiros, decorated inside and out with anticapitalist sociopolitical paintings, most by Siqueiros. It indicates quite strikingly the dichotomy of

Mexico when one knows that the hotel and the strongly anticapitalist Poliforum were both financed by a successful capitalist businessman, Manuel Suárez. Mario Pani designed the Hotel Condesa del Mar in Acapulco [1970-1971] and Juan Sordo Madaleno built the Hotel El Presidente on Cozumel, Quintana Roo [1969]. The two could hardly be more different: Pani's is essentially a large slab, enclosed by continuous balconies and their projecting eaves, above which slab a large off-centered cubic form provides a towering accent. Sordo Madaleno's solution, its masses reminiscent of Barragán's mode, hugs the ground level, rising no more than two stories (except for a decorative tower form) with its wings spread at right angles from the lobby and dining area.

Older buildings were endangered by enthusiasm for the new, by the problem of volcanic activity, and because of the subsoil. Ricardo de Robina has been the man particularly known for his understanding and care for the historic heritage of Mexico. He has lectured and written extensively on the subject and it is he who was responsible for the sensitive restoration of the church of Santiago de Tlatelolco, the cathedral of Cuernavaca, and many of Mexico's other historical monuments. There is increasingly widespread understanding of the need to preserve national monuments. The committee concerned with the renovation and restoration of the area of the National cathedral, the Zócalo, and the district San Lazaro east of it manifests the depth of concern for preservation as a reflection of national pride and as a pragmatic part of urban renewal.

The problems inherent in building on the varied terrains in Mexico City, from the lava of the Pedregal and University City to the lake bed of the city center, remain; and the occasional earthquakes or tremors increase the importance of the ongoing search for safe solutions. The several-stories-long well-patched crack on the north face of the Hotel María Isabel tells of the difficulties that architects face in this situation. To prevent damage from earthquakes and uncertain subsoil conditions, various techniques such as the flotation principle or building on concrete piles have been used with more or less successful results. The flotation principle as employed in Mario Pani's and Enrique del Moral's Hydraulic Resources building in 1950 has proven effective but is costly. Concrete piles have been useful. At Tlatelolco research with various kinds of piles led to two new types and a greater understanding of differences between, for example, metal and concrete piles. Sometimes piles have been combined with a hydraulic system. When the clay of the lake bed compresses because of the groundwater level being lowered by the city's need for, and thus use of, water, the building seems to rise; and steps must be added to keep it at street level. The hydraulic system actually allows the piles to be cut when necessary, in effect lowering the building to the level of the ground beneath it.

Most spectacular in this search for solutions has been the work at the Templo de Capuchinas, the Church of the Capuchins built in 1787 which is part of the complex containing the old and new [1976] Basilicas of the Virgin of Guadaloupe. Under the aegis of Ramírez Váquez, Secretary of Human Settlements and Public Works, the engineer Manuel González Flores was retained to implant his system of control *pilotis* and attempt to raise and straighten the building from a few feet at one side to more than ten feet at the other. One hundred and fifty-nine concrete piles were used ranging in height from about fifty feet to almost one hundred feet. The building was freed from its old foundations and literally lifted into the air and then slowly, over a period of seventy-five days, first leaned back and then straightened. This major feat substantially finished by 1978, the work of completing foundations and restoring the still stripped-down interior continues. The system includes ongoing maintenance to keep the building level. The new Basilica of the Virgin of Guadaloupe (by Ramírez-Vázquez, José Luis Bennlliure, Gabriel Chávez de la Mora, Alejandro Schoenhofer, and Javier Garcia Lascurain) [1976] was built using this *Pilotis Control* system for its foundation.

The restoration of the Iturbide Palace, Madero 17, Mexico, D.F., in 1972, and of the smaller house next door as administrative offices for Banamex, the Banco Nacional de Mexico, is one of the most beautiful projects of recycling and restoration that we have seen. Originally built between 1779 and 1785, Renaissance in plan, Spanish in the proportions of its elevation, and with Spanish and Mexican decoration, later changes had included installation of false floors when it was converted for use as a hotel. Ricardo Legorreta Vilchis and Associates restored the building leaving balconies and interior loggias with their decorative elements. In renovating the palace, Legorreta has roofed the whole with a broad tentlike section of a reverse tunnel vault that permitted the inclusion of high glass clerestories on two sides. Thus, work in the uppermost story is done in natural light. The former indoor chapel with its tiled canopy protruding into the top floor has been converted into a small and attractive conference room. Astonishingly, as we go towards the uppermost floor of the building, the interior decoration and furniture become increasingly of the twentieth century and the eighteenth- and nineteenth-century works of art give way to the spare lines of Josef Albers, to the sharply contemporary installations of Mathias Goeritz, and to the broad, solid furniture and bright colors that are contemporary Mexico's.

In 1964 Legorreta and Associates built the Chrysler Automex Factory in Toluca, State of Mexico. Here Legorreta's abilities in designing a new building are clearly recognizable. He wished to construct an industrial community in which economics and an aesthetic of Functionalism were integral to a Mexican architecture. For this purpose he used the think-tank method that he has developed so successfully—the team as a "collaboration, one mind working with others."[17] The result was the use of simple and strong design elements and textures that use sunlight to emphasize their forms. Two freestanding, large, abstract cones of different heights become the landmark, the logo, of this architectural complex. They are reminiscent of the 350- to 400-year-old "granaries" in Tacoleche (or Santa Monica) near Zacatacos in northwest Mexico, and thus lend the whole an additional indigenous element.

The Hotel Camino Real (fig. 29.7), a short walk from where the Paseo de la Reforma meets Chapultepec Park, opened in 1968. By architects Legorreta, Noé Castro, Carlos Varga, and Emilio Guerrero, it was one of the boldest statements made to that time in hotel design. A sense of expansive enclosure exists as one enters this low-rise building, with attention called to the walls by their broad, sensitively developed proportions, their striking colors contrasting from one surface to another, and by the wide monumental spaces channeled between them. The private accommodations are sequestered around a large, rectangular, beautifully landscaped courtyard to one side of and parallel with the more public spaces. In the latter a rectangular system of corridors encloses administrative offices and provides access to interior shops and restaurants.

The influence of Luis Barragán, a consultant for the project, is clear in the strong, bold, very simple elements that lead us to call this architecture "minimalist." Yet, because of its bold use of striking colors and the sophisticated juxtaposition of forceful elements it is almost opulent. Legorreta speaks of Barragán: "He built for specific problems that are basically esthetic problems. . . ."[18] He and his colleagues, often building on the architectural formulations of Barragán, at the same time are wrestling with the economics necessary for commercial buildings. They hope and believe they have successfully blended a variety of complex factors in their 1970s buildings such as the IBM factory in Guadalajara, Jalisco (Legorreta Arquitectos: Ricardo Legorreta, Noé Castro, Carlos Vargas, Emilio Guerrero) and the Camino Real Hotel at Cancún (Legorreta Arquitectos: Ricardo Legorreta, Noé Castro, Carlos Vargas, Emilio Guerrero). They have achieved economically realistic and functional buildings that are monumental and attractive and have become part of the continuum of Mexican architecture.

Hotel Camino Real at Cancún (fig. 29.7) proceeds much farther with the idea of raking walls than did the hotel at Mexico City. At Cancún the long, dramatic, swept-back wall of the guest-room wing recalls more strongly the fundamental sloping effect of such monuments of Mexico's past as the Pyramid of the Sun at Teotihuacán. Simultaneously, with the outer wall of each chamber recessed and with private balconies projecting to the sloped surface, a sunshade effect is created. Again employing large, essentially simple, geometric forms in the bright Mexican sunlight, Legorreta and Associates have designed a building complex that seems permanently part of its surroundings.

The careers of the partners Abraham Zabludovsky and Teodoro González de León parallel well the changes in thinking of the best of Mexican architects in the post-World War II era and exemplify the creative potential of the country. In the early fifties as young men in their twenties, their first buildings were careful, well-though-out applications of some of the most advanced architectural principles of the period. The ideas of Le Corbusier and the CIAM seem to have been of prime importance. By the sixties perceptions had changed. González de León states that, "In the fifties nobody thought that old and new could co-exist. In the sixties architecture came together within the existing cities."[19] In the sixties Zabludovsky saw problems with curtain walls because they needed to be made technically perfect, a difficult task in a land with a lack of skilled labor. Since, also, curtain walls were often not well suited to the climate, the partners came to prefer concrete and brick which they used in building their own houses late in the sixties. The Zabludovsky home of 1969 seems a more temperate parallel to the Brutalism of more northerly countries, while in the González de León home of the same year the simplicity, openness, and rectilinearity of the International Style persists, though large glass surfaces are framed by massive concrete.

The stepped-back urban houses of their Torres de Mixcoac [1968], an urban development of high rises for middle- and low-income families, would seem to recall formal inventions of Louis Kahn or the serial

29.7. Legorreta Architects: Richardo Legorreta, Noé Castro, Carlos Varga, and Emilio Guerrero. Hotel Camino Real. Cancún, Q.R. (Photograph: Julius Shulman, courtesy of the architects)

arrangements of the Dutch Structurists. The La Patera housing of 1969 with a series of two- to five-story buildings and some 1760 apartments is more variegated in its volumes and textures.

Zabludovsky and González de León have seriously explored the work of many other international architects such as Mies van der Rohe, I. M. Pei, Paul Rudolph, and Roche and Dinkeloo, as well as the Japanese Metabolists. Paul Heyer writes, "One senses that they see modern architecture as the manifestation of a new and progressive social order rather than any disciplining ideology."[20]

The INFONAVIT complex, headquarters of the Government Institute of Funds for Workers' Housing, distills the best in international and Mexican architecture, adapting it climatically and architecturally. Completed in 1973, the organization of the tall space of the central circulation area and the manner in which the large, wedgelike, plaza entry space cuts into a monumental facade seem to presage some of I. M. Pei's solutions for the 1978 National Gallery East Wing in Washington, D.C.

The Colegio de México (figs. 29.8 and 29.9) of 1975 is a more mature and complex unity of ideas, many of which were previously employed at the INFONAVIT building. At the Colegio these are combined with an emphasis on siting and landscaping suggesting an Organic approach. Predominantly horizontal in thrust, it is trapezoidal in plan with its longest side forming a forceful diagonal that borders upon and opens up the central atrium. Partly roofed by a series of small, translucent, plastic, tunnel vaults, the atrium is multileveled with broad staircases and varied plazas, and richly planted with rocky gardens and small trees. Large structural elements of reinforced concrete, huge lintels in space, unexpected volumetric recesses within solid masses, concrete sunshades with deeply recessed glass surfaces, all combine to emphasize both the continuity and the interplay of this masterful building with the space and the landscape of its environs.

The extraordinarily inventive architecture of Agustín Hernández is more widely varied, reflecting his own approach to building rather than any particular style. His theories of design and structure were developed during several years (from 1954 on) as head of design for CAPFCE and principal of the National University's project workshop (1957-1968). For Hernández, architectural space should facilitate man's actions just as the musculature that comprises

29.8. Abraham Zabludovsky and Teodoro González de León, architects. Colegio de México, view of the interior patio. Mexico, D.F., 1975. (Photograph: Julius Shulman, courtesy of Abraham Zabludovsky)

his formal, biological unity does. This architectural space should affect and reflect not only one's physical or biological existence but also one's psychological being. If an architect follows such theoretical and functional bases and the characteristics of a particular site are respected and expressed as well, then, almost inevitably, each work will be unique.

Whether in modest office buildings such as those at 104 Tokio Street and at 58 Praga Street (1968), [both in Mexico City]; in the design of private residences such as the Neckelmann and Hernández houses of the early to late 1970s; or in larger projects such as the almost Mendelsohnian IMSS Villa Obregón Hospital and the huge Heroico Colegio Militar (Heroic Military Academy) of Mexico

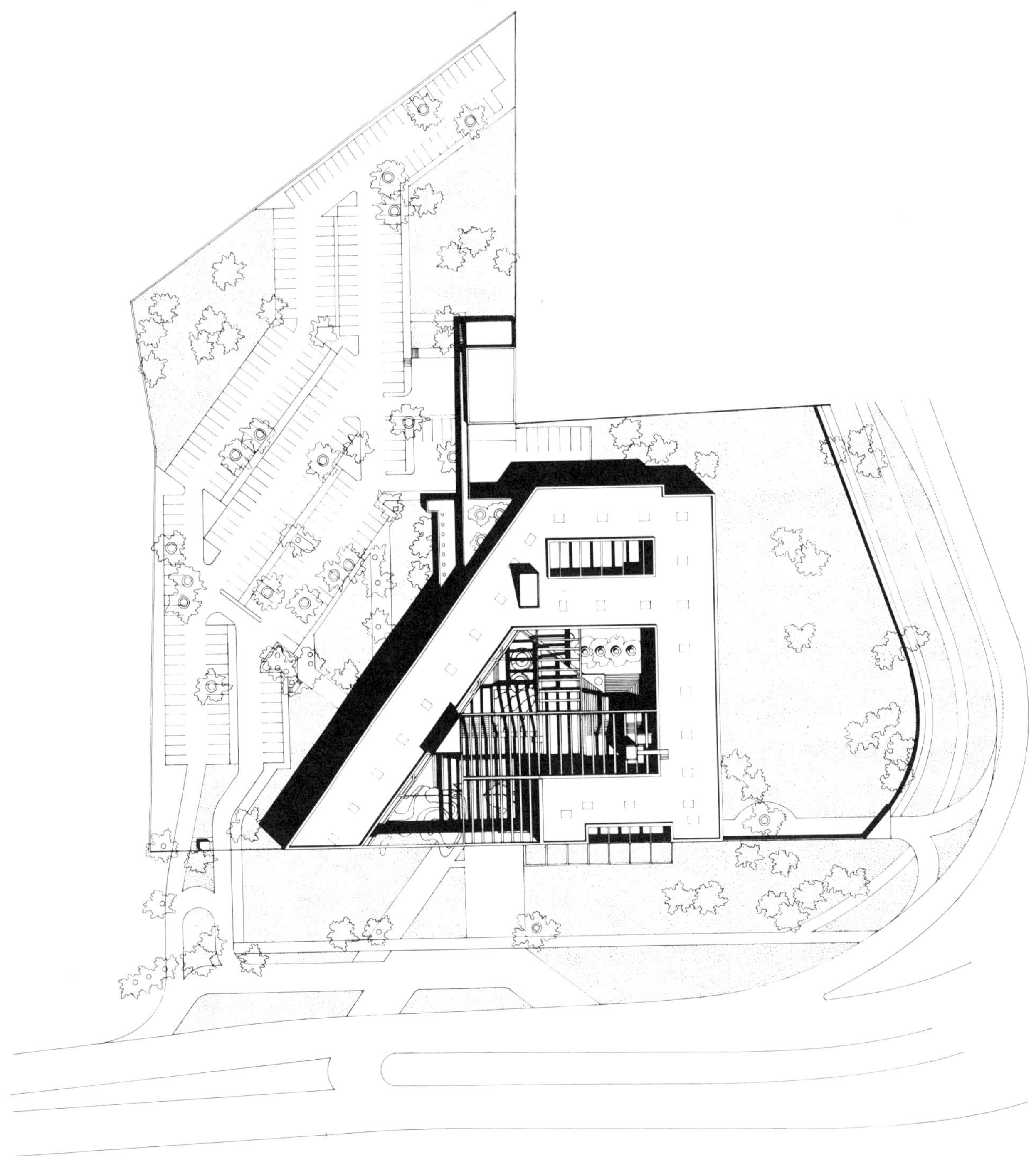

29.9. Abraham Zabludovsky and Teodoro González de León, architects. Colegio de México, site plan, Mexico, D.F., 1975. (Photograph: Courtesy of the architects)

[1971-1976] the stamp of Hernández's originality and his concern for structural excellence are evident. Though the Praga Street office building is part of a row of buildings in a crowded urban context, its facade is separated: it seems to hover upon a single pylon. It is formed between, but seems separate from, two elegantly thinned finlike elements that course the full depth of the building. In the Casa Hernández, built for the architect's sister, there is an innovative organic continuity of variegated, curving spaces at multiple levels, with the living room concluding in an inverted prismatic form, overlooking the valley beneath. Both the vast military college project and the school of the Ballet Folklórico de México (fig. 29.10) consist of volumes and masses that clearly incorporate Hernández's understanding of Mexico's

29.10. Agustín Hernández, architect. Ballet Folklórico of Mexico School. Central lobby. Mexico City, 1968-1970. (Photograph: G. Zamora, courtesy of the architect)

pre-Hispanic architecture while speaking in the language of contemporary Mexico and her future.

Hernández's own office tower [1976-1977], situated in the ravines of Bosques de las Lomas on the southwest of Mexico City, is the most sensational of all of his structures (fig. 29.11). One comes upon the gleaming one hundred foot-high, silvery, futuristic tower of marbleized reinforced concrete from below. It is securely anchored by cables that extend nearly forty feet into the rock of the forty-five-degree, sloped site. But entrance is from a higher bridge accessible by a looping, climbing roadway. For Hernández the form chosen was that of a tree. But this has been resolved into a cubiform trunk, supporting polyhedral modules above, in which large, interlocking, prismatic forms predominate. On the interior a metallic spiral staircase, reinforced by heavy coils, occupies the vestibule and leads up to the spacious two-storied atelier and offices, while on the uppermost level there is a small study. Hernández is undoubtedly the most creatively avant-garde of Mexico's established architects. For him the past and the present are, together, the foundation upon which to build into the future.

29.11. Agustín Hernández, architect. Architect's Workshop. Bosques de las Lomas, Mexico, D.F., 1976-1977. (Photograph: Courtesy of the architect)

A few buildings from the period of the late sixties on, not mentioned previously, include Salvador de Alba's unusual federal office block in Lagos de Moreno, Jalisco, and his auditorium annex to the Regional Normal School of Ciudad Guzmán [1967]; Horst Hartung's office building on Avenida Unión, Guadalajara, a city of some two million inhabitants; Eric E. Coufal's Industrial Bank of Jalisco and his Experimental Theater in Aqua Azul Park, also in the State of Jalisco; and Leopoldo Fernández Font's fluent organic spaces in the Church of the Resurrected Christ (Templo Cristo Resucitado), again in Guadalajara. In Monterrey, another city of two million people, two unusual solutions may be seen in Fernando Garza Treviño's raking ovoidal Cultural Center Alfa, and in Oscar Bulnes Valero's triangular system of two joined houses. Other buildings are Marco Antonio Garfias de los Santos's Centro de Difusión Cultural del Instituto Potosino de Bellas Artes (Center for Cultural Broadcasting of the Potosí Institute of Fine Arts), San Luis Potosí; the Sergio Mosiño Barreto and Manuel Solórzano Soto's circular residence in Irapuato, Guanajuato.

The Hotel Presidente Chapultepec [ca. 1977], Mexico, D.F., by Juan Sordo Madaleno and José A. Wiechers (fig. 29.12) is an elegant high-rise building of twin slabs; one forty stories, the other thirty-two stories high. Here the volumes work together as a beautiful sculpture. Luis Barragán's poetic architecture remains intensely interesting and influential. He, with Alberto Chauvet, built the Gilardi house (fig. 29.13), a small, three-floor building on a thirty foot by one hundred foot infill site at Tacubaya, Mexico, D.F., for which he won the prestigious Pritzker Architectural Prize in 1980. Here again he has built a home which is unlike any other, yet contains the elements of the quiet interior garden, the use of

29.12. Juan Sordo Madaleno and José A. Wiechers, architects. Hotel Presidente Chapultepec, Mexico, D.F., 1977. (Photograph: Courtesy of the architects)

bright color, especially dramatic in the pool area, sensitive emphases of light and shadow and, always, the whitewashed wall.

At the farflung campus of the National Autonomous University of Mexico, more than a mile to the south of the academic quadrangle, a new complex, including a theater and a library, was completed late in the seventies. The music hall, Sala Nezahualcóyotl, by Orso Núñez Ruiz Velasco and Arcadio Artis Espriú with Manuel Medina and Arturo Treviño, is a large structure recalling the international Brutalist style and is functionally well conceived. Christopher Jaffe, who was responsible for the acoustics of Denver's (U.S.) new auditorium, helped to perfect the interior qualities of this music hall in association with the Mexican acoustics specialist Eduardo Sad.

Nearby is an installation called the Center of Sculptural Space developed in 1979 by artists Mathias Goeritz, Helen Escobedo, Manuel Felguerez Hersua, Sebastian and Federico Silva. Rising from and encircling wild lava rock is a series of wedge-shaped, concrete forms radially arranged, suggesting the composition of an open-air amphitheater. Acoustically exciting, it has been the site of concerts both planned and impromptu and of modern performance works designed for the open air.

A concern for social programs has remained evident into the eighties. The National Institute of Mental Health by Manuel Rosen Morrison and Pedro Ramírez Vázquez; the IMSS Obstetrics and Gynecology Hospital Complex of Villa Obregón by Agustín Hernández, Alejandro Martos Lizárraga and Gonzolo Arenas; and the Cardiology Complex by José Villagrán García and Raúl F. Gutierrez are among the new hospitals. Alejandro Zohn's low-rise housing complex, Atemjac at Guadalajara, Jalisco, for INFONAVIT, is but one example of many developments. State sponsored agencies and firms continue to direct the construction of publicly needed buildings such as hospitals, markets, and schools. Though thousands of schools have been built, there is still a very real lack of facilities in many areas. The population of Mexico almost doubled from 1950 to 1970 alone, but the number of people receiving education from primary schools through the university level has increased from the 1930s at a much higher rate than has the population.[21] Cooperative efforts among the many different governmental offices, federal, regional, and local, and private concerns can cause delays. Moreover, while construction techniques have become more sophisticated and the number of buildings erected has been incredibly large, these have met needs on only a limited scale. The housing estates have been exceedingly important for improving the living standards of the spectrum of people called the middle class, but they have not substantially solved the problems of the poor. Some architects' solutions for this problem are mentioned below.

Urban problems have expanded as the urban population has increased from 35.1 percent of the whole population in 1940 to 64.9 percent in 1977.[22] With a large and continued daily influx of country people, Mexico City's population could, according to United Nations projections, be thirty-two million by the year 2000. With this in mind and for the well-being of the whole country there has been an increasing concentration of efforts to encourage the growth of other regions of Mexico. A first step has been the two-hundredfold growth of the highway system over the past forty years. A most important move was the

29.13. Luis Barragán with Alberto Chauvet, architects. The Francisco Gilardi House, Indoor-Outdoor Pool. Tacubaya, Mexico, D.F., 1976-1978. (Photograph: Courtesy of Luis Barragán and P. Ramírez Vázquez)

National Plan for Urban Development of 1978 which laid out the problems; suggested some steps for immediate solutions, such as indicating the amount of pesos to be invested in the next four years; and pointed out the areas that should be developed on the basis of a priority system. In addition, Mexico City has a master plan for streets and traffic worked out during the seventies under architect-planner Eduardo Terrazas.

Architects of all ages speak of their social concerns and have proposed varied methods for alleviating social problems. In Guadalajara, for instance, only 55 percent of the population lives in rental housing. Some 28 percent of the population has very low incomes and needs housing aid. Therefore, architect Hernández Davila suggested converting this group into builders of their own homes with government help.

Mario Pani is working on a variety of problems ranging from his project for renewing the 180 kilometers of canals at Xochimilco to his several urban-development proposals. He explains that each city has a city within that city which must be reconditioned, and that there also is the new city just outside the city. These are like separate human biological cells. He sees new communities encompassed by new fast-access roads to make cells of humanly scaled neighborhoods. This would be an infinitely expandable idea—"small cells make the elephant."

He also speaks of the need for "Urgency Cities," a name perhaps derived from the Spanish translation of Richard Neutra's "Rush City." What Pani has in mind is the need for dwelling places for the rural people who pour into Mexico City each day, housing that would be available for them for perhaps one or two years, till they became acclimated.

Pedro Ramírez Vázquez has demonstrated his solutions, for instance, with his system for school modules that has been used for twenty years. He states, "Mexico is a developing country with many social problems that are manageable. The most direct way to proceed is by the use of basic systematic modules geared to particular functions, modified by local and regional manifestations and permitting a degree of originality. There is room for some architectural individuality, but that is a by-product and not a goal."[23] He wants to develop major centers in addition to Mexico City and is encouraging architects to help in their development. He believes that the architect's role is to affirm the communal or national personality. Not only does he see architectural individuality as a by-product, but he also believes that architecture should not be exclusively concerned with beauty: harmony in a work is the result of its honesty.[24] One can certainly agree with this when the architect involved has a solid educational background and a great deal of talent. Otherwise, one may run the risk of a shoddy and stifling mediocrity.

In the architectural development of Mexico over the last forty years, as in other countries, many buildings raised have been commercial only and have had little intrinsic architectural or technological interest. But Mexico has also benefited from a rather large number of exciting and diverse architectural talents. These architects have learned from non-Mexican sources and from their own heritage, whether pre-Hispanic, colonial, or contemporary—as exemplified by Barragán among others.

In the eighties several common elements are clear. In rural areas particularly, the combination of traditional craftmanship, materials, and techniques of construction have allowed for continuity through the centuries. Residential, and even public, spaces are built with interior gardens for privacy or quiet, and distantly echo southern Spain. Light as an architectural element accentuates textural details and large architectural surfaces. The changing cast of shadows and light lends bold interests to the building in its environment; while bright colors add beauty and complexity, heightening the drama of architecture, land, water, and sky. Since the sixties, aspects of international Brutalist style have been embraced by many Mexican architects because its massive qualities are so well suited to the Mexican predilection for the monumental. Moreover, there is a sense of permanence in the large solid forms that look as if they had always been and would always remain part of the landscape.

Architecture in Mexico has evolved over the past forty years from a sometimes uncritical acceptance of Modernism, at times coupled with a self-conscious search for a national architecture. In recent years the best buildings, the ones that we accept as functionally and aesthetically superior, are confident, even audacious, integrations of elements that produce structures that are distinctively and uniquely Mexican.

Notes

1. Pedro Ramírez Vázquez, "Valores Invariables de la Arquitectura" (unpublished manuscript), p. 5.
2. Roberto de Robina, "L'Architecture moderne," *L'Architecture d'Aujourd'hui* 59 (1955): 13.
3. D.F. means *Distrito Federal* (Federal District) and includes most of Mexico City and its suburbs.
4. We are very much indebted to Mr. O'Gorman for discussing with us some of his penetrating views of developments in contemporary architecture.
5. Manuel Larrosa, "El Primer Multifamiliar cumple 30 Años," *Arquitectura México* 118 (1978): 92-103.
6. Max L. Cetto, *Modern Architecture in Mexico* (London: Alec Tiranti, 1961), p. 165.
7. Thirty-five percent of the population was covered by Social Security in 1980.
8. Irving Evan Myers, *Mexico's Modern Architecture* (New York: Architectural Book Publishing Co., 1952), p. 204.
9. Emilio Ambasz, *The Architecture of Luis Barragán* (New York: Museum of Modern Art, 1976), p. 11.
10. Cetto, *Modern Architecture*, p. 26.
11. Ibid., p. 29.
12. Ambasz, *Barragán*, p. 33.
13. In an interview in the fall, 1980, given at his offices, located in one of the condominium buildings. Another condominium of about the same time is just across the broad Paseo de la Reforma.
14. For a very short but interesting discussion on what hospital designing entails *see* Enrique Yáñez's introduction to a special issue on hospitals in *Arquitectura México* 103 (September 1970): 2.
15. Pedro Ramírez Vázquez, "La Industrializacion de la Arquitectura," *Arquitectos de México* 17 (March 1963): 24-28.
16. Juan O'Gorman, "Arquitectura en México Durante los Ultimos Treinta Años," *Arquitectura México* 100 (1969): 59.
17. Quoted in a section about the architect in *Arquitectura México* 100 (1969): 32.
18. C. Ray Smith quoting Legorreta in "The Mexican Minimalism of Ricardo Legorreta," *Architectural Record* 160 (October 1976): 104.
19. Paul Heyer, *Mexican Architecture: The Work of Abraham Zabludovsky and Teodoro González de León* (New York: Walker & Co., 1978), p. 17.
20. Heyer, *Mexican Architecture*, p. 46.
21. Pablo Gonzalez Casanova, "The Economic Development of Mexico," *Scientific American*, September 1980, p. 202.
22. Ibid., p. 195.
23. In an interview in Mexico City, 1980.
24. From an address before the *XIIIth Congreso Mundial UIA* (Thirteenth Congress of the International Union of Architects) held in Mexico, October 1978; quoted in *Arquitectura México* 119 (1978): 137.

Bibliography

BOOKS

Ambasz, Emilio. *The Architecture of Luis Barragán*. New York: Museum of Modern Art, 1976.

Arquitectura y Conservacion del Patrimonio Artistico Nacional. *Anuario de Arquitectura Mexicana* 1977. D.F., Mexico: Instituto Nacional de Bellas Artes, 1978.

______. *Anuario de Arquitectura Mexicana* 1978. D.F., Mexico: Instituto Nacional de Bellas Artes, 1979.

Born, Esther. *The New Architecture in Mexico, The Architectural Records*. New York: William Morrow and Co., 1937.

Bullrich, Francisco. *New Directions in Latin American Architecture*. New York: George Braziller, 1969.

Cetto, Max L. *Modern Architecture in Mexico* (in Spanish & English). London: Alec Tiranti, 1961.

Damaz, Paul. *Art in Latin American Architecture*. New York: Reinhold Publishing, 1963.

Heyer, Paul. *Mexican Architecture: The Work of Abraham Zabludovsky and Teodoro González de León* (in Spanish & English). New York: Walker & Co., 1978.

Hitchcock, Henry-Russell. *Latin American Architecture since 1945*. New York: Museum of Modern Art, 1972.

Myers, Irving Evan. *Mexico's Modern Architecture* (in Spanish & English). New York: Architectural Book Publishing Co., 1952 (in cooperation with the National Institute of Fine Arts of Mexico).

Neuvillate Ortíz, Alfonso de. *10 Arquitectos Mexicanos*. Mexico: Ediciones Galeria de Arte Misrachi, 1977.

Secretaria de Asentamientos Humanos y Obra Públicas, et al. *Plan Nacional de Desarrollo Urbano* (abbreviated version). D.F., Mexico: Editorial Roer, S.P., 1978 (introductory text by Lic. José López Portillo, President of Mexico).

Smith, Clive Bamford. *Builders in the Sun—Five Mexican Architects*. New York: Architectural Book Publishing Co., 1967.

Sociedad de Arquitectos Mexicanos Colegio Nacional de Arquitectos de México. *4000 Years of Mexican Architecture*. Edited by Pedro Ramírez Vázquez (in Spanish, English, French, German). Mexico: Libreros Mexicanos Unidos, S. de R.L. De C.U., 1956.

Trueblood, Beatrice. *Pedro Ramírez Vázquez* (in Spanish). Stuttgart: Karl Kramer Verlag, 1979.

JOURNALS

Ambasz, Emilio. "Imponderable Substance: Luis Barragán's Casa Gilardi in Mexico." *Progressive Architecture*, September 1980, pp. 38-41.

"Atelier di architettura in Messico, Architetto Augustín Hernández Navarro." *L'Architettura 25*, no. 6 (June 1979): 344-48.

Atoe, Wayne. "Thick, Tough, Malleable: The IBM Center in Mexico by Ricardo Legorreta." *Progressive Architecture*, September 1980, pp. 184-87.

Bowman, Peggy Cochrane. "Me Gusta Mucho Mexico." *American Institute of Architects Journal* 50 (October 1968): 46-58.

Brunati, M. and Cantoni, G. Carnevale. "Nuova Architettura in Mexico." *Casabella* 30, no. 310 (October 1966): 32-55.

"Centro di ricerche post-universitaria à Città del Messico, architetti, T. González de León, A. Zabludovsky." *L'Architettura* 25, no. 1 (January 1979): 26-32.

Cetto, Max L. et al. "Architecture Mexicaine, 1968-1978 " (English captions). *Techniques et Architecture* 320 (June 1978): 119-46.

"La Ciudad de México, no. IV, Sus Casas." *Artes de México* nos. 97/98 (1967): 9-110.

"Colegio de México" (English summary). *L'Architettura* 25, no. 1 (January 1979): 26-32.

"Designing for a Dry Climate (Barragán)." *Progressive Architecture* 52, August 1971, pp. 50-57.

"Everyman's Casa, Villa Florestas, Tijuana, Mexico." *Progressive Architecture*, July 1978, pp. 76-79.

"Everyman's Mexican Home: A Hotel in Mexico City by Architect Ricardo Legorreta. . . ." *Progressive Architecture*, June 1969, pp. 82-91.

Gerster, Giuseppe. "Juan O'Gorman's Haus Zerstört." *Werk* 57 (June 1970): 362-63.

Kaspé, M. Vladimir, Irving Nerubay et al. "Mexique." *L'Architecture d'Aujourd'hui* 109 (September 1963): 1-91.

Lifchez, Raymond. "A Brilliant Museum Reflects Mexico's Cultural Ambitions." *Architectural Record* 145 (June 1969): 76-80.

"Mexico: Special Issue." *Interiors* 123 (December 1963): 56-101 (esp. pp. 64-67, 84-88).

"Musée National d'anthropologie à Mexico" and "Musée National à Ciudad Juarez Mexique." *L'Architecture d'Aujourd'hui* 129 (December 1966/January 1967): 12-15; 16-17.

"An Olympic Preview down Mexico Way." *American Institute of Architects Journal* 49 (January 1968): 39-45.

Persitz, Alexandre, Vladimir Kaspé et al. "Architecture Mexicaine." *L'Architecture d'Aujourd'hui* 59 (April 1955): 1-97.

Ramírez Sotomayor, Jorge. "La Arquitectura Contemporanea de Jalisco." *Artes de México* nos. 94/95 (1967): 150-66.

Smith, C. Ray. "The Mexican Minimalism of Ricardo Legorreta." *Architectural Record* 160 (October 1976): 97-104.

Urbanski, Wolfgang. "XIII. Weltkongress und XIV. Generalversammlung der Internationalen Union der Architekten (U.I.A.) in Mexiko." *Architektur der D.D.R.* 28 (May 1979): 300-309.

Wright, Raymond L. W. "Architectural Practice in Mexico." *Progressive Architecture* 45 (February 1964): 154.

Yamazaki, Yasutaka. "Luis Barragán" (in Japanese with

English captions). *Architecture and Urbanism* 119 (August 1980): 3-32.

See also all issues of *Arquitectura México*, 1938-1979. For example: no. 100, "30 Años de la Revista" (digest and translation in English). *Arquitectura México* (April/July 1968): 1-109.

30

THE NETHERLANDS

H. WOUTER HUBERS
and HEERO MEINDERSMA

Introduction

Every building is an answer to a social demand, whether or not the demand was actually expressed in the client's list of requirements. Consequently, there is an important correlation between what people want to have built and the building itself, not only in its functioning but also in its form. A country gets the architecture it deserves. Requirements change in the course of time, and opinions are divided. The avant-garde in architecture, for example, has a very important role as eye-opener, signpost, and talking point, existing against a background of more anonymous-looking buildings. The rather drab mainstream of architecture, designed and constructed according to generally prevalent design concepts and building techniques creates the climate in which more spectacular buildings come into being. Thus, a chronological enumeration of the more or less famous buildings and their architects in the Netherlands since 1945 does not in itself give an adequate impression of the development of Dutch architecture during this period. It is also necessary to draw attention to less well known movements in design and to the social processes which helped to determine the development of architecture in the Netherlands.

After 1945 many of the factors influencing architecture in the Netherlands underwent great change. Some factors were a direct consequence of developments in the building industry itself: building technique, supply and demand in the construction market, relations between building partners, and so on, while there were also factors of a sociocultural nature such as taste, changes in the cultural pattern and, closely linked, the significance attributed to the forms of buildings.

From some 2.2 million units just after the war, the Dutch housing stock was doubled by 1975 to about 4.4 million units. The vastly increased supply of housing and other types of buildings over a mere thirty years was necessitated by the great shortage of buildings caused by the war, and by the population explosion which continued until well into the 1960s. (Although until the end of the sixties it was generally assumed that the Netherlands would have more than 20 million inhabitants by the year 2000, the population is now only expected to reach 14.5 million by 2000, owing to a sharp decrease in the birth rate). Housing in the Netherlands was long considered to be a question of production, not a matter of how and where it was best to build, but of how many houses could be built for a certain price.

There are few countries in the world where the government exerts as much influence on building as in the Netherlands, where government itself commissions more than 50 percent of the total building output. Since the Housing Act of 1902 nearly all building activity has been controlled by an increasingly complex system of permits and regulations. Even the architecture of a building or plans for its extension are subject to approval, and the system of governmental control has been greatly extended in scope since 1945. Although bureaucratic influence limits the freedom necessary for the development of new architectural forms and techniques, it does offer a certain amount of protection against the worst abuses. This moderating, leveling effect is unmistakably evident in Dutch architecture after 1945.

Translated from the original Dutch by Anne van Blaaderen.

The form of a building results from all of these factors and from the architect's personal contribution.

Before the Second World War the Dutch architectural world was characterized by a more or less clear division between traditional and modern. Such groups as De Stijl and de 8 en de Opbouw belonged to the Modern Movement. Names like Rietveld, Oud, Duiker, and Van Doesburg became international symbols of the Dutch avant-garde. The traditional architects, whether members of the Delft school or not, remained less well known.

This division between traditional and modern in Dutch architecture was causally linked to sociocultural and political differences in Dutch society that were especially clear before the Second World War and were based on one's relationship with specific religious denominations. From the cultural and politico-religious point of view three important groups may be distinguished, based not only on formal affiliation but also on the extent to which religion was allowed importance in other areas. The three originated in the movements of Catholicism, the Reformation, and Humanism. Although they cooperated in many areas, great rivalry was largely apparent, for example in the formation of political parties.

Dutch culture was also pervaded by these mainly religious differences. Important buildings have always been symbols of cultural power. Historically, the Catholics were closely involved in the development of traditional architecture, the Modern Movement was linked to Humanism, and an intermediate position was occupied by the sober Protestants.

One of the things which differentiates the traditionalist Delft school from the Modern Movement is its strong emphasis on the architectonic significance of the Medieval city and its buildings, the imperfection of which was considered to be a symbol of Christian unpretentiousness. Professor Granpré Molière, a Catholic and the most important theoretician of the Delft school, put it this way:

> The Christian also aims for the highest in his architecture, even if he does not consider it to be his most exalted task. Its main characteristic, however, is its freedom regarding the acceptance and application of imperfections. After all, everything is derived from dust and returns to it in the end. The Christian cannot ignore this. That is why he does not eschew crooked streets, slanting, overhanging houses, rough, weather-stained materials, uncertainty and improvisation.
>
> It seems to me that this principle had its richest and most fertile application in the Medieval city. In Dutch speaking areas this resulted in a separate style, especially in town planning. This town planning style was still deliberately adhered to at a time when people elsewhere, out of a blind perfectionism, began to bar all imperfections, being unwilling to accept anything but rectilinearity, parallelism and symmetry. Imperfection was affectedly retained for a while in the rubble gables of the early Renaissance but soon this too had to make way for the one-sided passion for perfection.[1]

The aversion of traditionalists such as Granpré Molière to modern architecture was based largely on the pursuit of abstraction and perfection that was expected to ensue from mechanical building methods. J. J. P. Oud (a member of the De Stijl group) often wrote about the relationship between the new, functional architecture and modern technique. Oud described the contrast of functional with traditional building:

> . . . a type of architecture which is rationally based on modern living conditions will contrast with present architecture in every respect. Above all, it will be functional without falling into dry rationalism, but it will immediately attain the highest in this functionalism. Contrasting as sharply as possible with the untechnical, shapeless and colourless products of immediate inspiration familiar to us, it will express its appointed tasks with complete subservience to function and an almost impersonal technical manner, in structures of clear form and pure proportion. Instead of the natural attractiveness of unworked materials, broken expanses of glass, diversified surfaces, turbid colour, mottled glazing, weather-stained walls, etc., it will unfold the charm of worked materials, clear glass, shining, rounded surfaces, glossy paint, glittering steel, brilliant colour, etc.[2]

The difference between the opinions of Granpré Molière and Oud as representatives of the traditionalist and modernist movements respectively is illustrated by their housing complexes in Rotterdam. In Tuindorp Vreewijk, built 1916-1919 by Granpré Molière, Verhagen, De Roos, and Overeijnden according to a street plan by Berlage, the craftsmanship in building with brick, tiles, and a great deal of wood lends a traditional atmosphere and seems as much indebted to the English garden city as to Medieval Dutch almshouse architecture. The residential area Kiefhoek, by Oud, was built at the end of the twenties. In the white, plastered blocks there is a strong horizontal articulation because of the banded windows on the first floor; there are no irregularities of planes, no tiled roofs; the front and back of the blocks are almost identical, and the only "decorative" concession is that the corners in the main street facade are rounded.

Wartime Developments

The war made the differences between traditionalist and functionalist camps smaller. In the first year of the German occupation (1940) the society Architectura et Amicitia (A et A) appointed a committee to continue the furtherance of architecture and the allied arts during the war. In order to present a more united front to the occupiers, representatives of such movements as the 8, the Delft school and the General Catholic Artists Society, were invited to sit on it, and contact between modernists (the 8), and traditionalists (Delft school) that would not have occurred in normal circumstances began. In the village of Doorn near Utrecht this committee organized three seminars (the Doornse Leergangen) oriented towards the bridging of ideological divergencies of opinion. Important participants from the various movements, including Professor M. J. Granpré Moliére and J. F. Berghoef (Delft school), and G. Rietveld and W. van Tijen (modernists), joined in discussion to try to settle disputes.

Cooperation between modernists and traditionalists brought about the realization of a construction plan for Rotterdam, which had been severely bombed in May 1940. Immediately after the heavy air raids the city corporation commissioned W. G. Witteveen, Director of Municipal Technical Services, to draw up a reconstruction plan. Completed in 1941 it proposed several important improvements in the traffic structure and moved the sluice system to the bank of the river Maas. In spite of these improvements, however, the plan was highly colored by restoration of the former urban infrastructure. In 1943 C. van Traa succeeded Witteveen and began to revise Witteveen's plan. Van Traa's advisors included J. H. van den Broek and W. van Tijen, both representatives of the new approach. At their suggestion, traditionalists like P. Verhagen (former colleague of Granpré Molière), H. M. Kraayenvanger, and A. van der Steur were called in. The master plan accepted by the Rotterdam corporation in 1946 took Witteveen's interventions as a starting point but augmented these upon very different spatial and functional bases.

A restoration mentality had given way to the desire for a modern city to be based on the principle of divisions of function. The master plan was highly flexible, allowing unforeseen future developments without hindrance. Perhaps this flexibility resulted from compromises between traditionalist and modernist advisors that enabled the plan to be completed in contrasting ways exemplified so well in van den Broek and Bakema's Lijnbaan complex. The modern Rotterdam master plan regarded by many as indicating a radical change in Dutch town planning was perhaps partly due to the spirit of the Doorn seminars.

Cooperation between traditionalists and modernists became impossible once again after the liberation. The Doorn conferences came to a halt, the question of handwork versus machine work being the greatest stumbling block, but the decision was made to publish a new magazine with the appropriate name, *Forum*. Its initial aims of continuing the Doorn discussions before a wider audience and preventing the various movements from returning to an isolation in separate magazines appear as yet unrealized.

Postwar Trends

Dutch architecture may be roughly considered in terms of conventional (the traditionalists), unconventional (the avant-garde), and neutral groups during each of four postwar periods.

RECONSTRUCTION (1945-ABOUT 1950)

The first years after the war were characterized by shortages: everything was in short supply, including buildings and building capacity, houses, and utilities as a direct result of the war. Poor building capacity was caused mainly by a lack of funds and of building materials. Against this background it is understandable that with the Reconstruction Act (1949) means were created to regulate building output and the building industry. The powerful system of government approvals then controlled building output and the nature and size of projects. The productive sector (docks and industries) was given priority.

At that time, shortages of imported building materials such as steel, glass, and wood were even greater than that of home-produced bricks, cement, and such. Moreover, the now well-known building machines and means of transport were absent. Builders were almost forced to use traditional building methods.

In these years the spirit of reconciliation which had affected Dutch architects and officials during the war soon ebbed away. When important posts were again filled, society was rapidly reorganized according to its prewar structure, and political and sociocultural distinctions became sharply drawn once more. W. van Tijen who, together with J. H. van den Broek, had involved the traditionalists in the reconstruction plan for Rotterdam, expressed his disappointment about this as late as 1972:

Right after the war, there were many people who sincerely wished to tackle the enormous tasks ahead in unison and undogmatically. Hence, Van den Broek and I requested Verhagen and Kraayvanger to cooperate in our task to advise Van Traa with regard to the Reconstruction-plan for Rotterdam. The other party thought differently. After the May-days they still occupied all important posts—certainly not without the influence of Molière—and censored the modernists like supervisors. I personally experienced this in Rotterdam. Later, only Verhagen gave the modernists a chance, at Nagele in Noordoostpolder. Even after the war Molière publicly spoke of "tearing the mask off modernism." I sharply reproached him then for saying this.[3]

As early as 1947 van Tijen drew up a balance sheet showing that reconstruction was to be carried out by traditional architects in sixty-four places and by modern architects in a mere eleven. Granpré Molière was professor in Delft until 1953, a period in which the ideology of traditionalism was defined by the Delft school. Well-known Delft school reconstruction plans were followed for instance at Middelburg, (fig. 30.1) Rhenen, and Zandvoort.

For large government commissions, preference was usually given to followers of the Delft school during this period, as for example the Amsterdam Tax Office building by G. Friedhof (a government architect at the time).

The Lijnbaan in Rotterdam was the first postwar building complex to be labelled as nonconformist [1949-1953]. Two considerations were involved: first, the extensive, traffic-free residential and business complex was a departure from the traditional type of street, both in design and function; and second, perhaps even more importantly, it was a demonstrative gesture, a symbol of the reconstruction of the heart of Rotterdam which had been ravaged by German bombardments. Unlike many smaller Dutch towns and villages destroyed in the war, where town plans, street profiles and, when possible, buildings were painstakingly reconstructed by traditional architects, the Lijnbaan came to symbolize new kinds of renewal (fig. 30.2). The flexibility

30.2. Johannes H. van den Broek and Jacob B. Bakema, architects. Lijnbaan Shopping Center. Rotterdam, 1949-1953. (Photograph: Courtesy of Stichting Wonen, G.v.d. Vlugt)

built into the Rotterdam reconstruction plan and its close relationship to the CIAM's principles of urban planning facilitated experimentation in the relation between public urban space here and the buildings which were placed in it.

Van Tijen cited the new village of Nagele in the Noordoostpolder as one of the few cases in which the traditionalists, as important government advisors, gave the modernists a chance to put their ideas into practice. Nagele was designed by a team of architects including Gerrit Rietveld, Johannes H. van den Broek, Jacob B. Bakema, and Aldo van Eyck. The extremely fine plan was still strongly influenced by the CIAM concept of division of functions. A broad, rectangular windbreak protects the entire village and, at the same time, visually separates it from the endless expanse of the flat polder. The space enclosed by the windbreak is like an interior in conception, with the buildings placed in it as if they were pieces of furniture in a room. This paradoxical relationship between interior and exterior was later to become one of the most familiar themes of the *Forum* group.

Although the differences between modernists and traditionalists became sharper again during the first postwar period, the desire to bridge over the contrasts in form had not entirely vanished. During the war the neofunctionalist architect A. Komter, a moderate, had played an important role in the at-

30.1. Delft School, Postwar reconstruction of Middleburg. (Photograph: Courtesy of Archiphoto, Amsterdam)

tempt at conciliation formed by the Doorn conferences. He had also been an advisor on the Rotterdam reconstruction plan and was one of the few people who attempted to express this compromise in his postwar plans. His design for a new clubhouse (the old one had been destroyed during the war) for the royal rowing and yachting club *De Hoop* on the Amstel in Amsterdam is a good example of this. (fig. 30.3). Later, such conciliatory architecture was termed, appropriately, the "shake hands" manner.

30.3. A. Komter, architect. Royal Rowing and Yachting Club, *De Hoop*. Clubhouse. Amsterdam, 1952. (Photograph: Courtesy of Hubers/Meindersma)

THE TRANSITION TOWARD AFFLUENCE
(ABOUT 1950-1960)

At the beginning of the fifties the reconstruction period was under way. Industry especially got many opportunities, partly as a result of Marshall Plan help, partly through the economic policy of the government. The socioeconomic and cultural aspects of Dutch society changed very much with economic growth, international contacts, and stable government paving the way for an affluent society. While the power structures changed, buildings continued to symbolize power, status, and success. The Netherlands changed from a predominantly agricultural country with important colonies into a modern trading and industrial state, without colonies, on the American model. Many architectural movements especially were greatly influenced by America—the economic example. Building materials were soon in ample supply again, so that it was no longer necessary to build in the traditional way. Thinking in numbers became increasingly important; and for mass production of buildings, especially houses, the production-line techniques of the automobile industry were imitated. Thinking in terms of increased scale did not stop at the number of houses to be built or the required production techniques: the buildings themselves became larger and, particularly, higher. It was, however, still too early for the large-scale application of industrial building techniques, in spite of the great shortages of buildings. The requisite funds were still needed in order to rebuild industry.

During the fifties and sixties the three tendencies that had been discernible in Dutch architecture began to disintegrate for a time. Many new social and technical developments resulted in new forms, and the differences between traditional and modern faded. It became apparent that the ideal models of both the Delft school and the CIAM needed modifying, though many people remained oblivious to the need for new points of departure in architectural design. The introduction of experimental new materials and building techniques, and design patterns influenced by personal preferences, appeared to be more important than the search for communal solutions. Liberation from the old dogmas as well as the reestablishment of international contacts gave rise to a large number of highly individual styles in design. Thus, J. J. Vriend, the most important Dutch critic of architecture until the seventies, could write of this period: "The concept of architecture taken for granted in our culture since the end of the nineteenth century, seems to have lost all significance."[4] Despite such important changes, the three main groups, traditionalist, nonconformist, and moderate, reemerged in the seventies as distinct.

In 1953 the Delft school lost its most important leader when Granpré Molière ended his career as professor in Delft. That the younger generation of the Delft school began to look for new forms, no longer eschewing modern building materials and methods, may be partially attributed to changed circumstances. Professor J. F. Berghoef, one of its most important members, went so far as to design a great number of dwellings in the preindustrial Airey building system (fig. 30.4), that was based on the

30.4. J. F. Berghoef and H. Klarenbeek, architects. Housing project in the Airey, small elements building system, 1957. (Photograph: Courtesy of Hubers/Meindersma)

superimposition of relatively small standardized elements, comparable to the well-known Lego toy system. Only at the end of the sixties was it supplanted by the large-element system. The Gelderland county hall in Arnhem by J. J. Vegter with its diverse cubical forms and surface textures may also be regarded as a largely successful attempt at modernization on the part of a traditionalist architect.

The social changes of the fifties brought about a modification of prewar assumptions concerning modern architecture. The foundations for the renewal of the original CIAM views, based on a highly analytical approach to problems in architecture and urban design, were laid during CIAM conferences in Bridgewater, England (1947), Dubrovnik, Yugoslavia (1956), and Otterloo, the Netherlands (1959). The most important Dutch spokesmen at these conferences were J. B. Bakema and Aldo van Eyck, who were members of the international Team X group of architects. They also became editors of the previously mentioned journal, *Forum*, in 1959. Van Eyck, in particular, was opposed to the CIAM's analytical approach to architectural problems, in which urban design, among other things, was regarded as a separate discipline. In Otterloo, he said: "Yes, we must stop stop splitting the making of a habitat into two disciplines—architecture and urbanism. . . . a house must be like a small city if it's to be a real house—a city like a large house if it's to be a real city. In fact, what is large without being small has no more real size than what is small without being large."[5]

The resistance of van Eyck, Bakema, and others to the CIAM doctrine took shape in the design movement known as Brutalism, the ideological significance and most important examples of which have been described in detail by Reyner Banham in *The New Brutalism*. In the Netherlands, the firm of van den Broek and Bakema built several important Brutalist buildings such as the reformed church at Nagele [1960], a particularly fine example.

In Amsterdam Aldo van Eyck designed his well-known orphanage [1955-1960] on a parcel of wasteland on the outskirts of Amsterdam (fig. 30.5). Instead of a spectacular, high building with lots of glass and primary colors, it was a highly introverted complex with as many as possible of its more or less private spaces at ground level. Most remarkable about the building was its construction according to a refined geometrical pattern that was spatially interpreted in terms of functional requirements. The striking roof construction of prefabricated concrete domes was in itself a turning point in thought concerning the creative possibilities of industrial building methods, and actually anticipated Structuralism, the important Dutch avant-garde movement of the sixties. Moreover, the building's many functional and decorative details (such as little built-in mirrors at child's eye level and passage lights placed outside of windows so that artificial light comes in also at night, to make the border between inside and outside less distinct) in fact indicate a break with modern functionalist tradition. Van Eyck's orphanage was soon given the nickname "Kaffir village," rightly referring to the African influence which, together with the theme "inside-outside," played such an important role in works of the *Forum* group.

30.5. Aldo van Eyck, architect. Orphanage. Amsterdam, 1955-1960. (Photograph: Courtesy of Hubers/Meindersma)

AFFLUENCE AND EXPANSION: THE SIXTIES

Around 1960 the economy started booming. Sacrifices for the benefit of the reconstruction, such as wage and price moderations, were no longer acceptable and a wage explosion at the beginning of the sixties began a period of expansion. People enjoyed the blessings of the consumer society.

At first all went well and even the housing problem was attended to at last. The Netherlands government's attempt to remedy the housing shortage created a building boom in the sixties, a decade sometimes referred to as the numerical nightmare. Great efforts were made to speed up production; and building firms had to introduce labor-saving techniques in order to be eligible for certain projects. Unlike the fifties, when industrial building techniques were mainly based on small elements and on-the-site rationalizations of the building process, the necessary increase of production could only be attained by means of large, factory-made building components. At first, building systems from France (Indeco-Coignet) and Denmark (Larsen Nielsen) were adopted for the purpose.

It was not realized that encouragement of the techniques of industrialization and standardization, and of factories for housing threatened not only to result in the creation of monopolies but also in an impoverishment of design. Large-scale design became a most important theme in Dutch architecture. In the future, houses and other buildings would have to be built in quantity from standard factory-made components which were to be simply assembled on the site. The superimposition of large components led almost automatically to high-rise building, and from then on a guaranteed regular turnover was necessary if the manufacture of housing was to function at its optimum. The construction of high-rise buildings was advocated as the solution for the problem of housing the 20 million population that was projected for Holland in the year 2000; and in turn all this led to a very considerable building bureaucracy.

Clearly the design of extensive new housing estates had to meet the stiff preliminary conditions of industrial builders and bureaucratic planners and consequently uniformity came about in residential, commercial, industrial, and utilitarian building. An overall increase in scale, conformity, and red tape were the banes of the building process. Traditional building and design seemed things of the past.

However, this period of unbridled expansion within uniformity of design did not last very long. Already halfway through the sixties the first cracks in the pattern of our self-satisfied welfare state started to show. The reactions provoked made it clear that the way decisions were made needed revision. Criticism of large-scale building came from the protest and resistance movements of the mid and late sixties. But it was still a question of finding solutions for regulating an affluent society. The artist Constant (Nieuwenhuys) created a furor with his New Babylon architectural project [1960], which consisted of models of cities and buildings for a future society in which nobody would have to work. Above all, the architectural movements of the sixties reflected an affluent society in both traditional and modern architecture.

During the sixties the traditionalism of the Delft school and its variants became a thing of the past. Conformity was no longer expressed as a reflection of tradition but represented new positions of authority and commercial success. Rotterdam's Euromast [built in 1960 by H. A. Maaskant] exemplifies this "demonstrative" architecture: after its completion the Euromast's height was increased so that it would remain the tallest building in Rotterdam, despite the competition of other high rises that were becoming so popular then in the Netherlands. The head office of the Bank of the Netherlands in Amsterdam, for instance [designed by M. F. Duint'jes and finished in [1969], was the first Dutch building with more than fifteen stories. Most high office buildings of the 1960s and into the 1970s were designed in an individual style to symbolize the success of the company involved, as for example, the Shell building (fig. 30.6), in Amsterdam [1970, designed by A. Staal].

30.6. A. Staal, architect. Shell Building, Amsterdam, 1969-1971. (Photograph: Courtesy of Archiphoto, Amsterdam)

Resistance to the conformist and bureaucratic philosophies of large-scale building expansion took shape socially and architecturally in the Provo movement. Nonconformist architects had never resigned themselves to gratuitous high-rise solutions for the greater need for space. The problem was, however, how to avoid being bound by the simple addition of quantities of uniform spaces.

The reaction to uniformity and mono Functionalism culminated in the new architectural movement of Structuralism which took Aldo van Eyck's orphanage [1957-1960] as a methodological archetype and used the Dutch magazine *Forum* as a mouthpiece.* Industrial building and functional adaptability, borrowed from Nikolaas John Habraken and the Stichting Architecten Research (SAR) among others, were taken as points of departure; and the search began for space-creating building components which would provide a large degree of freedom in design and functioning, despite the inevitable uniformity due to mass production. Herman Hertzberger, an important advocate of Structuralism, described it as "the interaction of form and programme. . . . In order to survive the transformation process everything that is built must be so formed that it can be plurally interpreted, that is to say, able to take on other implications and discard them again without its identity being affected. . . . A form must be interpretable so as to be able to play a changing role [and its implications incorporated as concealed possibilities] in such a way that they are present in the form of stimuli, suggested but not stated."[6]

In 1968 Aldo van Eyck was invited to enter a competition to design an extension for the town hall situated in the old city center of Deventer. His winning plan embodied an endorsement of the existing architecture of the city center, not so much by falling back on traditional ideas, though certain affinities to these cannot be entirely denied, as by recognizing the physical and functional significance of the existing city center. In connection with their reconstruction plan for the Nieuwmarkt neighborhood in Amsterdam, in 1970 van Eyck and his colleagues expressed their approach to urbanism:

> We believe that the old city centers, both spatially and physically, and for their own sakes are psychologically indispensable today, because they are there with their vivid colorfulness and privacy and because none of the new urban areas to date possess these essential qualities at all, not even in a modern idiom. They are unaccommodating, bare and sterile and therefore insufficiently liveable.
>
> As long as they remain this way, the city center will function as donor. Today, however, this task is too great for its size. Therefore, it is absolutely essential not only to keep the city center as large as possible, but also to prevent those qualities enabling it to function as donor, owing to the sterility of the suburbs, from being destroyed by the addition of mass.[7]

Building plans for the same Nieuwmarkt area and the city center of Zwolle reveal that careful adaptation to the existing urban framework is not possible with structuralistic design principles and system-built housing.

Van Eyck's vision, or what stood for it, quickly became popular. Small-scale thinking and traditional building structures began to replace demolition and large-scale new building not only in urban renewal but also in areas of new development. High-rise plans were quickly converted into small-scale, somewhat cozy, low-rise building designs so that housing factories that had flourished before were all but closed down by the mid-seventies.

Sharply increased bureaucratic influence during this period was not limited to the administrative and financial side of things, but also had its effects on design, especially in the field of housing. Pragmatic attempts to rationalize and increase the production of housing were unlike the government intervention respecting a Dutch cultural background which took place during the reconstruction period of the fifties. Not only governmental and large construction firms recommended the rationalization and automation of the building process to solve the growing demand for housing and other buildings. For the many architects who also looked toward the renaissance of the machine, Nicholaas J. Habraken was undoubtedly the most important theoretician. As director of the Stichting Architecten Research (SAR) he had great influence on the development of housing during the

*EDITOR'S NOTE: The Dutch Structuralists have sought to return the human factor to Functionalism and urban design by using basic architectural forms intended to encourage group interrelationships. Furthered at first in the 1950s and 1960s by research into the architectures of primitive peoples, Structuralism became an architectural movement in which relatively simple geometric forms were repeated to strengthen and clarify communication. With geometric constants of architectural design imbued with various meanings, changes in and expansion of the architectural organism could be accomplished so as to enrich rather than disturb ongoing human relationships. Though the Dutch Structuralists originally developed with no relation to the philosophy espoused by Claude Lévi-Strauss, they have come to recognize that there are many parallels between their architectural thinking and his philosophical theories. *W.S.*

sixties, the results of which are seen in the massive bureaucratic architecture of such residential areas as the Bijlmermeer in Amsterdam and the Ommoord in Rotterdam.

THE TURNAROUND OF THE SEVENTIES

The protest movement of the sixties and the call for a renewal of society accompanying it were largely based on the assumption that economic growth would continue: only the odd pessimist doubted this. The Club of Rome in 1972 and the oil crisis in the following year, however, drastically changed this outlook. During the seventies, shortages of energy and raw materials, widespread and probably lasting unemployment, economic stagnation, inequitable distribution of resources, and environmental pollution all became problems which diminished faith in the affluent society and in the "experts" who had underestimated its negative side effects.

Economic stagnation was an important factor in reviving interest in the past, which had been rather neglected as a result of thinking primarily in terms of "progress" during the two previous postwar decades. And the past was expressed by a superficial romanticizing of grandmother's days.

The wave of protests during the late sixties had paved the way for great public involvement in important social matters, including building. Architecture was no longer an autonomous process, with architects and other specialists alone in leading roles. Future users had to be considered as well. "What people would like" took tangible form in their participation at the design-stage, and made itself felt as well in cases where the users were not personally consulted. An aversion to design movements associated with specialized views and particular cultural traditions arose, almost as a matter of natural course. These were replaced by populist views in which for the most part architectural forms and urban patterns of the broad past were borrowed for, after all, these were considered as "beautiful" by a wide spectrum of the general public.

Symptomatic of the pause that occurred in architectural debate late in the sixties and into the seventies was the fact that Dutch architectural magazines then were filled mainly by the writings of social critics. It became apparent that industrial building methods were no longer needed to attain the necessary level of housing production, and urban renewal was viewed as the most important problem of architecture and urban design. Urban renewal, public participation, and the rejection of the post-modern architecture of the sixties were combined in so paradoxical a composition of societal demand that the concepts of traditionalism and nonconformism hardly seem significant in understanding the architecture of the seventies.

Traditionalism as an ideologically based movement in architecture had already begun to be more or less displaced in the late fifties by the "status-symbol" architecture of the expansion period, which often displayed classic characteristics. The great popularity enjoyed by the restoration of historical buildings expressed a new notion of traditionalism during the seventies in which the main focus was on pre-eighteenth-century architecture that was analogous to historical examples of the Delft school. The fortified town of Heusden, for example, was restored and returned to its seventeenth-century plan.

The avant-garde architecture of the seventies, unlike preceding periods, was typically multiformal. Many progressive architects were enthusiastic advocates of full client participation in building design, and this went hand in hand with the renewal of urban centers and old residential areas, where the users were known. After Aldo van Eyck and Theo Bosch made their plans for the Deventer town hall and the renewal of the Nieuwmarkt area in Amsterdam, conflicts between architects and inhabitants about design became rare, because extant structures were valued as a point of departure in urban renewal. A high point in the interpretation of a vernacular architecture for urban renewal is undoubtedly the home for unmarried mothers in Amsterdam by Also van Eyck [1979] (fig. 30.7) with its varied, often elegant design.

Attempts by Herman Hertzberger and others, including Piet Blom, Jaap van Stigt, Frank van Klingeren and Henk Klunder, to give industrialized building systems a multiform, yet individualized character exemplified Dutch Structuralism well into the seventies.[8] The best known of structuralist buildings is in Apeldoorn, where Hertzberger designed a large office complex [1970-1972] (fig. 30.8) and in Hengelo where Piet Blom built a complex of 168 municipal housing units [1972-1973] known as the Kasbah (fig. 30.9) because of its resemblance to North African town centers. Blom's buildings in particular created a fresh integration of residential with other functions in a high-density plan that was originally intended for an urban renewal area in Amsterdam. Urban renewal had begun to attract great interest at the end of the sixties, partly because with the end of the housing shortage apparently in sight it was viewed as a means of preventing the building industry from collapsing. With

30.7. Aldo van Eyck, architect. Home for unwed mothers. Amsterdam, 1979. (Photograph: Courtesy of Stichting Wonen, G.v.d. Vlugt)

30.8. Herman Hertzberger, architect. Centraal Beheer Office Building Complex. Apeldoorn, 1970-1972. (Photograph: Courtesy of Hubers/Meindersma)

Blom's Kasbah plan often serving to best exemplify it, Structuralism, for its versatility and its flexible allocation of functions, appeared to be the ideal architectural approach for urban renewal.

In the seventies despite the apparent absence of important conflicts about design between architects and the public, there was often a dilemma as to where the professional designer's control ended and that of the concerned users began. As a structuralist, Hertzberger tried to skirt this by designing a series of "shell" dwellings, for instance at Delft [1971], in such a way that their future inhabitants would be able to finish them in different ways themselves. Almost inevitably, this led to great discrepancies between on the one hand the building techniques and structuralist design-language of Hertzberger and on the other the more limited capacity for design and construction techniques of the do-it-yourselfer inhabitants.

During the seventies too a hesitant reaction to the energy shortage took the form of plans for active or passive solar power uses and many special constructions and installations designed to conserve energy. For the 1977 design competition for a new city hall in Lelystad the entry of F. L. Kristinsson-Reitsema employed parabolic roof channels of stainless steel as energy collectors and was most promising, but unfortunately the municipal council's conservative majority chose a more traditional plan. The well-known Dutch critic of architecture, Ruud Brouwers, described his disappontment at the lost opportunity:

> Had the Kristinsson plan been chosen it would have meant the construction at a competitive price compared with traditional building, of a building able to be heated the whole year round by solar energy, thanks to underground seasonal storage, for the first time in the northern hemisphere. It was not to be. Everything must always be done without risk and according to plan, so that nothing is actually possible.[9]

Unrelated to energy-conscious architecture in 1978 Rem Koolhaas of the Office of Metropolitan Architecture (OMA) and a virtual unknown in the Netherlands entered the competition for augmenting The Hague's Second Chamber of Holland's parliament (fig. 30.10) with a design of long, slender, geometrically neat buildings linked in places by long, narrow, bridgelike passageways. This broke completely with the type of architecture based upon restoration of the urban structure in its historic context. Though considered as the most noteworthy plan, Koolhaas's proposal was rejected. He has since become a prominent, highly original representative of Dutch architectural innovation.

30.9. Piet Blom, architect. "Kasbah" housing complex. Hengelo, 1972-1973. (Photograph: Courtesy of Stichting Wonen, G.v.d. Vlugt)

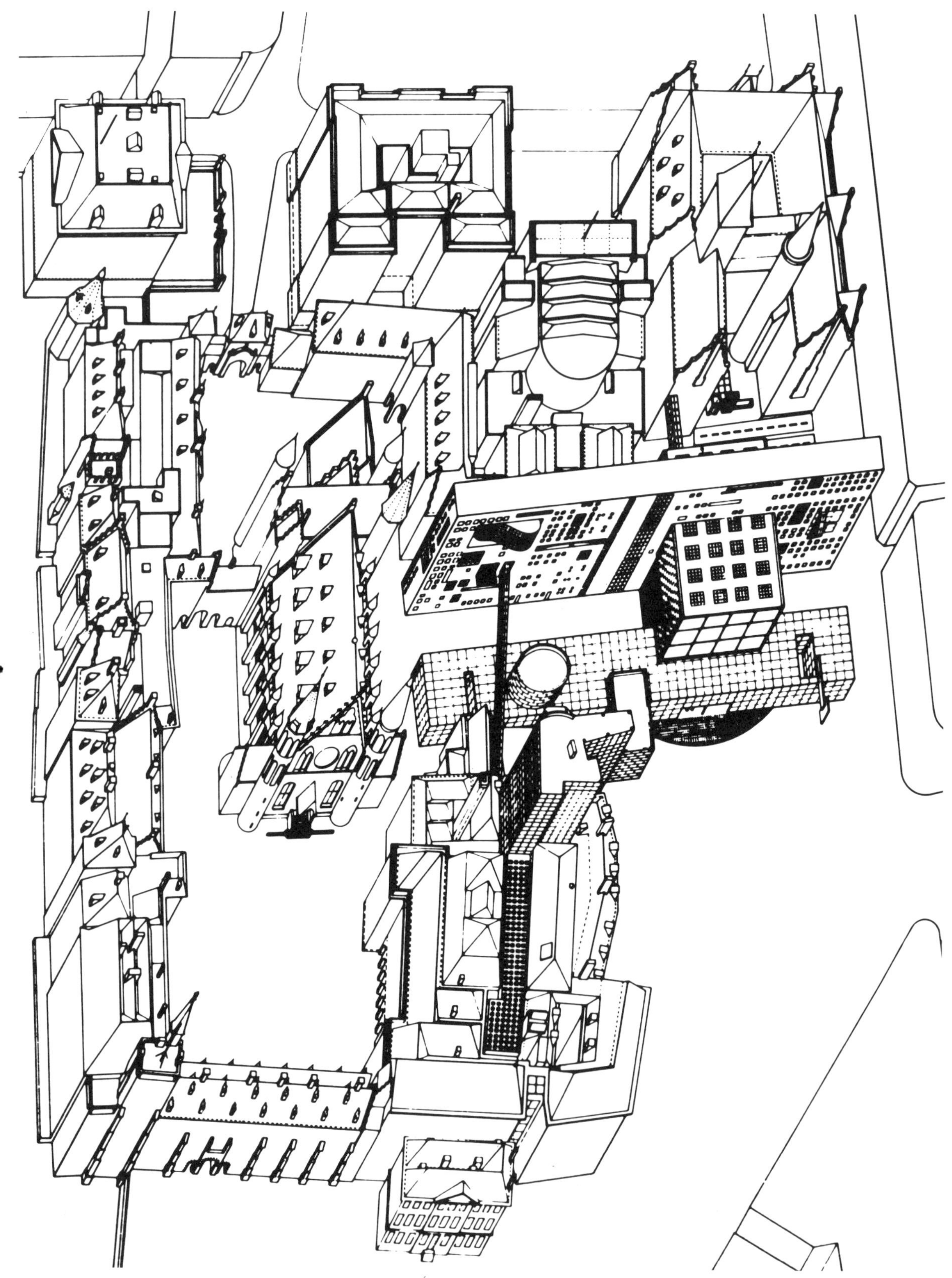

30.10. Rem Koolhaas, architect. Competition entry for augmentation of the Second Chamber of Parliament. The Hague, 1978. (Photograph: Courtesy of Archiphoto, Amsterdam)

The outer form of many buildings constructed during the past decade or so might lead one to believe that the days of the traditionalist Delft school had returned. Appearances, however, are deceptive.

Modern designs were developed in which such traditional building materials as brick, tiles, and much wood were employed only to satisfy popular taste. The same principle is evident in urban planning and design. The new satellite town of Amsterdam, Almere Haven in the Zuidelijke Flevoland polder, is a typical example. In 1971 the plan of the design team led by G. Frieling was adapted at the last moment to fit the current taste for nostalgia including even a copy of an Amsterdam canal.

Epilogue

Recently, there has been a significant revival of architectural debate after a decade in which Dutch architects, aside from the Structuralists, made virtually no contribution to theoretical discussion concerning what should be built and methods of construction. With the impetus coming mainly from abroad, there is a parallel with the situation in the fifties when the need for an approach equally free from the traditional and the most advanced modern was sought. Again, many important international contacts and influences are combined with much changed social conditions that require new architectural and planning solutions. During the fifties there seemed to be no limit to the developments of technology and to an affluence consequent upon it. Now, however, that prospect has been reversed. For the first time since the Second World War, incomes in the Netherlands are projected to decrease. Planning for decline may well require even greater inventiveness than did unlimited growth and expansion.

Remarkably enough now, architectural debate in the Netherlands seems detached from its social content, most likely in reaction to the seventies when design had to meet requirements arising from public participation. Competition designs in which the development and testing of ideas, like one of 1979-1980 for expanding the town hall in Usquert (designed originally by H. P. Berlage) will continue to play an important role in the ongoing discussion. The continuous thread of social awareness in the development of modern Dutch architecture is so important, however, that it cannot remain neglected for long. When taken up again, the altered social perspectives, such as a sharply declining occupancy rate, are likely to provoke a new critical analysis of the relations between quality and cost, given the different demand. Curtailment of construction and production costs are likely to be the most important factors in the development of design and building techniques during the eighties; and the increase of do-it-yourself activity may result in a lighter, less formal type of architecture. With the distinction between avant-garde and more traditional movements depending partly on the cultural differences in society, decreasing affluence is likely to exaggerate rather than lessen differences, and almost certainly this will be reflected in tomorrow's Dutch architecture.

Notes

1. *De eeuwige architectuur* (Amsterdam, 1957).
2. *Over de toekomstige Bouwkunst en haar architectonishe Mogelijheden* (1921).
3. W. van Tijen, *Plan* 6, 1972.
4. *Links Bouwen, Rechts Bouwen* (Amsterdam, 1974), p. 144.
5. Alison Smithson, *Team X Primer* (Cambridge, Mass.: MIT Press, 1968), p. 27.
6. Herman Hertzberger, *Forum* 16, no. 3 (1963).
7. Lectures given by Aldo van Eyck et al., "Post Academiale Cursus," Academie van Bouwkunst, Amsterdam, 1970.
8. Arnulf Lüchinger, "Strukturalismus line neue Strömung in der Architektur," *Bauen und Wohmer* 30, no. 1 (January 1976): 5-40. See also Editor's Note, p. 426.
9. Ruud Brouwers, *Wonen—TA/BK*, 1977, pp. 21-77.

Bibliography

BOOKS

Bouwen '20-40, Catalog, Stedelyk Van Abbemuseum. Eindhoven: 1971.

Blijstra, R. *Dutch Architecture after 1900*. Amsterdam: P. N. van Kampen and Zoon, N.V., 1966.

Brown, Theodore M. *The Work of G. Rietveld*. Cambridge, Mass.: MIT Press, 1958.

Fanelli, G. *Architettura Moderna in Olanda 1900-1940*. Florence: 1968 and The Hague: 1978.

Granpré Molière, M. J. *De Euwige Architectuur. I. De Hedendaagse Architectuur in het Licht der Geschiedenis*. Amsterdam: 1958.

Gubitosi, Camillo and Izzo, Alberto, eds., *Van den Broek/Bakema*. Rome: Officina Edizioni, 1976.

Habraken, Nikolaas J. *Supports, An Alternative to Mass Housing*. New York: Praeger, 1972.

Jaffé, Hans L. C. *De Stijl*. London: Thames and Hudson, 1970.

Joedicke, Jürgen. *Architektur und Städebau: Das Werk van den Broek und Bakema*. Stuttgart: Karl Krämer Verlag, 1963.

Oud, J. J. P. *Mijn Weg in 'De Stijl.'* The Hague Rotterdam: 1960.

Szénássy, István L. *Architectuur in Nederland*, 1960/1967. Amsterdam: Scheltema and Holkema, 1969.

Vriend, J. J. *Links Bouwen, Rechts Bouwen*. Amsterdam: Contract, 1974.

JOURNALS

"A. Bonnema: Office Building in Leeuwarden," *Architecture and Urbanism* 100 (January 1979): 75-84. (In Japanese; English photo captions)

"Architecture in the Netherlands—Special Issue." *Bauforum* 7 (January/February 1974). (In German)

"Un architetto e una città: Berlage ad Amsterdam." *Casabella* no. 249 (March 1961): 36-53.

Barbieri, S. Umberto. "Form and Planning: Some Aspects of Contemporary Dutch Architecture." *Dutch Art and Architecture Today* 4 (November 1978): 25-38.

Bindels, John et al. "Profile of a Growing City: Breda." *Bouw* 34, no. 10 (12 May 1979): 9-38. (In Dutch)

Brouwers, Ruud. "Wm. Quist Retires as 'Ryksbouwmeester' with Sure Cynicism." *Wonen TA/BK* 23 (December 1979): 9-15. (In Dutch)

Burns, L. S. "Relationship between Physical and Economic Planning." (Rotterdam) *Town Planning Review* 34 (January 1964): 269-84.

Castex, Jean and Panerai, Philippe. "The Amsterdam School; Urban Architecture and Social-Democratic Planning." *Architecture, Mouvement, Continuité* 40 (September 1976): 39-54. (In French)

"Centre de Minique d'Utrecht." *L'Architecture d'Aujourd'hui* 198 (September 1978): 48-53.

Dijk, Hans van. "Herman Hertzberger: Architectural Principles in the Decade of Humanism." *Dutch Art and Architecture Today* 6 (December 1979): 25-35.

Goetham, J. van. "Casa dei Ragazzi ad Amsterdam, A. van Eyck, Architect." *Architettura* 7 (October 1961): 386-402.

Grinberg, Donald I. "Modernist Housing and Its Critics: The Dutch Contributions." *Harvard Architecture Review* 1 (Spring 1980): 146-57.

Hartsuyker, Hendrik, ed. "Hollandische Architektur und Kunst der Gegenwart." *Werk* 38 (November 1951): 325-48.

Hertzberger, Herman. "A New Music Center at Utrecht." (In English, French, Italian) *Domus* 601 (December 1971): 9-20.

______. "Per gli studenti ad Amsterdam." *Domus* 454 (September 1967): 9-18.

Hubers, W. and Meindersma, H. "Variation and Monotony: Post-War Architecture in Holland." (In Dutch and English) *Forum* 26, no. 4/5 (1978): 5-60.

Jaffe, C. and Fischer, R. E. "3 Acoustic Designs from Europe." *Architectural Record* 166 (Mid-August 1979): 109-13.

Kloos, J. P. "The Dutch Melting-Pot: Recent Architecture in Holland. *Architectural Review* 103, no. 616 (April 1948): 137-56.

Liang Kho le Associates, ed. "Itinerario: Architettura Olandese 1900-1973." *Domus* 529 (December 1973): 1-8.

Lüchinger, Arnulf. "Strukturalismus—eine neue Strömung in der Architektur." *Bauen und Wohnen* 30, no. 1 (January 1976): 5-40.

______ and Hertzberger, Herman. "Herman Hertzberger, Dutch Architect." (In English and Japanese) *Architecture and Urbanism* 3, no. 75 (March 1977): 46-146.

Manacorda, Giuseppe and Nicoli, Antonio. "Olanda, Le iniziative economiche, legislative e sociali e i criteri tecnici e architettonici negli interventi di recupero." *Casabella* no. 442 (December 1978): 34-40.

Mulder, Jos De et al. "To Build for the District: Urban Renovation . . . " *A+* 62 (January/February 1980): 7-21. (In French)

"Municipio di Ede, Olanda." *Architettura* 23 (January 1978): 512-20.

Nicolin, Pierluigi. "Aldo van Eyck; the Web and the Labyrinth." (In English and Italian) *Lotus* 11 (1976): 105-27.

Patijn, Wytze. "Variation und Diversität: eine neue Form der Eintönigkeit?" *Werk Archithese* 65, no. 17/18 (May 1978): 15-20.

Pawley, M. "Agora, Holland's New-style Community Centre; F. van Klingeren, Architect." *Architectural Design* 39 (July 1969): 358-62.

______. "Mass housing . . . (Nikolaas Habraken)." *Architectural Design* 40 (January 1970): 32-38.

Perugini, G. "Costruzioni degli architetti Jacob Bakema e Johannes van den Broek." *Architettura* 5 (September 1959): 324-39.

Polano, Sergio and Barbiere, Umberto. "La Charte D'Athènes Réalisée ou le Silence de L'architecture (Bijlmermeer, Amsterdam)." *L'Architecture d'Aujourd'hui* 187 (October/November 1976): 2-6. (English Summary p. lvi)

Prak, N. Luning. "Material for the Modern Movement. Foundation of the CIAM . . . " *Parametro* 8, no. 58 (July/August 1977): 42-45. (In Italian)

Sandberg, W. "Centre Commercial pour piétons (van den Broek et Bakema) et Les grands magasins de Rotterdam (Breuer, Elzas and Schwarzman)." *Zodiac* 1 (1957): 139-58. (French and English summaries p. 275)

"Special Issue. Rotterdam: Does Urban Renewal Help against the Growth of Slums?" *Wonen—TA/BK* 9/10 (May 1979): 6-46. (In Dutch)

"Spijkenisse: Mirror of Dutch Housing Architecture (1950-1979)." *Architect* 10, no. 12 (December 1979): 93-98. (In Dutch)

Taylor, Brian Brace. "Nikolaas Habraken." *L'Architecture d'Aufourd'hui* 174 (July/August 1974): 66-73. (In English and French)

______. "Utopia: Cento anni di acqua potabile a Rotterdam: the conversion of an old water-tower." *Domus* 96 (July 1979): 33-38. (In Italian and English)

Veronesi, G. "Jacobus Johannes Pieter Oud, 1890-1963." *Zodiac* 12 (1963): 82-105.

Walraven, A. van. "La revisione e l'attuazione del piano di Amsterdam." *Urbanistica* 38 (March 1963): 13-44.

Wiekart, Karel. "Dutch Modern Architecture." *Museum Journal* 3 (September 1974): 98-104.

______. "Zeichensetzende Architektur: Town Hall in Terneuzen." *Bauen und Wohnen* 28, no. 2 (1974): 76.

SOME USEFUL JOURNALS

Architect (The Hague)
Bouw
Dutch Art and Architecture Today
Forum
Museum Journaal
Plan
Polytechnisch Tijdschrift
Wonen—TA/BK

31

NORWAY

NILS-OLE LUND

The Second World War hit Norway very badly. In April 1940 several towns on the west coast were bombed and burnt out and in the ensuing five years very little was built. Finally, during the German withdrawal from the northern part of the country in 1945 great destruction was wrought. Thus, just after the war problems of reconstruction became most urgent. Even before 1940 there had been a shortage of dwellings but available money had to be spent where the war damage was worst.

The postwar years were necessarily a period of rationing and restrictions. During the occupation, with its complete stagnation in the building industry, architects had survived in a state of hibernation though some planning was carried out for the reconstruction of the burnt-out cities. The layouts, designed then by the internationally well-known town planner, Sverre Pedersen, were based on principles derived from the classical revival period of the twenties. After the war his planning was considered as too formalistic and as a German import similar to Albert Speer's planning of Berlin, lacking the surveys and socioeconomical considerations which are integrated into Anglo-Saxon planning.

More important for postwar development was research carried out by a group of Oslo architects including Carsten Boysen and Odd Brochmann on the conditions of the housing stock of Oslo. During the war, when professional practice was impossible, architects and other specialists had studied the dwellings produced in the twenties and thirties. They gathered the opinions of people living in flats and documented housing standards, and flat sizes and plans. This survey was most influential on housing policy just after the war. The overall standard was raised, equipment was improved, and the three-room flat became the standard dwelling in state-subsidized housing.

The war had created a strong feeling of national solidarity which was the political basis for reforms. While, between the wars, housing had been mostly the responsibility of local authorities, after 1945 cooperative housing societies (NBBL and OBOS) took over. The government set up a state bank (*husbanken*) to finance new housing schemes and lower rents. A new school of architecture was established in Oslo (the first had been in Trondheim) and Norway got its first institute of building research. Though the period of recovery after the war produced quite a number of buildings, very few were of permanent architectural value. Among the reasons for quantity rather than quality were the many restrictions placed on the building industry, the scarcity of materials, and the overall weak economy.

In the late twenties and the thirties the Modern Movement, arriving in Scandinavia from Germany, Holland, and France (Le Corbusier), was overwhelmingly successful. The Stockholm Exhibition of 1930 in a sense marked its victory in the Nordic countries. The Modern Movement was forward-looking with its white, cubistic style. International in its outlook, it made use of new technology to help solve the problems of industrial societies. Its most important Norwegian architects were Lars Backer, Frithjof Reppen, Arne Korsmo, and Ove Bang.

It is not surprising that the attitude of the profession changed after the war. The buildings of the thirties with their flat roofs and plastered facades had been criticized for their lack of tradition and for being badly suited to the Nordic climate. As early as 1938 this change can be seen, for example, in the project by Odd and Karen Brochmann for the

Norwegian Pavilion at the World's Fair in New York and in the graceful Forest Crematorium at the Woodland Cemetery outside Stockholm at Emskede [1935-1940], designed by the architect of the Stockholm Exhibition, Erik Gunnar Asplund. Five years of occupation produced even stronger national feelings—feelings that had to be translated into Norway's architecture. In the late 1940s nearly everybody agreed that architecture should be more humane and less doctrinaire. This pragmatism, named Scandinavian Empiricism by the English, was an ideology well adapted to the restrictions and regulations imposed on the building industry by the government.

In planning there was the same vaguely defined but socially concerned approach. The master plan for Oslo prepared in 1950 under chief planner Erik Rolfsen was typical, with ideological influences from the Anglo-Saxon world and especially from Lewis Mumford whose book, *The Culture of Cities*, had been translated into Swedish in 1952. The master plan was made up of greenbelts, neighborhood units, and satellite towns connected with the inner city by a network of suburban railroads. As a special Norwegian feature the plan included a system of paths along which the people of Oslo could go skiing from the center to the hilly woodland around the town. The plan demonstrated little concern for the inner city and instead all the energy of the city planners was concentrated on the development of new settlements east of Oslo.

The first ten years after the war were a time of recovery, while during the next ten years Norway began to be a country of affluence. In the 1960s Norway joined in the overall boom of the Western economies and the standard of living rose at a very fast rate. The boom was accompanied by drastic changes in economic life and in settlement patterns. Though Norway is a vast country, 85 percent of its total area cannot be used for human settlement. Its four million inhabitants are spread unevenly mostly near the sea or in the more friendly valleys with the district around the Oslo fjord especially densely populated.

In the postwar period fewer and fewer people were earning their income from fishing, agriculture, and forestry and these industries stopped expanding. As centers of service and trade the towns have absorbed the influx of people from the countryside. At the same time there has been a push outwards from the cities, with people moving out into the suburbs as they searched for a higher standard of living than the inner city could offer. This movement was made possible by the automobile. While this trend can be seen everywhere in the Western world, in a country with a tradition of people making their living from the sea and from the land, abrupt change has created a great deal of social and political unrest. The opinion that the change is not worthwhile, that it endangers the best of the traditional Norwegian life-style, grows ever more common. The general feeling that growth is not always beneficial gained strength in the 1970s especially with the international debates on dwindling resources and environmental issues.

For the early 1950s, Norwegian architects may be grouped into three categories. The first, a Norwegian branch of CIAM called PAGON, was a very small group that consisted of very young, newly educated architects, keen on importing international trends to Norwegian soil. Projects designed by the PAGON team were very Miesian in their concern with order, structure, and clean detailing. Active members included among others, Christian Norberg-Schulz, Sverre Fehn, Odd Østbye, Gierg Grung, Hakon Mjelva, and Arne Korsmo, the only architect among them with professional experience dating from the period before the war. One of the few buildings erected while the group was together is the old peoples' home at Økern in Oslo, by architects, Geirg Grung and Sverre Fehn [1956]. A low, white, horizontal building, it is very powerful in its strict geometric order but a strangely modernistic environment for old people. Another project, three houses built on a slope north of Oslo in 1954, was designed by Arne Korsmo and Christian Norberg-Schulz, and included homes for themselves. These reflect a deep interest in the steel-frame structures of Mies van der Rohe and of Charles Eames's Santa Monica house of 1948. The various members of the PAGON group have now separated. Norberg-Schulz is known as a theorist; Sverre Fehn works more and more with a rather timeless, basic architecture as in his Norwegian Pavilion in Brussels [1958]; his Norwegian Art Pavilion in Venice [1962]; and the school in Skådalen outside Oslo [1968-1975]; and only Håkon Mjelva, for example, in the Økern center [1969], is still designing in the mainstream of the International Style.

In the second grouping, not a working group per se, were all the architects designing within the postwar tradition of Norwegian architecture, an architecture without any clear philosophy. A typical and especially well-known example of their work is the big housing project outside Oslo, Lambertsæter, built from 1951 to 1954.

The third group was started with the philosophy of one man. By the mid-1950s Knut Knutsen, a self-made architect about fifty years old, began to attract a whole school of followers with his philosophy of nature. The turning away from international, cubistic Functionalism that had been introduced into Scandinavia just before the war is evident in Knut Knutsen's two projects: the old-age home at Tåsen in Oslo [1939-1941] and the Sørmarka high school south of Oslo [1938]. The architecture in these projects is relaxed, unobtrusive, and difficult to describe, with blocks of linked buildings of varying heights and materials and many pitched roofs. In a country where one can often look down on buildings, the roof becomes a fifth facade. It is an architecture of repetition and rhythm where the buildings are stepped downhill in many directions. The complexity of the layout is accentuated by the choice of materials. In the high school the facade is made of wooden panels tinted dark brown, with whitewashed brickwork and tiles on the roof. In the old-age home at Tåsen the walls are plastered and painted in light colors and the roof is covered with corrugated eternite. This change from plastered concrete to bricks and wood is more than a mere shift of form; it reflects a change in attitude. Here is no architecture of abstract statements about form and functions but instead an architecture trying to cope with local problems and relying on traditional craftsmanship. Knut Knutsen plays a game in which the rules are difficult to define and the results are often mixed and blurred. So much depends on talent and often his complexity seems somewhat forced. In 1938 Knut Knutsen designed a house for himself and his family on a slope north of Oslo, overlooking a fjord. The layout copies the summer residence of Gunnar Asplund, built a year before near Stockholm, with the living room making the same shift of direction and connected to the bedroom wing by a flight of stairs. After the war Knutsen's house was doubled in size by the addition of a drawing office and a flat for use when the architect retired. The house seems almost a small village unto itself with each function announced by a change in height, direction, and materials. The bedroom is of a timber construction, the living room surrounded by brick walls, the rest a mixture of bricks and timber. The house is designed for a family whose life-style may change while the architectural atmosphere remains friendly and unpretentious. It is activating architecture that steps back and invites participation.

In 1947, only two years after the end of the war, an architectural competition was held in the small town of Vågåmo not far from Dovre in the middle of Norway. The program, a combined community center and city hall, included offices for the administration, a theater, a cinema, and an assembly hall near the old stave church. With many of the best traditional farm buildings still to be seen in Norway in the district of Vågå, it is not surprising that the first prize was given to Knut Knutsen whose project used the traditional layout with individual buildings around a courtyard. The program, which was never executed except for the administration building, remained more a framework for building than a full construction. Though the architecture was deliberately simple and humble in appearance, the handling of materials and forms was highly sophisticated with roofs varying in degrees of inclination. If there was any foreign influence on Knut Knutsen then, it was that of Frank Lloyd Wright. Building materials and construction systems were chosen sensibly so that local craftsmen could do the job. The whole building unfolds without strain, adapting itself to the existing environment by its small scale and its grouping of individual sections. The architect, however, is not imitating the forms of historical Norwegian log houses: his ideas come also from many other parts of the world where architecture is related organically to the landscape. As is common in Norwegian competitions, Knutsen's entry was given a descriptive title characterizing the project and the architect's attitude: "Quiet Movement, Hideaway, Suggestions."

In Knut Knutsen's thinking building must be subdivided into parts, each related to a certain function. When the parts are placed together the composition translates the rhythm of the surrounding landscape into architecture. Such a theory is particularly well suited to a country in which the landscape dominates man-made artifacts. For Knut Knutsen the Classical order was inhuman, invented as it was in a society where slavery was the basis for a democracy of the rich. A building should not try to impose itself on the natural setting, it ought to blend in and let the scene be determined by nature. A house should be neither an idea turned into stone or timber, nor a built piece of fashion; it should be a humble work of art filled with the excitement of form, space, and movement.

An architecture of simplicity corresponds to the relaxed life-style of a summer house. In 1948, when it was forbidden to erect summer houses in new materials, Knutsen built a residence for himself and his family near Portør (fig. 31.1) on the south coast of Norway. The house does not look like a home, or a house, since it takes its form from the rocks of the island. Without drawings the architect and local craftsmen nailed the summer house together out of used boards that were afterwards tarred. Hidden between rocks, the building is perhaps more a wooden shed than a real house, more camouflage than architecture. In such a house there are of course no

31.1. Knut Knutsen, architect. Summer residence at Portør, 1948. (Photograph: Courtesy of the architect)

modules, no Miesian order: order grows from the shape of the stony island and the used boards indicate the rules of the game. This architecture is genuinely organic, apparently grown from sheer necessity, but its straightforwardness of design reveals an architect whose sheer talent is stronger than any artifices of philosophy. The shape is thus nevertheless both sophisticated and controlled. The house reminds one of the American handmade house of the 1960s when puritanism went hand in hand with Californian affluence.

Knut Knutsen fought formal architecture and sought a kind of eternal architecture which could grow from man's essential needs. But at the same time he was gaining inspiration from abroad. In the late 1930s the inspiration came from Asplund, as Knutsen's own house documents. In the 1950s it was Frank Lloyd Wright's total philosophy that appeared close to that of Knutsen. From Frank Lloyd Wright he learned a feeling for continuous space and rhythmically arranged forms. Later, from Le Corbusier came an interest in light, in rough concrete surfaces, and in robust forms.

The influence from Frank Lloyd Wright can best be seen in the Norwegian Embassy in Stockholm which was built in 1952 on an idyllic site at Djurgården (fig. 31.2). The building has two parts—the living area and the office wing. The embassy has the quality of a big single family house. On the interior, a richly rhythmical interplay of varying spaces surrounds a large fireplace that is the key to the spatial organization, as in the prairie houses of Wright. The house is situated among trees near the sea, its overall form broken into parts in such a way that horizontal accents are stressed against a background of verticals. Only the framing of its windows echoes the slender pines around the building, for it is built mostly of bricks, copper, and tinted wood. Since diplomats represent their governments, their homes are usually formal exhibitions of national art and craftsmanship. The Norwegian Embassy, however, is not prestigious; the building is

31.2. Knut Knutsen, architect. Norwegian Embassy. Djurgården, Stockholm, 1952. (Photograph: Courtesy of the architect)

small and nothing reminds one of power and the elite. Architecture is seen as an act of liberation rather than merely a question of good manners or good education: architecture as art, not fashion. Traditional Japanese architecture and traditional Norwegian architecture appear to share this unusual mixture of intimacy, greatness, and adaptability.

Knut Knutsen's design philosophy is based less on strict rules than filled with contradictions. Since, like Alvar Aalto, he was not a man of letters, very few of his written statements were saved. His influence has been through his buildings and his teaching. For a long period of time he taught at the school of architecture in Oslo, training a whole generation of Norwegian architects in an Organic approach to building. During the fifties, in one of his few statements, criteria for what he calls the natural form of a house were set down as follows:

1) The expression of function, the wish to manifest forms of the room externally, as for instance in windows that are proportionate with the size of the room and that express the purpose of the room and the room's atmosphere.

2) It must be possible to enlarge and alter the house without losing its intrinsic value, quietness, spaciousness.

3) Every enterprise must be consigned the minimum of space, relinquishing the unnecessary.

4) Dimensions should be in accordance with the character and rhythm of the landscape, so that nature's variations are accentuated.

5) The countryside should be preserved as much as possible with building projects that are unobtrusive.

6) Design simply and naturally, as in everyday things, in accordance with material, construction, and climate.

7) Erect buildings requiring a minimum of maintenance and in such a way that the materials can be used again, and reduce heating requirements as much as possible.

8) Emphasize the nature of the materials and utilize them according to structure and form.

9) Protect available land by building the house, road, aerodrome, and so on, where ground cannot be cultivated.

10) Keep in mind the relationship which our country and others equally prosperous have to the rest of the world.

11) Liberate one's self from historical forms such as Baroque and Rococo, and set one's self free from the mentality behind the modes of expression that encouraged class distinction, gave rise to poverty, and caused much damage in the world.

Knut Knutsen's criteria for natural form, as with Frank Lloyd Wright's Organic architecture and Bruno Zevi's *Towards an Organic Architecture*, define the Organic principles which should rule a humanized architecture. Knutsen is concerned with more than houses, landscape, and architecture. His views include as well some of the broader and better-known arguments of the seventies concerning scarcity of resources, the need for the reuse of materials and buildings, the dangers of the exploitation of the Third World, and a distrust of modern technology. He counsels minimizing any harm to the environment.

With the large urban commissions of an affluent society, it became difficult for Knutsen to adjust his thinking. Designing in a town on a larger scale and in a very different setting meant that the inspiration of the rhythm of the landscape was gone. He had to cope instead with the artifacts of modern life. Around 1950 Knut Knutsen designed and executed two large hotels, one in Gjøvik and one in Oslo. The design of both shows a conflict between the ideals of the architect and the actual environment, as we may see in the latter. The Hotel Viking, planned for the Winter Olympiad of 1952, is near the main railway station in Oslo. Designed as a people's hotel its services were reduced to a bare minimum to accommodate as many as possible. There would be neither room service nor fine restaurants. With this reduced program Knut Knutsen insisted that the hotel be Norwegian in atmosphere. In contrast to the anonymity of much international hotel architecture he proposed that it have a local character in the way that light, colors, and materials were put together. Not the motifs but the architectural atmosphere would tell guests where they were. The relaxed simplicity of the interiors in the Viking Hotel carries conviction. Wooden furniture, colored textiles, shifting spaces—together they produce a people's architecture which is neither formal, nor sentimental, nor pretentious. The mixture of organic materials (copper, wood, and concrete) endows the building with a sense of friendliness. The building complex is composed of a tower block, a lower wing, and a two-story base. The skeleton construction is exposed concrete with infill of red bricks and tinted wooden windows. The main form's complexity corresponds to the chaotic city-shapes around the square. Unfortunately, the disintegration of the exterior comes about not as a translation of city forms but as an import of "natural" antiurban forms.

Knut Knutsen had great influence when, in the fifties, the next generation of Norwegian architects reacted against the vagueness of Norwegian postwar Empiricism. In the Organic approach of Knut Knutsen several found an architecture that was not clean and cool like the glass boxes of the International Style. Here was an architecture based not on national motifs but, rather, seeking "natural" forms wherever they could be found, whether in the anonymous villages of Greece and Italy, in traditional Japanese farmhouses, in the prairie houses of Frank Lloyd Wright, or in a city hall by Alvar Aalto.

Organic architecture was difficult to teach, especially in the late fifties, at a time of increasing industrialization in the building industry. The International Style of Mies van der Rohe, one of repetition and purity of structure, was much better suited for prefabricated buildings of great numbers of identical units. The architecture of Knut Knutsen cannot be a kind of ready-to-wear architecture. The best-known followers of Knutsen's philosophy include Are Vesterlid [Mesenlia school, Mesenlia, near Lillehammer, 1957, and the restaurant at the Folk Museum, Elverum, 1960], Per and Molle Cappelen [Institute of Social Research, Oslo, 1959], Trond Eliassen and Birger Lambertz-Nilssen [Maritime Museum, Oslo, 1961-1973, and Community Center, Sandefjord, 1975]. Theirs is an architecture of timber, bricks, and copper, sometimes seeming rather fragmented in its complexity but always at ease at the same time.

At the beginning of their careers, the internationally known Norwegian architects Kjell Lund and Nils Slaatto were designing similar architecture of decomposition (fig. 31.3). In their later works multiplicity is ordered by a strict geometry with a resulting architecture of dualism: tradition and experiment go hand in hand and variation marries order. Because of this dualism Lund and Slaatto have been able to work within the demands of the building industry without neglecting their own aesthetic. Their first major work, the Catholic church of Saint Hallvard in Oslo

31.3. Kjell Lund and Nils Slaatto, architects. Kjell Lund's house, 1964. (Photograph: Courtesy of the architects)

[1966] reflects a kind of romantic Brutalism in which the primary forms of the cube and the cylinder are "disturbed" through a delicate use of rough materials and a complicated fenestration. In the student union building in Oslo [1970], with functions obviously very different from those of the church, the same layout and combinations of monumental form with lively spaces are used to create a timeless architecture which embodies the needs of the present. In competitions for the National Bank in Oslo [1973] and the National Art Gallery in Oslo [1972] Lund and Slaatto have continued to develop an architecture based on a strict geometric grid-system, and the art gallery especially is very near in philosophy to Louis Kahn. In the headquarters of Veritas [1976], an institution for the classification of ships situated outside Oslo near the coast, the grid-system approach is used again to create a very human working environment, with each cube accentuated on the exterior and interior. The whole building complex, a factory and an office building, looks like a solid and very large block with single units, stepping up and down, in relation to the landscape and the older industrial buildings on the site.

From the fifties into the late seventies Norwegian architecture has grown more mature. For the moment Norway presents a most promising picture when compared with other Nordic countries. Three young architects, Are Telje, Fredrik Torp, and Knut Aasen [residential housing "Svendstuen" near Oslo, 1974, and police headquarters, Oslo, 1978] exemplify the best design for a Norwegian setting with their recreation and sports center for the handicapped at Beitostølen [1970] (fig. 31.4), situated at the upper edge of the woodland where the bare mountains start. In this new sort of building many kinds of handicapped people may take part in mountain sports. All functions are placed under one big, undulating roof that is covered with turf, mirrors the silhouette of the surrounding mountains, and follows the main direction of the valley. The staff's dwellings, of timber, are a modernized version of traditional Norwegian wooden architecture. Here again the mixture of romanticism and rationalism which is typical of the best architecture since Knut Knutsen points toward an organic architecture that is truly Norwegian.

31.4. Are Telje, Fredrik Torp and Knut Aasen, architects. Recreation and Sports Center at Beitostølen, 1970. (Photograph: Courtesy of the architects)

*Bibliography**

BOOKS

No competent books exist on new Norwegian architecture. The only relevant book is: *Treprisen—Ten Norwegian Prize-Winning Architects*. Oslo, 1978.

JOURNALS

"Architectures Nordiques: Norvège." *L'Architecture d'Aujourd'hui*, no. 134 (October 1967): 70-97.

Diamant-Berger, Renée, ed. "Pays Nordiques: Norvège." *L'Architecture d'Aujourd'hui*, no. 93 (December 1960): 69-89. (Introduction by Helge Abrahamsen)

"Knut Knutsen." *Byggekunst*, no. 8 (1953).

"Knutsen and Korsmo." *Byggekunst*, no. 6 (1972).

"Norse Art Center." *Progressive Architecture* 49 (October 1968): 82.

"Norwegian Architecture." *Byggekunst*, no. 5-6 (1956), no. 3 (1961), and no. 7-8 (1968).

"The PAGON-group." *Byggekunst*, no. 6 (1952).

Schimmerling, André, ed. "Norvège." *L'Architecture d'Aujourd'hui*, no. 54 (May 1954): 38-49. (Introduction by Helge Heiberg)

"Trondheim, Norvegia, 1967." *Casabella*, no. 354 (November 1974): 41-44.

*Compiled with the assistance of the editorial staff, Montreal.

32

POLAND

ZBIGNIEW PINIŃSKI

During the years since the Second World War the Polish architectural milieu has been characterized by changes and controversy that reflect strongly differing opinions. In 1945 Poland was faced with a dramatic situation which resulted from the immense destruction caused by the war and the enormity of construction necessary. In the ensuing years, a rather short span in the historic processes of development, Poland successfully accelerated a rich evolution of architectural form and thought. A certain enthusiastic atmosphere colored attempts to overcome difficulties and led to an architectural development in which there were diversely oriented approaches, a strict discipline of thought, and an economic outlook toward construction.

The years 1945-1949 called forth great efforts of rebuilding and reconstruction. Warsaw, for instance, had been almost completely destroyed and there was much discussion about moving Poland's capital. Instead, it was decided to rebuild (*see* Chapter 5, above) and town planning and reconstruction were given primary importance. Indeed, the rebuilding of Warsaw's historic areas was on a scale previously unknown anywhere. Critics complained that reconstruction was at the expense of other construction, especially residential housing, but now most would agree that the rich restoration of the fabric of Warsaw's architectural scene that resulted is altogether worthwhile.

In the forties, too, public buildings, though erected to provide economic, functional spaces, were often burdened with a great amount of decorative detail. For example, the Palace of the Bishops of Cracow in Warsaw, that since the nineteenth century had been a tenement house, was rebuilt from its seventeenth-century foundations as a Baroque structure with decoration closely emulating that of its origins and now houses the "Delta" Union of Aircraft and Engine Manufacturers. The 1949 architects' congress emphasized an architecture that was socialist in context and national in form. Given the needs and priorities of the period, a major effort in industrialized housing was emphasized and housing estates began to use basically flat, prefabricated units widely.

Through the fifties modern building methods were introduced, as in the steel construction of the Palace of Culture and Science, a Soviet gift. Newer materials were introduced on larger-scale projects while traditional techniques and materials were usually used on small-scale ones. Though socialist Realism was preferred, more functionally designed buildings such as the Central Department Store, Warsaw [1948-1952, by Z. Ihnatowicz and J. Romański] were also built.

The 1956 national architects congress underscored diversity by seeking guidelines that avoided ideological formulae to emphasize the practical approach rather than the theoretical. At this time also there was an increased interest in architectural accomplishments in much of the world beyond Poland's borders. "Mister Warsaw" awards have signaled both a growing public interest in architecture and some of the best achievements of construction in the capital city.

In the following discussion of important new Polish developments in architecture the examples have been selected with the intention of showing that they are based on very clear, almost axiomatic, intellectual conceptions that function relatively unaffected by other architectural premises.

In the midst of the almost archaeologically accurate efforts of restoration of the fifties in Warsaw, in 1958, a competition took place for the innovative reconstruction of the east side of Marszalkowska Street, Warsaw's busiest downtown boulevard before its destruction in the Second World War. The winner for the whole of the general design was Zbigniew Karpiński. Inevitably, the competition version (figs. 32.1, 32.2) varies from what was built between 1960 and 1970 since some ideas were changed over the decade or more of its full implementation. The competition version included two tall buildings on the outskirts of the complex that, due to decisions without the architect's consent, were eliminated. Karpiński's intentions were to locate a hotel to the south and a chemistry-ministry/foreign-commerce office building on the north. The two tall buildings would have played an important role in the whole east side complex as an optical linkage with the monumental Palace of Culture and Sciences in Parade Square, integrating that isolated, Stalinist-type skyscraper with the developing city center.

The Palace of Culture and Sciences, as the name indicates, is a sort of Centre Pompidou of the socialrealism epoch. Presented by the Soviet Union to the Polish nation, it was designed by Soviet architect L. W. Rudniev in 1952 and constructed within three years by Soviet construction teams. It was built on a site in the midtown district where Warsaw's dominant vertical thrust was to have been located, as clearly set forth in the theoretical works of one of the greatest contemporary Polish architects, Maciej Nowicki. Instead, as a consequence of the political climate of the early fifties that totally changed architectural trends in Polish architecture (to accord with the slogan "socialistic in content, national in form") the tall palace structure with its gigantic complex of mass-cultural functions was built. With a space of some 817,000 cubic meters and a height of 234 meters, the palace has 3,288 different rooms on its 42 levels and from its uppermost floors are some of the best views of the city.

The palace is the headquarters for the Polish Academy of Sciences and the UNESCO-Polish Committee, while also accommodating part of Warsaw

32.1 Zbigniew Karpiński et al., architects. East side of Marszalkowska Street project (1958), model viewed from the southwest; built 1960-1970, Warsaw. (Photograph: Courtesy of Z. Piniński)

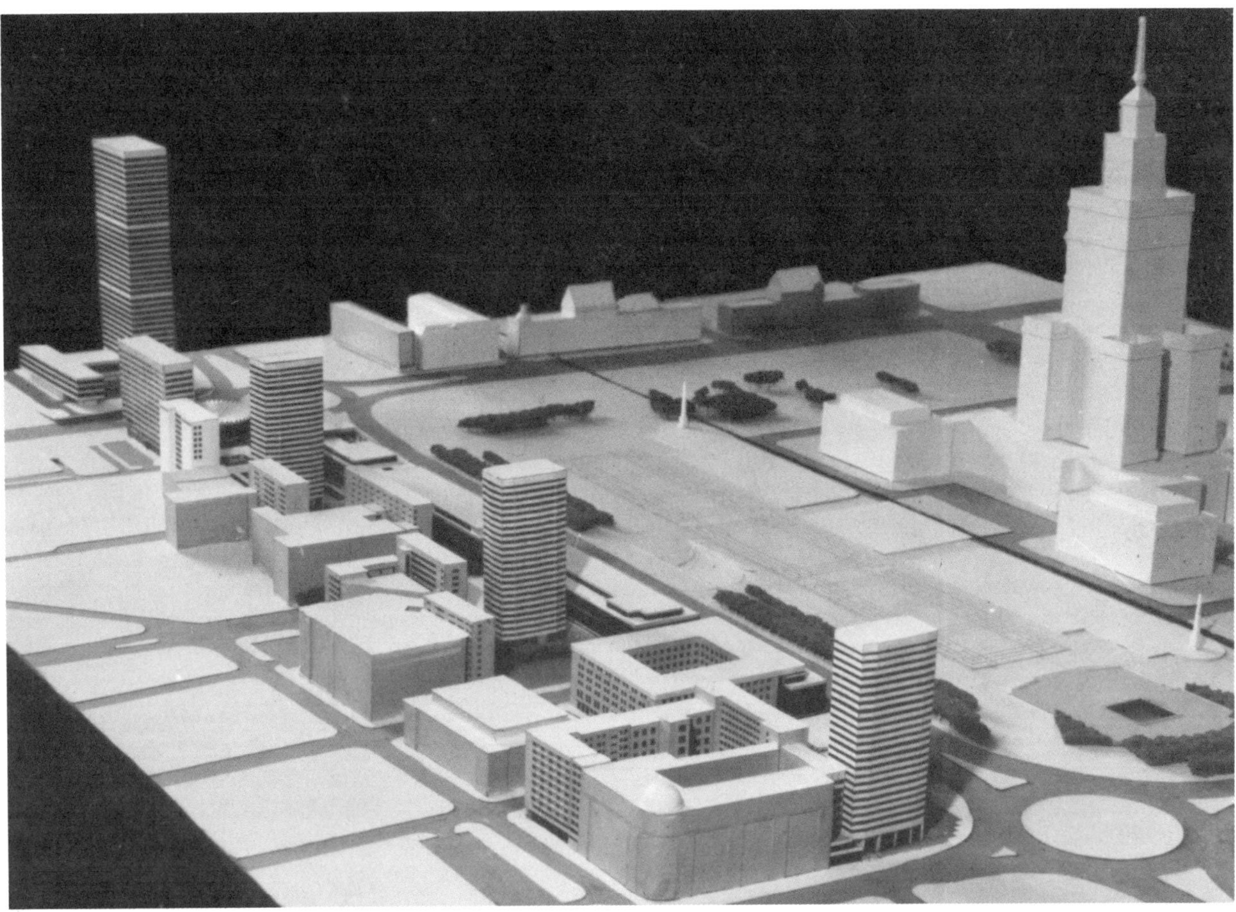

32.2. Zbigniew Karpiński et al., architects. Marszalkowska Street project, model viewed from northeast with Palace of Culture and Sciences of 1952-1955, Warsaw. (Photograph: Courtesy of Z. Piniński)

University. There is a huge Congress Hall with seating for 3,200, three theaters, three cinemas, a science museum, two restaurants, a TV studio, and a complex of youth hobby clubs called the Palace of Youth, all in a marble, stucco, and sandstone Social-Realist shell with Polish Renaissance elements. (Among others these latter elements recall the historical Cracow Cloth Market.) Though merging with the Warsaw skyline, the Palace of Culture and Sciences ought not be considered as an example of Polish architecture. Remaining nevertheless the highest building in Warsaw, any designing done in its vicinity must respect its enormous scale and be properly correlated with it, as indeed Zbigniew Karpiński had intended.

The northernmost and southernmost buildings of the Marszalkowska Street project were to have been as high as the palace's 140 meters-tall central tower, thus creating a complete and properly marked-out urban space. A second element of the plan, the three lower, rhythmically placed apartment houses within the complex are as tall as the four 80-meter-high elements that symmetrically adjoin the main tower of the palace. Finally, the long row of Karpiński's four department stores (each 22 meters tall) is correlated with the palace's numerous adjoining cubatures. Thus, Marszalkowska Street's modern, new, functionalist town-within-the-city consisted of major elements, the heights of which were interrelated with the previously built palace. The urban space envisioned by Karpiński with innovative buildings was to have been a harmoniously unified totality.

Not only were its two tallest buildings unrealized, but a hotel that has been erected in the place suggested by Karpiński varies in form from the hotel Karpiński had in mind. The Forum Hotel of the Intercontinental Hotel System was built in the years 1972-1973 according to a design done by Sten Samuelson, a Swedish contractor from Malmö. About 100 meters tall (instead of the 140 meters Karpiński anticipated) it has 33 levels with 752 rooms, 1,382 beds, and dining places for some 900 people in a building the proportions of which differ from Karpiński's tall, slender shaftlike design.

Along the east side of Marszalkowska Street an elongated terrain (about 70 meters x 600 meters with an area of about 45,000 square meters) has been built up with service, commercial, and catering functions. In twenty-three buildings (with a total volume of 640,000 cubic meters) 280,000 cubic meters are for commercial and service functions, 200,000 for apartment houses, 75,000 for office buildings, and the rest is for catering functions and entertainment facilities. According to Karpiński's planning, the program of commercial and service functions may be considered as supplementary to the cultural focus of the Palace of Culture and Sciences and to the program already existent in the midtown district beyond to the east (that is, where one finds the Philharmonic Hall, three cinemas, two hotels, two department stores, a bank, and grocery shops). Here also we see Karpiński's urbanistic integration of his East Side project with the three apartment houses acting as screens for the shopping streets and arranged perpendicularly toward the east.

In the 65 meters from Marszalkowska Street to these apartment houses, first we have a 15-meter-wide pedestrian pavement partly roofed by the 6-meter overhang of the upper level of the department stores to provide shelter from sun and rain for the window shoppers. Then on the ground level, there are 24 meters of department store, where commercial functions are located, and between the department stores and the apartment houses a 15-meter-wide pedestrian passage is parallel to Marszalkowska Street. The ground and first-floor levels of the apartment houses communicate with the pedestrian passage, and supply roads are routed beneath it in an innovation for Warsaw of which Karpiński is justly proud. Along the passage among numerous shopping and service facilities one finds ten coffee houses, two quick-service luncheonettes, two restaurants, a theater, and a panoramic-screen cinema. The intimate micro-atmosphere of the passage is largely due to such secondary architectural accoutrements as freestanding canopies permitting movement undisturbed by inconveniences of weather and areas of 45-centimeter-high flower beds with adjoining benches upon which people may relax. We should not lose sight of just how unusual all of this was when it was first designed in 1958.

In bringing this project to fruition, Zbigniew Karpiński worked with some of Poland's most talented architects. At the southern end of the complex, the tall hotel building that had been planned but has been replaced in actuality by the Forum Hotel, was designed by Karpiński with Zbigniew Waclawek. The fourteen-story, flatly shaped Foreign Trade Offices "Universal" building behind the rotunda and parallel to the long axis of the complex was designed by Jerzy Kowarski. The rotunda with banking services (fig. 32.1) was designed by J. Jakubowicz. Though in reality its roof is asymmetrical, the rotunda shape persists. Northward from the rotunda along Marszalkowska Street are two linked department stores, one for ladies, called "Sawa," and the other for men, called "Wars," designed by J. Jakubowicz and P. Zajlich. The third department store in the row, "Junior," was originally dedicated to younger clients when designed by Z. Waclawek. At the end of the shopping chain the "Sezam" cooperative department store designed by A. Sierakowski and T. Blażejewski is treated differently, aluminum-paneled in contrast with the glass-screened "Junior," "Sawa," and "Wars" buildings. Of the three tall apartment houses the two east of the department stores were designed by Z. Waclawek and J. Klewin. Other architects and other buildings were also included in the completion of this complex, so well suited from its inception for a city of Warsaw's size (some two million inhabitants). With many of its buildings sheathed in double glass panels, during the day a pleasant play of reflections is created, while in the evening light from within enlivens Warsaw's whole east side. The first State Prize was awarded for the design of the East Side of Marzalkowska Street, one of the most important and popular realizations of the last thirty years in Poland.

There were interesting architectural developments elsewhere in Poland during the years in which Warsaw was being recreated, particularly in the sixties. In Katowice, the capital of Silesia, the main industrial district located just before the foothills of Poland's Beskid Slaski Mountains, factories were built employing prefabricated-concrete constructional units. Large housing estates of low-rise, slab-type buildings were erected in relatively low-density groups in various parts of the city. Adjacent to a traffic circle in the city center a noteworthy, isolated setting was created in 1966-1967 by architect Wojciech Zablocki for three large (14.5-meter-high) bronze sculptures by sculptor Gustaw Zemla commemorating the Silesian uprisings of 1919, 1920, and 1921 against German occupiers.

Some 80 kilometers away from Katowice in the mountains at Ustroń-Zawodzie architects Henryk Buszko, Alexander Franta, and Tadeusz Szewczyk designed an 8,000-bed rehabilitation quarter between 1965 and 1969, the construction of which was begun in 1967. With ten buildings completed by 1980, eight in construction, and fourteen more planned, this is the largest of four major sanatoriums begun in the region during the sixties. All were fully planned in their sitings (fig. 32.3) before construction was undertaken and, in each, details and local materials such as the stone of the region and local lumber were employed to provide effects that were deliberately different from urban architecture. Site plans called for free-standing buildings, arranged in groups according to their forms, and in most low-rise, cubical structures are predominant. Buildings are introduced into mountainous terrains carefully so as not to overwhelm but instead to preserve the effect of an untouched landscape.

At the Zawodzie quarter (fig. 32.4) in Ustronie, the health resort seems much less crowded with buildings and their appurtenances than one would anticipate from the approximately 890,000 cubic meters per 180 hectares area that is occupied. In all directions one is amidst greenery in crisp mountain air. Pyramidal, reinforced-concrete buildings (fig. 32.5) entirely or partially on *pilotis* with large, glazed surfaces throughout framed in wood and with balconies for almost every room on the peripheries are built into the landscape and linked by walks and a looping utility roadway. Each building seems a man-made codification of a small mountain; yet with balconies providing sequences of horizontals all appear interrelated, not only with the terrain but also with each other. Though they certainly exceed the scale of traditional buildings in the area, the local architecture of the mountainous landscape of Silesia is consistently reflected in their forms (which are the result of years-long studies) and in their skillful siting.

Not far from Zawodzie's health resort, also near Ustronie, at Jaszowiec, architects J. Winnicki and Z. Winnicki, I. Kotela and Cz. Kotela designed a 2,500-bed sanatorium [1961-1965, completed by 1969] along similar conceptual lines. H. Buszko and A. Franta built a rest home for teachers [1964] that consists of a long low structure, with continuous loggias, following the topography of the site in two and three stories. Farther away, at the source of the Vistula River (that flows into Warsaw), also in the Silesian Beskids, W. Jacior and A. Piasecki were responsible [1963-1975] for a health resort at Partecznik near the old Vistula spa. A final example of this type of development is the sanatorium at Polanczyk at Solina Bay in the Bieszcady range of the eastern Carpathian mountains. Designed between 1968 and 1973 by W. Pankiewicz, S. Wantuch, U. Alda, and A. Pankiewicz, it was 60 percent complete in 1980.

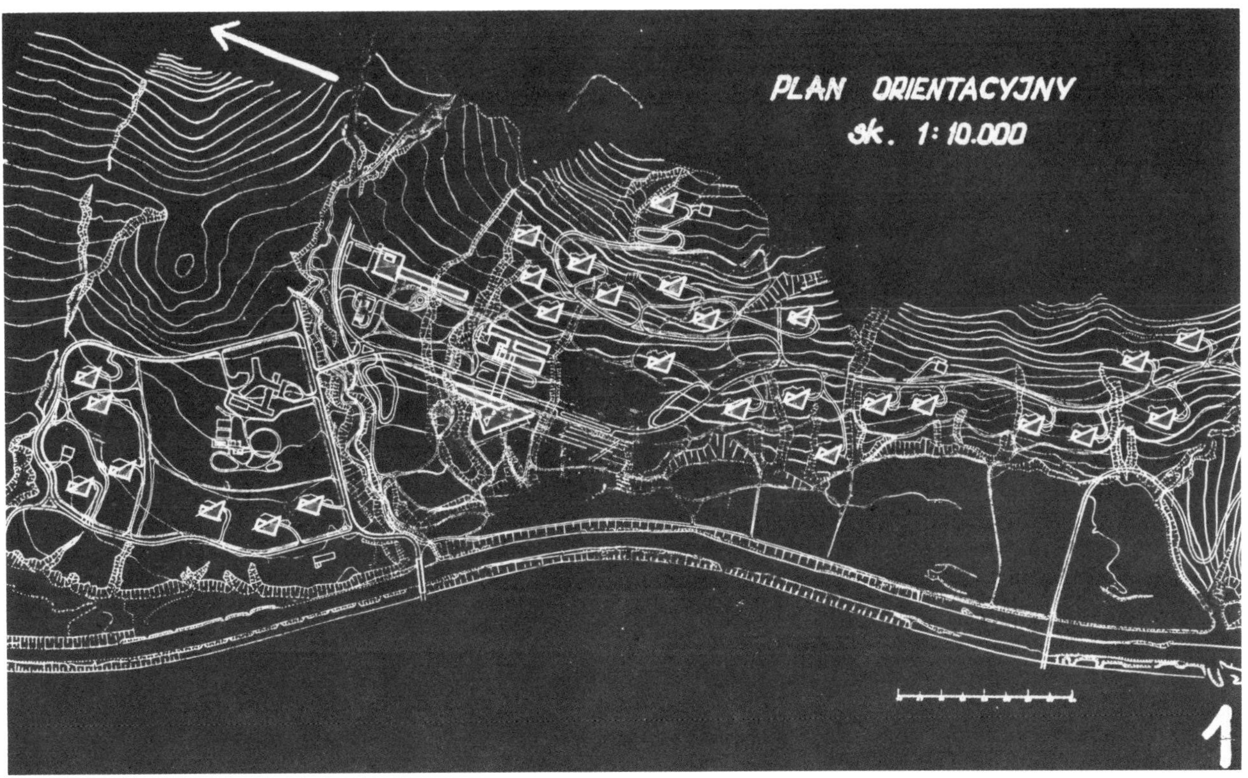

32.3. Henryk Buszko, Alexander Franta and Tadeusz Szewczyk, architects. Site plan of the Zawodzie Sanatorium area. Ustroń, Silesia, 1965-1980s. (Photograph: Courtesy of the architects)

32.4. Buszko, Franta and Szewczyk, architects. Partial view of the Zawodzie Sanatorium buildings. (Photograph: Courtesy of "Gwarek")

32.5. Buszko, Franta and Szewczyk, architects. Zawodzie Sanatorium buildings, detail of 32.4. (Photograph: Courtesy of "Gwarek")

This facility of some 3,000 beds provides the same social services as do the others and moreover emphasizes therapeutic and medical services.

In the context of contemporary Polish rustic architecture, the popular work of Stanislaw Karpiel, architect and outdoorsman of the Tatra Mountains, is typical of a relatively new interest in linkages with Polish traditional construction. Residing in his family's age-old, crude, wooden, villager's cottage, Karpiel specializes in an architecture of small buildings that often serve as vacation or weekend homes and that contrast with the rather uniform character of much modern architecture. Karpiel's creative work directly continues the centuries-long practices of numerous, nameless, carpenters who built shepherds' sheds and huts far up in the mountains, farm buildings across the landscape, and other necessary buildings in the villages. Such men knew their material intimately and understood well the effects of a very snowy, very windy climate in which drastic changes in temperature are frequent. Typical of Karpiel's little buildings are the Bartnik vacation home [1976] in the Beskidy mountains, essentially an A-frame, two-story, wooden structure on a stone basement-level and the somewhat larger Mlynarski weekend house [1972] in the Tatra Mountains. The Mlynarski house also employs the A-frame idea but with small, twin-gabled windows at the second-story level on its long sides and a broad, glazed area opening onto porches cut out of the shingled roofs at the first story, while its fairly high basement roots the cottage into the rolling terrain.

Changes from traditional form in Karpiel's houses reflect the needs of contemporary man and the functions of the holiday house. The proportions of these houses are taller; since the upper area is no longer used to store hay it is utilized for bedrooms; windows are enlarged; and loggias or balconies are more frequent. Within monospatial structures, open mezzanines are built as sleeping areas. Neither steel, reinforced concrete, nor modern thermo-insulating materials are employed: only traditional materials, and his craftsmanship with these is superb. In almost all of these houses the roofs, usually wooden-shingled, are steeply gabled so that melting snow may easily slide off and, as a unified structure, strong winds may be withstood. Because of his uncompromising adherence to traditional building principles, houses by Karpiel and others working in the same manner have become popular in contemporary Poland and have led to a revival of the long-neglected fine skills of woodworking.

Returning to the urban scene, after more than a decade of reconstruction in Poland, Josef Golab's elementary school on Rydel Street in Cracow [1960], though of six-stories, is so long and its horizontality is so repeatedly stressed by full, continuous, deep balustrades providing communication for traffic at each level that a dramatic, fluent, low-rise effect is achieved. In Lublin later in the 1960s, Wojcisch designed an excellent, multipurpose auditorium situated upon a hill in the vicinity of the restored, historic, center city. Its sweeping, hyperbolic, paraboloidal roof, anchored at two supports, provides an elegantly modern urban accent and permits walls of glass around the periphery of the building to further enhance its attractive qualities. Accommodating three thousand, with self-contained offices, with practice and preparation rooms as well as some storage capacity, it serves as theater, concert hall, and sports arena, all in one. In Cracow in the second half of the 1960s, the 700-bed Hotel Cracow was built as a long, low-rise slab of prefabricated, reinforced-cement, panel construction with curtain-wall facades of aluminum. The thousand-seat Kijow Cinema, built on the same site in conjunction with the hotel, records the effects of *architecture brût* in Cracow, departing somewhat from the rectilinearity stressed in the hotel, with impressively angled staircases leading to three entries framed by projecting slabs in boxlike fashion.*

In the realm of apartment housing Aleksander Markiewicz's high-rise design at 9 Wiejska Street in Warsaw [1961] deserves mention for its appearance of diversity within unity, upon a tree-lined urban site. More typical of slablike high-rise housing is the arrangement of many buildings in Warsaw's West Jerozolimskie Avenue complex, designed by Jerzy Baumiller and Jan Zdanowicz and built from 1964. Among the best of housing estates in Warsaw, however, may be the Kepa Potocka development with its three seventeen-story buildings and one long, nine-story apartment house. Built in 1965-1969, these were the results of a design by Boguslaw Chyliński, Hanna Graff-Chylińska, and Zbigniew Pawlowski with Barbara Tucholska having planned the green areas.

One of the architecturally most important and impressive of housing estates may be found at Wroclaw in southwestern Poland. Set back a short distance from the Odra River, the Grünwald Square complex (fig. 32.6) was designed in 1966-1967 by J. Hawrylak-Grabowska in collaboration with Z. Kowalski and W. Wasilewski and constructed between 1970 and 1975.

Some 2,150 people reside in its six sixteen-story buildings in apartments of from two to seven rooms, conveniently served by three adjacent, one- and two-story pavilions in which are the post office, catering, handicraft, and other specialty shops. On the first floor of the apartment buildings other shopping facilities may be found. In each apartment building

*For the buildings mentioned in this paragraph see the illustrations in *Casabella* no. 341 (October 1969): 1, 6-53.

32.6. J. Hawrylak-Grabowska with Z. Kowalski and W. Wasilewski, architects. Grünwald Square Housing Estate in 1979. Wroclaw, designed 1967 and built 1970-1975. (Photograph: Courtesy of Z. Piniński)

are two elevators, rubbish chute, laundry and drying facilities, a room for baby carriages and boxes for home-delivered milk and bread. On the top floor of each are multifunctional accommodations, including common rooms, club rooms, reading rooms and a gardenlike terrace for recreation.

J. Hawrylak-Grabowska wished to demonstrate in this group of buildings that a poetic level of architectural achievement could be attained employing prefabricated, reinforced-concrete elements. In each apartment building a modular grid, 3.90 x 4.20 meters, is basic to the skeleton of H-shaped, prefabricated, reinforced-concrete frames; and prefabricated cross-reinforced-concrete floor slabs were utilized throughout. In Poland comparatively flat, prefabricated slabs are used in great quantities for wall construction. At the Grünwald complex, however, for the first time special curving elements (fig. 32.7) made of insulated reinforced concrete were prefabricated for the curtain walls and balconies of the six apartment buildings in accord with the architect's wishes. Her obstinant and disciplined persistence, even insistence, brought her to her goal of reaching a poetics of prefabricated concrete in this apartment complex of 111,300 cubic meters space. The special, prefabricated facade elements so precisely designed by J. Hawrylak-Grabowska for the Grünwald Housing Estate have attracted considerable attention and are very much admired.

A recent addition to the historically eclectic architecture of the Warsaw Technical University, originally built at the turn of the century with Renaissance and Baroque elements and augmented in then-current styles into the 1920s, is the Chemical Technology Pavilion, designed by Zbigniew Piniński early in the 1970s. It was added to the Warsaw Technical University in two stages: the building itself was completed during 1972-1973 and a rectangular patio-courtyard was arranged in the small area between it and the existing Chemistry Department buildings behind it. The steel structure of this essentially cubiform four-story building is painted white and made visible: vertical girders on the principal

32.7. J. Hawrylak-Grabowska, architect. Curved prefabricated units of Grünwald Square Housing Estate. (Photograph: Courtesy of Z. Piniński)

facade project from the glass curtain wall and on the sides the horizontal beams are recessed, framing four oblong panels of ceramic tiles, one panel per story. This emphasis upon the building's skeletal structure together with the use of ceramic tiles in interrelated nonstructural patterns of design force a contrast with the adjacent buildings of the 1930s in which there are thick, brick, load-bearing exterior walls.

In a second stage of construction a communicative aspect was added to this building's exterior. In accord with the original design, symbols of the general formula for metallic organic chemistry (C-C-M-CC-M-CC) each about 1.5-meters high, were added in two diagonal patterns to a pair of girders of the principal facade (fig. 32.8). On the bottom left of one of the

32.8. Zbigniew Piniński, architect. Chemical Technology Pavilion, Technical University. Warsaw, 1972-1973 and 1978. (Photograph: Courtesy of the architect)

narrow sides a gate to a loading platform within is covered with a *sculpture verité*, a bas-relief of the front of a truck of the 1930s. When opened the two halves of this image move apart for they are fixed to the wings of the gate. Artistic elements also play a role within the building. Since its completion in 1973, the marble floors of the building, whether in halls, corridors, smoking rooms, or whatever, have played a role. Colorful marble reminders mark the traffic flow so that the floor's composition becomes a facetious bearer of data. In the smoking rooms at each level, separated from corridor and staircase by glazed partition walls, the function of the space is announced by a huge, red bas-relief of lips with a large cigarette located on a full back wall. In the Chemical Technology Pavilion modern architecture and modern art are one.

During the 1970s Poland's architects have continued to be prominent on the international scene, as they have been since the 1960s, with many Polish-designed buildings being constructed abroad. Summarizing briefly, the first major Polish international success occurred when, in the 1959 competition for the cultural center of Leopoldville, the Polish team of J. Z. Polak, J. Chyrosz, Z. Pawtowski, K. Lukasiewicz, and St. Wiland took second prize. This was followed by prizewinning efforts in competitions for a church in Denmark (by K. Brozek, W. Drozdziewicz, and T. Sunycha), a college in Dublin (by A. Weichert, Z. Pawtowski, J. Szpakowicz, and T. Krupinski), a project for the core of Tel Aviv (B. Perchal, J. Plesner, M. Turski) and many others. During the 1970s, M. Dunikowski, M. Mazurkiewicz, J. J. Meyssner, and W. Miecznikowski took first prize for their Damascus Public Library project [1974]. The third and fourth prize-winners for the National Opera House in Sofia [1974] were Polish teams, as was the second-prize team for the National Theater and Opera House at Damascus [1979]. The 1980s started off with Polish architectural teams taking both first and second prizes in the competition for Madrid's Islamic Cultural Center. Clearly in recent years the Polish contribution to contemporary architecture has assumed increasing importance.

The long epoch of architecture that consisted in the creation of individual, "unique" works is coming to an end. We have entered a postindustrial age, the center of which is neither machine, object, nor work of art, all of which are static, but rather the organization of life in the dynamics of a fast-changing world.

Bibliography

Alberti, Franco, ed., Vagnetti, Luigi, et al. "Polonia." *Casabella* 341 (October 1969): 1, 6-53. (In Italian and English)

Borusiewicz, W. *Preservation of Ancient Brick Structures* (*Konserwacja zabytków budownictwa murowego*). Polish edition, 1971.

Braun, J. *Częstochowa. Town Planning and Architecture (Urbanistyka i architecktura*). Polish edition, 1979.

Budrewicz, O. *Trip Across Poland. From Warsaw to Tatra Mountains* (*Podróż po Polsce—Od Warszawy do Tatr*). German edition, *Polereise von Warschau zur Tatra*, 1974.

Chrościcki, J. and Rottermund, Andrzej. *Atlas of Architecture of Warsaw* (*Atlas architektury Warszawy*), 1977. Foreign language editions: Polish, English, German, Russian.

Ciolek, G. *Polish Gardens* (*Ogrody polskie*). Polish edition, 1979.

Cydzik, J. and W. Fijalkowski. *Wilanów*, 1975. German edition, 1979.

Czerner, O. and Arczyński, S. *Wroclaw. Landscape and*

Architecture, 1975. Foreign language editions: Polish, English, German.

Dobrowolski St., R. and E. Kupiecki. *Warsaw of Today* (*Warszawa dzisiejsza*). Polish edition, 1974.

Dobrzycki, J. and E. Kupiecki. *Cracow*, 1974. Foreign language editions: Polish, German, French, Russian.

Gasiorowski, E. *Toruń. Landscape and Architecture*. Polish edition, 1974.

Gawarecki H., C. Gawdzik, and K. Jabloński. *Lublin. Landscape and Architecture*. Polish edition, 1972.

Giekżyński, W. *Poland from the Baltic Sea to Carpathian Mountains*, 1975. Foreign language editions: Polish, English, German, French, Russian.

Gliszczyński, J. and A. Chojnacka. *Katowice*. Polish edition, 1974.

Guerquin, B. *Castles in Poland* (*Zamki w Polsce*). Polish edition, 1975.

______. *Malbork Castle* (*Zamek w Malborku*). Polish edition, 1974.

Kostrowiccy, I. and J. *Poland. Nature-Architecture* (*Polska, Przyroda i architektura*), 1979. Edition: Polish, English, German, Russian.

Koziński, S. *A Concept of Urban Built Up* (*Koncepcja zabudowy miasta*). Polish edition, 1974.

Knox, Brian. *The Architecture of Poland*. New York: Praeger, 1971.

Maliszowa, B. *Town Centre, Selected Planning Issues* (*Śródmieście. Wybrane zagadnienia planowania*). Polish edition, 1974.

Modern Polish Town Planning (*Polska urbanistyka wspólczesna*). Polish edition, 1975.

Ostrowski, W. *Contemporary Town Planning* (*Urbanistyka wspólczesna*). Polish edition, 1975.

Pokropek, M. *Atlas of Folk Art and Folklore in Poland* (*Atlas sztuki ludowej i folkloru w Polsce*), 1978. Foreign language editions: Polish, English, French, German, Russian.

Sokolowski, Z. and Soktysik, M. *Plock. Town-Planning and Architecture* (*Plock. Urbanistyka i architektura*). Polish edition, 1975.

Stankiewicz, J. and Szermer B. *Gdańsk. Landscape and Architecture*. Polish edition, 1972.

Szafer, T. P. *Modern Polish Architecture* (*Nowa architektura polska*). Polish edition, 1972.

______. *New Polish Architecture Diary of the Period 1971-1976* (*Nowa architektura polska. Diariusz lat 1971-1976*). Polish edition.

Szczecin. Landscape and Architecture, 1977. Foreign language editions: Polish, German, English.

Tatarkiewicz, W. *Royal Lazienki Palace and its Sights* (*Lazienki królewskie i ich osobliwości*). Polish edition, 1975.

Warsaw—A Portrait of the City (*Warszawa—portret miasta*), 1979. Foreign language editions: Polish, English, German, French, Russian.

Wejchert, K. *A Town on the Stocks* (*Miasto na warsztacie*). Polish edition, 1974. Foreign language edition: English.

Zin, W. *With Pen and Charcoal. Part I* (*Piękno nie dostrzegane*). Polish edition, 1970.

______. *With Pen and Charcoal. Part II*. (*Piękno potężne*). Polish edition, 1972.

______. *With Pen and Charcoal. Part III—Beauty Lost* (*Piórkiem i weglem cz. III. Piękno ultracone*). Polish edition, 1975.

Zlat, M. and Arczyński, S. *Wroclaw, 1975*. Foreign language editions: Polish, English, French, German, Russian.

33

REPUBLIC OF SOUTH AFRICA

IVOR PRINSLOO

There is no consistent, representative, South African architecture any more than there is a unified South African culture. The reasons are, of course, the same. In typical fashion, indigenous traditions were neglected in the development of a local architecture and models from the colonists' countries of origin—mainly Holland and Britain—were copied. Though mostly imperfectly imitated, sometimes happy results led to fine regional styles derived from a blend of imported formal principles and the demands of local practice. Although South Africa is no longer a colony, there are powerful forces working against the development of a unified culture with a consequent erosion of the possibilities for a congruent and culturally appropriate architecture. Cultural integration between the many diverse and, in themselves, often culturally rich population groups is actively opposed by the dominant political ideology of separate developments. This is compounded by the fact that industrialization, urbanization, and the consequent modernization is rapidly breaking down any residual pockets of cultural uniformity in favor of the more universal dictates of the international market place. In this process, architecture itself has been progressively devalued and architectural styles have become mere commodities, now exhibiting a wider range of influences than the European ones upon which the beginnings of modern architecture were first based.

From about 1925 onwards, against the background of important local work by persons such as Gordon Leith, Prof. G. E. Pearse and others, the influence of contemporary movements abroad became particularly evident, especially those associated with the heroic period of the Modern Movement (*see* Gilbert Herbert, *Martienssen and the International Style*, 1975). This took place mainly through the architectural schools in Johannesburg and Cape Town and the then principal architectural journal, the *South African Architectural Record*. A. Stanley Furner, editor of the SAAR from 1926 to 1929, introduced most contemporary movements to the architectural profession. His students under the active leadership of Rex Martienssen (1905-1942) and recent immigrants from Europe, many of them Bauhaus graduates, responded to these influences; especially to Dutch architecture of the 1920s, the work of Gropius and others at the Bauhaus, the paintings of Léger and the cubists, and the early buildings of Mies van der Rohe and Le Corbusier. Following diverse activities by Martienssen and his colleagues, including visits to Europe, polemics, and the publishing of papers, these influences appeared in built form, initially in domestic architecture. The Munro house, Pretoria [McIntosh, 1932] was followed by others of which the Harris house, Johannesburg [Hanson, Tomkin, and Finkelstein, 1933] is a good example—a two-story white cube showing formal and spatial characteristics derived from Gropius and the early work of Mies van der Rohe. A rapid development of significant domestic architecture followed, culminating in the Stern house, Johannesburg [Martienssen, Fassler, and Cooke, 1935] which is a synthesis of many of the elements particular to the International Style. Considerably more plastic and sculptural than was common elsewhere, it included the use of *pilotis*, a roof terrace defined by parapet walls, a flying beam and metal pipe screens, and a use of color and transparency to manipulate space in particular formal relationships. These buildings, derived from the International Style, were controversial. There were also other influences which acted to transform local adaptations of the International Style by retaining its better qualities but adapting the particular, flat-roofed cubic imagery. Casa Bedo, Johannesburg [Cowlin and Ellis, 1936] is a house with a free plan form and Miesian spatial organization adapted to local conditions by wide eaves and a hipped roof reminiscent of Sir Herbert Baker and Frank Lloyd Wright. This adaptation is typical and produced a model for many houses of the next two decades. In particular, it influenced speculative builders with a resultant, fairly uniform pattern of built form in the residential suburbs. It is interesting to note that many of the early "pure" International Style buildings which were built locally have subsequently been changed by their owners into this later form by the addition of hipped, sloped roofs and overhanging eaves. One reason, among others, for this occurrence is often given as a technical failure of the flat roofs. This is only partly true; the real explanation has more to do with ordinary people and what they consider to be an appropriate style for domestic building.

A similar pattern of development occurred in other building types in which the formal tenets of the early International Style were developed to a significant degree of sophistication. Notable examples are in Johannesburg, Peterhouse [Martienssen, Fassler, and Cooke, 1936] and in Cape Town, the Cavalla Factory [Policansky, 1938]. However, as had happened in previous periods, local conditions, technology, and inventiveness led to adaptations towards a contemporary vernacular, quite diverse in style, but still securely within the traditions of the Modern Movement. Examples include, in Johannesburg, the 20th-Century-Fox cinema and offices [Hanson and others, 1937] and the innovative work, derived from German Expressionism, of W. B. Pabst; in Cape Town the work of P. E. Pahl, M. Policansky, Prof. L. Thornton Whyte and others; in Durban buildings such as the Technical College Clubhouse [Jackson and Park Ross, 1943]. In these cases the use of more traditional materials such as face bricks, the adaptation to the particular local climate and to the conventions of the building industry, all have acted to modify the architecture.

The changes in all aspects of architectural practice were, however, overshadowed by the advent of World War II in which South Africa took a major part in support of the Allies. This disrupted building considerably and later precipitated the country into a postwar building boom. During the war period most architects had the opportunity to reconsider their positions vis-à-vis an appropriate architectural language. The local experience with the International Style had not been entirely satisfactory due to technical failure and public rejection, and architects actively sought other modes of designing in the postwar period. At this time a new set of diverse influences entered the field; the influence of Scandinavian work, the gentler brick architecture of persons such as Dudok (both under the rubric of New Empiricism), and the recent work done in Brazil and made known to South Africans by the publication of *Brazil Builds* (Goodwin, 1943) with photographs by Kidder Smith. The Brazilian work in particular, had a wide and pervasive influence, especially in Pretoria with its hot climate, and on a group of architects who were culturally particularly receptive to a new, non-European architecture. The capital city of the country was the center of those pressures which sought to develop a particular South African identity and, in building, Brazilian models seemed more appropriate than European ones. The influence was mainly twofold: that relating to vernacular building, that is, seeing that vernacular building could provide a legitimate point of departure for modern building; and that relating to building form as such, in particular lessons from the Ministry of Education and Health Building, Rio de Janiero [Lucio Costa and others, with Le Corbusier, 1942]. The *brise-soleil*, the use of *pilotis*, and the use of a regular frame to contain the other elements, were particularly emulated. The Meat Board Building, Pretoria [Stauch and Partners, 1951] is a good example of the application of these ideas and the fact that the Institute of South African Architects gave an Award of Merit to it signifies the importance attributed to these ideas.

By the mid-1950s a fairly widespread contemporary vernacular had emerged—albeit one with regional differences—which some architects believed to be a corruption of both the best traditions of the past and the early promise of the Modern Movement. In order to reinstate architecture there were conscious attempts to generate new styles. For example, Fassler, Hanson, and others attempted to establish a neoclassical style based on the work of Auguste Perret and on lessons from the work of Sir Herbert Baker, Gordon Leith, and others. This and other attempts were not particularly effective as movements. The country was growing rapidly and the cities were eroded by pragmatic immediacy, with architects on the whole happy to follow the line of least resistance in meeting their clients' desires. There were, however, isolated exceptions.

Norman Eaton (1902-1966) developed a fine regional architecture, responding in each instance to local technology, climate, the dictates of the program, a well-developed knowledge of the formal tenets of western European architecture and, significantly, a sensitive understanding of the lessons of African vernacular architecture as well as a sense of what is spatially and formally appropriate in an African context [Clinton, 1975]. The Netherlands Bank Building, Pretoria [Eaton, 1953] is one of the country's finest buildings (fig. 33.1); a thoroughly well-resolved spatial and technical composition in which the elements of the building—brick surfaces, floors, details—are all the products of fine and well-directed craftsmanship. The Netherlands Bank Building in Durban [Eaton, 1966] responds to an entirely different climate and context, but is resolved in an equally appropriate manner. Eaton's work shows him to be an architect of major significance. His domestic work has equal authority, the best example being his Greenwood House [1950], and Anderson House [1949]. Other examples of regionally sensitive and appropriate architecture are to be found in Pretoria by John Templar and John Claasens, houses in Durban by Biermann and by Hallen, and the early houses of Revel Fox in the Cape (fig. 33.2); the latter offers a sensitive interpretation of the local vernacular. On the whole, however, the 1950s was a period of undistinguished building.

The next discernible wave of influence occurred in the early 1960s with the return to the country of a number of young architects who had done graduate study abroad, mainly in the United States with persons such as Louis Kahn, Romaldo Giurgola, Paul Rudolph, Robert Venturi, and others. Projects from this period show the spatial and formal qualities that are characteristic of much contemporary work done in other countries. Many innovative buildings that were designed showed the effect of these influences in their use of materials and their formal and spatial resolution. Recognizable influences include the following: plans that are ordered by means of geometrically regular forms, often set at 45° to site boundaries and often overlapping; the organization of functional elements into served and service spaces after the work of Louis Kahn; the deliberately rough

33.1. Norman Eaton, architect. Banking lobby of the Netherlands Bank Building. Pretoria, 1946-1953. (Photograph: Courtesy of Walt Verwey Studio Johannesburg)

33.2. Revel Fox, architect. Courtyard house. Worcester, The Cape, 1954. (Photograph: Ginger Odes, courtesy Revel Fox and Partners, Cape Town)

materials—broken bricks or red engineering bricks, exposed timber, off-the-shutter concrete, and so forth—following ideas based on Le Corbusier's later work and made current by James Stirling and Alison and Peter Smithson; the use of commercial imagery, and signs and graphics as major decorative and organizational elements, with reference to the work of the Venturis and others. Notable buildings that show these influences are, in Cape Town, the Truworths Factory [Uytenbogaardt, 1968]; in Johannesburg, the Robinson House [Meyer and Gallagher, 1966]; in Pretoria, Gruptel's Court [Meyer and others, 1965] and in Durban, Halls of Residence, University of Natal [Hallen and Dibb, 1968].

With continued rapid economic growth and prosperity in the latter part of the 1960s, foreign architects were invited by multinational corporations and local businesses to act as principal designers in major projects in the cities, especially in Johannesburg, the commercial capital of the country and a focus of foreign investment. The Carlton Centre [Skidmore, Owings and Merrill and others, 1966] is a large underground shopping area, an office tower, and a hotel and department—at one time the largest reinforced-concrete building complex in the world. It introduces a new scale into local city building and is stylistically in conformity with large city projects elsewhere, especially in North America. The Standard Bank Headquarters [Hentrich and Petschnigg and others, 1971] is a structurally innovative office building with floors suspended from the core so as to free the ground-floor level and thus contribute to the flow of space at the level of the plaza. The IBM Building [Philip Dowson and others, 1975] is a curved glass tower reminiscent of an early project for a glass tower by Mies van der Rohe. These buildings are good examples and all show the formal internationalism one finds in office buildings throughout the Western world. Even where foreign architects were not active in the design, work by local architects shows an international "likeness" in commercial buildings. The Trust Bank Centre, Cape Town [Colyn and Meiring, 1970] is a steel and glass tower on a podium in the manner of the New York work of Skidmore, Owings and Merrill and some of the later work of Mies van der Rohe. Commercial architecture continues to follow international models, and office buildings on the whole show, in spite of sometimes extravagant formal manipulation, a uniformity that is internationally ubiquitous: South African city centers are in parts quite indistinguishable from most city centers elsewhere, especially in North America. This distinct trend in commercial architecture has provided the model for local architecture in other building types, particularly public buildings.

The tendency is to build increasingly larger buildings which are completely out of scale with the city and which warrant examination and criticism that encompasses both the growing bureaucracy requiring such buildings as well as architectural styles which, although appropriate to that bureaucracy, do not add much to the ordinary enjoyment of their use by people. It is even questionable whether South

African society with its extensive underdevelopment can justify this mode of organization and consequent architecture. The reliance on necessarily simplistic geometries, prefabricated techniques, and rationalized building methods in many of these projects produces a uniformity which, coupled with their great size, makes for buildings and environments that are dehumanizing in effect.

The spate of very large hospitals being built at present shows similar characteristics, as do recent university campuses. The latter are particularly interesting as a type of building complex. They may be interpreted as a city in microcosm and show not only the urban qualities inherent in a particular architecture, but also the view of people in society implicit in that mode of design. The University of Port Elizabeth and the University of the North are both examples of a formal grouping that is typical of many campuses; a rectilinear geometry used to achieve formal arrangements with large open spaces between isolated buildings. The university as a megastructure can be seen in the Randse Afrikaanse Universiteit [Meyer and others, 1976] (fig. 33.3). The principal university departments and main functions are all in one building with Sant'Elia-like towers linked by walkways encircling a large open plaza from which the buildings radiate outwards. The plan form of the central plaza is clearly derived from Paul Rudolph's Boston Government Service Center and because of the large size of the project there is a different scale resulting in a very affirmative, aggressive group of buildings that have a tendency to be dominating in effect. The rather overwhelming nature of the buildings gives grounds for concern and adverse criticism, not of necessity directed only at architects. The buildings at RAU are competently handled and so are the other notable overscale buildings, the General Hospital, Johannesburg [Colyn and Meiring, 1978] and the New Civic Centre, Cape Town [Hannes van der Merwe, 1978], but there is a tendency in South African life to disregard humanistic values in the mode of organization of society with a consequent attitude to technology and to the scale and form of buildings that lead to an erosion of the environment.

At the other extreme, church architecture has been singularly innovative and appropriate, especially among the Afrikaans churches which have had little by way of architectural tradition to provide points of reference. Typical of the emergent genre is the Nederduitse Gereformeerde Kerk, Pretoria [Jan van Wyk, 1967] which is a well-scaled brick, concrete, and laminated timber building with a typical upwardly soaring, curved interior space terminating in a cone-shaped tower. Although this type of building has become more or less a norm for Protestant churches, the style is not yet universally used. The Nederduitse Gereformeerde Kerk in Welkom [Uytenbogaardt, 1964], for example, has a strong geometric and spatial order similar to that of Wright's Unity Temple. The most recent significant contribution to church architecture is the project for the Anglican Cathedral in Pietermaritzburg [Kammeyer and Rozendal, 1978], a cylinder articulated by an undulating wall which extends into the adjacent urban areas and achieves what promises to be a fine solution to city building in a small city. The freestanding wall acting as a second facade and used mainly to modulate scale is an element which has been extensively developed by Giurgola, Venturi, and Moore.

Theaters and concert halls show great diversity in their solution, although once again there is often nothing in the particular solution which testifies to its appropriateness in its immediate context. The Johannesburg Civic Theatre [Hermer, 1961] is a glass and concrete building with a distinctive pattern of concrete cruciform-shaped columns reminiscent of Latin American work, especially the President's Palace in Brazilia. The Nico Malan Opera House [Kent and others, 1971] is a rectilinear arrangement of concrete boxes which, in their formal juxtaposition and the resolution of the interior spaces, give the building complex a feeling similar to most new theaters in Europe, a true adaptation of a modified International Style with many references to international commercial architecture. The Baxter Theatre, University of Cape Town [Barnett and Broer, 1978], is a concert hall and theatre of curved forms in rough brick with corbels and pilasters and a number of stairs and galleries under a space-frame forming a parasol which is clad in cor-ten. This is a popular group of buildings which goes a long way toward being contextually appropriate.

As may be seen, there are some trends in, for example, the respective architectures of commerce and of certain public buildings, that are identifiable as having certain general tendencies the interpretation of which will always be a matter of opinion. As may also be seen, within certain building types, such as churches and theaters, the full complexity of present-day architecture shows itself with both indications of uniform stylistic tendencies and references to wide and diverse influences. Furthermore, as one approaches the present, so it becomes even more difficult to identify tendencies or trends. There are, however, isolated buildings designed with implicit or

33.3. Wilhelm Meyer, François Pienaar and Partners Inc., architects. Randse Afrikaanse Universiteit. Johannesburg, 1976. (Photograph: Courtesy of the architects)

even explicit intentions and stylistic characteristics which may in time prove to be the beginnings of coherent movements. In identifying some of these buildings we shall consider them in terms of their references and, if possible, in terms of their poetic content.

During the last decade there have been diverse local talents each attempting to build in a manner that revalidates architecture as architecture, doing so by a number of means: for example, finding a fresh point of departure by returning to the formal and spatial principles of the heroic period of the Modern Movement (such as in the work of Antoine and Adele de Sousa Santos in Cape Town) or referring to lessons from postwar Le Corbusier (such as in some of the work of R. S. Uytenbogaardt, also in Cape Town). The Werdmuller Centre, Claremont [Uytenbogaardt, 1977] is a shopping and office complex organized around an open, central, spiral ramp linking complex spaces and masses and finished in slate, off-the-shutter concrete, and exposed grey aggregate; the whole very skillfully articulated and reminiscent of the Visual Arts Center at Harvard. The Stekhoven House (fig. 33.4), Newlands [Antoine and Adele de Sousa Santos, 1972] takes the early International Style as its point of departure and refers to Alvar Aalto. Given the constraints of a difficult site, the

33.4. Antonia and Adele de Sousa Santos, architects. Steckhoven House, Newlands, 1972. (Photograph: Courtesy of William D. Parker)

design is resolved with an authority that makes it one of the seminal buildings in the country.

A distinctive architecture is emerging which refers to the images of high technology, the world of advertising media and manufacturing processes, an architecture that accepts the reality of the post-industrial commercial world and attempts to transcend it. Examples include, in the Transvaal, a recent award-winning building for Xerox S. A. Ltd. which is appropriately "slick" in its execution and imagery; and in Natal the work of architects such as Ferreira da Silva and Building Design Partnership. A very well-resolved example of this mode of architecture is the Huletts Head Office, Natal [Hallen and others, 1977]. This is a low-rise three-story office building with open-plan offices on the main floor. The building is a freestanding glass pavilion in a parklike setting, its quality as a pavilion emphasized by a podium consisting of a lower floor with battered sides. It has a deep roof overhang of curved reflective metal which also screens the glass walls from the sun.

Vernacular buildings and local historical precedent have also been a source of consistent architectural development, as in most of the influential work of Revel Fox and Gawie Fagan, both in Cape Town. Such concerns are augmented by important restoration work on some of the great Cape Dutch houses: for example, the eighteenth-century house at Boschendal restored by Fagan. Although restoration work is done as a matter of course by many architects, embodying principles of organization, the program, growing tendency for historical and vernacular building to become an explicit focus for the development of new styles of building. While the principal influences have been Cape Dutch architecture and a Cape vernacular of rural houses, the range of influence is expanding to include a wider range of historical periods, including for example, the legacy of Victorian building.

There is also evident a mode of design which is explicitly concerned with the dialogue between the contextual immediacy of the project and a diagram embodying principles of organization, the program, and so on. The possibility exists that an architecture may emerge from the dialogue between these sets of concerns; an architecture that would be archetypal, popular and, it is hoped, profound. After the work of Eaton this search is evident in some of the work of Bannie Britz such as the Marshall House, Benoni [1974], which is a rectangular brick box, with long, vertical, slit-windows, intersected by a triangle which opens the house out towards a lake. The imagery created is appropriate to its context and clearly transcends its references. Similar concerns are found in works such as the Ferndale House, Randburg [Prinsloo, 1965], the Saffer House, Geriston [Cooke, 1975], and the innovative and poetic houses of Stanley Saitowitz: the Fook house, Schoemansville [1975] (which has been described as a magic multicolored meccano house, a development of the traditional pitched-roofed box) and the Halfway House [1975 onwards] which is a very carefully sited house with curved roof forms and which makes reference in its inherent diagram and organization to traditional African architecture.

The latter part of the 1970s and beginning 1980s finds South Africa faced with unresolved problems of a divided plural and growing society. Much attention was and is being focused on the political and social situation of a large black population which has no political voice in the management of the country but whose growing awareness of their condition is making their demands for representation and equity more strident, and justifiably so. These problems are exacerbated by fluctuations in the economy which have materially affected the normal productive aspects of the country and thus the continued production of buildings. A great deal of attention is being directed at low-income group settlements as well as some attempts at a radical and critical appraisal of architecture and the role of the architect in a developing country. The considerable technical resources of the country are being marshalled towards massive housing programs. These may not, however, generate either a meaningful architecture or socially healthy and economically viable settlements, unless other tendencies are counteracted; for example, the legislation which excludes the ultimate user in determining significant parameters in his or her life is having a permanently damaging effect. Associated with these problems is a final discernible tendency—that of architects involved in community programs often suspending the dictates of architecture as architecture in the interests of meeting immediate needs.

On the whole, however, current issues are expressed by architects mainly in terms of the strategies and politics of professional survival although, behind the scenes, the battle lines are being drawn for a renewed consideration of the meaning of architecture in a developing society and the tenets of formal practice congruent with this meaning. What the dominant position is to be is unclear; whether towards a greater formalism seeking a revalidation of architecture by reference to the dictates of art history and the international media, or towards a greater realism seeking a more critical and humanistic response in architecture, or even towards greater pragmatism, remains to be seen.

Bibliography

BOOKS

Greig, D. *A Guide to Architecture in South Africa.* Cape Town: Howard Timmins, 1971.

Harrop-Allin, C. *Norman Eaton: Architect. A Study of the Work of the South African Architect Norman Eaton, 1902-1966.* 1975.

Herbert, Gilbert. *Martienssen and the International Style.* Cape Town: A. A. Balkema, 1975.

Lewcock, Ronald B. *Early Nineteenth Century Architecture in South Africa.* Cape Town: A. A. Balkema, 1963.

Pearse, Geoffrey E. *Eighteenth Century Architecture in South Africa.* London: Batsford, 1957.

Walton, J. *Homesteads and Villages of South Africa.* Cape Town: van Schaik, 1952.

USEFUL JOURNALS

Architect and Builder (Cartwright's Corner, Adderley Street, Cape Town).

Architecture S. A. (journal of the Institute of South African Architects).

Isilili sam sise Africa (a quarterly journal of architecture and human settlements by the School of Architecture, University of Cape Town).

34

SWEDEN

STEN SAMUELSON

Before we may discuss developments in Swedish architecture since 1940 we should consider briefly some relevant assumptions concerning architectural development. The term *architecture* is so complicated and multifaceted, varies so greatly from time to time and in different locations, and covers so wide and diverse a field that some attempt at a general, even if inadequate, definition seems necessary. More than any other form of cultural expression, architecture may be the materialization of the social, political, economic, technical, and aesthetic aims of a given time and place. Historical studies of architecture support and clarify this thesis, regardless of whether its expression found form in natural stone, wood, brick, steel, or concrete or in more or less brutal or sophisticated treatment of materials, quantities and qualities. The ambitions of a welfare state, unlike the monument builders who raised temples, pyramids, and castles, are expressed in pragmatic attempts to establish a broadly based high standard of building. Whether there is room here for individual expression by architects is an open question, although a partial answer may be found in this essay. The welfare state slowly and almost unnoticeably tends to move towards a bureaucratic condition in which development serves neither the individual nor his architectural environment. Instead, through cooperation of organizations at the federal and regional levels it tends to serve the bureaucratic apparatus. These obvious trends are reflected particularly in building of the 1960s and the first part of the 1970s, after which developments seem to have moved toward a more progressive architectural ideology.

Before describing developments in Swedish architecture during the period 1940-1980 we should look to the year 1930, since that marks the beginning of a whole new line of thought towards architecture in Sweden. The Stockholm Exhibition of 1930, an architectural manifestation that has had few parallels in history and whose national importance has perhaps no equivalent in other countries, must be seen as an expression of ideas that had their roots in the social development of the twenties and the aesthetic movements from the continent. The artistic and technical strength displayed then had and continues to have an extraordinary importance for Swedish architecture, planning, and design with architects such as Erik Gunnar Asplund, Sigurd Lewerentz, Sven Markelius, Arthur von Schmalensee, Uno Åhrén, and Eskil Sundahl. Architectural developments of the thirties were also dependent upon political support and a recognition of the historical connections between political ideas and new architectural viewpoints.

The functionalist architecture already evident in the twenties provided possibilities for a rational program of design and production. At the same time its rather frugal, formal expression and technical simplicity made it usable for socially desirable and politically necessary mass production of housing. Because of the concentration on social and welfare ideologies in the thirties, architects shifted their interest away from aesthetics. Thus within the victory of functionalist aesthetics per se, a loss of aesthetics in the greater sense was heralded. The followers of the initial development, moreover, utilized only what was both clearly visible and easily copied so that mostly facile stereotypes survived in both architecture and city planning. The beginning of the war in 1939 marked a strong reaction against European Functionalism for which German schools such as the Bauhaus had been the dominant sources of inspiration. Although Sweden remained neutral, international contacts were broken and shortages of material, transportation difficulties, and economic restraints developed. The openness of the architecture of the thirties was replaced by the use of more closed forms, forms perhaps more truly Swedish, apparently expressing a need for security. No doubt some problems inherent in functionalist architecture, including roof designs unsuitable for local climatic conditions, also contributed to this reaction. In city planning as well, basic changes in thinking occurred. A positive result of these was that the schematic, stereotyped plans of the prewar era were abandoned, not to be taken up again until the sixties and the seventies.

The architecture of the forties in Sweden reflected a balanced and humane synthesis of notions that were in reality not in opposition to the theoretical principles of Functionalism. Development from 1939 to 1949, in spite of its speed, was not as rapid as the explosive changes of later decades. The size of buildings in this period remained within human reason and there was time for contemplation and study down to the smallest of details. In special harmony with the conditions of this time were the architects Sven Bäckström and Leif Reinius, who were responsible for the Gröndal housing project in Stockholm built just after the war, perhaps the most interesting in its diversified and organic arrangement of terrace housing, low apartment blocks, and higher so-called point-buildings. This area together with Rosta in Örebro, because of their individuality are still experienced as fresh and coherent work which is not often surpassed. As early as the end of the thirties these architects had worked toward a natural accommodation of various materials. Their later work, often of extremely high quality, has a character that approaches decoration without the usual detrimental consequences.

In urban planning, environmental and social requirements were joined together in organic compositions, as in the plans for Vällingby and Årsta. In Vällingby, where the city plan dated from the war years on, Sven Markelius demonstrated that he was not only one of the great architects of the time but also one of the great city planners. In its integration of housing, industrial sites, commercial, social, and cultural buildings, Vällingby even today is exemplary, affording a textured variety of identities. Particularly in some of the later stages, however, the center of Vällingby [finished, 1954] shows deficiencies and an insecurity that led to extremes. The center's component architectural blocks are not always consistent with their meanings. Several of the later buildings must nevertheless be mentioned for their fine quality, particularly a housing project [1949-1955] by Paul Hedqvist and a very fine area of row houses [1955-1958] by Ragnar Uppman. These later buildings are extremely well accommodated to the landscape and often present exciting spatial solutions.

About the same time as Vällingby, Uno Åhrén brought forth some basic thought concerning the Stockholm suburb of Årsta in his well-known design for Årsta Center, which was completed later by the firm of the brothers Eric and Tore Ahlsén. Årsta Center illustrated powerful social ambitions that are seldom attempted even in new centers today, since commercial interests have gained control. The informal nature of its architecture allowed a great flexibility in design and future extensions, encouraged efforts to integrate art with architecture, and inspired the later architecture of the seventies.

The firm of Ancker, Gate, and Lindegren may be noted also as representative of the forties and later, with, among other projects, their fine city plan and well-detailed architecture in Lidingö that was so important for future planning. Sune Lindström's City Hall and Hotel in Karlskoga, Värmland, also must be mentioned as they relate to his later, almost formal-constructivist work. In southern Sweden, Sigurd Lewerentz had completed his crematorium in Malmö, while the developments of the talented Hans Westman proceeded steadily from his functionalistically strong Transformer Station toward a more human but also more decorative architecture, unfortunately often in clear opposition to Functionalism's demands for structural honesty.

The fifties were characterized by an optimistic belief in the possibilities of technology. At the same time, the architectural problems raised in the forties fell into the hands of second-rate architects, superficial copyists who built a banal architecture. In Sweden the fifties saw an exaggerated industrial expansion that led to an excessive movement of population and created an increased demand for building. In turn, year-round building became necessary in this cold land, and new demands arose for appropriate production techniques and working environments. Though we may speak of the overinflated Swedish social welfare program, we should recall that Sweden had developed in a few decades from a poor agrarian land with enormous overcrowding (four to eight persons per room) into a new welfare state. The new, rather exceptional, and in part unexpected requirements, however, paved the way for new production systems of prefabricated elements. New concrete building-systems were a natural development in a country where concrete has traditionally been an important material; and the "All-Beton" system, invented in Malmö in 1950, provided high production speeds so successfully that it was later exported throughout the entire world. The "All-Beton" (or "All-Concrete") system is really not a fully prefabricated system. The concrete is poured *in situ* in specially constructed forms, which are used over and over again. The surface of the forms can be a special type of plywood, steel, or other materials that will reflect the final result. Unfortunately, this and other, similar systems together with an increasing demand for economic returns on both machines and building cranes had a detrimental effect on many city-planning efforts. We should note here that city planner Sune Lindström tended at this time to become lost in a formalistic and technological planning aesthetic whereas his technical building projects, such as water tower designs, and other infrastructures, were developed beautifully and can be considered as art that remains unsurpassed today.

Technology was used to meet both political and economic objectives. Architecture became subordinated to technology and associated itself with the economic and technological rationales of the thirties. Unfortunately during the fifties there was no one such as Gunnar Asplund to shape the new technology in an artistic way. Furthermore, decisive economic power came to rest in the hands of the building contractors. The rather constructively designed architecture of the fifties found its best forms in southern Sweden, where volume and proportions were humanized and translated into scale and proportions that were seldom found in the other parts of the country. The new technocratic ideology, relatively little concerned with human conditions and environmental requirements and emanating from Stockholm and Gothenburg (Göteborg), was expressed by some of the country's best talents in terms extremely sympathetic to production. Thus, Arthur von Schmalensee's addition to the Chancellory in the Old City in Stockholm during this period was subjected to a great deal of criticism. And yet, since in its form and materials this building was designed to fit well into its surroundings, von Schmalensee would seem to have been the first modern architect in Stockholm to have dared to work with an older formal language. Hans Asplund was subjected to similar criticism for his Citizen's Building of the fifties in Eslöv, in which he strongly emphasized formal and aesthetic elements.

With few exceptions city planners of the fifties and later worked with the generally successful idea of designing satellite suburbs enclosed by concentric rings of housing areas. These areas included some high point-buildings, with structures of reduced height and forms in the centers in order to fit in with row houses or individual homes. Some of these developments were so large that unfortunately they have led to increased social segregation. In contrast, the city planning director of Malmö, Gunnar Lindman, worked toward a more unified, more integrated city, an idea that was abandoned after his time (1956) with very unfortunate consequences.

In the mid-1950s the Arton architectural firm designed two interesting housing areas, one in Lund, the other in the Elineberg area of Helsingborg. The Lund complex was accomplished with the help of Jørn Utzon, the Danish architect of the Kingohus [1956] development. Utzon's work and the cultural contact with Denmark have had great importance for the best of the architecture of southern Sweden. Ideas in city planning, building forms, and constructional details crossed the sound into Skåne, the old Danish part of Sweden, resulting in such projects as Arton's library in Helsingborg and strongly influencing Bengt Blasberg and Henrik Jais-Nielsen's work, particularly in the area around Helsingborg. In Skåne a strong attempt to increase density in housing while maintaining forms of low buildings showed components of Danish design clearly.

The landscape provides a different situation at Gothenburg, where Lennart Kvarnström and Jan Wallinder designed buildings that fit well into the special conditions of the site with rocks, sea, and lakes. At about the same time the Anglo-Swedish architect Ralph Erskine, a man of great talent, ability, and an innate understanding of nature and tradition, accomplished his first projects of village architecture as in his settlement for forest workers in Jädraas [1951]. His first major project, a ski hotel at Borgafjäll [1948-1950], was received at first with humorous acceptance, then evoked sharp criticism, and finally was admired, with all due justice, as a work of unique importance for this country. Many have seen Erskine's buildings in the subarctic conditions of northern Sweden as an expression of a new sort of Formalism rather than, it seems, as an attempt to develop a climatically conditioned regional architecture transformed by the personal aesthetic of a sensitive architect. His designs date from 1958, and realized projects are located, for instance, at Kiruna and Svappavaara (figs. 1.3 and 1.4)

While in general large building projects reflected mostly technological approaches, the significant architectural works occurred in the designs of churches, crematoriums, sports halls, and similar projects over which large, entrenched bureaucracies had no control. For instance, Sigurd Lewerentz, one of the architects involved with the Stockholm Exhibition of 1930, built an absolute masterpiece of a church in Skarpnäck [1960] (fig. 34.1), close to Stockholm, which has been very much admired for its firm feeling of eternity and its use of space, light,

34.1. Sigurd Lewerentz, architect. Church in Skarpnäck, Stockholm, 1960. (Photograph: Courtesy of Paal-Nils Nilssonito)

and materials. As at Skarpnäck, so at Klippan, another church designed by the aging Lewerentz became a place for architectural pilgrimages from afar. Its structural treatment is heavy, as if the Eternal had entered into the genial architect's service. Space is conquered and light becomes the servant of space, while weight becomes man's support in an uncertain world. Architecturally it is the ancient, trustworthy materials which emphasize and support this feeling. The spirit of Lewerentz's work of the twenties and thirties was brought to bear upon his masterwork in Klippan especially, where the idea of the mystical light and the whole concept of containment facilitate man's search for his God. Neither the obvious nor the apparent was emphasized by Lewerentz, for something more emerges.

In secularized, materialistic Sweden, during this decade of the fifties a greater number of churches was built than ever before, by such architects as Peter Celsing, Carl Nyrén, Bengt Lindroos, Anders Berg. Celsing's church of 1955 in Vällingby (figs. 34.2 and 34.3) and his extremely interesting creation in Sundsvall are particularly well known. The Vällingby building with its powerful and careful brickwork had a great influence on later Swedish churches. Outstanding in the work of younger architects is Alf Engström, Gunnar Landberg, Bengt Larsson, and Alvar Törneman's (ELLT's) crematorium of 1960 in Gävle (figs. 34.4 and 34.5). The building is a worthy heir of Gunnar Asplund's Forest Cemetery (begun in 1915), yet very unlike it. It is both an organism of nature and an independent individual entity. The columns are like the pine trees surrounding the building; they rise to support a floating roof set on an all-glass clerestory, while the landscape architecture by Per Friberg helps to complete its thorough integration with nature. I can recall few times when I have seen such harmony between nature and that which man has created.

At the beginning of the sixties an architectural vacuum appeared in city planning and in the art of urban building. A centralization of power, consisting of political and semipolitical movements linked in an unholy alliance with the large building contractors such as SIAB, SCG, and others, had rather disastrous effects on both architecture and the environment. There are few countries in which architecture and architects have been defamed as much as they were during those years in "democratic" Sweden. Reactions to this predominantly barren, dull type of building came in the seventies, seemingly to the complete surprise of the politicians, when average citizens refused to move into these "social-hygienic" slums, especially in the Stockholm, Gothenburg, and

34.2. Peter Celsing, architect. Church in Vällingby, exterior, 1955. (Photograph: Courtesy of Sune Sundahl)

34.3. Peter Celsing, architect. Church in Vällingby, interior, 1955. (Photograph: Courtesy of Sune Sundahl)

Malmö suburbs. Nevertheless, there was some city planning and architecture well worth mentioning during this period.

The Brittgården project in Tibro by Ralph Erskine (figs. 34.6 and 34.7) is a most important example, with its varied building types and climatic architecture largely of concrete and wood [1960-1962]. The concern with climate that Erskine showed first in northern Sweden's mining districts where the north wind was blocked by the buildings was demonstrated again here. He focused as much upon the problem of noise as climate and designed the inner part of the area, with its mixed building forms, so as to protect it from traffic noise. The result was a firm, logical, richly varied, and exciting environment.

The first important wedge in the fight against large, monotonous, point-building developments, where production methods were given priority but which disregarded human needs, was driven in by Lennart Kvarnström and Bertil Hultén with their Vivalla apartment house project [1962] in Örebro. Its importance was that it showed it was possible to build close to the ground and provide human environments within the economic framework of building production. As a final product, despite the careful consideration that went into it, this project of low structures represents a kind of additive thinking

34.4. Alf Engström, Gunnar Landberg, Bengt Larsson, Alvar Törneman (ELLT) architects. Chapel of Eternal Life, entrance. Gävle, 1960. (Photograph: Courtesy of Gunnar Landberg)

34.5. Alf Engström, Gunnar Landberg, Bengt Larsson, Alvar Törneman (ELLT) architects. Chapel of Eternal Life, interior. Gävle, 1960. (Photograph: Courtesy of Sune Sundahl)

34.6. Ralph Erskine, architect. Brittgården Housing, inner courts. Tibro, 1962. (Photograph: Courtesy of Sune Sundahl)

34.7. Ralph Erskine, architect. Brittgården Housing. Tibro, 1962. (Photograph: Courtesy of Mats Linden)

in which architectural qualities have been subordinated to other circumstances. Particularly Kvarnström moved from an earlier architecture of homes, as sophisticated as they are economical, and a very interesting student building in Gothenburg, towards an almost artificial and at times dry simplicity that seems to be a sort of synthetic "poor-communism" in one of the world's richest countries. In Örebro during the same period, Sidney White's office was making a new and important effort to design an integrated city center in stages over several decades. These architects, like the firm A4, relied primarily on programming and pseudotechnology over several years. Only in the latter part of the seventies do they reappear as architects, as we shall see, when their whole complex register is used in more aesthetic interpretations. In the shadow of population movements and of the broad urban restructuring and renewal programs in larger cities, there are a few architects who separated themselves from the prevalent demands of production-effective design at any aesthetic cost by insisting on high quality design and construction during this period.

Together Götaplatsen and the Avenue in Gothenburg comprise one of Sweden's most beautiful cityscapes. It is seldom that any building project seems to me to have been so seminal for future rebuilding and renewal as that of Helge Zimdahl's Avenue buildings. In his command over the Avenue's scale this fine architect points the way to a result that moves future urban renewal toward a level that is far above that found anywhere else in the world. In this effort he has been aided by the unaffected and natural work of the architect Sven Brolid. In their works these architects along with others such as Stig Axel Ancker, Bengt Gate, Sten Lindegren (AGL), and Nils Ahrbom and Nils Tesch reflected a search for quality which reached perhaps one of its finest examples in von Schmalensee's city hall in northern Kiruna, far north of the polar circle. The large hall and meeting place afford protection, have a firmness that seems to be part of the northern mountains, and demonstrate a feeling for the use of materials that imparts a reassuring sense of permanence.

Hans Asplund, one of the few architects who proceeds independently, showed an acceptance of a formal aesthetic in his NK (Nordiska Kompaniet) building, a large department store and parking garage in Stockholm [to 1964], as well as in his community hall in Eslöv [1957], an acceptance that few other architects care to admit. In the search for quality we must also acknowledge the work of Anders Tengbom, even though at times it has been reactionary in appearance. In his use of time-tested materials such as brick and natural stone, Tengbom hardly stands in the spotlight of progressive architecture, but his work reaches its architectural peak without resort to easy effects when it is deeply rooted in nature as in his educational building at Skogshem or in that inner city's other sensitively designed buildings.

One building which has not received its fair share of praise is the community hall in Örebro [1965] by the Ahlsén brothers. With its square plaza consisting of both cultural and commercial elements, this building presents one of the few examples in which work of our own day has enriched the content of the inner city in a new way. The exterior has the natural force of a Medieval residence, without overdoing it; the interior, an extremely interesting spatial concept. These two architects also have an unusually great talent for the integration of all architectural parts and even seem to build a creative sense of humor into their solutions. One may note, strangely enough, that in some cities and towns as at Örebro or Landskrona there is a genuine feeling for architecture. As at Örebro with the Ahlsén brothers, for example, so at Landskrona with the great, often misunderstood, and shy architect Inge Stolz, some excellent work has been accomplished.

In Lund in southern Sweden, as a contrast to Westman's more romantic architecture, there developed during the sixties and seventies a simpler architecture, the best of which is by Klas Anshelm. His art gallery [1957] in Lund is a particularly good, early indication of this style that is also exemplified by the "Landsting" building and the city hall in Lund. At the same time in the north a special relationship may be seen between the architect and his material in the work of Alexis-Franklin, since it seems hardly accidental that the material, in this case steel, harmonized with its surroundings.

The works of some of these architects during the sixties and the seventies led toward a simplified Brutalism. This ideology includes the idea that production of the architectural works required by a society can be facilitated through simplification. But Brutalism also demands excellence in artistic expression, for, as with all "isms," in the hands of second-rate and third-rate architects it becomes a false opportunistic doctrine, as found for instance in Gothenburg and Lund-Malmö.

Among Swedish architects two solitary men, Jan Gezelius and Per Friberg, are seldom mentioned. Yet their work, often dealing with problems of small-scale architecture, is outstanding; and their more traditional buildings, erected years before the traditional became popular, have a remarkable sense of permanence. Both command a deep knowledge of landscape and siting and use materials of earth and nature. Both teach landscape planning and architecture: Gezelius in Stockholm and Friberg in Skane. Jan Gezelius's architecture shows how nature and creativity can be interwoven with light in a wonderful way, as for example at the museum of Jokkmokk at the polar circle, built with A. Björklund [to 1966]. In his buildings wood is used lovingly. In the siting and building of Per Friberg's homes, such as at Skånör [1960], sensitive concern with placement and with details that work in the most simple, economical, and refreshing ways is evident, so that a strong sense of being close to nature is evoked.

If in the future Sweden were to be seen as typifying the role of the architect in the complex of problems involving the state and architecture, one would see in the seventies a time of reaction against high buildings and their disruptive environmental consequences; and one might become aware of how the entire apparatus of building production changed in form, first accommodating to and finally directing construction programs of additive houses ("villas") that became monotonous just as had been the case earlier with the point-building. This led to further social segregation rather than to a desirable societal integration.

Hopefully it would also be seen that the seventies signaled the beginning of a better understanding of our physical surroundings and their importance to our everyday life.

A paradox may also be perceived: "common art in architecture becomes dictatorship." Developments have again shown that politically inspired criticism of architecture as well as of other cultural areas is only in organic harmony with society's well-being if it serves human beings as individuals, families, or other clearly identifiable units. Wagnerian wholism within architecture is the result of political attitudes and ideologies that serve only a central, guardian mentality.

The first thoroughly studied, developed thoughts about a new architecture of city planning were effected in southern Sweden at Landskrona, where our Danish master Arne Jacobsen [design, 1961] and our Anglo-Swedish master Ralph Erskine [1968-1970] designed projects of unusual interest. New ideas included the notion of decentralization into understandable villages, each of which is itself completely integrated. With this concept, a humanistically accentuated architecture was provided in which social, service, and work places were integrated and personal identification once again became possible. The solution of the problem of identification and the reduction of the scale of building to understandable groupings are of prime importance, since city planning in this manner becomes both more flexible and better able to accommodate further development. The danger of a new romantic formalism remains, however, even with this model in which new viewpoints concerning social life, service facilities, care of the elderly, hospital service, and common activities were given priority. When such working models are applied to larger, more extensive groups, they ought to provide important possibilities for future design.

In the larger, more important architectural offices, there probably was too great a reliance upon formulating verbal programs and an overestimation of technological possibilities that must be more carefully controlled in the future. Typical of this is the group of architects called A4 which, with Ragnar Uppman, had done the extremely fine row housing in Vällingby and, with John Sjöström, had designed an outstanding building on Gotland for the Court of Law, which was quickly protected by law. Though during the sixties this office focused on the possibilities of modular technology, during the seventies its entire artistic register of knowledge was brought into play in the design of Landvetter Airport at Gothenburg [1977]. During the fifties and sixties Sidney White's architectural office showed itself thoroughly capable of taking mathematical problems and translating them functionally. Then in the seventies they shifted rather strongly towards more humanistic and expressive work of higher artistic quality. In general, in the seventies the larger offices and the more individual architects exhibited a broader formal range and a development towards greater expressions of personality that reflected the maturing of their design capabilties.*

Worked out in the forties, published in 1952 under architects Sven Markelius and Göran Sidenbladh, and revised since then, great interest has been focused on the plans for the center of Stockholm. Here problems of traffic and scale were considered paramount. Thus, the smaller outer areas of the center were designed with concern for communication, traffic, and volumetric requirements of the city rather than for people. Possibilities inherent in the physical character of Stockholm were largely ignored in the city plan. Many architectural problems recognized during the seventies came to be sharply focused in the city's center but not because of any planning successes. Whether successful or not, the city plan of Stockholm confronted problems common to both the large and small city's core. Rather than in its ideas as such, the fact that it was completed at all is remarkable, and enables this city plan to serve as an example for those who see it as a failure as well as for the few who see it as a proper solution.

Major criticisms may be made, particularly of the manner in which the whole idea of communication in the inner city is approached and in the lack of understanding of Stockholm's structure as well as of its historical background. In spite of the heaviness of so many buildings, such as the Royal Bank with its almost dictatorially imposing presence, there is a surprising lack of substance in the whole inner-city plan. Lacking natural roots in the city's architectural and historical development, the plan must be seen primarily as a response to the ideologies of the traffic planners of the fifties and sixties. While some architects attempt to approach the task of creating useful spaces within this elaborate apparatus in a superficial way, others seek support in older building types, such as Anders Tengbom's buildings, Carl Nyrén's bank building, Hans Asplund's addition to NK [1964] and Sven Markelius's Sweden building [1960], each of which is completely different in architectural character. Ultimately, Peter Celsing's work in Stockholm makes the best of a situation that is architecturally almost impossible.

*This may be seen, for instance, in the municipal library at Norrköping [1971] by Sten Samuelson Arkitektkontor AB (fig. 34.8)—ED.

34.8. Sten Samuelson, architect. Municipal Library. Norrköping, 1971. (Photograph: Courtesy of the architect)

It was easier to work with the planning of Gothenburg where a continuity of rooflines is still to be found. When both rooflines and continuity disappear, however, the same problematic situation will arise. In Malmö the problems of planning have been resolved by a slow development of the inner city, as exemplified by Carl-Axel Acking's bank building, which seems almost interwoven within its southern Swedish, middle-class surroundings. Smaller cities continue to suffer architecturally under the pressures of larger shopping centers and environments of almost impenetrable traffic.

Although efforts to involve prospective users in city planning in order to increase the viability of living in the city have been largely unsuccessful, one must view the latter part of the seventies and the early eighties in Sweden with optimism because of a generally increasing interest in the architecture of the city's living and working environments. One can look forward from this, hopefully, to a revaluation of the idea that only by means of analysis and programming can buildings become total architecture. This revaluation seen by centralists as something negative, is understood by others such as myself as something positive. One looks forward to a decrease in centralized bureaucracies, so that architects may once more turn their efforts fully toward creating a more truly organic architecture.

*Bibliography**

BOOKS

Backström, Sven and Stig, Alund, eds. *Fyrtiotalets Svenska Bostad* [*Swedish Housing of the Forties*]. Stockholm: Svenska Arkitekters Riksförbund, 1950. (In Swedish and English)

Bauen und Wohnen in Schweden 1930-1980. (catalog) Stockholm: Swedish Museum of Architecture, 1980.

Kidder-Smith, G. E. *Sweden Builds.* Stockholm: Albert Bonnier, 1950.

Kooperativa Förbundets Arkitektkontor, ed. *Swedish Cooperative Union and Wholesale Society's Architect's Office 1935-1949.* Part 1. Stockholm: Kooperativa Förbundets Bokförlag, 1949. (In Swedish and English)

*Compiled by the editorial staff, Montreal

Larsson, Mårten J., ed. *New Architecture in Sweden.* (National Association of Swedish Architects) New York: John Wiley and Sons, 1961. (In Swedish and English)

Paulsson, Thomas. *Skandinavian Architecture.* London: Leonard Hill, 1958.

Ray, Stefano. *Il contributo svedese all' architettura contemporary Swedish Architecture, 1968-1978.* Stockholm: Svenska Arkitekters Riksförbund, 1978.

Svenska Arkitekters Riksförbund. *SAR Guide to Contemporary Swedish Architecture, 1968-1978.* Stockholm: Svenska Arkitekters Riksförbund, 1978.

Wrede, Stuart. *The Architecture of Erik Gunnar Asplund.* Cambridge, Mass.: MIT Press, 1980.

JOURNALS

Arkitekur. (Swedish review of architecture, published ten times yearly, 1959 to date.)

"Casa del popolo a Stoccolma" (S. Markelius, architect). *L'Architettura* 7 (January 1962): 621.

Celant, G. "L'Architettura moderna nei paesi scandinavi, Capelli, Bologna, 1965." *Casabella* 297 (September 1965): 96.

Diamant-Berger, Renée. "Pays Nordiques: Suède. *L'Architecture d'Aujourd'hui* 93 (December 1960): XIII, XIX-XXXVII, 56-68.

______. "Sten Samuelson: Landskrona Town Hall, Landskrona, Sweden." *Architecture and Urbanism* 100 (January 1979): 105-114. (In Japanese; English photo captions)

______ and Cousin, Jean-Pierre, eds. "Architectures Nordiques: Suède." *L'Architecture d'Aujourd'hui* 134 (October 1967): XXXI-XXVIII, 46-56, 77-99. (English summary, CLXXIII-CLXXVI)

Egelius, Mats. "Ralph Erskine." *Architectural Design* 47 (November-December 1977): 751-853.

Hall, Thomas. "New Studies on Building Developments in the Metropolitan Area of Stockholm." *Konsthistorisk Tidskrift* 46 (August 1977): 72-76.

"Kulturhuset, Stockholm." *Architectural Review* 150 (October 1971): 198-205.

"New Stockholm Landmarks." *Architectural Review* 133 (February 1963): 112-18.

"Nouveau Centre Commercial de Stockholm." *L'Architecture d'Aujourd'hui* 101 (April 1962): 62-67.

"Space Frame in a Swedish Forest, A. Jacobsen, Architect." *Architectural Forum* 126 (January 1967): 104-7.

"Unité Résidentielle Brittgarden à Tibro, Suède." *L'Architecture d'Aujourd'hui* 120 (April 1963): 623.

"Voyage of Discovery: Sweden." *Interiors* 124 (June 1965): 63-107.

35

TURKEY

DOĞAN KUBAN

Background

When considering recent architectural history in countries where Western culture is not an integral part of their tradition and where industrialization was begun relatively late, the use of Western terms in an evaluation of architectural developments may be misleading. To consider aspects of modernization and its limits with clarity, therefore, we must dwell briefly upon the context in which it arose in Turkey.

During the centuries of the Ottoman Empire's ascendancy, Istanbul was a great cosmopolitan capital of the Mediterranean world. As early as the eighteenth century, the influence of Western culture, institutions, and art was introduced, slowly changing the traditional aspects of the society. Yet when the Turkish Republic was founded in 1923, the cultural outlook, the social structure, and the economy of the country had not yet reached the level of the Western model. The Republic took as its goal a total restructuring of its society. This process obviously encompassed a reorganization of the building field and brought a great many innovations in the education and training of architects and technicians, in the writing of new laws and regulations, in the development of building technology, and ended with a new social status for the architect.

All these developments gradually came into being during the first three decades of the Republic, or, if we include the early twentieth-century Ottoman beginnings, during the first half of this century.

The idea of Westernization, today rejected with some reluctance as an imitative process, gave rise to adaptation problems of great complexity in every facet of life, with changes in the physical environment being not the least important of them.

The repercussions of European eclecticism were visible in the development of the neo-Ottoman style during the last phase of the Empire. Begun as a curious interpretation of the so-called Saracenic manner and executed mostly by minority or foreign architects, it soon became a revival of the classical Ottoman style in the hands of Turkish architects, corresponding in spirit to the European revivals of the early nineteenth century. Very popular in the last decades of the Empire, it continued during the first years of the Republic.

Architectural Developments

FROM THE 1920s TO 1950

The International Style was introduced in the late 1920s and early 1930s by foreign architects, especially Germans. Representatives of modern architecture such as Ernst Egli, Clemens Holzmeister, Martin Elsaesser, Bruno Taut and planners such as Herman Jansen and Martin Wagner, among others, practiced in Turkey, and many also taught in Turkish schools of architecture; Egli and Taut, for instance, at the Academy of Fine Arts, Holzmeister at the Technical University.

The experiments of the Bauhaus were represented particularly by architects such as Ernst Egli and Martin Elsaesser. The official architect of government buildings, Clemens Holzmeister, fostered a personal taste for a Functionalism mixed with a sort of medieval austerity and monumentality, as can be seen in his building for the Turkish parliament, Ankara [1938]. Later, Bruno Taut brought in his personal interpretation of the modern, especially through his teachings at the Academy of Fine Arts in Istanbul. Simplicity, Functionalism, Rationalism, and economy became the catchwords of architectural theory. While Functionalism was predominantly espoused by architects in the early 1930s, its principles of design were applied usually only to official buildings. In the years between the founding of the Republic and the Second World War, the country had a very limited economic capacity for large-scale building programs, except in the capital. Thus, outside Ankara and Istanbul except for government buildings, vernacular architecture remained traditional in design. In time, however, the new building regulations and the new image of modernism represented by official taste practically destroyed the traditional building in large cities. First brick and then ferro-concrete gradually replaced wood, which was prohibited as a building material even in remote regions. Thus age-old construction methods were eventually to be abandoned.

The interpretation of modern forms (called cubic architecture in Turkey) was rather different from its European counterpart. The International Style had to be adapted to local building practices, especially in the use of materials. But universal clichés such as the terrace-roof, horizontal window bands, certain plan combinations and forms of stairs, new facilities such as the bathroom with a bathtub, and two-dimensional geometric play in different colors of plaster on the facades became the essential elements of a stereotyped modern style that radically changed the traditional appearance of Turkish cities.

Among examples of functionalist architecture before the Second World War are two buildings of S. H. Eldem, the office building of Satie at Istanbul, the General Directorate of the Tobacco Monopolies at Ankara [1930], buildings by Seyfi Arkan, the Ankara Exhibition Hall [1935] by Şevki Balmumcu, the Central Bank [1933] by Holzmeister, Sümerbank [1938] by Elsaesser and buildings by Egli, especially the İsmetpaşa Institute for Girls [1930] at Ankara. But soon these were followed by a rigid, monumental, sometimes forceful style, as in some buildings by Holzmeister and in the uninspiring buildings of the war years. The political ascendancy of authoritarian rule thus found its expression in the neoclassical and the pseudomonumental in Turkey as in other countries.

The most concentrated effort to create a building that expressed the new Turkish culture is to be observed in the entries for the competition held in 1942 for the mausoleum of Atatürk in Ankara. Modern versions of Medieval tomb-towers indicating a soul-searching for ancient roots, or monumental designs of eclectic character combining both Turco-Muslim and Classical Mediterranean elements represented the cultural mood of the time. The winning project by Emin Onat and Orhan Arda was a simplified version of the Hellenistic mausoleum, with a cavelike mystical interior which, however, was eliminated during construction. The adaptation of an old Anatolian form for the exterior of Atatürk's tomb was a clear statement of one of the fundamental tenets of the official doctrine that the Turks were the only true inheritors of the old cultures of Anatolia.

While modern neo-Classicism mushroomed in the West, the main centers of architectural training, the Academy of Fine Arts and the Department of Architecture of the Technical University at Istanbul, reintroduced a forced Classicism into their curriculums in the 1940s. Major elements of expression were stone revetment and arched openings, while building proportions were inspired by traditional models.

For more than a decade into the early 1950s, young Turkish architects prepared neoclassical designs for state-sponsored competitions. A frequent jury member, Paul Bonatz, the well-known architect of the Stuttgart train station, as an advisor to the Ministry of Education and later as professor at the Technical University helped further this trend with his work. In his remodeling of the exhibition hall at Ankara into an opera house, suitably reflecting a reemergent nationalist style, he used Ottoman architectural features such as arcades, mukarnas, capitals, and cornices. As the designer of the noted Saraçoglu Mahallesi housing complex for government employees at Ankara [1946], he used the classical plan. This so-called classical Turkish house, whose examples are to be found from the Balkans to eastern Asia Minor, is a building of mixed construction. The most common type has a ground floor in stone which is a service area and a first floor—*piano nobile*—which has a rather symmetrical scheme most often, with a semi-open veranda or a central hall. In most cases, upper floors have projections over the ground floors and rooms have well-established plans and built-in furniture.

A genuine interest in the Anatolian house tradition led some architects to try to imitate motifs from vernacular tradition. This trend was encouraged at architectural schools, and examples of domestic architecture that reflected older schemes came into vogue. Among the more notable examples are some houses by Sedat Hakki Eldem in Istanbul such as his famous Cafe House at Taşlik [1950] on the model of the traditional Turkish house (figs. 35.1 and 35.2), Cenap And's Ankara home [1952] by Emin Onat, with some features of traditional Ankara houses but also recalling the rustic house tradition of central

35.1. Sedat Hakki Eldem, architect. Coffee House at Taşlik. Istanbul, 1950. (Photograph: Courtesy of Erken Ewiroğlu)

European countries, and Nuri Çapa's house at Bebik, Istanbul, by Söylemezoğlu.

Two large educational complexes, the Department of Sciences at the University of Ankara [1940] and the Department of Letters and Sciences at the University of Istanbul [1943], both designed by Sedat Hakki Eldem and Emin Onat, are large-scale official examples of the neonational style. The latter building, except for some finesse in its details, is a particularly repressive, self-conscious example of unfunctional monumentalism and lacks respect for its environment.

This short lived, second neonationalist style, which did not last after the 1950s, was much more moderate in the use of old features and dispensed with many of the decorative aspects of the neo-Ottoman style of the early twentieth century. More importance was given to volume and plan, though elements such as arches and stone revetments, projecting upper floors, large eaves, and arcades were used to convey the spiritual continuity with tradition. One may say that this was a detour in the normal development of modern Turkish architecture and mostly political in character. No parallel cultural development accompanied this return to traditional sources. Although the Republic had always promoted national culture, education was essentially international in outlook.

After the collapse of fascism and the resurgence of the modern style, even the fiercest Classicists gave up their clichés and once again followed the interna-

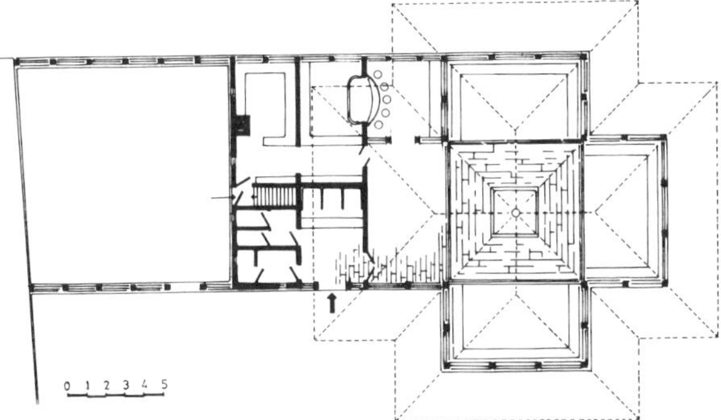

35.2. Sedat Hakki Eldem, architect. Plans of Coffee House at Taşlik. Istanbul, 1950. (Drawing: Courtesy of Nur Altinyildiz)

tional development. Influence from English-speaking cultures had already entered Turkey during the war. Two expositions, first of British architecture (1944) and then of British town planning (1947), which were prepared by the proponents of Rationalism, reawakened the latent ideas of Functionalism and led to a new vogue. The transition from neonational to postwar modern came rapidly. The modern masters, who found building opportunities all over the world, held sway over the architectural currents in Turkey where their ideas came to the fore in new projects. Since Turkish architects at that time had their own legal organizations and laws to protect their rights, works by foreign architects were restricted. New regulations were issued for the planning of cities, and standardization was instituted in many areas of building.

ARCHITECTURE IN THE 1950s

After the Second World War, Turkey underwent a great political transformation, in which one-party rule was abolished. The ensuing decade witnessed a great political euphoria, with the participation of the masses in the political process, the replacement of ruling bureaucrats by technicians and businessmen, and a rapid industrialization and urbanization.

A building boom that formulated a rather cheap version of modern architecture signaled the end of the old physiognomy of the cities. The few architects of that time participated fully and freely in bringing about physical changes of the urban environment with buildings that slavishly imitated international masters. Since steel was expensive, concrete was used as the main structural material. Curtain walls, though unfunctional and expensive for conditions in Turkey, were added to the repertory of design. Le Corbusier, Mies, and Aalto had their followers; Wright found less favor with Turkish architects although his ideas about architectural space received attention.

The postwar economic development released an experimental spirit that opened the way to freer and more imaginative design. The competition for the Palace of Justice at Istanbul, on the site of important archeological and historical remains near the old hippodrome, was won by Sedat Hakki Eldem and Emin Onat [1949]; for the municipality of Istanbul structure in the center of the old city, by Nevzat Erol [1953] and for the commercial center of Ulus at Ankara, by Beken, Bolak, and Bozkurt [1955].

The concepts of office towers, shopping centers, large unified glass facades, horizontal roofs, and freer planning were introduced. Although these ideas had been disseminated earlier in Turkish schools of architecture, they were not acted upon until the 1950s.

This was an era of complete surrender to the invasion of foreign ideas of design. Discussions concerning the true character of national design were abandoned. Generally reactionary in cultural and political behavior, the democratic regime opened all doors to Western and American ideas. Neither the social and economic implications of the rapid change in the traditional environment nor the possibilities of local technology were explored by architects. An interesting case that examplifies this attitude is the Hilton Hotel at Istanbul designed by Gordon Bunshaft from the firm of Skidmore, Owings and Merrill and his Turkish counterpart Sedat Hakki Eldem, who was responsible for the execution and the decorative details [1952]. The Istanbul Hilton set a new standard for building performance, though its negative influence probably outweighs its positive effects, since the project was designed according to American standards for which many materials and mechanical parts were imported. Apart from some elegant details designed by Eldem, it proved culturally and economically fatal for the development of a sensible, appropriate, architectural behavior interpreting the real potential of the country. Such situations are common in Third World countries.

After the 1950s mass immigration to the cities, foreign investment pumping the accelerated rate of building demands, and a government eager to create a new industrial image were responsible for profoundly altering the appearance of the cities. Because of a lack of experience and the lack of a developed building technology, the Western model was translated into an architectural language with an extremely provincial vocabulary. In the hands of simple, uneducated contractors of small-town origins, modern jargon was too easily converted into the most banal box-architecture that expressed a complete disregard for past architecture.

The 1950s, with its building boom may be thought of as an era in which a new architectural vocabulary was developed. For schools, hospitals, hotels, office buildings, housing developments, and new apartment buildings there were experiments with different dimensions and new forms. Among these experiments, the Divan Hotel by Rüknettin Güney [1956] and the Anadolu Club at Büyükada, Istanbul, by Turgur Cansever [1950] were particularly successful. Among new housing projects, one may point to Levent 4. in Istanbul [1954] by K. A. Aru and the Ataköy-I Housing Development [1959] designed by a group of architects for upper-middle-class families at Bakirköy, also in Istanbul.

ARCHITECTURE SINCE 1960

During the 1960s, Miesian or Corbusian approaches of the 1950s were replaced by a many-sided approach to form. The new spatial and structural experiences which became fashionable reflected post-Wrightian ideas influenced by Alvar Aalto, and reminiscences of the works of Kenzo Tange, Louis Kahn, Eero Saarinen, Paul Rudolph and Pier Luigi Nervi. Spatial structures, though never realized on a grand scale, and building complexes for industry tempted leading architects because they constituted a new ground for experiments with larger structures and modern materials.

Theoretical discussions of architectural styles lost their importance after 1960 as a consequence of a revolutionary change in the government. Subsequently, architects focused their attention on social issues. The creation of new governmental agencies dealing with housing, rural development, the urban and rural infrastructure, and the growing problems of urbanization and industrialization radicalized architectural thought.

With this new shift in attitudes and support by some politicians and administrators, planners and architects were still unable to check building for speculation which was responsible for the chaotic urban development. In most cases Turkish architecture in the 1960s became neither more rational nor beautiful.

Certain limitations in the areas of building technology and economic capacity determined the physiognomy of modern Turkish architecture, as for instance with the skyscraper. Defined in Turkish terms, a skyscraper is a building of fifteen to thirty stories. The office building at Kizilay by Enver Tokay (twenty-one stories), the Stad Hotel by Doğan Tekeli and Partners (nineteen stories) and similar skyscrapers at Ankara remain rare examples, although they have served to change the characteristic horizontal silhouette of the capital with its monumental government buildings. In Istanbul, the development of high-rise buildings from the early 1950s was followed by hotel towers such as the Sheraton Hotel by Aru, Süher, Emiroğlu, and others (twenty-one stories) and the Intercontinental Hotel by Fatin Uran (twenty-eight stories), both of which stand isolated like their counterparts in Ankara.

No matter which style or trend is followed, projects by Turkish architects tend to shy away from the daring dimensions and the technical virtuosity that one finds in the architectural experiments of wealthier countries. Since fifty-story skyscrapers or the use of the latest materials or experimentation with forms of fantasy are prohibitively costly, recent generations have taken a more modest approach and search not for dazzling solutions, but for rational and modest design.

Whereas in the 1950s good examples of modern architecture were found only within the boundaries of a few large cities, in the 1960s acceptable examples of modern buildings appeared in every corner of the country, though sporadically. Competitions for government buildings again produced good results that probably represent the better side of contemporary Turkish architecture. Deserving mention among these are the Government House of the province Artvin, designed by A. Aslaner, H. Güngören, and S. Gürel [1969]; the Karayollari Genel Müdürlüğü (General Directorate of Highways) [1967] by Fikret Cankut; the Vakiflar Genel Müdürlüğü (General Directorate of Religious Endowments) by Ertur Yener, Erdoğan Elmas, and Zafer Gülçür; the Bankalar Birliği (the Banks Union) [1970] at Ankara and the Türk Dil Kurumu (Turkish Language Association) [1979] by Cengiz Bekkaş, also at Ankara.

A sensitivity for but not imitation of traditional forms has become strong among many talented architects. One of the best examples of this trend, Turgur Cansever's building for the Turkish Historical Association at Ankara [1966] (fig. 35.3) exhibits a preference for a subtle play of architectural elements based on a fine sense of proportion and detailing and the use of materials which refer to tradition. Sedat Hakki Eldem, the champion for a free interpretation of traditional forms, has contributed to this trend with buildings such as the Atatürk Library at Istanbul [1973] (fig. 35.4) and the elegant Indian Embassy at Ankara [1965] which displays his preference for presenting forms and textures of tradition with a subdued modernism.

35.3. Turgur Cansever, architect. Turkish Historical Association Building. Ankara, 1966. (Photograph: Courtesy of Dr. Inci Aslanoğlu)

35.4. Sedat Hakki Eldem, architect. Atatürk Library. Istanbul, 1973. (Photograph: Courtesy of Erkin Ewiroğlu)

Respect for the dimensions of urban space and for the forms of the traditional environments have also attracted a growing interest in recent years. Buildings such as the Bazaar for Manufacturers at Istanbul by Doğan Tekeli and Sami Sisa [1960], and the library of the Istanbul University (fig. 35.5) by Hadi Şandor (under construction, 1979-1980) have demonstrated the possibility of a harmony of form and scale with the existing environment, without necessarily referring to traditional features. Again, S. H. Eldem's Social Insurance Agency at Zeyrek, Istanbul [1972], is one of the most relevant examples of this approach.

This new attitude towards design, in which the modern, now practically assimilated, meets with the reinterpretation of the past, looks back to the past not for models but rather for inspiration. Although the formal devices used are not always satisfactory, this group of buildings exhibits a continuing search for cultural identity, a sensitivity to the existing environment, and an awareness of appropriate technical means.

Large office buildings of business firms and administrative centers of important banks are now prominent in the Turkish cityscape. In metropolitan areas where architects have found economical means

35.5. Hadi Şandor, architect. Library of Istanbul University, under construction. Istanbul, 1979-1980. (Photograph: Courtesy of Erkin Ewiroğlu)

35.6. Ahmet Oral, architect. Yapi ve Kredi Bankasi at Tepebaşi. Istanbul, 1971. (Photograph: Courtesy of Erkin Ewiroğlu)

to experiment with new ideas and materials, the sumptuous headquarters of Yapi ve Kredi Bankaşi (fig. 35.6) at Tepebaşi by Ahmet Oral [1971], and that of Akbank by Sedat Hakki Eldem [1971], both at Istanbul; as well as the headquarters of İş Bankasi (Bank of Labor) at Ankara [1978], and the office buildings of the Chamber of Industry at Istanbul [1976] are examples to be mentioned. While some of these, such as Eldem's Akbank, concentrate on the elegance of facades, others such as the office building of the Chamber of Industry and the headquarters of the Bank of Labor, attempt to create a monumental plasticity of free volumes. The somewhat symbolic character required of these buildings compelled their designers to search for strong plastic expressions, however sometimes to the detriment of their functional aspects as commercial architecture. For one group of architects, of which Metin Hepgüler is typical with his Army Officers' House at Istanbul [designed in 1967], there is quite a characteristic concern for projecting volumetric elements and texture. More relevant instances of structures with free planning and open form are a dormitory building at Tandoğan Place, Ankara, by Şevki Vanli and Ersen Gömleksizoğlu, and two office buildings [one designed in 1969] for an advertising agency, İstanbul Reklam (fig. 35.7), the other a business center [1979] at Istanbul both by Günay Çilingiroğlu.

Another field of experimentation for architects has been large university campuses. The Middle East Technical University [1962], the Technical University

35.7. Günay Çilingiroğlu, architect. İstanbul Reklam Building, designed 1969. (Photograph: Courtesy of Erkin Ewiroğlu)

of Trabzon, the University of Diyarbakir, Ege University at Izmir, and the University of Erzurum [1956] are among the large-project commissions that have gone to the winners of national competitions. Most of these consist of a collection of individual buildings of various qualities and craftsmanship: the Middle East Technical University planned [1965] and mostly executed by Behruz Çinici, is a striking example of eclectic virtuosity in unequal quality in campus design. One of its earlier and most prominent buildings, the Department of Architecture and Urban Planning, is an early instance of an extensive use of *béton brut* in Turkey. Some projects, such as those for the University of Diyarbakir [1971] and the Istanbul Technical University [1972], both planned by Kemal Ahmet Aru and Associates, employ modular schemes first experimented with in Germany. The city campus of Hacettepe University at Ankara, planned by the university's own architectural office and that of the University of Istanbul, in occupying the old city cores have, unfortunately, destroyed the traditional character and dimensions of their environment while failing to contribute a distinguished character of their own.

Between 1950 and the 1970s Turkish industrial development and growth in the parallel building industry was rapid although not very coherent. Ferroconcrete remained the main structural material. Since industrialized building techniques were not developed enough for widespread utilization, the needs of the rapidly increasing population and of urbanization were met mainly by construction techniques of a semi-industrialized character. Ready-made elements are increasingly being used, but the fact that mechanization has not yet taken hold has proved to be a very serious handicap in keeping up with demands for housing. Aluminum and metal frame windows, various artificial stones for revetments and floors, insulation and electric equipment, and an overgrown paint industry, nevertheless, give architects a free hand to play with contemporary themes.

The Training of Architects

In the 1930s and the 1940s, as we have seen, the architectural authorities were at first Europeans who became influential through their teachings and practice. Later in the 1940s, Turkish architects, who in most cases were professors at the architectural schools, became prominent. After the 1950s, Turkish architects educated at Turkish schools finally replaced foreigners in practice, in education, and as advisors to adminstrations.

In town planning, foreign dominance was partly a necessity and partly imposed by the foreign credit mechanism, a situation which lasted until the late 1960s. After 1960 the universities and architectural schools were able to educate enough professionals in both architecture and urban planning so that presently, as with engineering and medicine, architecture is a field in which the average graduate of a Turkish institution can compete in international markets. The output of architectural schools is excessive now, and architects face difficulties in finding jobs.

In the early decades, programs of the architectural schools followed two directions: fine arts and engineering. The Academy of Fine Arts paraphrased the Western fine-arts tradition, but supplemented it with some new programs that were introduced as early as the 1920s by Ernst Egli; nevertheless, emphasis on visual experience remained the essential characteristic of the architects' training for a long time. The second path, represented by the Department of Architecture of the Istanbul Technical University, stressed technology rather than aesthetics in the curriculum. Though the architectural profession had its roots in traditional Turkish culture, Western techniques of engineering were accepted as representative of modern civilization and therefore claimed superiority in the minds of the people.

Thus the public image of the architect as a designer as opposed to an engineer had to be recreated. After the 1960s, however, architectural education became uniform in all schools of architecture and remains so today.

In the practical training of architects, the system of architectural competition has played an important role. This was one of the means by which priority was given to Turkish rather than foreign architects. The competition system, in spite of some of its disadvantages, offered great challenges for young, talented architects and it forced them, at the very least, to become familiar with the major buildings of the contemporary world, if not with the architectural theory. Later, it led the younger generations to criticize the imitative attitude of many prominent architects and, eventually, to a certain maturity of architectural taste.

Finally, an increase in the number of educational institutions, the publication of professional journals—one of the oldest, *Mimar* (*Architect*), has been issued since 1931—and critical writing on architecture have all helped to improve architectural practice and to make the development of architecture and town planning carry some weight in decision making.

The Changing Face of the Cities

Urban planning was initiated during the early years of the Republic in Ankara, the new capital, then a city of about 20,000 where the headquarters of the revolution had been established. The first plan was for a residential quarter, drawn up around 1924 by the German architect Hansler, which reproduced the layout of Potsdam; the housing units themselves were free imitations of contemporary German suburban dwellings. Another German town planner, Herman Jansen, prepared a master plan of the capital in 1928, envisaged for a population of 300,000. Developed along a central axis, the plan connected the old Ankara with the new and emphasized the monumental governmental quarter. Thus, immediately after the proclamation of the Republic in 1923, representative buildings of the old architectural style stood side by side with works under the strong influence of European models. New government buildings, such as the Ministry of Health by Theodor Post and the Ministry of War by Clemens Holzmeister [1930] were European buildings transplanted into the heart of Anatolia by European architects. Other government buildings designed by Holzmeister, new public buildings, and schools created a monumentality of a new kind, symbolizing the aspirations of the modern Turkish state.

From the 1930s on, every city was legally required to have a master plan and this became a fashionable way for architects to earn money. With a minumum of data and a superficial survey, many were able to produce new town plans which consisted mainly in the creation of a new axis, the widening of existing streets and the designation of areas for government buildings, business centers, schools, and parks. All was prepared without sufficient field studies and no consideration whatsoever was given to existing buildings nor to socioeconomical and cultural conditions.

In Istanbul, the French urban planner Henry

Proust had prepared a master plan only for the Old City and that was often reworked. The general plan of metropolitan areas has always been one step behind actual developments. Thus, partial plans, mostly under the influence of speculative developers, have guided various implementations. Neither in establishing qualifications, in the number of specialists, nor in its sociopolitical and economic structuring has Turkish society been able to cope adequately with the accelerated growth of metropolitan Istanbul. Instead of guiding development many plans, executed wholly or in part, have resulted in the outright destruction of the structure of the Old City, and vernacular architecture has been replaced by an unassimilated architectural pseudomodernism. The entire process of creating and implementing city plans has revealed the harsh inadequacies of a society in rapid transformation.

In the West, the growth of the city is controlled by an autonomous administration which is often sensitive to the pressure of a vocal, concerned citizenry, a tradition that can be traced to the Middle Ages. The idea of urban community in the Western sense was, however, rather amorphous in Ottoman history. The municipality as an institution was introduced in the second half of the nineteenth century and took root in the social and cultural structure of Turkish society only after 1950. Especially today, with more than half of the city population composed of recent immigrants of rural origin, it is difficult to create an urban consciousness concerned with finding solutions to urban plights. This situation greatly facilitates speculative, irrational disposal of urban land.

With an annual population increase of 1,000,000,Turkey requires a minimum of 200,000 new housing units per year, without taking into consideration the old or the obsolete. Since ready-made elements produced by private firms are more expensive than the traditional systems, unless used in the quantities required for large-scale projects, they have become items for luxury building instead of ordinary consumer goods. The approach to the rebuilding of the country since the founding of the Republic has been through a mixed economic system. The great infrastructures, roads, railroads, harbors, electricity, water, and irrigation, were realized by the state while building activity, especially in urban reconstruction and housing, has remained essentially within the domain of private enterprise. Importation of building materials steadily increased until the 1950s. Even after that time, when domestic production of basic materials such as cement and steel greatly increased and the state became more increasingly involved with low-cost housing, building construction remained in the hands of private firms. The obvious outcome of this situation has been an appalling chaos in city development, exorbitant prices for land and construction, high rents, and the inevitable belts of squatter housing that have grown up around the cities. Since most of the municipalities sold the land they owned, they now have practically no control over planning for growth.

Flight from the countryside is largely responsible for the increase of population in Turkish cities between 1950 and 1975, which was in some cases fourfold. On the outskirts of cities, the development of large areas of squatter housing has posed a serious problem with lasting implications. At first the single-story, single-room buildings put up by the squatters were executed with reused materials, mostly on state-owned land. These improvised rural buildings employ mainly scrap materials and follow no particular model. And they are often eventually replaced by cheap apartment houses developed by mediocre speculators.

In a short period of time, the population of the fringe areas exceeded that of the cities themselves, and, by their sheer size, created formidable pressure on city authorities. The municipalities and governments brought in some facilities and services, such as roads, water, and electricity, which although often minimal or inadequate served to create an even greater demand for buildings in these areas. Consequently, large agglomerations that were frighteningly irregular were developed around the old city cores. All agricultural land lying outside the cities was either occupied by emerging industries or destroyed by urban sprawl. The quality of urban space and urban life severely declined from the city dweller's point of view. For those people coming from rural areas and remote villages, however, the squatter areas were not as intolerable as one might suppose.

While agricultural land was being turned into suburban areas, old city centers were also gradually undergoing transformation. Some old quarters, abandoned by their original settlers and long-term residents, fell into slums, while others took on new life as high-density business centers. The traditional structures, in most cases in wood, were vacated and left to decay, in time to be replaced by new structures. High density and high-rise buildings have in fact become uncontrollable factors in new city development.

Ankara today, with a population ten times greater than the pre-Second World War period, sprawls over the barren landscape of the Anatolian plateau (fig. 35.8) and little of the symbolic spirit of the early Republican capital remains. The old administrative center is dwarfed by an enormous growth of new buildings with high rises scattered about. Most of the

35.8. View of urban sprawl at Gecekoudu, Ankara, in 1979. (Photograph: Courtesy of Dr. Sevgi Aktüre)

architecture of the 1930s and the early 1940s has also been washed away by newer buildings.

It was only in the late 1950s that some healthy developments in planning, involving moderating practices, finally appeared. The teaching of architecture and urban planning at architectural schools emphasized the new social and economic realities.

Although this has not yet proved a strong enough force to halt the mechanism of chaotic development that started after the 1950s, professionals and urban administrators have at least been made aware of the inadequacy and potential dangers of urban politics: the soaring land prices; the apparent impossibility of coping with the exigencies of an overgrown city population; the energy crisis; alienation and urban unrest. All of these have made a reevaluation of the situation an urgent necessity today.

Later in the 1960s, a growing interest in the past took shape as one aspect of the problem of cultural identity. A policy of preservation was introduced into city plans by law. New regulations introducing numerous building restrictions and new systems of control have one by one come into force.

In the 1970s, environmental control won wide support as a total approach to urban planning and architecture, but this was seen in physical terms and neglected architectural quality. One of the positive accomplishments that the concept of environmental control has fostered is a new consciousness of the importance of the Turkish historical heritage. For many years, the problem of preservation had been restricted to the restoration of great monuments. Even the fleeting recognition of the value of the Anatolian houses during the 1940s had been insufficient to rescue the best examples of Turkish vernacular architecture. Now, together with the need to modernize cities, historical continuity and cultural identity are being emphasized.

This last stage in the search for identity is the first conscious effort to synthesize what is regarded as Turkish with what is modern. It constitutes a search for a new architectural expression and is the outcome of the unceasing, restless process of change in contemporary architecture which has evolved now into a phase of postmodern eclecticism. Countries like Turkey cannot afford the extravagance of an individualism bent on inflicting untried forms on the building scene. The country needs inexpensive, unadventurous, sound architecture for its new urban population. Certainly, architects' fantasies still have a role of importance to play; yet no possible imaginative effort can fill the gap between the great demands of our society and idiosyncratic inventions.

To answer the immediate needs of the Turkish millions, a solid, realistic, and responsible approach to architecture, to urban planning, to preservation, to the creation of a human environment, and to the organization of building is requisite. This seems to be the real creative challenge for Turkish architects and planners of the near future.*

Bibliography

(Except for a few projects published in foreign journals, no relevant publication in European languages exists on modern Turkish architecture.)

Akçura, Tuğrul. *Türkiye Cumhuriyeti'nin Başkenti Hakkinda Monografik bir Araştirma*. Ankara, 1971.

Alsac, Üstün. *Türk Mimarlik Düşüncesinin Cumhuriyet Devrindeki Evrimi*. Trabzon, 1976.

Aru, K. Ahmet. "Türkiye'de Konut Politikasi." *Şehircilik Enstitüsü Dergisi*, Istanbul no. 1 (1970).

Eldem, S. Hakki. "Elli Yillik Cumhuriyet Mimarliği." *Mimarlik*, nos. 11-12 (1973).

Günce, Ergin. "Türkiye'de Planlamanin Tarihçesi." *Mimarlik*, no. 11 (1972), pp. 19-25.

İnkaya, Yilmaz. "Türkiye'de Cumhuriyet Devrinin Başindan Günümüze Kadar Konut Sorunu." *Mimarlik*, no. 9 (1972), pp. 50-65.

Keleş, Ruşen. *100 Soruda Türkiye'de Şehirleşme, Konut ve Gecekondu*. Istanbul, 1972.

Kortan, Enis. *Türkiye'de Mimarlik Hareketleri ve Eleştirisi 1950-1960*. Ankara: ÖDTÜ Mimarlik Fakültesi, Yayin No. 18, 1971.

———. *Türkiye'de Mimarlik Hareketleri ve Eleştirisi 1960-1970*. Ankara: ÖDTÜ Mimarlik Fakültesi, Yayin No. 23, 1974.

Kuban, Doğan. "Emin Onat ve Cumhuriyet Devri Mim-

*The architects and buildings in this text were selected only as representative of the main trends in the development of modern Turkish architecture.

arisi." *Mimarlik ve Sanat*, nos. 4-5 (1961), pp. 143-53 (with an English translation).

______. "Gelecek Açisindan Günümüz Mimari ve Şehircilik Uygulamalarinin Eleştirisi." *Mimarlik*, no. 7 (1968), pp. 13-30.

Özer, Bülent. "Mimaride Üslup, Bati ve Biz." *Mimarlik*, no. 11 (1965), pp. 17-27.

Tapan, Metin-Mete. *50 Yilin Türk Mimarisi*. Istanbul, 1973.

Taut, Bruno. *Mimari Biligisi*. Translated by Adnan Kolatan. Istanbul: Güzel Sanatlar Akademisi Yanini, 1958.

"Türk Mimarliği." Açik Oturum (Ankara). *Mimarlik*, no. 12 (1970), pp. 27-35.

"Türk Mimarliği." Açik Oturum (Istanbul). *Mimarlik*, no. 12 (1970), pp. 36-54.

Yildirim, Yavuz. "Cumhuriye Dönemi Ankara" sinda Mimari Biçim Endişesi. *Mimarlik*, nos. 11-12 (1973), pp. 26-44.

USEFUL JOURNALS

Arkitekt 1931-1979.

Mimarlik 1944 to date.

Yapi 1973-1979.

Journal of the Faculty of Architecture, Middle East Technical University (Turkish and English). 1975 to date.

36

UNION OF SOVIET SOCIALIST REPUBLICS

IGOR GOLOMSTOCK

Architectural Theory and Practice: 1945-1954

From 1945 into the mid-1950s, Soviet architecture brought to some degree of fruition ideological and stylistic principles that had first been formulated and practiced in the early thirties. In the early thirties, too, events occurred that shaped the creation and outlook of the Union of Soviet Architects. A resolution of the Central Commune of the Communist Party of Bolsheviks, 23 April 1932, that called for a reconstruction of "literary and art organizations" included all functionalist and constructivist architectural organizations, whatever their views had been in the twenties. Written clearly into the regulations of the new Union of Soviet Architects, however, was the statement: "Social realism is the basic method of Soviet architecture." The dogma of social realism as the single major direction for the development of the whole of Soviet artistic culture was so formulated in 1934 that the main task of any cultural worker became the "truthful presentation of reality in its revolutionary development." The Union of Soviet Architects, the Academy of Architecture of the USSR, founded in 1934, and the magazine, *Architecture of the USSR*, which became the only major publication in the field, were called upon to unite diverse architectural forces and guide them along the pathway of social realism. Already in its first issues, this journal mounted an attack upon architecture of "stone boxes" and the basic principles of modern Functionalism and Constructivism. More and more, these movements were equated with the architecture of a "creeping capitalism" and a "dehumanized, bourgeois society."

Soviet architectural theory opposed to Functionalism the principle of a humanistic architecture. This principle would reflect in its buildings the heroic struggle of the Soviet people toward a socialist society and the wisdom of the party and its leaders that guides this struggle. It declared that in the heritages of Russian and Classical architecture all the necessary sources of stylistic forms were available. From 1934 on architecture was treated not as an independent art in itself but as a part of materialistic culture. Along with the rest of Soviet art, it became part of an all-embracing system of political propaganda. During Stalin's time (d. March 5, 1953), this system of propaganda entered into and dominated all levels of the social organism.

The major implementation of Soviet architectural theory during the thirties was in the general plan for the reconstruction of Moscow, and in the construction of the Palace of the Soviets (by B. M. Iofan, V. Thchooko, and V. Gilfreikh), both of which were established in 1935 with a special resolution of the Soviet of the People's Commissars of the USSR and the Central Committee of the All-Union Communist Party of Bolsheviks. The purpose of the general plan was to give Moscow the solemn architectural appearance appropriate for the "capital of the state of victorious socialism and all progressive humanity." This appearance was centered in the Palace of the Soviets with its immense crowning figure of Lenin that exceeded in size any known in the history of sculpture. Gradually in the thirties, ideological factors began to outweigh the technological and economic in determining the artistic appearance of

Translated from the original Russian text by Elena Baranova, Côte St. Luc, Québec.

architecture. With an acceleration of the ideas of the thirties, the years from 1945 to 1954 in the Soviet Union constituted a time of purely ideological, totalitarian architecture.

The Second World War caused heavy damage to the stock of residential, public, and commercial buildings. According to official Soviet data 1,710 cities and towns and more than 70,000 villages were destroyed in the territory of the USSR. Such cities as Minsk, Stalingrad (now Volgograd), Sevastopol, and Vitebsk, as well as many others, were almost completely destroyed. Minsk, for instance, lost more than 75 percent of its habitable dwellings and major public buildings. Leningrad, Kiev, Rostov-on-the-Don, and Kalinin were among the very heavily damaged. Priority, therefore, was given to the reconstruction of the cities, and to accomplish this the Committee on Architectural Affairs of the Soviet of Ministers of the USSR was created as early as 1943.

In November 1945 the Soviet of the People's Commissars of the USSR issued a resolution "concerning the urgent sanctioning of the reconstruction of the fifteen oldest Russian cities." The major creative forces and means were put first towards the realization of the general plan for the reconstruction of Moscow, though that city had suffered much less than others. The general plan was renamed "Stalin's Plan" and given priority. Its purpose was to provide an appropriate facade for the Soviet state that would reflect architecturally the glory and power of Stalin's socialism. In the first place, Stalin's Plan for reconstructing Moscow was supposed to do away with the heritage of chaotic "capitalist" construction and present a new overall layout for the city based upon a new radial circulation system. The straightening of Moscow's major avenues, begun before the Second World War, was intended to link the ideological centers of the capital and the country—the Kremlin and Red Square—with the suburbs. In works of new construction major attention was given to buildings' facades in order to provide a festive, glorious character for the most important arteries and squares. Such motives inspired a great deal of sustained postwar construction in Moscow.

Most characteristic of postwar construction in the capital were so-called high-rise buildings, the initiative for which may also be attributed to Stalin. Usually the construction of high rises was planned for intersections of radiating avenues with the Sadovoe Koltso and the Moscow River. In their architecture each was to project the new socialist-Stalinist appearance, while emphasizing the city's new, radial, circular, unified plan in a system oriented around the great ideological centers of the Kremlin and the Palace of the Soviets. Thus, the appearance of the city as a whole came to be changed.

One of the first buildings to be completed was the Ministry of Foreign Affairs [1948-1952] on Smolensky Square. The goal of its architects, V. G. Gilfreikh and M. A. Minkus, was to show in its artistic image the conception of a growing pride of the Soviet people in their socialist state that had destroyed fascism and that had become even more powerful than before. The people's pride in the socialist motherland as the invincible stronghold of all of progressive and freedom-loving humanity was also to be expressed in the buildup of architectural elements. From a four to six-story base to fifteen-story towers on the four corners the design built towards a central twenty-seven-story, massive, vertically articulated tower that steps back toward the top in two stages to an octahedral tower with a tall, crowning spire. The principle of a centralized, towered architecture crowned with a spire and with masses diminishing towards the top was employed in such other high rises of the Stalinist period as: an apartment house of Kotelsnaia Quai [1948-1952] by architects D. N. Chechulin and A. K. Rostkowsky in which six-story corner towers adjoined three twenty-story buildings that were linked with the main, 153-meter-high construction with its tall spire; in an apartment building [1950-1954] by M. V. Posokhin and A. A. Mdoyants on Vosstania Place; in the enormous complex of the Moscow State University on Lenin's Hills [1949-1970] by L. V. Rudnev, S. E. Chernishov, P. V. Abrosomov, and A. F. Khrjkov; and in various hotels such as the Leningradskaya [1953] by L. M. Poliakov and A. L. Boretsky and the Ukraina [1957] by A. G. Mordvinov, V. K. Oltarjevsky, and other collaborators (fig. 36.1). The construction of Moscow's high rises came towards the end of a national campaign against cosmopolitanism and the admiration of the West [1947-1953]. During that period the national tradition and artistic heritage of Russia, which was called by Stalin "the most prominent among the nations of the USSR [and] the ruling force among the people of our country," was proclaimed as a source of inspiration for artists and architects alike.

The architectural theory of that time saw in tower construction the continuation and development of a major tradition of ancient Russian architecture, supposedly different from Western traditions of the Renaissance. The spires of high rises recalled both church architecture of the seventeenth century and the tops of the Kremlin's towers. Thus, the spires were supposed to link Moscow's new skyline with the Kremlin and the Palace of the Soviets. The new silhouette of the city could have been perceived, however, only upon a topographical map or from the

36.1. A. G. Mordvinov, V. K. Oltarjevsky et al., architects. Hotel Ukraine. Moscow, 1948/1950-1957. (Photograph: Andrey Ikonnikov et al., *Soviet Architecture Today: 1960 to the Early 1970's*, 1975. Courtesy of The Copyright Agency of the USSR)

air. All of this new construction was aimed not at an individual's understanding, but rather at some majestic viewpoint—and in itself this is a clearly distinguishing characteristic of a kind of cult architecture.

Reinforced-concrete construction was used for the first time in the USSR in this high-rise architecture. Its functional reality was concealed behind pompous facades, heavy with revetments of marble and granite, adorned with coats of arms and other sculptural reliefs, obelisks, multitudes of spires, towers, and Kremlinlike melon domes, all of which transformed contemporary buildings into strange hybrids of cult, fortress, and palace architecture. By the end of the forties these elements were found upon virtually all of the residential architecture of Moscow. Early in this period the world Classical heritage was set forth as a source of models for the new Soviet architecture. There was much building in the classical style of the seventeenth century and in the manner of the *palazzi* of the Italian Renaissance—with the architect-academician I. V. Joltowsky as the foremost advocate. In time, however, Soviet architecture turned toward the heavy forms of the Empire style with touches of earlier, historic Eastern and Russian architecture. The uses of cyclopean portals, as in the residential buildings on Smolenskaya Place and Kotelnucheskaya Quai, together with porches, massive columns, and pillars on facades, and marble, granite, and bronze as decorative materials, gave a pompous, ceremonial look to many of the capital's major buildings. In other cities the same kind of construction, but in less expensive materials, cast polychromed plaster and ceramics, for example, was helping to form major new avenues and broad boulevards.

Another realm of construction that was initiated under Stalin was very important during this period: Moscow's subway system. Its first section, opened in 1935, was accomplished in the then relatively reserved style of the new architecture. After the war, however, its purpose was proclaimed as "the creation of places for people which would express with great forcefulness the glory and beauty of Stalin's era, and care for the workers of the Soviet state." In other words, the architectural style of the subway, as with all other architecture of that period, had a quite clearly ideological and propagandistic content. The Komsomolskaya-Koltsevaya station [1952] was considered as the highest achievement in subway architecture. Its designer, A. V. Tchusev, also the creator of Lenin's mausoleum [1927-1930], had used Stalin's words at the beginning of the Second World War to explain its architectural image: "Let the examples of our glorious ancestors give us encouragement in this war—Alexander Nevsky, Dmitri Donskoy, Kusma Minim, Dmitri Pojarsky, Alexander Suvorov, Michael Kutuzov! Let us wrap ourselves in the victorious banner of the great Lenin." Tchusev gave a grandiose scope to the underground lobby and entrance halls of this station, employing huge columnar supports; mosaics of ceramic plaques in the ceiling by P. Korin that represent the victories of all of the Russian commanders mentioned by Stalin; the shine of gold, bronze, and other expensive decorative materials; friezes, and of course monumental sculptures of Stalin himself. With all of this, a utilitarian construction was transformed into a kind of museum of the glory of Russian armies. Another subway station, Kievskaya-Koltsevaya, was devoted to an expression of the "century-old, inviolable friendship between the Russian and Ukrainian people" in its decoration with Ukrainian ornament and in the subjects of its mosaics. This approach to architecture is typical of almost all of Moscow's subway stations built between 1945 and the mid-1950s. Serpukovskaya station [1952] by architect M. Ilin, on the other hand, was strongly criticized because its architecture "did not tell of any heroic event in the history of our people, did not immortalize or glorify either the beauty of today's Soviet people or the greatness of its movement toward a communistic tomorrow."[1]

The growth from year to year of the gigantomania and pomposity of Stalin's constructions can be followed very clearly in subway stations built between the mid-1940s and 1954. In the later examples from this time span, such as Kalujskaya or Kurskaya Koltsevaya [1951] by architects G. Zakharov and Z. Chernishova, lobbies at surface level that are used only to dispense tickets and that lead to the escalator are some twelve to fourteen meters high: their volumes exceed the analogous spaces of earlier stations by factors of between eight and ten.

In Leningrad immediately after the war large-scale work of restoration and new construction was begun with architect N. V. Baranov in charge. The architectural image of this city, formed in the eighteenth century as the historic capital of the Russian Empire, and its lesser ideological importance in Soviet times, led to a more careful handling of its extant structural system and to a less splendid style in the raising of new buildings. Among the most important constructions here in that period were the new Lenin Square, near Finliandsky station [N. V. Baranov, 1946-1960] with its large exit towards the Neva River and the monument of Lenin. In the middle of the athletic complex of the Primorsky Park of Victory that is situated in the delta of the Neva, the Kirov Stadium is inevitably architecturally dominant. Built between 1932 and 1950 by A. S. Nikolsky, N. N. Stepanov, and K. I. Kashin-Linde, it has a capacity of 80,000 spectators. In 1955 Leningrad's first section of subway system was opened.

Much more damaged, not only by the war's destruction but also by the effects of Stalinist theories of construction, were the older Russian cities of Minsk, Kiev, Stalingrad (now Volgograd), and Rostov-on-Don, among others. Government resolutions pointed out the need for replacement during the restoration of old Russian cities, and this meant not the reconstruction of the former image of the city but, instead, the creation in its place of new architectural organisms that were to be socialistic in their content and national in form. For this, the general plan of reconstruction of Minsk, worked out between 1944 and 1946 by Moscow architects A. V. Tchusev, N. Y. Kolli, A. G. Mordvinov, and Minsk's N. E. Trachtenberg, M. N. Androsov, and others, was typical. Moscow's example of a plan with a radial system of circulation, an idea having no relationship to Minsk, was employed as a model. According to theory, the architecture of the socialist city was supposed to reflect "great public ideas, ideas of the great revolutionary struggle, the peaceful, constructive labor of the Soviet people, their heroism and patriotism." And it was supposed to create an atmosphere of sunlight even in winter.[2] Priority was given here to a tradition of Russian, national city building that supposedly had always implemented within itself patriotic ideas, a tradition in which the center of the city was to be understood above all else as a "monumental chronicle of the glory and solemnity of the motherland." The chain of avenues linked with squares became an important trait of urban planning of the period. Its strictly axially based construction centralized the composition of squares in the city's ensemble. The ideal, central, urban complex consisted of a system of wide boulevards, framed by rows of solemn architecture with symmetrically arranged towerlike superstructures, ending in towering usually governmental buildings that were surmounted by single central spires. In general, construction, style, and form in Minsk's high rises were as in Moscow's.

The ideological character of these complexes was emphasized with the required monuments to Stalin, Lenin, and other leaders placed in the center of plazas, and by sculpted friezes, freestanding sculpture, and decorative elements upon the facades of buildings. The largest buildings were located around the square, the smaller ones on major avenues that opened into the square, and the least imposing upon streets in areas further removed from the square. The heights of buildings and the richness of their decoration depended upon the importance of the city in which they were located, with the highest and richest in the capitals. The best examples of new construction and reconstruction projects for old squares, partially finished before 1954-1956, are in the ensembles of Minsk and in Stalingrad, "hero city," where only the monumental stairway descending towards the Volga, by V. Simbirtsev and I. Fialko, was finished [1952-1953].

In rural architecture, as in the cities, major attention was given to the completion of public buildings. Cultural centers that served as places for official meetings and conventions were built in the centers of towns and villages and as a rule were decorated with large porticos and colonnades that recalled the monumental architecture of the capitals. In all, they looked like the estates of eighteenth- and nineteenth-century Russian Classicism and the Empire style.

Into the mid-1950s ideological expression also influenced the character of industrial architecture very much. Important industrial complexes built then became for the most part architectural monuments to the era of socialism and its creator, Stalin, and were known as "Stalin's Communist constructions." In June 1954 the most typical example of the technical, architectural accomplishment of Stalin's period, the Volga-Don River canal that bears Lenin's name, was opened. Completed in the record time of only four years, it had taken enormous sums of money and, as in many other important Communist constructions, large numbers of prisoners were used in forced labor. The complex was fronted by a gigantic statue of Stalin (by the sculptor, Tomsky) which was destroyed in the late 1950s. Each of its thirteen floodgates was in the form of a triumphal arch, faced with richly decorated reliefs and surmounted by a complete sculptural composition, while its hydrotechnical facilities repeated forms of Empire-style palace architecture.

Criticisms of the goals, costs, and quality of Stalinist constructions were published in the Soviet press in 1953-1954, only after the death of Stalin. But it is clear that towards the beginning of the 1950s the situation in Soviet architecture had taken on threatening aspects. Enormous funds went into the creation of exhibitionist-propagandist architecture. Ideological factors demanded an overlay of artistic representation and totally subjugated the utilitarian purposes of architecture. Very often upon facades rich sculptural decoration closed off windows with the result that the spaces behind them became almost unsuitable for living; sometimes two balconies were built for a single room, while in other instances one balcony would suffice for two entire apartments. The costs of external building-decoration from the mid-1940s into the early 1950s reached as high as 30 percent of the total for construction. With the extremely low technical level of achievement and an inevitably rapid deterioration, by the mid-1950s on the main avenues of the capital one found metallic nets projecting from ornate facades above the first-floor level to protect pedestrians from falling parts of decorative elements. With all of this and the concentration there had been upon towers, spires, engaged decorative elements, and huge halls, the percentage of useful living spaces was reduced to a minimum during a period of extreme shortages of living accommodations throughout the country.

According to the official norms for this period, each person was entitled to four square meters of living space, but in reality very few had even that. Most of the urban population lived in communal apartments with three to five people usually occupying one small room. For between five and ten of these rooms, there was only one kitchen and one bathrom. Most of the rural population lived in housing without running water, without sewage systems, and very often even without electricity. The situation was worse in even the largest of coal-mining centers. "In Stalino and Makeevka only central areas have canalization [sewage systems] and most miners' villages with two and three-story constructions do not have this."[3] According to the general plan for the reconstruction of the cities (that is, Moscow's), by far the greatest part of the extant living accommodations was slated for condemnation. However, since funds were not made available for decades, neither condemnation nor restoration, improvements nor major repairs could be undertaken, and the availability of habitable housing diminished across the land.

Nevertheless, as a purely cultural phenomenon, Soviet architecture from 1945 to 1954 may be regarded as the most interesting since the 1920s. In the development of Soviet artistic culture it was in this period that the ideology of Stalin's state found its best-defined and finished forms in a style of purely totalitarian twentieth-century architecture, a style that was analogous only to the architectural manner of the Nazis' Third Reich.

Architectural Developments in the Post-Stalin Period

Early in the 1950s the situation in Soviet architecture had become so catastrophic that only one month after Stalin's death in March 1953 the first official criticisms of the previous methods of construction and of architectural theory appeared in the Soviet press. Each month the flow of criticism increased until in 1954 it took on the characteristics of an official campaign that came to be called the struggle against exaggerations and extremes of decoration in architecture.

In December 1954 the All-Union Concilium of Builders, Architects, and Representatives of Industrial Ministries headed by N. Khrushchev took place in the great palace of the Kremlin. This was followed on 4 November 1955 by a resolution of the Central Committee of the Communist party of the USSR and the Council of Ministers of the USSR about elimination of extremes in planning and construction. The Concilium and the resolution sharply condemned the existing situation in architecture and the construction industry. In his speech N. Khrushchev pointed out that "architects are a stumbling block on the road toward the industrialization of the country."[4] As a means of overcoming the evident crisis he determined that individual building construction should be replaced by residential planning on a mass scale. "We should find a limited number of model houses, schools, hospitals, kindergartens, nurseries, stores and other buildings and begin mass construction only in accord with planned models."[5] These words of the USSR's leader determined the major line of development of Soviet architecture from 1955 on.

Before the war, residential planning on a mass scale was concerned almost exclusively with the construction of buildings of one or two stories. In the new Siberian cities and other northerly areas of the country (Angarsk, Kokhtla-Yarve, and so on) this had helped create residential areas within a very short time. In 1948 experimental residential construction of four- and five-story buildings was begun in Moscow's Peschanaya Street district. But at that time this type of construction was not coordinated: only individual building projects were erected, and these limited the possibilities of creating adequately functional residential precincts. There were so many types of ongoing projects that production and standardization of the elements of construction were slowed. As a result, in 1953 only 12 percent of industrial buildings, 37 percent of public construction, and 62 percent of residential architecture that were erected employed mass-production systems. The change to totally standardized residential buildings was possible for major housebuilding combines only in large block and large panel construction.

A resolution of 1955 was aimed at the construction of 402 new plants for the production of concrete over a three year period, mostly in the Moscow area. In 1959-1961 the first plants for residential construction were opened, and thereafter industrial, large-block (slab) building became the basic form for the development of Soviet architecture. As early as 1926-1927 slab-type housing blocks had been undertaken in Moscow and were developed together with Constructivist architecture that was unfortunately demolished in the early 1930s. During Stalin's time concrete was used in a way that imitated the color and texture of brickwork in large-scale slab buildings. After the war, however, the experience of large, slab-type residential construction was forgotten and the organizations that had successfully produced it before were not reestablished. Only in individual and experimental cases were such buildings erected. In 1947 the construction of the first five-story, slab-type apartment house in Moscow was begun by engineer G. Kuznetsov on Sokolnaya hill. Soon the methods developed there could be found in buildings erected on Novopeschanaya Street, Khoroshevsky Highway, and other districts of the capital. In the early 1950s the first non-frame-based slab-type apartment houses were built in Moscow and in Magnitogorsk in the Ural mountains. But this type of housing was immediately subjected to severe criticism for its constructivist style, and the next ones built were covered with decorations.

Post-Stalinist architecture at first consisted of volumes formed by blocks and slabs, with smooth surfaced facades that were adorned along the top and the base with traditional rows of spires, towers, and pediments, as for instance in M. V. Posokhin's and A. A. Mdoyants's apartment building project on the First Khoroshevskaya Street in Moscow. Gradually, the increasing demand for more economic construction forced the removal of extreme social-realist elements from architectural projects. In 1957 the Central Committee of the Communist Party of the USSR and the Council of Ministers of the USSR adopted another resolution that concerned development in the field of residential construction in the USSR which had as a goal ending the inadequacy of living space in the country in the following ten to twelve years. From that moment on, the development of Soviet architecture took two well-defined routes: 1) construction of mass-planned apartment housing with a minimum of the formerly standard decorative elements; and 2) individual planning of government and public buildings. The first route was expected to provide the population with living accommodations of at least minimum standards, while the second, as under Stalin, continued to create an ideological or totalitarian architecture.

The need for residential construction continued and brought about the creation of large residential boroughs within cities and satellite towns upon the perimeters of already extant cities. The main component of urban planning became the microdistrict with residential buildings placed freely around its center. The principle of free construction in these microdistricts was a change from the symmetry that had characterized previous planning. As in Western examples, the nucleus of the microdistrict was formed by a shopping area, with nearby buildings for the use of public and cultural organizations. When several microdistricts were clustered to form a residential borough of a city, hospitals, kindergartens, schools, and other necessary service organizations were supposed to have been built, though often there was quite some time lag between theory and practice.

One of the early experimental residential apartment complexes was constructed in 1956 in the New Cheremushki area of Moscow by architects N. Osterman, S. Liatchenko, and others. Based upon the principle of the slab building, its purpose was to test the reliability of new methods of concrete mass construction and of new ideas in planning. Soon after its introduction into that Moscow microdistrict, experimental construction of the same type was undertaken in other cities: the Tchemilovka area of Leningrad [1958-1964] by E. Levinson, D. Goldor, and others; the Second River district of Vladivostok [1962] by T. Drujinina and V. Simbirtsev, among others; in Stalingrad's Kirovsky and Krasnovtiaborsky districts; the Tchilinzar district in Tashkent, and various others. But the advantages of constructing in complexes remained for the most part upon the drafting board. The architectural appearance of these new districts and of newly built cities, such as Bratsk in Siberia, was marked by a severe economy of means and an increased pace of construction, both of which were dictated by the need to end the housing crisis and the technical primitivism of the past. Khruschchev's message on standardization was directly understood, and the socialist-economic system's state monopoly of the construction industry made possible a singular effort to effect his pronouncement of goals throughout the vast territory of the country. Yet, until the mid-1960s, the Soviet construction industry supplied even major cities like Moscow and Leningrad with only a minimal range of standardized elements. With them only one or two types of residential/apartment buildings were constructed—the four- or five-story grey slab-and-box, extended horizontally and much the same designs oriented vertically to form nine-story towers. With the kind of plastic contrasts afforded by these two types, both of which had been tried at New Cheremushki, Soviet city builders sought to organize enormous districts of residential apartments that had populations ranging from 10,000 to 100,000: the term *New Cheremushki* became a common noun that identified any new construction in the USSR from Mordovia in the middle-Volga region to the Far East and from the northern Urals south to the Caucasus mountains.

During the next decade, Soviet architecture accumulated experience in industrialized construction and slowly new methods were learned. The average height of constructions in reinforced concrete was increased, new choices for decoration in plastic and aluminum were made available, and there was an improvement in detail elements produced by industry. Exemplary among the new residential areas of the early 1960s are the buildings along Rublevsky highway by V. Gilfreikh and at Khimki-Khavrino by Selivanov, both in Moscow; in the Dachnoe district of Leningrad by V. Kamensky; the Rusinovsky residential area in Kiev by V. Ladny, and in the scientist's settlement at Novosibirsk by A. Mikailov, all of which were conglomerates of five-, nine-, and twelve-story buildings, differing from one another only in height or length. To conceal the dull appearance of this architecture, builders often employed a system of site planning in which the better and higher buildings were placed along major avenues as a decorative barrier.

Nevertheless, Soviet ideologues proclaimed these structures as examples of "the most advanced in the world" and as "truly socialist" architecture, just as the creations of Stalin's time had been touted ten years before. In 1964 during one of his speeches, N. Khrushchev went so far as to say that "the people of communism [that is, in the communist future as opposed to the socialist present] will live in the apartment houses built now."[6] Some architects understood these words of their leader as a signal to create an "architecture of the communist future."

In Moscow mass housing for small families and single people was begun. Buildings often had one-room apartments, but were without individual kitchens and bathroom facilities, both of which had to be shared. The architects of these projects, M. V. Posokhin and N. Ostermann for instance, saw in them a means of educating the Soviet person to collective, communist customs. Fortunately, in Moscow where people had suffered during many decades of communal living conditions, this type of "architecture of the future" was not very widely employed.

In the late 1960s the scandalous differences between the optimistic theories and the sad realities of Soviet architecture began to be strongly felt when enormous spaces across the country were filled with monotonous, technically and aesthetically poor architecture that would all too frequently become ramshackle soon after its completion. As a result of this, early in 1969 the Soviet press initiated a campaign of criticism against the low quality and grey appearance of architecture, a campaign that concluded with the 28 May 1969 resolution of the Central Committee of the Communist Party of the Soviet Union (hereinafter referred to as the CCCP) and the Council of Ministers of the USSR concerning measures that were to improve the quality of residential construction. After fifteen years of Soviet architectural development, "Methods of construction, residential planning decisions, and the external appearances of residences are stereotyped. The architecture in areas of mass residential construction is dull and unattractive."[7] This judgement was as true for the ideological architecture of that period as for individual constructions.

Although the architecture of Stalin's time had been condemned in 1954, the new rulers of the country maintained its ideological outlook almost untouched. Social realism is still considered today "the basic mode and major line" for the development of architecture as well as for other forms of the creative arts. Instead of the richness and solemnity of architectural forms that typified the greatness and strength of Stalin's state, during the 1960s strict simplicity of architectural configuration combined with usefulness and economy were claimed as showing that in a socialist architecture the Communist party and the government cared for the individual.

A sharp turn towards new principles was evident in the competition of 1956 for the new Palace of the Soviets in Moscow in which all major Soviet architects were involved. Instead of the huge towering monuments of the 1930s, the majority of projects submitted were flat boxes that seemed like contemporary exhibition halls or terminals blown into a gigantic size. Not one was built. One of the first projects to give life to the new direction was the Soviet Pavilion of the International Exhibition in Brussels in 1958 designed by architects Y. Abramov, A. L. Boretsky and A. Poliansky as a quadrilateral, glass building with a free flow of interior space. In the functional forms of this structure as well as in some of the buildings that followed, such as the Soviet pavilions at Expo '67 in Montreal and at Osaka-1970 by the architect M. V. Posokhin, Western critics often observed a revival of the great traditions of the Soviet architectural avant-garde of the 1920s. This is unlikely: the traditions of the Russian avant-garde of the first quarter of the century were very strongly criticized in the USSR and then were completely forgotten. In the West on the other hand the architectural ideas of V. Tatlin and El Lissitsky, and of some very few constructions accomplished then by K. Melnikov and I. Leonidov, were assimilated into the Modern Movement in architecture, became an integral part of it, and were developed toward new, more advanced technological and aesthetic levels. That being the case, when Soviet architects were faced with the need to replace their long-standard books on the distantly historic architecture of Russia and of the Italian Renaissance, instead of taking up the projects and plans of their ingenious countrymen that could have been found in the archives, they filled their drafting tables and workshops with the most recent American, English, and German architectural journals. In the post-Stalin years Moscow became a center, a so-called artistic laboratory, for both individual and standardized construction.

In 1960 M. V. Posokhin became the chief architect of Moscow and therefore of all of the USSR, a post he still holds today. The architect of the most pompous of Stalinist architecture, such as the many-storied building [1950-1954] on Vosstania Square in Moscow, Posokhin was one of the first to condemn the architectural extremes recognized after Stalin's death by holding himself and other leading Soviet architects responsible. During the period that followed, the cultural ideology of the immediate past was maintained and Posokhin and other architects of Stalin's time such as A. G. Mordvinov, D. N. Chechulin, and V. Gilfreikh found that they were able to continue their hold upon the leadership of Soviet architecture. The building up of Moscow was continued in accord with the reconstruction plan that had had as its goal the making of the capital into the exemplary socialist city.

Despite an enormous amount of residential construction on the outskirts, neither Moscow's center nor its many historic districts with their countless architectural monuments were saved from drastic changes. In the middle of the Kremlin in 1961, M. V. Posokhin and a group of his assistants put up a new Palace of Congresses (fig. 36.2), a severe rectangular structure of white Ural marble and glass with its windows framed in aluminum and with thin marble pylons repeated monotonously along its facades. In 1965 this architectural image was repeated almost identically by S. Fradkin in the house of government at the Moldavian capital of Kishenev. During construction of the Palace of Congresses in Moscow, not only were architectural monuments of the fifteenth through the nineteenth centuries destroyed but the entirety of the cultural stratification on its site was set into disarray and an enormous fortune of archaeological data was totally wasted. In the early 1960s too, construction of the Hotel Russia, described as the largest in the world, by the major Moscow architect D. N. Chechulin and several collaborators, did even greater harm to the architectural appearance of Moscow. Occupying the site of the former Chinatown which had been razed despite its architectural and historic monuments, this enormous box of a building consists of four huge oblong sides bordering a great open rectangular court into which there projects a single massive tower that is interlocked with and rises from one of the longer sides. Since the Hotel Russia is so huge in scale, and higher than the nearby walls of the Kremlin, it disrupts the harmony of the oldest part of the city—the Kremlin, Red Square, and the Church of Basil the Blissful.

Creation of immense residential areas around Moscow required new avenues of communication with the downtown area so that activities of reconstruction were intensified. Old streets were straightened and new roadways such as Kutusovsky Avenue [V. G. Gilfreikh, 1957] and Komsomolsky Avenue [A. G. Mordvinov, E. G. Vulikh, and N. P. Baranov, 1958-1965] were built up. The reconstruction of Sadovoe Koltso and the construction of a new circular highway around greater Moscow were completed. Finally, between 1964 and 1969, Kalininsky Prospect (fig. 36.3) was built by M. V. Posokhin, A. A. Mdoyants, and V. A. Svirskyl, cutting through the old Arbat, one of the most beautiful districts of

36.2. M. V. Posokhin, A. A. Mdoyants, E. Stamo, P. Steller and N. Shchepetilnikov, architects, with G. Lvov, A. Kondratyev, S. Shkolnikov and T. Melik-Arakelian, engineers. Kremlin Palace of Congresses. Moscow, 1961. (Photograph: Andrey Ikonnikov et al., *Soviet Architecture Today: 1960 to the Early 1970's*, 1975. Courtesy of The Copyright Agency of the USSR)

Old Moscow. This sadly typifies the Soviet approach to problems of urban building. "Progressive" ideological architecture took priority over the more important tasks of coordinating the old and the new, the useful and the economic, within a total urban ensemble.

One side of Kalininsky Prospect consists of a series of four twenty-two- to twenty-six-story buildings, arranged at an angle to the boulevard in a so-called booklike pattern. The frame and panel high rises repeat interesting variations and articulations upon slab architecture and are joined with one another at ground level by two-storied gallery spaces in which there are stores and offices. On the other side of Kalininsky Prospect, five high-rise apartment buildings, each consisting of two slightly offset vertical segments, are arranged at right angles to the street and in a monotonous row. Completing this complex a slight distance away, stands the glass high rise of the Council for Mutual Economic Aid (fig. 36.4) with its gently curving Y-shaped plan forming three wings [1969, M. V. Posokhin, A. A. Mdoyants, V. Svirskyl and others]. All in all, here is a closed system of building left purposely without any connection to the older, lower architecture that remains in the area. Almost a copy of downtown Detroit and American high-rise hotels, this complex seems a strange intervention in the historically formed fabric of the city. The same type of closed system is found in the reconstruction of Smolenskaya Square early in the 1970s: V. G. Gilfreikh arranged two glass hotel-tower slabs symmetrically across the square from one another and pointing at the Stalinist style high rise of the Ministry of Foreign Affairs that he also had designed [1948-1952].

The twenty-two-story Hotel Intourist on Gorky Street, by architects V. Voznesensky and Y. Sheverdiaev, was erected between 1968 and 1970, further disharmonizing the central ensemble of the capital, despite opposition among virtually all sections of the populace. Countless letters of protest were addressed to the government and the newspapers, and protests were heard in many speeches as well. It was criticized often by major architects in the press, and indirectly by a resolution of 25 May 1969 of the Council of Ministers of the USSR. The resolution was actually against the basic ideas contained in a new general plan for Moscow drawn up by the same Posokhin mentioned previously, a plan that meant further destruction of the old monuments in the capital of Russia. Z. Lioveiko, Posokhin's predecessor as head architect of Moscow, had already noted with dissatisfaction more than a decade before that "today, only from old photographs and archival documents may the appearance of old Moscow be known."[8]

36.3. M. V. Posokhin, A. A. Mdoyants and V. A. Svirskyl, architects. Kalininsky Prospect development. Moscow, 1964-1969. (Photograph: Andrey Ikonnikov et al., *Soviet Architecture Today: 1960 to the Early 1970's*, 1975. Courtesy of The Copyright Agency of the USSR)

36.4. M. V. Posokhin, A. A. Mdoyants and V. A. Svirskyl, architects. Council for Economic Aid Building. Moscow, 1969. (Photograph: Andrey Ikonnikov et al., *Soviet Architecture Today: 1960 to the Early 1970's*, 1975. Courtesy of The Copyright Agency of the USSR)

Growth of the New Architecture

The real significance of Moscow's new architecture was defined not only by its place within the urban ensemble but by the fact that the best examples of residential housing, government, and public buildings were to serve as models for construction in the rest of the country. It was in Moscow that new construction materials, new methods of decoration, and new ideas in urban planning as well as new styles of architecture were introduced into the mainstream of Soviet architecture, all to be reflected elsewhere in the land, usually in somewhat more simplified modes (fig. 36.5).

During the 1960s, modern Western architectural style was exemplified in Moscow's Hotel Younost [Y. Arndt, T. Bevsheva, V. Burovin, 1961], the Rossia cinema [Y. Sheverdiaev, E. Gadjinskaya, D. Solopov, 1961], and the first municipal airport terminal building in the USSR [D. Burdin, A. Artemev, Y. Ribakov, 1965]. All were framed, panelled boxes with almost infinitely adaptable interior spaces; all were repeated in the same building types that appeared soon after throughout the country. To discuss the new architecture of other Soviet cities, one would need, therefore, only to cite Moscow's types of construction complexes and residential areas. And these were far from being better than American or the average Western examples of architecture either in

36.5. A. Klimcochkin, D. Lsichkin and B. Oskin, architects. Shopping center with highrises. Zelenograd, Kazak Republic, 1969. (Photograph: Andrey Ikonnikov et al., *Soviet Architecture Today: 1960 to the Early 1970's* 1975. Courtesy of The Copyright Agency of the USSR)

their styles or in their technological aspects. Their national character was limited to ornamentation—with exceptions to be found in Armenia and to a lesser measure in Georgia. There, the widespread use of such local materials as pink tufa together with the long tradititions of church and fortress architecture helped to determine the unique appearance of new constructions. Outstanding among examples of this in Armenia are a depository for old manuscripts, called the Matendaran, built by M. Grigorian in 1959 at Erevan, and the Hotel Armenia and the House of Unions [1956-1958] by M. Grigorian and E. Sarapian, both of which structures are upon one of the major squares of Erevan.

The partial rehabilitation of the field of design in 1960 and experience gathered over the decades contributed far more positively to the quality of Soviet architecture than did the resolution of the CCCP of the Soviet Union and of the Council of Ministers of the USSR of 28 May 1969 concerning measures for improving the quality of residential construction. In Stalin's time, design—along with genetics, Einstein's theories, and computer technology—was seen solely as a reactionary, bourgeois, false science that had as its goal the inculcation of Formalism into creative fields. In 1962 the All-Union Research Institute of Technical Aesthetics began to function in Moscow, and branches were established in Leningrad, Tbilisi, Novossibirsk, and other cities throughout the country. Among the areas studied were general theory of the creation of form, methods of design for industrial and residential interiors, for technical and home appliances large and small, and also environmental planning. Within organizations that were project oriented, studios for artistic design were established; and with considerable consequence the study of design became part of architectural curriculums.

These developments first influenced industrial architecture. Indeed, the way had been prepared in the first years following Stalin's death when, with the removal of their rich ideological ornamentation, hydroelectric power plants at Bratskaya, Voljskaya, and Krasnoyarskaya came to resemble modern functional architecture. One of the few instances of technical and artistic innovation in Soviet architecture is the Ostankino Telecenter Tower of 1967 in Moscow, designed by architect D. Burdin and engineered by N. Nikitin in the shape of a grand upward-pointing needle. Constructed of reinforced concrete to a height of 533 meters, it is topped by a very tall, thin spire and has a slowly rotating observation deck within which are restaurants from which one may enjoy the view. The tower is supported by bundles of prestressed-concrete frames located within its narrow stem and rests lightly upon its outward-flaring concrete base of six arches borne upon piers. Its entirety forms an elegant silhouette that may be recognized from almost anywhere in Moscow. More and more in new construction, utilitarian, functional, and economic factors became primary design considerations and the former temple-like facades and palatial interiors gave way to smooth, glass surfaces and free, open, interior spaces. Nowhere was this more evident than in Moscow's Sheremetievo airport buildings [1964, by G. Elkin, M. Chesakov, and L. Ivanov] and New Kursky Station [1972, by G. Voloshinov, V. Evstigneev, and N. Panchinko], and in Leningrad's Pulkovo airport [1974, by A. Jukov, J. Verjbitsky, and G. Vlanin]. Somehow, despite the Soviet idea of the supposedly exceptional, socialistic character of these buildings, they looked very much like London's Heathrow airport. Nevertheless, they may be regarded as an important step forward, since their design was based upon the real needs of the consumer, the airport users, rather than upon the demonstration of any ideology. New subway stations, too, were more reserved and rationally designed in their spatial proportions and functions in Leningrad, Moscow, and Kiev.

Experience in production-line construction over the past twenty years has recently brought about an improvement approaching the average of Western standards of mass construction. In 1973, for instance, as a progressive element the use of basement levels as garages and their servicing by elevators was built into the residential structures of Moscow's new Chertanovo district. During the mid-1970s, methods of apartment house construction were sweepingly changed with the introduction of a completely standardized catalog of products. One of the first results of this could be seen in the twenty-two-story apartment dwellings erected in 1975 according to the plans of A. Sansonov and A. Bergelson in Moscow's new Troparevo district. There, plastic polychromed-relief and sheathing were employed for the first time. An increase in the average height of buildings and a new range of detailing permitted the planning of residential areas according to a more rationalist aesthetic, particularly in the Baltic republics as in Vilna's Landsy and Tarmunay districts, the former by V. Chekanayskas [completed 1975], the latter by B. Kasperavchene [1977]. In Vilna, the capital of Lithuania, and throughout the Baltic republics traditions of construction have remained closer to those of Western modern architecture.

In recent years, too, the design of some public

buildings has been improved. For instance, in place of the usual five-story barrackslike building used throughout the Soviet Union for schools and kindergartens, systems of linked pavilions were introduced to house different functions such as classrooms, workshops, and so on. The notion of interconnected buildings is also evident in the design of Moscow's State Tretiakovskaya Gallery. Underway in 1978 (M. Gruglov, Y. Sheverdiaev and N. Sukoyan, architects), it is the end product of construction begun in 1965 and will be joined to the exhibition halls of the Union of Soviet Artists to provide a combined floor space of 25,000 square meters. This is the first museum to have been constructed in the Soviet Union since the 1917 Bolshevik revolution.

Yet, the ideological goals of Soviet architecture remain unchanged: the humbling of the Soviet masses and the expression of the grandeur of the motherland, the Communist Party, and the approach of Communism. Instead of building these ideas into architectural works, they now take expression in special constructions that account for a large proportion of the building industry's achievements. Despite the severe cutback in construction announced in the 1950s, the flow of all sorts of memorials and monuments has continued to grow. The memorial complex dedicated to "The Heroes of the Battle of Stalingrad," situated upon the Mamaen Curgan, with its central figure of Mother Russia fifty-two meters high and strongly recalling the gigantomania of Stalin's time was accomplished by architects Y. Belopolsky and V. Demin with the sculptors E. Vutechich and V. Matrosov between 1963 and 1967. Architects M. Bartch and A. Kolchin working with the sculptor A. Faidish in Moscow created the hundred-meter-high monument commemorating the "Outstanding Achievements of the Soviet People in the Exploration of Space," continuing the idea expressed in the Circle of Glorious Battle around Leningrad, a complex of monuments erected upon the sites of World War II battles. Finally, in 1970 to commemorate the centennial of Lenin's birth, the entire downtown area of the city in which he was born, Ulyanovsk, was converted by architect B. Mesentsev into an enormous memorial with the Lenin Museum (fig. 36.6) in the middle of a square enclosed by modern buildings. To these few examples one should add the almost countless monuments to Lenin (figs. 36.7 and 36.8), to Marx, and to the "heroic feats of the Soviet people during World War II" that are required virtually in every city of the Soviet Union.

The last two decades have been a time of rapid construction in the USSR. With the building of huge new residential and industrial districts, the appearance of old Russian cities is changing. In the rate of growth of residential space and of industrialized construction the Soviet press proudly asserts that the USSR is the world's leader, ahead of the USA, West Germany, and France. Considering that the Soviet construction industry started from ground zero twenty years ago, this is very likely the truth. And decorative, ideological elements continue to accom-

36.6. B. Mesentsev, M. Konstantinov et al., architects. Lenin Memorial Complex. Ulyanvosk, 1970. (Photograph: Andrey Ikonnikov et al., *Soviet Architecture Today: 1960 to the Early 1970's*, 1975. Courtesy of The Copyright Agency of the USSR)

36.7. N. Ripinsky, L. Ukhobotov, Y. Ratushny et al., architects. Lenin Palace of the Arts. Alma-Ata, Tienshan, 1970. (Photograph: Andrey Ikonnikov et al., *Soviet Architecture Today: 1960 to the Early 1970's*, 1975. Courtesy of the Copyright Agency of the USSR)

36.8. N. Ripinsky et al., architect. Detail of façade of Lenin Palace of the Arts. Alma-Ata, Tienshan, 1970. (Photograph: Andrey Ikonnikov et al., *Soviet Architecture Today: 1960 to the Early 1970's*, 1975. Courtesy of the Copyright Agency of the USSR)

pany Soviet architecture in some measure. Socialist economic planning made it possible to concentrate enormous sums of money and substantial creative forces between 1960 and 1970 to produce exemplary complexes and constructions, such as the "Artek" summer colony (fig. 36.9) built on the south coast of the Crimea; the "Motherland of Shevchenko" village in the Ukraine; the city of Zelenograd, a suburb of Leningrad; and the Togliatti district of Moscow, as well as various apartment buildings, schools, nurseries, and factories.

But at the same time the same centralized socialist economic system, with its decision-making concentrated in the hands of the topmost members of the party apparatus, also made possible across the USSR construction at less expensive, lower standards. Thus, in 1969 a resolution of the CCCP of the Soviet Union and Council of Ministers of the USSR concerning regulation of rural constructions took note of a disastrous lack of housing in rural regions and indicated a necessary increase of housing in those areas. Until recently, the traditional Russian village consisted of post-and-lintel houses (*isba*) with adjoining plots of land (*duor*). Now, across the countryside, standard two- or three-story concrete boxes have been built. In a country that has almost one-third of the world's forest land, there is almost no wooden construction occurring. The traditional Russian village is being replaced by dull, suburbanlike housing.

Standardization of housing characterizes construction in widely different climatic belts, ranging even into Siberia and beyond the polar circle. Siberian cities such as Ust-Ulimsk (1974), or Nijnevartovsk (became a city in 1976), or the town of Poliarnie Zori hundreds of kilometers north of the polar circle are not different from cities of similar sizes in central and even southern Russia. Nevertheless, the research institutes and large design studios mentioned previously are now occupied primarily with problems of construction, taking into account climatic and other environmental differences in the various parts of the country. Unfortunately, however, there are many substantial barriers to bringing their solutions into actuality.

After the repeated traditional assertions of "new achievements" and "gigantic successes" of Soviet architecture, periodically the press published, typically, that "architecture of mass construction is not distinguished enough, and as a result new areas in cities all over the country look alike."[9] The huge amount of construction that has occurred in the Soviet Union during recent decades is like a drop in the ocean when compared with the real needs of the

36.9. A. Poliansky, V. Belov, M. Lifatov et al., architects. "Artek" summer colony. Crimea, 1960-1979. (Photograph: Andrey Ikonnikov et al., *Soviet Architecture Today: 1960 to the Early 1970's*, 1975. Courtesy of The Copyright Agency of the USSR)

country. And the promises, first of Khrushchev and then of Brezhnev, to provide the populace with at least minimal living conditions are as far from being realized today as they were when they were first uttered. Soviet architecture continues to be confronted with massive problems.

Notes

(All references are in Russian.)

1. *Architecture of the U.S.S.R.*, no. 4 (1952): 3.
2. Ibid., no. 11 (1952): 30.
3. Ibid., no. 12 (1955): 13.
4. Ibid., no. 2 (1955): 7.
5. Ibid.
6. *Pravda*, 26 July 1964.
7. *Architecture of the U.S.S.R.*, no. 8 (1969): 1.
8. Ibid., no. 11 (1957): 18.
9. Ibid. (1978): 2.

*Bibliography**

BOOKS

Cohen, Jean-Louis; De Michelis, Marco; Tafuri, Manifredo. *URSS 1917-1978. La Ville, l'Architecture.* (In French and Italian) Rome: L'Equerre, Paris and Officina Edizioni, 1979).

Ikonnikov, Andrey, et al. *Soviet Architecture Today: 1960's to the Early 1970's.* Leningard: Aurora Art Publishers, 1975.

Kopp, Anatole. *L'Architecture de la periόde Stalinienne.* Grenoble: Presses Universitaires de Grenoble, 1978.

Petrov, Anatolli N. *Architectural Monuments of Leningrad.* Leningrad: Gosudarstvennia inspektsiia po okhrane pamiatnikov Leningrada, 1972. (Summaries and captions in English.)

Schmidt, H. "Zur Geschichte der Sowjetarchitektur." In *Beiträge zur Architektur 1924-1964.* Berlin: D.D.R./Basel, 1965.

Senkevitch, Anatole, Jr. *Soviet Architecture, 1917-1962: A Bibliographical Guide to Source Material.* Charlottesville, Va.: University Press of Virginia, 1974.

Starr, S. Frederick. *Melnikov, Solo Architect in a Mass Society.* Princeton: Princeton University Press, 1978.

JOURNALS

Cousin, J. P. and Pontoizeau, Yvette, eds. "Architecture Soviètique." *L'Architecture d'Aujourd'hui* 147 (December 1969-January 1970): V-LXVIII, 1-109 (English summary, LXV-LXVIII).

de Seta, Cesare. Introduction to "La Città Olimpiche." *Casabella* 43 (March 1979): 54-59.

*Compiled by the editorial staff, Montreal

"Finland—Russia: Two Sides of a Gulf." *Progressive Architecture* 51 (March 1970): 71-73, 80-83, 87-99.

Huxtable, Ada Louise. "Soviet Architecture Today." *Architectural Forum* 127 (November 1967): 32-41.

Ketchum, Morris, Jr. and Dluhosch, Eric. "Behind the Iron Curtain." *American Institute of Architects Journal* 51 (April 1969): 70-78.

Kopp, Anatole. "Moscou 1917-1967, 50 années d'urbanisme dans une économie planifiée." *L'Architecture d'Aujourd'hui* 132 (June/July 1967): 66-71.

Kreis, Barbara. "Moskauer Monumentalarchitektur." *Bauwelt* 69, no. 25 (7 July 1978): 986-90.

Néret, Gilles. "Monuments de l'espace." *Connaissance des Arts* 318 (August 1978): 40-49.

Pica, Agnoldomenico. "Review of Vieri Quilici's *Mosca: Il nuovo Piano del 1971 e la sua realizzazione* (Milano: Gabriele Mazotta Editore, 1974)." *Domus* 537 (August 1974): 54.

Rossi, Sara. "Review of Vieri Quilici's *Architettura Sovietica Contemporanea* (Bologna: Editore Cappelli, 1965)." *L'Architettura* 11 (August 1965): 279.

Russell, Vernon George. "Looking Behind the Iron Curtain." *American Institute of Architects Journal* 57 (January 1972): 23-26.

Schmertz, Mildred F. "Architecture U.S.S.R." *Architectural Record* 153 (February 1963): 91-102.

Voriga, J. P. "L'Architecture et le Réalisme Socialiste." *L'Architecture d'Aujourd'hui* 158 (October 1971): 48-53.

OTHER USEFUL JOURNALS

Arkhitektura i stroitel'stvo [Architecture and construction] 1946 to date.

Arkhitektura S.S.S.R. [Architecture of the USSR] 1933 to date.

37

UNITED STATES OF AMERICA

EUGENE J. JOHNSON

Postwar American Architecture

In very broad terms, the decade following World War II saw the acceptance by United States corporations and universities, and eventually by the government, of the architecture invented by the great European masters of the 1920s and 1930s. Before the war, remarkably little International Style building had taken place in the United States, although two American architectural critics, Henry-Russell Hitchcock and Philip Johnson, had given the term currency in their 1932 book of the same name. Hitchcock and Johnson accomplished the removal of the radical social content from the architecture they described, so that it could become acceptable as a manifestation of advanced taste in the thirties and as the appropriate architectural garb of forward-thinking corporations in the forties and fifties. By the mid-fifties, however, boredom with the postwar version of the International Style had set in, as became clear in the writings of Philip Johnson, who in the interim had studied with Walter Gropius and Marcel Breuer at Harvard to become an architect. From the mid-fifties on a host of new ideas was tried out, with one new style succeeding another in a manner parallel to the emergence of Pop, Op, and Minimal Art in rapid succession in the sixties. At the end of that decade the whole process seemed to have come full circle, when a group of young architects revived the International Style of the twenties. In the seventies the bad economic climate created a situation in which many architects turned more and more to theoretical writings and to architectural drawing for its own sake. In this decade as well, the Miesian glass curtain, the bane of the energy conscious, made a startling comeback as the mirror glass skin, which looks back to Mies's glass skyscraper projects of the early twenties rather than to his work of the forties and fifties.

Throughout the entire period at least one thread has united all the disparate events: a sense of history from which no major architect who came of age in the postwar period has been free.* Indeed, differences of approach can often be most clearly defined by careful attention to differences in historical sources. Perhaps the greatest contribution that Philip Johnson has made to the whole period is his leadership in the vanguard of those who look back.

If one were to expect great architecture where there is great power, one might assume that in the postwar period the government of the United States commissioned buildings of high quality. Sadly, the reverse is the case. Indeed, many of the greatest failures of the period are the result of poor governmental choices. From the outlandish extravagance of the Sam Rayburn Office Building completed in 1965 under the supervision of J. George Stewart, Architect of the Capitol in Washington (which proves that among bureaucrats there is no taste about which to dispute) to the wholesale destruction of the hearts of numerous cities in the name of urban renewal, to the social and functional disaster of mass housing, most grimly exemplified by Minoru Yamasaki's Pruitt-Igoe Houses in St. Louis [1952-1955, destroyed 1972], government policies, even when well-

*This essay does not include work that is ultimately technological rather than architectural. Thus there is no discussion of that Yankee inventor *par excellence*, Buckminster Fuller.

intentioned, have largely produced very bad results.

Equally, architects have failed. In the profession arrogance is not unknown and singlemindedness of vision in the face of an enormously complex program has led to problems in the final product. It would be tiresome and ultimately pointless to enumerate the functional failures of functionalist architecture. Structurally, the most spectacular snafu (a word coined in World War II) of the period is I. M. Pei Associates's Hancock Tower in Boston [1971-1976], the Beauvais Cathedral of skyscrapers, which popped its oversized and undersecured glass panels all over the streets below. The Hancock is also arrogant in its insensitivity to the city around it.

The greatest successes of the period are found in four different areas of architectural activity. Immediately following the war the question of housing and particularly of the private house for the middle-class family dominated architectural thought. Particularly distinguished essays in the genre were the Case Study Houses, sponsored by John Entenza, built in the late forties in and around Los Angeles. Rather quickly, however, as the demand for housing began to be satisfied, other types came to the fore. The great corporations, in their urban office towers and their rural retreats for research (buildings for the active and contemplative life) were the first to adopt the modern idiom in large-scale commissions. Institutions of culture and learning, whose trustees were often the same people who were building new corporate structures, were quick to follow. Indeed, the increasing popular diffusion of culture and knowledge has been housed in a remarkable profusion of museums and research institutes. The fourth category of architectural activity is that dedicated to travel and the pursuit of pleasure. Regrettably, the areas of greatest new development for urban America—the suburb, the shopping center, the strip, and mass housing—have been little touched by architecture of genius or even architecture of competence. Still and all, the good buildings that have been built are an important gauge of what really counted in postwar America.

Frank Lloyd Wright (1867-1959)

Frank Lloyd Wright was, without doubt, the greatest American architect of the twentieth century. Discounted as a has-been in the early thirties, Wright reclaimed a place for himself in the forefront of twentieth-century architecture with the designs of Falling Water [1935] and the S. C. Johnson office building, Racine, Wisconsin [1936]. Both were heralded as masterpieces from the very beginning. Mies van der Rohe could say of him in 1940 "In his undiminished power he resembles a great tree in a wide landscape, which year after year attains a more noble crown," but Wright's postwar buildings have suffered something of a critical eclipse. Relatively little has been written on his last years, but recent publications indicate that the situation is changing, despite the fact that most of the primary material for serious research is kept under tight wraps by his widow. In the fifteen years before his death in 1959, Wright, in his seventies and eighties, produced more than one-third of his still standing structures, an output surpassed only by the prodigious and far more famous years between 1893 [Winslow House] and his trip to Europe in 1909.

Wright was always primarily a domestic architect. Residential structures make up over 90 percent of his work. Most of the more than one hundred houses and house projects of the postwar period are of the Usonian type, which began in 1936 with the first Jacobs house in Madison, Wisconsin. (The term itself comes from Samuel Butler's novel *Erewhon.*) These houses center on a work space, or kitchen, that divides sleeping from living areas. They are often simple in plan, an L or a long rectangle, and constructed of prefabricated wood sandwich-panels joined to masonry piers or walls. Glass is used abundantly to integrate interior and exterior. Basement and attic are eliminated, warmth is provided by radiant heat in the floors, and the roof is flat for the sake of economy, although in more expensive houses Wright allowed himself the luxury of expressive rooflines. This basic type could be modified by introducing 30-, 60-, or 120-degree angles in the plan, or by basing the plan on interlocking geometric elements: triangle, hexagon, or even circle. The geometric inventiveness displayed in these latter plans is astounding, as are the spatial complexities, unrivaled in almost any other domestic architecture. In comparison, however, to many of his great interiors of the first decade of the century, such as the Robie or Coonley living rooms, many of the late interiors have large expanses of unadorned surfaces that provide a remarkable, even noble, sense of repose. Two good examples are the living rooms of the Walter house, Quasqueton, Iowa [1945] and the Llewellyn Wright house, Bethesda, Maryland [1953].

A subcategory of the Usonian house is what Wright called the solar hemicycle. The first of these was the second house he designed, in 1943, for Herbert Jacobs (Middleton, Wisconsin). Its not quite semicircular plan opens, through a two-story glass wall, onto a sunken garden to the south. The dirt excavated to create the garden is piled up against the north wall to create an insulating berm against the winter winds of the hilltop site. Inside, the bedrooms and bath are on a balcony that overlooks the workspace and living room. This design then undergoes a number of complex variations, including the Llewellyn Wright house, and even appears as a part of the very grand "Tiranna," in New Canaan, Connecticut [1955], one of the few Wright houses of these years to be built on a truly large scale. There were, of course, projects for houses of pretentious size. At least one of these, the Martin house, to be attached to a hundred-foot cliff on the California coast, would have rivaled Falling Water in terms of dramatic integration of architecture and landscape.

In all of these houses Wright uses an almost infinite variety of materials. No architect, one suspects, has ever been quite so prodigal with nature's and industry's bounties for the purpose of building. Although Wright experimented widely with materials in the early phases of his career, nothing there prepares us for the rich outpouring of materials in ever-different combinations in the last years. Even rooflines match plans and materials in inventiveness, from the Usonian flat roofs to the teepee shape of such relative oddities as the Arnold Friedman house, Pecos, New Mexico [1945]. In all of this Wright seems never to have lost his sensitivity to the interaction of house and land—his unique ability to site a building—a talent that can be appreciated only by visiting the houses themselves.

The individuality of his houses grows directly out of Wright's philosophical commitment to individualism. He wrote of his house designs in the January, 1948, *Architectural Forum* "Each man's house is his own home. There is but one house like it and that house is his. His own devices, tastes and limitations are present in each instance, intelligently interpreted for him as an individual." Or, as Wright generalized in his 1956 introduction to a book about the Price Tower: "Organic architecture—natural architecture—is capable of infinite variety in concept and form but faithful always to principle. It is—in fact and in deed—itself principle. A natural architecture is true to the nature of the problem, to the nature of the site, of the materials, and of those for whom it is built—in short, of the Time and Place and Man."

From 1945 on Wright produced the lion's share of his public buildings: the Guggenheim Museum [New York City, 1943-1959]; S. C. Johnson Research Tower [Racine, Wisconsin, 1944]; First Unitarian Church [Madison, Wisconsin, 1947]; Morris Store [San Francisco, California, 1948]; Price Tower [Bartlesville, Oklahoma, 1952]; Beth Sholom Synagogue [Elkins Park, Pennsylvania, 1954]; Greek Orthodox Church of the Annunciation [Wauwatosa, Wisconsin, 1956]; Marin County Civic Center [San Rafael, California, 1957]; to name some of the most important; and there is also the Lindholm Service Station [Cloquet, Minnesota, 1956].

Like the houses, each public building is unique, a personal assessment on Wright's part of the building requirements coupled with often daring innovations in structure, to say nothing of form. They are as different as Mies's Chicago Lake Shore Drive Apartments [1951] and New York Seagram Building [1958] are alike. All this freedom of expression, of course, has to do with Wright's desire to give each building an emotional kick. The dramatically angled roof of the First Unitarian Church, for instance, seems to draw directly on German architecture between 1915 and 1925, as do the curving forms of the Guggenheim—*Time* magazine called it a "Naughty Nautilus"—and the angles of the synagogue, meant to hold the congregation in the cupped hands of God under an abstract metal and glass empyrean. Wright had already dipped into the expressionist past, and into the futurist past as well, in the Johnson office building. For Wright, Expressionism was a means to individualism, an idea he championed in the forties and fifties, the years of the man in the grey flannel suit. By then, he was a holdover from the American nineteenth century. In 1949 Philip Johnson aptly put it: "Does not Wright's work typify the exuberant individualism of an ever-expanding frontier?"

The Guggenheim Museum (fig. 37.1), Wright's most widely known building from these years, spans the whole of his postwar period. He first announced the design in 1944 as a building with a steel, marble, and glass exterior, with the pictures built into the interior—a far cry from the reinforced-concrete spiral that he presented to the press in the fall of 1945. Although the idea of a spiral museum owes something to Le Corbusier's Mundaneum project of the 1920s, and the spiral itself played a significant role in Wright's thinking from 1929 on, the Guggenheim design was radical. With it Wright, ever the brilliant self-publicist, got off to a very fast start from the postwar gate. The museum would have been the most remarkable building of the 1940s, anywhere, had it been built immediately and to Wright's original specifications. Instead, the final version was a compromise between the architect's intentions, the New York City building codes, and the project budget, as William Jordy has made clear in his splendid account of the building. Construction did not even begin until 1956, a year after Le Corbusier's epochal church at Ronchamp had been dedicated. When the building finally opened in 1959,

37.1. Frank Lloyd Wright, architect. Guggenheim Museum, interior. New York, 1945-1959. (Photograph: Courtesy of Robert E. Mates)

just after Wright died, it was seen as only one of several contemporary essays in the sculptural possibilities of reinforced concrete.

In the Guggenheim Wright sought to give his patron's collection of nonobjective paintings, including an unrivalled group of Kandinskys, an appropriate space. Ever the implacable enemy of the box, Wright wanted to replace the rectangularity of traditional gallery space, which he saw as related to the frame rather than to the painting, with a fluid space in which the pictures, hung without frames, could be seen to best advantage. We should take Wright's intentions seriously. He wanted a new kind of architectural space to house a new kind of pictorial space which, in the works of Kandinsky, was even more fluid than in the works of the Cubists with whose pictures Wright's early designs have often been compared. The spiral ramp, for Wright, created exactly the new spatial continuity he sought—a space without corners through which the visitor would "glide" in a state of perfect repose which, to Wright, did not imply stasis but motion. The protagonist of a short story that appeared in the *New Yorker* shortly after the museum opened, who rode down the ramp on a child's scooter, experienced Wright's space in a way very close to that intended by the master.

For Wright, architecture should provide repose, and thus well-being, an intention not far from the desire of his contemporary, Henri Matisse, to provide delight in his paintings. The public and private buildings both serve this end. Whereas the houses open out to nature, the public buildings turn inward, to create a protected and isolated world. From the early Unity Temple and Larkin building to the Guggenheim and Marin County buildings, this same theme prevails. In this regard, Wright was particularly specific about his intentions in his description of a 1940s hotel project for Dallas. The hotel was to be built around an interior court, to shut out urban chaos and commercialism. The project anticipates by a decade and more the work of John Portman.

In the buildings executed in the last five or so years of Wright's life the detailing is often poor and in some cases, such as the altar screen of the 1956 Greek Orthodox church, horrendous enough to sour one on the entire building. But despite Wright's loss of control over detail, the same building has a grandeur of scale and spatial conception that simply cannot be dismissed. The whole design is a brilliant play on the traditions of Byzantine architecture. The building is entered, like San Vitale at Ravenna, obliquely, but the plan is a Greek cross. Three of the arms hold parts of the congregation, while the fourth houses the sanctuary. The walls of the cross rise up to become four piers that support a circular balcony, reached by four circular staircases. Over this fusion of cross and circle, a favorite device of eleventh-century Byzantine architects, floats a gilded saucer-dome, seemingly as thin as the gold leaf that shimmers on its inner surface. Whereas eleventh-century Byzantine churches had cramped, vertical spaces, with the main dome restricted to the square bay at the center of the cross, the reinforced-concrete dome at Milwaukee-Wauwatosa stretches out in its Wrightian horizontality to enclose the whole 333-foot circumference of the building (note the triple Trinitarian connotations). The dome is separated from the balcony below by a glowing necklace of hollow, glass-ball windows, which makes the dome seem to be suspended from heaven, just as Procopius described the original shallow dome of the Hagia Sophia in Constantinople. Wright's courageous and imaginative confrontation here with the architecture of the past was very much in the forefront of what was happening in the architecture of the mid and late fifties, but, unlike Saarinen, Kahn, or Johnson, Wright made almost no concessions to European Modernism, particularly those varieties that had been imported into America in the preceding two decades. Perhaps it is the ultimate measure of Wright that to the end he was simultaneously his own man and still part of the vanguard.

If the Greek Orthodox church is Byzantine, the Marin County Civic Center buildings are Roman, two segments of an aqueduct flung between three low hills and hinged together by a dome that covers not a church but a centrally planned library. The dome recalls a host of American government buildings, from the Massachusetts State House and the Capitol at Washington on. But the domed library, presiding over a sprawling architectural complex, brings to mind Jefferson's University of Virginia. The relationship could hardly be accidental. Wright was philosophically the last of the great Jeffersonians. In the Marin County buildings, government and justice come under the aegis of knowledge. All three, *pace* Jefferson, are brought together in a bureaucratic village.

These California buildings are also very much of the present. The gilded, ball-fringe ornament that fairly drips from the roof—hopelessly cheap and tawdry from close up—reads brilliantly from a car speeding down the nearby freeway, and it did so some ten years before we were asked to learn from Las Vegas. The building is also meant to be approached by automobile. The visitor rolls up a driveway and emerges from his car under a vast, dark arch. A few steps up, a low door leads to a gloomy hall, filled by an escalator that cannot be avoided. The escalator lifts you up, as if you were a penny mechanically pulled through a slot, out of the darkness of the interior of a piggy bank into light. On that escalator one glides through space literally, in a way that can only be experienced conceptually on the Guggenheim ramp. That escalator is one of Wright's most brilliant uses of technology for architectural effect. It propels the visitor into the repose of the enclosed world of a three-story gallery, toplit by an enormous skylight, off of which the offices of the Marin County bureaucracy open. Although the concept of such galleries is hardly new (one thinks of such nineteenth-century urban amenities as the Galleria in Milan, or even of the covered shopping mall just beginning to emerge in the mid-fifties in such work as Victor Gruen's Northland at Detroit [1954]), it gives a wholly new twist to the architecture of modern government. Whatever else Wright was doing here, he was trying to make the image of government open and humane. He was trying to rectify, in his churches and in this, his only constructed government building, the widely felt failure of modern architecture which was, as Peter Blake said in 1959, "to develop convincing symbols of religion and government."

Ludwig Mies van der Rohe (1886-1969)

In the late 1930s, just as Wright's star began to rise again, a number of prominent architects fled Nazi Germany for the United States. Marcel Breuer, Walter Gropius, Mies van der Rohe, and to a lesser extent Erich Mendelsohn, came to play a dominant role in the profession, just as their scholarly counterparts came to play a major role in American intellectual life.

Of the architect immigrants, it was Mies who gave the most persuasive, coherent, and replicable vision of an architecture others might follow. In 1939 Mies was commissioned to design a new campus for the Armour Institute in Chicago, which soon became the Illinois Institute of Technology (IIT). Construction began in 1942, while the war was going on, with the Metals and Minerals Research Building, a clear obeisance to American factory buildings of the late 1930s, particularly Albert Kahn's Lady Esther plant of 1938, and, in a sense, an Americanized version of Gropius's factorylike workshops at the Bauhaus.

Mies's Alumni Hall [1945-1946], however, marked a decisive break with the straightforward steel and glass curtain wall enclosing a structural system of reinforced concrete. For Alumni Hall Mies designed a curtain wall that masqueraded, at least at first sight, as a structural frame of steel, with glass and brick infill. This subtle and elegant design cloaks a functionalist structural system in a skin that is different in kind from those of late-nineteenth-century, Chicago-school skyscrapers only in that Mies used a functionalist vocabulary instead of one derived from antiquity or the Renaissance. The kinship between Alumni Hall and Louis Sullivan's Wainwright Building in Saint Louis is remarkable, in that visually the number of supporting elements is doubled in the skin.

The metal-and-glass skyscraper, from Pietro Belluschi's Equitable Life Assurance Building of 1944-1947 in Portland, Oregon, to Philip Johnson's 1979 mirror-glass tower project in a Gothic vein for Pittsburgh Plate Glass, may well be the most singular contribution of the United States to world architecture in the postwar years. If nothing else, in no other country have so many buildings gone so high. Not just in New York and Chicago, but in every city of any size—Washington and Philadelphia excepted—the skyline has been dramatically transformed by the addition of rectangular towers clad in steel and glass. Lower Manhattan shows the most dramatic changes; its prewar pointed spires have been dwarfed by flat-topped rectangles, like Skidmore, Owings and Merrill's Chase Manhattan Bank and Yamasaki's World Trade Center. All of this, of course, reflects the enormous expansion of American corporations during this period, as well as the desire on the part of certain companies and organizations to build symbols of power and even of good taste. The office building has become to great corporations what the palace was to great Italian families in the Renaissance. And the contest for the tallest building mirrors the competition between Medieval Italian families for the tallest defensive tower. It is no accident that Phyllis Bronfman pointed to the patronage of the Medici and Gonzaga when she urged her father, Samuel Bronfman, to secure the services of a great architect for the building that Seagram's, the family company, planned to build in New York. The design that Mies produced for Seagram's [1954-1957] is probably the most distinguished exercise in the whole genre, and certainly the most widely imitated. Austere, impersonal, and lavishly bronzed, it sums up the power, personality, and wealth of the modern corporation, whose public philanthropy is symbolized by the piazza in front, with its paired fountains—private land donated to the urban populace. If the piazza and twin fountains call to mind the Palazzo Farnese in Rome, so be it, particularly when one looks out from the Seagram lobby across the open space to the Renaissance-revival facade of McKim, Mead and White's Racquet Club which quotes the garden facade of Palazzo Farnese! Mies set up a brilliant conversation between two classicizing buildings, bringing the nineteenth and twentieth centuries together without compromise on either part. Mies was in many ways *the* great classicist of this century. One might say that one of his major successes lay in fusing the principles of the great classical tradition of Western architecture with the raw technology of the modern age.

Mies was also, as a classicist should be, a great generalist, who sought the universal rather than the specific solution. The fact that all his tall buildings, from the Lake Shore Drive Apartments [1948-1951], through the design for Seagram's, the Chicago Federal Office Building and Courthouse [1964], and the Toronto Dominion Center [1969], look alike is one of their strong points, at least theoretically. No matter what function it might house—offices, apartments, courtrooms, or even jail cells—the tall building was simply the tall building. A cardinal point for Mies was that uses change, while the buildings that house them remain, not a bad point to recall in an age when conservation of resources has become urgent. The adaptable building requires adaptable interior spaces, which Mies sought to satisfy through "universal spaces," that could be modified almost infinitely, according to need. The great spans of Albert Kahn's factory interiors provided the structural basis for Mies's ideas. In 1942 he used a photograph of Kahn's Martin airplane factory as the basis for a drawing of the interior of a concert hall, changing the function by the addition of demountable planes, hung from the overhead truss system. Mies's great project for a Convention Hall [1953], rendered in one of his most splendid collages, marked the fulfillment of this notion. Chicago's McCormick Place On-The-Lake [C. F. Murphy Association, 1971] is only a pallid reminder of what Mies's grandiose scheme might have been.

The energy crisis of the 1970s produced a lot of sniping at Mies's achievements. He is accused of total indifference to energy problems. Such criticism is made with the help of hindsight and without careful attention to the buildings themselves. The forest of trees that forms a sunscreen on all but the north side of Crown Hall at IIT is clearly laid out on Mies's site plan, and the south face of Alumni Hall has far fewer windows than the less well-known north side, where a large two-story expanse of glass lights the major interior space.

Moreover, Mies was hardly insensitive to the

specifics of a particular site. The placement of the Farnsworth house [1945-1950] depends on the positions of the already existing trees. The Seagram building is successful urbanistically and symbolically precisely because it takes into account its own urban and historical context. In Mies, as in Palladio, the use of a general type is made more potent by adapting it to the particular circumstance.

The Farnsworth house at Plano, Illinois, is the first and, one suspects, greatest piece of minimal sculpture. Slipped between old trees on the banks of the Fox River, it may also be Mies's finest example of his notion that architecture should be "almost nothing." The rather ordinary midwestern landscape, with which the hovering horizontals of the house are sympathetic, dominates the architecture, as the Grand Tetons were to have overwhelmed the never-built Resor house for Jackson Hole. Mies's two-part scheme of house and terrace establishes a place in the continuum of space, marked by the horizontal floor planes, the roof plane, and eight vertical I-beams. The uninterrupted glass walls hardly exist. House and terrace, although attached, slip past each other with Stijl-ish ease; the places and beams are tangential, like the seat and legs of the Rietveld chair.

In contrast, Philip Johnson's 1949 glass house, indebted as it is to Mies, is an exercise in all-American bluntness. It does not hover. Its rhythmic patterns have no mannered syncopations. It is painted basic industrial black, instead of Greek Revival white. The two sections are ripped apart to make an abrupt and obvious contrast between the solid of the guest house and the void of the main house. The contrast, however, is not really between solid and void, but between opaque and transparent enclosures. The black steel chair-rail of the main house makes palpable the planes of clear glass and eliminates all ambiguity between inside and out.

Johnson has said that the brick podium and chimney of his house derive from burnt-out farmhouses, with only foundations and flues standing. As such, his chimney and podium are a ruin, like those built in eighteenth-century gardens, but a ruin that is the direct result of tragedy rather than the erosion of time. The glass walls enclose and preserve that ruin, as if it were a specimen in a bell jar. From inside one compares the repoussé effects of real trees with the same effect achieved by painted trees in Poussin's *Funeral of Phocion*, a picture about a good man brought to a tragic end. The Farnsworth house is not a *memento mori*; the Johnson house is.

The concept of the ruin in the garden is only one aspect of the overt historicism of Johnson's design. In his publication of the house, Johnson drew, for instance, a parallel between the siting of the main house and the placement of Athena's house, the Parthenon, on the Acropolis. Precociously, and perhaps a bit cheekily, Johnson sought here, in 1949, to reconcile modern architecture with carefully selected examples of the architecture of the past. Perhaps it was only possible for a man who had moved from critic to architect to make this first step. Was it also Johnson's literary bent that led him to design buildings with allusive qualities that recall the poetry of T. S. Eliot?

In the same year that Johnson built his house, the designer Charles Eames built a house for himself and his wife in Pacific Palisades, California, that shares an overt industrial vocabulary with the Johnson house. But there is a difference of intent between these two houses greater than the coast-to-coast distance that separates them physically. The Eames house is simply what it is, industrial components ordered out of a catalog and put together with a loving sense of proportion. Its message is the rather simple one that industrial components can be put together to provide a pleasant place for man and woman to live, surrounded not necessarily by high art (Barcelona chairs and Prussian), but by objects of lesser ambition that still give delight. The Eames house is as laid-back as the Johnson house is uptight. But both share an American directness of approach. Neither is self-consciously beautiful, in the manner of the Farnsworth house. Mies may have moved to America, but he never became American, any more than Picasso became French.

Eero Saarinen (1910-1961)

Eero Saarinen turned the steel and glass cage into the preferred vernacular of the American corporation and thus made modern architecture safe for plutocracy. Saarinen's opportunity came in the late 1940s, when his father, the distinguished architect Eliel Saarinen, received a commission from General Motors, a corporation of enormous size and power, to design a new technical center in Warren, Michigan. In the structure, General Motors wanted to convey the image of a corporation committed to the most forward-looking design and engineering. The first project, a kind of automotive Cranbrook, was clearly the work of Saarinen *père*, but the second design [1951] was that of *fils*—a collection of long, low, steel and glass buildings arranged on two sides of an enormous lake, set in a large park. The architecture was designed to be viewed from a passing automobile—the brilliantly colored planes of glazed brick at the ends of the long rectangles carrying across the "sublime," in a late-eighteenth-century sense, expanse of flat landscape. The buildings themselves made use of the newest in automobile technology, and by so doing led to dramatic changes in the technology of building. The neoprene seal, previously designed for windshields, was used to hold great panes of glass, on five-foot modules, in place and so revolutionized the application of glass to steel frames. Even the technological gloss of these buildings, their shiny surfaces, helped to convey the desired image. General Motors was, in a sense, the king of corporations. In these very years its president was telling the world, "What's good for General Motors is good for the USA." How fitting, then, for Saarinen to design a constructivist Versailles for a man whose remarks weren't all that different from *L'Etat, c'est moi.*

In 1944 Paul Zucker edited an important collection of essays, under the title *New Architecture and City Planning*, which included papers on the then widely discussed subject of monumentality. In one such endeavor Sigfried Giedion, deploring the lack of monumentality in orthodox modern architecture of the twenties, called for a new monumentality which rose naturally out of the architectural materials of the twentieth century. The GM Technical Center seemed to respond to that plea by fusing up-to-date technology with planning schemes derived from monumental complexes of the past. (There is a resulting confusion, however, of skinniness of parts and grandeur of scale.) In this light, the domed building designed to display the latest models of cars takes on a new significance. The dome's interior was painted white and lit from concealed lights at its base. Functionally, the dome could be justified as an attempt to cut down the glare that normally played over the surface of newly painted cars. Symbolically, the result is a Pantheon for Pontiacs. Instead of a coffered, and therefore visually heavy dome, the brightly lit interior surface appears almost completely insubstantial. Its aluminum exterior merges with the sky, so that there is really only the sense of the volume of the dome, not the mass, just as Giedion advocated. The actual structure, of course, is entirely concealed. The Saint Louis arch, also designed in the late 1940s but not built until much later, is precisely analogous—an ancient form, transformed by modern materials, into a twentieth-century monument in Giedion's terms.

The Tech Center [1949-1955] is the first of Saarinen's exercises in what one might call the *corporate villa.* He followed it with the great glass arc, on the brow of a hill, for IBM at Yorktown Heights, New York [1956]—taking a leaf from the book of Bath; with the great mirror-glass box set in an English garden for Bell Labs at Holmdell, New Jersey (deliciously like Andy Warhol's *Two Hundred Cans of Campbell Soup* in the vacuous repetition of identical units); and the Cor-Ten steel giant reaper for John Deere in Moline, Illinois [1961-1964]. The reaper is set in a romantic park; it is Leo Marx's *Machine in the Garden* (published 1964) reduced to one brilliant image. Shortly after GM moved to the country, other corporations followed suit. Skidmore, Owings and Merrill's Miesian buildings for Connecticut General Life [1954-1957] at Bloomfield, Connecticut, are an early example; the Architects Collaborative's (TAC's) giant prairie house for Johns Manville [1973-1976] in the foothills of the Colorado Rockies (twenty-two miles from Denver, in Jefferson County) a later one.

The success of the GM center also must have played a large role in the acceptance of the modern idiom, at long last, by the United States government in the Skidmore, Owings and Merrill (SOM) design for the Air Force Academy at Colorado Springs [1956]. If it was good enough for General Motors, then apparently it was good enough for the USAF. The simplified Miesian idiom SOM used here had the right forward-looking spirit for the newest of the armed services, the one that flew the great machines of the new technology. The outdoor spaces of the academy are even as wide and sublime as those of Saarinen's Versailles for GM. Saarinen's accent of a round dome, however, is replaced by the spiky Gothic silhouette of the chapel, cribbed, one suspects, from Bruno Taut's projected war memorial at Magdeburg. What a mistake those spikes were, in a situation where Miesian universality would have given each faith equal treatment, and where expressionist "excess" seems very much out of place.

The design of the Air Force chapel, not established in the original 1956 plan for the whole academy, reflects a growing interest in the use of concrete for expressive ends that matured in the 1950s. In his 1956 *Architecture, You and Me*, Sigfried Giedion noted this trend as it manifested itself in the design of concrete vaults, particularly those of Ronchamp, of Matthew Nowicki's Livestock Judging Pavilion, Raleigh, North Carolina [designed 1949], and Saarinen's Kresge Auditorium at MIT [designed in 1950, completed in 1955].

The publication date of Giedion's book, however, coincided with Saarinen's first truly bold experiments with expressive vaulted structures, the Ingalls Hockey Rink at Yale [1956-1958] and the TWA Terminal [1956-1962] at New York's then Idlewild, now

John F. Kennedy, Airport. For a number of critics and for Saarinen himself, the MIT auditorium was a failure; he criticized the fact that the one-eighth-sphere vault that covered the whole never seemed to get off the ground. With the designs of 1956 all that changed. The soaring concrete spine of the hockey rink, from which the roof was supported on suspended steel cables, gave at least one member of the hockey team the feeling that he wanted to "go, go, go." The TWA Terminal offers the most memorable image of flight any architect has produced. These two buildings unleashed the possibilities of an expressionist architecture of concrete for academic and commercial purposes, thereby doing for concrete what Saarinen had already done for steel and glass at the GM Technical Center.

Saarinen's attitude toward design was closely analogous to that of Wright: each building demanded its own particular solution; each design had to reflect the specific spirit of each commission. Saarinen's buildings were not equally successful in capturing the proper image and spirit, but even some of the least successful, such as the exterior of the women's dormitory at the University of Pensylvania [1957-1960] were in part saved by his sense of humor, a quality all too few architects are willing or even able to display in their buildings.

Saarinen's masterpiece is the terminal building for Dulles International Airport [1958-1962] (fig. 37.2) at Chantilly, Virginia, outside Washington: a monumental gateway, in the modern idiom, to the capital. Rising majestically out of the flat countryside, the broad, low structure echoes, in its strong horizontal roof supported by regularly spaced posts, the classical architecture of Washington and perhaps even the great porch of George Washington's house at nearby Mount Vernon. Indeed, the whole terminal is a porch. Departing or arriving, the traveler experiences the building as a semi-enclosed space that lies between the enclosed space of the airplane or of the bus that brings the traveler to the terminal proper and the open Virginia landscape that waits outside. The curve of the roof, aerodynamic in shape, moves up and away from the plane side, to underscore the opening up of space as one disembarks or the closing down as one boards. The reinforced concrete of the roof, suspended from cables and seemingly as thin as tent canvas, reflects the transient nature of the place and even, as Vincent Scully would have it, the tentative hold Americans have on their own land. The Baroque undulations of the glass walls that rise between the supporting piers add to the sense of movement and to the sense of joy. Dulles is that rare building that is both serious and joyous, monumental and liberating. Few buildings of this period, or even this century, are more satisfying. Saarinen's all-too-early death at age fifty-one, in 1961, was a tragic loss; he seemed only to have found his stride.

37.2. Eero Saarinen, architect. Dulles International Airport, Terminal Building. Chantilly, Virginia, 1962. (Photograph: Courtesy of the U.S. Department of Transportation)

Louis I. Kahn (1901-1974)

Like Saarinen, who was nine years his junior, Louis I. Kahn was born near the Baltic Sea and immigrated to the United States at an early age. Both finally reached national and international prominence in the fifties. More importantly, they shared a Wrightian sense that each building required its own solution. As Kahn put it, he always asked himself what the building wanted to be. They came, however, from economically widely different backgrounds. Saarinen's position was greatly enhanced by the fact that he was the son of a well-known architect, had a Yale education, and almost instant entry into important boardrooms. Kahn grew up in poverty; the only significant building he did for a large corporation was for Olivetti. Saarinen seems to have been a man who experienced flashes of brilliance. His best work shows a facility of design that few architects achieve. Kahn's work is marked by anguished struggles with the recalcitrant elements of his art, by a forthrightness that gives his buildings the force of moral imperatives.

Kahn's first building of national significance was the Yale Art Gallery (fig. 37.3), designed in 1951 after he had returned from a year in Rome. Its severe and uncompromising directness of structure and materials, recognized immediately by some Europeans with a Brutalist bent, marked a clear break with Miesian elegance, even though there is an abundance of Miesian ideas in the building. The interior is composed of large, flexible spaces, covered with 40-foot-square floor slabs of reinforced concrete, through the tetrahedral patterns of which pass the air ducts and wiring that make the building habitable and the installations of works of art flexible. These bare concrete forms are supported by equally bare (originally) concrete piers. In the center, two rows of these piers marked off a narrow rectangle in which the vertical services and circulation areas are concentrated. On the outside, to the east, the building is attached to an older masonry block, in collegiate Gothic style. On the south, along busy Chapel Street, the gallery presents a blind brick expanse save for the entrance. On the west, steel and glass windows span the intervals between the vertical concrete piers, but they are not attached to the floor slabs. On the north, steel and glass curtain walls, hung from the floor

37.3. Chapel Street, New Haven, Conn. (left to right): Louis I. Kahn, architect. Mellon Center for British Art, 1969-1974; Paul Rudolph, architect. Yale Art and Architecture Building, 1958-1963; Louis I. Kahn, architect. Yale Art Gallery, 1951-1953. (Photograph: Courtesy of John Stambaugh)

slabs, overlook a beautifully terraced court, an island of calm in which the visitor can enjoy the old buildings that surround the court to the north and east. Although the materials on the exterior all come out of Mies in Chicago, the way they are handled—pragmatically, in changing combinations in relation to the needs of individual sides, and even awkwardly, in the uncomfortable juxtaposition of curtain wall and support on the west wall—marks Kahn as a very different man from Mies, as a designer who reveals his unsolved problems with ruthless honesty and total disregard for beauty cheaply bought.

Even with the success of the Yale gallery, Kahn was not overwhelmed with commissions. Unfortunately, his greatest project of mid-decade, the Trenton, New Jersey, Jewish Community Center [1954-1959], was largely unrealized, although even unbuilt it was one of the seminal designs of the day. The power of the spatial conception was clear, even in wretched photographs of the model. The main building was to house multiple functions, including a social hall and a basketball court. For the most widely published version of the design, Kahn used a grid of piers set at 10-foot and 20-foot intervals to create 20-foot square bays, each surrounded by 10-foot wide interstices. The whole made a rectangle, 310 feet x 130 feet. All but four of the 20-foot bays were capped by truncated concrete pyramids, supported at their corners by brick piers and lit by square lanterns. (The unroofed bays became parts of open courtyards.) Each 20-foot bay, then, became a vertical unit complete in itself. In canonical modern design, interior space was conceived as that fragment of the continuum of all space captured between the parallel planes of floor and flat roof. The thin, widely spaced piers that supported the roof, in theory, were to make no impact on the interior. Walls, freed of their traditional role as supporting elements, could be arranged any way the architect chose, the result being the free plan. In Mies's designs of the fifties, such as Crown Hall and the Chicago Convention Hall project, the supports were banished to the periphery, leaving the interior wholly unpunctuated by structural elements. At Trenton, Kahn's bays, complete unto themselves from floor to vault, establish a wholly different spatial conception that looks back to the Beaux-Arts tradition, in which he was trained, and further still to Renaissance, Medieval, and Roman practices. For Kahn, the free plan, the flat roof, and the unobtrusive point support system were no longer valid. At the same time, by opting for a wholly masonry architecture, Kahn also discarded the metal frame.

Kahn's seemingly simple system here was greatly complicated by the need to accommodate the required functions within the grid. The social hall and the gym both required greater spans than the 20-foot bays provided, and the basketball court especially needed to be taller than the other spaces. To achieve wider spans, without sacrificing the sense of the grid, Kahn designed long, reinforced-concrete beams, spanning as much as 80 feet in the gym, that would support two or three pyramidal roof sections in a row. The brick piers were beefed up where necessary to take the greater load. The resulting tension between the grid and the accommodations made therein, in both two and three dimensions, produced a design of enormous complexity, with enough double functioning elements to please the sixteenth-century Mannerist, Giulio Romano. The architecture itself, unlike Giulio's, would have had a Spartan spareness of surface that would have made the rhythmic changes even more forceful because they would have been seen nude. At Trenton, the lack of ornamentation would have been Kahn's only concession to orthodox modern design.

Of the whole Trenton complex only the small Bath House was ever built, in 1955. The plan is a Greek cross, with twelve hollow piers of concrete block supporting four pyramidal roofs that cover the arms of the cross. The center space is unroofed; a circular patch of grass recalls the dome that would have covered it, were it a Renaissance church. The north and south arms are dressing rooms, for which the inner, hollow piers serve as entrances and the outer piers as cubicles for toilets. The eastern arm is a place to check valuables; the western arm, unwalled, leads to stairs that climb to the level of the swimming pool. Brilliantly, the bathhouse is a centrally planned composition turned axial and a symmetrical design modified to satisfy functional requirements. Visually it is a primitive shelter, a role symbolized by the emphatic pyramids of the roofs.

In 1957 Kahn left his teaching position at Yale to move to the University of Pennsylvania, for which in the same year he designed the Richards Medical Research Laboratories. In this building complex Kahn worked out for the first time, on a monumental scale, his concept of served and servant spaces—one of his most important contributions to architectural thought during these years.

Richards consists of three buildings that radiate from a core containing elevators, offices, and air-intake stacks. The core is poured concrete, built first to hold the prefabricated parts of the rest of the building as construction proceeded. The three radiating buildings, housing 40-foot-square lab spaces on seven floors, are built of precast concrete;

eight piers support the truss systems of the floors and roof. These open trusses, in turn, provide space for the pipes, wiring, and ventilation systems required by the labs. At the cantilevered corners the trusses are thinned down to make visible the fact that less is needed for support at those points. Attached to three sides of this rather Miesian cage are tall brick shafts that rise between the relatively skinny structural piers to house staircases and exhaust systems. These shafts, memories of a day in San Gimignano, overwhelm the thin skeleton of the labs with their powerfully archaic monumentality. As in Beaumarchais's play, *The Marriage of Figaro*, the servants are more interesting than those they serve. There are functional as well as visual problems with the buildings. The large expanses of glass, hung at the outer edges of the floor trusses, allow for all-too-successful solar heating of the labs, and the exposed trusses collect dust that falls into test tubes and ruins experiments. With all its faults, Richards represents a turning point for Kahn. The visual power of the towers seduced a number of architects, and the building brought him to the attention of Jonas Salk.

Salk, the inventor of the polio vaccine, wanted to build an institute for scientific research with a humane bent—he wanted, as he told Kahn, a place to which he could invite Picasso. Kahn responded to the man he felt to be his greatest client with one of his masterpieces—the result of creative interplay between two men of genius. The laboratory buildings that were erected between 1959 and 1965 were so expensive, however, that only a third of the entire project could be realized. Kahn's buildings may be severe in appearance but they were never cheap to construct.

The Salk Institute sits on a high bluff at the edge of the Pacific, just north of San Diego, like a walled city designed by the eighteenth-century architect, Boullée. Its squat, concrete towers, containing both stairs and vents, seem more like defenders than servants. On the inside Salk wanted the sense of a cloister; he had been deeply affected by the one at San Francesco of Assisi. Kahn gave him, however something closer to the Alhambra—a paved courtyard with a sliver of water running through a channel in its center, to spill down some Vignolesque steps of travertine to a lower terrace, where one can enjoy the culinary delights of the Salk Institute cafeteria. The images are, of course, jarring—a cafeteria in a walled garden that conjures up images of caliphs and popes at play, all put to the purposes of modern science. But such are the contradictions of a society in which democratized learning is supported by the foundations of merchant princes and the subscriptions of movie stars.

The conflicts inherent in the relationship between the skeletal frame and its skin had caused Kahn no end of trouble, both at Yale and at the University of Pennsylvania. At the Salk Institute and the contemporary Unitarian Church in Rochester, New York, Kahn solved this problem by uniting frame and skin in a continuous wall that supported and enclosed simultaneously. At the Salk Institute, the central court is flanked north and south by four-story towers that contain, on the second and fourth floors, studies for thirty-six scholars. On the floors below the studies are open porches for casual meetings between scholars, outside the inviolable privacy of the study cells. Both studies and porches are formed by reinforced-concrete slabs. The studies are enclosed by inserting teak and glass panels into the voids of this structural system. Each study has a wall canted into the courtyard at a 45-degree angle, to provide a view of the sea. As one moves through the courtyard, from east to west, the studies and porches open up into a panoply of Piranesian spaces, voids and solids, lights and darks, that screen the court from the main business at hand, the labs.

The labs are enormous universal spaces, roughly 60 feet x 250 feet, stacked three to the north and to the south of the court. The 11-foot-tall labs are spanned by a 9-foot system of vierendeel trusses that form servant floors over each lab. Through these floors run all the services that the labs need. Although the labs are completely enclosed on the outside by glass, there is no problem with heat; the walkways that surround the labs and service floors provide shade. Thus at Salk, Kahn solved the functional problems he created at Richards.

In the 1959 project for the American Consulate at Luanda, Angola, that never was built though it probably was the most distinguished design to come out of the 1950s State Department effort to upgrade the American image with good architecture, Kahn faced the problem of sun control squarely for the first time. From local traditions he came up with the notion of a two-roofed structure, one to keep the sun off, the other, below, to keep out the rain. Le Corbusier's High Court of Justice at Chandigarh (fig. 1.1) [1956] must also have been in his mind. To control glare he decided, as he put it, to wrap the building in a ruin, to encircle the main structure with perforated, freestanding walls, to filter the light and surround the interior space with a soft glow, rather than a harsh glare. He repeated this idea in his contemporary design for the meetinghouse at the Salk Institute, never constructed because money ran out. In the 1961-1970 designs for the Mikveh Israel Synagogue in Philadelphia, also unfortunately never built, he took the idea even further. There, great cylinders, cut into as if they were vertical rolls of Swiss cheese, would have formed illuminated buffer zones between inside and out. The whole system is startlingly close to the one Alberti designed for Sant' Andrea in Mantua. Perhaps the ultimate sunscreen in Kahn's work is the west facade of the Ayub Hospital [begun 1962] at Dacca, Bangladesh. There the vast portico is preceded by a light-filter of monumental brick walls and arches.

In the last decade or so of his career Kahn was able to rival Aalto as the great master of light in twentieth-century architecture. From the window seats and light hoods on the Unitarian Church at Rochester to the buildings at Dacca and Ahmedabad and the carrels at the Exeter Library [1967-1972; a man with a book goes to the light, said Kahn], his control of light became ever more masterful. By all accounts the natural lighting in the Kimbell Art Museum, Fort Worth [sketches 1967-1970; open to public 1972] is the very finest museum lighting to be found, anywhere. The light enters through slits at the tops of the barrel vaults and is thrown by baffles onto the under sides of the vaults.

With the mastery of light came simultaneously a power of formal expression that is only barely, and rarely, glimpsed in his work of the 1950s. The simple, rectangular, brick service towers of Richards are no match for the severe grandeur of the four great concrete circles that surround the central court of the Exeter library, to say nothing of the extraordinary play in three dimensions of brick piers and arches in the porch of the Dacca hospital. Indeed, it was often in the sunscreens that Kahn let himself go into flights of his own very restrained fancy (dare one say archaic Baroque?). From Luanda to Dacca there is an ever surer and freer mastery of a formal vocabulary of simple but large-scale, geometric forms.

New Haven is a special place for devotees of Kahn's work. He taught for a number of years at Yale. His galleries that frame Chapel Street, with Rudolph's Art and Architecture Building in between (fig. 37.3) form the termini of the important years of Kahn's career. Kahn designed the Mellon Center for British Art in 1969 (fig. 37.3), but it was not finished until after his death. Because none of his post-Mellon designs, except one house, was built, Mellon stands as his valedictory. In this building he returned with noble restraint to themes from earlier years: a white, reinforced-concrete frame, into which a dark skin—here stainless steel and tinted glass—is set; square bays covered by truncated pyramids; interruptions in the grid to indicate changes in function. The building is drastically simpler than any of its predecessors, more sure of itself, more in repose, more able to subsume the contradictions of functions in a great whole. It is almost as if Kahn here recollected his past in tranquillity, before moving on. One wonders if this building might have marked the beginning of an *ultima maniera*, of an architecture of renunciation. In 1974, before he had answered the questions posed by Mellon, a heart attack struck Kahn down in the miserable, new Pennsylvania Station in New York. If he had to meet his Maker in a waiting room, Louis Kahn at least deserved to do so in the Penn Station of McKim, Mead and White's great Beaux-Arts reconstruction of the Baths of Caracalla, destroyed only a few years earlier.

Action Architecture: The Fifties and Sixties

The late fifties and early sixties were a time of particularly great architectural ferment. The aggressive, rough-hewn structures designed in those years have tended to be lumped together under the term *Brutalism*, especially since the appearance of Reyner Banham's *The New Brutalism* in 1965, but Brutalism can make strange bedfellows. In April 1959, in an essay in *Architectural Forum*, G. M. Kallmann used the term *action architecture*, which has certain advantages in an American context. Kallmann's "action" obviously refers to the kind of New York painting developed by the almost mythic figure of Jackson Pollock and others in the previous ten years. Moreover, Kallmann's own Boston City Hall (fig. 37.4)—his firm, Kallmann, McKinnell and Knowles was the winner of the 1962 competition—may be taken as a paradigm of the whole phenomenon.

The basic source for action architecture, as for action painting, was French art, specifically surrealism, although the precise relationship between surrealist painting and sculpture, on the one hand, and architecture, on the other, has yet to be clarified. (One should not, of course, overlook the Catalonian connection—Gaudí for architecture and, later, Dalí and Miró for painting.) If, as Charles Jencks has rightly suggested, Ronchamp is a surrealist building, aspects of the surrealist vocabulary also appear at Marseille [1948-1952], at La Tourette [1957-1960], and in Le Corbusier's buildings in Chandigarh [1950-1965] and Ahmedabad [1956]. Corbusier's late works of the fifties appeared in an atmosphere prepared by action painters who had, in a sense, transformed the automatic writing of Parisian surrealists into monumental painting. There was the further attraction that action painting made the artist himself, his artistic personality, the centerpiece of the whole endeavor. At least some architects were eager to sign on for a similar artistic ego trip.

In his 1959 essay in *Architectural Forum*, Kallmann praised a housing project that "tears into the space that surrounds it, using violent horizontals

37.4. Kallmann, McKinnell and Knowles, architects. Boston City Hall. Boston, Mass., 1962-1969. (Photograph: Courtesy of Edith S. Sanderson)

and rocketlike excrescencies [*sic*] in a searing vision of ruthless energy unleashed," heady words to apply even to a great Pollock or Kline. Parallel with the aims of such masters, the new architecture, according to Kallmann, sought a space-matter continuum, in which weight was no longer banned from buildings. And he saw the forms of the building not preconceived, but growing "out of the manner of structuring, usually complex and composite." That is, the building was designed in a manner analogous to the way Pollock worked out a picture, one step suggesting the next.

In practice, of course, it is hard to do an abstract-expressionist or action building—structural and functional constraints on an architect are greater than they are on a painter. Nevertheless, similarities do obtain. The rectangle of Boston City Hall [1969] is marked off by rows of vertical concrete slabs, not always evenly spaced, that form the structural system, or the support for the work, analagous to the canvas of a picture. The support becomes the frame on which the architecture is developed. The space of the great plaza flows into the interior of the frame, the spaces of the structure project through the frame out into the space of the plaza, in a continuum of solids and voids, of space and mass.

Functionally, the building is divided into three parts, vertically. The lower floor, paved with the same brick as the plaza, is for the conduct of daily business—paying fees and getting licenses. The middle is the ceremonial section, with council chambers and mayoral suite. Here, the various space requirements allowed the architects to hang masses of varied size and shape from the frame and to project them out over the plaza below, in a seemingly random fashion that recalls directly the accidents of action painting. These heavy, hovering forms are visually the most arresting parts of the whole building. The third level, cantilevered in three steps out from the frame, and marked by the repetition of the same window forms all around, holds general office space. This level forms a strong contrast to the eccentric shapes of level two. Throughout the entire building there is an emphasis on process, on how materials and parts are used and joined, another aspect of action painting that not only Kallmann, but also Louis Kahn picked up.

Overall, many reminiscences of Medieval and Renaissance Italy in the building and its piazza seem to separate it from the a-traditional aims of the action painters. But even here there is a common link. In the late 1930s and early 1940s, following the lead of the surrealists, painters like Pollock and Rothko had delved deeply into myth as a means for understanding basic psychic impulses (Pollock's enigmatic *Guardians of the Secret* may be taken to stand for this phase of their work) and into the arts of preliterate peoples that seemed most forcefully to express those myths. For architects in the 1950s the spaces of Mediterranean towns and villages took on a similar quality of *Ur*-urbanity. The accidental shapes of the stepped streets of hill towns and island villages—Siena and Mykonos were two favored pilgrimage sites—and the space-mass continua of piazza, street, courtyard, loggia, and vaulted passageway, punctuated by towers breaking up into the sky, could be seen as actual experiences of action architecture, built marvelously by men expressing primordial needs to provide shelter and to establish communities. Better still, the surfaces were rough, the shapes primal, the joints between parts clearly expressed, and the play of forms dramatic. I. M. Pei's 1958 master plan for the whole Boston City Hall area, with its clear recollections of Medieval stepped streets, and of the Piazza del Campo in Siena, is a splendid expression of precisely this point of view. Pei's plan really cried out for the kind of city hall Kallmann and Company designed for it.

It is hard, however, to go back into prehistory for prototypical city halls, but one can return to the origins of the type itself in the Medieval towns of Italy like Siena. Thus the great three-story cornice at Boston recalls not only Corbusier's La Tourette, in itself an essay in modern medievalism, but also Medieval crenellations as well as the great Renaissance cornices of the Palazzo Medici and Palazzo Farnese. Overall, the asymmetrical play of projecting forms, the dramatic diagonals of exterior staircases, and the continuum established between piazza and interior echoes such splendid Medieval building complexes as the town palaces at Todi. Kahn's recollection of the towers of San Gimignano in the Richards labs shows a similar but more restrained impulse.

Functionally, of course, Boston City Hall has problems. The meanderings of Medieval streets do not provide a clear circulation pattern for a couple trying to find out where to get a marriage license or a dog tag. Moreover, as Robert Venturi has pointed out, Americans don't use urban spaces the same way Mediterranean peoples do, and the New England climate hardly makes outdoor life pleasant for most of the year. City Hall plaza often has a De Chirico emptiness that the planners never intended. Instead, urban life swirls around the periphery, where the shops and restaurants are, and around nearby Faneuil Hall and the remodelled Quincy Markets. Instead of an urban amenity, City Hall Plaza is often a windswept, ice-covered barrier to be negotiated when one has business in City Hall. This space does not stand alone as an urban failure. Lincoln Center in New York [1957-1966]—Michelangelo's Campidoglio, sadly revisited (Philip Johnson said all that needs to be said about it when he put Michelangelo's pavement pattern on the ceiling of his New York State Theater)—and the Trajanic expanse of Albany's Empire State Plaza [1962-1976] by Wallace K. Harrision and others (both Rockefeller projects that failed to understand the lesson of Rockefeller Center) are visually and functionally even worse. Perhaps Charles Moore's Piazza d'Italia in New Orleans, opened in 1978, will, thanks to the architect's wit, the New Orleans climate, and the ethnic origin of the clients, prove the exception to the rule that Italian piazzas should not be built in the USA.

Most of the works of Paul Rudolph—such as the Yale Art and Architecture building [1958-1963] (fig. 37.3), the project for the Graphic Arts Center in New York [1967], and the Southeast Massachusetts University campus at North Dartmouth [1968], to name some of the most outstanding—fall into the category of action architecture. Indeed, the Art and Architecture Building deserves pride of place as the first major example of the style. Designed in 1958, only a year after Kahn's Richards complex, it is a self-consciously aggressive statement about architecture and about the role of architecture in an urban context. Like Mies at Crown Hall, Rudolph was both client and architect, a situation always fraught with danger for the outcome of the building. One concern apparently uppermost in Rudolph's mind when he worked out his scheme for the building was its position on a street corner at the edge of the Yale campus. Thus the many stages of the design (all of which he published, so that the creative process could be admired by all) worried through the problems of turning the corner and of giving the building the necessary monumentality to make a decisive edge between Yale and New Haven. Where Kahn's buildings, which flank Rudolph's, accede to the flow of the street they face, Rudolph's sits like a triumphal arch, out of Wright, Le Corbusier, and van Doesburg, blocking the progress of vision.

The interior, broken up into an almost uncountable number of levels, exhibited at a fairly early stage Rudolph's love affair with Piranesi's *Prisons*. This interest was shared by any number of contemporary architects, who found in those prints a breathtaking space-mass continuum that Piranesi could only imagine but they, thanks to modern technology, could actually build. Functionally, the building was not a success, except for the architecture studios, and perhaps the library. In the lounges at Southern Methodist University (SMU) and the great galleries of the Boston Government Center [1962-1971] the Piranesian spaces are handled with much greater skill and far more dramatic effect, even though the appropriateness of such grandiose spaces for an employment office or the collection of welfare checks is debatable.

By the late 1960s this kind of overwhelming architecture came more and more to be questioned by new generations. Indeed the Art and Architecture Building became the Valhalla in the *Götterdämmerung* of this overbearing architecture, when students put its interior to the torch. Rightly or wrongly, Rudolph's building was seen to embody those values against which students at the end of the decade were revolting.

Action architecture was not Rudolph's province alone. To a greater or lesser degree, I. M. Pei, John Johansen, and Ulrich Franzen, to name only three, produced buildings in the same mold. Johansen's Clark University Library [1965-1969] at Worcester, Massachusetts, and his later Mummer's Theater [1966-1970] in Oklahoma City possess a convincing sense of actual movement and a most complex relationship between mass and surrounding space. Pei and Franzen picked up on some of Kahn's early schemes for the Richards servant towers, those with the most picturesque and top-heavy silhouettes. Indeed, Pei's San Gimignano-in-the-Rockies, the Atmospheric Research Center [1967] at Boulder, Colorado, has such a "futuristic" character that it could be used with great effect as a set in Woody Allen's film *Sleeper*. Even Pei's addition to the National Gallery in Washington [opened in 1978] continues many of the notions we have seen developed in these buildings. With its intersecting diagonals in plan reflecting the Washington street pattern, it is a discourse on the place of the building in an urban context. Inside, visions of Piranesi dance over one's head. On the exterior it works primarily as a piece of monumental urban sculpture. That one of the opening exhibitions should have been sculptures executed by David Smith in Spoleto, a Medieval Italian hill town, is more fitting than many have realized.

The architects attracted to this mode of expression in large number share a common master, Walter Gropius. Indeed, they are his rebellious children. They have developed, instead of the anonymity preached by Gropius, highly personal and, one might add, well-publicized styles. Not all of Gropius's students, however, fit this description. Those who have entered The Architects Collaborative (TAC), the firm he founded, have tended to do far more discrete designs. Benjamin Thompson, for example, was a member of TAC for a number of year before entering practice on his own in the mid-1960s. Thompson has developed a blend of Bauhaus planning techniques with a brick-and-concrete vocabulary derived from Le Corbusier's Maisons Jaoul and Stirling and Gowan's Ham Common [1955-1958] in a number of very successful buildings for New England educational institutions. Thompson's remodeling of the Quincy Markets [completed 1977] in Boston is in many ways a model of adaptive reuse, rivaled in excellence only by the somewhat earlier remodeling of Ghirardelli Square [1964-1968] in San Francisco by Lawrence Halprin and the firm of Bernardi and Emmons.

Architecture About Architecture: The Sixties and Seventies

In the richly varied years around 1960 architects sensed a certain chaos and lack of direction, so much so that *Progressive Architecture* devoted a good part of three issues in 1962 to the question of where are we going? As one might expect, no clear answers emerged. It was generally felt, however, that the rigors of the International Style, especially as it was practiced by Mies, had fallen into disfavor—partly, even, out of boredom.

A vigorous new direction that was emerging in these years, although not clearly recognized in 1962, was that pursued by, among others, some architects who had been students of Jean Labatut at Princeton during the late 1940s and 1950s, such as Robert Venturi and Charles Moore. Labatut, unlike Mies at IIT or Gropius at Harvard, was committed to no particular aspect of the Modern Movement, and so his students grew up in a far more permissive atmosphere. Unlike Gropius, he eagerly used history as a tool for teaching, particularly in his stress on such basics as scale, proportion and the relationship of the building to site, surroundings, and climate. But he clearly shared Giedion's interest in space-time phenomena, in that he particularly encouraged his students to deal with the problem of architecture as perceived from a moving automobile. Princeton, of course, is close to Philadelphia, and so students there saw a lot by Louis Kahn, whose Trenton Bath House was only a few miles away. Kahn's rejection of most of the basic tenets of the International Style in his work of the 1950s encouraged the younger architects to similar ends, but on their own terms, and his creative reworking of the past opened new doors. There also seems to have been at Princeton a keener awareness of the possibilities inherent in Aalto's postwar work than there was at any other American architectural school at the time.

Venturi's Guild House in Philadelphia [1960-1963] was the first major statement in the new genre. Although it has by now taken on something of the quality of a golden oldie, Guild House was a shocker in its day and rightly so. From a polemical point of view, Guild House was most important for what it was not. It was not an exercise in modern technology, nor in "modern" form, in the manner that such exercises had become acceptable in the 1950s. Worse still, from an orthodox, modern point of view, it was a low-cost housing block that had not a hint of Corbusier's Ville Radieuse about it. If Guild House owed any debt to a great modern master, it was to the Aalto of Baker Hall [1947-1948] at Massachusetts Institute of Technology (MIT). Indeed, Venturi appears to be the first American architect who took the lessons of Baker Hall to heart. Venturi designed a six-story, red-brick, block that fit easily into its old, semi-industrial neighborhood. It did not try to shame its neighbors by being a shining new tower, lifted on stilts above the common run of buildings. Nor did Venturi try for an interesting shape for its own sake. The form of the building was dictated largely by a desire to provide as many rooms as possible with a southern exposure and to relate the building closely to the street by means of the projecting central pavilion. The standard construction and aluminum windows ordered out of a catalogue talked about budget constraints, as well as about giving people the kinds of things they are used to, when designing a place for them to live. Wonder of wonders for low-cost housing, the people who live in it are actually happy. When asked, in the early 1970s, these people appeared unaware of the fact that they were living in a building having even the least interest to the architectural profession.

For the profession, however, there was plenty of interest. The whole south side builds up, with a kind of Baroque grandeur, to the central bay. There, at ground level, a knowing shift to white brick in the English manner gives pedestrian scale, while the importance of the entrance set back within the facade is emphasized by a single, centrally placed shaft of highly polished black granite before it. Above, Pop Art letters against the white brick read "Guild House," while a row of windows rises left and right to a round arch, behind which is placed a room for group television-watching. Over the false front that frames this window soars an anodized, aluminum TV antenna, like the statue of Mercury that flies over the central bay of the eighteenth-century German, Baroque facade at Schloss Pommersfelden. Venturi, who designed the antenna despite an engineer's warning that it would not work, meant it to be interpreted in two ways "as sculpture, in the manner of Lippold, and as symbol of the aged, who spend so much time looking at T.V." The irony is painful and drawn, one fears, a bit at the expense of the inhabitants, whether they understood or not.

The building itself also operates on at least two levels: as rather ordinary-looking low-cost housing, and as a statement about the symbolic possibilities inherent in the juxtaposition of carefully selected architectural and sculptural forms. The antenna is a piece of Pop sculpture, not different in kind from a Warhol Brillo Box or an Oldenburg Hamburger. It even carries the same connections with Abstract Expressionism that the Warhol and Oldenburg possess, even though the works themselves are in part direct attacks on the abstract-expressionist aesthetic. But Venturi's use of Pop sculpture, which one could mistake for a found object, in place of a Baroque acroterion gives the whole composition a complex twist that brings it closer to Jasper Johns, about whom Venturi wrote well in *Complexity and Contradiction in Architecture* (1966).

Guild House was followed swiftly by Charles Moore's own 1961 house in Orinda, California, and Venturi's house for his mother in Chestnut Hill, Pennsylvania [1962]. In both, historical forms are used for symbolic purposes, to speak about the idea of the house. The notion of shelter, as provided by an ample roof, is stressed in each. The Moore house has a sense of playfulness, an ironic inversion of forms for the sake of fun, that does not happen in the Venturi design. Moore's box, wearing a slightly askew Trenton Bath House roof, contains two sets of four columns in squares. The columns, of course, recall the four posts arranged around a circular hearth that characterized that *Ur*-domicile, the Mycenaean megaron. *Chez* Moore, however, the smaller set of columns surrounds a sunken bathtub—fire is replaced (quenched?) by water.

In the Venturi house the entrance hall, staircase, and fireplace engage in a battle to occupy a very small space. Each has to give way to the others, exemplifying Venturi's interest in a complex architecture in which forms accommodate themselves to the requirements of the program and the site. Kahn said that a wall has two parts, an inside and an outside. This notion was in direct contrast with the thinking of International Style architects. For Corbusier the enclosing planes of the Villa Stein [1927] were a "veil of masonry and glass." For Venturi and Moore, the wall became the battleground where the claims of inside and outside competed. The split wall could also be used as a means of controlling light, following, once again, Kahn's lead. One of the most beautifully lit interiors of the whole postwar period is Moore's Faculty Club [1968-1969] at the University of California at Santa Barbara. Direct sunlight is filtered through double walls to create a glowing envelope around the softly lit interior. The Faculty Club is also a wonderful architectural playhouse.

Inside futurist bridges, stuffed heads, neon banners, and a gilded ceiling from Hearst's Castle at San Simeon, and much more, are combined in a Pop-goes-the-Piranesi send-up of medievalizing men's clubs.

To these architects American vernacular architecture was a subject of great interest. The Venturi house refers to American colonial architecture, with its staircase attached to the large central chimney. Its street facade recalls McKim, Mead and White's Lowe House and, by inference, that whole splendid tradition of late-nineteenth-century, American domestic architecture that Scully labeled the Shingle Style. For the Sea Ranch [1964-1966] on the northern California coast, Moore and his partners Lyndon, Turnbull, and Whitaker, went back to the wooden mining structures of the Old West for appropriate forms to fit the landscape. Venturi's investigations of Las Vegas, abhorrent to the aesthetically squeamish, in part reflect the same interest in indigenous architecture, which seems to him and his associates at least as valid a source for architectural ideas, and even architectural symbols, as Rome or Mykonos.

Learning from Las Vegas (1972), of which Venturi was coauthor with Denise Scott Brown and Steven Izenour, was in many ways an investigation of the possibilities of symbolic content in architecture. The Las Vegas Strip provided an unusually rich site for field study, perhaps the richest available in 1968 when the work was actually carried out. The tawdriness of the subject led to widespread misunderstanding of the book, possibly by people who failed to go on to read its second and third parts. In the second section the authors took up the more general task of defining and defending "Ugly and Ordinary" architecture, borrowing a derogatory phrase Philip Johnson has used about Venturi's Brighton Beach housing project of 1968. They divided buildings into two general types: ducks and decorated sheds. The first, named in honor of a Long Island poultry shop shaped like a duck, looks like what it sells. The second is a simple shelter to which the symbols that make its functions clear are attached. According to the authors, Amiens Cathedral, with its richly carved facade, is a decorated shed, but it is also a duck because its plan is cruciform. The third part of the book discussed the recent work of Venturi and Rauch which, as is generally the unfortunate case, has largely remained in project form. The 1970 California City project, however, showed what the whole crew had learned from Las Vegas. Particularly apt was the proposed town hall, a mirror-glass cube (with the only successfully designed entrance into a mirrored curtain wall of which I know) that would have sparkled like a diamond in the desert sun and glowed electrically at night. It was a design in which Mies and Ledoux met Las Vegas, and no one came out the loser.

The acid test for the ideas propounded in *Learning from Las Vegas* came in 1977, when the firm was commissioned to design an enormous hotel/casino addition to the old Marlborough-Blenheim in Atlantic City, New Jersey (fig. 37.5) where gambling was voted in to bring the crumbling Boardwalk back to life. Here was the chance to give form to Las Vegas East. The old hotel was significant in its own right; it is the first large reinforced-concrete building in America built for other than industrial purposes. Just as the Boardwalk was an early, pedestrian version of the Strip, so the old hotel is an early Caesar's Palace (Las Vegas), about which much was made, with malicious wit, in *Learning from Las Vegas*. Both have Bernini-inspired forecourts, but the Marlborough-Blenheim, with its dome flanked by a pair of utterly useless blind towers, also recalls that quintessential assemblage of architectural forms put to symbolic purposes at Johann Fischer von Erlach's eighteenth-century Karlskirche in Vienna.

In Venturi's hands the old hotel became a sign, a symbol standing free in space, for the new casino. All that was needed was a new billboard, a reverse curve inserted in the old forecourt, to complete the act. The old hotel, inflected toward the "street," provided a human scale that made an easy transition to the monumental scale required by the program for the addition. The new part embraces the isolated old tower in three ascending terraces that lead back to the great segmental arc of the hotel, which, despite its size, modestly becomes a backdrop. Indeed, with its blue color, it is really a giant cyclorama. The bland surface of the hotel, in which the boring repetition of endlessly alike bays was stressed, is a foil for the quirkiness of the old, while the shifts in color over its smooth, glassy surfaces (shades of the Yale Mathematics Building) break it down to a more manageable scale and tend to merge the upper stories with the sky. The new hotel has a large vertical hole cut cleanly through the center, flanked by blank elevator shafts that rise to support a semicircular restaurant/nightclub spanning the void. As in the street facade of Venturi's mother's house, and at Sir John Vanbrugh's Blenheim Palace (1705), the split is sealed with a curve. The nightclub is a marvel of multiple meanings. It can be read as one of those ubiquitous revolving restaurants, cut in half and turned on its side. It is a triumphal arch on which triumphant words from British history can be inscribed in elegant Roman caps. It also provides a signboard for the display of those words—the upper parts of the curves are false fronts—that advertise the presence of

37.5. Venturi and Rauch, architects. Marlborough-Blenheim Hotel project. Atlantic City, N.J., model 1977. (Photograph: Courtesy of the architects)

the wholly profit-oriented establishment below. Finally, old and new hotels are tied together, with deadpan literalness, by giant strings of lightbulbs that look like huge fake pearls by day. The Marlborough-Blenheim was Venturi's biggest and most aptly awarded commission; would that it were to be built.

Venturi's sensitivity to the problem of shifting architectural scales, as exemplified by the Marlborough-Blenheim project, is not always shared by his contemporaries. Take, for example, one of the most widely published buildings of the 1970s, Cesar Pelli's Pacific Design Center in Los Angeles [1975] (fig. 37.6). An enormous building (one thinks instantly of the Crystal Palace) dropped down between a vast parking lot in the rear and Melrose Avenue, which is lined with old houses converted to shops, the Pacific Design Center literally overwhelms its neighbors, particularly when viewed from a still residential side street. Its nickname of the Blue Whale is not undeserved.

Whatever reservations one may have about Pelli's Pacific Design Center, it is visually spectacular. The combination of opaque, cobalt blue glass panels, dark brown, transparent glass panels, and glazed, blood-red tile creates a play of colors, reflections, and transparencies that makes a simple mirror-glass structure seem boring ever after. The Blue Whale is also an abstract symbol of what it sells: the architectural molding shape of the roofline vaguely suggests the home furnishings found within. If the building were only slightly purple, it could be called a mauvey duck.

37.6. Cesar Pelli, with Gruen Associates, architects. Pacific Design Center. Los Angeles, California, 1975-1976. (Photograph: Courtesy of Eugene Johnson)

Pelli's earlier Security Pacific National Bank branch (fig. 37.7) in downtown San Bernardino [1972] is far more successful, if less well published. Like those of many small American cities, San Bernardino's downtown has been ripped apart in an effort to make it competitive with suburban shopping centers. The old and new buildings, isolated from each other by parking lots, garages, and streets, no longer form a coherent, connected, urban landscape. Pelli's bank accepts this condition with grace. It stands alone, on a corner, blind on all sides save the north, where a glass wall lights the interior. The exterior is clad in glazed brick that approaches the blue grey color of a smoggy sky on a sunny day. At ground level a band of intense red orange brick runs along the south face and turns north to join the doors in the east and west faces. The color change establishes pedestrian scale. Along the south face a screen of lemon trees with deep, waxy green leaves and yellow fruit is set against the orange band. Above this lush display of citrus colors, the blue of the upper wall soars, scarcely distinguishable from the sky itself. A second row of trees separates the sidewalk from the street and provides blessed shade in San Bernardino's desert climate.

At ground level on the north side, neat rows of palm trees form *allées* that lead to drive-in windows, an elegant expression of the importance of the automobile for southern California architecture. One should note particularly Los Angeles's carwashes, where the *rite de lavage* often becomes an extraordinary architectural *rite de passage* for car and owner alike. The bank, in other words, takes into account its surroundings and the way people on foot and in cars will use it. The doors on the east and west faces lead from sidewalk and parking lot into a multi-storied lobby lit by the great wall of glass on the north. To the south are stacked office floors that open onto the lobby space and offer a spectacular view, on clear days, of the San Bernardino Mountains through the glazed north wall. But from the ground, the interior seems an enclosed oasis that shuts out the world, in a manner Wright himself might have planned. The ultmate delight of the interior is the use of color, which shades gently from orange and yellow at ground level through pale yellow to blue in the ceiling, a blue that is slightly more intense than the blue of the sky, as seen through the window. The juxtaposition of architectural and natural blues, both inside and out, raises issues of illusion and reality that one finds more often in paintings than in buildings.

The giant scale of Pelli's Blue Whale is common to many works of the late 1960s and 1970s—Dinkeloo and Roche's New Haven Coliseum [1967], or their Fine Arts Center at the University of Massachusetts at Amherst [opened 1975], or Gordon Bunshaft's 1979 design for a bank building in Jedda, Saudi Arabia, a twenty-eight-story skyscraper lit by three square windows, each seven stories high. Similarly, there is the ten-story colonnade at the base of Philip Johnson's 1978 design for the AT&T Building in New York—the facade of the Pazzi Chapel enlarged, in the manner of a Roy Lichtenstein comic-strip Pop painting, to something like ten times its actual size. All in all, these buildings have the vastness of a Boullée vision, gone slightly mad.

Just as the painting and sculpture of the 1960s and 1970s were marked by an extraordinary pluralism in the United States, so did architecture move off in a plethora of different directions. Almost as soon as the Venturi/Moore forces had gained a beachhead in the profession by attacking modernism, a younger group came along and revived the International Style white boxes of the 1920s. Richard Meier's Smith House in Darien, Connecticut, of 1965, followed swiftly by houses by Peter Eisenman, Michael Graves, and Charles Gwathmey, announced the new movement. These four, together with John Hejduk, were the subject of a private seminar at the Museum of Modern Art in 1969, and they were published as a group in 1972 in a volume called *Five Architects*. The most interesting aspect of their work, however, is not its revivalism, but rather the way in which Eisenman, Graves, and Hejduk in particular have tried to blur the distinctions between painting, sculpture, and architecture, directions shared by a number of contemporary painters and sculptors. If the sculptress Alice Aycock, for instance, does pieces that approach architecture, then it is equally true that Graves, and especially Eisenman, do houses that approach sculpture. Graves and Hejduk, on the other hand, are both painters *manqués*. Their drawings exist for their own sakes as painterly exercises in architectural form. It would be impossible to build an actual structure on the basis of one of Hejduk's synthetic, cubist drawings or one of Graves's Juan Gris-like collages.

The work of all three of these architects, however, runs the risk of becoming so self-referential and so totally involved with issues that have only to do with art or intellectual constructs, that they lose the touch with the real world that architecture alone among the arts demands. Eisenman's House number 6 [1977], already notorious in this regard, has a column as a permanent guest (but a dull dinner partner) at the dining table, a beam that forces adults to duck when ascending the staircase, and a perilous slit in the floor between the owners' beds in the upstairs bedroom. Graves's projected civic center [plans 1977-1978] that

37.7. Cesar Pelli, with Gruen Associates, architects. Security Pacific National Bank. San Bernardino, California, 1972-1976. (Photograph: Courtesy of Eugene Johnson)

will join Fargo, North Dakota and Moorhead, Minnesota by means of a bridge across the Red River, with its ever so *recherché* mannerist tricks, bids fair to be the most successful work the whole group has yet pulled off.

In many ways opposed to Eisenman's work is that of Christopher Alexander, whose *A Pattern Language* (1977), written with a kind of laid-back Bay Area (San Francisco) attitude, celebrates the program over all else. The final form of a house, for Alexander, is determined by the accretion of individually designed parts, created to serve particular needs of the user. If one detects in the book a certain nostalgia for Shingle-Style verandahs and all-sheltering roofs, that nostalgia is coupled with hardheaded thinking about the ways people use spaces and the psychological impact of architectural forms.

Still another direction is that taken by John Portman, hotel architect to the affluent traveler, and probably the most successful architect/entrepreneur in the whole history of architecture. Portman controls his own financing, so he can build whatever he pleases. His success is all the more remarkable in that it has continued through hard times, when other architects were forced to resort to teaching, or even to abandoning the profession entirely to make a living. Portman has a rare ability to popularize the modern idiom. While some of his details give one pause—the ubiquitous glass-bullet elevators outlined in white light bulbs, for instance—his spatial effects are grand. Certainly the lobby of the San Francisco Hyatt-Regency [opened 1975], a hollow pyramid surrounded by balconies that stack up inwardly, is one of the most exciting interiors of the decade. In certain self-contained architectural circles, however, it is all right to admire Disney World but very bad taste to praise Portman.

The 1970s have also seen the emergence of women, for the first time in recorded history, as full participants in the profession on more than a very occasional basis. A 1977 exhibition at the Brooklyn Museum attempted to trace the history of women architects in the United States, few though there have been. Increasingly large numbers of women have graduated from architectural schools in the last decade. If it is true, as Philip Johnson has suggested, that an architect's life begins at age forty-five, then we will have to wait for the new century before the impact of their work can be clearly felt, much less analyzed.

Increasingly, since World War II, architecture in the United States has become an academic discipline. Architecture schools operate within the contexts of universities, and professional training takes place in an intellectual atmosphere, where humanistic learning is stressed. Integrated into the curricula of most architecture schools is considerable study in the history of architecture. Such training cannot help but affect the ways architects practice. Moreover, a number of the most important architects of the period have also been teachers (Wright, Mies, Gropius, Kahn, Rudolph, Moore, Venturi, for instance), partly out of an interest in teaching itself and partly as a way of making ends meet when the commissions were few and far between.

Parallel to this academic direction which the profession has taken is a burgeoning interest in critical writing about architecture on the part of architects themselves. Johnson, Venturi, Moore, Robert Stern, and Eisenman stand out as practitioners of this genre; the first four write with notable clarity, Eisenman with unrivaled obscurity. The center of much of this activity is the Institute for Architecture and Urban Studies in New York, which Eisenman founded and still directs. The poor economic climate of the 1970s with all-too-few commissions coming along, especially for architects with an avant-garde bent, has also been conducive to extensive self-examination. Architects often turn to writing when they have nothing else to do—witness Frank Lloyd Wright in the early 1930s. The intellectualization of architecture parallels much that happened in the other arts in the late 1960s and 1970s, when the boundaries between artist and critic began to break down just as the boundaries between painting and sculpture often became blurred. For Venturi and Johnson, at least, it is clear that the importance of the practice of criticism by an artist goes back to their readings of T. S. Eliot, whom Venturi quoted in this regard in the preface to *Complexity and Contradiction*.

It is also Eliot, one suspects, who stands behind the healing of the rift with the past that has taken place in architecture in the postwar decades. His name crops up in Johnson's 1950 publication of his glass house, an article which signaled the emergence of a new sense of how the past might be used. And Venturi, again in *Complexity and Contradiction*, quoted Eliot's remarks about the necessity for a poet to be aware of tradition, so that he could also be aware of his own contemporaneity. If one event could be singled out as symbolic of the reconciliation of the past and present, it would be the New York Museum of Modern Art's (MOMA) exhibition of the architecture of the Ecole des Beaux-Arts in the fall of 1975. Accompanied by a scholarly volume that dwarfs any of the myriad catalogues on architecture produced by the same institution, the show presented precisely those architectural works that had been anathema to the founders of the Modern Movement. Almost entirely composed of project drawings, the show was also clearly a reflection of the current interest in the profession in paper architecture, and a clear parallel could be drawn between the use of the ancient orders on the part of Beaux-Arts designers, and the use of motifs from Le Corbusier's houses of the 1920s by the New York Five. Indeed, in the winter of 1978 MOMA showed a group of the most canonical Corbusier drawings of the 1920s, many of them familiar from the pages of volume I of the *Oeuvre complète*.

The impact of the Beaux-Arts show on the profession was swift. Architectural drawings by contemporary architects became one of the hottest items on the New York art gallery circuit, a development of undoubted economic benefit to architects who make interesting drawings. Philip Johnson's Renaissance (AT&T, New York City) and Gothic (Pittsburgh Plate Glass, Pittsburgh) skyscrapers followed in 1978 and 1979. In the enormously ambitious, if confusing, architectural show mounted by the Museum of Modern Art in the spring of 1979 called "Transformations," Kevin Roche's new design for a corporate villa on an extravagant Beaux-Arts plan was one of only a very few unexecuted projects allowed.

"Transformations" marked the first time the MOMA had put together a comprehensive exhibition of recent world architecture since its epochal 1932 International Exhibition of Modern Architecture. If the early show was singleminded in its aims, Transformations was muddled in its pluralism. As such, it probably presented a fair picture of architecture practiced around the globe today. It may help to clarify the American contribution to this confusion to put side by side two buildings (fig. 37.8) that seemingly have almost nothing in common: Dinkeloo and Roche's Knights of Columbus Tower [1969] and Moore, Lyndon, Turnbull, and Whitaker's high-rise housing for the elderly [1971], both in New Haven. The Knights tower is a castellated skyscraper, a monumental building in which the tile-covered, cylindrical towers at the four corners are contrasted with

37.8. Charles Moore et al., architects. Tower #1, Church Street South Housing. New Haven, Conn., 1971 (left in photo); Dinkeloo and Roche, architects. Knights of Columbus Building. New Haven, Conn., 1969 (right in photo). (Photograph: Courtesy of Moore, Grover, Harper)

the open, cor-ten steel trusses that span the distances between towers, support the interior floors, and hold up the glass walls. The building is a splendid exercise in the fusion of historical forms and modern technology, all in the service of a strong, monumental statement in an urban setting. Moore's tower, which sits across an expressway from Roche's, is an irregular octagon, faced in slightly rusticated cinder block, with increasingly large windows in the upper stories. It is clearly a cheap, antimonumental building, whose only celebration of modern technology is found in the individual air-conditioning vents that poke through the walls. Yet, Moore's building is a wry comment on the Knights' castle. Quite clearly, it is Roche's building, with the massive towers amputated. Both, then, are buildings that make reference to other buildings. In their very disparity, they strongly underscore the fact that architects in the USA, since World War II, have been designing architecture about architecture. Whatever theoretical positions they may hold, and however they may view the relative importance of *Utilitas*, *Firmitas*, *Venustas*, or other aspects of the builder's art, they are united by the conviction that a primary role of architecture is to discourse on the art itself.

Bibliography

Alexander, Chrisopher. *Notes on the Synthesis of Form*. Cambridge, Mass.: Harvard University Press, 1964.

Alexander, Christopher et al. *A Pattern Language*. New York: Oxford University Press, 1977.

Blankenship, Edward G. *The Airport*. New York: Praeger, 1974.

Bloomer, Kent C. and Moore, Charles W. *Body, Memory and Architecture*. New Haven: Yale University Press, 1977.

Carter, Peter. *Mies van der Rohe at Work*. New York: Praeger, 1974.

Cook, John W. and Klotz, Heinrich. *Conversations with Architects*. New York: Praeger, 1973.

Drew, Philip. *Third Generation: The Changing Meaning of Architecture*. New York: Praeger, 1972.

Frampton, Kenneth; Drexler, Arthur; and Rowe, Colin. *Five Architects: Eisenman, Graves, Gwathmey, Hejduk, Meier*. New York: Oxford University Press, 1975.

"Five on Five." *Architectural Forum*, May 1973, pp. 46-57.

Giedion, Sigfried. *Architecture, You and Me*. Cambridge, Mass.: Harvard University Press, 1958.

Glaeser, Ludwig. *Mies van der Rohe: Drawings in the Collection of the Museum of Modern Art*. New York: Museum of Modern Art, 1969.,

Heyer, Paul. *Architects on Architecture: New Directions in America*. New York: Walker, 1966.

Hitchcock, Henry-Russell and Drexler, Arthur, eds. *Built in USA: Post-war Architecture*. New York: Simon & Schuster, 1952.

Huxtable, Ada Louise. *Will They Ever Finish Bruckner Boulevard?* New York: Macmillan, 1970.

Jacobs, Jane. *The Death and Life of Great American Cities*. New York: Random House, 1961.

Jacobus, John M. *Twentieth-Century Architecture, The Middle Years 1940-1965*. New York: Praeger, 1966.

Jencks, Charles. *The Language of Post-Modern Architecture*. New York: Rizzoli, 1977.

______, and Baird, George, eds. *Meaning in Architecture*. New York: Braziller, 1970.

Johnson, Philip C. *Mies van der Rohe*. 1st ed. New York: Museum of Modern Art, 1947; 2d ed., rev., 1953; 3d ed., 1978.

______. *Writings*. New York: 1979.

Jordy, William H. *American Buildings and Their Architects: The Impact of European Modernism in the Mid-Twentieth Century*. Garden City, N.Y.: Doubleday, 1972.

McCoy, Esther. *Case Study Houses, 1945-1962*. 2d ed., rev. Los Angeles: Hennessey, 1977.

Maniera-Elia, Mario. *L'Archittetura del Dopoguerra in U.S.A.* Bologna: Editore Coppelli, 1966.

Moore, Charles; Allen, Gerald; and Lyndon, Donlyn. *The Place of Houses*. New York: Holt, Rinehart and Winston, 1974.

Newman, Oscar. *Defensible Space*. New York: Macmillan, 1973.

Ronner, Heinz; Jhaveri, Sharad; and Vasella, Alessandro. *Louis I. Kahn: Complete Works, 1935-1974*. Boulder, Colo.: Westview Press, 1977.

Rowe, Colin. *The Mathematics of the Ideal Villa, and Other Essays*. Cambridge, Mass.: MIT Press, 1976.

Rudofsky, Bernard. *Architecture Without Architects*. New York: Museum of Modern Art, 1964.

Saarinen, Eero (Saarinen, Aline, ed.). *Eero Saarinen on His Work*. 1st ed. New Haven: Yale University Press, 1962; 2d ed., 1968.

Scully, Vincent. *American Architecture and Urbanism*. New York: Praeger, 1969.

______. *The Shingle Style Today: or, The Historian's Revenge*. New York: Braziller, 1974.

Sergeant, John. *Frank Lloyd Wright's Usonian Houses*. New York: Whitney Library of Design, 1976.

Stern, Robert. *New Directions in American Architecture*. New York: Braziller, 1969.

Sweeney, Robert L. *Frank Lloyd Wright: An Annotated Bibliography*. Los Angeles: Hennessey and Ingalls, 1978.

Torre, Susana, ed. *Women in American Architecture: A Historic and Contemporary Perspective*. New York: Whitney Library of Design, 1977.

Venturi, Robert. *Complexity and Contradiction in Architecture. New York: Museum of Modern Art, 1966.*

______; Brown, Denise Scott; and Izenour, Steven. *Learning from Las Vegas*. 1st ed. Cambridge, Mass.: MIT Press, 1972; 2d ed., rev., 1977.

Wurmfeld, Michael. *Princeton's Beaux Arts and Its New Academicism, from Labatut to the Program of Geddes*. New York: 1977.

Zucker, Paul, ed. *New Architecture and City Planning*. New York: Philosophical Library, 1944.

38

VENEZUELA

ELIZABETH D. HARRIS

One man dominated architectural development in Venezuela since 1945 and remained at the fore with technically accomplished modern designs until his death in 1975. Carlos Rául Villanueva pioneered the implementation of advanced building standards and was a primary force in establishing architecture as a professon in Venezuela. Though at first he followed European precedents, Villanueva's eminent talent enabled him to remain aware yet independent of his European counterparts in projects that ranged from domiciles and skyscrapers to massive, government housing projects.

Other architects often stood in Villaneuva's shadow. They followed various international trends in the 1960s and combined their ideas with Latin-American innovations in the 1970s to create a distinctive Venezuelan interpretation of modern developments. The most recently completed urban complex in Caracas, Parque Central by Siso, Shaw and Associates, exhibited this new direction in architecture while continuing to pay attention to problems of urbanization, a major concern because of Venezuela's booming metropolitan populations.

Until the early years of this century Venezuela was a sparsely populated agricultural country. Rustic colonial architecture in adobe and brick pervaded the landscape due to the absence of more sophisticated building materials. Even with such limited resources these structures confronted the tropical climate with a natural logic by enhancing exteriors with decorative verandas, balconies, and extended eaves. In 1913 a sizable quantity of oil was discovered in the area of Lake Maracaibo, and modernization thrust itself upon the country. Overnight, Venezuela began to move toward the future. As in the Alaskan gold rush, farmers abandoned crops and Europeans flooded the country, all in search of their fortunes. The capital city of Caracas grew by leaps and bounds, turning into a bustling metropolitan area set picturesquely in a valley surrounded by mountains. With no plans for this sudden expansion the influx of population spread chaotically from the city to the edges of the valley.

Until the 1950s the city's constant demand for housing, offices, and schools led to spontaneous and inadequate solutions. The engineering and contracting offices responsible for most of the building proclaimed the slogan: "We design for you for nothing"[1] and concentrated their efforts on monumental structures, often producing rather utopian schemes. But, without careful financial forethought, housing projects were often left to rot when only half finished. Architects vied with contractors for government commissions. During the regime of Juan Vicente Gómez in the 1930s the exceptional talent of one architect, Carlos Rául Villanueva, was singled out.

Villanueva, born in 1900 in London, the son of a Venezuelan diplomat and a French mother, studied architecture at the Ecole des Beaux-Arts in Paris and returned to Caracas in 1928 to open his own office. Early in his career, he received several awards and soon became Overseer of Public Works under the Gómez regime. In that capacity his concern with the organization of the National Council for the Protection and Conservation of Historical Monuments put him in close touch with national architectural traditions and led him to his first, eclectically styled commissions. Unwilling to continue an antiquated status quo, in his architecture Villanueva soon began to respond to changing social requirements.

For Villanueva, the architectural process was one always in transition, adapting to society's needs and to the individuals it served. This challenging dynamic was reflected in his work because of his receptiveness to technical innovation and his belief in the primacy of spatial design. "I believe that the specific expression of architecture is the created space, the enjoyed space, enjoyed by man, the user of spaces. From the essential invention of space as the key to the entire project, the volumetric enclosure articulates itself. Volume and structure must be alive with color and texture, vibrant with mechanical equipment and services."[2] Faithful to these concepts, Villanueva balanced volumes that were often animated with color as they were interconnected within a structure, whether in an apartment building or a grand university auditorium.

Though economics played a major role in architectural conceptions, its importance varied from one project to another, whereas sun and rain acted as constant elemental forces of the tropical climate and always had to be taken into account. With the eyes of an inspired technician, Villanueva studied Venezuela's architectural problems, for " . . . only as a technician could he, the architect, fulfill his dreams as an intellectual. If these dreams become exceptionally rich, poetic and alive, this means that he also may become an artist."[3] In Villanueva's architectural studies he indeed responded to the elements as a resourceful artist. Le Corbusier had proposed the *brise-soleil* (sun breaker) in 1933 for an Algerian apartment building. Villanueva did not borrow the idea from Le Corbusier but arrived at his own solutions independently. To deflect the sun's rays he envisioned seven different approaches derived from his studies of colonial structures in Venezuela, from simple balcony projections or verandas to window lattices and immovable shutters. Villanueva took the lessons of vernacular architecture to heart, utilizing certain motifs and varying them according to specific needs of a site.

The first turning point in Villanueva's career came in 1939 with the abandonment of anachronistic revivals and a new concentration on modern functional forms. In his Gran Colombia School, Villanueva realized the modern vocabulary of Le Corbusier, Gropius, and the Bauhaus in smooth, geometric, concrete boxes with ribbon windows and patio extensions, supported by round or squared concrete columns (*pilotis*). Since Venezuela still lacked the technology for modern materials, especially for reinforced concrete, concrete frames were used without reinforcement and thus the walls of his school were as thick as its masonry. In this major government project distinguished and subtle modifications included smaller windows, covered walkways, and balconies added to keep the interior comfortable and to protect students from the harsh tropical sun.

Some of Villanueva's most inventive climatic adaptations were for his own homes. In a suburb outside of Caracas, his 1951 residence contrasted sharply with other houses in the area for it was neither an English Victorian villa nor a colonial hacienda. Built with a reinforced-concrete frame and a hollow brick infill, the exterior was finished in stucco to effect a simplicity not unlike colonial structures. While sloping eaves are to be found in many rural areas of Venezuela, here Villanueva straightened the eaves to form sharp horizontal extensions that shaded doors and windows, noticeably recessed from the facade. An innovative architectural statement vied with copies of the past in a neighborhood that remained sedate.

Within, space is divided functionally as part of the house is reserved for children and part for adults, with communal areas occupying the central portion. Interior spaces are defined as well by a colorfully articulated treatment of surfaces that includes ceramic tiled floors and displays of plants which add an atmosphere of a free exchange with the outdoors. A tropical garden becomes part of the house, separated from the living room by glass doors designed to remain open. The house remains cool because thick concrete walls isolate most of the interior from heat while the garden shades the western exposure from the intense afternoon sun, yet allows breezes to flow throughout the house. Finally, works by Alexander Calder, Hans Arp, Joan Miro, Anton Pevsner, László, Moholy-Nagy, Fernand Léger, and others bring the various visual arts together under one roof to complement the architect's effort.

Villanueva's summer home of 1958 in Caraballeda, near the beach on the Caribbean coast, offers us another look at his adaptations of form to the tropics. A very small house of reinforced concrete, it uses a sloping roof with a dramatic overhang to help drain off the rain from the heavy tropical storms so frequent in the area. The roof reaches far beyond the load bearing walls of the central structure thanks to careful mathematical calculations and effectively shields all openings from sun and rain. In the rear a modern-styled pergola—a wooden trellis derived from the indigenous construction of the tropics—shades the patio area. Throughout the bungalow no glass was used; instead, wooden shutters substitute for doors and windows, and separated cement slats closed off a hallway while allowing air to circulate. Villanueva found air conditioning objectionable and instead employed a continuation of high ceilings and open, well-aired spaces to provide comfortable living in heat and humidity.

Villanueva's early architectural education had not included city planning, though urban housing has been a major architectural concern in Venezuela since the boom period in the early decades of this century. In many Latin-American countries slums and shanties cover the hillsides around large metropolitan areas, since squatters settled wherever they could find space. Venezuela's lack of adequate housing made a deep impression on Villanueva after his appointment in 1928 to the Public Works Department, and he returned to France to attend the Institut d'Urbanisme at the University of Paris. Upon his return, he became chief architect and advisor for the Banco de Obreros (Worker's Bank) of Venezuela. Created to improve living conditions for the *obreros* who occupied the many shanty dwellings on the hillsides, the bank financed six low-cost housing projects prepared by Villanueva between 1940 and 1960. Usually he worked alone, but at times younger architects collaborated with him, and eventually his office became a workshop in which the younger generation both learned from and contributed to his ideas and designs.

El Silencio, built by Villanueva in 1941, was the first urban-renewal project in all of Latin America. Slums in the center of Caracas were razed to make way for high-rise apartments in a program that presented problems he would continue to face in other such housing projects. Even with a restricted budget, Villanueva's first attempt at public housing was quite successful, providing the necessary high-density housing complex with a complete communication system and various amenities for the community. But El Silencio's unity was destroyed in a manner that would be repeated in other countries: a highway was cut through the middle of the project to provide direct access from downtown Caracas to the outlying airport.

A majority of Villanueva's housing programs were constructed during the 1950s. Three projects in the Caracas area, El Paraiso completed in 1952, Cerro Piloto in 1954, and 23 de Enero in 1955, sparked redevelopment of slum areas in smaller towns such as Maracaibo, Ciudad Bolivar, and Maracay. The colorful shanties of Caracas's worst slums on the hills surrounding the city not only have the most magnificent views in Caracas but also benefit from cool breezes that the wealthy neighborhoods on flatter ground never enjoy. Beginning with such environmental advantages, Villanueva collaborated with Celis Cepero and José Mijares on the El Paraiso project. The slum was replaced by a series of high-density apartment blocks, built in reinforced concrete with standardized parts, to form a snakelike pattern descending the hillside, together with a well-integrated road system that curved around each structure. The project followed the principles of the 1933 CIAM (Congrès Internationaux d'Architecture Moderne) inspired by Le Corbusier's ideas of urban planning, but proceeded beyond them with a number of personalized additions. High-density structures were geared toward self-sufficiency, interspersed with gardens and joined by an intricate roadway. Sensitive to the original layout of dwellings on the hillside, the Venezuelan architects retained picturesque views for each apartment whenever possible and varied the facades of each structure, thereby avoiding the monotony so common in so many depersonalized urban complexes of the United States and Europe in the same period. Throughout the six- and fifteen-story buildings, standardized dimensions were maintained, but the colorful facades and the seemingly random placement of each block do not conform to CIAM concepts. With such details as brightly colored panel insets in red, white, blue, and green that covered the surfaces of the facades as additions reminiscent of their former homes, people became comfortable at their new location. Within the buildings, facilities such as kindergartens, shops, and laundries were made available, while playgrounds and schools were planned for the surrounding areas to help create self-sufficient communities. Certainly the comparison with Le Corbusier's Unité d'Habitation [1946-1952] in Marseille must be made: both complexes have similar stylistic qualities, accord with their milieux, and project a responsive determination to provide a clean, sanitary environment with open spaces for children to play in.

Near El Paraiso, Cerro Piloto [1954] was constructed in the same vernacular by Villanueva in collaboration with younger architects Guido Bermudez, Carlos Brando, and Juan Centella. A year later the largest housing development of his career, 23 de Enero, got under way when he teamed with Carlos Brando, José Manuel Mijares, and José Hoffman. El Silencio had occupied over seven city blocks and provided 747 living units. By 1956, through various government commissions, 33,462 units had been built, 180,000 people had been rehoused, and the enormous task of housing Venezuela's migrating population, one that still remains a formidable undertaking for the city of Caracas, was begun in earnest.[4] The redevelopment areas of the 1950s are now falling into disrepair, and the housing shortage and slum redevelopment of Caracas, where one-third of Venezuela's population lives, continue to present major architectural challenges.

After leaving Villanueva's atelier Guido Bermudez (b. 1925) established his career in collaboration with Carlos Brando and Juan Centella with the plan for the Unidad de Habitación at Caracas. As the name suggests, their twelve-story apartment design was taken from Le Corbusier, although it was distinguished by its much lighter and freer appearance. The interior used Le Corbusier's ideas about the functional division of space, with one story for the bedrooms, another for the living room, kitchen, and dining area, and with one balcony for each apartment. A gallery that occupied an entire floor in the apartment building was reserved for shops and internal communications to provide a communal gathering place. Although squared columns (*pilotis*) supported the ground floor, the facade pushed Corbusian motifs aside and introduced a lightness of syncopated variety, as brightly colored panels delineated the exterior facings below the windows. The project was funded by the Worker's Bank, where Villanueva's authority was paramount and thus it carried his stamp of approval.

The work of Martin Vegas Pacheco and José Miguel Galia, known as Vegas and Galia, reveals the impact of American architecture upon Venezuela during the 1950s. With no formal training in architecture available in Venezuela at that time, Vegas went to the United States to study with Mies van der Rohe at the Illinois Institute of Technology. Galia, on the other hand, studied with Julio Vilamajó, an outstanding Uruguayan architect whose independence and regionalist approach to modern architecture had distinguished his work as most progressive during the 1930s and 1940s. Mies's tenets of structural purity and truth to material, his steel I-beam construction, and his clean use of glass were retained by Vegas after his return to Venezuela. The Edificio Polar [1952] by Vegas and Galia in the Plaza Venezuela in Caracas is one of the best examples of Mies's influence in all of South America. Smaller and more compact than Mies's and Philip Johnson's Seagram Building [1957], it poses a fifteen-story tower upon a two-story horizontal base. Upon its exterior, structural divisions are articulated by Mies's dark mullions. The completely glass-skinned walls Mies preferred would have been most impractical in the tropical climate of Caracas, allowing the direct sunlight to heat the offices throughout the day. Thus plywood-backed aluminum panels in various patterns were substituted at calculated intervals. The surfaces of glass and aluminum shine in a way to maintain a homogeneous surface that suggests the salient structural lines of a Miesian formula.

In another fine work by Vegas and Galia, the Twin Morochos apartment building [1958] in Caracas, two structures perfectly square in plan, faced with a rich local brick, trimmed in concrete, and highlighted with wooden shutters, reflect Vilamajó's influence rather than Mies's.

Villanueva continued to work on government projects during the 1950s. The Ciudad Universitaria in Caracas was first established by royal Spanish decree in 1721. But not until the early 1940s were there plans to move it out of its antiquated convent quarters. A traditional Beaux-Arts design was first proposed by Villanueva and fortunately was never acted upon. In the late 1940s another plan was formulated which eventually led to Villanueva's more contemporary conception that was enacted. Construction of the major buildings took place during the mid-1950s and continued until 1965 when the School of Architecture was finished.

The campus spreads across five hundred acres with the most important university offices occupying the central core of the ground plan, while beyond that the campus has grown seemingly of its own volition. Because of Villanueva, a marvelous harmony pervades the campus; yet each building exists autonomously with structure following function. Reinforced concrete, the basic material employed, is highlighted with cement blocks perforated to let air in, but not the sun, and with glazed tiles in various colors to animate the outer surfaces of buildings. Over a mile of covered walkways, centrally placed gardens, sculpture, mosaics, and other works of art enhance the architecture.

Dynamic engineering with simple materials provides continuous communication between the campus buildings. Multipurpose walkways link buildings and often widen to become plazas with benches where students may stop and chat, shaded from the intense sun. Practically and aesthetically functional, these shaded passageways are comprised of free-form designs that add a sculptural, integrating quality to the campus. Canopies of prestressed concrete, including a most unusual corrugated wave, twenty-nine feet in width supported by columns every forty-nine feet, punctuate the covered walks. These pathways form the major arteries of the university. They seem to emerge organically from the landscape, as if nature herself had planned them, and allow an easy flow of traffic from one building to the next.

The covered plazas mentioned above, where students like to gather, contain many works of art, including sculptures by Hans Arp, Anton Pevsner, and Henri Laurens. Paintings and mosaics by Fernand Léger and Victor Vasarely, among others, decorate walls and passageways throughout the university. Villanueva admirably achieved his goal of making the campus of the University of Venezuela "one world through the synthesis of architecture and art."[5]

Of the many buildings planned and executed on this campus, the famous Aula Magna and the School of Architecture best exemplify his individualistic approach to architecture. Villanueva's structural self-consciousness and uses of unfinished materials differed from Le Corbusier's and helped define his originality. The Aula Magna [1952], with a seating capacity of 2600, has been recognized as a bold structural statement for its openly exposed exterior supports and as highly innovative for its use of Alexander Calder's floating acoustical discs (fig. 38.1). Visible as one approaches the Aula is the key to its structural design—a series of steel ribs, each sheathed in rough concrete. Radiating from a crossing element that frames the juncture of the performance area with the auditorium proper, they arch elegantly out over the audience's space. But the ribs cannot be seen within the hall, since the shell-like ceiling of the interior is suspended from them, and in turn Calder's multicolored mobile shields are suspended from the ceiling. The radiating ribs work in concert with the fan shape of the hall, and become prominently finlike as they move forward, revealed by the curvature of the roof that has descended more rapidly than the ribs. This major structural, expressively sculptural element is continued in a kind of counterpoint by fins of less striking dimensions that fan forward from the ribs onto the lower roof level of the wide, arching vestibule that fronts the auditorium. Within, the vestibule surprises the viewer with its striking plays of solids and voids, in large, rounded forms such as the heavy concrete ramps that curve upward to the auditorium itself. In this extraordinary accomplishment Villanueva's architecture has clearly fused with and become art.

The School of Architecture was founded in 1944, but not until Villanueva designed a structure with stimulating spaces for teaching early in the 1960s was

38.1. Carlos Raúl Villaneuva, architect. Aula Magna of the Central University of Venezuela, interior; acoustical discs by Alexander Calder. Caracas, 1952. (Photograph: Courtesy of Paolo Gasparini)

an adequate building constructed for it. Approaching the architecture building from the composition workshops (west) (fig. 38.2) it seems only a nine-story, oblong, cubicular structure with a rich surface articulation of *brise-soleil*. In fact it is conceived in a T-shaped plan, one wing of which is hidden from view. The hidden wing that extends east from the main portion of the building and contains the services ends in a low polygonal auditorium. To the north of this wing is a museum exhibition hall in a slightly larger scale. On the south flank of the projecting wing are the parking areas. Instead of the regularity that one might anticipate in one of Martin Vegas Pacheco's interpretations of Mies, here each element of the T-form building is resolved differently in terms of the scales and materials of its articulating surface designs. The asymmetrically placed eastern mass of the T is perhaps the most interesting, since Villanueva gave it the appearance of a varied, off-center cluster of rectangular-plan towers, the broadest of which is in the midst of the block and rises the highest. Though within the spaces of the upper stories a modular solution was adopted out of practical needs, a very different practicality called forth an effective variety of spaces in the many workshops of the lower level. A variety of colorful sun deflectors shades each exterior wall. Vertically strung concrete panels are arranged at right angles to, and project a short distance from, the tiled, windowless west wall of the school to provide shade for its many windows, while modulated blue panels enclose the short ends of the building. The polychromatic reflecting and absorbing effects upon the building's surfaces that seem so integral to its architectural design are the results of a carefully thought through program composed by the well-known Venezuelan painter, Alejandro Otero.

Villanueva's genius in maintaining a sense of simplicity in a sublimely sophisticated, structurally fascinating design, alive with color and texture, that functions well is evident in this School of Architecture building. With its completion in the mid-1960s, a suitable environment for educating architects, hence ultimately ensuring the future of the architectural profession in Venezuela, had been achieved.

38.2. Carlos Raúl Villaneuva, architect. Central University of Venezuela, shaded passage with rear façade of the School of Architecture. Caracas, 1965. (Photograph: Courtesy of Paolo Gasparini)

Two more works of the 1960s show Villanueva's ability to interpret structure and function poetically. Minimal art inspired his first total synthesis of art and architecture, the Venezuelan pavilion at Expo '67 in Montreal, Quebec (fig. 38.3). Two aluminum cubes painted in bright primary colors were linked by the lower, quite narrow, constricted mass of the translucent glass entrance area, all resting upon a solid podium. Pristine geometry and bright coloring interrupted only by the stark typography of the word "Venezuela" stimulated an uncanny dynamic of ambiguity between the few components of this design on the one hand and the ideas of sculpture and architecture on the other.

One of his last projects, the Museum of Fine Arts in Caracas [1968], exhibits Villanueva's lucid manipulation of volumes into a form that controls and directs function with an appearance of playful innovation. It appears that here a stronger sense of angular organization and a newly enriched, even idiosyncratic, formal vocabulary emerged from his previous year's consideration of minimal architecture. At the juncture of the major arms of the building (where one wishes to find a massing of towers perhaps similar to that in his School of Architecture project) new tower shapes are invented instead, each of different height, and they are spun off, dispersed from the central axis of the structure. A sense of unity is provided by the cubical capping of the slimmest turret nearest to the main juncture of the design. The notion of a dynamic of ambiguity, evident in his Expo '67 building, seems resolved anew, more richly articulated, yet with a clear formal impact.

Most of Villanueva's major commissions, his housing projects and university designs, were built during the mid-1950s when Colonel Marcos Pérez Jiménez was president, for under his regime public building programs boomed. During Jiménez's push for material progress, foreign investment in steel and power plants was encouraged. After abuses of public funds and restrictions of political liberty, the Jiménez dictatorship lost its hold. With the exile of Pérez Jiménez a decrease in public building projects led architects to realize that: "architecture was freer and more expansive until the old regime ended in 1958."[6] After 1958 the younger generation, although influenced by Villanueva, moved toward a new urban Rationalism. In response to the problems of Caracas, architects rejected isolated monumental structures and stylistic concepts from outside of Latin America. Tomas José Sanabria, Vegas and Galia, and Dirk Bornhorst led the way into the 1960s with designs that showed an awareness of and sensitivity to

38.3. Carlos Raúl Villaneuva, architect. Venezuelan Pavilion for Expo '67. Montreal, Quebec, 1967. (Photograph: Courtesy of Paolo Gasparini)

Venezuela's economic and social environment. Although most of these architects had studied elsewhere, they began to return to continental Latin American sources for inspiration, such as the ingeniously engineered structures of Mexican architect Félix Candela. Candela's concrete vaults, based on the geometry of the hyperbolic parabola, were easy to build and could be adapted efficiently to shelter homes or factories. In the 1970s these engineering techniques were combined with an emphasis on the textural qualities of concrete. New Rationalism moved into Brutalism when new building techniques allowed architects the freedom to utilize a variety of materials for functional and decorative purposes.

Dirk Bornhorst's Volkswagen Assembly Plant [1966], two well-lit yet cool structures in a large park near Caracas, reflect Candela's influence and the new Rationalism. Sawtoothed vaulting in the main building of the plant is posed six inches over the lateral walls to allow cool breezes to flow freely through the building. Nearby, in the other building, there is vaulting of reinforced concrete in the shape of mushroom shells supported by central stems. For this rationalistic and economical design with straightforward utilization of material and structural simplicity, Candela is the obvious source.

In the late 1960s Tomas José Sanabria's Banco Central de Venezuela in Caracas derived its design from international Brutalism but stepped beyond the use of exterior facing in raw materials to stylize the entire design with a heavy textural effect that joins particular parts to the whole. The site for this commercial bank and treasury complex was on a sloping street near older government buildings. Sanabria developed a structure which grows in broadening sections, expanding as it rises, and which is topped with an enclosed roof garden. A fortresslike base of textured concrete encloses the lower half of the building, built against the slope of the street. The glass-enclosed second story is faced with sungrids that overhang the base and in turn the third-story roof garden, enclosed with vertical ribs, caps the structure and overhangs the floor below. Monumental yet balanced in its massive proportions the building fits well with the surrounding eclectic structures.

Brutalist tendencies can also be clearly seen in houses of the late 1960s and 1970s in Venezuela. Updating Villanueva's ideas, the architectural firm of Carmona and Puig built the Toro House in Caracas [1966]. Although it was cubist in the sense of Villanueva's Caracas home [1951], these young architects used raw materials instead of smooth, painted concrete, and they integrated flower boxes and wooden shutters into the structure itself to give a warm, naturalistic feeling to the house. Wood and rich red brick, outlined against the concrete, elaborated the Brutalist vocabulary with a return to nature. Recessed openings with projecting wooden pergolas help maintain a comfortable temperature inside the dwelling year-round. Air flows freely through the pergolas and shutters, while light is diffused through sawtoothed skylights which allow only indirect light to enter and not the sun's intense rays. Here, combinations of rich materials, geometrically abstracted, manifest the maturation of Villanueva's influence on young Venezuelan architects.

International Brutalism fell to mannerist tendencies as reflected in the home that Susana Orias de Kovacs designed and built for herself in the Caracas area in 1966. Inside, three levels are cantilevered from a cylindrical core encircled by a staircase. Exterior spatial volumes are sharply angular and describe the irregular shape of rooms which jut out beyond the central plan. Windows appear to be punched out where needed, each decoratively divided with black mullions like a Mondrian painting. Exterior and interior walls are surfaced in rough concrete that has been whitewashed, while built-in furnishings retain their natural wood finish. Starkly effective, the home exhibits Kovacs's ability to maintain a simple directness even with a complex layering of space and volume.

In the 1970s Venezuela's architectural activity reached a climax in Caracas's ambitious Parque Central urban-revitalization project (fig. 38.4) by the architectural firm of Siso, Shaw and Associates. Daniel Shaw described it succinctly: "Since 1912 and the arrival of the automobile in Caracas, the transportation system has been unchanged. Our project is a departure from this system. In the Parque Central project, a community has been created providing all the facets of one's way of life. . . . This gives a vitality to the complex and avoids the common failing of monotony."[7] And indeed, it provides a variety of office spaces, urban housing, and a hotel for downtown Caracas. Just off Avenida Bolivar, the Parque Central complex covers an area of sixteen hectares with seven high-rise buildings, each forty-four-stories high, two office buildings fifty-six-stories high, and the Anauco-Hilton hotel. No more than a five-minute walk or ride connects Parque Central to all major parts of the city, thanks to the fine circulation system built into this urban construction program.

Such an alternative to suburban living would have delighted Le Corbusier with its high-density com-

38.4. Siso, Shaw and Associates, architects. Parque Central Complex in construction; with Anauco-Hilton (far left) completed. Caracas, 1978. (Photograph: Courtesy of Pascual de Leo)

munity that incorporated ideas from his "Contemporary City for Three Million Inhabitants." The first three floors of each building in this self-contained community form a common base. The first floor links offices with a plaza and entrances to the subway, the second story provides grocery stores and boutiques, the third floor is reserved for recreation and cultural activities, and from the fourth floor up are offices or apartments. On the top floor of each building, instead of penthouses, are schools, playgrounds, and social clubs to complete the scheme of urban community services.

One of the best designs in the Parque Central is the Residencias Anauco, Hilton-Caracas [1975], a skyscraper slab, cut off diagonally along the top and with long sides that slope outward in its lower portion. The immediate garden surroundings (fig. 38.5), designed by the distinguished Brazilian landscape architect, Roberto Burle-Marx, complement this elegant structure by transforming the urban area into a tropical paradise. Tall, monumental, shell-thin slabs enclose the short sides of the building left and right, punctuated only by a single vertical row of sparsely spaced windows. On the front and rear, a regular pattern of concrete balconies on almost every floor is broken at two levels to divide the design into three unequal sections superposed sequentially in diminishing heights. The front facade is topped by a broad surface of tiles beneath which is an arrangement of large, wide, two-storied windows. The top of a narrow, rectangular shaft interrupts this glazed upper terminus of the design and descends far beneath to fuse with the lower floors as they slope outward. With this device the facade received a simple, effective, central vertical accent.

At the base two ideas express a grounding for the hotel's design. First, the lower stories are recessed from the flaring surface of the building so that they are in shadow; and second, from the main flow of the building's form, vertical concrete strips are disposed in a very rapid rhythm across the lowest balconies to descend three stories. The quick sequence of tall,

38.5. Siso, Shaw and Associates, architects. Parque Central with detail of Anauco-Hilton and garden (Roberto Burle-Marx, landscape architect). Caracas, 1978. (Photograph: Courtesy of Pascual de Leo)

vertical strips forms a monumental screen that bridges the transition from the mass of this graceful building to the volume of its shaded lowest levels. Full advantage of the intense Caracas sunlight has been taken by articulating the broadest elements of the plan in terms of decorative screens and reflective surfaces versus recessed, shadowed volumes. The creative spirit of the new generation of architects educated in Venezuela has come of age in the design of the vastly scaled project of Parque Central.

Since 1948 when the first class of eleven architects graduated from the Ciudad Universitaria of Caracas, their number has continued to increase. But the demand for architects has become so incessant that now young architects often enter architectural firms before completing their degrees. Through the efforts of people like Oscar Tenreiro, who was a colleague and close friend of Carlos Rául Villanueva and currently heads the Architecture Department of the Ciudad Universitaria, architects are continuing to pursue aggressive approaches to building so that, as it was with Villanueva, dynamic design will continue to be associated with modern architecture in Venezuela.

Notes

1. Ray Smith, "After Corbu, What's Happening?" *Progressive Architecture* 47 (September 1966): 14.
2. Sibyl Moholy-Nagy, *Carlos Rául Villanueva and the Architecture of Venezuela* (London: Alec Tiranti, 1964), p. 169.
3. Ibid., p. 160.
4. Since the discovery of oil in Venezuela, peasants whose land was purchased by speculators have been moving into the capital. The government has attempted to house these migrants, but many still live in their slums.
5. Moholy-Nagy, *Villanueva*, p. 102.
6. Smith, "After Corbu," p. 12.
7. New York, *Hilton International News*, 1975.

Bibliography

BOOKS

Bullrich, Francisco. *Arquitectura Latinoamericana, 1930-70.* Barcelona: Editorial Gustavo Gili, S.A., 1970.

———. *New Directions in Latin American Architecture.* New York: George Braziller, 1969.

Hitchcock, Henry-Russell. *Latin American Architecture Since 1945.* New York: Museum of Modern Art, 1972.

Moholy-Nagy, Sibyl. *Carlos Rául Villanueva and the Architecture of Venezuela.* London: Alec Tiranti, 1964.

JOURNALS

Alfieri, Bruno. "New York, Caracas, Brasilia." *Zodiac II*, 1963, pp. 2-19.

"Auto Assembly Plant Set in Tree-Bounded Park." *Architectural Record* 141 (January 1967): 164-66.

Lumsden, Mary. "Caracas." *Architectural Forum*, 101 (November 1954), 152-55.

Moholy-Nagy, Sibyl. "Some Aspects of Latin American Architecture." *Progressive Architecture* 41 (April 1960): 135.

Négron, M. "A Caracas." *L'Architecture d'Aujourd'hui* 173 (May 1974): 52-71.

"Progress on the Helicoid." *Architectural Review* 128 (December 1960): 390.

Smith, Ray. "After Corbu, What's Happening?" *Progressive Architecture* 47 (September 1966): 140-61.

Villanueva, Carlos R. "Nouvelle Unités Residentielles au Venezuela." *L'Architecture d'Aujourd'hui* 20 (September 1950): 8-13.

APPENDIX A

EDUCATIONAL INSTITUTIONS FOR ARCHITECTURE AND PLANNING

Argentina

Faculty of Architecture and Urbanism, Federal University of Argentina at Buenos Aires.

Faculty of Architecture and Urbanism, Federal University of Argentina at Córdoba.

Faculty of Architecture, University of the Province of Mar del Plata, Mar del Plata.

Faculty of Architecture and Urbanism, University of Mendoza, Mendoza.

Faculty of Architecture, Federal University of Rosario, Rosario.

Faculty of Architecture, Federal University of Tucumán, San Miguel de Tucumán.

Australia

School of Architecture, South Australian Institute of Technology, Adelaide, South Australia 5000.

Department of Architecture, University of Adelaide, Adelaide, South Australia 5000.

School of Environment Design, Canberra College of Advanced Education, Belconnen, ACT 2616

Department of Architecture, Deakin University, Belmont, Victoria 3216.

Institute of Technology, Bentley, Western Australia 6102.

School of Architecture and Building, New South Wales Institute of Technology, Broadway, New South Wales 2007.

Urban Research Unit, Australian National University, Canberra, ACT 2600. Empirical studies of urban development in Australia with particular emphasis on the role played by government authorities and on the distributive effects of urban development.

Department of Environmental Design, Tasmanian College of Advanced Education, Hobart, Tasmania 7001.

Faculty of Architecture, University of New South Wales, Kensington, New South Wales 2033.

Graduate School of the Built Environment, Faculty of Architecture, University of New South Wales, Kensington, New South Wales, 2033. Research in those multidisciplinary areas concerned with the creating and managing of the built environment.

School of Health Administration. University of New South Wales, Kensington, New South Wales, 2033. Study of health administration including hospital design.

Faculty of Architecture, Royal Melbourne Institute of Technology, Melbourne, Victoria 3000.

Faculty of Architecture, University of Western Australia, Nedlands, Western Australia 6009.

School of Built Environment, Queensland Institute of Technology, North Quay, Queensland 4000.

Environmental Studies, c/o School of Biological Sciences, Macquarie University, North Ryde, New South Wales 2113. Study of environmental issues including urban microclimate.

School of Architecture, University of Melbourne, Parkville, Victoria 3052.

Faculty of Architecture, University of Queensland, St. Lucia, Queensland 4067.

Faculty of Architecture, University of Newcastle, Shortland, New South Wales 2307.

School of Architecture, University of Sydney, Sydney, New South Wales 2006.

Architectural Psychology Research Unit, Department of Architecture, University of Sydney, Sydney, New South Wales 2006. Research in all aspects of environmental psychology.

Department of Architectural Science, University of Sydney, New South Wales 2006. Research in all aspects of building including urban microclimate.

Planning Research Centre, Department of Town & Country Planning, University of Sydney, Sydney, New South Wales 2006. Fundamental research into physical planning and development.

Ian Buchan Fell Research Project on Housing, Faculty of Architecture, University of Sydney, Sydney, New South

Wales 2006. Research into the housing needs of various groups of people within the community.

Austria

Technische Hochschule Graz, Fakultät für Architektur, Graz.

Hochschule für Gestaltung, Linz an der Donau.

Universität Innsbruck, Fakultät für Architektur, Innsbruck.

Akademie der Bildenden Künste Wien, Meisterschulen für Architektur, Vienna.

Hochschule für Angewandte Kunst, Abteilung Architektur, Vienna.

Technische Universität Wien, Fakultät für Architektur, Vienna.

Belgium

Kroninklijke Academie voor schone Kunster van Antwerpen, 2000 Antwerp.

Académie Royale des Beaux Arts de Bruxelles, 1000 Brussels.

Ecole Nationale Supérieure d'Architecture et des Arts Visuels, 1050 Brussels.

Académie Royale des Beaux Arts de Gand, Koninklijke Academie voor schone Kunsten van Gent, 9000 Ghent.

Académie Royale des Beaux Arts de Liège, Ecole Supérieure d'Architecture, 4000 Liège.

Chaire d'Architecture, Université de Liège, 4000 Liège.

Académie Royale des Beaux Arts de Mons, 7000 Mons.

Bolivia

Escuela de Arquitectura, Universidad Mayor de San Simon, Cochabamba.

Escuela de Arquitectura, Universidad Mayor de San Andrés, La Paz.

Brazil

Escola de Arquitetura, Universidade Federal de Minas Gerais, Belo Horizonte, M.G.

Faculdade de Arquitetura e Urbanismo, Universidade de Brasilia, Brasilia, D.F.

Departamento de Arquitetura, Universidade Federal do Paranà, Curitiba, P.R.

Curso de Arquitetura e Urbanismo, Universidade Federal do Cearà, Fortaleza, C.E.

Escola da Arquitetura, Universidade Catolica de Goiàs, Goiània, G.O.

Faculdade de Arquitetura e Urbanismo Farias Brito, Guarulhos, S.P.

Faculdade de Arquitetura e Urbanismo, Universidade Estadual de Londrina, Londrina, P.R.

Faculdade de Arquitetura, Universidade Federal do Rio Grande do Sul, Porto Alegre, Rio Grande do Sul.

Faculdade de Arquitetura, Universidade Federal de Pernambuco, Recife, Pernambuco.

Faculdade de Arquitetura e Urbanismo, Universidade Federal de Rio de Janeiro, Rio de Janeiro, G.B.

Faculdade de Arquitetura, Universidade da Bahía, Salvador, Bahía.

Faculdade de Arquitetura e Urbanismo de Santos, Santos, S.P.

Faculdade de Arquitetura e Urbanismo, Universidade de São Paulo, São Paulo, S.P.

Canada

Faculty of Environmental Design, University of Calgary, Calgary, Alberta.

School of Architecture, Nova Scotia Technical College, Halifax, Nova Scotia.

School of Architecture, McGill University, Montreal, Quebec.

Ecole d'Architecture, Université de Montréal, Montréal, Québec.

School of Architecture, Carleton University, Ottawa, Ontario.

Ecole d'Architecture, Université Laval, Québec, Québec.

School of Architecture, University of Toronto, Toronto, Ontario.

School of Architecture, University of British Columbia, Vancouver, British Colombia.

School of Architecture, University of Waterloo, Waterloo, Ontario.

Faculty of Architecture, University of Manitoba, Winnipeg, Manitoba.

Chile

Facultad de Arquitectura, Universidad de Chile, Santiago.

Facultad de Arquitectura y Bellas Artes, Universidad Catolica de Chile, Santiago.

Facultad de Arquitectura, Universidad Católica de Valparaíso, Valparaíso.

China, People's Republic of

Qinghua University, Beijing.

South China Institute of Technology, Guangzhou, Guangzhou Province.

Harbin Architectural Engineering Institute, Harbin, Heilongjian Province.

Nanjing Institute of Technology, Nanjing, Jiangsu Province.

Tongji University, Shanghai.

Xian Metallurgy Institute, Xian, Shanxi Province.

Chongqing Architectural Engineering Institute, Chongqing, Sichuan Province.

Tianjin University, Tianjin.

Colombia

Facultad de Arquitectura, Universidad del Atlántico, Barranquilla.

Facultad de Arquitectura y Diseño, Pontificia Universidad Javeriana, Bogotá, D.E.

Facultad de Arquitectura, Universidad de los Andes, Bogotá, D.E.

Facultad de Arquitectura, Universidad Nacional de Colombia, Bogotá, D.E.

Facultad de Arquitectura, Universidad del Valle, Cali.

Facultad de Arquitectura, Universidad Nacional de Colombia, Medellín.

Cuba

Escuela de Arquitectura, Universidad de La Habana, Havana.

Czechoslovakia

Faculty of Architecture, Slovak Technical University, 800 43 Bratislava.

Faculty of Architecture, Technical University, 601 90 Brno.

Faculty of Architecture, Academy of Fine Arts, 170 22 Prague.

Faculty of Architecture, Technical University of Prague, Prague 2.

Denmark

Arkitekskolen i Aarhus, 8000 Aarhus C.

Kunstakademiets Arkitekskole, Det Kongelige Danske Kunstakademi, Copenhagen K.

Finland

Department of Architecture, Teknillinen Korkeakoulu, 02150 Espoo 15.

Department of Architecture, Teknillinen Korkeakoulu, 02150 Otaniemi.

Department of Architecture, Oulun Yliopisto, 90100 Oulu 10.

Department of Architecture, Tampereen Tecknillinen Korkeakoulu, 33100 Tampere 10.

France

Ecole spéciale d'architecture, 75014 Paris.

Unités pedagogiques d'architecture (awarding the title, "architecte diplômé par le Gouvernement"). Among the 9 U.P.A.s in the Paris area, divisions of the Ecole Nationale des Beaux-Arts:

U.P.A. no. 1, 75 272 Paris (at l'Ecole Nationale des Beaux-Arts).

U.P.A. No. 4, same address.

U.P.A. No. 9, same address.

U.P.A. No. 3, Petites Ecuries du Roy 2, 78000 Versailles.

Among the 14 others are:

U.P.A. de Nancy, 54600, Nancy.

U.P.A. de Marseille, 13288 Marseille.

U.P.A. de Rennes, 35000 Rennes.

U.P.A. de Strasbourg, 67000 Strasbourg.

Germany, Democratic Republic of (DDR)

Kunsthochschule Berlin, 112 Berlin.

Technische Universität Dresden, 8027 Dresden.

Hochschule für Architektur und Bauwesen Weimar, 53 Weimar.

Germany, Federal Republic of (BRD)

Architekturabteilung, Technische Hochschule Aachen, 51 Aachen.

Staatliche Hochschule für Bildende Künste, 1 Berlin 12.

Technische Fachhochschule Berlin, 1 Berlin 65.

Fachbereich 8, Technische Universität Berlin, Berlin.

Architekturabteilung, Technische Universität Braunschweig, 33 Braunschweig.

Fakultät für Architektur, Technische Hochschule Darmstadt, 61 Darmstadt.

Abteilung Architektur, Hochschule für Bildende Künste, Staatliche Kunstakademie Düsseldorf, 4 Düsseldorf.

Hochschule für Bildende Künste, 2 Hamburg 22.

Technische Universität, Fakultät für Bauwesen, 3 Hanover.

Technische Hochschule, 75 Karlsruhe.

Architekturabteilung, Technische Hochschule München, 8 Munich 2.

Architekturabteilung, Universität Stuttgart, 7 Stuttgart 1.

Great Britain

School of Architecture, University of Bath, Avon.

School of Architecture, University of Bristol, Bristol.

Centre for Land Use and Built Form, University of Cambridge, Cambridge.

School of Architecture, University of Cambridge, Cambridge.

School of Architecture, University of Edinburgh, Edinburgh.

School of Architecture, University of Liverpool, Liverpool.

The Architectural Association Inc., 34 Bedford Square, London WC1.

School of Architecture, Polytechnic of North London, London N7 8DB.

School of Architecture, University College London, Wates House, London WC1.

School of Architecture, University of Sheffield, Sheffield.

Institute of Advanced Architectural Studies, King's Manor, York.

Greece

Athens Center of Ekistics, Athens 136.

School of Architecture, National Technical University of Athens, Athens 146.

School of Architecture, Aristotle University of Salonica, Salonica.

Hungary

Faculty of Architecture, Budapest Technical University, 1111 Budapest XI.

Hungarian College of Arts and Crafts, 1121 Budapest XII.

India

The Chandigarh College of Architecture, Chandigarh.

School of Architecture, Ahmedabad 9, Gujerat.

Architecture Section, The Governmental College of Fine Arts and Architecture, Hyderabad 5000 28 AP.

Architecture Section, The Indian Institute of Technology, Kharagpur 721302.

Academy of Architecture, Bombay 25, Maharashtra.

Architecture Section, Bandra School of Art, Bombay 50 AS, Maharashtra.

Sir J. J. College of Architecture, Bombay, Maharashtra.

School of Planning and Architecture, New Delhi.

Israel

"Bezalel," Academy of Art and Design, Jerusalem.

Faculty of Architecture and Town Planning, Technion, Israel Institute of Technology, Haifa.

Italy

Facoltà di Architettura, Università di Firenze, Florence.

Facoltà di Architettura, Università di Genova, Genoa.

Facoltà di Architettura, Politecnico di Milano, Milan.

Facoltà di Architettura, Università di Napoli, Naples.

Facoltà di Architettura, Università di Palermo, Palermo.

Facoltà di Architettura della Libera Università "Gabriele d'Annunzio" di Pescara, Pescara.

Istituto Universitario di Architettura e Urbanistica di Reggio Calabria, Reggio Calabria.

Facoltà di Architettura, Università di Roma, Rome.

Facoltà di Architettura, Politecnico di Torino, Turin.

Istituto Universitario di Architettura di Venezia, Venice.

Japan

National Universities:
Hiroshima
Hokkaido
Kyoto
Kyushu
Nagoya
Osaka
Tohoku
Tokyo
Tokyo Geijutsu
Tokyo Kogyo
Prefectural or Municipal Universities:
Osaka Municipal
Tokyo Metropolitan
Private Universities:
Nihon (Tokyo and others)
Waseda (Tokyo)

Mexico

Escuela de Arquitectura, Universidad Autónoma de Morelos, Cuernavaca, Mor.

Escuela de Arquitectura, Instituto Tecnológico y de Estudios Superiores de Occidente, Guadalajara, Jal.

Instituto Tecnológico, Universidad de Guadalajara, Escuela de Arquitectura, Guadalajara, Jal.

Facultad de Arquitectura, Universidad de Guadalajara, Guadalajara, Jal.

Escuela de Arquitectura, Universidad de Guanajuato, Guanajuato, Gto.

Escuela de Arquitectura, Universidad de Yucatán, Mérida, Yuc.

Escuela de Arquitectura, Universidad Anáhuac, Lomas Anáhuac, México 10, D.F.

Escuela de Arquitectura, Universidad Iberoamericana, México, D.F.

Escuela Mexicana de Arquitectura, Universidad Nacional Autónoma de México, Ciudad Universitaria, México 10, D.F.

Escuela Méxicana de Arquitectura, Universidad de la Salle, México 18, D.F.

Escuela Superior de Ingenieria y Arquitectura, Instituto Politécnico Nacional, Zacatenco, México 14, D.F.

Escuela de Arquitectura, Instituto Tecnológico de Monterrey, Monterrey, N.L.

Facultad de Arquitectura, Universidad Autónoma de Nuevo León, Ciudad Universitaria, Monterrey, N.L.

Escuela de Arquitectura, Universidad Benito Juarez, Oaxaca, Oax.

Escuela de Arquitectura, Universidad Autónoma de Puebla, Puebla.

Facultad de Arquitectura, Universidad Autónoma de Tamaulipas, Ciudad Victoria, Tamps.

Facultad de Arquitectura, Universidad Veracruzana, Xalapa, Ver.

Netherlands

Academie van Bouwkunst, Amsterdam.

Research Instituut Gebouwde Omgeving (RIGO), Amsterdam.

Academie van Bouwkunst, Arnhem.

Afdeling Bouwkunde, Technische Hogeschool, Delft.

Afdeling Bouwkunde, Technische Hogeschool te Eindhoven, Eindhoven.

Academie van Bouwkunst, Groningen.

Academie van Bouwkunst, Maastricht.

Academie van Bouwkunst, Rotterdam.

Academie van Bouwkunst, Tilburg.

Norway

School of Architecture, Oslo. (Arkitekthøgskolen i Oslo, AHO), Oslo 1.

Department of Architecture, the Technical University of Norway, Trondheim (Norges Tekniske Høgskole, Trondheim), 7034 Trondheim.

Poland

Wydzial Architektury, Politechnika Krakowska, 31-121 Cracow.

Instytut Architektury i Urbanistyki, Politechnika Gdanska, 80-321 Gdansk.

Wydzial Budownictwa i Architektury, Politechnika Szczencinska, 70-310 Szczecin.

Instytut Urbanistyki i Architektury, 00-060 Warsaw.

Wydzial Architektury, Politechnika Warszawska, 00-659 Warsaw.

Wydzial Architektury, Politechnika Wroclawska, 50-137 Wroclaw.

South Africa

School of Architecture, University of the Orange Free State, Bloemfontein 9300.

School of Architecture, University of Cape Town, Cape Town 7700.

School of Architecture, University of Natal, Durban 4001.

School of Architecture, University of the Witwatersrand, Johannesburg 2001.

School of Architecture, Summerstrand Campus, University of Port Elizabeth, Port Elizabeth 6001.

School of Architecture, University of Pretoria, Pretoria 0001.

Spain

Escuela Técnica Superior de Arquitectura, Barcelona 14.

Escuela Técnica Superior de Arquitectura, Ciudad Universitaria, Madrid 3.

Escuela Técnica Superior de Arquitectura, Ciudad Universitaria de Navarra, Pamplona.

Escuela Técnica Superior de Arquitectura, Universidad, Politecnica de Valencia, Valencia 10.

Escuela Técnica Superior de Arquitectura, Facultad de Ciencias Exactas de la Facultad de Valladolid, Valladolid.

Sweden

School of Architecture, Chalmers University of Technology, 40220 Göteborg 5.

Institute of Architecture, The Institute of Technology, 522007 Lund.

Nordic Institute for Studies in Urban and Regional Planning (Nordiska Institutet för samhälls-planering) S-111 49 Stockholm.

Switzerland

Ecole d'Architecture de l'Université de Genève, 1205 Geneva.

Ecole Polytechnique Fédérale de Lausanne, 1007 Lausanne.

Abt. für Architektur. Eidgenossische Technische Hochschule (E.T.H.) Zürich, 8006 Zurich.

Turkey

Ankara State Academy of Engineering and Architecture, Department of Architecture, Ankara.

Middle East Technical University, Faculty of Architecture, Department of Architecture, Ankara.

Edirne State Academy of Engineering and Architecture, Department of Architecture, Edirne.

Istanbul State Academy of Engineering and Architecture, Department of Architecture, Istanbul.

Istanbul State Academy of Engineering and Architecture, Kadiköy School of Engineering, Istanbul.

Istanbul State Academy of Fine Arts, Department of Architecture, Istanbul.

Istanbul Technical University, Faculty of Architecture, Istanbul.

Istanbul Technical University, Faculty of Architecture and Engineering, Department of Architecture, Istanbul.

Ege University, Faculty of Fine Arts, Department of Environmental Design, Izmir.

Karadeniz Technical University, Faculty of Civil Engineering and Architecture, Department of Architecture, Karadeniz.

Konya State Academy of Engineering and Architecture, Department of Architecture, Konya.

Union of Soviet Socialist Republics

Kazakh Polytechnic Institute, Alma-Ata.

Azerbaïdjan Polytechnic Institute, Baku.

Tadjikistan Polytechnic Institute, Duchanbe.

Erevan Polytechnic Institute, Erevan.

Polytechnic Institute of Georgia, Georgia.

Kaunas Polytechnic Institute, Kaunas.

Kharkov Civil Engineering Institute, Kharkov.

Kiev State Art Institute, Kiev.

Leningrad Civil Engineering Institute, Leningrad.

Leningrad I. E. Repin Institute of the Arts, Leningrad.

Lvov Polytechnic Institute, Lvov.

Byelorussian Polytechnic Institute, Minsk.

All Union Research Institute of Technical Aesthetics, Moscow. (branches in other cities of the U.S.S.R.)

Novosibirsk Institute of Electrical Engineering, Novosibirsk.

Riga Polytechnic Institute, Riga.

Rostov-on-Don Civil Engineering Institute, Rostov/Don.

Urals S. M. Kirov Polytechnic Institute, Sverdlovsk.

Estonian S.S.R. State Arts Institute, Tallinn.

Tashkent Polytechnic Institute, Tashkent.

Tbilisi Academy of Arts, Tbilisi.

Lithuanian S.S.R. State Arts Institute, Vilnius.

United States of America

College of Architecture and Urban Planning, University of Michigan, Ann Arbor, MI.

College of Architecture, Georgia Institute of Technology, Atlanta, GA.

School of Environmental Design, Louisiana State University, Baton Rouge, LA.

College of Environmental Design, University of California, Berkeley, CA.

Department of Architecture, Harvard University, Cambridge, MA.

Department of Architecture, Massachusetts Institute of Technology, Cambridge, MA.

School of Architecture, University of Virginia, Charlottesville, VA.

College of Architecture, Planning and Design, Illinois Institute of Technology, Chicago, IL.

Department of Architecture, University of Illinois at Chicago Circle, Chicago, IL.

Department of Architecture, Cornell University, Ithaca, NY.

School of Architecture and Urban Planning, University of California, Los Angeles, CA.

School of Architecture, Yale University, New Haven, CT.

School of Architecture, Tulane University, New Orleans, LA.

School of Engineering and Architecture, CUNY City College, New York, NY.

Department of Architecture, Columbia University, New York, NY.

School of Architecture, Cooper Union, New York, NY.

Department of Architecture, University of Pennsylvania, Philadelphia, PA.

School of Architecture and Urban Planning, Princeton University, Princeton, NJ.

Department of Architecture, Rhode Island School of Design, Providence, RI.

School of Architecture, Washington University, St. Louis, MO.

School of Architecture and Environmental Design, California Polytechnic State University, San Luis Obispo, CA.

Department of Architecture, University of Illinois at Urbana-Champaign, Urbana, IL.

College of Architecture and Urban Planning, University of Washington, Seattle, WA.

School of Architecture, Rensselaer Polytechnic Institute, Troy, NY.

Venezuela

Departamento de Diseño y Estudios Urbanos, Universidad Simón Bolívar, Caracas, D.F.

Facultad de Arquitectura y Urbanismo, Universidad Central de Venezuela, Caracas.

Facultad de Arquitectura, Universidad del Zulia, Maracaibo.

Facultad de Arquitectura, Universidad de Los Andes, Mérida.

Appendix B
PROFESSIONAL SOCIETIES AND ASSOCIATIONS

Argentina

Federación Argentina de Sociedades de Arquitectos, Caseros 344, Córdoba, Argentina.

Sociedad Central de Arquitectos, Montevideo 938, piso 1019, Buenos Aires, Argentina

Australia

Australian Council of National Trusts, 14 Martin Place, Sydney, New South Wales 2000. Preservation and enhancement of national estate.

Australian Institute of Landscape Architects, 2a Mugga Way, Red Hill, ACT 2603. Professional organization of landscape architects.

Australian Institute of Urban Studies, P.O. Box 809, Canberra City, ACT 2601. Promotion and coordination of urban research.

Cement and Concrete Association of Australia, 147 Walker Street, North Sydney, New South Wales 2060. Interest in all aspects of concrete construction.

Inner Sydney Regional Council for Social Development Cooperative Ltd., P.O. Box J240, Brickfield Hill, New South Wales 2000. Most resident action groups do not maintain regular mailing addresses. However, this cooperative acts as a resource center and information exchange for inner-city community groups.

Royal Australian Institute of Architects, 2a Mugga Way, Red Hill, ACT 2603. Professional organization of architects.

Royal Australian Planning Institute, 19 London Circuit, Canberra City, ACT 2601. Professional organization of planners. Interests include advocacy planning.

Austria

Fachverband der Bauindustrie, Engelberggasse 4, Vienna 1030.

Österreichischer Ingenieur- und Architektverein (Association of Austrian Engineers and Architects), Eschenbachgasse 9, Vienna 1010.

Zentralvereinigung der Architekten Österreichs (Central Association of Austrian Architects), Salvatorgasse 10, Vienna 1.

Belgium

La Fédération Royale des Sociétés d'Architectes de Belgique.

Bolivia

ANEC (Asociación Nacional de Empresas Consultoras). Register of firms specializing in branches of engineering; includes architectural studios.

CAB (Colegio de Arquitectos de Bolivia). The national professional association of architects.

INALPRE (Instituto Nacional de Preinversiones). Register of firms specializing in urbanism and architecture.

Canada

Alberta Association of Architects, Duggan House, 10515 Saskatchewan Drive, Edmonton, Alberta T6E 4S1.

Architects' Association of New Brunswick, P.O. Box 910, Rothesay, New Brunswick E0G 2W0.

Architects' Association of Prince Edward Island, Box 1766, Charlottetown, Prince Edward Island.

Architectural Conservancy of Ontario, 191 College Street, Toronto, Ontario M5T 1P7.

Architectural Institute of British Columbia, 970 Richards Street, Vancouver, British Columbia V6B 3C1.

Association of Architectural Technologists of Ontario, Suite 105, 1027 Yonge Street, Toronto, Ontario M4W 2K9.

The British Columbia Society of Landscape Architects, 970 Richards Street, Vancouver, British Columbia V6B 3C1.

Canadian Conference of University Schools of Architecture, Carleton University, School of Architecture, Ottawa, Ontario K1S 5B6.

The Canadian Society of Landscape Architects, P.O. Box 3304, Station C,. Ottawa, Ontario K1Y 4J5.

Manitoba Assocation of Architects, 710-177 Lombard, Winnipeg, Manitoba R3B 0W9.

Montreal Architectural Society/Societé d'architecture de Montréal, 1825 Dorchester Boulevard West, Montréal, Québec H3H 1R4.

Newfoundland Association of Architects, Box E, 5204, St. John's, Newfoundland A1C 5V5.

Nova Scotia Association of Architects, Suite 630, 5991 Spring Garden Road, Halifax, Nova Scotia B3H 1Y6.

Ontario Association of Architects, 50 Park Road, Toronto, Ontario M4W 2N5.

Order of Architects of Quebec/Ordre des Architects du Québec, 1825 Dorchester Boulevard West, Montréal, Québec H3H 1R4.

The Royal Architectural Institute of Canada (RAIC)/L'Institut Royal d'Architecture du Canada, 151 Slater Street, Suite 1104, Ottawa, Ontario K1P 5H3.

Saskatchewan Association of Architects, LML Phoenix House, 226-20th Street East, Saskatoon, Saskatchewan S7K 0A6.

Society for the Study of Architecture in Canada, Box 2935, Station D, Ottawa, Ontario K1P 5W9.

Chile

Association of Chilean Architects, Santiago.

China, People's Republic of

The Academy of Building Research, Beijing.

The Architectural Society of China, Beijing.

The Central-South Design Institute of Industrial Buildings at Wuhan, Hubei Province.

The Northeastern Architectural Design Institute at Shenyang, Liaonin Province.

The Northwestern Architectural Design Institute at Xian, Shanxi Province.

Shanghai Design Institute of Industrial Buildings, Shanghai.

The Southwestern Design Institute of Industrial Buildings at Chengdu, Sichuan Province.

Colombia

Sociedad Colombiana de Arquitectos.

Czechoslovakia

The Block of Progressive Unions of Architects (BAPS). Supra-organization of groups of professional architects.

The Union of Czechoslovak Architects.

Denmark

Federation of Danish Architects, Bredgade 66, 1260 Copenhagen K.

Finland

Arkkitehtitoimisto KRT, Huvilakatu 14, 00150 Helsinki 15.

Finlands Arkitekförbund Unionkatu 30, 00100 Helsinki 10.

France

Académie d'Architecture, 9, place des Vosges, 75004 Paris.

Association des Ingénieurs Architectes, 2, rue des Petits Ponts, 92140 Clamart.

Conseil Supérieur de l'Ordre des Architectes, 10, rue Portalis, 75008 Paris.

Société des Architectes Diplômés par le Gouvernement, 100, rue du Cherche-Midi, 75279 Paris, Cédex 06.

Union Internationale des Architectes, 1, rue d'Ulm, 75005 Paris. Branches of this organization, headquartered in Paris, exist in several countries throughout the world.

Germany, Democratic Republic of (DDR)

Bund der Architekten der DDR, Breite Strasse 36, 102 Berlin.

Germany, Federal Republic of (BRD)

Bund Deutscher Architekten (BDA, The Association of German Architects) is the leading organization. Within this there are chapters in each of the federal provinces. Membership requires the indication of several completed, artistically qualified buildings. Organizations of architects exist in each federal province. Qualifications for membership are demonstrable completion of architectural education and three to ten years of practice. Only listed members may submit project for building.

Akademie der Künste (Architektur), Hanseatenweg 10, Berlin 21.

Deutscher Architekten-und Ingenieuverband e. V., 53 Theaterplatz 2, Bonn-Bad Godesberg 1.

Deutsche Gesellschaft für Bauingenieurwesen e. V. (Constructional Engineering), Barbarossaplatz 2, Karlsruhe 75.

Deutscher Verband für Wohnungswesen, Stadtebau und Raumplanung e. V. (German Federation for Housing and Planning), Wrangelstr. 12, 5 Cologne-Mühlheim.

Hauptverband der Deutschen Bauindustrie e.V., Abraham-Lincoln Strasse 30, Postfach 2966, Wiesbaden 6200.

Informationsverbundzentrum Raum und Bau der Fraunhofer Gesellschaft (Information Center of Planning and Construction), Silberburgstr. 119A, Stuttgart 7000.

Great Britain

The Architectural Association Incorporated, 34 Bedford Square, London WC1. Membership open to all those genuinely interested in architecture and related matters. Facilities include a library, slide library, exhibition and lecture rooms, and restaurant and bar. The association runs its own school of architecture (which is world renowned and the only one in Britain outside the publicly financed university and polytechnic framework of higher education), publishes a journal (*The Architectural Association Quarterly*), and has a program of lectures and exhibitions for members and the public.

Commonwealth Association of Architects, 17 Northumberland Avenue, London WC2N5AP. Branches of this organization, headquartered in London, exist in Commonwealth countries around the world.

The Royal Institute of British Architects, 66 Portland Place, London W1. The professional institute of British architects controls the standards of practice and education. Membership is open only to those who qualify by examination at schools of architecture recognized by the institute for such purposes in Britain, the Commonwealth, and the European Economic Community. Facilities include a library, exhibition and lecture rooms, and a cafeteria and bar. The institute publishes a monthly journal and has a program of lectures and exhibitions. It also runs a Clients Advisory Service.

Greece

Greek Architects' Association (SADAS), 3 Ipiti Street, Athens 118.

Technical Chamber of Greece, 4 Karageorgi Servias Street, Athens 125.

Hungary

Society of Hungarian Architects (MÉSZ), Dienes Lajos u. 2, 1088 Budapest VIII.

Scientific Society for Building (ÉTE), Kossuth Lajos tér 6-8, 1055 Budapest V.

Israel

Association of Engineers and Architects in Israel, 200 Dizengoff Street, Tel Aviv.

Italy

ANCE—Associazione Nazionale Costruttori Edili, Rome.

ANIAI—Associazione Nazionale Ingegneri e Architetti Italiani, Rome.

APAO—Associazione per l'Architettura Organica Rome (presently disbanded).

Collegio Costruttori Edili (provincial or regional).

Collegio Lombardo Architetti, Milan.

Consiglio Nazionale degli Architetti, Rome.

Consiglio Nazionale degli Ingegneri, Rome.

IACP—Istituto Autonomo Caso Popolari (provincial) Accademia di S. Luca, Rome.

INARCH—Istituto Nazionale di Architettura, Rome (divided into regional sections), Palazzo Taverna, Via di Monte Giordano 36, Rome.

INU—Istituto Nazionale di Urbanistica, Rome (divided into regional sections), Via S. Caterina da Siena 46, Rome.

Italia Nostra—Associazione Nazionale per la Tutela del Patrimonio Storico Artistico e Naturale della Nazione (National Association for the Preservation of the Historical, Artistic, and Natural Heritage of the Nation), Corso Vittorio Emanuele 287, Rome.

MIAR—Movimento Italiano per l'Architettura Razionale, Milan (presently disbanded).

Ordine Architetti (provincial).

Ordine Ingegneri (provincial).

SAIE—Salone Internazionale dell'Industrializzazione Edilizia, Bologna.

Sindacato Architetti Liberi Professionisti (provincial or regional).

Sindacato Ingegneri Liberi Professionisti (provincial or regional).

Societa Ingegneri e Architetti, Turin.

UIA—Union Internationale Architectes (Italian section, Rome), Rome.

Japan

Architectural Institute of Japan. Headquarters: Tokyo. This is the main scientific organization devoted to the advancement and development of science, technology, and art of architecture through mutual cooperation among its members. Membership includes architects, architectural engineers, architectural historians, and anyone in a related field.

The Building Center of Japan, Tokyo. Objectives and nature: (1) Documentation of technical information in building; (2) Cooperation and coordination with research organizations in building and related fields; (3) Contact with building centers in other countries.

Japan Architects Association. Headquarters: Tokyo. This is the Japan Section of the International Union of Architects (UIA). Membership is restricted to professional architects.

Mexico

Asociación de Ingenieros y Arquitectos de México (Association of Mexican Engineers and Architects), 3A Calle del Puente de Alvarado 58, Mexico, D.F.

El Colegio Nacional, Luis González Obregón 23, Mexico 1, D.F. Government body for the promulgation of national culture.

Sociedad de Arquitectos Mexicanos, Avenida Constituyentes Núm, 161, Mexico City.

Netherlands

Architectura et Amicitia (A et A), Waterlooplein 67, Amsterdam.

Koninklijke Maatschapp tot Bevordering der Bouwkunst Bond van Nederlandse Architecten (BNA) (Royal Institute of Dutch Architects), P.O.B. 19606, Keizersgracht 321, 1000 GP Amsterdam.

Norway

Association of Norwegian Architects (Norske Arkitekters Lansforbund) Josefine, gate 34, Oslo 3.

South Africa

Institute of Town and Regional Planners, P.O. Box 61019, Marshalltown, Johannesburg 2107.

South African Institute of Architects, P.O. Box 31750, Braamfontein, Johannesburg 2017.

Sweden

Royal Academy of Fine Arts, Fredsgatan 12, Box 16317, 103-26 Stockholm 16.

Svenska Arkitekters Riksforbund (National Association of Swedish Architects), Odengatan 3, 114 24 Stockholm.

Switzerland

Bund Schweizer Architekten—Federatión des Architectes Suisses, Hotelgasse 1, Berne 3011.

Societé Suisse des Ingenieurs et des Architectes, Selnaustr. 16, Zurich 8039.

Turkey

Chamber of Architects of Turkey, Ankara.

Society of Environmental Sciences, Ankara.

Society of Urban Planners, Ankara.

Society of Landscape Architects, Ankara.

Union of Soviet Socialist Republics

The Union of Soviet Architects, Moscow.

United States of America

American Institute of Architects (AIA), 1735 New York Avenue NW, Washington, DC 20006. (18 regional groups, 50 state groups, 221 local groups)

American Planning Association (formerly AIP and ASPO), 1776 Massachusetts Avenue NW, Washington, DC 20036.

American Society of Landscape Architects (ASLA), 1900 M Street NW, No. 750, Washington, DC 20036.

Association of Women in Architecture (AWA), 7440 University Drive, St. Louis, MO 63130.

Council of American Building Officials (CABO), 560 Georgetown Building, 2233 Wisconsin Avenue NW, Washington, DC 20007.

Metropolitan Association of Urban Designers and Environmental Planners (MAUDEP), P.O. Box 722, Church Street Station, New York, NY 10008.

National Association of Housing and Redevelopment Officials (NAHRO), 2600 Virginia NW, Washington, DC 20037.

Society of American Registered Architects, 2011 West Pershing Road, Chicago, IL 60609.

Society of Architectural Historians, 1700 Walnut Street, Room 716, Philadelphia, PA 19103.

Venezuela

Colegio de Arquitectos de Venezuela, Apdo. 5262, Caracas.

Federación Panamericana de Asociaciones de Arquitectos (FPAA), Avenida San Juan Besco Centro Altamira, Mezzanina Officinas 6Y7, Chacao, Caracas 106.

Justa Nacional Protectora y Conservadore del Patrimonio Histórico y Artístico de la Nación, Caracas.

APPENDIX C

AGENCIES CONCERNED WITH ARCHITECTURE AND PLANNING

Argentina

Instituto de Planeamiento Regional y Urbano, Mexico 625-piso 5, 1097 Buenos Aires.

Instituto Torcuato Di Tella, Center for Urban and Regional Studies, Buenos Aires.

Australia

NATIONAL

Albury-Wodonga Development Corporation, P.O. Box 913, Albury, New South Wales 2640. Responsibilities for the development of a growth center at Albury-Wodonga.

Architecture and Design Panel. The Australia Council, P.O. Box 302, North Sydney, New South Wales 2060. Promotion of an awareness of excellence in all aspects of design including engineering, industrial and architectural design.

Australian Heritage Commission, P.O. Box 1567, Canberra City, ACT 2601. Activities include the establishment and maintenance of the Register of the National Estate and encouragement of research and education programs.

C.S.I.R.O., Building Research Division, P.O. Box 56, Highett, Victoria 3190. Research activities from basic materials science and applied development studies, through structural engineering, thermal and acoustic behavior to operations, economics, urban planning, and social studies of the built environment.

C.S.I.R.O., Mechanical Engineering Division, P.O. Box 26, Highett, Victoria 3190. Activities include research in the fields of utilization of recoverable energy resources and human environmental engineering and noise control.

Department of Aboriginal Affairs, P.O. Box 17, Woden, ACT 2606. Responsibility for the development and administration of national policies directed to the advancement of the Aboriginal people and the coordination of programs.

Department of Housing and Construction, P.O. Box 111, Dickson, ACT 2602. Responsibility for national housing policy, policy for the building and construction industry, and for the planning, design, construction, and maintenance of Australian government buildings.

Department of National Development and Energy, P.O. Box 5, Canberra, ACT 2600. Responsibility for national energy policy. Interests include decentralization, urban planning, and development.

Department of Science and the Environment, P.O. Box 449, Woden, ACT 2606. Responsibility for national policy for science, technology, and the environment. Interests include conservation, management, and protection of the environment.

Department of Social Security, P.O. Box 1, Woden, ACT 2606. Providing income security and associated welfare services to the community and planning social advancement. Interests include aged persons' housing.

Experimental Building Station, P.O. Box 30, Chatswood, New South Wales 2067. Research into building technology and the application of research to the design of buildings for Australian conditions. Interests include climate control and sun control.

National Capital Development Commission, P.O. Box 373, Canberra City, ACT 2601. The planning and development of the City of Canberra as the national capital of Australia.

Schools Commission, P.O. Box 34, Woden, ACT 2606. Advisory role to Australian government on schools. Activities include the establishment of acceptable standards and the investigation of improved designs for school buildings.

LOCAL (in order of states)

Bathurst-Orange Development Corporation, P.O. Box 143, Bathurst, New South Wales 2795. Established to develop the growth center of Bathurst-Orange.

Department of Environment and Planning, Box 3927,

G.P.O., Sydney, New South Wales 2001. To promote and coordinate town and country planning and to secure the orderly and economic development and use of land.

Government Architect's Branch, NSW Department of Public Works, State Office Block, 47-90 Phillip Street, Sydney, New South Wales 2000. Design and construction of new state government buildings and major renovations of older government buildings. Particularly noted for development of new school designs.

Housing Commission of NSW, 203 Castlereagh Street, Sydney, New South Wales 2000. Provisions of housing for low-income earners. Activities include inner-city housing.

Architectural Branch, Department of Works, Executive Building, 100 George Street, Brisbane, Queensland 4000. State construction authority.

Planning and Environment Section, Coordinator General's Department, Executive Building, 100 George Street, Brisbane, Queensland 4000. State town planning authority.

Queensland Housing Commission, G.P.O. Box 690, Brisbane, Queensland 4000. State housing authority.

Architect-in-Chief, Public Buildings Department, State Administration Centre, Victoria Square, Adelaide, South Australia 5000. State construction authority.

State Planning Authority, G.R.E. Building, 50 Grenfell Street, Adelaide, South Australia 5000. State town planning authority.

South Australian Housing Trust, 17 Angas Street, Adelaide, South Australia 5000. State housing authority.

Construction Division, Department of Housing and Construction, 10 Murray Street, Hobart, Tasmania 7000. State construction authority.

Department of Planning and Development, Savings Bank of Tasmania Building, 39 Murray Street, Hobart, Tasmania 7000. State town planning authority.

Housing Division, Department of Housing and Construction, Farley Street, Glenorchy, Tasmania 7010. State housing authority.

Department of Public Works, 2 Treasury Place, Melbourne, Victoria 3002. State construction authority.

Housing Commission, Victoria, 179 Queen Street, Melbourne, Victoria 3000. State housing authority.

Town and Country Planning Board, 235 Queen Street, Melbourne, Victoria 3000. State town planning authority.

Architectural Division, Public Works Department, 2 Havelock Street, West Perth, Western Australia 6005. State construction authority.

State Housing Commission, 99 Plain Street, East Perth, Western Australia 6000. State housing authority.

Town Planning Board, Oakleigh Building, 22 St. George Terrace, Perth, Western Australia 6000. State planning authority.

Austria

Ministry of Building and Technology, Vienna.

Bolivia

Alcaldias Municipales (Mayors' offices) of each city.

CONAVI (Consejo Nacional de Vivienda) plans, finances, and constructs public housing. It is organized in various subcouncils concerned, for instance, with housing for the military, miners, factory workers, etc.

CONEPLAN (Ministerio de Planificación) assigns priorities to projects, assists in financial arrangements for regional and urban planning studies, and works throughout the country.

CONES (Consejo Nacional de Edificaciones Escolares) designs and supervises projects and works in the realm of education from elementary through normal school.

Corporaciones de Desarrollo—one in each of the nine administrative departments of Bolivia.

Ministry of Urbanism and Housing supervises and elaborates development plans.

SENDU (Secretaría Nacional de Desarrollo Urbano) provides technical assistance and assists in financial arrangements for municipal development throughout the country.

Canada

Canadian Centre for Architecture/Centre Canadien d'Architecture, 1440 St. Catherine West, Montreal, H3g 1R8.

Canadian Housing Design Council, CMHC National Office, Montreal Road, Ottawa, Ont. K1A 0P7.

Central Mortgage and Housing Corp. (CMHC), Montreal Road, Ottawa, Ont.

Construction Industry Development Council, 235 Queen St., Ottawa, Ont.

Heritage Canada, P.O. Box 1358, Station B, Ottawa, Ont. H1P 5R4.

Héritage Montréal, 318 Bonsecours, Montréal, Qué.

Housing and Urban Development Association of Canada, 15 Toronto St., 10th Floor, Toronto, Ont. M5C 2E3.

China, People's Republic of

Provincial, municipal, and autonomous regional agencies of all provinces, cities, and autonomous regions are entitled: Architectural Design Institute, Design Institute of City Planning, City Construction Bureau, Institute of Building Research, etc.

Colombia

Banco Central Hipotecario, Carrera 6 No. 51-32, Bogotá, D.E.

Caja de la Vivienda Popular, Calle 14 No. 7-19, piso 11, Bogotá, D.E.

Cámara Colombiana de la Construcción, Carrera 10 No. 19-65, oficina 1002, Bogotá, D.E.

Centro Nacional de Estudios de la Construcción (CENAC), Ciudad Universitaria, Carrera 30, Calle 45, Edificio Cinva.

Corporación Nacional de Turismo, Dirección de Assesoría y Proyectos, Calle 28 No. 13A-15, piso 16, Bogotá, D.E.

Instituto Colombiano de Construcciones Escolares, Centro Administrativo Nacional CAN, Edificio de Mineducación, piso 2°, Bogotá, D.E.

Instituto de Crédito Territorial (ICT), Carrera 13 No. 18-51, Bogotá, D.E.

Instituto de Desarrollo Urbano de Bogotá, Distrito Especial. Carrera 7 No. 20-99, Bogotá, D.E.

Ministerio de Obras Públicas y Transporte, Dirección General de Inmeubles Nacionales, Centro Administrativo Nacional CAN, Bogotá, D.E.

Cuba

Ministry of Construction, Havana. In socialist Cuba the Ministry of Construction is responsible by and large for design, construction, engineering, etc., has many regional offices, and closely integrates its policies with other strata of the bureaucracy, especially various planning boards.

Czechoslovakia

Institute of Architectural Studies and Standardization, Prague and Bratislava.

Institute of Building and Architecture of the Slovak Academy of Sciences.

Institute of Town and Country Planning.

Research Institute of Construction and Architecture.

State Institute for the Reconstruction of Historical Towns and Buildings, Prague.

Stavoprojekt(s)—Collective Architectural Design Institutes.

Denmark

Danish Town Planning Institution, Tordenskjoldsgade 10, 1055 Copenhagen.

France

Agence d'architecture de l'opération Maine-Montparnasse, 17, rue de l'Arrivée, 75015 Paris.

Agence d'urbanisme de l'agglomération bordelaise, 105, rue d'Ornano, 33000 Bordeaux.

Agence d'urbanisme de l'agglomération marseillaise, Parc Valmer, 272, corniche Kennedy, 13208 Marseille, Cédex 1.

Agence d'urbanisme de l'agglomération strasbourgeoise, 6, avenue du Général de Gaulle, 67000 Strasbourg.

Agence d'urbanisme de la communauté urbaine de Brest et son environnement, 13, rue Védrines, 29200 Brest.

Agence d'urbanisme de la région grenoblaise, Hôtel de Ville, Boulevard Jean Pain, B.P. 3, 38001 Grenoble.

Atelier normand d'aménagement urbain et rural, 32, rue d'Ernemont, 76000 Rouen.

Atelier Parisien d'urbanisme (APUR), 17, boulevard Morland, 75181 Paris, Cédex 04

Germany, Democratic Republic of (DDR)

Bauakademie der DDR, Plauener Strasse, 1125 Berlin.

Institut für Denkmalpflege in der DDR, Brüderstrasse 13, 102 Berlin.

Institut für Kulturbauten, Clara-Zetkin-Strasse 105, 108 Berlin.

Germany, Federal Republic of (BRD)

Bundesministerium für Raumordnung, Bauwesen, und Städtebau (Minister of Regional Planning, Construction, and Urbanism), Hausdorfstr. 105, Bonn. (Branches in all the federal provinces are part of the Ministry of the Interior)

Great Britain

The Building Centre, 26 Store Street, London WC1. The main purpose of the center is to provide information on building products and services. There is a permanent exhibition of materials and fittings and a library, information service, and bookshop. It is open to the public.

The Building Research Establishment, Garston near Watford. The official government center for all aspects of building research. It publishes papers and practical bulletins on its findings.

The Department of the Environment, 2 Marsham Street, London SW1. The ministry is responsible for all government buildings and also for the control of all environmental matters. In addition to the research carried out at the Building Research Establishment the department conducts other research and studies, particularly in the field of housing. The department embraces the Historic Monuments Division and its own design organization known as the Property Services Agency.

The Greater London Council Architect's Department, North Block, County Hall, London SE1, has an information service which is invaluable in visiting and studying buildings designed by or for the GLC. It also publishes regular reviews of its work and related studies.

Greece

Center for Programming and Economic Research (K.E.P.E.), 22 Hippocratous Street, Athens.

Greek Tourist Organization (E.O.T.), 2b Amerikis Street, Athens.

Ministry of Public Works, Department of the Athens Master Plan, Phidippidou 31, Athens.

Ministry of Public Works, Department of Housing, Pouliou and Amaliados Street, Athens.

National Statistical Service of Greece (E.S.Y.E.), 14-16 Lycourgou Street, Athens.

Organization for Workers' Housing, Studies Division, 37 Patision and Stournara Street, Athens 146.

Hungary

Hungarian Academy of Sciences, including the Committee of Architectural History and Theory, Committee of Building Sciences, Committee of Urbanistic Sciences, Münnich Ferenc u.7, 1051 Budapest V.

Israel

The Building Centre of Israel, P.O. Box 7102, Tel Aviv.

Building and Industry Research Institute of the Association of Engineers and Architects in Israel, 200 Dizengoff Street, Tel Aviv, P.O. Box 6572.

Desert Research Institute, Sdeh Boker, Negev.

Israel Ministry of Building and Housing, Hakirya Street D-4, Tel Aviv (Design Department): Hillel Street, Jerusalem (Ministry).

Israel Ministry of the Interior, Department of Planning, Hakirya, Jerusalem.

Settlement Study Center, Rehovot.

Technion: Center for Urban and Regional Studies, Haifa.

Technion: Research and Development Foundation, Building Research Station, Haifa.

Japan

Environmental Department, Prime Minister's Office, Department of Cultural Affairs, Ministry of Education. For cultural properties protection.

Industrial Science and Technology, Ministry of International Trade and Industry.

Japan Housing Corporation.

Ministry of Construction. For planning, city, housing, regional construction.

National Land Department, Prime Minister's Office. For planning, land adjustment within the boundaries of large cities.

Mexico

Comisión Federal de Electricidad, Ródano 4. México 5, D.F.

Fondo de la Vivienda del Instituto de Seguridad Social al Servicio de los Trabajadores del Estado. Balderas 58. México 1, D.F.

Instituto del Fondo Nacional de la Vivienda para los Trabajadores. Barranca del Muerto 280. México 19, D.F.

Instituto Nacional para el desarrollo de la comunidad rural y de la vivienda popular. Niños Heroes 139. México 7, D.F.

Secretaria de Agricultura y Recursos Hidraulicos. Insurgentes Sur 476. México 7, D.F.

Secretaría de Asentamientos Humanos y Obras Públicas. Constituyentes 947. México 10, D.F.

Netherlands

Architects' Registration Council, Keizersgracht 321, 1016EE, P.O. B19611, 1000 GP Amsterdam.

Dutch Documentation Center of Architecture (NDB), Nederlands Documentatiecentrum voor de Bouwkunst, Droogbak, 12 Amsterdam.

Government Department for the Preservation of Historical Monuments, Broederplein 41, Zeist.

Ministry of Culture (CRM)

Ministry of Housing and Planning (MURO).

Norway

Ministry of Environment (Miljøverndepartementet) Myntgaten 2, Oslo 1.

Ministry of Local Government and Labor (Kommunal-og arbeidsdepartementet) Pilestredet 33, Oslo 1.

Norwegian Building Research Institute (Norges byggforskningsinstitutt, NBI) Forskningsveien 3 b, Oslo 3.

Norwegian Institute of Urban and Regional Research (Norsk institutt for by-og regionforskning, NIBR) Nycoveien 1, Oslo 4.

Royal Norwegian Council for Scientific and Industrial Research (Norges teknisk-naturvitenskapelige forskningsraad NTNF) Sognsveien 72, Oslo 3.

Poland

"Bibrohut" (Design Office of Iron and Steel Industry), ul. Dubois 16, 44-100 Cliwice.

"Biprowlók" (Study and Design Office for Textile Industry), ul. Glówna 12, 90-050 Lódź. Design of light industry building.

"Bistyp" (Research and Design Center for Industrial Building), ul. Parkingowa 1, 00-518 Warsaw. Design and typification of industrial building, computer-aided design.

CTK (Center of Municipal Engineering), ul. Filtrowa 57, 02-056 Warsaw.

COBPBO (Research and Design Center for General Building, ul. Wierzbowa 11, 00-094 Warsaw. Design and typification of general building.

"Elektroprojekt" (Study and Design Office for Industrial Electrical Equipment), ul. Swietkrzyska 18, 00-052 Warsaw. Design of electrical installations and equipment in building.

"Energoprojekt" (Main Study and Design Office for Power Industry), ul. Krucza 6/14, 00-950 Warsaw.

Glówne Biuro Studiów i Projektów Górniczych (Main Study and Design Office for Mining Industry), 40-950 Katowice, Pl. Grunwaldzki 8-10. Design of mining building.

"Instalprojekt" (Design Office for Industrial Installations), ul. Świętokrzyska 18, 00-052 Warsaw. Design of industrial installations and ventilation systems in building.

Mostostal (Research and Design Center for Metal Structures), ul. Krucza 20-22, 00-926 Warsaw. Design of metal building structures.

"Prochem" (Enterprise for Design and Realization of Chemical Industry Projects), ul. Wspólna 32-46, 00-512 Warsaw. Design of chemical industry building.

"Transprojekt" (Central Design and Research Office for Road and Bridge), ul. Wileńska 10, 00-987 Warsaw. Design of road and bridge.

South Africa

Building Industries Federation.

Department of Community Development, Pretoria.

Department of Planning and Design, City Council of Cape Town.

National Building Research Steering Committee.

National Development and Management Foundation.

National Housing Commission.

Simon van der Stel Foundation, Raadsaal, Church Square, Pretoria.

South African Institute of Housing Management.

Sweden

The National Swedish Institute of Building Research, S-801 29 Gavle, Sweden.

Turkey

Iller Bankasi (Bank of Municipalities).

Master Plan Bureau of Metropolitan Istanbul, Ankara, Izmir, and Samsun.

Ministry of Construction and Planning.

Ministry of Public Works.

Union of Soviet Socialist Republics

The Academy of Architecture of the USSR. Moscow.

The All-Union Concilium of Builders, Architects, and Representatives of Industrial Ministries.

Committee on Architectural Affairs of the Soviet of Ministries of the USSR.

United States of America

Advisory Council on Historic Preservation, 1522 K St. NW, Washington,DC.

American Heritage Foundation, Old City Hall, 45 School St., Boston, MA 02108.

Architectural League of New York, 41 E. 65th St., New York, NY 10021.

Automated Procedures for Engineering Consultants (APEC), Miami Valley Tower, Suite 2100, Dayton, OH 45402.

Department of Housing and Urban Development, 451 7th St. SW, Washington, DC.

Federal Housing Administration, 451 7th St. SW, Washington, DC.

Frank Lloyd Wright Association, P.O. Box 2100, Oak Park, IL 60303.

Institute for Architecture and Urban Studies, 8 West 40th St., New York, NY 10018.

National Council of Architectural Registration Boards (NCARB), 1735 New York Ave. NW, Suite 700, Washington, DC 20006.

National Endowment for the Arts, Architectural and Environmental Arts, 2401 E St. NW, Washington, DC.

National Trust for Historic Preservation, 740 Jackson Pl. NW, Washington, DC.

Office of Preservation Services, National Trust for Historic Preservation, 1785 Massachusetts Ave. NW, Washington, DC 20036.

Venezuela

Dirección Géneral de Desarrollo Urbanistico del Ministerio del Desarrollo Urbano, Caracas.

INDEX TO BUILDINGS

Numbers in **boldface** indicate pages with illustrations.

GENERAL INDEX

Numbers in **boldface** indicate pages with illustrations.

ABOUT THE CONTRIBUTORS

MARLENE MILAN ACAYABA, a graduate of the School of Architecture and Planning of the University of São Paulo in 1973, worked at her husband's (Marcos Acayaba) office between 1972 and 1977, participating in several projects for residences and institutional buildings. After graduation she taught History of Architecture at the School of Architecture and Planning of Guarulhos until 1976. Now working towards a master's degree in history of architecture, her thesis subject is residential architecture in São Paulo from 1950 to 1970.

FRIEDRICH ACHLEITNER (b. 1930), architect, author, and educator, commands an unusually broad understanding of Austrian architecture of this century as attested by the numerous articles of architectural criticism that have issued from his pen since 1958. In 1965 he undertook the enormous task of systematically organizing knowledge of twentieth-century Austrian architecture into a three volume publication, *Österreichische Architektur im 20. Jahrhundert*, the first two volumes of which have appeared (1980, 1981). The third, on Vienna's architecture, is scheduled for publication in 1984. In 1953 Professor Achleitner received his diploma from Vienna's Akademie der Bildenden Künste after studying with the distinguished architect, Clemens Holzmeister, and launched his career as an architect in association with Johann Georg Gsteu. For a decade from 1962 he was also architecture critic for the Vienna daily newspaper, *Die Presse*. In 1963 he joined the faculty of the Akademie der Bildenden Künste, teaching the History of Architectural Construction and in 1968 became professor in that field at the same institution. Professor Achleitner has also offered courses at the Hochschule für Angewandte Kunst in Vienna since the early 1970s. Throughout the past score of years his architectural criticism has appeared and continues to appear in such journals as *Archithese*, *Alte und Moderne Kunst*, *Bau*, *Bauen und Wohnen*, *Domus*, *L'Architecture d'Aujourd'hui*, and *Bauwelt*.

JEAN BARTHELEMY (b. 1932) received his degree in civil engineering, specializing in construction, in 1956 at the University of Liège. In 1961 he took a degree in architectural engineering at the University of Louvain, having also studied under Professor Konrad Wachsmann (of the University of Southern California) at the 1960 Salzburg International Seminar in Architecture. In 1966 he was awarded the E. J. Van de Ven Biennial Prize in Architecture. Professor of Architecture at the Polytechnic Faculty of Mons since 1968, he successfully combines an active career as an architect and planner with teaching, and a broad range of publishing in such journals as *La Maison*, *Revue A+*, and the *Revue de la Fédération Royale des Sociétés d'Architectes de Belgique*.

CLAUDE BERGERON (Ph.D. Princeton University) teaches in the Department of Architecture at Laval University in Quebec City, is currently coeditor of RACAR (*Revue d'art canadienne/Canadian Art Review*), and secretary of the Society for the Promotion of Art History Publications in Canada.

JÁNOS BONTA has a broad-ranging knowledge of the contemporary architectural scene in the major cities of Hungary and a perspective upon that country's varied architectural developments during the past centuries. He is Professor at the Technical

University of Budapest and Director of its Institute of History and Theory of Architecture.

YVES BRUAND (b. 1926) gained a well-balanced view of architectural history and criticism during his studies in France (Sorbonne, Ecole des Chartes, Ecole du Louvre), in Rome at the French School (1952-1954) and in Madrid (1954-1955). From 1960 through 1969 he was Professor of Art History at the University of São Paolo in Brazil, returning to France in 1969 as professor at the University of Toulouse-le-Mirail. His doctoral dissertation *L'architecture contemporaine au Bresil* (1971) is a fundamental document of recent architectural history. Among the numerous articles he has published over the years, his principal interests have been in Medieval military architecture and the architecture of the twentieth century. Professor Bruand is currently Head of History of Art and Archaeology at the University of Toulouse-le-Mirail.

ROBERT BRUEGMANN worked with the Historic American Buildings Survey between 1973 and 1978 and has taught at the University of Pennsylvania and the Philadelphia College of Art. From 1977 he has taught Architectural History and Historic Preservation at the University of Illinois in Chicago. Since receiving his Ph.D. from the University of Pennsylvania in 1976, he has been a frequent contributor to such journals as *Planning Magazine*, *Preservation News*, and the *Journal of Architectural Education* published (1980) a book on the architecture of Benicia, an early California town established in 1846; and will soon publish a monograph on the Chicago architectural firm of Holabird and Roche/Holabird and Root. Professor Bruegmann has been the recipient of several honors including the Founders' Award of the Society of Architectural Historians for the best article published in its *Journal* of 1978.

FENG CHI-CHUNG (born in Kaifeng, China) studied at the Technical Higher School, Vienna, from 1936 to his graduation in 1941. Thereafter, he worked in several architectural offices in Vienna and returned to China after the Second World War. From 1947 to 1948 he was active as an architect and planner for the City Planning Board, Nanjing, and between 1949 and 1955 as an advisor of the City Planning Board, Shanghai, during which time he remained in active practice. In 1948 he became Professor of Architecture at Tongji University Shanghai. Professor Feng has been Dean of the School of Architecture at this university since 1956.

ADOLF CIBOROWSKI, Professor of Town Planning at Warsaw's Technical University, is recognized internationally for his expertise as an urban planner who has implemented strategies for the reconstruction and development of cities, including some largely destroyed during the Second World War. Chief architect of Warsaw (1956-1964), chief planner of the Polish National Housing Board (1950-1955), United Nations Project Manager for the Skopie (Yugoslavia) Reconstruction (1964-1969), and Deputy Director of the United Nations' Center for Housing, Building and Planning (1969-1973), he is currently Director of the Institute for Urban Design and Physical Planning at the Warsaw Technical University (1978-). Professor Ciborowski has consulted and lectured in various capacities throughout the world, directed United Nations seminars and meetings of international experts in urban development, is the bearer of Polish, Belgian, and Yugoslavian Orders, and has received the Fritz Schumacher award of the Federal Republic of Germany. Author of more than 250 publications in six languages, Professor Ciborowski's most recent book, *Environmental Policy* (in Polish), appeared in 1979.

SYLVIA FICHER worked at the Zezinho Magalhães Prado housing-complex project under the direction of architects João Batista Vilanova Artigas and Fabio Penteado until she graduated from the School of Architecture and Planning of the University of São Paulo in 1972. For two years after that, at Vilanova Artigas's office, she worked on such projects as the Porto Velho public high school (Rondônia) and the Jaú bus depot. In 1976 she went to the USA to take a master's degree in historic preservation at Columbia University. Back in Brazil since 1978, she is completing her Ph.D. at the School of Philosophy, Letters, and Social Sciences of the University of São Paulo, while teaching History of Brazilian Architecture at the School of Architecture and Planning of Santus and at the School of Fine Arts of São Paulo.

IGOR GOLOMSTOCK, art historian, has maintained his awareness of developments in Soviet architecture and art since leaving the Soviet Union and is frequently called upon for his knowledge of events there. In 1974 he was lecturer in Russian Studies at the University of Saint Andrews, Scotland, and presently holds the same post at the Taylorian Institute, Oxford University. A specialist in Renaissance and twentieth-century art and architecture, he is the author (with Andrei Sinyonsky) of a book on Picasso and of several monographs in Russian. While his primary interest remains modern Soviet architecture, perhaps best known of his publications in English now is *Unofficial Art from the Soviet Union* (London, 1977), coauthored with Alexander Glezer.

ELIZABETH D. HARRIS. As a doctoral candidate at the University of Chicago, Elizabeth Harris's initial contact with modern Latin American architecture was in 1974 during the tenure of a Fulbright Fellowship when she investigated the architecture and urban planning of Brasilia. At that time she travelled throughout South America, noting trends in contemporary architecture. Soon after she presented a graduate course, "Twentieth-Century Architecture and Urban Planning in Latin America," at the University of Wisconsin in Milwaukee. Her current research is focused upon Le Corbusier's trip to Brazil in 1936 and its ramifications. She presently resides in Rio de Janeiro.

GILBERT HERBERT is Mary Hill Swope Professor of Architecture at the Technion: Israel Institute of Technology, which he joined in 1968 having previously held teaching positions at the University of the Witwatersrand, Johannesburg and the University of Adelaide, South Australia. He was educated as an architect and planner at the University of the Witwatersrand (B. Arch., M. Arch., Dip. T.P.) and in the Art History Department of the University of South Africa (D. Litt. et Phil.) Dr. Herbert is the author of numerous papers on the theory and history of architecture and planning and of three books: *The Synthetic Vision of Walter Gropius* (1959); *Martienssen and the International Style* (1975); and *Pioneers of Prefabrication* (1978). For this work he was awarded the Architectural Writers and Critics Award of the South African Institute of Architects in 1979. In 1980-81 Professor Herbert lectured in Brazil, the United States, and Canada. Born in Johannesburg in 1924 Gilbert Herbert now lives in Israel with his wife and daughter.

H. WOUTER HUBERS (b. 1941) and **HEERO MEINDERSMA** (b. 1941) had worked together as part of a team on seven reports published since 1972 when they both began their association with the Research Instituut Gebouwde Omgeving (RIGO) in Amsterdam. Hubers attended the Academy of Architecture (at Waterlooplein 67), Amsterdam, between 1966 and 1977 after completing his studies in technical school in Amsterdam, and, since 1969 has maintained his own architectural office. Publications authored by him alone have been concerned particularly with housing in Amsterdam (1978). Meindersma attended the same Academy of Architecture (1965-1977) after technical school at Leeuwarden, and practiced architecture independently between 1969 and 1978, giving his time after that primarily to RIGO projects. His publications have ranged from an interest in the "Kasbah" at Hengelo (RIGO, 1978) to urban planning and architectural competitions in the Netherlands. Both authors are actively engaged, socially concerned architects.

EIZO INAGAKI (b. 1926), graduate of the University of Tokyo in 1948, has been a Professor of Japanese Architectural History at that same institution since 1973. He has spoken at architectural conferences frequently, contributed many articles to architectural journals, authored several books including *The Birth and Development of Modern Architecture in Japan* (1959) and *Shrines and Mausolea* (1968), and has coauthored *The Characteristics of Japanese Architecture* (1976).

EUGENE J. JOHNSON, Professor of Art and Chairman of the Department of Art at Williams College, Williamstown, Massachusetts, received his Ph.D. from the Institute of Fine Arts, New York University, in 1970. He is the author of *Sant'Andrea in Mantua, The Building History* (University Park, Pennsylvania, 1975) and is currently collaborating on a history of twentieth-century art, as author of the sections on architecture.

DOǦAN KUBAN (b. 1926) received his M. Architecture degree (1949) from the Istanbul Technical University, and began his academic career at the same university in 1952. After completing his doctoral dissertation (*An Essay on Turkish Baroque Architecture*, 1954) and his habilitation treatise (*The Development of Space in Classical Ottoman Architecture: A Comparison with Centralized Buildings of the Italian Renaissance*, 1957) also at the Istanbul Technical University, in 1961 he became chairman of the Department of History of Architecture and Restoration. A Fulbright research grant brought him to the University of Michigan as a visiting scholar in 1962-1963, and the following year he was Harvard Fellow at Dumbarton Oaks. Returned to Istanbul, he became full professor in 1965 with his thesis, *The Origins and Problems of Anatolian-Turkish Architecture*. From 1966 through 1977 Professor Kuban codirected the Harvard University-sponsored excavation and restoration of the Byzantine church, Kalenderhane, at Istanbul, a period broken by intervals as guest professor for History of Islamic Architecture at the University of Michigan (1967) and the University of Minnesota (1970). He was again Harvard Fellow at Dumbarton Oaks between 1977 and 1979; in 1980-1981 he was Visiting Aga Khan Professor of Architecture in the department of architecture at Massachusetts Institute of Technology. Since 1968 he has been a permanent member of Turkey's Superior Council of Monuments and from 1974 was also the director of the Institute of History of Architecture and Restoration. With his outstanding expertise in Islamic architecture he is a member of the steering committee for the Aga Khan Award for architecture. In addition to the works already mentioned Professor Kuban is the author of numerous articles and several books on architectural history, theory, criticism, and preservation of the historical environment.

NILS-OLE LUND (b. 1930) M.N.A.L., M.A.A., received his diploma of architecture in 1953 (Copenhagen) and practiced in Norway until 1973. He taught in the Department of Architecture at the Technical University, Trondheim, Norway, from 1963 until called in 1965 to a professorship at the school of Architecture in Aarhus, Denmark. In 1972 he became head of that school. Professor Lund has contributed articles to Danish and Norwegian architectural journals and published a book entitled *Teoridannelser i Arkiteturen* (1970). He is a member of the administrative council of the European Association for Architectural Education.

JAMES B. LYNCH, JR. (b. 1919). After completing his doctoral studies at Harvard University (1960) with a dissertation on the work of José Clemente Orozco, Professor Lynch continued to teach at Boston University until 1966, publishing on both Latin American and Italian Renaissance topics. In 1966 he accepted a professorship at the University of Maryland where he teaches now in the Department of Art. In the Latin American field he has published articles and reviews in the *Journal of Inter-American Studies*, the *Art of the Americas Bulletin*, the *Hispanic American Historical Review*, the *Art Journal* (on Cuban architecture, 1979), and has contributed to the *Encyclopedia of World Art* and McGraw-Hill's *Dictionary of Art*. Since 1968 among other activities Professor Lynch has served as contributing editor for the *Handbook of Latin American Studies*, consultant to the Library of Congress, and lecturer to the Foreign Service Institute of the U.S. State Department. He is presently gathering materials for a book on Cuban architecture.

SARAH McCUTCHEON's first-hand experiences of architecture during a stay in Finland in 1976 led, ultimately, to her participation in the writing of this chapter. Currently a student in Concordia University's M.F.A. program in Art History, she has contributed articles on art and architecture to such journals as *Arts Canada* and is completing a thesis relating to the architecture of nineteenth-century Montreal.

GUSTAVO MEDEIROS (b. 1939) distinguished himself in his architectural studies at the National University of Córdoba in Argentina where he was awarded a gold medal upon graduation in 1964. Returning to Bolivia, he taught at the University of Cochabamba until 1969. Particularly his work (at first with Franklin Anaya) in planning the University of Oruro from 1966 and in designing and supervising construction of many of its buildings to 1977 has brought him international recognition (*L'Architecture d'Aujourd'hui*, no. 173, 1974). Founder and director of the firm, Centro de Estudios y Proyectos Nueva Visión, in La Paz, he is largely responsible for the urban development and construction of "Los Pinos" in that city and for the large Laykacota Government Center project (not yet funded) for the center of La Paz. Professor at the University of La Paz since 1974, Medeiros has published a book (1975) on the University of Oruro and its place in urban and regional development and has also shown a concern for the historic buildings of Bolivia's capital in his carefully documented *La Paz: Casco Urbano Central (1977)*.

HEERO MEINDERSMA. *See* **H. WOUTERS HUBER**

RAMÓN ALFONSO MÉNDEZ is a leading architectural critic in Chile with an extraordinary knowledge of avant-garde developments since the thirties in that country. Professor at the University of Chile in Santiago for many years and practitioner of architecture as well, his publications include fundamental works on Chilean architecture in various journals and books.

WINFRIED NERDINGER (b. 1944) architectural engineer and critic of contemporary German art and architecture, was assistant at the Institute of Art

History of Munich's Technical University (1971-1975) and has pursued research on the Baūhaūs at Harvard University's Busch Reisinger Museum since September, 1979. He had been in charge of the "Architektursammlung" at the Technical University in Munich since 1975 and has published several articles on nineteenth- and twentieth-century art and architecture.

JOSÉ M. F. PASTOR, architect and urban and regional planner, has been Director of the (private) Institute of Urban and Regional Planning in Buenos Aires for a number of years. Among other accomplishments he replanned the city of San Juan, Argentina (population 40,000), that had been devastated in 1944 by an earthquake, and supervised the implementation of the first stage of its rebuilding (1949-1952). Mr. Pastor is concerned now especially with intra- and intergovernmental prerogatives for planning and building in response to the profound demographic changes that have occurred over the past thirty-five years and that are projected for the next quarter-century in the nations of South America.

JOSEF PECHAR, docent in architectural engineering, is Vice-Dean for Science and Research and occupies the Chair of Theory and Development of Architecture in the Faculty of Architecture at the Technical University of Prague.

DIMITRI PHILIPPIDES (b. 1938) has been Lecturer since 1975 at the School of Architecture and the National Technical University of Athens and has a private practice in architecture and planning. Philippides studied at the University of Michigan (Arch. D., 1973). A frequent contributor on Greek vernacular and modern architecture to European periodicals, he has translated A. Rapoport's *House Form and Culture* into Greek (1977) and has edited a forthcoming (1982) publication on Greek traditional architecture.

ZBIGNIEW PINIŃSKI (b. 1933), Professor at the Institute of Architectural Design, Faculty of Architecture of the Technical University at Warsaw (since 1978), studied at the Technical University of Cracow where he obtained the M.Sc. in Architecture and Planning (1951-1957), and went on to take the Ph.D. in these fields. He has been active as an architect, planner, and theorist. Of nearly thirty architectural and planning projects that he has accomplished, five were prizewinning entries in competitions. He has served as Dean of Architecture and Professor at the Technical University of Bialystock (1973-1978), has lectured widely (for instance, at Cambridge University's Faculty of Architecture and of History of Art, 1975, and the Technical University of Vienna, 1978), and has presented research reports at international seminars in Poland, Austria, and Spain. His theoretical considerations have been particularly in the realm of environmental and industrial planning and their methodologies. Between these and more specifically physical architectural concerns, Dr. Piniński has published over thirty articles and some fifteen technical reports, for the most part in Polish, but also in German and English.

IVOR PRINSLOO taught at the University of the Witwatersrand at Johannesburg before coming to the University of Cape Town where he is now Professor and Director of the School of Architecture. After a period of research toward the Ph.D. in Urban Planning at the University of California in Los Angeles and a tenure as Visiting Professor at the Facultad de la Arquitectura at La Plata, Argentina, he returned to Cape Town where he currently practices. Professor Prinsloo has contributed to various architectural publications and is editor of the University of Cape Town's new periodical, *Isilili sam sise Afrika. A Journal of Architecture and Human Settlements*, established in 1977.

MALCOLM QUANTRILL, the well-known architectural critic, studied at Liverpool University (B. Arch.) and the University of Pennsylvania (M. Arch., 1955); practiced in the Helsinki office of Arne Ervi and later in London (1960-1962). He was director of the Architectural Association in London (1967-1970) and first director of its Centre for Advanced Studies in Environment, among other activities, before his appointment in 1973 to the Polytechnic of North London. Quantrill has lectured as a visiting professor in the United States, Canada, Denmark, Austria, and Finland. Two decades after receiving his M. Arch., he took the Ph.D. at the Technical University of Wroclaw with a dissertation on concepts of urban space and conservation (1975). Head of the Department of Environmental Design at the Polytechnic of North London since 1973, and deputy editor of *Art International* (Lugano) since 1978, he has a number of publications to his credit, ranging from articles on Vienna's Karl Schwanzer (*Building Design*, March 1976), the current architectural scene in London (*London Magazine*, 1977), and Finnish architecture after Aalto (*Architectural Design*, June 1979) to books such as *Ritual and Response in Architecture* (1974) and the most recently published *Alvar Aalto: The Making of Finnish Architecture* (1981). In preparation by Professor Quantrill is *Adventures in Space: An Introduction to the Development of the Western Tradition in Architecture*. Since 1980, Dr. Quantrill has been Professor of Architecture and Urban Planning at the University of Jordan in Amman.

MARIO FEDERICO ROGGERO (b. 1919, Turin) received his degree in architecture from the Polytechnical University at Turin in 1944 and went on to distinguish himself as an architect, urban planner, and educator. Among his various honors have been prize winning projects ranging from new constructions to the recycling of historic buildings and the development of new plans for old towns and city centers. His works may be seen especially in and around Turin, at Bologna, and in many northwestern Italian locales. During the writing of his contribution to this volume one of his projects for a hotel was underway in Cairo, Egypt. In 1959 he returned to the Polytechnical University at Turin, four years later became Professor of Architecture, and since 1979 Professor Roggero has been Dean of the Faculty of Architecture. His efforts as architect and planner have appeared in many journals. Among his published critical studies are various essays on the relationships between historic and contemporary architecture in an urban context and a consideration of the architecture of Erich Mendelsohn.

JAIME SALCEDO SALCEDO (b. 1946 in Buga, Colombia) has been concerned with the architecture of Colombia and Latin America for over a decade. Architect of the Pontificia Universidad Javeriana at Bogotá (1970) and active in the restoration of historical monuments, he has lectured widely, been a UNESCO consultant in Peru and Mexico, and has advised officials of the Brazilian State of Pernambuco on conservation programs for their historical cities. Contributor of several essays on architectural history and restoration to various journals, Professor Salcedo is Director of the Institute of Aesthetic Investigations and of the Department of History of Architecture in the College of Architecture and Design of the Pontificia Universidad Javeriana, Bogotá.

STEN SAMUELSON, born in Lund, southern Sweden in 1926, graduated from the Royal University in Stockholm (1950) and soon entered into an architectural partnership with Fritz Jaenicke (1951-1964). While actively pursuing an important architectural practice, with his firm now employing 100 people, he has also taught since 1964 as Professor of Architecture at Lund University. Among Professor Samuelson's best-known architectural works are the Västra Fäladen housing complex of some 230 flats at Landskrona (1977-1978), the headquarters building of the Euroc concern in Malmö (1978), the Sweden Center Building in Tokyo (1971), a hospital in Helsingborg (1972-1974), and stadia in Göteborg (1957-1958) and Malmö (1957-1958).

EDITH S. SANDERSON's interest in modern architecture became evident during extended stays in Europe in 1971 and 1974 as one aspect of her broader concern with the economics of urbanism (Phi Beta Kappa, Florida State University, B.S. magna cum laude, 1976). Her interest developed further during travels in the United States, Mexico, and, especially, in Canada after 1976, reflected in her photographic essays on outstanding buildings.

WARREN SANDERSON (b. 1931) has lectured on architectural history and art for almost twenty years in American, Canadian, and German universities. His interest in modern and contemporary architectural history and theory first became evident in Chicago where he edited and otherwise contributed to a catalog of the works of Frank Lloyd Wright in Oak Park and River Forest, Illinois for the celebration of that great architect's centennial (1969). After studies at Boston University (B.A., M.A.), the University of Saarbrücken, and the Institute of Fine Arts of New York University (Ph.D.), Professor Sanderson taught at the University of Illinois in Chicago (1966-1970), Florida State University (1970-1976), as Visiting Professor (under the auspices of the *Deutsche Forschungsgemeinschaft*) at the University of Trier in the Federal Republic of Germany, and was Director of the Graduate Division of the Faculty of Fine Arts, Concordia University, Montreal (1979-1981). Presently Professor of Art History in the Faculty of Fine Arts at Concordia, Warren Sanderson has published articles and reviews in the *Journal of the Society of Architectural Historians*, the *Art Bulletin*, the *Trierer Zeitschrift für Geschichte und Kunst*, the *Jahrbuch der Berliner Museen*, and the *Transactions of the American Philosophical Society*, among others. A chapter on "Japanese Avant-Garde Architecture and the West" will appear in Friedhelm Lach's *The Avant-Garde and Semotics* (Indiana University Press, forthcoming). Recently he completed a review-article on Carolingian architecture for *Speculum* and is working on two books concerning twentieth-century architecture, a new synthesis of global developments and a reformulation of expressionist tendencies since the 1920s.

ROSALIE STALEY received the Ph.D. in Art Education from Pennsylvania State University in 1977 and has taught aesthetics of art and architecture and history of twentieth-century art and architecture at the University of Texas and Concordia University. Her publications in Canadian and American journals have been on contemporary art, in some cases relating both architecture and art to the aesthetics of Ernst Cassirer and Suzanne Langer. Her contribution to this volume is the result of long-standing interest and recent inquiry into the works of contemporary Finnish architects.

JENNIFER TAYLOR has lectured and published extensively on Australian and Japanese architecture. She began her architectural training in England, went on to graduate as Bachelor of Architecture from the University of Washington, Seattle, USA, and in 1969 was granted the Master of Architecture degree by the same university. A year later she joined the staff of the University of Sydney where currently as a Senior Lecturer she teaches architectural history and design. Mrs. Taylor has authored the book, *An Australian Identity: Houses in Sydney 1953-63*, coauthored the volume *John Andrews: Architecture a Performing Art*, and is at the moment preparing a book on recent developments in Australian architecture.

ROBERT W. WHITE (1942) holds an engineering degree from Cornell University (1965) and took his M. Architecture at Yale University (1969) with a thesis on simulation and gaming in housing design. He has designed many residences and mixed-use and housing projects in the United States and Canada. Recently he was design architect for the Canadian Embassy in Paris, for a luxury hotel in Hull, Quebec, and for several residences. In 1980 he received an award for an entry in the Low Energy Building Design Competition sponsored by the Canadian government. Professor White's design projects have been widely published, and articles by him have appeared in various building and engineering journals. A member of the faculty of the Centre for Building Studies of Concordia University in Montreal, Robert White is devoting considerable research to daylight design in large spaces and shadow studies as aids for predicting solar gain.

BRUNO ZEVI (b. 1918). During the years with which this volume is primarily concerned, Zevi has been an outstanding force in contemporary architectural criticism. Proponent of modern architecture and polemicist for Organic architecture and urbanism, Professor Zevi has made his views known as a distinguished lecturer in Europe, Asia, and the Americas and in important editorial capacities since 1941. A leader of the anti-Fascist *Giustizia e Libertà* movement, he left Italy for political reasons in 1939, returning in 1943 to join the Italian partisans. In the year after the Italian publication of his fundamental work, *Towards an Organic Architecture* (1945), he was instrumental in the establishing at Rome of the Association for an Organic Architecture. His efforts were paramount in offering an alternative to the Rationalists' approaches to architecture, first in Italy and then in Europe and South America during the decade following the Second World War. His personal influence upon architecture in South America was second only to Le Corbusier's before him. A frequent contributor to various architectural publications, Zevi was the editor of *Metron* (1945-1955) and now edits *L'Architettura: Cronache e Storia* (since 1955). Among his major books, which are too numerous to list here, *Architecture as Space* (1957), *Erich Mendelsohn: opera completa* (1970), *The Modern Language of Architecture* (1978), and the series *Cronache d'Architettura* (1970-1978) have had wide influence. Educated at the University of Rome and at Harvard University, Bruno Zevi has been Professor of the History of Architecture and Modern Architecture at the University of Rome (1948-1952) and the University of Venice (1948-1963). He currently occupies the Chair of History of Architecture in the Faculty of Architecture at the University of Rome.